OECD International Direct Investment Statistics 2019

2009-2018

OECD
BETTER POLICIES FOR BETTER LIVES

Please cite this publication as:
OECD (2020), *OECD International Direct Investment Statistics 2019*, OECD Publishing, Paris, *https://doi.org/10.1787/g2g9fb42-en*.

ISBN 978-92-64-31324-8 (print)
ISBN 978-92-64-31325-5 (pdf)

OECD International Direct Investment Statistics
ISSN 2307-4361 (print)
ISSN 2307-437X (online)

Corrigenda to publications may be found on line at: *www.oecd.org/about/publishing/corrigenda.htm*.

Table of contents

Conventional signs and abbreviations

Data in this publication are current up to 28 February 2020.

FDI flows and FDI positions are converted using average exchange rates and end of period exchange rates, respectively. Data in national currencies are available and can be accessed at: *http:/dx.doi.org/10.1787/idi-data-en*.

Signs and abbreviations

..	Not available
.	Decimal point
|	Break in series
c	Confidential data
d	Secondary confidentiality
-	Nil

Reporting and partner countries

OECD-Total	The OECD aggregate corresponds to the member country composition of the reporting period. 2010-2015: 34 member countries 2016-2017: 35 member countries, including Latvia 2018: 36 member countries, including Lithuania
European Union	EU27 for 2007 to 2012 and EU28 as from 2013.
ASEAN countries	Association of South-East Asian Nations. Brunei Darussalam, Indonesia, Cambodia, Lao People's Democratic Republic, Myanmar, Malaysia, Philippines, Singapore, Thailand, Viet Nam

International comparisons

INTERNATIONAL COMPARISONS

Table 1. Foreign direct investment inflows, US dollars

Million US dollars

	2009	2010	2011	2012	2013	2014	2015	2016	2017	2018
Australia[1]	31 668	36 442	58 907	59 540	56 273	58 505	28 274	45 519	42 289	60 425
Austria[2]	9 397	2 728	10 820	4 003	5 813	4 800	1 295	-8 401	14 926	2 211
Belgium	62 847	132 604	241 730	-26 383	-68 019	-41 191	-70 573	59 185	5 149	17 088
Canada	22 733	28 399	39 667	43 118	69 371	59 008	43 853	36 062	26 518	43 450
Chile[2]	..	..	..	30 428	21 015	23 100	20 913	12 345	6 053	5 704
Czech Republic[1]	2 929	6 147	2 323	8 000	3 641	5 492	465	9 814	9 518	9 479
Denmark[2]	1 428	-9 179	11 457	644	1 045	4 680	3 617	235	3 749	2 406
Estonia	1 840	1 509	1 006	1 566	771	684	36	1 058	1 917	1 474
Finland[1]	718	7 359	2 552	4 156	-106 |	18 547	2 109	8 573	2 858	-4 030
France[1]	30 735	13 891	31 671	16 069	34 264	2 669	45 355	23 055	29 812	37 286
Germany[1]	23 807	65 646	67 573	28 190	12 799 |	-3 005	30 563	12 614	33 190	11 917
Greece[1]	2 437	330	1 144	1 741	2 817	2 683	1 268	2 762	3 477	3 971
Hungary[2]	2 175	2 355	6 553	14 625	3 587	7 967	-14 545	-5 439	3 667	8 387
Iceland[2]	79	245	1 107	1 025	397	447	709	-427	-41	-282
Ireland	25 717	42 807	23 566	48 901 |	50 585	48 186	217 820	39 377	52 722	-28 073
Israel[1, 3]	4 607	6 985	8 653	9 018	11 842	6 049	11 336	11 988	18 169	20 789
Italy[1]	20 078	9 179	34 355	93	24 267 |	23 224	19 631	28 441	23 996	32 866
Japan	11 939	-1 252	-1 757	1 732	2 303	10 622	-2 251	19 357	10 976	9 856
Korea	9 022	9 497	9 773	9 496	6 083 |	-917	3 076	7 415	12 699	12 183
Latvia[1]	-21	420	1 469	1 113	901	893	734	257	667	995
Lithuania	-448	1 020	1 801	802	519	-183	1 054	436	1 027	1 093
Luxembourg[2]	20 667	35 661	13 302	19 997 |	19 332	24 645	32 757	24 391	-7 056	-20 083
Mexico[2]	17 967	27 157	25 571	21 775	48 214	30 261	35 648	30 644	33 596	33 615
Netherlands[2]	38 748	-7 185	24 391	20 121	51 096	45 018	178 950	30 645	60 231	114 235
New Zealand[1]	701	-61	4 229	3 502	1 860	2 437	-309	2 844	2 429	1 945
Norway	16 637	17 043	20 608	16 655	-5 916 |	19 504	-2 515	-3 900	-5 922	226
Poland	11 892	12 799	18 290	7 130	2 734	17 509	11 819	17 329	9 507	15 609
Portugal[2]	1 342	1 517	5 997	8 157	8 216	4 560	9 180	5 734	6 368	5 919
Slovak Republic[1]	-7	1 770	2 146	2 826	-604	-512	106	805	4 008	1 183
Slovenia[1]	-477	106	1 088	339	-151	1 050	1 675	1 245	896	1 368
Spain	13 632	40 331	32 412	24 667	28 342	22 571	8 557	31 538	38 724	44 982
Sweden	10 095	141	12 946	16 349	4 125	4 032	8 395	19 153	14 252	3 355
Switzerland	28 945	28 750	25 857	28 969	646	9 352 |	75 289	88 619	107 321	-53 150
Turkey[1]	8 585	9 086	16 136	13 743	13 565	12 973	18 903	13 707	11 478	13 025
United Kingdom	89 796	58 180	42 196	55 626	51 673	24 704	39 189	258 570	101 290	65 285
United States[1]	157 737	210 544	242 155	211 467	217 274	211 985	481 502	486 022	291 898	268 441
OECD total	**679 946**	**792 970**	**1 041 691**	**709 198**	**680 574**	**662 350**	**1 243 884**	**1 311 573**	**972 358**	**745 147**
European Union[4]	**444 794**	**465 501**	**643 372**	**335 621**	**271 038**	**279 168**	**568 578**	**581 171**	**445 532**	**348 936**
G20	**698 373**	**905 575**	**1 067 278**	**889 353**	**1 013 453**	**866 361**	**1 130 330**	**1 288 358**	**951 852**	**949 916**
of which:										
Non-OECD G20 countries	**274 307**	**438 805**	**501 032**	**428 504**	**477 367**	**436 332**	**386 589**	**326 953**	**334 110**	**361 568**
Argentina	4 017	11 333	10 840	15 324	9 822	5 065	11 759	3 260	11 517	11 873
Brazil	25 949	77 687	97 422	82 060	59 089	63 846	49 961	53 700	66 585	59 802
China	131 057	243 703	280 072	241 214	290 928	268 097	242 489	174 750	166 084	203 492
India	35 582	27 397	36 497	23 995	28 153	34 577	44 009	44 459	39 966	42 117
Indonesia	4 878	13 771	19 241	19 138	18 817	21 811	16 641	3 921	20 579	21 474
Russian Federation	27 752	31 668	36 868	30 188	53 397	29 152	11 858	37 176	25 954	13 228
Saudi Arabia	36 458	29 233	16 308	12 182	8 865	8 012	8 141	7 453	1 419	4 247
South Africa	8 614	4 015	3 785	4 403	8 296	5 772	1 729	2 235	2 007	5 334
World	**1 249 049**	**1 573 527**	**1 927 303**	**1 550 614**	**1 514 040**	**1 519 412**	**2 088 370**	**2 031 733**	**1 717 378**	**1 442 185**

.. Not available; | Break in series

Note: Detailed metadata at: *http://stats.oecd.org/OECDStat_Metadata/ShowMetadata.ashx?Dataset=FDI_AGGR_SUMM*.

1. Resident Special Purpose Entities (SPEs) are not present or not significant.
2. Data excludes Special Purpose Entities (SPEs).
3. Information on data for Israel: *http://oe.cd/israel-disclaimer*.
4. EU27 for 2007 to 2012 and EU28 as from 2013.

Source: OECD International Direct Investment Statistics (database): https://doi.org/10.1787/idi-data-en

Table 2. Foreign direct investment outflows, US dollars

Million US dollars

	2009	2010	2011	2012	2013	2014	2015	2016	2017	2018
Australia[1]	16 409	19 803	1 716	7 889	1 441	18 184	-10 220	328	3 320	3 634
Austria[2]	11 038	9 548	22 004	13 060	15 598	-665	6 915	-1 323	10 679	5 941
Belgium	40 454	60 335	54 135	79 719	26 217	26 189	57 563	36 337	33 528	27 647
Canada	39 660	34 721	52 144	55 875	57 364	60 273	67 467	69 518	78 338	49 869
Chile[2]	..	..	..	20 837	9 996	13 146	15 886	6 584	5 417	1 498
Czech Republic[1]	950	1 168	-328	1 794	4 021	1 620	2 488	2 182	7 557	5 277
Denmark[2]	3 690	1 368	11 278	7 349	7 162	8 249	9 424	10 112	9 520	1 137
Estonia	1 375	167	-1 455	1 054	516	42	132	486	873	49
Finland[1]	5 597	10 189	5 016	7 546	-2 306 |	1 742	-16 030	23 695	-738	11 363
France[1]	100 872	48 158	51 462	35 453	20 365	49 785	53 206	64 785	41 271	102 408
Germany[1]	68 548	125 453	78 002	62 188	39 505 |	83 977	99 023	60 344	88 075	63 280
Greece[1]	2 055	1 558	1 774	678	-785	3 015	1 578	-1 665	168	477
Hungary[2]	1 881	1 234	4 804	11 802	1 943	3 854	-16 118	-8 272	1 228	5 059
Iceland[2]	2 248	-2 368	18	-3 205	460	-257	-31	-1 147	-208	118
Ireland	26 617	22 350	-1 166	22 557 |	29 164	41 182	168 443	30 055	-2 043	723
Israel[1, 3]	1 751	7 944	7 401	2 276	3 858	4 526	10 969	14 579	6 153	6 117
Italy[1]	21 277	32 657	53 677	7 992	25 130 |	26 327	21 640	16 165	24 478	32 673
Japan	74 699	56 276	107 550	122 514	135 745	129 157	128 698	155 923	164 658	143 142
Korea	17 436	28 280	29 705	30 632	31 488 |	19 994	18 490	30 508	51 044	38 220
Latvia[1]	-63	20	61	193	413	517	68	147	132	190
Lithuania	555	42	750	540	132	9	369	51	68	671
Luxembourg[2]	6 709	20 842	9 052	805 |	23 917	37 271	27 033	21 752	30 564	2 016
Mexico[2]	9 861	14 372	13 282	22 882	15 544	6 332	10 663	628	3 833	7 831
Netherlands[2]	26 267	68 363	34 818	6 174	69 690	53 951	247 681	156 445	46 683	-18 830
New Zealand[1]	-1 001	716	2 682	-433	530	472	-59	196	227	425
Norway	19 159	23 238	19 901	19 791	6 213 |	32 939	30 947	3 092	-7 415	11 405
Poland	3 657	6 148	3 677	-2 660	-1 346	4 598	1 928	13 122	1 878	965
Portugal[2]	878	-10 064	13 627	-8 474	769	-3 260	4 810	980	-1 141	402
Slovak Republic[1]	904	946	491	-73	-313	43	6	95	1 323	234
Slovenia[1]	214	-19	200	-258	-214	275	267	290	338	267
Spain	16 334	38 393	45 248	-2 479	14 294	36 743	41 917	43 902	52 238	27 058
Sweden	26 205	20 364	29 912	28 977	30 279	9 162	13 045	4 703	25 512	16 818
Switzerland	26 428	85 718	48 098	43 572	38 568	-47 |	88 759	122 101	30 144	60 781
Turkey[1]	1 553	1 469	2 330	4 106	3 536	6 681	4 812	2 892	2 634	3 607
United Kingdom	28 993	48 075	95 578	20 767	40 483	-151 368	-66 827	-37 587	117 605	41 415
United States[1]	309 252	296 334	415 271	338 363	321 937	347 658	279 471	309 901	321 822	-68 407
OECD total	**912 463**	**1 073 799**	**1 212 717**	**959 800**	**971 315**	**872 316**	**1 304 412**	**1 151 902**	**1 149 762**	**585 481**
European Union[4]	**451 890**	**542 921**	**555 940**	**360 965**	**366 085**	**294 154**	**697 209**	**437 018**	**499 967**	**320 099**
G20	**779 344**	**850 148**	**1 033 844**	**815 939**	**856 607**	**814 823**	**821 722**	**918 907**	**1 117 533**	**582 441**
of which:										
Non-OECD G20 countries	**90 784**	**144 550**	**133 127**	**107 278**	**164 068**	**217 823**	**215 298**	**245 504**	**220 454**	**164 768**
Argentina	712	965	1 488	1 055	890	1 921	875	1 787	1 156	1 802
Brazil	-10 084	22 060	11 062	-8 425	-478	-3 261	-11 643	-5 901	19 040	-16 336
China	43 890	57 954	48 421	64 963	72 971	123 130	174 391	216 424	138 293	96 472
India	16 068	15 968	12 608	8 553	1 765	11 686	7 514	5 047	11 090	11 418
Indonesia	2 249	2 664	7 713	5 422	6 647	7 077	5 937	-12 215	2 077	8 052
Russian Federation	34 450	41 116	48 635	28 423	70 685	64 203	27 090	26 951	34 153	35 820
Saudi Arabia	2 177	3 907	3 430	4 402	4 943	5 396	5 390	8 936	7 280	22 987
South Africa	1 322	-84	-229	2 886	6 646	7 671	5 744	4 474	7 366	4 552
World	**1 193 087**	**1 450 621**	**1 597 719**	**1 316 062**	**1 366 292**	**1 423 298**	**1 734 613**	**1 580 387**	**1 586 980**	**887 715**

.. Not available; | Break in series

Note: Detailed metadata at: *http://stats.oecd.org/OECDStat_Metadata/ShowMetadata.ashx?Dataset=FDI_AGGR_SUMM.*

1. Resident Special Purpose Entities (SPEs) are not present or not significant.
2. Data excludes Special Purpose Entities (SPEs).
3. Information on data for Israel: *http://oe.cd/israel-disclaimer.*
4. EU27 for 2007 to 2012 and EU28 as from 2013.

Source: OECD International Direct Investment Statistics (database): https://doi.org/10.1787/idi-data-en

Table 3. Foreign direct investment inflows as a percentage of GDP

Per cent

	2009	2010	2011	2012	2013	2014	2015	2016	2017	2018
Australia[1]	3.1	2.8	3.8	3.7	3.6	4.0	2.3	3.5	3.0	4.2
Austria[2]	2.3	0.7	2.5	1.0	1.4	1.1	0.3	-2.1	3.6	0.5
Belgium	13.0	27.4	45.9	-5.3	-13.1	-7.8	-15.5	12.6	1.0	3.2
Canada	1.7	1.8	2.2	2.4	3.8	3.3	2.8	2.4	1.6	2.5
Chile[2]	..	..	..	11.4	7.5	8.9	8.6	4.9	2.2	1.9
Czech Republic[1]	1.4	3.0	1.0	3.9	1.7	2.6	0.2	5.0	4.4	3.9
Denmark[2]	0.4	-2.9	3.3	0.2	0.3	1.3	1.2	0.1	1.1	0.7
Estonia	9.4	7.7	4.3	6.8	3.1	2.6	0.2	4.4	7.2	4.9
Finland[1]	0.3	3.0	0.9	1.6	0.0 |	6.8	0.9	3.6	1.1	-1.5
France[1]	1.1	0.5	1.1	0.6	1.2	0.1	1.9	0.9	1.2	1.3
Germany[1]	0.7	1.9	1.8	0.8	0.3 |	-0.1	0.9	0.4	0.9	0.3
Greece[1]	0.7	0.1	0.4	0.7	1.2	1.1	0.6	1.4	1.7	1.8
Hungary[2]	1.7	1.8	4.7	11.4	2.7	5.7	-11.8	-4.3	2.6	5.4
Iceland[2]	0.6	1.8	7.3	7.0	2.5	2.5	4.1	-2.1	-0.2	-1.1
Ireland	10.9	19.3	9.9	21.7 |	21.2	18.6	74.7	13.1	15.7	-7.3
Israel[1, 3]	2.2	3.0	3.3	3.5	4.0	2.0	3.8	3.8	5.1	5.6
Italy[1]	0.9	0.4	1.5	0.0	1.1 |	1.1	1.1	1.5	1.2	1.6
Japan	0.2	0.0	0.0	0.0	0.0	0.2	-0.1	0.4	0.2	0.2
Korea	1.0	0.9	0.8	0.8	0.5 |	-0.1	0.2	0.5	0.8	0.8
Latvia[1]	-0.1	1.8	5.2	4.0	3.0	2.8	2.7	0.9	2.2	2.9
Lithuania	-1.2	2.7	4.1	1.9	1.1	-0.4	2.5	1.0	2.2	2.1
Luxembourg[2]	40.2	67.0	22.2	35.3 |	31.3	37.3	56.7	40.2	-11.0	-28.3
Mexico[2]	2.0	2.6	2.2	1.8	3.8	2.3	3.0	2.8	2.9	2.7
Netherlands[2]	4.5	-0.8	2.7	2.4	5.8	5.1	23.4	3.9	7.2	12.5
New Zealand[1]	0.6	0.0	2.5	2.0	1.0	1.2	-0.2	1.5	1.2	0.9
Norway	4.3	4.0	4.1	3.3	-1.1 |	3.9	-0.7	-1.1	-1.5	0.1
Poland	2.7	2.7	3.5	1.4	0.5	3.2	2.5	3.7	1.8	2.7
Portugal[2]	0.6	0.6	2.4	3.8	3.6	2.0	4.6	2.8	2.9	2.5
Slovak Republic[1]	0.0	2.0	2.2	3.0	-0.6	-0.5	0.1	0.9	4.2	1.1
Slovenia[1]	-0.9	0.2	2.1	0.7	-0.3	2.1	3.9	2.8	1.8	2.5
Spain	0.9	2.8	2.2	1.9	2.1	1.6	0.7	2.6	3.0	3.2
Sweden	2.3	0.0	2.3	3.0	0.7	0.7	1.7	3.7	2.6	0.6
Switzerland	5.3	4.9	3.7	4.3	0.1	1.3 |	11.1	13.2	15.8	-7.5
Turkey[1]	1.3	1.2	1.9	1.6	1.4	1.4	2.2	1.6	1.3	1.7
United Kingdom	3.7	2.4	1.6	2.1	1.9	0.8	1.4	9.7	3.8	2.3
United States[1]	1.1	1.4	1.6	1.3	1.3	1.2	2.6	2.6	1.5	1.3
OECD total	**1.6**	**1.8**	**2.2**	**1.5**	**1.4**	**1.3**	**2.7**	**2.7**	**1.9**	**1.4**
European Union[4]	**2.6**	**2.8**	**3.6**	**2.0**	**1.5**	**1.5**	**3.5**	**3.5**	**2.6**	**1.9**
G20	**1.5**	**1.8**	**1.9**	**1.5**	**1.7**	**1.4**	**1.9**	**2.2**	**1.5**	**1.4**
of which:										
Non-OECD G20 countries	**2.5**	**3.2**	**3.0**	**2.4**	**2.5**	**2.2**	**2.1**	**1.7**	**1.6**	**1.6**
Argentina	1.2	2.7	2.0	2.6	1.6	0.9	1.8	0.6	1.8	2.3
Brazil	1.6	3.5	3.7	3.3	2.4	2.6	2.8	3.0	3.2	3.1
China	2.6	4.0	3.7	2.8	3.0	2.6	2.2	1.6	1.4	1.5
India	2.7	1.6	2.0	1.3	1.5	1.7	2.1	2.0	1.5	1.6
Indonesia	0.8	1.8	2.2	2.1	2.1	2.4	1.9	0.4	2.0	2.1
Russian Federation	2.1	1.9	1.8	1.4	2.3	1.4	0.9	2.9	1.6	0.8
Saudi Arabia	8.5	5.5	2.4	1.7	1.2	1.1	1.2	1.2	0.2	0.5
South Africa	2.9	1.1	0.9	1.1	2.3	1.6	0.5	0.8	0.6	1.4

.. Not available; | Break in series

Note: Detailed metadata at: *http://stats.oecd.org/OECDStat_Metadata/ShowMetadata.ashx?Dataset=FDI_AGGR_SUMM.*

1. Resident Special Purpose Entities (SPEs) are not present or not significant.
2. Data excludes Special Purpose Entities (SPEs).
3. Information on data for Israel: *http://oe.cd/israel-disclaimer.*
4. EU27 for 2007 to 2012 and EU28 as from 2013.

Source: OECD International Direct Investment Statistics (database): https://doi.org/10.1787/idi-data-en

Table 4. Foreign direct investment outflows as a percentage of GDP

Per cent

	2009	2010	2011	2012	2013	2014	2015	2016	2017	2018
Australia[1]	1.6	1.5	0.1	0.5	0.1	1.2	-0.8	0.0	0.2	0.3
Austria[2]	2.8	2.4	5.1	3.2	3.6	-0.2	1.8	-0.3	2.6	1.3
Belgium	8.3	12.5	10.3	16.0	5.0	4.9	12.6	7.7	6.8	5.2
Canada	2.9	2.1	2.9	3.1	3.1	3.3	4.3	4.5	4.7	2.9
Chile[2]	..	..	..	7.8	3.6	5.0	6.5	2.6	2.0	0.5
Czech Republic[1]	0.5	0.6	-0.1	0.9	1.9	0.8	1.3	1.1	3.5	2.2
Denmark[2]	1.1	0.4	3.3	2.2	2.1	2.3	3.1	3.2	2.9	0.3
Estonia	7.0	0.9	-6.3	4.6	2.1	0.2	0.8	2.0	3.3	0.2
Finland[1]	2.2	4.1	1.8	2.9	-0.9 |	0.6	-6.9	9.9	-0.3	4.1
France[1]	3.7	1.8	1.8	1.3	0.7	1.7	2.2	2.6	1.6	3.7
Germany[1]	2.0	3.7	2.1	1.8	1.1 |	2.2	2.9	1.7	2.4	1.6
Greece[1]	0.6	0.5	0.6	0.3	-0.3	1.3	0.8	-0.9	0.1	0.2
Hungary[2]	1.4	0.9	3.4	9.2	1.4	2.8	-13.1	-6.6	0.9	3.2
Iceland[2]	17.1	-17.3	0.1	-21.8	2.9	-1.4	-0.2	-5.6	-0.9	0.5
Ireland	11.3	10.1	-0.5	10.0 |	12.2	15.9	57.8	10.0	-0.6	0.2
Israel[1, 3]	0.8	3.4	2.8	0.9	1.3	1.5	3.7	4.6	1.7	1.7
Italy[1]	1.0	1.5	2.3	0.4	1.2 |	1.2	1.2	0.9	1.3	1.6
Japan	1.4	1.0	1.7	2.0	2.6	2.7	2.9	3.2	3.4	2.9
Korea	1.9	2.6	2.5	2.5	2.4 |	1.4	1.3	2.2	3.3	2.4
Latvia[1]	-0.2	0.1	0.2	0.7	1.4	1.7	0.3	0.5	0.4	0.5
Lithuania	1.5	0.1	1.7	1.3	0.3	0.0	0.9	0.1	0.1	1.3
Luxembourg[2]	13.1	39.2	15.1	1.4 |	38.7	56.4	46.8	35.8	47.7	2.8
Mexico[2]	1.1	1.4	1.1	1.9	1.2	0.5	0.9	0.1	0.3	0.6
Netherlands[2]	3.0	8.1	3.9	0.7	7.9	6.1	32.4	20.0	5.6	-2.1
New Zealand[1]	-0.8	0.5	1.6	-0.2	0.3	0.2	0.0	0.1	0.1	0.2
Norway	5.0	5.4	4.0	3.9	1.2 |	6.6	8.0	0.8	-1.9	2.6
Poland	0.8	1.3	0.7	-0.5	-0.3	0.8	0.4	2.8	0.4	0.2
Portugal[2]	0.4	-4.2	5.6	-3.9	0.3	-1.4	2.4	0.5	-0.5	0.2
Slovak Republic[1]	1.0	1.1	0.5	-0.1	-0.3	0.0	0.0	0.1	1.4	0.2
Slovenia[1]	0.4	0.0	0.4	-0.6	-0.4	0.6	0.6	0.6	0.7	0.5
Spain	1.1	2.7	3.1	-0.2	1.1	2.7	3.5	3.6	4.0	1.9
Sweden	6.0	4.1	5.2	5.3	5.2	1.6	2.6	0.9	4.7	3.0
Switzerland	4.9	14.7	6.9	6.5	5.6	0.0 |	13.1	18.2	4.4	8.6
Turkey[1]	0.2	0.2	0.3	0.5	0.4	0.7	0.6	0.3	0.3	0.5
United Kingdom	1.2	2.0	3.6	0.8	1.5	-5.0	-2.3	-1.4	4.5	1.5
United States[1]	2.1	2.0	2.7	2.1	1.9	2.0	1.5	1.7	1.6	-0.3
OECD total	**2.1**	**2.4**	**2.5**	**2.0**	**2.0**	**1.8**	**2.8**	**2.4**	**2.3**	**1.1**
European Union[4]	**2.7**	**3.2**	**3.1**	**2.1**	**2.0**	**1.6**	**4.2**	**2.6**	**2.9**	**1.7**
G20	**1.7**	**1.7**	**1.8**	**1.4**	**1.4**	**1.3**	**1.4**	**1.6**	**1.8**	**0.9**
of which:										
Non-OECD G20 countries	**0.8**	**1.1**	**0.8**	**0.6**	**0.9**	**1.1**	**1.1**	**1.3**	**1.0**	**0.7**
Argentina	0.2	0.2	0.3	0.2	0.1	0.3	0.1	0.3	0.2	0.3
Brazil	-0.6	1.0	0.4	-0.3	0.0	-0.1	-0.6	-0.3	0.9	-0.9
China	0.9	1.0	0.6	0.8	0.8	1.2	1.6	1.9	1.1	0.7
India	1.2	0.9	0.7	0.5	0.1	0.6	0.4	0.2	0.4	0.4
Indonesia	0.4	0.4	0.9	0.6	0.7	0.8	0.7	-1.3	0.2	0.8
Russian Federation	2.6	2.5	2.4	1.3	3.1	3.1	2.0	2.1	2.2	2.3
Saudi Arabia	0.5	0.7	0.5	0.6	0.7	0.7	0.8	1.4	1.1	2.9
South Africa	0.4	0.0	-0.1	0.7	1.8	2.2	1.8	1.5	2.1	1.2

.. Not available; | Break in series

Note: Detailed metadata at: *http://stats.oecd.org/OECDStat_Metadata/ShowMetadata.ashx?Dataset=FDI_AGGR_SUMM.*

1. Resident Special Purpose Entities (SPEs) are not present or not significant.
2. Data excludes Special Purpose Entities (SPEs).
3. Information on data for Israel: *http://oe.cd/israel-disclaimer*.
4. EU27 for 2007 to 2012 and EU28 as from 2013.

Source: OECD International Direct Investment Statistics (database): https://doi.org/10.1787/idi-data-en

Table 5. Foreign direct investment inward positions (stocks), US dollars

At year end

Million US dollars

	2009	2010	2011	2012	2013	2014	2015	2016	2017	2018
Australia[1]	439 446	527 096	554 931	615 116	568 855	582 540	565 804	606 131	689 369	682 880
Austria[2]	174 486	166 478	158 863	171 697	186 591	182 785	165 845	156 671	202 992	208 561
Belgium[2]	..	..	..	..	557 245	496 519	520 992	517 401	556 011	524 711
Canada	867 470	983 889	862 698	953 503	982 529	994 712	864 233	903 454	963 383	852 196
Chile[2]	..	..	..	204 206	212 208	221 722	230 607	248 731	274 329	268 335
Czech Republic[1]	125 829	128 505	120 569	136 494	134 085	121 512	116 628	121 855	155 994	163 289
Denmark[2]	103 230	96 984	98 423	98 320	74 943	95 766	91 979	99 403	116 993	109 894
Estonia	15 842	15 551	16 349	18 934	22 017	20 900	18 918	19 667	23 927	24 828
Finland[1]	85 169	85 855	89 226	96 636	88 807 |	93 047	81 660	79 930	89 987	71 500
France[1]	648 065	630 692	698 832	680 337	761 383	700 027	687 394	694 881	818 545	824 987
Germany[1]	965 014	959 200	988 551	863 410 |	955 168	862 213	795 496	792 321	954 491	939 148
Greece[1]	42 101	35 025	29 058	24 763	25 850	24 567	26 951	24 615	33 404	34 851
Hungary[2]	98 898	91 020	85 615	104 401	109 150	100 411	86 254	82 701	93 497	95 173
Iceland[2]	8 622	11 784	12 656	10 367	7 367	7 889	7 851	9 841	10 130	9 138
Ireland	250 122	285 572	290 479	383 164 |	414 747	429 823	890 126	840 646	1 058 012	1 000 393
Israel[1, 3]	56 253	60 086	64 842	75 805	86 531	89 619	99 313	107 483	129 143	145 345
Italy[1]	364 456	328 055	355 108	363 586	364 965 |	352 482	340 477	352 626	424 743	426 411
Japan	200 151	214 890	225 785	205 754	170 713	171 664	174 146	196 614	202 441	204 780
Korea[2]	..	..	..	..	166 375	168 827	168 923	174 979	210 864	..
Latvia[1]	11 520	10 869	12 062	13 488	15 905	15 117	14 729	14 316	17 543	17 407
Lithuania	14 713	15 339	16 027	17 574	19 323	16 699	15 846	16 048	19 555	19 501
Luxembourg[2]	..	..	..	150 904	160 575	186 660	195 665	185 281	177 377	149 785
Mexico[2]	339 043	389 571	383 699	458 834	489 685	491 707	501 999	473 424	490 574	511 275
Netherlands[2]	646 343	588 071	610 643	628 120	797 556	1 082 570	1 398 628 |	1 411 222	1 692 688	1 685 058
New Zealand[1]	56 459	57 364	64 433	71 579	75 344	76 622	66 479	69 960	75 308	75 158
Norway[2]	..	..	..	..	190 836	173 127	147 487	147 524	145 488	134 928
Poland[2]	167 381	187 602	164 424	198 953	229 167	211 951	183 869	186 735	238 990	228 337
Portugal[2]	92 569	90 878	92 308	105 726	132 122	123 728	123 513	123 644	151 948	147 944
Slovak Republic[1]	52 541	50 327	51 978	55 118	58 022	49 738	46 016	47 592	59 510	58 441
Slovenia[1]	11 276	10 667	11 490	12 202	12 269	12 385	12 642	13 672	16 739	17 348
Spain[2]	..	..	..	..	638 731	587 426	553 237	556 756	664 646	684 770
Sweden[2]	..	..	..	..	359 801	293 526	291 338	293 910	339 860	319 767
Switzerland[2]	..	..	..	..	..	706 237	768 164	940 426	1 172 249	1 167 102
Turkey[1]	143 842	187 147	136 606	190 125	151 832	183 679	158 867	149 752	197 271	146 976
United Kingdom	1 026 351	1 068 143	1 157 485	1 440 525	1 512 648	1 581 494	1 530 652	1 460 578	1 805 842	1 930 435
United States[1]	2 995 459	3 422 293	3 498 726	3 915 804	4 948 418	5 456 888	5 731 383	6 586 391	7 844 202	7 432 134
OECD total	**12 320 529**	**13 202 264**	**13 472 121**	**14 735 462**	**16 360 526**	**16 966 523**	**17 674 113**	**18 707 180**	**22 118 046**	**21 523 648**
European Union[4]	**6 920 904**	**6 908 722**	**7 190 848**	**7 730 553**	**8 415 215**	**8 396 535**	**8 928 841**	**8 840 331**	**10 583 197**	**10 544 385**
G20	**10 803 768**	**12 322 432**	**12 785 891**	**13 905 842**	**15 408 778**	**15 964 718**	**15 843 916**	**17 113 749**	**19 464 679**	**18 955 534**
of which:										
Non-OECD G20 countries	**2 697 710**	**3 482 033**	**3 794 597**	**4 068 299**	**4 336 208**	**4 418 485**	**4 324 540**	**4 722 598**	**4 862 954**	**4 793 447**
Argentina	78 205	85 591	92 295	98 706	88 338	89 716	79 773	74 868	80 700	72 573
Brazil	367 183	640 330	649 126	664 208	627 789	601 490	429 843	563 539	623 021	568 741
China	1 314 771	1 569 604	1 906 908	2 068 027	2 331 238	2 599 102	2 696 344	2 755 147	2 725 662	2 762 349
India	171 437	205 603	206 373	224 987	226 549	265 838	282 617	318 320	377 287	386 172
Indonesia	..	160 735	184 804	211 635	230 799	217 487	222 410	249 859	231 492	225 501
Russian Federation	367 379	464 228	408 942	438 195	471 475	290 039	262 748	393 910	441 123	408 097
Saudi Arabia	148 089	176 378	186 758	199 032	207 897	215 909	224 050	231 502	227 566	231 603
South Africa	138 751	179 564	159 391	163 509	152 123	138 904	126 755	135 453	156 103	138 410
World	**18 265 115**	**20 383 056**	**21 299 846**	**23 439 786**	**25 713 952**	**26 752 536**	**27 569 831**	**29 298 301**	**33 793 193**	**33 318 997**

.. Not available; | Break in series

Note: Detailed metadata at: *http://stats.oecd.org/OECDStat_Metadata/ShowMetadata.ashx?Dataset=FDI_AGGR_SUMM*.

1. Resident Special Purpose Entities (SPEs) are not present or not significant.
2. Data excludes Special Purpose Entities (SPEs).
3. Information on data for Israel: *http://oe.cd/israel-disclaimer*.
4. EU27 for 2007 to 2012 and EU28 as from 2013.

Source: OECD International Direct Investment Statistics (database): https://doi.org/10.1787/idi-data-en

Table 6. Foreign direct investment outward positions (stocks), US dollars

At year end

Million US dollars

	2009	2010	2011	2012	2013	2014	2015	2016	2017	2018
Australia[1]	364 581	449 768	418 814	476 541	456 977	467 173	415 412	432 015	495 952	490 997
Austria[2]	176 779	187 857	199 307	215 786	238 357	224 039	210 510	202 757	239 801	238 905
Belgium[2]	..	..	..	..	565 311	554 624	582 582	599 380	706 197	586 104
Canada	892 342	998 466	891 619	972 042	1 131 177	1 125 917	1 112 689	1 290 015	1 526 996	1 366 192
Chile[2]	..	..	..	97 033	102 472	107 046	107 969	117 749	123 645	118 871
Czech Republic[1]	14 805	14 922	13 214	17 368	20 627	18 235	18 591	19 426	32 364	34 943
Denmark[2]	153 871	165 375	176 065	183 987	157 753	167 395	164 758	169 708	201 622	193 338
Estonia	6 262	5 545	4 805	6 064	6 827	6 216	6 039	6 299	7 807	7 919
Finland[1]	130 241	137 662	133 773	151 373	145 454 |	116 740	94 611	108 406	122 661	127 873
France[1]	1 120 571	1 172 979	1 247 922	1 272 327	1 325 443	1 294 151	1 268 228	1 284 859	1 466 602	1 507 862
Germany[1]	1 357 953	1 383 601	1 432 696	1 344 222 |	1 448 431	1 388 803	1 362 452	1 361 506	1 618 087	1 643 626
Greece[1]	39 457	42 623	48 041	44 960	36 300	32 431	27 288	18 006	20 104	19 554
Hungary[2]	22 937	23 613	27 557	39 165	39 929	40 533	35 537	25 019	30 058	30 697
Iceland[2]	10 180	11 466	11 521	12 305	9 503	8 415	7 637	6 058	5 269	5 263
Ireland	295 358	340 110	330 793	412 011 |	534 765	618 800	909 668	856 582	986 846	942 868
Israel[1, 3]	57 438	67 893	72 177	72 565	77 745	79 011	84 696	94 633	100 260	103 506
Italy[1]	486 424	489 654	519 660	534 980	533 906 |	477 456	456 619	456 380	547 578	554 280
Japan	740 965	831 110	955 854	1 037 700	1 118 009	1 152 007	1 228 767	1 315 221	1 497 525	1 567 161
Korea[2]	..	..	..	..	237 932	242 792	276 100	296 641	343 089	..
Latvia[1]	892	894	864	1 113	1 600	1 493	1 554	1 635	1 931	2 007
Lithuania	2 842	2 647	3 249	3 854	4 005	3 516	3 532	3 543	4 137	4 643
Luxembourg[2]	..	..	..	100 708	132 422	165 574	179 173	212 374	247 606	243 217
Mexico[2]	84 447	116 906	112 841	151 307	143 742	150 085	144 619	146 169	175 036	153 576
Netherlands[2]	965 222	968 130	996 012	1 001 416	1 147 501	1 612 101	2 031 456 |	2 205 837	2 531 182	2 380 454
New Zealand[1]	13 801	16 053	19 100	19 130	18 385	17 996	17 025	16 888	17 800	17 278
Norway[2]	..	..	..	..	181 736	162 028	172 432	192 013	200 887	196 080
Poland[2]	11 503	16 407	18 928	26 102	27 725	21 797	22 281	25 388	28 478	25 423
Portugal[2]	53 760	52 495	63 082	57 941	71 462	56 919	58 873	58 122	63 284	56 833
Slovak Republic[1]	3 152	3 456	4 021	4 765	4 830	2 820	2 462	2 631	4 590	4 585
Slovenia[1]	8 850	8 147	7 826	7 533	7 142	6 477	5 997	6 052	7 159	6 941
Spain[2]	..	..	..	..	572 343	519 308	505 765	495 217	570 596	544 368
Sweden[2]	..	..	..	..	414 533	377 441	338 754	338 481	370 533	370 293
Switzerland[2]	..	..	..	..	..	986 525	1 033 297	1 151 989	1 279 295	1 334 338
Turkey[1]	22 248	22 506	27 652	30 936	33 318	39 458	35 543	38 397	45 582	44 495
United Kingdom	1 643 017	1 686 191	1 728 556	1 693 955	1 796 164	1 681 283	1 605 443	1 567 989	1 773 656	1 788 180
United States[1]	4 322 122	4 809 587	4 514 327	5 222 874	6 254 171	6 320 124	6 059 271	6 412 138	7 828 747	6 452 718
OECD total	**15 663 667**	**16 952 191**	**17 014 234**	**18 214 984**	**20 091 888**	**20 246 642**	**20 587 641**	**21 535 523**	**25 222 961**	**23 508 476**
European Union[4]	**8 364 078**	**8 644 851**	**8 928 746**	**9 066 004**	**9 752 945**	**9 910 864**	**10 422 189**	**10 548 494**	**12 170 476**	**11 314 913**
G20	**12 032 967**	**13 150 484**	**13 196 386**	**14 316 875**	**16 070 559**	**16 149 880**	**15 960 095**	**16 997 319**	**20 375 232**	**18 999 007**
of which:										
Non-OECD G20 countries	**877 884**	**1 046 586**	**1 174 953**	**1 378 207**	**1 591 290**	**1 810 632**	**1 994 945**	**2 395 988**	**3 056 383**	**3 086 833**
Argentina	29 536	30 328	31 891	32 919	34 517	36 180	37 843	39 735	40 930	42 228
Brazil	133 523	149 333	159 809	203 897	203 799	209 993	184 909	203 186	239 630	208 431
China	245 750	317 210	424 780	531 943	660 480	882 640	1 095 909	1 357 390	1 809 040	1 899 012
India	80 943	96 911	109 519	118 072	119 838	132 741	139 038	144 086	155 176	166 594
Indonesia	..	6 672	6 204	12 401	19 350	25 396	29 351	59 134	65 928	72 742
Russian Federation	288 289	336 355	315 742	332 836	385 322	332 961	290 092	342 849	388 693	346 593
Saudi Arabia	22 621	26 528	29 958	34 359	39 303	44 699	63 121	73 973	84 437	105 063
South Africa	70 190	83 248	97 051	111 779	128 681	146 023	154 683	175 635	272 548	246 170
World	**18 470 052**	**20 180 169**	**20 605 633**	**22 367 457**	**24 676 154**	**25 385 044**	**26 119 435**	**27 617 990**	**32 506 820**	**30 346 200**

.. Not available; | Break in series

Note: Detailed metadata at: *http://stats.oecd.org/OECDStat_Metadata/ShowMetadata.ashx?Dataset=FDI_AGGR_SUMM*.

1. Resident Special Purpose Entities (SPEs) are not present or not significant.
2. Data excludes Special Purpose Entities (SPEs).
3. Information on data for Israel: *http://oe.cd/israel-disclaimer*.
4. EU27 for 2007 to 2012 and EU28 as from 2013.

Source: OECD International Direct Investment Statistics (database): https://doi.org/10.1787/idi-data-en

Table 7. Foreign direct investment inward positions (stocks), as a percentage of GDP
At year end

Per cent

	2009	2010	2011	2012	2013	2014	2015	2016	2017	2018
Australia[1]	43.3	40.6	35.9	38.7	36.9	39.8	45.3	46.2	48.7	47.1
Austria[2]	43.6	42.5	36.8	41.9	43.4	41.4	43.4	39.6	48.6	45.8
Belgium[2]	..	..	..	..	107.0	93.5	114.3	110.2	112.3	98.7
Canada	63.1	60.8	48.1	52.1	53.2	55.2	55.5	59.0	58.4	49.8
Chile[2]	..	..	..	76.4	76.2	85.1	94.5	99.4	98.8	90.0
Czech Republic[1]	61.0	61.9	52.9	65.8	64.0	58.5	62.4	62.5	72.2	66.6
Denmark[2]	32.1	30.1	28.6	30.1	21.8	27.1	30.4	31.9	35.5	31.2
Estonia	80.6	79.7	70.6	82.2	87.6	78.5	82.6	82.0	89.9	82.0
Finland[1]	33.9	34.6	32.6	37.6	32.9 |	34.1	35.1	33.4	35.7	26.1
France[1]	24.1	23.9	24.4	25.3	27.1	24.5	28.2	28.1	31.6	29.7
Germany[1]	28.2	28.1	26.3	24.4 |	25.5	22.1	23.5	22.7	25.8	23.5
Greece[1]	12.8	11.7	10.1	10.1	10.8	10.4	13.7	12.6	16.4	16.0
Hungary[2]	75.7	69.5	60.8	81.7	80.7	71.7	70.1	65.6	66.9	61.1
Iceland[2]	65.5	86.1	83.5	70.4	45.9	44.4	45.1	47.7	41.4	35.3
Ireland	105.8	128.5	122.3	170.3 |	173.9	166.3	305.4	279.7	316.0	261.5
Israel[1, 3]	27.1	25.7	24.8	29.5	29.6	29.0	33.1	33.7	36.6	39.2
Italy[1]	16.6	15.4	15.5	17.4	17.0 |	16.3	18.5	18.8	21.7	20.5
Japan	3.8	3.8	3.7	3.3	3.3	3.5	4.0	4.0	4.2	4.1
Korea[2]	..	..	..	..	12.7	12.0	12.2	12.4	13.8	..
Latvia[1]	44.0	45.7	42.4	48.0	52.6	48.2	54.6	51.7	57.6	49.9
Lithuania	39.3	41.3	36.8	41.0	41.6	34.4	38.2	37.3	41.1	36.6
Luxembourg[2]	..	..	..	266.2	260.1	282.4	338.8	305.3	277.1	211.3
Mexico[2]	37.7	36.8	32.5	38.2	38.4	37.4	42.9	43.9	42.4	41.8
Netherlands[2]	74.5	69.5	67.5	74.9	90.9	121.5	182.8 |	180.1	203.5	184.4
New Zealand[1]	46.5	39.1	38.2	40.6	39.5	38.2	37.5	37.2	37.2	36.7
Norway[2]	..	..	..	..	36.5	34.7	38.2	40.0	36.5	31.1
Poland[2]	38.1	39.1	31.1	39.8	43.7	38.9	38.5	39.6	45.4	39.0
Portugal[2]	38.0	38.2	37.7	48.9	58.4	53.9	62.0	59.9	68.8	61.5
Slovak Republic[1]	59.1	56.2	52.9	59.0	58.9	49.3	52.4	53.0	62.2	54.9
Slovenia[1]	22.4	22.2	22.4	26.3	25.5	24.8	29.3	30.6	34.5	32.0
Spain[2]	..	..	..	..	47.1	42.9	46.3	45.2	50.8	48.3
Sweden[2]	..	..	..	..	61.5	50.6	57.8	57.0	62.9	57.5
Switzerland[2]	..	..	..	..	..	99.6	113.0	140.1	172.4	165.5
Turkey[1]	22.3	24.2	16.4	21.8	16.0	19.7	18.5	17.3	23.1	19.1
United Kingdom	42.9	43.5	43.9	53.8	54.9	52.1	52.8	54.9	68.5	68.3
United States[1]	20.7	22.8	22.5	24.2	29.5	31.1	31.4	35.2	40.2	36.1
OECD total	**28.8**	**29.4**	**28.0**	**30.7**	**33.7**	**34.2**	**37.8**	**39.1**	**44.3**	**40.8**
European Union[4]	**41.1**	**41.3**	**39.8**	**45.4**	**46.7**	**45.1**	**54.4**	**53.5**	**61.1**	**56.4**
G20	**23.4**	**24.2**	**22.7**	**24.1**	**26.0**	**26.3**	**27.2**	**28.9**	**30.9**	**28.5**
of which:										
Non-OECD G20 countries	**24.5**	**25.4**	**22.9**	**23.0**	**23.0**	**22.6**	**23.0**	**25.0**	**23.1**	**21.3**
Argentina	23.3	20.1	17.4	17.0	14.4	15.8	12.4	13.4	12.6	14.0
Brazil	22.0	29.0	24.8	26.9	25.4	24.5	23.9	31.4	30.3	29.8
China	25.8	25.8	25.3	24.2	24.4	24.9	24.5	24.7	22.4	20.3
India	13.2	12.0	11.3	12.3	12.2	13.0	13.4	14.0	14.5	14.4
Indonesia	..	21.3	20.7	23.1	25.3	24.4	25.8	26.8	22.8	21.6
Russian Federation	27.9	28.3	19.9	19.8	20.5	14.1	19.2	30.7	28.0	25.9
Saudi Arabia	34.5	33.4	27.8	27.0	27.8	28.5	34.2	35.9	33.0	29.6
South Africa	46.9	47.8	38.3	41.3	41.5	39.6	39.9	45.7	44.7	37.6

.. Not available; | Break in series

Note: Detailed metadata at: *http://stats.oecd.org/OECDStat_Metadata/ShowMetadata.ashx?Dataset=FDI_AGGR_SUMM.*

1. Resident Special Purpose Entities (SPEs) are not present or not significant.
2. Data excludes Special Purpose Entities (SPEs).
3. Information on data for Israel: *http://oe.cd/israel-disclaimer.*
4. EU27 for 2007 to 2012 and EU28 as from 2013.

Source: OECD International Direct Investment Statistics (database): https://doi.org/10.1787/idi-data-en

Table 8. Foreign direct investment outward positions (stocks), as a percentage of GDP
At year end

Per cent

	2009	2010	2011	2012	2013	2014	2015	2016	2017	2018
Australia[1]	35.9	34.6	27.1	30.0	29.6	31.9	33.3	32.9	35.0	33.9
Austria[2]	44.2	47.9	46.2	52.7	55.4	50.7	55.1	51.3	57.5	52.5
Belgium[2]	..	..	..	..	108.5	104.5	127.8	127.6	142.7	110.2
Canada	64.9	61.7	49.7	53.2	61.2	62.4	71.5	84.3	92.5	79.8
Chile[2]	..	..	..	36.3	36.8	41.1	44.3	47.0	44.5	39.9
Czech Republic[1]	7.2	7.2	5.8	8.4	9.9	8.8	10.0	10.0	15.0	14.2
Denmark[2]	47.9	51.4	51.2	56.2	45.9	47.4	54.4	54.4	61.1	54.9
Estonia	31.9	28.4	20.7	26.3	27.2	23.4	23.4	26.3	29.3	26.1
Finland[1]	51.8	55.6	48.9	59.0	53.9 |	42.8	40.6	45.4	48.6	46.7
France[1]	41.7	44.4	43.6	47.4	47.2	45.4	52.0	52.0	56.7	54.3
Germany[1]	39.7	40.5	38.1	37.9 |	38.6	35.6	40.3	39.0	43.8	41.1
Greece[1]	12.0	14.2	16.7	18.3	15.1	13.7	13.9	9.2	9.9	9.0
Hungary[2]	17.6	18.0	19.6	30.6	29.5	28.9	23.9	19.9	21.5	19.7
Iceland[2]	77.3	83.8	76.0	83.6	59.3	47.4	43.9	29.4	21.5	20.3
Ireland	125.0	153.1	139.3	183.1 |	224.2	239.4	312.1	285.0	294.7	246.5
Israel[1, 3]	27.7	29.0	27.6	28.2	26.6	25.5	23.2	29.7	28.4	27.9
Italy[1]	22.2	22.9	22.7	25.6	24.9 |	22.1	24.9	24.3	28.0	26.6
Japan	14.2	14.6	15.5	16.7	21.7	23.8	23.0	26.7	30.8	31.5
Korea[2]	..	..	..	..	18.2	17.2	20.0	21.0	22.4	..
Latvia[1]	3.4	3.8	3.0	4.0	5.3	4.8	5.8	5.9	6.3	5.8
Lithuania	7.6	7.1	7.5	9.0	8.6	7.2	8.5	8.2	8.7	8.7
Luxembourg[2]	..	..	..	177.7	214.5	250.5	310.3	349.9	386.7	343.1
Mexico[2]	9.4	11.1	9.6	12.6	11.3	11.4	12.4	13.6	15.1	12.6
Netherlands[2]	111.2	114.4	110.2	119.4	130.9	180.9	265.5 |	281.5	304.3	260.5
New Zealand[1]	11.4	11.0	11.3	10.9	9.6	9.0	9.6	9.0	8.8	8.4
Norway[2]	..	..	..	..	34.8	32.5	44.7	52.1	50.4	45.2
Poland[2]	2.6	3.4	3.6	5.2	5.3	4.0	4.7	5.4	5.4	4.3
Portugal[2]	22.1	22.1	25.8	26.8	31.6	24.8	29.5	28.2	28.7	23.6
Slovak Republic[1]	3.5	3.9	4.1	5.1	4.9	2.8	2.8	2.9	4.8	4.3
Slovenia[1]	17.6	17.0	15.3	16.3	14.8	13.0	13.9	13.6	14.8	12.8
Spain[2]	..	..	..	..	42.2	37.9	42.3	40.2	43.6	38.4
Sweden[2]	..	..	..	..	70.9	65.0	67.3	65.6	68.5	66.6
Switzerland[2]	..	..	..	..	..	139.1	152.0	171.6	188.1	189.2
Turkey[1]	3.5	2.9	3.3	3.5	3.5	4.2	4.1	4.4	5.3	5.8
United Kingdom	68.6	68.7	65.6	63.3	65.2	55.4	55.4	59.0	67.2	63.3
United States[1]	29.9	32.1	29.0	32.2	37.3	36.1	33.2	34.3	40.1	31.4
OECD total	**36.6**	**37.8**	**35.3**	**37.9**	**41.4**	**40.8**	**44.0**	**45.0**	**50.5**	**44.6**
European Union[4]	**49.7**	**51.7**	**49.4**	**53.2**	**54.2**	**53.2**	**63.5**	**63.8**	**70.3**	**60.5**
G20	**26.0**	**25.8**	**23.4**	**24.8**	**27.2**	**26.6**	**27.4**	**28.7**	**32.4**	**28.6**
of which:										
Non-OECD G20 countries	**8.0**	**7.6**	**7.1**	**7.8**	**8.4**	**9.3**	**10.6**	**12.7**	**14.5**	**13.7**
Argentina	8.8	7.1	6.0	5.7	5.6	6.4	5.9	7.1	6.4	8.1
Brazil	8.0	6.8	6.1	8.3	8.2	8.6	10.3	11.3	11.7	10.9
China	4.8	5.2	5.6	6.2	6.9	8.5	9.9	12.2	14.9	14.0
India	6.2	5.7	6.0	6.5	6.5	6.5	6.6	6.3	6.0	6.2
Indonesia	..	0.9	0.7	1.4	2.1	2.9	3.4	6.3	6.5	7.0
Russian Federation	21.9	20.5	15.4	15.1	16.8	16.1	21.2	26.7	24.6	22.0
Saudi Arabia	5.3	5.0	4.5	4.7	5.3	5.9	9.6	11.5	12.3	13.4
South Africa	23.7	22.2	23.3	28.2	35.1	41.6	48.7	59.3	78.1	66.9

.. Not available; | Break in series

Note: Detailed metadata at: *http://stats.oecd.org/OECDStat_Metadata/ShowMetadata.ashx?Dataset=FDI_AGGR_SUMM.*

1. Resident Special Purpose Entities (SPEs) are not present or not significant.
2. Data excludes Special Purpose Entities (SPEs).
3. Information on data for Israel: *http://oe.cd/israel-disclaimer.*
4. EU27 for 2007 to 2012 and EU28 as from 2013.

Source: OECD International Direct Investment Statistics (database): https://doi.org/10.1787/idi-data-en

Table 9. Income on inward Foreign Direct Investment, US dollars

At year end

Million US dollars

	2009	2010	2011	2012	2013	2014	2015	2016	2017	2018
Australia[1]	26 176	39 894	45 666	35 683	33 996	29 806	24 066	27 528	37 319	44 418
Austria[2]	8 375	9 127	12 151	11 598	9 505	9 459	9 845	12 146	15 988	15 245
Belgium	14 951	32 634	24 464	27 461	26 890	34 389	28 819	33 268	26 434	36 634
Canada	26 856	40 075	45 524	48 209	47 319	47 786	34 640	31 001	37 795	41 472
Chile[2]	..	..	..	17 529	16 873	14 107	10 608	9 963	14 583	15 903
Czech Republic[1]	13 525	15 395	15 278	15 115	15 441	16 098	14 474	15 344	19 127	19 052
Denmark[2]	..	..	..	..	6 395	5 452	4 620	5 481	6 184	5 893
Estonia	1 022	1 639 |	2 053	1 818	1 846	1 916	1 385	1 591	1 712	1 869
Finland[1]	2 559	5 331	6 772	6 267	5 536 |	6 597	4 631	6 491	8 425	7 760
France[1]	21 024	29 143	19 745	30 551 |	26 824	24 900	26 923	29 484	33 001	32 750
Germany[1]	17 776	43 208	41 092	40 166	32 635 |	41 272	28 768	37 723	38 597	39 190
Greece[1]	674	-867	-2 139	-3 481	-332	522	1 157	1 150	1 452	1 552
Hungary[2]	5 708	6 714	7 955	7 530	6 828	9 484	8 855	7 682	10 581	10 917
Iceland[2]	-607	-249	116	751 |	-47 |	-47	31	-29	40	-26
Ireland	48 579	49 849	59 083	50 379 |	49 514	52 055	71 582	61 829	75 987	85 309
Israel[1, 3]	4 083	4 177	3 644	6 425	5 362	3 949	5 808	5 846	6 062	5 750
Italy[1]	17 663	16 725	20 810	12 486	10 059 |	11 199	11 685	14 147	19 621	20 315
Japan[1]	8 834	5 771	11 013	15 278	13 031	26 287 |	23 858	34 242	34 923	33 941
Korea[1]	..	..	..	..	7 580	-1 142	2 261	4 031	3 633	13 951
Latvia[1]	-1 428	188	633	1 004	1 077	1 040	1 155	1 187	1 399	1 872
Lithuania[1]	-1 066	516	1 558	1 245	1 184	684	1 642	1 722	1 980	2 242
Luxembourg[2]	..	..	..	8 364	8 525	12 833	11 694	14 051	12 002	10 395
Mexico[2]	9 186	9 970	14 346	19 292	30 337	22 278	18 121	17 120	18 473	22 197
Netherlands[2]	20 729	30 074	31 928	25 437	37 471 |	43 658	72 778	69 364	64 356	69 426
New Zealand[1]	3 555	4 722	5 819	6 185	6 758	7 330	5 849	5 534	7 207	6 952
Norway	11 377	13 477	16 400	17 688	15 179 |	7 757	6 038	7 061	10 943	12 677
Poland[1]	13 876	16 907	17 505	16 000	18 620	21 426	18 178	20 939	21 419	24 017
Portugal[2]	5 574	7 215	2 371	4 774	3 211	4 035	4 842	5 699	6 215	6 733
Slovak Republic[1]	3 562	5 102	6 279	4 079	3 297 |	3 949	4 421	4 411	4 330	4 774
Slovenia[1]	568 |	301	422	265	-1	-49	1 078	1 252	1 255	1 568
Spain	26 125	31 122	30 540	22 199	28 313	24 010	22 030	23 653	27 420	25 197
Sweden	16 789	23 256	21 430	19 443	21 065	23 603	22 053	21 836	22 166	24 105
Switzerland	36 566	35 947	36 212	40 637	33 750	73 369 |	59 800	70 912	98 751	105 010
Turkey[1]	2 933	2 871	2 931	2 655	3 678	2 363	3 563	3 137	3 280	3 198
United Kingdom	71 650	61 503	72 858	72 338	79 526	79 045	73 586	67 864	70 555	96 727
United States[1]	112 122	157 583	178 262	172 761	184 116	187 547	163 802	170 208	188 418	222 958
OECD total	**588 113**	**751 470**	**803 177**	**768 026**	**785 997**	**845 018**	**798 836**	**839 021**	**945 571**	**1 066 191**
European Union[4]	..	..	..	..	..	..	..	..	..	..
G20	..	..	..	..	..	..	..	..	..	..
of which:										
Non-OECD G20 countries	..	..	..	..	..	..	..	..	..	..
Argentina	..	..	..	..	..	..	..	..	..	..
Brazil	21 029	65 373	62 427	46 366	23 326	27 980	13 915	30 359	41 474	45 740
China	..	..	..	..	..	..	..	..	..	..
India	..	..	..	..	..	..	..	..	..	..
Indonesia	..	..	..	..	..	..	..	..	..	..
Russian Federation	..	..	..	..	..	..	..	..	..	..
Saudi Arabia	..	..	..	..	..	..	..	..	..	..
South Africa	..	..	..	..	..	..	..	..	..	..
World	..	..	..	..	..	..	..	..	..	..

.. Not available; | Break in series

Note: Detailed metadata at: *http://stats.oecd.org/OECDStat_Metadata/ShowMetadata.ashx?Dataset=FDI_AGGR_SUMM*.

1. Resident Special Purpose Entities (SPEs) are not present or not significant.
2. Data excludes Special Purpose Entities (SPEs).
3. Information on data for Israel: *http://oe.cd/israel-disclaimer*.
4. EU27 for 2007 to 2012 and EU28 as from 2013.

Source: OECD International Direct Investment Statistics (database): https://doi.org/10.1787/idi-data-en

Table 10. Income on outward Foreign Direct Investment, US dollars
At year end

Million US dollars

	2009	2010	2011	2012	2013	2014	2015	2016	2017	2018
Australia[1]	11 653	16 397	19 810	20 772	19 746	19 180	13 785	13 315	14 189	16 500
Austria[2]	9 780	12 644	15 127	13 963	14 106	11 648	10 823	15 536	15 260	16 648
Belgium	11 801	25 024	9 436	23 559	26 157	34 250	29 336	33 352	26 897	33 877
Canada	25 433	37 481	44 448	45 094	44 446	47 130	41 825	40 774	54 573	60 287
Chile[2]	..	..	..	4 170	4 398	5 384	3 779	3 379	4 074	4 203
Czech Republic[1]	820	1 093	1 187	2 251	1 320	1 589	1 861	2 015	4 665	2 975
Denmark[2]	..	..	..	..	12 430	13 709	12 126	12 027	12 996	14 022
Estonia	409	403 |	535	440	652	595	364	492	484	662
Finland[1]	8 576	10 946	10 698	10 144	7 867 |	10 942	7 373	7 889	8 837	10 208
France[1]	57 626	77 095	76 027	78 845 |	78 541	78 586	70 308	69 441	76 115	83 730
Germany[1]	66 596	83 489	101 941	81 156	89 600 |	89 590	84 951	97 529	100 267	113 620
Greece[1]	750	1 047	438	1 169	795	3 114	1 801	627	1 099	694
Hungary[2]	954	992	1 273	1 710	1 437	1 687	988	1 823	2 175	1 887
Iceland[2]	12	-27	572	-268 |	300 |	164	283	436	302	305
Ireland	12 805	18 989	21 295	13 905 |	16 389	17 675	11 765	14 640	17 470	15 297
Israel[1, 3]	2 648	3 720	4 517	4 194	4 239	5 188	6 575	6 453	5 955	7 639
Italy[1]	28 354	28 200	33 669	26 239	22 849 |	26 374	12 049	17 895	24 782	29 870
Japan[1]	45 814	38 261	58 880	68 079	68 225	100 236 |	96 359	110 503	120 301	125 065
Korea[1]	..	..	..	..	9 924	6 305	-124	9 055	10 259	13 066
Latvia[1]	-74	-29	58	82	97	54	153	117	218	158
Lithuania[1]	-38	60	56	100	165	120	135	145	150	300
Luxembourg[2]	..	..	..	7 192	6 831	6 200	4 646	5 588	6 457	5 731
Mexico[2]	2 027	6 567	6 904	6 779	8 076	7 332	3 430	3 193	4 764	5 228
Netherlands[2]	37 310	57 875	71 677	65 871	64 468 |	59 981	102 729	87 990	104 395	116 102
New Zealand[1]	190	594	342	679	572	707	511	741	523	373
Norway	3 875	10 944	8 263	11 065	8 667 |	13 770	9 073	6 772	8 408	12 005
Poland[1]	-1 142	528	-262	1 332	406	1 641	713	977	2 288	2 285
Portugal[2]	2 351	3 928	2 510	2 355	2 542	2 045	2 003	2 517	3 686	2 892
Slovak Republic[1]	511	495	441	216	273 |	811	350	206	391	371
Slovenia[1]	-146 |	-318	-54	-388	-552	-87	55	176	220	346
Spain	32 797	38 740	41 158	33 934	38 884	35 392	31 694	33 709	34 205	36 001
Sweden	24 569	34 394	33 851	32 720	34 882	36 148	26 830	25 633	30 744	32 957
Switzerland	48 231	72 271	49 358	64 148	61 238	90 614 |	91 013	90 756	99 840	106 142
Turkey[1]	182	681	220	98	273	314	224	202	298	957
United Kingdom	108 692	135 386	158 549	127 585	123 000	112 807	87 381	69 270	110 581	125 452
United States[1]	361 390	436 161	466 938	458 257	467 395	471 765	448 447	448 182	492 377	553 227
OECD total	**919 122**	**1 180 681**	**1 269 443**	**1 230 003**	**1 236 400**	**1 307 774**	**1 209 061**	**1 226 903**	**1 394 289**	**1 543 462**
European Union[4]	..	..	..	..	..	..	..	..	..	..
G20	..	..	..	..	..	..	..	..	..	..
of which:										
Non-OECD G20 countries	..	..	..	..	..	..	..	..	..	..
Argentina	..	..	..	..	..	..	-	..	..	..
Brazil	1 287	10 773	13 613	2 457	7 447	2 526	-2 398	7 878	17 332	4 835
China	..	..	..	..	..	..	-	..	..	..
India	..	..	..	..	..	..	-	..	..	..
Indonesia	..	..	..	..	..	..	-	..	..	..
Russian Federation	..	..	..	..	..	..	-	..	..	..
Saudi Arabia	..	..	..	..	..	..	-	..	..	..
South Africa	..	..	..	..	..	..	-	..	..	..
World	..	..	..	..	..	..	..	..	..	..

.. Not available; | Break in series

Note: Detailed metadata at: *http://stats.oecd.org/OECDStat_Metadata/ShowMetadata.ashx?Dataset=FDI_AGGR_SUMM.*

1. Resident Special Purpose Entities (SPEs) are not present or not significant.
2. Data excludes Special Purpose Entities (SPEs).
3. Information on data for Israel: *http://oe.cd/israel-disclaimer.*
4. EU27 for 2007 to 2012 and EU28 as from 2013.

Source: OECD International Direct Investment Statistics (database): https://doi.org/10.1787/idi-data-en

Table 11. Income on inward Foreign Direct Investment as a percentage of GDP
At year end

Per cent

	2009	2010	2011	2012	2013	2014	2015	2016	2017	2018
Australia[1]	2.6	3.1	3.0	2.2	2.2	2.0	1.9	2.1	2.6	3.1
Austria[2]	2.1	2.3	2.8	2.8	2.2	2.1	2.6	3.1	3.8	3.3
Belgium	3.1	6.7	4.6	5.5	5.2	6.5	6.3	7.1	5.3	6.9
Canada	2.0	2.5	2.5	2.6	2.6	2.6	2.2	2.0	2.3	2.4
Chile[2]	..	..	..	6.6	6.1	5.4	4.3	4.0	5.3	5.3
Czech Republic[1]	6.6	7.4	6.7	7.3	7.4	7.7	7.7	7.9	8.9	7.8
Denmark[2]	..	..	..	..	1.9	1.5	1.5	1.8	1.9	1.7
Estonia	5.2	8.4 |	8.9	7.9	7.3	7.2	6.0	6.6	6.4	6.2
Finland[1]	1.0	2.2	2.5	2.4	2.1 |	2.4	2.0	2.7	3.3	2.8
France[1]	0.8	1.1	0.7	1.1 |	1.0	0.9	1.1	1.2	1.3	1.2
Germany[1]	0.5	1.3	1.1	1.1	0.9 |	1.1	0.9	1.1	1.0	1.0
Greece[1]	0.2	-0.3	-0.7	-1.4	-0.1	0.2	0.6	0.6	0.7	0.7
Hungary[2]	4.4	5.1	5.7	5.9	5.0	6.8	7.2	6.1	7.6	7.0
Iceland[2]	-4.6	-1.8	0.8	5.1 |	-0.3 |	-0.3	0.2	-0.1	0.2	-0.1
Ireland	20.6	22.4	24.9	22.4 |	20.8	20.1	24.6	20.6	22.7	22.3
Israel[1, 3]	2.0	1.8	1.4	2.5	1.8	1.3	1.9	1.8	1.7	1.6
Italy[1]	0.8	0.8	0.9	0.6	0.5 |	0.5	0.6	0.8	1.0	1.0
Japan[1]	0.2	0.1	0.2	0.2	0.3	0.5 |	0.5	0.7	0.7	0.7
Korea[1]	..	..	..	..	0.6	-0.1	0.2	0.3	0.2	0.9
Latvia[1]	-5.5	0.8	2.2	3.6	3.6	3.3	4.3	4.3	4.6	5.4
Lithuania[1]	-2.8	1.4	3.6	2.9	2.6	1.4	4.0	4.0	4.2	4.2
Luxembourg[2]	..	..	..	14.8	13.8	19.4	20.3	23.2	18.7	14.7
Mexico[2]	1.0	0.9	1.2	1.6	2.4	1.7	1.5	1.6	1.6	1.8
Netherlands[2]	2.4	3.6	3.5	3.0	4.3 |	4.9	9.5	8.9	7.7	7.6
New Zealand[1]	2.9	3.2	3.5	3.5	3.5	3.6	3.3	2.9	3.6	3.4
Norway	2.9	3.1	3.3	3.5	2.9 |	1.6	1.6	1.9	2.7	2.9
Poland[1]	3.2	3.5	3.3	3.2	3.6	3.9	3.8	4.4	4.1	4.1
Portugal[2]	2.3	3.0	1.0	2.2	1.4	1.8	2.4	2.8	2.8	2.8
Slovak Republic[1]	4.0	5.7	6.4	4.4	3.3 |	3.9	5.0	4.9	4.5	4.5
Slovenia[1]	1.1 |	0.6	0.8	0.6	0.0	-0.1	2.5	2.8	2.6	2.9
Spain	1.8	2.2	2.1	1.7	2.1	1.8	1.8	1.9	2.1	1.8
Sweden	3.9	4.7	3.7	3.5	3.6	4.1	4.4	4.2	4.1	4.3
Switzerland	6.8	6.2	5.2	6.1	4.9	10.3 |	8.8	10.6	14.5	14.9
Turkey[1]	0.5	0.4	0.4	0.3	0.4	0.3	0.4	0.4	0.4	0.4
United Kingdom	3.0	2.5	2.8	2.7	2.9	2.6	2.5	2.6	2.7	3.4
United States[1]	0.8	1.1	1.1	1.1	1.1	1.1	0.9	0.9	1.0	1.1
OECD total	**1.4**	**1.7**	**1.7**	**1.6**	**1.6**	**1.7**	**1.7**	**1.7**	**1.9**	**1.9**
European Union[4]	..	..	..	..	..	..	..	..	..	..
G20	..	..	..	..	..	..	..	..	..	..
of which:										
Non-OECD G20 countries	..	..	..	..	..	..	..	..	..	..
Argentina	..	..	..	..	..	..	..	..	..	..
Brazil	1.3	3.0	2.4	1.9	0.9	1.1	0.8	1.7	2.0	2.4
China	..	..	..	..	..	..	..	..	..	..
India	..	..	..	..	..	..	..	..	..	..
Indonesia	..	..	..	..	..	..	..	..	..	..
Russian Federation	..	..	..	..	..	..	..	..	..	..
Saudi Arabia	..	..	..	..	..	..	..	..	..	..
South Africa	..	..	..	..	..	..	..	..	..	..

.. Not available; | Break in series

Note: Detailed metadata at: *http://stats.oecd.org/OECDStat_Metadata/ShowMetadata.ashx?Dataset=FDI_AGGR_SUMM.*

1. Resident Special Purpose Entities (SPEs) are not present or not significant.
2. Data excludes Special Purpose Entities (SPEs).
3. Information on data for Israel: *http://oe.cd/israel-disclaimer.*
4. EU27 for 2007 to 2012 and EU28 as from 2013.

Source: OECD International Direct Investment Statistics (database): https://doi.org/10.1787/idi-data-en

Table 12. Income on outward Foreign Direct Investment as a percentage of GDP

At year end

Per cent

	2009	2010	2011	2012	2013	2014	2015	2016	2017	2018
Australia[1]	1.1	1.3	1.3	1.3	1.3	1.3	1.1	1.0	1.0	1.1
Austria[2]	2.4	3.2	3.5	3.4	3.3	2.6	2.8	3.9	3.7	3.7
Belgium	2.4	5.2	1.8	4.7	5.0	6.5	6.4	7.1	5.4	6.4
Canada	1.9	2.3	2.5	2.5	2.4	2.6	2.7	2.7	3.3	3.5
Chile[2]	..	..	..	1.6	1.6	2.1	1.5	1.3	1.5	1.4
Czech Republic[1]	0.4	0.5	0.5	1.1	0.6	0.8	1.0	1.0	2.2	1.2
Denmark[2]	..	..	..	..	3.6	3.9	4.0	3.9	3.9	4.0
Estonia	2.1	2.1 |	2.3	1.9	2.6	2.2	1.6	2.1	1.8	2.3
Finland[1]	3.4	4.4	3.9	4.0	2.9 |	4.0	3.2	3.3	3.5	3.7
France[1]	2.1	2.9	2.7	2.9 |	2.8	2.8	2.9	2.8	2.9	3.0
Germany[1]	1.9	2.4	2.7	2.3	2.4 |	2.3	2.5	2.8	2.7	2.8
Greece[1]	0.2	0.3	0.2	0.5	0.3	1.3	0.9	0.3	0.5	0.3
Hungary[2]	0.7	0.8	0.9	1.3	1.1	1.2	0.8	1.4	1.6	1.2
Iceland[2]	0.1	-0.2	3.8	-1.8 |	1.9 |	0.9	1.6	2.1	1.2	1.2
Ireland	5.4	8.5	9.0	6.2 |	6.9	6.8	4.0	4.9	5.2	4.0
Israel[1, 3]	1.3	1.6	1.7	1.6	1.4	1.7	2.2	2.0	1.7	2.1
Italy[1]	1.3	1.3	1.5	1.3	1.1 |	1.2	0.7	1.0	1.3	1.4
Japan[1]	0.9	0.7	1.0	1.1	1.3	2.1 |	2.2	2.2	2.5	2.5
Korea[1]	..	..	..	..	0.8	0.4	0.0	0.6	0.7	0.8
Latvia[1]	-0.3	-0.1	0.2	0.3	0.3	0.2	0.6	0.4	0.7	0.5
Lithuania[1]	-0.1	0.2	0.1	0.2	0.4	0.2	0.3	0.3	0.3	0.6
Luxembourg[2]	..	..	..	12.7	11.1	9.4	8.0	9.2	10.1	8.1
Mexico[2]	0.2	0.6	0.6	0.6	0.6	0.6	0.3	0.3	0.4	0.4
Netherlands[2]	4.3	6.8	7.9	7.9	7.4 |	6.7	13.4	11.2	12.6	12.7
New Zealand[1]	0.2	0.4	0.2	0.4	0.3	0.4	0.3	0.4	0.3	0.2
Norway	1.0	2.6	1.7	2.2	1.7 |	2.8	2.4	1.8	2.1	2.8
Poland[1]	-0.3	0.1	0.0	0.3	0.1	0.3	0.2	0.2	0.4	0.4
Portugal[2]	1.0	1.7	1.0	1.1	1.1	0.9	1.0	1.2	1.7	1.2
Slovak Republic[1]	0.6	0.6	0.4	0.2	0.3 |	0.8	0.4	0.2	0.4	0.3
Slovenia[1]	-0.3 |	-0.7	-0.1	-0.8	-1.1	-0.2	0.1	0.4	0.5	0.6
Spain	2.2	2.7	2.8	2.6	2.9	2.6	2.7	2.7	2.6	2.5
Sweden	5.6	6.9	5.9	5.9	6.0	6.2	5.3	5.0	5.7	5.9
Switzerland	8.9	12.4	7.1	9.6	8.9	12.8 |	13.4	13.5	14.7	15.1
Turkey[1]	0.0	0.1	0.0	0.0	0.0	0.0	0.0	0.0	0.0	0.1
United Kingdom	4.5	5.5	6.0	4.8	4.5	3.7	3.0	2.6	4.2	4.4
United States[1]	2.5	2.9	3.0	2.8	2.8	2.7	2.5	2.4	2.5	2.7
OECD total	**2.2**	**2.6**	**2.7**	**2.5**	**2.5**	**2.6**	**2.6**	**2.6**	**2.8**	**2.9**
European Union[4]	..	..	..	..	..	..	..	..	..	..
G20	..	..	..	..	..	..	..	..	..	..
of which:										
Non-OECD G20 countries	..	..	..	..	..	..	..	..	..	..
Argentina	..	..	..	..	..	..	..	..	..	..
Brazil	0.1	0.5	0.5	0.1	0.3	0.1	-0.1	0.4	0.8	0.3
China	..	..	..	..	..	..	..	..	..	..
India	..	..	..	..	..	..	..	..	..	..
Indonesia	..	..	..	..	..	..	..	..	..	..
Russian Federation	..	..	..	..	..	..	..	..	..	..
Saudi Arabia	..	..	..	..	..	..	..	..	..	..
South Africa	..	..	..	..	..	..	..	..	..	..

.. Not available; | Break in series

Note: Detailed metadata at: *http://stats.oecd.org/OECDStat_Metadata/ShowMetadata.ashx?Dataset=FDI_AGGR_SUMM.*

1. Resident Special Purpose Entities (SPEs) are not present or not significant.
2. Data excludes Special Purpose Entities (SPEs).
3. Information on data for Israel: *http://oe.cd/israel-disclaimer.*
4. EU27 for 2007 to 2012 and EU28 as from 2013.

Source: OECD International Direct Investment Statistics (database): https://doi.org/10.1787/idi-data-en

Country tables

AUSTRALIA

Table 1. Foreign direct investment flows by country

Million US dollars

	Inward					Outward				
	2014	2015	2016	2017	2018	2014	2015	2016	2017	2018
WORLD	**58 504.6**	**28 274.1**	**45 519.2**	**42 289.1**	**60 425.0**	**18 183.7**	**-10 220.2**	**327.8**	**3 319.8**	**3 634.1**
OECD COUNTRIES	**21 283.6**	**19 891.1**	**35 529.6**	**31 135.0**	**49 136.5**	**8 640.7**	**-7 840.6**	**8 789.1**	**10 137.9**	**14 741.2**
Australia	-	-	-	-	-	-	-	-	-	-
Austria	.. c	.. c	.. c	.. c	.. c	.. c	.. c	.. c	.. c	.. c
Belgium	-658.9	-502.7	219.3	-115.0	424.3	.. c	.. c	-3.7	3.8	.. c
Canada	4 852.2	1 758.2	1 297.1	2 183.3	2 928.2	.. c	-530.5	209.6	869.8	5 186.4
Chile	.. c	.. c	.. c	.. c	-	108.2	136.0	37.9	94.3	114.3
Czech Republic	-1.8	0.8	-2.2	-0.8	.. c	.. c	3.0	.. c	.. c	-2.2
Denmark	.. c	.. c	.. c	.. c	85.2	.. c	.. c	.. c	-4.6	.. c
Estonia	.. c	.. c	.. c	-	-	.. c	.. c	.. c	.. c	.. c
Finland	.. c	.. c	.. c	.. c	133.7	.. c	.. c	3.0	-2.3	.. c
France	443.5	314.1	37.9	470.5	16 575.0	.. c	93.9	406.6	11.5	469.1
Germany	921.2	661.2	579.1	1 226.9	1 542.5	-729.2	.. c	507.7	570.9	599.1
Greece	.. c	.. c	.. c	.. c	.. c	.. c	.. c	.. c	.. c	.. c
Hungary	.. c	1.5	-0.7	.. c	.. c	.. c	.. c	.. c	.. c	.. c
Iceland	.. c	-	.. c	-	-	-	-	-	-	-
Ireland	96.4	2 356.3	-15.6	-1 612.4	233.8	.. c	-98.4	5.9	-226.8	3.7
Israel[1]	7.2	9.0	.. c	.. c	3.7	-	-	-	.. c	.. c
Italy	-36.1	.. c	-91.4	25.3	-94.9	.. c	.. c	1.5	.. c	2.2
Japan	-	10 058.6	-	-	-	-	33.1	-	-	-
Korea	446.2	7.5	839.2	.. c	702.2	.. c	20.3	.. c	.. c	308.5
Latvia	-	-	-	-	-	-	-	-	-	-
Lithuania	-	-	.. c	.. c	-	-	-	-	-	-
Luxembourg	-29.7	-220.9	2 732.5	2 544.3	-476.6	.. c	.. c	.. c	.. c	91.9
Mexico	-0.9	0.8	-	.. c	.. c	5.4	61.6	.. c	.. c	-65.7
Netherlands	8 265.7	2 494.6	2 028.5	3 197.2	-5 051.2	811.2	.. c	.. c	.. c	511.7
New Zealand	-262.3	369.7	681.6	-44.4	770.2	82.0	-232.9	899.4	846.0	-778.4
Norway	.. c	-0.8	.. c	-76.6	-44.1	.. c	.. c	.. c	.. c	.. c
Poland	1.8	-	.. c	.. c	-1.5	-2.7	.. c	.. c	.. c	.. c
Portugal	-	.. c	-	.. c	.. c	.. c	.. c	.. c	-	.. c
Slovak Republic	-	-	.. c	.. c	-	.. c	.. c	.. c	.. c	.. c
Slovenia	.. c	.. c	-	-	-	.. c	.. c	.. c	.. c	.. c
Spain	.. c	2.3	-4.5	-1.5	2.2	-	.. c	.. c	.. c	7.5
Sweden	559.8	200.6	85.5	50.6	281.6	.. c	.. c	.. c	-6.1	-40.3
Switzerland	-8 343.2	728.8	78.8	345.6	825.4	.. c	.. c	.. c	.. c	.. c
Turkey	-0.9	-	-	.. c	.. c	.. c	.. c	.. c	.. c	2.2
United Kingdom	-692.3	-11 857.4	12 071.7	11 205.5	8 396.2	4 543.9	4 970.3	643.7	2 089.8	9 566.7
United States	10 389.4	13 306.8	8 015.3	6 559.9	16 327.8	261.4	-6 173.3	5 045.7	2 879.1	643.9
EUROPE	..	..	..	..	..	..	..	..	..	..
Bulgaria	.. c	.. c	.. c	.. c	.. c	.. c	.. c	.. c	.. c	.. c
Croatia	.. c	.. c	.. c	.. c	.. c	.. c	.. c	.. c	.. c	.. c
Cyprus[2, 3]	.. c	.. c	.. c	-	-	.. c	.. c	.. c	-	.. c
Malta	.. c	.. c	.. c	-	.. c	-	-	.. c	.. c	.. c
Romania	.. c	.. c	.. c	-	-	.. c	.. c	0.7	.. c	.. c
Russian Federation	.. c	.. c	.. c	.. c	.. c	.. c	-0.8	10.4	.. c	29.9
Ukraine	-	-	-	-	-	.. c	.. c	.. c	.. c	.. c
AFRICA	..	..	..	..	..	..	..	..	..	..
Northern Africa	..	..	..	..	..	..	..	..	..	..
Algeria	.. c	.. c	.. c	.. c	.. c	-	-	-	-	-
Egypt	.. c	.. c	.. c	.. c	.. c	.. c	.. c	.. c	.. c	.. c
Libya	-	-	-	-	-	.. c	.. c	.. c	.. c	.. c
Morocco	.. c	.. c	.. c	.. c	-	.. c	.. c	.. c	.. c	-
Tunisia	.. c	.. c	.. c	.. c	.. c	-	-	-	-	-
Other African countries	..	..	..	..	..	..	..	..	..	..
Nigeria	.. c	.. c	.. c	.. c	.. c	.. c	.. c	.. c	.. c	.. c
South Africa	.. c	268.2	.. c	341.8	144.9	-233.5	54.1	-26.0	38.3	-156.9
AMERICA	..	..	..	..	..	..	..	..	..	..
Northern America	..	..	..	..	..	..	..	..	..	..
Central America and Caribbean countries	..	..	..	..	..	..	..	..	..	..
Bahamas	.. c	-11.3	.. c	.. c	.. c	.. c	.. c	.. c	.. c	.. c
Bermuda	.. c	.. c	952.9	3 476.9	2 911.0	.. c	.. c	-356.1	.. c	-7.5
Cayman Islands	.. c	.. c	.. c	49.0	-617.8	.. c	.. c	.. c	.. c	-895.6
Costa Rica	.. c	.. c	.. c	-	-	.. c	.. c	.. c	.. c	.. c
El Salvador	-	-	-	-	-	.. c	.. c	.. c	.. c	.. c
Guatemala	-	-	-	-	-	.. c	.. c	.. c	.. c	.. c
Honduras	-	-	-	-	-	-	-	.. c	.. c	.. c
Nicaragua	-	-	-	-	-	.. c	.. c	-	.. c	.. c
Panama	-	-	.. c	.. c	.. c	.. c	.. c	.. c	.. c	.. c
Virgin Islands, U.S.	-	-	-	.. c	.. c	-	-	-	-	-
South America	..	..	..	..	..	..	..	..	..	..
Argentina	.. c	.. c	.. c	-2.3	.. c	.. c	-48.1	.. c	.. c	-1.5
Bolivia	-	-	-	-	-	.. c	.. c	.. c	.. c	.. c
Brazil	-1.8	.. c	.. c	-6.1	.. c	595.8	450.1	124.1	334.9	-44.1
Colombia	.. c	.. c	.. c	.. c	.. c	.. c	12.0	-12.6	.. c	-38.8
Ecuador	-	-	-	-	-	.. c	.. c	.. c	29.1	.. c
Paraguay	-	-	-	-	-	-	-	-	-	-
Peru	.. c	.. c	.. c	.. c	.. c	.. c	21.8	.. c	.. c	15.7
Uruguay	-	-	-	-	-	.. c	.. c	.. c	.. c	.. c
Venezuela	.. c	.. c	.. c	.. c	.. c	.. c	.. c	.. c	.. c	.. c

AUSTRALIA

Table 1. Foreign direct investment flows by country *(cont.)*

Million US dollars

	Inward					Outward				
	2014	2015	2016	2017	2018	2014	2015	2016	2017	2018
ASIA	..	..	..	..	..	..	..	..	..	..
Near and Middle East	..	..	..	..	..	..	..	..	..	..
Gulf Arabian countries	..	..	..	..	..	..	..	..	..	..
Kuwait	.. c	1 813.1	.. c	.. c	.. c	.. c	.. c	.. c	.. c	.. c
Qatar	.. c	.. c	.. c	.. c	.. c	.. c	.. c	.. c	-	.. c
Saudi Arabia	.. c	-6.8	-89.9	.. c	.. c	-26.1	.. c	.. c	.. c	10.5
United Arab Emirates	.. c	-3 606.6	-136.0	95.0	90.4	-151.4	-335.1	19.3	.. c	127.0
Other Near and Middle East	..	..	..	..	..	..	..	..	..	..
Jordan	.. c	.. c	.. c	.. c	.. c	.. c	.. c	-	-	.. c
Other Asian countries	..	..	..	..	..	..	..	..	..	..
China	8 883.2	2 179.0	1 506.0	700.4	2 619.7	599.4	457.6	-266.9	-1 629.2	637.2
Hong Kong, China	2 530.2	2 409.6	1 089.0	1 851.5	568.5	589.5	-171.3	-487.6	234.5	35.9
India	21.6	-82.7	44.6	26.8	27.6	49.6	81.1	50.5	84.3	29.9
Indonesia	.. c	-16.5	7.4	.. c	1.5	94.6	-37.6	56.5	136.4	.. c
Iran, Islamic Republic of	.. c	.. c	.. c	.. c	.. c	-	-	-	-	-
Malaysia	521.9	740.1	131.6	1 056.0	121.8	560.7	240.4	176.2	68.2	67.2
Philippines	.. c	.. c	-	-7.7	-48.6	.. c	43.6	61.0	66.7	61.3
Singapore	3 868.8	355.4	-3 725.6	1 781.0	1 972.1	1 236.7	1 828.8	159.8	114.2	-238.3
Chinese Taipei	-7.2	15.0	-5.2	29.1	25.4	.. c	.. c	-7.4	.. c	.. c
Thailand	.. c	.. c	.. c	494.3	-146.4	-5.4	.. c	6.7	87.4	-0.7
Viet Nam	-2.7	-4.5	3.0	-1.5	1.5	168.6	23.3	6.7	28.4	.. c
AUSTRALIA, OCEANIA AND POLAR REGIONS	..	..	..	..	..	..	..	..	..	..
WORLD unallocated and confidential	**25 918.5**	**2 488.5**	**16 829.7**	**7 280.3**	**7 786.7**	**9 352.8**	**-11 191.7**	**-6 668.4**	**-3 400.3**	**-11 854.0**
European Union (EU28)	**3 252.2**	**-6 080.1**	**17 052.7**	**17 074.1**	**22 311.9**	**5 844.6**	**4 944.8**	**2 627.7**	**2 051.5**	**11 290.1**
G20 countries excl. European Union	**.. d**	**.. d**	**.. d**	**.. d**	**.. d**	**.. d**	**.. d**	**.. d**	**.. d**	**.. d**
G20 OECD countries	**16 322.3**	**.. d**	**22 748.8**	**.. d**	**.. d**	**.. d**	**.. d**	**.. d**	**.. d**	**16 712.5**
G20 Non-OECD countries	**.. d**	**.. d**	**.. d**	**.. d**	**.. d**	**.. d**	**.. d**	**.. d**	**.. d**	**.. d**
MENA countries	**.. d**	**.. d**	**.. d**	**.. d**	**.. d**	**.. d**	**.. d**	**.. d**	**.. d**	**.. d**
ASEAN countries	**4 156.3**	**1 475.7**	**-4 306.8**	**3 319.8**	**1 906.3**	**1 992.1**	**2 585.5**	**596.9**	**862.9**	**-3 460.8**

- Nil; .. Not available; c Confidential data; d Secondary Confidentiality

Note: Detailed metadata at: *http://stats.oecd.org/OECDStat_Metadata/ShowMetadata.ashx?Dataset=FDI_CTRY_IND_SUMM.*

1. Information on data for Israel: *http://oe.cd/israel-disclaimer.*
2. Note by Turkey: The information in this document with reference to "Cyprus" relates to the southern part of the Island. There is no single authority representing both Turkish and Greek Cypriot people on the Island. Turkey recognises the Turkish Republic of Northern Cyprus (TRNC). Until a lasting and equitable solution is found within the context of the United Nations, Turkey shall preserve its position concerning the "Cyprus issue".
3. Note by all the European Union Member States of the OECD and the European Union: The Republic of Cyprus is recognised by all members of the United Nations with the exception of Turkey. The information in this document relates to the area under the effective control of the Government of the Republic of Cyprus.

Source: OECD International Direct Investment Statistics (database): https://doi.org/10.1787/idi-data-en

Table 2. Foreign direct investment positions by country

At year end

Million US dollars

	Inward					Outward				
	2014	2015	2016	2017	2018	2014	2015	2016	2017	2018
WORLD	**582 533.1**	**565 804.0**	**606 131.0**	**689 369.0**	**682 880.4**	**467 167.1**	**415 412.4**	**432 015.2**	**495 952.0**	**490 996.6**
OECD COUNTRIES	**357 272.6**	**346 867.8**	**372 811.9**	**422 229.2**	**427 271.3**	**266 715.1**	**217 044.6**	**225 117.2**	**262 070.8**	**269 202.4**
Australia	-	-	-	-	-	-	-	-	-	-
Austria	.. c	.. c	.. c	.. c	.. c	.. c	.. c	.. c	.. c	.. c
Belgium	3 304.6	3 659.7	4 025.3	4 106.5	3 797.3	562.7	.. c	.. c	.. c	.. c
Canada	18 616.1	18 120.8	20 133.1	25 095.5	26 064.4	9 937.5	5 768.2	5 894.4	8 196.7	23 866.5
Chile	-5.7	.. c	.. c	.. c	.. c	1 218.0	.. c	1 159.2	1 259.7	1 289.5
Czech Republic	2.5	3.7	1.4	.. c	1.4	.. c	.. c	.. c	.. c	.. c
Denmark	.. c	.. c	.. c	.. c	723.5	.. c	3.7	.. c	.. c	.. c
Estonia	.. c	.. c	-	-	-	.. c	.. c	.. c	.. c	.. c
Finland	.. c	.. c	.. c	.. c	253.4	8.2	.. c	3.6	4.7	.. c
France	4 701.4	4 670.1	4 428.4	5 053.4	20 285.9	.. c	1 596.4	1 895.1	1 879.7	2 227.6
Germany	12 946.9	12 418.4	14 141.1	18 725.5	17 150.6	12 580.2	.. c	.. c	.. c	.. c
Greece	.. c	.. c	.. c	.. c	.. c	.. c	.. c	.. c	.. c	18.4
Hungary	.. c	.. c	.. c	-	0.7	.. c	.. c	.. c	.. c	.. c
Iceland	-	-	-	-	-	-	-	-	-	-
Ireland	648.8	3 016.0	2 925.5	1 514.7	1 302.2	.. c	.. c	.. c	-373.6	.. c
Israel[1]	.. c	.. c	.. c	.. c	.. c	-	-	-	.. c	.. c
Italy	770.2	.. c	430.5	537.4	427.7	.. c	101.6	112.9	178.6	.. c
Japan	-	67 160.8	-	-	-	-	.. c	-	-	-
Korea	2 593.5	2 321.9	3 159.9	3 572.3	3 662.5	554.5	.. c	589.7	669.2	818.0
Latvia	-	-	-	-	-	-	-	-	-	-
Lithuania	-	-	.. c	.. c	.. c	-	-	-	-	-
Luxembourg	2 409.7	2 045.0	4 592.6	7 355.1	6 294.5	.. c	1 296.1	1 191.8	1 783.0	.. c
Mexico	-	.. c	-	1.6	2.8	.. c	895.0	1 041.2	723.0	609.8
Netherlands	32 892.5	35 093.9	37 277.9	43 685.4	34 769.9	6 997.1	5 552.7	5 845.9	5 343.6	5 441.1
New Zealand	4 185.5	4 087.8	4 280.0	4 463.8	4 623.8	49 382.6	43 426.6	48 036.2	48 724.7	39 808.7
Norway	767.7	678.7	619.4	639.6	460.2	.. c	.. c	.. c	.. c	.. c
Poland	.. c	.. c	0.7	3.1	1.4	.. c	.. c	.. c	33.5	33.2
Portugal	-	.. c	.. c	-	.. c	.. c	2.9	8.7	10.1	8.5
Slovak Republic	-	-	.. c	-	-	.. c	.. c	.. c	.. c	.. c
Slovenia	.. c	-	-	-	-	.. c	.. c	.. c	.. c	.. c
Spain	.. c	.. c	.. c	.. c	.. c	.. c	.. c	31.8	28.1	33.2
Sweden	1 525.6	1 500.0	1 516.6	1 624.7	1 657.3	.. c	212.6	266.3	292.5	.. c
Switzerland	6 505.0	6 639.1	6 694.6	7 332.5	7 159.8	.. c	.. c	.. c	.. c	281.6
Turkey	.. c	.. c	.. c	.. c	.. c	.. c	.. c	91.2	.. c	.. c
United Kingdom	64 452.1	47 426.0	54 065.1	67 964.3	69 697.2	63 926.4	62 808.5	57 480.5	69 585.8	83 750.7
United States	134 238.0	134 369.8	140 751.1	150 932.8	151 250.0	109 386.8	79 378.2	87 319.1	99 532.8	85 163.0
EUROPE	..	..	..	..	..	..	..	..	..	..
Bulgaria	.. c	.. c	.. c	.. c	.. c	.. c	.. c	.. c	.. c	.. c
Croatia	.. c	.. c	-	.. c	-	.. c	.. c	.. c	.. c	.. c
Cyprus[2, 3]	.. c	.. c	-	-	-	.. c	.. c	.. c	.. c	.. c
Malta	.. c	.. c	-	-	-	.. c	.. c	.. c	.. c	.. c
Romania	.. c	.. c	.. c	.. c	.. c	.. c	.. c	.. c	.. c	.. c
Russian Federation	.. c	.. c	.. c	.. c	3.5	.. c	.. c	36.2	.. c	189.9
Ukraine	-	-	-	-	-	.. c	.. c	.. c	.. c	.. c
AFRICA	..	..	..	..	..	..	..	..	..	..
Northern Africa	..	..	..	..	..	..	..	..	..	..
Algeria	.. c	.. c	.. c	.. c	.. c	-	-	-	-	-
Egypt	.. c	.. c	.. c	.. c	.. c	.. c	.. c	5.8	.. c	.. c
Libya	-	-	-	-	-	.. c	.. c	.. c	-0.8	.. c
Morocco	.. c	.. c	.. c	-	-	.. c	.. c	-	.. c	.. c
Tunisia	.. c	.. c	.. c	.. c	-	.. c	.. c	.. c	.. c	.. c
Other African countries	..	..	..	..	..	..	..	..	..	..
Nigeria	.. c	.. c	.. c	.. c	.. c	.. c	.. c	.. c	.. c	.. c
South Africa	2 424.5	2 134.9	2 556.4	2 609.0	2 486.6	668.5	853.4	875.5	2 166.8	893.6
AMERICA	..	..	..	..	..	..	..	..	..	..
Northern America	..	..	..	..	..	..	..	..	..	..
Central America and Caribbean countries	..	..	..	..	..	..	..	..	..	..
Bahamas	903.0	.. c	1 424.0	1 511.6	.. c	.. c	.. c	.. c	.. c	.. c
Bermuda	33 679.9	26 103.6	25 310.4	29 872.9	28 077.4	.. c	24 097.3	24 045.6	.. c	.. c
Cayman Islands	1 919.3	1 869.7	4 119.4	4 390.5	3 318.7	.. c	.. c	.. c	.. c	.. c
Costa Rica	.. c	.. c	-	-	-	.. c	.. c	.. c	.. c	.. c
El Salvador	-	-	-	-	-	.. c	.. c	.. c	.. c	.. c
Guatemala	-	-	-	-	-	.. c	.. c	.. c	.. c	.. c
Honduras	-	-	-	-	-	-	-	.. c	.. c	.. c
Nicaragua	-	-	-	-	-	.. c	-	-	.. c	.. c
Panama	-	-	-	.. c	-	.. c	.. c	.. c	.. c	.. c
Virgin Islands, U.S.	-	-	-	.. c	-	-	-	-	-	-
South America	..	..	..	..	..	..	..	..	..	..
Argentina	.. c	.. c	.. c	.. c	.. c	155.0	174.6	170.8	287.8	.. c
Bolivia	-	-	-	-	-	.. c	.. c	.. c	.. c	.. c
Brazil	.. c	.. c	.. c	.. c	.. c	.. c	3 023.3	3 217.1	.. c	3 208.6
Colombia	.. c	.. c	.. c	.. c	.. c	107.4	.. c	91.9	157.6	152.5
Ecuador	-	-	-	-	-	.. c	.. c	.. c	103.0	.. c
Paraguay	-	-	-	-	-	-	-	-	-	-
Peru	.. c	.. c	.. c	.. c	.. c	146.8	157.8	200.4	232.4	223.0
Uruguay	-	-	-	-	-	.. c	.. c	4.3	.. c	.. c
Venezuela	.. c	.. c	.. c	.. c	.. c	.. c	.. c	.. c	.. c	.. c

Table 2. Foreign direct investment positions by country *(cont.)*

At year end

Million US dollars

	Inward					Outward				
	2014	2015	2016	2017	2018	2014	2015	2016	2017	2018
ASIA	..	..	..	..	..	..	..	..	..	..
Near and Middle East	..	..	..	..	..	..	..	..	..	..
Gulf Arabian countries	..	..	..	..	..	..	..	..	..	..
Kuwait	.. c	.. c	.. c	.. c	.. c	.. c	.. c	.. c	.. c	.. c
Qatar	.. c	.. c	.. c	.. c	.. c	.. c	-0.7	-2.9	-3.1	-2.8
Saudi Arabia	.. c	.. c	646.9	713.7	686.8	.. c	632.0	.. c	.. c	.. c
United Arab Emirates	5 552.8	1 325.3	1 186.0	1 708.9	1 211.9	.. c	-46.0	.. c	.. c	.. c
Other Near and Middle East	..	..	..	..	..	..	..	..	..	..
Jordan	.. c	.. c	.. c	.. c	.. c	.. c	.. c	.. c	.. c	-
Other Asian countries	..	..	..	..	..	..	..	..	..	..
China	26 134.0	26 100.7	27 997.8	29 932.1	28 306.7	10 307.5	10 150.5	9 672.9	10 390.8	9 556.7
Hong Kong, China	7 892.0	9 171.5	9 869.8	12 329.0	11 540.1	4 180.6	3 630.5	3 230.1	3 350.8	3 647.7
India	783.3	655.4	670.8	701.2	669.8	1 254.9	1 176.3	1 272.8	1 442.2	1 142.7
Indonesia	10.7	.. c	-	.. c	0.7	4 353.6	4 057.1	4 515.9	5 886.4	1 611.4
Iran, Islamic Republic of	-	.. c	.. c	-	.. c	-	-	-	-	-
Malaysia	7 850.1	7 926.5	8 879.2	10 443.0	9 839.8	5 128.7	4 027.3	4 036.9	4 619.0	4 235.6
Philippines	.. c	2.9	2.9	.. c	.. c	.. c	577.3	696.1	755.0	743.2
Singapore	22 877.8	21 305.6	16 851.7	20 269.9	19 780.5	10 761.0	13 677.9	14 549.9	15 749.2	17 248.0
Chinese Taipei	85.3	85.5	77.4	107.6	111.5	.. c	.. c	.. c	.. c	.. c
Thailand	3 739.3	4 105.4	3 369.8	4 243.0	4 108.6	515.1	1 088.6	1 265.6	1 364.2	978.3
Viet Nam	-	.. c	.. c	.. c	.. c	898.9	995.1	1 120.8	1 576.3	.. c
AUSTRALIA, OCEANIA AND POLAR REGIONS	..	..	..	..	..	..	..	..	..	..
WORLD unallocated and confidential	**176 439.0**	**103 730.5**	**185 832.1**	**208 884.6**	**204 088.8**	**173 442.0**	**145 091.0**	**139 555.0**	**196 638.3**	**193 059.7**
European Union (EU28)	**127 274.5**	**114 258.1**	**126 699.0**	**154 410.0**	**159 280.8**	**88 225.6**	**85 099.0**	**80 390.7**	**96 024.5**	**115 456.7**
G20 countries excl. European Union	.. d	.. d	.. d	.. d	.. d	.. d	.. d	.. d	.. d	.. d
G20 OECD countries	.. d	.. d	.. d	.. d	.. d	.. d	.. d	.. d	.. d	.. d
G20 Non-OECD countries	.. d	.. d	.. d	.. d	.. d	.. d	.. d	.. d	.. d	.. d
MENA countries	.. d	.. d	.. d	.. d	.. d	.. d	.. d	.. d	.. d	.. d
ASEAN countries	**34 540.3**	**33 330.9**	**29 104.2**	**34 947.4**	**33 682.9**	**24 140.9**	**25 581.9**	**27 463.8**	**31 543.6**	**27 987.0**

- Nil; .. Not available; c Confidential data; d Secondary Confidentiality

Note: Detailed metadata at: *http://stats.oecd.org/OECDStat_Metadata/ShowMetadata.ashx?Dataset=FDI_CTRY_IND_SUMM.*

1. Information on data for Israel: *http://oe.cd/israel-disclaimer*.
2. Note by Turkey: The information in this document with reference to "Cyprus" relates to the southern part of the Island. There is no single authority representing both Turkish and Greek Cypriot people on the Island. Turkey recognises the Turkish Republic of Northern Cyprus (TRNC). Until a lasting and equitable solution is found within the context of the United Nations, Turkey shall preserve its position concerning the "Cyprus issue".
3. Note by all the European Union Member States of the OECD and the European Union: The Republic of Cyprus is recognised by all members of the United Nations with the exception of Turkey. The information in this document relates to the area under the effective control of the Government of the Republic of Cyprus.

Source: OECD International Direct Investment Statistics (database): https://doi.org/10.1787/idi-data-en

AUSTRALIA

Table 3. Foreign direct investment income by country

Million US dollars

	Inward					Outward				
	2014	2015	2016	2017	2018	2014	2015	2016	2017	2018
WORLD	**29 806.2**	**24 065.7**	**27 528.4**	**37 318.6**	**44 417.7**	**19 179.7**	**13 784.7**	**13 315.2**	**14 188.8**	**16 500.3**
OECD COUNTRIES	**20 860.8**	**14 234.7**	**15 602.5**	**23 323.6**	**28 346.9**	**11 425.1**	**7 361.2**	**7 112.2**	**7 926.3**	**9 649.7**
Australia	-	-	-	-	-	-	-	-	-	-
Austria	.. c	.. c	.. c	.. c	.. c	.. c	.. c	.. c	.. c	.. c
Belgium	145.1	102.9	141.2	131.8	224.1	.. c	.. c	-	.. c	.. c
Canada	.. c	399.7	304.8	654.5	543.8	1 207.0	.. c	.. c	52.1	301.0
Chile	.. c	.. c	-	-	-	.. c	.. c	.. c	91.2	.. c
Czech Republic	-	-	-	-	-	.. c	.. c	.. c	.. c	-2.2
Denmark	.. c	.. c	.. c	.. c	.. c	.. c	1.5	.. c	.. c	.. c
Estonia	-	-	-	-	-	.. c	.. c	.. c	.. c	.. c
Finland	.. c	.. c	.. c	.. c	.. c	.. c	.. c	.. c	.. c	.. c
France	457.9	365.9	557.5	505.8	702.2	.. c	.. c	.. c	101.9	.. c
Germany	.. c	.. c	.. c	.. c	1 110.8	530.0	.. c	.. c	.. c	.. c
Greece	-	-	-	-	-	.. c	.. c	.. c	.. c	.. c
Hungary	-	-	-	-	-	.. c	.. c	.. c	.. c	.. c
Iceland	-	-	-	-	-	-	-	-	-	-
Ireland	67.6	182.6	263.1	.. c	.. c	-30.6	.. c	-14.9	.. c	.. c
Israel[1]	-	.. c	.. c	.. c	.. c	-	-	-	-	-
Italy	.. c	-5.3	.. c	.. c	.. c	1.8	.. c	.. c	.. c	.. c
Japan	-	3 246.7	-	-	-	-	.. c	-	-	-
Korea	.. c	.. c	119.7	.. c	396.7	.. c	.. c	-3.7	5.4	40.3
Latvia	-	-	-	-	-	-	-	-	-	-
Lithuania	-	-	-	-	-	-	-	-	-	-
Luxembourg	38.8	.. c	180.6	239.9	82.9	.. c	.. c	.. c	.. c	.. c
Mexico	-	-	-	-	-	.. c	.. c	.. c	95.8	.. c
Netherlands	1 316.9	741.6	726.2	1 403.2	2 083.4	.. c	406.5	.. c	.. c	.. c
New Zealand	-24.3	116.5	459.4	474.4	272.7	4 050.8	3 526.9	3 301.9	3 644.7	3 650.6
Norway	.. c	.. c	.. c	.. c	.. c	.. c	.. c	.. c	.. c	.. c
Poland	-	-	-	-	-	.. c	.. c	.. c	.. c	.. c
Portugal	-	-	-	-	-	.. c	.. c	.. c	-	-
Slovak Republic	-	-	-	-	-	.. c	.. c	.. c	.. c	.. c
Slovenia	-	-	-	-	-	.. c	.. c	.. c	.. c	.. c
Spain	.. c	-	-	-	.. c	.. c	10.5	.. c	.. c	.. c
Sweden	163.2	122.5	96.6	.. c	130.0	.. c	.. c	.. c	.. c	.. c
Switzerland	1 268.3	39.8	.. c	.. c	666.3	.. c	.. c	.. c	.. c	5.2
Turkey	-	-	-	-	-	.. c	.. c	.. c	.. c	.. c
United Kingdom	2 859.2	1 380.3	912.1	4 099.9	5 563.6	2 488.7	1 442.6	1 436.9	1 118.1	1 296.0
United States	7 663.6	6 104.9	6 224.6	7 957.7	9 516.7	2 477.0	711.5	903.9	1 570.2	2 914.0
EUROPE	..	..	..	..	..	..	..	..	..	..
Bulgaria	-	-	-	-	-	.. c	.. c	.. c	.. c	.. c
Croatia	-	-	-	-	-	.. c	.. c	.. c	.. c	.. c
Cyprus[2, 3]	.. c	-	-	-	-	-	-	.. c	-	.. c
Malta	.. c	.. c	.. c	-	.. c	-	-	-	.. c	-
Romania	-	-	-	-	-	.. c	.. c	-	.. c	.. c
Russian Federation	.. c	.. c	.. c	.. c	-	.. c	.. c	.. c	0.8	.. c
Ukraine	-	-	-	-	-	.. c	.. c	.. c	.. c	.. c
AFRICA	..	..	..	..	..	..	..	..	..	..
Northern Africa	..	..	..	..	..	..	..	..	..	..
Algeria	-	-	-	-	-	-	-	-	-	-
Egypt	-	-	-	-	-	.. c	.. c	.. c	.. c	.. c
Libya	-	-	-	-	-	.. c	.. c	.. c	.. c	-
Morocco	-	-	-	-	-	-	-	-	-	-
Tunisia	-	-	-	-	-	-	-	-	-	-
Other African countries	..	..	..	..	..	..	..	..	..	..
Nigeria	-	-	-	-	-	.. c	.. c	.. c	.. c	-
South Africa	94.6	.. c	168.7	105.8	125.5	.. c	11.3	14.1	-30.7	.. c
AMERICA	..	..	..	..	..	..	..	..	..	..
Northern America	..	..	..	..	..	..	..	..	..	..
Central America and Caribbean countries	..	..	..	..	..	..	..	..	..	..
Bahamas	.. c	.. c	.. c	.. c	.. c	-	-	.. c	-	-
Bermuda	806.7	845.3	1 575.1	1 949.6	2 950.6	.. c	.. c	.. c	.. c	.. c
Cayman Islands	169.5	130.7	.. c	216.9	224.1	.. c	168.3	.. c	.. c	.. c
Costa Rica	-	-	-	-	-	.. c	.. c	.. c	.. c	.. c
El Salvador	-	-	-	-	-	.. c	.. c	.. c	.. c	.. c
Guatemala	-	-	-	-	-	.. c	.. c	.. c	.. c	.. c
Honduras	-	-	-	-	-	-	-	.. c	.. c	.. c
Nicaragua	-	-	-	-	-	.. c	-	-	.. c	.. c
Panama	-	-	.. c	-	-	.. c	.. c	.. c	.. c	.. c
Virgin Islands, U.S.	-	-	-	-	-	-	-	-	-	-
South America	..	..	..	..	..	..	..	..	..	..
Argentina	.. c	.. c	.. c	.. c	.. c	.. c	-13.5	.. c	-3.1	.. c
Bolivia	-	-	-	-	-	.. c	.. c	.. c	.. c	.. c
Brazil	-	.. c	.. c	.. c	.. c	306.5	118.0	.. c	100.4	.. c
Colombia	-	-	-	-	-	.. c	.. c	-11.2	.. c	-10.5
Ecuador	-	-	-	-	-	.. c	.. c	.. c	.. c	.. c
Paraguay	-	-	-	-	-	-	-	-	-	-
Peru	-	-	-	-	-	.. c	.. c	.. c	.. c	.. c
Uruguay	-	-	-	-	-	.. c	.. c	.. c	.. c	.. c
Venezuela	-	-	-	-	-	.. c	.. c	.. c	.. c	.. c

Table 3. Foreign direct investment income by country *(cont.)*

Million US dollars

	Inward					Outward				
	2014	2015	2016	2017	2018	2014	2015	2016	2017	2018
ASIA	..	..	..	..	..	..	..	..	..	..
Near and Middle East	..	..	..	..	..	..	..	..	..	..
Gulf Arabian countries	..	..	..	..	..	..	..	..	..	..
Kuwait	-	.. c	.. c	11.5	.. c	.. c	.. c	.. c	.. c	-
Qatar	.. c	.. c	.. c	.. c	.. c	.. c	.. c	.. c	-	-
Saudi Arabia	.. c	.. c	.. c	-31.4	.. c	.. c	0.8	.. c	.. c	.. c
United Arab Emirates	202.8	112.0	94.4	158.6	114.3	-2.7	20.3	2.2	.. c	9.7
Other Near and Middle East	..	..	..	..	..	..	..	..	..	..
Jordan	.. c	.. c	.. c	.. c	.. c	-	-	-	-	-
Other Asian countries	..	..	..	..	..	..	..	..	..	..
China	.. c	28.6	136.0	456.7	1 623.2	183.9	237.0	492.8	171.7	236.1
Hong Kong, China	935.6	833.3	825.8	959.5	1 151.9	366.0	319.3	208.9	198.5	239.0
India	.. c	.. c	40.1	.. c	.. c	78.4	.. c	65.4	70.5	.. c
Indonesia	.. c	.. c	-	-	-	.. c	69.1	61.7	162.5	268.2
Iran, Islamic Republic of	-	-	-	-	-	-	-	-	-	-
Malaysia	.. c	.. c	84.7	.. c	.. c	.. c	.. c	.. c	219.2	184.5
Philippines	.. c	-	-	-	-	66.7	53.3	54.3	.. c	.. c
Singapore	379.5	777.7	.. c	799.3	723.1	1 260.1	976.0	396.2	.. c	571.5
Chinese Taipei	.. c	.. c	3.0	11.5	.. c	.. c	.. c	.. c	.. c	-0.7
Thailand	.. c	-56.4	.. c	.. c	-211.4	16.2	.. c	29.0	35.3	14.2
Viet Nam	-	-	-	-	-	41.5	.. c	10.4	.. c	44.1
AUSTRALIA, OCEANIA AND POLAR REGIONS	..	..	..	..	..	..	..	..	..	..
WORLD unallocated and confidential	**13 191.8**	**7 348.4**	**14 439.2**	**15 706.2**	**16 423.4**	**5 185.7**	**4 964.3**	**6 084.1**	**6 472.5**	**6 382.3**
European Union (EU28)	**6 298.9**	**4 324.9**	**3 930.0**	**8 040.5**	**10 434.8**	**3 626.3**	**2 877.0**	**2 659.6**	**2 335.0**	**2 624.2**
G20 countries excl. European Union	**.. d**	**.. d**	**.. d**	**.. d**	**.. d**	**.. d**	**.. d**	**.. d**	**.. d**	**.. d**
G20 OECD countries	**.. d**	**.. d**	**.. d**	**.. d**	**.. d**	**.. d**	**.. d**	**.. d**	**.. d**	**.. d**
G20 Non-OECD countries	**.. d**	**.. d**	**.. d**	**.. d**	**.. d**	**.. d**	**.. d**	**.. d**	**.. d**	**.. d**
MENA countries	**.. d**	**.. d**	**.. d**	**.. d**	**.. d**	**.. d**	**.. d**	**.. d**	**.. d**	**.. d**
ASEAN countries	**857.2**	**1 133.8**	**1 233.2**	**964.1**	**792.6**	**1 953.3**	**1 639.5**	**849.6**	**1 405.5**	**1 304.3**

- Nil; .. Not available; c Confidential data; d Secondary Confidentiality

Note: Detailed metadata at: *http://stats.oecd.org/OECDStat_Metadata/ShowMetadata.ashx?Dataset=FDI_CTRY_IND_SUMM.*

1. Information on data for Israel: *http://oe.cd/israel-disclaimer.*
2. Note by Turkey: The information in this document with reference to "Cyprus" relates to the southern part of the Island. There is no single authority representing both Turkish and Greek Cypriot people on the Island. Turkey recognises the Turkish Republic of Northern Cyprus (TRNC). Until a lasting and equitable solution is found within the context of the United Nations, Turkey shall preserve its position concerning the "Cyprus issue".
3. Note by all the European Union Member States of the OECD and the European Union: The Republic of Cyprus is recognised by all members of the United Nations with the exception of Turkey. The information in this document relates to the area under the effective control of the Government of the Republic of Cyprus.

Source: OECD International Direct Investment Statistics (database): https://doi.org/10.1787/idi-data-en

AUSTRALIA

Table 4. Foreign direct investment flows by industrial sector

Million US dollars

	Inward					Outward				
	2014	2015	2016	2017	2018	2014	2015	2016	2017	2018
All FDI activities	**58 504.6**	**28 274.1**	**45 519.2**	**42 289.1**	**60 425.0**	**18 183.7**	**-10 220.2**	**327.8**	**3 319.8**	**3 634.1**
Agriculture, forestry and fishing	**.. c**	**.. c**	**.. c**	**308.8**	**-366.0**	**.. c**	**.. c**	**.. c**	**.. c**	**.. c**
Mining and quarrying	**49 106.7**	**10 962.5**	**23 738.2**	**15 139.1**	**12 632.4**	**28 215.3**	**-13 542.7**	**300.3**	**-465.2**	**1 116.8**
Extraction activities	..	..	..	..	..	..	..	..	..	..
Manufacturing	**1 627.9**	**2 587.0**	**3 527.1**	**6 472.5**	**5 907.2**	**2 235.4**	**6 006.5**	**3 305.6**	**4 805.7**	**4 403.5**
of which:										
Food products, beverages and tobacco	..	..	..	..	..	..	..	..	..	..
Textiles, wood and paper products; printing	..	..	..	..	..	..	..	..	..	..
Chemical, rubber, plastic, non-metallic mineral products	..	..	..	..	..	..	..	..	..	..
Metal and machinery products, except electrical equipment	..	..	..	..	..	..	..	..	..	..
Motor vehicles, trailers, semi-trailers, other transport equipment	..	..	..	..	..	..	..	..	..	..
Other manufacturing	..	..	..	..	..	..	..	..	..	..
Electricity, gas, steam and air conditioning supply	**626.5**	**2 235.3**	**-762.7**	**2 889.9**	**1 139.2**	**.. c**	**.. c**	**20.8**	**388.5**	**462.4**
Water supply; sewerage, waste management and remediation activities	..	..	..	..	..	..	..	..	..	..
Construction	**2 834.0**	**-811.5**	**553.8**	**1 395.5**	**1 194.4**	**-1 955.1**	**-544.0**	**264.6**	**460.6**	**685.7**
Services	**3 260.3**	**15 105.6**	**23 133.1**	**17 494.1**	**36 595.2**	**-195.6**	**9 635.6**	**3 857.9**	**6 123.1**	**4 758.3**
Wholesale and retail trade; repair of motor vehicles and motorcycles	3 874.2	-2 097.1	1 887.3	738.0	3 020.8	-102.8	915.2	997.5	-296.6	1 524.6
Transportation and storage	882.5	5 677.4	2 966.6	-52.1	149.4	25.2	151.8	-198.5	-246.8	-331.7
Accommodation and food service activities	1 419.7	-823.5	-25.3	236.8	1 753.2	.. c	.. c	3.7	90.4	.. c
Information and communication	-1 595.5	782.9	-385.8	1 316.6	2 146.1	.. c	.. c	-427.4	313.4	319.7
Financial and insurance activities	-11 716.2	3 971.7	3 892.1	7 345.4	24 569.4	-1 284.5	4 724.6	3 180.0	5 185.8	2 583.1
Activities of holding companies	..	..	..	..	..	..	..	..	..	..
Real estate activities	10 655.3	.. c	.. c	.. c	5 122.1	192.9	.. c	-334.5	2 263.0	386.9
Professional, scientific and technical activities	-172.2	340.4	832.5	766.3	-200.9	.. c	60.1	.. c	-294.3	-107.6
Administrative and support service activities	-572.4	-250.2	.. c	360.2	475.8	-338.9	.. c	263.9	-80.5	147.9
Public administration; activities of households and of extraterritorial organisations	.. c	.. c	.. c	.. c	.. c	-	.. c	-	-	-
Education	-	.. c	.. c	.. c	.. c	-	.. c	.. c	.. c	.. c
Human health and social work activities	418.2	-825.0	1 449.5	482.8	-26.9	1 960.5	-204.4	503.2	.. c	440.7
Arts, entertainment and recreation	1.8	.. c	.. c	.. c	.. c	.. c	.. c	.. c	.. c	.. c
Other services	.. c	.. c	.. c	.. c	-9.0	-	-	-	-	.. c
Not allocated and confidential	**1 049.2**	**-1 804.8**	**-4 670.3**	**-1 410.8**	**3 322.6**	**-10 116.3**	**-11 775.5**	**-7 421.4**	**-7 993.0**	**-7 792.6**
Private real estate activities	..	..	..	..	..	..	..	..	..	..

- Nil; .. Not available; c Confidential data

Note: Detailed metadata at: *http://stats.oecd.org/OECDStat_Metadata/ShowMetadata.ashx?Dataset=FDI_CTRY_IND_SUMM.*

Source: OECD International Direct Investment Statistics (database): https://doi.org/10.1787/idi-data-en

AUSTRALIA

Table 5. Foreign direct investment positions by industrial sector

At year end

Million US dollars

	Inward					Outward				
	2014	2015	2016	2017	2018	2014	2015	2016	2017	2018
All FDI activities	**582 533.1**	**565 804.0**	**606 131.0**	**689 369.0**	**682 880.4**	**467 167.1**	**415 412.4**	**432 015.2**	**495 952.0**	**490 996.6**
Agriculture, forestry and fishing	**1 266.4**	**2 344.6**	**2 372.6**	**2 783.7**	**2 232.5**	**.. c**	**.. c**	**.. c**	**.. c**	**.. c**
Mining and quarrying	**242 649.6**	**229 291.3**	**243 304.6**	**268 004.8**	**257 987.0**	**128 540.1**	**83 761.2**	**91 384.2**	**101 582.6**	**105 174.3**
Extraction activities	..	..	..	..	..	..	..	..	..	..
Manufacturing	**70 816.9**	**66 141.6**	**68 521.7**	**79 397.1**	**75 981.8**	**65 704.6**	**70 271.8**	**68 969.6**	**88 653.0**	**101 904.3**
of which:										
Food products, beverages and tobacco	..	..	..	..	..	..	..	..	..	..
Textiles, wood and paper products; printing	..	..	..	..	..	..	..	..	..	..
Chemical, rubber, plastic, non-metallic mineral products	..	..	..	..	..	..	..	..	..	..
Metal and machinery products, except electrical equipment	..	..	..	..	..	..	..	..	..	..
Motor vehicles, trailers, semi-trailers, other transport equipment	..	..	..	..	..	..	..	..	..	..
Other manufacturing	..	..	..	..	..	..	..	..	..	..
Electricity, gas, steam and air conditioning supply	**10 510.0**	**11 635.9**	**11 457.3**	**15 899.7**	**15 300.0**	**6 216.3**	**3 509.2**	**3 374.1**	**3 906.1**	**4 211.6**
Water supply; sewerage, waste management and remediation activities	..	..	..	..	..	..	..	..	..	..
Construction	**15 536.2**	**12 793.9**	**14 607.8**	**19 006.3**	**15 843.5**	**8 918.9**	**6 426.5**	**6 494.9**	**7 716.2**	**5 628.9**
Services	**174 760.0**	**174 028.6**	**195 276.4**	**224 882.6**	**239 174.9**	**158 338.0**	**153 393.0**	**155 839.4**	**171 875.0**	**153 586.3**
Wholesale and retail trade; repair of motor vehicles and motorcycles	48 131.8	38 614.0	38 901.6	42 643.3	39 996.5	4 487.3	4 493.3	5 321.3	4 628.3	5 205.4
Transportation and storage	11 135.0	15 468.0	17 976.1	15 575.2	13 758.5	2 483.6	2 987.5	2 924.0	2 861.7	2 452.7
Accommodation and food service activities	6 674.8	5 291.2	5 045.6	5 303.0	6 172.4	.. c	62.8	58.6	128.7	57.2
Information and communication	20 527.1	19 313.9	18 188.1	19 856.5	18 980.1	1 964.4	2 333.6	1 360.3	2 010.0	2 096.3
Financial and insurance activities	41 760.5	46 550.0	47 799.6	57 600.0	75 895.7	126 707.8	120 508.5	123 236.6	137 117.2	119 251.8
Activities of holding companies	..	..	..	..	..	..	..	..	..	..
Real estate activities	38 397.7	42 450.5	54 720.0	70 845.5	72 593.9	10 102.4	11 74[illegible].8	11 984.1	14 756.3	14 189.7
Professional, scientific and technical activities	3 105.3	3 303.1	3 907.4	5 173.5	4 576.5	.. c	2 12[illegible].7	2 069.5	1 925.7	1 809.7
Administrative and support service activities	1 502.6	1 136.1	2 730.1	3 175.3	3 283.5	.. c	.. c	.. c	.. c	2 400.5
Public administration; activities of households and of extraterritorial organisations	.. c	.. c	.. c	.. c	592.2	-	-	-	-	-
Education	-	.. c	.. c	.. c	.. c	-	.. c	.. c	.. c	.. c
Human health and social work activities	2 986.3	1 299.0	2 551.4	3 102.7	2 776.0	5 586.4	4 287.3	4 591.9	4 682.2	4 852.5
Arts, entertainment and recreation	190.3	.. c	.. c	.. c	.. c	.. c	.. c	.. c	.. c	.. c
Other services	.. c	.. c	219.2	.. c	.. c	-	-	-	-	.. c
Not allocated and confidential	**66 993.9**	**69 568.2**	**70 590.4**	**79 394.7**	**76 360.8**	**99 449.3**	**98 050.7**	**105 953.0**	**122 219.0**	**120 491.2**
Private real estate activities	..	..	..	..	..	..	..	..	..	..

- Nil; .. Not available; c Confidential data

Note: Detailed metadata at: *http://stats.oecd.org/OECDStat_Metadata/ShowMetadata.ashx?Dataset=FDI_CTRY_IND_SUMM.*

Source: OECD International Direct Investment Statistics (database): https://doi.org/10.1787/idi-data-en

Table 6. Foreign direct investment income by industrial sector

Million US dollars

	Inward					Outward				
	2014	2015	2016	2017	2018	2014	2015	2016	2017	2018
All FDI activities	**29 806.2**	**24 065.7**	**27 528.4**	**37 318.6**	**44 417.7**	**19 179.7**	**13 784.7**	**13 315.2**	**14 188.8**	**16 500.3**
Agriculture, forestry and fishing	**.. c**	**48.8**	**107.8**	**105.8**	**.. c**	**.. c**	**-**	**-**	**-**	**.. c**
Mining and quarrying	**9 261.8**	**5 158.9**	**4 975.8**	**12 391.8**	**17 935.3**	**5 587.7**	**-81.9**	**-164.3**	**2 207.8**	**2 092.3**
Extraction activities	..	..	..	..	..	..	..	..	..	..
Manufacturing	**5 550.7**	**3 850.0**	**4 670.3**	**4 534.4**	**4 697.8**	**3 128.7**	**2 993.5**	**2 993.4**	**3 330.5**	**3 775.3**
of which:										
Food products, beverages and tobacco	..	..	..	..	..	..	..	..	..	..
Textiles, wood and paper products; printing	..	..	..	..	..	..	..	..	..	..
Chemical, rubber, plastic, non-metallic mineral products	..	..	..	..	..	..	..	..	..	..
Metal and machinery products, except electrical equipment	..	..	..	..	..	..	..	..	..	..
Motor vehicles, trailers, semi-trailers, other transport equipment	..	..	..	..	..	..	..	..	..	..
Other manufacturing	..	..	..	..	..	..	..	..	..	..
Electricity, gas, steam and air conditioning supply	**630.1**	**507.9**	**815.4**	**.. c**	**1 203.4**	**249.7**	**193.9**	**.. c**	**.. c**	**.. c**
Water supply; sewerage, waste management and remediation activities	**..**	**..**	**..**	**..**	**..**	**..**	**..**	**..**	**..**	**..**
Construction	**1 102.4**	**.. c**	**.. c**	**1 203.2**	**1 290.8**	**547.1**	**.. c**	**.. c**	**422.3**	**.. c**
Services	**11 086.2**	**11 665.8**	**14 171.6**	**15 693.2**	**17 206.2**	**6 799.2**	**7 549.8**	**6 985.1**	**4 890.0**	**6 568.3**
Wholesale and retail trade; repair of motor vehicles and motorcycles	2 018.2	2 194.0	2 583.1	1 970.3	3 686.4	328.1	616.9	197.0	-87.4	184.5
Transportation and storage	-116.3	337.4	767.9	633.8	819.5	-40.6	121.7	20.1	108.1	50.8
Accommodation and food service activities	557.1	571.0	799.8	784.0	667.1	.. c	.. c	.. c	.. c	.. c
Information and communication	641.8	822.8	984.2	1 186.3	1 263.2	231.7	87.9	82.5	-76.6	-28.4
Financial and insurance activities	4 771.9	3 428.5	3 736.0	4 825.7	4 983.2	5 100.1	5 462.5	5 491.0	3 827.9	5 135.6
Activities of holding companies	..	..	..	..	..	..	..	..	..	..
Real estate activities	2 571.7	.. c	.. c	.. c	.. c	.. c	540.2	.. c	.. c	.. c
Professional, scientific and technical activities	272.2	139.8	161.3	-20.7	-145.7	.. c	.. c	.. c	.. c	.. c
Administrative and support service activities	42.4	107.4	139.7	153.3	111.3	.. c	.. c	.. c	.. c	.. c
Public administration; activities of households and of extraterritorial organisations	.. c	72.1	.. c	.. c	.. c	-	.. c	-	-	.. c
Education	-	-	.. c	.. c	.. c	-	.. c	.. c	.. c	.. c
Human health and social work activities	244.3	212.6	191.0	187.8	160.6	.. c	436.5	.. c	.. c	.. c
Arts, entertainment and recreation	.. c	.. c	.. c	.. c	.. c	.. c	.. c	.. c	.. c	.. c
Other services	.. c	.. c	.. c	.. c	.. c	-	-	-	-	-
Not allocated and confidential	**2 175.1**	**2 834.2**	**2 787.5**	**3 390.3**	**2 084.1**	**2 867.3**	**3 129.5**	**3 501.1**	**3 338.2**	**4 064.4**
Private real estate activities	..	..	..	..	..	..	..	..	..	..

- Nil; .. Not available; c Confidential data

Note: Detailed metadata at: *http://stats.oecd.org/OECDStat_Metadata/ShowMetadata.ashx?Dataset=FDI_CTRY_IND_SUMM.*

Source: OECD International Direct Investment Statistics (database): https://doi.org/10.1787/idi-data-en

AUSTRIA

Table 1. Foreign direct investment flows by country

Million US dollars

	Inward					Outward				
	2014	2015	2016	2017	2018	2014	2015	2016	2017	2018
WORLD	**4 578.7**	**1 487.5**	**-8 500.5**	**14 921.7**	**2 084.3**	**-723.1**	**7 027.2**	**-2 031.4**	**10 228.8**	**5 868.1**
OECD COUNTRIES	**4 467.3**	**3 124.8**	**-8 340.2**	**7 038.7**	**5 673.3**	**8 143.8**	**4 321.7**	**8 929.6**	**6 060.2**	**2 865.6**
Australia	433.9	54.4	-11.1	-55.2	-72.0	127.4	175.3	119.4	86.8	606.6
Austria	-	-	-	-	-	-	-	-	-	-
Belgium	-1 549.7	410.4	14.4	665.1	-1 312.4	-579.8	257.3	454.5	-273.9	-348.2
Canada	18.6	-44.4	25.4	230.0	-40.1	-594.4	-117.6	-184.7	-391.2	139.3
Chile	38.5	-149.8	-2.2	-3.4	-3.5	-175.1	-1.1	17.7	-	14.2
Czech Republic	73.0	66.6	28.8	3.4	66.1	472.3	676.7	-1 019.6	554.6	473.3
Denmark	197.7	-119.8	-426.8	-	-	-35.8	43.3	12.2	-78.9	-1.2
Estonia	-	-	-3.3	-	-	10.6	83.2	18.8	-77.8	98.0
Finland	-447.1	25.5	44.2	57.5	-69.6	-134.0	44.4	91.8	113.9	22.4
France	1 162.3	1 090.4	-315.2	7.9	-214.8	2 656.2	-55.5	19.9	310.0	85.0
Germany	-617.0	-1 559.6	938.8	4 137.1	5 745.3	-1 068.1	602.3	1 282.8	1 889.3	-1 950.9
Greece	33.2	299.5	38.7	48.5	-351.7	-102.2	49.9	85.1	3.4	-317.5
Hungary	-19.9	219.6	-8.8	-80.0	5.9	-283.9	733.2	-832.7	335.9	-668.0
Iceland	1.3	-1.1	1.1	13.5	-	1.3	-	-	-	-3.5
Ireland	445.8	-1 013.9	696.7	-811.6	1 019.7	-9.3	31.1	86.3	31.6	-44.8
Israel[1]	-14.6	-8.9	-10.0	-1.1	-2.4	-9.3	-8.9	-2.2	4.5	4.7
Italy	-1 072.0	1 279.0	-7 566.1	666.2	394.2	-449.8	563.5	811.7	-168.0	671.5
Japan	18.6	-68.8	80.7	287.5	-53.1	33.2	46.6	31.0	-9.0	10.6
Korea	-208.3	11.1	364.9	319.0	1 328.9	179.1	10.0	-43.1	-10.1	120.4
Latvia	..	..	..	..	..	..	..	..	..	..
Lithuania	..	..	..	..	..	..	..	..	..	..
Luxembourg	1 582.9	1 558.5	2 051.3	110.5	2 013.5	-406.0	-215.2	800.6	-232.2	1 854.1
Mexico	57.1	-16.6	-33.2	196.1	-7.1	-8.0	155.3	174.7	131.9	121.6
Netherlands	4 712.8	1 232.4	-2 337.7	355.1	-5 132.8	6 876.7	-1 009.4	6 886.0	5 024.2	-1 148.4
New Zealand	-	2.2	-	-1.1	-5.9	34.5	-287.3	-31.0	-34.9	321.0
Norway	-45.1	18.9	-33.2	19.2	69.6	593.1	185.2	191.3	-804.9	-787.2
Poland	-46.4	83.2	-5.5	144.3	-76.7	-51.7	82.1	558.4	1 079.9	-186.5
Portugal	-15.9	-5.5	18.8	7.9	-	46.4	10.0	-1.1	32.7	-18.9
Slovak Republic	127.4	-93.2	-36.5	-379.9	456.7	-510.8	287.3	5.5	-479.1	-13.0
Slovenia	-142.0	56.6	-117.2	-62.0	31.9	-65.0	183.0	-81.8	320.1	-30.7
Spain	-120.7	-46.6	-97.3	-11.3	224.2	67.7	94.3	194.6	280.7	345.8
Sweden	-8.0	54.4	70.8	157.8	112.1	70.3	208.5	21.0	411.5	-112.1
Switzerland	689.9	-516.9	1 237.4	951.4	717.6	480.3	653.4	1 237.4	-799.2	1 860.0
Turkey	192.4	218.5	180.3	231.1	44.8	567.9	271.9	-2 687.2	-1 252.4	207.7
United Kingdom	-711.2	98.7	-808.4	857.9	1 190.8	-1 069.4	-16.6	826.1	-210.8	-107.4
United States	-299.9	-10.0	-2 326.7	-1 028.1	-407.2	1 479.4	646.7	-213.4	248.0	1 664.1
EUROPE	**5 223.6**	**3 269.0**	**-6 914.7**	**13 042.5**	**4 088.3**	**2 099.0**	**5 748.2**	**4 073.9**	**7 960.8**	**303.3**
Bulgaria	-71.6	-85.4	195.7	30.4	7.1	-180.4	345.0	-1 933.0	-308.9	-42.5
Croatia	131.4	-25.5	16.6	-94.7	54.3	-578.5	-271.9	-1 803.6	58.6	1.2
Cyprus[2, 3]	..	..	..	..	..	..	..	..	..	..
Malta	..	..	..	..	..	..	..	..	..	..
Romania	-253.4	13.3	-10.0	-	-10.6	-1 401.1	1 325.6	-1 015.2	756.4	675.1
Russian Federation	244.1	-164.2	-25.4	6 417.5	-1 071.6	327.7	454.8	-517.5	1 364.0	5.9
Ukraine	19.9	119.8	14.4	-7.9	9.4	-1 405.1	541.3	-222.3	-13.5	-159.3
AFRICA	**1 517.8**	**-855.2**	**276.5**	**1 288.5**	**178.2**	**98.2**	**-108.7**	**-35.4**	**144.3**	**-70.8**
Northern Africa	13.3	3.3	-3.3	-24.8	-	-21.2	31.1	-54.2	28.2	22.4
Algeria	..	..	..	..	..	..	..	..	..	..
Egypt	..	..	..	..	..	..	..	..	..	..
Libya	-	-	-	-	-	..	..	..	..	..
Morocco	..	..	..	..	..	..	..	..	..	..
Tunisia	..	..	..	..	..	..	..	..	..	..
Other African countries	..	..	..	..	..	..	..	..	..	..
Nigeria	..	..	..	..	..	..	..	..	..	..
South Africa	..	..	..	..	..	..	..	..	..	..
AMERICA	**-1 961.0**	**-379.4**	**-2 345.5**	**-77.8**	**-2 178.7**	**-3 663.3**	**359.4**	**-7 431.2**	**351.7**	**2 204.7**
Northern America	-281.3	-54.4	-2 301.2	-798.1	-447.3	885.0	529.1	-398.1	-143.2	1 803.4
Central America and Caribbean countries	-2 194.5	71.0	174.7	1 404.6	-37.8	-4 588.0	-306.2	-7 227.7	441.9	146.3
Bahamas	..	..	-	-	..	..	..	..	..	..
Bermuda	..	..	..	..	..	..	..	..	..	..
Cayman Islands	..	..	..	..	..	..	..	..	..	..
Costa Rica	..	..	..	..	..	..	..	..	..	..
El Salvador	-	-	-	-	-	-	-	-	-	-
Guatemala	-	-	..	..	..	..	..	..	..	..
Honduras	-	-	-	-	-	..	..	..	..	..
Nicaragua	-	-	-	-	-	..	..	..	..	..
Panama	..	..	..	..	..	..	..	..	..	..
Virgin Islands, U.S.	-	..	..	..	..	-	-	-	-	-
South America	514.8	-396.0	-219.0	-684.3	-1 693.6	39.8	136.4	194.6	53.0	254.9
Argentina	-4.0	3.3	-1.1	7.9	17.7	17.2	12.2	121.6	18.0	24.8
Bolivia	-	-	-	..	..	..	..	..	..	..
Brazil	408.7	-244.0	-105.1	-688.8	-1 691.3	99.5	117.6	-39.8	47.3	173.5
Colombia	..	..	..	..	..	..	..	..	..	..
Ecuador	..	-	-	..	..	..	..	..	..	..
Paraguay	-	-	-	-	-	..	..	..	..	-
Peru	..	..	..	..	..	..	..	..	..	..
Uruguay	..	..	..	..	..	..	..	..	..	..
Venezuela	..	..	..	..	..	..	..	..	..	..

Table 1. Foreign direct investment flows by country *(cont.)*

Million US dollars

	Inward					Outward				
	2014	2015	2016	2017	2018	2014	2015	2016	2017	2018
ASIA	**-635.5**	**-556.9**	**492.1**	**724.8**	**74.4**	**579.8**	**1 132.6**	**1 255.1**	**1 720.2**	**2 504.4**
Near and Middle East	-354.3	-391.6	-152.6	86.8	-882.8	195.0	448.1	548.5	45.1	1 116.5
Gulf Arabian countries	-341.0	-383.8	-139.3	86.8	-881.6	242.8	453.7	528.6	55.2	1 095.2
Kuwait	..	..	..	..	..	-	-	-	-	..
Qatar	..	-	..	..	..	..	..	..	..	..
Saudi Arabia	..	..	..	..	..	..	..	..	..	..
United Arab Emirates	..	..	..	..	..	..	..	..	..	..
Other Near and Middle East	-14.6	-6.7	-13.3	-	-1.2	-49.1	-4.4	19.9	-10.1	22.4
Jordan	..	..	..	..	..	..	..	..	..	..
Other Asian countries	-280.0	-165.3	644.7	638.0	958.3	386.1	684.4	706.6	1 675.1	1 386.8
China	-65.0	62.1	2.2	22.5	138.1	-229.5	140.9	268.7	592.9	624.3
Hong Kong, China	-203.0	-99.8	147.1	-134.1	-112.1	4.0	108.7	206.8	242.4	166.4
India	-6.6	8.9	-1.1	-	-21.2	102.2	49.9	86.3	39.5	140.4
Indonesia	-1.3	-1.1	-3.3	3.4	-1.2	26.5	-16.6	21.0	-5.6	36.6
Iran, Islamic Republic of	..	..	..	..	..	..	..	..	..	..
Malaysia	..	..	..	..	..	..	..	..	..	..
Philippines	-	-	-2.2	-	-	15.9	6.7	8.8	9.0	3.5
Singapore	406.0	48.8	-5.5	-19.2	2.4	208.3	72.1	7.7	1 030.3	207.7
Chinese Taipei	..	..	..	..	..	..	..	..	..	..
Thailand	-216.3	-126.5	-88.5	-23.7	-420.2	-	306.2	28.8	-232.2	55.5
Viet Nam	..	..	..	..	..	..	..	..	..	..
AUSTRALIA, OCEANIA AND POLAR REGIONS	**433.9**	**56.6**	**-11.1**	**-56.4**	**-79.1**	**163.2**	**-117.6**	**87.4**	**51.9**	**927.7**
WORLD unallocated and confidential	**..**	**-46.6**	**2.2**	**-**	**1.2**	**..**	**13.3**	**18.8**	**-**	**-1.2**
European Union (EU28)	**3 700.4**	**3 452.0**	**-8 227.4**	**5 451.5**	**4 264.1**	**1 992.8**	**4 066.6**	**6 032.3**	**9 428.5**	**-966.6**
G20 countries excl. European Union	**1 015.0**	**-143.1**	**-9 319.9**	**12 939.9**	**5 519.9**	**2 276.8**	**3 046.0**	**127.2**	**2 748.3**	**2 576.4**
G20 OECD countries	**-1 025.6**	**1 051.6**	**-9 470.3**	**5 849.4**	**7 909.8**	**1 854.8**	**2 220.7**	**136.0**	**624.5**	**1 569.7**
G20 Non-OECD countries	**2 040.6**	**-1 194.7**	**150.4**	**7 090.5**	**-2 388.8**	**421.9**	**826.4**	**-8.8**	**2 123.8**	**1 007.9**
MENA countries	**-327.7**	**-379.4**	**-146.0**	**62.0**	**-881.6**	**228.2**	**484.7**	**473.3**	**69.9**	**1 123.6**
ASEAN countries	**187.1**	**-76.5**	**-45.3**	**-3.4**	**-400.1**	**278.6**	**369.4**	**103.9**	**789.1**	**343.4**

- Nil; .. Not available

Note: Data excludes resident Special Purpose Entities (SPEs). Detailed metadata at: *http://stats.oecd.org/OECDStat_Metadata/ShowMetadata.ashx?Dataset=FDI_CTRY_IND_SUMM*.

1. Information on data for Israel: *http://oe.cd/israel-disclaimer*.
2. Note by Turkey: The information in this document with reference to "Cyprus" relates to the southern part of the Island. There is no single authority representing both Turkish and Greek Cypriot people on the Island. Turkey recognises the Turkish Republic of Northern Cyprus (TRNC). Until a lasting and equitable solution is found within the context of the United Nations, Turkey shall preserve its position concerning the "Cyprus issue".
3. Note by all the European Union Member States of the OECD and the European Union: The Republic of Cyprus is recognised by all members of the United Nations with the exception of Turkey. The information in this document relates to the area under the effective control of the Government of the Republic of Cyprus.

Source: OECD International Direct Investment Statistics (database): https://doi.org/10.1787/idi-data-en

Table 2. Foreign direct investment positions by country
At year end

Million US dollars

	Inward					Outward				
	2014	2015	2016	2017	2018	2014	2015	2016	2017	2018
WORLD	**175 755.5**	**159 723.5**	**150 648.3**	**196 133.4**	**201 892.6**	**218 116.7**	**205 235.7**	**196 996.9**	**232 706.9**	**232 394.1**
OECD COUNTRIES	**127 957.6**	**122 621.7**	**113 170.7**	**141 902.1**	**147 023.1**	**155 625.8**	**148 300.5**	**152 926.1**	**180 702.8**	**179 607.3**
Australia	57.1	54.4	67.5	87.6	79.0	2 090.7	2 061.2	2 130.3	2 551.0	2 870.4
Austria	3 008.5	2 423.5	2 342.2	5 155.9	5 798.0	-	-	-	-	-
Belgium	971.3	823.1	765.3	891.1	920.5	1 751.9	1 653.8	2 004.8	1 921.3	1 485.0
Canada	2 497.4	2 920.0	3 706.1	4 439.9	4 963.4	1 402.3	1 260.8	986.6	512.1	600.0
Chile	165.1	1.1	1.1	1.2	1.1	156.6	141.5	159.2	167.9	162.6
Czech Republic	25.5	197.1	254.0	206.3	311.4	14 593.5	14 398.5	11 573.7	14 570.6	14 773.3
Denmark	230.7	201.4	179.2	218.3	195.8	204.0	154.6	176.0	277.0	262.2
Estonia	-	-	-8.4	1.2	1.1	361.8	254.8	246.7	203.9	289.7
Finland	809.8	731.6	728.4	838.3	616.0	550.0	544.4	615.6	804.7	790.0
France	3 942.2	4 604.2	3 677.7	5 865.9	5 666.4	4 565.0	4 148.1	4 177.3	4 940.0	4 799.6
Germany	45 400.1	45 058.2	44 714.9	56 338.5	60 326.3	28 454.9	26 27[illegible].1	28 231.3	35 520.5	34 850.0
Greece	467.4	664.1	758.9	899.5	479.7	336.3	335.3	376.3	417.4	234.7
Hungary	88.6	155.7	190.8	207.5	216.4	8 853.2	7 952.1	6 870.5	8 163.8	7 054.0
Iceland	-	-	-	-	-	1.2	4.4	4.2	6.0	4.6
Ireland	347.2	341.9	662.0	722.0	486.6	190.6	179.6	179.2	251.9	196.9
Israel[2]	20.6	18.5	160.2	266.3	111.1	15.8	7.6	5.3	9.6	14.9
Italy	20 404.2	18 500.8	10 314.1	11 662.3	11 573.2	2 447.6	2 469.2	3 163.3	3 788.7	4 577.5
Japan	2 578.7	2 102.3	2 142.9	2 823.2	2 862.4	91.1	133.9	175.0	171.5	184.3
Korea	193.0	189.4	227.7	255.5	1 534.2	1 324.6	1 196.5	1 105.7	1 166.9	1 234.3
Latvia	..	..	..	..	..	..	..	..	..	..
Lithuania	..	..	..	..	..	..	..	..	..	..
Luxembourg	2 264.3	2 394.1	3 321.4	3 328.1	4 329.1	10 867.4	11 665.8	12 643.6	14 292.4	15 545.0
Mexico	2 496.2	1 779.0	1 660.2	2 729.7	2 150.2	565.8	675.0	717.8	889.9	1 009.8
Netherlands	6 013.4	8 135.0	4 421.8	5 540.9	8 141.7	25 254.5	20 751.2	25 500.2	36 103.4	33 565.4
New Zealand	1 381.6	-	-	-	-	471.1	124.1	97.0	62.4	365.2
Norway	329.0	235.2	248.8	310.6	285.1	2 855.6	2 572.7	2 792.2	2 203.2	1 336.2
Poland	34.0	9.8	16.9	25.2	8.0	5 016.7	4 849.2	5 051.1	7 031.7	6 371.7
Portugal	30.4	68.6	85.4	88.8	82.4	199.1	261.3	227.7	297.4	265.6
Slovak Republic	52.2	25.0	24.2	28.8	27.5	6 694.5	6 541.1	6 250.7	7 266.7	7 033.4
Slovenia	156.6	167.7	122.3	154.7	154.6	2 493.8	3 358.7	2 843.9	3 642.4	3 515.0
Spain	821.9	1 020.1	1 242.8	1 452.4	739.6	1 074.5	1 071.3	1 183.7	1 560.3	1 716.3
Sweden	962.8	793.7	918.1	1 036.2	1 187.3	1 331.9	1 552.5	1 535.8	1 772.6	1 480.4
Switzerland	8 901.8	7 989.1	9 112.5	13 261.0	12 621.9	7 197.2	8 315.7	9 551.0	8 546.4	10 316.0
Turkey	195.5	206.9	218.2	247.1	241.6	6 002.5	4 881.9	3 580.7	1 790.6	1 548.0
United Kingdom	4 663.4	5 259.7	5 716.2	6 682.7	6 815.9	7 832.2	7 618.9	8 187.0	7 778.8	7 380.4
United States	18 448.2	15 551.4	15 170.2	16 128.6	14 088.6	10 376.9	10 890.6	10 451.1	11 849.4	13 496.7
EUROPE	**127 666.3**	**124 238.4**	**113 256.0**	**148 287.4**	**151 856.0**	**179 384.5**	**167 276.0**	**166 382.4**	**197 311.1**	**192 007.1**
Bulgaria	-	4.4	278.3	317.8	311.4	4 834.5	4 593.4	3 152.7	3 238.2	3 050.1
Croatia	-7.3	-	1.1	3.6	2.3	5 589.7	5 264.0	3 959.1	4 552.7	4 387.5
Cyprus[3, 4]	..	..	..	..	..	..	..	..	..	..
Malta	..	..	..	..	..	..	..	..	..	..
Romania	-	56.6	55.9	68.4	66.4	10 828.6	9 527.5	8 282.9	10 100.7	10 317.2
Russian Federation	23 944.5	21 389.2	20 206.6	30 197.9	27 789.1	6 808.7	5 693.0	4 966.8	6 103.4	5 164.9
Ukraine	19.4	18.5	42.2	45.6	52.7	1 178.9	997.3	331.0	488.1	332.0
AFRICA	**6 165.2**	**1 948.8**	**1 924.7**	**3 004.3**	**3 068.5**	**1 092.7**	**887.3**	**820.1**	**993.0**	**878.2**
Northern Africa	-	-	-	-	-1.1	242.8	234.1	172.9	293.8	305.7
Algeria	-	-	-	-	..	..	..	..	..	..
Egypt	..	..	-	..	..	..	..	..	..	..
Libya	-	-	-	-	-	..	..	..	..	..
Morocco	-	-	-	-	-	..	..	..	..	..
Tunisia	-	-	-	-	-	..	..	..	..	..
Other African countries	..	..	..	..	..	..	..	..	..	..
Nigeria	-	-	..	-	-	..	..	..	..	..
South Africa	..	..	..	..	..	..	..	..	..	..
AMERICA	**27 104.8**	**21 442.6**	**21 840.4**	**26 765.4**	**24 290.1**	**24 004.0**	**23 296.7**	**15 143.9**	**16 569.9**	**18 605.5**
Northern America	20 945.7	18 471.4	18 877.4	20 568.5	19 052.0	11 779.2	12 151.3	11 437.8	12 361.5	14 096.6
Central America and Caribbean countries	2 796.1	1 793.1	1 666.5	2 579.8	2 240.7	10 588.2	9 623.3	1 933.2	2 360.3	2 588.7
Bahamas	..	..	-	-	..	..	..	..	..	..
Bermuda	..	..	..	..	..	..	..	..	..	..
Cayman Islands	..	..	-	-	..	..	..	..	..	..
Costa Rica	..	..	-	-	-	..	..	..	..	..
El Salvador	-	-	-	-	-	-	-	-	-	-
Guatemala	-	-	-	-	-	..	..	..	..	..
Honduras	-	-	-	-	-	..	..	..	..	..
Nicaragua	-	-	-	-	-	..	..	..	..	..
Panama	..	..	..	..	..	..	..	..	..	..
Virgin Islands, U.S.	-	..	-	-	-	-	-	-	-	-
South America	3 363.1	1 176.9	1 296.5	3 617.2	2 997.5	1 636.6	1 522.0	1 773.0	1 848.2	1 920.1
Argentina	26.7	50.1	49.5	62.4	713.3	99.6	98.0	92.8	106.7	84.7
Bolivia	-	-	-	-	-	..	..	..	..	..
Brazil	3 162.7	1 118.1	1 239.6	3 552.4	2 275.0	1 294.2	1 077.8	1 173.2	1 334.9	1 344.2
Colombia	-	-	-	-	-	..	..	..	..	..
Ecuador	-	-	-	-	-	..	..	..	..	..
Paraguay	-	-	-	-	-	..	..	..	..	-
Peru	-	-	-	-	..	..	..	..	..	..
Uruguay	..	-	-	-	-	..	..	..	..	..
Venezuela	..	..	..	..	..	..	..	..	..	..

Table 2. Foreign direct investment positions by country *(cont.)*

At year end

Million US dollars

	Inward					Outward				
	2014	2015	2016	2017	2018	2014	2015	2016	2017	2018
ASIA	**13 054.0**	**11 746.3**	**13 276.1**	**17 663.7**	**22 291.0**	**11 067.7**	**11 573.2**	**12 422.3**	**15 217.1**	**17 665.4**
Near and Middle East	5 767.0	5 549.3	6 269.6	8 725.1	12 452.5	4 045.4	4 559.6	4 986.8	5 805.9	6 931.5
Gulf Arabian countries	5 736.6	5 527.5	6 108.4	8 457.7	12 340.3	3 970.1	4 498.6	4 921.5	5 724.4	6 831.9
Kuwait	..	..	..	..	..	-	-	-	-	..
Qatar	-	-	-	-	-	..	..	..	..	..
Saudi Arabia	..	..	..	..	..	..	..	..	..	..
United Arab Emirates	..	..	..	..	..	..	..	..	..	..
Other Near and Middle East	29.1	20.7	162.3	267.5	112.2	75.3	61.0	65.4	81.6	100.8
Jordan	..	..	..	..	..	..	..	..	..	..
Other Asian countries	7 287.0	6 198.1	7 005.4	8 939.8	9 839.7	7 022.4	7 013.6	7 435.4	9 411.1	10 732.8
China	661.7	484.5	375.3	903.1	941.2	2 445.2	2 481.2	2 615.2	3 445.7	4 189.4
Hong Kong, China	3 306.0	2 802.4	3 301.4	3 500.8	3 052.4	575.5	679.4	877.0	1 232.9	1 370.5
India	140.8	138.3	123.3	328.6	353.8	364.2	427.9	450.1	645.2	738.5
Indonesia	-	-	-	-	-	239.2	211.2	226.6	226.7	254.2
Iran, Islamic Republic of	..	..	-	..	..	..	..	..	..	..
Malaysia	..	..	..	..	..	..	..	..	..	..
Philippines	1.2	1.1	-	-	-	63.1	74.0	79.1	79.2	77.9
Singapore	403.1	457.3	610.3	568.5	545.0	1 443.6	1 281.4	1 290.2	1 805.0	1 975.0
Chinese Taipei	..	..	..	..	..	..	..	..	..	..
Thailand	-	-	-	16.8	17.2	146.9	310.3	331.0	249.5	306.8
Viet Nam	-	-	-	-	-	..	..	..	..	..
AUSTRALIA, OCEANIA AND POLAR REGIONS	**1 437.5**	**54.4**	**67.5**	**87.6**	**79.0**	**2 567.8**	**2 189.4**	**2 228.3**	**2 615.7**	**3 236.8**
WORLD unallocated and confidential	**327.8**	**292.9**	**283.5**	**325.0**	**308.0**	**..**	**13.1**	**-**	**-**	**1.1**
European Union (EU28)	**93 052.3**	**93 426.2**	**82 307.4**	**103 460.1**	**109 931.3**	**147 824.0**	**137 523.1**	**139 249.5**	**171 018.2**	**166 214.8**
G20 countries excl. European Union	**135 158.5**	**121 521.0**	**111 744.5**	**145 581.7**	**145 704.1**	**76 810.0**	**72 022.9**	**72 912.4**	**83 385.7**	**84 870.6**
G20 OECD countries	**100 875.9**	**96 225.4**	**87 616.7**	**107 260.7**	**110 298.8**	**65 155.9**	**61 611.3**	**62 907.1**	**70 961.9**	**72 551.0**
G20 Non-OECD countries	**34 282.5**	**25 294.5**	**24 127.8**	**38 320.9**	**35 405.3**	**11 654.1**	**10 411.5**	**10 005.3**	**12 425.0**	**12 319.7**
MENA countries	**5 745.1**	**5 528.6**	**6 108.4**	**8 457.7**	**12 340.3**	**4 239.6**	**4 759.9**	**5 118.6**	**6 054.2**	**7 180.0**
ASEAN countries	**404.3**	**462.7**	**689.4**	**716.0**	**696.1**	**2 134.4**	**2 063.1**	**2 139.8**	**2 642.1**	**2 928.8**

- Nil; .. Not available

Note: Data excludes resident Special Purpose Entities (SPEs). Detailed metadata at: *http://stats.oecd.org/OECDStat_Metadata/ShowMetadata.ashx?Dataset=FDI_CTRY_IND_SUMM.*

1. Inward FDI positions are allocated according to the ultimate investing country. Detailed metadata at: *http://stats.oecd.org/OECDStat_Metadata/ShowMetadata.ashx?Dataset=FDI_CTRY_IND_SUMM.*
2. Information on data for Israel: *http://oe.cd/israel-disclaimer.*
3. Note by Turkey: The information in this document with reference to "Cyprus" relates to the southern part of the Island. There is no single authority representing both Turkish and Greek Cypriot people on the Island. Turkey recognises the Turkish Republic of Northern Cyprus (TRNC). Until a lasting and equitable solution is found within the context of the United Nations, Turkey shall preserve its position concerning the "Cyprus issue".
4. Note by all the European Union Member States of the OECD and the European Union: The Republic of Cyprus is recognised by all members of the United Nations with the exception of Turkey. The information in this document relates to the area under the effective control of the Government of the Republic of Cyprus.

Source: OECD International Direct Investment Statistics (database): https://doi.org/10.1787/idi-data-en

AUSTRIA

Table 3. Foreign direct investment income by country

Million US dollars

	Inward					Outward				
	2014	2015	2016	2017	2018	2014	2015	2016	2017	2018
WORLD	**9 229.1**	**9 651.7**	**11 956.2**	**15 794.2**	**15 040.7**	**11 442.2**	**10 661.1**	**15 376.5**	**15 095.3**	**16 474.7**
OECD COUNTRIES	**8 222.1**	**9 462.0**	**10 632.5**	**13 050.4**	**11 928.5**	**6 391.1**	**6 815.3**	**9 847.4**	**9 533.3**	**9 991.7**
Australia	5.3	7.8	10.0	11.3	11.8	155.2	129.8	123.9	147.7	295.1
Austria	-	-	-	-	-	-	-	-	-	-
Belgium	79.6	30.0	130.5	73.3	38.9	91.5	83.2	129.4	137.5	69.6
Canada	-9.3	16.6	16.6	-6.8	11.8	-38.5	147.5	224.5	-143.2	24.8
Chile	-	-	-	-	-	-26.5	-6.7	13.3	-3.4	14.2
Czech Republic	1.3	6.7	4.4	22.5	18.9	2 100.3	1 846.9	1 712.9	1 924.2	1 954.4
Denmark	46.4	-56.6	27.6	28.2	29.5	10.6	4.4	21.0	10.1	9.4
Estonia	-	-	-3.3	-	-	5.3	-1.1	14.4	20.3	-
Finland	27.9	64.3	63.0	55.2	35.4	17.2	26.6	54.2	77.8	29.5
France	-50.4	287.3	253.2	200.7	313.9	119.4	187.5	94.0	-128.5	85.0
Germany	3 587.6	2 794.2	3 680.2	4 781.9	4 910.9	1 479.4	1 134.8	954.3	2 409.0	1 830.5
Greece	25.2	-48.8	38.7	47.3	28.3	-41.1	-23.3	-3.3	-5.6	11.8
Hungary	17.2	63.2	44.2	44.0	16.5	-406.0	1 122.6	680.1	1 050.6	15.3
Iceland	-	-	-	-	-	-	-	-	-	1.2
Ireland	15.9	16.6	34.3	-21.4	53.1	21.2	33.3	27.6	28.2	7.1
Israel[1]	-	-	-	-	-	-4.0	-3.3	-	-1.1	2.4
Italy	-2 275.4	474.8	412.5	812.8	435.5	-345.0	62.1	76.3	11.3	116.8
Japan	2.7	1.1	50.9	49.6	61.4	15.9	10.0	2.2	6.8	13.0
Korea	-	-5.5	-10.0	3.4	60.2	136.7	105.4	189.1	99.2	170.0
Latvia	..	..	..	..	..	..	..	..	..	..
Lithuania	..	..	..	..	..	..	..	..	..	..
Luxembourg	264.0	311.7	1 402.2	12.4	1 256.9	-25.2	-470.3	732.1	-307.7	703.4
Mexico	-27.9	7.8	7.7	10.1	10.6	110.1	134.2	152.6	121.7	99.1
Netherlands	3 437.7	3 088.2	2 069.0	4 775.1	2 811.3	203.0	-786.5	1 091.5	383.3	1 358.4
New Zealand	18.6	-	-	-	-	33.2	-144.2	58.6	48.5	5.9
Norway	87.6	13.3	-16.6	-13.5	20.1	5.3	-219.6	19.9	19.2	135.7
Poland	-15.9	-4.4	-2.2	-12.4	-22.4	372.8	471.4	329.5	455.4	495.7
Portugal	-	7.8	28.8	15.8	7.1	10.6	23.3	14.4	-	7.1
Slovak Republic	181.8	16.6	-	3.4	4.7	768.2	641.2	755.3	695.5	600.7
Slovenia	-1.3	-	-	2.3	3.5	-485.6	286.2	305.2	402.4	186.5
Spain	157.9	92.1	81.8	87.9	72.0	107.5	144.2	232.2	151.1	44.8
Sweden	185.8	186.4	191.3	158.9	112.1	173.8	142.0	160.3	220.9	38.9
Switzerland	1 164.9	688.9	1 406.6	1 084.4	1 007.9	916.8	713.3	901.3	98.1	791.9
Turkey	199.0	156.4	194.6	193.9	37.8	330.4	251.8	170.3	170.2	18.9
United Kingdom	892.9	560.2	362.7	423.9	347.0	65.0	93.2	-69.7	742.9	214.8
United States	204.3	684.4	150.4	206.3	231.3	510.8	662.2	660.2	664.0	639.7
EUROPE	**7 759.1**	**8 824.2**	**10 810.6**	**13 110.1**	**13 606.8**	**4 087.8**	**7 862.5**	**12 057.9**	**11 928.8**	**11 241.6**
Bulgaria	-	-1.1	110.6	22.5	20.1	-84.9	526.9	291.9	143.2	245.5
Croatia	-2.7	-10.0	-11.1	-10.1	-8.3	116.8	-231.8	334.0	223.2	331.6
Cyprus[2, 3]	..	..	..	..	..	..	..	..	..	..
Malta	..	..	..	..	..	..	..	..	..	..
Romania	-5.3	-3.3	-4.4	-2.3	-1.2	-777.5	531.3	525.3	860.1	943.0
Russian Federation	-273.3	-52.1	-102.8	87.9	1 828.2	597.1	902.9	927.8	1 197.2	413.1
Ukraine	-78.3	-33.3	-42.0	-22.5	1.2	-1 228.6	-106.5	112.8	152.2	18.9
AFRICA	**18.6**	**-225.2**	**43.1**	**478.0**	**192.4**	**71.6**	**-25.6**	**-43.1**	**59.7**	**46.0**
Northern Africa	-1.3	-1.1	-1.1	-1.1	-2.4	5.3	6.7	-58.6	-3.4	13.0
Algeria	-	-	..	..	..	..	..	..	..	..
Egypt	..	..	..	..	..	..	..	..	..	..
Libya	-	-	..	..	..	..	..	..	..	..
Morocco	-	-	..	..	..	..	..	..	..	..
Tunisia	..	..	..	..	..	..	..	..	..	..
Other African countries	..	..	..	..	..	..	..	..	..	..
Nigeria	-	-	..	..	..	..	..	..	..	..
South Africa	..	..	..	..	..	..	..	..	..	..
AMERICA	**650.1**	**758.7**	**-171.4**	**846.6**	**563.0**	**5 394.7**	**1 171.4**	**1 427.6**	**824.0**	**1 057.5**
Northern America	193.7	701.1	167.0	199.5	243.1	472.3	809.8	884.7	520.8	663.3
Central America and Caribbean countries	412.6	153.1	139.3	231.1	125.1	4 768.5	311.7	457.8	266.0	259.6
Bahamas	..	-	..	..	..	..	..	..	..	..
Bermuda	..	..	..	..	..	..	..	..	..	..
Cayman Islands	..	..	..	..	..	..	..	..	..	..
Costa Rica	..	-	..	..	..	..	..	..	..	..
El Salvador	-	-	..	..	..	-	-	..	..	..
Guatemala	-	-	..	..	..	..	..	..	..	..
Honduras	-	-	..	..	..	..	..	..	..	..
Nicaragua	-	-	..	..	..	..	..	..	..	..
Panama	..	..	..	..	..	..	..	..	..	..
Virgin Islands, U.S.	-	..	..	..	..	-	-	..	..	..
South America	43.8	-95.4	-477.7	416.0	194.7	153.9	49.9	85.1	37.2	134.5
Argentina	-1.3	-	-	37.2	23.6	8.0	25.5	18.8	7.9	7.1
Bolivia	-	-	..	..	..	-	-	..	..	..
Brazil	43.8	-95.4	-477.7	378.8	171.1	39.8	33.3	15.5	15.8	92.1
Colombia	-	-	..	..	..	..	..	..	..	..
Ecuador	-	-	..	..	..	..	..	..	..	..
Paraguay	-	-	..	..	..	..	..	..	..	..
Peru	-	-	..	..	..	..	..	..	..	..
Uruguay	-	-	..	..	..	..	..	..	..	..
Venezuela	..	-	..	..	..	..	..	..	..	..

Table 3. Foreign direct investment income by country *(cont.)*

Million US dollars

	Inward					Outward				
	2014	2015	2016	2017	2018	2014	2015	2016	2017	2018
ASIA	**778.8**	**331.7**	**1 261.7**	**1 341.5**	**664.5**	**1 698.3**	**1 692.7**	**1 764.9**	**2 097.8**	**3 834.5**
Near and Middle East	522.8	55.5	875.8	939.0	262.0	786.8	868.6	834.9	762.0	1 595.7
Gulf Arabian countries	529.4	64.3	888.0	945.8	262.0	818.6	864.1	831.6	768.8	1 578.0
Kuwait	..	..	..	..	..	-	-	..	..	..
Qatar	-	-	..	..	..	..	..	..	..	..
Saudi Arabia	..	..	..	..	..	..	..	..	..	..
United Arab Emirates	..	..	..	..	..	..	..	..	..	..
Other Near and Middle East	-6.6	-8.9	-12.2	-6.8	-	-31.8	4.4	2.2	-6.8	17.7
Jordan	..	..	..	..	..	..	..	..	..	..
Other Asian countries	254.7	276.2	385.9	402.4	402.5	911.5	825.3	930.0	1 335.8	2 237.7
China	-2.7	-1.1	-1.1	-7.9	3.5	500.2	545.8	504.3	1 148.7	1 514.2
Hong Kong, China	256.1	275.1	289.7	322.4	233.7	66.3	48.8	23.2	99.2	109.8
India	-	-	-	-	-	22.6	26.6	24.3	38.3	63.7
Indonesia	-	-	-	-	-	-5.3	3.3	17.7	14.7	21.2
Iran, Islamic Republic of	..	..	..	..	..	..	..	..	..	..
Malaysia	..	..	..	..	..	..	..	..	..	..
Philippines	-	-	-1.1	-	-	10.6	13.3	16.6	14.7	11.8
Singapore	4.0	8.9	3.3	-4.5	1.2	84.9	82.1	79.6	-131.9	247.8
Chinese Taipei	..	..	..	..	..	..	..	..	..	..
Thailand	-5.3	-4.4	-4.4	-2.3	-1.2	15.9	33.3	29.9	18.0	37.8
Viet Nam	-	-	..	..	..	..	..	..	..	..
AUSTRALIA, OCEANIA AND POLAR REGIONS	**22.6**	**7.8**	**8.8**	**11.3**	**11.8**	**189.7**	**-14.4**	**183.6**	**196.1**	**301.0**
WORLD unallocated and confidential	**..**	**-45.5**	**3.3**	**6.8**	**2.4**	**..**	**-24.4**	**-14.4**	**-11.3**	**-5.9**
European Union (EU28)	**6 659.1**	**8 061.0**	**9 182.8**	**11 635.7**	**10 630.2**	**3 717.7**	**5 885.7**	**9 210.4**	**9 705.8**	**9 337.9**
G20 countries excl. European Union	**2 319.2**	**4 612.3**	**4 596.9**	**7 659.8**	**8 661.6**	**3 750.8**	**4 480.3**	**4 102.6**	**6 523.5**	**5 669.8**
G20 OECD countries	**2 527.5**	**4 986.1**	**5 128.8**	**6 687.0**	**6 433.4**	**2 542.1**	**2 918.5**	**2 578.8**	**4 102.1**	**3 507.6**
G20 Non-OECD countries	**-208.3**	**-372.7**	**-533.0**	**972.8**	**2 228.3**	**1 208.7**	**1 561.8**	**1 523.8**	**2 421.4**	**2 162.2**
MENA countries	**522.8**	**55.5**	**875.8**	**937.9**	**258.5**	**825.3**	**869.7**	**773.0**	**762.0**	**1 598.0**
ASEAN countries	**-1.3**	**6.7**	**54.2**	**30.4**	**9.4**	**142.0**	**124.2**	**174.7**	**-68.8**	**357.6**

- Nil; .. Not available

Note: Data excludes resident Special Purpose Entities (SPEs). Detailed metadata at: *http://stats.oecd.org/OECDStat_Metadata/ShowMetadata.ashx?Dataset=FDI_CTRY_IND_SUMM.*

1. Information on data for Israel: *http://oe.cd/israel-disclaimer.*
2. Note by Turkey: The information in this document with reference to "Cyprus" relates to the southern part of the Island. There is no single authority representing both Turkish and Greek Cypriot people on the Island. Turkey recognises the Turkish Republic of Northern Cyprus (TRNC). Until a lasting and equitable solution is found within the context of the United Nations, Turkey shall preserve its position concerning the "Cyprus issue".
3. Note by all the European Union Member States of the OECD and the European Union: The Republic of Cyprus is recognised by all members of the United Nations with the exception of Turkey. The information in this document relates to the area under the effective control of the Government of the Republic of Cyprus.

Source: OECD International Direct Investment Statistics (database): https://doi.org/10.1787/idi-data-en

AUSTRIA

Table 4. Foreign direct investment flows by industrial sector

Million US dollars

	Inward					Outward				
	2014	2015	2016	2017	2018	2014	2015	2016	2017	2018
All FDI activities	**4 578.7**	**1 487.5**	**-8 500.5**	**14 921.7**	**2 084.3**	**-723.1**	**7 027.2**	**-2 031.4**	**10 228.8**	**5 868.1**
Agriculture, forestry and fishing	**-1.3**	**-1.1**	**-1.1**	**-1.1**	**1.2**	**-25.2**	**-2.2**	**110.6**	**14.7**	**-68.5**
Mining and quarrying	**15.9**	**76.5**	**64.1**	**-189.4**	**151.1**	**214.9**	**-572.4**	**-796.2**	**-1 209.6**	**-47.2**
Extraction activities	..	..	..	..	..	..	..	..	..	..
Manufacturing	**1 796.5**	**619.0**	**483.2**	**354.0**	**1 298.2**	**-1 462.1**	**2 88[illegible].9**	**2 566.6**	**2 338.0**	**2 851.4**
of which:										
Food products, beverages and tobacco	132.7	-53.2	360.5	-80.0	-263.2	-622.3	109.8	68.6	92.4	-232.5
Textiles, wood and paper products; printing	-21.2	-106.5	-22.1	-	-3.5	-169.8	303.9	831.6	1 481.2	578.3
Chemical, rubber, plastic, non-metallic mineral products	1 430.3	-178.6	-19.9	157.8	11.8	-899.6	695.5	57.5	-462.2	1 338.4
Metal and machinery products, except electrical equipment	8.0	563.5	-7.7	325.8	129.8	586.4	1 083.7	-230.0	298.7	996.1
Motor vehicles, trailers, semi-trailers, other transport equipment	301.2	-203.0	434.6	-120.6	1 074.0	387.4	558.0	1 006.3	800.4	109.8
Other manufacturing	-53.1	596.8	-262.1	69.9	349.3	-743.0	132.0	833.8	128.5	61.4
Electricity, gas, steam and air conditioning supply	**-55.7**	**113.1**	**-8.8**	**102.6**	**-4.7**	**946.0**	**-142.0**	**52.0**	**-1 778.8**	**352.9**
Water supply; sewerage, waste management and remediation activities	**-1.3**	**4.4**	**2.2**	**-**	**-9.4**	**222.9**	**58.8**	**58.6**	**-25.9**	**4.7**
Construction	**-82.3**	**-2.2**	**34.3**	**200.7**	**312.8**	**163.2**	**-331.7**	**-786.2**	**-206.3**	**-142.8**
Services	**2 905.7**	**676.7**	**-9 216.0**	**14 453.8**	**335.2**	**-883.6**	**5 124.8**	**-3 909.1**	**9 279.7**	**2 299.1**
Wholesale and retail trade; repair of motor vehicles and motorcycles	1 854.8	-1 930.1	2 502.5	2 988.4	102.7	1 913.2	1 94[illegible].2	1 668.7	1 698.8	67.3
Transportation and storage	379.5	-237.4	409.2	41.7	43.7	104.8	[illegible].1	110.6	225.5	2.4
Accommodation and food service activities	-8.0	-21.1	-87.4	14.7	-22.4	-374.2	179.7	-66.4	-199.5	34.2
Information and communication	569.2	-718.8	1 016.3	-720.3	-2 093.7	-553.3	378.3	-110.6	590.7	-66.1
Financial and insurance activities	-1 113.2	3 455.4	-8 222.9	-1 357.2	-813.2	-4 878.6	3 407.7	-8 549.2	-384.4	3 952.6
Activities of holding companies	-2 065.8	1 748.2	-311.8	-1 379.8	-1 485.9	-2 240.9	-5[illegible].0	-2 634.1	-1 189.3	4 661.9
Real estate activities	660.7	485.9	-682.3	2 198.2	1 068.1	136.7	-307.3	-253.2	567.0	-793.1
Professional, scientific and technical activities	800.1	-464.8	-4 017.5	10 990.9	1 746.7	2 767.7	-63[illegible].2	2 961.4	7 038.7	-1 091.7
Administrative and support service activities	-256.1	112.0	-106.2	273.9	351.7	-43.8	108.7	275.4	-390.0	55.5
Public administration; activities of households and of extraterritorial organisations	-	-	-	-	-	1.3	-[illegible].1	-1.1	5.6	1.2
Education	..	..	..	..	..	..	..	..	..	..
Human health and social work activities	..	..	..	..	..	..	..	..	..	..
Arts, entertainment and recreation	6.6	2.2	-31.0	22.5	-46.0	5.3	10.0	59.7	128.5	129.8
Other services	14.6	-7.8	-1.1	-5.6	-1.2	-10.6	28.8	-42.0	7.9	5.9
Not allocated and confidential	**1.3**	**1.1**	**141.5**	**1.1**	**-**	**100.8**	**10.0**	**672.3**	**1 817.2**	**618.4**
Private real estate activities	..	-	..	..	..	..	-	..	..	..

- Nil; .. Not available

Note: Data excludes resident Special Purpose Entities (SPEs). Detailed metadata at: *http://stats.oecd.org/OECDStat_Metadata/ShowMetadata.ashx?Dataset=FDI_CTRY_IND_SUMM.*

Source: OECD International Direct Investment Statistics (database): https://doi.org/10.1787/idi-data-en

Table 5. Foreign direct investment positions by industrial sector
At year end

Million US dollars

	Inward					Outward				
	2014	2015	2016	2017	2018	2014	2015	2016	2017	2018
All FDI activities	**175 755.5**	**159 723.5**	**150 648.3**	**196 133.4**	**201 892.6**	**218 116.7**	**205 235.7**	**196 996.9**	**232 706.9**	**232 394.1**
Agriculture, forestry and fishing	**23.1**	**17.4**	**21.1**	**22.8**	**22.9**	**119.0**	**101.3**	**83.3**	**103.1**	..
Mining and quarrying	**228.3**	**280.9**	**403.7**	**266.3**	**403.0**	**8 672.3**	**7 995.6**	**6 124.2**	**7 230.8**	..
Extraction activities	..	..	..	..	..	..	..	..	..	..
Manufacturing	**16 123.2**	**14 734.9**	**14 262.7**	**16 207.7**	**17 196.0**	**39 741.1**	**38 175.3**	**39 284.3**	**45 710.0**	..
of which:										
Food products, beverages and tobacco	1 541.9	1 371.8	1 696.0	1 745.0	1 646.4	1 134.0	1 199.8	1 559.0	1 948.9	..
Textiles, wood and paper products; printing	1 008.9	816.5	919.2	1 037.4	986.9	4 673.1	4 632.6	5 516.0	6 856.6	..
Chemical, rubber, plastic, non-metallic mineral products	5 543.6	4 592.3	4 047.6	4 454.3	4 262.7	15 507.7	14 196.0	13 321.4	14 688.2	..
Metal and machinery products, except electrical equipment	3 491.8	3 644.0	3 324.5	4 365.6	4 538.6	8 481.7	8 653.2	8 363.0	9 628.2	..
Motor vehicles, trailers, semi-trailers, other transport equipment	3 038.9	2 438.8	2 492.9	2 764.5	3 682.2	2 535.0	2 911.3	3 760.9	5 153.5	..
Other manufacturing	1 498.2	1 871.5	1 781.4	1 842.2	2 080.4	7 408.4	6 582.5	6 765.0	7 434.6	..
Electricity, gas, steam and air conditioning supply	**903.3**	**776.3**	**807.4**	**1 262.9**	**1 079.7**	**5 514.4**	**4 531.3**	**4 305.9**	**2 759.7**	..
Water supply; sewerage, waste management and remediation activities	**81.3**	**74.0**	**78.0**	**91.1**	**77.9**	**974.9**	**700.1**	**710.4**	**814.3**	..
Construction	**163.9**	**136.1**	**387.9**	**466.5**	**751.1**	**3 944.6**	**3 437.1**	**2 706.9**	**3 028.3**	..
Services	**158 232.4**	**143 703.9**	**134 557.8**	**177 816.0**	**182 362.0**	**159 161.2**	**150 301.6**	**142 510.8**	**173 752.7**	..
Wholesale and retail trade; repair of motor vehicles and motorcycles	21 153.3	15 906.4	18 748.8	25 600.9	25 292.0	26 877.7	27 506.8	28 932.2	32 536.6	..
Transportation and storage	1 418.1	1 024.5	1 531.6	2 223.6	2 161.7	1 284.5	1 176.9	1 292.3	1 622.7	..
Accommodation and food service activities	409.2	354.9	303.6	442.6	400.7	272.0	607.5	595.6	682.4	..
Information and communication	4 266.3	2 792.6	3 649.2	3 112.3	2 700.9	4 043.0	3 323.9	3 100.0	4 201.2	..
Financial and insurance activities	32 165.2	31 829.1	22 282.1	26 037.4	24 090.9	79 103.5	74 683.7	64 026.6	74 707.4	..
Activities of holding companies	5 578.8	6 565.1	6 343.4	8 737.1	6 865.1	35 561.0	34 315.7	32 799.6	39 002.2	..
Real estate activities	4 012.6	4 065.3	3 869.5	7 615.7	8 265.4	5 933.3	5 345.7	6 417.2	7 745.3	..
Professional, scientific and technical activities	91 830.9	83 415.4	81 512.6	109 462.7	115 011.5	37 180.6	33 511.2	33 278.2	46 459.6	..
Administrative and support service activities	2 826.4	4 180.7	2 530.8	3 157.8	4 324.5	3 367.9	3 061.5	3 754.6	4 377.5	..
Public administration; activities of households and of extraterritorial organisations	-	-	-	-	-	17.0	17.4	17.9	25.2	..
Education	..	..	..	..	..	..	..	..	..	..
Human health and social work activities	..	..	..	..	..	..	..	..	..	..
Arts, entertainment and recreation	98.3	95.8	91.7	122.3	72.1	925.1	856.8	878.0	1 143.0	..
Other services	29.1	16.3	14.8	9.6	8.0	120.2	137.2	99.1	112.7	..
Not allocated and confidential	-	-	**129.7**	-	-	**-10.9**	**-6.5**	**-5.3**	**677.6**	..
Private real estate activities	..	-	..	..	..	..	-	..	..	..

- Nil; .. Not available

Note: Data excludes resident Special Purpose Entities (SPEs). Detailed metadata at: *http://stats.oecd.org/OECDStat_Metadata/ShowMetadata.ashx?Dataset=FDI_CTRY_IND_SUMM.*

Source: OECD International Direct Investment Statistics (database): https://doi.org/10.1787/idi-data-en

AUSTRIA

Table 6. Foreign direct investment income by industrial sector

Million US dollars

	Inward					Outward				
	2014	2015	2016	2017	2018	2014	2015	2016	2017	2018
All FDI activities	**9 229.1**	**9 651.7**	**11 956.2**	**15 794.2**	**15 040.7**	**11 442.2**	**10 661.1**	**15 376.5**	**15 095.3**	**16 474.7**
Agriculture, forestry and fishing	**-1.3**	**-1.1**	**-1.1**	**-1.1**	**1.2**	**-1.3**	**-5.5**	**1.1**	**-**	**14.2**
Mining and quarrying	**13.3**	**6.7**	**67.5**	**87.9**	**75.5**	**-61.0**	**-1 139.2**	**-748.6**	**259.3**	**336.4**
Extraction activities	..	..	..	..	..	..	..	..	..	..
Manufacturing	**1 910.6**	**1 817.0**	**2 001.5**	**1 869.0**	**2 876.2**	**3 948.5**	**4 288.4**	**5 229.5**	**4 709.7**	**4 905.0**
of which:										
Food products, beverages and tobacco	281.3	359.4	382.6	361.9	292.7	140.6	146.4	165.9	180.4	119.2
Textiles, wood and paper products; printing	73.0	122.0	108.4	139.8	107.4	756.3	907.4	1 271.7	1 370.8	959.5
Chemical, rubber, plastic, non-metallic mineral products	383.4	342.8	527.5	417.1	526.4	1 633.3	1 878.0	2 191.8	1 790.1	2 330.9
Metal and machinery products, except electrical equipment	838.5	617.9	666.8	783.5	967.8	976.5	732.1	764.1	553.5	801.4
Motor vehicles, trailers, semi-trailers, other transport equipment	226.9	-16.6	270.9	9.0	590.1	120.7	110.9	238.9	281.8	335.2
Other manufacturing	106.1	391.6	45.3	157.8	393.0	321.1	513.6	597.1	533.2	358.8
Electricity, gas, steam and air conditioning supply	**-14.6**	**36.6**	**27.6**	**136.4**	**35.4**	**-122.1**	**107.6**	**13.3**	**86.8**	**135.7**
Water supply; sewerage, waste management and remediation activities	**4.0**	**6.7**	**11.1**	**25.9**	**2.4**	**18.6**	**72.1**	**38.7**	**65.4**	**47.2**
Construction	**18.6**	**1.1**	**-2.2**	**18.0**	**43.7**	**550.6**	**313.9**	**267.6**	**128.5**	**171.1**
Services	**7 301.3**	**7 784.8**	**9 851.8**	**13 656.9**	**12 006.4**	**7 106.3**	**7 023.8**	**10 573.9**	**9 844.4**	**10 856.8**
Wholesale and retail trade; repair of motor vehicles and motorcycles	2 380.3	2 490.3	2 177.4	3 261.2	3 176.0	2 422.7	2 757.6	2 730.3	3 670.4	2 667.3
Transportation and storage	136.7	143.1	168.1	139.8	217.2	110.1	130.9	133.8	162.3	69.6
Accommodation and food service activities	-31.8	-4.4	29.9	12.4	1.2	-38.5	31.1	66.4	24.8	16.5
Information and communication	456.4	351.6	482.1	411.5	266.7	-208.3	281.8	90.7	111.6	199.5
Financial and insurance activities	-839.9	854.1	1 604.6	2 356.0	604.3	477.6	4 364.9	5 180.8	4 793.1	5 361.7
Activities of holding companies	1 157.0	615.6	1 130.2	1 289.6	190.0	961.9	664.4	2 119.9	496.0	2 218.8
Real estate activities	120.7	232.9	143.8	214.2	311.6	-195.0	-97.6	186.9	343.8	282.1
Professional, scientific and technical activities	4 818.9	3 458.7	4 859.0	7 079.2	7 313.8	4 163.5	-778.7	1 861.1	1 101.3	1 929.7
Administrative and support service activities	269.3	251.8	385.9	178.1	110.9	355.6	307.3	291.9	-375.4	234.9
Public administration; activities of households and of extraterritorial organisations	-	-	-	-	-	-1.3	-1.1	-1.1	-1.1	1.2
Education	..	..	..	..	..	..	..	..	..	..
Human health and social work activities	..	..	..	..	..	..	..	..	..	..
Arts, entertainment and recreation	-10.6	5.5	-2.2	4.5	-	13.3	35.5	50.9	12.4	75.5
Other services	1.3	-1.1	-1.1	-4.5	1.2	-2.7	-3.3	-11.1	9.0	8.3
Not allocated and confidential	**-2.7**	**-**	**-**	**1.1**	**-**	**2.7**	**-**	**1.1**	**1.1**	**8.3**
Private real estate activities	..	-	..	..	..	..	-	..	..	..

- Nil; .. Not available

Note: Data excludes resident Special Purpose Entities (SPEs). Detailed metadata at: *http://stats.oecd.org/OECDStat_Metadata/ShowMetadata.ashx?Dataset=FDI_CTRY_IND_SUMM.*

Source: OECD International Direct Investment Statistics (database): *https://doi.org/10.1787/idi-data-en*

BELGIUM

Table 1. Foreign direct investment flows by country

Million US dollars

	Inward					Outward				
	2014	2015	2016	2017	2018	2014	2015	2016	2017	2018
WORLD	**-13 465.6**	**51 524.1**	**68 178.7**	**4 212.6**	**17 028.2**	**-4 126.3**	**44 194.1**	**40 165.9**	**34 746.9**	**31 312.4**
OECD COUNTRIES	**-9 440.1**	**.. d**	**65 172.0**	**3 082.0**	**22 903.3**	**6 501.3**	**43 496.4**	**41 489.6**	**30 063.1**	**..**
Australia	784.1	-109.8	-259.9	598.6	343.4	.. d	.. d	8.8	899.6	..
Austria	.. d	469.2	404.7	-372.0	413.1	30.5	-84.3	17.7	-363.0	..
Belgium	-	-	-	-	-	-	-	-	-	..
Canada	-398.0	74.3	325.1	465.6	246.7	2.7	.. d	317.4	126.3	..
Chile	-66.3	.. d	-12.2	45.1	-43.7	.. d	73.2	-84.0	31.6	..
Czech Republic	.. d	.. d	.. c	.. c	.. c	.. d	.. d	722.1	652.7	..
Denmark	130.0	-30.0	-151.5	-77.8	239.6	.. d	126.5	27.6	169.1	..
Estonia	.. d	.. d	8.8	-6.8	-7.1	.. d	-6.7	11.1	6.8	..
Finland	-851.8	-1 015.0	-96.2	-1 370.8	1 692.4	120.7	11.1	37.6	49.6	..
France	1 133.1	1 032.7	11 004.1	-510.7	6 943.2	525.4	-825.3	5 402.0	4 978.0	..
Germany	-2 933.5	7 509.7	-1 407.7	-10 686.5	-1 061.0	.. d	.. d	-1 307.1	692.1	..
Greece	-175.1	81.0	-8.8	30.4	-33.0	-17.2	.. d	.. c	.. c	..
Hungary	41.1	-383.8	1 403.3	-2 199.3	-1 714.9	.. d	.. d	76.3	292.0	..
Iceland	.. d	.. d	.. c	.. c	.. c	.. d	.. d	.. c	.. c	..
Ireland	-122.1	3 708.3	3 518.7	7 002.6	4 384.5	-504.2	.. d	-353.9	148.8	..
Israel[1]	.. d	.. d	-76.3	-25.9	13.0	-37.2	22.2	12.2	30.4	..
Italy	5 461.1	-3 711.6	907.9	375.4	172.3	-53.1	.. d	745.3	1 129.5	..
Japan	1 192.8	1 330.0	2 961.4	421.6	2 038.2	443.1	-26.6	447.9	-395.7	..
Korea	.. d	87.6	137.1	181.5	529.9	471.0	92.1	25.4	154.4	..
Latvia	.. d	.. d	.. c	.. c	.. c	-2.7	3.3	-14.4	12.4	..
Lithuania	.. d	.. d	.. c	.. c	.. c	.. d	.. d	1.1	1.1	..
Luxembourg	164.5	1 767.1	14 935.3	6 815.5	-5 960.1	.. d	.. d	12 966.9	25 214.7	..
Mexico	23.9	393.8	-63.0	3.4	-115.7	.. d	.. d	-21 045.0	4 716.5	..
Netherlands	-12 880.5	-3 284.5	-19 941.4	16.9	1 999.3	5 078.9	.. d	6 772.1	844.3	..
New Zealand	-29.2	-21.1	115.0	-41.7	1.2	-2.7	-	-64.1	135.3	..
Norway	-2 417.4	-6 289.5	-8 077.0	-1 707.8	3 421.5	443.1	246.3	307.4	-64.3	..
Poland	-1 606.7	102.1	116.1	395.7	-13.0	.. d	.. d	179.1	563.6	..
Portugal	37.2	1 517.5	226.7	27.1	-53.1	.. d	.. d	335.1	-223.2	..
Slovak Republic	54.4	.. d	147.1	-19.2	-46.0	.. d	.. d	-44.2	128.5	..
Slovenia	.. d	.. d	-15.5	-1.1	60.2	233.5	-159.7	98.4	104.8	..
Spain	-948.7	240.7	2 707.1	-515.2	460.3	.. d	165.3	822.7	292.0	..
Sweden	4 715.4	-2 231.8	4 525.0	-3 492.3	-10 374.1	.. d	.. d	61.9	1 322.3	..
Switzerland	2 708.0	42 036.6	1 842.3	2 632.2	3 406.1	.. d	.. d	-122.7	4.5	..
Turkey	.. d	- d	10.0	-116.1	72.0	.. d	916.3	1 300.5	-102.6	..
United Kingdom	-4 198.0	4 577.9	6 184.9	573.8	-544.1	.. d	.. d	.. c	.. c	..
United States	-537.3	895.2	43 172.6	3 645.6	18 838.7	.. d	.. d	-60 143.8	1 268.2	..
EUROPE	**-9 763.8**	**45 497.5**	**19 181.7**	**-1 625.5**	**899.3**	**9 383.0**	**38 962.8**	**122 805.5**	**24 736.8**	**..**
Bulgaria	14.6	-10.0	31.0	4.5	-13.0	.. d	.. d	89.6	730.5	..
Croatia	- d	.. d	5.5	-	3.5	.. d	.. d	21.0	6.8	..
Cyprus[2, 3]	.. d	39.9	174.7	-48.5	232.5	.. d	.. d	303.0	1 016.8	..
Malta	.. d	.. d	39.8	651.6	-671.5	.. d	11.1	21.0	12.4	..
Romania	45.1	-3.3	-4.4	80.0	-79.1	.. d	.. d	140.4	77.8	..
Russian Federation	-124.7	275.1	128.3	-84.5	345.8	.. d	.. d	211.2	-205.2	..
Ukraine	.. d	5.5	6.6	1.1	-10.6	.. d	.. d	-3.3	4.5	..
AFRICA	**-238.8**	**110.9**	**-598.3**	**457.7**	**72.0**	**.. d**	**.. d**	**294.2**	**651.6**	**..**
Northern Africa	14.6	-20.0	-22.1	48.5	34.2	.. d	.. d	394.8	340.4	..
Algeria	.. d	.. d	.. c	.. c	.. c	-1.3	-	-1.1	-1.1	..
Egypt	.. d	.. d	-7.7	42.8	21.2	.. d	.. d	362.7	284.1	..
Libya	.. d	- d	.. c	.. c	.. c	- d	.. d	.. c	.. c	..
Morocco	.. d	.. d	.. c	.. c	.. c	.. d	124.2	33.2	53.0	..
Tunisia	.. d	.. d	.. c	.. c	.. c	15.9	5.5	-	4.5	..
Other African countries	-253.4	130.9	-577.2	408.1	36.6	-1 766.0	508.0	-100.6	312.3	..
Nigeria	.. d	.. d	.. c	.. c	.. c	13.3	10.0	32.1	11.3	..
South Africa	-297.2	.. d	66.4	230.0	64.9	260.1	82.1	28.8	99.2	..
AMERICA	**-4 358.5**	**3 615.1**	**43 824.0**	**3 370.5**	**16 105.3**	**.. d**	**3 871.3**	**-80 869.2**	**6 605.8**	**..**
Northern America	-935.4	970.6	43 496.6	4 111.1	19 085.3	.. d	.. d	-59 826.4	1 394.4	..
Central America and Caribbean countries	-2 818.1	1 649.5	-59.7	-214.2	-5 072.6	.. d	.. d	-21 046.1	4 610.5	..
Bahamas	.. d	-	.. c	.. c	.. c	.. d	.. d	.. c	.. c	..
Bermuda	2 676.1	.. d	.. c	.. c	.. c	.. d	3.3	-4.4	58.6	..
Cayman Islands	.. d	-8.9	-77.4	2.3	-253.7	.. d	.. d	-17.7	-27.1	..
Costa Rica	.. d	.. d	.. c	.. c	.. c	2.7	-1.1	-1.1	-1.1	..
El Salvador	- d	.. d	.. c	.. c	.. c	1.3	.. d	.. c	.. c	..
Guatemala	.. d	.. d	.. c	.. c	.. c	-	- d	.. c	.. c	..
Honduras	- d	-	-	-	-	- d	- d	.. c	.. c	..
Nicaragua	- d	.. d	.. c	.. c	.. c	-	-	.. c	.. c	..
Panama	.. d	- d	5.5	-20.3	-131.0	.. d	.. d	.. c	.. c	..
Virgin Islands, U.S.	- d	- d	-	-1.1	-1.2	-	-	-	-	..
South America	-606.3	995.0	387.0	-526.4	2 092.5	358.2	.. d	3.3	600.8	..
Argentina	114.1	-18.9	.. c	.. c	.. c	.. d	.. d	52.0	2.3	..
Bolivia	-	-	-	-2.3	-	-	- d	-	-	..
Brazil	-709.8	1 080.4	677.9	-441.9	1 891.9	.. d	.. d	-60.8	455.4	..
Colombia	.. d	.. d	-3.3	-22.5	21.2	11.9	.. d	29.9	19.2	..
Ecuador	.. d	- d	-6.6	-	2.4	4.0	.. d	.. c	.. c	..
Paraguay	-	-	-1.1	-	-	- d	- d	.. c	.. c	..
Peru	-4.0	.. d	.. c	.. c	.. c	.. d	.. d	.. c	.. c	..
Uruguay	.. d	.. d	.. c	.. c	.. c	-1.3	.. d	3.3	-10.1	..
Venezuela	.. d	-1.1	.. c	.. c	.. c	.. d	-1.1	-77.4	-49.6	..

Table 1. Foreign direct investment flows by country *(cont.)*

Million US dollars

	Inward					Outward				
	2014	2015	2016	2017	2018	2014	2015	2016	2017	2018
ASIA	**299.9**	**2 373.8**	**5 912.9**	**1 454.2**	**-357.6**	**.. d**	**.. d**	**-2 014.8**	**1 391.0**	..
Near and Middle East	-384.8	.. d	-298.6	19.2	-348.2	.. d	.. d	147.1	299.9	..
Gulf Arabian countries	-61.0	.. d	-16.6	45.1	-348.2	.. d	.. d	148.2	269.4	..
Kuwait	.. d	.. d	.. c	.. c	.. c	.. d	-	-	-	..
Qatar	.. d	.. d	6.6	73.3	-4.7	.. d	93.2	-10.0	-5.6	..
Saudi Arabia	.. d	.. d	-28.8	13.5	4.7	.. d	.. d	60.8	5.6	..
United Arab Emirates	.. d	44.4	2.2	-101.5	-382.4	91.5	146.4	97.3	278.4	..
Other Near and Middle East	-323.7	.. d	.. c	.. c	.. c	-26.5	22.2	-1.1	29.3	..
Jordan	.. d	.. d	.. c	.. c	.. c	.. d	4.4	.. c	.. c	..
Other Asian countries	684.6	2 085.4	6 211.4	1 435.0	-9.4	.. d	.. d	-2 161.9	1 091.2	..
China	-862.4	451.5	319.6	60.9	813.2	635.5	.. d	-46.4	1.1	..
Hong Kong, China	179.1	493.6	1 872.2	20.3	-3 119.3	.. d	.. d	-2 960.3	-134.1	..
India	.. d	.. d	-42.0	25.9	182.9	.. d	.. d	278.7	266.0	..
Indonesia	-63.7	94.3	-23.2	4.5	1.2	-853.1	-18.9	164.8	227.7	..
Iran, Islamic Republic of	.. d	.. d	.. c	.. c	.. c	- d	.. d	.. c	.. c	..
Malaysia	-31.8	.. d	.. c	.. c	.. c	.. d	.. d	67.5	208.5	..
Philippines	-1.3	-1.1	.. c	.. c	.. c	23.9	-6.7	19.9	4.5	..
Singapore	149.9	178.6	457.8	581.7	-587.7	.. d	.. d	-353.9	627.9	..
Chinese Taipei	-41.1	68.8	39.8	37.2	-21.2	18.6	18.9	-6.6	-11.3	..
Thailand	59.7	-629.0	.. c	.. c	.. c	.. d	55.5	61.9	9.0	..
Viet Nam	- d	.. d	-1.1	-3.4	-4.7	-6.6	34.4	6.6	276.2	..
AUSTRALIA, OCEANIA AND POLAR REGIONS	**594.4**	**-104.3**	**-139.3**	**554.6**	**332.8**	**.. d**	**.. d**	**-49.8**	**1 360.6**	..
WORLD unallocated and confidential	**1.3**	**31.1**	**-2.2**	**1.1**	**-23.6**	**.. d**	**.. d**	**-**	**1.1**	..
European Union (EU28)	**-9 603.3**	**9 428.7**	**25 383.2**	**-2 326.7**	**-6 298.8**	**9 088.5**	**37 610.6**	**121 102.5**	**25 120.1**	..
G20 countries excl. European Union	**-1 369.2**	**14 052.1**	**63 831.7**	**-5 377.1**	**30 947.7**	**-7 284.1**	**17 543.0**	**20 416.9**	**1 460.9**	..
G20 OECD countries	**655.4**	**12 082.1**	**62 971.4**	**-5 047.9**	**27 463.7**	**-7 851.9**	**17 069.3**	**19 726.9**	**608.7**	..
G20 Non-OECD countries	**-2 024.7**	**1 970.1**	**860.3**	**-329.2**	**3 484.0**	**566.5**	**.. d**	**690.0**	**852.2**	..
MENA countries	**-33.2**	**189.7**	**-38.7**	**93.6**	**-326.9**	**.. d**	**.. d**	**505.4**	**602.0**	..
ASEAN countries	**95.5**	**-397.1**	**931.1**	**677.5**	**-406.0**	**.. d**	**.. d**	**-2.2**	**1 339.2**	..

- Nil; .. Not available; c Confidential data; d Secondary Confidentiality

Note: Data excludes resident Special Purpose Entities (SPEs). Detailed metadata at: *http://stats.oecd.org/OECDStat_Metadata/ShowMetadata.ashx?Dataset=FDI_CTRY_IND_SUMM.*

1. Information on data for Israel: *http://oe.cd/israel-disclaimer*.
2. Note by Turkey: The information in this document with reference to "Cyprus" relates to the southern part of the Island. There is no single authority representing both Turkish and Greek Cypriot people on the Island. Turkey recognises the Turkish Republic of Northern Cyprus (TRNC). Until a lasting and equitable solution is found within the context of the United Nations, Turkey shall preserve its position concerning the "Cyprus issue".
3. Note by all the European Union Member States of the OECD and the European Union: The Republic of Cyprus is recognised by all members of the United Nations with the exception of Turkey. The information in this document relates to the area under the effective control of the Government of the Republic of Cyprus.

Source: OECD International Direct Investment Statistics (database): https://doi.org/10.1787/idi-data-en

BELGIUM

Table 2. Foreign direct investment positions by country

At year end

Million US dollars

	Inward					Outward				
	2014	2015	2016	2017	2018	2014	2015	2016	2017	2018
WORLD	**496 545.0**	**520 992.9**	**517 401.7**	**583 051.1**	**524 712.6**	**554 653.1**	**582 582.5**	**599 379.2**	**706 661.1**	**586 103.7**
OECD COUNTRIES	**491 936.3**	**.. d**	**507 827.6**	**571 567.5**	**519 640.5**	**525 242.7**	**.. d**	**573 158.0**	**674 429.1**	**558 486.4**
Australia	-781.9	-797.0	-1 033.0	-425.8	-292.0	784.3	2 035.9	2 224.1	2 962.3	1 390.0
Austria	683.5	1 200.9	1 412.5	1 180.1	1 412.9	821.9	696.8	635.6	297.4	427.1
Belgium	-	-	-	-	-	-	-	-	-	-
Canada	-781.9	-312.5	-144.4	165.5	611.4	520.8	1 008.2	1 540.0	2 161.2	2 312.8
Chile	.. d	8.7	24.2	201.5	.. c	1 180.1	1 004.9	1 019.3	1 254.5	1 185.0
Czech Republic	1 512.8	.. d	3 388.8	5 170.3	2 600.2	4 440.0	4 707.7	6 267.5	7 265.5	7 098.7
Denmark	983.4	1 327.2	748.4	833.5	998.4	400.7	688.1	561.8	883.9	816.4
Estonia	-14.6	.. d	9.5	2.4	-4.6	14.6	15.2	7.4	31.2	8.0
Finland	2 354.1	1 399.0	1 345.0	834.7	1 782.7	539.1	634.7	598.7	485.7	516.4
France	130 485.4	115 236.8	127 166.6	133 574.0	136 551.4	40 884.8	36 172.0	41 659.1	46 169.3	58 196.7
Germany	10 674.4	15 651.6	10 587.1	1 314.5	12 267.0	12 931.4	.. d	9 343.3	12 180.4	14 894.7
Greece	547.6	603.2	599.8	880.3	617.1	238.0	.. d	774.7	1 605.9	1 135.8
Hungary	3 834.1	3 051.7	4 297.5	2 049.7	308.0	1 754.4	1 822.5	1 852.0	3 181.8	3 076.5
Iceland	27.9	.. d	-	-	-2.3	29.1	28.3	112.8	145.1	3.4
Ireland	-6 593.8	-2 297.2	1 769.8	8 524.8	12 316.2	5 411.2	7 073.5	6 589.0	6 764.2	5 500.3
Israel[1]	-51.0	.. d	-71.7	-84.0	-79.0	46.1	44.6	64.3	36.0	49.2
Italy	136.0	-1 050.6	1 411.4	2 261.9	2 238.4	9 461.5	9 442.6	9 295.9	10 981.1	11 351.0
Japan	14 086.0	13 285.8	15 879.6	18 689.1	19 613.0	1 836.9	1 932.5	2 631.0	2 409.5	2 431.9
Korea	944.6	966.8	1 054.1	1 397.2	1 757.5	1 346.4	292.9	336.3	652.4	913.7
Latvia	.. d	-12.0	.. c	-1.2	.. c	24.3	31.6	10.5	37.2	59.5
Lithuania	.. d	.. d	-8.4	-	1.1	10.9	10.9	6.3	7.2	-3.4
Luxembourg	152 925.6	143 213.9	127 452.3	155 038.4	134 599.3	155 788.5	169 294.5	140 822.2	199 493.9	149 528.3
Mexico	-1 244.5	-704.4	-660.9	-713.6	-629.7	17 144.3	.. d	-4 890.9	-2.4	693.8
Netherlands	184 087.9	185 607.0	156 584.8	170 479.7	129 498.5	200 889.8	216 541.1	228 930.1	245 362.2	198 465.8
New Zealand	-125.1	-128.5	-6.3	-38.4	-69.8	13.4	10.9	-14.8	161.9	681.2
Norway	8 929.7	3 572.1	-4 635.8	-4 998.8	-1 691.1	695.7	513.9	756.8	575.7	614.8
Poland	-3 438.3	-3 002.7	-2 209.3	-2 090.4	-1 959.0	.. d	.. d	2 777.5	3 683.1	3 432.6
Portugal	-2 166.0	-443.1	-163.4	-146.3	-154.6	914.2	2 541.1	2 709.0	3 147.0	390.4
Slovak Republic	.. d	.. d	266.7	284.2	243.9	1 515.2	1 368.5	1 322.9	1 731.8	1 777.0
Slovenia	.. d	.. d	-21.1	-24.0	.. c	757.6	680.5	675.7	756.8	724.8
Spain	-4 157.1	-3 514.4	-375.3	-229.1	1 165.6	4 011.4	3 909.6	4 341.7	4 914.8	6 249.1
Sweden	11 134.5	7 923.8	11 575.8	8 136.2	5 093.9	990.7	732.7	748.4	1 063.8	53.8
Switzerland	3 313.3	44 021.8	43 837.9	52 555.8	49 552.3	1 918.3	2 151.3	1 569.5	4 430.3	4 121.8
Turkey	71.6	-42.5	-14.8	-52.8	-34.3	2 620.0	2 616.2	3 767.3	3 637.6	3 286.0
United Kingdom	-7 179.0	-3 011.4	4 119.3	4 941.2	3 374.2	24 663.2	34 476.9	142 859.7	136 410.4	79 149.3
United States	-8 654.1	-9 404.5	3 629.2	11 854.2	17 366.6	27 795.6	22 250.4	-38 736.2	-30 443.8	-2 042.6
EUROPE	**491 887.8**	**513 532.9**	**490 791.6**	**542 918.0**	**492 380.4**	**480 760.5**	**514 788.2**	**614 905.7**	**704 474.7**	**561 244.6**
Bulgaria	88.6	68.6	95.9	112.7	-13.7	296.2	377.8	474.3	1 596.3	1 417.4
Croatia	-14.6	-10.9	-6.3	-8.4	-3.4	259.8	545.5	470.1	668.0	830.1
Cyprus[2, 3]	1 080.5	774.1	845.4	927.1	956.0	2 480.4	.. d	2 246.2	3 476.9	5 242.7
Malta	.. d	.. d	781.1	1 550.7	897.6	.. d	.. d	32.7	49.2	45.8
Romania	-24.3	-28.3	-42.2	-50.4	-109.9	1 005.3	837.2	1 425.1	1 348.0	1 632.7
Russian Federation	-309.6	-59.9	44.3	-20.4	6.9	1 960.8	.. d	1 203.8	1 192.1	258.8
Ukraine	-17.0	-9.8	-5.3	-3.6	-13.7	-7.3	.. d	-2.1	-2.4	18.3
AFRICA	**-471.1**	**-233.0**	**-796.9**	**-254.3**	**-96.2**	**1 781.1**	**2 202.5**	**2 049.1**	**2 669.7**	**1 836.5**
Northern Africa	35.2	14.2	-3.2	44.4	.. c	535.4	452.9	645.1	1 241.3	978.9
Algeria	.. d	.. d	2.1	2.4	-	6.1	16.3	15.8	22.8	9.2
Egypt	.. d	.. d	-34.8	4.8	43.5	276.8	215.6	446.9	791.6	728.2
Libya	8.5	.. d	4.2	1.2	2.3	-	3.3	3.2	3.6	3.4
Morocco	.. d	26.1	21.1	31.2	96.2	204.0	185.1	151.8	387.4	211.8
Tunisia	- d	.. d	.. c	.. c	9.2	47.4	32.7	27.4	34.8	26.3
Other African countries	-505.1	-248.2	-793.7	-298.6	-247.3	1 245.7	1 749.6	1 404.0	1 428.4	857.6
Nigeria	.. d	.. d	.. c	.. c	.. c	75.3	432.2	73.8	78.0	65.3
South Africa	-693.3	.. d	-431.1	-219.5	-144.3	250.1	235.2	320.4	305.8	-50.4
AMERICA	**-12 289.1**	**-10 009.8**	**4 536.7**	**13 203.4**	**7 206.3**	**50 657.1**	**44 118.7**	**-37 018.0**	**-22 076.0**	**5 491.2**
Northern America	-9 437.2	-9 716.9	3 485.8	12 019.7	17 976.9	28 316.5	23 258.6	-37 196.2	-28 282.6	270.2
Central America and Caribbean countries	1 334.3	2 695.7	3 413.1	3 596.8	-942.3	17 252.4	.. d	-4 766.5	32.4	596.5
Bahamas	-	-	7.4	8.4	-	2.4	2.2	2.1	-	-
Bermuda	.. d	.. d	3 106.4	3 263.4	-1 212.5	-	.. d	85.4	142.7	91.6
Cayman Islands	195.5	167.7	1 191.1	1 273.7	1 046.5	.. d	32.7	8.4	2.4	2.3
Costa Rica	.. d	.. d	.. c	.. c	144.3	.. d	- d	-	-1.2	-
El Salvador	-1.2	-	-	-1.2	-	4.9	4.4	5.3	6.0	5.7
Guatemala	.. d	.. d	1.1	-	-1.1	1.2	1.1	1.1	1.2	-
Honduras	-	-	-	-	-	3.6	3.3	4.2	-129.5	-216.4
Nicaragua	-	-	-	-	-	-	-	11.6	13.2	18.3
Panama	-111.7	-113.2	-95.9	-115.1	-242.7	-8.5	-3.3	1.1	-6.0	-1.1
Virgin Islands, U.S.	-	-	-	-	-1.1	-	-	-	-	-
South America	-4 187.4	-2 988.6	-2 362.2	-2 413.0	-9 828.3	5 088.3	4 572.7	4 944.7	6 172.9	4 624.5
Argentina	574.3	486.7	239.3	202.7	356.1	.. d	.. d	1 634.9	1 741.4	161.4
Bolivia	-	-	-	-	-	2.4	2.2	1.1	1.2	1.1
Brazil	-4 873.4	-3 416.4	-2 540.3	-2 751.3	-764.8	1 873.4	.. d	1 562.1	2 314.7	2 173.1
Colombia	.. d	.. d	-40.1	-57.6	-34.3	21.9	19.6	128.6	255.5	1 150.7
Ecuador	-15.8	-14.2	-13.7	-14.4	-13.7	7.3	14.2	7.4	12.0	14.9
Paraguay	-	-	-	-	-	-	-	33.7	60.0	77.9
Peru	- d	.. d	-10.5	.. c	.. c	.. d	.. d	600.8	620.1	601.1
Uruguay	.. d	.. d	-6.3	-	-	19.4	15.2	10.5	9.6	8.0
Venezuela	.. d	.. d	-22.1	12.0	51.5	23.1	68.6	-53.8	-95.9	-748.8

Table 2. Foreign direct investment positions by country *(cont.)*

At year end

Million US dollars

	Inward					Outward				
	2014	2015	2016	2017	2018	2014	2015	2016	2017	2018
ASIA	**18 016.0**	**18 290.7**	**23 561.7**	**27 302.7**	**25 273.6**	**20 653.1**	**19 420.8**	**17 215.1**	**18 117.1**	**14 625.6**
Near and Middle East	.. d	148.1	91.7	149.9	-295.4	1 697.3	.. d	2 257.8	1 922.5	1 931.5
Gulf Arabian countries	.. d	-98.0	75.9	127.1	-265.6	919.1	.. d	1 432.5	1 164.5	1 173.6
Kuwait	-	.. d	-23.2	-	-	-	-	-	-	-
Qatar	.. d	.. d	3.2	66.0	59.5	.. d	66.4	56.9	54.0	93.9
Saudi Arabia	.. d	.. d	-40.1	-26.4	-21.8	40.1	.. d	71.7	72.0	83.6
United Arab Emirates	.. d	.. d	186.6	116.3	-306.8	911.8	1 193.3	1 295.5	1 021.8	993.8
Other Near and Middle East	199.1	.. d	15.8	22.8	-29.8	778.2	786.1	825.3	758.0	758.0
Jordan	-	-	-	-	-1.1	734.5	734.9	745.2	696.8	692.7
Other Asian countries	18 161.7	18 142.6	23 470.0	27 152.8	25 569.0	18 955.7	17 309.7	14 957.3	16 194.5	12 694.1
China	-1 946.2	-1 020.1	-412.1	-624.9	420.2	2 278.9	2 406.1	2 094.4	2 498.2	2 064.3
Hong Kong, China	5 406.4	5 470.9	6 592.2	6 598.7	3 095.9	7 210.5	6 559.6	3 639.7	3 276.6	2 686.1
India	174.8	155.7	52.7	193.1	364.1	1 498.2	.. d	1 303.9	1 471.6	1 212.5
Indonesia	.. d	.. d	25.3	32.4	35.5	63.1	238.4	495.4	761.6	699.6
Iran, Islamic Republic of	-	- d	-	-	-3.4	1.2	10.9	-	14.4	13.7
Malaysia	191.8	136.1	163.4	127.1	56.1	318.1	.. d	472.2	735.2	846.1
Philippines	.. d	12.0	.. c	.. c	-20.6	57.1	35.9	311.0	63.6	65.3
Singapore	-416.4	-204.7	313.1	783.2	155.7	.. d	3 363.1	2 779.6	3 490.0	1 361.3
Chinese Taipei	-32.8	33.8	72.7	112.7	84.7	59.5	68.6	76.9	39.6	50.4
Thailand	-108.1	-710.9	-302.5	-179.9	6.9	310.8	515.0	353.1	386.2	316.0
Viet Nam	-6.1	-4.4	-4.2	-4.8	-9.2	13.4	49.0	21.1	251.9	13.7
AUSTRALIA, OCEANIA AND POLAR REGIONS	**-598.6**	**-589.0**	**-693.6**	**-119.9**	**-30.9**	**802.5**	**2 052.3**	**2 227.3**	**3 475.7**	**2 905.9**
WORLD unallocated and confidential	**-**	**1.1**	**2.1**	**1.2**	**-20.6**	**-1.2**	**-**	**-**	**-**	**-**
European Union (EU28)	**479 888.8**	**466 027.2**	**451 644.4**	**495 563.7**	**444 698.9**	**473 407.9**	**508 222.1**	**607 433.3**	**693 635.2**	**552 079.2**
G20 countries excl. European Union	**130 642.0**	**125 515.5**	**158 933.3**	**169 793.7**	**193 071.9**	**149 533.4**	**145 368.5**	**178 715.1**	**197 479.0**	**179 180.2**
G20 OECD countries	**137 756.6**	**129 820.4**	**161 996.4**	**173 006.7**	**192 821.2**	**139 990.6**	**137 067.0**	**170 028.5**	**187 120.4**	**172 577.3**
G20 Non-OECD countries	**-7 113.4**	**-4 304.8**	**-3 063.1**	**-3 213.0**	**250.7**	**9 542.8**	**8 301.6**	**8 686.6**	**10 357.4**	**6 602.9**
MENA countries	**-217.3**	**4.4**	**162.3**	**279.4**	**-64.1**	**2 189.0**	**2 517.1**	**2 824.9**	**3 102.7**	**2 848.6**
ASEAN countries	**-440.7**	**-794.8**	**201.3**	**759.2**	**222.1**	**4 601.4**	**4 710.9**	**4 551.5**	**5 776.0**	**3 207.0**

- Nil; .. Not available; c Confidential data; d Secondary Confidentiality

Note: Data excludes resident Special Purpose Entities (SPEs). Detailed metadata at: *http://stats.oecd.org/OECDStat_Metadata/ShowMetadata.ashx?Dataset=FDI_CTRY_IND_SUMM.*

1. Information on data for Israel: *http://oe.cd/israel-disclaimer.*
2. Note by Turkey: The information in this document with reference to "Cyprus" relates to the southern part of the Island. There is no single authority representing both Turkish and Greek Cypriot people on the Island. Turkey recognises the Turkish Republic of Northern Cyprus (TRNC). Until a lasting and equitable solution is found within the context of the United Nations, Turkey shall preserve its position concerning the "Cyprus issue".
3. Note by all the European Union Member States of the OECD and the European Union: The Republic of Cyprus is recognised by all members of the United Nations with the exception of Turkey. The information in this document relates to the area under the effective control of the Government of the Republic of Cyprus.

Source: OECD International Direct Investment Statistics (database): https://doi.org/10.1787/idi-data-en

BELGIUM

Table 3. Foreign direct investment income by country

Million US dollars

	Inward					Outward				
	2014	2015	2016	2017	2018	2014	2015	2016	2017	2018
WORLD	**22 222.4**	**20 682.2**	**31 450.8**	**26 833.5**	**42 567.0**	**18 898.8**	**12 695.5**	**32 119.9**	**24 680.4**	**38 648.6**
OECD COUNTRIES	**22 333.8**	**.. d**	**31 321.5**	**26 541.5**	**42 381.7**	**19 522.4**	**11 327.8**	**30 771.9**	**22 437.2**	**35 751.2**
Australia	-37.2	-6.7	-24.3	-40.6	-8.3	103.5	163.1	4.4	624.5	-157.0
Austria	2.7	42.2	118.3	99.2	76.7	110.1	69.9	52.0	89.1	151.1
Belgium	-	-	-	-	-	-	-	-	-	-
Canada	-10.6	-15.5	60.8	51.9	54.3	.. d	.. d	78.5	69.9	112.1
Chile	.. d	.. d	-16.6	-29.3	-20.1	-15.9	36.6	28.8	22.5	-3.5
Czech Republic	13.3	6.7	3.3	3.4	14.2	.. d	.. d	799.5	762.0	909.9
Denmark	.. d	.. d	67.5	72.1	107.4	.. d	58.8	27.6	63.1	85.0
Estonia	- d	-	-	-	-	-	.. d	3.3	4.5	4.7
Finland	74.3	228.5	2.2	505.0	269.1	34.5	26.6	96.2	31.6	7.1
France	6 036.9	5 738.2	7 862.4	8 760.0	10 003.5	-73.0	1 327.8	3 345.1	2 404.5	2 592.9
Germany	1 038.9	1 487.5	1 607.9	3 151.8	2 364.0	.. d	.. d	290.8	1 087.8	6 780.4
Greece	-4.0	-11.1	-2.2	-1.1	-11.8	-8.0	-16.6	-10.0	84.5	88.5
Hungary	61.0	49.9	46.4	-2.3	-	.. d	.. d	214.5	190.5	260.8
Iceland	.. d	.. d	.. c	.. c	.. c	- d	.. d	3.3	4.5	3.5
Ireland	63.7	145.3	222.3	-3.4	107.4	.. d	.. d	395.9	591.8	770.7
Israel[1]	.. d	.. d	-8.8	-12.4	-20.1	-18.6	24.4	18.8	32.7	-
Italy	-513.5	-337.2	-73.0	-18.0	-48.4	-520.1	55.5	662.4	1 139.7	420.2
Japan	1 350.7	1 041.6	822.7	-32.7	2 024.1	41.1	-224.1	113.9	127.4	201.8
Korea	.. d	.. d	57.5	93.6	105.0	26.5	73.2	57.5	67.6	92.1
Latvia	- d	- d	-	-	-	1.3	1.1	3.3	3.4	3.5
Lithuania	.. d	.. d	.. c	.. c	.. c	1.3	1.1	1.1	1.1	1.2
Luxembourg	6 375.2	5 027.2	9 896.1	-289.7	7 227.7	6 324.8	1 835.8	1 073.8	7 166.0	7 328.0
Mexico	.. d	.. d	-19.9	-44.0	-54.3	.. d	.. d	822.7	-47.3	11.8
Netherlands	6 931.1	5 756.0	8 477.3	8 712.7	14 791.7	7 028.0	.. d	11 435.4	372.0	6 939.7
New Zealand	-6.6	-6.7	-2.2	-	-2.4	1.3	1.1	66.4	-12.4	36.6
Norway	58.4	-2.2	-56.4	1 586.1	162.9	55.7	25.5	35.4	21.4	10.6
Poland	-134.0	-103.2	-73.0	-32.7	-18.9	.. d	.. d	320.7	253.6	252.6
Portugal	-8.0	-	42.0	-2.3	-	.. d	.. d	499.8	293.1	86.2
Slovak Republic	- d	- d	-1.1	-1.1	-1.2	.. d	.. d	123.9	95.8	75.5
Slovenia	- d	- d	-	-1.1	-1.2	.. d	.. d	118.3	108.2	131.0
Spain	42.5	1.1	120.5	38.3	81.4	.. d	.. d	494.3	290.8	177.0
Sweden	557.3	316.1	749.8	1 502.6	940.6	.. d	.. d	84.0	177.0	64.9
Switzerland	-69.0	686.6	754.2	811.6	518.1	.. d	.. d	-245.5	96.9	55.5
Turkey	-13.3	.. d	4.4	-18.0	-24.8	39.8	143.1	217.8	414.8	509.9
United Kingdom	363.5	475.9	230.0	981.9	2 155.1	.. d	.. d	10 470.0	6 663.3	8 560.1
United States	110.1	318.4	457.8	697.8	1 589.8	1 378.5	768.7	-928.9	-855.6	-813.2
EUROPE	**20 960.6**	**19 486.4**	**30 000.0**	**25 804.3**	**38 713.6**	**17 059.8**	**9 632.8**	**31 049.4**	**22 743.8**	**37 083.7**
Bulgaria	-1.3	-1.1	-1.1	-	-	.. d	.. d	26.5	74.4	76.7
Croatia	.. d	- d	-	-	-	.. d	.. d	34.3	18.0	21.2
Cyprus[2, 3]	.. d	7.8	58.6	16.9	22.4	.. d	.. d	193.5	-37.2	249.0
Malta	.. d	.. d	-19.9	-51.9	-41.3	10.6	8.9	8.8	9.0	8.3
Romania	.. d	.. d	-3.3	-3.4	-5.9	.. d	.. d	95.1	133.0	132.2
Russian Federation	-14.6	-28.8	-25.4	-15.8	-24.8	.. d	.. d	174.7	172.5	354.1
Ukraine	- d	- d	.. c	.. c	.. c	.. d	.. d	-6.6	5.6	13.0
AFRICA	**-26.5**	**-26.6**	**-22.1**	**-7.9**	**-1.2**	**-1 840.3**	**-431.5**	**-277.6**	**251.4**	**1 109.4**
Northern Africa	6.6	2.2	2.2	4.5	3.5	.. d	-312.8	-32.1	96.9	55.5
Algeria	- d	- d	-	-	-	1.3	2.2	3.3	2.3	3.5
Egypt	- d	- d	-1.1	-	-	.. d	.. d	-153.7	45.1	-3.5
Libya	- d	- d	-	-	-	- d	- d	-	-	-
Morocco	.. d	.. d	.. c	.. c	.. c	.. d	.. d	105.1	37.2	40.1
Tunisia	- d	- d	-	-	-	19.9	14.4	12.2	12.4	14.2
Other African countries	-30.5	-28.8	-24.3	-12.4	-4.7	.. d	-118.7	-245.5	154.4	1 055.1
Nigeria	.. d	- d	.. c	.. c	.. c	42.5	11.1	13.3	20.3	920.6
South Africa	-13.3	.. d	-8.8	-3.4	-1.2	26.5	36.6	29.9	37.2	17.7
AMERICA	**-122.1**	**65.4**	**347.2**	**578.3**	**1 476.5**	**2 536.8**	**2 022.2**	**301.9**	**-207.4**	**-203.0**
Northern America	99.5	302.8	518.6	748.5	1 645.2	1 345.4	753.2	-849.3	-785.7	-701.1
Central America and Caribbean countries	-31.8	.. d	32.1	29.3	-26.0	.. d	.. d	828.3	-24.8	33.0
Bahamas	-	-	-	-	-	- d	- d	-	-	-
Bermuda	21.2	17.7	.. c	.. c	.. c	-	.. d	3.3	13.5	14.2
Cayman Islands	.. d	-2.2	14.4	15.8	23.6	.. d	- d	-	-	-
Costa Rica	-4.0	- d	.. c	.. c	.. c	-	-	-1.1	-	-
El Salvador	- d	- d	-	-	-	.. d	.. d	1.1	1.1	1.2
Guatemala	- d	- d	.. c	.. c	.. c	-	-	-	-	-
Honduras	- d	-	-	-	-	- d	- d	-	-1.1	-2.4
Nicaragua	- d	-	-	-	-	-	-	1.1	4.5	5.9
Panama	.. d	.. d	-	-	-	.. d	- d	.. c	.. c	.. c
Virgin Islands, U.S.	- d	-	-	-	-	-	-	-	-	-
South America	-191.1	-247.4	-203.5	-199.5	-141.6	152.6	277.3	324.0	600.8	466.2
Argentina	-	.. d	-	-2.3	-1.2	.. d	.. d	40.9	-6.8	22.4
Bolivia	-	-	-	-	-	- d	- d	-	-	-1.2
Brazil	-165.8	-223.0	-184.7	-164.6	-120.4	21.2	.. d	94.0	443.0	180.6
Colombia	.. d	.. d	-1.1	-	-2.4	-1.3	-	16.6	19.2	4.7
Ecuador	- d	- d	-	-	-	4.0	3.3	1.1	1.1	-
Paraguay	-	-	-	-	-	- d	- d	1.1	3.4	3.5
Peru	- d	- d	.. c	.. c	.. c	.. d	.. d	.. c	.. c	.. c
Uruguay	- d	- d	.. c	.. c	.. c	.. d	.. d	5.5	11.3	9.4
Venezuela	- d	-	-	-2.3	-	-1.3	.. d	-52.0	-53.0	81.4

Table 3. Foreign direct investment income by country (cont.)

Million US dollars

	Inward					Outward				
	2014	2015	2016	2017	2018	2014	2015	2016	2017	2018
ASIA	**1 456.8**	**1 170.3**	**1 152.3**	**498.3**	**2 388.8**	**1 037.5**	**1 307.8**	**968.7**	**1 278.3**	**778.9**
Near and Middle East	-1.3	-11.1	4.4	-4.5	11.8	.. d	.. d	170.3	91.3	27.1
Gulf Arabian countries	.. d	.. d	13.3	9.0	31.9	.. d	.. d	110.6	38.3	-4.7
Kuwait	-	-	-	-	-	-	-	-	-	-
Qatar	- d	- d	.. c	.. c	.. c	.. d	.. d	-6.6	-5.6	-16.5
Saudi Arabia	- d	.. d	.. c	.. c	.. c	.. d	.. d	17.7	4.5	11.8
United Arab Emirates	14.6	.. d	14.4	10.1	34.2	49.1	52.1	99.5	53.0	-1.2
Other Near and Middle East	-14.6	.. d	-8.8	-12.4	-20.1	.. d	.. d	59.7	53.0	31.9
Jordan	- d	-	-	-	-	.. d	.. d	32.1	11.3	13.0
Other Asian countries	1 458.1	1 181.4	1 147.8	502.8	2 378.1	927.4	1 117.0	798.4	1 188.1	753.0
China	79.6	75.4	241.1	223.2	187.7	.. d	.. d	14.4	129.6	3.5
Hong Kong, China	58.4	75.4	86.3	245.7	86.2	455.1	737.0	310.7	323.5	145.2
India	.. d	.. d	-19.9	-13.5	-11.8	.. d	.. d	103.9	129.6	33.0
Indonesia	-2.7	.. d	-1.1	-1.1	-	.. d	.. d	28.8	55.2	40.1
Iran, Islamic Republic of	-	- d	-	-	-	-	.. d	4.4	4.5	4.7
Malaysia	2.7	-1.1	-2.2	-1.1	5.9	.. d	.. d	59.7	95.8	99.1
Philippines	- d	-	-	-	-	.. d	4.4	11.1	12.4	7.1
Singapore	-25.2	-13.3	-24.3	-10.1	-11.8	.. d	.. d	-16.6	255.9	66.1
Chinese Taipei	1.3	.. d	2.2	2.3	-	14.6	16.6	8.8	2.3	3.5
Thailand	.. d	.. d	-14.4	-6.8	-7.1	.. d	.. d	46.4	21.4	33.0
Viet Nam	- d	- d	-	-	-	1.3	2.2	-	-	-4.7
AUSTRALIA, OCEANIA AND POLAR REGIONS	**-43.8**	**-14.4**	**-26.5**	**-40.6**	**-10.6**	**106.1**	**165.3**	**76.3**	**614.4**	**-122.7**
WORLD unallocated and confidential	**-2.7**	**1.1**	**-**	**1.1**	**-**	**-1.3**	**-1.1**	**1.1**	**-**	**2.4**
European Union (EU28)	**21 005.7**	**18 843.0**	**29 329.9**	**23 442.7**	**38 104.6**	**16 677.7**	**9 298.9**	**30 859.2**	**22 067.4**	**36 177.3**
G20 countries excl. European Union	**8 186.3**	**8 492.5**	**10 985.3**	**13 606.1**	**18 184.8**	**3 926.0**	**4 227.4**	**15 639.7**	**12 661.5**	**18 976.8**
G20 OECD countries	**8 309.7**	**8 707.7**	**10 985.3**	**13 583.6**	**18 157.7**	**3 603.6**	**3 690.5**	**15 134.4**	**11 696.5**	**18 312.3**
G20 Non-OECD countries	**-122.1**	**-215.2**	**1.1**	**22.5**	**26.0**	**323.7**	**538.0**	**505.4**	**964.9**	**665.6**
MENA countries	**25.2**	**.. d**	**16.6**	**13.5**	**35.4**	**-273.3**	**-143.1**	**118.3**	**148.8**	**79.1**
ASEAN countries	**-38.5**	**-27.7**	**-42.0**	**-18.0**	**-13.0**	**132.7**	**297.3**	**140.4**	**438.5**	**240.8**

- Nil; .. Not available; c Confidential data; d Secondary Confidentiality

Note: Data excludes resident Special Purpose Entities (SPEs). Detailed metadata at: *http://stats.oecd.org/OECDStat_Metadata/ShowMetadata.ashx?Dataset=FDI_CTRY_IND_SUMM.*

1. Information on data for Israel: *http://oe.cd/israel-disclaimer.*
2. Note by Turkey: The information in this document with reference to "Cyprus" relates to the southern part of the Island. There is no single authority representing both Turkish and Greek Cypriot people on the Island. Turkey recognises the Turkish Republic of Northern Cyprus (TRNC). Until a lasting and equitable solution is found within the context of the United Nations, Turkey shall preserve its position concerning the "Cyprus issue".
3. Note by all the European Union Member States of the OECD and the European Union: The Republic of Cyprus is recognised by all members of the United Nations with the exception of Turkey. The information in this document relates to the area under the effective control of the Government of the Republic of Cyprus.

Source: OECD International Direct Investment Statistics (database): https://doi.org/10.1787/idi-data-en

Table 4. Foreign direct investment flows by industrial sector

Million US dollars

	Inward					Outward				
	2014	2015	2016	2017	2018	2014	2015	2016	2017	2018
All FDI activities	**-13 465.6**	**51 524.1**	**68 178.7**	**4 212.6**	**17 028.2**	**-4 126.3**	**44 194.1**	**40 165.9**	**34 746.9**	**31 312.4**
Agriculture, forestry and fishing	**10.6**	**-13.3**	**2.2**	**-3.4**	**944.2**	**-4.0**	**8.9**	**-5.5**	**1.1**	**1.2**
Mining and quarrying	**.. d**	**-**	**-**	**169.1**	**-**	**6.6**	**276.2**	**-497.6**	**53.0**	**375.3**
Extraction activities	-	-	-	-	-	-	-	-	-	-
Manufacturing	**1 634.6**	**54 145.3**	**11 350.2**	**-9 542.3**	**-1 205.0**	**5 572.5**	**31 614.0**	**3 827.3**	**1 819.4**	**-3 648.1**
of which:										
Food products, beverages and tobacco	-311.8	-958.4	2 281.3	-3 094.4	304.5	71.6	-84.3	2 085.6	308.9	2 115.0
Textiles, wood and paper products; printing	-282.6	.. d	101.7	175.9	-249.0	-290.6	1 027.2	236.6	331.4	26.0
Chemical, rubber, plastic, non-metallic mineral products	3 874.2	57 679.4	5 607.7	-7 955.1	-5 738.2	2 629.7	29 499.7	288.6	169.1	-1 624.0
Metal and machinery products, except electrical equipment	-935.4	-1 927.9	74.1	1 096.8	5 169.4	2 072.4	-1 093.7	938.8	657.2	-4 390.4
Motor vehicles, trailers, semi-trailers, other transport equipment	111.5	-74.3	1 623.4	571.5	178.2	723.1	.. d	520.8	112.7	260.8
Other manufacturing	-821.3	1 064.9	1 662.1	-335.9	-868.6	364.9	592.3	-243.3	239.0	-35.4
Electricity, gas, steam and air conditioning supply	**4 589.4**	**-4 952.9**	**-4 599.1**	**3 624.2**	**984.3**	**.. d**	**-477.0**	**1 056.1**	**2 918.5**	**1 032.7**
Water supply; sewerage, waste management and remediation activities	**-66.3**	**13.3**	**-112.8**	**42.8**	**-540.5**	**8.0**	**.. d**	**-18.8**	**-39.5**	**-22.4**
Construction	**-358.2**	**380.5**	**-382.6**	**441.9**	**664.5**	**337.0**	**144.2**	**-95.1**	**490.4**	**-75.5**
Services	**-18 391.9**	**2 254.0**	**62 415.1**	**11 751.8**	**22 867.9**	**-8 763.4**	**12 162.0**	**35 780.2**	**29 056.5**	**38 882.3**
Wholesale and retail trade; repair of motor vehicles and motorcycles	-2 202.5	5 666.1	7 904.5	2 096.7	-1 148.4	-2 071.1	6 494.7	533.0	506.1	-7 100.2
Transportation and storage	1 360.0	477.0	254.3	-196.1	-833.2	.. d	.. d	455.6	828.5	-695.1
Accommodation and food service activities	.. d	.. d	37.6	152.2	94.4	724.4	-6.7	95.1	216.4	54.3
Information and communication	451.1	1 256.8	3 822.8	429.5	488.6	1 730.1	280.6	338.4	1 229.9	-675.1
Financial and insurance activities	-12 421.4	1 642.8	10 456.7	7 410.7	11 675.9	-7 625.1	-10 407.1	-13 526.5	30 480.2	32 384.0
Activities of holding companies	-2 300.7	4 816.4	-13 570.7	-1 202.8	75.5	-4 696.8	-9 696.1	-30 043.1	11 872.4	11 646.4
Real estate activities	-1 053.5	119.8	1 332.5	-92.4	-2 086.6	-431.2	66.6	899.0	-156.7	-251.4
Professional, scientific and technical activities	-7 028.0	-6 241.8	41 210.9	2 161.0	13 657.5	-1 301.6	15 516.4	48 179.8	-2 715.6	14 881.4
Administrative and support service activities	1 726.2	-752.1	-2 416.2	-143.2	986.7	74.3	394.9	-1 081.5	993.1	207.7
Public administration; activities of households and of extraterritorial organisations	-	-	-	-	-	4.0	7.8	1.1	-2 315.4	35.4
Education	-	-	-	-	-	-	.. d	1.1	1.1	-
Human health and social work activities	.. d	-	-	34.9	30.7	-1.3	-	-	-	-
Arts, entertainment and recreation	39.8	88.7	-25.4	-25.9	44.8	.. d	- d	-	5.6	4.7
Other services	9.3	-8.9	-163.7	-75.5	-43.7	5.3	77.6	-115.0	-15.8	35.4
Not allocated and confidential	**..**	**.. d**	**-14.4**	**-41.7**	**-4 900.3**	**..**	**.. d**	**119.4**	**447.5**	**-5 233.1**
Private real estate activities	**.. d**	**.. d**	**-479.9**	**-2 229.7**	**-1 786.9**	**-**	**-**	**-**	**-**	**-**

- Nil; .. Not available; d Secondary Confidentiality

Note: Data excludes resident Special Purpose Entities (SPEs). Detailed metadata at: *http://stats.oecd.org/OECDStat_Metadata/ShowMetadata.ashx?Dataset=FDI_CTRY_IND_SUMM.*

Source: *OECD International Direct Investment Statistics (database): https://doi.org/10.1787/idi-data-en*

BELGIUM

Table 5. Foreign direct investment positions by industrial sector
At year end

Million US dollars

	Inward					Outward				
	2014	2015	2016	2017	2018	2014	2015	2016	2017	2018
All FDI activities	**496 545.0**	**520 992.9**	**517 401.7**	**583 051.1**	**524 712.6**	**554 653.1**	**582 582.5**	**599 379.2**	**706 661.1**	**586 103.7**
Agriculture, forestry and fishing	**166.3**	**145.9**	**.. d**	**.. d**	..	**42.5**	**35.9**	**5.3**	**6.0**	..
Mining and quarrying	**307.2**	**300.5**	**250.9**	**.. d**	..	**4 280.9**	**5 265.1**	**4 550.4**	**4 601.8**	..
Extraction activities	-	-	-	-	..	-	-	-	-	..
Manufacturing	**103 162.1**	**148 903.6**	**142 889.2**	**154 717.0**	..	**93 519.7**	**112 978.8**	**119 590.0**	**145 107.9**	..
of which:										
Food products, beverages and tobacco	10 404.8	9 297.8	8 780.4	10 124.7	..	16 674.4	16 881.9	26 508.9	32 736.9	..
Textiles, wood and paper products; printing	5 546.0	4 458.4	4 208.9	4 820.1	..	1 727.7	2 252.6	2 363.2	2 500.6	..
Chemical, rubber, plastic, non-metallic mineral products	65 289.4	117 469.8	110 265.6	117 134.8	..	49 381.1	69 504.6	63 177.0	74 672.6	..
Metal and machinery products, except electrical equipment	13 404.9	11 040.8	11 550.5	14 119.7	..	19 685.4	16 805.7	19 568.9	26 547.1	..
Motor vehicles, trailers, semi-trailers, other transport equipment	1 129.1	928.7	1 620.1	2 494.6	..	446.8	394.1	979.2	1 571.1	..
Other manufacturing	7 387.8	5 708.2	6 464.6	6 023.0	..	5 604.3	7 138.8	6 993.8	7 078.4	..
Electricity, gas, steam and air conditioning supply	**40 898.2**	**32 155.7**	**14 817.1**	**18 354.5**	..	**37 240.1**	**32 501.9**	**20 636.7**	**28 714.3**	..
Water supply; sewerage, waste management and remediation activities	**1 744.7**	**1 632.0**	**1 419.8**	**1 686.3**	..	**650.8**	**523.7**	**597.7**	**558.9**	..
Construction	**3 121.5**	**3 253.1**	**2 583.5**	**2 985.1**	..	**1 214.1**	**1 984.8**	**1 997.5**	**2 822.0**	..
Services	**325 644.7**	**316 591.2**	**322 023.8**	**363 424.1**	..	**403 572.9**	**416 545.5**	**436 127.3**	**479 938.8**	..
Wholesale and retail trade; repair of motor vehicles and motorcycles	36 679.2	37 419.7	42 686.8	52 196.0	..	26 891.1	29 968.4	31 281.8	31 990.9	..
Transportation and storage	4 333.1	3 725.6	3 602.8	4 164.1	..	2 621.2	3 402.3	3 177.0	5 163.1	..
Accommodation and food service activities	2 737.8	2 524.8	2 654.2	2 347.1	..	1 174.0	1 022.3	1 029.8	1 351.6	..
Information and communication	3 619.2	4 156.8	8 008.9	10 036.0	..	11 243.8	10 478.0	11 070.9	12 180.4	..
Financial and insurance activities	132 563.9	128 049.0	125 992.4	139 022.5	..	121 547.2	100 2[illegible]5.6	79 222.1	97 419.0	..
Activities of holding companies	65 538.3	70 659.8	69 405.5	70 552.9	..	79 234.6	63 162.8	36 950.6	48 812.7	..
Real estate activities	4 951.1	6 047.9	7 845.5	8 452.9	..	4 714.4	4 568.3	2 980.9	3 251.4	..
Professional, scientific and technical activities	122 474.8	117 679.9	114 280.6	131 869.8	..	221 778.4	254 009.8	297 704.2	321 729.4	..
Administrative and support service activities	17 611.7	16 376.7	16 215.9	14 587.4	..	5 810.7	5 348.9	1 757.1	5 907.9	..
Public administration; activities of households and of extraterritorial organisations	-	-	-	-	..	7 250.6	6 929.8	7 487.1	26.4	..
Education	97.1	87.1	84.3	95.9	..	- d	.. d	.. d	.. d	..
Human health and social work activities	38.9	26.1	326.8	271.0	..	2.4	1.1	.. d	33.6	..
Arts, entertainment and recreation	267.1	230.8	253.0	284.2	..	197.9	175.3	181.3	211.1	..
Other services	272.0	266.7	72.7	99.5	..	343.6	421.3	200.3	668.0	..
Not allocated and confidential	..	**-209.0**	**.. d**	**.. d**	..	..	**7[illegible]9.7**	**-650.4**	**189.5**	..
Private real estate activities	**19 940.4**	**18 219.9**	**17 768.5**	**20 491.7**	..	**13 163.3**	**12 027.2**	**11 728.7**	**13 527.2**	..

- Nil; .. Not available; d Secondary Confidentiality

Note: Data excludes resident Special Purpose Entities (SPEs). Detailed metadata at: *http://stats.oecd.org/OECDStat_Metadata/ShowMetadata.ashx?Dataset=FDI_CTRY_IND_SUMM.*

Source: OECD International Direct Investment Statistics (database): *https://doi.org/10.1787/idi-data-en*

BELGIUM

Table 6. Foreign direct investment income by industrial sector

Million US dollars

	Inward					Outward				
	2014	2015	2016	2017	2018	2014	2015	2016	2017	2018
All FDI activities	**22 222.4**	**20 682.2**	**31 450.8**	**26 833.5**	**42 567.0**	**18 898.8**	**12 695.5**	**32 119.9**	**24 680.4**	**38 648.6**
Agriculture, forestry and fishing	**27.9**	**.. d**	**-13.3**	**10.1**	**-5.9**	**15.9**	**14.4**	**-17.7**	**4.5**	**2.4**
Mining and quarrying	**4.0**	**.. d**	**-64.1**	**306.6**	**-26.0**	**322.4**	**-96.5**	**85.1**	**1 466.6**	**280.9**
Extraction activities	-	-	-	-	-	-	-	-	-	-
Manufacturing	**8 222.1**	**6 688.9**	**11 927.5**	**-1 637.9**	**12 649.6**	**8 161.1**	**3 006.1**	**8 360.1**	**-1 205.1**	**3 528.9**
of which:										
Food products, beverages and tobacco	615.6	553.5	644.7	-2 439.4	476.8	18.6	-166.4	263.2	-50.7	-131.0
Textiles, wood and paper products; printing	197.7	96.5	216.7	306.6	1 582.7	62.4	.. d	147.1	196.1	161.7
Chemical, rubber, plastic, non-metallic mineral products	4 492.5	4 394.9	9 062.3	-3 237.5	6 337.8	6 675.1	1 100.4	6 170.5	-3 309.7	1 652.3
Metal and machinery products, except electrical equipment	1 755.3	918.5	1 373.4	2 564.5	2 335.7	510.8	1 069.3	1 155.6	1 648.1	1 396.2
Motor vehicles, trailers, semi-trailers, other transport equipment	533.4	295.1	266.5	441.9	310.4	-34.5	15.5	82.9	148.8	129.8
Other manufacturing	626.2	430.4	362.7	727.1	1 605.1	930.1	533.6	540.8	161.2	319.8
Electricity, gas, steam and air conditioning supply	**10.6**	**.. d**	**658.0**	**58.6**	**526.4**	**-156.6**	**.. d**	**-141.5**	**-181.5**	**-57.8**
Water supply; sewerage, waste management and remediation activities	**34.5**	**150.9**	**88.5**	**-29.3**	**42.5**	**-152.6**	**-78.8**	**5.5**	**-4.5**	**17.7**
Construction	**213.6**	**320.6**	**10.0**	**103.7**	**177.0**	**-1 292.3**	**-37.7**	**-144.9**	**101.5**	**146.3**
Services	**13 396.6**	**13 474.2**	**16 930.2**	**10 366.4**	**14 873.1**	**11 598.8**	**9 500.8**	**22 231.6**	**20 910.8**	**28 743.1**
Wholesale and retail trade; repair of motor vehicles and motorcycles	2 832.7	2 306.2	4 093.8	2 500.3	1 652.3	1 580.2	590.1	1 836.8	1 176.9	2 364.0
Transportation and storage	356.9	244.0	171.4	-41.7	297.4	142.0	163.1	128.3	63.1	160.5
Accommodation and food service activities	126.0	45.5	68.6	93.6	23.6	11.9	-44.4	-17.7	-122.9	-7.1
Information and communication	226.9	260.7	376.0	308.9	93.2	-386.1	-227.4	499.8	82.3	276.2
Financial and insurance activities	3 664.6	7 031.6	7 905.6	7 721.8	10 492.2	5 035.2	4 866.3	6 929.1	4 980.3	8 252.1
Activities of holding companies	-2 113.6	1 443.2	1 167.8	191.6	2 217.6	2 692.1	2 339.4	3 248.9	337.1	5 109.2
Real estate activities	433.9	398.2	-420.2	555.7	-924.1	228.2	191.9	113.9	249.1	238.4
Professional, scientific and technical activities	4 914.4	2 528.0	3 072.0	778.9	2 486.7	4 967.5	2 927.3	10 903.5	13 973.6	16 936.2
Administrative and support service activities	808.0	637.8	1 612.3	-1 582.7	721.1	423.2	276.2	802.8	355.1	468.5
Public administration; activities of households and of extraterritorial organisations	-	-	-	-	-	.. d	.. d	1 015.2	19.2	-23.6
Education	.. d	.. d	6.6	6.8	7.1	.. d	.. d	3.3	1.1	2.4
Human health and social work activities	.. d	.. d	-4.4	-4.5	-1.2	-	-1.1	4.4	7.9	7.1
Arts, entertainment and recreation	22.6	21.1	36.5	24.8	23.6	1.3	-	10.0	6.8	-2.4
Other services	10.6	1.1	11.1	4.5	2.4	9.3	35.5	3.3	116.1	68.5
Not allocated and confidential	**..**	**.. d**	**1 914.2**	**17 655.3**	**14 330.2**	**..**	**.. d**	**1 741.7**	**3 588.1**	**5 987.3**
Private real estate activities	**-**	**-**	**-**	**-**	**-**	**-**	**-**	**-**	**-**	**-**

- Nil; .. Not available; d Secondary Confidentiality

Note: Data excludes resident Special Purpose Entities (SPEs). Detailed metadata at: *http://stats.oecd.org/OECDStat_Metadata/ShowMetadata.ashx?Dataset=FDI_CTRY_IND_SUMM.*

Source: OECD International Direct Investment Statistics (database): https://doi.org/10.1787/idi-data-en

CANADA

Table 1. Foreign direct investment flows by country

Million US dollars

	Inward					Outward				
	2014	2015	2016	2017	2018	2014	2015	2016	2017	2018
WORLD	**59 137.3**	**45 630.9**	**36 061.7**	**26 518.8**	**43 449.6**	**60 542.2**	**67 862.0**	**69 518.0**	**78 338.3**	**49 868.8**
OECD COUNTRIES	..	..	..	..	..	..	..	..	..	..
Australia	..	..	-415.5	-34.8	1 949.8	..	..	1 598.6	-334.8	2 433.3
Austria	..	..	..	..	..	..	..	..	..	..
Belgium	..	..	..	..	..	..	..	..	..	..
Canada	-	-	..	..	..	-	-	..	..	..
Chile	..	..	..	..	..	..	..	..	..	..
Czech Republic	..	..	..	..	..	..	..	..	..	..
Denmark	..	..	..	..	..	..	..	..	..	..
Estonia	..	..	..	..	..	..	..	..	..	..
Finland	..	..	..	..	..	..	..	..	..	..
France	..	..	417.3	736.4	2 791.6	..	..	-98.4	584.6	137.9
Germany	..	..	369.6	585.3	370.0	..	..	1 381.9	-228.0	963.4
Greece	..	..	..	..	..	..	..	..	..	..
Hungary	..	..	..	..	..	..	..	..	..	..
Iceland	..	..	..	..	..	..	..	..	..	..
Ireland	..	..	..	..	..	..	..	..	..	..
Israel[1]	..	..	..	..	..	..	..	..	..	..
Italy	..	..	..	..	..	..	..	..	..	..
Japan	..	..	1 080.8	527.8	476.3	..	..	-308.5	-839.4	226.1
Korea	..	..	..	..	..	..	..	..	..	..
Latvia	..	..	..	..	..	..	..	..	..	..
Lithuania	..	..	..	..	..	..	..	..	..	..
Luxembourg	..	..	1 420.8	1 896.1	327.4	..	..	-2 506.2	-601.7	3 636.0
Mexico	..	..	-50.8	192.4	23.9	..	..	1 390.0	894.9	923.8
Netherlands	..	..	4 341.5	-1 678.4	3 466.2	..	..	1 419.6	1 151.4	898.7
New Zealand	..	..	..	..	..	..	..	..	..	..
Norway	..	..	..	..	..	..	..	..	..	..
Poland	..	..	..	..	..	..	..	..	..	..
Portugal	..	..	..	..	..	..	..	..	..	..
Slovak Republic	..	..	..	..	..	..	..	..	..	..
Slovenia	..	..	..	..	..	..	..	..	..	..
Spain	..	..	..	..	..	..	..	..	..	..
Sweden	..	..	..	..	..	..	..	..	..	..
Switzerland	..	..	9 559.0	-2 851.1	2 828.6	..	..	-455.7	2 303.2	1 729.1
Turkey	..	..	..	..	..	..	..	..	..	..
United Kingdom	..	..	-1 712.3	2 573.4	2 166.8	..	..	9 073.1	6 251.2	7 631.4
United States	18 761.7	34 506.0	18 669.1	14 583.6	18 295.7	41 035.6	47 446.2	55 928.0	67 638.9	25 864.5
EUROPE	..	..	..	..	..	..	..	..	..	..
Bulgaria	..	..	..	..	..	..	..	..	..	..
Croatia	..	..	..	..	..	..	..	..	..	..
Cyprus[2, 3]	..	..	..	..	..	..	..	..	..	..
Malta	..	..	..	..	..	..	..	..	..	..
Romania	..	..	..	..	..	..	..	..	..	..
Russian Federation	..	..	..	..	..	..	..	..	..	..
Ukraine	..	..	..	..	..	..	..	..	..	..
AFRICA	..	..	..	..	..	..	..	..	..	..
Northern Africa	..	..	..	..	..	..	..	..	..	..
Algeria	..	..	..	..	..	..	..	..	..	..
Egypt	..	..	..	..	..	..	..	..	..	..
Libya	..	..	..	..	..	..	..	..	..	..
Morocco	..	..	..	..	..	..	..	..	..	..
Tunisia	..	..	..	..	..	..	..	..	..	..
Other African countries	..	..	..	..	..	..	..	..	..	..
Nigeria	..	..	..	..	..	..	..	..	..	..
South Africa	..	..	..	..	..	..	..	..	..	..
AMERICA	..	..	..	..	..	..	..	..	..	..
Northern America	..	..	..	..	..	..	..	..	..	..
Central America and Caribbean countries	..	..	..	..	..	..	..	..	..	..
Bahamas	..	..	..	..	..	..	..	..	..	..
Bermuda	..	..	..	..	..	..	..	..	..	..
Cayman Islands	..	..	245.5	173.8	1 527.5	..	..	2 622.9	2 971.2	-3 157.7
Costa Rica	..	..	..	..	..	..	..	..	..	..
El Salvador	..	..	..	..	..	..	..	..	..	..
Guatemala	..	..	..	..	..	..	..	..	..	..
Honduras	..	..	..	..	..	..	..	..	..	..
Nicaragua	..	..	..	..	..	..	..	..	..	..
Panama	..	..	..	..	..	..	..	..	..	..
Virgin Islands, U.S.	..	..	..	..	..	..	..	..	..	..
South America	..	..	..	..	..	..	..	..	..	..
Argentina	..	..	..	..	..	..	..	..	..	..
Bolivia	..	..	..	..	..	..	..	..	..	..
Brazil	..	..	439.9	1 124.2	1 129.8	..	..	-76.1	129.7	726.0
Colombia	..	..	..	..	..	..	..	..	..	..
Ecuador	..	..	..	..	..	..	..	..	..	..
Paraguay	..	..	..	..	..	..	..	..	..	..
Peru	..	..	..	..	..	..	..	..	..	..
Uruguay	..	..	..	..	..	..	..	..	..	..
Venezuela	..	..	..	..	..	..	..	..	..	..

CANADA

Table 1. Foreign direct investment flows by country *(cont.)*

Million US dollars

	Inward					Outward				
	2014	2015	2016	2017	2018	2014	2015	2016	2017	2018
ASIA	..	..	..	..	..	..	..	..	..	..
Near and Middle East	..	..	..	..	..	..	..	..	..	..
Gulf Arabian countries	..	..	..	..	..	..	..	..	..	..
Kuwait	..	..	..	..	..	..	..	..	..	..
Qatar	..	..	..	..	..	..	..	..	..	..
Saudi Arabia	..	..	..	..	..	..	..	..	..	..
United Arab Emirates	..	..	..	..	..	..	..	..	..	..
Other Near and Middle East	..	..	..	..	..	..	..	..	..	..
Jordan	..	..	..	..	..	..	..	..	..	..
Other Asian countries	..	..	..	..	..	..	..	..	..	..
China	..	..	5 654.8	703.4	2 645.7	..	..	968.3	1 218.3	613.4
Hong Kong, China	..	..	1 154.4	58.8	1 538.7	..	..	666.9	2 069.9	508.1
India	..	..	..	..	..	..	..	..	..	..
Indonesia	..	..	..	..	..	..	..	..	..	..
Iran, Islamic Republic of	..	..	..	..	..	..	..	..	..	..
Malaysia	..	..	..	..	..	..	..	..	..	..
Philippines	..	..	..	..	..	..	..	..	..	..
Singapore	..	..	..	..	..	..	..	..	..	..
Chinese Taipei	..	..	..	..	..	..	..	..	..	..
Thailand	..	..	..	..	..	..	..	..	..	..
Viet Nam	..	..	..	..	..	..	..	..	..	..
AUSTRALIA, OCEANIA AND POLAR REGIONS	..	..	..	..	..	..	..	..	..	..
WORLD unallocated and confidential	**40 375.7**	**11 124.9**	**-5 405.0**	..	**25 153.9**	**19 506.7**	**20 413.8**	**-6 937.0**	..	**24 004.3**
European Union (EU28)	..	..	..	..	..	..	..	..	..	..
G20 countries excl. European Union	..	..	..	..	..	..	..	..	..	..
G20 OECD countries	..	..	..	..	..	..	..	..	..	..
G20 Non-OECD countries	..	..	..	..	..	..	..	..	..	..
MENA countries	..	..	..	..	..	..	..	..	..	..
ASEAN countries	..	..	..	..	..	..	..	..	..	..

- Nil; .. Not available

Note: Detailed metadata at: *http://stats.oecd.org/OECDStat_Metadata/ShowMetadata.ashx?Dataset=FDI_CTRY_IND_SUMM.*

1. Information on data for Israel: *http://oe.cd/israel-disclaimer.*
2. Note by Turkey: The information in this document with reference to "Cyprus" relates to the southern part of the Island. There is no single authority representing both Turkish and Greek Cypriot people on the Island. Turkey recognises the Turkish Republic of Northern Cyprus (TRNC). Until a lasting and equitable solution is found within the context of the United Nations, Turkey shall preserve its position concerning the "Cyprus issue".
3. Note by all the European Union Member States of the OECD and the European Union: The Republic of Cyprus is recognised by all members of the United Nations with the exception of Turkey. The information in this document relates to the area under the effective control of the Government of the Republic of Cyprus.

Source: OECD International Direct Investment Statistics (database): https://doi.org/10.1787/idi-data-en

CANADA

Table 2. Foreign direct investment positions by country
At year end

Million US dollars

	Inward					Outward				
	2014	2015	2016	2017	2018	2014	2015	2016	2017	2018
WORLD	**642 013.1**	**565 687.9**	**603 759.3**	**663 136.9**	**642 809.0**	**728 686.1**	**754 236.6**	**823 098.7**	**927 266.6**	**944 849.6**
OECD COUNTRIES	**..**	**..**	**510 685.4**	**561 860.6**	**..**	**528 808.5**	**551 341.5**	**611 581.6**	**697 789.0**	**718 470.5**
Australia	5 276.3	5 172.0	7 319.9	6 910.0	..	18 993.0	18 649.9	29 026.0	34 974.7	29 935.0
Austria	782.0	285.4	1 455.2	1 440.9	..	1 032.8	906.1	4 811.1	5 958.6	5 685.2
Belgium	2 706.3	1 685.7	1 664.1	2 064.2	..	553.5	627.5	731.6	1 703.0	1 565.0
Canada	5 233.2	5 321.5	6 439.6	11 442.5	..	-	-	..	..	..
Chile	263.8	279.6	530.6	376.9	..	16 175.5	11 355.2	20 140.4	28 450.9	24 288.5
Czech Republic	..	..	..	..	..	279.3	36.7	913.9	395.4	371.2
Denmark	664.7	425.6	706.3	646.4	..	112.9	298.9	1 001.0	1 410.7	1 367.8
Estonia	..	..	..	..	..	..	33.0	95.9	308.3	284.3
Finland	2 289.9	603.3	420.8	837.9	..	824.2	1 042.6	1 256.8	1 418.9	1 362.0
France	14 165.0	8 338.2	11 681.5	14 135.2	..	4 852.1	4 130.8	6 662.9	7 169.5	7 221.5
Germany	14 897.8	16 653.2	18 610.6	21 448.9	..	7 955.0	7 654.0	16 480.2	15 974.1	14 502.1
Greece	..	..	..	..	..	..	18.8	224.2	281.3	286.0
Hungary	..	..	..	..	..	3 095.1	4 350.0	4 043.8	4 359.8	3 696.5
Iceland	..	..	..	..	..	.. c	82.9	..	174.9	155.0
Ireland	2 465.7	2 742.8	4 445.1	7 874.1	..	11 354.4	11 224.6	9 550.9	8 364.9	7 223.6
Israel[1]	538.8	324.4	846.2	992.7	..	1 299.3	801.7	1 168.2	1 805.5	-452.5
Italy	4 501.3	3 887.3	3 602.0	4 191.5	..	357.8	350.0	1 159.1	2 061.8	2 083.3
Japan	28 161.9	27 344.7	28 801.6	31 447.7	..	5 030.6	3 281.2	4 231.5	5 717.8	6 013.9
Korea	3 336.5	1 379.3	2 262.9	2 895.4	..	430.2	1 020.9	1 602.2	2 099.2	2 345.6
Latvia	..	..	..	..	..	..	2.2	4.9	2.6	1.9
Lithuania	..	..	..	..	..	.. c	331.7	344.6	387.6	357.7
Luxembourg	14 204.7	11 355.5	14 640.5	17 894.2	..	47 745.5	51 572.0	99 411.9	113 108.6	76 610.0
Mexico	1 439.8	1 375.0	2 255.7	2 258.0	..	11 864.8	12 129.7	21 198.0	26 569.7	23 175.7
Netherlands	30 656.1	25 450.9	20 498.1	15 824.5	..	17 554.1	22 771.8	37 439.9	45 874.9	34 708.4
New Zealand	..	..	..	..	..	458.7	491.0	919.6	1 479.4	1 470.0
Norway	6 953.2	6 226.9	5 644.6	5 688.1	..	1 111.3	1 025.5	2 179.8	2 631.9	2 703.1
Poland	2 190.7	1 369.9	2 018.0	2 247.2	..	70.7	813.8	336.4	498.1	471.7
Portugal	..	..	..	..	..	11.2	170.3	104.8	140.2	136.6
Slovak Republic	..	..	..	..	..	15.5	3.9	-41.1	5.4	9.0
Slovenia	..	..	..	..	..	..	..	..	..	..
Spain	288.0	3 775.3	3 900.4	4 053.0	..	3 115.8	3 048.4	7 267.5	5 865.6	6 297.7
Sweden	1 928.6	2 083.8	1 747.5	1 951.6	..	1 521.7	4 186.6	6 087.8	3 607.5	3 343.4
Switzerland	13 301.1	15 638.0	20 058.1	23 187.6	..	5 818.6	-175.7	-1 190.5	3 651.7	7 182.6
Turkey	..	..	..	..	..	640.6	699.4	1 263.9	2 318.9	1 363.8
United Kingdom	44 750.4	34 830.9	38 114.8	41 670.2	..	65 353.9	66 803.7	96 444.4	107 298.2	105 575.5
United States	327 964.5	294 034.0	312 802.9	339 358.1	..	298 718.0	322 967.0	513 066.0	576 174.5	553 796.5
EUROPE	**162 339.9**	**139 817.9**	**152 762.2**	**170 555.8**	**..**	**.. c**	**196 129.3**	**206 260.3**	**228 616.7**	**232 940.5**
Bulgaria	..	..	..	..	..	4.3	6.2	..	21.6	19.9
Croatia	..	..	..	..	..	..	-1.0	..	..	..
Cyprus[2, 3]	3 062.3	2 246.4	1 384.7	2 141.2	..	2 741.6	3 321.5	5 640.7	4 242.3	2 764.7
Malta	..	..	..	..	..	506.9	448.6	..	..	..
Romania	..	..	..	..	..	117.3	142.0	813.5	1 071.8	971.5
Russian Federation	2 370.9	1 813.6	1 988.1	2 763.5	..	2 426.1	1 253.6	1 820.9	2 360.5	2 025.7
Ukraine	..	..	..	..	..	..	399.2	..	..	..
AFRICA	**3 175.3**	**2 437.9**	**1 385.5**	**1 546.4**	**..**	**2 869.2**	**3 180.6**	**4 554.9**	**5 545.5**	**5 028.1**
Northern Africa	..	..	..	..	..	.. c	..	..	..	..
Algeria	..	..	..	..	..	.. c	11.5	7.4	8.4	7.8
Egypt	..	..	..	..	..	87.1	0.4	-18.8	-43.0	-63.8
Libya	..	..	..	..	..	..	..	..	..	..
Morocco	..	..	..	..	..	3.4	-2.8	8.2	27.9	30.6
Tunisia	..	..	..	..	..	25.0	122.1	159.8	107.3	87.0
Other African countries	..	..	..	..	..	.. c	..	..	..	..
Nigeria	..	..	..	..	..	528.5	515.7	808.9	796.7	735.1
South Africa	2 190.7	1 040.5	564.9	598.2	..	2 455.4	1 407.0	2 763.9	2 794.4	2 206.7
AMERICA	**365 059.1**	**327 026.0**	**346 476.1**	**378 331.5**	**..**	**.. c**	**..**	**552 785.1**	**625 101.2**	**641 414.0**
Northern America	..	..	..	..	..	..	322 994.5	..	..	..
Central America and Caribbean countries	..	..	..	..	..	.. c	..	..	..	..
Bahamas	..	..	..	..	..	16 309.2	14 788.7	18 617.4	19 998.3	20 687.0
Bermuda	785.4	774.6	596.3	722.5	..	27 517.9	31 393.3	42 560.2	47 087.8	37 319.8
Cayman Islands	86.2	1 187.1	1 143.0	1 001.1	..	31 792.4	28 834.3	42 839.1	44 268.9	41 307.2
Costa Rica	..	..	..	..	..	-71.6	26.8	7.7	128.2	116.4
El Salvador	..	..	..	..	..	379.3	697.5	710.9	498.9	460.4
Guatemala	..	..	..	..	..	3.4	19.9	18.2	-4.1	8.6
Honduras	..	..	..	..	..	205.2	230.3	127.8	691.1	672.9
Nicaragua	..	..	..	..	..	.. c	251.4	704.5	548.7	504.5
Panama	..	..	..	..	..	1 113.9	3 521.6	6 547.2	9 402.1	8 417.2
Virgin Islands, U.S.	..	..	..	..	..	..	-	..	..	..
South America	..	..	..	..	..	.. c	..	..	..	..
Argentina	..	..	..	..	..	1 643.2	2 380.1	4 413.2	2 745.3	1 086.7
Bolivia	..	..	..	..	..	110.4	114.9	153.0	155.9	145.7
Brazil	28 369.7	23 541.9	22 035.7	22 176.5	..	12 105.4	8 564.9	15 929.1	19 995.0	17 347.6
Colombia	..	..	..	..	..	1 846.7	2 656.3	4 491.8	4 727.2	4 592.6
Ecuador	..	..	..	..	..	-	705.5	2 087.8	2 695.9	2 740.1
Paraguay	..	..	..	..	..	..	..	..	..	..
Peru	..	..	..	..	..	10 153.5	9 565.8	15 022.5	15 569.6	14 900.6
Uruguay	..	..	..	..	..	765.6	546.3	399.2	782.5	736.9
Venezuela	..	..	..	..	..	319.0	329.4	-35.7	339.1	5.4

Table 2. Foreign direct investment positions by country *(cont.)*

At year end

Million US dollars

	Inward					Outward				
	2014	2015	2016	2017	2018	2014	2015	2016	2017	2018
ASIA	..	..	..	..	..	.. c	..	..	..	..
Near and Middle East	..	..	..	..	..	.. c	..	..	..	..
Gulf Arabian countries	..	..	..	..	..	.. c	..	..	..	..
Kuwait	1 113.0	1 659.7	1 483.8	1 732.1	..	..	0.0	0.0	0.0	14.2
Qatar	..	..	..	..	..	..	0.6	0.2	0.2	0.2
Saudi Arabia	..	..	..	..	..	25.0	96.1	14.5	132.4	119.9
United Arab Emirates	9 212.0	8 357.7	7 672.5	7 965.5	..	31.0	-193.0	324.0	-162.0	-65.2
Other Near and Middle East	..	..	..	..	..	..	..	..	..	..
Jordan	..	..	..	..	..	..	-	..	..	..
Other Asian countries	..	..	..	..	..	..	..	..	..	..
China	24 320.2	17 449.4	18 662.4	21 597.6	..	6 927.3	7 407.6	13 015.8	15 331.8	15 489.4
Hong Kong, China	12 459.7	7 794.8	8 544.3	9 604.0	..	4 315.0	5 298.4	6 701.8	6 263.2	6 695.6
India	4 762.5	3 139.5	3 931.8	4 706.7	..	589.7	920.1	1 831.1	2 242.1	2 540.2
Indonesia	521.6	308.5	295.9	312.4	..	3 365.8	2 340.1	3 555.1	3 955.8	3 856.7
Iran, Islamic Republic of	..	..	..	..	..	..	..	..	..	..
Malaysia	2 675.2	6 342.5	7 346.8	7 122.8	..	445.7	682.4	1 104.2	1 180.7	1 114.5
Philippines	..	..	..	..	..	968.2	1 268.7	2 486.7	2 596.1	2 475.5
Singapore	2 508.0	631.5	389.1	368.5	..	2 778.7	3 087.6	4 216.8	5 957.4	5 805.4
Chinese Taipei	..	..	..	..	..	..	83.3	182.5	173.6	688.3
Thailand	..	..	..	..	..	167.3	103.3	256.2	340.6	165.9
Viet Nam	..	..	..	..	..	-95.7	-55.0	184.1	113.3	219.1
AUSTRALIA, OCEANIA AND POLAR REGIONS	..	..	..	..	..	..	..	..	..	..
WORLD unallocated and confidential	**111 438.9**	**96 406.1**	**15 578.3**	**17 048.1**	..	**9 673.2**	**906.5**	**-28 103.4**	**-32 085.0**	..
European Union (EU28)	..	..	**102 512.0**	**121 298.7**	..	**160 930.3**	**184 284.9**	**170 555.8**	**184 511.7**	**188 918.4**
G20 countries excl. European Union	..	..	..	..	..	**443 733.9**	**462 056.2**	..	..	..
G20 OECD countries	..	..	..	..	..	**414 196.1**	**437 686.6**	..	..	..
G20 Non-OECD countries	..	..	..	..	..	**29 537.9**	**24 369.5**	**43 343.6**	**49 557.3**	**44 673.1**
MENA countries	..	..	..	..	..	.. c	..	..	..	..
ASEAN countries	..	..	..	..	..	..	..	..	..	..

- Nil; .. Not available; c Confidential data

Note: Inward FDI positions are allocated according to the ultimate investing country. Inward FDI positions by immediate counterpart country are available for the most recent year in the *OECD FDI database according to BMD4*. Detailed metadata at: *http://stats.oecd.org/OECDStat_Metadata/ShowMetadata.ashx?Dataset=FDI_CTRY_IND_SUMM*.

1. Information on data for Israel: *http://oe.cd/israel-disclaimer*.
2. Note by Turkey: The information in this document with reference to "Cyprus" relates to the southern part of the Island. There is no single authority representing both Turkish and Greek Cypriot people on the Island. Turkey recognises the Turkish Republic of Northern Cyprus (TRNC). Until a lasting and equitable solution is found within the context of the United Nations, Turkey shall preserve its position concerning the "Cyprus issue".
3. Note by all the European Union Member States of the OECD and the European Union: The Republic of Cyprus is recognised by all members of the United Nations with the exception of Turkey. The information in this document relates to the area under the effective control of the Government of the Republic of Cyprus.

Source: OECD International Direct Investment Statistics (database): https://doi.org/10.1787/idi-data-en

Table 3. Foreign direct investment income by country

Million US dollars

	Inward					Outward				
	2014	2015	2016	2017	2018	2014	2015	2016	2017	2018
WORLD	**47 094.2**	**34 466.1**	**31 001.1**	**37 795.4**	**41 472.2**	**46 641.6**	**40 014.9**	**40 774.1**	**54 572.7**	**60 286.9**
OECD COUNTRIES	..	..	..	..	..	..	..	..	..	..
Australia	..	..	..	..	..	..	..	..	..	..
Austria	..	..	..	..	..	..	..	..	..	..
Belgium	..	..	..	..	..	..	..	..	..	..
Canada	-	-	..	..	..	-	-	..	..	..
Chile	..	..	..	..	..	..	..	..	..	..
Czech Republic	..	..	..	..	..	..	..	..	..	..
Denmark	..	..	..	..	..	..	..	..	..	..
Estonia	..	..	..	..	..	..	..	..	..	..
Finland	..	..	..	..	..	..	..	..	..	..
France	..	..	..	..	..	..	..	..	..	..
Germany	..	..	..	..	..	..	..	..	..	..
Greece	..	..	..	..	..	..	..	..	..	..
Hungary	..	..	..	..	..	..	..	..	..	..
Iceland	..	..	..	..	..	..	..	..	..	..
Ireland	..	..	..	..	..	..	..	..	..	..
Israel[1]	..	..	..	..	..	..	..	..	..	..
Italy	..	..	..	..	..	..	..	..	..	..
Japan	1 783.3	451.4	565.9	591.9	998.8	401.9	-36.0	-123.8	1 010.0	151.4
Korea	..	..	..	..	..	..	..	..	..	..
Latvia	..	..	..	..	..	..	..	..	..	..
Lithuania	..	..	..	..	..	..	..	..	..	..
Luxembourg	..	..	..	..	..	..	..	..	..	..
Mexico	..	..	..	..	..	..	..	..	..	..
Netherlands	..	..	..	..	..	..	..	..	..	..
New Zealand	..	..	..	..	..	..	..	..	..	..
Norway	..	..	..	..	..	..	..	..	..	..
Poland	..	..	..	..	..	..	..	..	..	..
Portugal	..	..	..	..	..	..	..	..	..	..
Slovak Republic	..	..	..	..	..	..	..	..	..	..
Slovenia	..	..	..	..	..	..	..	..	..	..
Spain	..	..	..	..	..	..	..	..	..	..
Sweden	..	..	..	..	..	..	..	..	..	..
Switzerland	..	..	..	..	..	..	..	..	..	..
Turkey	..	..	..	..	..	..	..	..	..	..
United Kingdom	4 119.7	2 238.9	3 035.8	2 942.5	2 511.5	8 541.7	5 558.2	6 768.6	4 027.1	5 566.9
United States	21 219.3	22 184.2	15 744.4	16 553.1	18 826.2	22 455.9	19 047.2	13 734.5	23 359.8	25 550.6
EUROPE	..	..	..	..	..	..	..	..	..	..
Bulgaria	..	..	..	..	..	..	..	..	..	..
Croatia	..	..	..	..	..	..	..	..	..	..
Cyprus[2, 3]	..	..	..	..	..	..	..	..	..	..
Malta	..	..	..	..	..	..	..	..	..	..
Romania	..	..	..	..	..	..	..	..	..	..
Russian Federation	..	..	..	..	..	..	..	..	..	..
Ukraine	..	..	..	..	..	..	..	..	..	..
AFRICA	..	..	..	..	..	..	..	..	..	..
Northern Africa	..	..	..	..	..	..	..	..	..	..
Algeria	..	..	..	..	..	..	..	..	..	..
Egypt	..	..	..	..	..	..	..	..	..	..
Libya	..	..	..	..	..	..	..	..	..	..
Morocco	..	..	..	..	..	..	..	..	..	..
Tunisia	..	..	..	..	..	..	..	..	..	..
Other African countries	..	..	..	..	..	..	..	..	..	..
Nigeria	..	..	..	..	..	..	..	..	..	..
South Africa	..	..	..	..	..	..	..	..	..	..
AMERICA	..	..	..	..	..	..	..	..	..	..
Northern America	..	..	..	..	..	..	..	..	..	..
Central America and Caribbean countries	..	..	..	..	..	..	..	..	..	..
Bahamas	..	..	..	..	..	..	..	..	..	..
Bermuda	..	..	..	..	..	..	..	..	..	..
Cayman Islands	..	..	..	..	..	..	..	..	..	..
Costa Rica	..	..	..	..	..	..	..	..	..	..
El Salvador	..	..	..	..	..	..	..	..	..	..
Guatemala	..	..	..	..	..	..	..	..	..	..
Honduras	..	..	..	..	..	..	..	..	..	..
Nicaragua	..	..	..	..	..	..	..	..	..	..
Panama	..	..	..	..	..	..	..	..	..	..
Virgin Islands, U.S.	..	..	..	..	..	..	..	..	..	..
South America	..	..	..	..	..	..	..	..	..	..
Argentina	..	..	..	..	..	..	..	..	..	..
Bolivia	..	..	..	..	..	..	..	..	..	..
Brazil	..	..	..	..	..	..	..	..	..	..
Colombia	..	..	..	..	..	..	..	..	..	..
Ecuador	..	..	..	..	..	..	..	..	..	..
Paraguay	..	..	..	..	..	..	..	..	..	..
Peru	..	..	..	..	..	..	..	..	..	..
Uruguay	..	..	..	..	..	..	..	..	..	..
Venezuela	..	..	..	..	..	..	..	..	..	..

CANADA

Table 3. Foreign direct investment income by country *(cont.)*

Million US dollars

	Inward					Outward				
	2014	2015	2016	2017	2018	2014	2015	2016	2017	2018
ASIA	..	..	..	..	..	..	..	..	..	..
Near and Middle East	..	..	..	..	..	..	..	..	..	..
Gulf Arabian countries	..	..	..	..	..	..	..	..	..	..
Kuwait	..	..	..	..	..	..	..	..	..	..
Qatar	..	..	..	..	..	..	..	..	..	..
Saudi Arabia	..	..	..	..	..	..	..	..	..	..
United Arab Emirates	..	..	..	..	..	..	..	..	..	..
Other Near and Middle East	..	..	..	..	..	..	..	..	..	..
Jordan	..	..	..	..	..	..	..	..	..	..
Other Asian countries	..	..	..	..	..	..	..	..	..	..
China	..	..	..	..	..	..	..	..	..	..
Hong Kong, China	..	..	..	..	..	..	..	..	..	..
India	..	..	..	..	..	..	..	..	..	..
Indonesia	..	..	..	..	..	..	..	..	..	..
Iran, Islamic Republic of	..	..	..	..	..	..	..	..	..	..
Malaysia	..	..	..	..	..	..	..	..	..	..
Philippines	..	..	..	..	..	..	..	..	..	..
Singapore	..	..	..	..	..	..	..	..	..	..
Chinese Taipei	..	..	..	..	..	..	..	..	..	..
Thailand	..	..	..	..	..	..	..	..	..	..
Viet Nam	..	..	..	..	..	..	..	..	..	..
AUSTRALIA, OCEANIA AND POLAR REGIONS	..	..	..	..	..	..	..	..	..	..
WORLD unallocated and confidential	19 971.9	9 591.6	..	..	..	15 242.1	15 444.7	..	..	..
European Union (EU28)	..	..	..	..	..	..	..	..	..	..
G20 countries excl. European Union	..	..	..	..	..	..	..	..	..	..
G20 OECD countries	..	..	..	..	..	..	..	..	..	..
G20 Non-OECD countries	..	..	..	..	..	..	..	..	..	..
MENA countries	..	..	..	..	..	..	..	..	..	..
ASEAN countries	..	..	..	..	..	..	..	..	..	..

- Nil; .. Not available

Note: Detailed metadata at: *http://stats.oecd.org/OECDStat_Metadata/ShowMetadata.ashx?Dataset=FDI_CTRY_IND_SUMM.*

1. Information on data for Israel: *http://oe.cd/israel-disclaimer.*
2. Note by Turkey: The information in this document with reference to "Cyprus" relates to the southern part of the Island. There is no single authority representing both Turkish and Greek Cypriot people on the Island. Turkey recognises the Turkish Republic of Northern Cyprus (TRNC). Until a lasting and equitable solution is found within the context of the United Nations, Turkey shall preserve its position concerning the "Cyprus issue".
3. Note by all the European Union Member States of the OECD and the European Union: The Republic of Cyprus is recognised by all members of the United Nations with the exception of Turkey. The information in this document relates to the area under the effective control of the Government of the Republic of Cyprus.

Source: OECD International Direct Investment Statistics (database): https://doi.org/10.1787/idi-data-en

CANADA

Table 4. Foreign direct investment flows by industrial sector

Million US dollars

	Inward					Outward				
	2014	2015	2016	2017	2018	2014	2015	2016	2017	2018
All FDI activities	**59 137.3**	**45 630.9**	**36 061.7**	**26 518.8**	**43 449.6**	**60 542.2**	**67 862.0**	**69 518.0**	**78 338.3**	**49 868.8**
Agriculture, forestry and fishing	..	..	..	..	..	..	..	..	..	..
Mining and quarrying	**15 266.6**	**2 924.2**	**8 255.9**	**-7 189.6**	**4 456.4**	**8 310.9**	**-12 959.4**	**11 613.4**	**-2 322.3**	**7 588.2**
Extraction activities	..	..	..	..	..	..	..	..	..	..
Manufacturing	**10 935.1**	**3 263.7**	**2 740.4**	**9 415.2**	**13 670.4**	**7 741.5**	**19 952.2**	**4 075.4**	**-2 740.2**	**5 315.4**
of which:										
Food products, beverages and tobacco	..	..	..	..	..	..	..	..	..	..
Textiles, wood and paper products; printing	..	..	..	..	..	..	..	..	..	..
Chemical, rubber, plastic, non-metallic mineral products	..	..	..	..	..	..	..	..	..	..
Metal and machinery products, except electrical equipment	..	..	..	..	..	..	..	..	..	..
Motor vehicles, trailers, semi-trailers, other transport equipment	..	..	..	..	..	..	..	..	..	..
Other manufacturing	..	..	..	..	..	..	..	..	..	..
Electricity, gas, steam and air conditioning supply	..	..	..	..	..	..	..	..	..	..
Water supply; sewerage, waste management and remediation activities	..	..	..	..	..	..	..	..	..	..
Construction	..	..	..	..	..	..	..	..	..	..
Services	..	..	..	..	..	..	..	..	..	..
Wholesale and retail trade; repair of motor vehicles and motorcycles	..	..	..	..	..	..	..	..	..	..
Transportation and storage	7 235.4	7 653.9	8 649.8	9 904.2	5 888.7	-1 325.2	1 652.2	17 092.9	43 579.6	13 804.8
Accommodation and food service activities	..	..	..	..	..	..	..	..	..	..
Information and communication	..	..	..	..	..	..	..	..	..	..
Financial and insurance activities	2 792.6	444.3	7 115.5	3 767.5	3 287.7	14 804.0	42 321.1	19 132.0	21 809.0	19 238.8
Activities of holding companies	..	..	..	..	..	..	..	..	..	..
Real estate activities	..	..	..	..	..	..	..	..	..	..
Professional, scientific and technical activities	13 935.0	11 108.5	4 320.2	2 526.0	2 475.9	20 228.1	9 423.5	-794.6	7 271.3	4 794.7
Administrative and support service activities	..	..	..	..	..	..	..	..	..	..
Public administration; activities of households and of extraterritorial organisations	..	..	..	..	..	..	..	..	..	..
Education	..	..	..	..	..	..	..	..	..	..
Human health and social work activities	..	..	..	..	..	..	..	..	..	..
Arts, entertainment and recreation	..	..	..	..	..	..	..	..	..	..
Other services	..	..	..	..	..	..	..	..	..	..
Not allocated and confidential	**8 972.6**	**20 236.3**	**25 065.4**	**24 293.2**	**25 322.8**	**10 783.0**	**7 432.5**	**53 829.2**	**83 400.9**	**36 965.2**
Private real estate activities	..	..	..	..	..	..	..	..	..	..

.. Not available

Note: Detailed metadata at: *http://stats.oecd.org/OECDStat_Metadata/ShowMetadata.ashx?Dataset=FDI_CTRY_IND_SUMM.*

Source: *OECD International Direct Investment Statistics (database): https://doi.org/10.1787/idi-data-en*

CANADA

Table 5. Foreign direct investment positions by industrial sector
At year end

Million US dollars

	Inward					Outward				
	2014	2015	2016	2017	2018	2014	2015	2016	2017	2018
All FDI activities	**642 013.1**	**565 687.9**	**603 759.3**	**663 136.9**	**642 809.0**	**728 686.1**	**754 206.6**	**823 098.7**	**927 266.6**	**944 849.6**
Agriculture, forestry and fishing	**322.4**	**307.1**	**107.5**	**144.7**	..	**2 213.1**	**1 919.8**	**2 432.1**	**1 699.7**	..
Mining and quarrying	**150 135.4**	**121 970.4**	**128 794.0**	**137 988.9**	**128 687.9**	**149 791.4**	**135 925.6**	**139 518.1**	**146 773.1**	**142 751.4**
Extraction activities	105 653.1	106 750.7	110 904.9	118 490.4	110 725.4	54 463.3	76 402.5	76 560.7	79 396.9	83 753.2
Manufacturing	**170 984.6**	**130 824.4**	**135 076.1**	**146 897.5**	**148 340.8**	**59 577.6**	**59 023.1**	**67 044.4**	**74 232.4**	**75 706.4**
of which:										
Food products, beverages and tobacco	25 578.9	20 377.9	40 505.1	40 199.7	45 170.8	8 824.0	12 462.4	22 515.7	27 713.3	28 801.1
Textiles, wood and paper products; printing	9 630.1	7 843.9	9 463.4	13 852.4	13 235.8	3 624.5	2 356.2	5 153.9	5 293.6	7 159.5
Chemical, rubber, plastic, non-metallic mineral products	76 852.3	60 877.9	69 323.7	72 525.3	71 311.0	13 825.3	11 437.9	11 788.9	12 127.6	11 631.6
Metal and machinery products, except electrical equipment	37 449.8	21 432.8	12 814.4	14 026.9	15 601.0	15 844.5	12 518.1	13 876.1	13 699.0	13 657.4
Motor vehicles, trailers, semi-trailers, other transport equipment	13 443.4	13 422.7	14 454.4	16 408.5	16 108.1	14 691.8	11 720.4	14 796.3	16 535.2	16 415.5
Other manufacturing	8 030.0	6 869.9	-11 484.9	-10 115.3	-13 085.9	2 767.5	8 527.5	-1 086.5	-1 136.2	-1 958.8
Electricity, gas, steam and air conditioning supply	..	**1 794.8**	**1 557.0**	**1 199.2**	**993.7**	..	**19 913.3**	**23 957.6**	**30 220.5**	**32 659.8**
Water supply; sewerage, waste management and remediation activities	..	..	..	..	..	..	..	..	..	..
Construction	**4 602.1**	**3 174.1**	**4 845.0**	**5 665.3**	**6 305.1**	**434.5**	**619.9**	**1 853.1**	**3 524.6**	**4 622.9**
Services	**303 846.0 e**	**303 605.5 e**	**331 109.0 e**	**368 014.6 e**	**347 989.8 e**	**482 003.6 e**	**518 263.7 e**	**570 010.9 e**	**652 982.0 e**	**642 640.3 e**
Wholesale and retail trade; repair of motor vehicles and motorcycles	80 633.7	67 195.1	76 747.0	84 540.2	82 151.4	15 653.9	21 244.9	28 031.5	28 623.3	28 133.0
Transportation and storage	6 684.2	6 343.2	7 906.7	10 884.7	10 423.4	23 108.0	24 583.8	35 114.4	53 079.4	61 916.3
Accommodation and food service activities	3 576.2	2 560.7	3 009.3	3 148.9	3 183.8	2 235.5	3 057.1	2 044.2	2 655.6	2 635.2
Information and communication	4 740.1	4 215.3	4 874.7	3 120.7	..	30 475.9	29 538.3	34 336.3	35 113.4	..
Financial and insurance activities	85 576.3	83 708.8	215 557.1	241 803.7	227 260.3	265 836.7	274 206.6	404 099.7	455 128.3	471 101.0
Activities of holding companies	..	..	123 683.1	133 688.0	..	..	..	115 943.4	139 498.6	..
Real estate activities	6 194.5	7 338.9	8 783.1	10 184.1	11 019.5	36 861.8	45 101.9	46 785.1	57 397.1	57 036.0
Professional, scientific and technical activities	116 441.1	132 243.5	14 231.1	14 332.4	13 951.5	107 831.7	120 531.1	19 599.8	20 985.0	21 818.9
Administrative and support service activities	..	..	..	..	..	..	..	..	..	..
Public administration; activities of households and of extraterritorial organisations	..	..	..	..	..	..	..	..	..	..
Education	..	..	..	..	..	..	..	..	..	..
Human health and social work activities	..	..	..	..	..	..	..	..	..	..
Arts, entertainment and recreation	..	..	..	..	..	..	..	..	..	..
Other services	..	..	..	..	..	..	..	..	..	..
Not allocated and confidential	**12 122.6**	..	**2 270.8 e**	**3 226.6 e**	**10 491.6 e**	**34 665.9**	..	**18 282.5 e**	**17 834.1 e**	**46 468.8 e**
Private real estate activities	..	..	..	..	..	..	..	..	..	..

.. Not available; e Estimated value

Note: Detailed metadata at: *http://stats.oecd.org/OECDStat_Metadata/ShowMetadata.ashx?Dataset=FDI_CTRY_IND_SUMM.*

Source: OECD International Direct Investment Statistics (database): https://doi.org/10.1787/idi-data-en

CANADA

Table 6. Foreign direct investment income by industrial sector

Million US dollars

	Inward					Outward				
	2014	2015	2016	2017	2018	2014	2015	2016	2017	2018
All FDI activities	**47 094.2**	**34 466.1**	**31 001.1**	**37 795.4**	**41 472.2**	**46 641.6**	**40 014.9**	**40 774.1**	**54 572.7**	**60 286.9**
Agriculture, forestry and fishing	..	..	..	..	..	..	..	..	..	..
Mining and quarrying	..	..	..	..	..	..	..	..	..	..
Extraction activities	..	..	..	..	..	..	..	..	..	..
Manufacturing	..	..	..	..	..	..	..	..	..	..
of which:										
Food products, beverages and tobacco	..	..	..	..	..	..	..	..	..	..
Textiles, wood and paper products; printing	..	..	..	..	..	..	..	..	..	..
Chemical, rubber, plastic, non-metallic mineral products	..	..	..	..	..	..	..	..	..	..
Metal and machinery products, except electrical equipment	..	..	..	..	..	..	..	..	..	..
Motor vehicles, trailers, semi-trailers, other transport equipment	..	..	..	..	..	..	..	..	..	..
Other manufacturing	..	..	..	..	..	..	..	..	..	..
Electricity, gas, steam and air conditioning supply	..	..	..	..	..	..	..	..	..	..
Water supply; sewerage, waste management and remediation activities	..	..	..	..	..	..	..	..	..	..
Construction	..	..	..	..	..	..	..	..	..	..
Services	..	..	..	..	..	..	..	..	..	..
Wholesale and retail trade; repair of motor vehicles and motorcycles	..	..	..	..	..	..	..	..	..	..
Transportation and storage	..	..	..	..	..	..	..	..	..	..
Accommodation and food service activities	..	..	..	..	..	..	..	..	..	..
Information and communication	..	..	..	..	..	..	..	..	..	..
Financial and insurance activities	..	..	..	..	..	..	..	..	..	..
Activities of holding companies	..	..	..	..	..	..	..	..	..	..
Real estate activities	..	..	..	..	..	..	..	..	..	..
Professional, scientific and technical activities	..	..	..	..	..	..	..	..	..	..
Administrative and support service activities	..	..	..	..	..	..	..	..	..	..
Public administration; activities of households and of extraterritorial organisations	..	..	..	..	..	..	..	..	..	..
Education	..	..	..	..	..	..	..	..	..	..
Human health and social work activities	..	..	..	..	..	..	..	..	..	..
Arts, entertainment and recreation	..	..	..	..	..	..	..	..	..	..
Other services	..	..	..	..	..	..	..	..	..	..
Not allocated and confidential	**47 094.2**	**..**	**31 001.1**	**37 795.4**	**41 472.2**	**46 641.6**	**..**	**40 774.1**	**54 572.7**	**60 286.9**
Private real estate activities	..	..	..	..	..	..	..	..	..	..

.. Not available

Note: Detailed metadata at: *http://stats.oecd.org/OECDStat_Metadata/ShowMetadata.ashx?Dataset=FDI_CTRY_IND_SUMM.*

Source: *OECD International Direct Investment Statistics (database): https://doi.org/10.1787/idi-data-en*

Table 1. Foreign direct investment flows by country

Million US dollars

	Inward					Outward				
	2014	2015	2016	2017	2018	2014	2015	2016	2017	2018
WORLD	**5 491.9**	**465.2**	**9 814.5**	**9 517.9**	**9 478.9**	**1 619.5**	**2 488.1**	**2 181.7**	**7 557.0**	**5 277.3**
OECD COUNTRIES	**.. c**	**264.4**	**.. c**	**.. c**	**9 764.7**	**1 912.1**	**1 943.3**	**.. c**	**3 372.3**	**2 917.6**
Australia	30.4	-20.7	31.3	23.3	-2.8	.. c	-31.8	.. c	.. c	-1.4
Austria	276.5	-115.8	-188.5	861.0	741.7	-17.1	4.0	5.5	17.1	-5.2
Belgium	-1 494.3	-237.0	-484.9	-739.0	3 024.6	26.8	7.7	-17.2	0.6	3.7
Canada	-27.1	25.4	-53.1	8.3	-2.6	3.4	-7.3	-3.0	7.3	14.5
Chile	-1.8	0.6	0.0	0.0	-0.3	0.1	0.0	0.1	.. c	4.5
Czech Republic	-	-	-	-	-	-	-	-	-	-
Denmark	62.6	149.6	73.0	6.7	-91.8	0.7	-0.3	0.4	2.0	0.9
Estonia	-3.6	-0.7	4.0	2.3	4.3	-0.8	1.8	-1.5	0.6	-0.9
Finland	-2.4	-12.9	13.1	57.6	40.2	0.0	.. c	20.5	2.2	3.4
France	677.4	221.1	707.3	416.4	1 082.0	42.1	64.8	42.5	8.0	23.9
Germany	2 811.4	1 003.5	2 535.1	4 553.2	2 783.8	684.0	276.2	-227.7	234.5	358.2
Greece	-13.4	2.8	-4.4	-10.5	-0.1	.. c	23.4	0.2	-937.4	0.0
Hungary	8.3	-77.6	20.0	126.4	28.7	112.4	-7.2	-29.8	175.5	242.4
Iceland	.. c	1.7	.. c	.. c	2.9	0.0	0.0	0.0	0.0	0.0
Ireland	255.2	138.8	41.3	-184.2	31.3	2.7	145.1	-294.8	-368.3	-326.6
Israel[1]	30.0	20.3	52.2	-0.5	8.6	-	-	-	.. c	.. c
Italy	47.3	134.2	739.9	325.4	511.7	-19.0	13.6	-89.2	151.3	-74.0
Japan	142.3	92.9	97.1	122.1	197.7	-11.5	-0.1	0.1	.. c	0.4
Korea	353.6	479.6	167.6	478.2	67.2	.. c	.. c	-0.5	.. c	.. c
Latvia	0.5	-0.7	9.1	4.4	6.9	1.0	1.1	3.7	11.2	-3.3
Lithuania	0.0	4.3	-6.1	4.5	-9.9	-1.3	-1.6	-0.2	5.5	0.6
Luxembourg	2 221.8	1 208.6	1 015.7	2 493.6	-227.1	5.2	848.7	379.0	2 785.0	303.8
Mexico	1.9	-66.8	-19.5	-44.4	21.5	3.5	1.0	-6.0	2.3	-10.0
Netherlands	819.8	-2 272.3	2 044.1	-2 043.9	1 114.1	-779.7	89.5	464.0	2 330.7	1 354.5
New Zealand	-5.5	3.3	-1.7	0.6	1.2	-	-	-	-	0.1
Norway	-13.5	-5.4	99.9	-13.9	31.9	-	.. c	50.6	7.8	6.6
Poland	-159.7	427.3	450.9	997.5	442.0	-175.6	145.4	-67.5	240.6	531.2
Portugal	-15.6	25.3	-27.6	11.2	-36.6	5.0	0.1	0.2	-0.2	0.0
Slovak Republic	142.2	-164.5	361.2	-232.3	-107.3	1 241.6	387.5	607.2	-1 148.4	399.5
Slovenia	7.5	-32.9	1.1	-0.5	7.6	86.5	-94.7	233.9	-9.9	15.6
Spain	-1 943.6	-159.0	215.0	77.3	-104.2	15.1	6.7	-1.1	15.1	-3.4
Sweden	51.6	-125.1	246.2	261.8	18.2	19.1	-0.7	3.7	4.8	92.0
Switzerland	-153.4	-650.0	426.1	1 190.3	50.0	-23.7	44.6	-45.5	-19.0	-7.9
Turkey	-2.9	7.3	2.8	-9.6	1.7	12.8	-30.8	-44.0	56.4	-71.6
United Kingdom	20.3	1 157.7	-620.1	-583.0	-48.3	-35.0	-11.9	8.6	-283.2	26.7
United States	-9.7	-895.0	81.4	-303.0	165.8	12.5	67.9	-29.2	48.1	39.6
EUROPE	**.. c**	**.. c**	**8 666.3**	**9 273.3**	**9 691.0**	**1 405.4**	**2 497.0**	**2 182.8**	**7 331.9**	**4 792.2**
Bulgaria	10.0	-12.0	6.0	4.2	-3.8	74.6	-78.2	77.6	48.8	-38.5
Croatia	-7.7	8.5	3.4	3.3	3.6	336.1	-210.5	-63.2	103.0	-1.7
Cyprus[2, 3]	939.1	-403.5	1 099.5	1 657.7	75.9	91.7	594.9	693.2	3 667.1	704.6
Malta	87.7	99.0	-194.5	16.4	32.2	11.4	-4.8	28.3	23.2	23.0
Romania	-6.7	-9.4	20.5	-14.7	7.7	-882.8	229.9	348.5	150.9	1 128.9
Russian Federation	190.1	110.4	-1.3	-123.8	147.8	-13.7	-9.4	33.4	51.3	73.6
Ukraine	-0.2	13.4	35.4	13.0	14.9	-8.5	-16.3	-1.4	3.8	-16.2
AFRICA	**-2.0**	**.. c**	**.. c**	**.. c**	**.. c**	**.. c**	**.. c**	**.. c**	**.. c**	**47.8**
Northern Africa	11.0	.. c	.. c	.. c	.. c	.. c	.. c	.. c	.. c	19.8
Algeria	0.1	.. c	.. c	.. c	.. c	-	-	-	-	-
Egypt	3.6	-0.6	3.8	-3.8	-1.7	.. c	.. c	.. c	.. c	.. c
Libya	-	-	-	-	-	-	-	-	-	-
Morocco	-0.5	-1.2	-0.9	-2.7	142.9	-	-	-	-	-
Tunisia	7.8	-2.8	0.1	0.4	0.1	0.5	0.4	-0.1	-0.9	.. c
Other African countries	-13.0	1.0	-0.6	11.9	-16.3	0.0	-1.0	5.6	23.9	28.1
Nigeria	.. c	.. c	.. c	-2.4	.. c	-	-	-0.2	0.0	-0.2
South Africa	-2.7	-5.4	2.2	16.7	-1.7	0.0	0.0	5.6	23.9	28.3
AMERICA	**.. c**	**.. c**	**.. c**	**-405.1**	**71.5**	**48.5**	**46.5**	**-38.0**	**91.7**	**48.0**
Northern America	-36.8	-869.6	28.3	-294.7	163.2	16.0	60.6	-32.2	55.4	54.2
Central America and Caribbean countries	139.7	141.8	-29.3	-112.3	40.3	30.4	-8.8	-7.1	3.4	.. c
Bahamas	-19.0	62.3	28.8	27.1	9.7	-	-	-	-	-
Bermuda	2.1	18.0	-0.6	-24.6	0.7	-	-	-	-	-
Cayman Islands	-6.9	1.1	-4.3	0.6	1.4	-	-	-	-	-
Costa Rica	.. c	.. c	.. c	.. c	.. c	-	0.0	-0.1	0.0	.. c
El Salvador	.. c	.. c	-	.. c	.. c	-	-	-	-	-
Guatemala	-	-	-	0.0	-	-	-	-	-	-
Honduras	-	.. c	.. c	.. c	0.0	-	-	-	-	-
Nicaragua	0.4	.. c	.. c	.. c	.. c	-	-	-	-	-
Panama	16.0	-0.8	10.2	-11.4	2.5	-	-	-	-	-
Virgin Islands, U.S.	-	-	-	-	-	-	-	-	-	-
South America	.. c	.. c	.. c	1.8	-132.0	2.1	-5.3	1.2	32.9	.. c
Argentina	-9.4	7.9	0.5	2.7	1.7	.. c	.. c	.. c	.. c	.. c
Bolivia	-	-	-	-	.. c	-	-	-	-	-
Brazil	-4.9	-1.5	5.3	0.3	-133.4	-8.2	-2.5	-1.0	0.2	-0.9
Colombia	0.9	0.3	0.3	-0.9	-0.3	-	-	0.5	-0.3	0.2
Ecuador	.. c	.. c	.. c	.. c	0.0	-	-	-	-	-
Paraguay	-	-	-	-	0.1	-	-	-	-	-
Peru	0.0	0.2	-0.2	.. c	-0.2	-	-	0.4	-0.1	0.4
Uruguay	-	-	-	-	.. c	-	-	-	-	-
Venezuela	-1.5	-	-	-	-	-	-	-	-	-

CZECH REPUBLIC

Table 1. Foreign direct investment flows by country (*cont.*)

Million US dollars

	Inward					Outward				
	2014	2015	2016	2017	2018	2014	2015	2016	2017	2018
ASIA	**.. c**	**695.9**	**.. c**	**.. c**	**-396.4**	**.. c**	**.. c**	**55.8**	**131.5**	**390.7**
Near and Middle East	.. c	-78.0	.. c	.. c	23.6	.. c	.. c	78.3	151.7	58.4
Gulf Arabian countries	.. c	-45.9	0.9	-8.9	14.2	.. c	.. c	-2.4	.. c	.. c
Kuwait	.. c	.. c	.. c	.. c	-	-	-	-	-	-
Qatar	0.0	-0.1	.. c	.. c	0.9	-	-	-	-	-
Saudi Arabia	1.8	1.5	2.5	-5.1	3.1	.. c	.. c	-	-	0.2
United Arab Emirates	9.0	15.5	-7.8	-4.6	14.6	3.1	-0.2	-2.4	2.3	-6.6
Other Near and Middle East	97.6	-32.1	.. c	.. c	9.4	3.1	-3.6	80.7	.. c	.. c
Jordan	1.4	-	-1.2	1.3	.. c	-	-	-	-	-
Other Asian countries	544.0	773.9	1 108.1	508.5	-420.0	91.8	-3.4	-22.5	-20.2	332.3
China	-4.1	277.1	512.0	-59.6	-694.6	48.1	0.1	-45.4	-32.8	393.8
Hong Kong, China	-21.9	-59.4	46.2	-9.0	-90.0	.. c	.. c	0.3	0.1	0.2
India	-0.2	-14.7	-108.9	-23.2	3.3	53.8	-0.1	21.2	8.4	-82.9
Indonesia	-0.1	0.2	-0.4	-0.4	-2.3	-	-	-0.3	-0.1	-0.4
Iran, Islamic Republic of	-	-0.3	0.3	-	0.0	-	-	-	-	-
Malaysia	1.0	-4.3	10.9	1.3	-2.4	-	-	-	-	.. c
Philippines	2.0	-0.5	0.0	1.7	-2.3	-	-	-	-	-
Singapore	79.5	53.9	121.5	-9.0	116.3	.. c	.. c	.. c	.. c	0.4
Chinese Taipei	-47.6	-31.2	209.3	-7.5	-5.3	-	-	-	0.4	.. c
Thailand	43.5	-24.9	-11.5	12.0	-1.5	0.0	0.0	0.1	0.0	0.4
Viet Nam	0.7	-1.8	-1.2	2.8	-3.0	-6.1	-1.0	0.8	6.7	-0.4
AUSTRALIA, OCEANIA AND POLAR REGIONS	**24.9**	**-17.4**	**31.3**	**117.5**	**-1.3**	**.. c**	**-31.8**	**.. c**	**.. c**	**-1.3**
WORLD unallocated and confidential	**.. d**	**.. d**	**.. d**	**.. d**	**.. d**	**.. d**	**.. d**	**.. d**	**.. d**	**-0.2**
European Union (EU28)	**4 792.1**	**957.1**	**8 080.3**	**8 072.5**	**9 327.4**	**.. c**	**.. c**	**2 124.8**	**7 230.3**	**4 759.5**
G20 countries excl. European Union	**4 215.4**	**2 514.8**	**4 081.5**	**4 794.5**	**4 101.7**	**775.1**	**.. c**	**-334.5**	**.. c**	**718.1**
G20 OECD countries	**4 044.9**	**2 139.2**	**3 669.9**	**4 986.9**	**4 777.7**	**696.1**	**.. c**	**.. c**	**224.2**	**.. c**
G20 Non-OECD countries	**170.4**	**375.6**	**411.7**	**-192.4**	**-676.0**	**79.0**	**-12.1**	**.. c**	**.. c**	**.. c**
MENA countries	**.. c**	**-50.4**	**4.2**	**-13.9**	**155.4**	**26.9**	**-5.7**	**.. c**	**-26.4**	**13.3**
ASEAN countries	**124.5**	**22.9**	**.. c**	**8.6**	**105.0**	**.. c**	**.. c**	**.. c**	**.. c**	**.. c**

- Nil; .. Not available; c Confidential data; d Secondary Confidentiality

Note: Detailed metadata at: *http://stats.oecd.org/OECDStat_Metadata/ShowMetadata.ashx?Dataset=FDI_CTRY_IND_SUMM.*

1. Information on data for Israel: *http://oe.cd/israel-disclaimer.*
2. Note by Turkey: The information in this document with reference to "Cyprus" relates to the southern part of the Island. There is no single authority representing both Turkish and Greek Cypriot people on the Island. Turkey recognises the Turkish Republic of Northern Cyprus (TRNC). Until a lasting and equitable solution is found within the context of the United Nations, Turkey shall preserve its position concerning the "Cyprus issue".
3. Note by all the European Union Member States of the OECD and the European Union: The Republic of Cyprus is recognised by all members of the United Nations with the exception of Turkey. The information in this document relates to the area under the effective control of the Government of the Republic of Cyprus.

Source: OECD International Direct Investment Statistics (database): https://doi.org/10.1787/idi-data-en

CZECH REPUBLIC

Table 2. Foreign direct investment positions by country

At year end

Million US dollars

	Inward					Outward				
	2014	2015	2016	2017	2018	2014	2015	2016	2017	2018
WORLD	**121 511.8**	**116 627.8**	**121 854.6**	**155 994.1**	**163 288.6**	**18 235.5**	**18 591.4**	**19 426.3**	**32 364.1**	**34 943.0**
OECD COUNTRIES	**114 217.1**	**109 917.7**	**113 133.7**	**145 348.9**	**153 045.4**	**14 355.7**	**14 588.6**	**14 557.3**	**22 431.2**	**26 639.3**
Australia	120.3	89.5	88.1	103.2	90.3	.. c	.. c	-	.. c	.. c
Austria	13 166.6	11 904.1	11 581.3	13 659.9	13 826.0	37.6	37.6	41.1	72.7	53.7
Belgium	5 146.3	5 006.7	4 974.1	5 314.4	5 353.4	230.2	211.4	184.5	212.5	207.7
Canada	384.8	393.3	390.3	488.6	529.7	20.0	25.1	.. c	28.3	26.2
Chile	2.1	1.5	1.3	1.6	1.5	0.0	-	-0.2	.. c	.. c
Czech Republic	7 475.1	9 132.4	9 482.4	22 133.1	28 974.9	-	-	-	-	-
Denmark	665.7	717.6	869.2	927.5	854.4	5.9	0.3	5.8	8.6	-0.8
Estonia	-	-	.. c	3.3	5.3	0.3	0.8	0.7	2.6	0.2
Finland	326.8	266.8	356.8	489.6	463.5	0.0	.. c	5.0	7.0	8.0
France	8 276.9	8 957.7	10 620.3	12 579.8	12 299.3	153.5	202.5	233.8	286.8	233.6
Germany	30 319.8	27 595.1	26 097.5	31 225.7	32 791.0	1 293.9	1 004.1	492.8	857.5	567.5
Greece	78.2	61.7	.. c	4.6	4.1	989.6	910.3	881.3	3.8	4.2
Hungary	271.9	193.4	244.8	382.7	379.6	155.6	138.9	132.0	430.8	367.1
Iceland	23.5	17.4	.. c	.. c	.. c	0.0	0.0	0.0	0.0	0.0
Ireland	68.7	289.4	576.9	586.5	380.0	757.5	873.2	511.2	188.8	90.6
Israel[1]	292.5	228.4	607.5	733.3	674.6	-	-	-	.. c	.. c
Italy	4 912.0	5 612.5	5 676.6	6 222.4	6 295.0	43.8	55.2	-37.2	119.7	114.2
Japan	2 211.1	2 676.8	2 519.3	3 284.3	3 382.3	.. c	0.0	.. c	.. c	0.1
Korea	1 611.4	2 056.6	2 294.0	3 174.2	2 899.5	.. c	.. c	.. c	.. c	.. c
Latvia	.. c	.. c	15.2	25.3	22.7	6.5	8.3	8.3	26.5	16.3
Lithuania	.. c	.. c	.. c	2.8	2.7	-0.1	1.4	1.4	7.3	-1.6
Luxembourg	2 937.7	3 259.8	1 838.7	1 978.9	1 988.2	22.2	660.2	952.7	6 180.9	9 775.5
Mexico	.. c	.. c	293.2	.. c	.. c	9.6	11.0	4.6	7.0	7.1
Netherlands	6 628.7	6 399.4	8 392.4	10 505.4	11 036.0	6 242.3	6 349.8	6 581.6	9 636.3	8 613.9
New Zealand	.. c	.. c	-	-	-	-	-	-	-	-
Norway	96.3	82.2	120.7	147.6	136.0	-	.. c	.. c	131.7	67.2
Poland	1 679.5	1 693.4	2 038.8	3 869.4	3 884.7	317.5	368.2	645.1	794.8	1 208.6
Portugal	33.0	40.0	49.3	67.0	42.7	4.6	4.2	4.3	4.7	4.6
Slovak Republic	3 615.1	3 051.2	2 766.9	1 986.1	2 099.6	3 346.4	3 131.3	3 085.1	2 888.4	2 763.3
Slovenia	63.0	42.2	34.9	34.6	26.7	83.6	-1.3	211.1	218.9	103.6
Spain	3 365.7	1 016.5	1 102.0	1 325.8	1 306.9	24.4	30.7	28.6	48.6	72.4
Sweden	1 208.5	1 037.4	946.2	1 307.3	1 316.2	19.4	19.1	22.4	29.8	19.2
Switzerland	3 513.4	3 242.4	4 657.7	6 157.6	6 668.0	-0.3	44.7	1.0	-19.6	1 246.8
Turkey	1.6	2.4	.. c	2.6	2.5	233.1	109.6	44.1	83.3	42.8
United Kingdom	5 930.5	5 350.9	5 604.1	5 949.8	5 569.8	310.8	304.0	314.1	58.0	409.0
United States	9 625.0	9 278.4	8 867.5	10 321.0	9 404.8	38.1	97.7	69.7	85.2	616.4
EUROPE	**105 298.1**	**99 618.3**	**.. c**	**133 052.4**	**141 636.4**	**17 623.5**	**18 043.6**	**.. c**	**31 190.6**	**.. c**
Bulgaria	11.2	9.2	10.4	9.0	10.1	568.8	438.7	482.7	742.0	678.6
Croatia	.. c	.. c	17.1	37.8	35.0	349.3	65.0	1.9	114.5	243.7
Cyprus[2, 3]	4 122.2	3 338.1	4 096.8	4 424.5	4 431.4	1 069.8	1 539.2	1 923.5	5 890.9	3 582.6
Malta	313.2	363.7	363.1	440.8	447.3	30.4	13.5	42.8	53.6	.. c
Romania	13.6	2.7	3.8	3.3	4.0	366.5	670.4	1 039.0	1 211.2	1 392.1
Russian Federation	715.8	656.5	799.6	955.7	711.1	194.5	162.4	192.7	272.5	369.5
Ukraine	52.6	62.8	89.6	117.0	93.3	32.0	-0.6	4.2	9.7	12.1
AFRICA	**91.1**	**.. c**	**43.2**	**.. c**	**54.2**	**.. c**	**.. c**	**.. c**	**.. c**	**138.0**
Northern Africa	3.9	.. c	5.7	.. c	.. c	.. c	.. c	.. c	.. c	.. c
Algeria	-	-	-	-	-	-	-	-	-	-
Egypt	3.9	.. c	.. c	.. c	.. c	.. c	.. c	.. c	.. c	.. c
Libya	-	-	-	-	-	-	-	-	-	-
Morocco	-	-	-	-	-	-	-	-	-	-
Tunisia	-	-	.. c	-	-	0.2	0.9	0.8	-0.4	0.9
Other African countries	87.3	168.1	37.5	14.6	.. c	1.5	0.0	2.7	28.0	.. c
Nigeria	-	-	-	-	-	-	-	-0.3	-	-
South Africa	88.9	168.7	.. c	-	.. c	0.0	0.0	3.1	28.0	49.3
AMERICA	**.. c**	**.. c**	**.. c**	**12 143.3**	**11 234.8**	**115.1**	**165.2**	**.. c**	**180.6**	**688.6**
Northern America	10 009.8	9 671.7	9 257.8	10 809.7	9 934.5	58.1	122.8	.. c	113.5	642.6
Central America and Caribbean countries	722.4	711.7	1 042.3	1 329.7	1 296.4	42.6	33.4	4.5	24.5	49.7
Bahamas	183.3	168.2	191.9	.. c	.. c	-	-	-	-	-
Bermuda	18.5	27.5	65.3	68.9	62.8	-	-	-	-	-
Cayman Islands	83.3	77.7	290.4	448.9	425.4	-	-	-	-	-
Costa Rica	-	-	-	.. c	.. c	-	1.5	-0.1	-	-
El Salvador	-	-	-	-	-	-	-	-	-	-
Guatemala	-	-	-	-	-	-	-	-	-	-
Honduras	-	-	-	-	-	-	-	-	-	-
Nicaragua	-	-	-	-	-	-	-	-	-	-
Panama	26.2	-7.0	-53.3	-65.1	-39.4	-	-	-	-	-
Virgin Islands, U.S.	-	-	-	-	-	-	-	-	-	-
South America	.. c	.. c	.. c	4.0	3.9	14.5	9.0	9.7	42.6	-3.7
Argentina	-	-	-	-	-	.. c	.. c	.. c	.. c	.. c
Bolivia	-	-	-	-	-	-	-	-	-	-
Brazil	.. c	.. c	1.8	2.3	2.4	2.1	0.0	0.1	-0.3	-0.7
Colombia	-	-	-	-	-	-	-	0.4	-	0.4
Ecuador	-	-	.. c	-	-	-	-	-	-	-
Paraguay	-	-	-	-	-	-	-	-	-	-
Peru	-	-	-	-	-	-	-	0.0	-	0.1
Uruguay	-	-	-	-	-	-	-	-	-	-
Venezuela	-	-	-	-	-	-	-	-	-	-

CZECH REPUBLIC

Table 2. Foreign direct investment positions by country *(cont.)*

At year end

Million US dollars

	Inward					Outward				
	2014	2015	2016	2017	2018	2014	2015	2016	2017	2018
ASIA	**5 104.0**	**6 124.1**	**7 656.0**	**10 526.7**	**10 132.6**	**.. c**	**240.3**	**.. c**	**858.8**	**.. c**
Near and Middle East	346.8	283.3	.. c	.. c	.. c	.. c	88.1	.. c	713.9	678.9
Gulf Arabian countries	40.9	44.1	.. c	100.7	86.8	.. c	1.2	.. c	.. c	.. c
Kuwait	.. c	.. c	6.9	6.3	5.7	-	-	-	-	-
Qatar	-	-	-	-	-	-	-	-	-	-
Saudi Arabia	.. c	.. c	7.2	.. c	.. c	.. c	-	-	-	-
United Arab Emirates	33.7	38.1	66.2	81.4	66.2	0.9	1.2	.. c	1.3	1.2
Other Near and Middle East	305.8	239.2	632.3	.. c	.. c	171.2	86.9	186.9	.. c	.. c
Jordan	1.3	1.2	-	1.5	1.4	-	-	-	-	-
Other Asian countries	4 757.2	5 840.8	.. c	.. c	.. c	159.6	152.2	153.4	144.9	.. c
China	204.0	370.7	794.3	1 100.9	881.2	91.8	85.3	64.0	39.2	421.4
Hong Kong, China	-17.8	-17.6	191.7	244.8	231.1	.. c	.. c	5.2	5.2	6.0
India	168.2	190.9	97.1	91.6	86.5	45.5	48.7	68.7	80.7	184.9
Indonesia	-	-	-	-	-	-	-	0.2	-	-
Iran, Islamic Republic of	-	-	-	-	-	-	-	-	-	-
Malaysia	.. c	.. c	.. c	.. c	.. c	-	-	-	-	-
Philippines	-	-	-	-	-	-	-	-	-	0.2
Singapore	.. c	.. c	392.7	824.7	990.6	.. c	.. c	.. c	.. c	.. c
Chinese Taipei	455.8	421.4	554.6	833.7	765.4	-	-	-	0.4	0.4
Thailand	1.3	.. c	-	-	-	0.0	0.0	0.0	-	.. c
Viet Nam	5.3	5.1	5.1	6.4	6.1	12.2	10.7	11.5	18.1	16.7
AUSTRALIA, OCEANIA AND POLAR REGIONS	**.. c**	**.. c**	**95.9**	**.. c**	**.. c**	**.. c**	**.. c**	**-**	**.. c**	**.. c**
WORLD unallocated and confidential	**.. d**	**.. d**	**.. d**	**.. d**	**.. d**	**.. d**	**.. d**	**.. d**	**.. d**	**.. d**
European Union (EU28)	**100 638.5**	**95 350.3**	**97 761.2**	**125 497.2**	**133 850.4**	**16 430.2**	**.. c**	**17 795.8**	**30 097.5**	**.. c**
G20 countries excl. European Union	**.. c**	**.. c**	**64 159.4**	**75 830.8**	**.. c**	**2 454.1**	**.. c**	**.. c**	**.. c**	**.. c**
G20 OECD countries	**.. c**	**.. c**	**.. c**	**.. c**	**.. c**	**2 119.0**	**1 809.1**	**1 142.0**	**1 525.0**	**2 012.4**
G20 Non-OECD countries	**1 243.6**	**1 457.7**	**.. c**	**.. c**	**1 721.5**	**335.1**	**.. c**	**.. c**	**.. c**	**.. c**
MENA countries	**46.1**	**47.3**	**94.9**	**108.6**	**94.5**	**111.6**	**.. c**	**86.2**	**67.5**	**90.2**
ASEAN countries	**90.3**	**112.6**	**.. c**	**.. c**	**.. c**	**.. c**	**.. c**	**.. c**	**.. c**	**-98.3**

- Nil; .. Not available; c Confidential data; d Secondary Confidentiality

Note: Inward FDI positions are allocated according to the ultimate investing country. Detailed metadata at: *http://stats.oecd.org/OECDStat_Metadata/ShowMetadata.ashx?Dataset=FDI_CTRY_IND_SUMM.*

1. Information on data for Israel: *http://oe.cd/israel-disclaimer.*
2. Note by Turkey: The information in this document with reference to "Cyprus" relates to the southern part of the Island. There is no single authority representing both Turkish and Greek Cypriot people on the Island. Turkey recognises the Turkish Republic of Northern Cyprus (TRNC). Until a lasting and equitable solution is found within the context of the United Nations, Turkey shall preserve its position concerning the "Cyprus issue".
3. Note by all the European Union Member States of the OECD and the European Union: The Republic of Cyprus is recognised by all members of the United Nations with the exception of Turkey. The information in this document relates to the area under the effective control of the Government of the Republic of Cyprus.

Source: OECD International Direct Investment Statistics (database): https://doi.org/10.1787/idi-data-en

Table 3. Foreign direct investment income by country

Million US dollars

	Inward					Outward				
	2014	2015	2016	2017	2018	2014	2015	2016	2017	2018
WORLD	**16 098.5**	**14 473.5**	**15 343.8**	**19 127.2**	**19 052.2**	**1 588.9**	**1 860.9**	**2 014.9**	**4 665.4**	**2 974.8**
OECD COUNTRIES	**14 990.7**	**13 878.2**	**.. c**	**.. c**	**18 503.3**	**1 367.9**	**1 622.0**	**1 585.0**	**3 715.0**	**2 093.8**
Australia	2.1	1.6	2.6	2.9	4.9	-0.5	0.0	-	.. c	.. c
Austria	2 236.1	1 945.5	1 982.7	2 029.7	2 217.7	1.4	-0.7	2.2	3.0	5.0
Belgium	1 062.8	977.6	1 003.2	804.4	1 436.6	2.4	3.6	2.8	3.3	4.1
Canada	-1.7	6.1	7.7	6.9	9.4	.. c	.. c	.. c	-2.2	14.6
Chile	-	-	-	-	-	-	-	0.1	-	.. c
Czech Republic	-	-	-	-	-	-	-	-	-	-
Denmark	89.4	88.7	99.5	92.0	115.9	0.9	0.1	0.7	1.0	1.3
Estonia	.. c	.. c	-1.3	1.9	2.4	0.1	0.3	-1.4	0.5	-0.8
Finland	39.0	44.9	54.6	45.6	67.5	-	0.0	4.4	2.0	4.3
France	1 250.2	1 060.4	1 187.1	1 316.2	1 088.1	2.7	11.6	10.7	11.2	4.3
Germany	2 628.5	2 163.2	2 666.0	2 984.8	3 932.3	68.7	333.3	34.3	286.9	9.6
Greece	.. c	.. c	-0.4	.. c	-0.1	-	-	-	0.1	0.4
Hungary	59.8	-5.7	102.6	-5.1	58.7	4.2	7.9	-1.0	60.8	32.4
Iceland	0.0	0.0	-	-	-	0.0	0.0	0.0	0.0	0.0
Ireland	51.0	29.7	0.7	-8.9	16.8	0.2	8.2	-1.3	2.0	3.1
Israel[1]	3.6	1.1	4.6	3.2	5.0	-	-	-	.. c	.. c
Italy	103.8	134.4	373.8	493.2	532.0	-8.2	8.4	-0.1	1.8	9.5
Japan	200.4	149.7	151.9	117.0	105.8	.. c	.. c	.. c	.. c	-0.2
Korea	478.7	300.3	413.9	351.8	411.6	-	-	-0.5	-0.6	-
Latvia	.. c	.. c	3.4	4.6	5.6	4.0	4.8	1.3	13.3	7.1
Lithuania	-0.5	.. c	.. c	1.7	5.7	0.3	0.1	-0.2	-0.3	-0.1
Luxembourg	1 612.4	1 946.6	1 786.1	4 721.1	3 038.7	1.2	-17.8	3.9	1 342.0	384.4
Mexico	-0.9	.. c	-2.4	-3.4	-6.9	0.2	0.7	1.2	1.1	1.4
Netherlands	2 885.0	2 915.5	2 982.4	3 518.3	3 297.8	558.6	656.9	1 314.7	1 620.3	1 223.7
New Zealand	.. c	.. c	-	-	0.2	-	-	-	-	-
Norway	7.1	15.1	30.3	20.9	35.1	-	-	1.9	.. c	6.1
Poland	156.4	279.7	286.7	209.3	346.7	19.8	-70.6	-21.4	66.9	120.9
Portugal	2.2	0.6	-19.1	-13.4	-19.4	-	-	.. c	0.0	0.0
Slovak Republic	372.7	396.8	300.5	325.8	391.7	707.9	670.8	213.5	221.5	259.1
Slovenia	8.5	5.4	11.3	8.3	8.9	7.6	13.4	16.5	20.4	21.6
Spain	121.1	112.7	96.2	106.7	119.5	1.7	2.5	2.3	2.2	4.5
Sweden	223.7	218.4	224.5	203.8	161.4	-0.4	.. c	.. c	-0.1	-2.0
Switzerland	592.4	470.0	483.3	670.7	506.3	0.2	0.1	0.1	0.7	0.4
Turkey	0.6	1.3	.. c	1.1	1.6	-11.6	-28.8	-26.7	25.8	-39.9
United Kingdom	370.4	506.8	297.9	315.6	413.1	3.7	5.0	1.5	2.0	10.1
United States	437.4	113.8	191.0	190.9	198.4	3.9	14.8	7.2	12.7	8.8
EUROPE	**15 014.7**	**13 966.3**	**.. c**	**18 552.8**	**18 288.9**	**1 537.1**	**.. c**	**1 928.8**	**4 637.3**	**2 786.6**
Bulgaria	.. c	-	-1.3	.. c	-0.6	-22.5	27.3	26.1	44.8	37.0
Croatia	-0.1	2.3	2.0	1.0	6.4	36.5	-0.2	-0.7	1.5	1.3
Cyprus[2, 3]	1 138.2	664.6	572.2	710.2	490.6	288.2	267.4	307.4	683.2	425.2
Malta	9.8	-1.8	28.3	52.4	46.5	28.3	12.9	25.9	.. c	38.1
Romania	-0.4	-0.2	0.3	-0.4	9.2	-235.2	-106.9	-50.7	95.0	97.6
Russian Federation	-7.9	-3.5	7.8	8.1	-27.6	6.4	-32.2	-10.7	44.7	70.9
Ukraine	-1.7	-2.3	-0.3	-0.3	6.6	0.3	-3.2	1.2	1.1	2.7
AFRICA	**.. c**	**.. c**	**.. c**	**-3.8**	**.. c**	**.. c**	**.. c**	**.. c**	**.. c**	**.. c**
Northern Africa	.. c	.. c	0.1	0.3	16.9	.. c	.. c	.. c	.. c	.. c
Algeria	-	-	-	-	-	-	-	-	-	-
Egypt	0.1	.. c	.. c	.. c	.. c	.. c	.. c	.. c	.. c	.. c
Libya	-	-	-	-	-	-	-	-	-	-
Morocco	-	-	-	.. c	.. c	-	-	-	-	-
Tunisia	.. c	0.0	.. c	-	.. c	0.0	0.0	0.0	0.0	0.1
Other African countries	-4.3	-3.3	.. c	-4.1	.. c	0.0	0.0	2.6	1.1	1.1
Nigeria	-	-	-	-	-	-	-	-0.2	-	-0.2
South Africa	-	-	-	-	-	0.0	0.0	2.6	1.2	1.3
AMERICA	**442.9**	**.. c**	**200.8**	**.. c**	**205.8**	**.. c**	**.. c**	**.. c**	**13.0**	**25.4**
Northern America	435.7	119.9	198.7	197.8	207.7	.. c	.. c	.. c	10.5	23.4
Central America and Caribbean countries	7.2	-11.9	2.2	3.5	-2.0	12.9	2.7	1.1	1.4	1.3
Bahamas	.. c	2.1	11.1	8.0	9.8	-	-	-	-	-
Bermuda	.. c	1.6	0.6	0.7	0.6	-	-	-	-	-
Cayman Islands	2.2	0.6	1.4	1.1	1.4	-	-	-	-	-
Costa Rica	-	-	-	-	-	-	0.0	-0.1	-	-0.1
El Salvador	-	-	-	-	-	-	-	-	-	-
Guatemala	-	-	-	-	-	-	-	-	-	-
Honduras	-	-	-	-	-	-	-	-	-	-
Nicaragua	0.0	.. c	.. c	.. c	.. c	-	-	-	-	-
Panama	-3.7	-5.4	-8.2	1.1	-3.3	-	-	-	-	-
Virgin Islands, U.S.	-	-	-	-	-	-	-	-	-	-
South America	0.0	.. c	0.0	.. c	0.1	0.1	-0.9	-1.0	1.2	0.7
Argentina	.. c	-	-	-	.. c	.. c	.. c	.. c	-	.. c
Bolivia	-	-	-	-	-	-	-	-	-	-
Brazil	.. c	.. c	.. c	.. c	.. c	-0.3	-1.3	-1.3	-0.9	-1.2
Colombia	-	-	-	-	-	-	-	0.2	-	0.2
Ecuador	-	-	.. c	-	.. c	-	-	-	-	-
Paraguay	-	-	-	-	-	-	-	-	-	-
Peru	-	-	-	-	-	-	-	0.3	-	0.2
Uruguay	-	-	-	-	-	-	-	-	-	-
Venezuela	-	-	-	-	-	-	-	-	-	-

Table 3. Foreign direct investment income by country *(cont.)*

Million US dollars

	Inward					Outward				
	2014	2015	2016	2017	2018	2014	2015	2016	2017	2018
ASIA	**644.2**	**401.9**	**.. c**	**.. c**	**537.9**	**23.4**	**-0.4**	**.. c**	**2.4**	**.. c**
Near and Middle East	.. c	.. c	.. c	.. c	.. c	24.9	3.2	.. c	30.9	64.6
Gulf Arabian countries	17.3	.. c	2.1	.. c	.. c	-0.1	0.1	.. c	.. c	.. c
Kuwait	-	-	-	-	-	-	-	-	-	-
Qatar	-	-	-	-	-	-	-	-	-	-
Saudi Arabia	-	-	.. c	-	0.2	-	-	-	-	-
United Arab Emirates	-0.1	0.6	2.1	-0.9	2.9	-0.1	0.1	.. c	0.0	0.0
Other Near and Middle East	.. c	1.1	.. c	4.7	5.5	25.0	3.1	66.5	.. c	.. c
Jordan	-	-	-	-	-	-	-	-	-	-
Other Asian countries	.. c	.. c	572.8	370.7	.. c	-1.5	-3.6	-11.9	-28.5	.. c
China	-7.6	-4.4	-17.9	-111.8	-37.7	-2.2	-6.7	-11.9	-31.7	23.9
Hong Kong, China	-64.4	-53.9	3.9	5.8	8.3	.. c	.. c	.. c	.. c	0.1
India	0.4	-14.5	1.0	-0.8	3.7	1.7	3.6	1.2	4.1	10.0
Indonesia	-	-	-	-	-	-	-	-0.4	-	-0.3
Iran, Islamic Republic of	-	-	-	-	-	-	-	-	-	-
Malaysia	.. c	.. c	.. c	.. c	1.2	-	-	-	-	-
Philippines	.. c	.. c	.. c	.. c	.. c	-	-	-	-	-
Singapore	13.5	13.9	9.6	2.6	11.2	.. c	.. c	.. c	.. c	.. c
Chinese Taipei	-0.3	8.4	9.1	3.7	22.4	-	-	-	-0.2	-0.1
Thailand	0.4	-	0.8	1.0	1.8	-	-	0.1	-	0.1
Viet Nam	-	-	-	-	-	-0.4	-	-	0.3	0.9
AUSTRALIA, OCEANIA AND POLAR REGIONS	**.. c**	**.. c**	**.. c**	**2.5**	**.. c**	**-0.5**	**0.0**	**-**	**.. c**	**.. c**
WORLD unallocated and confidential	**.. d**	**.. d**	**.. d**	**.. d**	**.. d**	**.. d**	**- d**	**.. d**	**- d**	**.. d**
European Union (EU28)	**14 418.9**	**13 485.3**	**.. c**	**17 918.9**	**17 789.7**	**1 472.1**	**.. c**	**1 891.9**	**.. c**	**2 701.4**
G20 countries excl. European Union	**5 454.4**	**4 414.1**	**.. c**	**.. c**	**6 629.0**	**.. c**	**.. c**	**.. c**	**356.1**	**122.6**
G20 OECD countries	**5 469.6**	**.. c**	**.. c**	**5 776.9**	**6 690.3**	**62.1**	**347.0**	**45.2**	**338.7**	**.. c**
G20 Non-OECD countries	**-15.2**	**.. c**	**-9.1**	**.. c**	**-61.3**	**.. c**	**.. c**	**.. c**	**17.4**	**.. c**
MENA countries	**.. c**	**0.1**	**2.2**	**-0.7**	**20.0**	**.. c**	**.. c**	**3.6**	**11.5**	**63.4**
ASEAN countries	**14.6**	**14.6**	**11.5**	**4.5**	**.. c**	**.. c**	**.. c**	**.. c**	**.. c**	**.. c**

- Nil; .. Not available; c Confidential data; d Secondary Confidentiality

Note: Detailed metadata at: *http://stats.oecd.org/OECDStat_Metadata/ShowMetadata.ashx?Dataset=FDI_CTRY_IND_SUMM.*

1. Information on data for Israel: *http://oe.cd/israel-disclaimer.*
2. Note by Turkey: The information in this document with reference to “Cyprus” relates to the southern part of the Island. There is no single authority representing both Turkish and Greek Cypriot people on the Island. Turkey recognises the Turkish Republic of Northern Cyprus (TRNC). Until a lasting and equitable solution is found within the context of the United Nations, Turkey shall preserve its position concerning the “Cyprus issue”.
3. Note by all the European Union Member States of the OECD and the European Union: The Republic of Cyprus is recognised by all members of the United Nations with the exception of Turkey. The information in this document relates to the area under the effective control of the Government of the Republic of Cyprus.

Source: OECD International Direct Investment Statistics (database): https://doi.org/10.1787/idi-data-en

Table 4. Foreign direct investment flows by industrial sector

Million US dollars

	Inward					Outward				
	2014	2015	2016	2017	2018	2014	2015	2016	2017	2018
All FDI activities	**5 491.9**	**465.2**	**9 814.5**	**9 517.9**	**9 478.9**	**1 619.5**	**2 488.1**	**2 181.7**	**7 557.0**	**5 277.3**
Agriculture, forestry and fishing	**15.6**	**.. c**	**26.6**	**-19.1**	**5.7**	**.. c**	**.. c**	**10.7**	**0.5**	**.. c**
Mining and quarrying	**.. c**	**.. c**	**.. c**	**.. c**	**-41.2**	**3.2**	**-0.4**	**4.9**	**1.6**	**-0.4**
Extraction activities	.. c	-50.6	3.9	12.9	2.1	-	-	-	-	-
Manufacturing	**2 569.3**	**2 006.8**	**2 310.9**	**1 595.5**	**1 547.3**	**574.8**	**-344.8**	**260.1**	**444.3**	**548.8**
of which:										
Food products, beverages and tobacco	.. c	.. c	393.5	-5.3	.. c	.. c	.. c	.. c	.. c	-8.7
Textiles, wood and paper products; printing	318.1	.. c	308.2	.. c	127.0	15.1	-0.5	-29.0	29.0	.. c
Chemical, rubber, plastic, non-metallic mineral products	.. c	518.6	305.0	355.0	.. c	47.1	.. c	.. c	177.5	.. c
Metal and machinery products, except electrical equipment	.. c	756.0	284.7	210.8	.. c	.. c	.. c	.. c	-38.1	-59.3
Motor vehicles, trailers, semi-trailers, other transport equipment	1 042.5	326.3	732.7	.. c	-160.9	8.2	-42.4	.. c	.. c	535.7
Other manufacturing	.. c	137.9	.. c	.. c	479.7	102.9	.. c	.. c	302.7	-48.3
Electricity, gas, steam and air conditioning supply	**-1 006.1**	**78.4**	**540.2**	**309.5**	**1 747.4**	**-346.9**	**-373.8**	**.. c**	**.. c**	**.. c**
Water supply; sewerage, waste management and remediation activities	**-108.0**	**.. c**	**.. c**	**.. c**	**-42.3**	**-0.6**	**0.0**	**0.2**	**-0.2**	**-**
Construction	**335.8**	**.. c**	**.. c**	**450.2**	**-100.6**	**-21.6**	**262.4**	**543.9**	**233.9**	**10.5**
Services	**4 789.3**	**-325.6**	**6 869.8**	**6 917.1**	**6 424.0**	**1 410.6**	**2 915.4**	**1 071.5**	**6 954.9**	**3 911.7**
Wholesale and retail trade; repair of motor vehicles and motorcycles	.. c	-376.7	419.1	.. c	.. c	.. c	-31.1	38.3	.. c	579.4
Transportation and storage	.. c	46.1	-240.2	.. c	183.3	29.4	-409.7	.. c	80.6	297.4
Accommodation and food service activities	20.8	177.3	.. c	.. c	.. c	-	-1.3	3.2	-0.3	.. c
Information and communication	57.1	-1 897.8	.. c	.. c	-104.8	50.6	.. c	-955.5	398.0	400.5
Financial and insurance activities	.. c	1 390.9	2 068.7	.. c	.. c	1 333.7	.. c	.. c	5 931.1	.. c
Activities of holding companies	-19.6	622.0	.. c	.. c	2 226.5	1 152.4	3 960.6	1 780.9	.. c	.. c
Real estate activities	.. c	.. c	.. c	1 507.2	1 460.1	-81.7	225.7	-48.4	131.3	61.0
Professional, scientific and technical activities	2 733.2	133.7	1 011.5	.. c	.. c	.. c	-711.8	-0.8	341.3	.. c
Administrative and support service activities	.. c	.. c	.. c	267.4	116.9	2.1	49.6	-13.5	.. c	.. c
Public administration; activities of households and of extraterritorial organisations	-	-	-	-	-	-	-	-	-	-
Education	.. c	.. c	-3.1	2.0	-1.7	-	-	-	-	-
Human health and social work activities	42.6	-7.5	9.1	.. c	40.5	-0.2	0.3	-	-	0.1
Arts, entertainment and recreation	-7.5	96.6	-0.1	33.3	7.8	8.8	2.8	0.1	5.1	9.2
Other services	.. c	.. c	.. c	.. c	12.4	15.1	8.7	-4.3	.. c	.. c
Not allocated and confidential	**9.8**	**.. c**	**.. c**	**.. c**	**.. c**	**0.0**	**.. c**	**.. c**	**.. c**	**.. c**
Private real estate activities	**-210.2**	**-245.3**	**299.0**	**139.9**	**-64.9**	**-**	**6.4**	**-3.3**	**27.3**	**-2.5**

- Nil; c Confidential data

Note: Detailed metadata at: *http://stats.oecd.org/OECDStat_Metadata/ShowMetadata.ashx?Dataset=FDI_CTRY_IND_SUMM.*

Source: OECD International Direct Investment Statistics (database): https://doi.org/10.1787/idi-data-en

Table 5. Foreign direct investment positions by industrial sector
At year end

Million US dollars

	Inward					Outward				
	2014	2015	2016	2017	2018	2014	2015	2016	2017	2018
All FDI activities	**121 511.8**	**116 627.8**	**121 854.6**	**155 994.1**	**163 288.6**	**18 235.5**	**18 597.4**	**19 426.3**	**32 364.1**	**34 943.0**
Agriculture, forestry and fishing	**256.1**	**.. c**	**319.4**	**.. c**	**413.9**	**.. c**	**53.9**	**61.7**	**69.8**	**38.5**
Mining and quarrying	**1 442.8**	**.. c**	**.. c**	**672.9**	**641.6**	**4.6**	**7.4**	**14.9**	**14.7**	**24.5**
Extraction activities	367.8	283.6	265.4	353.7	343.1	-	-	-	-	-
Manufacturing	**40 624.2**	**38 352.3**	**38 458.9**	**45 505.7**	**46 528.2**	**2 065.2**	**1 458.5**	**1 581.3**	**2 421.3**	**2 636.4**
of which:										
Food products, beverages and tobacco	.. c	4 122.0	.. c	5 032.5	.. c	.. c	214.8	.. c	.. c	276.9
Textiles, wood and paper products; printing	2 446.4	2 388.4	2 689.1	3 237.8	3 158.5	.. c	126.8	98.2	200.9	.. c
Chemical, rubber, plastic, non-metallic mineral products	5 104.8	5 343.1	5 724.8	.. c	6 358.4	716.3	.. c	.. c	955.0	.. c
Metal and machinery products, except electrical equipment	9 640.3	9 665.7	.. c	11 892.9	.. c	.. c	.. c	.. c	276.6	259.5
Motor vehicles, trailers, semi-trailers, other transport equipment	12 897.0	10 312.9	9 627.7	.. c	12 830.2	.. c	.. c	.. c	.. c	.. c
Other manufacturing	6 981.3	.. c	6 469.6	7 976.8	7 989.8	.. c	.. c	85.8	.. c	217.6
Electricity, gas, steam and air conditioning supply	**.. c**	**3 560.7**	**3 859.4**	**4 747.7**	**4 999.2**	**1 137.1**	**.. c**	**.. c**	**779.2**	**1 236.6**
Water supply; sewerage, waste management and remediation activities	**799.3**	**.. c**	**935.9**	**.. c**	**.. c**	**0.7**	**0.8**	**1.9**	**2.1**	**1.7**
Construction	**.. c**	**.. c**	**1 733.0**	**2 551.9**	**.. c**	**.. c**	**409.4**	**832.5**	**1 382.4**	**1 328.9**
Services	**69 800.9**	**69 047.3**	**73 030.0**	**97 525.3**	**104 056.6**	**.. c**	**15 219.9**	**15 146.9**	**26 560.5**	**28 795.8**
Wholesale and retail trade; repair of motor vehicles and motorcycles	13 028.3	.. c	.. c	13 789.2	14 989.0	844.8	629.4	.. c	867.6	.. c
Transportation and storage	2 033.4	1 927.3	.. c	.. c	.. c	861.9	.. c	.. c	275.1	253.9
Accommodation and food service activities	437.0	.. c	.. c	.. c	.. c	29.7	-28.5	-22.8	32.4	.. c
Information and communication	6 078.4	.. c	7 109.2	8 686.1	.. c	223.1	197.7	.. c	-626.9	-517.4
Financial and insurance activities	30 819.7	31 828.9	32 849.8	.. c	.. c	.. c	.. c	14 545.4	.. c	26 903.2
Activities of holding companies	5 352.3	5 896.9	7 123.5	15 236.4	17 272.0	9 077.6	12 095.1	12 799.5	.. c	.. c
Real estate activities	.. c	.. c	.. c	.. c	16 458.5	-199.3	0.2	-41.1	141.1	.. c
Professional, scientific and technical activities	6 737.1	5 927.4	6 730.1	.. c	12 572.3	1 454.8	312.4	478.6	.. c	854.2
Administrative and support service activities	1 325.8	1 363.1	1 211.0	1 838.4	1 566.7	-26.7	16.2	-6.9	.. c	8.7
Public administration; activities of households and of extraterritorial organisations	-	-	-	-	-	-	-	-	-	-
Education	.. c	21.0	33.0	42.9	39.6	-	-	-	-	-
Human health and social work activities	.. c	.. c	217.6	.. c	267.3	-	-	-	-	-
Arts, entertainment and recreation	.. c	.. c	76.7	.. c	.. c	70.9	74.6	70.4	83.7	.. c
Other services	203.9	.. c	.. c	.. c	.. c	34.0	35.8	30.6	.. c	.. c
Not allocated and confidential	**0.2**	**.. c**	**.. c**	**.. c**	**.. c**	**97.0**	**.. c**	**.. c**	**651.9**	**423.9**
Private real estate activities	**3 051.1**	**2 563.5**	**2 822.1**	**3 618.3**	**3 517.1**	**449.4**	**413.4**	**400.2**	**481.9**	**456.7**

- Nil; c Confidential data

Note: Detailed metadata at: *http://stats.oecd.org/OECDStat_Metadata/ShowMetadata.ashx?Dataset=FDI_CTRY_IND_SUMM.*

Source: OECD International Direct Investment Statistics (database): https://doi.org/10.1787/idi-data-en

Table 6. Foreign direct investment income by industrial sector

Million US dollars

	Inward					Outward				
	2014	2015	2016	2017	2018	2014	2015	2016	2017	2018
All FDI activities	**16 098.5**	**14 473.5**	**15 343.8**	**19 127.2**	**19 052.2**	**1 588.9**	**1 860.9**	**2 014.9**	**4 665.4**	**2 974.8**
Agriculture, forestry and fishing	**.. c**	**4.6**	**8.5**	**.. c**	**6.1**	**.. c**	**-**	**2.9**	**2.1**	**.. c**
Mining and quarrying	**.. c**	**-156.3**	**-171.3**	**.. c**	**-4.3**	**3.3**	**.. c**	**0.5**	**0.7**	**-0.3**
Extraction activities	87.3	37.1	.. c	1.7	2.9	-	-	-	-	-
Manufacturing	**7 441.1**	**7 005.8**	**7 025.9**	**6 923.6**	**6 013.1**	**153.1**	**37.4**	**140.8**	**170.5**	**298.9**
of which:										
Food products, beverages and tobacco	420.6	495.4	.. c	.. c	354.8	39.8	.. c	.. c	.. c	.. c
Textiles, wood and paper products; printing	342.9	347.9	461.7	433.5	482.7	.. c	2.5	5.8	29.2	66.3
Chemical, rubber, plastic, non-metallic mineral products	1 459.4	1 320.2	1 536.9	1 263.4	1 175.6	.. c	.. c	.. c	50.7	29.5
Metal and machinery products, except electrical equipment	.. c	1 087.4	942.3	1 096.2	.. c	.. c	5.1	31.4	.. c	.. c
Motor vehicles, trailers, semi-trailers, other transport equipment	2 447.7	2 712.9	2 484.4	2 612.8	1 728.4	.. c	-21.8	.. c	.. c	.. c
Other manufacturing	1 223.4	.. c	1 075.4	.. c	1 092.2	31.2	51.3	.. c	10.1	.. c
Electricity, gas, steam and air conditioning supply	**.. c**	**.. c**	**641.1**	**510.0**	**819.3**	**-312.6**	**31.6**	**.. c**	**48.4**	**.. c**
Water supply; sewerage, waste management and remediation activities	**.. c**	**.. c**	**137.3**	**161.9**	**172.1**	**0.0**	**-**	**0.7**	**0.9**	**1.0**
Construction	**121.9**	**.. c**	**191.8**	**.. c**	**179.0**	**17.6**	**.. c**	**-23.1**	**92.0**	**-9.1**
Services	**8 357.6**	**7 291.6**	**7 506.3**	**11 054.3**	**11 863.0**	**1 727.6**	**.. c**	**1 671.5**	**4 342.0**	**2 699.2**
Wholesale and retail trade; repair of motor vehicles and motorcycles	1 151.1	.. c	1 709.0	.. c	2 122.5	.. c	141.6	-10.8	.. c	-38.8
Transportation and storage	188.0	193.3	278.7	.. c	340.6	.. c	.. c	.. c	.. c	29.7
Accommodation and food service activities	12.1	98.5	.. c	.. c	60.1	-	-	0.8	0.6	.. c
Information and communication	690.5	683.5	879.5	944.8	984.3	37.9	114.1	.. c	61.1	52.9
Financial and insurance activities	.. c	.. c	.. c	6 428.6	5 480.3	1 604.5	1 520.2	1 402.7	.. c	.. c
Activities of holding companies	1 618.9	739.1	.. c	3 350.4	1 784.7	1 597.8	1 502.9	1 349.1	.. c	.. c
Real estate activities	.. c	338.6	.. c	.. c	1 668.1	-2.6	0.2	28.4	.. c	-2.7
Professional, scientific and technical activities	.. c	824.1	332.4	757.9	.. c	.. c	13.3	63.4	.. c	.. c
Administrative and support service activities	115.4	.. c	97.8	139.9	118.5	0.4	-0.1	27.5	.. c	.. c
Public administration; activities of households and of extraterritorial organisations	-	-	-	-	-	-	-	-	-	-
Education	.. c	.. c	2.1	4.5	-2.5	-	-	-	-	-
Human health and social work activities	.. c	-30.6	21.8	.. c	26.3	-0.1	0.5	-	-	0.1
Arts, entertainment and recreation	-3.4	5.5	29.3	.. c	17.7	1.2	2.0	15.7	20.5	18.9
Other services	1.0	10.9	.. c	.. c	.. c	-1.4	-	0.7	3.8	.. c
Not allocated and confidential	**-3.7**	**.. c**	**4.3**	**.. c**	**3.5**	**0.0**	**.. c**	**.. c**	**8.7**	**.. c**
Private real estate activities	**-**	**-**	**-**	**-**	**0.5**	**-**	**-**	**-**	**-**	**-2.5**

- Nil; c Confidential data

Note: Detailed metadata at: *http://stats.oecd.org/OECDStat_Metadata/ShowMetadata.ashx?Dataset=FDI_CTRY_IND_SUMM.*

Source: OECD International Direct Investment Statistics (database): https://doi.org/10.1787/idi-data-en

DENMARK

Table 1. Foreign direct investment flows by country

Million US dollars

	Inward					Outward				
	2014	2015	2016	2017	2018	2014	2015	2016	2017	2018
WORLD	**4 677.1**	**2 995.2**	**235.0**	**3 749.3**	**2 405.8**	**8 248.2**	**8 707.7**	**10 111.9**	**9 519.8**	**1 136.8**
OECD COUNTRIES	**4 063.2**	**2 880.7**	**188.7**	**3 989.1**	**1 593.4**	**8 235.7**	**7 503.2**	**7 635.1**	**9 008.6**	**-1 862.0**
Australia	-21.7	2.1	-3.4	5.3	-7.3	-448.3	-60.2	-56.9	-58.0	-439.5
Austria	11.0	16.2	0.1	-6.5	-12.5	-3.2	-35.4	.. d	-56.7	-45.0
Belgium	.. d	4.5	17.2	177.8	83.8	148.3	138.7	341.0	-218.7	-73.2
Canada	-8.9	1.6	-5.5	2.3	-4.8	104.1	46.2	89.0	145.3	120.4
Chile	2.5	0.7	-1.5	0.5	-1.7	46.1	-11.4	69.2	43.3	37.2
Czech Republic	8.0	4.8	-7.6	1.2	-5.4	74.0	171.9	5.8	30.0	-104.7
Denmark	-	-	-	-	-	-	-	-	-	-
Estonia	1.2	1.2	-28.2	.. d	-50.7	22.1	12.3	59.4	-169.3	-1.0
Finland	.. d	.. d	.. d	.. d	469.8	1 698.8	578.9	-337.6	-2 854.4	-491.6
France	-277.8	302.4	-316.9	.. d	-1 987.8	147.0	397.0	340.5	322.2	326.3
Germany	-128.5	245.6	-280.8	96.2	298.3	509.7	2 630.8	746.9	5 267.8	-1 953.3
Greece	41.8	0.9	-3.0	1.7	-3.6	35.4	-16.1	8.0	10.6	32.0
Hungary	-90.6	11.7	87.1	55.9	-22.7	181.2	32.4	235.8	146.5	172.2
Iceland	-1.1	3.0	-2.1	-17.6	-41.0	18.9	7.6	10.4	92.1	65.9
Ireland	-104.1	-465.5	38.8	-47.4	285.7	24.9	4.0	227.9	-34.7	-620.9
Israel[1]	0.5	0.3	-1.3	1.1	-2.5	8.7	59.0	-2.7	11.7	-5.4
Italy	28.5	57.7	22.4	154.0	-42.8	-149.9	-3.3	218.5	263.9	29.1
Japan	.. d	.. d	.. d	.. d	74.3	68.9	54.3	82.0	-119.2	140.8
Korea	4.1	1.9	-5.9	3.2	-7.1	-13.5	32.6	20.8	32.1	10.0
Latvia	3.2	1.5	-2.4	24.1	-2.4	-4.4	13.2	-20.4	-54.2	20.1
Lithuania	3.9	1.9	-3.3	0.5	-3.5	-235.5	19.0	67.5	-57.0	41.0
Luxembourg	-1 273.4	940.6	-3 052.2	-3 942.3	-4 062.2	50.5	.. d	275.0	-57.4	.. d
Mexico	4.3	9.1	10.8	18.5	-4.3	-0.7	113.3	142.2	42.1	92.2
Netherlands	239.6	-1 532.8	-743.2	2 720.0	1 297.7	-33.3	330.4	732.8	165.9	-1 552.9
New Zealand	1.2	-0.7	-2.4	2.9	0.3	20.5	3.7	15.2	-2.7	7.4
Norway	2 710.2	1 043.2	504.2	232.7	4 590.8	1 467.4	82.8	-136.4	759.8	-4 246.3
Poland	19.9	9.7	-22.3	0.5	9.0	-60.5	187.2	493.1	-10.8	145.9
Portugal	2.3	1.2	-2.2	0.3	-2.4	-215.2	-49.1	18.4	23.6	255.8
Slovak Republic	2.8	1.3	-1.3	-	-2.1	-9.6	42.5	-13.7	17.0	-10.1
Slovenia	1.2	0.4	-0.1	-0.8	-	-9.6	-	-2.1	-1.2	-4.1
Spain	145.1	129.4	.. d	410.3	6.7	89.3	167.9	701.8	219.2	524.6
Sweden	-235.8	1 686.7	-1 303.9	-817.5	1 769.1	1 047.2	474.3	-504.8	351.7	5 187.8
Switzerland	1 693.3	-547.0	106.8	-332.5	-707.2	593.6	1 201.6	.. d	348.8	-245.7
Turkey	28.5	3.3	-6.7	1.5	-7.3	17.4	81.9	11.9	-17.4	54.6
United Kingdom	350.1	273.3	2 795.1	490.8	251.2	2 382.2	1 727.8	4 227.7	4 148.4	-1 305.9
United States	-1 352.3	-69.3	1 175.9	80.3	-562.0	423.4	-793.9	286.4	221.8	1 771.1
EUROPE	**5 533.3**	**2 839.1**	**-728.3**	**3 580.5**	**2 299.4**	**7 874.2**	**8 275.8**	**6 730.0**	**9 490.6**	**-4 029.1**
Bulgaria	-	0.4	-0.9	0.2	-1.0	2.0	-14.4	-10.8	33.6	71.9
Croatia	-	-	-	-	-	-7.5	14.0	6.7	18.8	23.8
Cyprus[2, 3]	1.2	-40.1	9.5	-29.7	10.1	57.7	-17.4	14.3	27.0	-18.4
Malta	23.7	-38.5	.. d	.. d	-3.6	-1.6	.. d	-	-	0.3
Romania	2.3	1.0	-2.1	0.9	-2.4	-18.2	12.3	2.5	311.7	-128.3
Russian Federation	58.6	16.2	11.7	-75.6	0.3	7.5	-196.7	-239.8	287.0	293.0
Ukraine	1.6	0.6	-1.6	0.9	-1.9	2.1	4.3	18.1	30.6	15.8
AFRICA	**7.8**	**2.7**	**-4.2**	**4.4**	**-8.7**	**-318.6**	**197.3**	**17.4**	**-187.4**	**485.3**
Northern Africa	2.5	0.7	-3.7	2.9	-4.8	-194.4	-77.3	101.2	-238.6	.. d
Algeria	1.1	0.1	-1.0	0.8	-1.3	.. d	-35.5	43.1	.. d	.. d
Egypt	0.7	0.3	-1.9	1.5	-2.5	2.1	-43.9	66.6	-104.2	17.7
Libya	-	-	-	-	-	-0.5	-	-	-	-
Morocco	0.7	0.3	-0.7	0.6	-1.0	-	2.2	-8.3	.. d	.. d
Tunisia	-	-	-	-	-	-	-0.3	-0.1	0.2	0.2
Other African countries	5.3	1.9	-0.4	1.5	-3.8	-124.4	274.5	-83.9	51.2	41.3
Nigeria	2.7	1.3	-1.2	-0.2	-1.1	-12.8	44.0	-4.5	-28.3	11.6
South Africa	0.9	0.4	-2.2	1.7	-2.9	22.2	13.7	43.2	197.2	-22.5
AMERICA	**-1 159.2**	**-37.5**	**1 162.9**	**117.1**	**-610.1**	**812.1**	**-142.7**	**1 863.8**	**448.5**	**1 956.8**
Northern America	-1 346.9	-40.1	1 162.1	97.1	-597.9	516.7	-744.2	323.0	372.0	1 854.8
Central America and Caribbean countries	16.2	26.5	.. d	16.2	6.3	166.1	598.3	1 727.7	-98.6	-192.8
Bahamas	5.9	13.2	-13.8	-19.1	0.3	0.9	-0.3	-	-	-0.6
Bermuda	2.3	.. d	.. d	16.4	9.7	-38.3	-66.5	.. d	14.2	11.6
Cayman Islands	-	0.4	-0.1	0.2	0.2	31.0	.. d	-36.1	44.2	.. d
Costa Rica	-	-	-	-	-	3.9	.. d	.. d	.. d	.. d
El Salvador	-	-	-	-	-	-2.0	-	-	-	-
Guatemala	-	-	-	-	-	-	-0.9	0.7	-0.9	-0.5
Honduras	-	-	-	-	-	-6.4	-8.0	-5.6	10.6	0.2
Nicaragua	-	-	-	-	-	1.4	-1.9	-0.3	-0.9	-0.6
Panama	-	-	0.3	0.3	0.3	.. d	.. d	-57.1	2.9	33.4
Virgin Islands, U.S.	-	-	-	-	-	-	-0.6	-	-0.2	-
South America	171.7	.. d	-8.5	.. d	-18.4	129.4	3.1	-187.1	175.1	294.6
Argentina	4.4	-21.6	-1.5	-0.2	-1.3	8.4	-54.7	-63.9	5.9	112.8
Bolivia	-	-	-	-	-	0.5	-	-0.1	-0.2	-1.0
Brazil	18.0	.. d	.. d	.. d	-13.3	166.9	59.5	-161.5	-34.2	124.2
Colombia	1.8	0.4	-0.7	0.6	-1.0	14.4	0.1	-8.5	1.5	1.0
Ecuador	-	-	-	-	-	-0.5	0.3	-	.. d	5.7
Paraguay	-	-	-	-	-	-	-	-	-	-
Peru	0.7	0.3	-0.1	-0.3	-	17.6	-	-12.9	0.9	19.0
Uruguay	.. d	0.3	-0.9	0.6	-1.1	37.6	-3.4	0.1	-9.2	8.2
Venezuela	-	-	-	-	-	.. d	12.8	-9.5	-0.6	-12.0

Table 1. Foreign direct investment flows by country *(cont.)*

Million US dollars

	Inward					Outward				
	2014	2015	2016	2017	2018	2014	2015	2016	2017	2018
ASIA	**74.4**	**92.5**	**.. d**	**-97.7**	**598.6**	**268.2**	**390.6**	**1 684.5**	**-75.9**	**3 208.4**
Near and Middle East	5.3	4.5	-13.4	8.6	-16.8	-175.5	-84.3	31.2	-730.7	106.4
Gulf Arabian countries	4.3	3.9	-10.4	6.4	-12.0	-189.2	-135.9	34.9	-744.5	97.4
Kuwait	-2.0	0.7	-0.4	-0.2	0.3	-1.2	0.6	1.6	2.4	3.0
Qatar	2.0	1.0	-0.9	-0.2	-0.8	.. d	.. d	19.3	.. d	11.6
Saudi Arabia	2.0	1.0	-4.9	3.6	-6.3	26.9	23.9	14.1	1.1	19.6
United Arab Emirates	2.1	0.9	-3.3	2.4	-4.1	-46.5	0.6	16.9	-38.0	65.1
Other Near and Middle East	0.9	0.6	-3.1	2.3	-4.8	13.7	51.4	-3.7	13.9	9.0
Jordan	-	0.1	-0.7	0.6	-1.0	-	1.2	1.5	-1.7	9.2
Other Asian countries	69.1	88.0	.. d	-106.3	615.3	443.5	474.8	1 653.4	655.0	3 101.8
China	37.0	34.3	-29.9	2.3	-30.6	-282.8	79.1	347.7	56.7	47.7
Hong Kong, China	5.3	25.6	-6.1	-5.2	.. d	-16.0	-348.8	24.1	-30.1	61.0
India	5.0	2.2	-3.3	-0.2	-3.2	154.8	-25.9	93.5	-	339.9
Indonesia	14.2	0.7	-1.2	-	-1.1	0.9	21.7	-6.8	10.3	10.3
Iran, Islamic Republic of	0.4	0.1	-1.3	1.1	-1.7	-2.1	4.5	55.7	28.2	4.0
Malaysia	8.9	4.6	-1.5	0.5	-1.7	31.5	24.8	72.7	47.6	67.3
Philippines	-8.4	0.1	-1.0	0.8	-1.3	2.0	20.2	-24.8	-0.8	-7.9
Singapore	-14.2	-18.1	.. d	25.3	-36.7	359.0	784.6	1 107.3	671.8	1 663.4
Chinese Taipei	2.8	1.3	-2.5	0.5	-2.7	2.5	4.9	9.8	15.1	106.6
Thailand	1.4	1.2	-16.9	-7.0	-10.3	71.7	-212.3	-121.4	-174.0	175.7
Viet Nam	4.4	1.2	-2.8	0.8	-3.0	-25.1	4.6	-17.2	8.9	2.2
AUSTRALIA, OCEANIA AND POLAR REGIONS	**-20.6**	**1.3**	**-5.8**	**8.3**	**-7.0**	**-449.0**	**72.1**	**-192.5**	**-141.0**	**-466.8**
WORLD unallocated and confidential	**241.3**	**97.1**	**.. d**	**136.6**	**133.7**	**61.2**	**-85.3**	**8.8**	**-15.0**	**-17.7**
European Union (EU28)	**1 031.9**	**2 327.4**	**-1 335.1**	**3 761.1**	**-1 723.6**	**5 721.6**	**6 615.5**	**7 848.5**	**7 843.6**	**724.3**
G20 countries excl. European Union	**.. d**	**.. d**	**.. d**	**.. d**	**-2 057.8**	**3 145.2**	**4 147.1**	**6 135.5**	**10 772.8**	**-229.2**
G20 OECD countries	**.. d**	**.. d**	**.. d**	**.. d**	**-1 999.5**	**3 040.4**	**4 226.5**	**6 109.1**	**10 248.9**	**-1 154.2**
G20 Non-OECD countries	**139.9**	**.. d**	**.. d**	**.. d**	**-58.3**	**104.8**	**-79.4**	**26.4**	**523.9**	**925.0**
MENA countries	**7.3**	**4.9**	**-15.6**	**10.6**	**-19.0**	**.. d**	**.. d**	**139.5**	**.. d**	**.. d**
ASEAN countries	**6.2**	**-10.3**	**-108.0**	**20.1**	**-54.2**	**539.1**	**671.5**	**1 028.6**	**683.8**	**2 404.1**

- Nil; .. Not available; d Secondary Confidentiality

Note: Data excludes resident Special Purpose Entities (SPEs). Detailed metadata at: *http://stats.oecd.org/OECDStat_Metadata/ShowMetadata.ashx?Dataset=FDI_CTRY_IND_SUMM.*

1. Information on data for Israel: *http://oe.cd/israel-disclaimer.*
2. Note by Turkey: The information in this document with reference to "Cyprus" relates to the southern part of the Island. There is no single authority representing both Turkish and Greek Cypriot people on the Island. Turkey recognises the Turkish Republic of Northern Cyprus (TRNC). Until a lasting and equitable solution is found within the context of the United Nations, Turkey shall preserve its position concerning the "Cyprus issue".
3. Note by all the European Union Member States of the OECD and the European Union: The Republic of Cyprus is recognised by all members of the United Nations with the exception of Turkey. The information in this document relates to the area under the effective control of the Government of the Republic of Cyprus.

Source: OECD International Direct Investment Statistics (database): https://doi.org/10.1787/idi-data-en

Table 2. Foreign direct investment positions by country
At year end

Million US dollars

	Inward					Outward				
	2014	2015	2016	2017	2018	2014	2015	2016	2017	2018
WORLD	**95 766.5**	**91 978.8**	**99 403.4**	**116 993.1**	**109 894.0**	**167 394.9**	**164 757.8**	**169 708.2**	**201 621.5**	**193 338.2**
OECD COUNTRIES	**91 109.9**	**86 914.3**	**93 622.7**	**110 717.0**	**103 395.4**	**132 211.1**	**131 524.2**	**134 466.7**	**165 941.7**	**160 055.2**
Australia	-84.0	14.5	9.2	12.2	3.4	1 910.0	2 095.9	2 000.3	2 050.7	1 480.4
Austria	90.0	309.5	236.5	229.4	217.7	150.3	206.0	219.3	282.1	209.8
Belgium	783.3	756.4	822.1	1 219.3	1 217.3	644.6	1 095.6	974.1	700.9	778.9
Canada	303.2	139.5	30.1	67.3	58.9	1 597.7	1 314.1	1 095.6	1 115.1	1 246.3
Chile	-18.5	1.5	0.1	0.6	-0.8	348.0	319.6	346.5	403.4	278.2
Czech Republic	13.9	30.2	38.6	44.0	37.6	904.9	886.1	997.8	1 118.9	1 006.2
Denmark	-	-	-	-	-	-	-	-	-	-
Estonia	-11.1	5.6	-17.2	69.8	17.6	293.7	243.8	272.1	265.6	236.4
Finland	3 830.8	3 484.3	4 690.6	2 562.9	7 947.8	6 921.0	6 473.1	6 248.4	3 447.3	3 188.2
France	3 082.8	3 969.0	3 805.2	7 332.0	5 745.9	6 216.2	5 901.3	6 111.3	7 428.5	7 420.3
Germany	4 781.1	4 670.1	5 145.8	6 338.9	6 182.2	11 822.3	14 553.4	15 171.4	25 401.8	23 132.3
Greece	-31.7	-3.5	-7.5	-9.5	-12.4	232.8	234.1	219.6	235.4	223.3
Hungary	-81.0	-60.0	5.5	102.1	75.6	628.8	649.8	852.4	1 172.6	1 237.7
Iceland	82.3	62.5	66.9	50.7	8.6	826.8	951.1	871.6	1 102.3	1 372.8
Ireland	1 811.0	1 385.8	1 555.6	1 569.7	2 712.7	1 492.6	1 222.0	1 358.9	1 537.6	1 193.8
Israel[1]	37.2	21.5	28.1	28.8	25.0	53.4	105.7	114.1	136.4	123.0
Italy	229.5	465.6	483.2	736.8	627.5	1 146.6	1 091.7	1 352.8	1 708.0	1 587.9
Japan	.. d	.. d	.. d	.. d	.. d	862.4	896.0	992.7	911.9	1 067.7
Korea	12.9	-5.0	-9.8	16.6	9.1	304.2	362.2	268.4	325.1	316.7
Latvia	6.5	11.0	9.9	.. d	8.1	299.1	354.3	279.6	309.5	317.8
Lithuania	5.4	12.2	15.5	.. d	.. d	568.2	545.5	577.6	639.2	649.6
Luxembourg	11 478.4	11 449.9	14 934.5	12 779.9	9 784.0	1 038.5	881.4	995.3	1 168.7	1 459.2
Mexico	101.9	.. d	.. d	.. d	-10.9	645.8	656.7	689.2	815.3	904.4
Netherlands	13 938.5	10 530.2	10 385.5	16 682.0	16 709.5	10 790.0	10 044.9	11 616.5	14 867.7	11 626.2
New Zealand	-4.1	-4.5	43.4	55.9	53.5	115.2	112.2	167.7	122.3	118.4
Norway	9 219.5	9 623.4	10 008.9	12 306.2	12 263.6	7 340.3	6 304.7	6 282.0	9 589.5	7 644.7
Poland	35.6	58.7	61.1	46.1	55.5	3 307.4	3 115.4	3 839.0	4 353.8	4 147.9
Portugal	9.1	6.6	15.9	7.4	5.2	313.7	233.8	350.5	492.8	480.1
Slovak Republic	4.9	6.9	21.1	19.2	16.7	559.2	533.7	548.4	641.0	613.2
Slovenia	8.0	7.8	7.4	8.4	8.4	36.6	33.4	36.3	43.3	35.4
Spain	1 527.6	1 618.4	1 149.0	1 712.7	1 873.5	2 998.0	3 043.5	3 605.7	4 322.4	5 070.7
Sweden	24 920.8	22 250.1	20 240.3	23 697.8	18 666.3	27 216.3	27 177.3	25 608.3	29 445.7	31 327.1
Switzerland	3 252.5	2 421.5	3 557.7	3 434.4	2 587.4	5 481.6	5 062.1	3 922.3	4 502.8	3 956.3
Turkey	5.2	13.8	9.5	11.0	4.4	532.4	545.3	525.5	575.6	556.8
United Kingdom	5 716.2	7 371.6	9 431.7	11 955.8	11 224.5	20 246.2	20 833.8	21 918.4	30 039.8	27 780.5
United States	5 812.2	5 829.6	6 287.6	6 881.3	4 655.8	15 233.8	14 323.0	14 613.8	15 308.2	17 266.6
EUROPE	**86 142.5**	**81 616.0**	**88 774.2**	**104 830.9**	**99 696.0**	**114 352.1**	**114 533.5**	**117 257.5**	**149 335.8**	**139 838.9**
Bulgaria	-	1.5	0.7	1.0	0.2	113.7	95.9	84.1	126.9	187.0
Croatia	-0.2	-	-	-	-	158.3	147.9	162.5	248.1	253.1
Cyprus[2, 3]	363.6	254.5	396.6	230.0	233.5	234.6	131.8	117.4	132.6	62.1
Malta	595.9	592.5	435.7	143.0	130.8	25.2	83.7	64.5	90.4	86.4
Romania	-2.6	1.0	7.7	1.3	-0.8	408.7	380.4	298.7	752.8	586.3
Russian Federation	76.0	96.5	.. d	.. d	.. d	811.1	481.8	277.8	663.4	751.8
Ukraine	-2.8	-0.6	-0.4	-1.5	-3.1	159.0	151.5	192.5	199.6	212.1
AFRICA	**-11.8**	**-3.5**	**-6.8**	**58.3**	**47.2**	**2 085.8**	**1 725.8**	**1 851.0**	**1 751.2**	**1 993.7**
Northern Africa	-10.8	-10.7	-9.6	-12.4	-16.7	1 101.9	1 032.4	1 087.2	773.9	1 119.9
Algeria	-0.5	-2.8	-3.8	-3.5	-4.6	.. d	.. d	.. d	.. d	.. d
Egypt	-5.4	-4.8	-3.1	-6.6	-8.7	391.9	348.0	369.5	173.3	184.8
Libya	0.5	-	-	-	-	-2.6	0.1	0.1	0.2	0.2
Morocco	-5.2	-3.1	-2.7	-2.6	-3.4	42.1	38.1	21.3	123.6	.. d
Tunisia	-	-	-	-	-	4.9	8.2	8.8	7.6	6.7
Other African countries	-1.1	7.2	2.8	70.7	64.0	983.9	693.3	763.8	977.3	873.9
Nigeria	8.2	12.3	4.5	5.0	4.0	-7.2	37.8	45.2	12.9	19.5
South Africa	-6.7	-6.4	-4.8	-6.9	-9.4	344.9	297.4	348.4	624.5	517.5
AMERICA	**6 691.4**	**6 556.8**	**7 095.2**	**7 816.4**	**5 380.4**	**22 363.3**	**20 047.1**	**21 295.2**	**22 175.5**	**24 587.2**
Northern America	6 429.6	6 275.1	6 609.9	7 288.5	5 006.3	16 997.3	15 829.1	15 832.3	16 586.2	18 587.1
Central America and Caribbean countries	297.5	263.4	478.3	520.3	383.5	2 553.3	2 235.0	3 699.5	3 768.4	4 287.7
Bahamas	.. d	.. d	.. d	.. d	.. d	50.2	16.4	9.5	9.5	9.4
Bermuda	.. d	.. d	86.2	131.0	141.3	.. d	.. d	85.8	107.0	114.9
Cayman Islands	29.1	.. d	-78.8	-82.5	-70.7	525.2	770.0	600.5	.. d	.. d
Costa Rica	-	-	-	-	-	27.6	124.7	.. d	.. d	.. d
El Salvador	-	-	-	-	-	2.1	2.1	1.1	1.1	1.1
Guatemala	-	-	-	-	-	1.1	0.3	0.7	-0.3	-1.2
Honduras	-	-	-	-	-	34.8	.. d	.. d	.. d	.. d
Nicaragua	-	-	-	-	-	18.3	13.3	14.5	15.0	13.5
Panama	6.5	4.7	.. d	.. d	.. d	.. d	54.6	-21.0	-28.4	3.8
Virgin Islands, U.S.	-	-	-	-	-	2.5	1.9	-	1.5	1.4
South America	-35.4	18.3	7.1	7.9	-9.4	2 812.9	1 983.0	1 763.6	1 820.8	1 712.4
Argentina	.. d	.. d	.. d	.. d	.. d	634.8	175.0	116.3	147.1	150.3
Bolivia	-	-	-	-	-	1.5	1.5	1.4	1.8	-0.5
Brazil	-26.3	.. d	.. d	3.1	-9.7	1 623.6	1 284.6	1 048.4	912.7	976.8
Colombia	4.9	1.6	-2.8	-2.6	-3.4	54.2	55.2	78.7	96.3	92.3
Ecuador	-	-	-	-	-	3.3	2.8	2.1	.. d	.. d
Paraguay	-	-	-	-	-	2.0	1.6	2.0	2.7	2.6
Peru	3.8	3.4	3.3	3.4	3.4	88.2	84.8	73.3	75.2	92.8
Uruguay	-4.6	-2.9	-3.3	-2.9	-3.8	56.0	50.2	54.4	42.5	41.1
Venezuela	0.3	0.4	-	-	-	1.1	7.5	40.4	45.4	-11.7

Table 2. Foreign direct investment positions by country *(cont.)*

At year end

Million US dollars

	Inward					Outward				
	2014	2015	2016	2017	2018	2014	2015	2016	2017	2018
ASIA	**776.3**	**1 739.7**	**1 402.8**	**1 695.8**	**2 316.5**	**25 589.2**	**25 262.1**	**26 292.0**	**25 266.8**	**24 412.7**
Near and Middle East	26.6	12.9	24.8	48.2	29.5	1 322.1	1 245.4	1 371.8	785.6	902.8
Gulf Arabian countries	-7.2	-3.5	3.0	25.8	12.7	1 199.9	1 077.3	1 211.0	591.8	709.1
Kuwait	7.5	7.8	6.5	7.2	7.2	9.1	9.4	10.9	9.5	11.7
Qatar	10.8	8.6	5.0	5.5	4.4	.. d	.. d	.. d	88.4	61.2
Saudi Arabia	-18.3	-12.7	-15.0	26.4	18.7	165.6	169.7	197.8	188.6	207.5
United Arab Emirates	-4.4	-5.0	9.5	-10.3	-13.8	254.4	245.8	348.4	266.6	277.0
Other Near and Middle East	33.7	16.4	21.8	22.4	16.7	122.2	168.1	160.6	193.8	193.7
Jordan	-	-2.1	-2.7	-2.4	-3.2	0.8	16.5	18.0	16.8	25.6
Other Asian countries	749.7	1 726.8	1 378.0	1 647.5	2 286.9	24 267.2	24 016.7	24 920.2	24 481.2	23 509.7
China	174.6	179.2	310.5	312.8	134.5	3 783.9	4 154.5	4 362.4	4 229.9	3 957.1
Hong Kong, China	23.4	.. d	237.6	390.0	1 143.4	3 794.1	3 255.6	3 068.3	2 800.4	2 690.6
India	-8.3	22.0	61.7	15.0	12.0	769.6	744.5	820.8	810.6	942.0
Indonesia	0.5	5.1	3.8	4.2	3.2	142.6	143.2	142.9	119.2	109.5
Iran, Islamic Republic of	-3.4	-2.8	-5.0	-4.7	-5.8	40.7	44.8	101.1	142.9	141.9
Malaysia	107.8	.. d	30.8	25.6	23.0	992.7	777.2	922.3	1 024.2	1 185.8
Philippines	-34.6	-2.6	-3.8	-3.4	-4.6	76.3	146.0	161.4	146.4	127.3
Singapore	196.2	101.2	100.8	189.6	139.7	12 140.4	12 458.9	13 205.5	13 170.3	12 152.3
Chinese Taipei	29.4	33.7	36.9	109.9	102.5	36.3	59.3	47.9	58.3	143.0
Thailand	-16.5	7.8	.. d	.. d	.. d	956.8	703.2	569.7	435.7	504.2
Viet Nam	2.3	4.1	1.1	1.5	-1.1	108.0	120.4	118.8	127.3	116.3
AUSTRALIA, OCEANIA AND POLAR REGIONS	**-88.1**	**10.2**	**52.9**	**73.8**	**62.3**	**2 009.5**	**2 317.4**	**2 124.0**	**2 064.4**	**1 471.0**
WORLD unallocated and confidential	**2 256.0**	**2 059.6**	**2 085.0**	**2 517.8**	**2 391.6**	**994.9**	**866.9**	**888.4**	**1 027.8**	**1 034.6**
European Union (EU28)	**73 106.2**	**69 184.9**	**73 871.1**	**87 660.5**	**83 502.3**	**98 767.6**	**100 215.4**	**103 881.6**	**130 972.8**	**124 897.4**
G20 countries excl. European Union	**.. d**	**.. d**	**.. d**	**.. d**	**.. d**	**68 793.6**	**70 030.0**	**72 054.1**	**93 376.1**	**90 372.4**
G20 OECD countries	**.. d**	**.. d**	**.. d**	**.. d**	**.. d**	**60 517.5**	**62 579.4**	**64 739.4**	**85 680.0**	**82 759.9**
G20 Non-OECD countries	**.. d**	**.. d**	**.. d**	**.. d**	**.. d**	**8 275.7**	**7 450.7**	**7 314.7**	**7 696.1**	**7 612.5**
MENA countries	**-21.4**	**-19.5**	**-12.8**	**6.8**	**-12.1**	**.. d**	**.. d**	**.. d**	**.. d**	**.. d**
ASEAN countries	**255.5**	**131.5**	**252.9**	**338.3**	**265.7**	**14 665.8**	**14 497.8**	**15 280.0**	**15 237.0**	**14 307.9**

- Nil; .. Not available; d Secondary Confidentiality

Note: Data excludes resident Special Purpose Entities (SPEs). Detailed metadata at: *http://stats.oecd.org/OECDStat_Metadata/ShowMetadata.ashx?Dataset=FDI_CTRY_IND_SUMM.*

1. Information on data for Israel: *http://oe.cd/israel-disclaimer.*
2. Note by Turkey: The information in this document with reference to "Cyprus" relates to the southern part of the Island. There is no single authority representing both Turkish and Greek Cypriot people on the Island. Turkey recognises the Turkish Republic of Northern Cyprus (TRNC). Until a lasting and equitable solution is found within the context of the United Nations, Turkey shall preserve its position concerning the "Cyprus issue".
3. Note by all the European Union Member States of the OECD and the European Union: The Republic of Cyprus is recognised by all members of the United Nations with the exception of Turkey. The information in this document relates to the area under the effective control of the Government of the Republic of Cyprus.

Source: OECD International Direct Investment Statistics (database): https://doi.org/10.1787/idi-data-en

DENMARK

Table 3. Foreign direct investment income by country

Million US dollars

	Inward					Outward				
	2014	2015	2016	2017	2018	2014	2015	2016	2017	2018
WORLD	**5 452.2**	**4 606.0**	**5 481.4**	**6 184.4**	**5 880.3**	**13 709.6**	**12 131.8**	**12 061.1**	**12 990.7**	**14 022.2**
OECD COUNTRIES	**5 407.3**	**4 450.7**	**5 340.7**	**6 054.4**	**5 759.2**	**10 223.2**	**10 2[illegible]3.1**	**9 531.7**	**10 906.6**	**11 282.3**
Australia	-6.6	3.3	3.3	3.0	2.2	138.6	97.4	104.1	28.3	75.2
Austria	9.3	24.5	15.2	4.7	5.7	53.0	29.7	23.8	27.9	38.2
Belgium	19.0	25.1	36.5	55.0	70.5	142.7	62.2	69.8	112.4	102.6
Canada	-6.2	11.4	4.2	5.5	6.7	89.7	122.2	75.2	100.1	78.4
Chile	-2.7	-	-	-	-	62.3	47.6	79.6	24.2	25.3
Czech Republic	0.2	0.1	0.7	0.9	1.1	68.3	69.0	87.8	68.2	115.9
Denmark	-	-	-	-	-	-	-	-	-	-
Estonia	-0.7	-	0.1	0.2	0.2	73.1	[illegible]5.5	39.4	61.5	56.4
Finland	66.0	156.4	99.7	217.7	484.4	550.1	483.2	385.8	365.4	296.5
France	318.8	249.9	240.4	549.2	549.6	464.3	532.3	394.2	628.9	512.2
Germany	220.9	393.3	559.4	418.7	459.7	572.9	626.3	444.5	996.1	1 142.9
Greece	-4.4	-	-	-	-	1.8	-10.9	23.6	18.3	24.2
Hungary	-	-	-	-	-	51.3	58.9	76.8	129.2	112.5
Iceland	11.0	4.5	4.2	3.5	2.9	13.7	9.5	12.2	19.7	23.6
Ireland	-37.4	68.5	168.3	166.0	88.9	166.8	99.2	83.6	272.8	187.7
Israel[1]	2.1	..	..	..	..	1.4	..	..	..	..
Italy	15.8	46.7	23.8	35.4	31.0	-40.4	81.3	77.1	133.8	157.8
Japan	.. d	.. d	-78.4	-105.0	-28.2	75.8	77.9	94.2	82.9	85.2
Korea	0.5	0.4	-	0.5	1.1	17.6	24.1	32.1	23.2	43.7
Latvia	-	-	0.1	24.2	0.2	21.7	17.4	23.5	17.6	32.8
Lithuania	0.2	0.3	0.4	0.6	0.5	94.3	17.7	56.0	70.9	146.0
Luxembourg	325.5	256.0	497.3	414.6	239.6	95.0	48.2	94.6	61.2	85.4
Mexico	3.2	8.2	14.3	16.4	-	69.2	65.3	63.9	103.9	79.4
Netherlands	1 492.9	-313.0	282.6	453.8	465.0	230.8	104.2	383.6	391.6	368.9
New Zealand	-	-	-0.9	5.6	5.4	30.8	14.3	21.7	6.7	-2.1
Norway	-24.6	608.9	573.6	858.3	977.6	871.4	646.2	588.6	745.7	674.0
Poland	-1.1	14.9	-3.1	0.5	31.2	223.7	251.4	291.1	248.1	299.2
Portugal	0.4	0.3	0.6	2.1	0.2	33.1	30.9	21.7	45.0	50.1
Slovak Republic	0.2	-	0.9	0.9	0.6	59.6	46.1	45.8	53.0	57.8
Slovenia	0.2	-	-	0.2	0.2	23.8	19.3	20.9	13.0	9.8
Spain	168.9	157.9	61.2	306.9	194.8	69.1	217.4	-11.1	198.0	118.0
Sweden	1 610.3	1 413.0	1 332.1	976.6	842.0	1 441.6	978.2	1 142.8	1 260.6	1 736.3
Switzerland	132.4	206.5	232.4	285.1	138.4	2 354.5	2 776.6	2 341.2	2 120.0	1 815.3
Turkey	-2.3	-	0.1	0.2	0.2	49.5	88.3	43.5	19.5	50.2
United Kingdom	466.5	484.3	706.2	694.7	623.1	1 623.5	1 326.6	1 547.1	1 466.1	1 452.9
United States	620.1	633.3	564.3	657.9	562.9	544.3	1 172.4	805.7	1 059.3	1 226.6
EUROPE	**4 807.9**	**3 836.8**	**4 986.8**	**5 540.0**	**5 279.6**	**9 465.7**	**8 819.7**	**8 579.7**	**9 872.0**	**10 157.8**
Bulgaria	-	-	-	-	-	1.8	5.8	2.8	4.8	7.8
Croatia	-	-	-	-	-	-0.7	21.6	21.1	25.0	26.9
Cyprus[2, 3]	24.2	18.0	33.1	43.5	32.9	42.4	29.3	19.9	12.9	20.4
Malta	1.8	14.3	88.8	8.6	7.3	2.1	1.6	4.9	4.7	5.5
Romania	-	-	0.3	0.2	-	26.3	28.7	14.6	42.3	62.6
Russian Federation	1.6	1.2	32.1	10.1	20.6	78.3	61.7	30.0	63.2	108.0
Ukraine	..	..	..	..	..	..	..	..	..	..
AFRICA	**0.4**	**-**	**0.6**	**1.2**	**4.3**	**341.2**	**146.0**	**112.3**	**269.3**	**296.8**
Northern Africa	-	-	0.1	0.2	-	.. d	132.6	119.9	.. d	.. d
Algeria	..	..	..	..	..	..	..	..	..	..
Egypt	-	-	0.1	0.2	-	12.8	17.5	28.4	18.9	5.1
Libya	..	..	..	..	..	..	..	..	..	..
Morocco	-	-	-	-	-	0.5	1.5	0.1	3.6	4.6
Tunisia	..	..	..	..	..	..	..	..	..	..
Other African countries	0.4	-	0.4	1.1	4.3	-94.5	13.4	-7.4	100.4	83.0
Nigeria	-	-	-	-	-	0.9	1.3	5.8	8.5	0.3
South Africa	-	-	0.3	0.3	-	31.5	18.6	15.9	50.1	44.3
AMERICA	**634.8**	**692.2**	**602.6**	**692.8**	**589.7**	**997.6**	**1 437.7**	**1 050.1**	**1 456.1**	**1 563.3**
Northern America	639.8	658.7	576.5	669.1	570.5	637.9	1 301.0	872.7	1 167.3	1 283.6
Central America and Caribbean countries	17.3	39.7	22.0	23.8	19.6	34.4	59.9	49.9	180.3	125.1
Bahamas	..	..	..	..	..	..	..	..	..	..
Bermuda	..	..	..	..	..	..	..	..	..	..
Cayman Islands	..	..	..	..	..	..	..	..	..	..
Costa Rica	..	..	..	..	..	..	..	..	..	..
El Salvador	..	..	..	..	..	..	..	..	..	..
Guatemala	..	..	..	..	..	..	..	..	..	..
Honduras	..	..	..	..	..	..	..	..	..	..
Nicaragua	..	..	..	..	..	..	..	..	..	..
Panama	..	..	..	..	..	..	..	..	..	..
Virgin Islands, U.S.	..	..	..	..	..	..	..	..	..	..
South America	-22.2	-6.1	4.2	-	-0.5	325.3	76.7	127.3	108.6	154.6
Argentina	-2.0	-	-	-	-	124.1	-4.0	2.2	-17.7	48.2
Bolivia	..	..	..	..	..	..	..	..	..	..
Brazil	-11.2	-6.1	4.3	-0.2	-0.5	177.4	10.7	52.3	107.4	61.8
Colombia	..	..	..	..	..	..	..	..	..	..
Ecuador	..	..	..	..	..	..	..	..	..	..
Paraguay	..	..	..	..	..	..	..	..	..	..
Peru	..	..	..	..	..	..	..	..	..	..
Uruguay	-6.4	-	-	-	-	-2.0	-5.1	-8.2	-5.0	1.6
Venezuela	-	-	-	-	-	-58.0	-1.0	0.7	-0.2	-2.9

DENMARK

Table 3. Foreign direct investment income by country *(cont.)*

Million US dollars

	Inward					Outward				
	2014	2015	2016	2017	2018	2014	2015	2016	2017	2018
ASIA	**15.8**	**73.6**	**-111.0**	**-58.3**	**-1.3**	**2 733.7**	**1 614.5**	**2 191.6**	**1 354.2**	**1 937.1**
Near and Middle East	2.3	1.8	2.5	3.9	3.3	.. d	282.4	208.9	32.0	65.4
Gulf Arabian countries	-	-	0.9	2.1	1.3	.. d	276.1	202.2	24.8	59.2
Kuwait	..	..	..	..	..	..	..	..	..	..
Qatar	..	..	..	..	..	..	..	..	..	..
Saudi Arabia	..	..	..	..	..	..	..	..	..	..
United Arab Emirates	..	..	..	..	..	..	..	..	..	..
Other Near and Middle East	2.1	1.8	1.8	2.0	2.1	8.7	6.2	6.7	7.1	6.0
Jordan	..	..	..	..	..	..	..	..	..	..
Other Asian countries	13.5	72.0	-113.5	-62.3	-4.6	2 013.1	1 332.1	1 982.8	1 322.4	1 871.7
China	2.0	17.1	4.2	3.9	3.0	427.3	350.3	538.7	401.6	576.7
Hong Kong, China	3.0	26.8	3.6	5.3	27.9	175.5	147.2	239.3	67.7	154.9
India	2.8	0.7	1.0	2.4	0.3	87.6	45.6	44.6	28.9	72.7
Indonesia	-2.1	-	-	-	-	33.3	21.9	11.3	24.7	29.0
Iran, Islamic Republic of	..	..	..	..	..	..	..	..	..	..
Malaysia	28.5	43.0	1.5	1.2	1.4	81.0	69.7	104.3	88.0	100.6
Philippines	-1.6	-	-	-	-	4.1	7.1	1.2	5.8	1.0
Singapore	-29.4	-12.8	-51.1	19.4	-15.5	588.9	432.7	610.5	283.3	488.0
Chinese Taipei	1.6	1.8	1.9	6.5	8.2	6.8	10.7	-6.2	2.7	37.7
Thailand	-1.8	-	3.9	3.5	-3.0	.. d	37.9	205.6	143.7	144.3
Viet Nam	..	..	..	..	..	..	..	..	..	..
AUSTRALIA, OCEANIA AND POLAR REGIONS	**-6.8**	**3.3**	**2.4**	**8.8**	**8.1**	**169.6**	**111.8**	**126.1**	**35.7**	**73.7**
WORLD unallocated and confidential	**-**	**0.1**	**-**	**-0.2**	**-0.2**	**1.8**	**2.1**	**1.3**	**3.3**	**-6.5**
European Union (EU28)	**4 697.0**	**3 011.0**	**4 144.8**	**4 374.7**	**4 128.8**	**6 092.5**	**5 190.6**	**5 385.7**	**6 728.9**	**7 226.7**
G20 countries excl. European Union	**.. d**	**.. d**	**..**	**..**	**..**	**..**	**..**	**..**	**..**	**..**
G20 OECD countries	**.. d**	**.. d**	**2 037.4**	**2 276.3**	**2 208.3**	**3 605.1**	**4 214.2**	**3 681.6**	**4 642.1**	**4 904.6**
G20 Non-OECD countries	**..**	**..**	**..**	**..**	**..**	**..**	**..**	**..**	**..**	**..**
MENA countries	**..**	**..**	**..**	**..**	**..**	**.. d**	**..**	**..**	**..**	**..**
ASEAN countries	**-6.4**	**30.2**	**-45.8**	**24.2**	**-17.1**	**1 189.2**	**648.7**	**1 034.8**	**693.6**	**890.3**

- Nil; .. Not available; d Secondary Confidentiality

Note: Data excludes resident Special Purpose Entities (SPEs). Detailed metadata at: *http://stats.oecd.org/OECDStat_Metadata/ShowMetadata.ashx?Dataset=FDI_CTRY_IND_SUMM.*

1. Information on data for Israel: *http://oe.cd/israel-disclaimer.*
2. Note by Turkey: The information in this document with reference to "Cyprus" relates to the southern part of the Island. There is no single authority representing both Turkish and Greek Cypriot people on the Island. Turkey recognises the Turkish Republic of Northern Cyprus (TRNC). Until a lasting and equitable solution is found within the context of the United Nations, Turkey shall preserve its position concerning the "Cyprus issue".
3. Note by all the European Union Member States of the OECD and the European Union: The Republic of Cyprus is recognised by all members of the United Nations with the exception of Turkey. The information in this document relates to the area under the effective control of the Government of the Republic of Cyprus.

Source: OECD International Direct Investment Statistics (database): https://doi.org/10.1787/idi-data-en

DENMARK

Table 4. Foreign direct investment flows by industrial sector

Million US dollars

	Inward					Outward				
	2014	2015	2016	2017	2018	2014	2015	2016	2017	2018
All FDI activities	**4 677.1**	**2 995.2**	**235.0**	**3 749.3**	**2 405.8**	**8 248.2**	**8 707.7**	**10 111.9**	**9 519.8**	**1 136.8**
Agriculture, forestry and fishing	-	-	-	-	-	**48.2**	**17.0**	**13.5**	**17.0**	**50.7**
Mining and quarrying	**.. d**	**.. d**	**463.2**	**.. d**	**.. d**	**.. d**	**585.7**	**1 905.4**	**.. d**	**.. d**
Extraction activities	.. d	.. d	456.3	.. d	.. d	.. d	585.1	1 905.4	.. d	.. d
Manufacturing	**-594.3**	**3 001.3**	**-648.7**	**1 031.2**	**57.0**	**1 356.7**	**927.2**	**-642.1**	**985.6**	**1 374.8**
of which:										
Food products, beverages and tobacco	235.1	226.0	-16.3	84.4	538.5	-815.3	260.7	1 400.6	1 050.9	637.4
Textiles, wood and paper products; printing	-31.5	-6.8	-0.4	-7.0	1.6	51.4	90.4	154.4	60.6	-31.5
Chemical, rubber, plastic, non-metallic mineral products	-833.1	1 639.5	-62.3	-171.5	-302.2	177.3	501.7	-1 698.8	-407.2	996.1
Metal and machinery products, except electrical equipment	72.3	1 158.1	-613.2	980.6	-161.1	.. d	-381.5	-390.3	273.1	-285.1
Motor vehicles, trailers, semi-trailers, other transport equipment	6.2	-2.7	9.7	-1.4	65.4	6.4	22.0	14.0	9.4	27.7
Other manufacturing	-43.4	-12.6	34.2	145.7	-85.2	-439.2	434.2	-122.0	-1.2	30.4
Electricity, gas, steam and air conditioning supply	**.. d**	**-179.6**	**.. d**	**.. d**	**-56.5**	**128.5**	**300.1**	**588.6**	**.. d**	**.. d**
Water supply; sewerage, waste management and remediation activities	**-0.5**	-	**-5.8**	**6.7**	**6.3**	**-0.2**	**-0.6**	**-0.6**	-	**0.3**
Construction	**55.4**	**8.0**	**34.9**	**13.9**	**-30.4**	**104.7**	**126.5**	**-33.1**	**-20.4**	**-25.7**
Services	**1 914.5**	**369.0**	**1 028.6**	**-3 351.1**	**3 350.8**	**7 142.0**	**6 147.3**	**8 079.7**	**7 055.8**	**965.7**
Wholesale and retail trade; repair of motor vehicles and motorcycles	404.4	489.6	79.5	43.0	-356.9	32.6	-1 565.6	620.1	483.4	54.0
Transportation and storage	129.0	710.3	-136.8	-89.7	-2.7	606.0	1 433.5	403.8	.. d	81.3
Accommodation and food service activities	15.8	0.7	-13.5	-39.5	-3.8	-	-	-	-	-
Information and communication	-666.9	-179.6	-349.9	-140.0	51.5	.. d	-85.3	-353.2	-104.1	.. d
Financial and insurance activities	1 316.0	835.6	2 906.3	-3 946.5	-225.5	2 435.3	5 373.4	4 602.0	499.4	877.2
Activities of holding companies	..	..	..	..	..	..	..	..	..	..
Real estate activities	8.7	67.5	40.9	65.3	187.4	3.4	99.8	165.4	.. d	.. d
Professional, scientific and technical activities	454.2	-1 251.7	-431.4	555.2	366.7	984.0	545.5	2 484.3	1 409.3	2 250.6
Administrative and support service activities	285.5	-149.3	-1 105.1	134.7	.. d	398.8	297.1	194.0	246.8	296.7
Public administration; activities of households and of extraterritorial organisations	.. d	.. d	23.6	36.5	-38.6	19.9	6.5	-83.9	55.0	-8.9
Education	-	-	-	-	-	-	-	-	-	-
Human health and social work activities	-9.3	-8.5	-20.4	-11.2	35.6	.. d	35.1	47.2	.. d	20.1
Arts, entertainment and recreation	63.9	-0.6	10.3	18.3	-18.8	-	7.3	-	-	-
Other services	5.0	22.3	25.0	22.7	29.3	-	-	-	-	-0.6
Not allocated and confidential	**.. d**	**.. d**	**.. d**	**.. d**	**.. d**	**.. d**	**.. d**	**239.3**	**.. d**	**.. d**
Private real estate activities	**.. d**	**.. d**	**.. d**	**.. d**	**.. d**	**.. d**	**.. d**	**-38.9**	**.. d**	**.. d**

- Nil; .. Not available; d Secondary Confidentiality

Note: Data excludes resident Special Purpose Entities (SPEs). Detailed metadata at: *http://stats.oecd.org/OECDStat_Metadata/ShowMetadata.ashx?Dataset=FDI_CTRY_IND_SUMM.*

Source: OECD International Direct Investment Statistics (database): https://doi.org/10.1787/idi-data-en

Table 5. Foreign direct investment positions by industrial sector

At year end

Million US dollars

	Inward					Outward				
	2014	2015	2016	2017	2018	2014	2015	2016	2017	2018
All FDI activities	**95 766.5**	**91 978.8**	**99 403.4**	**116 993.1**	**109 894.0**	**167 394.9**	**164 757.8**	**169 708.2**	**201 621.5**	**193 338.2**
Agriculture, forestry and fishing	**.. d**	**98.4**	**60.4**	**109.5**	..	**338.0**	**302.6**	**299.5**	**329.4**	..
Mining and quarrying	**.. d**	**1 856.1**	**2 045.1**	**.. d**	..	**.. d**	**.. d**	**.. d**	**.. d**	..
Extraction activities	.. d	1 824.5	2 011.4	.. d	..	.. d	.. d	.. d	.. d	..
Manufacturing	**10 163.7**	**10 008.2**	**9 545.3**	**12 052.1**	..	**48 017.9**	**42 303.2**	**40 222.5**	**44 120.0**	..
of which:										
Food products, beverages and tobacco	2 668.3	2 678.8	2 732.5	3 266.9	..	25 529.8	24 079.8	23 521.3	27 492.5	..
Textiles, wood and paper products; printing	321.3	291.2	294.2	389.0	..	644.3	722.4	834.6	973.0	..
Chemical, rubber, plastic, non-metallic mineral products	2 724.7	3 437.5	3 337.8	3 634.0	..	12 075.0	8 106.6	6 838.7	5 828.4	..
Metal and machinery products, except electrical equipment	2 209.3	2 266.2	1 927.0	3 354.9	..	8 129.0	8 192.2	7 942.1	8 617.0	..
Motor vehicles, trailers, semi-trailers, other transport equipment	30.7	22.7	27.4	44.9	..	168.1	139.4	200.2	201.0	..
Other manufacturing	2 209.5	1 311.9	1 226.2	1 362.2	..	1 471.6	1 062.8	885.6	1 008.3	..
Electricity, gas, steam and air conditioning supply	**2 456.8**	**2 230.9**	**2 806.1**	**912.4**	..	**8 854.2**	**8 162.5**	**7 658.2**	**.. d**	..
Water supply; sewerage, waste management and remediation activities	**3.9**	**.. d**	**.. d**	**.. d**	..	**6.2**	**8.3**	**13.2**	**13.5**	..
Construction	**78.6**	**72.0**	**137.8**	**257.3**	..	**87.7**	**243.6**	**172.3**	**264.5**	..
Services	**69 977.5**	**70 941.1**	**77 816.6**	**90 709.1**	..	**95 108.8**	**103 903.7**	**101 698.3**	**123 988.8**	..
Wholesale and retail trade; repair of motor vehicles and motorcycles	11 515.8	11 659.0	12 222.0	12 979.2	..	12 596.5	11 103.2	12 162.0	13 471.3	..
Transportation and storage	2 362.5	3 138.8	2 830.5	2 969.4	..	18 509.5	18 977.7	9 985.7	14 972.2	..
Accommodation and food service activities	112.9	156.1	172.7	323.8	..	31.4	33.1	33.2	62.5	..
Information and communication	6 021.3	5 577.3	5 061.0	6 065.0	..	2 970.9	2 433.5	2 156.0	2 488.5	..
Financial and insurance activities	39 375.6	41 361.6	45 588.1	51 257.3	..	36 309.0	45 444.2	48 435.9	57 509.2	..
Activities of holding companies	..	..	..	..	..	..	..	..	..	..
Real estate activities	2 016.2	2 155.9	2 352.4	3 771.3	..	1 815.1	2 364.9	2 523.0	3 175.9	..
Professional, scientific and technical activities	5 691.7	4 455.8	4 615.6	6 752.7	..	18 714.7	19 165.0	22 024.3	24 197.0	..
Administrative and support service activities	3 456.7	3 165.6	5 649.7	7 077.5	..	2 322.0	2 541.0	2 561.7	5 914.9	..
Public administration; activities of households and of extraterritorial organisations	.. d	.. d	.. d	.. d	..	.. d	.. d	.. d	.. d	..
Education	0.7	0.7	-18.6	-21.4	..	12.3	16.7	23.5	21.3	..
Human health and social work activities	0.3	-11.9	-15.5	11.0	..	.. d	.. d	.. d	.. d	..
Arts, entertainment and recreation	-2.9	-19.8	-3.8	11.3	..	5.2	61.1	58.0	69.9	..
Other services	57.2	62.8	63.5	.. d	..	36.1	45.1	78.1	71.8	..
Not allocated and confidential	**.. d**	**.. d**	**.. d**	**.. d**	..	**.. d**	**.. d**	**.. d**	**.. d**	..
Private real estate activities	**.. d**	**.. d**	**.. d**	**.. d**	..	**.. d**	**.. d**	**.. d**	**.. d**	..

.. Not available; d Secondary Confidentiality

Note: Data excludes resident Special Purpose Entities (SPEs). Detailed metadata at: *http://stats.oecd.org/OECDStat_Metadata/ShowMetadata.ashx?Dataset=FDI_CTRY_IND_SUMM.*

Source: *OECD International Direct Investment Statistics (database): https://doi.org/10.1787/idi-data-en*

Table 6. Foreign direct investment income by industrial sector

Million US dollars

	Inward					Outward				
	2014	2015	2016	2017	2018	2014	2015	2016	2017	2018
All FDI activities	**5 452.2**	**4 606.0**	**5 481.4**	**6 184.4**	**5 880.3**	**13 709.6**	**12 131.8**	**12 061.1**	**12 990.7**	**14 022.2**
Agriculture, forestry and fishing	**7.5**	**17.7**	**12.8**	**15.1**	**12.4**	**22.6**	**21.7**	**22.3**	**25.3**	**22.7**
Mining and quarrying	**327.7**	**-337.2**	**-234.0**	**-59.2**	**62.9**	**.. d**	**.. d**	**429.4**	**.. d**	**.. d**
Extraction activities	320.2	-349.7	-253.3	-72.7	59.6	.. d	.. d	.. d	.. d	.. d
Manufacturing	**195.8**	**1 050.3**	**1 127.4**	**1 340.2**	**1 232.0**	**4 621.5**	**4 651.3**	**4 672.0**	**4 433.2**	**4 488.3**
of which:										
Food products, beverages and tobacco	373.9	318.3	275.0	334.3	338.0	1 103.6	706.6	1 021.9	1 045.2	1 273.8
Textiles, wood and paper products; printing	15.8	14.1	22.7	16.2	22.0	61.6	73.5	70.7	69.5	61.0
Chemical, rubber, plastic, non-metallic mineral products	-377.3	328.6	391.5	404.9	257.2	2 783.6	2 902.6	2 705.5	2 552.2	2 310.1
Metal and machinery products, except electrical equipment	-8.4	115.5	204.0	302.8	510.0	538.0	812.7	769.7	610.0	693.0
Motor vehicles, trailers, semi-trailers, other transport equipment	6.6	4.3	3.9	7.3	12.8	22.1	20.5	16.2	19.4	19.3
Other manufacturing	185.1	269.7	230.1	274.8	91.7	112.8	135.6	88.0	137.1	131.1
Electricity, gas, steam and air conditioning supply	**55.2**	**-30.3**	**69.5**	**53.5**	**64.5**	**940.4**	**230.6**	**296.7**	**382.8**	**.. d**
Water supply; sewerage, waste management and remediation activities	**-0.5**	**18.9**	**-4.0**	**5.8**	**8.2**	**0.2**	**-0.1**	**-**	**0.9**	**1.3**
Construction	**57.1**	**77.5**	**72.4**	**63.3**	**46.4**	**-10.3**	**5.1**	**2.7**	**6.8**	**19.5**
Services	**4 312.2**	**3 564.2**	**4 316.1**	**4 714.2**	**4 340.2**	**7 214.1**	**6 630.2**	**6 570.5**	**7 366.3**	**8 347.5**
Wholesale and retail trade; repair of motor vehicles and motorcycles	801.1	673.4	944.2	1 112.7	1 017.7	1 328.8	883.1	1 006.0	1 145.3	1 181.9
Transportation and storage	183.7	90.1	-192.5	28.5	-134.6	874.0	448.7	465.0	424.4	1 065.5
Accommodation and food service activities	17.1	15.9	19.5	0.8	29.1	1.8	2.2	1.9	4.2	4.6
Information and communication	187.2	153.9	115.7	-43.3	188.5	249.0	149.9	125.5	211.6	144.0
Financial and insurance activities	2 198.7	2 019.1	2 718.5	2 729.7	2 313.5	3 129.9	3 102.1	3 060.7	3 402.3	3 639.8
Activities of holding companies	..	..	..	..	..	..	..	..	..	..
Real estate activities	105.2	65.0	119.0	178.7	236.5	90.6	81.5	108.6	121.3	152.4
Professional, scientific and technical activities	657.1	211.4	334.0	267.8	286.8	1 205.4	1 603.3	1 549.0	1 642.7	1 644.4
Administrative and support service activities	165.3	312.8	251.5	427.2	370.0	203.3	272.8	209.0	339.5	503.5
Public administration; activities of households and of extraterritorial organisations	-	-	-	-	-	19.9	6.5	-24.5	1.4	-45.0
Education	-	-	0.3	0.9	1.3	0.5	1.0	0.9	1.4	1.4
Human health and social work activities	-28.8	-0.7	-19.8	-12.9	0.6	.. d	.. d	61.8	64.2	46.4
Arts, entertainment and recreation	0.7	0.6	0.6	0.8	1.0	0.7	0.4	3.6	3.9	4.3
Other services	24.7	22.6	25.3	23.3	30.1	1.8	2.4	3.0	4.1	4.3
Not allocated and confidential	**497.3**	**244.9**	**121.2**	**51.5**	**113.7**	**.. d**	**.. d**	**67.6**	**.. d**	**.. d**
Private real estate activities	-	-	-	-	-	-	-	-	-	-

- Nil; .. Not available; d Secondary Confidentiality

Note: Data excludes resident Special Purpose Entities (SPEs). Detailed metadata at: *http://stats.oecd.org/OECDStat_Metadata/ShowMetadata.ashx?Dataset=FDI_CTRY_IND_SUMM.*

Source: *OECD International Direct Investment Statistics (database): https://doi.org/10.1787/idi-data-en*

ESTONIA

Table 1. Foreign direct investment flows by country

Million US dollars

	Inward					Outward				
	2014	2015	2016	2017	2018	2014	2015	2016	2017	2018
WORLD	**683.7**	**35.5**	**1 058.2**	**1 916.8**	**1 474.4**	**42.0**	**182.1**	**486.5**	**872.6**	**48.9**
OECD COUNTRIES	**243.4**	**-45.0**	**860.2**	**1 577.6**	**1 188.4**	**176.6**	**274.8**	**415.1**	**879.3**	**-62.7**
Australia	-6.1	-0.2	1.2	6.2	12.8	2.2	2.5	0.7	-0.6	0.4
Austria	11.8	118.0	16.0	-54.6	62.4	0.3	1.6	-0.4	0.0	0.2
Belgium	-6.1	25.9	17.3	11.2	14.9	0.0	0.2	5.6	3.0	-0.2
Canada	5.0	-2.7	-0.7	-6.5	9.3	-0.6	0.0	0.0	0.1	0.1
Chile	0.0	0.0	0.0	0.0	0.0	.. c	.. c	.. c	.. c	.. c
Czech Republic	9.4	3.6	4.3	8.2	-0.5	-1.0	3.8	4.5	2.9	2.0
Denmark	252.1	-106.0	76.0	1.2	33.3	1.1	43.0	7.3	-48.3	2.1
Estonia	-	-	-	-	-	-	-	-	-	-
Finland	17.0	192.0	381.0	139.5	320.5	88.8	44.7	64.2	809.0	124.2
France	9.6	93.6	42.8	49.6	2.7	12.4	3.3	6.3	6.3	21.4
Germany	7.5	-62.2	8.0	126.7	180.9	-27.0	2.6	17.7	2.0	5.7
Greece	0.1	0.0	0.4	0.8	0.5	0.2	0.0	0.2	0.0	.. c
Hungary	4.4	-0.3	1.4	-0.4	3.1	-0.1	2.4	1.0	-0.2	0.7
Iceland	1.3	16.9	4.6	5.7	6.8	0.0	0.0	0.0	0.0	10.1
Ireland	-9.7	21.2	-4.5	-108.9	173.0	4.9	4.0	-10.1	-3.2	-0.7
Israel[1]	-0.6	0.7	0.1	1.5	5.0	2.8	0.3	-0.1	0.8	-0.2
Italy	9.0	9.1	19.9	-9.0	-16.2	9.7	3.0	11.9	-0.3	2.4
Japan	-0.1	0.0	10.6	5.4	20.0	-	.. c	-	-	.. c
Korea	-0.1	0.0	0.2	-1.1	-0.2	-	-	-	-	.. c
Latvia	132.9	-12.5	117.4	43.3	61.9	124.7	135.3	106.6	14.5	233.9
Lithuania	49.4	52.5	26.2	93.8	31.3	-411.6	112.4	-69.7	131.9	24.1
Luxembourg	-184.2	217.1	-17.4	109.6	1 111.3	13.7	-0.4	0.9	-0.2	45.7
Mexico	0.2	0.0	0.0	-0.4	-0.1	-	.. c	0.2	.. c	.. c
Netherlands	71.7	-79.1	15.1	-104.6	-640.1	-31.6	109.8	6.9	8.0	-637.4
New Zealand	0.0	0.0	1.7	0.5	0.5	.. c	.. c	.. c	.. c	.. c
Norway	171.2	-204.2	-250.2	37.3	-278.0	3.4	41.1	2.3	14.8	8.1
Poland	91.9	6.7	29.0	2.7	60.4	35.8	-19.8	79.2	11.0	17.0
Portugal	0.0	-11.2	5.1	9.4	-0.3	2.2	0.0	22.5	-12.9	2.9
Slovak Republic	13.0	0.3	0.3	3.3	3.4	0.1	1.2	0.5	-0.6	0.5
Slovenia	0.1	-0.2	0.1	0.2	0.7	.. c	0.0	-	-0.2	0.8
Spain	3.4	3.9	1.5	-3.9	17.2	15.2	15.0	22.8	21.2	18.7
Sweden	-226.4	-322.7	293.9	711.3	-165.5	28.5	35.6	30.5	-13.8	19.3
Switzerland	-44.0	-4.8	20.5	40.4	65.5	-7.0	1.3	-0.4	-0.8	-4.1
Turkey	-0.4	1.6	-2.6	3.2	7.4	0.1	0.2	0.2	0.0	0.6
United Kingdom	10.9	10.5	36.4	546.6	42.8	17.3	0.7	28.1	66.0	23.7
United States	31.9	27.3	30.9	3.1	41.8	5.2	-21.5	5.8	0.3	14.7
EUROPE	**564.5**	**92.3**	**958.1**	**1 732.7**	**1 347.0**	**29.7**	**196.9**	**458.5**	**816.8**	**-6.2**
Bulgaria	0.3	-0.3	0.8	0.0	1.6	1.4	-2.4	-	4.9	3.4
Croatia	-0.1	-0.5	1.1	-0.1	-0.5	1.8	0.1	0.4	1.5	2.1
Cyprus[2, 3]	-12.6	93.5	-51.8	-66.1	116.3	74.0	-166.1	32.6	-182.8	-37.3
Malta	3.5	5.7	27.1	12.5	9.2	3.3	-5.0	11.4	5.8	-7.1
Romania	0.1	-0.3	1.5	2.3	1.1	20.9	-8.5	15.0	-5.0	10.8
Russian Federation	151.3	-31.9	74.8	49.8	46.3	11.8	4.8	47.0	21.5	1.7
Ukraine	-17.6	25.1	44.6	56.9	53.9	15.7	-4.5	-15.8	-18.3	69.6
AFRICA	**2.3**	**-0.4**	**-7.4**	**9.2**	**1.1**	**1.9**	**-0.3**	**-0.9**	**-1.9**	**11.4**
Northern Africa	0.0	-0.1	0.0	0.4	0.6	1.6	.. c	.. c	0.3	1.4
Algeria	.. c	.. c	.. c	0.0	0.1	-	-	-	-	-
Egypt	0.0	0.0	0.0	0.3	0.5	0.0	-	-	0.1	0.5
Libya	-	-	-	-	.. c	-	-	-	-	-
Morocco	0.0	-	-	0.0	0.0	.. c	.. c	.. c	.. c	.. c
Tunisia	-	-0.1	0.0	0.0	0.0	-	-	-	-	-
Other African countries	2.3	-0.3	-7.5	8.8	0.5	0.3	.. c	-1.0	-2.1	10.1
Nigeria	-	.. c	.. c	0.0	0.0	-	-	-	.. c	.. c
South Africa	0.2	0.0	0.2	0.0	-0.5	0.1	-	.. c	.. c	2.5
AMERICA	**95.8**	**-66.4**	**57.9**	**-87.4**	**19.3**	**6.0**	**-20.9**	**5.9**	**1.4**	**16.0**
Northern America	36.9	24.6	30.2	-3.4	51.1	4.7	-21.5	5.8	0.4	14.8
Central America and Caribbean countries	59.8	-92.1	26.4	-85.0	-32.4	0.7	0.3	0.0	0.4	0.7
Bahamas	0.2	0.0	0.4	-0.2	0.1	-	-	.. c	-	-
Bermuda	.. c	.. c	-	.. c	-	-	-	-	-	-
Cayman Islands	-6.1	11.3	-5.2	-10.7	4.0	-	0.3	-	-	-
Costa Rica	.. c	.. c	0.1	-0.1	-	-	-	-	-	-
El Salvador	-	-	-	.. c	.. c	-	-	-	-	-
Guatemala	-	-	-	-	-	-	-	-	-	-
Honduras	-	-	-	.. c	.. c	-	-	-	-	-
Nicaragua	-	-	-	.. c	.. c	-	-	-	-	-
Panama	5.0	-1.8	8.2	1.6	-0.2	0.2	0.2	-0.1	0.1	0.1
Virgin Islands, U.S.	-	-	-	.. c	.. c	-	-	-	-	-
South America	-0.9	1.1	1.2	1.0	0.6	0.6	0.4	0.1	0.6	0.5
Argentina	0.0	0.0	-	0.0	0.0	.. c	-	.. c	-	.. c
Bolivia	.. c	.. c	0.3	.. c	.. c	-	-	-	-	-
Brazil	-0.7	0.9	0.8	0.7	0.4	.. c	0.7	0.3	0.2	0.6
Colombia	-	0.0	0.1	0.0	0.0	-	-	-	-	-
Ecuador	.. c	-	0.1	0.0	0.1	-	0.0	-	-	.. c
Paraguay	-	-	-	.. c	-	-	-	-	-	-
Peru	-	.. c	0.1	0.1	0.1	-	-	-	-	-
Uruguay	0.0	0.0	-	0.0	0.0	-	.. c	.. c	.. c	.. c
Venezuela	.. c	0.0	-	-	0.0	-	-	-	-	-

Table 1. Foreign direct investment flows by country (*cont.*)

Million US dollars

	Inward					Outward				
	2014	2015	2016	2017	2018	2014	2015	2016	2017	2018
ASIA	**25.8**	**7.0**	**10.1**	**253.1**	**90.3**	**2.0**	**3.7**	**22.3**	**56.6**	**26.5**
Near and Middle East	1.7	3.7	1.0	210.4	14.9	-0.4	4.1	16.0	59.3	29.2
Gulf Arabian countries	1.8	0.5	0.3	206.1	6.3	-6.2	-6.8	-0.4	2.4	5.9
Kuwait	-	-	.. c	0.0	0.0	-	-	-	-	-
Qatar	0.2	0.1	.. c	0.0	0.0	-	-	-	-	-
Saudi Arabia	.. c	0.0	0.0	0.0	0.0	-	-	-	-	-
United Arab Emirates	1.5	0.1	0.8	206.1	6.0	-5.7	-8.3	2.7	3.1	4.2
Other Near and Middle East	-0.1	3.3	0.7	4.3	8.6	5.9	10.9	16.4	56.9	23.3
Jordan	0.1	.. c	.. c	0.1	0.1	.. c	.. c	.. c	.. c	.. c
Other Asian countries	24.1	3.3	9.2	42.7	75.4	2.4	-0.4	6.2	-2.7	-2.7
China	9.6	-7.2	-8.6	5.6	8.5	-0.2	[illegible]	0.1	0.1	0.6
Hong Kong, China	-1.3	2.0	12.6	8.6	17.1	.. c	.. c	4.8	-4.7	0.4
India	2.2	3.6	-0.9	1.6	-0.6	.. c	-0.3	.. c	2.6	.. c
Indonesia	-0.2	0.0	0.0	0.0	0.1	-	-	-	0.2	0.1
Iran, Islamic Republic of	-	0.0	0.1	0.1	0.1	-	-	-	-	-
Malaysia	2.1	0.1	0.2	0.3	0.1	-	-	-	.. c	-
Philippines	0.0	0.1	0.1	0.3	0.2	.. c	-	-	0.1	-
Singapore	6.1	2.1	-4.5	17.8	16.9	-0.6	-1.2	-0.1	-2.8	-2.5
Chinese Taipei	0.0	0.0	0.2	0.7	0.9	-	.. c	.. c	-	-
Thailand	-0.1	-	-0.8	-2.0	3.1	0.6	0.4	0.6	0.3	-0.2
Viet Nam	0.0	0.0	0.1	0.0	0.1	.. c	.. c	.. c	-	-
AUSTRALIA, OCEANIA AND POLAR REGIONS	**-5.8**	**1.1**	**38.9**	**8.1**	**14.4**	**2.3**	**2.6**	**0.6**	**-0.4**	**1.2**
WORLD unallocated and confidential	**1.2**	**1.8**	**0.7**	**1.0**	**2.2**	**0.0**	**-**	**0.0**	**-**	**0.0**
European Union (EU28)	**258.8**	**258.5**	**1 048.8**	**1 524.7**	**1 425.5**	**-15.1**	**316.5**	**396.1**	**820.4**	**-121.1**
G20 countries excl. European Union	**229.8**	**42.4**	**213.0**	**781.6**	**355.3**	**31.8**	**-2.5**	**119.6**	**99.3**	**74.7**
G20 OECD countries	**67.4**	**77.0**	**146.7**	**723.9**	**301.2**	**19.3**	**-9.1**	**71.1**	**74.2**	**69.7**
G20 Non-OECD countries	**162.4**	**-34.6**	**66.3**	**57.7**	**54.2**	**12.5**	**6.6**	**48.5**	**25.1**	**5.0**
MENA countries	**2.4**	**0.5**	**0.0**	**206.3**	**6.9**	**-4.6**	**-6.1**	**-0.4**	**41.4**	**11.1**
ASEAN countries	**7.8**	**2.4**	**-4.9**	**16.3**	**20.5**	**0.0**	**-0.3**	**0.4**	**-2.0**	**-2.7**

- Nil; c Confidential data

Note: Detailed metadata at: *http://stats.oecd.org/OECDStat_Metadata/ShowMetadata.ashx?Dataset=FDI_CTRY_IND_SUMM.*

1. Information on data for Israel: *http://oe.cd/israel-disclaimer*.
2. Note by Turkey: The information in this document with reference to "Cyprus" relates to the southern part of the Island. There is no single authority representing both Turkish and Greek Cypriot people on the Island. Turkey recognises the Turkish Republic of Northern Cyprus (TRNC). Until a lasting and equitable solution is found within the context of the United Nations, Turkey shall preserve its position concerning the "Cyprus issue".
3. Note by all the European Union Member States of the OECD and the European Union: The Republic of Cyprus is recognised by all members of the United Nations with the exception of Turkey. The information in this document relates to the area under the effective control of the Government of the Republic of Cyprus.

Source: OECD International Direct Investment Statistics (database): https://doi.org/10.1787/idi-data-en

Table 2. Foreign direct investment positions by country
At year end

Million US dollars

	Inward					Outward				
	2014	2015	2016	2017	2018	2014	2015	2016	2017	2018
WORLD	**20 972.1**	**18 956.5**	**19 740.8**	**23 896.4**	**24 828.0**	**6 216.6**	**6 038.9**	**6 299.3**	**7 806.7**	**7 918.8**
OECD COUNTRIES	**17 071.6**	**15 469.8**	**16 427.9**	**20 078.5**	**..**	**1 241.0**	**1 476.8**	**2 776.6**	**3 675.5**	**5 469.9**
Australia	24.8	22.6	19.8	29.8	..	10.1	2.5	3.1	2.9	4.7
Austria	389.6	396.0	325.3	357.7	..	2.8	4.0	3.5	3.9	4.8
Belgium	76.1	74.9	80.3	96.9	..	2.8	2.7	45.8	4.0	3.6
Canada	73.7	50.2	66.9	84.1	..	0.8	0.5	0.4	0.6	0.7
Chile	.. c	.. c	0.0	0.0	..	0.1	0.1	0.1	0.2	0.2
Czech Republic	9.2	10.7	11.5	13.6	..	4.7	7.0	11.2	16.5	23.9
Denmark	527.7	490.1	487.7	587.1	..	6.4	47.6	53.4	10.1	11.7
Estonia	1 399.1	1 285.5	1 418.8	1 864.3	..	-	-	-	-	-
Finland	4 279.2	4 180.0	4 370.8	5 332.3	..	342.8	443.7	462.9	917.6	713.9
France	303.4	379.7	444.2	573.7	..	42.3	42.0	46.2	54.9	71.7
Germany	744.9	575.1	588.0	681.6	..	66.0	59.8	71.3	61.3	60.1
Greece	37.8	26.1	28.6	30.7	..	1.6	2.3	2.4	2.7	2.5
Hungary	4.7	4.7	5.3	9.3	..	0.8	3.1	4.1	4.5	4.9
Iceland	43.2	40.5	40.9	52.4	..	0.0	0.0	0.0	0.0	.. c
Ireland	74.7	59.9	52.3	61.5	..	13.6	15.8	5.7	2.2	1.4
Israel[1]	10.3	10.3	8.4	8.7	..	3.0	1.0	2.3	3.5	3.1
Italy	137.9	131.6	172.4	179.6	..	117.7	108.3	119.6	92.4	90.0
Japan	110.1	130.5	136.6	161.9	..	-	0.2	0.2	0.2	0.2
Korea	.. c	0.0	0.1	0.0	..	0.1	0.1	0.0	0.1	0.1
Latvia	334.7	316.0	446.4	472.0	..	1 030.1	1 060.4	1 102.6	1 392.1	1 643.7
Lithuania	678.4	691.1	722.7	896.4	..	1 135.0	1 281.4	1 210.1	1 606.4	1 581.6
Luxembourg	422.1	452.4	455.6	640.6	..	13.8	10.6	21.2	24.0	57.6
Mexico	0.1	0.1	0.0	0.0	..	0.3	0.3	0.5	1.0	1.6
Netherlands	659.3	509.6	541.9	551.4	..	134.9	239.8	232.4	266.2	290.1
New Zealand	0.4	0.6	1.9	2.7	..	0.1	0.1	0.0	4.5	4.4
Norway	1 045.8	905.6	895.3	1 238.3	..	44.2	84.7	44.8	68.6	71.2
Poland	42.0	46.3	91.1	135.4	..	75.4	51.3	124.8	153.5	163.1
Portugal	1.9	2.0	0.4	4.8	..	3.6	3.2	24.6	14.4	16.5
Slovak Republic	15.9	18.2	20.3	24.5	..	25.9	24.2	22.7	25.2	24.5
Slovenia	-0.1	-0.1	-0.1	-0.1	..	0.1	0.1	0.1	-0.2	0.5
Spain	22.3	7.4	30.1	43.1	..	81.3	74.1	83.5	122.9	139.8
Sweden	5 268.9	4 304.5	4 354.6	5 262.4	..	73.2	87.8	109.5	144.2	158.9
Switzerland	240.8	228.6	249.0	291.1	..	23.1	30.3	28.9	31.4	43.2
Turkey	5.1	5.2	6.0	8.7	..	2.4	2.3	2.4	2.7	3.2
United Kingdom	408.8	399.8	370.2	458.1	..	25.9	32.3	47.2	131.3	134.6
United States	691.6	721.3	707.4	820.3	..	121.1	95.0	99.0	116.4	127.8
EUROPE	**18 922.6**	**17 053.1**	**17 844.9**	**21 660.0**	**..**	**5 983.0**	**5 843.3**	**6 078.0**	**7 459.2**	**7 559.2**
Bulgaria	0.3	1.0	1.4	1.8	..	48.0	37.7	33.9	42.0	44.6
Croatia	0.1	0.3	0.4	0.6	..	28.9	25.1	24.9	28.4	28.5
Cyprus[2, 3]	384.7	355.0	368.6	401.9	..	1 738.2	1 401.9	1 403.8	1 394.1	1 274.4
Malta	22.7	23.1	42.5	48.5	..	23.9	22.5	33.3	52.3	44.0
Romania	0.1	1.2	2.3	3.9	..	50.0	25.5	38.1	37.3	37.7
Russian Federation	953.8	738.7	769.7	827.1	..	249.9	222.1	250.4	330.3	298.3
Ukraine	175.2	171.5	195.7	242.5	..	336.9	248.6	251.8	265.6	323.2
AFRICA	**13.4**	**9.2**	**16.2**	**43.1**	**..**	**16.3**	**15.2**	**15.3**	**15.5**	**29.2**
Northern Africa	0.2	0.3	0.8	1.9	..	14.1	13.3	13.4	15.5	16.1
Algeria	-	-	0.0	0.0	..	-	-	-	-	-
Egypt	0.2	0.2	0.7	1.7	..	0.7	0.7	0.7	0.8	1.3
Libya	-	0.1	0.0	0.1	..	-	-	-	-	-
Morocco	0.0	0.0	0.0	0.0	..	13.3	12.6	12.7	14.6	14.8
Tunisia	-	-	.. c	0.0	..	0.1	0.0	0.0	0.1	0.1
Other African countries	13.2	9.0	15.4	41.2	..	2.2	1.9	1.9	-0.1	13.1
Nigeria	0.6	0.5	0.6	0.7	..	-	-	-	.. c	.. c
South Africa	1.0	1.0	0.9	0.7	..	0.1	0.1	0.2	0.6	2.9
AMERICA	**1 130.4**	**1 023.6**	**1 101.2**	**1 196.3**	**..**	**140.1**	**114.0**	**115.2**	**135.9**	**147.8**
Northern America	765.3	771.5	774.4	904.4	..	121.9	95.5	99.5	117.0	128.5
Central America and Caribbean countries	362.3	250.2	323.8	287.5	..	5.0	4.4	1.7	2.3	2.8
Bahamas	2.1	1.3	1.7	2.0	..	-	-	0.0	0.0	0.0
Bermuda	0.3	0.4	0.3	0.5	..	-	-	-	-	-
Cayman Islands	.. c	.. c	.. c	.. c	..	-	0.3	0.2	0.3	0.3
Costa Rica	.. c	.. c	0.0	0.0	..	0.0	0.0	0.0	0.0	0.0
El Salvador	-	0.0	0.4	0.8	..	-	-	-	-	-
Guatemala	-	-	-	-	..	-	-	-	-	-
Honduras	-	-	-	.. c	..	-	-	-	-	-
Nicaragua	-	-	-	.. c	..	-	-	-	-	-
Panama	22.2	16.8	26.5	13.8	..	0.3	0.4	0.2	0.2	0.1
Virgin Islands, U.S.	-	-	-	.. c	..	-	-	-	-	-
South America	2.8	1.9	3.1	4.5	..	13.2	14.1	14.1	16.6	16.5
Argentina	0.6	0.5	0.5	0.5	..	0.1	0.1	0.1	0.1	0.2
Bolivia	0.3	0.3	0.3	0.5	..	-	-	-	-	-
Brazil	0.3	0.4	0.6	0.8	..	12.8	13.8	14.0	16.1	16.0
Colombia	-	0.1	0.1	0.2	..	-	-	-	-	-
Ecuador	0.3	0.5	1.5	2.4	..	-	0.0	0.0	0.0	0.1
Paraguay	-	-	-	.. c	..	-	-	-	-	-
Peru	-	-	-	.. c	..	0.1	0.1	-	-	-
Uruguay	0.0	0.0	0.0	0.0	..	.. c	.. c	.. c	.. c	-
Venezuela	.. c	0.0	-	-	..	-	.. c	.. c	.. c	.. c

Table 2. Foreign direct investment positions by country *(cont.)*

At year end

Million US dollars

	Inward					Outward				
	2014	2015	2016	2017	2018	2014	2015	2016	2017	2018
ASIA	**295.3**	**323.8**	**331.0**	**613.6**	..	**67.0**	**63.7**	**87.6**	**188.7**	**172.8**
Near and Middle East	17.2	20.4	19.7	26.6	..	12.8	14.6	34.6	103.8	130.5
Gulf Arabian countries	4.8	6.4	7.3	9.0	..	-1.6	-8.0	-7.3	-6.3	-0.5
Kuwait	0.2	0.1	0.2	0.2	..	-	-	-	-	-
Qatar	0.4	0.6	0.6	0.8	..	-	-	-	-	-
Saudi Arabia	1.1	1.1	1.5	1.4	..	-	-	-	-	-
United Arab Emirates	1.8	2.8	3.7	5.1	..	-3.8	-11.5	-8.5	-6.5	-2.4
Other Near and Middle East	12.4	14.1	12.5	17.6	..	14.4	22.7	41.9	110.1	131.1
Jordan	.. c	.. c	.. c	0.0	..	.. c	.. c	.. c	.. c	.. c
Other Asian countries	278.1	303.4	311.2	587.0	..	54.3	49.0	53.0	84.9	42.3
China	5.4	5.8	12.2	14.3	..	3.4	4.6	4.5	5.2	4.6
Hong Kong, China	30.6	37.2	46.5	51.0	..	0.5	0.5	5.0	24.6	13.1
India	-0.2	0.2	0.2	215.0	..	0.6	0.4	1.4	4.2	3.3
Indonesia	.. c	0.1	0.1	0.2	..	0.3	0.3	0.3	0.6	0.6
Iran, Islamic Republic of	0.2	0.2	0.3	0.5	..	-	-	-	-	-
Malaysia	5.2	5.6	6.3	7.9	..	-	-	-	0.1	0.1
Philippines	0.0	0.1	0.2	0.3	..	0.1	0.0	0.0	0.2	0.2
Singapore	113.1	109.1	92.1	115.3	..	3.5	2.1	1.6	2.5	1.4
Chinese Taipei	0.0	0.0	0.3	0.9	..	0.1	0.1	0.1	0.1	0.1
Thailand	0.0	0.2	0.6	0.3	..	5.6	5.4	5.7	6.8	6.3
Viet Nam	-	.. c	.. c	0.0	..	.. c	.. c	.. c	.. c	-
AUSTRALIA, OCEANIA AND POLAR REGIONS	**-5.1**	**-1.7**	**32.7**	**48.5**	..	**10.2**	**2.6**	**3.2**	**7.4**	**9.7**
WORLD unallocated and confidential	**615.5**	**548.4**	**414.8**	**334.9**	..	-	-	-	**0.0**	**0.0**
European Union (EU28)	**16 246.6**	**14 741.9**	**15 433.6**	**18 733.3**	..	**5 089.6**	**5 114.0**	**5 338.7**	**6 604.0**	**6 628.7**
G20 countries excl. European Union	**3 462.6**	**3 163.7**	**3 297.3**	**4 057.9**	..	**654.0**	**584.6**	**660.8**	**820.7**	**820.7**
G20 OECD countries	**2 500.5**	**2 416.0**	**2 511.6**	**2 997.9**	..	**386.8**	**343.2**	**390.0**	**463.7**	**494.8**
G20 Non-OECD countries	**962.1**	**747.7**	**785.7**	**1 059.9**	..	**267.2**	**241.4**	**270.8**	**356.9**	**326.0**
MENA countries	**5.9**	**7.4**	**13.2**	**17.9**	..	**12.7**	**5.5**	**6.1**	**46.3**	**59.7**
ASEAN countries	**118.3**	**115.0**	**99.3**	**124.0**	..	**9.5**	**3.3**	**8.1**	**10.6**	**8.8**

- Nil; .. Not available; c Confidential data

Note: Inward FDI positions are allocated according to the ultimate investing country. Detailed metadata at: *http://stats.oecd.org/OECDStat_Metadata/ShowMetadata.ashx?Dataset=FDI_CTRY_IND_SUMM.*

1. Information on data for Israel: *http://oe.cd/israel-disclaimer*.
2. Note by Turkey: The information in this document with reference to "Cyprus" relates to the southern part of the Island. There is no single authority representing both Turkish and Greek Cypriot people on the Island. Turkey recognises the Turkish Republic of Northern Cyprus (TRNC). Until a lasting and equitable solution is found within the context of the United Nations, Turkey shall preserve its position concerning the "Cyprus issue".
3. Note by all the European Union Member States of the OECD and the European Union: The Republic of Cyprus is recognised by all members of the United Nations with the exception of Turkey. The information in this document relates to the area under the effective control of the Government of the Republic of Cyprus.

Source: OECD International Direct Investment Statistics (database): https://doi.org/10.1787/idi-data-en

ESTONIA

Table 3. Foreign direct investment income by country

Million US dollars

	Inward					Outward				
	2014	2015	2016	2017	2018	2014	2015	2016	2017	2018
WORLD	**1 916.4**	**1 385.0**	**1 591.0**	**1 712.4**	**1 869.0**	**594.8**	**364.5**	**492.4**	**484.5**	**681.8**
OECD COUNTRIES	**1 611.8**	**1 171.6**	**1 348.1**	**1 425.5**	**1 565.2**	**33.5**	**12.6**	**190.0**	**222.1**	**458.7**
Australia	0.4	0.5	1.3	10.6	12.0	1.9	0.6	0.2	0.0	0.1
Austria	9.7	19.2	13.9	28.8	28.2	-0.1	0.1	0.1	0.0	0.1
Belgium	8.1	6.3	7.3	14.5	15.5	0.1	0.1	0.6	0.5	2.6
Canada	7.3	0.2	1.7	0.1	-0.1	0.0	0.0	0.0	0.0	0.0
Chile	-	-	.. c	-	-	0.0	0.0	0.0	0.0	0.0
Czech Republic	5.8	2.0	4.0	9.1	2.3	0.4	0.2	0.5	0.3	1.1
Denmark	47.9	43.3	33.5	34.9	26.4	1.8	1.7	4.3	4.0	-0.1
Estonia	-	-	-	-	-	-	-	-	-	-
Finland	422.0	307.2	383.1	381.9	376.8	-5.7	-13.5	5.2	71.4	132.6
France	22.0	18.1	25.4	32.1	39.5	0.0	1.4	0.9	1.6	1.2
Germany	40.0	34.3	27.8	48.6	64.1	7.3	0.4	1.7	0.5	3.2
Greece	0.0	0.0	0.2	0.8	0.9	0.0	0.0	1.4	0.0	0.0
Hungary	2.1	0.2	0.4	1.6	2.9	0.0	0.1	0.2	0.2	0.6
Iceland	5.5	11.7	9.5	7.9	9.7	0.0	0.0	-	-	-
Ireland	0.4	1.2	0.4	-1.3	2.0	0.3	0.7	0.5	0.2	-0.1
Israel[1]	1.0	1.1	1.8	1.7	1.3	0.0	0.0	0.0	0.0	0.0
Italy	3.2	4.3	4.7	3.7	6.0	-0.3	-0.2	-0.4	-0.7	1.3
Japan	0.1	0.2	0.4	0.6	5.5	-	0.0	0.0	0.0	0.0
Korea	-	-	.. c	-	-	0.0	0.0	-	0.0	-
Latvia	47.8	35.8	31.5	54.6	39.4	111.7	91.0	115.7	106.9	121.0
Lithuania	40.0	59.7	41.9	71.9	53.9	235.9	133.3	105.5	126.6	152.4
Luxembourg	-1.3	26.9	18.2	30.3	15.2	1.2	0.9	3.3	4.2	3.0
Mexico	0.0	0.0	0.0	0.0	0.1	0.0	0.0	0.0	0.0	0.0
Netherlands	185.8	123.7	133.3	83.9	120.9	-0.2	26.2	39.8	0.5	5.0
New Zealand	0.0	0.0	0.0	0.0	0.0	-	0.0	0.0	0.1	0.1
Norway	50.9	56.1	30.6	35.6	44.0	-1.9	-4.0	0.8	1.0	0.7
Poland	5.0	9.9	16.8	11.2	10.0	3.0	0.8	-0.1	0.8	6.3
Portugal	0.3	0.4	2.8	5.7	-3.3	0.0	0.0	0.0	0.1	0.5
Slovak Republic	1.9	0.1	0.3	3.2	3.4	-0.7	0.0	0.5	0.7	1.6
Slovenia	.. c	.. c	0.0	0.3	0.4	-0.2	0.0	0.0	-	0.4
Spain	5.8	7.9	4.5	5.0	6.4	6.8	5.1	6.1	4.9	6.4
Sweden	727.6	413.7	536.9	541.6	526.2	15.6	9.0	8.4	13.8	9.5
Switzerland	12.5	19.8	19.7	20.0	25.8	-2.9	0.2	0.6	7.9	7.9
Turkey	-0.3	1.7	-2.1	0.7	0.3	0.1	0.1	0.1	0.1	0.1
United Kingdom	24.8	40.6	32.7	53.0	96.4	8.2	-3.9	-0.2	3.1	2.1
United States	23.4	20.9	7.4	4.7	33.3	-1.3	-13.7	-0.3	-0.1	-0.8
EUROPE	**1 843.5**	**1 339.6**	**1 547.5**	**1 656.6**	**1 755.8**	**584.9**	**375.6**	**488.1**	**481.9**	**671.2**
Bulgaria	0.3	0.0	0.3	0.4	0.7	2.6	3.1	0.9	1.0	2.0
Croatia	-0.1	0.2	0.3	0.3	0.2	0.1	0.1	0.4	0.0	0.2
Cyprus[2, 3]	44.0	25.8	34.2	33.6	115.2	175.0	93.6	107.6	96.6	92.6
Malta	1.3	0.3	14.0	4.6	10.9	3.2	4.8	6.5	3.8	15.8
Romania	0.0	0.0	1.6	2.0	1.6	2.7	0.7	0.1	7.4	1.4
Russian Federation	90.7	23.1	80.6	70.9	46.8	18.1	10.7	29.5	6.0	3.7
Ukraine	14.7	20.2	30.1	51.0	50.8	-4.0	2.1	3.5	3.7	78.9
AFRICA	**0.1**	**0.2**	**-0.4**	**-1.8**	**1.0**	**2.3**	**-0.3**	**0.6**	**0.2**	**1.1**
Northern Africa	0.0	0.0	0.1	0.3	0.7	1.6	0.7	0.6	0.2	1.0
Algeria	.. c	.. c	0.0	0.0	0.1	-	-	-	-	-
Egypt	0.0	0.0	0.0	0.3	0.6	0.0	0.0	0.0	0.0	0.0
Libya	-	0.0	0.0	0.0	0.0	-	-	-	-	-
Morocco	-	-	-	0.0	0.0	1.6	0.7	0.5	0.2	0.9
Tunisia	-	-	-	-	-	0.0	0.0	0.0	0.0	0.0
Other African countries	0.1	0.2	-0.5	-2.2	0.3	0.6	-1.0	0.0	0.0	0.1
Nigeria	0.0	0.0	0.0	0.0	0.0	-	-	-	-	.. c
South Africa	0.0	0.0	0.1	-0.1	-0.2	0.0	0.0	0.0	0.0	0.0
AMERICA	**61.7**	**33.0**	**31.2**	**11.1**	**47.1**	**5.1**	**-11.5**	**1.3**	**0.1**	**-0.5**
Northern America	30.7	21.1	9.1	4.8	33.2	-1.3	-13.6	-0.3	-0.1	-0.8
Central America and Caribbean countries	30.9	11.6	21.6	5.9	13.6	5.4	1.7	1.1	0.0	0.0
Bahamas	-0.1	-0.1	0.0	-0.2	.. c	-	-	-	0.0	0.0
Bermuda	0.1	0.1	0.0	0.0	0.0	-	-	-	-	-
Cayman Islands	-1.5	13.9	9.0	7.6	7.8	-	0.0	0.0	0.0	0.0
Costa Rica	.. c	.. c	-	.. c	0.0	0.1	0.0	0.0	0.0	0.0
El Salvador	-	-	0.0	0.0	0.0	-	-	-	-	-
Guatemala	-	-	-	-	-	-	-	-	-	-
Honduras	-	-	-	-	-	-	-	-	-	-
Nicaragua	-	-	-	-	-	-	-	-	-	-
Panama	5.3	2.1	11.5	3.1	-0.2	0.0	0.0	0.0	0.0	0.0
Virgin Islands, U.S.	-	-	-	-	-	-	-	-	-	-
South America	0.1	0.2	0.5	0.3	0.3	1.0	0.4	0.5	0.1	0.3
Argentina	0.0	0.0	0.0	-	0.0	0.0	0.0	0.0	0.0	0.0
Bolivia	0.1	0.1	0.4	0.3	0.2	-	-	-	-	-
Brazil	0.0	0.0	0.0	-0.1	-0.1	1.0	0.4	0.5	0.1	0.3
Colombia	-	0.0	0.0	0.0	0.0	-	-	-	-	-
Ecuador	0.0	0.0	0.0	0.1	0.1	-	-	0.0	-	0.0
Paraguay	-	-	-	-	-	-	-	-	-	-
Peru	-	.. c	.. c	.. c	.. c	0.0	0.0	-	0.0	-
Uruguay	-	-	-	0.0	0.0	.. c	-	-	-	-
Venezuela	-	-	-	-	-	-	-	-	-	-

Table 3. Foreign direct investment income by country (cont.)

Million US dollars

	Inward					Outward				
	2014	2015	2016	2017	2018	2014	2015	2016	2017	2018
ASIA	**10.0**	**7.8**	**8.7**	**33.3**	**49.4**	**0.7**	**0.0**	**2.2**	**2.2**	**9.7**
Near and Middle East	0.9	3.2	3.9	8.4	9.0	0.0	0.5	1.6	1.2	8.2
Gulf Arabian countries	0.2	0.3	0.5	3.9	5.7	-0.1	-0.6	0.0	-1.1	0.6
Kuwait	0.0	0.0	0.0	0.0	0.0	-	-	-	-	-
Qatar	0.0	0.0	0.0	0.0	0.0	-	-	-	-	-
Saudi Arabia	0.0	0.0	0.0	0.0	0.0	-	-	-	-	-
United Arab Emirates	0.1	0.2	0.4	3.8	5.6	-0.2	-0.2	-0.3	-0.4	-0.1
Other Near and Middle East	0.7	2.9	3.4	4.4	3.2	0.1	0.1	1.6	2.3	7.6
Jordan	.. c	.. c	.. c	.. c	0.0	-	-	-	-	-
Other Asian countries	9.0	4.6	4.8	25.0	40.4	0.7	-0.5	0.6	1.0	1.5
China	0.1	0.3	0.2	0.7	3.2	0.3	0.0	-0.1	0.0	0.0
Hong Kong, China	-5.9	-5.3	1.6	0.4	-11.6	0.0	0.0	0.2	0.5	0.2
India	0.0	0.7	0.1	0.3	0.3	0.2	-0.2	0.0	0.3	0.0
Indonesia	.. c	.. c	0.0	0.0	0.0	0.0	0.0	0.0	0.0	0.0
Iran, Islamic Republic of	-	0.0	0.1	0.0	0.0	-	-	-	-	-
Malaysia	2.1	0.0	0.0	0.1	0.1	-	-	-	-	-
Philippines	-	0.1	-	0.2	0.3	0.0	0.0	0.0	0.0	0.0
Singapore	8.9	6.1	6.6	15.8	33.0	0.1	0.0	-0.1	0.0	0.1
Chinese Taipei	-	-	-0.1	-0.3	0.8	0.0	0.0	0.0	0.0	0.0
Thailand	.. c	0.0	0.1	0.1	0.2	0.2	0.2	0.2	0.2	0.2
Viet Nam	-	.. c	.. c	.. c	.. c	-	.. c	-	-	-
AUSTRALIA, OCEANIA AND POLAR REGIONS	**-0.6**	**2.5**	**2.3**	**11.9**	**13.6**	**1.9**	**0.6**	**0.2**	**0.1**	**0.2**
WORLD unallocated and confidential	**1.7**	**2.0**	**1.6**	**1.3**	**2.1**	**0.0**	**0.0**	**0.0**	**0.0**	**-**
European Union (EU28)	**1 644.5**	**1 181.1**	**1 370.1**	**1 456.4**	**1 561.9**	**568.8**	**355.8**	**409.5**	**448.4**	**562.6**
G20 countries excl. European Union	**211.6**	**145.0**	**180.3**	**226.0**	**307.2**	**35.5**	**-4.2**	**32.0**	**11.0**	**11.2**
G20 OECD countries	**120.8**	**120.8**	**99.2**	**154.1**	**257.0**	**15.9**	**-15.2**	**2.0**	**4.6**	**7.2**
G20 Non-OECD countries	**90.8**	**24.2**	**81.1**	**71.9**	**50.2**	**19.6**	**11.0**	**29.9**	**6.4**	**4.0**
MENA countries	**0.3**	**0.3**	**0.7**	**4.5**	**6.6**	**1.5**	**0.1**	**0.5**	**-0.9**	**1.6**
ASEAN countries	**11.1**	**6.2**	**6.7**	**16.2**	**33.6**	**0.3**	**0.2**	**0.1**	**0.1**	**0.3**

- Nil; c Confidential data

Note: Detailed metadata at: *http://stats.oecd.org/OECDStat_Metadata/ShowMetadata.ashx?Dataset=FDI_CTRY_IND_SUMM.*

1. Information on data for Israel: *http://oe.cd/israel-disclaimer.*
2. Note by Turkey: The information in this document with reference to "Cyprus" relates to the southern part of the Island. There is no single authority representing both Turkish and Greek Cypriot people on the Island. Turkey recognises the Turkish Republic of Northern Cyprus (TRNC). Until a lasting and equitable solution is found within the context of the United Nations, Turkey shall preserve its position concerning the "Cyprus issue".
3. Note by all the European Union Member States of the OECD and the European Union: The Republic of Cyprus is recognised by all members of the United Nations with the exception of Turkey. The information in this document relates to the area under the effective control of the Government of the Republic of Cyprus.

Source: OECD International Direct Investment Statistics (database): https://doi.org/10.1787/idi-data-en

Table 4. Foreign direct investment flows by industrial sector

Million US dollars

	Inward					Outward				
	2014	2015	2016	2017	2018	2014	2015	2016	2017	2018
All FDI activities	**683.7**	**35.5**	**1 058.2**	**1 916.8**	**1 474.4**	**42.0**	**182.1**	**486.5**	**872.6**	**48.9**
Agriculture, forestry and fishing	**12.5**	**26.0**	**28.1**	**32.5**	**26.7**	**0.9**	**-0.4**	**4.2**	**2.9**	**20.1**
Mining and quarrying	**19.9**	**-4.3**	**-3.4**	**-3.2**	**3.7**	**69.5**	**-150.0**	**29.6**	**-51.3**	**1.6**
Extraction activities	.. c	0.0	0.4	0.1	0.1	61.8	-150.1	29.6	-49.9	1.6
Manufacturing	**-128.6**	**167.1**	**215.4**	**858.6**	**245.0**	**-4.0**	**217.1**	**164.5**	**586.6**	**216.8**
of which:										
Food products, beverages and tobacco	-32.7	59.3	11.3	62.4	61.6	-4.3	46.5	8.2	-35.7	1.2
Textiles, wood and paper products; printing	65.8	22.4	95.8	27.8	126.2	-6.2	148.9	5.3	-31.8	71.7
Chemical, rubber, plastic, non-metallic mineral products	12.1	26.9	-77.6	-15.1	39.5	14.2	-7.6	2.5	-2.4	17.9
Metal and machinery products, except electrical equipment	-122.1	-13.3	-0.5	73.4	4.8	-12.5	6.9	10.2	1.5	18.2
Motor vehicles, trailers, semi-trailers, other transport equipment	-74.1	30.9	88.5	705.6	24.0	3.2	12.2	112.0	649.5	50.8
Other manufacturing	22.3	41.1	97.8	4.5	-11.0	1.6	10.3	26.2	5.5	57.0
Electricity, gas, steam and air conditioning supply	**-76.9**	**-51.6**	**-28.4**	**5.0**	**10.8**	**23.1**	**22.0**	**38.1**	**10.9**	**9.4**
Water supply; sewerage, waste management and remediation activities	**5.2**	**-11.3**	**-2.0**	**19.1**	**6.0**	**.. c**	**.. c**	**.. c**	**.. c**	**.. c**
Construction	**-5.0**	**17.6**	**45.2**	**-2.9**	**-59.6**	**24.3**	**14.8**	**-54.7**	**31.9**	**33.3**
Services	**856.2**	**-108.1**	**803.4**	**1 007.8**	**1 241.7**	**-110.2**	**78.0**	**281.2**	**266.3**	**-266.8**
Wholesale and retail trade; repair of motor vehicles and motorcycles	422.8	194.3	182.3	334.4	187.3	34.4	23.0	39.8	40.0	150.4
Transportation and storage	40.3	26.7	2.0	-3.9	157.8	8.7	43.6	11.2	-53.9	28.3
Accommodation and food service activities	11.8	1.6	9.0	2.6	-0.3	-0.7	-1.8	-1.8	25.5	11.1
Information and communication	52.9	22.3	70.5	142.9	-19.1	-470.5	3.7	-15.0	32.6	44.0
Financial and insurance activities	550.0	-427.4	427.6	344.1	1 176.6	168.4	-109.2	15.4	290.3	80.8
Activities of holding companies	102.4	5.4	82.5	-14.2	473.6	26.3	-59.7	-16.1	104.5	2.3
Real estate activities	106.0	24.9	14.9	-29.2	-20.4	100.8	109.0	93.5	72.9	-8.6
Professional, scientific and technical activities	-404.9	-34.1	-12.7	57.2	364.8	58.1	24.1	37.6	-13.3	-614.8
Administrative and support service activities	67.6	72.8	104.9	140.6	-627.8	-39.9	-56.6	56.5	-114.5	-26.3
Public administration; activities of households and of extraterritorial organisations	-	-	-	-	-	-	-	-	.. c	.. c
Education	0.1	1.1	1.7	1.5	1.9	.. c	0.1	.. c	0.9	.. c
Human health and social work activities	1.3	-1.3	-2.9	-0.1	-1.3	.. c	3.4	-0.1	-0.3	.. c
Arts, entertainment and recreation	6.5	5.4	2.2	14.9	20.7	30.5	34.0	20.6	6.1	20.5
Other services	2.0	5.5	3.7	3.0	1.6	-0.4	4.7	23.5	-19.6	49.0
Not allocated and confidential	**0.3**	**0.0**	**0.0**	**0.0**	**0.0**	**.. c**	**.. c**	**.. c**	**.. c**	**.. c**
Private real estate activities	-	-	-	-	-	-	-	-	-	-

- Nil; c Confidential data

Note: Detailed metadata at: *http://stats.oecd.org/OECDStat_Metadata/ShowMetadata.ashx?Dataset=FDI_CTRY_IND_SUMM.*

Source: *OECD International Direct Investment Statistics (database): https://doi.org/10.1787/idi-data-en*

Table 5. Foreign direct investment positions by industrial sector
At year end

Million US dollars

	Inward					Outward				
	2014	2015	2016	2017	2018	2014	2015	2016	2017	2018
All FDI activities	**20 972.1**	**18 956.5**	**19 740.8**	**23 896.4**	**24 828.0**	**6 216.6**	**6 038.9**	**6 299.3**	**7 806.7**	**7 918.8**
Agriculture, forestry and fishing	**402.7**	**381.5**	**367.2**	**428.0**	**499.9**	**13.7**	**14.2**	**21.6**	**36.8**	**52.4**
Mining and quarrying	**93.9**	**81.6**	**76.6**	**80.9**	**88.2**	**160.2**	**76.1**	**101.6**	**109.5**	**105.7**
Extraction activities	0.0	0.1	0.5	0.5	0.5	153.3	69.9	97.2	105.9	102.4
Manufacturing	**2 545.8**	**2 599.9**	**2 661.9**	**3 156.0**	**3 207.9**	**670.4**	**830.0**	**1 009.0**	**1 217.3**	**1 377.9**
of which:										
Food products, beverages and tobacco	549.9	584.7	572.9	690.9	719.6	41.0	88.1	111.9	102.3	93.1
Textiles, wood and paper products; printing	701.5	656.8	688.6	812.8	874.6	165.9	303.5	296.3	305.9	359.1
Chemical, rubber, plastic, non-metallic mineral products	290.1	381.2	287.1	331.6	351.5	128.3	103.6	110.3	111.3	119.5
Metal and machinery products, except electrical equipment	363.4	332.6	305.9	403.8	359.2	43.0	57.0	89.5	59.2	87.6
Motor vehicles, trailers, semi-trailers, other transport equipment	94.3	115.1	195.2	230.0	241.1	253.1	226.8	328.1	556.9	413.2
Other manufacturing	546.7	529.5	612.3	686.9	661.9	39.1	50.9	72.9	81.7	305.4
Electricity, gas, steam and air conditioning supply	**297.4**	**210.7**	**167.2**	**181.4**	**190.6**	**93.5**	**118.1**	**172.2**	**168.7**	**166.2**
Water supply; sewerage, waste management and remediation activities	**166.5**	**141.6**	**134.9**	**140.2**	**126.5**	**.. c**	**.. c**	**.. c**	**.. c**	**3.0**
Construction	**207.1**	**173.3**	**202.8**	**304.0**	**233.4**	**326.7**	**289.5**	**258.6**	**379.8**	**426.3**
Services	**16 735.9**	**14 858.1**	**15 523.6**	**18 953.2**	**19 654.3**	**4 345.4**	**4 237.9**	**4 231.9**	**5 247.2**	**5 108.0**
Wholesale and retail trade; repair of motor vehicles and motorcycles	2 922.2	2 596.9	2 498.6	3 004.6	2 896.5	516.2	485.2	504.1	663.5	735.6
Transportation and storage	1 101.3	991.9	927.4	987.2	1 095.2	241.7	264.5	238.9	200.9	199.1
Accommodation and food service activities	107.7	111.0	108.9	134.5	118.9	94.7	85.6	91.5	84.7	88.1
Information and communication	423.5	670.2	689.9	966.7	1 255.0	55.9	76.1	87.5	111.8	143.7
Financial and insurance activities	6 094.7	4 900.6	5 424.8	6 807.7	7 539.7	1 001.0	947.8	845.8	1 340.1	1 061.4
Activities of holding companies	1 149.1	638.6	1 058.9	1 006.2	958.2	204.0	169.5	137.3	222.1	170.4
Real estate activities	3 532.7	3 417.7	3 514.1	4 279.4	4 449.9	692.4	774.2	868.2	1 206.9	1 293.5
Professional, scientific and technical activities	1 818.6	1 430.4	1 614.2	1 782.4	1 577.2	82.6	116.2	149.9	142.0	114.0
Administrative and support service activities	659.6	666.7	674.1	891.2	618.5	1 531.7	1 326.4	1 332.8	1 383.1	1 295.5
Public administration; activities of households and of extraterritorial organisations	-	-	-	-	-	-	-	-	.. c	.. c
Education	3.8	2.0	3.5	6.2	6.0	.. c	0.3	0.3	1.8	.. c
Human health and social work activities	35.5	29.5	28.9	32.3	29.9	.. c	.. c	.. c	.. c	.. c
Arts, entertainment and recreation	24.2	25.3	25.5	43.2	56.7	.. c	153.9	78.0	94.5	113.4
Other services	12.1	15.8	13.7	17.7	10.8	1.6	5.9	30.9	13.6	59.2
Not allocated and confidential	**451.4**	**470.9**	**532.5**	**683.5**	**827.1**	**.. c**	**.. c**	**.. c**	**.. c**	**679.3**
Private real estate activities	-	-	-	-	-	-	-	-	-	-

- Nil; c Confidential data

Note: Detailed metadata at: *http://stats.oecd.org/OECDStat_Metadata/ShowMetadata.ashx?Dataset=FDI_CTRY_IND_SUMM.*

Source: OECD International Direct Investment Statistics (database): https://doi.org/10.1787/idi-data-en

Table 6. Foreign direct investment income by industrial sector

Million US dollars

	Inward					Outward				
	2014	2015	2016	2017	2018	2014	2015	2016	2017	2018
All FDI activities	**1 916.4**	**1 385.0**	**1 591.0**	**1 712.4**	**1 869.0**	**594.8**	**364.5**	**492.4**	**484.5**	**681.8**
Agriculture, forestry and fishing	**1.5**	**22.5**	**9.3**	**14.1**	**23.1**	**0.1**	**-0.3**	**0.3**	**-0.5**	**1.8**
Mining and quarrying	**7.7**	**3.3**	**3.6**	**6.9**	**8.6**	**0.8**	**.. c**	**29.7**	**1.4**	**0.2**
Extraction activities	.. c	0.0	0.5	0.1	0.1	.. c	.. c	.. c	1.2	0.2
Manufacturing	**337.7**	**255.3**	**298.2**	**313.1**	**311.2**	**54.1**	**16.3**	**49.3**	**73.9**	**126.0**
of which:										
Food products, beverages and tobacco	53.4	38.2	44.0	54.0	53.7	3.5	0.6	1.8	2.7	2.9
Textiles, wood and paper products; printing	91.6	70.4	80.5	69.2	80.8	25.9	10.4	26.8	23.3	14.7
Chemical, rubber, plastic, non-metallic mineral products	14.4	28.9	42.8	31.0	47.4	0.1	-16.9	-2.8	-3.9	-0.5
Metal and machinery products, except electrical equipment	76.2	35.1	43.2	50.8	40.2	-1.3	1.7	-1.0	1.1	5.7
Motor vehicles, trailers, semi-trailers, other transport equipment	25.4	28.4	15.2	48.0	24.1	15.0	16.7	13.9	41.4	47.7
Other manufacturing	76.8	54.4	72.4	60.2	65.0	11.0	3.8	10.5	9.2	55.6
Electricity, gas, steam and air conditioning supply	**15.2**	**8.4**	**17.6**	**14.3**	**17.9**	**2.6**	**12.0**	**10.0**	**9.7**	**16.0**
Water supply; sewerage, waste management and remediation activities	**11.5**	**8.1**	**13.7**	**15.4**	**11.3**	**.. c**	**.. c**	**.. c**	**.. c**	**.. c**
Construction	**20.5**	**-1.9**	**32.4**	**-3.8**	**5.3**	**25.1**	**31.6**	**18.5**	**16.8**	**16.1**
Services	**1 521.8**	**1 089.3**	**1 216.3**	**1 352.4**	**1 491.7**	**492.9**	**288.1**	**357.8**	**362.6**	**498.7**
Wholesale and retail trade; repair of motor vehicles and motorcycles	381.3	234.4	284.8	319.6	313.1	29.8	29.1	61.6	43.2	104.5
Transportation and storage	90.0	83.3	59.5	51.2	78.2	-28.8	-23.8	-19.8	-6.1	2.3
Accommodation and food service activities	18.7	10.8	14.3	16.4	15.8	-2.4	-1.4	-3.6	-3.0	-0.5
Information and communication	62.0	111.5	79.6	100.9	102.7	56.0	2.2	2.3	11.7	13.5
Financial and insurance activities	539.0	360.6	522.2	493.5	622.9	183.4	101.8	113.5	112.6	171.1
Activities of holding companies	53.5	35.6	79.0	31.9	90.4	4.1	2.2	29.3	4.6	9.4
Real estate activities	178.7	160.3	140.7	145.8	146.4	32.3	32.0	38.0	63.8	57.1
Professional, scientific and technical activities	150.1	74.6	47.5	117.4	105.4	10.7	13.3	13.9	18.3	14.5
Administrative and support service activities	94.1	50.3	60.0	90.4	85.9	171.3	92.7	106.0	94.8	105.6
Public administration; activities of households and of extraterritorial organisations	-	-	-	-	-	-	-	-	.. c	.. c
Education	0.1	0.3	1.1	1.4	1.6	.. c	.. c	.. c	.. c	.. c
Human health and social work activities	3.8	2.1	3.8	3.4	5.4	.. c	.. c	.. c	.. c	.. c
Arts, entertainment and recreation	0.1	-4.2	-1.7	7.7	13.6	40.7	42.5	45.5	27.4	.. c
Other services	4.1	5.2	4.5	4.6	0.6	-0.1	0.0	0.0	0.1	.. c
Not allocated and confidential	**0.5**	**-**	**0.0**	**0.0**	**0.0**	**.. c**	**.. c**	**.. c**	**.. c**	**.. c**
Private real estate activities	-	-	-	-	-	-	-	-	-	-

- Nil; c Confidential data

Note: Detailed metadata at: *http://stats.oecd.org/OECDStat_Metadata/ShowMetadata.ashx?Dataset=FDI_CTRY_IND_SUMM.*

Source: OECD International Direct Investment Statistics (database): https://doi.org/10.1787/idi-data-en

FINLAND

Table 1. Foreign direct investment flows by country

Million US dollars

	Inward					Outward				
	2014	2015	2016	2017	2018	2014	2015	2016	2017	2018
WORLD	**18 547.2**	**2 108.7**	**8 573.5**	**2 857.6**	**-2 425.4**	**1 742.1**	**-16 079.9**	**23 694.6**	**-738.4**	**10 950.1**
OECD COUNTRIES	**18 276.5**	**2 396.0**	**8 751.5**	**2 567.9**	**-4 195.7**	**3 395.3**	**-13 594.0**	**21 749.4**	**-4 135.9**	**10 652.7**
Australia	.. d	-1.1	.. d	-5.6	13.0	-27.9	179.7	-88.5	-138.7	147.5
Austria	-205.7	-259.6	112.8	-16.9	246.7	-335.7	42.2	-4.4	-65.4	148.7
Belgium	248.1	158.6	149.3	-208.5	165.2	-1 779.2	-2 326.1	778.5	-3 039.1	2 021.7
Canada	.. d	.. d	-1 133.5	-14.7	-34.2	8.0	-1 023.8	134.9	-359.6	1 025.6
Chile	-	-3.3	-	-21.4	20.1	33.2	.. d	3.3	-11.3	107.4
Czech Republic	1.3	-3.3	17.7	20.3	-10.6	47.8	-4.4	25.4	58.6	73.2
Denmark	1 524.5	-871.9	43.1	417.1	441.4	-91.5	97.6	975.3	441.9	-192.4
Estonia	50.4	-14.4	-29.9	683.1	100.3	189.7	33.3	107.3	657.2	304.5
Finland	-	-	-	-	-	-	-	-	-	-
France	-92.9	-3.3	-35.4	243.5	-62.6	727.1	213.0	13 415.9	-11 931.0	-1 050.4
Germany	-439.2	897.4	557.3	372.0	172.3	-1 183.5	790.9	-767.4	-465.6	-173.5
Greece	-	-	-	1.1	.. d	-	2.2	-3.3	55.2	-4.7
Hungary	-	-	5.5	4.5	-20.1	-127.4	-28.8	1.1	10.1	11.8
Iceland	-2.7	12.2	.. c	-	.. c	-	-5.5	-1.1	-	-1.2
Ireland	488.3	230.7	-23.2	84.5	-439.0	-1 118.5	-195.2	-1 257.3	582.8	1 811.6
Israel[1]	.. c	298.4	.. d	40.6	-54.3	139.3	.. c	3.3	25.9	23.6
Italy	33.2	55.5	174.7	21.4	152.2	-480.3	494.7	52.0	-449.8	516.9
Japan	92.9	309.5	-3 132.8	-4.5	416.6	-55.7	-15.5	-7.7	328.0	-82.6
Korea	2.7	12.2	-	7.9	34.2	-98.2	26.6	-19.9	-27.1	21.2
Latvia	151.3	-1.1	-24.3	7.9	11.8	5.3	-10.0	7.7	18.0	34.2
Lithuania	2.7	-2.2	-6.6	-3.4	-2.4	79.6	10.0	61.9	119.5	49.6
Luxembourg	5 645.5	-3 101.5	8 525.9	2 944.4	-180.6	351.6	457.0	1 306.0	-240.1	67.3
Mexico	.. d	.. d	-7.7	2.3	-1.2	26.5	-1.1	-88.5	108.2	370.6
Netherlands	5 644.2	867.4	638.1	1 940.0	-2 146.8	3 366.1	-12 035.5	4 201.0	14 293.8	-146.3
New Zealand	.. c	.. c	.. d	3.4	-3.5	-	-	8.8	-48.5	24.8
Norway	315.8	479.2	397.0	177.0	420.2	49.1	2 970.6	-70.8	-262.7	545.3
Poland	33.2	17.7	55.3	-4.5	5.9	-43.8	-82.1	140.4	102.6	-114.5
Portugal	-	-	6.6	-5.6	-1.2	18.6	7.8	3.3	-5.6	72.0
Slovak Republic	30.5	.. c	47.6	6.8	-49.6	-5.3	20.0	7.7	-15.8	-29.5
Slovenia	-	-	-	-	.. d	-9.3	-1.1	-4.4	6.8	2.4
Spain	6.6	-2.2	15.5	-30.4	47.2	96.9	13.3	82.9	237.9	-7.1
Sweden	2 251.6	2 361.6	656.9	-2 561.2	-3 486.4	2 835.3	-5 355.5	3 347.3	386.7	2 152.7
Switzerland	47.8	-46.6	606.0	-267.2	400.1	3 172.4	-2 619.0	-1 417.7	-51.9	30.7
Turkey	-1.3	24.4	-	2.3	8.3	42.5	3 161.4	105.1	81.2	-67.3
United Kingdom	1 998.1	261.8	399.2	-65.4	-769.5	-435.2	487.0	-765.2	589.6	53.1
United States	159.2	274.0	756.4	-1 205.1	408.4	-1 914.6	1 062.7	1 539.3	-5 008.5	2 904.5
EUROPE	**17 948.8**	**489.2**	**12 383.1**	**3 989.4**	**-3 609.1**	**5 754.3**	**-13 874.7**	**20 653.5**	**1 516.2**	**6 110.0**
Bulgaria	-	-	-	-	-	-	1.1	-1.1	2.3	9.4
Croatia	-	-	-	-	-	1.3	.. d	-2.2	1.1	5.9
Cyprus[2, 3]	51.7	-102.1	12.2	22.5	1 345.5	106.1	17.7	5.5	1.1	1.2
Malta	2.7	.. c	.. c	-3.4	.. d	15.9	.. c	69.7	16.9	-3.5
Romania	-	-3.3	.. d	-1.1	-2.4	-18.6	-10.0	2.2	-32.7	24.8
Russian Federation	299.9	-520.2	376.0	219.8	44.8	352.9	126.5	176.9	239.0	112.1
Ukraine	-	-	-	-	1.2	-104.8	-13.3	-36.5	10.1	3.5
AFRICA	**14.6**	**10.0**	**35.4**	**-41.7**	**-3.5**	**34.5**	**16.6**	**-6.6**	**110.5**	**35.4**
Northern Africa	-	-	-	-	-2.4	-	1.1	-2.2	34.9	22.4
Algeria	-	-	-	-	-	-	-	-	-	-
Egypt	-	-	-	-	-3.5	-	-1.1	-	27.1	16.5
Libya	-	-	-	-	-	-	-	-	-	-
Morocco	-	-	-	-	-	-	2.2	-2.2	4.5	9.4
Tunisia	-	-	-	-	-	-	-	-	3.4	-3.5
Other African countries	14.6	10.0	35.4	-41.7	-1.2	34.5	14.4	-5.5	75.5	13.0
Nigeria	-	-	-	-	-	-1.3	-1.1	-1.1	3.4	22.4
South Africa	.. d	.. d	1.1	-1.1	-2.4	23.9	-	2.2	53.0	1.2
AMERICA	**388.7**	**920.7**	**-629.2**	**-1 135.2**	**691.6**	**-3 029.1**	**-2 585.7**	**3 133.9**	**-3 520.5**	**4 300.7**
Northern America	524.1	722.1	-377.1	-1 219.7	374.1	-1 906.6	37.7	1 674.2	-5 368.1	3 930.1
Central America and Caribbean countries	-123.4	210.8	-247.7	98.1	297.4	-1 446.2	-2 567.9	1 618.9	1 720.2	375.3
Bahamas	-	-	-	.. c	24.8	.. d	.. d	-	-	-
Bermuda	.. d	.. c	.. c	.. c	.. c	.. c	.. c	1 703.0	1 614.2	.. d
Cayman Islands	.. c	.. c	.. c	.. c	-5.9	-	-	-	-	-
Costa Rica	-	-	-	-	-	-	-	-	2.3	-1.2
El Salvador	-	-	-	-	-	-	-	-	-1.1	.. d
Guatemala	-	-	-	-	-	.. d	-	-	-3.4	-1.2
Honduras	-	-	-	-	-	.. d	3.3	4.4	1.1	.. d
Nicaragua	-	-	-	-	-	-	-	-	-	-
Panama	-	-	-	-	-	-1.3	1.1	-3.3	-1.1	-1.2
Virgin Islands, U.S.	-	-	-	-	-	-	-	-	-	-
South America	-11.9	-11.1	-4.4	-13.5	20.1	325.1	-55.5	-159.2	126.3	-4.7
Argentina	.. d	.. d	-10.0	9.0	-1.2	-10.6	-2.2	-2.2	18.0	-1.2
Bolivia	-	-	-	-	-	-	-	-	1.1	-
Brazil	.. d	-8.9	-	3.4	-	-53.1	-112.0	-282.0	98.1	100.3
Colombia	-	-	-	-	-	-	-	-	19.2	72.0
Ecuador	-	-	-	-	-	.. c	.. c	-8.8	-6.8	-1.2
Paraguay	-	-	-	-	-	-	-	-	2.3	-
Peru	-	.. d	-	-1.1	-1.2	2.7	5.5	-2.2	-6.8	21.2
Uruguay	-	-	4.4	-3.4	1.2	360.9	26.6	133.8	14.7	-305.7
Venezuela	-	-	-	-	-	.. c	-	-1.1	-	-1.2

Table 1. Foreign direct investment flows by country *(cont.)*

Million US dollars

	Inward					Outward				
	2014	2015	2016	2017	2018	2014	2015	2016	2017	2018
ASIA	**216.3**	**651.1**	**-3 157.1**	**48.5**	**491.0**	**-988.5**	**184.1**	**-7.7**	**1 343.7**	**328.1**
Near and Middle East	102.2	294.0	-46.4	49.6	-16.5	192.4	232.9	146.0	136.4	30.7
Gulf Arabian countries	.. d	-4.4	-53.1	9.0	36.6	45.1	215.2	134.9	118.4	5.9
Kuwait	-	-	-	-	1.2	-	-	-	-2.3	-1.2
Qatar	-	-	-	-2.3	3.5	.. c	2.2	3.3	14.7	2.4
Saudi Arabia	-	-4.4	-54.2	21.4	30.7	-	25.5	27.6	86.8	-77.9
United Arab Emirates	1.3	-1.1	1.1	-9.0	3.5	1.3	159.7	14.4	-82.3	62.6
Other Near and Middle East	.. c	298.4	6.6	40.6	-53.1	147.3	17.7	10.0	16.9	24.8
Jordan	-	-	-	-	-	-	-	-	-	-2.4
Other Asian countries	114.1	358.3	-3 109.6	-2.3	507.5	-1 180.8	-49.9	-153.7	1 207.3	297.4
China	-10.6	21.1	8.8	-46.2	5.9	-1 379.9	-539.1	109.5	213.1	66.1
Hong Kong, China	.. c	.. c	4.4	45.1	28.3	-21.2	112.0	-130.5	10.1	-51.9
India	9.3	3.3	13.3	11.3	-10.6	4.0	88.7	-2.2	381.0	54.3
Indonesia	-	-	-	-1.1	-10.6	54.4	43.3	40.9	-15.8	115.7
Iran, Islamic Republic of	-	-	-	-	-	.. c	.. c	.. c	19.2	-38.9
Malaysia	-	-	1.1	-2.3	-1.2	-8.0	6.7	-22.1	32.7	5.9
Philippines	-	-	-	-1.1	-	-5.3	3.3	-8.8	4.5	-
Singapore	-2.7	-3.3	-11.1	-13.5	47.2	429.9	206.3	-19.9	174.7	1.2
Chinese Taipei	.. d	.. d	-1.1	1.1	-3.5	-	.. c	-36.5	7.9	-3.5
Thailand	-	-	-	-2.3	1.2	46.4	14.4	-1.1	95.8	225.4
Viet Nam	-	-	-	-	-	-131.4	-	-5.5	9.0	4.7
AUSTRALIA, OCEANIA AND POLAR REGIONS	**-22.6**	**-4.4**	**-**	**-2.3**	**9.4**	**-27.9**	**180.8**	**-77.4**	**-187.1**	**175.9**
WORLD unallocated and confidential	**1.3**	**42.2**	**-58.6**	**-1.1**	**-4.7**	**-1.3**	**-1.1**	**-1.1**	**-1.1**	**-**
European Union (EU28)	**17 418.1**	**553.5**	**11 098.1**	**3 865.4**	**-4 470.7**	**2 246.3**	**-17 492.0**	**21 899.8**	**1 335.8**	**5 637.9**
G20 countries excl. European Union	**2 373.6**	**1 768.2**	**-2 085.6**	**-429.5**	**394.2**	**-4 402.3**	**5 005.0**	**13 579.6**	**-16 198.9**	**4 029.3**
G20 OECD countries	**2 084.4**	**2 276.2**	**-2 421.8**	**-645.9**	**337.5**	**-3 393.9**	**5 375.5**	**13 508.8**	**-17 273.1**	**3 659.9**
G20 Non-OECD countries	**290.6**	**-508.0**	**336.2**	**215.3**	**57.8**	**-1 008.4**	**-369.4**	**70.8**	**1 074.3**	**369.4**
MENA countries	**1.3**	**-4.4**	**-53.1**	**9.0**	**34.2**	**51.7**	**218.5**	**134.9**	**146.5**	**27.1**
ASEAN countries	**-2.7**	**-3.3**	**-8.8**	**-19.2**	**36.6**	**387.4**	**272.9**	**-17.7**	**297.6**	**350.5**

- Nil; .. Not available; c Confidential data; d Secondary Confidentiality

Note: Detailed metadata at: *http://stats.oecd.org/OECDStat_Metadata/ShowMetadata.ashx?Dataset=FDI_CTRY_IND_SUMM.*

1. Information on data for Israel: *http://oe.cd/israel-disclaimer.*
2. Note by Turkey: The information in this document with reference to "Cyprus" relates to the southern part of the Island. There is no single authority representing both Turkish and Greek Cypriot people on the Island. Turkey recognises the Turkish Republic of Northern Cyprus (TRNC). Until a lasting and equitable solution is found within the context of the United Nations, Turkey shall preserve its position concerning the "Cyprus issue".
3. Note by all the European Union Member States of the OECD and the European Union: The Republic of Cyprus is recognised by all members of the United Nations with the exception of Turkey. The information in this document relates to the area under the effective control of the Government of the Republic of Cyprus.

Source: OECD International Direct Investment Statistics (database): https://doi.org/10.1787/idi-data-en

FINLAND

Table 2. Foreign direct investment positions by country

At year end

Million US dollars

	Inward					Outward				
	2014	2015	2016	2017	2018	2014	2015	2016	2017	2018
WORLD	**93 052.3**	**81 660.3**	**79 930.4**	**89 986.8**	**71 499.9**	**116 746.6**	**94 610.8**	**108 406.2**	**122 661.3**	**127 872.7**
OECD COUNTRIES	**87 179.7**	**77 404.5**	**68 168.0**	**76 454.8**	**60 053.8**	**110 849.8**	**92 311.4**	**103 610.2**	**113 506.8**	**118 049.0**
Australia	.. c	.. c	.. c	.. c	19.5	301.1	423.5	431.1	411.4	454.5
Austria	155.4	-66.4	-50.6	-80.4	40.1	46.1	98.0	121.2	-32.4	4.6
Belgium	117.8	100.2	170.8	155.9	131.7	6 376.5	3 240.1	3 350.9	1 650.3	3 281.4
Canada	2 164.7	2 536.7	1 085.7	1 256.9	2 545.2	2 445.2	1 413.2	1 634.9	1 129.8	1 625.8
Chile	-	-	-	-	-	155.4	144.8	148.6	217.1	263.3
Czech Republic	-	-	9.5	.. c	.. c	191.8	176.4	161.3	241.1	301.1
Denmark	6 314.5	4 782.8	5 656.2	6 622.7	3 535.6	1 144.9	1 502.5	2 076.5	3 087.1	8 264.3
Estonia	35.2	19.6	27.4	115.1	69.8	2 252.2	2 081.7	2 106.0	2 632.5	3 583.7
Finland	7 450.9	6 561.8	4 711.7	3 192.6	877.0	-	-	-	-	-
France	1 654.8	1 641.8	1 687.6	2 094.0	2 326.5	1 654.8	1 702.8	14 709.6	3 811.5	2 593.3
Germany	3 018.3	3 051.7	2 997.8	7 569.0	7 983.7	1 725.2	2 086.0	2 151.4	2 367.5	2 779.9
Greece	-	-	-	-	-	.. d	.. d	9.5	52.8	46.9
Hungary	-	-	-	-	-	63.1	31.6	36.9	33.6	30.9
Iceland	117.8	.. c	.. c	.. c	.. c	.. c	.. c	.. d	2.4	6.9
Ireland	1 115.8	184.0	1 373.5	1 737.8	2 066.6	13 213.1	12 131.7	9 971.5	12 187.6	12 812.0
Israel[1]	.. c	.. c	.. c	1 661.1	1 086.6	137.2	.. c	.. c	166.7	179.8
Italy	573.1	634.7	937.1	1 077.0	1 199.9	-162.7	292.9	332.0	-10.8	414.5
Japan	.. d	2 059.9	1 467.3	2 019.7	950.3	-37.6	-37.0	-43.2	311.8	224.4
Korea	-	-	-	.. d	49.2	114.1	130.6	109.6	195.5	158.0
Latvia	-	-	-	.. c	-	241.6	186.2	258.2	221.9	148.8
Lithuania	-	-	-	-	-	462.6	385.4	286.7	458.1	454.5
Luxembourg	2 666.2	2 732.7	2 330.6	2 807.6	2 453.6	3 321.8	1 623.3	2 687.9	2 369.9	2 325.4
Mexico	-	-	-	-	-	106.8	83.8	74.8	181.1	458.0
Netherlands	11 032.5	9 304.3	8 122.7	4 317.6	3 335.2	22 316.4	13 921.6	19 254.8	37 856.8	33 501.3
New Zealand	.. d	.. d	-	.. d	9.2	19.4	17.4	.. d	-21.6	27.5
Norway	1 520.1	1 354.4	971.9	1 314.5	1 483.9	1 370.7	2 409.4	2 452.8	2 203.2	5 512.9
Poland	.. c	.. c	43.2	.. c	.. c	1 650.0	1 387.0	1 098.3	1 593.9	1 379.7
Portugal	41.3	.. c	3.2	73.2	73.3	24.3	17.4	40.1	19.2	90.5
Slovak Republic	-	-	-	-	-	176.0	180.7	165.5	103.1	32.1
Slovenia	-	-	-	-	-	12.1	9.8	6.3	14.4	37.8
Spain	230.7	424.6	308.8	381.4	420.2	938.5	906.9	940.2	1 290.5	1 198.8
Sweden	29 840.2	33 199.8	29 237.9	27 312.3	16 032.7	36 939.0	31 497.0	29 774.4	32 383.1	26 165.6
Switzerland	788.0	1 168.2	879.1	1 156.2	985.8	4 514.0	1 436.0	-483.8	596.1	466.0
Turkey	.. d	.. d	.. d	49.2	51.5	185.8	2 798.0	1 997.5	2 432.2	1 826.2
United Kingdom	959.1	740.3	746.3	1 101.0	2 585.3	2 435.5	2 154.6	818.0	1 851.8	2 223.5
United States	15 273.4	6 792.6	5 332.6	10 308.2	9 617.6	7 196.0	8 310.3	7 051.8	1 958.5	5 175.2
EUROPE	**72 245.0**	**68 972.2**	**63 101.1**	**63 286.2**	**48 291.7**	**104 542.5**	**85 146.4**	**97 972.0**	**113 256.2**	**113 123.4**
Bulgaria	-	-	-	-	-	14.6	15.2	6.3	9.6	17.2
Croatia	-	-	-	-	-	.. d	.. d	-	2.4	8.0
Cyprus[2, 3]	.. c	13.1	.. d	6.0	33.2	-10.9	-1.1	1.1	7.2	8.0
Malta	465.0	.. c	.. c	.. c	317.2	377.6	344.0	360.5	427.0	405.3
Romania	-	-	-	-	-	109.3	84.9	83.3	58.8	57.2
Russian Federation	2 091.9	1 408.8	1 428.3	1 713.8	1 569.7	2 652.8	2 297.2	2 886.1	2 852.0	2 852.1
Ukraine	-	-	-	-	-	66.8	76.2	150.7	194.3	63.0
AFRICA	**224.6**	**178.6**	**.. d**	**115.1**	**71.0**	**131.1**	**149.2**	**160.2**	**386.2**	**415.6**
Northern Africa	-	-	-	-	-	1.2	3.3	5.3	42.0	74.4
Algeria	-	-	-	-	-	-	-	-	1.2	11.5
Egypt	-	-	-	-	-	1.2	-	-	26.4	42.4
Libya	-	-	-	-	-	-	-	-	-	-
Morocco	-	-	-	-	-	.. d	3.3	5.3	12.0	19.5
Tunisia	-	-	-	-	-	-	-	-	2.4	2.3
Other African countries	224.6	178.6	242.4	115.1	71.0	129.9	147.0	154.9	343.0	340.1
Nigeria	-	-	-	-	-	1.2	-1.1	-1.1	10.8	32.1
South Africa	224.6	178.6	242.4	22.8	19.5	60.7	72.9	69.6	203.9	185.5
AMERICA	**17 632.4**	**9 560.2**	**6 740.8**	**14 173.7**	**13 953.5**	**9 319.4**	**6 840.5**	**7 618.8**	**3 749.1**	**8 613.5**
Northern America	17 438.1	9 329.3	6 418.3	11 566.3	12 162.8	9 640.0	9 723.5	8 686.6	3 088.3	6 802.2
Central America and Caribbean countries	194.3	230.8	322.5	2 607.3	1 790.7	-1 038.1	-3 436.0	-1 961.6	-466.5	514.1
Bahamas	-	-	-	-	103.0	.. c	.. c	2.1	.. c	-
Bermuda	.. d	.. d	.. d	104.3	29.8	-1 335.5	.. c	-2 085.0	-689.6	35.5
Cayman Islands	.. c	.. c	.. c	2 503.0	1 657.9	-	-	-	-	-
Costa Rica	-	-	-	-	-	-	-	-	1.2	-1.1
El Salvador	-	-	-	-	-	-	-	-	.. d	.. d
Guatemala	-	-	-	-	-	-	-	-	-3.6	-4.6
Honduras	-	-	-	-	-	.. c	.. c	.. c	.. c	.. c
Nicaragua	-	-	-	-	-	-	-	-	-	-
Panama	-	-	-	-	-	.. d	.. d	.. d	21.6	9.2
Virgin Islands, U.S.	-	-	-	-	-	-	-	-	-	-
South America	-	-	-	-	-	716.3	552.0	894.9	1 127.4	1 298.4
Argentina	-	-	-	-	-	23.1	16.3	12.6	36.0	29.8
Bolivia	-	-	-	-	-	-	-	-	1.2	1.1
Brazil	-	-	-	-	-	526.9	348.4	455.4	681.2	863.3
Colombia	-	-	-	-	-	-	-	.. c	32.4	96.2
Ecuador	-	-	-	-	-	23.1	25.0	16.9	16.8	20.6
Paraguay	-	-	-	-	-	-	-	-	1.2	-
Peru	-	-	-	-	-	47.4	45.7	44.3	64.8	85.9
Uruguay	-	-	-	-	-	-60.7	-27.2	214.0	78.0	-64.1
Venezuela	-	-	-	-	-	-	-	.. d	1.2	-1.1

Table 2. Foreign direct investment positions by country *(cont.)*

At year end

Million US dollars

	Inward					Outward				
	2014	2015	2016	2017	2018	2014	2015	2016	2017	2018
ASIA	**2 917.5**	**2 921.1**	**9 828.2**	**12 374.7**	**9 156.2**	**2 427.0**	**2 028.3**	**2 187.2**	**4 870.5**	**5 226.7**
Near and Middle East	559.7	548.7	558.7	2 395.1	1 788.4	343.6	362.5	540.7	766.4	743.1
Gulf Arabian countries	.. d	.. d	.. d	734.0	701.9	189.4	227.5	395.3	591.3	554.2
Kuwait	-	-	-	-	-	-	-	-	-2.4	-3.4
Qatar	-	-	-	-	-	4.9	5.4	9.5	26.4	25.2
Saudi Arabia	-	-	-	-	-	138.4	149.2	187.6	353.8	264.5
United Arab Emirates	539.1	532.4	539.7	734.0	701.9	58.3	56.6	94.9	64.8	106.5
Other Near and Middle East	.. c	.. c	.. c	1 661.1	1 086.6	154.2	133.9	145.5	176.3	190.1
Jordan	-	-	-	-	-	-	-	-	-	-2.3
Other Asian countries	2 356.6	2 372.3	9 269.5	9 979.6	7 366.6	2 083.4	1 666.8	1 646.5	4 104.1	4 483.6
China	-	-	7 790.7	7 109.6	6 008.7	43.7	-328.8	-318.3	190.7	332.0
Hong Kong, China	-	-	-	.. c	24.0	-208.8	-213.4	-296.2	-279.4	-246.2
India	-	-	-	747.2	251.9	171.2	121.9	188.7	435.4	485.5
Indonesia	-	-	-	-	-	14.6	67.5	104.4	189.5	289.7
Iran, Islamic Republic of	-	-	-	-	-	-61.9	.. c	.. c	-21.6	-59.5
Malaysia	-	-	-	-	-	69.2	68.6	47.4	130.7	119.1
Philippines	-	-	-	-	-	6.1	8.7	1.1	.. d	2.3
Singapore	.. c	.. c	.. c	21.6	99.6	1 731.3	1 667.9	1 653.8	2 425.0	2 515.5
Chinese Taipei	.. c	301.6	-	-	-17.2	.. c	.. d	.. d	42.0	32.1
Thailand	-	-	-	-	-	205.2	202.5	178.1	334.6	550.7
Viet Nam	-	-	-	-	-	3.6	3.3	33.7	55.2	26.3
AUSTRALIA, OCEANIA AND POLAR REGIONS	**32.8**	**28.3**	**.. c**	**36.0**	**28.6**	**326.6**	**446.4**	**468.0**	**399.4**	**493.5**
WORLD unallocated and confidential	**-**	**-**	**.. d**	**1.2**	**-1.1**	**-**	**-**	**-**	**-**	**-**
European Union (EU28)	**65 705.9**	**63 883.5**	**58 834.2**	**58 967.4**	**43 564.2**	**95 651.7**	**76 051.2**	**90 808.5**	**104 685.8**	**102 166.2**
G20 countries excl. European Union	**28 009.3**	**19 092.0**	**23 765.2**	**35 154.7**	**35 179.8**	**19 595.6**	**22 103.4**	**32 853.4**	**19 581.4**	**23 234.5**
G20 OECD countries	**25 691.6**	**17 505.7**	**14 303.8**	**25 561.3**	**27 330.0**	**15 961.8**	**19 358.7**	**29 266.4**	**14 640.2**	**17 933.4**
G20 Non-OECD countries	**2 316.5**	**1 586.3**	**9 461.4**	**9 592.2**	**7 849.8**	**3 632.6**	**2 744.7**	**3 587.0**	**4 941.2**	**5 301.1**
MENA countries	**539.1**	**532.4**	**539.7**	**734.0**	**701.9**	**201.5**	**241.7**	**413.2**	**640.4**	**634.3**
ASEAN countries	**.. c**	**.. c**	**.. c**	**21.6**	**99.6**	**2 028.8**	**2 019.6**	**2 018.6**	**3 153.0**	**3 516.1**

- Nil; .. Not available; c Confidential data; d Secondary Confidentiality

Note: Inward FDI positions are allocated according to the ultimate investing country. Detailed metadata at: *http://stats.oecd.org/OECDStat_Metadata/ShowMetadata.ashx?Dataset=FDI_CTRY_IND_SUMM.*

1. Information on data for Israel: *http://oe.cd/israel-disclaimer.*
2. Note by Turkey: The information in this document with reference to "Cyprus" relates to the southern part of the Island. There is no single authority representing both Turkish and Greek Cypriot people on the Island. Turkey recognises the Turkish Republic of Northern Cyprus (TRNC). Until a lasting and equitable solution is found within the context of the United Nations, Turkey shall preserve its position concerning the "Cyprus issue".
3. Note by all the European Union Member States of the OECD and the European Union: The Republic of Cyprus is recognised by all members of the United Nations with the exception of Turkey. The information in this document relates to the area under the effective control of the Government of the Republic of Cyprus.

Source: OECD International Direct Investment Statistics (database): https://doi.org/10.1787/idi-data-en

FINLAND

Table 3. Foreign direct investment income by country

Million US dollars

	Inward					Outward				
	2014	2015	2016	2017	2018	2014	2015	2016	2017	2018
WORLD	**6 596.8**	**4 631.2**	**6 491.2**	**8 425.2**	**7 741.1**	**10 942.0**	**7 373.3**	**7 889.0**	**8 836.7**	**10 207.7**
OECD COUNTRIES	**6 470.7**	**4 554.6**	**6 489.0**	**8 303.5**	**7 653.7**	**9 838.1**	**6 566.8**	**7 260.9**	**7 703.8**	**9 536.2**
Australia	-	-	-	-1.1	-	29.2	23.3	-17.7	40.6	60.2
Austria	29.2	-	64.1	92.4	109.8	59.7	33.3	50.9	64.3	123.9
Belgium	41.1	38.8	42.0	29.3	-14.2	403.3	122.0	98.4	347.2	-20.1
Canada	19.9	-362.7	5.5	16.9	4.7	152.6	-32.2	85.1	102.6	98.0
Chile	-	-	-	-	-	46.4	33.3	26.5	16.9	20.1
Czech Republic	-	-	4.4	2.3	-1.2	45.1	3[illegible].1	38.7	56.4	44.8
Denmark	598.4	457.0	332.9	520.8	619.6	179.1	22[illegible].9	237.8	629.0	315.1
Estonia	-63.7	-17.7	-40.9	9.0	-20.1	265.4	255.1	193.5	294.2	322.2
Finland	-	-	-	-	-	-	-	-	-	-
France	123.4	48.8	89.6	85.7	125.1	14.6	9[illegible].0	-3.3	42.8	66.1
Germany	464.4	490.3	321.8	342.7	266.7	285.3	106.5	-261.0	-157.8	-8.3
Greece	-	-	-	-	-	1.3	3.3	4.4	11.3	5.9
Hungary	-	-	1.1	-	1.2	1.3	-1.1	2.2	13.5	15.3
Iceland	1.3	15.5	-	-	-5.9	4.0	3.3	3.3	-	2.4
Ireland	14.6	15.5	13.3	12.4	-5.9	171.2	64.3	122.7	120.6	92.1
Israel[1]	-2.7	7.8	6.6	40.6	9.4	-27.9	7.8	11.1	11.3	10.6
Italy	66.3	102.1	121.6	147.7	165.2	5.3	15.5	34.3	-50.7	72.0
Japan	130.0	350.5	180.3	162.3	182.9	-4.0	1.1	-	-31.6	16.5
Korea	-	-	-	4.5	4.7	11.9	16.6	7.7	11.3	15.3
Latvia	-	-	-	-	2.4	8.0	11.1	22.1	40.6	31.9
Lithuania	-	-	-	-	-	25.2	42.2	26.5	36.1	66.1
Luxembourg	-2 181.2	-2 313.9	779.6	710.2	257.3	128.7	186.4	105.1	102.6	67.3
Mexico	-	-	-	-	-	13.3	18.9	-68.6	12.4	47.2
Netherlands	3 382.0	1 891.3	520.8	1 485.7	1 575.6	2 096.3	1 812.5	2 552.3	1 789.0	1 455.2
New Zealand	-	-	-	-	-	-	-	1.1	-	5.9
Norway	151.3	129.8	148.2	112.7	211.3	159.2	44.4	226.7	46.2	328.1
Poland	-10.6	-8.9	2.2	3.4	3.5	149.9	119.8	125.0	202.9	172.3
Portugal	-	-	-	-	-	8.0	-	6.6	7.9	9.4
Slovak Republic	-	2.2	6.6	7.9	2.4	10.6	11.1	7.7	9.0	13.0
Slovenia	-	-	-	-	-	4.0	3.3	2.2	2.3	9.4
Spain	15.9	12.2	6.6	4.5	9.4	22.6	36.6	74.1	30.4	54.3
Sweden	3 062.2	3 232.4	3 435.8	3 948.8	3 543.0	4 646.4	3 109.3	3 079.7	3 182.3	4 764.5
Switzerland	120.7	133.1	216.7	168.0	178.2	110.1	88.7	97.3	93.6	88.5
Turkey	1.3	2.2	1.1	1.1	1.2	18.6	325.0	118.3	184.9	110.9
United Kingdom	368.8	230.7	146.0	312.3	303.3	268.0	275.1	121.6	130.8	214.8
United States	136.7	99.8	87.4	84.5	122.7	555.9	-461 5	154.8	346.1	846.2
EUROPE	**6 261.1**	**4 498.1**	**6 179.4**	**8 047.6**	**7 443.6**	**9 511.7**	**7 325 6**	**7 379.2**	**7 690.2**	**8 880.0**
Bulgaria	-	-	-	-	-	5.3	5 5	-	1.1	-7.1
Croatia	-	-	-	-	-	-	-	-	-	-
Cyprus[2, 3]	57.1	23.3	18.8	25.9	42.5	126.0	2 2	1.1	2.3	2.4
Malta	25.2	8.9	17.7	14.7	29.5	17.2	32 2	29.9	10.1	-2.4
Romania	-	-	-	-	-	-27.9	-6 7	2.2	5.6	4.7
Russian Federation	-1.3	7.8	-65.2	4.5	61.4	370.2	301 7	231.1	425.0	453.2
Ukraine	-	-	-	-	-	-88.9	-21 1	23.2	19.2	8.3
AFRICA	**-**	**-**	**-**	**1.1**	**1.2**	**27.9**	**11.1**	**4.4**	**10.1**	**4.7**
Northern Africa	-	-	-	-	-	-	-1 1	-	4.5	-4.7
Algeria	-	-	-	-	-	-	-	-	-	-1.2
Egypt	-	-	-	-	-	-	-1 1	-	2.3	-2.4
Libya	-	-	-	-	-	-	-	-	-	-
Morocco	-	-	-	-	-	-	-	-	2.3	1.2
Tunisia	-	-	-	-	-	-	-	-	-1.1	-2.4
Other African countries	-	-	-	1.1	1.2	27.9	11 1	4.4	5.6	9.4
Nigeria	-	-	-	-	-	-	-	-	-	1.2
South Africa	-	-	-	-	-	18.6	1 1	4.4	2.3	2.4
AMERICA	**197.7**	**-236.3**	**120.5**	**170.2**	**103.9**	**764.2**	**-535.8**	**-220.1**	**587.3**	**887.5**
Northern America	155.2	-261.8	91.8	101.5	128.6	708.5	-493.6	240.0	448.7	944.2
Central America and Caribbean countries	41.1	26.6	28.8	68.8	-24.8	23.9	36.6	-57.5	23.7	53.1
Bahamas	-	-	-	48.5	24.8	2.7	8.9	-	-	-
Bermuda	-	7.8	8.8	1.1	1.2	2.7	2.2	3.3	1.1	1.2
Cayman Islands	41.1	17.7	19.9	16.9	13.0	-	-	-	-	-
Costa Rica	-	-	-	-	-	-	-	-	-	-
El Salvador	-	-	-	-	-	-	-	-	-	-
Guatemala	-	-	-	-	-	-	-	-	-	-
Honduras	-	-	-	-	-	-	3.3	4.4	1.1	1.2
Nicaragua	-	-	-	-	-	-	-	-	-	-
Panama	-	-	-	-	-	-	1.1	-1.1	7.9	-
Virgin Islands, U.S.	-	-	-	-	-	-	-	-	-	-
South America	-	-	-	-	-	31.8	-78.8	-402.5	115.0	-109.8
Argentina	-	-	-	-	-	2.7	2.2	4.4	4.5	-3.5
Bolivia	-	-	-	-	-	-	-	-	-	-
Brazil	-	-	-	-	-	-39.8	-125.3	-319.6	28.2	-7.1
Colombia	-	-	-	-	-	-	-	-	1.1	-
Ecuador	-	-	-	-	-	11.9	7.8	-8.8	-1.1	-2.4
Paraguay	-	-	-	-	-	-	-	-	-	-
Peru	-	-	-	-	-	5.3	7.8	10.0	6.8	9.4
Uruguay	-	-	-	-	-	2.7	-4.4	-113.9	59.7	-127.5
Venezuela	-	-	-	-	-	2.7	-	-	-	-

Table 3. Foreign direct investment income by country *(cont.)*

Million US dollars

	Inward					Outward				
	2014	2015	2016	2017	2018	2014	2015	2016	2017	2018
ASIA	**138.0**	**368.3**	**190.2**	**207.4**	**193.6**	**609.0**	**549.1**	**743.1**	**508.4**	**369.4**
Near and Middle East	-2.7	7.8	6.6	40.6	9.4	29.2	92.1	98.4	58.6	27.1
Gulf Arabian countries	-	-	-	-	-	54.4	85.4	87.4	51.9	17.7
Kuwait	-	-	-	-	-	-	-	-	-	-
Qatar	-	-	-	-	-	11.9	2.2	6.6	6.8	-5.9
Saudi Arabia	-	-	-	-	-	8.0	43.3	52.0	28.2	23.6
United Arab Emirates	-	-	-	-	-	19.9	31.1	22.1	11.3	-1.2
Other Near and Middle East	-2.7	7.8	6.6	40.6	9.4	-23.9	5.5	12.2	7.9	9.4
Jordan	-	-	-	-	-	-	-	-	-	-2.4
Other Asian countries	140.6	360.5	184.7	166.8	184.1	578.5	458.1	643.6	449.8	342.3
China	-	-	-	-	-	42.5	37.7	127.2	-181.5	-62.6
Hong Kong, China	-	-	-	1.1	-10.6	164.5	148.6	-36.5	-37.2	-81.4
India	6.6	6.7	-	-7.9	-11.8	27.9	14.4	-15.5	56.4	23.6
Indonesia	-	-	-	-	-	2.7	-	15.5	-7.9	16.5
Iran, Islamic Republic of	-	-	-	-	-	-34.5	-1.1	-3.3	-4.5	-11.8
Malaysia	-	-	-	-	-	6.6	4.4	11.1	-14.7	-3.5
Philippines	-	-	-	-	-	2.7	2.2	1.1	2.3	-
Singapore	4.0	3.3	4.4	7.9	20.1	297.2	226.3	561.8	645.9	429.6
Chinese Taipei	-	-	-	-	-	1.3	1.1	-33.2	2.3	-
Thailand	-	-	-	-	-	50.4	2.2	3.3	6.8	16.5
Viet Nam	-	-	-	-	-	-	-	-4.4	1.1	2.4
AUSTRALIA, OCEANIA AND POLAR REGIONS	**-**	**-**	**-**	**-1.1**	**-**	**30.5**	**23.3**	**-16.6**	**41.7**	**66.1**
WORLD unallocated and confidential	**-**	**1.1**	**1.1**	**-**	**-1.2**	**-1.3**	**-**	**-1.1**	**-1.1**	**-**
European Union (EU28)	**6 009.0**	**4 226.3**	**5 881.9**	**7 754.5**	**7 015.2**	**8 922.6**	**6 586.8**	**6 677.0**	**6 923.7**	**7 885.0**
G20 countries excl. European Union	**1 316.2**	**977.3**	**886.9**	**1 153.2**	**1 226.2**	**1 784.5**	**655.6**	**268.7**	**988.6**	**1 985.1**
G20 OECD countries	**1 310.9**	**961.7**	**952.1**	**1 156.6**	**1 176.7**	**1 352.0**	**380.5**	**170.3**	**633.5**	**1 537.8**
G20 Non-OECD countries	**6.6**	**14.4**	**-65.2**	**-3.4**	**48.4**	**432.5**	**275.1**	**98.4**	**355.1**	**447.3**
MENA countries	**-**	**-**	**-**	**-**	**-**	**57.1**	**83.2**	**87.4**	**51.9**	**10.6**
ASEAN countries	**4.0**	**3.3**	**4.4**	**7.9**	**20.1**	**359.6**	**234.1**	**588.3**	**632.4**	**460.3**

- Nil

Note: Detailed metadata at: *http://stats.oecd.org/OECDStat_Metadata/ShowMetadata.ashx?Dataset=FDI_CTRY_IND_SUMM.*

1. Information on data for Israel: *http://oe.cd/israel-disclaimer.*
2. Note by Turkey: The information in this document with reference to "Cyprus" relates to the southern part of the Island. There is no single authority representing both Turkish and Greek Cypriot people on the Island. Turkey recognises the Turkish Republic of Northern Cyprus (TRNC). Until a lasting and equitable solution is found within the context of the United Nations, Turkey shall preserve its position concerning the "Cyprus issue".
3. Note by all the European Union Member States of the OECD and the European Union: The Republic of Cyprus is recognised by all members of the United Nations with the exception of Turkey. The information in this document relates to the area under the effective control of the Government of the Republic of Cyprus.

Source: OECD International Direct Investment Statistics (database): https://doi.org/10.1787/idi-data-en

FINLAND

Table 4. Foreign direct investment flows by industrial sector

Million US dollars

	Inward					Outward				
	2014	2015	2016	2017	2018	2014	2015	2016	2017	2018
All FDI activities	**18 547.2**	**2 108.7**	**8 573.5**	**2 857.6**	**-2 425.4**	**1 742.1**	**-16 079.9**	**23 694.6**	**-738.4**	**10 950.1**
Agriculture, forestry and fishing	-	-	-	-	.. c	**-1.3**	**1.1**	**-2.2**	.. c	.. c
Mining and quarrying	**-2.7**	**254.0**	**-1 302.7**	**-124.0**	.. d	**-6.6**	**-8.9**	**167.0**	.. d	.. d
Extraction activities	-2.7	254.0	-1 302.7	-124.0	93.2	-6.6	-8.9	167.0	-1.1	60.2
Manufacturing	**5 025.9**	**-1 907.9**	**2 754.6**	**2 058.4**	**-2 198.7**	**1 917.2**	**-11 460.9**	**19 691.5**	**-2 345.8**	**5 122.2**
of which:										
Food products, beverages and tobacco	33.2	7.8	-117.2	160.1	67.3	104.8	64.3	-285.3	207.4	282.1
Textiles, wood and paper products; printing	205.7	-3.3	173.6	-16.9	-1 711.3	1 586.8	392.7	426.8	184.9	-714.0
Chemical, rubber, plastic, non-metallic mineral products	740.3	1 129.2	882.5	366.4	-525.2	678.0	-74.3	846.0	205.2	507.5
Metal and machinery products, except electrical equipment	3 876.9	-3 219.1	1 291.6	1 595.1	-230.1	-483.0	-11 691.6	18 451.8	-2 672.8	4 054.1
Motor vehicles, trailers, semi-trailers, other transport equipment	75.6	-120.9	366.0	-62.0	118.0	-1.3	-23.3	2.2	16.9	79.1
Other manufacturing	95.5	299.5	157.0	15.8	81.4	33.2	-128.7	248.8	-288.6	914.7
Electricity, gas, steam and air conditioning supply	**-505.5**	.. c	**210.1**	**195.0**	**79.1**	**-1 722.2**	**-8 153.1**	**1 081.5**	**928.9**	**3 618.6**
Water supply; sewerage, waste management and remediation activities	**-4.0**	.. d	**-3.3**	**-2.3**	**8.3**	**2.7**	**-54.4**	**-136.0**	**184.9**	**17.7**
Construction	**-164.5**	**58.8**	**-297.5**	**-127.4**	**-161.7**	**-396.7**	**-203.0**	**-195.7**	**-74.4**	**616.1**
Services	**14 151.5**	**3 575.2**	**7 212.2**	**528.7**	**-263.2**	**1 378.5**	**3 771.5**	**3 088.6**	**445.3**	**1 470.6**
Wholesale and retail trade; repair of motor vehicles and motorcycles	1 313.5	-1 414.3	-380.4	1 677.4	-192.4	-4.0	65.4	227.8	-232.2	63.7
Transportation and storage	185.8	20.0	284.2	134.1	249.0	-61.0	140.9	16.6	-45.1	48.4
Accommodation and food service activities	.. d	17.7	-6.6	80.0	15.3	13.3	.. c	-	-	-
Information and communication	6 153.6	-505.8	9 870.6	-1 737.1	241.9	-1 654.5	-1 815.9	43.1	-1 281.7	-715.2
Financial and insurance activities	1 109.2	4 784.2	-2 866.3	-2 558.9	-731.7	611.6	1 235.7	2 236.0	1 614.2	705.8
Activities of holding companies	160.5	734.3	-2 822.1	86.8	-225.4	-37.2	85.4	211.2	326.9	82.6
Real estate activities	1 429.0	235.2	263.2	2 371.8	552.3	108.8	3 098.2	12.2	-57.5	572.4
Professional, scientific and technical activities	3 728.3	631.2	27.6	84.5	-31.9	1 723.5	604.5	289.7	-75.5	136.9
Administrative and support service activities	201.7	-224.1	-64.1	343.8	-256.1	473.7	12.2	136.0	-10.1	357.6
Public administration; activities of households and of extraterritorial organisations	-	-	-	-	-	161.9	412.6	127.2	545.6	280.9
Education	-	-	-	-	-	-	-	-	-	-
Human health and social work activities	.. d	37.7	87.4	127.4	-105.0	1.3	-	-12.2	2.3	-
Arts, entertainment and recreation	.. c	-6.7	-4.4	7.9	-3.5	-	.. c	-6.6	-18.0	-2.4
Other services	-	-	-	-	-	4.0	1.1	19.9	2.3	21.2
Not allocated and confidential	**-1.3**	**128.7**	-	**-1.1**	**110.9**	**-53.1**	-	-	**5.6**	**105.0**
Private real estate activities	**47.8**	-	-	**330.3**	-	**623.6**	-	-	**117.2**	-

- Nil; .. Not available; c Confidential data; d Secondary Confidentiality

Note: Detailed metadata at: *http://stats.oecd.org/OECDStat_Metadata/ShowMetadata.ashx?Dataset=FDI_CTRY_IND_SUMM.*

Source: OECD International Direct Investment Statistics (database): *https://doi.org/10.1787/idi-data-en*

Table 5. Foreign direct investment positions by industrial sector

At year end

Million US dollars

	Inward					Outward				
	2014	2015	2016	2017	2018	2014	2015	2016	2017	2018
All FDI activities	**93 052.3**	**81 660.3**	**79 930.4**	**89 986.8**	**71 499.9**	**116 746.6**	**94 610.8**	**108 406.2**	**122 661.3**	**127 872.7**
Agriculture, forestry and fishing	-	-	-	-	.. c	**149.3**	.. c	.. c	.. c	.. c
Mining and quarrying	**2 181.7**	**2 456.2**	**1 853.1**	**2 401.1**	.. d	**585.2**	.. d	.. d	.. d	.. d
Extraction activities	2 181.7	2 456.2	1 853.1	2 401.1	2 413.6	585.2	505.2	436.4	477.3	585.1
Manufacturing	**30 161.9**	**21 722.4**	**23 635.5**	**34 032.1**	**25 413.3**	**57 683.1**	**40 485.6**	**57 161.4**	**64 925.6**	**62 057.5**
of which:										
Food products, beverages and tobacco	1 396.2	1 986.9	1 256.5	1 527.9	1 566.3	3 094.7	2 878.6	1 639.1	2 079.6	2 170.8
Textiles, wood and paper products; printing	1 836.9	2 348.4	3 492.1	4 108.9	2 122.7	14 013.1	11 865.0	12 492.9	13 474.5	12 421.6
Chemical, rubber, plastic, non-metallic mineral products	8 366.4	8 019.6	7 982.5	9 425.5	8 615.8	7 358.7	6 509.5	7 279.4	8 732.3	8 449.7
Metal and machinery products, except electrical equipment	16 309.0	6 824.2	9 202.1	16 392.4	10 234.7	30 623.2	17 371.8	34 582.1	38 118.3	34 950.8
Motor vehicles, trailers, semi-trailers, other transport equipment	161.5	119.8	306.7	435.4	597.7	-23.1	-33.8	5.3	197.9	208.4
Other manufacturing	2 093.1	2 423.5	1 394.5	2 140.8	2 276.2	2 616.4	1 894.4	1 162.6	2 323.1	3 856.2
Electricity, gas, steam and air conditioning supply	**-104.4**	**3 119.2**	**3.2**	**1 283.3**	**1 227.4**	**16 869.9**	**11 488.3**	**11 238.5**	**14 346.4**	**16 289.2**
Water supply; sewerage, waste management and remediation activities	.. d	**19.6**	**16.9**	**16.8**	**26.3**	**190.6**	**450.7**	**63.2**	**239.9**	**247.3**
Construction	**483.2**	**731.6**	**659.9**	**899.5**	**841.5**	**1 120.6**	**419.2**	**322.5**	**321.4**	**997.3**
Services	**58 972.5**	**52 462.7**	**52 648.9**	**49 737.3**	**40 005.7**	**37 733.0**	**38 949.4**	**36 933.7**	**39 660.6**	**45 085.9**
Wholesale and retail trade; repair of motor vehicles and motorcycles	6 792.9	4 351.7	3 593.3	6 110.6	5 374.4	2 401.5	2 916.7	2 422.3	2 619.3	3 405.1
Transportation and storage	594.9	553.1	874.9	1 113.0	1 187.3	.. d	875.3	441.7	435.4	385.8
Accommodation and food service activities	492.9	455.1	381.6	549.3	572.5	.. c	.. c	.. c	-	-
Information and communication	7 755.7	8 859.0	14 733.8	14 074.1	12 944.8	8 139.3	10 639.1	7 353.2	6 874.6	6 000.7
Financial and insurance activities	29 087.4	28 289.6	25 317.8	14 137.7	6 648.7	7 591.8	5 464.3	21 625.4	24 288.8	28 492.1
Activities of holding companies	.. d	1 463.3	.. d	199.1	147.7	688.4	491.0	1 065.7	1 379.2	1 303.0
Real estate activities	4 974.2	4 264.6	3 540.6	8 728.7	8 202.4	524.5	1 780.1	1 414.6	1 212.5	1 777.0
Professional, scientific and technical activities	6 614.4	3 488.3	1 848.8	2 356.7	2 040.3	15 742.0	14 622.8	1 196.4	1 279.7	1 130.1
Administrative and support service activities	2 315.3	1 892.2	1 473.6	2 122.8	1 859.4	2 021.5	1 725.6	1 408.2	1 674.3	2 238.4
Public administration; activities of households and of extraterritorial organisations	-	-	-	-	-	59.5	458.4	626.1	1 147.8	1 353.3
Education	-	-	-	-	-	-	-	-	-	-
Human health and social work activities	295.0	273.3	874.9	526.5	1 161.0	.. c	.. c	325.7	-	158.0
Arts, entertainment and recreation	48.6	35.9	9.5	16.8	14.9	-	.. d	.. d	34.8	24.0
Other services	-	-	-	-	-	68.0	64.2	82.2	92.3	121.4
Not allocated and confidential	**76.5**	-	**1.1**	-	.. c	**-4.9**	**647.8**	**586.1**	**652.4**	.. c
Private real estate activities	**1 280.9**	**1 148.6**	**1 112.0**	**1 616.7**	**1 543.4**	**2 419.7**	**2 169.8**	**2 100.8**	**2 515.0**	**2 401.0**

- Nil; .. Not available; c Confidential data; d Secondary Confidentiality

Note: Detailed metadata at: *http://stats.oecd.org/OECDStat_Metadata/ShowMetadata.ashx?Dataset=FDI_CTRY_IND_SUMM.*

Source: OECD International Direct Investment Statistics (database): https://doi.org/10.1787/idi-data-en

FINLAND

Table 6. Foreign direct investment income by industrial sector

Million US dollars

	Inward					Outward				
	2014	2015	2016	2017	2018	2014	2015	2016	2017	2018
All FDI activities	**6 596.8**	**4 631.2**	**6 491.2**	**8 425.2**	**7 741.1**	**10 942.0**	**7 373.3**	**7 889.0**	**8 836.7**	**10 207.7**
Agriculture, forestry and fishing	-	-	-	-	1.2	**-1.3**	1.1	**-2.2**	1.1	**36.6**
Mining and quarrying	**11.9**	**-392.7**	**-63.0**	**36.1**	**116.8**	**-8.0**	**22.2**	**21.0**	**14.7**	**33.0**
Extraction activities	11.9	-392.7	-63.0	36.1	116.8	-8.0	22.2	21.0	14.7	33.0
Manufacturing	**4 016.2**	**931.8**	**1 819.1**	**3 048.1**	**3 089.8**	**4 674.3**	**2 387.1**	**2 466.0**	**4 566.6**	**4 619.4**
of which:										
Food products, beverages and tobacco	180.4	181.9	125.0	217.6	310.4	108.8	246.3	128.3	175.9	131.0
Textiles, wood and paper products; printing	118.1	147.5	188.0	267.2	231.3	1 021.6	610.1	1 200.9	1 400.1	1 069.3
Chemical, rubber, plastic, non-metallic mineral products	1 675.7	1 247.9	1 033.9	1 057.4	1 301.8	823.9	686.6	1 153.4	820.7	1 022.1
Metal and machinery products, except electrical equipment	1 574.9	-1 382.1	204.6	1 203.9	738.8	2 535.5	764.3	-269.8	2 179.0	2 201.1
Motor vehicles, trailers, semi-trailers, other transport equipment	50.4	-21.1	-85.1	7.9	55.5	-1.3	-1.1	-1.1	2.3	5.9
Other manufacturing	417.9	757.6	352.8	293.1	453.2	185.8	79.9	254.3	-11.3	190.0
Electricity, gas, steam and air conditioning supply	**-50.4**	**-115.4**	**-55.3**	**293.1**	**134.5**	**1 069.4**	**658.9**	**374.9**	**560.3**	**794.3**
Water supply; sewerage, waste management and remediation activities	**-4.0**	**-3.3**	**-5.5**	**2.3**	**1.2**	**1.3**	**-35.5**	**10.0**	**2.3**	**1.2**
Construction	**45.1**	**126.5**	**-18.8**	**47.3**	**69.6**	**659.4**	**686.6**	**559.5**	**280.7**	**279.7**
Services	**2 576.6**	**4 083.2**	**4 813.7**	**4 998.3**	**4 327.9**	**4 541.6**	**3 651.7**	**4 460.9**	**3 411.1**	**4 442.3**
Wholesale and retail trade; repair of motor vehicles and motorcycles	760.2	454.8	613.7	617.7	636.1	218.9	203.0	310.7	227.7	166.4
Transportation and storage	-23.9	43.3	82.9	121.7	139.3	120.7	10.0	49.8	-9.0	8.3
Accommodation and food service activities	23.9	13.3	32.1	39.5	17.7	13.3	12.2	-	-	-
Information and communication	-1 563.0	325.0	860.3	1 098.0	922.9	636.9	612.3	1 387.8	392.3	311.6
Financial and insurance activities	2 826.1	2 961.7	2 855.2	2 360.5	1 671.2	1 284.3	768.7	2 376.4	2 456.3	3 539.5
Activities of holding companies	217.6	656.7	504.3	25.9	-56.7	103.5	51.0	49.8	80.0	190.0
Real estate activities	95.5	138.7	170.3	387.8	504.0	29.2	76.5	103.9	90.2	31.9
Professional, scientific and technical activities	229.5	74.3	66.4	116.1	164.1	2 104.3	1 848.0	96.2	18.0	116.8
Administrative and support service activities	232.2	116.5	112.8	162.3	253.7	112.8	89.9	100.6	195.0	236.0
Public administration; activities of households and of extraterritorial organisations	-	-	-	-	-	13.3	22.2	35.4	36.1	26.0
Education	-	-	-	-	-	-	-	-	-	-
Human health and social work activities	-6.6	-44.4	26.5	100.3	24.8	-	-	-	-	-
Arts, entertainment and recreation	2.7	1.1	-5.5	-5.6	-7.1	-	-	-3.3	-7.9	-4.7
Other services	-	-	-	-	-	9.3	6.7	4.4	11.3	11.8
Not allocated and confidential	**1.3**	**1.1**	**1.1**	-	-	**5.3**	**1.1**	**-1.1**	-	**1.2**
Private real estate activities	-	-	-	-	-	-	-	-	-	-

- Nil

Note: Detailed metadata at: *http://stats.oecd.org/OECDStat_Metadata/ShowMetadata.ashx?Dataset=FDI_CTRY_IND_SUMM.*

Source: *OECD International Direct Investment Statistics (database): https://doi.org/10.1787/idi-data-en*

FRANCE

Table 1. Foreign direct investment flows by country

Million US dollars

	Inward					Outward				
	2014	2015	2016	2017	2018	2014	2015	2016	2017	2018
WORLD	**2 669.5**	**45 354.4**	**23 054.3**	**29 811.7**	**37 285.5**	**49 785.1**	**53 205.8**	**64 784.9**	**41 270.4**	**102 407.6**
OECD COUNTRIES	**6 526.5**	**38 489.2**	**22 293.5**	**28 124.2**	**37 285.5**	**42 336.5**	**44 911.8**	**55 650.8**	**41 552.2**	**102 407.6**
Australia	244.1	174.2	497.6	-547.9	-256.1	1 342.7	78.8	-742.0	1 675.1	6 759.1
Austria	-319.8	-393.8	142.7	81.2	-1 371.4	25.2	1 134.8	181.4	335.9	1 267.6
Belgium	-594.4	4 128.7	-5 049.2	417.1	-500.4	-3 922.0	-1 919.0	8 497.2	-13 043.6	2 641.3
Canada	39.8	-556.9	320.7	1 364.0	1 661.7	1 068.1	230.7	369.3	1 830.7	-2 191.7
Chile	350.3	120.9	74.1	11.3	..	258.7	402.7	-94.0	1 749.5	1 131.8
Czech Republic	-582.5	-221.9	102.8	-120.6	-67.3	342.3	188.6	421.3	417.1	575.9
Denmark	-711.2	429.3	320.7	196.1	109.8	183.1	1 453.1	424.6	901.8	4 376.3
Estonia	..	..	..	..	..	..	..	..	..	..
Finland	339.7	-176.4	13 714.5	-11 200.5	-2 379.3	-208.3	248.5	34.3	1 201.7	-429.6
France	-	-	-	-	-	-	-	-	-	-
Germany	-2 433.3	5 961.2	5 461.7	10 157.8	2 733.4	-585.1	3 456.5	10 055.3	7 722.9	-1 007.9
Greece	..	..	-70.8	240.1	-267.9	-63.7	201.9	77.4	-197.3	-115.7
Hungary	-10.6	18.9	10.0	15.8	204.2	-260.1	105.4	-209.0	-280.7	587.7
Iceland	-33.2	..	..	..	..	..	..	..	..	..
Ireland	6 724.2	-1 812.5	-750.9	1 198.3	-1 906.1	2 560.7	2 940.7	-2 332.2	2 831.7	2 343.9
Israel[1]	-87.6	-7.8	59.7	49.6	28.3	130.0	179.7	243.3	-169.1	118.0
Italy	5.3	1 368.8	3 314.2	465.6	1 562.6	2 818.1	7 401.0	13 788.6	2 631.0	31 930.8
Japan	514.8	129.8	1 006.3	1 111.5	577.1	2 018.0	37.7	1 712.9	2 937.7	1 971.0
Korea	65.0	309.5	237.8	77.8	382.4	143.3	241.8	-531.9	648.2	764.8
Latvia	-	-1.1	..	..	..	..	39.9	..	..	..
Lithuania	..	..	..	..	..	54.4	-1 048.3	-32.1	32.7	38.9
Luxembourg	7 195.2	2 434.8	13 760.9	-3 415.6	28 995.6	-3 449.6	3 783.7	-3 212.4	12 751.7	-1 979.2
Mexico	78.3	-313.9	161.5	-74.4	-212.4	-54.4	-577.9	127.2	1 544.4	308.0
Netherlands	-2 790.2	-6 681.1	-4 129.2	2 978.2	6 565.6	18 013.8	3 947.9	4 009.7	6 490.8	26 203.2
New Zealand	..	..	78.5	-7.9	-62.6	25.2	92.1	36.5	-12.4	33.0
Norway	207.0	292.8	76.3	240.1	627.9	1 444.9	-7.8	-412.5	-1 892.7	-1 648.8
Poland	-79.6	-754.3	-806.1	968.3	233.7	2 118.9	1 432.1	1 184.3	-480.2	1 262.8
Portugal	-6.6	323.9	123.9	217.6	-148.7	818.6	949.5	-614.8	162.3	48.4
Slovak Republic	..	..	-18.8	..	..	772.2	-76.5	131.6	65.4	410.7
Slovenia	..	..	..	..	..	13.3	-51.0	34.3	116.1	43.7
Spain	-6 242.5	2 126.5	-241.1	3 156.4	972.5	-870.4	3 673.9	4 780.5	-195.0	1 553.2
Sweden	-424.6	1 180.3	802.8	20.3	-125.1	-338.3	-127.6	834.9	3 628.7	107.4
Switzerland	-5 942.7	22 381.6	2 109.9	189.4	4 054.1	-5 202.3	-513.6	3 236.8	1 588.3	7 599.4
Turkey	..	217.4	-105.1	-95.8	-4.7	224.2	603.4	-474.4	651.6	546.4
United Kingdom	9 652.4	14 600.1	-972.0	20 597.5	5 923.5	11 582.9	7 351.1	-1 291.6	11 745.0	13 286.9
United States	1 367.9	-6 761.0	-7 935.4	-211.9	-9 835.9	11 309.5	8 012.2	15 409.7	-5 824.6	-9 675.4
EUROPE	**4 248.4**	**46 619.0**	**27 703.2**	**25 768.2**	**45 783.1**	**25 993.1**	**36 703.3**	**43 957.8**	**38 851.3**	**91 104.7**
Bulgaria	..	..	..	..	..	-244.1	67.7	207.9	-68.8	69.6
Croatia	..	..	..	..	..	-21.2	42.2	28.8	-475.7	-1.2
Cyprus[2, 3]	-314.4	644.5	-149.3	232.2	147.5	-8.0	1 296.7	653.5	-45.1	492.2
Malta	-118.1	495.8	179.1	-653.8	454.4	-656.8	45.5	71.9	24.8	74.4
Romania	..	..	..	..	..	82.3	234.1	89.6	230.0	554.7
Russian Federation	453.8	139.8	-94.0	352.8	-118.0	1 176.9	890.7	3 626.0	1 650.3	417.8
Ukraine	..	..	..	..	..	-303.8	-2.2	170.3	60.9	92.1
AFRICA	**342.3**	**-249.6**	**-631.4**	**276.2**	**-1 212.1**	**-283.9**	**7 671.7**	**303.0**	**-2 344.7**	**-4 827.1**
Northern Africa	396.7	1.1	-371.6	-34.9	47.2	-4 172.7	904.0	820.5	125.1	-808.5
Algeria	139.3	125.3	-328.4	44.0	-18.9	-46.4	245.1	70.8	205.2	334.0
Egypt	82.3	-14.4	-8.8	-77.8	-132.2	510.8	-239.6	160.3	-664.0	-704.6
Libya	14.6	1.1	8.8	6.8	5.9	88.9	-128.7	14.4	..	-348.2
Morocco	179.1	-51.0	-43.1	-25.9	147.5	-4 922.4	834.2	505.4	786.8	-102.7
Tunisia	-18.6	..	1.1	18.0	46.0	195.0	193.0	69.7	144.3	14.2
Other African countries	-54.4	-250.7	-259.9	311.1	-1 260.5	3 888.8	6 767.6	-517.5	-2 469.8	-4 018.6
Nigeria	..	..	..	..	..	898.2	-278.4	235.5	-307.7	-295.1
South Africa	..	..	150.4	-219.8	16.5	1 150.3	754.3	181.4	91.3	-388.3
AMERICA	**1 241.9**	**-7 181.4**	**-8 503.8**	**1 144.2**	**-7 938.2**	**14 252.4**	**3 317.8**	**22 464.9**	**4 417.8**	**8 475.2**
Northern America	1 407.7	-7 317.8	-7 614.7	1 152.1	-8 174.2	12 377.6	8 242.9	15 779.1	-3 993.9	-11 867.1
Central America and Caribbean countries	-439.2	-118.7	-940.0	-42.8	494.5	-4 535.0	149.8	3 250.0	2 522.8	17 021.1
Bahamas	..	..	..	..	..	-1 233.9	631.2	-53.1	..	..
Bermuda	..	..	-140.4	..	..	-2 705.3	-110.9	1 093.7	472.3	16 682.4
Cayman Islands	103.5	-112.0	-38.7	16.9	122.7	..	43.3	2 190.6	-36.1	-70.8
Costa Rica	..	..	..	..	..	..	..	..	..	..
El Salvador	..	..	..	..	..	..	..	..	..	..
Guatemala	..	..	..	..	..	..	..	..	..	..
Honduras	..	..	..	..	..	..	..	..	..	..
Nicaragua	..	..	..	..	..	..	..	..	..	..
Panama	98.2	23.3	-	29.3	-11.8	524.1	221.9	-282.0	166.8	123.9
Virgin Islands, U.S.	-	-	-	-	-	..	..	..	..	..
South America	..	254.0	50.9	34.9	-258.5	6 409.7	-5 074.9	3 435.8	5 888.9	3 321.1
Argentina	..	..	..	..	..	825.3	431.5	-66.4	452.0	-241.9
Bolivia	..	..	..	..	..	58.4	-401.6	-23.2	421.6	-50.7
Brazil	25.2	122.0	-31.0	143.2	136.9	5 231.5	-5 851.4	2 239.3	2 641.2	1 173.1
Colombia	..	..	..	..	..	-31.8	203.0	68.6	-19.2	227.8
Ecuador	-13.3	..	-	..	..	..	..	..	..	..
Paraguay	..	..	..	..	..	..	..	..	..	..
Peru	..	..	..	..	..	15.9	17.7	1 427.6	491.5	48.4
Uruguay	..	..	..	..	..	33.2	-24.4	5.5	-107.1	-4.7
Venezuela	..	..	..	..	..	8.0	240.7	-96.2	275.1	917.0

Table 1. Foreign direct investment flows by country *(cont.)*

Million US dollars

	Inward					Outward				
	2014	2015	2016	2017	2018	2014	2015	2016	2017	2018
ASIA	**-4 535.0**	**4 846.4**	**3 891.4**	**3 163.1**	**787.2**	**8 492.8**	**4 939.5**	**-1 118.0**	**-3 169.9**	**1 216.8**
Near and Middle East	-5 890.9	2 776.5	612.6	1 720.2	-383.6	1 411.7	-1 468.7	1 089.2	-650.4	1 709.0
Gulf Arabian countries	-6 095.3	1 697.2	801.7	569.3	-695.1	1 276.4	-2 067.7	884.7	-617.7	898.1
Kuwait	1.3	..	..	..	188.8	..	..	5.5	..	98.0
Qatar	-152.6	787.6	1 425.4	862.4	-770.7	77.0	-397.1	353.9	-1 743.9	1 235.7
Saudi Arabia	-107.5	237.4	38.7	28.2	-3.5	1 491.3	969.5	278.7	-436.3	505.1
United Arab Emirates	-5 814.0	738.8	-557.3	-304.4	-90.9	-481.6	-536.9	257.7	1 539.8	-396.6
Other Near and Middle East	204.3	1 079.3	-189.1	1 150.9	311.6	136.7	599.0	204.6	-32.7	812.0
Jordan	..	..	..	..	..	2.7	25.5	-7.7	-5.6	315.1
Other Asian countries	1 356.0	2 069.9	3 277.7	1 442.9	1 170.8	7 081.1	6 408.2	-2 207.2	-2 520.6	-492.2
China	-70.3	620.1	226.7	157.8	179.4	1 934.5	826.4	593.8	-153.3	-213.6
Hong Kong, China	1 312.2	17.7	1 612.3	951.4	330.5	189.7	1 802.6	-2 101.1	-523.1	193.6
India	..	91.0	-86.3	-32.7	-20.1	1 061.4	1 096.0	-246.6	421.6	225.4
Indonesia	..	..	173.6	382.1	67.3	298.5	-518.0	-632.5	-1 135.2	-1 079.9
Iran, Islamic Republic of	525.4	-480.3	-54.2	177.0	-203.0	-53.1	-136.4	-73.0	109.3	-88.5
Malaysia	..	-	-1.1	232.2	22.4	256.1	-164.2	-39.8	-91.3	282.1
Philippines	..	1 251.2	-8.8	..	..	-388.7	-49.9	-869.2	32.7	-87.3
Singapore	-1 222.0	339.4	94.0	-254.8	-92.1	1 373.2	611.2	178.0	-2 241.0	-807.3
Chinese Taipei	47.8	-4.4	39.8	20.3	-4.7	88.9	62.1	36.5	83.4	134.5
Thailand	376.8	..	42.0	-69.9	-20.1	514.8	-1 192.5	200.2	-559.1	-776.6
Viet Nam	-153.9	..	..	..	-8.3	49.1	-127.6	-75.2	130.8	-11.8
AUSTRALIA, OCEANIA AND POLAR REGIONS	**270.7**	**156.4**	**597.1**	**-542.2**	**-131.0**	**1 340.1**	**567.9**	**-800.6**	**3 517.1**	**6 438.1**
WORLD unallocated and confidential	**1 101.2**	**1 163.6**	**-2.2**	**2.3**	**-3.5**	**-9.3**	**5.5**	**-22.1**	**-1.1**	**-**
European Union (EU28)	**9 393.7**	**23 719.4**	**25 597.7**	**25 426.7**	**41 075.2**	**28 786.0**	**36 809.8**	**37 707.6**	**36 523.5**	**84 445.9**
G20 countries excl. European Union	**9 502.5**	**16 402.7**	**2 365.4**	**33 680.5**	**2 786.5**	**43 038.3**	**25 454.2**	**44 397.9**	**29 094.8**	**43 089.8**
G20 OECD countries	**9 404.3**	**15 128.1**	**1 986.1**	**32 843.0**	**2 531.6**	**29 867.3**	**26 835.3**	**38 424.2**	**25 563.1**	**42 692.1**
G20 Non-OECD countries	**98.2**	**1 274.5**	**379.3**	**836.4**	**256.1**	**13 171.0**	**-1 379.9**	**5 973.7**	**3 531.7**	**397.7**
MENA countries	**-5 419.9**	**2 766.5**	**165.9**	**1 601.8**	**-323.4**	**-2 831.4**	**-1 110.4**	**1 747.2**	**-379.9**	**591.3**
ASEAN countries	**-996.4**	**1 386.6**	**291.9**	**-1 026.9**	**-63.7**	**2 195.8**	**604.5**	**-1 198.7**	**-5 840.4**	**-2 888.0**

- Nil; .. Not available

Note: Detailed metadata at: *http://stats.oecd.org/OECDStat_Metadata/ShowMetadata.ashx?Dataset=FDI_CTRY_IND_SUMM.*

1. Information on data for Israel: *http://oe.cd/israel-disclaimer.*
2. Note by Turkey: The information in this document with reference to "Cyprus" relates to the southern part of the Island. There is no single authority representing both Turkish and Greek Cypriot people on the Island. Turkey recognises the Turkish Republic of Northern Cyprus (TRNC). Until a lasting and equitable solution is found within the context of the United Nations, Turkey shall preserve its position concerning the "Cyprus issue".
3. Note by all the European Union Member States of the OECD and the European Union: The Republic of Cyprus is recognised by all members of the United Nations with the exception of Turkey. The information in this document relates to the area under the effective control of the Government of the Republic of Cyprus.

Source: OECD International Direct Investment Statistics (database): https://doi.org/10.1787/idi-data-en

Table 2. Foreign direct investment positions by country

At year end

Million US dollars

	Inward					Outward				
	2014	2015	2016	2017	2018	2014	2015	2016	2017	2018
WORLD	**700 064.6**	**687 394.7**	**694 881.4**	**818 545.2**	**824 987.4**	**1 294 220.9**	**1 268 227.5**	**1 284 859.3**	**1 466 602.3**	**1 507 861.2**
OECD COUNTRIES	**660 183.9**	**635 455.6**	**635 961.8**	**744 415.9**	..	**1 080 173.8**	**1 061 566.7**	**1 069 930.4**	**1 236 098.6**	**1 507 861.2**
Australia	3 383.7	4 105.6	3 484.8	2 909.6	..	14 086.0	12 640.2	12 319.0	12 377.1	18 452.0
Austria	1 583.2	1 437.1	1 744.5	1 681.5	..	2 132.0	2 783.9	2 853.4	3 499.6	4 531.7
Belgium	45 724.2	40 031.6	46 226.4	46 279.7	..	185 139.3	166 371.3	165 440.1	178 348.5	174 665.7
Canada	6 519.7	6 797.0	7 132.9	12 770.4	..	11 107.8	9 781.2	12 018.6	12 368.7	9 175.6
Chile	373.9	474.7	765.3	901.9	..	1 466.6	1 820.4	1 767.7	3 810.3	4 790.5
Czech Republic	129.9	..	183.4	218.3	..	10 221.5	9 421.9	8 511.6	10 001.2	9 918.7
Denmark	5 385.7	5 315.2	4 775.0	5 676.4	..	4 718.0	7 407.7	7 817.0	9 985.6	13 793.2
Estonia	..	..	..	..	..	..	..	..	..	..
Finland	1 834.5	1 651.6	20 905.5	12 367.5	..	897.2	1 192.2	1 092.0	2 573.8	1 994.5
France	32 915.5	46 694.6	42 307.4	58 325.7	..	-	-	-	-	-
Germany	82 772.5	80 557.4	72 064.9	87 776.4	..	61 707.8	61 591.7	62 205.1	83 809.1	81 423.2
Greece	163.9	..	246.7	295.0	..	1 504.3	1 479.6	1 610.6	1 727.0	1 540.0
Hungary	..	..	120.2	319.0	..	3 545.2	3 411.0	3 210.7	3 716.7	3 991.3
Iceland	251.3	192.7	154.9	173.9	..	..	..	..	..	..
Ireland	6 385.0	6 720.7	5 303.0	5 942.7	..	22 997.5	23 325.0	19 622.6	24 822.5	25 730.5
Israel[1]	739.4	680.5	953.9	1 157.4	..	2 929.6	2 995.1	3 138.0	3 262.2	3 076.5
Italy	21 329.3	22 089.3	24 305.9	30 486.9	..	55 756.3	57 632.0	65 369.5	78 496.0	104 191.7
Japan	19 860.2	19 314.1	16 865.2	19 904.1	..	25 929.5	28 202.5	27 856.0	29 884.9	28 801.2
Korea	919.1	1 129.0	331.0	446.2	..	4 594.2	4 689.2	4 202.6	5 088.8	5 618.3
Latvia	148.1	129.6	..	..	..	..	236.3	..	..	..
Lithuania	..	..	..	..	..	299.9	206.9	157.1	262.7	274.8
Luxembourg	54 289.7	24 682.6	33 639.7	40 155.9	..	52 588.7	50 607.5	46 858.9	66 035.0	60 088.2
Mexico	1 302.7	1 082.2	1 424.1	1 319.3	..	3 303.6	2 646.7	2 569.8	5 243.5	5 587.4
Netherlands	55 928.7	50 586.8	46 167.4	41 554.3	..	139 333.8	130 150.2	134 564.1	158 010.3	177 364.3
New Zealand	140.8	123.0	129.7	183.5	..	376.4	408.3	428.0	362.2	376.7
Norway	2 911.4	3 048.4	2 187.2	3 698.7	..	8 504.8	7 242.2	6 882.0	5 485.7	3 529.9
Poland	..	-1 220.5	-1 538.9	-405.4	..	16 957.3	16 775.2	17 193.0	19 216.8	19 155.0
Portugal	994.3	1 035.4	1 704.4	2 055.6	..	4 237.2	4 280.9	3 742.0	4 358.4	4 256.9
Slovak Republic	..	..	..	..	..	471.1	341.9	450.1	575.7	944.6
Slovenia	..	..	..	..	..	661.7	518.2	635.6	633.2	648.0
Spain	11 098.1	12 675.0	15 922.8	21 661.1	..	47 130.1	45 978.2	49 303.3	59 353.6	57 166.2
Sweden	6 910.7	7 143.2	6 407.7	8 998.6	..	3 733.4	4 666.3	5 598.2	8 895.4	8 468.1
Switzerland	65 097.6	82 888.4	85 522.3	96 995.7	..	44 392.4	42 635.8	44 511.4	50 706.4	57 364.3
Turkey	195.5	277.6	269.8	256.7	..	4 720.4	4 228.6	3 788.3	4 672.6	3 940.9
United Kingdom	78 614.2	84 679.4	74 732.8	99 040.5	..	133 347.0	129 384.9	116 238.0	142 089.2	148 098.2
United States	152 084.2	130 959.2	121 413.5	141 153.8	..	211 671.0	226 904.7	238 007.8	246 521.9	237 188.0
EUROPE	**481 242.5**	**477 213.9**	**486 007.2**	**566 303.7**	..	**827 627.7**	**792 676.1**	**796 403.5**	**948 805.5**	**997 046.0**
Bulgaria	..	..	..	..	..	769.7	733.8	994.0	1 083.0	1 108.3
Croatia	..	..	..	..	..	813.4	770.8	748.4	209.9	208.4
Cyprus[2, 3]	879.0	859.0	319.4	301.0	..	981.0	1 494.8	1 408.2	1 468.0	1 876.6
Malta	610.7	272.2	967.6	380.2	..	715.1	666.3	657.7	963.1	1 024.7
Romania	..	..	183.4	227.9	..	4 705.9	4 699.0	4 519.9	5 178.7	5 358.4
Russian Federation	2 248.5	2 256.9	1 073.0	995.4	..	10 442.5	10 071.9	17 820.2	19 327.2	20 883.9
Ukraine	..	..	..	..	..	494.1	426.8	570.3	801.2	862.1
AFRICA	**5 391.8**	**4 695.7**	**9 495.1**	**10 755.6**	..	**60 008.1**	**62 084.9**	**60 422.7**	**61 775.0**	**53 023.8**
Northern Africa	1 807.8	1 518.8	3 072.6	3 629.2	..	20 537.7	18 289.6	16 715.5	18 749.1	17 271.6
Algeria	729.7	830.7	496.5	574.5	..	2 637.0	2 449.6	2 855.5	2 784.8	3 041.0
Egypt	201.5	..	183.4	251.9	..	4 107.3	3 650.5	1 988.0	1 593.9	890.8
Libya	160.3	..	..	..	..	902.1	751.2	421.6	..	-309.1
Morocco	585.2	476.9	1 853.1	2 145.6	..	11 094.4	10 496.5	10 591.3	13 310.1	12 759.3
Tunisia	129.9	..	461.7	562.5	..	1 796.9	941.8	857.0	1 014.6	889.6
Other African countries	3 580.4	3 173.7	6 422.5	7 126.4	..	39 471.6	43 795.3	43 707.2	43 025.9	35 752.2
Nigeria	..	..	..	..	..	10 338.1	9 927.1	11 545.3	11 141.8	10 744.2
South Africa	2 552.0	2 259.1	2 579.3	2 345.9	..	2 134.4	2 303.8	2 588.8	2 603.7	2 049.5
AMERICA	**167 196.1**	**143 683.2**	**135 828.0**	**162 061.6**	..	**272 718.4**	**275 976.0**	**296 572.2**	**317 926.4**	**317 988.3**
Northern America	158 608.8	137 760.5	128 544.3	153 924.2	..	222 778.9	236 685.9	250 026.4	258 890.6	246 363.6
Central America and Caribbean countries	7 948.7	5 320.6	5 524.4	5 892.3	..	9 879.1	9 417.5	11 229.1	15 197.9	33 319.2
Bahamas	..	..	..	..	..	-389.7	488.8	440.6	..	..
Bermuda	4 036.9	2 307.0	2 346.4	3 000.7	..	4 123.1	2 812.2	3 757.8	5 513.3	23 091.4
Cayman Islands	866.9	655.4	591.3	187.1	..	..	581.4	1 940.6	1 731.8	1 668.2
Costa Rica	..	..	..	..	..	..	..	..	..	..
El Salvador	..	..	..	..	..	..	..	..	..	..
Guatemala	..	..	..	..	..	..	..	..	..	..
Honduras	..	..	..	..	..	..	..	..	..	..
Nicaragua	..	..	..	..	..	..	..	..	..	..
Panama	183.3	373.4	307.8	369.4	..	638.6	839.4	687.3	674.0	803.8
Virgin Islands, U.S.	..	..	..	..	..	..	..	..	..	..
South America	638.6	602.1	1 759.2	2 245.1	..	40 060.4	29 872.6	35 316.7	43 837.9	38 305.5
Argentina	..	..	123.3	148.7	..	3 188.2	3 465.4	3 032.6	3 819.9	2 155.9
Bolivia	..	..	..	..	..	795.2	414.8	806.4	831.1	782.0
Brazil	..	..	528.1	815.5	..	30 624.5	20 078.4	25 305.2	29 695.4	27 088.4
Colombia	..	..	..	..	..	1 151.0	1 203.0	904.4	900.7	1 071.7
Ecuador	166.3	..	131.8	152.3	..	..	..	..	..	..
Paraguay	..	..	..	..	..	..	..	..	..	..
Peru	..	..	..	..	..	148.1	140.4	1 247.0	1 120.2	1 123.2
Uruguay	..	..	..	..	..	337.5	283.1	288.8	203.9	183.2
Venezuela	..	..	..	..	..	2 082.2	2 311.4	1 813.0	3 328.1	869.0

Table 2. Foreign direct investment positions by country *(cont.)*

At year end

Million US dollars

	Inward					Outward				
	2014	2015	2016	2017	2018	2014	2015	2016	2017	2018
ASIA	**38 808.7**	**42 967.9**	**45 882.8**	**59 126.9**	..	**118 879.8**	**123 546.0**	**118 080.5**	**122 693.7**	**118 676.4**
Near and Middle East	8 315.4	10 371.3	12 174.6	14 507.1	..	13 000.6	12 261.3	12 576.2	14 054.9	15 676.7
Gulf Arabian countries	6 605.9	8 737.1	10 120.2	9 660.6	..	8 933.3	7 762.7	7 861.3	8 692.7	9 888.9
Kuwait	..	..	139.1	225.5	..	..	..	108.6	..	211.8
Qatar	3 561.0	4 214.5	5 328.3	6 441.6	..	2 808.2	3 154.1	3 296.1	1 707.8	3 054.7
Saudi Arabia	570.6	1 035.4	527.0	593.7	..	4 197.1	5 592.8	5 382.1	5 113.9	5 795.7
United Arab Emirates	2 276.4	3 323.9	3 990.7	2 255.9	..	-386.1	-953.7	-797.9	1 817.0	1 425.5
Other Near and Middle East	1 709.5	1 634.2	2 055.4	4 846.5	..	4 067.2	4 493.6	4 714.9	5 362.2	5 786.6
Jordan	..	..	..	..	..	218.5	227.5	261.4	278.2	546.1
Other Asian countries	30 493.3	32 595.5	33 708.2	44 621.0	..	105 879.2	111 284.7	105 504.4	108 638.8	103 000.9
China	4 072.1	5 456.7	7 131.9	12 056.8	..	25 567.7	24 859.0	24 350.2	25 307.0	24 015.3
Hong Kong, China	2 932.1	3 342.4	4 148.8	5 232.7	..	11 016.7	12 172.0	10 327.8	11 266.5	11 430.0
India	167.5	372.3	527.0	539.7	..	4 958.4	5 762.7	5 762.6	6 671.9	6 332.7
Indonesia	128.7	..	870.7	790.4	..	3 331.5	2 684.8	2 711.1	1 480.0	318.3
Iran, Islamic Republic of	593.7	247.1	237.2	299.8	..	870.5	719.7	728.4	825.1	812.9
Malaysia	122.6	139.4	338.4	644.0	..	1 062.3	865.5	744.2	957.1	1 238.8
Philippines	..	..	..	..	..	803.7	1 176.9	402.7	353.8	269.1
Singapore	671.4	1 363.1	1 513.7	2 471.8	..	11 600.7	12 054.4	10 478.6	11 352.8	10 248.5
Chinese Taipei	208.8	162.2	153.9	262.7	..	545.1	642.4	585.0	725.6	834.7
Thailand	666.5	631.5	1 082.5	1 399.6	..	3 282.9	1 909.6	2 011.2	1 709.0	872.5
Viet Nam	-151.8	..	148.6	175.1	..	721.2	717.5	593.4	723.2	768.3
AUSTRALIA, OCEANIA AND POLAR REGIONS	**3 656.9**	**4 458.4**	**3 766.2**	**3 314.9**	..	**15 003.8**	**13 953.2**	**13 409.9**	**15 436.6**	**21 158.7**
WORLD unallocated and confidential	**3 768.6**	**14 375.6**	**13 902.2**	**16 982.5**	..	**-17.0**	**-8.7**	**-29.5**	**-34.8**	**-32.1**
European Union (EU28)	**408 388.0**	**385 971.7**	**396 907.3**	**463 572.8**	..	**755 490.7**	**726 168.8**	**720 838.0**	**865 425.8**	**908 034.1**
G20 countries excl. European Union	**409 701.7**	**409 228.1**	**377 689.5**	**472 676.9**	..	**610 666.8**	**612 520.4**	**631 527.4**	**714 571.8**	**731 115.2**
G20 OECD countries	**399 897.8**	**397 685.4**	**364 331.2**	**454 389.5**	..	**526 223.7**	**537 702.8**	**544 575.7**	**620 551.7**	**642 476.5**
G20 Non-OECD countries	**9 803.9**	**11 542.7**	**13 358.3**	**18 286.2**	..	**84 443.1**	**74 817.6**	**86 951.6**	**94 021.3**	**88 638.7**
MENA countries	**9 370.4**	**11 206.3**	**14 362.8**	**17 061.6**	..	**30 368.3**	**26 979.9**	**25 685.7**	**28 692.7**	**28 831.0**
ASEAN countries	**1 591.7**	**2 387.6**	**4 188.9**	**5 753.2**	..	**21 558.8**	**22 243.9**	**19 810.3**	**17 453.8**	**14 165.3**

- Nil; .. Not available

Note: Inward FDI positions are allocated according to the ultimate investing country. Inward FDI positions by immediate counterpart country are available for the most recent year in the *OECD FDI database according to BMD4*. Detailed metadata at: *http://stats.oecd.org/OECDStat_Metadata/ShowMetadata.ashx?Dataset=FDI_CTRY_IND_SUMM.*

1. Information on data for Israel: *http://oe.cd/israel-disclaimer.*
2. Note by Turkey: The information in this document with reference to "Cyprus" relates to the southern part of the Island. There is no single authority representing both Turkish and Greek Cypriot people on the Island. Turkey recognises the Turkish Republic of Northern Cyprus (TRNC). Until a lasting and equitable solution is found within the context of the United Nations, Turkey shall preserve its position concerning the "Cyprus issue".
3. Note by all the European Union Member States of the OECD and the European Union: The Republic of Cyprus is recognised by all members of the United Nations with the exception of Turkey. The information in this document relates to the area under the effective control of the Government of the Republic of Cyprus.

Source: OECD International Direct Investment Statistics (database): https://doi.org/10.1787/idi-data-en

FRANCE

Table 3. Foreign direct investment income by country

Million US dollars

	Inward					Outward				
	2014	2015	2016	2017	2018	2014	2015	2016	2017	2018
WORLD	**24 821.5**	**26 922.9**	**29 483.6**	**33 000.8**	**32 749.9**	**78 585.6**	**70 308.4**	**69 441.6**	**76 115.4**	**83 729.5**
OECD COUNTRIES	..	..	..	..	..	..	..	..	..	..
Australia	..	..	..	..	..	..	..	..	..	..
Austria	..	..	..	..	..	..	..	..	..	..
Belgium	1 500.6	3 088.2	3 294.3	3 297.3	2 931.7	7 732.5	6 552.4	7 248.7	4 531.6	4 423.5
Canada	9.3	61.0	54.2	89.1	77.9	-187.1	321.7	1 036.2	-603.1	-126.3
Chile	..	..	..	..	..	..	..	..	..	..
Czech Republic	8.0	16.6	16.6	-1.1	-4.7	1 237.9	1 159.2	974.2	1 051.7	1 078.7
Denmark	..	..	..	..	..	..	..	..	..	..
Estonia	..	..	..	..	..	..	..	..	..	..
Finland	..	..	..	..	..	..	..	..	..	..
France	-	-	-	-	-	-	-	-	-	-
Germany	2 510.3	2 261.8	2 247.0	3 015.4	2 549.3	4 621.2	4 190.8	5 174.2	6 030.9	6 069.9
Greece	..	..	..	..	..	..	..	..	..	..
Hungary	..	..	..	..	..	..	..	..	..	..
Iceland	..	..	..	..	..	..	..	..	..	..
Ireland	489.6	215.2	126.1	136.4	103.9	1 885.4	2 021.1	1 541.5	1 474.5	1 454.0
Israel[1]	..	..	..	..	..	..	..	..	..	..
Italy	431.2	629.0	994.1	475.7	725.8	1 845.6	2 303.9	3 731.1	4 272.3	4 253.5
Japan	484.3	572.4	535.2	483.6	463.8	3 309.0	1 986.7	3 550.8	3 965.7	3 884.1
Korea	..	..	..	..	..	..	..	..	..	..
Latvia	..	..	..	..	..	..	..	..	..	..
Lithuania	..	..	..	..	..	..	..	..	..	..
Luxembourg	3 433.7	3 825.8	4 075.0	4 963.4	5 339.3	2 627.0	2 109.8	2 599.8	2 561.2	2 693.3
Mexico	..	..	..	..	..	..	..	..	..	..
Netherlands	7 065.1	5 880.2	6 679.2	7 053.3	6 866.5	7 568.0	6 665.6	6 190.4	4 618.4	5 119.8
New Zealand	..	..	..	..	..	..	..	..	..	..
Norway	92.9	177.5	118.3	168.0	167.6	1 930.5	814.2	637.0	419.3	414.3
Poland	-188.4	-85.4	-107.3	-143.2	-127.5	1 334.7	1 250.1	954.3	1 366.3	1 275.8
Portugal	-63.7	88.7	103.9	57.5	46.0	455.1	607.9	464.4	490.4	496.9
Slovak Republic	..	..	..	..	..	..	..	..	..	..
Slovenia	..	..	..	..	..	..	..	..	..	..
Spain	935.4	1 002.8	1 071.5	1 361.7	1 328.9	2 830.0	2 587.9	3 060.9	4 497.8	4 495.5
Sweden	283.9	307.3	391.5	642.5	645.6	414.0	216.3	408.1	559.1	538.2
Switzerland	2 045.9	2 409.3	2 654.0	1 752.9	2 070.1	4 745.9	4 532.4	5 463.9	6 522.4	6 239.8
Turkey	2.7	2.2	3.3	3.4	2.4	427.2	367.2	263.2	772.2	735.3
United Kingdom	2 681.4	2 650.0	4 122.5	3 938.7	4 147.3	7 256.2	5 554.1	6 108.6	6 874.1	7 730.4
United States	2 298.0	2 941.8	2 073.4	2 583.7	2 549.3	5 483.6	9 131.4	5 539.1	5 988.1	11 074.0
EUROPE	..	..	..	..	..	..	..	..	..	..
Bulgaria	..	..	..	..	..	..	..	..	..	..
Croatia	..	..	..	..	..	..	..	..	..	..
Cyprus[2, 3]	..	..	..	..	..	..	..	..	..	..
Malta	..	..	..	..	..	..	..	..	..	..
Romania	-1.3	-	-1.1	-1.1	-2.4	345.0	416.0	538.5	724.8	704.6
Russian Federation	62.4	22.2	1.1	47.3	37.8	347.6	52.1	1 119.1	1 300.9	1 249.9
Ukraine	..	..	..	..	..	..	..	..	..	..
AFRICA	..	..	..	..	..	..	..	..	..	..
Northern Africa	..	..	..	..	..	..	..	..	..	..
Algeria	..	..	..	..	..	..	..	..	..	..
Egypt	..	..	..	..	..	..	..	..	..	..
Libya	..	..	..	..	..	..	..	..	..	..
Morocco	6.6	18.9	17.7	2.3	4.7	563.9	637.8	404.7	393.4	433.1
Tunisia	..	..	..	..	..	..	..	..	..	..
Other African countries	..	..	..	..	..	..	..	..	..	..
Nigeria	..	..	..	..	..	..	..	..	..	..
South Africa	..	..	..	..	..	..	..	..	..	..
AMERICA	..	..	..	..	..	..	..	..	..	..
Northern America	..	..	..	..	..	..	..	..	..	..
Central America and Caribbean countries	..	..	..	..	..	..	..	..	..	..
Bahamas	..	..	..	..	..	..	..	..	..	..
Bermuda	..	..	..	..	..	..	..	..	..	..
Cayman Islands	..	..	..	..	..	..	..	..	..	..
Costa Rica	..	..	..	..	..	..	..	..	..	..
El Salvador	..	..	..	..	..	..	..	..	..	..
Guatemala	..	..	..	..	..	..	..	..	..	..
Honduras	..	..	..	..	..	..	..	..	..	..
Nicaragua	..	..	..	..	..	..	..	..	..	..
Panama	..	..	..	..	..	..	..	..	..	..
Virgin Islands, U.S.	..	..	..	..	..	..	..	..	..	..
South America	..	..	..	..	..	..	..	..	..	..
Argentina	..	..	..	..	..	..	..	..	..	..
Bolivia	..	..	..	..	..	..	..	..	..	..
Brazil	-4.0	-1.1	-5.5	-1.1	-	1 325.5	252.9	938.8	918.7	1 002.0
Colombia	..	..	..	..	..	..	..	..	..	..
Ecuador	..	..	..	..	..	..	..	..	..	..
Paraguay	-	-	..	..	..	..	..	..	..	..
Peru	..	..	..	..	..	..	..	..	..	..
Uruguay	..	..	..	..	..	..	..	..	..	..
Venezuela	..	..	..	..	..	..	..	..	..	..

Table 3. Foreign direct investment income by country *(cont.)*

Million US dollars

	Inward					Outward				
	2014	2015	2016	2017	2018	2014	2015	2016	2017	2018
ASIA	..	..	..	..	..	..	..	..	..	..
Near and Middle East	..	..	..	..	..	..	..	..	..	..
Gulf Arabian countries	..	..	..	..	..	..	..	..	..	..
Kuwait	..	..	..	..	..	..	..	..	..	..
Qatar	..	..	..	..	..	..	..	..	..	..
Saudi Arabia	..	..	..	..	..	..	..	..	..	..
United Arab Emirates	..	..	..	..	..	..	..	..	..	..
Other Near and Middle East	..	..	..	..	..	..	..	..	..	..
Jordan	..	..	..	..	..	..	..	..	..	..
Other Asian countries	..	..	..	..	..	..	..	..	..	..
China	47.8	-13.3	1.1	15.8	49.6	2 130.8	2 796.5	988.6	1 659.3	1 684.2
Hong Kong, China	84.9	92.1	144.9	329.2	288.0	1 955.7	1 469.8	1 071.5	1 532.0	1 543.7
India	-6.6	-4.4	-3.3	-5.6	-4.7	168.5	399.3	275.4	290.8	290.3
Indonesia	-	-	-64.1	1.1	4.7	957.9	544.6	374.9	472.3	467.4
Iran, Islamic Republic of	..	..	..	..	..	..	..	..	..	..
Malaysia	..	..	..	..	..	..	..	..	..	..
Philippines	..	..	..	..	..	..	..	..	..	..
Singapore	39.8	-54.4	23.2	18.0	20.1	2 007.4	1 517.5	270.9	1 784.5	1 851.8
Chinese Taipei	..	..	..	..	..	..	..	..	..	..
Thailand	..	..	..	..	..	..	..	..	..	..
Viet Nam	..	..	..	..	..	..	..	..	..	..
AUSTRALIA, OCEANIA AND POLAR REGIONS	..	..	..	..	..	..	..	..	..	..
WORLD unallocated and confidential	..	..	..	..	..	..	..	..	..	..
European Union (EU28)	**19 607.3**	**20 565.7**	**24 236.4**	**25 333.1**	**25 059.6**	**41 616.0**	**38 546.9**	**41 311.5**	**41 721.3**	**42 969.4**
G20 countries excl. European Union	..	..	..	..	..	..	..	..	..	..
G20 OECD countries	..	..	..	..	..	..	..	..	..	..
G20 Non-OECD countries	..	..	..	..	..	..	..	..	..	..
MENA countries	..	..	..	..	..	..	..	..	..	..
ASEAN countries	..	..	..	..	..	..	..	..	..	..

- Nil; .. Not available

Note: Detailed metadata at: *http://stats.oecd.org/OECDStat_Metadata/ShowMetadata.ashx?Dataset=FDI_CTRY_IND_SUMM.*

1. Information on data for Israel: *http://oe.cd/israel-disclaimer.*
2. Note by Turkey: The information in this document with reference to "Cyprus" relates to the southern part of the Island. There is no single authority representing both Turkish and Greek Cypriot people on the Island. Turkey recognises the Turkish Republic of Northern Cyprus (TRNC). Until a lasting and equitable solution is found within the context of the United Nations, Turkey shall preserve its position concerning the "Cyprus issue".
3. Note by all the European Union Member States of the OECD and the European Union: The Republic of Cyprus is recognised by all members of the United Nations with the exception of Turkey. The information in this document relates to the area under the effective control of the Government of the Republic of Cyprus.

Source: OECD International Direct Investment Statistics (database): https://doi.org/10.1787/idi-data-en

Table 4. Foreign direct investment flows by industrial sector

Million US dollars

	Inward					Outward				
	2014	2015	2016	2017	2018	2014	2015	2016	2017	2018
All FDI activities	**2 669.5**	**45 354.4**	**23 054.3**	**29 811.7**	**37 285.5**	**49 785.1**	**53 205.8**	**64 784.9**	**41 270.4**	**102 407.6**
Agriculture, forestry and fishing	**1.3**	**26.6**	**113.9**	**59.7**	**89.7**	**-27.9**	**155.3**	**-131.6**	**81.2**	**-68.5**
Mining and quarrying	**506.8**	**-288.4**	**-134.9**	**349.5**	**859.2**	**-4 010.9**	**12 299.5**	**4 397.9**	**-7 555.0**	**2 705.1**
Extraction activities	485.6	-296.2	-136.0	405.8	599.6	-4 026.8	12 294.0	4 399.0	-7 573.0	2 705.1
Manufacturing	**-900.9**	**-4 221.9**	**8 033.8**	**-1 874.6**	**20 128.6**	**19 081.9**	**-4 329.5**	**16 377.3**	**15 449.2**	**42 022.9**
of which:										
Food products, beverages and tobacco	-2 340.5	-593.5	-3 915.7	3 741.4	371.8	-5 877.7	2 478.1	3 229.0	13 298.4	5 510.4
Textiles, wood and paper products; printing	1 803.1	26.6	513.1	-372.0	-924.1	2 073.8	-216.3	915.6	-2 190.3	469.7
Chemical, rubber, plastic, non-metallic mineral products	-6 365.9	3 263.5	984.2	8 833.3	-5 488.0	3 021.1	117.6	6 261.2	-7 812.0	3 160.6
Metal and machinery products, except electrical equipment	1 204.7	2 285.1	12 446.1	-8 650.7	440.2	-191.1	-2 463.7	8 010.6	5 955.4	-1 194.4
Motor vehicles, trailers, semi-trailers, other transport equipment	6 769.3	-1 044.9	-393.7	-2 679.5	695.1	8 774.0	3 808.1	-263.2	6 852.7	669.2
Other manufacturing	-1 972.9	-8 158.6	-1 600.1	-2 748.3	25 033.6	11 281.7	-8 054.4	-1 776.0	-656.1	33 406.1
Electricity, gas, steam and air conditioning supply	**-517.4**	**829.7**	**1 255.1**	**-464.4**	**-486.3**	**6 440.2**	**1 797.0**	**803.9**	**-728.2**	**1 777.4**
Water supply; sewerage, waste management and remediation activities	**-42.5**	**24.4**	**49.8**	**-319.0**	**50.7**	**-3 228.1**	**1 198.0**	**2.2**	**-65.4**	**957.2**
Construction	**-8.0**	**16 924.0**	**1 359.1**	**-2 992.9**	**-246.7**	**2 158.7**	**-1 026.1**	**-764.1**	**-5 489.8**	**234.9**
Services	**16 413.7**	**25 407.7**	**-2 208.3**	**30 804.9**	**14 383.3**	**23 321.0**	**44 645.6**	**40 132.7**	**38 453.4**	**33 747.2**
Wholesale and retail trade; repair of motor vehicles and motorcycles	2 104.3	2 376.0	212.3	3 812.4	-1 500.1	3 145.8	4 411.5	4 821.4	2 227.5	8 059.7
Transportation and storage	-2 652.2	2 134.2	1 351.3	3 115.8	-134.5	-437.8	1 812.5	-360.5	-399.1	-406.0
Accommodation and food service activities	-341.0	-549.1	2 440.6	-315.6	-858.0	609.0	173.0	2 612.0	7 657.5	-3 908.9
Information and communication	810.7	2 072.1	557.3	2 282.7	1 418.6	3 082.1	2 978.4	116.1	1 607.5	7 510.9
Financial and insurance activities	14 160.8	13 513.0	-11 714.0	16 830.1	17 559.3	8 600.2	12 863.0	26 855.0	19 838.8	395.4
Activities of holding companies	9 056.7	4 495.8	-5 298.0	6 444.6	9 307.2	2 329.8	2 794.2	819.4	4 536.1	3 183.1
Real estate activities	6 121.8	8 722.1	-2 011.5	-459.9	18.9	5 267.3	13 164.7	3 758.7	2 214.0	24 582.8
Professional, scientific and technical activities	-159.2	-1 724.9	3 773.1	4 039.0	1 163.7	3 458.9	4 169.7	1 586.9	3 749.3	311.6
Administrative and support service activities	-3 884.8	-56.6	2 275.8	89.1	-4 009.2	-892.9	4 022.2	560.7	1 336.9	-2 721.6
Public administration; activities of households and of extraterritorial organisations	-	-	..	..	..	..	..	201.3	225.5	-13.0
Education	37.2	-6.7	266.5	436.3	-73.2	..	..	..	..	-
Human health and social work activities	185.8	-748.8	512.0	307.7	581.8	488.3	1 213.5	-84.0	101.5	-77.9
Arts, entertainment and recreation	35.8	-320.6	130.5	658.3	223.1	..	..	..	..	..
Other services	-2.7	..	..	..	-	67.7	23.3	50.9	-84.5	15.3
Not allocated and confidential	**-12 783.6**	**6 652.2**	**14 585.9**	**4 248.7**	**2 506.8**	**6 050.2**	**-1 534.1**	**3 966.6**	**1 125.0**	**21 031.5**
Private real estate activities	-	-	-	-	-	-	-	-	-	-

- Nil; .. Not available

Note: Detailed metadata at: *http://stats.oecd.org/OECDStat_Metadata/ShowMetadata.ashx?Dataset=FDI_CTRY_IND_SUMM.*

Source: *OECD International Direct Investment Statistics (database): https://doi.org/10.1787/idi-data-en*

Table 5. Foreign direct investment positions by industrial sector
At year end

Million US dollars

	Inward					Outward				
	2014	2015	2016	2017	2018	2014	2015	2016	2017	2018
All FDI activities	**700 064.6**	**687 394.7**	**694 881.4**	**818 545.2**	**824 987.4**	**1 294 220.9**	**1 268 227.5**	**1 284 859.3**	**1 466 602.3**	**1 507 861.2**
Agriculture, forestry and fishing	**451.6**	**496.5**	**678.8**	**856.3**	**878.2**	**329.0**	**499.7**	**393.2**	**407.8**	**327.5**
Mining and quarrying	**1 692.5**	**4 272.2**	**4 899.3**	**5 611.7**	**4 316.5**	**93 558.5**	**103 472.0**	**113 755.7**	**105 212.3**	**99 744.7**
Extraction activities	1 438.7	4 058.8	4 707.5	5 371.8	3 832.2	93 547.6	103 462.2	113 755.7	105 169.1	99 684.0
Manufacturing	**186 970.2**	**166 421.3**	**179 479.3**	**196 752.2**	**202 513.2**	**389 846.3**	**373 918.3**	**380 503.8**	**418 938.6**	**448 797.8**
of which:										
Food products, beverages and tobacco	35 166.4	32 898.2	26 577.4	31 796.6	31 237.7	66 435.6	60 243.9	61 354.5	87 273.9	90 369.8
Textiles, wood and paper products; printing	8 356.7	7 163.9	7 447.0	7 150.4	6 345.3	16 890.6	15 648.3	15 642.5	14 326.0	15 490.0
Chemical, rubber, plastic, non-metallic mineral products	74 929.4	71 850.8	75 444.3	92 344.7	86 720.9	126 416.9	135 303.2	137 969.9	159 120.9	159 053.1
Metal and machinery products, except electrical equipment	18 496.8	17 823.6	36 895.8	32 625.3	22 114.7	35 834.2	27 742.0	41 073.0	28 752.7	25 443.1
Motor vehicles, trailers, semi-trailers, other transport equipment	17 643.3	16 751.2	14 685.4	20 100.7	18 815.0	62 083.0	67 343.5	62 618.3	69 838.1	67 683.8
Other manufacturing	32 378.8	19 932.5	18 427.3	12 733.3	37 279.6	82 184.9	67 637.5	61 845.7	59 627.0	90 758.0
Electricity, gas, steam and air conditioning supply	**4 219.0**	**3 713.7**	**4 382.8**	**5 421.0**	**5 440.8**	**97 727.8**	**89 245.5**	**85 793.2**	**95 949.9**	**93 540.2**
Water supply; sewerage, waste management and remediation activities	**390.9**	**621.7**	**719.9**	**682.4**	**632.0**	**4 611.2**	**5 516.6**	**4 973.1**	**5 777.2**	**6 095.7**
Construction	**11 831.4**	**22 391.9**	**22 863.9**	**23 455.3**	**22 228.1**	**32 547.6**	**27 436.0**	**22 586.7**	**18 674.7**	**17 121.6**
Services	**489 165.7**	**475 276.0**	**454 420.8**	**554 393.1**	**563 212.7**	**649 722.0**	**641 045.2**	**647 115.0**	**787 951.5**	**802 458.2**
Wholesale and retail trade; repair of motor vehicles and motorcycles	50 795.5	51 325.0	46 885.2	54 588.6	52 305.9	97 871.0	91 222.6	95 101.7	116 367.2	123 572.2
Transportation and storage	8 325.1	9 737.6	9 967.3	12 760.9	13 319.2	8 033.7	8 999.5	8 656.1	9 907.7	9 177.9
Accommodation and food service activities	6 563.4	5 684.3	7 609.4	8 667.5	7 972.3	11 818.0	12 861.2	12 998.8	21 664.7	15 397.3
Information and communication	15 714.1	16 681.5	18 234.4	24 291.2	24 112.7	82 765.2	79 499.2	75 413.7	83 187.8	85 982.4
Financial and insurance activities	193 979.2	189 669.0	172 687.9	203 358.1	212 401.0	322 542.7	311 113.8	322 707.9	377 319.5	377 352.9
Activities of holding companies	78 366.5	75 523.1	74 580.0	93 872.6	100 345.8	32 661.7	35 098.5	34 721.2	44 726.6	50 156.9
Real estate activities	158 174.2	152 710.9	143 840.0	173 948.2	173 035.3	69 538.8	76 129.6	74 232.1	87 534.2	107 208.6
Professional, scientific and technical activities	40 303.3	35 528.6	39 808.2	50 271.0	48 278.0	50 002.7	52 194.9	48 424.2	77 071.2	72 907.0
Administrative and support service activities	8 773.1	8 761.0	9 265.3	17 476.6	22 444.5	4 306.4	5 457.8	5 912.3	10 764.0	7 011.7
Public administration; activities of households and of extraterritorial organisations	..	..	..	..	..	..	..	256.1	531.3	494.6
Education	1 240.8	1 087.6	1 368.2	2 013.7	2 035.7	..	..	..	..	..
Human health and social work activities	3 948.3	3 193.3	3 723.0	5 700.4	5 894.2	2 170.8	2 938.5	2 757.5	2 947.9	2 702.1
Arts, entertainment and recreation	1 100.0	726.2	904.4	1 133.4	1 243.4	..	..	..	..	..
Other services	165.1	..	..	..	..	534.2	512.8	546.0	522.9	518.7
Not allocated and confidential	**5 343.3**	**14 201.4**	**27 436.5**	**31 373.2**	**25 766.0**	**25 878.5**	**27 094.2**	**29 738.6**	**33 690.3**	**39 775.6**
Private real estate activities	-	-	-	-	-	-	-	-	-	-

- Nil; .. Not available

Note: Detailed metadata at: *http://stats.oecd.org/OECDStat_Metadata/ShowMetadata.ashx?Dataset=FDI_CTRY_IND_SUMM.*

Source: OECD International Direct Investment Statistics (database): https://doi.org/10.1787/idi-data-en

Table 6. Foreign direct investment income by industrial sector

Million US dollars

	Inward					Outward				
	2014	2015	2016	2017	2018	2014	2015	2016	2017	2018
All FDI activities	**24 821.5**	**26 922.9**	**29 483.6**	**33 000.8**	**32 749.9**	**78 585.6**	**70 308.4**	**69 441.6**	**76 115.4**	**83 729.5**
Agriculture, forestry and fishing	..	..	..	..	-	..	..	..	..	-
Mining and quarrying	..	..	..	..	..	..	..	..	..	..
Extraction activities	..	..	..	..	..	..	..	..	..	..
Manufacturing	..	..	..	..	..	..	..	..	..	..
of which:										
Food products, beverages and tobacco	..	..	..	..	..	..	..	..	..	..
Textiles, wood and paper products; printing	..	..	..	..	..	..	..	..	..	..
Chemical, rubber, plastic, non-metallic mineral products	..	..	..	..	..	..	..	..	..	..
Metal and machinery products, except electrical equipment	..	..	..	..	..	..	..	..	..	..
Motor vehicles, trailers, semi-trailers, other transport equipment	..	..	..	..	..	..	..	..	..	..
Other manufacturing	..	..	..	..	..	..	..	..	..	..
Electricity, gas, steam and air conditioning supply	..	..	..	..	..	..	..	..	..	..
Water supply; sewerage, waste management and remediation activities	..	..	..	..	..	..	..	..	..	..
Construction	..	..	..	..	..	..	..	..	..	..
Services	..	..	..	..	..	..	..	..	..	..
Wholesale and retail trade; repair of motor vehicles and motorcycles	..	..	..	..	..	..	..	..	..	..
Transportation and storage	..	..	..	..	..	..	..	..	..	..
Accommodation and food service activities	..	..	..	..	..	..	..	..	..	..
Information and communication	..	..	..	..	..	..	..	..	..	..
Financial and insurance activities	..	..	..	..	..	..	..	..	..	..
Activities of holding companies	..	..	..	..	..	..	..	..	..	..
Real estate activities	..	..	..	..	..	..	..	..	..	..
Professional, scientific and technical activities	..	..	..	..	..	..	..	..	..	..
Administrative and support service activities	..	..	..	..	..	..	..	..	..	..
Public administration; activities of households and of extraterritorial organisations	-	-	-	-	-	..	-	-	..	..
Education	..	..	..	..	..	..	..	..	..	..
Human health and social work activities	..	..	..	..	..	..	..	..	..	..
Arts, entertainment and recreation	..	..	..	..	..	..	..	..	..	-
Other services	..	..	..	..	-	..	..	..	..	..
Not allocated and confidential	..	..	..	..	..	..	..	..	..	..
Private real estate activities	-	-	-	-	-	-	-	-	-	-

- Nil; .. Not available

Note: Detailed metadata at: *http://stats.oecd.org/OECDStat_Metadata/ShowMetadata.ashx?Dataset=FDI_CTRY_IND_SUMM.*

Source: OECD International Direct Investment Statistics (database): https://doi.org/10.1787/idi-data-en

GERMANY

Table 1. Foreign direct investment flows by country

Million US dollars

	Inward					Outward				
	2014	2015	2016	2017	2018	2014	2015	2016	2017	2018
WORLD	**-3 005.2**	**30 562.4**	**12 614.2**	**33 190.2**	**11 916.7**	**83 976.4**	**99 022.7**	**60 343.9**	**88 074.6**	**63 279.8**
OECD COUNTRIES	**-4 213.9**	**39 868.0**	**16 754.4**	**32 375.2**	**13 190.1**	**73 622.1**	**82 656.7**	**51 385.6**	**74 438.1**	**50 270.3**
Australia	-866.4	-116.5	-148.2	259.3	-282.1	213.6	800.9	171.4	1 906.2	2 002.8
Austria	1 166.2	3 025.0	-603.8	567.0	378.9	2 983.9	-1 147.0	4 502.9	4 422.3	1 084.6
Belgium	-5 167.8	-5 721.6	293.0	-8 864.8	-4 853.1	2 937.5	8 723.2	-3 974.3	-18 353.1	-2 792.4
Canada	37.2	-368.3	503.2	-12.4	-29.5	-213.6	674.5	993.0	644.8	1 294.7
Chile	345.0	2.2	11.1	-54.1	-205.4	-280.0	668.9	-69.7	250.3	113.3
Czech Republic	-406.0	-88.7	61.9	117.2	-395.4	3 096.7	290.6	2 145.3	2 080.9	1 649.9
Denmark	-490.9	1 798.1	-1 246.3	5 529.3	-436.7	-1 030.9	-449.3	-371.6	807.1	501.6
Estonia	-45.1	-12.2	23.2	11.3	-18.9	98.2	-104.3	22.1	102.6	60.2
Finland	-652.8	248.5	-288.6	-1 057.4	16.5	460.4	593.5	-351.7	822.9	550.0
France	-350.3	-175.3	5 061.4	5 647.6	555.9	1 846.9	-631.2	-236.6	7 738.7	3 015.5
Germany	-	-	-	-	-	-	-	-	-	-
Greece	-179.1	-114.3	-12.2	36.1	-46.0	195.0	63.2	244.4	771.1	496.9
Hungary	-145.9	-119.8	-25.4	-253.6	192.4	1 442.2	228.5	1 550.4	-2 809.2	-1 210.9
Iceland	57.1	8.9	-8.8	-1.1	1.2	2.7	17.7	26.5	47.3	73.2
Ireland	2 020.7	1 961.2	-3 141.7	1 483.5	2 486.7	2 574.0	198.6	872.5	-2 896.0	13 325.9
Israel[1]	66.3	163.1	133.8	57.5	175.9	497.5	130.9	288.6	237.9	-15.3
Italy	1 313.5	-481.4	645.8	-1 121.6	1 233.3	70.3	961.7	3 231.2	259.3	2 459.6
Japan	541.3	2 474.8	1 903.1	2 321.0	601.9	-173.8	-2 816.4	1 711.8	-200.7	-211.3
Korea	1 226.0	162.0	717.7	152.2	10.6	800.1	684.4	471.1	933.4	-610.2
Latvia	-11.9	-2.2	3.3	-31.6	4.7	165.8	2.2	22.1	28.2	67.3
Lithuania	65.0	-11.1	-12.2	-24.8	-38.9	-75.6	66.6	140.4	-28.2	70.8
Luxembourg	6 709.6	14 629.0	-2 624.1	596.3	2 895.1	11 723.5	12 183.0	11 200.9	31 003.3	14 913.3
Mexico	411.3	-281.8	90.7	-76.7	218.3	1 175.5	1 764.8	1 361.3	3 193.6	1 936.7
Netherlands	-32 497.0	10 577.9	3 404.8	11 050.6	9 373.3	20 505.5	27 710.5	2 460.5	-3 049.3	-15 656.8
New Zealand	-18.6	-54.4	-10.0	7.9	-10.6	184.4	28.8	-	-15.8	194.7
Norway	-184.4	-150.9	240.0	292.0	-192.4	431.2	1 375.5	-742.0	884.9	-777.8
Poland	-245.5	190.8	-303.0	-115.0	414.3	420.6	2 437.0	3 056.5	2 397.7	1 900.2
Portugal	-96.9	-15.5	59.7	-63.1	-75.5	525.4	-45.5	831.6	156.7	398.9
Slovak Republic	74.3	383.8	182.5	-223.2	-135.7	-521.4	-120.9	138.2	810.5	-85.0
Slovenia	-5.3	-3.3	-3.3	16.9	9.4	406.0	203.0	7.7	34.9	206.5
Spain	1 808.4	921.8	1 392.2	499.4	4 372.7	-447.1	717.7	2 573.3	5 623.9	8 894.1
Sweden	-1 972.9	-437.0	-1 070.4	8 312.5	-6 115.9	8 163.7	7 575.2	1 069.3	3 490.0	4 331.4
Switzerland	4 172.7	6 699.9	8 336.8	4 187.8	11 315.9	5 599.0	690.0	4 026.3	2 480.0	433.1
Turkey	159.2	208.5	-53.1	186.0	-482.7	999.1	1 083.7	538.5	1 364.0	1 878.9
United Kingdom	14 710.1	2 761.0	3 312.0	-7 998.0	-618.4	-1 268.4	-1 863.6	1 555.9	5 053.5	-2 818.4
United States	4 292.2	1 792.6	-82.9	10 916.5	-7 129.7	10 204.3	20 083.7	12 057.9	24 216.0	12 594.1
EUROPE	**-8 108.0**	**33 914.6**	**10 345.0**	**17 411.8**	**18 242.7**	**54 416.9**	**63 782.6**	**33 839.4**	**46 423.2**	**38 234.4**
Bulgaria	4.0	38.8	101.7	29.3	54.3	-132.7	184.1	220.1	201.8	192.4
Croatia	13.3	6.7	33.2	-37.2	8.3	213.6	35.6	134.9	292.0	292.7
Cyprus[2, 3]	287.9	98.7	214.5	34.9	90.9	-4.0	303.4	79.6	-587.3	284.4
Malta	45.1	55.5	56.4	14.7	-132.2	-2 276.8	1 205.9	-4 755.1	250.3	-1 138.9
Romania	-5.3	12.2	28.8	49.6	-18.9	555.9	484.7	1 058.3	-15.8	912.3
Russian Federation	1 056.1	543.5	-228.9	-1 421.5	-972.5	-4 343.9	521.4	1 906.4	1 692.0	3 429.7
Ukraine	53.1	-49.9	-47.6	-9.0	11.8	-294.5	-105.5	-70.8	130.8	-170.0
AFRICA	**-691.3**	**-17.7**	**-60.8**	**481.3**	**-16.5**	**666.0**	**694.4**	**1 930.8**	**1 379.8**	**2 400.6**
Northern Africa	-22.6	-17.7	-6.6	91.3	-56.7	22.6	269.6	1 181.0	664.0	1 594.5
Algeria	-1.3	-1.1	1.1	5.6	-5.9	167.2	276.2	314.1	402.4	411.9
Egypt	-19.9	-7.8	-12.2	51.9	-34.2	-5.3	293.4	685.6	96.9	-214.8
Libya	-	-	-16.6	-1.1	18.9	-188.4	-303.9	-213.4	155.6	-53.1
Morocco	5.3	-3.3	13.3	11.3	1.2	46.4	10.0	384.8	-21.4	1 397.4
Tunisia	-6.6	-5.5	8.8	22.5	-36.6	1.3	-11.1	11.1	31.6	53.1
Other African countries	-668.7	-1.1	-55.3	390.0	38.9	644.8	426.0	748.6	715.8	806.1
Nigeria	-130.0	7.8	39.8	12.4	8.3	63.7	56.6	42.0	-24.8	2.4
South Africa	-525.4	1.1	-95.1	394.5	48.4	408.7	350.5	716.6	500.5	716.4
AMERICA	**3 205.5**	**-5 699.4**	**-1 400.0**	**13 492.3**	**-7 525.1**	**11 722.2**	**26 429.3**	**12 075.6**	**27 482.8**	**16 163.1**
Northern America	4 329.3	1 423.2	420.2	10 904.1	-7 160.4	9 992.0	20 703.3	13 051.0	24 860.8	13 888.8
Central America and Caribbean countries	-1 300.3	-7 063.8	-1 839.0	2 522.8	-22.4	1 858.8	2 095.4	489.9	2 422.5	709.3
Bahamas	155.2	173.0	5.5	58.6	-1 015.0	2.7	7.8	4.4	-	5.9
Bermuda	-1 264.4	-5 141.4	-1 084.8	-126.3	-614.9	5.3	14.4	115.0	-29.3	279.7
Cayman Islands	-525.4	-1 478.6	-713.3	558.0	-2 241.2	544.0	410.4	-999.7	-985.2	-1 488.3
Costa Rica	-9.3	6.7	-	-1.1	-1.2	-13.3	3.3	16.6	-38.3	-60.2
El Salvador	-	-	-	-1.1	-3.5	-	3.3	-5.5	-5.6	-27.1
Guatemala	6.6	-	2.2	1.1	-2.4	-8.0	3.3	-13.3	4.5	-4.7
Honduras	2.7	2.2	2.2	1.1	-3.5	-2.7	8.9	-3.3	-13.5	2.4
Nicaragua	18.6	-10.0	-	-	-	8.0	8.9	-	-21.4	8.3
Panama	-15.9	-56.6	-3.3	30.4	-22.4	127.4	84.3	-27.6	182.6	108.6
Virgin Islands, U.S.	-	-	-	-	-	-	-	-	-	-
South America	175.1	-59.9	19.9	66.5	-342.3	-128.7	3 630.6	-1 466.3	198.4	1 565.0
Argentina	-51.7	-65.4	43.1	40.6	-14.2	286.6	458.1	210.1	731.6	342.3
Bolivia	-	1.1	-	-	1.2	5.3	7.8	-91.8	-	5.9
Brazil	-147.3	43.3	-34.3	48.5	-109.8	766.9	1 907.9	-991.9	-559.1	-64.9
Colombia	4.0	-6.7	-11.1	4.5	-31.9	4.0	114.3	178.0	152.2	153.4
Ecuador	-	-2.2	-	-2.3	7.1	-542.7	54.4	18.8	29.3	29.5
Paraguay	6.6	-	8.8	1.1	-2.4	-8.0	-	2.2	15.8	24.8
Peru	2.7	-2.2	1.1	-2.3	-8.3	33.2	83.2	73.0	50.7	109.8
Uruguay	18.6	-8.9	-11.1	1.1	-9.4	75.6	257.8	1.1	146.5	1 206.2
Venezuela	-4.0	-22.2	12.2	29.3	30.7	-469.7	52.1	-820.5	-625.6	-339.9

GERMANY

Table 1. Foreign direct investment flows by country *(cont.)*

Million US dollars

	Inward					Outward				
	2014	2015	2016	2017	2018	2014	2015	2016	2017	2018
ASIA	**3 464.2**	**2 535.8**	**3 906.9**	**1 580.4**	**1 464.7**	**16 779.9**	**7 290.1**	**12 323.3**	**10 900.7**	**4 281.8**
Near and Middle East	-802.7	-154.2	201.3	205.2	-121.6	1 133.1	854.1	949.9	1 236.6	297.4
Gulf Arabian countries	-888.9	-323.9	49.8	140.9	-302.1	469.7	758.7	617.1	1 072.0	291.5
Kuwait	14.6	12.2	11.1	-15.8	-9.4	55.7	-8.9	74.1	92.4	11.8
Qatar	-55.7	-300.6	123.9	299.9	-207.7	-99.5	102.1	127.2	-5.6	-336.4
Saudi Arabia	-65.0	53.2	-140.4	-164.6	-17.7	-13.3	64.3	359.4	-3.4	-276.2
United Arab Emirates	-794.7	-96.5	69.7	41.7	-49.6	583.8	634.5	-65.2	909.7	887.5
Other Near and Middle East	86.2	169.7	151.5	64.3	180.6	663.4	95.4	334.0	164.6	5.9
Jordan	4.0	-6.7	7.7	2.3	1.2	91.5	-1.1	1.1	-15.8	-24.8
Other Asian countries	4 267.0	2 690.0	3 705.6	1 375.3	1 586.2	15 646.8	6 435.9	11 372.3	9 664.1	3 984.4
China	2 019.4	103.2	327.3	-222.1	-50.7	11 385.2	6 081.0	8 398.8	6 202.2	365.9
Hong Kong, China	358.2	25.5	422.4	-387.8	836.8	432.5	271.8	437.9	-120.6	270.3
India	-25.2	-21.1	-48.7	-41.7	-140.4	1 263.1	1 773.7	1 495.1	1 215.2	1 218.0
Indonesia	15.9	25.5	23.2	-33.8	15.3	156.6	13.3	99.5	282.9	435.5
Iran, Islamic Republic of	122.1	-5.5	15.5	72.1	136.9	898.2	25.5	264.3	-551.2	144.0
Malaysia	98.2	130.9	67.5	-200.7	8.3	257.4	205.2	555.1	583.9	367.0
Philippines	-14.6	-5.5	4.4	2.3	-13.0	-63.7	58.8	-351.7	213.1	232.5
Singapore	49.1	-219.6	147.1	-497.1	94.4	-696.6	166.4	-2 603.1	-22.5	299.8
Chinese Taipei	4.0	59.9	70.8	15.8	38.9	614.3	53.2	112.8	211.9	809.6
Thailand	-10.6	-27.7	-109.5	-11.3	70.8	398.0	-281.8	385.9	580.5	269.1
Viet Nam	-2.7	3.3	4.4	7.9	-15.3	-9.3	79.9	107.3	108.2	29.5
AUSTRALIA, OCEANIA AND POLAR REGIONS	**-881.0**	**-169.7**	**-172.5**	**208.5**	**-279.7**	**391.4**	**826.4**	**175.8**	**1 889.3**	**2 201.1**
WORLD unallocated and confidential	**5.3**	**-1.1**	**-4.4**	**15.8**	**30.7**	**-**	**-**	**-1.1**	**-1.1**	**-1.2**
European Union (EU28)	**-14 054.7**	**29 526.3**	**5 543.5**	**14 205.8**	**9 201.0**	**52 628.4**	**59 813.6**	**27 429.0**	**38 609.0**	**31 906.1**
G20 countries excl. European Union	**23 750.8**	**6 658.9**	**11 795.9**	**8 873.9**	**-7 163.9**	**23 563.8**	**31 858.0**	**34 049.5**	**55 170.8**	**27 709.2**
G20 OECD countries	**21 474.1**	**5 975.6**	**11 949.6**	**10 273.9**	**-5 922.3**	**13 654.0**	**20 687.7**	**21 855.6**	**45 108.8**	**21 542.5**
G20 Non-OECD countries	**2 276.8**	**683.3**	**-153.7**	**-1 400.1**	**-1 241.6**	**9 909.8**	**11 170.3**	**12 194.0**	**10 062.0**	**6 166.6**
MENA countries	**-899.6**	**-345.0**	**60.8**	**240.1**	**-355.2**	**521.4**	**983.9**	**1 801.4**	**1 731.5**	**1 867.1**
ASEAN countries	**118.1**	**-82.1**	**131.6**	**-737.2**	**159.3**	**41.1**	**252.9**	**-1 802.5**	**1 748.4**	**1 602.7**

- Nil

Note: Detailed metadata at: *http://stats.oecd.org/OECDStat_Metadata/ShowMetadata.ashx?Dataset=FDI_CTRY_IND_SUMM.*

1. Information on data for Israel: *http://oe.cd/israel-disclaimer.*
2. Note by Turkey: The information in this document with reference to "Cyprus" relates to the southern part of the Island. There is no single authority representing both Turkish and Greek Cypriot people on the Island. Turkey recognises the Turkish Republic of Northern Cyprus (TRNC). Until a lasting and equitable solution is found within the context of the United Nations, Turkey shall preserve its position concerning the "Cyprus issue".
3. Note by all the European Union Member States of the OECD and the European Union: The Republic of Cyprus is recognised by all members of the United Nations with the exception of Turkey. The information in this document relates to the area under the effective control of the Government of the Republic of Cyprus.

Source: OECD International Direct Investment Statistics (database): https://doi.org/10.1787/idi-data-en

GERMANY

Table 2. Foreign direct investment positions by country

At year end

Million US dollars

	Inward					Outward				
	2014	2015	2016	2017	2018	2014	2015	2016	2017	2018
WORLD	**859 564.6**	**781 743.1**	**794 510.4**	**957 467.0**	**939 148.2**	**1 398 632.3**	**1 369 209.6**	**1 367 630.4**	**1 645 169.1**	**1 643 627.2**
OECD COUNTRIES	.. d	**734 250.4**	**740 795.8**	**886 950.1**	..	**1 164 727.4**	**1 143 407.7**	**1 135 030.0**	**1 377 444.2**	**1 377 837.2**
Australia	3 722.4	3 246.6	4 354.4	5 115.1	..	13 265.3	11 603.7	11 963.7	14 484.3	14 989.7
Austria	27 324.5	24 989.7	23 894.8	28 881.0	..	48 188.8	44 631.5	50 981.3	66 045.8	66 659.0
Belgium	14 120.0	11 479.6	10 011.6	12 130.0	..	42 896.6	40 618.4	35 196.6	21 261.7	21 250.3
Canada	6 888.8	.. d	.. d	.. d	..	16 771.6	13 905.3	14 705.4	16 608.3	16 738.0
Chile	.. c	620.6	1 499.9	563.7	..	1 941.3	1 984.8	.. d	.. d	.. d
Czech Republic	1 267.5	808.9	855.9	989.4	..	19 727.9	18 904.7	20 343.6	27 005.3	27 230.4
Denmark	7 518.9	7 646.2	8 241.8	9 375.2	..	6 502.7	5 242.2	6 134.7	7 606.1	6 930.4
Estonia	4.9	3.3	5.3	8.4	..	-21.9	4.4	23.2	128.3	199.2
Finland	3 740.6	3 071.3	2 875.5	4 407.5	..	3 372.8	3 078.9	2 937.7	3 785.1	4 348.5
France	59 195.9	54 028.3	53 257.1	70 020.4	..	78 366.5	72 999.5	70 393.2	101 826.6	97 062.1
Germany	68 773.9	62 546.5	71 940.6	88 746.7	..	-	..	-	-	-
Greece	72.8	67.5	76.9	51.6	..	5 049.4	4 497.6	5 065.9	7 052.1	6 718.6
Hungary	71.6	66.4	99.1	111.5	..	15 396.0	13 728.9	13 877.9	18 336.5	15 714.4
Iceland	399.4	397.4	16.9	18.0	..	18.2	57.7	.. d	.. d	.. d
Ireland	8 360.3	7 584.1	5 347.3	5 124.7	..	10 034.5	10 260.2	10 209.8	13 049.9	25 389.3
Israel[1]	6 283.0	5 585.2	5 062.7	5 958.3	..	977.4	1 094.2	1 197.4	1 442.8	1 432.3
Italy	40 730.6	35 062.6	33 599.7	35 765.2	..	40 064.1	31 816.0	32 880.8	39 173.7	38 026.1
Japan	37 229.2	36 272.2	37 322.7	42 181.6	..	9 414.1	6 525.9	8 340.9	9 528.7	9 821.4
Korea	5 735.4	4 536.7	5 755.2	6 295.3	..	8 944.3	9 208.5	8 271.3	10 453.3	9 837.4
Latvia	9.7	9.8	.. c	14.4	..	693.3	769.7	649.3	816.7	857.6
Lithuania	.. c	2.2	.. c	.. c	..	1 053.8	724.0	953.9	1 077.0	897.6
Luxembourg	55 098.3	54 835.1	53 514.3	60 084.0	..	148 809.8	139 543.8	136 757.7	176 811.0	185 967.5
Mexico	.. d	.. d	.. d	.. d	..	9 546.5	8 260.2	9 058.7	12 854.4	15 659.5
Netherlands	56 614.7	51 801.9	46 522.6	54 118.5	..	103 715.7	120 076.2	133 641.8	173 359.3	165 679.0
New Zealand	1 223.8	55.5	.. d	.. d	..	539.1	508.4	663.0	1 577.1	1 722.0
Norway	2 855.6	2 155.7	2 241.0	3 001.9	..	7 356.2	7 277.1	6 929.5	6 928.5	6 272.0
Poland	689.6	432.2	716.8	813.1	..	31 773.0	29 566.7	29 132.5	37 765.7	37 926.5
Portugal	446.8	445.3	416.4	412.6	..	3 624.1	3 166.0	3 359.3	4 378.7	5 044.7
Slovak Republic	1.2	1.1	1.1	1.2	..	4 588.1	3 881.3	3 158.0	4 180.9	4 436.7
Slovenia	87.4	84.9	76.9	67.2	..	1 124.3	1 198.7	1 135.2	1 478.8	1 635.0
Spain	21 512.6	25 955.4	24 900.4	29 593.4	..	55 989.4	49 805.1	48 540.1	63 602.8	65 500.3
Sweden	14 286.3	15 486.1	14 714.9	17 912.0	..	17 433.3	25 171.5	23 485.8	27 332.7	26 331.6
Switzerland	63 104.1	54 352.7	59 685.9	70 117.5	..	36 397.5	34 801.3	38 921.7	45 445.0	41 985.3
Turkey	801.3	1 585.2	1 612.7	1 960.9	..	10 984.0	9 992.4	9 351.7	10 584.1	9 306.2
United Kingdom	106 889.4	89 879.2	92 148.2	103 998.6	..	168 541.4	151 477.4	140 717.8	159 872.9	144 218.0
United States	194 859.4	171 474.1	171 626.4	219 305.6	..	243 397.9	268 515.0	254 632.7	289 683.4	299 314.2
EUROPE	**566 818.4**	**520 013.1**	**527 565.1**	**622 904.8**	..	**914 261.0**	**873 252.0**	**873 344.6**	**1 074 952.0**	**1 063 023.8**
Bulgaria	.. c	.. c	.. c	.. c	..	1 676.7	1 734.3	1 926.8	2 217.6	2 303.6
Croatia	.. c	.. c	.. c	-	..	2 297.1	2 164.4	2 160.9	2 528.2	2 926.5
Cyprus[2, 3]	757.6	1 475.2	1 300.7	1 633.5	..	1 125.5	1 694.1	215.0	-795.2	954.9
Malta	500.2	370.2	721.0	470.1	..	13 602.8	13 850.8	9 407.6	10 519.3	8 946.6
Romania	6.1	6.5	6.3	.. c	..	6 921.6	7 060.4	7 802.3	8 989.0	9 143.6
Russian Federation	5 724.5	7 914.0	8 730.9	11 602.3	..	16 946.4	14 918.9	18 945.9	21 971.7	21 750.6
Ukraine	.. d	135.0	.. c	.. c	..	4 399.9	2 880.8	2 679.5	2 868.8	3 036.4
AFRICA	**2 529.0**	**1 699.5**	**1 514.7**	**1 598.7**	..	**10 743.6**	**8 916.7**	**10 170.8**	**11 496.8**	**14 418.4**
Northern Africa	88.6	236.3	198.2	104.3	..	2 651.6	2 403.9	2 624.6	2 786.0	5 825.5
Algeria	3.6	3.3	3.2	3.6	..	295.0	389.8	533.4	599.7	1 118.6
Egypt	.. c	.. c	56.9	.. d	..	1 333.1	1 367.4	1 573.7	1 587.9	2 129.6
Libya	.. c	167.7	134.9	.. c	..	241.6	-57.7	-255.1	-209.9	417.9
Morocco	.. c	.. c	.. c	.. c	..	468.6	411.5	536.5	567.3	1 915.5
Tunisia	1.2	1.1	.. d	1.2	..	312.0	292.9	237.2	241.1	243.9
Other African countries	2 440.3	1 463.3	1 316.5	1 495.6	..	8 092.0	6 513.9	7 546.1	8 710.7	8 592.9
Nigeria	.. c	.. c	.. c	.. c	..	384.9	381.1	374.2	316.6	297.7
South Africa	2 433.1	1 464.3	1 308.1	.. d	..	6 114.2	4 843.8	5 764.7	6 766.6	6 472.4
AMERICA	**208 468.3**	**185 536.2**	**185 547.6**	**234 773.3**	..	**305 389.9**	**321 532.9**	**310 884.4**	**352 528.2**	**359 905.0**
Northern America	201 748.2	178 657.6	179 464.5	228 383.3	..	260 169.5	282 420.3	269 338.0	306 291.7	316 052.2
Central America and Caribbean countries	5 565.4	5 210.7	2 931.4	4 384.7	..	20 812.1	16 474.7	16 394.0	19 412.3	20 653.8
Bahamas	7.3	.. c	.. c	6.0	..	108.1	103.4	106.5	136.7	138.5
Bermuda	1 619.6	1 457.8	1 368.2	2 076.0	..	2 164.7	2 112.1	1 794.0	1 789.4	2 188.0
Cayman Islands	1 147.3	1 730.0	-546.0	-597.3	..	2 532.6	1 921.5	1 418.8	717.2	-817.5
Costa Rica	-	-	-	-	..	109.3	127.4	190.8	145.1	49.2
El Salvador	-	-	-	-	..	129.9	119.3	117.0	111.5	60.7
Guatemala	-	-	4.2	4.8	..	89.8	105.5	98.0	100.7	91.6
Honduras	-	-	-	-	..	65.6	79.5	84.3	116.3	40.1
Nicaragua	-	-	-	-	..	55.8	67.5	.. d	.. d	.. d
Panama	.. c	.. c	.. c	.. c	..	4 902.5	2 669.5	2 534.0	2 669.7	2 794.8
Virgin Islands, U.S.	1.2	1.1	1.1	1.2	..	.. c	.. c	.. c	.. c	.. c
South America	1 154.6	1 666.8	3 150.6	2 006.5	..	24 408.3	22 636.3	25 152.3	26 823.0	23 199.0
Argentina	2.4	2.2	2.1	2.4	..	2 805.8	2 499.7	2 286.3	2 720.1	2 254.4
Bolivia	-	-	-	-	..	139.6	168.3	84.3	80.4	84.7
Brazil	1 016.2	1 028.9	1 620.1	1 404.4	..	15 541.7	13 490.5	14 884.6	16 048.2	13 957.0
Colombia	.. c	3.3	3.2	3.6	..	1 219.0	1 127.3	1 342.9	1 593.9	1 605.2
Ecuador	-	-	-	1.2	..	286.5	324.4	326.8	358.6	348.1
Paraguay	-	-	-	-	..	185.8	156.3	173.9	212.3	219.8
Peru	2.4	2.2	3.2	3.6	..	611.9	627.1	714.7	694.4	762.5
Uruguay	.. c	.. c	13.7	18.0	..	412.8	687.0	770.5	823.9	2 055.2
Venezuela	8.5	7.6	8.4	9.6	..	1 237.2	1 558.0	2 297.9	1 492.0	-593.1

Table 2. Foreign direct investment positions by country *(cont.)*

At year end

Million US dollars

	Inward					Outward				
	2014	2015	2016	2017	2018	2014	2015	2016	2017	2018
ASIA	**76 801.5**	**71 192.2**	**75 274.6**	**93 251.4**	..	**154 354.6**	**153 341.3**	**160 563.9**	**190 075.6**	**189 740.1**
Near and Middle East	.. d	17 895.5	16 689.2	18 860.6	..	7 106.1	7 609.1	8 090.0	10 931.9	11 977.3
Gulf Arabian countries	14 491.5	12 252.6	11 551.6	12 829.2	..	5 011.8	5 587.4	5 991.4	8 859.4	9 690.9
Kuwait	337.5	327.7	322.5	373.0	..	137.2	163.3	220.3	260.3	257.6
Qatar	7 568.7	6 874.3	6 660.7	8 287.4	..	211.3	271.1	300.4	359.8	349.2
Saudi Arabia	.. d	365.8	378.4	428.2	..	1 439.9	1 476.3	1 613.8	1 527.9	1 407.1
United Arab Emirates	3 762.5	2 780.6	2 343.2	2 257.1	..	3 048.6	3 574.3	3 462.6	6 423.6	7 347.1
Other Near and Middle East	.. d	5 642.9	5 136.5	6 031.4	..	2 094.3	2 021.8	2 098.7	2 072.4	2 286.5
Jordan	2.4	3.3	5.3	.. c	..	173.6	167.7	158.1	134.3	116.8
Other Asian countries	.. d	53 296.7	58 585.4	74 390.7	..	147 248.5	145 731.1	152 473.9	179 143.7	177 762.8
China	4 537.1	4 935.2	7 611.5	16 754.6	..	71 871.1	72 182.9	77 044.4	91 752.2	87 757.0
Hong Kong, China	1 025.9	853.6	1 265.9	1 446.4	..	5 729.3	5 930.3	5 402.1	6 504.0	7 228.1
India	3 747.9	.. d	2 874.5	3 268.2	..	21 331.7	24 132.8	25 177.6	28 907.4	28 051.3
Indonesia	.. c	.. c	3.2	.. c	..	2 558.1	2 573.8	2 743.8	3 085.9	3 391.3
Iran, Islamic Republic of	1 623.3	1 673.4	1 710.8	1 772.6	..	574.3	248.2	406.9	434.2	482.0
Malaysia	696.9	755.6	770.5	901.9	..	4 642.7	3 924.9	4 412.4	5 238.7	5 930.8
Philippines	-	-	-	.. c	..	1 001.6	1 032.1	1 022.5	1 243.7	1 370.5
Singapore	677.5	386.5	341.5	548.1	..	14 653.0	13 846.5	12 935.6	13 971.0	14 496.2
Chinese Taipei	417.7	542.2	609.3	827.5	..	1 535.8	1 935.8	1 922.6	2 295.5	3 023.8
Thailand	61.9	52.3	186.6	194.3	..	3 054.7	2 554.2	2 996.7	3 750.3	3 987.9
Viet Nam	.. c	.. c	.. c	.. c	..	586.4	636.9	708.3	804.7	841.5
AUSTRALIA, OCEANIA AND POLAR REGIONS	**4 946.2**	**3 303.2**	**4 609.5**	**4 937.6**	..	**13 883.2**	**12 167.7**	**12 666.8**	**16 117.8**	**16 764.4**
WORLD unallocated and confidential	**1.2**	**-1.1**	**-1.1**	**1.2**	..	**-**	**-1.1**	**-**	**-1.2**	**-224.4**
European Union (EU28)	**488 175.0**	**448 199.2**	**445 338.9**	**524 856.1**	..	**832 548.4**	**797 669.0**	**791 088.9**	**979 406.3**	**972 299.1**
G20 countries excl. European Union	**543 797.8**	**485 193.3**	**502 493.9**	**618 099.1**	..	**737 903.3**	**720 423.5**	**708 777.3**	**837 849.6**	**820 013.7**
G20 OECD countries	**.. d**	**466 323.4**	**479 965.2**	**583 173.4**	..	**599 294.3**	**584 305.9**	**560 316.2**	**665 068.4**	**654 972.5**
G20 Non-OECD countries	**.. d**	**18 869.9**	**22 528.7**	**34 925.6**	..	**138 608.9**	**136 117.6**	**148 461.1**	**172 781.2**	**165 041.2**
MENA countries	**14 611.7**	**12 521.5**	**11 805.6**	**12 985.1**	..	**8 024.0**	**8 372.3**	**8 992.3**	**12 017.3**	**16 045.3**
ASEAN countries	**1 546.8**	**1 302.1**	**1 332.4**	**1 718.6**	..	**26 514.7**	**24 587.9**	**24 840.3**	**28 123.1**	**30 022.9**

- Nil; .. Not available; c Confidential data; d Secondary Confidentiality

Note: Inward FDI positions are allocated according to the ultimate investing country. Detailed metadata at: *http://stats.oecd.org/OECDStat_Metadata/ShowMetadata.ashx?Dataset=FDI_CTRY_IND_SUMM.*

1. Information on data for Israel: *http://oe.cd/israel-disclaimer.*
2. Note by Turkey: The information in this document with reference to "Cyprus" relates to the southern part of the Island. There is no single authority representing both Turkish and Greek Cypriot people on the Island. Turkey recognises the Turkish Republic of Northern Cyprus (TRNC). Until a lasting and equitable solution is found within the context of the United Nations, Turkey shall preserve its position concerning the "Cyprus issue".
3. Note by all the European Union Member States of the OECD and the European Union: The Republic of Cyprus is recognised by all members of the United Nations with the exception of Turkey. The information in this document relates to the area under the effective control of the Government of the Republic of Cyprus.

Source: OECD International Direct Investment Statistics (database): https://doi.org/10.1787/idi-data-en

GERMANY

Table 3. Foreign direct investment income by country

Million US dollars

	Inward					Outward				
	2014	2015	2016	2017	2018	2014	2015	2016	2017	2018
WORLD	**41 271.1**	**28 767.6**	**37 723.1**	**38 597.7**	**39 190.4**	**89 590.0**	**84 950.6**	**97 529.6**	**100 267.2**	**113 619.7**
OECD COUNTRIES	**37 716.6**	**27 528.6**	**37 521.8**	**37 883.0**	**38 308.7**	**60 656.8**	**63 957.8**	**74 997.2**	**75 233.9**	**85 709.9**
Australia	-143.3	-21.1	67.5	73.3	73.2	691.3	438.2	488.8	821.8	933.6
Austria	2 564.7	1 984.5	1 909.8	2 313.2	2 326.2	3 476.2	3 493.1	4 117.0	4 969.0	5 610.8
Belgium	1 621.3	2 232.9	964.3	642.5	581.8	3 007.8	2 501.4	1 706.3	1 698.8	1 921.4
Canada	58.4	114.3	90.7	93.6	101.5	883.6	723.2	881.3	722.6	827.3
Chile	-	-16.6	-38.7	-55.2	-55.5	-14.6	16.6	140.4	191.6	197.1
Czech Republic	157.9	-30.0	282.0	244.6	252.6	2 160.0	1 943.4	2 092.2	2 229.7	2 542.2
Denmark	2 128.2	986.1	670.1	532.1	555.9	195.0	73.2	520.8	521.9	564.1
Estonia	-	-	-	-	4.7	17.2	13.3	18.8	14.7	17.7
Finland	106.1	8.9	71.9	117.2	85.0	407.3	311.7	346.1	341.6	396.6
France	5 216.9	2 959.5	5 948.2	4 908.1	5 037.2	2 022.0	2 524.7	3 027.8	3 167.6	3 597.3
Germany	-	-	-	-	-	-	-	-	-	-
Greece	13.3	1.1	-	29.3	24.8	322.4	296.2	188.0	349.5	384.8
Hungary	46.4	32.2	39.8	23.7	23.6	1 167.6	1 286.7	973.1	1 092.3	1 254.6
Iceland	2.7	3.3	1.1	1.1	1.2	-5.3	-1.1	-	-	-
Ireland	854.5	382.7	853.7	874.8	932.4	782.8	274.0	692.2	994.3	1 097.6
Israel[1]	77.0	77.6	67.5	91.3	92.1	43.8	54.4	78.5	73.3	79.1
Italy	2 778.3	2 046.6	2 054.6	3 777.5	3 886.5	1 816.4	2 049.9	2 042.5	2 220.7	2 509.1
Japan	294.5	491.4	233.3	877.0	881.6	1 570.9	910.7	1 171.1	693.3	786.0
Korea	124.7	351.6	211.2	213.1	210.1	1 232.6	917.4	1 099.2	1 108.1	1 259.3
Latvia	-	-1.1	1.1	-	-1.2	54.4	51.0	37.6	48.5	55.5
Lithuania	2.7	1.1	2.2	3.4	1.2	106.1	62.1	21.0	76.7	61.4
Luxembourg	4 979.4	355.0	756.4	1 398.9	1 599.2	5 031.2	4 708.8	7 852.5	8 909.9	10 011.8
Mexico	-34.5	-89.9	-7.7	-23.7	-22.4	631.6	897.4	897.9	872.5	1 004.4
Netherlands	5 845.8	7 013.9	8 970.5	8 702.5	8 949.6	5 560.6	14 069.9	8 052.6	7 759.0	9 101.9
New Zealand	2.7	2.2	1.1	2.3	2.4	91.5	72.1	116.1	142.0	157.0
Norway	172.5	129.8	29.9	-86.8	-85.0	551.9	-271.8	356.1	454.3	485.1
Poland	203.0	142.0	258.8	290.8	344.6	3 230.7	2 489.2	2 654.0	2 560.0	2 962.4
Portugal	8.0	6.7	-15.5	-21.4	-20.1	532.0	453.1	414.7	461.1	528.7
Slovak Republic	2.7	4.4	8.8	11.3	15.3	449.8	521.4	593.8	579.4	660.9
Slovenia	17.2	16.6	29.9	31.6	31.9	122.1	133.4	134.9	144.3	162.9
Spain	1 766.0	1 203.6	2 179.6	2 313.2	2 313.2	1 901.3	2 154.2	2 428.4	3 262.3	3 734.2
Sweden	1 665.1	353.9	-577.2	1 039.3	944.2	1 468.8	1 454.2	4 844.6	5 023.1	5 698.1
Switzerland	3 559.8	2 422.6	6 860.6	5 231.7	5 191.8	4 395.6	4 691.1	5 822.2	4 705.2	5 316.9
Turkey	84.9	41.0	53.1	60.9	61.4	1 113.2	1 133.2	790.7	1 120.5	1 273.5
United Kingdom	367.5	1 879.1	2 447.2	766.5	682.2	4 317.4	2 873.6	5 622.0	2 988.4	3 219.6
United States	3 175.0	2 442.6	3 098.5	3 408.9	3 285.7	11 482.0	10 770.9	14 794.9	14 992.7	17 297.3
EUROPE	**36 271.7**	**24 515.8**	**33 550.8**	**33 425.8**	**33 990.3**	**49 108.4**	**51 932.3**	**60 628.1**	**61 426.0**	**69 514.9**
Bulgaria	21.2	11.1	12.2	21.4	21.2	86.2	47.7	152.6	144.3	165.2
Croatia	-4.0	6.7	11.1	5.6	11.8	156.6	143.4	235.5	201.8	227.8
Cyprus[2, 3]	651.5	227.4	91.8	82.3	80.3	59.7	63.8	143.8	148.8	168.8
Malta	73.0	26.6	49.8	12.4	14.2	1 298.9	-10.0	411.4	540.0	618.4
Romania	6.6	3.3	15.5	20.3	21.2	705.9	687.7	991.9	998.8	1 135.4
Russian Federation	816.0	232.9	-103.9	435.1	441.4	2 335.1	1 417.6	2 974.7	2 858.8	3 055.6
Ukraine	5.3	1.1	1.1	-3.4	-2.4	-211.0	-109.8	-84.0	-121.7	-122.7
AFRICA	**107.5**	**-112.0**	**196.8**	**151.1**	**141.6**	**881.0**	**633.4**	**1 255.1**	**1 144.2**	**1 437.5**
Northern Africa	8.0	-1.1	16.6	2.3	2.4	119.4	74.3	368.2	397.9	613.7
Algeria	5.3	-	-	-	-	71.6	123.1	195.7	169.1	207.7
Egypt	2.7	-1.1	15.5	1.1	1.2	103.5	147.5	247.7	241.2	417.8
Libya	-1.3	-	-	-	-	-151.3	-250.7	-140.4	-25.9	-27.1
Morocco	-	-	-	-	-	58.4	26.6	49.8	-4.5	-4.7
Tunisia	-	1.1	1.1	1.1	-	37.2	27.7	15.5	18.0	20.1
Other African countries	99.5	-110.9	179.1	149.9	139.3	761.6	559.1	888.0	745.1	825.0
Nigeria	23.9	-	-5.5	1.1	1.2	22.6	27.7	-13.3	-12.4	-14.2
South Africa	63.7	-100.9	190.2	136.4	127.5	642.2	470.3	826.1	692.1	773.0
AMERICA	**4 105.1**	**3 537.4**	**3 757.6**	**3 984.9**	**4 045.8**	**15 381.5**	**13 099.3**	**15 225.0**	**15 771.6**	**18 116.4**
Northern America	3 232.1	2 556.9	3 190.3	3 502.4	3 388.4	12 367.0	11 493.1	15 677.3	15 715.3	18 124.6
Central America and Caribbean countries	853.1	982.8	604.9	534.3	703.4	3 186.9	2 142.0	162.6	193.9	229.0
Bahamas	163.2	26.6	3.3	21.4	21.2	4.0	5.5	1.1	1.1	1.2
Bermuda	468.4	394.9	266.5	215.3	212.4	330.4	301.7	257.7	263.8	304.5
Cayman Islands	172.5	585.7	258.8	211.9	193.6	1 967.6	746.5	-1 066.0	-1 040.5	-1 188.5
Costa Rica	-	-	-	-	-	-5.3	-1.1	-11.1	-25.9	-30.7
El Salvador	-	-	-	-	-	4.0	4.4	-1.1	-3.4	-3.5
Guatemala	-	-	-	-	-	5.3	34.4	-3.3	5.6	7.1
Honduras	-	-	-	-	-	11.9	11.1	23.2	23.7	27.1
Nicaragua	-	-	-	-	-	2.7	2.2	3.3	2.3	2.4
Panama	-8.0	-4.4	-4.4	-4.5	-4.7	189.7	120.9	53.1	93.6	107.4
Virgin Islands, U.S.	-	-	-	-	-	-	-	-	-	-
South America	19.9	-2.2	-37.6	-51.9	-46.0	-171.2	-535.8	-613.7	-137.5	-237.2
Argentina	-	-2.2	-4.4	-3.4	-3.5	102.2	69.9	247.7	236.7	275.0
Bolivia	-	-	-	-	-	15.9	15.5	4.4	6.8	8.3
Brazil	18.6	16.6	7.7	7.9	11.8	-234.8	-761.0	-757.5	-751.9	-931.2
Colombia	-	-	-	-	-	45.1	59.9	40.9	94.7	109.8
Ecuador	-	-	-	-	-	22.6	28.8	17.7	25.9	27.1
Paraguay	-	-	-1.1	-	-	5.3	-5.5	-1.1	2.3	2.4
Peru	-	1.1	1.1	1.1	-	74.3	85.4	90.7	87.9	101.5
Uruguay	1.3	-	-2.2	-1.1	-1.2	33.2	47.7	28.8	31.6	38.9
Venezuela	-	1.1	1.1	1.1	1.2	-217.6	-87.6	-420.2	-57.5	-59.0

Table 3. Foreign direct investment income by country *(cont.)*

Million US dollars

	Inward					Outward				
	2014	2015	2016	2017	2018	2014	2015	2016	2017	2018
ASIA	**927.4**	**941.8**	**540.8**	**1 171.2**	**1 190.8**	**23 433.7**	**18 859.7**	**20 039.8**	**21 125.0**	**23 618.6**
Near and Middle East	222.9	87.6	192.4	187.1	191.2	1 052.1	966.2	1 003.0	781.2	769.5
Gulf Arabian countries	143.3	4.4	121.6	82.3	83.8	914.2	922.9	836.0	614.4	612.5
Kuwait	10.6	6.7	15.5	16.9	14.2	45.1	11.1	40.9	89.1	50.7
Qatar	128.7	3.3	118.3	86.8	86.2	30.5	18.9	29.9	4.5	5.9
Saudi Arabia	-6.6	1.1	-18.8	-19.2	-20.1	447.1	475.9	296.4	90.2	61.4
United Arab Emirates	14.6	4.4	7.7	1.1	5.9	374.2	374.9	382.6	351.7	401.3
Other Near and Middle East	79.6	83.2	70.8	106.0	107.4	138.0	43.3	167.0	166.8	157.0
Jordan	-	-	1.1	-	1.2	10.6	7.8	32.1	22.5	4.7
Other Asian countries	704.5	853.0	348.3	983.0	1 000.8	22 381.6	17 893.5	19 037.9	20 344.9	22 849.1
China	152.6	-52.1	-44.2	-25.9	-22.4	13 672.5	10 702.2	11 905.3	13 154.1	14 769.3
Hong Kong, China	14.6	-8.9	-87.4	-68.8	-60.2	1 714.2	1 426.5	1 140.1	1 171.2	1 336.0
India	-45.1	-7.8	-26.5	-27.1	-28.3	934.1	1 023.8	911.2	1 214.1	1 482.4
Indonesia	-2.7	-	1.1	1.1	1.2	480.3	382.7	366.0	485.9	557.1
Iran, Islamic Republic of	59.7	26.6	66.4	67.6	67.3	327.7	72.1	74.1	129.6	86.2
Malaysia	30.5	17.7	46.4	30.4	29.5	362.2	498.1	591.6	572.7	633.8
Philippines	-	1.1	1.1	1.1	1.2	74.3	62.1	19.9	207.4	238.4
Singapore	57.1	18.9	-69.7	-103.7	-96.8	1 196.8	1 166.9	706.6	445.3	501.6
Chinese Taipei	9.3	8.9	8.8	11.3	10.6	216.3	208.5	167.0	240.1	275.0
Thailand	10.6	7.8	12.2	10.1	9.4	382.1	353.9	529.7	568.1	650.3
Viet Nam	-4.0	-2.2	-2.2	-1.1	-	51.7	58.8	179.1	111.6	109.8
AUSTRALIA, OCEANIA AND POLAR REGIONS	**-140.6**	**-17.7**	**53.1**	**59.7**	**60.2**	**786.8**	**523.6**	**606.0**	**966.1**	**1 094.1**
WORLD unallocated and confidential	**-**	**-97.6**	**-376.0**	**-195.0**	**-238.4**	**-1.3**	**-97.6**	**-224.5**	**-165.7**	**-161.7**
European Union (EU28)	**31 093.3**	**21 854.7**	**27 036.4**	**28 141.1**	**28 719.5**	**40 456.4**	**44 693.3**	**50 316.3**	**51 446.3**	**58 409.1**
G20 countries excl. European Union	**12 918.9**	**10 302.8**	**14 197.7**	**14 660.1**	**14 704.4**	**44 139.6**	**37 032.7**	**47 586.0**	**46 688.1**	**52 749.9**
G20 OECD countries	**11 922.5**	**10 215.2**	**14 196.6**	**14 155.1**	**14 196.9**	**25 760.9**	**23 251.2**	**30 816.1**	**28 708.2**	**32 707.4**
G20 Non-OECD countries	**996.4**	**87.6**	**1.1**	**505.0**	**507.5**	**18 378.7**	**13 781.5**	**16 769.9**	**17 979.9**	**20 042.5**
MENA countries	**151.3**	**7.8**	**139.3**	**96.9**	**96.8**	**1 003.1**	**969.5**	**1 244.1**	**1 049.5**	**1 252.2**
ASEAN countries	**92.9**	**43.3**	**-10.0**	**-62.0**	**-55.5**	**2 556.7**	**2 534.7**	**2 404.1**	**2 503.7**	**2 702.7**

- Nil

Note: Detailed metadata at: *http://stats.oecd.org/OECDStat_Metadata/ShowMetadata.ashx?Dataset=FDI_CTRY_IND_SUMM.*

1. Information on data for Israel: *http://oe.cd/israel-disclaimer.*
2. Note by Turkey: The information in this document with reference to "Cyprus" relates to the southern part of the Island. There is no single authority representing both Turkish and Greek Cypriot people on the Island. Turkey recognises the Turkish Republic of Northern Cyprus (TRNC). Until a lasting and equitable solution is found within the context of the United Nations, Turkey shall preserve its position concerning the "Cyprus issue".
3. Note by all the European Union Member States of the OECD and the European Union: The Republic of Cyprus is recognised by all members of the United Nations with the exception of Turkey. The information in this document relates to the area under the effective control of the Government of the Republic of Cyprus.

Source: OECD International Direct Investment Statistics (database): https://doi.org/10.1787/idi-data-en

Table 4. Foreign direct investment flows by industrial sector

Million US dollars

	Inward					Outward				
	2014	2015	2016	2017	2018	2014	2015	2016	2017	2018
All FDI activities	**-3 005.2**	**30 562.4**	**12 614.2**	**33 190.2**	**11 916.7**	**83 976.4**	**99 022.7**	**60 343.9**	**88 074.6**	**63 279.8**
Agriculture, forestry and fishing	**-35.6**	**37.8**	**3.8**	**30.1**	..	**75.2**	**29.8**	**-28.2**	**-50.7**	..
Mining and quarrying	**-117.8**	**-36.1**	**111.3**	**43.6**	..	**1 191.3**	**581.4**	**1 090.6**	**1 992.3**	..
Extraction activities	80.8	105.4	10.4	37.6	..	68.0	-479.9	98.5	1 470.0	..
Manufacturing	**4 397.7**	**4 573.2**	**-326.4**	**12 826.3**	..	**18 963.8**	**26 276.1**	**3 554.4**	**4 713.4**	..
of which:										
Food products, beverages and tobacco	-283.6	267.5	998.1	-411.2	..	-242.8	-136.9	-312.3	-211.4	..
Textiles, wood and paper products; printing	633.0	135.6	-64.2	-127.9	..	260.3	37.8	-12.1	226.2	..
Chemical, rubber, plastic, non-metallic mineral products	2 509.2	1 962.7	-2 639.6	4 869.0	..	6 832.7	6 203.2	-380.1	1 455.0	..
Metal and machinery products, except electrical equipment	-554.4	547.0	-252.3	1 531.9	..	-1 954.4	5 828.5	2 806.6	-3 953.1	..
Motor vehicles, trailers, semi-trailers, other transport equipment	1 218.4	1 275.7	395.2	5 915.9	..	9 521.1	17 051.9	4 652.6	4 095.2	..
Other manufacturing	875.0	384.7	1 236.4	1 048.6	..	4 546.9	-2 702.5	-3 200.3	3 101.4	..
Electricity, gas, steam and air conditioning supply	**541.4**	**5 353.4**	**-7 506.8**	**-1 025.8**	..	**1 622.5**	**-2 682.1**	**-7 811.1**	**273.5**	..
Water supply; sewerage, waste management and remediation activities	**23.0**	**59.2**	**35.1**	**15.0**	..	**191.9**	**216.9**	**111.0**	**29.1**	..
Construction	**634.3**	**386.2**	**524.4**	**317.3**	..	**308.8**	**281.7**	**78.8**	**-14.6**	..
Services	**-17 502.0**	**13 588.4**	**4 121.8**	**19 649.1**	..	**31 300.5**	**45 115.3**	**20 879.5**	**47 167.0**	..
Wholesale and retail trade; repair of motor vehicles and motorcycles	1 076.0	-2 314.1	1 244.4	3 964.9	..	1 555.5	-842.8	2 939.2	7 884.3	..
Transportation and storage	-20.3	244.2	-551.4	4 241.4	..	2 086.0	1 295.7	-3 048.3	823.8	..
Accommodation and food service activities	2.9	-80.3	16.5	544.7	..	161.3	62.9	70.4	49.6	..
Information and communication	-26 861.1	1 553.6	-2 306.0	-1 826.3	..	15 491.6	5 739.3	-5 228.9	444.9	..
Financial and insurance activities	-1 208.0	4 916.6	-1 420.3	-11 934.0	..	-5 447.7	17 458.4	15 448.3	17 598.7	..
Activities of holding companies	-330.6	2 840.5	-4 000.2	-6 603.9	..	-5 887.1	5 306.0	9 283.9	1 690.6	..
Real estate activities	-93.8	1 504.0	-20.4	6 436.8	..	-412.9	392.5	-382.2	253.2	..
Professional, scientific and technical activities	8 962.2	6 707.8	6 177.1	18 510.8	..	17 895.9	22 977.7	9 195.0	21 869.7	..
Administrative and support service activities	695.1	901.1	875.8	-437.1	..	133.9	-1 259.9	1 795.3	-1 427.5	..
Public administration; activities of households and of extraterritorial organisations	-1.7	1.5	4.6	4.3	..	-259.7	-723.2	11.5	-310.6	..
Education	0.9	5.5	19.0	5.3	..	13.1	12.3	-9.1	0.4	..
Human health and social work activities	-90.3	5.3	18.8	50.2	..	3.4	0.9	9.4	1.2	..
Arts, entertainment and recreation	27.1	143.3	33.3	83.0	..	83.3	4.3	79.8	-10.5	..
Other services	9.0	-0.2	30.5	5.1	..	-3.3	-2.9	-0.7	-10.1	..
Not allocated and confidential	**9 465.1**	**5 480.4**	**14 393.9**	**505.3**	**11 916.7**	**30 024.7**	**30 350.4**	**41 873.5**	**31 840.7**	**63 279.8**
Private real estate activities	**-411.3**	**1 120.1**	**1 257.2**	**829.3**	..	**297.8**	**-1 146.6**	**595.4**	**2 124.0**	..

.. Not available

Note: Detailed metadata at: *http://stats.oecd.org/OECDStat_Metadata/ShowMetadata.ashx?Dataset=FDI_CTRY_IND_SUMM.*

Source: *OECD International Direct Investment Statistics (database): https://doi.org/10.1787/idi-data-en*

Table 5. Foreign direct investment positions by industrial sector
At year end

Million US dollars

	Inward					Outward				
	2014	2015	2016	2017	2018	2014	2015	2016	2017	2018
All FDI activities	**859 564.6**	**781 743.1**	**794 510.4**	**957 467.0**	**939 148.2**	**1 398 632.3**	**1 369 209.6**	**1 367 630.4**	**1 645 169.1**	**1 643 627.2**
Agriculture, forestry and fishing	**194.3**	**181.8**	**335.2**	**341.8**	..	**2 662.5**	**2 640.2**	**2 718.5**	**3 391.7**	..
Mining and quarrying	**499.0**	**153.5**	**2 109.2**	**528.9**	..	**9 200.5**	**8 209.0**	**7 578.8**	**7 126.4**	..
Extraction activities	235.5	-19.6	1 834.1	265.1	..	8 796.2	7 929.2	7 142.4	6 596.3	..
Manufacturing	**43 490.3**	**42 703.3**	**40 651.4**	**59 786.5**	..	**216 148.7**	**195 268.4**	**207 732.7**	**253 595.6**	..
of which:										
Food products, beverages and tobacco	4 023.5	4 213.4	3 687.2	5 151.1	..	5 809.5	5 960.8	6 068.3	7 814.8	..
Textiles, wood and paper products; printing	6 377.7	3 009.3	4 339.6	4 739.7	..	5 484.1	5 330.4	5 025.8	6 213.7	..
Chemical, rubber, plastic, non-metallic mineral products	14 617.8	16 707.7	16 038.8	22 739.3	..	60 457.3	44 548.7	47 308.9	58 159.0	..
Metal and machinery products, except electrical equipment	13 351.5	14 317.9	14 714.9	15 329.8	..	52 579.0	52 372.3	55 578.2	62 829.2	..
Motor vehicles, trailers, semi-trailers, other transport equipment	-620.4	-566.1	-2 861.8	3 572.8	..	52 382.3	48 897.1	52 905.0	71 454.8	..
Other manufacturing	5 741.5	5 020.1	4 732.8	8 252.6	..	39 436.4	38 157.9	40 846.4	47 122.8	..
Electricity, gas, steam and air conditioning supply	**8 084.7**	**8 231.9**	**7 424.9**	**8 124.3**	..	**23 084.9**	**18 329.9**	**13 382.5**	**15 880.3**	..
Water supply; sewerage, waste management and remediation activities	**414.0**	**420.3**	**416.4**	**452.1**	..	**2 011.8**	**1 488.3**	**1 545.3**	**1 556.7**	..
Construction	**1 443.6**	**1 644.0**	**792.7**	**2 563.0**	..	**2 105.2**	**1 609.1**	**2 079.7**	**2 278.7**	..
Services	**779 759.4**	**703 984.8**	**717 454.4**	**854 659.4**	..	**955 660.6**	**963 449.1**	**957 855.0**	**1 157 864.0**	..
Wholesale and retail trade; repair of motor vehicles and motorcycles	42 659.8	42 561.8	43 973.9	57 637.3	..	107 237.8	107 732.2	113 203.3	138 413.3	..
Transportation and storage	7 187.5	6 561.8	8 046.8	9 374.0	..	8 158.8	6 814.4	7 031.7	11 686.3	..
Accommodation and food service activities	1 592.9	1 428.4	1 534.7	1 982.5	..	1 710.7	1 814.9	1 760.3	1 829.0	..
Information and communication	45 488.7	35 860.6	36 232.7	35 403.0	..	19 874.8	20 088.2	21 608.5	29 546.7	..
Financial and insurance activities	306 748.4	285 777.9	284 748.6	339 420.7	..	581 949.7	582 034.8	507 963.5	587 951.5	..
Activities of holding companies	236 471.5	226 884.0	221 776.1	259 743.3	..	538 508.0	517 573.2	454 265.8	542 740.5	..
Real estate activities	25 690.4	24 980.9	23 540.6	24 617.4	..	27 685.1	27 331.5	27 663.1	34 039.3	..
Professional, scientific and technical activities	348 384.8	305 542.7	317 975.1	382 943.2	..	188 975.9	197 033.2	257 246.8	329 420.7	..
Administrative and support service activities	1 597.8	538.9	567.1	2 271.5	..	13 141.4	12 080.6	12 629.9	15 015.6	..
Public administration; activities of households and of extraterritorial organisations	.. c	.. c	.. c	.. c	..	.. c	.. c	.. c	24.0	..
Education	.. d	-2.2	20.0	32.4	..	.. d	34.8	32.7	48.0	..
Human health and social work activities	.. d	251.5	265.6	346.6	..	6 471.2	8 093.6	8 298.7	9 419.5	..
Arts, entertainment and recreation	194.3	301.6	348.9	425.8	..	154.2	126.3	150.7	165.5	..
Other services	.. d	.. d	.. d	.. d	..	.. d	.. d	.. d	304.6	..
Not allocated and confidential	**1.2**	**-2.2**	**-**	**-**	**939 148.2**	**-**	**-2.2**	**-**	**-1.2**	**1 643 627.2**
Private real estate activities	**25 678.2**	**24 425.7**	**25 326.2**	**31 011.0**	..	**187 758.1**	**178 217.7**	**174 738.1**	**203 476.9**	..

- Nil; .. Not available; c Confidential data; d Secondary Confidentiality

Note: Detailed metadata at: *http://stats.oecd.org/OECDStat_Metadata/ShowMetadata.ashx?Dataset=FDI_CTRY_IND_SUMM.*

Source: OECD International Direct Investment Statistics (database): https://doi.org/10.1787/idi-data-en

Table 6. Foreign direct investment income by industrial sector

Million US dollars

	Inward					Outward				
	2014	2015	2016	2017	2018	2014	2015	2016	2017	2018
All FDI activities	**41 271.1**	**28 767.6**	**37 723.1**	**38 597.7**	**39 190.4**	**89 590.0**	**84 950.6**	**97 529.6**	**100 267.2**	**113 619.7**
Agriculture, forestry and fishing	**4.5**	**4.3**	**4.0**	**4.1**	..	**12.7**	**20.0**	**6.3**	**17.3**	..
Mining and quarrying	**6.5**	**3.7**	**4.8**	**-2.2**	..	**755.6**	**572.9**	**621.5**	**193.2**	..
Extraction activities	0.6	0.8	0.8	-4.7	..	728.4	546.1	604.6	174.0	..
Manufacturing	**3 905.2**	**3 098.3**	**2 333.9**	**2 751.2**	..	**15 293.3**	**12 785.0**	**16 361.5**	**21 908.5**	..
of which:										
Food products, beverages and tobacco	651.1	736.5	302.5	603.0	..	874.3	437.1	327.9	508.0	..
Textiles, wood and paper products; printing	312.5	167.0	195.1	144.2	..	277.0	248.3	209.7	260.3	..
Chemical, rubber, plastic, non-metallic mineral products	387.8	464.1	506.3	372.3	..	2 181.8	2 854.3	2 252.0	3 398.1	..
Metal and machinery products, except electrical equipment	1 811.8	1 303.2	1 399.6	1 490.4	..	4 065.1	2 800.4	3 578.2	3 258.9	..
Motor vehicles, trailers, semi-trailers, other transport equipment	174.1	137.3	-19.5	-0.2	..	5 980.5	3 817.9	7 789.5	11 987.4	..
Other manufacturing	568.0	290.3	-50.0	141.5	..	1 914.7	2 586.8	2 204.1	2 495.7	..
Electricity, gas, steam and air conditioning supply	**321.0**	**736.0**	**335.6**	**1 012.4**	..	**778.5**	**679.1**	**337.2**	**-50.3**	..
Water supply; sewerage, waste management and remediation activities	**6.1**	**6.2**	**-0.6**	**2.6**	..	**12.4**	**9.7**	**15.7**	**10.5**	..
Construction	**1 493.5**	**1 055.4**	**860.8**	**701.5**	..	**315.0**	**234.8**	**292.6**	**225.5**	..
Services	**24 632.7**	**20 951.1**	**26 001.1**	**17 678.5**	..	**37 520.7**	**36 903.7**	**34 595.9**	**42 045.1**	..
Wholesale and retail trade; repair of motor vehicles and motorcycles	2 686.8	2 230.4	2 056.4	2 408.8	..	1 008.7	1 318.3	1 539.7	1 062.2	..
Transportation and storage	122.8	138.7	206.9	548.5	..	1 519.2	682.3	510.7	1 514.2	..
Accommodation and food service activities	58.4	60.0	96.8	18.9	..	1.7	2.1	3.3	2.5	..
Information and communication	406.1	330.9	557.3	567.3	..	-587.1	-133.9	44.3	460.9	..
Financial and insurance activities	2 356.1	2 606.2	5 736.2	5 438.2	..	9 150.9	10 689.0	19 560.5	28 009.4	..
Activities of holding companies	89.0	963.4	3 443.5	4 331.9	..	349.0	1 991.9	13 096.8	20 045.8	..
Real estate activities	780.5	493.9	430.6	757.5	..	249.8	214.2	260.0	125.9	..
Professional, scientific and technical activities	17 978.6	14 794.7	16 576.5	7 728.8	..	25 605.0	23 835.8	12 398.4	10 675.4	..
Administrative and support service activities	200.7	210.8	204.9	103.1	..	262.1	195.8	124.8	51.3	..
Public administration; activities of households and of extraterritorial organisations	37.9	75.0	88.9	94.0	..	319.2	105.0	152.9	119.3	..
Education	-0.3	0.0	0.1	0.1	..	-16.9	-13.1	-16.6	-12.1	..
Human health and social work activities	-0.5	4.2	0.0	0.0	..	0.9	1.6	0.0	0.8	..
Arts, entertainment and recreation	4.8	5.8	7.4	12.5	..	7.1	11.6	16.1	25.2	..
Other services	0.7	0.4	39.0	0.8	..	-	1.0	1.9	10.0	..
Not allocated and confidential	**9 022.3**	**1 223.8**	**6 472.3**	**14 599.4**	**39 190.4**	**29 396.5**	**29 774.6**	**41 385.3**	**31 296.3**	**113 619.7**
Private real estate activities	**1 879.0**	**1 688.8**	**1 711.3**	**1 850.2**	..	**5 505.3**	**3 966.0**	**3 913.6**	**4 621.0**	..

- Nil; .. Not available

Note: Detailed metadata at: *http://stats.oecd.org/OECDStat_Metadata/ShowMetadata.ashx?Dataset=FDI_CTRY_IND_SUMM.*

Source: *OECD International Direct Investment Statistics (database): https://doi.org/10.1787/idi-data-en*

GREECE

Table 1. Foreign direct investment flows by country

Million US dollars

	Inward					Outward				
	2014	2015	2016	2017	2018	2014	2015	2016	2017	2018
WORLD	**2 683.4**	**1 267.8**	**2 762.4**	**3 477.4**	**3 970.8**	**3 015.3**	**1 577.9**	**-1 665.4**	**168.0**	**476.6**
OECD COUNTRIES	**1 901.0**	**1 003.5**	**1 925.6**	**2 864.7**	**2 371.6**	**945.1**	**537.6**	**-2 404.6**	**302.6**	**86.2**
Australia	3.6	2.6	5.4	7.9	16.3	0.6	0.9	-0.2	-0.3	-2.0
Austria	84.0	-30.2	7.3	-1.7	2.5	7.0	3.4	-7.2	-7.2	-2.3
Belgium	-151.0	15.0	-18.1	37.0	163.0	1.9	1.2	-1.0	-0.6	-0.3
Canada	470.5	710.9	205.6	183.8	176.7	0.2	0.0	0.0	-0.1	0.1
Chile	-	-	-	-	-	-	-	-	-	-
Czech Republic	4.8	-5.3	6.5	5.2	18.6	-11.5	-7.1	-6.9	-7.7	-7.1
Denmark	39.0	4.9	-3.8	-3.1	-18.1	0.2	0.1	-	-1.0	-1.9
Estonia	0.6	0.1	0.6	0.6	0.6	-	-	-	-	-
Finland	0.5	0.2	-2.1	4.8	-15.1	-	-	-	-0.6	-0.7
France	-104.5	-130.6	144.2	-46.2	-28.9	10.2	-0.2	-3.0	8.2	-10.9
Germany	138.8	123.6	242.3	715.4	541.6	-126.8	7.8	12.4	12.5	5.1
Greece	-	-	-	-	-	-	-	-	-	-
Hungary	0.7	-0.1	0.6	0.3	8.8	-	-1.3	0.6	0.6	0.2
Iceland	-	0.0	0.0	-0.3	-1.0	-	-	-	-	-
Ireland	25.7	9.2	-15.4	26.2	-66.4	0.3	-0.1	11.0	-	-
Israel[1]	1.7	2.5	3.2	32.1	28.3	-	0.0	0.7	-	0.9
Italy	26.8	102.0	84.0	133.4	341.5	142.6	13.7	-2.7	13.1	-44.8
Japan	-0.4	-0.7	-0.6	-4.7	-3.8	-8.9	-0.5	-0.3	-0.3	-0.4
Korea	-	1.3	1.3	-0.6	-0.2	-5.2	-	-	-	-
Latvia	1.8	1.1	1.6	1.1	2.3	-	-	-	-	-
Lithuania	-	0.0	0.0	0.1	0.8	-	-	-	-	-
Luxembourg	529.4	-151.3	810.7	111.8	406.7	215.8	18.7	55.1	95.5	55.6
Mexico	-	0.1	0.0	0.5	1.9	-	-	-	0.0	-
Netherlands	-2.3	317.3	99.5	489.9	-91.7	-235.5	135.6	-38.3	29.4	-61.7
New Zealand	-0.1	-	0.0	0.5	1.5	-	-	-	-	-
Norway	9.4	10.9	-0.3	1.8	4.9	-	-	0.0	-0.4	-0.8
Poland	1.1	0.1	1.7	5.1	2.9	-39.8	5.2	5.9	4.8	-7.8
Portugal	0.3	0.1	0.0	6.5	-2.3	0.3	0.2	0.6	0.5	-0.4
Slovak Republic	-	0.1	0.4	0.7	1.9	-	-0.3	-0.3	-0.3	-0.3
Slovenia	-0.1	-0.1	0.7	0.6	-1.4	0.3	0.2	1.3	2.6	3.0
Spain	-25.9	138.4	109.3	47.0	30.7	4.1	4.3	11.6	0.3	0.2
Sweden	-3.3	-4.2	4.5	1.6	18.9	-0.1	0.2	0.7	-5.4	-3.6
Switzerland	56.3	-66.9	152.3	849.3	552.8	-5.7	-16.8	-0.8	22.6	5.3
Turkey	7.4	-1.4	5.8	44.7	35.6	1 013.0	791.6	-2 467.4	58.0	57.0
United Kingdom	-151.7	79.7	14.6	175.2	159.3	-1.5	-437.9	-118.1	8.5	31.0
United States	939.8	-124.5	63.5	38.4	82.3	-16.3	18.7	141.8	70.3	72.6
EUROPE	**978.7**	**513.1**	**1 990.1**	**3 082.9**	**3 070.2**	**2 939.5**	**1 464.6**	**-2 084.1**	**-3.2**	**365.6**
Bulgaria	2.5	-4.1	35.7	24.0	33.3	685.9	553.6	259.6	-545.7	42.7
Croatia	-	0.0	0.2	0.1	-0.1	-	0.0	2.6	0.5	0.5
Cyprus[2, 3]	422.1	91.2	285.2	413.8	810.2	840.9	436.3	51.6	391.3	811.6
Malta	4.9	1.8	4.6	11.1	24.8	20.6	90.9	2.8	-0.1	-0.2
Romania	1.1	1.1	2.2	-0.5	6.7	239.8	-104.5	52.6	-0.8	-354.3
Russian Federation	35.3	22.4	14.8	18.9	11.8	50.9	38.9	38.6	39.1	42.7
Ukraine	1.2	0.1	0.3	0.0	0.2	-35.8	-36.4	-3.7	-2.8	-2.2
AFRICA	**-19.4**	**-12.1**	**-11.4**	**-4.9**	**-13.2**	**7.5**	**-2.6**	**12.9**	**0.9**	**-12.2**
Northern Africa	1.3	1.0	2.6	7.3	8.7	11.7	0.5	0.1	0.5	0.0
Algeria	-	-	-	-	-	-	-	-	0.1	-
Egypt	1.3	0.9	2.0	7.3	8.7	11.7	0.5	0.3	0.4	0.2
Libya	-	-	-	-	-	-	0.0	-0.2	0.0	-0.3
Morocco	-	-	0.3	-	-	-	-	-	-	-
Tunisia	-	0.1	0.3	-	-	-	0.0	0.0	-	-
Other African countries	-20.7	-13.1	-14.0	-12.2	-22.0	-4.2	-3.0	12.8	0.5	-12.1
Nigeria	-	-	-	-	0.9	-	-	-	-	-
South Africa	0.1	0.0	0.0	0.5	0.8	-4.4	-3.0	-	0.2	-11.9
AMERICA	**1 492.6**	**640.4**	**364.1**	**229.7**	**141.7**	**-64.0**	**-71.1**	**107.3**	**21.7**	**-92.5**
Northern America	1 410.2	586.4	269.1	222.3	259.0	-16.1	18.7	141.8	70.2	72.7
Central America and Caribbean countries	82.4	54.1	94.9	7.3	-118.9	-48.6	-89.9	-34.8	-48.4	-164.7
Bahamas	0.9	0.3	1.6	3.8	2.5	-	0.2	-	-	-
Bermuda	97.8	64.6	106.3	17.6	7.0	-	-	-	-13.9	-
Cayman Islands	-1.5	2.4	-0.4	0.1	-0.3	3.3	-68.4	-2.4	-30.5	-31.8
Costa Rica	-	-	-	-	-	-	-	-	-	-
El Salvador	-	-	-	-	-	-	-	-	-	-
Guatemala	-	-	-	-	0.0	-	-	-	-	-0.1
Honduras	-	0.1	-	-	-	-	-	-	-	-
Nicaragua	-	-	-	-	-	-	-	-	-	-
Panama	-4.5	-0.2	0.5	-0.8	0.1	0.1	-	-0.1	-	-
Virgin Islands, U.S.	-	-	-	-	-	-	-	-	-	-
South America	-	0.0	0.1	0.2	1.7	0.7	0.1	0.3	0.0	-0.5
Argentina	-	-	-	-	0.5	-	-	-	-	-
Bolivia	-	-	-	-	-	-	-	-	-	-
Brazil	-	0.0	-	0.2	0.4	0.7	0.1	0.3	-0.1	-0.6
Colombia	-	-	-	-	-	-	-	0.1	0.1	0.1
Ecuador	-	-	-	-	-	-	-	-	-	-
Paraguay	-	-	-	-	-	-	-	-	-	-
Peru	-	-	-	-	0.4	-	-	-	-	-
Uruguay	-	-	0.1	-	0.3	-	-	-	-	-
Venezuela	-	-	-	-	-	-	-	-	-	-

GREECE

Table 1. Foreign direct investment flows by country *(cont.)*

Million US dollars

	Inward					Outward				
	2014	2015	2016	2017	2018	2014	2015	2016	2017	2018
ASIA	**236.2**	**130.6**	**420.0**	**169.7**	**755.3**	**131.7**	**185.7**	**298.8**	**149.0**	**217.7**
Near and Middle East	177.5	73.4	33.1	85.8	96.1	-60.9	-33.8	13.2	45.1	42.7
Gulf Arabian countries	132.4	59.3	18.4	25.7	31.5	-59.3	-32.8	17.2	45.6	44.4
Kuwait	-	1.1	1.0	4.9	1.4	0.3	0.2	-	-	-
Qatar	60.8	31.8	9.2	2.5	1.9	0.1	0.8	16.7	44.9	36.6
Saudi Arabia	1.6	10.8	2.4	1.1	3.9	-	-	-0.1	-	-
United Arab Emirates	69.3	13.3	2.9	13.6	20.7	-59.7	-33.7	0.6	0.9	7.8
Other Near and Middle East	45.1	14.1	14.7	60.1	64.6	-1.6	-1.0	-4.0	-0.6	-1.7
Jordan	1.1	1.1	2.9	4.6	4.5	1.2	-	-	-	-2.3
Other Asian countries	58.8	57.2	386.9	84.0	659.2	192.6	219.5	285.5	104.0	175.0
China	22.6	20.7	32.4	53.7	254.2	-0.1	0.2	0.4	0.7	10.9
Hong Kong, China	36.6	35.1	350.6	29.2	370.5	206.7	219.9	285.5	103.6	164.4
India	0.1	0.1	0.3	0.0	1.3	-	0.0	0.0	0.0	0.0
Indonesia	-	-	0.0	-	-	-	-	-	-	-
Iran, Islamic Republic of	-	-	0.0	1.5	2.8	-	-	-	-	-
Malaysia	-	-	0.2	0.2	0.3	-	-	-	-	-
Philippines	-	-	-	-	-	-	-	-	-	-
Singapore	1.3	0.0	1.3	2.9	28.1	-	-	-	-	-
Chinese Taipei	-	-	0.1	-	3.0	-0.3	-	-	-	-
Thailand	-	0.1	0.0	0.2	-	-	-	-	-	-
Viet Nam	-	-	-	-	0.3	-	-	-	-	-
AUSTRALIA, OCEANIA AND POLAR REGIONS	**-4.8**	**-4.4**	**-0.9**	**-0.6**	**13.8**	**0.6**	**0.9**	**-0.2**	**-0.5**	**-2.0**
WORLD unallocated and confidential	**0.0**	**0.2**	**0.5**	**0.5**	**3.0**	**0.0**	**0.4**	**0.0**	**0.0**	**0.0**
European Union (EU28)	**845.2**	**560.0**	**1 817.0**	**2 159.8**	**2 351.1**	**1 754.5**	**719.9**	**290.8**	**-1.8**	**453.9**
G20 countries excl. European Union	**1 390.0**	**816.9**	**816.1**	**1 322.3**	**1 595.3**	**1 055.0**	**430.2**	**-2 398.3**	**209.6**	**149.0**
G20 OECD countries	**1 330.3**	**763.0**	**766.2**	**1 247.8**	**1 322.4**	**1 007.9**	**394.1**	**-2 437.4**	**169.8**	**107.9**
G20 Non-OECD countries	**59.7**	**53.9**	**49.8**	**74.4**	**272.9**	**47.1**	**36.1**	**39.1**	**39.9**	**41.1**
MENA countries	**176.1**	**70.7**	**31.9**	**60.4**	**73.2**	**-49.4**	**-33.1**	**13.0**	**45.8**	**42.0**
ASEAN countries	**1.3**	**0.1**	**1.5**	**3.4**	**28.8**	**-**	**-**	**-**	**-**	**-**

- Nil

Note: Detailed metadata at: *http://stats.oecd.org/OECDStat_Metadata/ShowMetadata.ashx?Dataset=FDI_CTRY_IND_SUMM.*

1. Information on data for Israel: *http://oe.cd/israel-disclaimer.*
2. Note by Turkey: The information in this document with reference to "Cyprus" relates to the southern part of the Island. There is no single authority representing both Turkish and Greek Cypriot people on the Island. Turkey recognises the Turkish Republic of Northern Cyprus (TRNC). Until a lasting and equitable solution is found within the context of the United Nations, Turkey shall preserve its position concerning the "Cyprus issue".
3. Note by all the European Union Member States of the OECD and the European Union: The Republic of Cyprus is recognised by all members of the United Nations with the exception of Turkey. The information in this document relates to the area under the effective control of the Government of the Republic of Cyprus.

Source: OECD International Direct Investment Statistics (database): https://doi.org/10.1787/idi-data-en

Table 2. Foreign direct investment positions by country
At year end

Million US dollars

	Inward					Outward				
	2014	2015	2016	2017	2018	2014	2015	2016	2017	2018
WORLD	**21 550.3**	**24 082.0**	**24 614.9**	**33 404.1**	**34 851.3**	**29 415.1**	**24 419.0**	**18 005.9**	**20 104.3**	**19 554.2**
OECD COUNTRIES	**24 968.9**	**25 225.0**	**24 961.0**	**33 380.5**	**33 764.3**	**10 811.6**	**8 194.0**	**4 570.0**	**5 863.0**	**6 127.8**
Australia	-6.0	-5.0	-4.5	9.8	19.6	2.2	2.0	1.9	11.7	11.3
Austria	325.7	255.2	351.7	507.5	292.7	894.8	688.6	625.6	722.2	416.6
Belgium	1 201.4	1 415.9	1 450.0	801.5	1 296.8	-20.0	4.5	47.9	153.1	148.6
Canada	1 135.5	748.9	591.1	876.3	722.0	2.6	2.3	-	17.4	15.7
Chile	0.0	0.0	0.0	0.0	0.0	-	-	-	0.2	0.2
Czech Republic	-0.2	-0.1	-0.3	13.6	21.9	0.9	0.1	-0.4	0.2	0.0
Denmark	99.6	89.7	86.6	194.2	190.8	7.7	7.1	5.0	2.0	-1.8
Estonia	0.0	0.0	0.0	5.3	5.6	-	-	-	0.1	0.1
Finland	11.5	2.7	12.0	50.1	52.5	-	-	-	1.1	0.6
France	1 836.6	2 060.0	1 464.2	1 743.3	1 706.0	28.6	18.0	26.0	69.0	64.6
Germany	5 532.1	5 559.1	5 226.2	7 721.0	7 927.0	154.9	185.9	232.4	366.7	368.4
Greece	-	-	-	-	-	-	-	-	-	-
Hungary	67.0	60.5	39.0	44.8	14.9	3.1	-0.8	0.4	1.9	2.0
Iceland	1.3	1.1	1.1	1.7	1.7	-	-	-	-	-
Ireland	466.6	376.2	410.6	474.4	447.6	13.3	11.5	11.4	13.8	13.3
Israel[1]	38.1	36.1	34.9	46.5	64.0	0.0	0.0	-	0.5	3.6
Italy	940.6	920.0	1 024.3	1 241.4	1 644.4	614.7	533.8	339.7	568.5	574.5
Japan	35.1	46.8	44.7	47.1	42.0	12.4	11.3	-0.6	12.9	12.3
Korea	4.8	4.9	8.2	20.2	12.4	-6.8	-6.1	-12.5	-14.9	-14.2
Latvia	0.0	0.0	0.0	12.8	13.9	-	-	-	0.3	0.3
Lithuania	0.0	0.0	0.0	3.5	3.9	-	-	-	0.1	0.1
Luxembourg	5 842.4	4 766.5	5 634.6	7 731.4	7 565.4	-121.7	406.9	-192.6	-383.6	-345.3
Mexico	-6.2	-25.8	-25.0	-27.9	-25.6	-	-	-	-	-
Netherlands	4 456.9	4 980.6	5 014.6	5 763.3	5 443.1	1 168.9	2 137.1	2 034.0	2 185.0	2 023.9
New Zealand	-0.1	-0.1	-0.1	0.8	1.6	-	-	-	0.7	0.7
Norway	60.9	52.5	59.4	37.3	24.6	33.3	29.9	29.0	6.8	7.1
Poland	-9.1	-4.6	5.1	15.2	10.8	-281.1	-125.6	51.7	44.5	50.9
Portugal	0.2	1.4	0.6	1.5	2.5	6.1	5.5	4.7	5.4	4.9
Slovak Republic	-1.8	-2.9	-5.8	-5.4	-3.9	-3.6	-7.1	-6.6	-6.5	-6.0
Slovenia	-1.6	7.8	5.7	6.9	22.2	15.0	13.6	11.9	20.0	20.9
Spain	1 253.7	835.5	818.6	865.6	767.9	133.2	118.2	125.9	154.0	110.7
Sweden	136.3	107.0	101.2	143.3	132.0	4.3	4.2	3.9	10.0	8.4
Switzerland	1 411.0	1 781.4	1 928.8	3 408.4	3 558.0	-36.4	-32.6	0.6	92.9	98.8
Turkey	26.8	13.4	6.7	42.6	59.7	6 479.5	3 589.7	143.5	153.5	272.8
United Kingdom	-847.5	342.2	106.5	549.3	757.8	-507.3	-1 547.9	-1 253.0	-784.3	-239.4
United States	957.2	798.1	570.3	1 036.7	968.5	2 212.8	2 143.9	2 340.3	2 438.0	2 503.4
EUROPE	**17 654.4**	**21 225.6**	**21 772.7**	**29 790.5**	**31 192.4**	**23 975.5**	**19 318.6**	**12 646.7**	**13 554.8**	**13 306.9**
Bulgaria	1.8	1.9	-8.0	4.9	72.5	1 994.7	1 766.4	1 328.0	1 474.7	1 459.8
Croatia	-12.7	-1.4	0.0	0.4	-0.1	60.8	56.3	62.7	6.9	5.8
Cyprus[2, 3]	-5 192.3	-2 484.2	-2 040.2	-1 728.8	-985.3	6 078.0	5 435.7	4 500.8	4 971.6	5 031.4
Malta	0.5	1.2	1.4	-38.9	-36.6	346.0	561.2	-4.7	-0.8	-2.3
Romania	-12.1	-6.3	-3.2	5.7	9.9	3 537.1	2 828.9	2 486.5	1 792.6	1 785.9
Russian Federation	41.2	36.3	27.3	102.7	110.6	99.2	89.0	86.1	77.6	75.9
Ukraine	-2.3	-1.9	-0.2	2.4	2.3	96.5	53.4	37.8	46.8	44.3
AFRICA	**100.6**	**72.2**	**62.9**	**64.5**	**45.3**	**813.1**	**518.2**	**91.1**	**302.3**	**338.8**
Northern Africa	-2.4	-0.2	-0.2	8.6	13.6	714.8	439.1	18.5	279.7	332.8
Algeria	0.0	0.0	0.0	0.0	0.0	-	-	-	-	-
Egypt	-1.1	0.0	-0.1	8.3	13.1	709.8	438.7	12.9	278.9	332.3
Libya	-0.1	-	-	-	-	5.1	0.5	0.3	0.3	0.0
Morocco	-1.0	0.0	0.0	0.2	0.2	0.0	0.0	5.4	0.2	0.2
Tunisia	-0.2	-0.2	-0.2	0.2	0.3	0.0	-0.1	-0.1	0.3	0.3
Other African countries	103.0	72.4	63.2	55.8	31.7	98.3	79.0	72.6	22.5	6.0
Nigeria	0.0	0.0	0.0	0.0	0.5	29.0	26.0	25.2	0.3	0.3
South Africa	-0.1	-0.2	-0.1	0.7	1.0	37.7	24.6	19.8	16.5	2.7
AMERICA	**2 845.6**	**2 102.7**	**1 837.9**	**2 239.4**	**2 103.1**	**3 428.4**	**3 256.2**	**3 383.2**	**3 802.5**	**3 573.0**
Northern America	2 092.7	1 547.0	1 161.4	1 913.0	1 690.5	2 215.4	2 146.3	2 340.3	2 455.4	2 519.1
Central America and Caribbean countries	752.7	556.5	679.0	299.7	413.5	1 212.5	1 109.7	1 042.8	1 193.1	915.2
Bahamas	-	-	-	0.9	1.0	-	-	-	1.0	1.0
Bermuda	459.2	295.7	500.3	1.0	1.5	1.2	-	-	-	-
Cayman Islands	39.1	118.1	23.2	13.2	12.8	502.9	504.5	490.9	131.5	125.6
Costa Rica	-	-	-	-	-	-	-	-	0.1	0.1
El Salvador	-	-	-	-	-	-	-	-	-	-
Guatemala	-	0.0	0.0	-0.1	0.0	-	-	-	-	0.3
Honduras	-	-0.3	-0.3	-0.3	-0.3	-	-	-	-	-
Nicaragua	-	-	-	-	-	-	-	-	-	-
Panama	93.7	81.7	91.4	147.2	141.8	11.0	9.8	9.5	12.3	1.5
Virgin Islands, U.S.	-	-	-	-	-	-	-	-	-	-
South America	0.2	-0.8	-2.5	26.8	-0.9	0.5	0.2	-	154.0	138.6
Argentina	1.3	0.4	-0.7	-0.8	-0.5	-	-	-	0.5	0.5
Bolivia	-	-	-	-	-	-	-	-	0.0	0.0
Brazil	-0.3	-1.1	-1.6	27.6	-0.5	0.5	0.2	-	151.9	136.5
Colombia	-0.1	-0.1	-0.2	-0.2	-0.2	-	-	-	1.0	1.0
Ecuador	-	-	-	0.0	-	-	-	-	0.1	0.1
Paraguay	-	-	-	-	-	-	-	-	-	-
Peru	-0.6	-	-	0.0	0.0	-	-	-	0.1	0.1
Uruguay	0.0	-	0.0	0.1	0.2	-	-	-	0.3	0.3
Venezuela	-0.1	-	-	0.0	0.0	-	-	-	-	-

Table 2. Foreign direct investment positions by country *(cont.)*

At year end

Million US dollars

	Inward					Outward				
	2014	2015	2016	2017	2018	2014	2015	2016	2017	2018
ASIA	**899.6**	**636.1**	**909.5**	**1 246.0**	**1 433.4**	**1 195.9**	**1 324.1**	**1 883.0**	**2 391.5**	**2 282.9**
Near and Middle East	306.2	156.9	217.4	235.4	283.0	56.7	-19.3	33.4	48.0	48.4
Gulf Arabian countries	265.8	113.4	177.9	98.7	114.1	9.4	-27.5	25.5	35.0	28.9
Kuwait	-	-	-	4.0	4.8	-	-	-	-	-
Qatar	39.0	22.7	33.4	63.0	62.3	-11.9	-	0.0	0.2	0.3
Saudi Arabia	-0.1	0.0	-0.4	10.8	12.8	-	-	-	0.0	0.0
United Arab Emirates	226.9	90.8	144.9	14.5	26.0	10.7	-37.2	14.9	20.5	21.3
Other Near and Middle East	40.4	43.4	39.5	136.7	168.9	47.3	8.2	7.9	13.0	19.5
Jordan	-0.9	0.2	1.0	8.1	10.3	3.1	-	-	0.9	4.8
Other Asian countries	593.5	479.2	692.0	1 010.6	1 150.3	1 139.2	1 343.4	1 849.6	2 343.5	2 234.5
China	13.7	6.4	10.1	128.8	256.0	24.0	39.2	24.1	22.3	21.4
Hong Kong, China	472.9	361.6	574.9	744.3	751.5	1 087.7	1 280.0	1 823.5	2 316.4	2 208.0
India	0.3	0.8	0.4	0.8	0.8	14.3	12.8	12.4	0.0	0.0
Indonesia	0.0	0.0	0.0	0.1	0.1	9.9	8.9	8.6	0.3	0.3
Iran, Islamic Republic of	62.3	53.0	48.6	56.7	56.6	-	-	-	-	-
Malaysia	0.3	0.1	0.3	0.7	0.9	-0.7	-1.0	-1.1	-1.1	-1.1
Philippines	-	0.0	0.0	-	-	0.0	0.0	0.0	0.1	0.1
Singapore	0.2	2.1	1.6	4.3	19.4	-0.4	-0.4	-0.8	2.4	2.4
Chinese Taipei	0.1	0.2	0.1	0.1	1.8	-0.7	-0.7	-1.9	-2.1	-2.0
Thailand	0.6	0.5	0.5	0.7	0.7	-1.9	-2.1	-2.5	-1.4	-1.3
Viet Nam	0.0	-	0.0	0.0	0.2	-	-	-	-	-
AUSTRALIA, OCEANIA AND POLAR REGIONS	**50.1**	**45.3**	**31.8**	**47.7**	**61.2**	**2.2**	**2.0**	**1.9**	**13.4**	**12.9**
WORLD unallocated and confidential	**-**	**0.0**	**-**	**16.0**	**15.9**	**-0.2**	**0.0**	**0.0**	**39.9**	**39.6**
European Union (EU28)	**16 095.6**	**19 283.8**	**19 695.3**	**26 127.9**	**27 376.1**	**14 128.5**	**13 102.1**	**10 441.2**	**11 388.2**	**11 496.7**
G20 countries excl. European Union	**9 665.0**	**10 505.1**	**9 047.7**	**13 530.6**	**14 214.0**	**9 179.3**	**5 107.7**	**1 968.7**	**3 107.6**	**3 806.6**
G20 OECD countries	**9 609.0**	**10 462.5**	**9 012.7**	**13 259.9**	**13 833.8**	**8 993.7**	**4 953.0**	**1 817.7**	**2 838.6**	**3 569.3**
G20 Non-OECD countries	**56.0**	**42.6**	**35.0**	**270.7**	**380.2**	**185.6**	**174.7**	**151.0**	**269.0**	**237.3**
MENA countries	**264.4**	**116.4**	**181.6**	**196.1**	**229.4**	**768.7**	**417.4**	**49.6**	**317.7**	**368.2**
ASEAN countries	**1.1**	**2.7**	**2.3**	**5.9**	**21.4**	**6.9**	**5.3**	**4.2**	**8.2**	**8.4**

- Nil

Note: Detailed metadata at: *http://stats.oecd.org/OECDStat_Metadata/ShowMetadata.ashx?Dataset=FDI_CTRY_IND_SUMM.*

1. Information on data for Israel: *http://oe.cd/israel-disclaimer.*
2. Note by Turkey: The information in this document with reference to "Cyprus" relates to the southern part of the Island. There is no single authority representing both Turkish and Greek Cypriot people on the Island. Turkey recognises the Turkish Republic of Northern Cyprus (TRNC). Until a lasting and equitable solution is found within the context of the United Nations, Turkey shall preserve its position concerning the "Cyprus issue".
3. Note by all the European Union Member States of the OECD and the European Union: The Republic of Cyprus is recognised by all members of the United Nations with the exception of Turkey. The information in this document relates to the area under the effective control of the Government of the Republic of Cyprus.

Source: OECD International Direct Investment Statistics (database): https://doi.org/10.1787/idi-data-en

Table 3. Foreign direct investment income by country

Million US dollars

	Inward					Outward				
	2014	2015	2016	2017	2018	2014	2015	2016	2017	2018
WORLD	**520.9**	**1 156.8**	**1 149.8**	**1 451.9**	**1 551.9**	**3 113.9**	**1 801.5**	**627.5**	**1 098.5**	**694.2**
OECD COUNTRIES	**460.5**	**1 017.5**	**922.0**	**1 325.3**	**1 426.1**	**1 070.6**	**719.6**	**200.7**	**360.7**	**472.2**
Australia	0.3	0.1	0.1	0.1	0.1	0.1	0.1	0.1	0.2	0.2
Austria	69.0	-29.0	-10.2	-9.1	-9.2	4.5	36.5	-6.0	-7.4	-2.2
Belgium	-105.9	-26.7	-11.9	61.2	63.3	11.8	0.8	3.2	1.1	3.8
Canada	76.0	146.8	192.4	179.8	172.5	3.6	2.7	2.8	2.5	3.8
Chile	-	0.0	0.0	0.0	0.0	-	0.0	0.0	0.0	0.0
Czech Republic	2.7	40.3	1.1	-0.1	0.2	-6.0	-6.1	-6.4	-5.8	-5.4
Denmark	28.0	5.1	4.8	5.9	6.6	-	0.0	0.0	-0.3	0.4
Estonia	-	0.0	0.0	0.0	0.0	1.9	0.9	1.3	1.3	2.6
Finland	0.8	0.7	-2.2	4.2	11.5	-	-	-	-0.6	-0.7
France	28.7	17.6	14.9	27.3	66.5	8.0	3.3	2.5	7.5	1.5
Germany	213.3	238.6	207.0	291.9	231.0	114.8	19.9	32.9	52.1	44.0
Greece	-	-	-	-	-	-	-	-	-	-
Hungary	-	0.0	0.0	0.0	0.0	-0.1	-1.3	0.6	0.6	0.3
Iceland	-	0.0	0.0	0.0	-0.1	-	0.0	0.0	0.0	0.0
Ireland	-14.6	7.4	-13.7	20.6	4.9	-	0.0	0.1	0.2	1.4
Israel[1]	1.2	1.0	0.9	1.1	0.5	0.5	0.3	0.3	0.3	1.0
Italy	55.2	133.6	104.7	45.8	59.1	2.9	11.8	15.6	27.1	36.1
Japan	-0.1	-0.7	-0.3	-4.4	-4.0	-0.3	-0.3	-0.3	-0.3	-0.3
Korea	0.5	0.0	0.0	-0.6	7.0	-	0.0	-	-	0.0
Latvia	-	0.0	0.0	0.0	0.0	0.3	0.2	0.1	0.1	0.1
Lithuania	-	-	-	0.0	0.0	-	0.0	-	-	-
Luxembourg	-166.0	-142.9	116.3	180.0	458.1	20.2	30.5	56.9	65.7	42.3
Mexico	-	0.0	-	0.0	-	-	0.0	-	-	-
Netherlands	70.8	265.0	-18.6	223.8	212.6	-234.6	131.0	-70.3	-14.0	43.8
New Zealand	-	-	-	0.0	0.0	-	0.0	0.0	0.0	0.0
Norway	7.7	10.0	-1.3	-0.2	0.4	0.5	0.2	0.1	-0.7	-0.4
Poland	0.3	0.2	0.0	0.3	0.3	-40.7	4.4	5.9	3.4	2.9
Portugal	-	0.0	0.0	0.1	1.0	0.4	0.2	0.9	0.5	-0.4
Slovak Republic	0.4	0.2	0.1	0.1	0.1	0.1	-0.2	-0.2	-0.2	-0.1
Slovenia	-0.1	0.3	-0.1	-0.1	-1.4	0.1	0.2	1.9	3.1	3.1
Spain	19.5	155.3	110.1	73.4	78.9	5.2	4.2	3.3	2.5	7.2
Sweden	6.1	4.3	5.6	2.8	12.4	-0.1	0.3	0.3	-3.8	-2.9
Switzerland	37.7	7.4	-28.0	83.0	115.9	70.9	52.1	47.0	77.9	88.6
Turkey	-0.7	-3.8	-1.8	-2.1	-2.2	1 012.9	800.5	47.4	61.6	53.6
United Kingdom	105.1	169.2	212.5	115.3	-88.3	41.7	-401.9	-100.7	14.0	66.4
United States	24.7	17.7	39.4	25.3	28.5	52.3	29.4	161.4	72.3	81.5
EUROPE	**444.9**	**1 003.6**	**925.7**	**1 303.6**	**1 386.3**	**2 927.3**	**1 671.2**	**206.7**	**947.7**	**527.3**
Bulgaria	1.1	-1.0	-0.7	-0.5	-0.3	716.1	539.4	124.0	330.7	-1.5
Croatia	-	0.0	0.0	0.0	0.0	-	0.0	0.4	0.4	0.4
Cyprus[2, 3]	77.2	170.2	249.9	201.8	190.1	774.0	436.2	-77.1	254.4	172.4
Malta	-	0.0	0.0	-6.4	-6.7	33.3	91.9	12.5	0.1	7.6
Romania	9.7	0.1	0.2	0.4	0.2	209.9	-101.5	17.6	-34.9	-63.0
Russian Federation	2.1	1.2	-2.6	-6.7	-6.3	50.8	39.3	41.9	40.2	44.0
Ukraine	-	0.0	0.0	-	0.0	-34.5	-36.1	-3.1	-1.9	-1.2
AFRICA	**-20.6**	**-12.6**	**-12.9**	**-15.8**	**-25.5**	**8.6**	**-0.8**	**2.1**	**3.1**	**1.4**
Northern Africa	-	0.0	0.0	0.0	0.0	11.8	0.5	0.1	2.1	-0.1
Algeria	-	-	-	-	-	-	0.0	0.0	0.0	0.0
Egypt	-	0.0	0.0	0.0	0.0	11.8	0.4	0.3	0.4	0.2
Libya	-	-	0.0	0.0	0.0	-	0.0	-0.2	0.0	-0.3
Morocco	-	-	-	-	0.0	-	0.1	-	1.7	-
Tunisia	-	-	-	0.0	-	-	0.0	0.0	-	-
Other African countries	-20.6	-12.6	-12.9	-15.8	-25.5	-3.2	-1.3	1.9	1.0	1.5
Nigeria	-	0.0	-	-	-	-	-	-	-	-
South Africa	0.3	0.0	0.0	0.0	0.0	-4.0	-3.0	0.0	0.1	0.0
AMERICA	**74.2**	**153.6**	**215.2**	**188.2**	**184.4**	**25.5**	**-56.9**	**132.2**	**41.9**	**53.1**
Northern America	100.7	164.5	231.9	205.0	201.0	55.9	32.1	164.2	74.8	85.2
Central America and Caribbean countries	-27.2	-11.2	-16.8	-17.1	-17.3	-45.1	-89.0	-32.0	-33.0	-32.7
Bahamas	-	0.0	-	-	-	1.7	1.0	2.6	1.2	2.8
Bermuda	-11.4	-0.1	-0.1	0.0	-0.2	-	0.0	0.0	0.0	0.0
Cayman Islands	-1.5	2.4	-0.4	-0.3	-0.3	2.3	-68.4	-2.4	-30.4	-31.5
Costa Rica	-	0.0	0.0	0.0	0.0	-	0.0	0.0	0.0	0.0
El Salvador	-	-	-	-	-	-	0.0	0.0	0.0	0.0
Guatemala	-	0.0	0.0	0.0	0.0	-	0.0	0.0	0.0	-0.1
Honduras	-	0.0	0.0	0.0	0.0	-	-	-	-	-
Nicaragua	-	0.0	0.0	-	0.0	-	0.0	-	-	-
Panama	-4.4	-0.7	-3.7	-2.7	-2.9	1.1	0.3	0.1	0.3	0.2
Virgin Islands, U.S.	-	-	-	-	-	-	-	-	-	-
South America	0.7	0.3	0.1	0.2	0.7	14.7	0.0	0.0	0.1	0.5
Argentina	-	0.0	0.0	0.0	0.0	-	0.0	-	-	0.0
Bolivia	-	0.0	0.0	0.0	0.0	-	0.0	0.0	0.0	0.0
Brazil	0.7	0.2	0.1	0.2	0.7	14.7	0.0	0.0	-0.3	-1.0
Colombia	-	0.0	-	-	-	-	0.0	-	-	-
Ecuador	-	-	-	-	-	-	0.0	0.0	0.0	0.0
Paraguay	-	0.0	0.0	0.0	0.0	-	0.0	0.0	0.0	0.0
Peru	-	-	0.0	-	-	-	0.0	0.0	0.5	1.5
Uruguay	-	0.1	-	-	-	-	0.0	-	-	-
Venezuela	-	-	-	0.0	0.0	-	-	-	-	-

Table 3. Foreign direct investment income by country (cont.)

Million US dollars

	Inward					Outward				
	2014	2015	2016	2017	2018	2014	2015	2016	2017	2018
ASIA	**30.1**	**19.0**	**28.3**	**-13.8**	**16.0**	**150.9**	**187.0**	**285.7**	**105.1**	**110.0**
Near and Middle East	0.1	-7.2	-6.0	-5.9	-10.9	-57.1	-33.5	0.6	4.1	4.0
Gulf Arabian countries	-2.4	-8.9	-7.0	-7.0	-11.5	-58.1	-33.2	1.3	2.4	3.2
Kuwait	-	-	-	-	0.0	-	-	-	-	-
Qatar	1.6	-12.5	-0.5	-0.4	-2.6	-	0.0	-	0.0	0.8
Saudi Arabia	-	0.0	0.0	0.0	0.0	-	0.1	0.0	-	-
United Arab Emirates	-3.8	3.6	-6.6	-6.8	-9.0	-58.1	-33.3	1.3	2.4	2.4
Other Near and Middle East	2.4	1.7	1.0	1.2	0.6	1.1	-0.3	-0.7	1.7	0.8
Jordan	-	-	0.0	0.0	0.0	-	0.0	0.0	0.0	0.0
Other Asian countries	30.0	26.2	34.3	-8.0	26.9	208.0	220.5	285.1	101.1	106.0
China	-	0.4	1.8	0.2	20.3	0.1	0.1	0.1	0.1	0.3
Hong Kong, China	29.6	26.4	32.7	-3.1	3.5	207.6	220.1	284.7	100.0	105.0
India	-	-	-	-	0.0	-	0.0	0.0	0.3	0.1
Indonesia	-	-	-	-	-	-	0.0	0.0	0.0	0.0
Iran, Islamic Republic of	-	-	-	0.0	0.0	-	-	0.0	-	-
Malaysia	-	0.0	0.0	0.0	0.0	-	0.0	-	0.1	0.1
Philippines	-	-	-	-	-	-	-	-	-	0.1
Singapore	-	0.1	0.0	-	0.0	0.3	0.5	0.5	0.7	0.3
Chinese Taipei	-	-	-	-	0.0	0.3	0.0	0.0	0.2	0.4
Thailand	-	-	-	-	-	-	0.0	-	-	0.0
Viet Nam	-	0.0	-	-	0.0	-	0.0	0.0	0.0	0.0
AUSTRALIA, OCEANIA AND POLAR REGIONS	**-7.9**	**-6.8**	**-6.3**	**-10.2**	**-11.2**	**0.7**	**0.6**	**0.6**	**0.2**	**1.0**
WORLD unallocated and confidential	**0.1**	**0.0**	**0.0**	**-0.1**	**2.0**	**0.9**	**0.5**	**0.2**	**0.4**	**1.5**
European Union (EU28)	**401.2**	**1 008.5**	**969.9**	**1 238.7**	**1 290.9**	**1 663.6**	**800.7**	**19.3**	**697.6**	**360.1**
G20 countries excl. European Union	**506.0**	**720.9**	**768.3**	**672.0**	**485.0**	**1 297.7**	**502.1**	**203.7**	**277.3**	**330.0**
G20 OECD countries	**503.0**	**719.1**	**769.0**	**678.3**	**470.3**	**1 236.0**	**465.6**	**161.7**	**236.9**	**286.6**
G20 Non-OECD countries	**3.1**	**1.8**	**-0.7**	**-6.3**	**14.7**	**61.7**	**36.5**	**42.1**	**40.4**	**43.4**
MENA countries	**-1.9**	**-8.9**	**-7.0**	**-7.0**	**-11.4**	**-45.8**	**-33.1**	**0.7**	**6.1**	**3.1**
ASEAN countries	**-**	**0.2**	**0.0**	**0.0**	**0.0**	**0.3**	**0.5**	**0.5**	**0.8**	**0.6**

\- Nil

Note: Detailed metadata at: *http://stats.oecd.org/OECDStat_Metadata/ShowMetadata.ashx?Dataset=FDI_CTRY_IND_SUMM.*

1. Information on data for Israel: *http://oe.cd/israel-disclaimer.*
2. Note by Turkey: The information in this document with reference to "Cyprus" relates to the southern part of the Island. There is no single authority representing both Turkish and Greek Cypriot people on the Island. Turkey recognises the Turkish Republic of Northern Cyprus (TRNC). Until a lasting and equitable solution is found within the context of the United Nations, Turkey shall preserve its position concerning the "Cyprus issue".
3. Note by all the European Union Member States of the OECD and the European Union: The Republic of Cyprus is recognised by all members of the United Nations with the exception of Turkey. The information in this document relates to the area under the effective control of the Government of the Republic of Cyprus.

Source: OECD International Direct Investment Statistics (database): https://doi.org/10.1787/idi-data-en

Table 4. Foreign direct investment flows by industrial sector

Million US dollars

	Inward					Outward				
	2014	2015	2016	2017	2018	2014	2015	2016	2017	2018
All FDI activities	**2 683.4**	**1 267.8**	**2 762.4**	**3 477.4**	**3 970.8**	**3 015.3**	**1 577.9**	**-1 665.4**	**168.0**	**476.6**
Agriculture, forestry and fishing	**2.8**	**1.7**	**5.2**	**10.3**	**17.2**	**5.1**	**-5.0**	**-0.3**	**7.5**	**0.3**
Mining and quarrying	**180.7**	**156.8**	**128.6**	**128.0**	**37.9**	**-125.2**	**-1.8**	**35.3**	**10.2**	**1.2**
Extraction activities	263.6	9.0	-6.1	20.8	26.9	1.1	0.1	0.1	10.1	6.8
Manufacturing	**-430.0**	**8.0**	**50.1**	**311.6**	**364.9**	**-25.2**	**-6.3**	**188.3**	**126.6**	**74.6**
of which:										
Food products, beverages and tobacco	-46.0	22.4	54.7	68.2	-5.5	13.6	5.1	28.7	41.8	35.8
Textiles, wood and paper products; printing	-18.7	1.4	3.3	-6.2	5.9	10.9	-4.1	1.3	2.3	5.1
Chemical, rubber, plastic, non-metallic mineral products	-268.4	0.4	20.3	179.5	350.8	-8.0	-8.2	22.3	4.8	5.5
Metal and machinery products, except electrical equipment	-120.2	-3.5	-3.1	29.0	19.0	-29.7	-22.5	-21.8	31.7	-1.0
Motor vehicles, trailers, semi-trailers, other transport equipment	2.2	4.5	4.5	0.7	0.2	0.3	-	-	0.8	-
Other manufacturing	21.2	-17.1	-29.6	40.5	-5.6	-12.3	23.5	157.8	45.0	29.1
Electricity, gas, steam and air conditioning supply	**1.7**	**-35.7**	**19.6**	**465.4**	**85.6**	**10.0**	**9.4**	**7.5**	**27.3**	**47.7**
Water supply; sewerage, waste management and remediation activities	**-0.5**	**0.9**	**0.0**	**1.0**	**1.0**	**3.0**	**5.2**	**4.1**	**0.8**	**-1.6**
Construction	**-45.8**	**22.4**	**39.1**	**-15.6**	**-77.0**	**-20.4**	**17.7**	**100.2**	**116.5**	**78.5**
Services	**2 712.7**	**947.3**	**2 308.8**	**2 200.3**	**2 756.4**	**3 161.3**	**1 579.0**	**-2 030.8**	**-125.2**	**272.4**
Wholesale and retail trade; repair of motor vehicles and motorcycles	-124.7	94.7	97.2	100.7	133.1	289.8	312.0	402.6	150.5	301.2
Transportation and storage	38.4	107.0	600.6	1 455.9	870.4	7.2	44.0	6.5	8.7	-50.9
Accommodation and food service activities	210.7	15.6	488.6	123.1	137.2	0.5	0.2	6.6	1.0	-0.8
Information and communication	404.8	-119.0	-165.5	-132.9	301.6	-36.3	-60.0	-189.4	-144.5	-147.4
Financial and insurance activities	1 292.7	650.3	886.6	516.4	721.9	2 983.8	1 292.6	-2 305.7	-334.3	47.9
Activities of holding companies	194.9	102.3	153.8	49.7	300.2	307.3	278.2	-240.5	365.1	291.7
Real estate activities	634.5	135.0	162.6	78.3	844.3	-61.0	-42.4	-7.1	138.6	102.0
Professional, scientific and technical activities	69.2	-28.7	10.1	24.0	-123.1	-26.7	30.8	-22.0	-2.8	9.3
Administrative and support service activities	60.6	59.0	50.6	52.8	56.2	6.1	5.2	-36.8	53.1	5.7
Public administration; activities of households and of extraterritorial organisations	-	-	-	-	-	-	-	-	-	-
Education	3.4	0.1	4.2	-0.1	0.0	-1.4	-	-	-0.1	-
Human health and social work activities	-14.0	-5.6	30.9	20.6	-89.3	-2.7	-3.3	-6.2	-3.8	-4.3
Arts, entertainment and recreation	135.7	35.0	131.9	-35.7	-100.1	-0.1	-0.1	151.7	8.7	9.7
Other services	-1.3	3.9	11.0	-2.8	4.2	2.3	0.0	-31.0	-0.2	0.0
Not allocated and confidential	**42.7**	**34.6**	**45.8**	**6.8**	**11.6**	**-0.6**	**-6.9**	**31.6**	**0.0**	**-1.3**
Private real estate activities	**219.1**	**131.7**	**165.4**	**369.5**	**773.3**	**7.4**	**-13.4**	**-1.2**	**4.2**	**4.7**

- Nil

Note: Detailed metadata at: *http://stats.oecd.org/OECDStat_Metadata/ShowMetadata.ashx?Dataset=FDI_CTRY_IND_SUMM.*

Source: OECD International Direct Investment Statistics (database): https://doi.org/10.1787/idi-data-en

Table 5. Foreign direct investment positions by industrial sector
At year end

Million US dollars

	Inward					Outward				
	2014	2015	2016	2017	2018	2014	2015	2016	2017	2018
All FDI activities	**21 550.3**	**24 082.0**	**24 614.9**	**33 404.1**	**34 851.3**	**29 415.1**	**24 419.0**	**18 005.9**	**20 104.3**	**19 554.2**
Agriculture, forestry and fishing	**303.6**	**286.2**	**260.7**	**327.6**	**313.6**	**71.4**	**60.5**	**56.1**	**63.0**	**60.1**
Mining and quarrying	**521.9**	**387.5**	**1 222.2**	**1 403.1**	**1 346.3**	**26.2**	**24.0**	**22.4**	**32.5**	**18.2**
Extraction activities	224.6	209.2	101.2	111.6	113.2	12.4	11.2	10.8	19.3	5.6
Manufacturing	**7 334.9**	**7 579.7**	**8 005.2**	**9 072.8**	**9 148.8**	**3 539.7**	**3 220.5**	**2 956.4**	**3 455.2**	**3 853.0**
of which:										
Food products, beverages and tobacco	2 185.8	1 858.0	1 867.2	2 097.2	2 078.7	251.9	258.8	207.1	278.1	279.0
Textiles, wood and paper products; printing	154.6	133.5	119.0	132.2	124.1	100.4	46.4	39.4	63.8	60.3
Chemical, rubber, plastic, non-metallic mineral products	2 931.4	2 940.7	3 009.9	4 339.3	4 270.7	293.8	77.9	136.7	150.1	217.5
Metal and machinery products, except electrical equipment	1 330.4	1 485.5	1 526.1	848.1	1 164.9	599.1	517.2	483.9	372.0	381.8
Motor vehicles, trailers, semi-trailers, other transport equipment	2.0	11.8	11.4	11.3	0.3	-	-	-	5.3	5.1
Other manufacturing	730.7	1 150.3	1 471.7	1 644.6	1 510.1	2 294.7	2 320.2	2 089.3	2 585.9	2 909.4
Electricity, gas, steam and air conditioning supply	**3 028.2**	**2 983.0**	**2 529.6**	**3 103.2**	**2 929.6**	**164.8**	**181.4**	**174.8**	**220.8**	**245.6**
Water supply; sewerage, waste management and remediation activities	**40.9**	**34.6**	**37.0**	**35.4**	**34.5**	**25.8**	**23.1**	**22.4**	**25.5**	**25.3**
Construction	**412.1**	**425.1**	**241.4**	**337.2**	**383.5**	**34.8**	**59.2**	**98.3**	**116.8**	**137.2**
Services	**9 848.2**	**12 313.1**	**12 237.3**	**17 180.0**	**17 947.0**	**25 543.7**	**20 780.2**	**14 607.9**	**15 190.6**	**14 174.9**
Wholesale and retail trade; repair of motor vehicles and motorcycles	5 543.7	5 432.4	5 447.0	5 782.3	5 483.4	3 192.9	3 157.9	3 683.9	4 910.7	4 511.1
Transportation and storage	886.7	875.8	1 769.0	3 552.6	4 015.2	750.1	203.4	187.1	212.7	202.4
Accommodation and food service activities	931.4	812.1	874.9	1 039.1	1 030.6	54.7	47.4	41.8	39.7	31.3
Information and communication	5 299.7	4 378.0	4 137.7	5 926.0	5 946.2	2 300.3	2 295.2	1 768.8	1 420.3	1 594.6
Financial and insurance activities	-8 171.0	-4 537.5	-4 369.9	-4 743.9	-3 410.8	17 990.4	14 540.8	8 013.3	7 469.1	6 786.6
Activities of holding companies	1 009.6	799.8	716.9	644.8	1 349.5	5 258.3	4 817.1	4 864.3	4 096.5	3 906.2
Real estate activities	1 706.8	2 588.1	2 103.9	2 316.0	2 119.4	421.4	185.3	382.6	367.4	372.1
Professional, scientific and technical activities	798.9	692.7	273.6	333.7	332.4	448.7	-32.9	189.4	389.3	331.8
Administrative and support service activities	676.8	661.1	711.4	1 050.0	981.6	154.8	177.8	136.9	157.6	134.2
Public administration; activities of households and of extraterritorial organisations	1.5	-	1.7	2.0	1.9	-	-	-	-	-
Education	0.7	0.6	0.9	1.0	0.9	-	-	-	-	-
Human health and social work activities	241.6	137.9	84.1	298.9	206.3	19.9	13.2	15.7	17.4	15.3
Arts, entertainment and recreation	1 914.0	1 262.5	1 194.0	1 612.0	1 229.8	193.3	173.3	167.8	191.0	182.3
Other services	17.2	9.4	9.0	10.3	10.1	17.2	15.7	20.7	15.5	13.0
Not allocated and confidential	**60.5**	**72.8**	**81.4**	**105.6**	**172.0**	**8.6**	**70.0**	**67.7**	**-421.4**	**-363.4**
Private real estate activities	**-**	**-**	**-**	**1 839.2**	**2 576.1**	**0.0**	**-**	**-**	**1 421.2**	**1 403.2**

- Nil

Note: Detailed metadata at: *http://stats.oecd.org/OECDStat_Metadata/ShowMetadata.ashx?Dataset=FDI_CTRY_IND_SUMM.*

Source: OECD International Direct Investment Statistics (database): https://doi.org/10.1787/idi-data-en

Table 6. Foreign direct investment income by industrial sector

Million US dollars

	Inward					Outward				
	2014	2015	2016	2017	2018	2014	2015	2016	2017	2018
All FDI activities	**520.9**	**1 156.8**	**1 149.8**	**1 451.9**	**1 551.9**	**3 113.9**	**1 801.5**	**627.5**	**1 098.5**	**694.2**
Agriculture, forestry and fishing	**5.0**	**1.5**	**1.6**	**2.7**	**3.4**	**1.8**	**-1.5**	**0.1**	**0.2**	**0.1**
Mining and quarrying	**74.2**	**1.1**	**-6.1**	**74.0**	**10.2**	**83.2**	**4.1**	**1.8**	**12.8**	**5.4**
Extraction activities	-51.3	0.6	27.6	108.0	46.4	2.7	1.4	0.9	3.7	4.6
Manufacturing	**-183.6**	**174.4**	**103.9**	**332.8**	**593.3**	**-42.4**	**23.4**	**142.1**	**142.1**	**175.3**
of which:										
Food products, beverages and tobacco	103.0	127.5	65.2	85.3	136.4	3.6	5.8	6.4	44.7	50.0
Textiles, wood and paper products; printing	-9.8	12.3	-1.3	-14.1	-7.8	6.6	38.2	1.2	1.9	2.6
Chemical, rubber, plastic, non-metallic mineral products	-133.1	46.6	73.1	233.6	443.7	-15.3	-11.0	4.3	3.9	11.1
Metal and machinery products, except electrical equipment	-160.3	-4.0	-9.5	26.5	3.7	-25.7	-33.2	-22.3	-9.9	-9.3
Motor vehicles, trailers, semi-trailers, other transport equipment	2.2	4.3	7.0	0.0	-0.3	-	-	-	-	0.1
Other manufacturing	14.5	-12.4	-30.6	1.5	17.5	-11.7	23.6	152.4	101.4	120.9
Electricity, gas, steam and air conditioning supply	**119.8**	**2.7**	**34.2**	**109.9**	**-21.9**	**8.9**	**7.7**	**12.8**	**2.9**	**-8.2**
Water supply; sewerage, waste management and remediation activities	**0.1**	**0.2**	**0.0**	**1.0**	**1.0**	**0.9**	**0.8**	**0.8**	**0.8**	**0.0**
Construction	**17.6**	**0.6**	**17.2**	**34.7**	**34.6**	**-72.4**	**6.9**	**50.7**	**59.4**	**76.5**
Services	**355.9**	**877.3**	**931.5**	**841.3**	**858.8**	**3 013.9**	**1 670.8**	**301.0**	**789.5**	**351.1**
Wholesale and retail trade; repair of motor vehicles and motorcycles	87.6	126.8	206.3	180.4	265.2	272.6	285.2	354.5	165.0	175.3
Transportation and storage	113.3	181.6	174.0	136.9	176.3	212.9	57.7	89.6	129.7	190.7
Accommodation and food service activities	-12.7	-15.7	-14.9	-15.4	-10.6	2.6	2.0	1.9	4.4	5.2
Information and communication	-107.1	-17.9	-64.1	27.7	138.4	-17.5	-36.6	-187.7	-152.2	-147.6
Financial and insurance activities	260.7	424.1	448.8	364.5	332.2	2 764.0	1 353.6	37.5	207.3	48.6
Activities of holding companies	194.9	87.5	145.8	18.4	98.8	307.3	297.9	-86.4	-183.2	-50.2
Real estate activities	29.6	32.2	58.1	28.5	42.8	-212.4	-55.3	5.3	39.5	21.8
Professional, scientific and technical activities	31.8	-20.3	-8.6	26.1	30.6	-24.0	34.0	-20.8	-2.4	16.1
Administrative and support service activities	12.2	17.4	19.0	31.7	37.5	4.8	4.9	6.7	391.7	17.4
Public administration; activities of households and of extraterritorial organisations	-	-	-	-	-	-	-	-	-	-
Education	0.1	0.1	-0.1	-0.1	5.8	2.3	-	-	-	-
Human health and social work activities	-17.2	-3.4	29.0	-23.0	-26.4	-10.1	-2.3	-2.8	-2.9	-3.1
Arts, entertainment and recreation	-43.8	151.7	69.2	82.7	-145.9	16.6	27.7	16.8	9.4	26.9
Other services	1.3	0.6	14.9	1.3	12.8	2.3	0.0	0.1	0.1	-0.1
Not allocated and confidential	**132.1**	**98.7**	**67.2**	**55.2**	**69.7**	**112.2**	**81.7**	**103.5**	**76.1**	**72.0**
Private real estate activities	**0.4**	**0.3**	**0.4**	**0.3**	**2.9**	**7.8**	**7.6**	**14.7**	**14.7**	**21.8**

- Nil

Note: Detailed metadata at: *http://stats.oecd.org/OECDStat_Metadata/ShowMetadata.ashx?Dataset=FDI_CTRY_IND_SUMM.*

Source: OECD International Direct Investment Statistics (database): https://doi.org/10.1787/idi-data-en

HUNGARY

Table 1. Foreign direct investment flows by country

Million US dollars

	Inward					Outward				
	2014	2015	2016	2017	2018	2014	2015	2016	2017	2018
WORLD	**7 967.0**	**-14 544.6**	**-5 438.6**	**3 666.9**	**8 386.8**	**3 854.1**	**-16 117.7**	**-8 272.2**	**1 228.0**	**5 058.6**
OECD COUNTRIES	**6 566.3**	**-7 902.9**	**-6 730.6**	**1 811.6**	**8 124.7**	**2 327.1**	**-16 476.6**	**1 277.8**	**-942.1**	**4 051.2**
Australia	-9.6	10.0	13.6	-47.1	21.9	4.7	-12.0	9.7	-18.8	10.3
Austria	1 467.7	1 145.8	-186.2	258.8	481.3	8.6	-23.2	23.8	2.7	29.8
Belgium	390.5	-408.3	299.5	-278.2	1 805.3	97.6	50.4	77.9	-2 841.3	0.2
Canada	139.9	28.3	8.6	-57.6	-66.1	.. c	.. c	9.4	12.2	11.4
Chile	-0.8	-0.2	3.5	2.0	1.2	.. c	.. c	.. c	.. c	.. c
Czech Republic	34.9	42.4	131.8	186.3	76.0	79.1	-34.6	-3.3	297.9	-98.8
Denmark	276.6	50.1	147.1	148.3	109.9	-	.. c	.. c	.. c	.. c
Estonia	0.4	0.0	-0.1	0.3	0.3	-0.5	-0.6	-0.3	0.5	0.0
Finland	-143.3	-22.0	1.3	-15.0	9.1	-0.2	-0.3	0.1	0.0	0.0
France	36.7	-1 545.4	1 912.5	382.0	506.0	17.2	-20.6	3.9	23.4	14.1
Germany	1 141.0	-2 189.9	3 707.4	-1 705.7	-816.2	9.4	49.2	115.2	22.3	-2.6
Greece	4.5	-4.4	50.7	1.4	-4.3	0.0	0.0	0.1	0.4	-0.2
Hungary	-	-	-	-	-	-	-	-	-	-
Iceland	3.6	-1.5	-1.1	-3.7	1.8	-	-	-	.. c	.. c
Ireland	-119.9	5 757.4	-4 021.9	69.0	837.5	21.7	10.7	1.2	440.4	1 361.6
Israel[1]	-13.2	863.1	-25.2	-2 104.5	-45.4	.. c	546.1	317.2	360.6	152.9
Italy	255.2	308.9	1 387.8	46.8	-181.0	-41.2	-24.3	371.1	5.1	59.4
Japan	391.3	-467.1	118.2	173.1	224.5	1.2	-0.5	3.1	1.0	1.4
Korea	185.0	169.6	185.8	264.3	896.2	16.1	22.6	16.5	11.5	-1.2
Latvia	0.1	-0.2	-4.6	-1.3	-0.4	-0.3	1.5	-0.3	0.3	-0.1
Lithuania	3.0	-1.6	3.5	1.9	-2.2	1.0	1.0	1.3	0.7	0.7
Luxembourg	-24.8	-13 183.7	-164.3	539.3	905.9	190.5	-2 200.1	215.6	-164.1	-40.4
Mexico	-17.3	-414.9	74.1	-12.3	-39.0	16.2	229.5	85.5	18.4	18.7
Netherlands	3 248.9	5 066.5	-9 255.4	2 018.1	620.3	902.2	52.1	-62.3	183.2	1 641.7
New Zealand	11.9	-0.9	-9.9	2.2	1.0	-	-	-	-	-
Norway	248.6	-19.5	-14.2	10.5	-417.0	-	.. c	.. c	.. c	.. c
Poland	25.4	100.9	124.2	764.7	-9.8	55.8	51.3	51.0	395.8	111.6
Portugal	-282.5	-43.3	-9.5	18.7	-3.1	0.8	-40.2	-4.5	-0.3	0.2
Slovak Republic	15.6	-42.9	-3.9	-15.5	-24.4	130.8	277.8	162.4	21.2	-182.2
Slovenia	-0.5	5.6	5.3	-1.9	1.8	-13.0	-72.5	1.3	4.1	31.8
Spain	-122.1	-15.6	37.4	3.0	180.3	49.9	83.8	118.3	164.1	151.5
Sweden	-85.6	73.6	33.9	-46.9	30.9	0.0	-0.5	0.5	.. c	0.6
Switzerland	-317.1	-1 116.2	134.7	2 255.2	49.0	-279.3	-15 532.0	17.4	176.1	-268.4
Turkey	-4.9	-2.0	11.4	9.2	-7.9	-12.2	1.5	-23.8	-1.6	-3.8
United Kingdom	-444.3	995.4	-882.4	-1 398.6	-734.4	21.9	18.8	21.0	36.1	14.8
United States	274.8	-3 042.8	-540.6	346.9	3 715.5	804.7	62.0	-249.9	-94.0	1 034.8
EUROPE	**6 329.4**	**-4 716.1**	**-5 978.5**	**3 728.9**	**3 594.8**	**2 162.1**	**-16 988.9**	**1 799.7**	**271.3**	**4 231.3**
Bulgaria	-16.7	-11.3	3.7	3.0	11.8	64.2	17.5	-42.8	-25.3	736.7
Croatia	26.3	-221.7	-4.8	-18.8	17.2	122.5	7.2	163.7	725.3	188.9
Cyprus[2, 3]	36.1	-59.2	0.4	20.2	-37.5	236.5	38.7	354.1	192.5	104.8
Malta	-27.5	349.0	-117.8	48.5	-480.5	138.7	23.1	-22.0	120.7	64.0
Romania	7.5	-26.4	23.2	28.7	4.2	149.8	170.3	-21.7	190.3	117.1
Russian Federation	601.2	-25.8	154.1	62.3	163.2	56.1	-32.1	71.7	199.4	30.1
Ukraine	104.6	99.2	57.8	52.3	9.2	222.1	121.4	191.5	61.3	66.0
AFRICA	**611.7**	**274.6**	**311.7**	**306.1**	**163.6**	**.. c**	**43.1**	**10.5**	**1.9**	**-6.4**
Northern Africa	-1.4	-8.3	5.6	4.7	3.7	-	.. c	-0.4	-0.5	-2.7
Algeria	-0.1	-0.2	0.1	0.6	0.1	-	-	-	-	-
Egypt	-0.2	-2.3	1.7	5.3	1.9	-	.. c	.. c	.. c	.. c
Libya	-	-	-	-	-	-	-	-	-	-
Morocco	-0.6	-5.2	3.4	-2.2	1.6	-	-	-	.. c	.. c
Tunisia	-0.4	-0.4	0.4	1.1	0.2	-	-	-	-	-
Other African countries	613.0	282.9	306.1	301.4	159.9	.. c	43.2	.. c	.. c	.. c
Nigeria	0.0	-0.2	-0.3	0.3	0.1	-	-	-	-	-
South Africa	0.2	7.1	-2.7	-2.8	0.4	-	.. c	.. c	.. c	.. c
AMERICA	**171.1**	**-10 743.2**	**-374.1**	**1 621.5**	**2 614.7**	**1 476.4**	**276.2**	**-10 421.6**	**545.7**	**672.6**
Northern America	414.7	-3 014.5	-532.0	289.3	3 649.5	828.8	90.0	-240.5	-81.7	1 046.2
Central America and Caribbean countries	-256.5	-7 743.7	145.7	1 325.6	-928.1	617.8	132.9	-10 260.9	566.4	-429.8
Bahamas	0.7	0.6	.. c	6.1	0.7	-	-	-	-	-
Bermuda	2.6	0.5	-1.3	1.5	0.9	-	-	-	-	-
Cayman Islands	-42.4	99.6	230.0	252.2	14.3	-	-	-	.. c	.. c
Costa Rica	0.1	0.0	0.0	-0.1	0.0	-	-	-	-	-
El Salvador	.. c	.. c	.. c	-	.. c	-	-	-	-	-
Guatemala	.. c	.. c	.. c	.. c	0.0	-	-	-	-	-
Honduras	0.2	0.4	-0.5	0.0	0.1	-	-	-	-	-
Nicaragua	-	-	-	-	-	-	-	-	-	-
Panama	-6.3	15.9	-26.5	-2.1	3.8	.. c	.. c	.. c	.. c	.. c
Virgin Islands, U.S.	-	-	-	-	-	-	-	-	-	-
South America	13.0	15.0	12.1	6.6	-106.7	29.8	53.3	79.7	60.9	56.2
Argentina	-1.5	-0.7	0.6	0.5	1.5	.. c	.. c	.. c	.. c	.. c
Bolivia	-	-	.. c	-	-	-	-	-	-	-
Brazil	16.2	8.6	5.0	-4.1	1.0	16.9	37.0	70.4	76.5	57.1
Colombia	0.2	0.3	0.4	-0.3	-113.2	.. c	.. c	.. c	.. c	.. c
Ecuador	.. c	-0.1	0.2	-0.1	0.2	-	-	.. c	-	-
Paraguay	-	.. c	.. c	.. c	.. c	-	-	-	-	-
Peru	0.4	-1.6	1.9	0.2	0.4	.. c	.. c	.. c	.. c	-
Uruguay	2.7	-0.3	0.3	0.3	0.0	.. c	.. c	-	.. c	.. c
Venezuela	-4.5	9.2	0.1	8.1	0.0	-	-	-	-	-

Table 1. Foreign direct investment flows by country *(cont.)*

Million US dollars

	Inward					Outward				
	2014	2015	2016	2017	2018	2014	2015	2016	2017	2018
ASIA	**1 039.9**	**524.3**	**470.8**	**-2 075.3**	**1 408.1**	**210.5**	**563.2**	**329.0**	**427.6**	**150.3**
Near and Middle East	7.7	886.0	117.4	-2 166.1	-44.3	224.6	552.6	337.4	383.9	169.0
Gulf Arabian countries	18.0	28.3	146.2	-58.6	-3.3	4.5	6.0	20.1	23.3	15.8
Kuwait	.. c	.. c	0.0	.. c	0.0	-	-	.. c	-	-
Qatar	-5.8	-2.8	-0.5	-0.7	-3.0	-	-	-	-	-
Saudi Arabia	-0.3	0.9	1.2	0.5	0.1	-	-	-	-	-
United Arab Emirates	21.1	30.9	147.6	-59.2	-2.2	.. c	.. c	.. c	.. c	.. c
Other Near and Middle East	-10.3	857.6	-28.8	-2 107.5	-41.1	220.2	546.7	317.3	360.5	153.2
Jordan	.. c	.. c	0.0	.. c	.. c	-	-	-	-	-
Other Asian countries	1 032.2	-361.6	353.5	90.8	1 452.4	-14.1	10.5	-8.4	43.7	-18.7
China	0.8	22.8	80.9	8.7	59.0	3.3	-3.4	7.9	3.3	-2.9
Hong Kong, China	230.8	-9.9	9.5	-280.0	309.0	-21.7	-8.6	28.8	20.1	-67.2
India	51.7	-141.9	-64.9	-0.5	1.6	1.2	0.0	-1.1	0.6	-0.7
Indonesia	2.7	-3.1	-3.5	4.7	0.7	-	-	-	-	-
Iran, Islamic Republic of	-	-	.. c	.. c	.. c	-	-	-	-	-
Malaysia	32.7	31.1	-22.1	3.3	24.4	.. c	.. c	.. c	-	-
Philippines	7.7	2.4	-0.8	23.5	4.6	-	-	.. c	.. c	-
Singapore	93.8	55.7	13.6	-63.3	-18.0	-22.2	-9.5	-71.2	-0.3	48.9
Chinese Taipei	26.8	-29.1	40.8	-54.8	-51.2	.. c	.. c	.. c	.. c	.. c
Thailand	8.2	-0.3	-1.2	-3.1	8.5	.. c	-	-	-	-
Viet Nam	0.4	-0.9	-0.2	0.7	-3.4	.. c	.. c	-	-	-
AUSTRALIA, OCEANIA AND POLAR REGIONS	**0.9**	**5.3**	**3.8**	**-44.9**	**185.2**	**4.7**	**-12.0**	**9.7**	**-18.8**	**10.3**
WORLD unallocated and confidential	**-186.2**	**110.4**	**127.7**	**130.5**	**420.3**	**.. d**	**0.7**	**0.5**	**0.3**	**0.5**
European Union (EU28)	**5 703.0**	**-3 880.4**	**-6 781.3**	**1 057.0**	**3 304.0**	**2 243.1**	**-1 563.2**	**1 525.0**	**-204.1**	**4 305.3**
G20 countries excl. European Union	**2 618.7**	**-6 282.0**	**6 167.3**	**-1 929.7**	**3 746.9**	**952.6**	**415.2**	**530.6**	**280.9**	**1 236.6**
G20 OECD countries	**1 947.6**	**-6 149.9**	**5 996.4**	**-1 999.0**	**3 519.6**	**862.2**	**354.3**	**361.8**	**15.6**	**1 157.4**
G20 Non-OECD countries	**671.0**	**-132.1**	**170.9**	**69.3**	**227.3**	**90.3**	**60.9**	**168.8**	**265.3**	**79.2**
MENA countries	**19.6**	**14.6**	**151.8**	**-57.2**	**3.2**	**3.5**	**5.8**	**19.7**	**22.8**	**13.1**
ASEAN countries	**145.4**	**84.9**	**-14.1**	**-34.4**	**16.8**	**-24.6**	**-9.7**	**-71.2**	**-0.3**	**48.9**

- Nil; .. Not available; c Confidential data; d Secondary Confidentiality

Note: Data excludes resident Special Purpose Entities (SPEs). Detailed metadata at: *http://stats.oecd.org/OECDStat_Metadata/ShowMetadata.ashx?Dataset=FDI_CTRY_IND_SUMM.*

1. Information on data for Israel: *http://oe.cd/israel-disclaimer*.
2. Note by Turkey: The information in this document with reference to "Cyprus" relates to the southern part of the Island. There is no single authority representing both Turkish and Greek Cypriot people on the Island. Turkey recognises the Turkish Republic of Northern Cyprus (TRNC). Until a lasting and equitable solution is found within the context of the United Nations, Turkey shall preserve its position concerning the "Cyprus issue".
3. Note by all the European Union Member States of the OECD and the European Union: The Republic of Cyprus is recognised by all members of the United Nations with the exception of Turkey. The information in this document relates to the area under the effective control of the Government of the Republic of Cyprus.

Source: OECD International Direct Investment Statistics (database): https://doi.org/10.1787/idi-data-en

HUNGARY

Table 2. Foreign direct investment positions by country

At year end

Million US dollars

	Inward					Outward				
	2014	2015	2016	2017	2018	2014	2015	2016	2017	2018
WORLD	**100 410.8**	**86 253.7**	**82 701.0**	**93 497.3**	**95 172.7**	**40 533.1**	**35 536.9**	**25 018.8**	**30 058.2**	**30 696.7**
OECD COUNTRIES	**90 561.3**	**75 892.9**	**70 880.2**	**78 742.7**	**..**	**18 712.0**	**15 709.4**	**14 722.5**	**16 657.1**	**17 075.7**
Australia	19.1	25.2	28.9	6.6	..	.. c	1.6	33.6	31.9	8.1
Austria	6 210.7	5 969.9	6 608.4	8 245.5	..	121.6	78.2	93.7	97.6	114.6
Belgium	1 242.1	1 295.4	1 499.5	1 623.5	..	3 877.2	3 521.7	3 469.1	2 081.7	8.3
Canada	395.4	381.4	352.3	421.3	..	26.3	53.1	18.6	7.0	-7.9
Chile	-	-	-	-	..	-	.. c	.. c	.. c	.. c
Czech Republic	270.2	336.1	384.8	545.5	..	420.8	374.8	329.9	737.0	598.5
Denmark	775.7	709.4	781.3	995.1	..	-	.. c	.. c	.. c	.. c
Estonia	-	-	-	10.3	..	1.1	0.6	0.3	0.8	0.8
Finland	109.5	80.0	74.2	103.9	..	0.9	0.5	1.1	1.3	1.2
France	5 032.9	4 522.2	4 711.2	5 123.2	..	61.3	40.8	41.9	48.5	73.2
Germany	26 416.4	24 172.2	24 020.3	23 709.6	..	91.7	154.7	199.7	227.3	216.8
Greece	3.6	3.2	3.1	3.5	..	0.3	0.2	0.2	0.7	0.5
Hungary	647.0	394.2	322.9	564.5	..	-	-	-	-	-
Iceland	3.3	2.1	-	-	..	-	-	-	.. c	.. c
Ireland	202.4	246.0	275.4	359.8	..	90.4	140.0	137.5	592.3	1 282.0
Israel[2]	11 663.0	11 205.0	931.1	1 266.7	..	.. c	4 548.9	3 177.7	3 180.0	2 422.6
Italy	3 356.5	2 944.4	3 209.0	3 879.4	..	36.0	5.3	397.3	449.0	752.2
Japan	2 323.1	2 282.8	2 563.0	3 208.1	..	3.4	2.5	5.7	6.7	8.0
Korea	1 157.1	1 241.8	1 438.1	2 000.3	..	494.7	512.5	551.0	645.9	575.6
Latvia	-	-	-	-	..	0.5	1.8	0.8	2.7	2.5
Lithuania	2.5	3.0	3.5	3.6	..	4.0	3.9	4.3	6.9	7.7
Luxembourg	1 390.3	1 273.7	1 366.1	1 689.7	..	3 230.3	1 048.8	1 230.6	1 124.6	1 164.3
Mexico	173.8	148.6	162.8	202.1	..	42.2	234.5	136.7	164.2	153.5
Netherlands	2 274.0	2 299.1	2 285.3	2 709.7	..	1 183.0	3.7	-167.0	364.9	2 020.5
New Zealand	57.6	51.4	36.7	41.6	..	-	-	-	-	-
Norway	845.5	548.4	514.4	586.3	..	-	.. c	.. c	.. c	.. c
Poland	184.0	263.5	237.9	434.6	..	381.0	376.5	429.4	1 409.2	1 394.9
Portugal	175.5	88.1	76.2	99.1	..	41.1	0.7	-3.8	-4.1	-3.9
Slovak Republic	67.0	53.8	81.2	100.3	..	1 717.9	2 142.7	2 445.7	2 779.1	2 612.3
Slovenia	-5.4	-1.2	4.9	9.0	..	55.0	15.5	16.5	24.4	53.9
Spain	686.9	706.2	701.9	700.8	..	862.5	882.3	994.6	1 337.2	1 401.5
Sweden	344.9	368.6	463.3	579.4	..	1.3	0.1	0.2	.. c	0.2
Switzerland	1 624.9	1 798.1	1 855.0	2 095.1	..	496.9	509.0	285.9	593.2	387.5
Turkey	63.7	53.5	53.5	63.1	..	73.2	58.3	27.1	23.2	12.7
United Kingdom	4 087.1	3 617.1	3 046.9	3 790.3	..	47.8	65.8	70.2	97.8	143.3
United States	18 763.2	8 812.6	12 790.4	13 574.6	..	1 227.8	935.6	796.8	628.4	1 664.6
EUROPE	**59 066.9**	**54 680.3**	**56 534.3**	**63 044.8**	**..**	**23 376.3**	**18 430.5**	**19 513.7**	**23 981.4**	**24 907.7**
Bulgaria	-0.2	-0.8	9.8	16.5	..	1 069.2	974.3	897.9	1 031.8	1 671.0
Croatia	6.3	11.8	12.6	25.4	..	3 734.6	2 939.6	2 952.7	4 284.9	4 269.9
Cyprus[3, 4]	921.1	816.2	973.0	1 064.3	..	3 147.8	2 665.2	3 008.0	3 060.5	3 167.5
Malta	163.9	258.1	402.9	222.3	..	127.5	138.0	128.5	199.6	273.4
Romania	162.1	131.8	146.0	259.4	..	1 159.6	1 226.4	1 181.9	1 555.6	1 447.8
Russian Federation	551.3	465.3	640.6	817.9	..	467.2	330.3	463.8	783.0	623.3
Ukraine	593.1	491.8	456.3	554.6	..	4.2	-52.8	116.2	157.3	220.7
AFRICA	**256.7**	**239.7**	**274.7**	**278.4**	**..**	**6.3**	**56.6**	**6.0**	**6.3**	**1.0**
Northern Africa	0.5	0.5	0.1	0.1	..	.. c	4.6	2.7	2.6	-0.7
Algeria	-	-	-	-	..	-	-	-	-	-
Egypt	0.5	0.5	0.1	0.1	..	.. c	.. c	.. c	2.2	.. c
Libya	-	-	-	-	..	.. c	.. c	.. c	.. c	-
Morocco	-	-	-	-	..	-	-	-	.. c	.. c
Tunisia	-	-	-	-	..	-	-	-	-	-
Other African countries	256.2	239.2	274.6	278.3	..	.. c	52.0	.. c	.. c	.. c
Nigeria	-	-	-	-	..	-	-	-	-	-
South Africa	17.3	24.9	48.6	60.6	..	-	.. c	.. c	.. c	.. c
AMERICA	**19 448.5**	**9 374.8**	**13 345.5**	**14 442.3**	**..**	**12 095.4**	**11 365.1**	**1 100.9**	**1 524.2**	**2 058.5**
Northern America	19 158.6	9 193.9	13 142.7	13 995.9	..	1 254.2	988.7	815.4	635.4	1 656.7
Central America and Caribbean countries	281.0	172.8	193.1	435.8	..	10 669.0	10 301.1	144.1	684.1	175.9
Bahamas	2.4	2.0	1.9	6.8	..	-	-	-	-	-
Bermuda	-4.4	-0.1	2.6	0.6	..	-	-	-	-	-
Cayman Islands	64.9	43.4	39.3	34.5	..	-	-	-	.. c	.. c
Costa Rica	-	-	-	-	..	-	-	-	-	-
El Salvador	-	-	-	-	..	-	-	-	-	-
Guatemala	-	-	-	-	..	-	-	-	-	-
Honduras	-	-	-	-	..	-	-	-	-	-
Nicaragua	-	-	-	-	..	-	-	-	-	-
Panama	8.2	-21.1	13.6	13.2	..	.. c	.. c	.. c	.. c	.. c
Virgin Islands, U.S.	-	-	-	-	..	-	-	-	-	-
South America	8.9	8.1	9.7	10.6	..	172.2	75.4	141.4	204.7	225.9
Argentina	6.4	5.8	5.6	6.3	..	.. c	.. c	.. c	.. c	.. c
Bolivia	-	-	-	-	..	-	-	-	-	-
Brazil	-	-	1.8	1.5	..	152.5	44.0	109.6	194.1	220.7
Colombia	-	-	-	-	..	.. c	.. c	.. c	.. c	.. c
Ecuador	-	-	-	-	..	-	-	.. c	-	-
Paraguay	-	-	-	-	..	-	-	-	-	-
Peru	-	-	-	-	..	.. c	.. c	.. c	-	-
Uruguay	2.5	2.4	2.3	2.8	..	.. c	.. c	.. c	.. c	.. c
Venezuela	-	-	-	-	..	-	-	-	-	-

Table 2. Foreign direct investment positions by country (*cont.*)
At year end

Million US dollars

	Inward					Outward				
	2014	2015	2016	2017	2018	2014	2015	2016	2017	2018
ASIA	**18 833.4**	**19 276.5**	**10 009.1**	**12 716.7**	**..**	**5 016.6**	**5 668.4**	**4 351.1**	**4 501.0**	**3 710.4**
Near and Middle East	11 851.5	11 415.6	1 345.0	1 655.7	..	4 167.9	4 833.2	3 481.0	3 511.3	2 733.8
Gulf Arabian countries	178.8	208.1	411.6	386.4	..	55.0	275.3	294.5	322.6	302.2
Kuwait	-	-	-	-	..	-	-	-	-	-
Qatar	-10.8	-7.0	-8.0	-9.5	..	-	-	-	-	-
Saudi Arabia	10.1	10.2	6.3	7.0	..	-	-	-	-	-
United Arab Emirates	179.5	204.9	413.3	388.8	..	4.1	4.4	.. c	90.0	82.7
Other Near and Middle East	11 672.7	11 207.5	933.4	1 269.3	..	4 112.9	4 558.0	3 186.5	3 188.8	2 431.6
Jordan	-	-	-	-	..	-	-	-	-	-
Other Asian countries	6 981.9	7 860.9	8 664.1	11 061.0	..	848.7	835.2	870.0	989.7	976.7
China	1 268.3	1 951.7	1 933.8	1 987.2	..	36.0	30.4	35.8	40.8	37.9
Hong Kong, China	170.9	144.3	177.6	209.0	..	-28.9	-35.2	-19.9	-2.0	-22.6
India	1 637.5	1 798.0	2 200.4	2 676.1	..	25.6	24.3	23.1	25.4	23.7
Indonesia	-	-	-	-	..	-	-	-	-	-
Iran, Islamic Republic of	-	-	-	-	..	-	-	-	-	-
Malaysia	31.6	25.0	26.0	30.7	..	.. c	.. c	.. c	.. c	.. c
Philippines	-	-	-	-	..	-	-	.. c	-	-
Singapore	93.4	158.7	22.9	-56.1	..	286.8	290.2	254.8	245.9	327.3
Chinese Taipei	294.7	207.9	299.7	978.7	..	.. c	.. c	.. c	.. c	.. c
Thailand	8.3	53.3	5.1	9.1	..	.. c	-	-	-	-
Viet Nam	-	-	-	-	..	.. c	.. c	.. c	.. c	.. c
AUSTRALIA, OCEANIA AND POLAR REGIONS	**82.6**	**78.5**	**65.7**	**48.2**	**..**	**.. c**	**1.6**	**33.6**	**31.9**	**8.1**
WORLD unallocated and confidential	**2 722.7**	**2 603.8**	**2 471.8**	**2 967.0**	**..**	**.. d**	**14.7**	**13.6**	**13.3**	**11.0**
European Union (EU28)	**54 727.1**	**50 562.2**	**51 701.8**	**56 868.3**	**..**	**21 464.4**	**16 802.7**	**17 862.4**	**21 511.2**	**22 675.4**
G20 countries excl. European Union	**65 279.2**	**52 457.5**	**57 213.3**	**61 535.2**	**..**	**2 825.5**	**2 570.0**	**2 943.6**	**3 385.4**	**4 510.4**
G20 OECD countries	**61 788.3**	**48 201.5**	**52 376.2**	**55 978.7**	**..**	**2 126.3**	**2 064.5**	**2 278.5**	**2 329.9**	**3 600.0**
G20 Non-OECD countries	**3 490.9**	**4 255.9**	**4 837.1**	**5 556.5**	**..**	**699.2**	**505.5**	**665.1**	**1 055.5**	**910.3**
MENA countries	**188.9**	**211.1**	**414.0**	**389.1**	**..**	**55.5**	**279.9**	**297.2**	**325.2**	**301.5**
ASEAN countries	**133.2**	**237.1**	**54.1**	**-16.4**	**..**	**278.3**	**282.8**	**247.7**	**237.3**	**319.2**

- Nil; .. Not available; c Confidential data; d Secondary Confidentiality

Note: Data excludes resident Special Purpose Entities (SPEs). Detailed metadata at: *http://stats.oecd.org/OECDStat_Metadata/ShowMetadata.ashx?Dataset=FDI_CTRY_IND_SUMM*.

1. Data excludes resident Special Purpose Entities (SPEs). Inward FDI positions are allocated according to the ultimate investing country. Inward FDI positions by immediate counterpart country are available for the most recent year in the *OECD FDI database according to BMD4*. Detailed metadata at: *http://stats.oecd.org/OECDStat_Metadata/ShowMetadata.ashx?Dataset=FDI_CTRY_IND_SUMM*.
2. Information on data for Israel: *http://oe.cd/israel-disclaimer*.
3. Note by Turkey: The information in this document with reference to "Cyprus" relates to the southern part of the Island. There is no single authority representing both Turkish and Greek Cypriot people on the Island. Turkey recognises the Turkish Republic of Northern Cyprus (TRNC). Until a lasting and equitable solution is found within the context of the United Nations, Turkey shall preserve its position concerning the "Cyprus issue".
4. Note by all the European Union Member States of the OECD and the European Union: The Republic of Cyprus is recognised by all members of the United Nations with the exception of Turkey. The information in this document relates to the area under the effective control of the Government of the Republic of Cyprus.

Source: OECD International Direct Investment Statistics (database): https://doi.org/10.1787/idi-data-en

Table 3. Foreign direct investment income by country

Million US dollars

	Inward					Outward				
	2014	2015	2016	2017	2018	2014	2015	2016	2017	2018
WORLD	**9 484.3**	**8 855.2**	**7 682.1**	**10 580.6**	**10 917.0**	**1 687.4**	**988.0**	**1 822.6**	**2 175.2**	**1 887.3**
OECD COUNTRIES	**8 563.2**	**7 742.7**	**6 183.6**	**8 984.7**	**9 075.3**	**771.3**	**653.7**	**1 019.5**	**1 169.1**	**868.6**
Australia	10.5	-1.1	21.3	1.1	-0.2	.. c	.. c	.. c	0.8	9.2
Austria	1 549.0	1 667.6	855.8	981.8	1 220.4	7.4	22.9	-0.5	9.8	17.3
Belgium	61.8	18.2	17.0	137.4	191.4	66.6	59.7	52.3	1.4	1.5
Canada	10.6	32.7	29.9	38.6	8.1	.. c	.. c	.. c	4.4	4.7
Chile	.. c	.. c	.. c	.. c	.. c	-	-	-	.. c	.. c
Czech Republic	16.1	-13.3	45.6	42.8	48.4	68.1	66.1	24.2	23.9	-11.6
Denmark	67.0	66.6	118.2	155.7	200.6	-	.. c	.. c	.. c	.. c
Estonia	-	-	-	-	-	-0.5	-0.2	-0.3	0.0	-0.1
Finland	4.8	5.3	7.7	9.7	19.6	0.1	0.1	0.0	0.1	-0.1
France	574.6	386.5	535.1	598.3	514.1	16.5	5.4	5.6	12.4	12.4
Germany	1 491.9	1 294.8	1 229.8	1 985.8	2 117.6	2.7	17.2	9.7	23.2	12.9
Greece	-1.7	-1.0	-0.9	-	0.0	-	-	0.0	0.0	-0.4
Hungary	-	-	-	-	-	-	-	-	-	-
Iceland	.. c	.. c	-	-	-	-	-	-	.. c	.. c
Ireland	114.8	100.7	188.6	158.5	314.5	16.5	14.8	1.4	-1.7	140.9
Israel[1]	-8.6	-15.2	8.3	7.1	-70.8	.. c	287.0	320.6	297.5	132.0
Italy	92.4	93.2	287.7	221.9	149.0	-99.7	-67.3	-7.6	-6.9	23.9
Japan	85.9	82.3	98.5	122.0	124.0	0.3	0.9	3.0	1.5	1.8
Korea	178.4	173.0	158.3	178.9	155.0	105.8	107.7	108.2	102.1	70.9
Latvia	-	-	-	-	-	1.3	0.2	-1.1	-1.5	-2.3
Lithuania	3.0	3.8	5.0	3.2	6.6	-1.3	-1.8	-3.1	-4.1	-5.3
Luxembourg	648.5	507.5	348.1	857.2	886.6	113.7	89.9	79.3	76.6	33.3
Mexico	.. c	-14.0	-24.2	-17.2	-18.6	8.9	15.0	82.6	14.3	13.8
Netherlands	2 153.9	2 155.9	1 250.1	1 600.1	1 695.7	19.2	-314.5	-21.0	173.9	96.3
New Zealand	.. c	.. c	.. c	.. c	.. c	-	-	-	-	-
Norway	86.7	89.8	96.5	117.5	0.7	-	.. c	-	-	-
Poland	27.9	31.5	45.5	45.4	19.3	40.7	28.4	32.6	76.5	47.0
Portugal	91.9	60.2	58.4	62.8	62.0	0.0	2.3	3.0	0.1	0.1
Slovak Republic	4.5	13.1	29.2	19.2	28.8	77.6	324.3	275.8	212.1	198.8
Slovenia	3.0	3.3	5.3	6.3	6.3	17.6	11.6	7.4	11.4	9.7
Spain	146.2	127.7	165.4	230.7	173.0	-0.1	0.3	-0.4	19.5	4.6
Sweden	69.5	65.0	68.9	72.9	94.5	-0.3	-0.3	.. c	.. c	.. c
Switzerland	235.3	270.9	164.5	834.5	587.8	21.7	-62.0	58.4	135.8	92.3
Turkey	8.8	5.0	7.1	5.0	8.5	.. c	.. c	-7.2	-2.8	-3.1
United Kingdom	415.9	364.3	410.7	516.8	464.3	22.3	15.4	14.3	17.9	31.7
United States	420.1	173.2	-31.9	-6.3	68.2	33.0	26.4	-26.7	-34.0	-64.5
EUROPE	**8 172.1**	**7 661.0**	**6 518.4**	**9 322.0**	**9 535.7**	**977.2**	**580.8**	**1 189.7**	**1 697.9**	**1 667.1**
Bulgaria	-0.7	-1.0	-1.2	-0.7	0.0	148.8	183.7	154.7	136.8	169.3
Croatia	16.1	5.8	-3.2	3.6	12.2	95.0	-31.1	84.9	171.6	152.5
Cyprus[2, 3]	118.1	75.3	112.5	329.2	271.5	268.1	154.6	277.0	266.8	401.9
Malta	29.8	41.1	132.2	38.6	41.5	0.0	23.1	23.8	120.1	64.9
Romania	18.7	15.0	15.0	5.4	-10.3	28.0	25.5	47.4	68.8	38.7
Russian Federation	-2.6	-2.0	8.8	14.2	-17.4	-13.6	-37.6	39.7	48.3	56.0
Ukraine	.. c	1.5	-0.5	0.1	0.3	146.2	-30.0	5.4	61.3	54.0
AFRICA	**137.9**	**275.2**	**319.4**	**281.3**	**157.9**	**-**	**.. c**	**13.4**	**3.7**	**-7.0**
Northern Africa	.. c	.. c	0.0	0.0	-	-	.. c	-0.5	-0.6	-2.8
Algeria	-	-	-	-	-	-	-	-	-	-
Egypt	-	-	-	-	-	-	.. c	.. c	.. c	.. c
Libya	-	-	-	-	-	-	-	-	-	-
Morocco	-	-	-	-	-	-	-	-	.. c	.. c
Tunisia	.. c	.. c	.. c	.. c	-	-	-	-	-	-
Other African countries	137.9	275.7	319.4	281.4	157.9	-	.. c	.. c	.. c	.. c
Nigeria	-	-	-	-	-	-	-	-	-	-
South Africa	.. c	.. c	.. c	.. c	.. c	-	-	.. c	.. c	.. c
AMERICA	**736.2**	**305.0**	**207.5**	**189.1**	**163.1**	**351.7**	**-21.2**	**138.0**	**42.0**	**-1.7**
Northern America	430.7	205.8	-2.0	32.4	76.3	33.0	26.5	-21.2	-29.6	-59.8
Central America and Caribbean countries	305.4	99.1	209.6	156.6	87.1	301.5	-86.7	83.0	18.4	15.3
Bahamas	0.7	.. c	.. c	1.4	1.5	-	-	-	-	-
Bermuda	-0.1	-0.1	.. c	.. c	.. c	-	-	-	-	-
Cayman Islands	62.6	113.5	206.9	96.3	62.4	-	-	-	-	-
Costa Rica	-	-	-	-	-	-	-	-	-	-
El Salvador	-	-	-	-	-	-	-	-	-	-
Guatemala	-	-	-	-	-	-	-	-	-	-
Honduras	-	-	-	-	-	-	-	-	-	-
Nicaragua	-	-	-	-	-	-	-	-	-	-
Panama	-2.3	-5.2	4.2	10.3	3.8	.. c	.. c	.. c	.. c	.. c
Virgin Islands, U.S.	-	-	-	-	-	-	-	-	-	-
South America	0.1	0.1	-0.1	0.2	-0.3	17.2	39.1	76.2	53.3	42.8
Argentina	-	-	-	-	-	.. c	.. c	.. c	.. c	.. c
Bolivia	-	-	-	-	-	-	-	-	-	-
Brazil	.. c	.. c	.. c	.. c	.. c	15.4	32.7	73.2	50.6	45.6
Colombia	-	-	-	-	.. c	.. c	.. c	.. c	.. c	.. c
Ecuador	-	-	-	-	-	-	-	-	-	-
Paraguay	-	-	-	-	-	-	-	-	-	-
Peru	-	-	-	-	-	-	-	-	-	-
Uruguay	.. c	.. c	.. c	.. c	-	.. c	.. c	-	-	-
Venezuela	-	-	-	-	-	-	-	-	-	-

Table 3. Foreign direct investment income by country *(cont.)*

Million US dollars

	Inward					Outward				
	2014	2015	2016	2017	2018	2014	2015	2016	2017	2018
ASIA	**357.5**	**274.2**	**344.5**	**414.0**	**429.1**	**341.8**	**425.6**	**481.1**	**430.5**	**218.8**
Near and Middle East	58.7	-16.0	10.3	-15.9	-53.3	227.9	299.2	360.0	321.9	159.8
Gulf Arabian countries	64.4	-0.8	2.1	-22.9	17.6	6.4	12.0	39.2	24.8	28.6
Kuwait	-	-	-	-	-	-	-	.. c	-	-
Qatar	.. c	.. c	.. c	.. c	.. c	-	-	-	-	-
Saudi Arabia	-	-	-	.. c	-	-	-	-	-	-
United Arab Emirates	70.2	3.8	5.3	-18.6	25.1	.. c	.. c	.. c	.. c	.. c
Other Near and Middle East	-5.8	-15.2	8.2	7.0	-70.9	221.4	287.2	320.8	297.1	131.2
Jordan	-	-	-	-	-	-	-	-	-	-
Other Asian countries	298.9	290.2	334.2	429.9	482.4	114.0	126.4	121.1	108.6	59.0
China	0.7	10.9	46.4	55.3	72.0	1.9	2.4	3.3	-2.5	0.7
Hong Kong, China	3.5	-5.2	6.9	23.1	90.1	-0.8	.. c	.. c	-2.5	-46.9
India	.. c	1.2	1.9	5.6	4.0	2.0	1.0	0.6	1.3	1.7
Indonesia	-	-	-	-	-	-	-	-	-	-
Iran, Islamic Republic of	-	-	-	-	-	-	-	-	-	-
Malaysia	4.1	1.7	1.8	0.8	.. c	.. c	.. c	.. c	-	-
Philippines	.. c	.. c	.. c	.. c	.. c	-	-	-	-	-
Singapore	20.8	24.7	19.7	26.2	27.2	5.0	3.6	3.7	7.0	30.5
Chinese Taipei	-	-	-	.. c	.. c	.. c	.. c	.. c	.. c	.. c
Thailand	.. c	.. c	.. c	.. c	.. c	-	-	-	-	-
Viet Nam	-	-	-	-	-	.. c	.. c	-	-	-
AUSTRALIA, OCEANIA AND POLAR REGIONS	**12.6**	**-2.5**	**10.7**	**1.8**	**0.2**	**.. c**	**.. c**	**.. c**	**0.8**	**9.2**
WORLD unallocated and confidential	**68.1**	**342.2**	**281.7**	**372.4**	**631.1**	**.. d**	**.. d**	**.. d**	**0.3**	**0.9**
European Union (EU28)	**7 717.1**	**7 087.4**	**5 926.4**	**8 082.2**	**8 527.4**	**908.3**	**630.1**	**1 059.6**	**1 409.2**	**1 438.6**
G20 countries excl. European Union	**3 288.5**	**2 599.3**	**2 779.1**	**3 719.8**	**3 648.4**	**108.5**	**127.9**	**320.9**	**237.8**	**212.8**
G20 OECD countries	**3 291.4**	**2 589.8**	**2 722.2**	**3 644.8**	**3 590.0**	**100.9**	**123.0**	**187.4**	**132.9**	**113.7**
G20 Non-OECD countries	**-2.9**	**9.4**	**56.9**	**75.0**	**58.5**	**7.6**	**4.9**	**133.5**	**104.9**	**99.1**
MENA countries	**67.3**	**-1.3**	**2.0**	**-22.9**	**17.7**	**6.5**	**11.5**	**38.8**	**24.2**	**25.8**
ASEAN countries	**30.4**	**27.9**	**23.7**	**50.9**	**43.7**	**4.6**	**3.4**	**3.6**	**7.0**	**30.5**

- Nil; .. Not available; c Confidential data; d Secondary Confidentiality

Note: Data excludes resident Special Purpose Entities (SPEs). Detailed metadata at: *http://stats.oecd.org/OECDStat_Metadata/ShowMetadata.ashx?Dataset=FDI_CTRY_IND_SUMM.*

1. Information on data for Israel: *http://oe.cd/israel-disclaimer.*
2. Note by Turkey: The information in this document with reference to "Cyprus" relates to the southern part of the Island. There is no single authority representing both Turkish and Greek Cypriot people on the Island. Turkey recognises the Turkish Republic of Northern Cyprus (TRNC). Until a lasting and equitable solution is found within the context of the United Nations, Turkey shall preserve its position concerning the "Cyprus issue".
3. Note by all the European Union Member States of the OECD and the European Union: The Republic of Cyprus is recognised by all members of the United Nations with the exception of Turkey. The information in this document relates to the area under the effective control of the Government of the Republic of Cyprus.

Source: OECD International Direct Investment Statistics (database): https://doi.org/10.1787/idi-data-en

Table 4. Foreign direct investment flows by industrial sector

Million US dollars

	Inward					Outward				
	2014	2015	2016	2017	2018	2014	2015	2016	2017	2018
All FDI activities	**7 967.0**	**-14 544.6**	**-5 438.6**	**3 666.9**	**8 386.8**	**3 854.1**	**-16 117.7**	**-8 272.2**	**1 228.0**	**5 058.6**
Agriculture, forestry and fishing	**68.6**	**45.3**	**10.5**	**42.8**	**-40.0**	**-15.4**	**0.1**	**-0.1**	**-0.7**	**-0.3**
Mining and quarrying	**14.6**	**-9.6**	**-19.0**	**0.7**	**86.4**	**328.4**	**-192.6**	**22.6**	**143.4**	**-185.2**
Extraction activities	..	..	..	..	..	..	..	..	..	..
Manufacturing	**2 758.2**	**-13 886.7**	**16 552.9**	**1 350.5**	**3 259.0**	**529.9**	**1 323.9**	**1 478.4**	**1 203.7**	**-2.0**
of which:										
Food products, beverages and tobacco	-37.3	109.0	151.4	50.9	-477.8	7.6	13.7	5.6	7.7	-0.4
Textiles, wood and paper products; printing	161.3	198.9	524.3	91.6	25.5	8.4	-17.8	5.1	5.2	76.2
Chemical, rubber, plastic, non-metallic mineral products	669.5	-324.5	964.6	1 313.4	1 382.6	364.3	544.7	825.6	168.3	160.4
Metal and machinery products, except electrical equipment	781.7	-14 774.4	14 054.3	2 634.9	1 333.6	125.3	212.8	501.1	849.7	-91.3
Motor vehicles, trailers, semi-trailers, other transport equipment	494.4	577.4	548.2	-2 698.9	438.2	2.6	555.3	87.0	117.1	-161.9
Other manufacturing	688.7	326.8	310.1	-41.3	556.9	21.7	15.1	54.0	55.8	15.0
Electricity, gas, steam and air conditioning supply	**-657.4**	**97.2**	**-243.1**	**-454.5**	**-515.3**	**3.2**	**12.1**	**-18.0**	**23.9**	**-30.3**
Water supply; sewerage, waste management and remediation activities	**-38.2**	**-13.8**	**2.3**	**9.0**	**-1.9**	**-0.6**	**0.8**	**0.6**	**1.6**	**-0.3**
Construction	**-78.1**	**6.7**	**121.7**	**-27.6**	**101.0**	**-15.3**	**-39.1**	**24.7**	**-4.4**	**2.1**
Services	**5 675.3**	**-1 037.7**	**-22 150.2**	**2 404.9**	**5 173.5**	**2 829.9**	**-17 461.6**	**-10 141.4**	**-576.1**	**4 802.6**
Wholesale and retail trade; repair of motor vehicles and motorcycles	465.4	441.9	-166.6	663.5	1 479.0	303.5	-15 813.4	-153.8	214.4	173.9
Transportation and storage	62.1	246.8	630.9	327.6	-120.6	-4.6	16.6	30.9	13.4	80.2
Accommodation and food service activities	-33.7	49.0	60.5	64.4	-9.5	4.7	-0.5	-17.5	-71.1	-0.7
Information and communication	240.2	698.5	-340.0	-395.1	13.4	346.7	227.0	53.4	-19.8	-25.0
Financial and insurance activities	2 984.5	473.8	-9 860.4	23.8	3 220.3	1 574.6	864.9	596.2	-827.5	2 091.0
Activities of holding companies	535.3	618.0	-10 430.7	-63.0	3 037.9	1 154.5	226.4	155.0	394.5	1 412.0
Real estate activities	99.7	0.0	-97.5	122.9	342.9	23.0	39.8	6.8	-6.0	31.0
Professional, scientific and technical activities	1 309.1	-2 557.4	-3 715.1	90.3	921.7	-106.0	-2 616.9	221.6	57.1	-78.1
Administrative and support service activities	537.1	-371.9	-8 754.4	1 429.4	-702.6	652.8	-186.5	-10 887.7	58.8	2 532.5
Public administration; activities of households and of extraterritorial organisations	-	-	-	-	-	-	-	-	-	-
Education	-0.9	-0.8	-0.4	3.3	12.8	-	-	1.2	0.1	0.8
Human health and social work activities	13.8	8.1	9.8	9.1	3.6	0.8	-0.2	2.0	1.0	0.7
Arts, entertainment and recreation	-1.9	-9.3	5.3	54.3	11.4	14.2	4.6	2.8	2.6	-0.2
Other services	-0.2	-16.4	77.8	11.5	1.1	20.2	3.1	2.7	1.0	-3.5
Not allocated and confidential	**0.0**	**0.0**	**0.0**	**0.0**	**0.0**	**4.6**	**4.5**	**0.0**	**0.0**	**0.3**
Private real estate activities	**224.0**	**254.0**	**286.2**	**341.1**	**324.1**	**189.5**	**234.2**	**361.1**	**436.5**	**471.7**

- Nil; .. Not available

Note: Data excludes resident Special Purpose Entities (SPEs). Detailed metadata at: *http://stats.oecd.org/OECDStat_Metadata/ShowMetadata.ashx?Dataset=FDI_CTRY_IND_SUMM.*

Source: OECD International Direct Investment Statistics (database): https://doi.org/10.1787/idi-data-en

Table 5. Foreign direct investment positions by industrial sector

At year end

Million US dollars

	Inward					Outward				
	2014	2015	2016	2017	2018	2014	2015	2016	2017	2018
All FDI activities	**100 410.8**	**86 253.7**	**82 701.0**	**93 497.3**	**95 172.7**	**40 533.1**	**35 536.9**	**25 018.8**	**30 058.2**	**30 696.7**
Agriculture, forestry and fishing	**573.1**	**554.5**	**547.3**	**672.5**	**588.1**	**3.9**	**3.5**	**3.3**	**3.1**	**2.7**
Mining and quarrying	**244.1**	**203.3**	**229.0**	**377.9**	**418.4**	**3 986.3**	**3 037.0**	**2 887.1**	**3 273.1**	**2 896.5**
Extraction activities	..	..	..	..	..	..	..	..	..	..
Manufacturing	**24 932.2**	**9 329.4**	**24 494.8**	**39 255.5**	**37 470.6**	**7 188.9**	**8 269.3**	**7 846.0**	**9 927.8**	**9 355.7**
of which:										
Food products, beverages and tobacco	2 058.6	2 185.6	2 301.3	2 718.4	2 194.3	26.4	40.2	42.2	67.8	47.6
Textiles, wood and paper products; printing	1 242.9	1 342.5	1 805.7	2 198.9	1 964.1	86.7	72.4	70.0	83.2	150.9
Chemical, rubber, plastic, non-metallic mineral products	6 880.1	5 958.4	6 561.9	8 736.4	9 552.7	5 694.1	6 236.1	5 631.0	5 699.8	5 296.1
Metal and machinery products, except electrical equipment	6 063.8	-8 926.8	4 686.8	7 686.4	8 360.6	944.5	940.0	1 391.7	2 588.6	2 620.8
Motor vehicles, trailers, semi-trailers, other transport equipment	4 657.3	4 794.9	5 089.6	13 424.1	11 011.6	52.3	594.7	295.3	992.7	768.1
Other manufacturing	4 029.5	3 974.8	4 049.6	4 491.4	4 387.3	384.9	386.0	415.8	495.7	472.1
Electricity, gas, steam and air conditioning supply	**2 472.8**	**2 707.7**	**2 392.4**	**2 276.4**	**1 475.0**	**91.8**	**58.7**	**23.5**	**41.6**	**10.4**
Water supply; sewerage, waste management and remediation activities	**93.2**	**54.1**	**62.7**	**88.1**	**79.8**	**36.7**	**17.5**	**16.6**	**17.9**	**10.7**
Construction	**769.2**	**766.5**	**931.3**	**1 115.6**	**1 137.2**	**27.1**	**2.5**	**15.2**	**25.6**	**23.1**
Services	**68 860.3**	**69 822.3**	**50 688.9**	**45 290.2**	**49 248.0**	**25 327.0**	**20 169.3**	**9 904.0**	**11 673.7**	**12 995.2**
Wholesale and retail trade; repair of motor vehicles and motorcycles	9 380.6	8 685.1	8 074.2	9 793.1	10 401.9	2 020.6	1 709.9	1 544.0	1 921.9	1 985.1
Transportation and storage	1 432.7	1 482.3	1 925.3	2 597.1	2 498.5	59.5	60.3	64.1	85.6	95.9
Accommodation and food service activities	544.8	574.5	695.1	902.6	921.4	183.5	163.4	137.6	77.3	68.3
Information and communication	5 513.4	5 543.6	5 117.6	4 963.6	4 621.7	624.3	447.7	470.9	453.1	236.8
Financial and insurance activities	15 792.8	15 326.4	6 459.3	7 896.7	10 487.6	8 062.8	6 666.8	7 065.1	8 291.2	7 544.7
Activities of holding companies	9 909.1	10 041.2	118.4	4.3	2 793.7	2 446.8	1 231.0	1 397.4	2 179.6	3 498.2
Real estate activities	6 233.9	5 673.7	5 743.4	6 947.7	8 243.7	95.0	103.7	98.4	136.9	157.4
Professional, scientific and technical activities	25 097.3	19 739.4	15 887.2	6 275.6	6 530.1	2 907.5	324.7	401.6	538.5	482.7
Administrative and support service activities	4 667.8	12 602.0	6 631.1	5 657.1	5 294.1	11 341.0	10 655.3	78.9	114.8	2 375.3
Public administration; activities of households and of extraterritorial organisations	-	-	-	-	-	-	-	-	-	-
Education	26.5	23.2	23.5	31.4	46.9	-	-	1.2	1.5	2.3
Human health and social work activities	50.0	54.6	61.2	81.0	71.1	3.9	3.4	4.4	7.1	7.4
Arts, entertainment and recreation	81.5	73.2	28.1	88.3	76.3	13.0	17.0	19.9	23.8	22.4
Other services	38.8	44.2	42.7	55.7	54.9	15.8	17.3	17.8	22.0	17.0
Not allocated and confidential	**-**	**-**	**0.0**	**-**	**0.0**	**0.4**	**0.3**	**0.3**	**0.4**	**0.3**
Private real estate activities	**2 465.8**	**2 815.9**	**3 354.5**	**4 421.1**	**4 755.6**	**3 870.9**	**3 978.7**	**4 322.7**	**5 095.0**	**5 402.0**

- Nil; .. Not available

Note: Data excludes resident Special Purpose Entities (SPEs). Detailed metadata at: *http://stats.oecd.org/OECDStat_Metadata/ShowMetadata.ashx?Dataset=FDI_CTRY_IND_SUMM.*

Source: OECD International Direct Investment Statistics (database): https://doi.org/10.1787/idi-data-en

HUNGARY

Table 6. Foreign direct investment income by industrial sector

Million US dollars

	Inward					Outward				
	2014	2015	2016	2017	2018	2014	2015	2016	2017	2018
All FDI activities	**9 484.3**	**8 855.2**	**7 682.1**	**10 580.6**	**10 917.0**	**1 687.4**	**988.0**	**1 822.6**	**2 175.2**	**1 887.3**
Agriculture, forestry and fishing	**59.5**	**35.0**	**38.9**	**55.9**	**55.4**	**0.1**	**0.0**	**0.0**	**0.0**	**0.0**
Mining and quarrying	**23.7**	**7.0**	**4.6**	**30.3**	**52.0**	**98.2**	**-182.5**	**33.3**	**229.2**	**140.4**
Extraction activities	..	..	..	..	..	..	..	..	..	..
Manufacturing	**3 850.0**	**3 515.0**	**3 784.6**	**5 093.7**	**4 963.5**	**392.5**	**764.7**	**868.9**	**952.6**	**538.4**
of which:										
Food products, beverages and tobacco	231.1	205.2	336.8	253.5	275.7	3.9	6.6	1.8	15.1	-3.1
Textiles, wood and paper products; printing	167.7	134.1	171.8	155.5	233.1	12.9	9.7	10.1	12.2	3.3
Chemical, rubber, plastic, non-metallic mineral products	1 282.5	1 252.0	1 325.0	2 023.8	1 721.0	203.4	549.1	607.0	584.3	304.0
Metal and machinery products, except electrical equipment	910.9	791.0	712.9	1 068.0	1 131.7	127.6	158.5	188.0	255.1	245.1
Motor vehicles, trailers, semi-trailers, other transport equipment	737.9	711.0	749.0	1 045.5	972.3	9.3	2[illegible].4	27.9	31.2	-42.5
Other manufacturing	520.0	421.8	489.1	547.4	629.6	35.3	19.4	34.1	54.7	31.5
Electricity, gas, steam and air conditioning supply	**151.8**	**112.1**	**156.7**	**116.1**	**114.4**	**3.3**	**-2.7**	**-16.5**	**-7.1**	**0.4**
Water supply; sewerage, waste management and remediation activities	**8.0**	**3.1**	**7.5**	**11.0**	**9.8**	**1.5**	**1.7**	**2.6**	**3.2**	**-0.2**
Construction	**7.9**	**110.5**	**127.8**	**113.2**	**106.3**	**-10.7**	**-21.9**	**26.8**	**4.5**	**4.3**
Services	**5 383.4**	**5 072.6**	**3 562.0**	**5 160.3**	**5 615.6**	**978.3**	**205.4**	**669.7**	**780.4**	**954.2**
Wholesale and retail trade; repair of motor vehicles and motorcycles	762.7	976.1	1 068.2	1 408.4	1 524.0	219.9	222.9	224.9	207.8	247.0
Transportation and storage	416.2	358.1	496.6	455.4	592.9	-11.3	-4.4	-12.9	-16.9	-17.0
Accommodation and food service activities	11.5	48.1	58.4	88.8	97.2	5.0	6.7	7.7	4.8	-0.7
Information and communication	750.2	561.1	531.6	513.0	645.7	49.2	45.8	16.7	41.7	21.3
Financial and insurance activities	934.0	448.7	560.9	1 072.7	1 168.7	437.4	-15.5	379.9	501.9	598.9
Activities of holding companies	271.9	-97.8	6.7	230.8	243.7	100.1	-146.5	112.7	200.9	300.1
Real estate activities	76.4	120.4	148.7	427.5	357.2	15.7	18.8	1.9	1.6	10.2
Professional, scientific and technical activities	785.7	617.2	285.5	274.5	530.7	-62.7	31.8	6.8	61.7	9.3
Administrative and support service activities	1 567.2	1 874.1	369.6	885.9	662.3	294.6	-109.8	38.9	-26.5	86.9
Public administration; activities of households and of extraterritorial organisations	-	-	-	-	-	-	-	-	-	-
Education	2.6	1.6	1.7	5.0	8.4	-	-	-0.1	0.1	0.8
Human health and social work activities	11.4	11.6	9.3	11.0	8.0	0.9	0.8	0.9	1.0	0.7
Arts, entertainment and recreation	15.8	19.1	28.8	12.8	16.3	14.2	5.1	2.9	2.6	-0.2
Other services	49.8	36.6	2.7	5.1	4.2	15.4	3.1	1.9	0.4	-3.0
Not allocated and confidential	**0.0**	**-**	**0.0**	**0.0**	**0.0**	**0.0**	**0.0**	**0.0**	**0.0**	**0.0**
Private real estate activities	**-**	**-**	**-**	**-**	**-**	**224.2**	**223.3**	**237.8**	**212.4**	**249.7**

- Nil; .. Not available

Note: Data excludes resident Special Purpose Entities (SPEs). Detailed metadata at: *http://stats.oecd.org/OECDStat_Metadata/ShowMetadata.ashx?Dataset=FDI_CTRY_IND_SUMM.*

Source: OECD International Direct Investment Statistics (database): https://doi.org/10.1787/idi-data-en

ICELAND

Table 1. Foreign direct investment flows by country

Million US dollars

	Inward					Outward				
	2014	2015	2016	2017	2018	2014	2015	2016	2017	2018
WORLD	**447.4**	**708.7**	**-427.2**	**-41.4**	**-316.4**	**-257.2**	**-31.3**	**-1 147.3**	**-208.3**	**148.0**
OECD COUNTRIES	**352.2**	**597.6**	**-679.8**	**154.3**	**-325.9**	**-231.1**	**-280.9**	**-1 171.4**	**-291.8**	**88.8**
Australia	-27.5	7.7	-5.2	87.2	-0.8	-3.2	274.6	-3.8	-6.6	0.5
Austria	0.6	7.4	1.8	-4.3	3.0	0.0	-	-	-	-
Belgium	-14.6	-10.6	36.7	-1.4	0.0	0.1	0.2	0.3	0.1	0.0
Canada	103.5	106.3	-134.7	44.9	0.0	0.5	1.2	-44.5	-29.5	0.2
Chile	-	1.5	-	-	-	3.7	2.2	4.6	6.1	5.9
Czech Republic	4.2	-0.6	5.2	-3.9	-3.0	0.0	0.0	0.0	0.0	0.0
Denmark	40.8	10.3	30.7	174.3	55.7	11.7	11.7	5.7	-3.5	1.0
Estonia	-	-	-	-	-	-2.5	2.1	4.9	4.1	3.7
Finland	3.4	2.5	5.8	21.5	9.1	-2.1	-60.1	-25.3	-2.1	-3.9
France	53.8	8.0	25.7	-75.8	-	0.0	5.0	0.0	-47.9	-6.5
Germany	-7.6	71.3	-12.3	27.8	40.3	-16.3	13.1	21.2	8.0	7.7
Greece	-3.8	1.8	12.8	-12.3	-	-0.1	0.0	0.0	0.0	0.0
Hungary	2.0	1.7	1.4	-2.5	0.0	-1.3	-0.1	-0.2	-1.9	0.8
Iceland	-	-	-	-	-	-	-	-	-	-
Ireland	61.5	32.7	69.1	-135.5	-72.4	0.7	0.5	0.9	0.9	0.2
Israel[1]	-	-	-0.4	-0.3	0.3	-	-	-	-	-
Italy	12.3	9.0	-26.5	-3.9	-7.1	-0.1	0.0	0.0	0.0	0.0
Japan	-	-	-	-	-	3.9	1.9	0.0	-	-
Korea	-	0.3	-	-	244.5	-	-	0.0	0.0	0.0
Latvia	0.6	1.0	0.9	2.1	2.8	-42.3	-22.7	1.3	15.8	11.0
Lithuania	1.0	1.0	0.7	0.1	-	-4.6	-4.4	0.8	1.0	1.5
Luxembourg	60.5	-478.9	-444.7	-553.2	-293.4	-399.6	-9.5	-3.9	25.3	30.9
Mexico	-1.8	-3.6	-2.8	7.4	-	0.2	0.4	-0.3	0.3	-0.2
Netherlands	165.1	515.3	-506.8	-841.9	32.9	109.6	-192.1	20.7	-45.6	-119.6
New Zealand	-	-	-	-	-	0.4	-0.1	0.4	0.3	0.6
Norway	7.0	36.7	85.5	-14.6	26.6	7.2	-314.5	-41.1	-3.9	-52.6
Poland	-	-	-	0.2	-0.4	2.2	0.0	0.1	0.3	0.2
Portugal	-	-	-	-	-	0.0	0.0	0.0	-	-
Slovak Republic	2.3	-0.2	2.8	-	-	0.5	0.6	0.3	-0.3	-0.6
Slovenia	-	-	-	-	-	-	-	-	-	-
Spain	5.1	0.9	-1.8	-2.2	-10.6	9.8	27.4	-207.7	-8.6	3.4
Sweden	34.0	-1.8	-4.5	-80.3	-35.7	-42.6	-89.1	-132.7	-160.8	-6.7
Switzerland	-333.8	5.8	151.9	-1 275.8	-306.7	56.0	-43.6	-6.5	-10.4	179.5
Turkey	3.8	-5.6	9.1	-0.1	0.8	-1.3	-4.2	3.0	0.1	0.2
United Kingdom	91.2	255.3	116.6	-144.2	35.5	56.6	94.5	-771.2	-45.7	-32.1
United States	90.3	24.2	-96.4	2 941.3	-47.4	-25.4	-2.9	2.3	13.7	63.8
EUROPE	**244.1**	**528.4**	**-211.4**	**-3 138.8**	**-507.3**	**-245.1**	**-310.4**	**-1 095.6**	**-246.4**	**31.1**
Bulgaria	5.2	-0.5	-5.0	-6.6	-1.2	-	-	-	-	-
Croatia	-	-	-0.1	2.6	-1.9	-	-	-	0.1	-
Cyprus[2, 3]	-3.1	-0.4	-3.2	-6.5	-6.2	-2.6	274.3	-38.9	11.4	0.2
Malta	55.2	74.0	278.9	-207.5	-0.7	-	-	0.1	-	-
Romania	0.1	1.0	-1.1	0.5	-0.8	0.0	0.1	0.0	0.0	-0.1
Russian Federation	0.1	-1.0	0.0	-1.2	19.2	3.2	-2.6	-2.0	-2.5	-0.4
Ukraine	-5.8	0.0	5.7	-	-	-	-	-	-	-
AFRICA	**-**	**-**	**0.1**	**1.5**	**-0.3**	**0.2**	**-0.2**	**-0.2**	**0.1**	**0.5**
Northern Africa	-	-	-	-	-	0.0	0.0	-	-	-
Algeria	-	-	-	-	-	-	-	-	-	-
Egypt	-	-	-	-	-	-	-	-	-	-
Libya	-	-	-	-	-	-	-	-	-	-
Morocco	-	-	-	-	-	0.0	0.0	-	-	-
Tunisia	-	-	-	-	-	-	-	-	-	-
Other African countries	-	-	0.1	1.5	-0.3	0.2	-0.2	-0.2	0.1	0.5
Nigeria	-	-	-	-	-	-	-	-	-	-
South Africa	-	-	0.1	0.4	-0.3	0.2	-0.2	-0.2	0.0	0.2
AMERICA	**187.0**	**132.6**	**-223.1**	**2 998.5**	**-49.7**	**-20.4**	**0.6**	**-68.8**	**-10.4**	**66.8**
Northern America	193.8	130.5	-231.1	2 986.2	-47.4	-24.8	-1.5	-42.1	-15.8	63.9
Central America and Caribbean countries	2.4	10.5	-2.3	6.5	-2.3	0.3	0.2	-30.9	-0.4	-3.6
Bahamas	-0.1	12.6	-	-	-	-	-	-	-	-
Bermuda	-	0.6	-0.7	1.3	0.4	-	-	0.7	-2.0	0.4
Cayman Islands	4.3	-	-	-2.5	-2.5	0.1	-0.2	-31.2	0.9	-4.0
Costa Rica	-	-	-	-	-	-	-	-	-	-
El Salvador	-	-	-	-	-	-	-	-	-	-
Guatemala	-	-	-	-	-	-	-	-	-	-
Honduras	-	-	-	-	-	-	-	-	-	-
Nicaragua	-	-	-	-	-	-	-	-	-	-
Panama	-	-	-	-	-	-	-	-	-	-
Virgin Islands, U.S.	-	-	-	-	-	-	-	-	-	-
South America	-9.1	-8.4	10.2	5.8	0.0	4.1	1.9	4.3	5.8	6.4
Argentina	-	-	-	-	-	-	-	-	-	-
Bolivia	-	-	-	-	-	-	-	-	-	-
Brazil	-9.1	-9.9	10.2	5.8	0.0	0.1	0.0	-0.2	-0.1	0.6
Colombia	-	-	-	-	-	-	-	-	-	0.0
Ecuador	-	-	-	-	-	-	-	-	-	-
Paraguay	-	-	-	-	-	-	-	-	-	-
Peru	-	-	-	-	-	-	-	-	-	-
Uruguay	-	-	-	-	-	0.3	-0.3	-0.1	-0.1	-0.1
Venezuela	-	-	-	-	-	-	-	-	-	-

Table 1. Foreign direct investment flows by country (cont.)

Million US dollars

	Inward					Outward				
	2014	2015	2016	2017	2018	2014	2015	2016	2017	2018
ASIA	**14.6**	**17.2**	**-1.5**	**6.4**	**244.1**	**10.9**	**4.2**	**5.8**	**6.7**	**2.0**
Near and Middle East	7.3	1.6	-3.6	6.4	0.3	0.0	0.0	0.1	0.0	0.0
Gulf Arabian countries	7.3	1.6	-3.3	6.7	-	0.0	0.0	0.0	0.0	0.0
Kuwait	-	-	-	-	-	-	-	-	-	-
Qatar	-	-	-	-	-	-	-	-	-	-
Saudi Arabia	-	-	-	1.9	-	-	-	-	-	-
United Arab Emirates	7.3	1.6	-3.3	4.9	-	0.0	0.0	0.0	0.0	0.0
Other Near and Middle East	-	-	-0.4	-0.3	0.3	-	-	0.1	0.0	0.0
Jordan	-	-	-	-	-	-	-	-	-	-
Other Asian countries	7.3	15.6	2.1	0.0	243.9	10.9	4.2	5.7	6.7	2.0
China	-0.5	13.8	-2.0	-0.7	-0.7	6.9	1.9	3.1	6.1	1.1
Hong Kong, China	4.9	0.0	-6.4	-6.3	-0.2	-0.5	0.2	2.3	0.2	0.2
India	-	0.0	0.0	-	-	0.0	-0.1	0.0	-	-
Indonesia	-	-	0.1	-	-	0.0	-	-	-	-
Iran, Islamic Republic of	-	-	-	-	-	-	-	-	-	-
Malaysia	-	-	-0.1	0.1	-	-	-	-	0.1	0.0
Philippines	-	-	-	-	-	-	-	-	-	-
Singapore	-3.2	-2.9	3.0	4.5	-0.1	0.3	0.0	0.1	0.0	0.0
Chinese Taipei	-	-	-	0.0	-	-	-	-	-	-
Thailand	6.2	4.4	7.5	2.3	0.3	0.4	0.2	0.2	0.2	0.2
Viet Nam	-	-	-	-	-	-	-	-	0.0	0.4
AUSTRALIA, OCEANIA AND POLAR REGIONS	**-27.5**	**7.7**	**-5.2**	**87.2**	**-0.8**	**-2.8**	**274.5**	**-3.4**	**-6.3**	**1.1**
WORLD unallocated and confidential	**29.2**	**22.6**	**13.8**	**3.9**	**-2.5**	**0.0**	**0.0**	**14.9**	**48.1**	**46.6**
European Union (EU28)	**569.8**	**500.3**	**-416.7**	**-1 853.1**	**-254.2**	**-322.7**	**51.4**	**-1 123.6**	**-249.2**	**-108.8**
G20 countries excl. European Union	**308.4**	**475.9**	**-117.9**	**2 890.7**	**284.1**	**25.4**	**382.7**	**-792.4**	**-104.2**	**35.0**
G20 OECD countries	**317.9**	**473.0**	**-126.3**	**2 884.5**	**265.9**	**15.1**	**383.6**	**-793.1**	**-107.7**	**33.5**
G20 Non-OECD countries	**-9.5**	**2.9**	**8.5**	**6.2**	**18.2**	**10.3**	**-1.0**	**0.7**	**3.5**	**1.5**
MENA countries	**7.3**	**1.6**	**-3.3**	**6.7**	**-**	**0.0**	**0.0**	**0.0**	**0.0**	**0.0**
ASEAN countries	**2.9**	**1.5**	**10.5**	**6.9**	**0.2**	**0.7**	**0.1**	**0.3**	**0.4**	**0.6**

- Nil

Note: Data excludes resident Special Purpose Entities (SPEs). Detailed metadata at: *http://stats.oecd.org/OECDStat_Metadata/ShowMetadata.ashx?Dataset=FDI_CTRY_IND_SUMM.*

1. Information on data for Israel: *http://oe.cd/israel-disclaimer.*
2. Note by Turkey: The information in this document with reference to "Cyprus" relates to the southern part of the Island. There is no single authority representing both Turkish and Greek Cypriot people on the Island. Turkey recognises the Turkish Republic of Northern Cyprus (TRNC). Until a lasting and equitable solution is found within the context of the United Nations, Turkey shall preserve its position concerning the "Cyprus issue".
3. Note by all the European Union Member States of the OECD and the European Union: The Republic of Cyprus is recognised by all members of the United Nations with the exception of Turkey. The information in this document relates to the area under the effective control of the Government of the Republic of Cyprus.

Source: OECD International Direct Investment Statistics (database): https://doi.org/10.1787/idi-data-en

Table 2. Foreign direct investment positions by country

At year end

Million US dollars

	Inward					Outward				
	2014	2015	2016	2017	2018	2014	2015	2016	2017	2018
WORLD	**7 888.8**	**7 851.0**	**9 841.0**	**10 129.9**	**9 138.0**	**8 414.9**	**7 636.6**	**6 058.2**	**5 268.6**	**5 262.8**
OECD COUNTRIES	**7 172.2**	**7 152.8**	**9 091.9**	**9 500.3**	**8 529.0**	**7 141.2**	**6 177.3**	**5 022.9**	**4 684.5**	**4 661.4**
Australia	-	-	-	-	0.0	2.3	239.9	240.1	-162.7	12.1
Austria	20.5	26.6	16.0	16.7	17.8	-	-	-	-	-
Belgium	3.8	4.3	4.9	5.3	4.8	0.0	0.0	0.1	17.1	16.4
Canada	151.5	157.7	195.4	190.2	196.8	108.3	102.5	35.6	12.0	11.2
Chile	-	1.1	-	-	-	28.0	29.5	32.6	39.2	44.1
Czech Republic	-	-	-	-	-	0.1	0.1	0.2	0.2	0.2
Denmark	443.2	451.7	424.6	467.8	473.6	41.8	70.5	84.8	109.1	59.7
Estonia	-	-	-	-	-	17.9	22.4	30.8	38.9	43.0
Finland	1.3	0.8	2.6	9.8	8.9	217.1	120.3	81.3	83.2	80.8
France	6.3	8.5	15.1	18.9	24.2	2.6	1.8	8.2	82.7	71.3
Germany	83.6	104.8	83.4	97.7	122.0	89.2	107.0	128.5	137.1	135.9
Greece	-	-	-	-	-	0.6	0.3	0.2	0.2	0.2
Hungary	-	-	-	-	-	1.7	1.0	1.5	1.0	1.7
Iceland	85.9	62.7	116.3	69.4	40.8	-	-	-	-	-
Ireland	86.5	39.1	57.7	63.2	56.7	9.6	9.1	9.1	12.4	12.1
Israel[2]	1.3	1.3	2 788.6	2 789.5	2 327.4	-	-	-	-	-
Italy	4.0	4.3	6.0	5.6	6.0	-0.1	0.0	0.0	0.0	0.0
Japan	-	-	-	-	-	16.1	14.8	5.6	5.8	6.0
Korea	-	-	-	-	227.9	-	-	8.2	8.2	8.2
Latvia	37.6	-9.5	48.8	64.2	63.7	112.5	53.9	51.7	69.8	82.7
Lithuania	-	-	-	-	-	33.3	23.2	17.8	29.0	29.2
Luxembourg	168.5	136.3	568.5	329.2	380.6	882.2	690.1	290.2	158.1	158.1
Mexico	-	-	-	-	-	0.0	0.4	0.1	0.3	0.1
Netherlands	102.2	118.3	162.6	265.6	235.9	2 719.9	2 513.5	2 532.7	3 033.8	2 772.3
New Zealand	-	-	-	-	-	2.3	1.8	2.1	2.6	3.0
Norway	105.5	109.9	239.5	282.1	253.5	412.7	120.6	124.5	186.2	131.1
Poland	-	-	-	-	-	0.7	0.2	0.1	0.5	0.7
Portugal	-	-	-	-	-	0.0	0.0	-	-	-
Slovak Republic	-	-	-	-	-	6.1	6.1	6.2	-0.4	-1.0
Slovenia	-	-	-	-	-	-	-	-	-	-
Spain	85.8	84.7	10.3	-1.7	0.6	72.1	91.4	47.1	45.8	47.2
Sweden	29.1	42.7	31.1	32.6	76.9	623.1	371.7	207.0	62.7	53.4
Switzerland	29.0	32.8	68.1	118.0	76.9	52.2	-0.7	-7.0	-59.0	111.3
Turkey	-	-	-	-	-	17.1	7.1	4.9	11.3	11.0
United Kingdom	724.2	744.4	1 648.7	2 016.0	1 596.7	1 777.9	1 636.1	1 076.3	752.0	663.5
United States	5 040.0	5 020.9	2 603.7	2 660.1	2 337.2	39.5	20.1	20.4	36.4	96.2
EUROPE	**2 168.6**	**2 126.3**	**3 664.8**	**3 977.5**	**3 549.8**	**7 481.0**	**6 528.8**	**5 449.8**	**5 093.0**	**4 813.7**
Bulgaria	-	-	-	-	-	-	-	-	-	-
Croatia	-	-	-	-	-	-	-	-	0.1	0.1
Cyprus[3, 4]	59.5	56.6	76.2	29.9	28.0	160.9	556.1	526.1	109.6	119.4
Malta	26.4	41.8	53.1	54.6	48.5	-	-	0.1	0.1	0.1
Romania	-	-	-	-	-	0.4	0.5	0.5	0.6	-
Russian Federation	0.3	0.3	0.3	0.4	0.3	40.8	30.6	32.0	36.1	33.7
Ukraine	-	-	-	-	-	-	-	-	-	-
AFRICA	**-**	**-**	**-**	**2.4**	**1.9**	**1.0**	**1.3**	**1.0**	**1.7**	**1.9**
Northern Africa	-	-	-	-	-	0.4	0.4	-	-	-
Algeria	-	-	-	-	-	-	-	-	-	-
Egypt	-	-	-	-	-	-	-	-	-	-
Libya	-	-	-	-	-	-	-	-	-	-
Morocco	-	-	-	-	-	0.4	0.4	-	-	-
Tunisia	-	-	-	-	-	-	-	-	-	-
Other African countries	-	-	-	2.4	1.9	0.6	0.9	1.0	1.7	1.9
Nigeria	-	-	-	-	-	-	-	-	-	-
South Africa	-	-	-	1.3	0.9	0.6	0.9	1.0	1.0	0.9
AMERICA	**5 275.3**	**5 259.6**	**2 884.2**	**2 887.9**	**2 565.2**	**463.7**	**438.0**	**102.8**	**102.5**	**162.7**
Northern America	5 191.5	5 178.6	2 799.1	2 850.2	2 533.9	147.8	123.0	56.0	48.4	107.4
Central America and Caribbean countries	83.8	79.9	85.1	37.6	31.3	287.0	285.0	14.1	15.0	10.9
Bahamas	8.9	4.8	-	-	-	-	-	-	-	-
Bermuda	2.1	2.7	3.1	3.4	3.0	4.8	4.8	5.9	7.3	7.7
Cayman Islands	72.6	71.1	81.7	34.0	28.2	33.3	31.2	8.0	6.9	2.4
Costa Rica	-	-	-	-	-	-	-	-	-	-
El Salvador	-	-	-	-	-	-	-	-	-	-
Guatemala	-	-	-	-	-	-	-	-	-	-
Honduras	-	-	-	-	-	-	-	-	-	-
Nicaragua	-	-	-	-	-	-	-	-	-	-
Panama	0.2	0.2	0.2	0.2	0.2	-	-	-	-	-
Virgin Islands, U.S.	-	-	-	-	-	-	-	-	-	-
South America	-	1.1	-	-	-	28.9	30.0	32.7	39.1	44.5
Argentina	-	-	-	-	-	-	-	-	-	-
Bolivia	-	-	-	-	-	-	-	-	-	-
Brazil	-	-	-	-	-	0.3	0.2	0.0	-0.1	0.4
Colombia	-	-	-	-	-	-	-	-	-	-
Ecuador	-	-	-	-	-	-	-	-	-	-
Paraguay	-	-	-	-	-	-	-	-	-	-
Peru	-	-	-	-	-	-	-	-	-	-
Uruguay	-	-	-	-	-	0.7	0.3	0.1	0.0	0.0
Venezuela	-	-	-	-	-	-	-	-	-	-

Table 2. Foreign direct investment positions by country *(cont.)*

At year end

Million US dollars

	Inward					Outward				
	2014	2015	2016	2017	2018	2014	2015	2016	2017	2018
ASIA	**180.9**	**183.4**	**2 981.1**	**2 965.5**	**2 754.8**	**64.0**	**63.3**	**74.5**	**83.8**	**82.4**
Near and Middle East	1.3	1.3	2 788.6	2 791.4	2 329.1	1.0	0.9	0.8	0.0	0.0
Gulf Arabian countries	-	-	-	1.9	1.7	1.0	0.9	0.7	0.0	0.0
Kuwait	-	-	-	-	-	-	-	-	-	-
Qatar	-	-	-	-	-	-	-	-	-	-
Saudi Arabia	-	-	-	1.9	1.7	-	-	-	-	-
United Arab Emirates	-	-	-	-	-	1.0	0.9	0.7	0.0	0.0
Other Near and Middle East	1.3	1.3	2 788.6	2 789.5	2 327.4	-	-	0.1	0.0	0.0
Jordan	-	-	-	-	-	-	-	-	-	-
Other Asian countries	179.6	182.1	192.5	174.1	425.7	63.0	62.4	73.6	83.7	82.4
China	116.5	125.7	143.8	124.0	150.6	43.1	43.7	58.2	67.0	64.7
Hong Kong, China	24.4	24.3	29.4	23.7	21.1	0.6	0.6	0.7	0.9	1.1
India	-	-	-	-	-	0.1	0.0	0.0	-	-
Indonesia	-	-	-	-	-	0.0	-	-	-	-
Iran, Islamic Republic of	-	-	-	-	-	-	-	-	-	-
Malaysia	-	-	-	-	-	-	-	-	0.2	0.2
Philippines	-	-	-	-	-	-	-	-	-	-
Singapore	38.7	32.0	19.3	26.3	26.1	2.5	2.6	0.0	0.3	0.3
Chinese Taipei	-	-	-	-	-	-	-	-	-	-
Thailand	-	-	-	-	-	0.7	0.8	1.0	1.3	1.5
Viet Nam	-	-	-	-	-	-	-	-	0.0	0.4
AUSTRALIA, OCEANIA AND POLAR REGIONS	**-**	**-**	**-**	**-**	**0.0**	**4.7**	**241.7**	**242.2**	**-160.2**	**15.0**
WORLD unallocated and confidential	**264.2**	**281.7**	**310.9**	**296.7**	**266.3**	**400.4**	**363.5**	**188.0**	**147.7**	**187.1**
European Union (EU28)	**1 882.6**	**1 855.4**	**3 209.5**	**3 475.5**	**3 145.0**	**6 769.7**	**6 275.2**	**5 100.5**	**4 743.5**	**4 346.9**
G20 countries excl. European Union	**6 126.4**	**6 166.6**	**4 696.4**	**5 116.1**	**4 664.3**	**2 137.7**	**2 205.0**	**1 619.0**	**987.1**	**1 115.2**
G20 OECD countries	**6 009.6**	**6 040.5**	**4 552.3**	**4 988.5**	**4 510.7**	**2 052.9**	**2 129.6**	**1 527.9**	**883.2**	**1 015.4**
G20 Non-OECD countries	**116.8**	**126.0**	**144.2**	**127.6**	**153.5**	**84.8**	**75.4**	**91.1**	**104.0**	**99.8**
MENA countries	**-**	**-**	**-**	**1.9**	**1.7**	**1.4**	**1.3**	**0.7**	**0.0**	**0.0**
ASEAN countries	**38.7**	**32.0**	**19.3**	**26.3**	**26.1**	**3.2**	**3.4**	**1.0**	**1.8**	**2.4**

- Nil

Note: Data excludes resident Special Purpose Entities (SPEs). Detailed metadata at: *http://stats.oecd.org/OECDStat_Metadata/ShowMetadata.ashx?Dataset=FDI_CTRY_IND_SUMM.*

1. Inward FDI positions are allocated according to the ultimate investing country. Detailed metadata at *http://stats.oecd.org/OECDStat_Metadata/ShowMetadata.ashx?Dataset=FDI_CTRY_IND_SUMM.*
2. Information on data for Israel: *http://oe.cd/israel-disclaimer.*
3. Note by Turkey: The information in this document with reference to "Cyprus" relates to the southern part of the Island. There is no single authority representing both Turkish and Greek Cypriot people on the Island. Turkey recognises the Turkish Republic of Northern Cyprus (TRNC). Until a lasting and equitable solution is found within the context of the United Nations, Turkey shall preserve its position concerning the "Cyprus issue".
4. Note by all the European Union Member States of the OECD and the European Union: The Republic of Cyprus is recognised by all members of the United Nations with the exception of Turkey. The information in this document relates to the area under the effective control of the Government of the Republic of Cyprus.

Source: OECD International Direct Investment Statistics (database): https://doi.org/10.1787/idi-data-en

ICELAND

Table 3. Foreign direct investment income by country

Million US dollars

	Inward					Outward				
	2014	2015	2016	2017	2018	2014	2015	2016	2017	2018
WORLD	**-47.3**	**31.2**	**-29.2**	**40.4**	**-27.3**	**164.1**	**283.4**	**435.8**	**302.1**	**303.8**
OECD COUNTRIES	**-22.0**	**58.4**	**-18.5**	**49.1**	**..**	**134.7**	**260.1**	**390.9**	**270.0**	**..**
Australia	-7.5	-6.4	-4.1	-1.7	..	0.3	-2.9	-5.3	-0.2	..
Austria	-3.1	-2.8	3.1	6.1	..	-	-	-	-	..
Belgium	-1.4	-1.2	-0.1	0.3	..	0.1	0.2	0.3	0.1	..
Canada	-7.6	-0.8	-1.9	0.0	..	0.5	1.3	5.3	0.7	..
Chile	-	-	-	-	..	4.1	-5.4	5.5	6.3	..
Czech Republic	0.0	0.0	-0.2	0.0	..	-	-	-	-	..
Denmark	18.9	10.2	13.1	12.1	..	3.7	24.6	24.4	22.4	..
Estonia	-	-	-	-	..	0.7	2.0	4.9	4.3	..
Finland	0.1	3.7	9.0	9.2	..	1.9	0.1	-0.8	0.9	..
France	0.3	0.1	-0.1	-0.1	..	0.7	0.6	0.1	2.2	..
Germany	-8.5	-4.1	0.6	-1.1	..	4.1	22.6	16.1	7.7	..
Greece	-0.6	0.0	0.0	-	..	-0.1	0.0	0.0	0.0	..
Hungary	-0.2	-0.1	0.0	0.0	..	-1.0	0.5	-0.5	-1.2	..
Iceland	-	-	-	-	..	-	-	-	-	..
Ireland	3.9	0.2	7.0	12.6	..	0.6	0.5	0.6	0.7	..
Israel[1]	-	-	-	-	..	-	-	-	-	..
Italy	1.9	-4.5	0.9	-3.1	..	-	-	-	-	..
Japan	-	-	-	-	..	0.5	0.2	0.0	-	..
Korea	-	-	-	-	..	-	-	0.0	0.0	..
Latvia	0.6	1.0	3.2	2.9	..	8.0	4.1	7.4	11.2	..
Lithuania	-0.2	-0.1	-0.1	0.0	..	2.1	2.2	1.1	1.5	..
Luxembourg	39.3	99.4	134.6	-25.2	..	23.9	20.0	16.9	24.3	..
Mexico	-0.2	-0.3	-0.5	-0.5	..	-	-	-	-	..
Netherlands	99.3	70.2	65.1	97.8	..	4.0	62.9	117.5	112.6	..
New Zealand	-	-	-	-	..	0.2	0.1	0.0	0.1	..
Norway	15.2	21.7	-0.5	7.9	..	11.2	2.6	3.5	31.9	..
Poland	-	-	-	-	..	0.0	-	0.0	0.0	..
Portugal	-	-	-	-	..	-	-	-	-	..
Slovak Republic	0.1	-0.1	-0.1	-	..	0.6	0.5	0.4	-	..
Slovenia	-	-	-	-	..	-	-	-	-	..
Spain	0.5	0.4	-1.8	-3.8	..	16.2	24.2	3.5	3.1	..
Sweden	15.2	-4.9	-17.4	-49.7	..	15.7	4.1	2.0	-1.7	..
Switzerland	2.8	4.5	-25.8	94.6	..	0.6	-0.1	0.1	0.2	..
Turkey	-0.3	-0.8	-0.9	-0.1	..	-1.3	-4.2	3.0	0.1	..
United Kingdom	-17.7	-11.5	39.8	2.7	..	45.4	105.1	181.5	37.1	..
United States	-172.6	-114.4	-241.5	-112.0	..	2.1	0.5	4.6	7.3	..
EUROPE	**138.0**	**157.5**	**216.2**	**157.2**	**..**	**153.6**	**287.2**	**418.0**	**278.5**	**..**
Bulgaria	-	-	-	-	..	-	-	-	-	..
Croatia	-	-	-	-	..	-	-	-	-	..
Cyprus[2, 3]	-3.1	0.4	-1.5	-6.5	..	1.2	5.0	11.0	-2.8	..
Malta	-18.0	-14.8	-7.2	-1.0	..	-	-	-	-	..
Romania	-	-	-	-	..	0.1	0.1	0.1	0.1	..
Russian Federation	-3.9	-3.5	-2.5	-2.6	..	1.6	-3.7	-2.0	-2.5	..
Ukraine	-0.4	-0.3	-0.2	-	..	-	-	-	-	..
AFRICA	**-**	**-**	**-**	**-0.3**	**..**	**-0.1**	**0.3**	**-0.1**	**0.1**	**..**
Northern Africa	-	-	-	-	..	-	-	-	-	..
Algeria	-	-	-	-	..	-	-	-	-	..
Egypt	-	-	-	-	..	-	-	-	-	..
Libya	-	-	-	-	..	-	-	-	-	..
Morocco	-	-	-	-	..	-	-	-	-	..
Tunisia	-	-	-	-	..	-	-	-	-	..
Other African countries	-	-	-	-0.3	..	-0.1	0.3	-0.1	0.1	..
Nigeria	-	-	-	-	..	-	-	-	-	..
South Africa	-	-	-	-0.3	..	-0.1	0.3	-0.1	0.1	..
AMERICA	**-181.0**	**-123.4**	**-247.2**	**-115.5**	**..**	**6.8**	**-3.2**	**16.9**	**20.3**	**..**
Northern America	-180.1	-115.2	-243.4	-112.0	..	2.6	2.0	9.8	8.0	..
Central America and Caribbean countries	-0.3	-6.1	-1.9	-2.8	..	0.1	0.1	1.6	6.0	..
Bahamas	-0.1	-5.8	-	-	..	-	-	-	-	..
Bermuda	-	-	-1.4	0.4	..	-	-	0.7	0.5	..
Cayman Islands	-	-	-	-2.5	..	0.1	0.1	0.9	5.4	..
Costa Rica	-	-	-	-	..	-	-	-	-	..
El Salvador	-	-	-	-	..	-	-	-	-	..
Guatemala	-	-	-	-	..	-	-	-	-	..
Honduras	-	-	-	-	..	-	-	-	-	..
Nicaragua	-	-	-	-	..	-	-	-	-	..
Panama	-	0.0	0.0	0.0	..	-	-	-	-	..
Virgin Islands, U.S.	-	-	-	-	..	-	-	-	-	..
South America	-0.6	-2.1	-2.0	-0.7	..	4.1	-5.4	5.5	6.3	..
Argentina	-	-	-	-	..	-	-	-	-	..
Bolivia	-	-	-	-	..	-	-	-	-	..
Brazil	-0.6	-2.1	-2.0	-0.7	..	-	-	-	-	..
Colombia	-	-	-	-	..	-	-	-	-	..
Ecuador	-	-	-	-	..	-	-	-	-	..
Paraguay	-	-	-	-	..	-	-	-	-	..
Peru	-	-	-	-	..	-	-	-	-	..
Uruguay	-	-	-	-	..	-	-	-	-	..
Venezuela	-	-	-	-	..	-	-	-	-	..

Table 3. Foreign direct investment income by country *(cont.)*

Million US dollars

	Inward					Outward				
	2014	2015	2016	2017	2018	2014	2015	2016	2017	2018
ASIA	**-0.2**	**0.4**	**-2.7**	**0.8**	..	**3.3**	**2.0**	**3.5**	**1.6**	..
Near and Middle East	-0.5	-0.3	-0.1	-0.1	..	0.0	0.0	0.0	0.0	..
Gulf Arabian countries	-0.5	-0.3	-0.1	-0.1	..	0.0	0.0	0.0	0.0	..
Kuwait	-	-	-	-	..	-	-	-	-	..
Qatar	-	-	-	-	..	-	-	-	-	..
Saudi Arabia	-	-	-	-	..	-	-	-	-	..
United Arab Emirates	-0.5	-0.3	-0.1	-0.1	..	0.0	0.0	0.0	0.0	..
Other Near and Middle East	-	-	-	-	..	-	-	0.0	0.0	..
Jordan	-	-	-	-	..	-	-	-	-	..
Other Asian countries	0.2	0.6	-2.6	0.9	..	3.3	2.0	3.5	1.6	..
China	0.0	-0.2	-2.0	-0.7	..	2.0	1.4	3.0	1.2	..
Hong Kong, China	0.0	0.5	0.4	-1.1	..	0.8	0.2	0.2	0.2	..
India	-	-	-	-	..	0.0	-0.1	-	-	..
Indonesia	-	-	-	-	..	-	-	-	-	..
Iran, Islamic Republic of	-	-	-	-	..	-	-	-	-	..
Malaysia	-	-	0.0	0.0	..	-	-	-	0.0	..
Philippines	-	-	-	-	..	-	-	-	-	..
Singapore	0.2	0.2	-1.2	2.4	..	0.1	0.1	0.1	0.0	..
Chinese Taipei	-	-	-	-	..	-	-	-	-	..
Thailand	0.0	0.1	0.2	0.3	..	0.0	0.2	0.1	0.2	..
Viet Nam	-	-	-	-	..	-	-	-	-	..
AUSTRALIA, OCEANIA AND POLAR REGIONS	**-7.5**	**-6.4**	**-4.1**	**-1.7**	..	**0.5**	**-2.8**	**-5.3**	**-0.1**	..
WORLD unallocated and confidential	**3.5**	**3.1**	**8.7**	**-0.1**	..	**0.0**	**0.0**	**2.8**	**1.7**	..
European Union (EU28)	**127.4**	**141.5**	**247.9**	**53.5**	..	**128.0**	**273.1**	**386.3**	**222.5**	..
G20 countries excl. European Union	**-216.6**	**-148.5**	**-214.1**	**-120.1**	..	**55.8**	**121.1**	**206.1**	**53.6**	..
G20 OECD countries	**-212.1**	**-142.8**	**-207.6**	**-115.8**	..	**52.3**	**123.3**	**205.2**	**54.8**	..
G20 Non-OECD countries	**-4.5**	**-5.7**	**-6.5**	**-4.2**	..	**3.5**	**-2.1**	**1.0**	**-1.2**	..
MENA countries	**-0.5**	**-0.3**	**-0.1**	**-0.1**	..	**0.0**	**0.0**	**0.0**	**0.0**	..
ASEAN countries	**0.2**	**0.3**	**-1.0**	**2.6**	..	**0.1**	**0.3**	**0.2**	**0.2**	..

- Nil; .. Not available

Note: Data excludes resident Special Purpose Entities (SPEs). Detailed metadata at: *http://stats.oecd.org/OECDStat_Metadata/ShowMetadata.ashx?Dataset=FDI_CTRY_IND_SUMM.*

1. Information on data for Israel: *http://oe.cd/israel-disclaimer.*
2. Note by Turkey: The information in this document with reference to "Cyprus" relates to the southern part of the Island. There is no single authority representing both Turkish and Greek Cypriot people on the Island. Turkey recognises the Turkish Republic of Northern Cyprus (TRNC). Until a lasting and equitable solution is found within the context of the United Nations, Turkey shall preserve its position concerning the "Cyprus issue".
3. Note by all the European Union Member States of the OECD and the European Union: The Republic of Cyprus is recognised by all members of the United Nations with the exception of Turkey. The information in this document relates to the area under the effective control of the Government of the Republic of Cyprus.

Source: OECD International Direct Investment Statistics (database): https://doi.org/10.1787/idi-data-en

Table 4. Foreign direct investment flows by industrial sector

Million US dollars

	Inward					Outward				
	2014	2015	2016	2017	2018	2014	2015	2016	2017	2018
All FDI activities	**447.4**	**708.7**	**-427.2**	**-41.4**	**-316.4**	**-257.2**	**-31.3**	**-1 147.3**	**-208.3**	**148.0**
Agriculture, forestry and fishing	**37.2**	**1.3**	**40.4**	**10.1**	**-1.2**	**6.8**	**21.0**	**-22.3**	**34.7**	**23.3**
Mining and quarrying	**0.2**	**30.9**	**2.7**	**-0.9**	**42.6**	-	-	-	-	-
Extraction activities	-	30.9	0.3	-0.9	42.5	-	-	-	-	-
Manufacturing	**-104.4**	**-82.7**	**-96.3**	**98.3**	**99.9**	**26.4**	**133.4**	**97.5**	**3.3**	**80.8**
of which:										
Food products, beverages and tobacco	-0.7	-2.6	-3.6	14.4	2.8	1.4	-220.5	-26.6	1.3	1.3
Textiles, wood and paper products; printing	-	-	-	-	-	2.5	0.4	77.5	23.1	20.1
Chemical, rubber, plastic, non-metallic mineral products	-8.9	-19.5	-20.8	0.4	148.6	13.9	298.1	10.9	-6.6	0.6
Metal and machinery products, except electrical equipment	-99.2	-114.8	-95.4	-18.1	76.3	1.5	59.8	39.8	79.4	60.9
Motor vehicles, trailers, semi-trailers, other transport equipment	-	-	-	-	-	-0.3	-0.1	-0.7	-	-
Other manufacturing	4.4	54.2	23.5	101.7	-127.9	7.4	-4.4	-3.4	-93.9	-2.1
Electricity, gas, steam and air conditioning supply	**8.6**	**13.5**	**1.8**	**-60.9**	**10.5**	**6.5**	**1.1**	**0.4**	**0.8**	**0.8**
Water supply; sewerage, waste management and remediation activities	**0.0**	**0.0**	**0.1**	**0.8**	**-23.6**	-	-	-	-	-
Construction	**0.7**	**1.6**	**15.1**	**8.6**	**-14.3**	**-4.0**	**54.5**	**-409.5**	**4.9**	**4.3**
Services	**499.5**	**740.0**	**-391.1**	**-98.0**	**-427.7**	**-292.9**	**-241.3**	**-825.8**	**-260.8**	**36.4**
Wholesale and retail trade; repair of motor vehicles and motorcycles	647.5	-2 218.0	681.0	3 217.0	-275.9	-14.3	52.8	40.2	7.8	30.7
Transportation and storage	-1.6	-1.3	1.6	-2.5	-0.4	34.1	9.7	35.3	47.4	23.7
Accommodation and food service activities	-	-	29.6	-3.4	37.4	0.3	-4.4	-1.7	-17.8	-
Information and communication	8.6	38.8	18.7	136.7	28.2	2.8	0.4	-1.6	-33.9	-0.7
Financial and insurance activities	-237.2	2 880.5	-1 176.1	-3 460.0	-286.9	-265.9	-155.0	-411.0	-247.0	-55.8
Activities of holding companies	-235.9	2 883.4	-841.0	-3 446.5	-468.1	-257.2	-82.0	-407.2	-244.9	-58.4
Real estate activities	32.5	23.8	15.3	8.1	8.7	-54.8	-45.9	-96.7	-5.3	37.8
Professional, scientific and technical activities	32.1	21.8	35.3	11.3	36.5	5.2	-87.3	-236.0	-4.0	5.1
Administrative and support service activities	17.6	-5.6	3.9	-4.9	24.9	-4.7	-12.6	-14.9	-8.5	-4.9
Public administration; activities of households and of extraterritorial organisations	-	-	-	-	-	-	-	-	-	-
Education	-	-	-0.5	-0.3	-0.3	-	-	-	-	-
Human health and social work activities	-	-	-	-	-	4.4	1.2	-139.4	-	-
Arts, entertainment and recreation	-	-	-	0.0	-	-	-	-	0.4	0.5
Other services	-	-	-	-	-	-	-	-	-	-
Not allocated and confidential	**5.7**	**4.0**	**0.0**	**0.6**	**-2.7**	**0.0**	**0.2**	**12.3**	**8.9**	**2.4**
Private real estate activities	-	-	-	-	-	-	-	-	-	-

- Nil

Note: Data excludes resident Special Purpose Entities (SPEs). Detailed metadata at: *http://stats.oecd.org/OECDStat_Metadata/ShowMetadata.ashx?Dataset=FDI_CTRY_IND_SUMM.*

Source: OECD International Direct Investment Statistics (database): https://doi.org/10.1787/idi-data-en

Table 5. Foreign direct investment positions by industrial sector

At year end

Million US dollars

	Inward					Outward				
	2014	2015	2016	2017	2018	2014	2015	2016	2017	2018
All FDI activities	**7 888.8**	**7 851.0**	**9 841.0**	**10 129.9**	**9 138.0**	**8 414.9**	**7 636.6**	**6 058.2**	**5 268.6**	**5 262.8**
Agriculture, forestry and fishing	**70.4**	**67.4**	**147.8**	**189.8**	**175.1**	**145.1**	**126.8**	**124.4**	**173.6**	**202.7**
Mining and quarrying	**41.8**	**36.2**	**39.8**	**39.8**	**64.3**	-	-	-	-	-
Extraction activities	-	36.2	27.4	39.8	55.0	-	-	-	-	-
Manufacturing	**1 484.6**	**1 362.1**	**1 238.4**	**1 243.8**	**1 331.7**	**1 299.0**	**1 585.7**	**1 573.7**	**821.0**	**1 001.6**
of which:										
Food products, beverages and tobacco	98.8	92.6	97.9	120.4	113.8	198.7	73.1	13.2	14.5	14.5
Textiles, wood and paper products; printing	-	-	-	-	-	45.5	10[illegible].7	144.7	156.5	168.8
Chemical, rubber, plastic, non-metallic mineral products	137.9	118.6	108.3	88.8	191.7	244.1	680.6	669.7	-150.0	24.8
Metal and machinery products, except electrical equipment	920.5	778.1	648.3	618.2	606.9	549.7	559.5	583.9	729.5	734.9
Motor vehicles, trailers, semi-trailers, other transport equipment	-	-	-	-	-	0.7	0.4	-	-	-
Other manufacturing	327.3	372.7	383.9	416.2	419.3	260.4	170.4	162.2	70.6	58.6
Electricity, gas, steam and air conditioning supply	**182.2**	**182.0**	**184.8**	**183.6**	**190.9**	**43.4**	**43.6**	**53.0**	**57.1**	**54.9**
Water supply; sewerage, waste management and remediation activities	**19.6**	**19.2**	**22.1**	**24.5**	-	-	-	-	-	-
Construction	**1.2**	**4.1**	**37.4**	**46.2**	**30.8**	**305.4**	**159.2**	**19.1**	**17.4**	**21.8**
Services	**5 922.7**	**6 021.7**	**7 991.8**	**8 193.8**	**7 160.6**	**6 221.4**	**5 357.3**	**4 054.0**	**3 999.0**	**3 800.6**
Wholesale and retail trade; repair of motor vehicles and motorcycles	2 925.0	145.5	734.3	1 419.8	1 070.8	508.8	605.4	673.6	666.4	644.1
Transportation and storage	41.4	34.0	31.3	35.0	29.1	356.2	244.5	263.5	303.5	300.5
Accommodation and food service activities	2.3	2.2	4.3	14.8	18.3	10.7	19.2	0.3	0.3	0.3
Information and communication	110.8	158.5	207.6	334.8	193.7	29.6	27.8	32.8	10.9	10.6
Financial and insurance activities	2 395.7	5 192.3	6 405.2	5 709.3	5 196.4	4 503.8	3 752.1	2 872.9	2 846.9	2 621.1
Activities of holding companies	2 368.0	5 160.9	6 046.8	5 004.5	4 387.9	4 368.3	3 707.9	2 834.2	2 804.3	2 577.8
Real estate activities	264.5	285.8	318.5	353.2	325.2	361.1	215.4	119.9	132.4	162.3
Professional, scientific and technical activities	41.2	80.4	151.9	179.0	194.7	237.2	314.1	59.7	6.2	11.4
Administrative and support service activities	141.9	122.9	133.6	142.9	127.9	107.8	65.4	31.2	30.9	48.4
Public administration; activities of households and of extraterritorial organisations	-	-	-	-	-	-	-	-	-	-
Education	-	-	5.0	5.1	4.6	-	-	-	-	-
Human health and social work activities	-	-	-	-	-	106.2	113.3	-	-	-
Arts, entertainment and recreation	-	-	-	0.0	0.0	-	-	-	1.4	1.8
Other services	-	-	-	-	-	-	-	-	-	-
Not allocated and confidential	**166.4**	**158.3**	**178.9**	**208.4**	**184.6**	**400.5**	**363.9**	**234.1**	**200.5**	**181.2**
Private real estate activities	-	-	-	-	-	-	-	-	-	-

- Nil

Note: Data excludes resident Special Purpose Entities (SPEs). Detailed metadata at: *http://stats.oecd.org/OECDStat_Metadata/ShowMetadata.ashx?Dataset=FDI_CTRY_IND_SUMM.*

Source: *OECD International Direct Investment Statistics (database): https://doi.org/10.1787/idi-data-en*

ICELAND

Table 6. Foreign direct investment income by industrial sector

Million US dollars

	Inward					Outward				
	2014	2015	2016	2017	2018	2014	2015	2016	2017	2018
All FDI activities	**-47.3**	**31.2**	**-29.2**	**40.4**	**-27.3**	**164.1**	**283.4**	**435.8**	**302.1**	**303.8**
Agriculture, forestry and fishing	**-0.7**	**-0.3**	**-0.4**	**-3.3**	**-3.2**	**7.4**	**21.4**	**27.5**	**20.5**	**20.2**
Mining and quarrying	**0.2**	**0.0**	**-0.2**	**-0.9**	**5.5**	**-**	**-**	**-**	**-**	**-**
Extraction activities	-	0.0	-0.2	-0.9	5.4	-	-	-	-	-
Manufacturing	**19.4**	**-29.7**	**-46.3**	**-73.5**	**-118.8**	**54.9**	**75.0**	**121.0**	**129.4**	**166.3**
of which:										
Food products, beverages and tobacco	-4.5	-2.8	-1.3	2.8	3.3	1.5	1.7	1.4	1.3	1.3
Textiles, wood and paper products; printing	-	-	-	-	-	3.5	1.5	14.4	19.5	19.3
Chemical, rubber, plastic, non-metallic mineral products	-7.2	-53.3	-36.5	-92.8	-113.0	13.9	-7.2	10.9	-0.4	0.6
Metal and machinery products, except electrical equipment	23.3	13.2	-33.1	-4.1	-26.9	21.5	70.5	76.9	111.0	147.9
Motor vehicles, trailers, semi-trailers, other transport equipment	-	-	-	-	-	-	-0.1	-	-	-
Other manufacturing	7.8	13.1	24.5	20.6	17.8	14.5	8.7	17.3	-2.0	-2.7
Electricity, gas, steam and air conditioning supply	**12.0**	**16.5**	**1.8**	**4.1**	**10.5**	**1.2**	**1.1**	**0.4**	**0.8**	**0.8**
Water supply; sewerage, waste management and remediation activities	**0.0**	**0.0**	**0.1**	**0.8**	**-**	**-**	**-**	**-**	**-**	**-**
Construction	**-0.6**	**0.2**	**1.1**	**-14.3**	**-14.1**	**-2.8**	**48.9**	**123.1**	**4.8**	**4.8**
Services	**-77.6**	**44.5**	**14.7**	**130.2**	**95.6**	**103.3**	**136.9**	**161.5**	**144.0**	**109.3**
Wholesale and retail trade; repair of motor vehicles and motorcycles	117.9	-45.1	-103.0	-119.1	14.8	29.7	38.3	31.3	26.5	30.2
Transportation and storage	-1.1	-1.2	1.1	-0.4	-0.4	30.6	22.8	35.3	25.0	24.6
Accommodation and food service activities	-	0.0	-0.1	2.3	4.1	0.3	0.3	-2.0	-	-
Information and communication	-1.5	4.0	13.5	8.5	8.4	-2.0	3.4	3.3	4.5	-0.9
Financial and insurance activities	-223.3	55.1	76.5	209.6	39.7	29.7	59.9	92.0	90.4	59.6
Activities of holding companies	-222.0	59.2	74.6	191.1	26.0	26.9	56.3	90.8	85.5	57.6
Real estate activities	2.2	4.2	6.2	7.3	7.2	10.9	8.0	9.1	2.0	1.4
Professional, scientific and technical activities	8.4	3.0	4.7	11.4	11.2	9.2	9.9	1.8	0.4	-1.1
Administrative and support service activities	19.7	24.5	16.2	10.8	10.8	-9.8	-10.1	-14.1	-5.1	-5.0
Public administration; activities of households and of extraterritorial organisations	-	-	-	-	-	-	-	-	-	-
Education	-	-	-0.5	-0.3	-0.3	-	-	-	-	-
Human health and social work activities	-	-	-	-	-	4.8	4.3	4.8	-	-
Arts, entertainment and recreation	-	-	-	-	-	-	-	-	0.4	0.4
Other services	-	-	-	-	-	-	-	-	-	-
Not allocated and confidential	**0.0**	**0.0**	**0.0**	**-2.7**	**-2.7**	**0.0**	**0.2**	**2.3**	**2.4**	**2.4**
Private real estate activities	**-**	**-**	**-**	**-**	**-**	**-**	**-**	**-**	**-**	**-**

- Nil

Note: Data excludes resident Special Purpose Entities (SPEs). Detailed metadata at: *http://stats.oecd.org/OECDStat_Metadata/ShowMetadata.ashx?Dataset=FDI_CTRY_IND_SUMM.*

Source: OECD International Direct Investment Statistics (database): https://doi.org/10.1787/idi-data-en

IRELAND

Table 1. Foreign direct investment flows by country

Million US dollars

	Inward					Outward				
	2014	2015	2016	2017	2018	2014	2015	2016	2017	2018
WORLD	**48 185.0**	**217 818.1**	**39 375.2**	**52 722.4**	**-28 071.5**	**41 180.8**	**168 442.6**	**30 056.4**	**-2 043.7**	**727.0**
OECD COUNTRIES	**36 835.6**	**141 354.4**	**-51 120.2**	**37 331.8**	**-104 719.7**	**30 226.9**	**155 159.2**	**11 446.4**	**-32 593.8**	**-57 047.1**
Australia	483.0	-806.4	-1 280.5	790.2	-378.9	188.4	326.1	-358.3	39.5	165.2
Austria	156.6	-170.8	129.4	69.9	-88.5	104.8	-8.9	-225.6	-126.3	267.9
Belgium	2 930.9	6 319.5	4 772.8	-1 586.1	13 368.3	244.1	392.7	-709.9	565.9	886.3
Canada	380.8	-1 074.9	-1 058.3	-1 867.9	-1 166.1	145.9	579.0	118.3	326.9	119.2
Chile	.. c	-81.0	-57.5	-78.9	5.9	.. c	.. c	10.0	9.0	.. c
Czech Republic	.. c	.. c	-157.0	10.1	66.1	-	37.7	.. c	22.5	.. c
Denmark	494.9	-35.5	-531.9	-466.7	-20.1	38.5	67.7	.. c	101.5	337.5
Estonia	.. c	.. c	1.1	-	1.2	-	-	-	-	.. c
Finland	-1 150.3	761.0	-142.7	40.6	-41.3	.. c	.. c	.. c	-76.7	.. c
France	-4 882.6	4 184.1	1 866.6	2 790.0	6 569.1	80.9	196.3	418.0	1 406.8	-507.5
Germany	18.6	-1 896.8	2 813.2	-886.0	2 786.5	326.4	-62.1	-1 073.8	-423.9	-750.6
Greece	.. c	.. c	.. c	-158.9	141.6	14.6	-6.7	7.7	.. c	-7.1
Hungary	.. c	30.0	.. c	.. c	.. c	-193.7	106.5	807.3	.. c	.. c
Iceland	-	.. c	.. c	.. c	.. c	.. c	.. c	.. c	.. c	.. c
Ireland	-	.. c	-	.. c	-	-	-	-154.8	-	-
Israel[1]	-425.9	569.1	14.4	33.8	63.7	.. c	.. c	119.4	158.9	-90.9
Italy	494.9	2 337.2	2 306.8	1 856.6	1 809.3	-27.9	-117.6	-629.2	98.1	-564.1
Japan	2 443.9	-1 236.8	586.1	-2 614.1	4 563.9	114.1	3 943.4	428.0	-1 650.3	330.5
Korea	1 261.8	.. c	.. c	164.6	-443.8	49.1	.. c	321.8	-6.8	89.7
Latvia	.. c	-	.. c	3.4	.. c	.. c	-	.. c	.. c	.. c
Lithuania	.. c	.. c	.. c	.. c	.. c	-5.3	.. c	19.9	.. c	24.8
Luxembourg	5 132.0	.. c	-61 160.0	64 617.3	-69 841.9	48 430.4	63 727.1	-8 409.8	-91 038.2	33 644.5
Mexico	-520.1	-16.6	-424.6	.. c	.. c	-100.8	-99.8	-125.0	189.4	-15.3
Netherlands	16 886.0	8 790.9	7 410.2	26 319.5	-113 702.3	3 688.5	5 254.6	4 833.6	31 481.2	-88 740.7
New Zealand	116.8	-122.0	.. c	64.3	-101.5	.. c	21.1	6.6	-1.1	1.2
Norway	-164.5	25.5	186.9	20.3	638.5	-42.5	66.6	.. c	-38.3	-348.2
Poland	53.1	15.5	112.8	-32.7	100.3	-15.9	5.5	28.8	33.8	5.9
Portugal	-283.9	143.1	183.6	251.4	10.6	42.5	-13.9	-49.8	30.4	-76.7
Slovak Republic	-26.5	-26.6	-55.3	-18.0	-37.8	.. c	3.7	.. c	-18.0	.. c
Slovenia	.. c	.. c	.. c	.. c	-3.5	-	-	-	-	.. c
Spain	3 956.5	-1 196.9	-759.7	1 821.7	2 827.8	173.8	113.5	67.5	-209.7	-179.4
Sweden	-2 498.3	215.2	1 087.0	-426.1	-1 130.7	27.9	.. c	471.1	.. c	-138.1
Switzerland	-1 366.6	4 823.1	42 488.1	626.8	11 160.2	.. c	6 253.2	-3 384.9	1 821.7	.. c
Turkey	5.3	46.6	-95.1	-147.7	334.0	63.7	.. c	-163.7	151.1	.. c
United Kingdom	3 757.5	-1 592.9	-17 207.8	5 254.2	-19 751.0	-1 044.2	2 157.5	12 006.0	2 265.8	2 764.1
United States	9 145.5	84 810.9	-61 299.3	-59 817.4	86 524.3	-5 449.1	69 739.3	7 802.7	4 073.9	-6 482.9
EUROPE	**25 937.4**	**88 714.4**	**106 699.1**	**114 122.4**	**-182 452.5**	**36 673.7**	**82 472.5**	**591.6**	**-28 036.3**	**-14 635.9**
Bulgaria	6.6	-3.3	.. c	-3.4	3.5	.. c	.. c	1.1	.. c	3.5
Croatia	.. c	-4.4	-16.6	.. c	.. c	.. c	.. c	.. c	.. c	.. c
Cyprus[2, 3]	-155.2	-205.2	.. c	.. c	.. c	.. c	.. c	.. c	6.8	5.9
Malta	.. c	-74.3	-165.9	.. c	.. c	.. c	.. c	.. c	.. c	.. c
Romania	30.5	-4.4	14.4	9.0	23.6	14.6	81.0	-70.8	13.5	73.2
Russian Federation	-4.0	583.5	1 090.3	127.4	190.0	-47.8	13.3	182.5	7.9	-338.7
Ukraine	.. c	.. c	11.1	2.3	.. c	.. c	.. c	.. c	.. c	.. c
AFRICA	**.. c**	**.. c**	**-96.2**	**121.7**	**82.6**	**.. c**	**21.1**	**.. c**	**45.1**	**.. c**
Northern Africa	-92.9	.. c	.. c	68.8	-47.2	5.3	.. c	.. c	-2.3	.. c
Algeria	.. c	-	.. c	.. c	4.7	-	-	-	.. c	-
Egypt	-86.2	43.3	60.8	40.6	15.3	2.7	.. c	.. c	.. c	3.5
Libya	.. c	.. c	.. c	.. c	.. c	-	-	-	-	-
Morocco	.. c	.. c	.. c	.. c	.. c	1.3	.. c	.. c	.. c	2.4
Tunisia	.. c	.. c	.. c	-2.3	.. c	-	-	.. c	.. c	.. c
Other African countries	.. c	.. c	.. c	53.0	128.6	.. c	.. c	.. c	47.3	.. c
Nigeria	.. c	.. c	45.3	11.3	2.4	.. c	-	.. c	-	8.3
South Africa	.. c	332.8	380.4	89.1	83.8	.. c	-13.3	-22.1	40.6	36.6
AMERICA	**29 716.1**	**94 538.0**	**-55 142.1**	**-35 596.9**	**128 780.8**	**2 328.5**	**72 228.7**	**19 726.9**	**-5 317.3**	**-1 599.2**
Northern America	9 523.7	83 736.0	-62 357.6	-61 685.3	85 358.2	-5 300.5	70 316.1	7 921.0	4 400.9	-6 363.7
Central America and Caribbean countries	20 237.5	11 032.7	7 215.5	26 099.7	43 748.4	7 634.3	.. c	11 437.6	.. c	4 549.7
Bahamas	.. c	.. c	206.8	.. c	623.2	.. c	-	-	-	-
Bermuda	14 533.6	4 214.1	6 736.7	1 420.4	49 427.6	5 924.1	3 089.3	.. c	-4 191.2	5 324.0
Cayman Islands	1 011.0	3 881.3	1 781.5	.. c	-2 402.9	-42.5	-1 365.5	588.3	-5 755.8	.. c
Costa Rica	4.0	.. c	.. c	38.3	64.9	.. c	1.1	.. c	37.2	.. c
El Salvador	.. c	-	.. c	.. c	.. c	-	-	-	-	-
Guatemala	-	-	.. c	-	-	-	-	-	-	-
Honduras	-	-	.. c	-	.. c	-	-	-	-	-
Nicaragua	-	-	.. c	.. c	-	-	-	-	-	-
Panama	-49.1	42.2	103.9	36.1	.. c	.. c	-	-4.4	36.1	56.7
Virgin Islands, U.S.	-	-	-	.. c	-	-	-	-	-	-
South America	-46.4	-230.7	1.1	-13.5	-323.4	-5.3	.. c	367.1	.. c	213.6
Argentina	6.6	-55.5	23.2	-21.4	22.4	25.2	24.4	29.9	31.6	49.6
Bolivia	-	-	.. c	.. c	.. c	-	-	-	-	-
Brazil	-26.5	-99.8	171.4	81.2	-203.0	-27.9	175.3	-86.3	-330.3	16.5
Colombia	10.6	.. c	-182.5	-16.9	-133.4	-	-	.. c	.. c	.. c
Ecuador	.. c	17.7	.. c	6.8	.. c	-	-	.. c	-	-
Paraguay	-	.. c	.. c	.. c	-	-	-	-	-	-
Peru	-19.9	1.1	-33.2	10.1	-79.1	-	3.3	.. c	.. c	.. c
Uruguay	.. c	-2.2	-5.5	-	.. c	-	-	-	-	-
Venezuela	.. c	-	.. c	7.9	68.5	.. c	.. c	.. c	-	.. c

Table 1. Foreign direct investment flows by country *(cont.)*

Million US dollars

	Inward					Outward				
	2014	2015	2016	2017	2018	2014	2015	2016	2017	2018
ASIA	**-5 044.4**	**8 543.5**	**-12 911.6**	**-1 615.4**	**22 523.3**	**1 354.7**	**10 320.6**	**-2 007.1**	**.. c**	**4 674.9**
Near and Middle East	-931.4	629.0	-1 333.6	-395.7	-190.0	196.4	485.9	-59.7	137.5	749.4
Gulf Arabian countries	-505.5	100.9	-909.0	-418.2	-263.2	.. c	.. c	-179.1	-19.2	.. c
Kuwait	-	.. c	.. c	3.4	.. c	-	-	.. c	-	-
Qatar	.. c	.. c	.. c	.. c	.. c	-	.. c	.. c	.. c	-
Saudi Arabia	.. c	.. c	-161.5	.. c	-443.8	2.7	.. c	.. c	.. c	61.4
United Arab Emirates	-184.4	363.8	-538.5	-248.0	199.5	31.8	15.5	202.4	11.3	.. c
Other Near and Middle East	-423.2	525.8	-423.5	24.8	74.4	.. c	.. c	118.3	157.8	.. c
Jordan	.. c	.. c	.. c	.. c	1.2	-	.. c	.. c	.. c	.. c
Other Asian countries	-4 111.7	7 915.7	-11 576.9	-1 220.8	22 714.5	1 160.9	9 834.7	-1 948.5	.. c	3 925.4
China	86.2	1 474.2	2 097.8	120.6	-81.4	455.1	-22.2	.. c	.. c	.. c
Hong Kong, China	.. c	-384.9	268.7	266.0	3.5	-14.6	.. c	-479.9	.. c	.. c
India	.. c	-715.5	-217.8	31.6	149.9	49.1	44.4	-10.0	9.0	-42.5
Indonesia	.. c	73.2	.. c	.. c	-4.7	-	.. c	.. c	.. c	.. c
Iran, Islamic Republic of	.. c	-	.. c	-	-	127.4	106.5	-	-	-
Malaysia	15.9	-6.7	6.6	11.3	16.5	.. c	.. c	.. c	1.1	.. c
Philippines	128.7	14.4	-61.9	-45.1	16.5	.. c	.. c	.. c	.. c	.. c
Singapore	.. c	7 982.3	-14 155.7	962.7	.. c	452.4	1 611.8	248.8	.. c	-194.7
Chinese Taipei	46.4	100.9	2.2	-87.9	-155.8	14.6	.. c	25.4	31.6	18.9
Thailand	.. c	8.9	.. c	-18.0	-87.3	.. c	.. c	.. c	-6.8	.. c
Viet Nam	.. c	.. c	.. c	.. c	-1.2	-	8.9	16.6	.. c	1.2
AUSTRALIA, OCEANIA AND POLAR REGIONS	**598.4**	**-929.6**	**.. c**	**859.0**	**-486.3**	**193.7**	**348.3**	**-350.5**	**38.3**	**166.4**
WORLD unallocated and confidential	**-2 928.2**	**26 580.1**	**.. d**	**-25 168.5**	**3 480.5**	**624.9**	**3 059.3**	**.. d**	**32 711.1**	**11 524.8**
European Union (EU28)	**25 945.3**	**54 290.6**	**-28 657.5**	**98 602.2**	**-201 424.5**	**52 905.7**	**73 949.0**	**7 187.9**	**-51 835.2**	**-62 145.6**
G20 countries excl. European Union	**..**	**..**	**.. d**	**.. d**	**..**	**..**	**..**	**.. d**	**.. d**	**..**
G20 OECD countries	**12 588.6**	**..**	**.. d**	**.. d**	**..**	**-5 653.4**	**..**	**18 744.9**	**6 470.5**	**..**
G20 Non-OECD countries	**..**	**..**	**.. d**	**.. d**	**-286.8**	**..**	**..**	**.. d**	**.. d**	**..**
MENA countries	**..**	**..**	**.. d**	**.. d**	**..**	**..**	**..**	**.. d**	**.. d**	**..**
ASEAN countries	**.. c**	**8 051.0**	**-14 402.3**	**.. c**	**.. c**	**362.2**	**1 679.4**	**-372.7**	**.. c**	**436.7**

- Nil; .. Not available; c Confidential data; d Secondary Confidentiality

Note: Detailed metadata at: *http://stats.oecd.org/OECDStat_Metadata/ShowMetadata.ashx?Dataset=FDI_CTRY_IND_SUMM.*

1. Information on data for Israel: *http://oe.cd/israel-disclaimer.*
2. Note by Turkey: The information in this document with reference to "Cyprus" relates to the southern part of the Island. There is no single authority representing both Turkish and Greek Cypriot people on the Island. Turkey recognises the Turkish Republic of Northern Cyprus (TRNC). Until a lasting and equitable solution is found within the context of the United Nations, Turkey shall preserve its position concerning the "Cyprus issue".
3. Note by all the European Union Member States of the OECD and the European Union: The Republic of Cyprus is recognised by all members of the United Nations with the exception of Turkey. The information in this document relates to the area under the effective control of the Government of the Republic of Cyprus.

Source: OECD International Direct Investment Statistics (database): https://doi.org/10.1787/idi-data-en

Table 2. Foreign direct investment positions by country
At year end

Million US dollars

	Inward					Outward				
	2014	2015	2016	2017	2018	2014	2015	2016	2017	2018
WORLD	**429 846.0**	**890 125.2**	**840 646.1**	**1 058 012.7**	**1 000 391.6**	**618 834.1**	**909 667.9**	**856 581.6**	**986 845.8**	**942 868.1**
OECD COUNTRIES	**340 559.9**	**765 318.5**	**639 685.9**	**870 374.2**	**729 646.2**	**491 002.7**	**797 432.8**	**711 684.4**	**798 833.1**	**716 519.3**
Australia	1 168.0	480.1	-731.5	403.0	120.2	5 917.5	1 829.1	.. c	1 364.8	516.4
Austria	490.5	299.4	448.0	480.9	387.0	148.1	136.1	.. c	-217.1	-38.9
Belgium	5 973.4	10 843.8	9 638.5	7 419.0	21 189.6	7 243.3	7 787.7	.. c	1 686.3	1 636.1
Canada	4 222.6	1 973.9	2 496.0	425.8	-823.2	2 522.9	2 350.6	2 463.4	2 500.6	1 820.5
Chile	.. c	-98.0	-161.3	-136.7	-121.4	23.1	.. c	31.6	40.8	.. c
Czech Republic	.. c	17.4	-132.8	12.0	73.3	358.2	497.6	.. c	-67.2	250.7
Denmark	2 365.1	1 434.9	506.0	130.7	-55.0	122.6	167.7	.. c	-116.3	200.4
Estonia	.. c	.. c	1.1	1.2	1.1	.. c	.. c	.. c	.. c	.. c
Finland	-1 011.3	-203.6	-183.4	-101.9	-137.4	1 175.2	1 253.1	-763.2	-847.9	-91.6
France	18 576.9	20 562.9	20 509.1	23 816.3	24 066.9	3 128.7	2 97[illegible].1	3 319.3	5 361.0	4 294.7
Germany	8 927.3	3 928.1	4 759.1	7 140.8	7 169.7	6 355.8	5 246.8	3 725.1	3 871.4	4 021.1
Greece	.. c	40.3	.. c	.. c	232.4	1.2	.. c	100.1	-217.1	-210.7
Hungary	.. c	.. c	.. c	.. c	.. c	27 261.4	25 814.9	.. c	.. c	.. c
Iceland	.. c	.. c	.. c	.. c	.. c	.. c	.. c	.. c	.. c	.. c
Ireland	-	-	-	.. c	-	-	96.9	.. c	.. c	.. c
Israel[1]	-463.8	123.0	128.6	151.1	-83.6	.. c	.. c	.. c	.. c	.. c
Italy	7 562.6	8 373.4	8 216.5	10 142.7	9 947.3	247.7	1 234.6	549.2	682.4	12.6
Japan	2 770.6	1 907.5	2 539.3	421.0	4 434.4	1 426.6	5 797.5	6 232.7	3 882.2	4 159.6
Korea	2 202.4	.. c	4 837.1	5 111.5	638.9	214.9	460.5	.. c	758.0	820.9
Latvia	.. c	.. c	.. c	.. c	5.7	-	-	.. c	.. c	.. c
Lithuania	.. c	15.2	40.1	34.8	8.0	-4.9	-5.4	.. c	25.2	46.9
Luxembourg	85 839.3	152 394.1	.. c	268 463.7	189 482.5	214 482.9	462 149.2	423 202.3	339 971.2	378 574.5
Mexico	139.6	101.3	-321.5	.. c	-404.2	694.5	926.5	695.7	941.5	910.2
Netherlands	92 525.3	100 641.3	89 640.6	110 159.5	-16 507.9	54 975.7	56 332.1	57 785.4	181 039.8	79 456.1
New Zealand	.. c	45.7	80.1	139.1	35.5	99.6	.. c	.. c	353.8	.. c
Norway	191.8	386.5	591.3	813.1	1 103.7	-59.5	6.5	.. c	.. c	101.9
Poland	-123.8	-94.7	24.2	-24.0	50.4	331.4	302.7	.. c	375.4	586.2
Portugal	252.5	427.9	629.3	952.3	613.7	.. c	.. c	.. c	.. c	.. c
Slovak Republic	44.9	7.6	-47.4	-72.0	.. c	160.3	.. c	959.2	961.9	245.0
Slovenia	.. c	.. c	.. c	-6.0	-10.3	.. c	.. c	.. c	.. c	.. c
Spain	15 251.5	12 201.4	8 403.1	11 107.0	12 500.6	.. c	.. c	.. c	.. c	7 919.6
Sweden	2 448.8	2 476.9	3 085.3	2 655.3	1 510.2	847.4	1 882.4	.. c	6 608.3	6 304.1
Switzerland	11 638.4	13 802.9	60 657.7	86 613.1	79 366.8	-8 322.7	-6 112.1	-18 538.0	-15 808.3	3 973.0
Turkey	29.1	.. c	.. c	.. c	-108.8	2 008.1	1 920.5	.. c	.. c	1 183.9
United Kingdom	56 208.0	56 807.8	78 050.0	70 197.9	60 901.1	94 325.9	98 851.4	99 266.4	106 291.7	98 323.8
United States	23 908.1	375 156.2	235 690.9	233 552.4	331 213.6	63 187.8	112 705.5	92 687.9	111 362.4	106 361.3
EUROPE	**319 909.3**	**396 315.7**	**497 426.0**	**729 005.8**	**511 159.8**	**434 097.8**	**693 740 9**	**630 141.2**	**708 088.3**	**661 542.2**
Bulgaria	.. c	18.5	-	-4.8	-	.. c	.. c	.. c	.. c	.. c
Croatia	2.4	.. c	.. c	-4.8	.. c	.. c	.. c	.. c	.. c	.. c
Cyprus[2, 3]	694.5	343.0	.. c	.. c	.. c	423.7	344 0	.. c	844.3	842.7
Malta	2 708.7	1 986.9	.. c	467.7	335.5	.. c	.. c	.. c	.. c	.. c
Romania	-21.9	-22.9	-8.4	2.4	27.5	263.5	285 2	.. c	225.5	224.4
Russian Federation	1 685.2	1 495.9	2 422.3	2 680.5	2 688.3	.. c	403 9	.. c	604.5	285.1
Ukraine	.. c	.. c	-15.8	.. c	.. c	.. c	.. c	.. c	.. c	.. c
AFRICA	**-1 499.4**	**81.7**	**4.2**	**.. c**	**.. c**	**412.8**	**390 9**	**.. c**	**-227.9**	**-476.3**
Northern Africa	-54.6	.. c	.. c	-4.8	.. c	354.5	311 4	.. c	.. c	92.7
Algeria	.. c	.. c	-	.. c	-4.6	-	-	-	.. c	.. c
Egypt	-87.4	-24.0	44.3	-46.8	-29.8	239.2	214 5	-	.. c	.. c
Libya	.. c	.. c	.. c	.. c	-11.5	-	-	-	-	-
Morocco	.. c	.. c	.. c	54.0	-6.9	116.6	96 9	83.3	93.5	92.7
Tunisia	.. c	-	-	.. c	.. c	-	-	.. c	.. c	-
Other African countries	-1 444.8	.. c	.. c	.. c	.. c	57.1	79 5	.. c	.. c	-569.0
Nigeria	.. c	-6.5	24.2	-10.8	-9.2	.. c	.. c	.. c	.. c	.. c
South Africa	-342.4	9.8	418.5	61.2	145.4	36.4	32 7	5.3	51.6	92.7
AMERICA	**87 931.2**	**453 350.0**	**308 094.2**	**320 768.8**	**459 539.7**	**160 977.5**	**165 850.8**	**170 419.5**	**181 131.0**	**178 485.2**
Northern America	28 130.7	377 131.2	238 187.0	233 977.0	330 390.4	65 710.7	115 056 1	95 151.3	113 863.0	108 181.8
Central America and Caribbean countries	60 193.9	76 844.9	70 498.6	86 959.7	129 615.3	94 644.0	50 141 5	74 008.6	66 319.3	69 169.9
Bahamas	.. c	.. c	.. c	.. c	11 932.7	-	-	-	-	-
Bermuda	46 355.6	54 299.4	48 187.0	29 124.5	76 518.2	70 130.1	29 632.0	53 506.9	50 314.2	55 439.7
Cayman Islands	5 175.7	11 024.5	12 142.9	45 767.6	40 667.5	.. c	19 175.8	.. c	.. c	.. c
Costa Rica	.. c	.. c	.. c	-70.8	-2.3	.. c	.. c	.. c	105.5	17.2
El Salvador	.. c	.. c	.. c	-	.. c	-	-	-	-	-
Guatemala	-	-	-2.1	-2.4	-2.3	-	-	-	-	-
Honduras	-	-	.. c	.. c	.. c	-	-	-	-	-
Nicaragua	-	-	.. c	-	-	-	-	-	-	-
Panama	-319.3	.. c	.. c	.. c	.. c	.. c	.. c	.. c	54.0	106.5
Virgin Islands, U.S.	-	-	-	.. c	.. c	-	-	-	-	-
South America	-394.6	-626.0	-591.3	-167.9	-466.0	621.6	653.2	1 260.7	948.7	1 132.4
Argentina	-43.7	-61.0	-47.4	-67.2	-40.1	.. c	116.5	.. c	.. c	194.6
Bolivia	.. c	-	.. c	.. c	-	-	-	-	-	-
Brazil	.. c	-263.5	-131.8	-133.1	-327.5	.. c	572.7	744.2	398.2	395.0
Colombia	75.3	-38.1	.. c	254.3	112.2	.. c	.. c	.. c	.. c	.. c
Ecuador	-18.2	.. c	.. c	-	-8.0	-	-	.. c	.. c	.. c
Paraguay	-	-	.. c	.. c	.. c	-	-	-	-	-
Peru	.. c	.. c	.. c	-10.8	.. c	-	.. c	.. c	.. c	.. c
Uruguay	.. c	.. c	.. c	-8.4	-5.7	-	-	-	-	-
Venezuela	.. c	-164.4	.. c	-63.6	17.2	.. c	.. c	.. c	.. c	.. c

Table 2. Foreign direct investment positions by country *(cont.)*

At year end

Million US dollars

	Inward					Outward				
	2014	2015	2016	2017	2018	2014	2015	2016	2017	2018
ASIA	**9 179.8**	**13 510.1**	**.. c**	**6 856.6**	**25 224.4**	**5 003.3**	**23 483.9**	**21 248.0**	**69 186.9**	**73 226.5**
Near and Middle East	-576.7	-1 145.3	.. c	-2 326.7	-1 394.6	546.3	1 563.4	1 414.6	1 602.3	1 859.4
Gulf Arabian countries	-114.1	-1 267.3	-2 174.6	-2 485.0	-1 329.3	354.5	.. c	.. c	.. c	.. c
Kuwait	-1.2	-2.2	.. c	.. c	.. c	-	-	.. c	-	-
Qatar	.. c	.. c	.. c	.. c	.. c	-	.. c	.. c	.. c	.. c
Saudi Arabia	-8.5	.. c	.. c	.. c	.. c	4.9	-1.1	.. c	7.2	55.0
United Arab Emirates	-69.2	80.6	-462.7	-630.8	974.4	.. c	.. c	.. c	110.3	798.0
Other Near and Middle East	-462.6	121.9	.. c	158.3	-65.3	191.8	.. c	.. c	.. c	.. c
Jordan	.. c	.. c	.. c	.. c	.. c	-	-	-	.. c	.. c
Other Asian countries	9 757.7	14 655.4	5 633.0	9 183.3	26 620.1	4 457.0	21 921.6	19 833.5	67 584.6	71 367.1
China	-261.0	.. c	.. c	.. c	6 752.9	1 541.9	.. c	.. c	.. c	.. c
Hong Kong, China	705.4	313.6	634.6	855.1	804.9	348.4	.. c	5 621.4	.. c	.. c
India	.. c	-252.6	-470.1	-796.4	-571.3	240.4	72.9	44.3	50.4	-6.9
Indonesia	.. c	5.4	.. c	7.2	-2.3	.. c	.. c	.. c	.. c	.. c
Iran, Islamic Republic of	.. c	.. c	-	-	-	-	-	-	-	-
Malaysia	-8.5	-22.9	3.2	-39.6	-20.6	46.1	56.6	.. c	.. c	16.0
Philippines	9.7	20.7	-41.1	8.4	24.0	.. c	-	.. c	.. c	5.7
Singapore	3 768.6	.. c	-4 653.7	-4 852.5	13 740.6	693.3	984.2	1 219.6	.. c	.. c
Chinese Taipei	177.3	310.3	315.2	209.9	45.8	30.4	52.3	.. c	97.1	98.5
Thailand	.. c	-26.1	-44.3	-	-97.3	.. c	.. c	.. c	.. c	-
Viet Nam	.. c	-	.. c	-	1.1	-	8.7	.. c	13.2	14.9
AUSTRALIA, OCEANIA AND POLAR REGIONS	**1 334.3**	**525.9**	**-653.5**	**544.5**	**153.4**	**6 017.1**	**2 176.4**	**.. c**	**1 718.6**	**1 028.2**
WORLD unallocated and confidential	**12 990.9**	**26 341.9**	**.. d**	**724.4**	**4 031.4**	**12 325.5**	**24 025.0**	**.. d**	**26 948.9**	**29 062.3**
European Union (EU28)	**300 236.0**	**374 145.9**	**339 587.9**	**544 762.5**	**319 453.9**	**429 172.2**	**682 620.6**	**630 117.0**	**683 589.6**	**600 849.6**
G20 countries excl. European Union	..	..	**.. d**	**.. d**	..	..	..	**.. d**	**.. d**	..
G20 OECD countries	**125 715.2**	..	**.. d**	**.. d**	**437 155.9**	**180 030.4**	**234 296.1**	**.. d**	**.. d**	**222 425.0**
G20 Non-OECD countries	..	..	**.. d**	**.. d**	..	..	..	**.. d**	**.. d**	..
MENA countries	..	..	**.. d**	**.. d**	..	..	..	**.. d**	**.. d**	..
ASEAN countries	**3 608.3**	**9 568.9**	**.. c**	**.. c**	**.. c**	**654.4**	**1 102.9**	**688.3**	**.. c**	**.. c**

- Nil; .. Not available; c Confidential data; d Secondary Confidentiality

Note: Detailed metadata at: *http://stats.oecd.org/OECDStat_Metadata/ShowMetadata.ashx?Dataset=FDI_CTRY_IND_SUMM.*

1. Information on data for Israel: *http://oe.cd/israel-disclaimer.*
2. Note by Turkey: The information in this document with reference to "Cyprus" relates to the southern part of the Island. There is no single authority representing both Turkish and Greek Cypriot people on the Island. Turkey recognises the Turkish Republic of Northern Cyprus (TRNC). Until a lasting and equitable solution is found within the context of the United Nations, Turkey shall preserve its position concerning the "Cyprus issue".
3. Note by all the European Union Member States of the OECD and the European Union: The Republic of Cyprus is recognised by all members of the United Nations with the exception of Turkey. The information in this document relates to the area under the effective control of the Government of the Republic of Cyprus.

Source: OECD International Direct Investment Statistics (database): https://doi.org/10.1787/idi-data-en

Table 3. Foreign direct investment income by country

Million US dollars

	Inward					Outward				
	2014	2015	2016	2017	2018	2014	2015	2016	2017	2018
WORLD	**54 464.6**	**71 584.0**	**61 827.9**	**75 764.9**	**85 256.7**	**20 477.6**	**11 762.6**	**14 638.9**	**17 361.1**	**15 296.8**
OECD COUNTRIES	**34 954.2**	**36 967.3**	**38 457.4**	**49 354.1**	**59 524.4**	**14 893.2**	**14 581.3**	**15 449.5**	**15 750.2**	**16 067.5**
Australia	-14.6	.. c	.. c	22.5	-15.3	.. c	42.2	91.8	-12.4	-14.2
Austria	.. c	.. c	12.2	4.5	-	8.0	4.4	15.5	-1.1	13.0
Belgium	1 491.3	1 620.6	1 217.5	2 008.8	3 539.5	-42.5	7.7	79.6	39.5	30.7
Canada	-26.5	14.4	35.4	-48.5	-127.5	123.4	34.4	-25.4	4.5	-5.9
Chile	-	.. c	-2.2	.. c	-	-	-	-	-	-
Czech Republic	-	-	-	-	-	.. c	6.6	.. c	-11.3	.. c
Denmark	104.8	166.4	89.6	74.4	.. c	.. c	.. c	11.1	6.8	16.5
Estonia	-	-	-	-	-	-	-	-	-	-
Finland	.. c	.. c	13.3	11.3	9.4	.. c	2.2	-	.. c	.. c
France	2 522.2	2 399.3	2 255.9	2 437.2	2 775.9	151.3	48.8	142.7	140.9	43.7
Germany	1 069.4	881.9	758.6	352.8	939.5	196.4	255.1	268.7	165.7	-135.7
Greece	-	-	-	.. c	.. c	.. c	.. c	.. c	.. c	.. c
Hungary	.. c	4.4	.. c	.. c	.. c	.. c	.. c	.. c	.. c	.. c
Iceland	.. c	.. c	-	.. c	.. c	-	.. c	-	-	-
Ireland	-	.. c	-	-	-	-	-	-	.. c	-
Israel[1]	-	-	-	-	-	.. c	.. c	.. c	.. c	107.4
Italy	2 037.9	1 978.9	1 659.8	1 652.6	1 670.0	35.8	-73.2	67.5	16.9	61.4
Japan	-45.1	13.3	419.1	406.9	535.8	17.2	4.4	-11.1	-20.3	.. c
Korea	99.5	.. c	85.1	67.6	5.9	.. c	.. c	.. c	.. c	.. c
Latvia	-	-	-	-	-	-	-	-	.. c	-
Lithuania	-	-	-	-	-	-	-	-	-	-
Luxembourg	4 878.6	4 657.8	4 598.0	11 272.7	13 512.3	6 838.3	8 481.4	10 401.4	9 696.8	9 974.0
Mexico	-	-	-1.1	-4.5	-7.1	.. c	.. c	45.3	.. c	.. c
Netherlands	9 612.6	13 148.1	12 987.9	7 436.6	6 540.8	2 505.0	2 142.0	2 981.3	4 123.5	5 399.5
New Zealand	-	-	-	4.5	-	.. c	.. c	.. c	.. c	.. c
Norway	.. c	.. c	.. c	-301.0	136.9	.. c	.. c	1.1	4.5	8.3
Poland	-	-	-	-	-	4.0	8.9	1.1	19.2	7.1
Portugal	-115.4	112.0	71.9	32.7	40.1	.. c	.. c	.. c	-6.8	.. c
Slovak Republic	-	-	-	-	-	-	.. c	.. c	.. c	.. c
Slovenia	-	-	-	-	-	-	-	-	-	-
Spain	685.9	168.6	246.6	558.0	544.1	.. c	-10.0	45.3	-6.8	-
Sweden	201.7	168.6	188.0	181.5	201.8	31.8	14.4	96.2	50.7	27.1
Switzerland	5 296.5	6 703.3	8 283.8	9 189.5	13 556.0	.. c	-397.1	-1 003.0	.. c	.. c
Turkey	-	-	-	.. c	.. c	.. c	.. c	26.5	.. c	.. c
United Kingdom	3 086.1	4 266.2	4 133.6	4 438.1	4 246.4	1 382.5	604.5	424.6	2 207.2	2 542.2
United States	4 026.8	411.5	684.5	8 332.8	11 091.7	1 624.0	1 859.1	498.7	-1 226.5	-2 202.3
EUROPE	**31 750.0**	**54 418.2**	**42 523.5**	**51 193.8**	**57 944.1**	**14 065.3**	**13 742.7**	**16 078.7**	**18 749.9**	**19 183.3**
Bulgaria	-	-	-	-	-	.. c	.. c	-	.. c	.. c
Croatia	.. c	-	-	-	-	-	-	-	-	-
Cyprus[2, 3]	.. c	.. c	.. c	.. c	.. c	-21.2	-	.. c	.. c	.. c
Malta	42.5	33.3	29.9	32.7	36.6	.. c	.. c	.. c	.. c	.. c
Romania	-	-	-	-	-	.. c	.. c	18.8	10.1	3.5
Russian Federation	-	-	.. c	.. c	1.2	.. c	.. c	.. c	.. c	.. c
Ukraine	-	-	-	-	-	.. c	.. c	.. c	.. c	.. c
AFRICA	**10.6**	**11.1**	**12.2**	**.. c**	**14.2**	**.. c**	**.. c**	**.. c**	**.. c**	**.. c**
Northern Africa	-	-	-	-	-	.. c	.. c	-	.. c	.. c
Algeria	-	-	-	-	-	-	-	-	-	-
Egypt	-	-	-	-	-	.. c	.. c	-	-	-
Libya	-	-	-	-	-	-	-	-	-	-
Morocco	-	-	-	-	-	-	-	-	-	-
Tunisia	-	-	-	-	-	-	-	-	.. c	.. c
Other African countries	10.6	11.1	12.2	.. c	14.2	-	-	.. c	-	.. c
Nigeria	-	-	-	-	-	-	-	.. c	.. c	-
South Africa	.. c	.. c	11.1	.. c	.. c	-	-	-	-	-
AMERICA	**21 760.6**	**16 677.8**	**18 402.1**	**22 968.1**	**25 337.0**	**5 844.5**	**3 740.4**	**3 290.9**	**2 165.5**	**907.6**
Northern America	3 998.9	424.8	721.0	8 283.2	10 964.2	1 748.7	1 894.6	473.3	-1 222.0	-2 209.4
Central America and Caribbean countries	17 763.0	16 252.9	17 685.5	14 686.1	.. c	.. c	1 770.4	2 729.2	3 270.2	.. c
Bahamas	.. c	.. c	.. c	.. c	.. c	-	-	-	.. c	-
Bermuda	15 316.4	12 073.2	13 110.7	8 614.6	8 242.7	2 170.6	888.5	1 272.8	1 749.5	.. c
Cayman Islands	2 597.9	4 400.4	4 472.0	5 631.8	5 073.8	.. c	859.7	1 405.5	.. c	.. c
Costa Rica	-	-	.. c	.. c	-	-	.. c	4.4	.. c	-
El Salvador	-	-	-	-	-	-	-	-	-	-
Guatemala	-	-	-	-	-	-	-	-	-	-
Honduras	-	-	-	-	-	-	-	-	-	-
Nicaragua	-	-	-	-	-	-	-	-	-	-
Panama	-13.3	.. c	-11.1	-1.1	4.7	-	-	-	-	-
Virgin Islands, U.S.	-	-	-	-	-	-	-	-	-	-
South America	-	-	-4.4	-1.1	.. c	.. c	76.5	88.5	117.2	.. c
Argentina	-	-	-	-	-	.. c	33.3	32.1	.. c	.. c
Bolivia	-	-	-	-	-	-	-	-	-	-
Brazil	-	-	.. c	-	.. c	5.3	.. c	54.2	.. c	.. c
Colombia	-	-	-	-	-	-	-	-	-	-
Ecuador	-	-	-	-	-	-	-	-	-	-
Paraguay	-	.. c	-	.. c	-	-	-	-	-	-
Peru	-	-	-	-	-	-	.. c	-	.. c	-
Uruguay	-	-	-	-	-	-	-	-	-	-
Venezuela	-	-	-	-	-	-	-	-	.. c	-

Table 3. Foreign direct investment income by country *(cont.)*

Million US dollars

	Inward					Outward				
	2014	2015	2016	2017	2018	2014	2015	2016	2017	2018
ASIA	**282.6**	**391.6**	**677.9**	**1 139.7**	**1 677.1**	**760.2**	**.. c**	**.. c**	**.. c**	**.. c**
Near and Middle East	.. c	8.9	7.7	7.9	-24.8	-13.3	10.0	.. c	.. c	178.2
Gulf Arabian countries	.. c	.. c	7.7	6.8	-26.0	.. c	.. c	.. c	.. c	.. c
Kuwait	-	-	-	-	-	-	-	-	-	-
Qatar	-	-	-	-	-	-	-	-	-	-
Saudi Arabia	-	-	-	-	-	-	-	.. c	-	.. c
United Arab Emirates	.. c	.. c	7.7	6.8	.. c	.. c	.. c	-	.. c	.. c
Other Near and Middle East	-	.. c	-	-	-	.. c	.. c	.. c	.. c	.. c
Jordan	-	.. c	-	-	-	-	-	-	-	.. c
Other Asian countries	.. c	381.6	670.1	1 132.9	1 701.9	773.5	.. c	.. c	.. c	.. c
China	-	.. c	.. c	.. c	.. c	.. c	.. c	.. c	.. c	.. c
Hong Kong, China	.. c	.. c	.. c	.. c	.. c	.. c	4.4	2.2	-11.3	8.3
India	-	-	.. c	.. c	.. c	69.0	.. c	18.8	15.8	.. c
Indonesia	-	-	-	-	-	-	-	-	-	-
Iran, Islamic Republic of	-	-	-	-	-	.. c	.. c	-	-	-
Malaysia	.. c	-	-	-	-	-	-	-	-	-
Philippines	.. c	-	-	-	-	.. c	-	-	-	-
Singapore	17.2	89.9	99.5	138.7	.. c	.. c	.. c	.. c	11.3	2.4
Chinese Taipei	-	-	-	-	-	.. c	.. c	.. c	.. c	.. c
Thailand	-	-	-	-	-	-	-	-	-	-
Viet Nam	-	-	-	-	-	-	-	-	-	-
AUSTRALIA, OCEANIA AND POLAR REGIONS	**-11.9**	**.. c**	**.. c**	**23.7**	**-11.8**	**84.9**	**48.8**	**99.5**	**-7.9**	**-20.1**
WORLD unallocated and confidential	**672.7**	**85.4**	**.. d**	**439.6**	**296.2**	**-277.3**	**-5 788.1**	**.. d**	**-3 541.9**	**-5 014.8**
European Union (EU28)	**25 618.9**	**29 638.4**	**28 608.9**	**31 754.0**	**34 288.9**	**12 745.1**	**13 379.9**	**16 209.2**	**18 116.3**	**18 739.5**
G20 countries excl. European Union	**..**	**..**	**.. d**	**.. d**	**..**	**..**	**..**	**.. d**	**.. d**	**..**
G20 OECD countries	**12 755.7**	**..**	**.. d**	**.. d**	**..**	**..**	**..**	**.. d**	**.. d**	**..**
G20 Non-OECD countries	**..**	**..**	**.. d**	**.. d**	**..**	**..**	**..**	**.. d**	**.. d**	**..**
MENA countries	**..**	**..**	**7.7**	**6.8**	**..**	**..**	**..**	**.. d**	**.. d**	**..**
ASEAN countries	**17.2**	**89.9**	**102.8**	**138.7**	**.. c**	**.. c**	**.. c**	**15.5**	**.. c**	**2.4**

- Nil; .. Not available; c Confidential data; d Secondary Confidentiality

Note: Detailed metadata at: *http://stats.oecd.org/OECDStat_Metadata/ShowMetadata.ashx?Dataset=FDI_CTRY_IND_SUMM.*

1. Information on data for Israel: *http://oe.cd/israel-disclaimer.*
2. Note by Turkey: The information in this document with reference to "Cyprus" relates to the southern part of the Island. There is no single authority representing both Turkish and Greek Cypriot people on the Island. Turkey recognises the Turkish Republic of Northern Cyprus (TRNC). Until a lasting and equitable solution is found within the context of the United Nations, Turkey shall preserve its position concerning the "Cyprus issue".
3. Note by all the European Union Member States of the OECD and the European Union: The Republic of Cyprus is recognised by all members of the United Nations with the exception of Turkey. The information in this document relates to the area under the effective control of the Government of the Republic of Cyprus.

Source: OECD International Direct Investment Statistics (database): https://doi.org/10.1787/idi-data-en

Table 4. Foreign direct investment flows by industrial sector

Million US dollars

	Inward					Outward				
	2014	2015	2016	2017	2018	2014	2015	2016	2017	2018
All FDI activities	**48 185.0**	**217 818.1**	**39 375.2**	**52 722.4**	**-28 071.5**	**41 180.8**	**168 442.6**	**30 056.4**	**-2 043.7**	**727.0**
Agriculture, forestry and fishing	.. c	.. c	.. c	.. c	.. c	-	-	-	-	-
Mining and quarrying	.. c	.. c	-	.. c	.. c	.. c	.. c	.. c	.. c	.. c
Extraction activities	-	-	-	-	-	-	-	-	-	-
Manufacturing	**2 907.0**	**23 021.6**	**-3 059.8**	**-40 928.9**	**64 342.0**	**4 607.9**	**4 89[illegible].8**	**4 749.5**	**3 760.6**	**12 663.8**
of which:										
Food products, beverages and tobacco	-3 753.5	89.9	-410.3	-109.3	.. c	-1 925.2	-66.6	358.3	.. c	193.6
Textiles, wood and paper products; printing	.. c	.. c	.. c	-	-	.. c	.. c	.. c	.. c	.. c
Chemical, rubber, plastic, non-metallic mineral products	6 200.1	7 018.3	12 029.2	-8 361.0	22 319.1	.. c	.. c	.. c	.. c	.. c
Metal and machinery products, except electrical equipment	-179.1	.. c	.. c	.. c	.. c	559.9	170.8	.. c	.. c	.. c
Motor vehicles, trailers, semi-trailers, other transport equipment	.. c	.. c	.. c	.. c	.. c	-	.. c	.. c	.. c	-
Other manufacturing	739.0	1 985.6	1 066.0	1 938.9	4 462.4	.. c	442.6	-97.3	16.9	1 775.1
Electricity, gas, steam and air conditioning supply	.. c	.. c	.. c	.. c	.. c	.. c	.. c	.. c	.. c	.. c
Water supply; sewerage, waste management and remediation activities	-	-	-	-	-	-	-	-	-	-
Construction	-	-	-	-	-	-	-	-	-	-
Services	**45 956.0**	**194 743.2**	**42 325.6**	**93 448.3**	**-93 273.9**	**34 333.3**	**160 920.7**	**23 942.3**	**-8 973.1**	**-13 737.8**
Wholesale and retail trade; repair of motor vehicles and motorcycles	2 991.9	3 237.9	.. c	31 392.2	.. c	725.8	1 975.6	1 925.2	-1 792.4	-610.2
Transportation and storage	.. c	.. c	.. c	.. c	.. c	.. c	.. c	.. c	.. c	.. c
Accommodation and food service activities	-	-	-	-	-	-	-	-	-	-
Information and communication	6 921.9	9 404.3	7 806.0	90 701.2	-65 734.7	2 779.6	2 991.7	-1 297.1	.. c	.. c
Financial and insurance activities	.. c	104 400.4	6 564.2	5 056.9	-21 036.2	-11 868.1	.. c	14 734.0	8 090.4	-13 442.7
Activities of holding companies	-148.6	3 130.3	-1 812.5	1 630.0	-2 981.2	34.5	175.3	-754.2	2 427.0	.. c
Real estate activities	-	-	-	-	-	-	-	-	-	-
Professional, scientific and technical activities	13 420.5	51 088.2	18 794.6	.. c	-2 840.8	42 648.3	80 381.6	2 079.0	-59 940.3	55 580.1
Administrative and support service activities	7 473.8	.. c	1 533.8	-3 125.9	-2 059.5	-1 215.3	.. c	797.3	.. c	2 641.3
Public administration; activities of households and of extraterritorial organisations	-	-	-	-	-	-	-	-	-	-
Education	-	-	-	-	-	-	-	-	-	-
Human health and social work activities	-	-	-	-	-	-	-	-	-	-
Arts, entertainment and recreation	-	-	-	-	-	.. c	.. c	.. c	.. c	.. c
Other services	-	-	-	-	-	-	-	-	-	-
Not allocated and confidential	.. c	.. c	.. c	.. c	.. c	.. c	.. c	.. c	.. c	.. c
Private real estate activities	-	-	-	-	-	-	-	-	-	-

- Nil; c Confidential data

Note: Detailed metadata at: *http://stats.oecd.org/OECDStat_Metadata/ShowMetadata.ashx?Dataset=FDI_CTRY_IND_SUMM.*

Source: *OECD International Direct Investment Statistics (database): https://doi.org/10.1787/idi-data-en*

IRELAND

Table 5. Foreign direct investment positions by industrial sector

At year end

Million US dollars

	Inward					Outward				
	2014	2015	2016	2017	2018	2014	2015	2016	2017	2018
All FDI activities	**429 846.0**	**890 125.2**	**840 646.1**	**1 058 012.7**	**1 000 391.6**	**618 834.1**	**909 667.9**	**856 581.6**	**986 845.8**	**942 868.1**
Agriculture, forestry and fishing	.. c	.. c	.. c	.. c	.. c	-	-	-	-	-
Mining and quarrying	.. c	.. c	.. c	.. c	.. c	.. c	.. c	.. c	.. c	.. c
Extraction activities	-	-	-	-	-	-	-	-	-	-
Manufacturing	**94 742.3**	**346 463.8**	**338 813.1**	**323 992.6**	**360 203.8**	**56 665.7**	**61 224.8**	**66 143.1**	**87 474.2**	**97 420.4**
of which:										
Food products, beverages and tobacco	7 316.2	6 550.9	5 640.4	5 044.4	.. c	18 615.8	22 185.1	20 756.8	.. c	.. c
Textiles, wood and paper products; printing	.. c	.. c	-	-	-	.. c	.. c	.. c	.. c	.. c
Chemical, rubber, plastic, non-metallic mineral products	57 283.7	68 160.0	75 389.5	88 749.1	90 865.6	.. c	.. c	.. c	.. c	.. c
Metal and machinery products, except electrical equipment	8 576.4	.. c	.. c	.. c	.. c	.. c	.. c	.. c	.. c	.. c
Motor vehicles, trailers, semi-trailers, other transport equipment	.. c	.. c	.. c	.. c	.. c	-	.. c	.. c	.. c	.. c
Other manufacturing	20 099.4	17 171.5	15 863.8	20 788.0	20 953.7	10 827.3	10 055.5	.. c	10 560.1	11 294.9
Electricity, gas, steam and air conditioning supply	**1 318.5**	**1 289.1**	**.. c**	**.. c**	**.. c**	**.. c**	**.. c**	**.. c**	**.. c**	**.. c**
Water supply; sewerage, waste management and remediation activities	-	-	-	-	-	-	-	-	-	-
Construction	-	-	-	-	-	-	-	-	-	-
Services	**333 475.6**	**542 177.5**	**500 819.0**	**732 762.1**	**639 032.5**	**540 484.5**	**820 501.9**	**758 951.2**	**865 181.1**	**819 425.2**
Wholesale and retail trade; repair of motor vehicles and motorcycles	20 097.0	17 702.8	18 194.4	52 753.7	50 184.3	22 685.5	15 996.7	16 775.6	19 342.8	15 064.1
Transportation and storage	.. c	.. c	.. c	.. c	.. c	.. c	.. c	.. c	.. c	.. c
Accommodation and food service activities	-	-	-	-	-	-	-	-	-	-
Information and communication	17 750.1	20 554.2	20 304.6	198 402.5	133 494.4	1 569.8	4 987.5	3 578.6	.. c	.. c
Financial and insurance activities	.. c	275 921.6	255 443.2	.. c	.. c	45 026.1	93 710.4	96 473.1	105 693.2	104 727.5
Activities of holding companies	22 995.1	23 430.6	22 537.2	24 346.4	21 470.1	10 202.1	9 313.0	7 573.5	9 648.6	9 226.0
Real estate activities	.. c	.. c	.. c	.. c	.. c	.. c	.. c	.. c	.. c	.. c
Professional, scientific and technical activities	19 743.7	118 391.9	137 960.4	121 421.2	118 184.1	407 301.4	609 615.7	555 569.7	507 453.8	543 179.5
Administrative and support service activities	77 411.0	107 810.6	67 058.1	75 790.4	69 406.9	22 487.6	55 463.3	43 842.1	42 764.5	31 952.1
Public administration; activities of households and of extraterritorial organisations	-	-	-	-	-	-	-	-	-	-
Education	-	-	-	-	-	-	-	-	-	-
Human health and social work activities	-	-	-	-	-	-	-	-	-	-
Arts, entertainment and recreation	-	-	-	-	-	.. c	.. c	.. c	.. c	.. c
Other services	-	-	-	-	-	-	-	-	-	-
Not allocated and confidential	**.. c**	**.. c**	**.. c**	**.. c**	**.. c**	**.. c**	**.. c**	**.. c**	**.. c**	**.. c**
Private real estate activities	-	-	-	-	-	-	-	-	-	-

- Nil; c Confidential data

Note: Detailed metadata at: *http://stats.oecd.org/OECDStat_Metadata/ShowMetadata.ashx?Dataset=FDI_CTRY_IND_SUMM.*

Source: OECD International Direct Investment Statistics (database): https://doi.org/10.1787/idi-data-en

IRELAND

Table 6. Foreign direct investment income by industrial sector

Million US dollars

	Inward					Outward				
	2014	2015	2016	2017	2018	2014	2015	2016	2017	2018
All FDI activities	**54 464.6**	**71 584.0**	**61 827.9**	**75 764.9**	**85 256.7**	**20 477.6**	**11 762.6**	**14 638.9**	**17 361.1**	**15 296.8**
Agriculture, forestry and fishing	**.. c**	**.. c**	**.. c**	**.. c**	**.. c**	-	-	-	-	-
Mining and quarrying	**.. c**	**.. c**	**.. c**	**.. c**	**.. c**	**.. c**	**.. c**	**.. c**	**.. c**	**.. c**
Extraction activities	-	-	-	-	-	-	-	-	-	-
Manufacturing	**25 455.8**	**46 930.7**	**35 241.6**	**42 271.4**	**49 025.1**	**1 413.0**	**-3 803.7**	**-3 473.4**	**-2 141.8**	**-3 295.2**
of which:										
Food products, beverages and tobacco	7 319.9	6 719.9	6 375.1	3 587.0	3 962.0	638.2	579.1	529.7	.. c	.. c
Textiles, wood and paper products; printing	.. c	.. c	.. c	-	-	.. c	556.9	.. c	.. c	.. c
Chemical, rubber, plastic, non-metallic mineral products	11 878.7	15 142.5	16 080.9	21 823.9	28 691.1	.. c	.. c	.. c	-39.5	.. c
Metal and machinery products, except electrical equipment	1 149.0	.. c	8 734.9	12 636.7	12 323.9	.. c	.. c	.. c	.. c	.. c
Motor vehicles, trailers, semi-trailers, other transport equipment	.. c	.. c	.. c	.. c	.. c	-	-	.. c	.. c	.. c
Other manufacturing	4 968.8	4 524.7	4 035.2	.. c	.. c	75.6	119.8	-	-234.5	-266.7
Electricity, gas, steam and air conditioning supply	**.. c**	**53.2**	**.. c**	**.. c**	**.. c**	**130.0**	**39.9**	**.. c**	**-83.4**	**.. c**
Water supply; sewerage, waste management and remediation activities	-	-	-	-	-	-	-	-	-	-
Construction	-	-	-	-	-	-	-	-	-	-
Services	**28 874.9**	**24 584.6**	**24 096.0**	**33 309.7**	**36 053.3**	**18 056.3**	**14 745.4**	**17 443.3**	**17 939.4**	**16 638.7**
Wholesale and retail trade; repair of motor vehicles and motorcycles	3 129.9	.. c	829.4	.. c	.. c	1 093.3	48.8	97.3	428.4	122.7
Transportation and storage	.. c	.. c	.. c	.. c	.. c	.. c	.. c	-	.. c	.. c
Accommodation and food service activities	-	-	-	-	-	-	-	-	-	-
Information and communication	10 295.9	9 163.6	8 431.9	12 257.9	13 053.2	-29.2	-345.0	-360.5	-130.8	-326.9
Financial and insurance activities	8 938.6	6 939.5	7 267.5	7 559.5	5 296.8	1 362.6	827.5	893.5	1 122.8	-876.9
Activities of holding companies	603.7	600.1	914.5	1 105.9	339.9	640.8	437.0	686.7	976.2	260.8
Real estate activities	-	-	-	-	-	-	-	-	-	-
Professional, scientific and technical activities	1 654.5	2 143.1	3 626.0	2 839.6	3 756.6	15 209.0	14 154.2	16 497.8	15 956.5	17 415.3
Administrative and support service activities	4 897.2	4 881.9	4 021.9	7 782.7	9 945.7	197.7	-16.6	274.2	273.9	60.2
Public administration; activities of households and of extraterritorial organisations	-	-	-	-	-	-	-	-	-	-
Education	-	-	-	-	-	-	-	-	-	-
Human health and social work activities	-	-	-	-	-	-	-	-	-	-
Arts, entertainment and recreation	-	-	-	-	-	.. c	.. c	.. c	.. c	.. c
Other services	-	-	-	-	-	-	-	-	-	-
Not allocated and confidential	**.. c**	**.. c**	**120.5**	**.. c**	**.. c**	**.. c**	**.. c**	**1 352.4**	**.. c**	**.. c**
Private real estate activities	-	-	-	-	-	-	-	-	-	-

- Nil; c Confidential data

Note: Detailed metadata at: *http://stats.oecd.org/OECDStat_Metadata/ShowMetadata.ashx?Dataset=FDI_CTRY_IND_SUMM.*

Source: OECD International Direct Investment Statistics (database): https://doi.org/10.1787/idi-data-en

ISRAEL

Table 1. Foreign direct investment flows by country

Million US dollars

	Inward					Outward				
	2014	2015	2016	2017	2018	2014	2015	2016	2017	2018
WORLD	**6 049.0**	**11 337.0**	**11 988.0**	**18 169.0**	**20 789.0**	**4 525.0**	**10 969.0**	**14 579.0**	**6 153.4**	**6 117.0**
OECD COUNTRIES	**2 106.4**	**3 668.0**	**6 374.0**	**.. d**	**9 546.0**	**2 946.8**	**8 088.0**	**11 850.0**	**.. d**	**3 304.0**
Australia	-2.7	.. c	-	.. c	..	87.4	96.0	79.0	76.1	41.0
Austria	..	-	-	-	..	0.6	-	-	..	..
Belgium	120.3	63.0	-22.0	-342.6	-7.0	26.5	-591.0	-	3.7	6.0
Canada	-132.5	102.0	61.0	178.9	-500.0	62.7	-71.0	125.0	327.0	108.0
Chile	..	-	-	..	..	.. c	.. c	-	.. c	..
Czech Republic	..	-	-	..	..	3.1	9.0	-3.0	-0.6	-2.0
Denmark	.. c	-	-	.. c	.. c	.. c	.. c	.. c	.. c	.. c
Estonia	..	-	-	..	..	..	-	-	..	..
Finland	..	-	-	..	..	.. c	.. c	10.0	.. c	.. c
France	101.5	372.0	114.0	-67.1	-77.0	-15.9	2.0	-20.0	-16.6	94.0
Germany	257.5	25.0	-5.0	29.8	26.0	151.3	134.0	115.0	265.6	-430.0
Greece	..	-	-	..	..	2.7	1.0	2.0	-4.6	-1.0
Hungary	.. c	.. c	.. c	.. c	.. c	-339.9	-88.0	-15.0	-9.7	37.0
Iceland	.. c	.. c	.. c	.. c	.. c	..	-	-	.. c	..
Ireland	.. c	.. c	.. c	.. c	.. c	..	-	-	.. c	.. c
Israel[1]	-	-	-	..	..	-	-	-	..	..
Italy	.. c	.. c	.. c	.. c	.. c	..	3.0	-8.0	12.6	19.0
Japan	29.0	12.0	137.0	1 058.6	152.0	561.2	162.0	96.0	41.3	1 369.0
Korea	..	-	-	..	..	24.4	21.0	19.0	18.7	16.0
Latvia	..	-	-	..	..	.. c	.. c	.. c	..	..
Lithuania	..	-	-	..	..	25.8	-	-	-	.. c
Luxembourg	58.0	-33.0	672.0	-293.3	-394.0	-1.3	242.0	178.0	75.8	34.0
Mexico	.. c	.. c	34.0	30.5	1 553.0	..	4.0	-6.0	4.2	3.0
Netherlands	-1 363.3	480.0	1 746.0	384.5	-119.0	1 327.5	7 756.0	9 875.0	3 426.6	2 051.0
New Zealand	..	-	-	..	..	..	.. c	-	-	..
Norway	.. c	.. c	-	..	..	.. c	.. c	.. c	.. c	.. c
Poland	.. c	.. c	.. c	.. c	.. c	18.1	111.0	15.0	-34.2	-8.0
Portugal	..	-	-	..	..	..	-	-	-	..
Slovak Republic	..	-	-	..	..	..	-	-	..	..
Slovenia	..	-	-	..	..	..	-	-	..	..
Spain	..	.. c	-	..	..	-2.0	-34.0	-47.0	8.4	91.0
Sweden	..	176.0	65.0	-38.8	-1.0	-0.6	1.0	-5.0	.. c	.. c
Switzerland	201.0	113.0	26.0	-142.2	13.0	138.5	165.0	85.0	51.2	-295.0
Turkey	.. c	.. c	.. c	.. c	.. c	13.8	5.0	6.0	12.0	8.0
United Kingdom	68.8	72.0	260.0	607.6	-821.0	972.6	631.0	-79.0	172.2	-191.0
United States	2 243.9	1 596.0	2 818.0	1 747.5	9 464.0	-195.5	-807.0	1 407.0	143.6	253.0
EUROPE	**-11.1**	**1 800.0**	**3 371.0**	**7 274.1**	**-748.0**	**2 292.9**	**8 913.0**	**10 213.0**	**4 670.1**	**1 629.0**
Bulgaria	..	-	-	..	..	50.5	30.0	26.0	20.8	10.0
Croatia	..	-	-	..	..	.. c	.. c	-	..	..
Cyprus[2, 3]	..	-	-	.. c	.. c	-92.3	-288.0	-140.0	79.2	-9.0
Malta	..	-	-	..	..	..	-	-	..	..
Romania	..	-	-	..	..	-2.1	13.0	-11.0	4.5	13.0
Russian Federation	.. c	.. c	-	..	..	54.0	75.0	70.0	45.7	26.0
Ukraine	..	-	-	..	..	52.2	61.0	55.0	46.8	14.0
AFRICA	**-**	**-**	**-**	**-**	**..**	**-2.7**	**-5.0**	**-23.0**	**-0.5**	**5.0**
Northern Africa	-	-	-	-	..	-	-	-	..	..
Algeria	..	-	-	..	..	..	-	-	..	..
Egypt	..	-	-	..	..	..	-	-	..	..
Libya	..	-	-	..	..	..	-	-	..	..
Morocco	..	-	-	..	..	..	-	-	..	..
Tunisia	..	-	-	..	..	..	-	-	..	..
Other African countries	-	-	-	-	..	-3.7	-3.0	-15.0	..	5.0
Nigeria	..	-	-	..	..	.. c	.. c	-	.. c	.. c
South Africa	..	-	-	..	..	1.8	4.0	2.0	4.7	3.0
AMERICA	**2 379.2**	**1 425.0**	**2 726.0**	**3 188.8**	**11 932.0**	**238.4**	**-529.0**	**1 973.0**	**655.8**	**692.0**
Northern America	2 111.5	1 698.0	2 879.0	..	8 964.0	-132.9	-878.0	1 532.0	470.5	361.0
Central America and Caribbean countries	188.8	-398.0	-159.0	..	2 959.0	263.6	322.0	333.0	..	158.0
Bahamas	..	-	-	..	..	..	-	-	..	..
Bermuda	25.0	-37.0	15.0	.. c	.. c	.. c	.. c	.. c	-	..
Cayman Islands	172.4	-364.0	-209.0	1 260.8	1 195.0	267.9	319.0	256.0	.. c	122.0
Costa Rica	..	-	-	..	..	.. c	.. c	.. c	.. c	34.0
El Salvador	..	-	-	..	..	..	-	-	..	..
Guatemala	..	-	-	..	..	..	-	-	..	..
Honduras	..	-	-	..	..	..	-	-	..	..
Nicaragua	..	-	-	..	..	..	-	-	..	..
Panama	-8.6	3.0	1.0	0.8	-9.0	.. c	.. c	-	.. c	..
Virgin Islands, U.S.	.. c	.. c	-	.. c	..	-4.6	-1.0	75.0	.. c	.. c
South America	-	-	-	..	9.0	14.7	22.0	17.0	..	173.0
Argentina	..	-	-	..	..	.. c	.. c	-1.0	.. c	.. c
Bolivia	..	-	-	..	..	..	-	-	..	..
Brazil	..	-	-	..	..	14.7	22.0	18.0	13.6	174.0
Colombia	..	-	-	..	..	.. c	.. c	-	0.5	.. c
Ecuador	..	-	-	..	..	.. c	.. c	-	.. c	.. c
Paraguay	..	-	-	..	..	..	-	-	..	..
Peru	..	-	-	..	..	.. c	.. c	-	.. c	.. c
Uruguay	.. c	.. c	.. c	.. c	..	.. c	-	-	..	..
Venezuela	..	-	-	..	..	..	-	-	..	..

Table 1. Foreign direct investment flows by country *(cont.)*

Million US dollars

	Inward					Outward				
	2014	2015	2016	2017	2018	2014	2015	2016	2017	2018
ASIA	**321.3**	**2 144.0**	**674.0**	**1 235.2**	**721.0**	**784.6**	**518.0**	**297.0**	**185.4**	**1 491.0**
Near and Middle East	-	-	-	..	..	-	-	-1.0	..	..
Gulf Arabian countries	-	-	-	..	..	-	-	-	..	..
Kuwait	..	-	-	..	..	..	-	-	..	..
Qatar	..	-	-	..	..	..	-	-	..	..
Saudi Arabia	..	-	-	..	..	..	-	-	..	..
United Arab Emirates	..	-	-	..	..	..	-	-	..	..
Other Near and Middle East	..	-	-	..	..	-	-	-1.0	..	..
Jordan	..	-	-	..	..	..	-	-	..	..
Other Asian countries	321.3	2 144.0	674.0	..	721.0	758.6	482.0	298.0	..	1 491.0
China	..	107.0	161.0	85.6	534.0	22.4	85.0	-2.0	3.3	25.0
Hong Kong, China	14.5	7.0	2.0	.. c	.. c	13.3	-7.0	14.0	18.0	-25.0
India	..	.. c	-	.. c	.. c	128.8	135.0	108.0	55.4	55.0
Indonesia	..	-	-	..	..	.. c	.. c	-	-	..
Iran, Islamic Republic of	..	-	-	..	..	..	-	-	-	..
Malaysia	..	-	-	..	..	.. c	.. c	-	.. c	.. c
Philippines	..	-	-	..	..	.. c	.. c	-	.. c	.. c
Singapore	277.7	2 018.0	374.0	68.3	33.0	-8.4	-2.0	1.0	7.4	3.0
Chinese Taipei	..	-	-	..	..	25.8	-	24.0	.. c	.. c
Thailand	..	-	-	..	..	-8.9	88.0	1.0	5.0	..
Viet Nam	..	-	-	..	..	.. c	.. c	12.0	2.8	26.0
AUSTRALIA, OCEANIA AND POLAR REGIONS	**-2.7**	**-**	**-29.0**	**..**	**..**	**87.4**	**96.0**	**81.0**	**76.1**	**41.0**
WORLD unallocated and confidential	**3 362.3**	**5 968.0**	**5 246.0**	**6 470.9**	**8 884.0**	**1 124.4**	**1 976.0**	**2 038.0**	**566.6**	**2 259.0**
European Union (EU28)	**.. c**	**.. c**	**3 339.0**	**.. d**	**-796.0**	**.. c**	**.. c**	**9 921.0**	**.. d**	**1 802.0**
G20 countries excl. European Union	**.. c**	**.. c**	**3 645.0**	**.. d**	**10 277.0**	**.. c**	**.. c**	**1 929.0**	**.. d**	**1 573.0**
G20 OECD countries	**2 640.6**	**2 190.0**	**3 484.0**	**.. d**	**9 744.0**	**1 661.9**	**180.0**	**1 734.0**	**1 056.5**	**1 290.0**
G20 Non-OECD countries	**.. c**	**.. c**	**161.0**	**.. d**	**533.0**	**.. c**	**.. c**	**195.0**	**.. d**	**283.0**
MENA countries	**..**	**-**	**-**	**..**	**..**	**..**	**-**	**-**	**..**	**..**
ASEAN countries	**..**	**2 018.0**	**374.0**	**..**	**33.0**	**.. c**	**.. c**	**14.0**	**.. d**	**29.0**

- Nil; .. Not available; c Confidential data; d Secondary Confidentiality

Note: Detailed metadata at: *http://stats.oecd.org/OECDStat_Metadata/ShowMetadata.ashx?Dataset=FDI_CTRY_IND_SUMM.*

1. Information on data for Israel: *http://oe.cd/israel-disclaimer*.
2. Note by Turkey: The information in this document with reference to "Cyprus" relates to the southern part of the Island. There is no single authority representing both Turkish and Greek Cypriot people on the Island. Turkey recognises the Turkish Republic of Northern Cyprus (TRNC). Until a lasting and equitable solution is found within the context of the United Nations, Turkey shall preserve its position concerning the "Cyprus issue".
3. Note by all the European Union Member States of the OECD and the European Union: The Republic of Cyprus is recognised by all members of the United Nations with the exception of Turkey. The information in this document relates to the area under the effective control of the Government of the Republic of Cyprus.

Source: OECD International Direct Investment Statistics (database): https://doi.org/10.1787/idi-data-en

Table 2. Foreign direct investment positions by country

At year end

Million US dollars

	Inward					Outward				
	2014	2015	2016	2017	2018	2014	2015	2016	2017	2018
WORLD	**89 619.0**	**99 313.0**	**107 483.0**	**129 143.0**	**145 345.0**	**79 012.0**	**84 696.0**	**94 633.0**	**100 260.0**	**103 506.0**
OECD COUNTRIES	**46 584.7**	**46 415.0**	**50 293.0**	**.. d**	**67 865.0**	**57 422.7**	**63 195.0**	**68 899.0**	**.. d**	**77 344.0**
Australia	107.5	.. c	-	.. c	..	805.4	805.0	822.0	848.9	754.0
Austria	..	-	-	..	..	12.8	-	-	..	..
Belgium	266.4	324.0	384.0	158.5	149.0	690.8	157.0	151.0	176.8	176.0
Canada	5 440.0	3 959.0	3 835.0	4 708.3	3 373.0	2 596.4	2 197.0	2 461.0	2 772.8	2 602.0
Chile	..	-	-	..	..	.. c	.. c	-	.. c	.. c
Czech Republic	..	-	-	..	..	29.8	36.0	32.0	39.4	37.0
Denmark	.. c	-	-	.. c	.. c	.. c	.. c	.. c	.. c	.. c
Estonia	..	-	-	..	..	..	-	-	..	..
Finland	..	-	-	..	..	.. c	.. c	.. c	.. c	.. c
France	518.0	829.0	853.0	823.8	706.0	138.1	138.0	46.0	22.6	129.0
Germany	404.6	468.0	489.0	513.8	554.0	1 398.9	1 433.0	1 583.0	1 991.7	1 295.0
Greece	..	-	-	..	..	16.4	15.0	16.0	14.3	12.0
Hungary	.. c	.. c	.. c	.. c	.. c	278.7	95.0	73.0	100.6	60.0
Iceland	.. c	.. c	.. c	.. c	.. c	..	-	-	.. c	..
Ireland	.. c	.. c	.. c	.. c	.. c	..	-	.. c	.. c	.. c
Israel[1]	-	-	-	..	..	-	-	-	..	..
Italy	.. c	.. c	.. c	.. c	.. c	125.1	125.0	115.0	139.1	101.0
Japan	125.5	-	359.0	1 462.5	1 578.0	1 653.5	1 807.0	1 763.0	1 758.6	3 028.0
Korea	..	-	-	..	..	251.4	243.0	237.0	238.8	..
Latvia	..	-	-	..	..	.. c	.. c	.. c	..	..
Lithuania	..	-	-	..	..	242.0	-	-	.. c	.. c
Luxembourg	2 651.5	2 854.0	3 522.0	3 343.2	3 226.0	624.1	1 055.0	1 349.0	1 727.1	1 461.0
Mexico	.. c	.. c	321.0	386.0	1 895.0	25.6	34.0	26.0	28.5	31.0
Netherlands	10 194.6	10 332.0	12 375.0	13 474.3	12 201.0	32 248.9	37 708.0	45 089.0	48 895.1	48 508.0
New Zealand	..	-	-	..	..	..	-	-	-	..
Norway	.. c	.. c	-	..	..	.. c	.. c	.. c	.. c	.. c
Poland	.. c	.. c	.. c	.. c	.. c	105.3	200.0	250.0	305.5	279.0
Portugal	..	-	-	..	..	..	-	-	-	.. c
Slovak Republic	..	-	-	..	..	..	-	-	..	..
Slovenia	..	-	-	..	..	..	-	-	..	..
Spain	..	.. c	-	..	..	62.8	31.0	-10.0	-2.7	108.0
Sweden	886.6	1 054.0	1 081.0	950.8	452.0	11.4	10.0	6.0	.. c	.. c
Switzerland	2 922.0	1 696.0	1 740.0	1 724.4	1 759.0	1 665.0	1 731.0	2 244.0	2 348.4	3 218.0
Turkey	.. c	.. c	.. c	.. c	.. c	582.3	784.0	711.0	864.5	587.0
United Kingdom	2 392.1	2 264.0	2 442.0	2 642.3	2 445.0	2 003.2	2 909.0	2 239.0	2 175.6	2 079.0
United States	15 299.8	16 853.0	18 680.0	21 043.6	29 781.0	11 364.9	10 776.0	10 517.0	11 133.2	11 998.0
EUROPE	**26 231.8**	**25 997.0**	**27 767.0**	**35 588.4**	**33 138.0**	**44 661.4**	**51 397.0**	**55 871.0**	**63 714.5**	**62 363.0**
Bulgaria	..	-	-	..	..	495.9	254.0	253.0	247.4	216.0
Croatia	..	-	-	..	..	.. c	.. c	-	..	..
Cyprus[2, 3]	..	-	-	..	.. c	914.0	387.0	230.0	367.4	293.0
Malta	..	-	-	..	..	..	-	-	..	..
Romania	..	-	-	..	..	81.0	73.0	75.0	70.6	83.0
Russian Federation	.. c	.. c	-	..	..	553.8	562.0	606.0	596.3	524.0
Ukraine	..	-	-	..	..	487.4	488.0	504.0	518.8	446.0
AFRICA	**-**	**-**	**-**	**-**	**..**	**-21.3**	**-21.0**	**-125.0**	**-129.4**	**-187.0**
Northern Africa	-	-	-	-	..	-	-	-	..	..
Algeria	..	-	-	..	..	..	-	-	..	..
Egypt	..	-	-	..	..	..	-	-	..	..
Libya	..	-	-	..	..	..	-	-	..	..
Morocco	..	-	-	..	..	..	-	-	..	..
Tunisia	..	-	-	..	..	..	-	-	..	..
Other African countries	-	-	-	-	..	25.7	28.0	-37.0	..	-187.0
Nigeria	..	-	-	..	..	.. c	.. c	5.0	.. c	.. c
South Africa	..	-	-	..	..	..	12.0	13.0	18.8	19.0
AMERICA	**29 107.1**	**28 200.0**	**30 493.0**	**35 370.6**	**45 813.0**	**17 100.2**	**15 717.0**	**16 976.0**	**17 729.3**	**17 552.0**
Northern America	20 739.8	20 812.0	22 515.0	25 751.9	33 154.0	13 961.2	12 973.0	12 978.0	13 905.9	14 600.0
Central America and Caribbean countries	7 777.3	6 732.0	7 949.0	..	12 495.0	998.7	1 565.0	2 399.0	..	2 845.0
Bahamas	..	-	-	..	..	..	-	-	..	..
Bermuda	1 451.1	351.0	518.0	.. c	..	.. c	.. c	.. c	.. c	..
Cayman Islands	6 293.9	6 337.0	7 067.0	8 485.8	9 801.0	963.7	1 264.0	1 471.0	1 639.0	.. c
Costa Rica	..	-	-	..	..	.. c	.. c	.. c	.. c	.. c
El Salvador	..	-	-	..	..	..	-	-	..	..
Guatemala	..	-	-	..	..	..	-	-	..	..
Honduras	..	-	-	..	..	..	-	-	..	..
Nicaragua	..	-	-	..	..	..	-	-	..	..
Panama	32.4	44.0	37.0	37.5	36.0	.. c	.. c	-	.. c	.. c
Virgin Islands, U.S.	.. c	.. c	6.0	-	..	9.5	267.0	369.0	.. c	.. c
South America	.. c	-	-	..	164.0	126.3	81.0	104.0	..	107.0
Argentina	..	-	-	..	..	.. c	.. c	-3.0	-2.5	-3.0
Bolivia	..	-	-	..	..	..	-	-	..	..
Brazil	..	-	-	..	..	126.3	81.0	107.0	108.2	94.0
Colombia	..	-	-	..	..	.. c	.. c	-	..	..
Ecuador	..	-	-	..	..	.. c	.. c	.. c	.. c	.. c
Paraguay	..	-	-	..	..	..	-	-	..	..
Peru	..	-	-	..	..	.. c	.. c	.. c	.. c	.. c
Uruguay	.. c	.. c	.. c	.. c	..	.. c	-	-	..	..
Venezuela	..	-	-	..	..	..	-	-	..	..

Table 2. Foreign direct investment positions by country *(cont.)*
At year end

Million US dollars

	Inward					Outward				
	2014	2015	2016	2017	2018	2014	2015	2016	2017	2018
ASIA	**6 043.1**	**5 171.0**	**5 860.0**	**7 982.1**	**8 696.0**	**3 993.9**	**4 159.0**	**4 228.0**	**4 199.3**	**5 893.0**
Near and Middle East	-	-	-	..	..	0.8	-	21.0	..	..
Gulf Arabian countries	-	-	-	..	..	-	-	-	..	..
Kuwait	..	-	-	..	..	..	-	-	..	..
Qatar	..	-	-	..	..	..	-	-	..	..
Saudi Arabia	..	-	-	..	..	..	-	-	..	..
United Arab Emirates	..	-	-	..	..	..	-	-	..	..
Other Near and Middle East	-	-	-	..	..	0.8	-	21.0	..	..
Jordan	..	-	-	..	..	..	-	-	..	..
Other Asian countries	6 043.1	5 155.0	5 852.0	..	8 696.0	3 991.1	3 905.0	3 720.0	..	5 893.0
China	..	77.0	373.0	3 575.5	4 260.0	207.8	469.0	218.0	228.4	848.0
Hong Kong, China	206.3	270.0	30.0	44.6	46.0	299.8	296.0	308.0	333.0	306.0
India	16.6	.. c	-	.. c	.. c	1 036.6	1 047.0	1 130.0	1 052.8	989.0
Indonesia	..	-	-	..	..	.. c	.. c	-	.. c	.. c
Iran, Islamic Republic of	..	-	-	..	..	..	-	-	..	..
Malaysia	..	-	-	..	..	.. c	.. c	-	.. c	.. c
Philippines	..	-	-	..	..	.. c	.. c	.. c	.. c	.. c
Singapore	5 694.8	4 808.0	5 090.0	2 893.3	2 809.0	28.5	29.0	30.0	39.4	40.0
Chinese Taipei	..	-	-	..	..	..	-	.. c	.. c	.. c
Thailand	..	-	-	..	..	23.9	14.0	15.0	21.3	6.0
Viet Nam	..	-	-	..	..	.. c	.. c	19.0	19.3	45.0
AUSTRALIA, OCEANIA AND POLAR REGIONS	**107.5**	**-**	**-**	**..**	**52.0**	**805.4**	**805.0**	**826.0**	**848.9**	**754.0**
WORLD unallocated and confidential	**28 129.4**	**39 945.0**	**43 363.0**	**50 201.9**	**57 646.0**	**12 472.4**	**12 639.0**	**16 857.0**	**13 897.4**	**17 131.0**
European Union (EU28)	**.. c**	**.. c**	**25 227.0**	**.. d**	**29 710.0**	**.. c**	**.. c**	**50 792.0**	**.. d**	**55 769.0**
G20 countries excl. European Union	**.. c**	**.. c**	**27 732.0**	**.. d**	**44 899.0**	**.. c**	**.. c**	**22 591.0**	**.. d**	**25 075.0**
G20 OECD countries	**24 794.9**	**24 956.0**	**27 351.0**	**.. d**	**40 636.0**	**20 944.7**	**21 251.0**	**20 520.0**	**21 974.0**	**22 604.0**
G20 Non-OECD countries	**.. c**	**.. c**	**381.0**	**.. d**	**4 263.0**	**.. c**	**.. c**	**2 071.0**	**.. d**	**2 471.0**
MENA countries	**..**	**-**	**-**	**..**	**..**	**..**	**-**	**-**	**..**	**..**
ASEAN countries	**..**	**4 808.0**	**5 090.0**	**..**	**2 809.0**	**.. c**	**.. c**	**69.0**	**.. d**	**95.0**

- Nil; .. Not available; c Confidential data; d Secondary Confidentiality

Note: Detailed metadata at: *http://stats.oecd.org/OECDStat_Metadata/ShowMetadata.ashx?Dataset=FDI_CTRY_IND_SUMM.*

1. Information on data for Israel: *http://oe.cd/israel-disclaimer*.
2. Note by Turkey: The information in this document with reference to "Cyprus" relates to the southern part of the Island. There is no single authority representing both Turkish and Greek Cypriot people on the Island. Turkey recognises the Turkish Republic of Northern Cyprus (TRNC). Until a lasting and equitable solution is found within the context of the United Nations, Turkey shall preserve its position concerning the "Cyprus issue".
3. Note by all the European Union Member States of the OECD and the European Union: The Republic of Cyprus is recognised by all members of the United Nations with the exception of Turkey. The information in this document relates to the area under the effective control of the Government of the Republic of Cyprus.

Source: OECD International Direct Investment Statistics (database): https://doi.org/10.1787/idi-data-en

Table 4. Foreign direct investment flows by industrial sector

Million US dollars

	Inward					Outward				
	2014	2015	2016	2017	2018	2014	2015	2016	2017	2018
All FDI activities	**6 049.0**	**11 337.0**	**11 988.0**	**18 169.0**	**20 789.0**	**4 525.0**	**10 969.0**	**14 579.0**	**6 153.4**	**6 117.0**
Agriculture, forestry and fishing	**37.8**	-	**-1.0**	**36.0**	**14.0**	**0.5**	-	**15.0**	**1.1**	**20.0**
Mining and quarrying	**-80.2**	-	**-194.0**	**309.7**	**680.0**	**265.2**	-	**-200.0**	**-114.3**	**-270.0**
Extraction activities	-80.2	-	-194.0	309.7	680.0	265.2	-	-200.0	4.3	..
Manufacturing	**1 223.2**	**1 695.0**	**2 870.0**	**3 003.9**	**4 441.0**	**4 055.7**	**9 958.0**	**12 136.0**	**4 266.8**	**3 166.0**
of which:										
Food products, beverages and tobacco	81.5	144.0	24.0	-15.1	23.0	-0.8	-2.0	1.0	209.6	41.0
Textiles, wood and paper products; printing	69.9	204.0	27.0	49.7	20.0	129.2	85.0	147.0	64.4	201.0
Chemical, rubber, plastic, non-metallic mineral products	817.5	410.0	566.0	180.7	3 187.0	3 187.1	9 454.0	11 403.0	3 709.4	3 096.0
Metal and machinery products, except electrical equipment	-94.7	899.0	1 495.0	2 911.5	1 149.0	675.0	265.0	556.0	272.5	-175.0
Motor vehicles, trailers, semi-trailers, other transport equipment	-10.1	27.0	33.0	6.9	24.0	-18.7	34.0	9.0	-34.2	-5.0
Other manufacturing	359.0	11.0	725.0	-129.8	38.0	84.0	122.0	20.0	44.8	8.0
Electricity, gas, steam and air conditioning supply	**15.8**	**846.0**	**46.0**	**-19.8**	**-9.0**	**2.0**	**122.0**	**56.0**	**-69.3**	.. c
Water supply; sewerage, waste management and remediation activities	**2.6**	**2.0**	**3.0**	**4.8**	**-45.0**	**0.1**	**6.0**	**-3.0**	-	.. c
Construction	**51.0**	**-1.0**	**115.0**	**19.4**	**527.0**	**-112.0**	**-34.0**	**-101.0**	**89.7**	**128.0**
Services	**4 799.5**	**5 630.0**	**6 319.0**	**12 052.1**	**15 343.0**	**-647.1**	**-782.0**	**1 299.0**	**3 954.0**	**1 551.0**
Wholesale and retail trade; repair of motor vehicles and motorcycles	115.0	110.0	284.0	157.4	113.0	-117.2	-597.0	51.0	581.8	44.0
Transportation and storage	16.1	-24.0	-23.0	14.6	59.0	269.6	-75.0	-12.0	33.1	-27.0
Accommodation and food service activities	-5.2	16.0	27.0	37.8	43.0	15.2	12.0	36.0	323.3	53.0
Information and communication	2 387.7	1 984.0	2 847.0	3 052.5	3 434.0	-14.6	125.0	71.0	64.7	44.0
Financial and insurance activities	692.0	1 611.0	1 132.0	448.8	8 571.0	-737.4	-200.0	1 019.0	2 288.6	642.0
Activities of holding companies	..	..	..	831.1	8 643.0	..	..	..	715.5	518.0
Real estate activities	-148.8	293.0	168.0	349.8	536.0	-106.4	-122.0	125.0	532.7	640.0
Professional, scientific and technical activities	1 711.3	1 362.0	1 837.0	1 872.8	2 231.0	35.1	94.0	-11.0	101.8	17.0
Administrative and support service activities	5.8	264.0	-	6 095.0	52.0	2.1	-20.0	-16.0	-1.1	-12.0
Public administration; activities of households and of extraterritorial organisations	-	-	-	-	..	-	-	-	-	..
Education	9.9	5.0	2.0	8.0	14.0	-0.5	1.0	11.0	7.1	-1.0
Human health and social work activities	5.8	-34.0	35.0	17.1	6.0	11.2	5.0	15.0	15.8	25.0
Arts, entertainment and recreation	6.3	36.0	4.0	-2.4	12.0	1.4	1.0	8.0	2.0	..
Other services	3.5	7.0	6.0	4.7	3.0	-5.7	-6.0	2.0	-3.0	4.0
Not allocated and confidential	**-0.6**	**3 165.0**	**2 830.0**	**2 763.0**	**-162.0**	**960.6**	**1 699.0**	**1 377.0**	**-1 974.6**	.. c
Private real estate activities	-	-	-	-	..	-	-	-	-	..

- Nil; .. Not available; c Confidential data

Note: The statistical data for Israel are supplied by and under the responsibility of the relevant Israeli authorities. The use of such data by the OECD is without prejudice to the status of the Golan Heights, East Jerusalem and Israeli settlements in the West Bank under the terms of international law.

Note: Detailed metadata at: *http://stats.oecd.org/OECDStat_Metadata/ShowMetadata.ashx?Dataset=FDI_CTRY_IND_SUMM.*

Source: OECD International Direct Investment Statistics (database): https://doi.org/10.1787/idi-data-en

Table 5. Foreign direct investment positions by industrial sector

At year end

Million US dollars

	Inward					Outward				
	2014	2015	2016	2017	2018	2014	2015	2016	2017	2018
All FDI activities	**89 619.0**	**99 313.0**	**107 483.0**	**129 143.0**	**145 345.0**	**79 012.0**	**84 696.0**	**94 633.0**	**100 260.0**	**103 506.0**
Agriculture, forestry and fishing	**217.5**	**-**	**260.0**	**280.6**	**286.0**	**5.0**	**-**	**25.0**	**14.4**	**195.0**
Mining and quarrying	**1 810.6**	**-**	**1 552.0**	**1 862.3**	**2 599.0**	**1 385.1**	**-**	**1 126.0**	**1 030.1**	**870.0**
Extraction activities	1 810.6	-	1 552.0	1 859.6	2 596.0	1 385.1	-	1 126.0	39.6	..
Manufacturing	**29 564.8**	**30 233.0**	**30 944.0**	**33 424.7**	**37 462.0**	**47 974.3**	**53 723.0**	**60 386.0**	**65 069.4**	**65 193.0**
of which:										
Food products, beverages and tobacco	1 445.2	125.0	1 611.0	1 695.2	1 625.0	1 012.6	803.0	749.0	1 581.5	1 176.0
Textiles, wood and paper products; printing	1 781.6	2 477.0	855.0	988.0	819.0	707.2	803.0	894.0	1 112.2	1 132.0
Chemical, rubber, plastic, non-metallic mineral products	6 493.5	6 765.0	5 540.0	..	8 549.0	38 538.7	44 658.0	52 970.0	56 524.4	58 010.0
Metal and machinery products, except electrical equipment	18 072.5	18 602.0	20 106.0	22 913.2	24 133.0	6 946.9	6 587.0	4 887.0	4 808.3	4 164.0
Motor vehicles, trailers, semi-trailers, other transport equipment	377.0	416.0	449.0	445.2	467.0	151.7	183.0	185.0	384.4	309.0
Other manufacturing	1 395.0	1 848.0	2 383.0	1 840.2	1 869.0	617.2	689.0	701.0	658.6	402.0
Electricity, gas, steam and air conditioning supply	**112.9**	**964.0**	**1 027.0**	**1 049.5**	**1 047.0**	**739.9**	**871.0**	**934.0**	**1 093.0**	**-74.0**
Water supply; sewerage, waste management and remediation activities	**23.0**	**24.0**	**28.0**	**33.0**	**-11.0**	**0.3**	**20.0**	**18.0**	**18.5**	**26.0**
Construction	**832.9**	**815.0**	**868.0**	**901.7**	**1 262.0**	**1 692.7**	**898.0**	**910.0**	**1 780.6**	**661.0**
Services	**48 497.9**	**56 515.0**	**62 242.0**	**77 766.3**	**89 610.0**	**17 661.1**	**17 952.0**	**19 906.0**	**29 225.8**	**23 499.0**
Wholesale and retail trade; repair of motor vehicles and motorcycles	1 864.3	2 011.0	2 939.0	3 164.5	3 196.0	769.6	181.0	310.0	549.0	409.0
Transportation and storage	192.5	222.0	151.0	177.9	287.0	216.5	-88.0	-117.0	0.2	-157.0
Accommodation and food service activities	134.3	283.0	466.0	597.9	725.0	214.6	144.0	259.0	669.5	256.0
Information and communication	18 104.7	22 174.0	22 952.0	26 461.9	28 004.0	1 320.7	1 381.0	1 338.0	2 001.2	2 173.0
Financial and insurance activities	9 014.6	11 209.0	12 544.0	14 094.8	21 154.0	10 994.8	12 190.0	13 821.0	19 732.5	15 060.0
Activities of holding companies	..	..	..	10 614.3	17 801.0	..	..	..	14 073.6	12 848.0
Real estate activities	3 489.8	4 209.0	4 365.0	5 429.5	4 767.0	3 794.4	3 751.0	3 862.0	5 540.5	4 813.0
Professional, scientific and technical activities	14 697.0	14 885.0	16 971.0	19 792.0	21 912.0	296.8	253.0	292.0	516.8	304.0
Administrative and support service activities	649.3	1 115.0	1 471.0	7 633.9	7 874.0	20.1	5.0	-31.0	100.7	-108.0
Public administration; activities of households and of extraterritorial organisations	-	-	-	.. c	..	-	-	-	.. c	..
Education	58.9	48.0	82.0	90.4	104.0	-3.0	2.0	16.0	32.9	9.0
Human health and social work activities	151.3	130.0	164.0	178.1	183.0	0.6	-6.0	7.0	43.5	-13.0
Arts, entertainment and recreation	80.5	164.0	64.0	67.9	77.0	43.9	33.0	46.0	33.8	44.0
Other services	60.7	65.0	73.0	77.3	80.0	-7.9	106.0	103.0	0.5	-14.0
Not allocated and confidential	**8 559.4**	**10 762.0**	**10 562.0**	**13 824.9**	**13 090.0**	**9 553.5**	**11 232.0**	**11 328.0**	**2 028.2**	**13 136.0**
Private real estate activities	**-**	**-**	**-**	**-**	**..**	**-**	**-**	**-**	**-**	**..**

- Nil; .. Not available; c Confidential data

Note: The statistical data for Israel are supplied by and under the responsibility of the relevant Israeli authorities. The use of such data by the OECD is without prejudice to the status of the Golan Heights, East Jerusalem and Israeli settlements in the West Bank under the terms of international law.

Note: Detailed metadata at: *http://stats.oecd.org/OECDStat_Metadata/ShowMetadata.ashx?Dataset=FDI_CTRY_IND_SUMM.*

Source: OECD International Direct Investment Statistics (database): https://doi.org/10.1787/idi-data-en

ITALY

Table 1. Foreign direct investment flows by country

Million US dollars

	Inward					Outward				
	2014	2015	2016	2017	2018	2014	2015	2016	2017	2018
WORLD	**23 224.2**	**19 630.8**	**28 440.8**	**23 995.9**	**32 865.7**	**26 327.2**	**21 639.9**	**16 164.8**	**24 478.4**	**32 673.2**
OECD COUNTRIES	**24 386.6**	**17 185.7**	**28 509.7**	**23 571.6**	**31 122.3**	**18 174.9**	**10 636.9**	**4 114.4**	**13 985.5**	**18 599.1**
Australia	77.2	17.1	66.2	34.4	89.3	161.7	121.3	45.8	177.4	202.6
Austria	581.3	-335.0	321.5	105.2	82.9	1 073.2	173.7	-9 176.9	709.2	311.0
Belgium	5 043.2	-4 390.8	-2 813.9	1 102.5	115.9	110.3	1 572.7	2 926.1	-3 876.6	-2 311.7
Canada	-46.2	-24.9	-56.1	261.8	70.1	5.3	255.0	75.0	390.8	595.6
Chile	127.6	-42.5	7.0	-246.8	-5.4	238.9	69.9	-12.3	9 808.8	166.1
Czech Republic	176.0	22.0	55.2	75.9	-0.9	-50.0	12.6	3 459.4	10.5	-230.6
Denmark	1 486.8	300.4	-764.2	44.6	-104.6	-242.9	482.4	456.6	-181.0	-82.4
Estonia	17.8	-0.4	-29.2	-6.5	-49.0	17.0	2.2	-5.3	15.8	-2.4
Finland	-560.6	-139.0	62.8	146.4	-320.5	843.1	-31.4	152.7	1.8	-202.4
France	6 900.6	6 802.2	18 029.3	-1 577.7	35 211.3	6 747.7	1 668.8	1 009.7	1 107.6	2 599.8
Germany	3 034.8	1 575.3	4 884.2	2 714.2	3 054.7	1 225.0	-190.4	-15.3	-2 132.3	2 404.1
Greece	17.0	-40.4	76.5	-140.6	-29.9	452.1	177.3	150.3	80.9	506.2
Hungary	-207.8	-585.9	200.7	17.0	116.0	-17.5	559.2	142.4	-35.8	145.9
Iceland	0.1	-46.1	18.6	28.3	0.2	-1.0	65.4	-11.2	-66.6	-10.7
Ireland	-1 421.9	-232.1	70.0	1 940.2	78.2	1 868.8	3 950.9	-336.2	-50.9	886.2
Israel[1]	97.0	-64.0	41.1	59.0	-21.9	220.6	194.9	292.4	414.6	178.2
Italy	-	-	-	-	-	-	-	-	-	-
Japan	587.2	1 120.8	278.8	163.4	176.6	-382.4	116.3	293.1	42.0	54.4
Korea	557.2	-188.0	-112.9	134.6	519.8	61.6	-65.3	133.5	36.7	278.3
Latvia	-4.8	6.4	7.1	4.2	-1.8	-14.3	-1.0	48.2	3.2	2.7
Lithuania	3.9	0.3	0.0	-1.3	3.6	-2.4	11.6	-14.4	-1.9	0.0
Luxembourg	-1 122.6	4 114.8	-3 325.6	8 131.6	-13 801.2	3 369.4	733.8	6 909.7	12 629.1	429.6
Mexico	-41.1	219.1	98.9	-84.7	51.1	94.5	226.7	121.4	337.1	429.1
Netherlands	3 168.3	2 677.9	528.0	4 287.1	844.0	-479.6	-5 639.7	-4 234.1	340.1	-460.2
New Zealand	10.8	1.2	0.6	-2.2	-2.2	1.0	6.6	34.7	14.1	12.2
Norway	-1 202.5	-371.4	403.7	121.2	384.8	148.0	110.1	1 420.1	180.8	283.7
Poland	38.5	31.0	-14.6	-91.5	114.2	411.8	1 071.6	-207.2	-2 207.3	-12.0
Portugal	-33.7	23.0	52.1	60.4	12.3	-940.0	34.5	124.3	163.6	208.3
Slovak Republic	-11.6	-76.2	-17.0	-22.0	27.7	209.9	26.1	-3 449.1	826.3	-87.7
Slovenia	2.2	40.4	46.2	28.6	4.8	120.3	42.1	332.2	12.4	128.5
Spain	-283.2	1 235.1	820.2	601.5	444.1	-1 288.3	1 293.0	-387.1	-7 105.1	8 170.4
Sweden	84.3	-72.7	478.4	730.1	186.9	261.6	332.3	87.4	-45.1	179.0
Switzerland	1 945.1	2 238.8	259.8	3 453.9	890.6	2 156.6	712.8	-939.2	222.7	-431.8
Turkey	566.7	47.9	-317.2	-0.1	23.7	-138.2	777.4	3 545.3	652.7	568.9
United Kingdom	4 156.3	3 863.5	7 443.1	1 714.2	3 753.1	2 439.1	-269.3	1 960.5	992.8	-286.6
United States	641.7	-535.3	1 710.5	-216.5	-796.0	-522.6	2 043.5	-832.5	515.3	3 976.9
EUROPE	**20 830.8**	**17 600.8**	**25 794.9**	**24 274.1**	**30 498.2**	**20 718.6**	**10 226.4**	**10 867.8**	**5 199.9**	**16 683.4**
Bulgaria	6.8	0.1	23.6	-5.1	6.5	256.1	141.7	1 141.2	1 240.3	163.7
Croatia	11.7	11.8	39.5	24.9	35.5	290.9	102.9	2 081.0	104.1	268.4
Cyprus[2, 3]	-38.9	29.6	223.4	-245.3	-671.9	102.6	-8.3	-3.0	7.1	-2.9
Malta	-1 418.8	497.6	-617.6	314.2	120.6	-19.9	-57.4	35.2	-42.0	-68.1
Romania	-28.6	38.6	-26.9	103.8	-96.6	180.9	274.3	788.5	501.8	3 339.2
Russian Federation	-79.5	139.4	-437.2	415.2	-63.6	1 464.3	1 025.5	2 424.6	938.8	683.0
Ukraine	1.1	28.1	-8.6	6.4	-6.5	-154.7	33.9	-26.9	-206.7	-302.5
AFRICA	**234.1**	**-39.4**	**320.4**	**74.2**	**-42.8**	**4 876.9**	**4 344.2**	**2 687.1**	**2 711.1**	**3 343.0**
Northern Africa	267.1	-8.3	100.7	29.8	22.5	3 993.7	3 780.0	1 279.7	2 130.5	1 947.6
Algeria	50.7	39.8	64.1	16.2	68.1	1 806.2	1 835.6	920.0	981.0	1 060.0
Egypt	23.7	-15.2	28.2	-6.1	7.6	1 249.5	1 654.9	236.1	794.3	283.3
Libya	171.1	1.5	-13.6	10.0	-52.7	209.4	1.3	-44.1	17.7	30.1
Morocco	19.4	-28.8	13.3	9.8	14.2	106.7	118.5	14.8	72.0	202.6
Tunisia	2.2	-5.5	8.7	0.0	-14.7	621.9	169.7	153.0	265.4	371.5
Other African countries	-33.1	-31.1	219.7	44.4	-65.3	883.2	564.2	1 407.4	580.6	1 395.4
Nigeria	9.3	1.9	27.6	0.1	-0.3	327.7	88.0	346.5	279.5	671.0
South Africa	0.7	-64.0	177.0	25.7	14.5	540.7	396.9	485.3	231.4	101.2
AMERICA	**770.8**	**-271.2**	**1 899.3**	**-537.1**	**241.5**	**722.0**	**3 834.1**	**127.4**	**12 295.5**	**6 071.7**
Northern America	595.5	-560.2	1 654.4	45.3	-725.9	-517.3	2 298.5	-757.5	906.1	4 572.4
Central America and Caribbean countries	-57.3	219.1	21.7	-460.5	494.4	-174.6	602.4	677.8	1 380.3	322.3
Bahamas	1.4	0.0	0.0	0.0	0.0	-11.8	0.5	0.5	0.3	0.2
Bermuda	17.2	-12.0	-0.3	-10.7	9.7	0.3	-10.4	-27.2	135.4	-5.4
Cayman Islands	-21.3	249.0	-241.7	-16.7	-15.0	-5.0	2.4	1.0	-23.5	-14.0
Costa Rica	0.0	4.5	2.3	2.4	2.3	-31.8	1.0	19.6	11.9	112.7
El Salvador	0.0	0.0	0.0	0.0	29.9	0.4	-0.3	1.0	-0.9	-0.2
Guatemala	-48.8	41.7	0.5	0.4	0.5	4.1	6.9	22.3	-42.9	5.2
Honduras	0.0	0.0	0.0	0.0	0.0	3.2	5.6	-4.3	-0.8	-2.3
Nicaragua	0.1	0.0	0.0	0.0	0.0	-1.3	-0.5	0.0	0.1	0.0
Panama	25.8	-59.7	-8.2	0.3	2.3	-71.2	-84.7	-34.6	109.5	-562.0
Virgin Islands, U.S.	-	-	-	-	-	0.1	-0.1	-	-	-
South America	232.5	69.9	223.2	-121.9	473.1	1 413.9	933.2	207.0	10 009.1	1 176.9
Argentina	104.6	3.4	129.9	81.8	121.1	340.7	245.5	-1 171.1	271.2	62.4
Bolivia	3.9	1.7	2.7	4.4	3.1	8.7	-1.4	2.9	3.1	4.2
Brazil	165.4	245.3	55.7	45.0	70.8	706.8	481.2	1 552.3	273.8	863.5
Colombia	3.4	0.1	21.1	5.7	-0.9	-31.8	37.7	81.0	90.7	36.0
Ecuador	-5.4	10.4	1.5	3.9	1.9	-15.3	-40.1	-11.2	5.5	4.0
Paraguay	0.4	0.3	0.1	-0.3	0.2	-1.6	0.9	0.2	0.3	0.3
Peru	-6.1	-1.9	24.5	9.3	10.4	-5.3	43.7	44.8	45.3	176.1
Uruguay	-171.0	-147.7	88.5	-118.2	262.5	6.8	11.7	-1.8	4.4	-9.9
Venezuela	9.7	0.9	-107.6	93.3	9.5	162.0	83.9	-262.2	-528.0	-156.1

Table 1. Foreign direct investment flows by country (*cont.*)

Million US dollars

	Inward					Outward				
	2014	2015	2016	2017	2018	2014	2015	2016	2017	2018
ASIA	**1 120.1**	**1 931.6**	**290.8**	**-64.4**	**2 128.3**	**4 352.7**	**3 134.4**	**2 450.9**	**3 914.4**	**6 358.9**
Near and Middle East	249.5	307.6	78.8	126.2	86.8	2 955.2	9.4	2 621.3	1 364.0	1 826.8
Gulf Arabian countries	146.5	372.4	37.6	67.3	105.2	2 416.3	-462.9	2 211.8	724.0	1 238.7
Kuwait	-162.6	852.5	-1.3	1.7	-9.3	279.1	-808.5	123.1	828.8	262.4
Qatar	-16.7	-48.4	-26.1	27.6	16.2	-1 198.2	-763.2	107.9	283.6	-118.4
Saudi Arabia	3.1	9.0	6.9	72.3	2.7	1 611.8	552.9	-148.3	-487.8	-359.3
United Arab Emirates	324.1	-420.0	51.7	-33.7	114.8	1 446.2	377.4	1 831.4	309.0	1 154.6
Other Near and Middle East	103.0	-64.8	41.2	58.9	-18.4	538.8	472.3	409.5	639.9	588.1
Jordan	0.5	0.4	0.4	-0.3	1.0	192.4	129.7	44.5	74.1	-132.8
Other Asian countries	870.6	1 624.0	212.0	-190.6	2 041.4	1 397.6	3 125.0	-170.4	2 550.4	4 532.0
China	65.2	59.8	-124.6	-400.7	1 303.4	-275.0	538.5	357.3	686.4	1 861.2
Hong Kong, China	-87.3	296.0	57.4	-239.2	-31.5	237.4	113.0	-1 523.1	86.9	-56.3
India	-85.8	115.8	-47.7	20.2	15.4	1 301.0	1 151.2	-18.3	291.5	189.2
Indonesia	4.7	-2.2	1.1	-1.2	1.0	-226.1	16.5	57.7	537.5	71.5
Iran, Islamic Republic of	4.4	-0.3	34.9	1.0	2.6	28.4	252.0	-123.9	-43.6	-177.9
Malaysia	17.4	-14.8	6.4	16.9	-1.1	237.5	244.7	223.7	722.9	436.9
Philippines	2.3	1.9	-0.1	0.7	2.3	16.8	6.5	3.2	9.3	473.2
Singapore	-278.4	-1.5	-10.7	118.6	-119.3	232.1	225.5	103.1	101.4	366.1
Chinese Taipei	-7.1	122.3	-79.6	-55.0	82.6	11.6	21.0	-13.7	4.1	0.5
Thailand	34.5	41.2	11.3	-5.1	6.7	-93.5	-39.7	-42.4	59.4	171.8
Viet Nam	-2.2	0.1	-0.6	-1.6	-3.2	147.3	105.4	93.8	132.3	256.6
AUSTRALIA, OCEANIA AND POLAR REGIONS	**88.4**	**18.5**	**67.1**	**32.3**	**86.8**	**-15.9**	**140.7**	**40.5**	**355.5**	**216.2**
WORLD unallocated and confidential	**180.2**	**390.5**	**68.2**	**216.7**	**-46.3**	**-4 327.1**	**-40.0**	**-8.9**	**2.0**	**0.1**
European Union (EU28)	**19 597.0**	**15 397.6**	**25 752.7**	**20 056.6**	**29 135.6**	**16 925.1**	**6 466.1**	**3 976.9**	**3 068.7**	**15 995.9**
G20 countries excl. European Union	**16 613.0**	**13 404.4**	**31 785.9**	**3 401.9**	**43 619.0**	**15 155.8**	**9 092.1**	**9 875.9**	**4 862.7**	**14 295.8**
G20 OECD countries	**16 434.5**	**12 897.8**	**32 024.7**	**3 143.6**	**42 153.7**	**9 691.6**	**4 683.9**	**6 336.5**	**2 120.0**	**10 823.0**
G20 Non-OECD countries	**178.5**	**506.6**	**-238.8**	**258.3**	**1 465.3**	**5 464.2**	**4 408.2**	**3 539.4**	**2 742.7**	**3 472.7**
MENA countries	**415.1**	**364.2**	**139.2**	**97.2**	**129.7**	**6 647.4**	**3 438.2**	**3 556.1**	**2 886.7**	**2 957.0**
ASEAN countries	**-230.1**	**38.5**	**66.0**	**141.8**	**-107.6**	**307.7**	**585.9**	**443.6**	**1 563.3**	**1 788.7**

\- Nil

Note: Detailed metadata at: *http://stats.oecd.org/OECDStat_Metadata/ShowMetadata.ashx?Dataset=FDI_CTRY_IND_SUMM.*

1. Information on data for Israel: *http://oe.cd/israel-disclaimer.*
2. Note by Turkey: The information in this document with reference to "Cyprus" relates to the southern part of the Island. There is no single authority representing both Turkish and Greek Cypriot people on the Island. Turkey recognises the Turkish Republic of Northern Cyprus (TRNC). Until a lasting and equitable solution is found within the context of the United Nations, Turkey shall preserve its position concerning the "Cyprus issue".
3. Note by all the European Union Member States of the OECD and the European Union: The Republic of Cyprus is recognised by all members of the United Nations with the exception of Turkey. The information in this document relates to the area under the effective control of the Government of the Republic of Cyprus.

Source: OECD International Direct Investment Statistics (database): https://doi.org/10.1787/idi-data-en

Table 2. Foreign direct investment positions by country

At year end

Million US dollars

	Inward					Outward				
	2014	2015	2016	2017	2018	2014	2015	2016	2017	2018
WORLD	**352 501.4**	**340 477.1**	**352 626.2**	**424 743.1**	**426 410.8**	**477 481.9**	**456 619.5**	**456 380.4**	**547 577.5**	**554 279.6**
OECD COUNTRIES	**258 808.0**	**258 838.7**	**282 861.8**	**336 621.5**	**312 775.6**	**377 510.8**	**354 248.8**	**338 716.9**	**405 727.5**	**407 840.7**
Australia	463.2	218.1	587.2	3.9	7.0	2 193.6	2 141.9	2 246.0	2 844.8	2 688.3
Austria	5 054.2	4 737.4	3 960.9	4 163.6	4 104.3	30 358.8	27 311.3	18 268.5	20 986.6	20 092.4
Belgium	4 518.4	2 668.5	4 047.3	3 656.4	1 810.9	13 334.5	13 202.1	14 468.4	10 672.5	8 013.9
Canada	708.6	777.0	1 040.3	1 605.3	1 903.5	1 846.0	1 743.7	2 068.5	2 723.9	3 259.7
Chile	355.5	283.3	266.1	0.2	-115.9	1 993.6	1 956.4	1 794.0	13 467.1	11 124.1
Czech Republic	196.0	219.6	585.9	775.5	158.9	914.9	879.3	3 696.9	4 361.7	4 119.2
Denmark	3 188.6	3 142.6	2 661.3	2 560.0	2 219.3	1 529.6	1 711.0	1 971.0	2 104.7	2 179.7
Estonia	58.0	82.1	59.1	-	-	34.6	35.8	32.2	56.5	88.8
Finland	1 171.4	184.2	247.1	560.4	304.7	2 060.4	1 959.2	1 862.4	1 820.6	1 793.2
France	61 243.9	51 578.5	58 481.4	63 308.5	49 785.9	26 848.2	25 724.3	26 415.8	32 418.1	35 056.0
Germany	26 206.8	22 366.9	33 032.3	39 738.7	35 315.7	40 228.4	38 260.1	37 048.3	42 944.3	44 132.3
Greece	-	-	-	0.0	-	2 916.7	2 840.9	2 957.5	3 739.8	3 887.4
Hungary	28.3	10.9	111.7	151.3	284.8	920.0	1 407.0	2 572.0	1 593.8	2 870.6
Iceland	-	-	-	-	-	-25.7	44.1	33.8	-31.4	3.6
Ireland	842.1	683.5	1 387.5	3 557.0	2 203.6	10 859.4	13 181.9	9 351.2	9 745.4	8 893.8
Israel[1]	46.8	103.7	156.5	252.5	273.5	786.6	859.9	1 602.2	2 279.4	1 792.7
Italy	23 526.6	32 732.4	33 128.2	32 382.3	31 135.1	-	-	-	-	-
Japan	7 008.4	7 104.1	4 646.9	11 113.6	8 825.0	1 690.3	1 245.3	1 507.7	1 859.9	2 017.8
Korea	820.2	545.6	596.3	1 225.2	1 572.1	1 243.3	1 088.1	1 183.0	1 444.7	1 716.9
Latvia	-	-	-	-	-	21.2	24.8	76.6	96.0	94.4
Lithuania	-	-	-	0.0	-	15.5	25.4	33.8	38.9	45.8
Luxembourg	29 533.5	19 495.6	25 704.5	25 893.6	25 820.5	19 544.4	20 494.5	25 480.2	46 329.0	44 903.3
Mexico	-	-	177.6	176.9	54.2	1 468.3	1 441.3	1 784.7	2 183.3	2 522.1
Netherlands	20 568.5	16 483.1	19 368.6	17 535.7	12 588.6	81 870.5	66 185.9	59 628.1	64 437.8	64 348.3
New Zealand	-	-	-	782.4	302.1	36.1	33.5	44.4	64.1	53.2
Norway	-52.0	-599.4	532.0	616.8	532.3	798.5	819.1	978.0	1 224.8	1 445.3
Poland	137.0	120.1	101.0	-10.4	127.4	12 904.6	11 342.7	9 623.9	8 313.8	8 058.1
Portugal	178.7	323.5	307.0	330.0	412.7	1 943.1	1 733.1	2 098.3	2 526.4	2 903.3
Slovak Republic	-	-	-	0.0	-	4 231.9	3 659.5	646.6	1 586.8	1 418.3
Slovenia	-	-	51.8	0.7	1.1	1 183.1	1 139.5	1 303.8	1 268.3	1 458.0
Spain	7 002.8	6 271.4	4 967.1	5 289.2	3 876.7	41 880.8	37 973.9	33 982.5	35 783.5	40 184.5
Sweden	1 806.0	2 206.8	1 004.1	2 988.7	2 613.9	1 312.2	1 783.7	1 603.1	1 796.3	1 758.7
Switzerland	21 350.9	19 707.5	18 533.4	25 084.4	32 557.9	10 700.6	10 917.4	9 941.7	11 709.6	9 881.8
Turkey	305.6	288.3	-	1.3	13.3	5 365.8	5 341.1	8 283.1	8 527.9	7 769.5
United Kingdom	4 975.1	32 016.8	32 979.6	46 767.8	44 297.5	25 234.3	24 295.9	19 503.1	26 403.5	24 851.2
United States	37 564.7	35 086.6	34 139.1	46 109.7	49 789.0	29 303.2	31 495.4	34 659.3	38 444.0	42 414.2
EUROPE	**216 918.4**	**219 094.8**	**243 847.4**	**279 230.2**	**254 520.8**	**361 938.9**	**337 118.6**	**323 587.4**	**376 763.5**	**376 628.4**
Bulgaria	69.8	64.7	-	0.0	-	803.3	1 094.4	2 261.3	2 926.0	2 446.3
Croatia	0.4	0.4	-	-	-	963.2	883.5	3 138.5	3 353.8	3 329.7
Cyprus[2, 3]	289.4	199.2	517.2	344.9	272.9	163.9	141.5	141.5	160.2	149.5
Malta	-	-	-	7.5	152.6	693.9	460.5	530.6	568.7	391.1
Romania	-0.8	-1.0	-1.3	-8.4	66.4	5 206.8	4 833.2	6 556.0	7 288.2	9 513.6
Russian Federation	3 168.3	2 393.3	478.3	2 219.6	1 712.3	8 966.5	9 078.6	11 514.0	13 238.5	12 240.9
Ukraine	823.0	827.2	-	592.1	652.4	793.7	745.9	684.6	586.0	318.9
AFRICA	**243.4**	**212.1**	**157.4**	**964.2**	**452.6**	**18 830.1**	**21 412.1**	**22 576.5**	**27 942.1**	**29 432.6**
Northern Africa	215.9	190.4	151.1	183.5	-	16 172.5	18 602.4	18 780.7	23 400.9	24 167.9
Algeria	-	-	-	-	-	7 246.9	8 389.1	9 016.2	11 176.6	11 529.1
Egypt	-	-	-	-	-	6 822.9	7 760.3	7 380.2	9 155.9	8 971.1
Libya	210.5	185.0	146.2	177.9	-	186.1	310.1	263.6	317.5	332.3
Morocco	5.4	5.4	5.0	5.6	-	465.9	607.2	524.0	677.3	965.6
Tunisia	-	-	-	-	-	1 450.6	1 535.8	1 596.8	2 073.7	2 369.7
Other African countries	27.5	21.6	6.3	780.7	452.6	2 657.6	2 809.6	3 795.8	4 541.2	5 264.7
Nigeria	-	-	-	-	-	469.4	503.6	837.8	1 239.0	1 823.3
South Africa	27.5	21.6	6.3	780.7	452.6	1 094.1	1 335.6	1 634.1	2 014.9	1 999.3
AMERICA	**40 563.3**	**46 168.2**	**45 224.3**	**60 165.5**	**64 994.0**	**47 793.9**	**49 505.5**	**57 647.6**	**77 918.9**	**80 514.3**
Northern America	38 273.3	35 863.6	35 179.4	47 714.9	51 692.5	31 149.2	33 239.0	36 727.9	41 167.8	45 673.9
Central America and Caribbean countries	1 488.9	9 617.6	9 346.0	12 393.1	13 172.4	2 557.7	3 193.0	4 272.9	6 027.4	6 195.8
Bahamas	-	-	-	-	-	4.3	4.4	4.7	5.6	5.6
Bermuda	556.1	586.9	-	83.1	199.0	5.8	6.6	3.0	135.8	122.4
Cayman Islands	-19.5	8 137.9	8 962.0	10 611.6	11 358.5	0.9	3.2	4.0	-20.5	-33.1
Costa Rica	-	-	-	-	-	231.1	231.9	362.9	240.3	377.5
El Salvador	-	-	-	-	-	0.5	0.3	7.8	7.0	6.8
Guatemala	-	-	-	-	-	172.5	195.9	162.5	484.2	488.6
Honduras	-	-	-	-	-	18.2	29.7	15.1	9.1	6.4
Nicaragua	-	-	-	-	-	1.3	0.7	0.6	0.8	0.7
Panama	40.6	11.5	8.7	65.5	21.3	231.8	227.7	414.3	534.6	-16.5
Virgin Islands, U.S.	-	-	-	-	-	0.1	-	-	-	-
South America	801.1	687.0	698.9	57.5	129.1	14 087.0	13 073.5	16 646.8	30 723.6	28 644.6
Argentina	-88.4	-153.0	92.3	49.6	36.5	1 659.5	1 488.2	1 223.5	1 563.5	1 635.8
Bolivia	-	-	-	-	-	34.7	28.9	30.9	29.3	31.6
Brazil	192.2	220.9	337.2	3.0	205.0	7 652.5	6 878.0	10 969.9	13 269.7	13 054.9
Colombia	-	-	-	0.2	-	258.9	283.3	570.1	434.6	443.8
Ecuador	-	-	-	-	-	93.6	63.9	35.9	44.0	49.6
Paraguay	-	-	-	0.1	-	8.0	7.6	8.0	8.9	10.7
Peru	-	-	-	0.2	-	296.7	341.2	374.8	537.9	690.2
Uruguay	341.7	335.8	3.2	4.2	3.6	44.9	52.0	48.5	59.5	53.6
Venezuela	-	-	-	-	-	2 051.6	1 981.8	1 612.9	1 297.5	1 510.6

Table 2. Foreign direct investment positions by country *(cont.)*

At year end

Million US dollars

	Inward					Outward				
	2014	2015	2016	2017	2018	2014	2015	2016	2017	2018
ASIA	**14 727.1**	**11 613.3**	**13 249.1**	**25 274.1**	**23 016.5**	**45 245.0**	**45 855.7**	**50 028.5**	**61 585.3**	**64 523.9**
Near and Middle East	5 721.1	2 646.4	2 427.1	3 465.2	3 048.3	22 365.7	21 383.7	23 986.0	27 916.5	27 942.6
Gulf Arabian countries	5 672.5	2 537.0	2 270.6	2 965.7	2 795.2	19 749.4	18 597.5	20 413.9	23 154.0	23 396.2
Kuwait	4 094.2	1 644.4	455.7	537.8	681.8	2 697.3	1 634.1	1 699.5	2 503.1	2 648.3
Qatar	868.9	539.9	1 373.0	2 136.2	1 576.9	1 336.9	821.9	950.9	1 204.0	1 086.8
Saudi Arabia	501.6	286.1	145.8	238.5	474.6	6 216.6	6 027.6	5 831.4	5 810.2	5 278.3
United Arab Emirates	207.9	66.7	296.1	53.2	61.9	8 456.8	8 955.9	10 421.0	12 093.0	12 622.2
Other Near and Middle East	48.6	109.4	156.5	499.5	253.1	2 616.3	2 786.1	3 572.1	4 762.5	4 546.4
Jordan	-	-	-	-	-	934.1	966.5	981.1	1 191.9	1 008.8
Other Asian countries	9 006.0	8 966.9	10 822.0	21 809.0	19 968.1	22 879.4	24 472.0	26 042.5	33 668.8	36 581.3
China	316.7	623.8	3 556.6	5 791.0	5 455.5	8 575.8	8 592.7	8 480.6	10 858.2	11 808.1
Hong Kong, China	22.4	45.0	692.8	-56.5	13.6	1 601.9	2 398.0	2 842.6	4 067.4	4 334.7
India	317.2	177.2	364.4	909.2	899.9	4 897.0	5 726.2	6 106.2	7 373.6	7 020.1
Indonesia	178.8	-	-	-	-	185.2	173.8	262.9	808.1	838.3
Iran, Islamic Republic of	28.1	25.8	58.0	68.0	-	1 414.6	1 519.2	1 316.6	1 594.3	1 594.5
Malaysia	-17.7	-14.6	57.2	-	-	664.2	824.6	1 059.3	1 987.0	2 306.1
Philippines	-	-	-	-	-	55.3	59.9	64.0	72.4	533.3
Singapore	78.0	204.4	190.7	1 646.6	1 638.7	596.9	558.0	689.1	745.8	977.6
Chinese Taipei	252.6	254.3	334.4	432.3	942.4	56.4	67.9	80.3	69.2	70.6
Thailand	1.3	1.3	1.3	33.5	-	426.3	360.9	317.0	346.8	420.8
Viet Nam	-	-	-	0.0	-	361.4	451.8	553.6	749.0	771.0
AUSTRALIA, OCEANIA AND POLAR REGIONS	**463.2**	**218.1**	**587.2**	**786.3**	**309.0**	**2 232.9**	**2 190.9**	**2 266.1**	**3 056.0**	**2 883.4**
WORLD unallocated and confidential	**79 585.9**	**63 170.7**	**49 560.8**	**58 322.7**	**83 117.8**	**1 441.1**	**536.6**	**274.3**	**311.6**	**297.1**
European Union (EU28)	**190 594.9**	**195 587.2**	**222 702.3**	**249 993.2**	**217 553.5**	**327 978.3**	**302 584.8**	**285 252.1**	**333 321.1**	**336 981.4**
G20 countries excl. European Union	**167 437.2**	**186 284.2**	**203 789.7**	**252 424.9**	**231 934.6**	**174 668.6**	**172 077.7**	**180 722.1**	**214 731.2**	**220 303.9**
G20 OECD countries	**162 823.2**	**182 714.3**	**198 808.7**	**242 433.2**	**222 698.2**	**135 421.5**	**132 777.1**	**134 699.6**	**159 794.5**	**166 428.2**
G20 Non-OECD countries	**4 614.0**	**3 569.9**	**4 981.0**	**9 991.7**	**9 236.4**	**39 247.2**	**39 300.7**	**46 022.5**	**54 936.7**	**53 875.8**
MENA countries	**5 890.2**	**2 733.2**	**2 421.8**	**3 396.1**	**2 774.8**	**37 385.9**	**38 643.4**	**40 662.5**	**48 263.8**	**48 983.9**
ASEAN countries	**240.4**	**191.1**	**440.1**	**2 173.7**	**2 135.6**	**2 415.9**	**2 569.1**	**3 085.9**	**4 868.9**	**6 011.9**

- Nil

Note: Inward FDI positions are allocated according to the ultimate investing country. Detailed metadata at: *http://stats.oecd.org/OECDStat_Metadata/ShowMetadata.ashx?Dataset=FDI_CTRY_IND_SUMM.*

1. Information on data for Israel: *http://oe.cd/israel-disclaimer.*
2. Note by Turkey: The information in this document with reference to "Cyprus" relates to the southern part of the Island. There is no single authority representing both Turkish and Greek Cypriot people on the Island. Turkey recognises the Turkish Republic of Northern Cyprus (TRNC). Until a lasting and equitable solution is found within the context of the United Nations, Turkey shall preserve its position concerning the "Cyprus issue".
3. Note by all the European Union Member States of the OECD and the European Union: The Republic of Cyprus is recognised by all members of the United Nations with the exception of Turkey. The information in this document relates to the area under the effective control of the Government of the Republic of Cyprus.

Source: OECD International Direct Investment Statistics (database): https://doi.org/10.1787/idi-data-en

Table 3. Foreign direct investment income by country

Million US dollars

	Inward					Outward				
	2014	2015	2016	2017	2018	2014	2015	2016	2017	2018
WORLD	**11 199.1**	**11 685.3**	**14 146.7**	**19 620.5**	**20 315.2**	**26 374.4**	**12 048.9**	**17 894.9**	**24 781.8**	**29 870.1**
OECD COUNTRIES	**11 413.8**	**11 788.9**	**14 015.2**	**19 607.3**	**20 289.3**	**21 575.7**	**10 457.2**	**15 165.6**	**20 785.8**	**25 188.3**
Australia	16.3	9.7	9.7	18.7	36.2	237.5	26.5	80.6	155.6	108.1
Austria	189.6	-26.1	281.6	213.3	162.9	1 033.1	741.6	874.8	926.8	931.9
Belgium	728.9	574.4	66.4	728.2	112.1	343.5	192.5	298.5	437.3	388.0
Canada	-10.8	-12.4	4.6	23.5	42.4	137.8	60.8	150.6	125.4	173.1
Chile	7.9	6.4	5.6	6.1	-0.1	202.1	5.9	12.9	524.9	734.1
Czech Republic	26.7	32.0	28.4	49.6	47.2	122.6	113.3	770.7	381.2	329.0
Denmark	242.7	279.7	237.1	274.0	51.7	20.9	-3.3	-11.6	9.2	15.3
Estonia	-1.6	-0.9	-30.6	-2.3	-1.8	1.4	0.9	1.3	0.9	1.6
Finland	8.1	5.3	11.6	-1.8	-0.4	147.5	121.4	170.8	170.4	73.2
France	3 194.5	3 357.0	2 873.2	3 337.7	4 347.8	694.0	309.1	1 606.3	1 294.6	1 625.3
Germany	1 155.2	1 897.7	1 773.7	2 181.4	1 425.0	2 142.1	2 045.9	1 826.5	2 047.3	2 565.9
Greece	5.0	6.1	6.5	9.3	13.5	60.5	90.3	67.0	91.8	78.6
Hungary	-88.9	-118.6	30.0	-32.4	11.5	105.3	76.6	85.6	83.6	131.5
Iceland	-	-	-1.1	-0.7	-	-1.1	-2.4	-41.8	1.3	0.3
Ireland	79.1	12.9	6.9	87.6	62.3	1 451.4	1 656.0	1 245.0	1 482.7	1 645.5
Israel[1]	19.2	-0.7	-0.5	1.8	4.2	6.6	42.2	130.5	98.8	211.6
Italy	-	-	-	-	-	-	-	-	-	-
Japan	224.1	170.1	248.4	356.9	224.7	102.1	-8.5	47.7	66.1	60.1
Korea	61.1	71.9	86.3	149.8	97.1	29.7	-0.4	13.6	26.0	8.6
Latvia	-0.2	-0.2	-0.1	0.0	0.1	-0.3	-0.1	0.4	3.3	4.2
Lithuania	-0.1	0.0	0.0	0.0	-0.1	0.6	0.0	1.5	1.4	1.7
Luxembourg	1 855.7	1 250.4	1 273.0	3 378.2	3 221.1	2 090.0	2 436.2	1 625.9	1 308.1	1 708.8
Mexico	-12.8	-7.3	-2.6	-0.5	-3.0	185.8	68.5	108.6	26.1	-38.2
Netherlands	3 639.4	2 538.2	4 379.8	4 197.2	6 244.2	6 072.4	-2 109.1	1 874.7	4 085.7	7 844.5
New Zealand	0.1	0.1	0.2	0.1	0.0	3.8	4.4	10.5	8.9	4.7
Norway	-16.9	-5.6	-15.9	-61.8	11.4	121.1	74.5	-13.7	44.1	18.5
Poland	0.7	0.4	1.1	0.7	-2.0	1 199.2	995.5	1 134.0	795.3	589.7
Portugal	-84.9	25.8	56.6	13.6	65.3	58.4	93.7	-11.0	113.7	128.0
Slovak Republic	5.5	2.6	0.9	0.5	-0.1	176.3	99.3	95.0	117.7	174.3
Slovenia	0.0	39.2	50.8	0.1	1.0	88.3	76.6	94.3	116.3	141.1
Spain	367.0	715.4	425.1	827.1	379.8	711.2	1 423.4	1 093.8	2 679.2	2 889.3
Sweden	121.8	209.9	188.1	144.5	292.8	125.5	203.1	120.5	64.7	107.2
Switzerland	336.1	709.8	615.9	1 619.3	1 033.9	190.0	135.5	290.0	235.1	612.6
Turkey	-12.2	3.7	5.5	-2.3	-2.5	673.9	342.1	471.5	667.7	494.5
United Kingdom	-700.1	-181.3	1 007.8	1 545.7	2 100.7	1 448.1	394.2	1 120.2	1 677.0	694.7
United States	57.0	223.2	391.3	543.9	310.4	1 594.9	750.7	-178.2	918.9	731.0
EUROPE	**11 077.4**	**11 448.6**	**13 385.7**	**18 490.0**	**19 769.0**	**20 109.5**	**10 370.5**	**16 041.7**	**20 709.4**	**25 133.5**
Bulgaria	0.7	1.0	10.3	0.3	0.6	265.9	224.0	225.2	237.0	247.2
Croatia	-0.6	-0.5	-0.5	-0.1	0.6	33.7	20.8	92.9	236.9	243.0
Cyprus[2, 3]	3.3	-18.7	-1.0	3.3	5.2	-5.3	-1.3	-0.8	-0.6	0.5
Malta	-36.8	18.1	28.3	-8.1	10.4	37.4	-49.1	-10.4	-25.9	-40.0
Romania	-0.7	-1.1	-1.9	2.5	14.9	211.1	175.9	270.5	420.2	356.8
Russian Federation	104.3	47.1	7.6	-12.3	129.5	173.9	208.0	475.6	811.4	936.8
Ukraine	-0.7	-0.5	0.1	-0.2	-0.1	4.8	-14.3	11.8	-8.4	1.0
AFRICA	**-8.5**	**-14.5**	**-14.7**	**-4.2**	**-31.4**	**1 088.7**	**504.0**	**495.5**	**736.8**	**898.1**
Northern Africa	16.4	-9.7	-3.6	0.6	-30.1	401.9	145.3	236.4	324.3	328.1
Algeria	-1.1	-0.6	-0.6	-0.1	-0.8	166.9	-75.3	36.2	95.9	39.0
Egypt	14.8	-9.6	-0.4	0.4	0.1	242.3	195.1	119.6	104.0	93.6
Libya	3.0	0.4	-1.8	0.8	-15.6	-86.0	-2.7	-0.3	-2.6	81.0
Morocco	-0.3	0.1	-0.7	-0.5	-0.4	33.1	5.7	42.8	73.6	50.6
Tunisia	0.0	0.0	-0.2	-0.1	-13.4	45.6	22.5	38.2	53.3	63.9
Other African countries	-24.9	-4.8	-11.1	-4.8	-1.4	686.8	358.7	259.1	412.6	570.0
Nigeria	-0.7	-0.9	-0.5	0.0	1.0	80.2	19.7	-37.1	33.4	22.4
South Africa	-9.4	-5.0	-6.7	-3.2	-2.9	218.4	118.9	70.0	67.2	21.8
AMERICA	**52.3**	**218.5**	**383.9**	**564.2**	**210.3**	**2 642.7**	**54.8**	**-690.1**	**1 063.7**	**1 575.4**
Northern America	46.2	210.7	395.9	567.3	352.7	1 732.7	811.5	-27.6	1 044.3	904.1
Central America and Caribbean countries	-7.5	-0.4	-26.7	-25.5	-45.2	134.2	-42.8	64.3	111.0	29.6
Bahamas	0.0	0.0	-	-	-	1.1	-	-	-	-
Bermuda	0.1	0.4	-23.2	0.1	-0.3	0.3	-0.2	-23.4	0.9	8.1
Cayman Islands	-0.4	-0.6	5.5	-22.3	-32.4	-	-	-	-	-0.7
Costa Rica	-	-0.1	0.0	0.0	-	2.3	5.6	18.8	1.1	2.0
El Salvador	-	-	-	-	-	0.0	0.0	0.0	0.0	0.0
Guatemala	-	-0.9	-	-	-	14.9	11.2	31.9	18.6	23.7
Honduras	-	-	-	-	-	1.8	1.6	1.0	0.1	-5.8
Nicaragua	-	-	-	-	-	0.0	0.0	0.0	-	0.0
Panama	1.6	2.0	0.2	0.0	0.0	-139.6	-135.1	-96.4	33.4	29.1
Virgin Islands, U.S.	-	-	-	-	-	0.0	0.0	-	-	-
South America	13.6	8.1	14.7	22.3	-97.2	775.8	-713.9	-726.8	-91.6	641.7
Argentina	-1.7	-1.8	-2.8	-2.6	-2.5	219.0	143.5	179.1	119.7	94.1
Bolivia	0.0	0.0	0.0	-0.1	0.0	0.7	9.2	3.4	0.1	0.0
Brazil	16.5	9.2	20.3	28.5	-84.9	273.9	-731.6	-714.0	-330.5	-2.9
Colombia	-0.6	-0.4	-0.4	-0.1	0.0	-46.6	-10.4	60.3	-8.8	-19.3
Ecuador	0.0	-0.2	0.0	0.0	0.0	4.9	0.9	5.2	0.1	1.5
Paraguay	-	-	-	0.0	0.0	-1.6	-1.8	-0.5	0.3	-0.2
Peru	-0.4	-0.4	-0.5	0.0	0.1	5.1	3.4	-7.9	-1.2	33.5
Uruguay	-7.9	-4.3	-7.3	-5.4	-9.6	0.5	0.0	-1.3	-3.3	-10.1
Venezuela	-0.2	-0.3	-0.1	-4.1	-0.4	116.6	-134.6	-263.6	-392.0	-188.9

Table 3. Foreign direct investment income by country *(cont.)*

Million US dollars

	Inward					Outward				
	2014	2015	2016	2017	2018	2014	2015	2016	2017	2018
ASIA	**61.9**	**24.2**	**383.5**	**553.0**	**330.9**	**2 282.1**	**1 088.6**	**1 956.7**	**2 108.4**	**2 149.4**
Near and Middle East	-20.8	-215.9	10.6	7.6	11.2	330.6	200.7	318.7	487.2	323.1
Gulf Arabian countries	-40.0	-215.3	11.1	5.9	7.1	317.1	152.6	187.1	397.9	47.5
Kuwait	-32.1	-19.3	0.0	0.0	1.6	38.6	0.4	0.1	294.4	1.9
Qatar	5.9	7.4	7.0	6.8	8.0	82.7	20.9	12.0	-19.4	-46.6
Saudi Arabia	-0.2	-0.3	-0.2	-0.2	0.0	129.6	84.2	137.9	53.4	31.4
United Arab Emirates	-14.5	-203.4	4.4	-0.7	-2.5	55.6	46.7	37.5	41.6	60.7
Other Near and Middle East	19.1	-0.6	-0.5	1.8	4.1	13.5	48.1	131.6	89.3	275.7
Jordan	-	-	-	-	0.0	-0.1	2.1	-0.2	-1.1	31.4
Other Asian countries	82.8	240.1	372.9	545.3	319.7	1 951.5	888.0	1 638.0	1 621.1	1 826.3
China	-14.1	-1.6	2.7	-20.8	-12.3	689.8	463.3	809.5	1 010.9	956.7
Hong Kong, China	-167.0	-4.6	8.5	10.5	6.9	151.2	-0.9	154.0	135.5	250.6
India	-4.1	-5.4	-1.9	-2.9	-2.8	707.9	122.2	221.5	209.2	237.6
Indonesia	-0.1	0.1	-0.1	0.0	-0.1	37.4	3.1	27.8	11.4	10.3
Iran, Islamic Republic of	-0.2	0.1	0.4	0.3	1.6	9.8	1.4	12.3	-93.5	-87.3
Malaysia	-0.2	-0.3	-0.5	-0.6	-0.1	64.0	58.7	84.2	42.5	7.9
Philippines	0.0	0.0	0.0	-0.1	-0.1	-1.1	1.4	0.3	2.4	2.4
Singapore	-13.1	11.4	12.2	45.5	1.1	73.0	42.4	72.2	26.9	49.1
Chinese Taipei	-0.1	-0.2	2.0	1.3	-0.8	6.4	3.7	3.5	-0.8	1.4
Thailand	-2.7	-0.7	0.4	0.1	-0.2	6.5	15.7	23.6	76.6	54.3
Viet Nam	0.0	-0.1	-0.1	-0.1	-0.2	23.1	95.2	121.1	53.1	83.7
AUSTRALIA, OCEANIA AND POLAR REGIONS	**16.4**	**9.9**	**9.8**	**18.9**	**36.3**	**247.1**	**31.0**	**91.1**	**163.5**	**112.8**
WORLD unallocated and confidential	**-0.4**	**-1.2**	**-1.6**	**-1.3**	**0.0**	**4.4**	**0.1**	**0.1**	**0.1**	**0.9**
European Union (EU28)	**10 710.3**	**10 618.6**	**12 703.0**	**16 950.4**	**18 566.2**	**18 634.8**	**9 327.4**	**14 661.6**	**18 756.0**	**22 876.8**
G20 countries excl. European Union	**4 063.5**	**5 574.5**	**6 416.8**	**8 141.3**	**8 602.9**	**9 695.5**	**4 400.5**	**6 454.8**	**8 957.4**	**8 708.8**
G20 OECD countries	**3 972.4**	**5 532.3**	**6 397.8**	**8 154.8**	**8 578.8**	**7 245.7**	**3 988.9**	**5 247.4**	**7 004.6**	**6 423.0**
G20 Non-OECD countries	**91.1**	**42.1**	**19.0**	**-13.6**	**24.0**	**2 449.8**	**411.5**	**1 207.4**	**1 952.8**	**2 285.8**
MENA countries	**-23.6**	**-225.0**	**7.5**	**6.4**	**-23.0**	**720.1**	**304.6**	**425.1**	**722.2**	**421.6**
ASEAN countries	**-16.2**	**10.1**	**12.0**	**46.5**	**2.6**	**209.7**	**215.5**	**329.3**	**213.0**	**207.8**

- Nil

Note: Detailed metadata at: *http://stats.oecd.org/OECDStat_Metadata/ShowMetadata.ashx?Dataset=FDI_CTRY_IND_SUMM.*

1. Information on data for Israel: *http://oe.cd/israel-disclaimer.*
2. Note by Turkey: The information in this document with reference to "Cyprus" relates to the southern part of the Island. There is no single authority representing both Turkish and Greek Cypriot people on the Island. Turkey recognises the Turkish Republic of Northern Cyprus (TRNC). Until a lasting and equitable solution is found within the context of the United Nations, Turkey shall preserve its position concerning the "Cyprus issue".
3. Note by all the European Union Member States of the OECD and the European Union: The Republic of Cyprus is recognised by all members of the United Nations with the exception of Turkey. The information in this document relates to the area under the effective control of the Government of the Republic of Cyprus.

Source: OECD International Direct Investment Statistics (database): https://doi.org/10.1787/idi-data-en

Table 4. Foreign direct investment flows by industrial sector

Million US dollars

	Inward					Outward				
	2014	2015	2016	2017	2018	2014	2015	2016	2017	2018
All FDI activities	**23 224.2**	**19 630.8**	**28 440.8**	**23 995.9**	**32 865.7**	**26 327.2**	**21 639.9**	**16 164.8**	**24 478.4**	**32 673.2**
Agriculture, forestry and fishing	**-399.5**	**-334.4**	**448.3**	**408.0**	**67.9**	**35.6**	**3.5**	**50.6**	**-73.7**	**59.8**
Mining and quarrying	**-103.9**	**459.4**	**-372.5**	**2 196.2**	**-148.2**	**2 122.3**	**-3 491.1**	**-3 407.4**	**2 068.5**	**-240.2**
Extraction activities	-125.2	472.5	-372.5	2 198.1	-148.2	2 106.6	-3 712.2	-3 380.1	2 068.1	-238.4
Manufacturing	**7 525.3**	**1 606.9**	**5 184.9**	**9 130.0**	**8 480.8**	**9 011.7**	**12 894.0**	**10 408.6**	**7 250.6**	**12 290.5**
of which:										
Food products, beverages and tobacco	457.6	183.7	1 721.0	-76.2	-315.4	997.6	1 109.6	339.8	831.6	524.1
Textiles, wood and paper products; printing	-75.3	1 811.0	-1 313.9	346.6	-469.3	48.0	942.2	-993.1	298.2	425.6
Chemical, rubber, plastic, non-metallic mineral products	3 427.0	1 368.8	305.6	3 882.9	-167.8	1 551.3	273.6	631.4	1 092.6	3 620.7
Metal and machinery products, except electrical equipment	4 119.4	-163.1	277.6	2 351.7	5 906.0	2 245.5	8 661.7	4 827.0	5 549.7	4 889.0
Motor vehicles, trailers, semi-trailers, other transport equipment	135.0	-2 208.7	-1 448.8	179.1	2 767.5	2 714.2	397.6	4 811.2	-200.2	738.4
Other manufacturing	-538.3	615.2	5 643.4	2 445.8	759.8	1 455.0	1 509.3	792.4	-321.3	2 092.7
Electricity, gas, steam and air conditioning supply	**3 351.8**	**599.0**	**-983.3**	**-45.7**	**886.8**	**-234.9**	**206.9**	**-3 158.1**	**1 551.2**	**3 104.9**
Water supply; sewerage, waste management and remediation activities	**350.6**	**-707.5**	**-120.8**	**-20.8**	**-36.5**	**-5.6**	**9.7**	**-3.3**	**29.5**	**-30.6**
Construction	**-46.1**	**-327.2**	**-847.8**	**137.9**	**111.4**	**5 766.3**	**582.7**	**2 636.5**	**3 765.0**	**8 623.1**
Services	**10 334.5**	**16 485.8**	**23 288.9**	**10 311.5**	**21 536.3**	**8 468.1**	**11 143.2**	**10 257.5**	**10 110.3**	**9 006.9**
Wholesale and retail trade; repair of motor vehicles and motorcycles	2 873.8	1 339.3	3 673.6	3 717.7	-1 435.3	-741.0	-1 231.2	2 075.6	110.4	3 835.6
Transportation and storage	-142.5	1 190.6	225.0	-769.7	1 304.8	585.2	248.9	-293.0	807.3	-790.6
Accommodation and food service activities	-1.1	-66.1	657.5	-330.8	179.8	135.7	8.2	-30.7	-356.4	183.3
Information and communication	541.6	10 835.8	509.6	182.4	-7.0	533.2	-314.9	-849.3	393.9	2 619.2
Financial and insurance activities	5 240.6	7 734.5	9 882.5	4 731.8	182.2	6 506.1	11 478.5	9 897.5	6 914.3	-3 838.5
Activities of holding companies	1 706.9	85.3	-4 279.2	284.0	1 249.9	-3 392.8	-3 348.5	3 014.9	325.5	-128.9
Real estate activities	2 781.2	-2 424.5	945.1	1 126.0	-391.7	-589.5	631.1	-241.0	254.0	383.7
Professional, scientific and technical activities	109.8	-3 489.4	5 933.2	228.4	18 734.6	1 648.1	-153.4	1 815.2	1 100.2	2 679.2
Administrative and support service activities	-992.6	1 752.7	1 255.2	680.7	3 142.4	1 242.9	339.8	-1 946.1	872.3	912.1
Public administration; activities of households and of extraterritorial organisations	-	-	-	-	138.8	-347.6	74.3	57.4	-19.8	2 929.4
Education	-82.3	0.0	-0.1	-	-	-5.4	0.8	-2.2	-1.9	-7.3
Human health and social work activities	-56.1	-11.5	19.4	18.1	30.0	38.3	17.0	-39.4	-25.9	-72.0
Arts, entertainment and recreation	-6.2	-594.3	-118.0	686.4	-471.6	-536.0	32.5	-187.6	55.2	172.7
Other services	68.1	218.7	305.9	40.5	129.5	-2.1	11.5	1.3	6.7	0.1
Not allocated and confidential	**0.0**	**0.0**	**0.0**	**0.0**	**0.0**	**0.0**	**0.0**	**0.0**	**0.0**	**0.0**
Private real estate activities	**2 211.4**	**1 848.8**	**1 843.1**	**1 878.8**	**1 967.1**	**1 163.7**	**291.0**	**-619.7**	**-222.9**	**-141.1**

- Nil

Note: Detailed metadata at: *http://stats.oecd.org/OECDStat_Metadata/ShowMetadata.ashx?Dataset=FDI_CTRY_IND_SUMM.*

Source: OECD International Direct Investment Statistics (database): https://doi.org/10.1787/idi-data-en

Table 5. Foreign direct investment positions by industrial sector
At year end

Million US dollars

	Inward					Outward				
	2014	2015	2016	2017	2018	2014	2015	2016	2017	2018
All FDI activities	**352 501.4**	**340 477.1**	**352 626.2**	**424 743.1**	**426 410.8**	**477 481.9**	**456 619.5**	**456 380.4**	**547 577.5**	**554 279.6**
Agriculture, forestry and fishing	**1 888.6**	**1 209.5**	**1 254.4**	**2 164.8**	**1 746.3**	**490.7**	**655.0**	**541.8**	**531.2**	**704.5**
Mining and quarrying	**3 047.0**	**3 288.1**	**2 771.2**	**3 138.5**	**3 505.6**	**1 556.4**	**-1 758.6**	**-3 435.0**	**3 665.2**	**5 904.0**
Extraction activities	2 873.9	3 277.0	2 771.2	3 138.5	3 505.6	1 117.7	-2 283.1	-3 599.5	3 635.6	2 671.0
Manufacturing	**85 684.8**	**83 141.0**	**92 095.8**	**118 455.3**	**111 127.2**	**115 492.6**	**118 515.6**	**125 553.4**	**154 183.5**	**156 495.2**
of which:										
Food products, beverages and tobacco	16 360.3	16 657.9	17 642.0	19 755.0	16 024.1	8 291.8	8 694.4	9 274.3	11 370.0	9 808.3
Textiles, wood and paper products; printing	1 524.4	5 754.8	2 337.0	3 644.6	2 950.7	4 972.7	5 423.8	4 137.6	4 694.3	5 000.9
Chemical, rubber, plastic, non-metallic mineral products	26 258.4	23 660.3	23 144.1	30 069.6	25 092.1	16 913.1	15 846.0	18 255.5	20 485.5	23 081.3
Metal and machinery products, except electrical equipment	20 788.9	20 160.8	21 661.9	31 012.2	32 625.6	59 480.6	62 864.3	64 057.4	77 722.6	79 598.4
Motor vehicles, trailers, semi-trailers, other transport equipment	13 261.4	9 423.0	14 758.4	18 019.1	18 861.9	12 098.1	10 925.7	14 893.1	18 215.5	16 197.3
Other manufacturing	7 491.4	7 484.4	12 552.4	15 954.8	15 572.8	13 736.3	14 761.5	14 935.4	21 695.6	22 809.1
Electricity, gas, steam and air conditioning supply	**5 650.2**	**4 467.9**	**4 444.9**	**6 160.7**	**4 347.7**	**6 076.5**	**5 457.5**	**6 638.7**	**5 790.1**	**7 121.4**
Water supply; sewerage, waste management and remediation activities	**1 327.2**	**517.5**	**413.7**	**453.4**	**456.3**	**149.9**	**144.9**	**157.9**	**83.3**	**65.5**
Construction	**4 913.2**	**4 111.8**	**3 272.6**	**4 790.3**	**4 249.7**	**34 994.2**	**32 353.9**	**36 078.0**	**43 940.9**	**50 405.1**
Services	**225 409.6**	**220 137.2**	**223 761.4**	**259 574.3**	**270 421.1**	**295 243.7**	**279 211.8**	**269 361.2**	**314 669.1**	**309 688.0**
Wholesale and retail trade; repair of motor vehicles and motorcycles	29 331.1	29 318.0	34 988.9	42 779.8	47 171.1	33 097.4	30 140.9	33 006.2	33 939.0	38 971.0
Transportation and storage	11 081.0	11 577.1	11 172.3	13 318.6	12 690.4	5 128.5	5 098.4	4 930.8	6 610.3	6 656.9
Accommodation and food service activities	2 014.2	1 912.5	2 493.1	2 341.2	3 623.7	1 950.0	1 651.2	1 432.5	1 374.3	2 201.4
Information and communication	16 530.6	27 928.7	25 519.3	27 943.1	27 769.8	7 072.2	6 081.8	6 088.7	5 607.9	5 334.2
Financial and insurance activities	51 887.4	56 116.2	40 681.7	45 975.5	40 574.1	218 507.1	209 645.6	203 772.1	240 929.7	226 567.5
Activities of holding companies	27 742.2	24 550.1	4 226.3	3 883.0	4 768.2	137 697.3	128 167.8	125 687.5	125 777.7	122 938.1
Real estate activities	14 976.3	12 033.5	17 142.5	22 241.1	21 777.7	2 677.4	3 536.3	3 653.9	5 273.9	5 586.6
Professional, scientific and technical activities	86 986.6	70 970.6	77 692.3	87 400.4	97 587.8	20 655.3	20 050.6	14 409.8	17 420.2	17 736.5
Administrative and support service activities	10 014.4	9 244.0	12 224.2	14 409.7	15 475.4	1 328.3	1 059.2	-798.9	106.9	1 412.8
Public administration; activities of households and of extraterritorial organisations	-	-	-	-	135.9	360.1	331.7	425.9	324.4	3 017.5
Education	-88.4	7.8	-	-	-	10.8	7.8	-2.5	-1.9	7.5
Human health and social work activities	287.2	194.5	193.5	119.3	195.4	104.8	121.0	92.3	123.8	134.1
Arts, entertainment and recreation	758.6	98.5	539.0	1 427.3	1 470.3	4 311.3	1 427.3	2 255.8	2 752.8	1 714.7
Other services	1 630.6	736.0	1 114.9	1 618.4	1 949.5	40.6	60.2	94.7	207.9	347.3
Not allocated and confidential	**0.0**	**0.0**	**0.0**	**0.0**	**0.0**	**784.8**	**783.7**	**749.6**	**841.2**	**1 140.4**
Private real estate activities	**24 580.9**	**23 604.0**	**24 612.2**	**30 005.9**	**30 556.8**	**22 693.2**	**21 255.6**	**20 734.8**	**23 873.0**	**22 755.4**

- Nil

Note: Detailed metadata at: *http://stats.oecd.org/OECDStat_Metadata/ShowMetadata.ashx?Dataset=FDI_CTRY_IND_SUMM.*

Source: *OECD International Direct Investment Statistics (database): https://doi.org/10.1787/idi-data-en*

Table 6. Foreign direct investment income by industrial sector

Million US dollars

	Inward					Outward				
	2014	2015	2016	2017	2018	2014	2015	2016	2017	2018
All FDI activities	**11 199.1**	**11 685.3**	**14 146.7**	**19 620.5**	**20 315.2**	**26 374.4**	**12 048.9**	**17 894.9**	**24 781.8**	**29 870.1**
Agriculture, forestry and fishing	**-16.3**	**-99.0**	**-40.3**	**98.7**	**27.1**	**19.4**	**4.8**	**2.8**	**34.6**	**-14.9**
Mining and quarrying	**605.1**	**183.3**	**-184.7**	**-48.2**	**263.1**	**115.4**	**2 262.8**	**70.1**	**42.9**	**560.2**
Extraction activities	575.9	183.1	-184.7	-48.2	263.1	81.3	2 166.0	69.7	42.6	562.6
Manufacturing	**3 664.3**	**2 736.6**	**4 037.7**	**7 010.3**	**7 078.6**	**9 031.6**	**5 034.1**	**7 555.1**	**8 295.1**	**8 163.7**
of which:										
Food products, beverages and tobacco	726.2	639.9	831.5	879.6	1 064.8	582.8	382.1	679.5	805.8	640.0
Textiles, wood and paper products; printing	83.3	169.8	-31.8	-0.2	87.3	389.0	255.7	307.7	232.4	199.4
Chemical, rubber, plastic, non-metallic mineral products	1 860.1	1 511.9	2 106.2	2 587.1	2 047.2	1 987.4	1 042.5	1 987.7	1 937.5	1 765.0
Metal and machinery products, except electrical equipment	48.5	622.8	883.4	1 897.8	1 767.6	3 090.7	1 441.5	2 232.0	2 284.9	2 450.9
Motor vehicles, trailers, semi-trailers, other transport equipment	-177.7	-1 126.3	-682.3	80.2	-678.1	2 019.2	1 036.7	1 474.4	1 713.1	1 257.8
Other manufacturing	1 123.9	918.6	930.7	1 565.8	2 789.7	962.5	875.7	873.8	1 321.4	1 850.7
Electricity, gas, steam and air conditioning supply	**278.3**	**286.2**	**-69.0**	**216.4**	**293.3**	**-60.4**	**-114.9**	**-252.6**	**75.1**	**27.0**
Water supply; sewerage, waste management and remediation activities	**-81.0**	**-5.7**	**-34.8**	**-16.5**	**-50.4**	**6.5**	**-0.1**	**6.0**	**-2.0**	**2.4**
Construction	**57.0**	**54.6**	**38.9**	**24.6**	**-148.8**	**843.0**	**-827.7**	**-244.1**	**710.1**	**432.7**
Services	**6 691.8**	**8 529.3**	**10 398.8**	**12 335.2**	**12 852.4**	**16 418.8**	**5 690.0**	**10 757.6**	**15 626.1**	**20 698.9**
Wholesale and retail trade; repair of motor vehicles and motorcycles	1 752.0	2 412.6	2 352.1	3 654.4	4 057.7	409.7	691.9	1 077.4	1 404.3	1 990.3
Transportation and storage	-84.5	306.2	843.4	1 031.0	1 384.4	175.0	-6.7	273.3	287.0	36.6
Accommodation and food service activities	176.8	100.5	37.1	-74.4	-14.4	150.2	158.9	210.0	215.2	180.8
Information and communication	1 147.1	345.8	1 491.4	1 078.8	969.3	-586.3	-923.7	-343.2	192.8	66.1
Financial and insurance activities	1 884.9	3 952.2	2 885.8	2 731.6	1 291.6	13 959.9	5 814.6	8 407.7	12 865.0	17 206.0
Activities of holding companies	-1 139.9	948.0	210.5	189.2	609.1	7 021.2	388.9	1 963.1	5 422.2	8 945.3
Real estate activities	-564.5	-791.9	1 129.1	128.8	1 576.9	281.6	184.5	142.8	370.5	281.8
Professional, scientific and technical activities	2 702.1	1 213.6	1 069.1	2 996.4	2 796.5	1 931.5	-381.5	861.2	169.8	632.3
Administrative and support service activities	-105.9	732.4	694.9	844.2	1 096.6	23.8	112.0	80.2	112.5	40.8
Public administration; activities of households and of extraterritorial organisations	-	-	-	-	-1.0	35.7	13.9	7.2	8.6	0.4
Education	-87.4	0.2	-	-	-	-3.0	-3.0	0.6	-1.3	0.0
Human health and social work activities	-57.4	-8.7	8.7	18.1	5.9	-0.6	4.2	-5.2	-9.4	-6.4
Arts, entertainment and recreation	-243.4	-91.1	-141.8	-88.3	-436.3	24.3	16.5	45.1	9.5	259.7
Other services	172.0	357.5	28.9	14.4	125.1	16.9	8.4	0.6	1.4	10.5
Not allocated and confidential	**0.0**	**0.0**	**0.0**	**0.0**	**0.0**	**0.2**	**0.0**	**0.0**	**0.0**	**0.0**
Private real estate activities	-	-	-	-	-	-	-	-	-	-

- Nil

Note: Detailed metadata at: *http://stats.oecd.org/OECDStat_Metadata/ShowMetadata.ashx?Dataset=FDI_CTRY_IND_SUMM.*

Source: OECD International Direct Investment Statistics (database): https://doi.org/10.1787/idi-data-en

Table 1. Foreign direct investment flows by country

Million US dollars

	Inward					Outward				
	2014	2015	2016	2017	2018	2014	2015	2016	2017	2018
WORLD	**12 040.8**	**2 976.6**	**17 749.5**	**10 975.6**	**9 856.3**	**130 963.4**	**136 295.5**	**151 287.1**	**164 658.4**	**143 142.3**
OECD COUNTRIES	**6 674.4**	**-864.7**	**10 116.4**	**5 569.6**	**7 659.0**	**84 039.3**	**92 921.6**	**113 752.1**	**113 071.8**	**75 520.8**
Australia	448.1	371.0	442.2	310.6	101.6	4 625.2	6 725.2	4 399.5	4 054.1	1 023.6
Austria	-8.4	7.8	11.5	37.5	10.7	43.5	75.4	14.3	279.1	-66.2
Belgium	-271.3	-29.5	70.7	-161.6	603.5	546.6	923.6	1 918.5	1 263.0	1 687.4
Canada	-11.4	-38.2	-52.4	55.2	50.2	1 864.9	1 277.1	676.2	921.8	2 486.9
Chile	-5.0	2.2	1.5	2.0	2.0	392.1	80.3	-201.7	-81.1	224.6
Czech Republic	-	-	-	-6.4	1.0	137.4	343.9	142.2	175.5	223.8
Denmark	43.1	0.1	91.2	11.3	60.5	158.1	-214.4	-162.9	313.7	176.0
Estonia	-	-	-	-	2.0	-	-	-	2.0	1.1
Finland	2.1	-1.1	-21.1	37.4	-438.7	160.1	117.3	-4 089.1	918.4	784.2
France	1 409.6	2 190.7	4 719.0	3 494.7	3 134.2	1 200.3	844.4	1 175.9	1 520.4	952.2
Germany	-354.6	-4 396.8	581.7	-1 006.2	-1 131.5	1 826.2	2 949.8	1 509.1	2 695.0	2 224.4
Greece	-9.4	-	-	-	-	0.2	0.1	-0.4	-1.0	-2.3
Hungary	-3.1	4.9	0.4	27.0	-	25.9	-4.6	125.9	135.5	180.8
Iceland	4.5	-0.9	-	-	1.2	3.1	-	-	7.3	8.9
Ireland	-1 514.0	-1 235.5	511.0	-1 457.0	-41.9	533.3	-782.2	2 572.1	2 007.1	6 354.2
Israel[1]	283.9	-28.7	-64.5	23.8	1 248.4	27.2	31.7	193.5	1 115.0	81.8
Italy	-86.4	257.4	24.1	97.8	-69.8	302.1	687.2	454.7	-152.7	1 103.8
Japan	-	-	-	-	-	-	-	-	-	-
Korea	764.8	904.9	581.8	937.0	1 889.8	3 277.8	1 562.6	1 631.6	1 635.3	4 766.2
Latvia	-	-	-	-	-	1.1	-	0.7	0.4	-
Lithuania	-	-	-	-	-	-	-	-	-	-
Luxembourg	-301.2	-1 065.2	1 004.3	1 358.6	-731.4	2 365.7	1 560.3	1 020.6	6 057.6	-436.6
Mexico	-2.4	-2.7	-	-	2.0	1 191.1	1 222.4	1 886.6	1 324.1	1 317.4
Netherlands	-1 181.4	-1 233.6	-940.9	-185.0	-442.2	4 475.4	7 268.4	3 585.0	14 843.9	7 810.9
New Zealand	33.0	-7.0	-26.3	-19.0	-1.3	1 164.0	123.2	400.0	339.7	312.1
Norway	-103.2	-139.3	-151.8	179.6	-160.7	238.4	-33.0	340.6	-175.6	312.4
Poland	-	-	-	0.3	-	18.9	-69.6	144.6	72.6	17.5
Portugal	77.3	-	-6.2	-67.6	0.9	28.4	8.8	92.6	6.7	12.8
Slovak Republic	-	-	0.9	-	2.0	-12.9	-3.3	48.4	22.1	27.1
Slovenia	-	-	-	-	-	4.6	26.6	-0.2	-16.4	-37.0
Spain	112.1	38.4	2.0	33.1	-226.4	905.2	544.4	800.4	290.0	4 260.4
Sweden	-1 381.8	-273.6	-87.4	263.1	181.2	1 510.1	2 479.2	247.2	967.7	1 288.7
Switzerland	696.6	-215.8	762.4	-2 613.6	-2 160.8	26.0	-569.2	1 935.7	-1 485.9	-303.4
Turkey	-	-	0.4	0.8	-	316.3	442.4	509.8	526.1	272.7
United Kingdom	1 198.0	839.5	-1 296.8	101.1	1 067.3	7 387.0	16 421.5	41 413.2	25 991.1	18 042.9
United States	6 834.9	3 186.3	3 958.8	4 115.2	4 705.3	49 297.4	49 001.6	50 967.7	47 499.6	20 411.7
EUROPE	**-1 690.1**	**-5 277.3**	**5 422.5**	**153.2**	**-316.4**	**22 746.8**	**33 225.2**	**53 766.4**	**56 456.8**	**46 340.7**
Bulgaria	-	-	-	0.7	-	0.4	-	-63.0	73.3	-3.6
Croatia	-	-	-	-	-	0.8	0.2	-0.1	0.1	0.6
Cyprus[2, 3]	16.0	2.0	-0.4	0.4	2.4	-226.9	1.4	3.0	96.7	12.0
Malta	-	-	1.1	0.8	0.9	-2.3	-2.1	-26.4	0.1	14.7
Romania	-	-	0.4	-	-	27.0	15.9	22.2	10.1	83.0
Russian Federation	2.1	-0.5	2.7	3.6	1.4	378.4	465.4	108.1	148.7	343.5
Ukraine	0.6	-	-	-	-	51.5	31.2	28.4	25.7	34.0
AFRICA	**11.7**	**-4.4**	**34.7**	**6.5**	**4.9**	**1 554.3**	**1 481.2**	**-555.5**	**1 720.4**	**1 574.0**
Northern Africa	-0.7	0.4	-	-	-	55.2	53.1	-15.9	127.4	38.9
Algeria	-	-	-	-	-	3.5	-	-	10.4	28.8
Egypt	-0.7	0.4	-	-	-	57.3	43.9	-21.1	112.2	-6.7
Libya	-	-	-	-	-	-	-	-	-	-
Morocco	-	-	-	-	-	-0.5	9.2	5.3	4.8	16.3
Tunisia	-	-	-	-	-	-5.1	-	-	-	0.5
Other African countries	12.3	-4.9	34.7	6.5	4.9	1 499.1	1 425.1	-539.6	1 593.0	1 535.1
Nigeria	-	-	-	-	-	7.7	9.6	7.3	1.5	4.1
South Africa	4.7	-0.5	0.7	-3.1	-0.6	1 680.7	1 037.9	928.2	1 060.5	1 255.3
AMERICA	**7 665.0**	**3 454.9**	**4 833.5**	**7 447.1**	**8 798.7**	**57 498.8**	**59 489.2**	**77 855.5**	**60 168.6**	**47 044.9**
Northern America	6 823.5	3 148.1	3 906.5	4 170.4	4 755.5	51 162.2	50 213.7	51 643.9	48 421.4	22 898.6
Central America and Caribbean countries	801.2	267.5	944.8	3 294.8	4 051.6	2 717.1	9 204.4	25 455.0	12 595.9	21 307.1
Bahamas	2.1	2.0	-	2.3	-	-10.6	25.1	-281.7	40.9	83.6
Bermuda	2.4	78.7	-18.2	26.4	-65.0	1 120.9	310.4	-315.2	7 395.9	85.2
Cayman Islands	642.5	140.9	748.6	3 225.3	3 674.8	987.3	7 855.2	20 485.0	3 882.0	16 777.9
Costa Rica	-	-	-	-	-	-	-	-1.1	1.0	0.3
El Salvador	-	-	-	-	-	1.5	1.9	2.3	1.5	1.7
Guatemala	-	-	-	-	-	-	-	-	-	-
Honduras	-	-	-	-	-	-	-	-	-	-
Nicaragua	-	-	-	-	-	-	-	-	-	-
Panama	0.3	7.0	14.2	6.0	25.7	-794.8	-474.0	91.6	-233.0	119.0
Virgin Islands, U.S.	1.3	-	1.8	-3.1	-	-2.1	1.4	-2.1	-4.8	-5.7
South America	40.3	39.3	-17.8	-18.1	-8.4	3 619.4	66.0	756.7	-848.7	2 839.2
Argentina	45.3	-7.0	-19.2	-17.4	-18.6	84.8	13.5	122.4	579.0	457.8
Bolivia	-	-	-	-	-	-185.3	-0.4	-	-	-
Brazil	-	44.6	-	-2.6	8.2	3 170.6	-204.7	835.9	-1 380.3	2 196.3
Colombia	-	-	-	-	-	26.4	21.5	5.6	28.7	41.5
Ecuador	-	-	-	-	-	0.1	-	-0.7	-	-
Paraguay	-	-	-	-	-	35.5	-12.0	-7.4	33.4	-6.4
Peru	-	-0.4	-	-	-	105.6	100.5	94.6	120.0	148.7
Uruguay	-	-	-	-	-	11.4	207.1	35.0	-105.2	-180.1
Venezuela	-	-	-	-	-	-21.7	-144.7	-127.1	-43.2	-43.2

Table 1. Foreign direct investment flows by country *(cont.)*

Million US dollars

	Inward					Outward				
	2014	2015	2016	2017	2018	2014	2015	2016	2017	2018
ASIA	**5 546.7**	**4 426.9**	**7 009.9**	**3 129.9**	**1 288.1**	**43 122.4**	**34 397.8**	**14 223.4**	**40 338.2**	**48 323.5**
Near and Middle East	286.3	38.6	43.1	100.9	1 384.2	654.2	522.0	682.2	2 012.6	770.1
Gulf Arabian countries	2.4	66.6	107.5	77.1	135.8	626.2	489.3	489.7	897.6	686.8
Kuwait	-	-	-	-	0.3	19.1	10.3	1.8	1.7	1.7
Qatar	-	-	-	-	-	-48.3	164.1	40.0	73.7	14.1
Saudi Arabia	14.9	53.0	58.6	55.4	77.0	873.0	482.5	267.4	169.2	333.5
United Arab Emirates	-18.6	13.6	48.9	17.1	56.0	-225.9	-168.9	147.6	644.3	412.2
Other Near and Middle East	283.9	-28.0	-64.5	23.8	1 248.4	28.0	32.7	192.5	1 115.0	83.4
Jordan	-	-	-	-	-	0.9	0.0	-	-	-
Other Asian countries	5 260.4	4 388.3	6 966.9	3 029.0	-96.1	42 468.2	33 875.8	13 541.1	38 325.6	47 553.4
China	331.3	83.7	278.7	600.7	447.7	10 444.5	9 454.8	9 811.3	10 727.6	10 421.9
Hong Kong, China	1 601.0	872.3	1 226.8	-99.6	749.4	2 563.6	2 636.2	1 967.3	2 841.6	2 158.0
India	-8.5	24.7	0.4	5.6	-4.6	2 414.9	-1 055.2	4 104.3	1 477.0	3 203.6
Indonesia	6.6	20.8	38.9	195.8	-2.6	4 843.5	3 150.4	2 985.4	3 637.1	3 211.2
Iran, Islamic Republic of	-	-	-	-	-	-	1.4	2.7	-	2.5
Malaysia	20.8	46.6	15.7	36.9	20.0	1 227.1	2 970.7	1 458.4	975.8	724.7
Philippines	15.0	12.1	-4.5	17.7	12.5	931.6	1 529.0	2 288.1	1 089.5	972.1
Singapore	1 326.1	1 845.6	2 450.3	526.8	-3 679.2	8 179.1	7 007.6	-18 361.5	6 790.3	12 572.1
Chinese Taipei	1 195.7	547.8	2 281.6	741.1	438.3	918.7	444.9	1 411.2	1 195.1	1 697.4
Thailand	5.4	43.3	102.1	72.9	47.4	5 445.5	3 760.2	4 085.4	5 438.2	5 424.3
Viet Nam	-0.9	0.3	1.7	0.1	1.0	1 637.8	1 445.5	1 658.9	2 007.0	1 829.9
AUSTRALIA, OCEANIA AND POLAR REGIONS	**507.6**	**376.5**	**449.0**	**238.4**	**114.8**	**6 042.6**	**7 703.4**	**5 998.5**	**5 017.1**	**-150.8**
WORLD unallocated and confidential	**0.0**	**0.0**	**0.0**	**0.5**	**-33.9**	**-1.5**	**-1.3**	**-1.2**	**957.4**	**9.9**
European Union (EU28)	**-2 253.4**	**-4 894.4**	**4 665.4**	**2 580.0**	**1 984.7**	**21 416.1**	**33 132.5**	**50 948.3**	**57 571.8**	**44 712.6**
G20 countries excl. European Union	**10 597.0**	**3 530.9**	**9 319.6**	**8 943.9**	**10 257.0**	**95 178.5**	**94 423.8**	**123 787.0**	**102 433.4**	**74 025.0**
G20 OECD countries	**10 200.6**	**3 312.1**	**8 958.8**	**8 106.0**	**9 749.0**	**71 288.1**	**81 074.5**	**104 624.1**	**86 014.7**	**52 601.7**
G20 Non-OECD countries	**396.4**	**218.8**	**360.7**	**837.9**	**508.0**	**23 890.4**	**13 349.4**	**19 162.9**	**16 418.7**	**21 423.2**
MENA countries	**1.7**	**67.8**	**107.5**	**77.1**	**135.8**	**682.2**	**545.4**	**473.8**	**1 025.0**	**726.8**
ASEAN countries	**1 372.6**	**1 967.4**	**2 605.7**	**850.2**	**-3 598.8**	**22 691.3**	**20 610.6**	**-5 621.8**	**20 230.5**	**25 138.4**

- Nil

Note: Detailed metadata at: *http://stats.oecd.org/OECDStat_Metadata/ShowMetadata.ashx?Dataset=FDI_CTRY_IND_SUMM.*

1. Information on data for Israel: *http://oe.cd/israel-disclaimer.*
2. Note by Turkey: The information in this document with reference to "Cyprus" relates to the southern part of the Island. There is no single authority representing both Turkish and Greek Cypriot people on the Island. Turkey recognises the Turkish Republic of Northern Cyprus (TRNC). Until a lasting and equitable solution is found within the context of the United Nations, Turkey shall preserve its position concerning the "Cyprus issue".
3. Note by all the European Union Member States of the OECD and the European Union: The Republic of Cyprus is recognised by all members of the United Nations with the exception of Turkey. The information in this document relates to the area under the effective control of the Government of the Republic of Cyprus.

Source: OECD International Direct Investment Statistics (database): https://doi.org/10.1787/idi-data-en

Table 2. Foreign direct investment positions by country
At year end

Million US dollars

	Inward					Outward				
	2014	2015	2016	2017	2018	2014	2015	2016	2017	2018
WORLD	**171 663.6**	**174 146.0**	**196 613.9**	**202 441.1**	**204 780.1**	**1 152 006.4**	**1 228 766.5**	**1 315 221.1**	**1 497 525.0**	**1 567 161.1**
OECD COUNTRIES	..	..	..	..	..	**760 116.5**	**825 579.1**	**886 155.2**	**1 005 386.9**	**1 031 719.6**
Australia	..	..	..	667.9	785.3	60 651.8	66 927.8	65 442.8	68 041.5	64 137.6
Austria	..	..	..	..	..	..	..	..	..	..
Belgium	..	..	..	1 311.4	751.4	17 866.6	16 904.9	17 439.5	20 514.5	21 784.2
Canada	..	..	..	1 378.9	1 384.6	16 659.0	16 075.6	15 840.7	16 439.6	17 079.4
Chile	..	..	..	..	..	..	..	..	..	..
Czech Republic	..	..	..	..	..	..	..	..	..	..
Denmark	..	..	..	..	..	..	..	..	..	..
Estonia	..	..	..	..	..	..	..	..	..	..
Finland	..	..	..	..	..	..	..	..	..	..
France	..	..	..	39 072.7	44 660.6	12 701.1	12 369.6	12 799.6	15 330.6	15 201.6
Germany	..	..	..	8 109.0	10 544.1	15 914.3	17 169.5	18 057.7	23 074.2	22 704.1
Greece	..	..	..	..	..	..	..	..	..	..
Hungary	..	..	..	..	..	..	..	..	..	..
Iceland	..	..	..	..	..	..	..	..	..	..
Ireland	..	..	..	..	..	..	..	..	..	..
Israel[1]	..	..	..	..	..	..	..	..	..	..
Italy	..	..	..	632.4	578.0	2 906.8	3 466.3	3 621.4	3 395.0	4 140.7
Japan	..	..	..	..	..	0.0	-	..	-	-
Korea	..	..	..	6 243.0	6 752.6	31 641.1	31 428.7	32 028.8	36 771.6	38 791.6
Latvia	..	..	..	..	..	..	..	..	..	..
Lithuania	..	..	..	..	..	..	..	..	..	..
Luxembourg	..	..	..	4 584.4	4 610.3	8 040.7	10 231.1	9 532.4	15 162.9	12 652.3
Mexico	..	..	..	234.6	258.8	5 799.1	7 357.9	8 794.5	10 377.8	11 921.8
Netherlands	..	..	..	8 130.9	6 600.3	93 170.6	99 814.4	94 713.0	114 317.0	114 949.5
New Zealand	..	..	..	338.8	342.0	3 404.9	3 060.7	3 396.2	3 730.2	3 909.9
Norway	..	..	..	..	..	..	..	..	..	..
Poland	..	..	..	..	..	..	..	..	..	..
Portugal	..	..	..	..	..	..	..	..	..	..
Slovak Republic	..	..	..	..	..	..	..	..	..	..
Slovenia	..	..	..	..	..	..	..	..	..	..
Spain	..	..	..	-182.5	-857.0	1 966.6	2 396.2	2 910.4	3 206.4	7 358.1
Sweden	..	..	..	425.4	497.7	2 676.0	4 676.6	4 336.6	5 572.4	6 999.2
Switzerland	..	..	..	9 805.8	9 779.4	6 520.2	6 071.3	8 285.1	8 082.2	6 726.2
Turkey	..	..	..	..	..	..	..	..	..	..
United Kingdom	..	..	..	6 362.6	2 618.3	73 876.6	86 153.6	118 135.2	151 633.6	153 793.6
United States	..	..	..	71 722.9	61 043.2	375 621.3	413 342.0	445 853.6	479 995.3	490 843.0
EUROPE	..	..	..	**83 039.9**	**86 856.8**	**265 481.1**	**286 386.4**	**312 439.5**	**387 489.8**	**405 329.4**
Bulgaria	..	..	..	..	..	..	..	..	..	..
Croatia	..	..	..	..	..	..	..	..	..	..
Cyprus[2, 3]	..	..	..	..	..	..	..	..	..	..
Malta	..	..	..	..	..	..	..	..	..	..
Romania	..	..	..	..	..	..	..	..	..	..
Russian Federation	..	..	..	51.4	52.7	1 679.3	1 806.0	1 503.9	1 576.5	1 523.4
Ukraine	..	..	..	..	..	..	..	..	..	..
AFRICA	..	..	..	**92.7**	**93.0**	**9 929.8**	**8 898.2**	**10 008.6**	**7 793.2**	**8 728.2**
Northern Africa	..	..	..	..	..	..	..	..	..	..
Algeria	..	..	..	..	..	..	..	..	..	..
Egypt	..	..	..	..	..	..	..	..	..	..
Libya	..	..	..	..	..	..	..	..	..	..
Morocco	..	..	..	..	..	..	..	..	..	..
Tunisia	..	..	..	..	..	..	..	..	..	..
Other African countries	..	..	..	..	..	..	..	..	..	..
Nigeria	..	..	..	..	..	..	..	..	..	..
South Africa	..	..	..	3.8	5.1	7 196.7	7 154.5	8 229.6	6 199.5	6 910.1
AMERICA	..	..	..	**78 573.0**	**69 264.3**	**464 701.1**	**499 646.7**	**549 724.5**	**596 208.4**	**621 629.7**
Northern America	..	..	..	73 101.8	62 427.9	392 280.3	429 417.5	461 694.3	496 434.9	507 922.3
Central America and Caribbean countries	..	..	..	..	..	..	..	..	..	..
Bahamas	..	..	..	..	..	..	..	..	..	..
Bermuda	..	..	..	..	..	..	..	..	..	..
Cayman Islands	..	..	..	5 423.7	8 931.9	12 600.5	15 359.0	31 340.5	35 222.3	46 552.2
Costa Rica	..	..	..	..	..	..	..	..	..	..
El Salvador	..	..	..	..	..	..	..	..	..	..
Guatemala	..	..	..	..	..	..	..	..	..	..
Honduras	..	..	..	..	..	..	..	..	..	..
Nicaragua	..	..	..	..	..	..	..	..	..	..
Panama	..	..	..	..	..	..	..	..	..	..
Virgin Islands, U.S.	..	..	..	..	..	..	..	..	..	..
South America	..	..	..	..	..	..	..	..	..	..
Argentina	..	..	..	..	..	..	..	..	..	..
Bolivia	..	..	..	..	..	..	..	..	..	..
Brazil	..	..	..	-1 169.7	-3 095.6	30 738.3	24 763.5	24 467.1	21 659.2	21 265.6
Colombia	..	..	..	..	..	..	..	..	..	..
Ecuador	..	..	..	..	..	..	..	..	..	..
Paraguay	..	..	..	..	..	..	..	..	..	..
Peru	..	..	..	..	..	..	..	..	..	..
Uruguay	..	..	..	..	..	..	..	..	..	..
Venezuela	..	..	..	..	..	..	..	..	..	..

Table 2. Foreign direct investment positions by country *(cont.)*

At year end

Million US dollars

	Inward					Outward				
	2014	2015	2016	2017	2018	2014	2015	2016	2017	2018
ASIA	..	..	..	**38 398.7**	**46 846.4**	**345 174.2**	**359 992.3**	**369 450.9**	**429 113.7**	**459 868.5**
Near and Middle East	..	..	..	1 290.4	-372.4	5 880.0	6 779.5	6 990.5	9 012.6	8 597.7
Gulf Arabian countries	..	..	..	..	..	..	..	..	..	..
Kuwait	..	..	..	..	..	..	..	..	..	..
Qatar	..	..	..	..	..	..	..	..	..	..
Saudi Arabia	..	..	..	-778.3	-3 104.3	4 112.2	4 921.6	4 850.9	4 897.0	5 202.8
United Arab Emirates	..	..	..	1 430.4	561.5	199.7	280.5	563.6	1 445.3	1 976.5
Other Near and Middle East	..	..	..	..	..	..	..	..	..	..
Jordan	..	..	..	..	..	..	..	..	..	..
Other Asian countries	..	..	..	37 108.3	47 218.8	339 294.2	353 212.8	362 460.4	420 101.1	451 270.8
China	..	..	..	1 593.8	2 340.1	103 164.9	107 575.6	108 230.4	117 568.0	121 537.8
Hong Kong, China	..	..	..	6 541.9	7 620.1	22 231.3	23 908.3	27 538.7	29 957.1	31 869.1
India	..	..	..	164.4	188.7	13 649.8	14 089.4	17 934.7	22 145.1	24 340.4
Indonesia	..	..	..	30.2	28.0	23 558.8	24 414.0	27 001.5	30 343.0	30 191.7
Iran, Islamic Republic of	..	..	..	..	..	4.7	6.1	8.8	9.1	11.8
Malaysia	..	..	..	292.3	305.6	13 453.0	13 358.2	12 618.5	14 096.4	16 326.7
Philippines	..	..	..	64.8	96.8	11 087.7	12 303.3	13 740.9	15 023.0	14 411.0
Singapore	..	..	..	13 939.3	20 792.6	44 556.1	48 957.0	39 563.3	59 361.9	71 332.4
Chinese Taipei	..	..	..	7 967.4	8 802.0	11 217.0	11 307.9	12 359.6	14 382.2	14 673.1
Thailand	..	..	..	135.0	121.5	51 213.8	50 019.5	53 797.8	61 409.8	66 845.1
Viet Nam	..	..	..	1.5	3.9	11 925.2	13 146.6	14 517.8	15 621.7	16 894.4
AUSTRALIA, OCEANIA AND POLAR REGIONS	..	..	..	**1 171.9**	**1 318.6**	**66 717.3**	**73 839.9**	**73 593.6**	**76 915.9**	**71 601.1**
WORLD unallocated and confidential	..	..	..	**1 164.8**	**400.9**	**2.9**	**2.9**	**4.0**	**4.1**	**4.2**
European Union (EU28)	..	..	..	..	..	**251 665.9**	**272 982.7**	**298 349.4**	**373 327.7**	**390 675.7**
G20 countries excl. European Union	..	..	..	..	..	..	..	..	..	..
G20 OECD countries	..	..	..	..	..	..	..	..	..	..
G20 Non-OECD countries	..	..	..	..	..	..	..	..	..	..
MENA countries	..	..	..	..	..	..	..	..	..	..
ASEAN countries	..	..	..	..	..	**156 713.4**	**163 967.2**	**163 435.0**	**198 170.1**	**218 865.1**

- Nil; .. Not available

Note: Inward FDI positions are allocated according to the ultimate investing country. Inward FDI positions by immediate counterpart country are available for more geographic details and for 2014 onwards in the *OECD FDI database according to BMD4*. Detailed metadata at: *http://stats.oecd.org/OECDStat_Metadata/ShowMetadata.ashx?Dataset=FDI_CTRY_IND_SUMM.*

1. Information on data for Israel: *http://oe.cd/israel-disclaimer.*
2. Note by Turkey: The information in this document with reference to "Cyprus" relates to the southern part of the Island. There is no single authority representing both Turkish and Greek Cypriot people on the Island. Turkey recognises the Turkish Republic of Northern Cyprus (TRNC). Until a lasting and equitable solution is found within the context of the United Nations, Turkey shall preserve its position concerning the "Cyprus issue".
3. Note by all the European Union Member States of the OECD and the European Union: The Republic of Cyprus is recognised by all members of the United Nations with the exception of Turkey. The information in this document relates to the area under the effective control of the Government of the Republic of Cyprus.

Source: OECD International Direct Investment Statistics (database): https://doi.org/10.1787/idi-data-en

Table 3. Foreign direct investment income by country

Million US dollars

	Inward					Outward				
	2014	2015	2016	2017	2018	2014	2015	2016	2017	2018
WORLD	**26 287.5**	**23 857.9**	**32 634.0**	**34 923.3**	**33 941.5**	**100 236.0**	**96 358.7**	**105 867.5**	**120 300.6**	**125 065.1**
OECD COUNTRIES	**22 942.3**	**19 930.5**	**28 694.7**	**29 740.6**	**27 929.7**	**56 231.5**	**53 905.8**	**57 586.0**	**63 138.4**	**65 516.3**
Australia	119.0	150.4	93.4	109.5	53.9	3 104.9	1 997.5	3 452.5	7 423.5	7 189.1
Austria	..	..	..	..	..	..	..	..	..	..
Belgium	113.2	107.2	89.9	136.8	123.2	400.8	711.8	1 007.3	1 037.4	629.0
Canada	7.1	-28.0	12.0	56.1	61.5	1 374.6	1 138.3	1 097.7	1 635.5	1 255.8
Chile	..	..	..	..	..	..	..	..	..	..
Czech Republic	..	..	..	..	..	..	..	..	..	..
Denmark	..	..	..	..	..	..	..	..	..	..
Estonia	..	..	..	..	..	..	..	..	..	..
Finland	..	..	..	..	..	..	..	..	..	..
France	4 526.7	4 387.7	5 341.1	5 459.0	5 582.3	581.4	768.1	605.5	637.4	772.7
Germany	1 296.3	1 151.1	1 124.8	1 973.2	1 922.6	933.5	964.5	941.5	2 296.7	2 177.5
Greece	..	..	..	..	..	..	..	..	..	..
Hungary	..	..	..	..	..	..	..	..	..	..
Iceland	..	..	..	..	..	..	..	..	..	..
Ireland	..	..	..	..	..	..	..	..	..	..
Israel[1]	..	..	..	..	..	..	..	..	..	..
Italy	23.7	8.2	10.8	13.2	21.1	175.3	125.4	131.2	149.0	172.1
Japan	-	..	..	-	-	-	..	..	-	-
Korea	522.7	425.2	492.1	645.0	669.6	2 409.1	2 428.8	2 639.0	2 748.9	2 934.4
Latvia	..	..	..	..	..	..	..	..	..	..
Lithuania	..	..	..	..	..	..	..	..	..	..
Luxembourg	940.6	526.0	980.0	680.4	1 296.4	302.2	299.3	384.2	485.6	554.8
Mexico	0.7	0.7	1.2	3.3	0.3	274.8	422.0	592.3	690.5	726.9
Netherlands	3 873.9	2 750.6	7 945.2	5 907.7	5 619.7	8 577.1	8 943.9	7 745.4	8 212.9	9 836.1
New Zealand	38.8	8.2	-2.8	-3.3	14.6	160.1	199.9	218.7	185.5	209.3
Norway	..	..	..	..	..	..	..	..	..	..
Poland	..	..	..	..	..	..	..	..	..	..
Portugal	..	..	..	..	..	..	..	..	..	..
Slovak Republic	..	..	..	..	..	..	..	..	..	..
Slovenia	..	..	..	..	..	..	..	..	..	..
Spain	63.7	11.5	3.3	3.0	6.5	138.4	153.9	186.3	270.7	276.4
Sweden	161.5	73.7	207.3	64.0	14.6	199.6	298.3	349.8	403.3	563.0
Switzerland	2 073.0	1 095.4	1 485.8	1 611.3	1 787.2	219.5	43.9	133.0	53.8	57.6
Turkey	..	..	..	..	..	..	..	..	..	..
United Kingdom	686.2	526.8	1 078.5	1 060.7	910.6	6 334.9	4 575.6	5 201.1	6 312.8	6 805.9
United States	8 402.3	7 752.7	9 373.1	11 713.5	9 632.3	29 770.5	29 948.4	32 054.7	28 899.6	29 649.8
EUROPE	**13 991.5**	**11 757.1**	**18 785.6**	**17 206.4**	**17 506.2**	**19 568.4**	**18 335.9**	**17 927.9**	**21 844.4**	**23 983.2**
Bulgaria	..	..	..	..	..	..	..	..	..	..
Croatia	..	..	..	..	..	..	..	..	..	..
Cyprus[2, 3]	..	..	..	..	..	..	..	..	..	..
Malta	..	..	..	..	..	..	..	..	..	..
Romania	..	..	..	..	..	..	..	..	..	..
Russian Federation	0.3	-	1.0	-	0.3	198.2	100.8	36.4	261.9	382.1
Ukraine	..	..	..	..	..	..	..	..	..	..
AFRICA	**26.1**	**3.5**	**7.1**	**9.8**	**12.9**	**858.5**	**822.6**	**680.0**	**548.9**	**594.5**
Northern Africa	..	..	..	..	..	..	..	..	..	..
Algeria	..	..	..	..	..	..	..	..	..	..
Egypt	..	..	..	..	..	..	..	..	..	..
Libya	..	..	..	..	..	..	..	..	..	..
Morocco	..	..	..	..	..	..	..	..	..	..
Tunisia	..	..	..	..	..	..	..	..	..	..
Other African countries	..	..	..	..	..	..	..	..	..	..
Nigeria	..	..	..	..	..	..	..	..	..	..
South Africa	-	-	0.1	0.5	-	561.2	323.2	183.9	221.0	324.5
AMERICA	**9 240.5**	**8 925.7**	**10 324.9**	**12 394.8**	**10 689.8**	**35 028.7**	**35 010.1**	**38 256.8**	**38 513.4**	**39 673.9**
Northern America	8 409.4	7 724.7	9 385.1	11 769.5	9 693.7	31 145.1	31 085.7	33 152.4	30 535.1	30 905.7
Central America and Caribbean countries	..	..	..	..	..	..	..	..	..	..
Bahamas	..	..	..	..	..	..	..	..	..	..
Bermuda	..	..	..	..	..	..	..	..	..	..
Cayman Islands	667.3	933.3	748.2	383.8	310.5	1 162.9	2 974.3	3 835.4	3 948.8	4 103.3
Costa Rica	..	..	..	..	..	..	..	..	..	..
El Salvador	..	..	..	..	..	..	..	..	..	..
Guatemala	..	..	..	..	..	..	..	..	..	..
Honduras	..	..	..	..	..	..	..	..	..	..
Nicaragua	..	..	..	..	..	..	..	..	..	..
Panama	..	..	..	..	..	..	..	..	..	..
Virgin Islands, U.S.	..	..	..	..	..	..	..	..	..	..
South America	..	..	..	..	..	..	..	..	..	..
Argentina	..	..	..	..	..	..	..	..	..	..
Bolivia	..	..	..	..	..	..	..	..	..	..
Brazil	0.9	1.5	-	-	-	971.5	-643.7	-213.0	1 910.7	2 157.4
Colombia	..	..	..	..	..	..	..	..	..	..
Ecuador	..	..	..	..	..	..	..	..	..	..
Paraguay	..	..	..	..	..	..	..	..	..	..
Peru	..	..	..	..	..	..	..	..	..	..
Uruguay	..	..	..	..	..	..	..	..	..	..
Venezuela	..	..	..	..	..	..	..	..	..	..

Table 3. Foreign direct investment income by country *(cont.)*

Million US dollars

	Inward					Outward				
	2014	2015	2016	2017	2018	2014	2015	2016	2017	2018
ASIA	**2 871.5**	**3 010.7**	**3 423.3**	**5 204.7**	**5 663.6**	**41 407.8**	**39 873.3**	**45 107.9**	**51 522.6**	**53 110.8**
Near and Middle East	-128.2	-92.7	-56.0	25.2	10.7	2 352.1	1 101.5	1 127.4	1 398.7	1 228.9
Gulf Arabian countries	..	..	..	..	..	..	..	..	..	..
Kuwait	..	..	..	..	..	..	..	..	..	..
Qatar	..	..	..	..	..	..	..	..	..	..
Saudi Arabia	-	-	-	-	-	1 825.3	464.7	611.1	693.0	966.9
United Arab Emirates	0.9	0.7	0.8	7.1	8.1	362.4	612.2	511.5	760.7	292.8
Other Near and Middle East	..	..	..	..	..	..	..	..	..	..
Jordan	..	..	..	..	..	..	..	..	..	..
Other Asian countries	2 999.7	3 103.4	3 479.3	5 179.5	5 652.9	39 055.7	38 771.7	43 980.4	50 123.9	51 881.9
China	64.7	31.6	41.4	71.0	117.3	12 483.5	12 669.9	14 757.1	16 687.4	18 190.0
Hong Kong, China	633.3	487.0	771.2	1 015.5	1 070.5	2 467.4	2 803.0	3 180.8	3 911.8	2 518.0
India	6.4	3.9	5.0	16.9	-	572.7	1 057.7	1 421.3	2 009.6	2 275.9
Indonesia	17.9	1.8	58.8	6.5	1.9	2 255.4	1 771.7	2 210.6	3 174.7	2 854.2
Iran, Islamic Republic of	-	-	-	-	-	-	-	-	-	3.2
Malaysia	119.9	27.6	13.6	59.3	47.3	2 070.3	1 548.0	1 527.8	1 391.2	1 335.2
Philippines	0.0	1.0	0.4	-	0.0	1 426.4	1 362.9	1 403.5	1 452.2	1 596.0
Singapore	1 412.7	1 937.5	1 869.2	3 056.0	3 410.1	4 795.1	5 248.6	5 621.3	5 452.1	5 606.7
Chinese Taipei	184.7	164.7	188.8	288.6	305.0	2 229.6	1 945.4	1 770.8	2 465.0	3 336.2
Thailand	33.3	14.5	30.6	15.6	28.7	7 036.2	6 447.6	7 573.6	8 828.9	9 119.8
Viet Nam	2.9	0.9	3.1	1.7	2.2	1 098.2	1 249.0	1 635.4	1 729.4	1 863.9
AUSTRALIA, OCEANIA AND POLAR REGIONS	**157.9**	**161.0**	**93.0**	**107.7**	**69.0**	**3 372.6**	**2 314.5**	**3 894.9**	**7 871.4**	**7 702.7**
WORLD unallocated and confidential	**0.0**	**0.0**	**-**	**0.0**	**-**	**0.0**	**1.3**	**0.0**	**0.0**	**0.0**
European Union (EU28)	**11 913.2**	**10 641.8**	**17 288.9**	**15 582.9**	**15 705.8**	**18 498.4**	**17 936.8**	**17 705.6**	**21 132.1**	**23 093.0**
G20 countries excl. European Union	..	..	..	..	..	..	..	..	..	..
G20 OECD countries	..	..	..	..	..	..	..	..	..	..
G20 Non-OECD countries	..	..	..	..	..	..	..	..	..	..
MENA countries	..	..	..	..	..	..	..	..	..	..
ASEAN countries	**1 588.0**	**1 986.0**	**1 980.4**	**3 142.3**	**3 490.1**	**18 794.9**	**17 654.6**	**19 978.1**	**22 054.2**	**22 391.7**

- Nil; .. Not available

Note: Detailed metadata at: *http://stats.oecd.org/OECDStat_Metadata/ShowMetadata.ashx?Dataset=FDI_CTRY_IND_SUMM.*

1. Information on data for Israel: *http://oe.cd/israel-disclaimer.*
2. Note by Turkey: The information in this document with reference to "Cyprus" relates to the southern part of the Island. There is no single authority representing both Turkish and Greek Cypriot people on the Island. Turkey recognises the Turkish Republic of Northern Cyprus (TRNC). Until a lasting and equitable solution is found within the context of the United Nations, Turkey shall preserve its position concerning the "Cyprus issue".
3. Note by all the European Union Member States of the OECD and the European Union: The Republic of Cyprus is recognised by all members of the United Nations with the exception of Turkey. The information in this document relates to the area under the effective control of the Government of the Republic of Cyprus.

Source: OECD International Direct Investment Statistics (database): https://doi.org/10.1787/idi-data-en

JAPAN

Table 4. Foreign direct investment flows by industrial sector

Million US dollars

	Inward					Outward				
	2014	2015	2016	2017	2018	2014	2015	2016	2017	2018
All FDI activities	**12 040.8**	**2 976.6**	**17 749.5**	**10 975.6**	**9 856.3**	**130 963.4**	**136 295.5**	**151 287.1**	**164 658.4**	**143 142.3**
Agriculture, forestry and fishing	**-1.2**	**10.6**	**0.6**	**8.2**	**50.5**	**1 667.2**	**281.4**	**53.1**	**-66.9**	**67.1**
Mining and quarrying	**10.7**	**14.5**	**15.9**	**164.6**	**29.9**	**5 407.0**	**4 813.2**	**4 045.9**	**792.6**	**7 810.4**
Extraction activities	..	..	..	..	..	..	..	..	..	..
Manufacturing	**4 214.1**	**2 505.1**	**11 219.7**	**10 035.6**	**13 242.3**	**65 506.7**	**51 038.8**	**52 899.4**	**56 378.6**	**54 849.8**
of which:										
Food products, beverages and tobacco	1 190.3	180.4	438.4	262.6	215.4	18 821.3	3 565.1	2 976.9	9 997.8	336.2
Textiles, wood and paper products; printing	51.1	119.0	36.0	22.4	-30.6	2 809.2	1 418.2	2 757.8	1 019.5	2 834.6
Chemical, rubber, plastic, non-metallic mineral products	..	..	..	..	..	..	..	..	..	..
Metal and machinery products, except electrical equipment	..	..	..	..	..	..	..	..	..	..
Motor vehicles, trailers, semi-trailers, other transport equipment	1 303.5	-1 038.8	3 750.2	3 444.8	2 769.3	9 721.5	12 897.5	12 508.4	9 012.3	12 722.1
Other manufacturing	..	..	..	..	..	..	..	..	..	..
Electricity, gas, steam and air conditioning supply	..	..	..	..	..	..	..	..	..	..
Water supply; sewerage, waste management and remediation activities	..	..	..	..	..	..	..	..	..	..
Construction	**-15.0**	**62.5**	**136.0**	**47.5**	**-205.1**	**408.8**	**387.8**	**1 630.1**	**1 655.0**	**2 463.4**
Services	**6 519.5**	**-685.7**	**5 169.0**	**-174.5**	**-3 936.5**	**55 275.3**	**77 273.1**	**89 155.6**	**100 445.7**	**71 696.2**
Wholesale and retail trade; repair of motor vehicles and motorcycles	-2 447.3	-3 940.6	-2 411.8	-5 214.5	-6 428.0	18 619.8	13 600.8	18 768.1	27 830.5	14 037.0
Transportation and storage	-854.3	586.5	1 520.7	707.5	20.8	1 575.6	8 099.6	2 291.3	1 068.9	2 098.7
Accommodation and food service activities	..	..	..	..	..	..	..	..	..	..
Information and communication	1 732.6	1 015.4	968.7	-233.8	-2 674.8	7 753.0	11 808.8	16 901.9	22 777.5	38 946.9
Financial and insurance activities	7 516.1	1 516.3	3 313.8	1 713.4	4 401.0	19 226.4	34 621.1	8 502.0	33 365.8	24 933.3
Activities of holding companies	..	..	..	..	..	..	..	..	..	..
Real estate activities	224.9	-135.0	308.5	466.0	835.3	1 529.2	3 716.5	5 119.7	6 387.7	4 602.3
Professional, scientific and technical activities	..	..	..	..	..	..	..	..	..	..
Administrative and support service activities	..	..	..	..	..	..	..	..	..	..
Public administration; activities of households and of extraterritorial organisations	..	..	..	..	..	..	..	..	..	..
Education	..	..	..	..	..	..	..	..	..	..
Human health and social work activities	..	..	..	..	..	..	..	..	..	..
Arts, entertainment and recreation	..	..	..	..	..	..	..	..	..	..
Other services	..	..	..	..	..	..	..	..	..	..
Not allocated and confidential	**1 312.8**	**1 069.5**	**1 208.4**	**894.3**	**675.3**	**2 698.4**	**2 501.1**	**3 503.1**	**5 453.3**	**6 255.3**
Private real estate activities	..	..	..	..	..	..	..	..	..	..

.. Not available

Note: Detailed metadata at: *http://stats.oecd.org/OECDStat_Metadata/ShowMetadata.ashx?Dataset=FDI_CTRY_IND_SUMM.*

Source: OECD International Direct Investment Statistics (database): https://doi.org/10.1787/idi-data-en

Table 5. Foreign direct investment positions by industrial sector
At year end

Million US dollars

	Inward					Outward				
	2014	2015	2016	2017	2018	2014	2015	2016	2017	2018
All FDI activities	**171 663.6**	**174 146.0**	**196 613.9**	**202 441.1**	**204 780.1**	**1 152 006.4**	**1 228 766.5**	**1 315 221.1**	**1 497 525.0**	**1 567 161.1**
Agriculture, forestry and fishing	**77.9**	**78.4**	**81.5**	**80.9**	**132.7**	**3 589.2**	**3 210.6**	**3 275.7**	**2 984.2**	**2 957.5**
Mining and quarrying	**46.4**	**59.8**	**117.6**	**274.3**	**160.0**	**94 520.7**	**94 435.8**	**83 214.4**	**77 565.0**	**77 152.2**
Extraction activities	..	..	..	..	..	..	..	..	..	..
Manufacturing	**69 632.0**	**73 483.9**	**81 159.7**	**88 042.3**	**94 829.7**	**521 497.3**	**535 640.1**	**554 005.7**	**617 584.7**	**626 268.5**
of which:										
Food products, beverages and tobacco	2 426.2	2 268.7	2 557.5	2 520.5	2 181.4	70 197.0	74 357.1	72 039.4	83 580.4	82 484.1
Textiles, wood and paper products; printing	295.9	398.4	467.2	479.2	453.2	16 352.0	16 062.8	17 042.1	17 714.1	20 012.7
Chemical, rubber, plastic, non-metallic mineral products	..	..	..	..	..	..	..	..	..	..
Metal and machinery products, except electrical equipment	..	..	..	..	..	..	..	..	..	..
Motor vehicles, trailers, semi-trailers, other transport equipment	23 064.5	22 435.6	26 011.5	29 057.8	31 181.1	105 192.4	108 728.0	114 617.1	125 618.1	126 467.3
Other manufacturing	..	..	..	..	..	..	..	..	..	..
Electricity, gas, steam and air conditioning supply	**..**	**..**	**..**	**..**	**..**	**..**	**..**	**..**	**..**	**..**
Water supply; sewerage, waste management and remediation activities	**..**	**..**	**..**	**..**	**..**	**..**	**..**	**..**	**..**	**..**
Construction	**202.3**	**270.3**	**780.1**	**579.4**	**367.3**	**5 767.8**	**5 504.6**	**6 898.9**	**7 760.8**	**9 094.5**
Services	**91 922.2**	**89 370.8**	**102 234.8**	**100 064.8**	**94 190.1**	**497 318.3**	**558 702.1**	**632 298.9**	**747 724.3**	**804 736.8**
Wholesale and retail trade; repair of motor vehicles and motorcycles	13 627.3	8 932.6	11 181.4	6 367.8	-1 496.0	160 456.2	173 966.9	182 152.0	210 584.8	225 079.1
Transportation and storage	1 089.2	1 580.6	3 693.8	3 563.3	3 949.8	13 607.1	21 302.5	18 025.5	16 791.5	17 694.6
Accommodation and food service activities	..	..	..	..	..	..	..	..	..	..
Information and communication	4 933.7	6 814.4	7 414.3	7 737.9	6 008.8	61 477.4	70 163.4	80 071.0	101 658.3	128 595.1
Financial and insurance activities	63 602.5	61 944.8	66 484.9	66 522.6	69 415.8	214 322.7	241 153.5	260 295.5	304 659.9	327 948.1
Activities of holding companies	..	..	..	..	..	..	..	..	..	..
Real estate activities	2 944.3	3 227.7	3 454.0	3 845.2	4 962.8	17 247.0	19 699.6	24 473.3	30 170.0	33 396.6
Professional, scientific and technical activities	..	..	..	..	..	..	..	..	..	..
Administrative and support service activities	..	..	..	..	..	..	..	..	..	..
Public administration; activities of households and of extraterritorial organisations	..	..	..	..	..	..	..	..	..	..
Education	..	..	..	..	..	..	..	..	..	..
Human health and social work activities	..	..	..	..	..	..	..	..	..	..
Arts, entertainment and recreation	..	..	..	..	..	..	..	..	..	..
Other services	..	..	..	..	..	..	..	..	..	..
Not allocated and confidential	**9 782.8**	**10 882.8**	**12 240.1**	**13 399.4**	**15 100.3**	**29 313.1**	**31 273.4**	**35 527.6**	**43 906.0**	**46 951.6**
Private real estate activities	**..**	**..**	**..**	**..**	**..**	**..**	**..**	**..**	**..**	**..**

.. Not available

Note: Detailed metadata at: *http://stats.oecd.org/OECDStat_Metadata/ShowMetadata.ashx?Dataset=FDI_CTRY_IND_SUMM.*

Source: OECD International Direct Investment Statistics (database): https://doi.org/10.1787/idi-data-en

Table 6. Foreign direct investment income by industrial sector

Million US dollars

	Inward					Outward				
	2014	2015	2016	2017	2018	2014	2015	2016	2017	2018
All FDI activities	**26 287.5**	**23 857.9**	**32 634.0**	**34 923.3**	**33 941.5**	**100 236.0**	**96 358.7**	**105 867.5**	**120 300.6**	**125 065.1**
Agriculture, forestry and fishing	**5.9**	**8.9**	**0.1**	**3.7**	**28.0**	**79.3**	**46.4**	**55.8**	**106.8**	**142.1**
Mining and quarrying	**3.5**	**3.2**	**4.9**	**31.9**	**15.1**	**5 696.0**	**1 833.0**	**2 637.9**	**8 750.9**	**9 021.7**
Extraction activities	..	..	..	..	..	..	..	..	..	..
Manufacturing	**9 521.6**	**7 764.5**	**12 640.5**	**12 744.2**	**12 646.5**	**52 716.1**	**48 053.5**	**51 807.8**	**58 402.7**	**61 015.3**
of which:										
Food products, beverages and tobacco	1 285.0	926.4	1 162.3	1 022.5	1 064.7	3 024.2	3 879.3	2 768.5	3 852.4	4 335.5
Textiles, wood and paper products; printing	35.9	28.0	36.0	42.3	31.7	518.9	843.1	763.5	938.6	1 019.1
Chemical, rubber, plastic, non-metallic mineral products	..	..	..	..	..	..	..	..	..	..
Metal and machinery products, except electrical equipment	..	..	..	..	..	..	..	..	..	..
Motor vehicles, trailers, semi-trailers, other transport equipment	3 378.0	3 533.9	4 215.1	3 952.8	4 326.3	17 120.4	15 772.6	16 820.8	17 380.5	18 255.1
Other manufacturing	..	..	..	..	..	..	..	..	..	..
Electricity, gas, steam and air conditioning supply	..	..	..	..	..	..	..	..	..	..
Water supply; sewerage, waste management and remediation activities	..	..	..	..	..	..	..	..	..	..
Construction	**62.4**	**185.0**	**86.4**	**112.6**	**-79.3**	**583.8**	**454.4**	**547.2**	**564.0**	**665.3**
Services	**15 801.0**	**15 071.5**	**18 497.9**	**20 748.2**	**19 949.9**	**38 778.7**	**43 442.6**	**48 240.9**	**49 488.7**	**51 441.6**
Wholesale and retail trade; repair of motor vehicles and motorcycles	2 507.5	3 148.5	3 063.8	4 713.1	3 596.8	15 553.6	18 349.0	19 693.9	21 018.6	21 812.0
Transportation and storage	45.2	57.4	60.6	2 285.4	131.4	1 606.9	2 569.4	2 276.2	1 822.4	1 998.1
Accommodation and food service activities	..	..	..	..	..	..	..	..	..	..
Information and communication	2 402.7	1 501.1	4 345.9	3 881.2	2 323.5	1 237.7	901.4	2 942.7	4 772.1	4 739.5
Financial and insurance activities	9 567.5	9 405.9	9 282.3	8 589.1	12 565.3	16 955.8	17 187.3	18 151.0	16 819.1	16 717.1
Activities of holding companies	..	..	..	..	..	..	..	..	..	..
Real estate activities	277.3	177.2	274.3	280.0	264.4	659.3	680.4	729.2	931.8	958.5
Professional, scientific and technical activities	..	..	..	..	..	..	..	..	..	..
Administrative and support service activities	..	..	..	..	..	..	..	..	..	..
Public administration; activities of households and of extraterritorial organisations	..	..	..	..	..	..	..	..	..	..
Education	..	..	..	..	..	..	..	..	..	..
Human health and social work activities	..	..	..	..	..	..	..	..	..	..
Arts, entertainment and recreation	..	..	..	..	..	..	..	..	..	..
Other services	..	..	..	..	..	..	..	..	..	..
Not allocated and confidential	**893.1**	**824.8**	**1 404.2**	**1 282.8**	**1 381.2**	**2 382.1**	**2 523.9**	**2 577.9**	**2 987.5**	**2 779.0**
Private real estate activities	..	..	..	..	..	..	..	..	..	..

.. Not available

Note: Detailed metadata at: *http://stats.oecd.org/OECDStat_Metadata/ShowMetadata.ashx?Dataset=FDI_CTRY_IND_SUMM.*

Source: OECD International Direct Investment Statistics (database): https://doi.org/10.1787/idi-data-en

KOREA

Table 1. Foreign direct investment flows by country

Million US dollars

	Inward					Outward				
	2014	2015	2016	2017	2018	2014	2015	2016	2017	2018
WORLD	**3 381.2**	**2 804.7**	**7 263.0**	**11 531.5**	**13 267.2**	**19 994.0**	**18 489.6**	**30 507.5**	**43 463.9**	**45 232.6**
OECD COUNTRIES	**4 217.7**	**972.8**	**4 619.0**	**6 407.4**	**7 131.6**	**7 638.0**	**7 447.0**	**12 486.8**	**20 259.0**	**19 455.3**
Australia	-433.0	5.5	2.0	33.7	2 004.2	1 441.4	679.9	817.6	-715.4	485.9
Austria	-236.5	-166.4	118.0	5.0	-4.0	8.6	.. c	12.3	41.3	1 290.4
Belgium	-11.6	-17.3	9.0	63.4	13.5	338.0	101.8	43.2	122.9	262.6
Canada	-2.5	191.0	153.0	124.2	-221.0	136.7	-1 354.6	293.9	-4.7	98.2
Chile	-10.2	4.8	9.0	-	0.1	39.3	-11.6	24.5	196.6	104.3
Czech Republic	-1.0	-	-	0.2	0.1	150.0	343.0	22.7	436.5	238.4
Denmark	148.1	38.9	-13.0	-7.8	3.7	23.4	.. c	.. c	12.0	2.7
Estonia	-	-	-	13.2	1.1	.. c	-	-	-	0.0
Finland	38.4	12.3	27.0	12.5	-22.3	0.6	6.9	.. c	36.5	-17.0
France	-1 471.2	2.4	387.0	55.8	635.5	-669.5	923.7	-21.0	119.2	490.7
Germany	303.9	252.8	-3.0	704.7	-255.1	71.3	153.7	280.1	556.4	503.5
Greece	-9.3	-	-	-	-	.. c	.. c	.. c	0.4	0.5
Hungary	407.7	47.0	27.0	3.7	-	87.0	98.9	125.8	432.0	378.9
Iceland	7.8	1.9	1.0	-0.2	-	.. c	.. c	.. c	0.0	189.3
Ireland	2.9	-245.1	84.0	163.8	500.0	-181.8	34.4	.. c	1 509.2	157.1
Israel[1]	3.8	1.9	2.0	1.9	10.8	11.3	.. c	.. c	-0.3	26.1
Italy	140.6	37.6	68.0	60.9	8.4	-37.8	98.0	-1.4	119.0	86.2
Japan	443.9	634.2	1 052.0	1 362.6	1 050.9	506.1	1 469.3	181.2	524.1	779.6
Korea	-	-	-	-	-	-	-	-	-	-
Latvia	-	-	-	-	1.2	.. c	.. c	.. c	0.2	-
Lithuania	0.0	-	-	0.2	0.1	.. c	-	-	-	0.0
Luxembourg	-1 009.5	189.6	92.0	186.5	146.8	879.0	315.5	639.0	879.8	2 634.0
Mexico	33.3	29.2	24.0	-	10.1	-326.5	220.2	-66.2	516.8	98.0
Netherlands	1 015.1	-343.0	616.0	1 113.7	133.1	559.8	1 157.9	-377.0	35.8	464.4
New Zealand	2 847.9	-	1.0	-2.6	-1.3	3.4	-0.7	9.8	-13.4	23.1
Norway	295.7	-111.2	107.0	46.7	1.1	-338.4	.. c	.. c	27.5	2.3
Poland	-0.9	-	3.0	-	0.5	-352.6	138.2	-155.9	239.4	438.9
Portugal	-74.8	3.1	13.0	0.4	-	4.3	.. c	.. c	48.7	15.6
Slovak Republic	-1.2	-	-	0.1	0.1	149.3	113.4	197.2	-107.6	133.6
Slovenia	-0.7	-	-	-	-	.. c	.. c	.. c	0.6	0.8
Spain	-86.2	33.6	45.0	6.8	1 389.7	-9.3	52.6	47.9	44.2	92.5
Sweden	-240.6	105.7	190.0	2.2	-244.8	44.2	.. c	.. c	41.0	13.0
Switzerland	429.6	253.6	401.0	185.8	26.3	14.4	134.2	94.1	65.6	135.9
Turkey	5.1	-	1.0	0.5	5.0	137.0	37.9	580.7	193.0	240.6
United Kingdom	-176.4	-810.2	153.0	1 151.8	-149.0	-396.9	-1 402.1	688.3	1 463.9	2 595.1
United States	1 859.5	821.0	1 050.0	1 118.2	2 087.0	5 344.9	4 263.9	9 100.3	13 437.9	7 490.7
EUROPE	**-1 749.1**	**-98.1**	**2 814.0**	**5 191.0**	**3 567.4**	**-95.8**	**2 442.1**	**3 348.8**	**7 424.9**	**11 228.4**
Bulgaria	-0.3	-	-	-	-	3.6	15.3	41.8	-21.7	-6.7
Croatia	0.0	-	-	-	-	.. c	-	-	-	-
Cyprus[2, 3]	-0.4	-	-	4.1	0.7	0.3	23.0	.. c	-224.6	-83.5
Malta	-1 213.8	557.5	427.0	1 405.1	1 370.2	.. c	-	-	-	14.2
Romania	0.4	-	-	-	-	-61.7	-50.6	.. c	84.5	3.8
Russian Federation	-23.7	-	-	2.0	5.7	-857.9	18.0	687.4	513.3	461.6
Ukraine	-1.0	-	-	10.1	0.0	0.0	.. c	.. c	0.3	2.9
AFRICA	**-190.1**	**-**	**-**	**11.2**	**5.5**	**85.0**	**-539.2**	**-453.8**	**232.2**	**65.3**
Northern Africa	-9.0	-	-	2.2	1.9	20.9	-9.8	-350.2	69.4	60.6
Algeria	-0.4	-	-	-	-	0.4	2.1	.. c	-0.7	1.8
Egypt	-3.2	-	-	1.1	0.8	-2.3	-12.6	.. c	36.1	23.1
Libya	-4.6	-	-	0.9	0.9	1.7	0.3	.. c	4.8	2.1
Morocco	-0.5	-	-	0.2	0.2	21.7	.. c	.. c	25.5	29.6
Tunisia	-0.3	-	-	-	-	.. c	.. c	.. c	3.7	4.0
Other African countries	-181.9	-	-	8.8	3.6	64.1	-529.4	-103.6	162.8	4.6
Nigeria	-34.1	-	-	0.3	0.9	50.2	-12.7	.. c	217.2	37.6
South Africa	-9.5	-	-	0.1	-	9.5	42.7	23.5	14.8	43.2
AMERICA	**2 104.8**	**1 145.9**	**2 103.0**	**2 342.2**	**3 152.1**	**8 571.5**	**4 339.9**	**13 441.6**	**19 126.8**	**13 699.1**
Northern America	1 857.0	1 012.0	1 203.0	1 242.3	1 866.0	5 481.6	2 909.3	9 394.2	13 433.2	7 588.9
Central America and Caribbean countries	247.0	129.1	891.0	1 098.2	1 285.7	1 634.2	2 473.6	2 471.8	3 755.1	5 005.7
Bahamas	-7.8	3.5	2.0	14.3	-	.. c	.. c	-	-	38.2
Bermuda	318.5	299.5	330.0	747.9	133.4	-41.5	-5.1	.. c	2.2	-26.6
Cayman Islands	121.0	-301.0	486.0	174.1	460.4	1 962.0	2 229.0	2 526.0	3 016.6	4 321.7
Costa Rica	0.2	-	-	-	-	-0.5	.. c	.. c	-1.5	2.2
El Salvador	-	-	-	-	-	4.9	.. c	.. c	-0.6	0.4
Guatemala	0.0	-	-	-	-	-2.3	1.3	.. c	13.9	2.0
Honduras	-	-	-	-	-	0.0	.. c	.. c	-2.1	-6.2
Nicaragua	-	-	-	-	-	-2.8	-2.4	.. c	3.0	9.1
Panama	-35.0	9.1	9.0	-4.5	0.7	95.3	2.3	-168.5	-194.5	18.4
Virgin Islands, U.S.	11.7	87.5	40.0	-	-	.. c	-	.. c	-	-
South America	-9.4	4.8	9.0	1.2	0.4	1 455.8	-1 043.0	1 575.6	1 938.5	1 104.5
Argentina	0.6	-	-	-	-	4.5	5.2	.. c	-1.0	337.1
Bolivia	0.2	-	-	-	-	-2.4	.. c	.. c	51.1	-1.2
Brazil	-0.8	-	-	1.1	-	1 021.0	-1 314.9	1 308.2	1 571.0	439.0
Colombia	0.0	-	-	-	-	-5.6	4.0	.. c	5.8	-12.8
Ecuador	-	-	-	-	-	-1.8	.. c	.. c	6.0	0.0
Paraguay	-1.0	-	-	-	0.1	0.1	.. c	.. c	0.2	0.5
Peru	-0.8	-	-	0.1	0.3	400.2	282.8	182.4	108.8	237.7
Uruguay	2.6	-	-	-	-	.. c	.. c	.. c	-	-
Venezuela	0.1	-	-	-	-	0.2	.. c	.. c	0.0	-0.1

Table 1. Foreign direct investment flows by country *(cont.)*

Million US dollars

	Inward					Outward				
	2014	2015	2016	2017	2018	2014	2015	2016	2017	2018
ASIA	**821.8**	**1 699.9**	**2 291.0**	**3 946.5**	**4 543.5**	**9 800.0**	**11 313.4**	**13 199.5**	**17 362.6**	**19 638.1**
Near and Middle East	-1 307.4	-6.5	82.0	26.9	99.0	-443.5	46.3	396.3	495.0	464.2
Gulf Arabian countries	-1 297.4	-8.4	80.0	22.5	86.0	-451.5	16.1	358.8	450.8	374.9
Kuwait	-0.2	-	-	-	1.3	0.4	.. c	.. c	1.3	-
Qatar	0.0	-	-	0.1	-	1.0	1.3	0.6	0.2	0.0
Saudi Arabia	-1 311.0	299.4	86.0	-	4.4	-508.1	-35.8	373.0	176.8	476.1
United Arab Emirates	21.0	-315.5	-17.0	1.7	0.2	-1.5	73.9	-79.3	234.9	-121.7
Other Near and Middle East	-10.0	1.9	2.0	4.3	13.0	8.0	30.3	37.5	44.1	89.3
Jordan	-8.4	-	-	0.6	0.3	-3.4	.. c	.. c	4.9	2.9
Other Asian countries	2 121.4	1 706.4	2 209.0	3 919.6	4 444.5	10 244.0	11 267.0	12 803.2	16 867.6	19 173.9
China	312.0	106.9	347.0	148.3	758.4	4 337.3	3 725.9	6 271.3	5 891.8	6 305.2
Hong Kong, China	246.1	353.1	313.0	1 194.6	931.5	250.8	1 648.1	-173.9	1 724.3	2 761.6
India	75.2	308.2	153.0	0.6	0.5	485.0	664.2	612.1	919.2	1 985.8
Indonesia	6.4	0.6	2.0	4.1	0.5	276.1	172.2	633.7	553.1	533.6
Iran, Islamic Republic of	-0.3	-	-	0.1	1.9	2.1	.. c	.. c	-12.1	-47.3
Malaysia	-310.0	-58.2	-70.0	142.7	15.2	178.7	147.0	607.9	711.0	217.6
Philippines	1.3	-55.7	-16.0	3.3	0.4	-84.8	-13.9	-187.3	486.8	-1 156.1
Singapore	1 379.1	364.8	425.0	1 020.5	1 441.8	1 470.3	1 987.0	1 840.8	2 704.7	2 362.4
Chinese Taipei	105.1	52.4	3.0	26.1	228.3	44.5	64.1	17.2	104.2	178.4
Thailand	-3.4	-	-	5.3	3.1	359.5	244.3	233.4	84.4	345.8
Viet Nam	-7.0	-	-	1.1	1.9	1 315.9	1 126.8	2 295.6	3 339.7	4 353.6
AUSTRALIA, OCEANIA AND POLAR REGIONS	**2 439.5**	**7.1**	**4.0**	**40.6**	**1 998.7**	**1 633.0**	**933.5**	**971.5**	**-682.6**	**601.6**
WORLD unallocated and confidential	**-45.7**	**49.8**	**51.0**	**0.0**	**0.0**	**-**	**0.0**	**0.0**	**-**	**-**
European Union (EU28)	**-2 477.4**	**-301.7**	**2 243.0**	**4 946.0**	**3 529.3**	**613.6**	**2 119.5**	**1 808.5**	**5 869.5**	**9 709.8**
G20 countries excl. European Union	**-247.7**	**1 878.6**	**3 475.0**	**4 768.3**	**5 945.4**	**10 974.2**	**8 367.3**	**21 759.4**	**25 849.2**	**23 450.2**
G20 OECD countries	**703.2**	**1 163.5**	**2 887.0**	**4 612.2**	**5 176.0**	**6 206.8**	**5 089.8**	**11 853.5**	**16 210.2**	**12 868.6**
G20 Non-OECD countries	**-950.8**	**715.1**	**588.0**	**156.2**	**769.5**	**4 767.5**	**3 277.5**	**9 906.0**	**9 639.0**	**10 581.6**
MENA countries	**-1 320.1**	**-8.4**	**80.0**	**27.1**	**90.2**	**-434.1**	**9.1**	**12.5**	**525.1**	**438.4**
ASEAN countries	**1 065.6**	**251.5**	**341.0**	**1 177.3**	**1 462.9**	**3 818.0**	**3 859.4**	**5 853.5**	**8 286.0**	**7 094.0**

- Nil; c Confidential data

Note: Data excludes resident Special Purpose Entities (SPEs). Detailed metadata at: *http://stats.oecd.org/OECDStat_Metadata/ShowMetadata.ashx?Dataset=FDI_CTRY_IND_SUMM.*

1. Information on data for Israel: *http://oe.cd/israel-disclaimer.*
2. Note by Turkey: The information in this document with reference to "Cyprus" relates to the southern part of the Island. There is no single authority representing both Turkish and Greek Cypriot people on the Island. Turkey recognises the Turkish Republic of Northern Cyprus (TRNC). Until a lasting and equitable solution is found within the context of the United Nations, Turkey shall preserve its position concerning the "Cyprus issue".
3. Note by all the European Union Member States of the OECD and the European Union: The Republic of Cyprus is recognised by all members of the United Nations with the exception of Turkey. The information in this document relates to the area under the effective control of the Government of the Republic of Cyprus.

Source: OECD International Direct Investment Statistics (database): https://doi.org/10.1787/idi-data-en

Table 2. Foreign direct investment positions by country
At year end

Million US dollars

	Inward					Outward				
	2014	2015	2016	2017	2018	2014	2015	2016	2017	2018
WORLD	**168 827.2**	**168 923.7**	**174 978.0**	**210 863.5**	**213 966.3**	**242 791.7**	**276 100.1**	**296 641.0**	**343 088.5**	**383 982.9**
OECD COUNTRIES	**142 929.2**	**135 470.0**	**135 601.7**	**157 266.9**	**161 400.1**	**98 219.8**	**118 311.7**	**126 418.8**	**148 737.9**	**166 676.3**
Australia	1 065.3	776.5	577.8	764.2	1 808.8	9 566.1	10 373.0	11 401.7	11 037.0	11 763.7
Austria	819.5	464.7	533.8	649.8	190.0	196.5	209.4	217.4	321.9	315.3
Belgium	406.2	201.1	359.3	602.5	595.0	1 468.1	1 524.0	1 482.1	1 777.6	1 956.4
Canada	1 026.5	1 500.1	2 201.9	2 344.7	1 842.4	4 680.4	3 935.6	3 735.1	3 883.0	4 135.4
Chile	16.4	1.2	24.9	15.7	-7.1	248.8	195.2	159.7	351.5	589.7
Czech Republic	-3.0	-2.5	-2.6	1.1	-33.2	2 021.0	2 221.1	1 989.3	3 046.0	3 032.1
Denmark	459.6	447.3	549.2	223.5	406.9	38.6	28.5	30.8	39.6	35.6
Estonia	-	-	-	12.8	25.7	.. c	.. c	.. c	0.1	0.1
Finland	248.4	117.3	177.8	128.2	125.5	2.7	9.5	11.2	53.2	32.6
France	5 672.7	5 315.6	4 205.1	5 375.6	6 122.5	128.1	772.7	626.5	997.6	1 064.7
Germany	6 312.0	6 772.7	6 950.6	8 306.5	9 457.2	4 113.6	3 381.8	3 242.2	4 045.4	4 409.3
Greece	3.5	0.5	19.4	5.9	9.9	.. c	.. c	.. c	8.1	8.4
Hungary	4 041.4	3 790.8	3 589.3	3 582.3	3 759.6	1 115.5	1 074.7	344.3	1 836.2	1 858.3
Iceland	12.3	1.3	14.0	38.4	18.4	.. c	.. c	.. c	3.0	192.2
Ireland	1 733.6	1 262.5	823.6	-53.3	1 989.3	427.4	1 193.7	1 202.2	3 008.9	2 991.5
Israel[1]	41.9	20.9	14.1	76.1	110.0	13.7	9.6	16.4	6.8	19.0
Italy	437.5	197.9	325.4	567.0	1 024.9	374.3	498.7	628.3	717.1	908.9
Japan	47 867.8	44 596.0	43 315.1	47 519.3	54 761.4	2 549.1	4 812.8	5 090.4	5 612.0	7 089.4
Korea	-	-	-	-	-	-	-	-	-	-
Latvia	-	-	-	-	1.2	.. c	.. c	.. c	5.8	5.8
Lithuania	0.0	0.0	0.0	0.2	0.3	0.7	.. c	.. c	0.5	0.5
Luxembourg	325.4	1 279.9	1 296.9	1 804.4	1 229.6	2 288.9	3 844.3	3 791.2	4 893.8	6 183.1
Mexico	181.8	155.5	152.2	190.3	244.3	1 951.5	2 968.7	2 504.0	3 196.8	3 047.3
Netherlands	16 117.1	15 359.4	17 549.6	27 591.7	21 609.7	8 114.6	12 444.4	11 694.9	8 572.3	8 398.8
New Zealand	2 852.2	8.9	34.6	55.8	366.5	99.8	171.4	200.0	145.0	187.3
Norway	1 476.9	916.7	738.0	767.2	666.1	380.0	.. c	-270.0	11.8	13.2
Poland	5.9	7.4	9.4	9.6	9.1	1 068.7	1 199.2	828.8	1 209.9	1 677.0
Portugal	58.9	166.9	169.9	186.0	218.2	59.3	.. c	.. c	184.7	203.5
Slovak Republic	-1.1	0.1	-0.9	-0.7	-18.6	2 638.3	2 489.6	2 437.7	2 613.5	2 605.0
Slovenia	6.2	5.3	5.4	5.3	13.0	.. c	.. c	.. c	9.0	8.8
Spain	655.8	514.4	510.6	428.8	520.6	840.9	818.3	826.1	987.6	955.3
Sweden	1 779.7	2 158.6	2 307.8	2 099.5	1 847.0	235.9	270.5	243.2	416.1	401.1
Switzerland	3 906.3	3 491.6	3 418.4	5 055.0	3 902.8	154.5	940.6	354.4	335.3	443.5
Turkey	22.4	11.0	27.4	34.8	-57.6	813.1	885.6	1 198.6	865.4	1 194.5
United Kingdom	13 320.5	13 003.1	13 952.0	14 941.4	16 209.0	5 310.7	5 352.3	4 888.5	7 627.9	10 352.4
United States	32 059.7	32 927.3	31 751.9	33 937.3	32 431.9	47 312.2	56 038.7	67 395.1	80 918.8	90 626.1
EUROPE	**61 239.2**	**61 797.5**	**63 544.6**	**82 239.7**	**79 191.3**	**36 571.6**	**44 551.7**	**43 031.6**	**52 276.5**	**57 277.2**
Bulgaria	1.5	1.1	1.0	1.0	1.0	153.5	231.7	235.3	141.8	135.1
Croatia	0.0	0.0	-	-	0.0	0.1	0.4	.. c	0.4	0.4
Cyprus[2, 3]	0.6	1.2	1.3	1.3	13.0	531.5	338.4	551.0	148.4	53.6
Malta	3 354.2	6 228.0	5 942.5	9 790.9	9 265.8	.. c	.. c	.. c	0.3	-9.7
Romania	0.6	-	-0.6	3.2	-1.5	84.8	71.5	197.4	610.8	113.5
Russian Federation	35.5	48.3	42.9	47.5	-8.8	2 047.2	1 373.9	2 482.6	2 617.5	3 051.6
Ukraine	1.3	1.5	1.3	1.4	1.4	135.8	163.0	158.4	203.4	162.4
AFRICA	**80.2**	**183.7**	**140.0**	**145.0**	**281.2**	**2 378.9**	**1 786.0**	**1 431.8**	**2 932.2**	**3 106.8**
Northern Africa	14.9	17.0	11.0	12.5	15.6	365.4	491.5	272.0	475.0	495.7
Algeria	0.1	-	0.1	0.1	0.1	1.5	3.8	4.4	2.6	62.5
Egypt	5.8	6.7	5.4	5.7	6.8	80.0	90.3	-128.6	-1.9	-2.6
Libya	8.0	8.9	5.0	6.0	7.2	278.9	387.2	383.0	393.0	369.3
Morocco	1.4	1.4	0.6	0.8	1.5	-0.3	5.5	5.5	70.5	54.3
Tunisia	-0.3	-	-0.1	0.0	0.0	.. c	.. c	.. c	10.7	12.2
Other African countries	64.4	165.9	128.8	132.3	265.5	2 013.4	1 294.5	1 159.9	2 454.5	2 612.8
Nigeria	43.5	40.5	7.4	8.3	18.0	194.4	136.7	43.1	450.1	476.2
South Africa	-2.3	2.5	-1.7	0.5	1.0	180.4	172.1	202.9	214.9	223.4
AMERICA	**36 209.7**	**37 208.5**	**38 506.1**	**45 533.0**	**40 084.6**	**70 515.4**	**81 340.2**	**97 541.5**	**114 957.7**	**130 672.6**
Northern America	33 086.1	34 427.4	33 953.8	36 282.0	34 274.3	51 992.5	59 974.3	71 130.1	84 801.8	94 761.5
Central America and Caribbean countries	3 083.1	2 708.7	4 469.9	9 175.2	5 882.3	11 722.7	16 131.6	18 262.5	21 034.3	25 940.1
Bahamas	33.2	40.4	47.0	31.6	52.0	.. c	.. c	.. c	1.9	28.7
Bermuda	397.1	27.3	710.6	1 748.6	480.7	1 273.4	1 189.3	.. c	824.0	889.6
Cayman Islands	1 128.8	1 093.2	1 813.6	5 223.2	3 111.5	6 847.1	10 014.0	12 483.8	15 076.3	18 875.1
Costa Rica	0.1	0.1	0.1	0.1	0.1	39.4	32.2	34.4	27.4	44.2
El Salvador	-	0.0	-	-	-	43.1	.. c	.. c	46.8	45.6
Guatemala	0.0	2.3	2.3	2.1	2.2	18.5	51.6	45.3	56.1	49.4
Honduras	-	-	-	-	-	15.9	20.4	20.8	21.0	14.8
Nicaragua	-	-	-	-	-	30.5	30.6	27.1	32.9	18.0
Panama	232.5	175.9	183.9	210.5	28.9	961.8	1 198.3	1 065.8	891.5	1 408.2
Virgin Islands, U.S.	-	-	-	-	-	.. c	.. c	.. c	0.4	0.4
South America	30.2	66.2	73.4	69.7	-76.5	6 800.2	5 233.6	8 148.6	9 121.5	9 971.1
Argentina	0.1	5.0	2.9	4.9	-14.5	37.2	43.4	39.7	40.8	378.1
Bolivia	0.2	0.2	-	-	-	14.6	9.8	83.1	133.9	12.7
Brazil	-3.3	50.5	44.0	47.7	-55.2	4 705.9	3 025.5	5 656.4	6 141.1	6 274.0
Colombia	0.2	0.3	0.1	0.1	-0.5	212.0	221.2	211.9	251.8	222.3
Ecuador	-	-	-	-	0.0	17.1	26.2	15.2	36.8	36.8
Paraguay	8.6	3.4	0.8	0.7	0.9	0.4	3.3	.. c	3.8	6.6
Peru	0.6	1.0	0.6	0.4	0.7	1 538.0	1 698.2	1 970.0	2 132.2	2 421.1
Uruguay	7.4	4.6	0.1	0.1	-0.1	.. c	0.6	.. c	28.0	28.0
Venezuela	0.1	0.0	0.0	0.0	-0.6	3.4	10.2	.. c	1.4	1.8

Table 2. Foreign direct investment positions by country *(cont.)*

At year end

Million US dollars

	Inward					Outward				
	2014	2015	2016	2017	2018	2014	2015	2016	2017	2018
ASIA	**67 188.6**	**68 758.6**	**71 968.2**	**82 017.6**	**92 143.2**	**122 642.1**	**136 180.1**	**141 198.9**	**159 831.6**	**178 848.4**
Near and Middle East	958.9	1 806.5	2 193.0	3 155.9	2 398.6	336.8	1 753.9	1 590.2	2 476.9	2 600.9
Gulf Arabian countries	896.0	1 762.9	2 166.3	3 058.0	2 257.2	312.0	1 681.5	1 482.2	2 340.8	2 383.4
Kuwait	0.3	12.2	12.5	11.0	12.5	19.3	27.5	22.6	22.8	20.6
Qatar	0.1	0.3	0.1	0.1	0.2	4.7	12.0	12.1	10.3	14.2
Saudi Arabia	631.8	1 528.1	1 667.4	2 617.7	1 840.9	-877.0	-590.8	-472.2	95.7	210.2
United Arab Emirates	77.7	34.8	309.7	211.2	174.1	501.0	871.0	942.6	1 185.1	1 210.9
Other Near and Middle East	62.9	43.5	26.7	97.9	141.4	24.8	72.5	108.0	136.1	217.6
Jordan	13.9	14.5	6.8	12.8	11.6	7.2	12.1	15.0	19.1	17.4
Other Asian countries	66 221.9	66 945.6	69 771.6	78 858.4	89 740.5	122 305.3	134 426.2	139 604.8	157 350.9	176 243.6
China	2 692.0	4 655.9	5 576.7	5 661.1	8 147.7	67 614.4	67 885.7	69 240.6	77 477.5	77 603.8
Hong Kong, China	4 502.6	5 000.1	6 151.3	6 706.6	7 098.4	11 397.2	13 293.4	12 363.3	13 411.7	15 404.7
India	960.6	833.0	1 106.1	650.5	569.9	3 968.9	4 268.9	5 081.2	5 409.0	12 442.7
Indonesia	29.2	64.2	65.8	60.9	63.2	5 135.0	6 437.1	6 963.7	7 041.3	7 735.4
Iran, Islamic Republic of	82.1	74.9	68.6	80.1	80.0	-7.1	-4.0	22.4	-19.6	-27.8
Malaysia	1 873.9	1 367.5	1 318.0	1 730.7	2 285.9	3 526.2	3 964.9	4 184.0	5 110.6	5 474.4
Philippines	24.4	217.3	165.1	691.2	186.4	2 651.5	2 790.3	2 346.0	2 856.1	1 718.9
Singapore	7 767.2	9 278.9	11 585.3	15 034.3	15 437.3	7 269.4	9 683.1	10 843.1	13 938.5	16 181.9
Chinese Taipei	218.1	647.8	339.9	623.2	899.2	1 044.7	873.2	746.6	953.5	1 051.1
Thailand	5.5	7.0	-10.3	0.5	25.1	2 547.4	2 633.3	3 084.4	3 085.3	3 618.7
Viet Nam	7.4	2.9	-36.1	-26.6	7.6	9 359.4	11 421.2	12 555.8	15 705.7	20 377.0
AUSTRALIA, OCEANIA AND POLAR REGIONS	**4 109.5**	**958.6**	**803.2**	**911.3**	**2 266.1**	**10 683.7**	**12 242.1**	**13 437.3**	**13 090.6**	**14 078.0**
WORLD unallocated and confidential	**0.0**	**16.9**	**16.9**	**16.9**	**0.0**	**0.0**	**0.0**	**-**	**0.0**	**0.0**
European Union (EU28)	**55 756.7**	**57 293.3**	**59 275.7**	**76 264.6**	**74 590.5**	**31 229.9**	**38 110.0**	**35 616.3**	**43 274.3**	**47 697.3**
G20 countries excl. European Union	**112 309.9**	**112 443.1**	**111 963.4**	**123 071.9**	**134 388.9**	**159 611.0**	**171 635.7**	**189 905.2**	**217 939.0**	**242 510.8**
G20 OECD countries	**107 966.2**	**105 255.6**	**103 459.4**	**113 981.1**	**123 844.7**	**76 799.0**	**89 013.7**	**100 710.4**	**118 901.1**	**134 591.7**
G20 Non-OECD countries	**4 343.7**	**7 187.5**	**8 504.0**	**9 090.8**	**10 544.2**	**82 812.1**	**82 615.0**	**89 194.8**	**99 037.9**	**107 919.1**
MENA countries	**931.9**	**1 802.4**	**2 189.7**	**3 092.1**	**2 362.1**	**683.7**	**2 193.7**	**1 777.5**	**2 835.6**	**2 904.6**
ASEAN countries	**9 721.5**	**10 959.6**	**13 105.0**	**17 501.5**	**18 023.7**	**33 849.4**	**40 710.4**	**44 390.6**	**52 463.1**	**60 325.3**

- Nil; c Confidential data

Note: Data excludes resident Special Purpose Entities (SPEs). Detailed metadata at: *http://stats.oecd.org/OECDStat_Metadata/ShowMetadata.ashx?Dataset=FDI_CTRY_IND_SUMM*.

1. Information on data for Israel: *http://oe.cd/israel-disclaimer*.
2. Note by Turkey: The information in this document with reference to "Cyprus" relates to the southern part of the Island. There is no single authority representing both Turkish and Greek Cypriot people on the Island. Turkey recognises the Turkish Republic of Northern Cyprus (TRNC). Until a lasting and equitable solution is found within the context of the United Nations, Turkey shall preserve its position concerning the "Cyprus issue".
3. Note by all the European Union Member States of the OECD and the European Union: The Republic of Cyprus is recognised by all members of the United Nations with the exception of Turkey. The information in this document relates to the area under the effective control of the Government of the Republic of Cyprus.

Source: OECD International Direct Investment Statistics (database): https://doi.org/10.1787/idi-data-en

KOREA

Table 3. Foreign direct investment income by country

Million US dollars

	Inward					Outward				
	2014	2015	2016	2017	2018	2014	2015	2016	2017	2018
WORLD	**-1 017.6**	**2 225.8**	**3 997.0**	**3 615.4**	**4 402.0**	**6 305.4**	**-124.1**	**9 054.5**	**10 090.4**	**9 629.2**
OECD COUNTRIES	**-917.1**	**1 899.9**	**3 098.0**	**3 505.4**	**3 512.6**	**1 428.8**	**-2 776.0**	**46.6**	**1 285.6**	**2 110.9**
Australia	-	-6.3	2.0	-	0.4	-79.0	-79.0	-359.5	-1 244.7	383.3
Austria	-0.2	-10.5	86.0	0.1	0.0	6.7	.. c	.. c	8.4	37.1
Belgium	-	-6.6	1.0	8.0	4.2	-3.0	61.8	.. c	68.4	36.6
Canada	-4.2	32.1	78.0	4.3	-	-463.1	-1 803.0	-305.2	-85.0	-210.9
Chile	-	2.5	10.0	-	-	-0.3	-42.0	-12.6	12.2	-0.6
Czech Republic	-	-	-	-	-	425.2	294.5	406.5	410.7	354.6
Denmark	-	-1.7	-1.0	5.6	2.3	-3.3	.. c	.. c	1.7	2.2
Estonia	-	-	-	-	-	.. c	-	-	.. c	-
Finland	-6.1	-2.4	15.0	-	-	-2.7	.. c	.. c	-0.1	-2.4
France	-49.7	133.6	134.0	97.7	90.2	.. c	127.7	0.2	51.0	32.9
Germany	-69.9	169.8	213.0	564.1	705.4	44.8	90.9	197.8	152.7	217.2
Greece	-	-	-	-	-	.. c	.. c	.. c	.. c	0.5
Hungary	-	7.0	12.0	8.6	-	91.1	90.5	.. c	419.5	-7.9
Iceland	-	0.9	-	-	-	.. c	.. c	.. c	.. c	-0.6
Ireland	-0.7	-40.8	66.0	0.0	231.2	-117.4	.. c	.. c	-2.7	-3.9
Israel[1]	-	0.0	3.0	0.1	0.0	-0.7	.. c	.. c	-0.3	-6.0
Italy	-3.9	-2.7	10.0	2.5	56.0	81.9	90.2	55.8	54.4	48.8
Japan	-515.2	551.0	643.0	1 041.1	575.3	118.8	14.9	64.1	141.3	85.3
Korea	-	-	-	-	-	-	-	-	-	-
Latvia	-	-	-	-	-	.. c	.. c	.. c	.. c	-
Lithuania	-	-	-	-	-	.. c	-	-	.. c	-
Luxembourg	-	66.3	83.0	0.1	-	131.8	138.6	-123.5	-13.2	401.9
Mexico	-2.0	12.9	21.0	-	1.7	-216.0	-801.4	-459.7	-99.0	-58.1
Netherlands	-46.9	-57.5	344.0	253.6	78.4	-69.6	48.9	-158.9	89.3	150.1
New Zealand	-	-	2.0	2.8	-	-58.8	-11.6	.. c	0.4	16.5
Norway	-17.9	5.6	20.0	183.2	5.1	-370.5	.. c	.. c	.. c	-4.4
Poland	-	-	1.0	-	-	89.2	115.9	60.5	38.9	-24.4
Portugal	-	1.8	3.0	-	-	4.3	.. c	.. c	9.8	15.2
Slovak Republic	-	-	-	-	-	563.3	344.2	382.8	367.6	399.5
Slovenia	-	-	-	-	-	.. c	.. c	.. c	.. c	0.2
Spain	-	6.7	36.0	-	0.9	-1.9	41.5	40.7	59.7	16.1
Sweden	-2.4	14.6	104.0	71.4	29.2	38.4	.. c	.. c	29.5	30.8
Switzerland	-101.7	216.6	249.0	59.9	30.9	0.2	.. c	.. c	9.5	8.0
Turkey	-	-	1.0	0.2	-	48.5	-113.7	-122.1	86.4	69.2
United Kingdom	-17.4	179.3	234.0	759.0	116.3	-526.5	-146.1	-31.3	323.9	345.1
United States	-78.9	627.7	728.0	443.1	1 585.0	1 739.9	-1 029.4	464.8	367.9	-220.8
EUROPE	**-326.8**	**898.8**	**1 766.0**	**2 014.1**	**1 352.6**	**-442.9**	**809.6**	**1 221.5**	**2 472.5**	**2 480.7**
Bulgaria	-	-	-	-	-	3.6	15.1	48.9	1.4	-3.6
Croatia	-	-	-	-	-	.. c	-	-	.. c	-
Cyprus[2, 3]	-	-	-	-	-	-32.9	.. c	.. c	-213.0	-99.5
Malta	-10.0	180.2	115.0	-	2.5	.. c	-	-	.. c	-0.5
Romania	-	-	-	-	-	-112.7	.. c	.. c	13.9	-10.9
Russian Federation	-	-	-	-	-	-727.5	-122.5	583.8	453.6	477.1
Ukraine	-	-	-	-	-	-	-	.. c	-	-0.2
AFRICA	**-**	**-**	**-**	**-**	**-**	**-197.7**	**-667.5**	**-562.4**	**-45.3**	**6.8**
Northern Africa	-	-	-	-	-	-19.1	-20.7	-367.7	40.7	26.8
Algeria	-	-	-	-	-	-	.. c	.. c	-0.7	-0.7
Egypt	-	-	-	-	-	-10.1	.. c	.. c	37.4	22.2
Libya	-	-	-	-	-	-	.. c	.. c	-1.3	-0.6
Morocco	-	-	-	-	-	-11.3	.. c	.. c	-0.1	-0.8
Tunisia	-	-	-	-	-	.. c	.. c	.. c	.. c	6.7
Other African countries	-	-	-	-	-	-178.6	-646.8	-194.8	-86.0	-20.0
Nigeria	-	-	-	-	-	-39.7	.. c	.. c	-0.7	45.3
South Africa	-	-	-	-	-	4.8	43.7	19.9	15.1	46.6
AMERICA	**-89.1**	**579.9**	**804.0**	**447.7**	**1 598.8**	**1 838.7**	**-4 217.9**	**730.0**	**1 168.9**	**90.4**
Northern America	-83.1	659.8	806.0	447.3	1 585.0	1 276.8	-2 832.4	159.6	282.9	-431.7
Central America and Caribbean countries	-6.0	-82.4	-12.0	0.3	13.7	-57.5	-600.6	-274.3	-163.0	61.2
Bahamas	-	1.3	2.0	-	-	.. c	-	-	.. c	15.0
Bermuda	-0.1	-3.9	-4.0	0.3	-	110.8	82.7	.. c	48.3	49.4
Cayman Islands	0.0	-81.8	-46.0	0.0	12.0	104.6	106.9	64.2	-103.7	19.8
Costa Rica	-	-	-	-	-	-0.5	.. c	.. c	-1.6	1.3
El Salvador	-	-	-	-	-	4.9	.. c	.. c	.. c	2.6
Guatemala	-	-	-	-	-	-0.8	.. c	.. c	0.1	0.5
Honduras	-	-	-	-	-	0.0	.. c	.. c	-2.1	-7.2
Nicaragua	-	-	-	-	-	-2.7	.. c	.. c	-2.2	-1.6
Panama	-	1.3	3.0	-	-	-17.1	-18.3	-40.1	1.7	41.1
Virgin Islands, U.S.	-	-12.6	12.0	-	-	.. c	-	-	.. c	-
South America	-	2.5	10.0	-	-	619.5	-784.9	844.7	1 049.0	461.0
Argentina	-	-	-	-	-	4.2	.. c	.. c	0.3	-46.9
Bolivia	-	-	-	-	-	0.2	.. c	.. c	1.1	-1.0
Brazil	-	-	-	-	-	629.5	-734.1	859.8	1 040.8	516.2
Colombia	-	-	-	-	-	-6.2	1.6	.. c	-1.0	-0.8
Ecuador	-	-	-	-	-	-4.3	.. c	.. c	-	-
Paraguay	-	-	-	-	-	-0.3	.. c	.. c	.. c	-0.1
Peru	-	-	-	-	-	-2.9	.. c	.. c	-4.3	-5.8
Uruguay	-	-	-	-	-	.. c	.. c	.. c	.. c	-
Venezuela	-	-	-	-	-	-	-	-	.. c	-

Table 3. Foreign direct investment income by country *(cont.)*

Million US dollars

	Inward					Outward				
	2014	2015	2016	2017	2018	2014	2015	2016	2017	2018
ASIA	**-601.7**	**717.3**	**1 389.0**	**1 150.8**	**1 450.2**	**5 272.1**	**4 018.0**	**8 035.5**	**7 709.2**	**6 608.8**
Near and Middle East	-7.0	59.4	72.0	39.5	91.6	-1 156.5	-710.1	-550.3	-103.6	55.0
Gulf Arabian countries	-7.0	59.4	69.0	39.4	91.6	-1 151.7	-708.6	-552.6	-105.3	69.3
Kuwait	-	-	-	-	-	0.0	.. c	.. c	-	-
Qatar	-	-	-	-	-	0.0	.. c	.. c	-	-
Saudi Arabia	0.0	66.7	51.0	-	-	-1 328.4	-709.5	-485.3	-182.1	131.5
United Arab Emirates	-0.2	-19.0	8.0	0.1	-	-63.3	20.4	-64.1	72.6	-64.4
Other Near and Middle East	-	0.0	3.0	0.1	0.0	.. c	-1.5	2.3	1.8	-14.4
Jordan	-	-	-	-	-	-4.0	.. c	.. c	5.5	-2.2
Other Asian countries	-594.7	657.8	1 317.0	1 111.3	1 358.6	6 428.7	4 728.1	8 585.8	7 812.7	6 553.8
China	-0.5	4.3	136.0	0.8	56.3	4 288.7	3 547.7	6 111.4	4 235.5	3 730.7
Hong Kong, China	-4.7	35.0	249.0	4.6	16.1	-76.6	-22.5	-141.5	-726.7	-443.9
India	-	-37.8	64.0	-	-	262.3	502.2	520.4	480.0	972.8
Indonesia	-	0.1	2.0	-	-	-0.6	-267.5	271.6	73.7	218.6
Iran, Islamic Republic of	-	-	-	-	-	2.1	.. c	.. c	-13.8	-47.3
Malaysia	-	61.0	21.0	0.3	-0.9	112.6	128.6	387.2	377.8	349.1
Philippines	-	-19.0	-19.0	-	-	141.5	52.1	-342.0	-95.4	-1 295.7
Singapore	-74.0	90.1	189.0	64.6	711.8	688.8	889.5	947.0	1 297.5	1 064.2
Chinese Taipei	-0.2	-26.9	32.0	-	-	61.8	64.6	15.1	78.9	101.0
Thailand	-	-	-	-	-	193.6	186.1	203.8	141.0	173.5
Viet Nam	-	-	-	-	-	102.2	-122.9	528.3	1 831.6	1 699.2
AUSTRALIA, OCEANIA AND POLAR REGIONS	**-**	**-6.2**	**4.0**	**2.8**	**0.4**	**-164.8**	**-68.3**	**-370.1**	**-1 214.9**	**442.5**
WORLD unallocated and confidential	**0.0**	**36.0**	**34.0**	**0.0**	**0.0**	**-**	**0.0**	**-**	**-**	**-**
European Union (EU28)	**-207.3**	**637.1**	**1 456.0**	**1 770.8**	**1 316.6**	**570.2**	**1 102.4**	**875.0**	**1 871.4**	**1 935.8**
G20 countries excl. European Union	**-741.7**	**1 730.5**	**2 317.0**	**2 912.8**	**3 186.7**	**3 839.4**	**-1 383.7**	**7 383.2**	**5 865.9**	**6 738.4**
G20 OECD countries	**-741.2**	**1 697.3**	**2 064.0**	**2 912.0**	**3 130.4**	**706.2**	**-3 648.9**	**-495.0**	**-251.1**	**691.8**
G20 Non-OECD countries	**-0.5**	**33.2**	**253.0**	**0.8**	**56.3**	**3 133.1**	**2 265.2**	**7 878.2**	**6 117.0**	**6 046.6**
MENA countries	**-7.0**	**59.4**	**69.0**	**39.4**	**91.6**	**-1 175.0**	**-728.6**	**-918.1**	**-59.2**	**94.0**
ASEAN countries	**-74.1**	**132.3**	**193.0**	**64.9**	**710.9**	**1 200.0**	**829.8**	**1 994.9**	**3 605.3**	**2 147.1**

- Nil; c Confidential data

Note: Data excludes resident Special Purpose Entities (SPEs). Detailed metadata at: *http://stats.oecd.org/OECDStat_Metadata/ShowMetadata.ashx?Dataset=FDI_CTRY_IND_SUMM.*

1. Information on data for Israel: *http://oe.cd/israel-disclaimer.*
2. Note by Turkey: The information in this document with reference to "Cyprus" relates to the southern part of the Island. There is no single authority representing both Turkish and Greek Cypriot people on the Island. Turkey recognises the Turkish Republic of Northern Cyprus (TRNC). Until a lasting and equitable solution is found within the context of the United Nations, Turkey shall preserve its position concerning the "Cyprus issue".
3. Note by all the European Union Member States of the OECD and the European Union: The Republic of Cyprus is recognised by all members of the United Nations with the exception of Turkey. The information in this document relates to the area under the effective control of the Government of the Republic of Cyprus.

Source: OECD International Direct Investment Statistics (database): https://doi.org/10.1787/idi-data-en

KOREA

Table 4. Foreign direct investment flows by industrial sector

Million US dollars

	Inward					Outward				
	2014	2015	2016	2017	2018	2014	2015	2016	2017	2018
All FDI activities	**3 381.2**	**2 804.7**	**7 263.0**	**11 531.5**	**13 267.2**	**19 994.0**	**18 489.6**	**30 507.5**	**43 463.9**	**45 232.6**
Agriculture, forestry and fishing	**9.0**	**0.7**	**2.0**	**5.0**	**-28.5**	**31.3**	**69.7**	**59.0**	**81.9**	**118.1**
Mining and quarrying	**-4.4**	**7.3**	**13.0**	**0.1**	**1.6**	**2 553.8**	**-3 384.0**	**-1 106.0**	**-1 126.1**	**873.2**
Extraction activities	-4.4	-	-	0.1	-	2 438.7	-1 281.6	-1 029.0	-1 102.4	298.5
Manufacturing	**-848.9**	**1 507.4**	**3 909.0**	**5 180.9**	**5 245.3**	**7 759.7**	**7 794.6**	**11 758.0**	**14 631.2**	**17 421.0**
of which:										
Food products, beverages and tobacco	-63.7	-958.9	154.0	150.3	142.6	143.3	392.0	587.9	570.3	578.5
Textiles, wood and paper products; printing	9.5	-61.9	111.0	73.5	30.4	312.5	306.9	489.0	411.4	178.8
Chemical, rubber, plastic, non-metallic mineral products	1 106.0	2 436.5	2 839.0	2 120.7	2 049.5	2 196.6	1 321.7	1 778.6	1 540.4	1 849.2
Metal and machinery products, except electrical equipment	-8 443.6	-189.1	-44.0	1 901.5	964.2	3 002.9	2 059.6	5 578.1	7 756.9	10 163.9
Motor vehicles, trailers, semi-trailers, other transport equipment	4 274.0	-1 032.3	-139.0	524.3	1 873.1	1 884.2	2 608.3	2 108.2	3 221.2	2 293.9
Other manufacturing	2 268.9	1 313.1	988.0	410.6	185.4	220.2	1 106.1	1 216.3	1 131.0	2 356.7
Electricity, gas, steam and air conditioning supply	**21.4**	**7.4**	**50.0**	**-135.9**	**160.0**	**445.9**	**1 805.8**	**781.0**	**1 206.7**	**1 006.0**
Water supply; sewerage, waste management and remediation activities	**-27.2**	**-5.8**	**10.0**	**149.2**	**1.5**	**17.5**	**12.7**	**3.0**	**174.8**	**442.2**
Construction	**-70.0**	**2.6**	**-33.0**	**11.8**	**14.7**	**-757.1**	**-105.4**	**778.0**	**638.1**	**885.8**
Services	**4 301.2**	**1 285.1**	**3 312.0**	**6 320.4**	**7 872.8**	**9 942.8**	**12 296.2**	**18 234.0**	**27 855.9**	**24 486.3**
Wholesale and retail trade; repair of motor vehicles and motorcycles	480.0	755.3	1 029.0	1 042.4	936.6	1 885.4	2 910.9	4 504.0	11 682.8	5 605.9
Transportation and storage	306.9	464.6	315.0	192.6	116.7	504.6	238.2	1 002.0	1 027.2	718.3
Accommodation and food service activities	-776.0	625.6	770.0	808.3	281.1	237.5	179.6	401.0	208.9	109.6
Information and communication	968.1	540.4	511.0	756.1	2 821.9	410.9	376.7	1 191.0	2 174.6	851.0
Financial and insurance activities	39.8	-749.2	151.0	2 100.2	2 057.5	5 359.1	6 043.7	5 343.0	9 506.9	12 837.0
Activities of holding companies	-1 725.6	387.0	580.0	76.4	656.6	4 198.3	1 226.8	479.3	1 105.3	1 648.6
Real estate activities	513.6	-278.7	148.0	912.3	906.9	923.5	1 998.1	4 995.8	2 521.1	3 448.2
Professional, scientific and technical activities	4 199.7	-34.1	309.0	400.6	128.3	242.3	136.0	519.0	458.5	948.7
Administrative and support service activities	-1 613.9	-	-	72.2	377.7	315.1	348.2	176.9	-335.8	-203.7
Public administration; activities of households and of extraterritorial organisations	-0.2	-	-	-	-	0.1	1.0	-	258.0	-
Education	-40.9	45.9	21.0	13.7	11.7	-2.3	25.0	11.1	125.6	12.8
Human health and social work activities	-1.8	-	-	-	-	11.3	44.9	68.9	175.4	181.5
Arts, entertainment and recreation	27.3	-55.3	-14.0	16.0	233.3	49.4	-8.6	9.0	5.4	-26.0
Other services	323.6	-29.4	72.0	5.8	1.1	6.0	2.5	12.7	47.4	3.0
Not allocated and confidential	**0.0**	**0.0**	**-**	**0.0**	**0.0**	**-**	**0.0**	**0.1**	**1.3**	**0.0**
Private real estate activities	..	..	-	-	-	..	-	-	-	-

- Nil; .. Not available

Note: Data excludes resident Special Purpose Entities (SPEs). Detailed metadata at: *http://stats.oecd.org/OECDStat_Metadata/ShowMetadata.ashx?Dataset=FDI_CTRY_IND_SUMM.*

Source: OECD International Direct Investment Statistics (database): https://doi.org/10.1787/idi-data-en

Table 5. Foreign direct investment positions by industrial sector
At year end

Million US dollars

	Inward					Outward				
	2014	2015	2016	2017	2018	2014	2015	2016	2017	2018
All FDI activities	**168 827.2**	**168 923.7**	**174 978.0**	**210 863.5**	**213 966.3**	**242 791.7**	**276 180.1**	**296 641.0**	**343 088.5**	**383 982.9**
Agriculture, forestry and fishing	**221.6**	**153.1**	**200.6**	**235.3**	**203.1**	**662.6**	**855.5**	**842.0**	**910.0**	**1 031.1**
Mining and quarrying	**46.8**	**21.5**	**11.1**	**44.8**	**42.8**	**37 987.9**	**37 533.6**	**35 209.0**	**34 055.1**	**33 676.6**
Extraction activities	46.8	14.0	3.0	44.8	2.9	28 605.9	28 624.9	26 806.4	25 601.9	24 678.8
Manufacturing	**65 199.7**	**62 916.4**	**66 721.2**	**79 861.6**	**82 015.7**	**96 768.5**	**102 287.2**	**110 985.0**	**135 266.9**	**135 519.5**
of which:										
Food products, beverages and tobacco	1 560.4	3 166.5	3 296.2	4 817.0	4 134.5	3 229.0	3 279.2	4 319.6	4 152.1	4 414.1
Textiles, wood and paper products; printing	1 599.5	1 375.3	1 606.6	1 359.0	2 538.0	4 824.9	5 205.7	5 729.7	6 424.2	5 536.3
Chemical, rubber, plastic, non-metallic mineral products	23 768.5	25 445.6	27 498.5	37 225.6	33 422.9	10 703.0	12 833.1	13 725.1	15 259.1	17 859.3
Metal and machinery products, except electrical equipment	13 791.3	18 020.9	18 067.2	20 369.9	23 757.8	42 257.1	44 940.0	50 536.8	60 291.8	65 102.0
Motor vehicles, trailers, semi-trailers, other transport equipment	15 638.5	7 060.1	8 216.7	7 099.0	8 347.5	26 832.2	26 545.9	25 735.6	37 816.9	28 616.6
Other manufacturing	8 841.4	7 848.0	8 036.1	8 991.1	9 815.0	8 922.3	9 403.4	10 938.4	11 322.7	13 991.3
Electricity, gas, steam and air conditioning supply	**751.1**	**1 012.6**	**1 002.9**	**1 053.8**	**1 139.1**	**3 085.7**	**4 262.3**	**5 013.0**	**6 391.2**	**7 258.2**
Water supply; sewerage, waste management and remediation activities	**103.3**	**92.2**	**146.3**	**194.0**	**245.2**	**-73.7**	**30.6**	**18.0**	**166.2**	**612.0**
Construction	**154.8**	**1 310.3**	**1 306.1**	**1 801.4**	**1 635.7**	**665.1**	**1 922.7**	**1 813.0**	**2 987.7**	**3 578.6**
Services	**102 349.9**	**103 417.5**	**105 589.9**	**127 672.5**	**128 684.8**	**103 695.7**	**129 287.2**	**142 758.0**	**163 309.9**	**202 305.4**
Wholesale and retail trade; repair of motor vehicles and motorcycles	16 438.7	12 813.3	15 313.1	20 940.9	24 163.6	41 313.5	44 506.5	47 874.0	54 164.8	72 349.1
Transportation and storage	3 999.3	3 025.3	3 169.6	3 698.0	2 923.4	2 658.7	2 678.1	4 519.0	4 133.2	5 150.7
Accommodation and food service activities	13 309.3	13 480.6	14 584.0	17 937.6	15 987.5	1 763.7	2 043.3	2 351.0	3 048.4	2 574.5
Information and communication	7 058.1	6 747.2	4 579.9	7 382.6	7 689.8	2 356.5	3 736.8	5 495.0	6 366.3	6 403.3
Financial and insurance activities	48 042.4	52 747.3	54 129.8	61 630.1	60 792.7	40 226.7	57 409.5	54 265.0	68 982.9	84 638.0
Activities of holding companies	-1 725.6	0.2	1.4	3 079.2	2 867.6	23 788.3	16 317.3	7 876.2	8 907.4	10 350.3
Real estate activities	4 460.7	7 068.3	6 858.3	8 658.4	10 578.0	10 693.7	11 788.9	15 477.1	17 270.3	21 094.7
Professional, scientific and technical activities	8 310.7	4 312.4	4 737.2	3 491.0	2 599.7	1 251.2	1 472.6	8 205.0	3 845.8	4 625.0
Administrative and support service activities	-	1 289.8	1 432.9	1 982.3	2 262.8	2 056.0	4 079.7	2 754.5	3 350.1	3 274.1
Public administration; activities of households and of extraterritorial organisations	-	0.1	-	-	0.1	16.6	17.7	17.7	17.7	17.7
Education	142.4	222.9	193.8	260.1	249.0	155.4	200.3	204.4	222.4	253.3
Human health and social work activities	16.9	11.3	12.0	12.0	1.9	229.5	193.5	426.7	611.0	674.0
Arts, entertainment and recreation	188.8	1 257.1	454.7	1 398.8	710.3	711.8	875.9	888.0	964.1	927.1
Other services	382.5	442.0	124.6	280.6	726.1	262.3	284.3	281.8	332.9	323.9
Not allocated and confidential	**0.0**	**-0.2**	**0.1**	**0.1**	**0.0**	**-**	**1.0**	**2.7**	**1.3**	**1.3**
Private real estate activities	..	..	-	-	-	-	-	-	-	-

- Nil; .. Not available

Note: Data excludes resident Special Purpose Entities (SPEs). Detailed metadata at: *http://stats.oecd.org/OECDStat_Metadata/ShowMetadata.ashx?Dataset=FDI_CTRY_IND_SUMM.*

Source: *OECD International Direct Investment Statistics (database): https://doi.org/10.1787/idi-data-en*

Table 6. Foreign direct investment income by industrial sector

Million US dollars

	Inward					Outward				
	2014	2015	2016	2017	2018	2014	2015	2016	2017	2018
All FDI activities	**-1 017.6**	**2 225.8**	**3 997.0**	**3 615.4**	**4 402.0**	**6 305.4**	**-124.1**	**9 054.5**	**10 090.4**	**9 629.2**
Agriculture, forestry and fishing	**-1.3**	**0.6**	**3.0**	**4.5**	**-**	**-49.1**	**-43.0**	**0.3**	**13.6**	**6.9**
Mining and quarrying	**-**	**13.7**	**10.0**	**0.6**	**1.3**	**-653.0**	**-5 337.7**	**-2 267.0**	**-1 637.2**	**-18.3**
Extraction activities	-	-	-	0.6	-	-402.4	-3 520.2	-1 951.5	-1 717.3	-347.7
Manufacturing	**-443.6**	**941.7**	**2 107.0**	**2 869.2**	**3 515.4**	**6 347.9**	**3 949.9**	**8 963.0**	**9 774.4**	**6 177.0**
of which:										
Food products, beverages and tobacco	-50.9	119.0	144.0	147.4	155.3	-58.0	20.8	224.1	0.1	8.2
Textiles, wood and paper products; printing	-1.9	-0.6	118.0	22.4	81.8	79.0	96.1	27.4	73.6	-77.0
Chemical, rubber, plastic, non-metallic mineral products	-176.3	345.8	661.0	1 860.1	2 169.2	838.5	512.1	834.5	734.4	238.0
Metal and machinery products, except electrical equipment	-36.6	50.0	305.0	587.4	732.5	2 454.8	896.9	5 109.3	6 913.9	5 792.3
Motor vehicles, trailers, semi-trailers, other transport equipment	-171.7	335.5	760.0	104.4	61.9	3 239.4	2 194.5	2 204.1	1 544.1	-296.4
Other manufacturing	-6.1	92.0	119.0	146.8	314.7	-205.9	229.4	563.7	508.3	511.9
Electricity, gas, steam and air conditioning supply	**-7.3**	**51.2**	**51.0**	**52.4**	**96.3**	**216.7**	**171.7**	**161.3**	**378.2**	**311.4**
Water supply; sewerage, waste management and remediation activities	**-0.1**	**-4.4**	**-3.0**	**0.2**	**-**	**5.0**	**0.6**	**13.5**	**11.7**	**19.2**
Construction	**-**	**45.3**	**50.0**	**5.5**	**-**	**-1 505.2**	**-897.0**	**-532.0**	**-54.3**	**252.6**
Services	**-565.4**	**1 177.6**	**1 779.0**	**682.9**	**789.1**	**1 943.0**	**2 031.5**	**2 715.5**	**1 604.0**	**2 880.4**
Wholesale and retail trade; repair of motor vehicles and motorcycles	-93.4	157.1	558.0	325.4	205.8	1 656.9	2 232.3	2 049.6	1 234.6	2 968.4
Transportation and storage	-14.6	276.6	192.0	211.0	18.5	110.4	192.3	199.2	140.6	168.5
Accommodation and food service activities	-319.8	128.5	172.0	1.7	55.3	-26.5	-64.9	-12.9	-76.2	-181.8
Information and communication	-12.5	316.4	305.0	5.3	2.4	109.2	-250.5	52.8	-9.1	-278.3
Financial and insurance activities	-74.1	188.7	325.0	81.9	475.5	7.0	-452.2	-41.0	180.9	23.9
Activities of holding companies	-	37.2	47.0	44.1	9.6	312.1	-580.8	-31.9	26.2	60.9
Real estate activities	-17.7	22.0	96.0	1.0	25.8	-40.5	108.8	211.1	111.5	312.0
Professional, scientific and technical activities	-28.8	100.8	129.0	44.5	1.4	-56.3	20.8	286.5	6.7	-120.1
Administrative and support service activities	-	-	2.0	11.8	4.2	176.0	320.9	-24.9	124.6	29.1
Public administration; activities of households and of extraterritorial organisations	-	-	-	-	-	-	-	-	-	-
Education	-	9.5	5.0	0.3	-	-2.7	-4.5	-8.5	-2.3	-19.4
Human health and social work activities	-	-	-	-	-	-6.2	-4.6	19.3	-1.9	68.5
Arts, entertainment and recreation	-	-24.8	-12.0	-	-	16.2	-66.4	-15.0	-103.7	-86.7
Other services	-4.5	2.8	7.0	-	-	-0.5	-0.5	-0.7	-1.7	-3.6
Not allocated and confidential	**0.0**	**0.0**	**-**	**0.0**	**0.0**	**-**	**0.0**	**0.1**	**0.0**	**0.0**
Private real estate activities	..	..	-	-	-	..	-	-	-	-

- Nil; .. Not available

Note: Data excludes resident Special Purpose Entities (SPEs). Detailed metadata at: *http://stats.oecd.org/OECDStat_Metadata/ShowMetadata.ashx?Dataset=FDI_CTRY_IND_SUMM.*

Source: OECD International Direct Investment Statistics (database): https://doi.org/10.1787/idi-data-en

LATVIA

Table 1. Foreign direct investment flows by country

Million US dollars

	Inward					Outward				
	2014	2015	2016	2017	2018	2014	2015	2016	2017	2018
WORLD	**894.3**	**734.3**	**257.7**	**666.2**	**993.7**	**517.4**	**67.7**	**147.1**	**130.8**	**190.0**
OECD COUNTRIES	**254.7**	**193.0**	**-71.9**	**329.2**	**606.6**	**184.4**	**-66.6**	**97.3**	**64.3**	**41.3**
Australia	-	-	-	-	-	-	-	-	-	-
Austria	-46.4	25.5	108.4	-6.8	13.0	.. c	.. c	.. c	2.3	-
Belgium	-9.3	2.2	-7.7	1.1	7.1	-	-	-	-	-
Canada	-6.6	5.5	6.6	3.4	-	-4.0	.. c	-	-	-
Chile	-	-	-	-	-	-	-	-	-	-
Czech Republic	1.3	2.2	1.1	-	-	.. c	-	.. c	.. c	-
Denmark	22.6	5.5	33.2	44.0	-34.2	2.7	2.2	12.2	11.3	13.0
Estonia	-10.6	41.0	79.6	19.2	269.1	50.4	-23.3	42.0	5.6	13.0
Finland	-103.5	-3.3	13.3	-57.5	-47.2	1.3	4.4	-	-6.8	5.9
France	5.3	4.4	7.7	16.9	15.3	.. c	-4.4	.. c	2.3	3.5
Germany	156.6	16.6	-122.7	-9.0	31.9	2.7	2.2	-	-1.1	-10.6
Greece	-	-	-	-	-	-	-	-	-	-
Hungary	-27.9	-238.5	-	1.1	-	-	-	-	-	.. c
Iceland	-14.6	2.2	-6.6	22.5	-55.5	.. c	-	.. c	-	1.2
Ireland	-	-1.1	6.6	32.7	-30.7	-	-	-	-	-
Israel[1]	4.0	-2.2	1.1	1.1	4.7	-	-	-	-	1.2
Italy	-	-4.4	44.2	2.3	3.5	-	3.3	-	-	-
Japan	-	-	-	-	-	-	-	-	-	-
Korea	15.9	5.5	-7.7	-37.2	-2.4	-	-	-	-	-
Latvia	-	-	-	-	-	-	-	-	-	-
Lithuania	-75.6	73.2	61.9	148.8	27.1	203.0	25.5	37.6	55.2	28.3
Luxembourg	138.0	51.0	207.9	71.0	230.1	4.0	-1.1	1.1	-10.1	-3.5
Mexico	-	-	-	.. c	-1.2	-	-	.. c	.. c	.. c
Netherlands	43.8	206.3	-8.8	2.3	-147.5	122.1	5.5	-	-	-
New Zealand	-15.9	.. c	-	-	-	-	-	-	-	-
Norway	51.7	62.1	6.6	-597.5	3.5	-2.7	-	-	-	-
Poland	26.5	16.6	13.3	22.5	10.6	1.3	11.1	-15.5	-3.4	5.9
Portugal	-	-	-	-	-	.. c	.. c	.. c	-	-
Slovak Republic	-	-	-	-1.1	-	26.5	.. c	.. c	44.0	-31.9
Slovenia	-	-	-	-	-	-	-	-	-	-
Spain	1.3	-	-1.1	-	233.7	-2.7	3.3	6.6	4.5	1.2
Sweden	92.9	-82.1	-456.7	870.3	212.4	-1.3	1.1	2.2	16.9	8.3
Switzerland	-70.3	32.2	71.9	-45.1	4.7	-14.6	-71.0	17.7	-44.0	-20.1
Turkey	5.3	-	1.1	-1.1	3.5	-	-	-	-	-
United Kingdom	-	34.4	-60.8	-22.5	-139.3	-2.7	1.1	2.2	-5.6	-
United States	-9.3	10.0	-3.3	-3.4	-5.9	1.3	17.7	18.8	44.0	35.4
EUROPE	**760.2**	**491.4**	**101.7**	**617.7**	**860.4**	**520.1**	**-2.2**	**101.7**	**74.4**	**96.8**
Bulgaria	6.6	-	1.1	3.4	1.2	-	-	-	-	1.2
Croatia	-	-	-	-	-	-	.. c	-	-	-
Cyprus[2, 3]	90.2	110.9	3.3	-81.2	-115.7	-8.0	74.3	-4.4	-27.1	-49.6
Malta	35.8	15.5	-68.6	45.1	8.3	-	-33.3	.. c	.. c	77.9
Romania	-	-	-	-3.4	4.7	.. c	-	.. c	1.1	.. c
Russian Federation	383.4	106.5	175.8	127.4	351.7	123.4	14.4	15.5	14.7	17.7
Ukraine	18.6	1.1	17.7	12.4	5.9	-	-4.4	-4.4	-4.5	18.9
AFRICA	**-5.3**	**-**	**7.7**	**5.6**	**1.2**	**-**	**-**	**-**	**-**	**1.2**
Northern Africa	-	-	-	-	-	-	-	-	-	-
Algeria	-	-	-	-	-	-	-	-	-	-
Egypt	-	-	-	-	-	-	-	-	-	-
Libya	-	-	-	-	-	-	-	-	-	-
Morocco	-	-	-	-	-	-	-	-	-	-
Tunisia	-	-	-	-	-	-	-	-	-	-
Other African countries	-4.0	-	7.7	5.6	1.2	-	-	-	-	1.2
Nigeria	-	-	-	-	-	-	-	-	-	-
South Africa	-	-	-	-	-	-	-	-	-	-
AMERICA	**-8.0**	**1.1**	**-23.2**	**-11.3**	**-10.6**	**-2.7**	**17.7**	**38.7**	**46.2**	**26.0**
Northern America	-15.9	15.5	3.3	-	-5.9	-2.7	16.6	18.8	44.0	35.4
Central America and Caribbean countries	9.3	-14.4	-26.5	-11.3	-4.7	-	-	19.9	.. c	-9.4
Bahamas	-	-	-	-	-	-	-	-	-	-
Bermuda	-	-	-	-	-	-	-	-	-	-
Cayman Islands	.. c	.. c	.. c	.. c	.. c	-	-	-	-	-
Costa Rica	-	-	-	-	-	-	-	-	-	-
El Salvador	-	-	-	-	-	-	-	-	-	-
Guatemala	-	-	-	-	-	-	-	-	-	-
Honduras	-	-	-	-	-	-	-	-	-	-
Nicaragua	-	-	-	-	-	-	-	-	-	-
Panama	-	-	-2.2	-3.4	-1.2	-	-	-	-	-
Virgin Islands, U.S.	-	-	-	-	-	-	-	-	-	-
South America	-	-	-	-	-	-	-	-	-	-
Argentina	-	-	-	-	-	-	-	-	-	-
Bolivia	-	-	-	-	-	-	-	-	-	-
Brazil	-	-	-	-	-	-	-	-	-	-
Colombia	-	-	-	-	-	-	-	-	-	-
Ecuador	-	-	-	-	-	-	-	-	-	-
Paraguay	-	-	-	-	-	-	-	-	-	-
Peru	-	-	-	-	-	-	-	-	-	-
Uruguay	-	-	-	-	-	-	-	-	-	-
Venezuela	-	-	-	-	-	-	-	-	-	-

Table 1. Foreign direct investment flows by country *(cont.)*

Million US dollars

	Inward					Outward				
	2014	2015	2016	2017	2018	2014	2015	2016	2017	2018
ASIA	**87.6**	**35.5**	**48.7**	**-27.1**	**28.3**	**10.6**	**42.2**	**-**	**-12.4**	**13.0**
Near and Middle East	14.6	2.2	29.9	-12.4	2.4	2.7	41.0	1.1	-13.5	13.0
Gulf Arabian countries	-	-	2.2	-2.3	-1.2	-	39.9	.. c	.. c	9.4
Kuwait	-	-	-	-	-	-	-	-	-	-
Qatar	-	-	-	-	-	-	-	-	-	-
Saudi Arabia	-	-	-	-2.3	-	-	-	-	-	-
United Arab Emirates	-	-	2.2	-1.1	-1.2	-	39.9	.. c	.. c	.. c
Other Near and Middle East	14.6	2.2	28.8	-9.0	3.5	2.7	1.1	10.0	-	2.4
Jordan	-	-	-	-	-	-	-	-	-	-
Other Asian countries	73.0	32.2	17.7	-14.7	26.0	8.0	1.1	-1.1	1.1	-
China	33.2	7.8	4.4	4.5	10.6	-	-	-1.1	-	-
Hong Kong, China	-	-	-	-	2.4	-	-	-	-	-
India	-	-	-	-	-	-	-	-	-	-
Indonesia	-	-	-	-	-	-	-	-	-	-
Iran, Islamic Republic of	-	-	-	-	-	-	-	-	-	-
Malaysia	-	.. c	-	-	-	-	-	.. c	-	-
Philippines	-	-	-	-	-	-	-	-	-	-
Singapore	4.0	18.9	5.5	4.5	1.2	-	-	-	-	-
Chinese Taipei	-	-	-	-	-	-	-	-	-	-
Thailand	-	-	-	-	-	-	-	-	-	-
Viet Nam	-	-	12.2	5.6	5.9	-	-	-	-	-
AUSTRALIA, OCEANIA AND POLAR REGIONS	**-15.9**	**-2.2**	**-**	**-1.1**	**-1.2**	**-**	**-**	**-**	**-**	**-**
WORLD unallocated and confidential	**75.6**	**208.5**	**122.7**	**82.3**	**115.7**	**-10.6**	**10.0**	**6.6**	**22.5**	**53.1**
European Union (EU28)	**388.7**	**282.9**	**-184.7**	**1 108.1**	**553.5**	**403.3**	**53.2**	**65.2**	**87.9**	**64.9**
G20 countries excl. European Union	**583.8**	**184.1**	**46.4**	**78.9**	**265.5**	**119.4**	**34.4**	**48.7**	**55.2**	**34.2**
G20 OECD countries	**168.5**	**71.0**	**-133.8**	**-50.7**	**-96.8**	**-4.0**	**18.9**	**35.4**	**40.6**	**17.7**
G20 Non-OECD countries	**416.6**	**114.3**	**180.3**	**129.6**	**361.1**	**123.4**	**14.4**	**14.4**	**14.7**	**16.5**
MENA countries	**-**	**-**	**2.2**	**-2.3**	**-1.2**	**-**	**39.9**	**.. c**	**-13.5**	**9.4**
ASEAN countries	**4.0**	**17.7**	**17.7**	**10.1**	**7.1**	**-**	**-**	**.. c**	**-**	**-**

- Nil; c Confidential data

Note: Detailed metadata at: *http://stats.oecd.org/OECDStat_Metadata/ShowMetadata.ashx?Dataset=FDI_CTRY_IND_SUMM.*

1. Information on data for Israel: *http://oe.cd/israel-disclaimer.*
2. Note by Turkey: The information in this document with reference to "Cyprus" relates to the southern part of the Island. There is no single authority representing both Turkish and Greek Cypriot people on the Island. Turkey recognises the Turkish Republic of Northern Cyprus (TRNC). Until a lasting and equitable solution is found within the context of the United Nations, Turkey shall preserve its position concerning the "Cyprus issue".
3. Note by all the European Union Member States of the OECD and the European Union: The Republic of Cyprus is recognised by all members of the United Nations with the exception of Turkey. The information in this document relates to the area under the effective control of the Government of the Republic of Cyprus.

Source: OECD International Direct Investment Statistics (database): https://doi.org/10.1787/idi-data-en

Table 2. Foreign direct investment positions by country

At year end

Million US dollars

	Inward					Outward				
	2014	2015	2016	2017	2018	2014	2015	2016	2017	2018
WORLD	**15 118.0**	**14 729.5**	**14 316.4**	**17 542.6**	**17 405.5**	**1 493.3**	**1 553.6**	**1 633.8**	**1 929.7**	**2 007.1**
OECD COUNTRIES	**10 523.8**	**9 990.2**	**9 358.1**	**11 464.4**	**12 635.7**	**825.6**	**690.3**	**805.3**	**993.0**	**1 393.4**
Australia	-	2.2	1.1	-	-	-	-	-	-	-
Austria	200.3	207.9	215.0	235.1	239.3	13.4	8.7	10.5	13.2	11.5
Belgium	30.4	31.6	53.8	34.8	57.2	-	-	-	-	1.1
Canada	25.5	17.4	12.6	14.4	14.9	1.2	-	-	-	1.1
Chile	-	-	-	-	-	-	-	-	-	-
Czech Republic	17.0	15.2	14.8	13.2	20.6	1.2	1.1	6.3	4.8	3.4
Denmark	693.3	622.8	629.3	704.0	645.8	3.6	10.9	22.1	25.2	14.9
Estonia	872.9	1 044.1	1 011.9	1 563.9	1 739.2	150.5	135.0	176.0	226.7	194.6
Finland	420.1	436.6	413.2	405.4	424.8	7.3	16.3	14.8	19.2	14.9
France	98.3	87.1	95.9	115.1	169.5	13.4	9.8	7.4	7.2	2.3
Germany	888.7	787.2	643.0	783.2	862.1	24.3	14.2	12.6	32.4	46.9
Greece	-	-	-	2.4	-	-	-	-	-	-
Hungary	263.5	1.1	1.1	13.2	11.5	-	-	-	-	2.3
Iceland	78.9	62.1	102.2	103.1	44.7	1.2	1.1	-	-	1.1
Ireland	15.8	15.2	7.4	54.0	19.5	3.6	4.4	-	-	-
Israel[1]	41.3	65.3	29.5	37.2	63.0	-	-	1.1	2.4	3.4
Italy	32.8	33.8	101.2	91.1	106.5	-	14.2	13.7	15.6	-
Japan	-	-	1.1	-	-	-	-	-	-	-
Korea	51.0	50.1	40.1	10.8	8.0	-	-	-	-	-
Latvia	-	-	-	-	-	-	-	-	-	-
Lithuania	598.6	712.0	754.7	1 143.0	1 116.3	264.7	294.0	339.4	460.5	541.6
Luxembourg	423.7	474.7	685.1	951.1	1 045.3	142.1	116.5	112.8	117.5	114.5
Mexico	-	-	-	1.2	-2.3	-	-	9.5	15.6	-
Netherlands	1 216.5	1 334.8	1 274.4	1 464.4	1 245.7	111.7	106.7	103.3	117.5	113.4
New Zealand	46.1	27.2	27.4	30.0	25.2	-	-	-	-	-
Norway	922.7	811.1	752.6	355.0	597.7	23.1	10.9	12.6	32.4	18.3
Poland	51.0	66.4	70.6	105.5	114.5	47.4	54.4	65.4	62.4	38.9
Portugal	-	-	-	-	-	31.6	1.1	-	-	-
Slovak Republic	1.2	3.3	2.1	1.2	3.4	18.2	22.9	20.0	67.2	34.3
Slovenia	-	-	-	-	-	1.2	2.2	2.1	3.6	3.4
Spain	15.8	6.5	2.1	9.6	226.7	6.1	5.4	9.5	10.8	12.6
Sweden	3 206.4	2 854.7	2 254.7	3 320.9	3 054.7	7.3	10.9	21.1	27.6	17.2
Switzerland	207.6	197.1	238.2	310.6	248.5	191.8	96.9	111.7	67.2	49.2
Turkey	29.1	24.0	30.6	34.8	16.0	-	1.1	-	1.2	2.3
United Kingdom	491.7	544.4	441.7	520.5	326.3	19.4	25.0	30.6	33.6	28.6
United States	182.1	166.6	205.5	173.9	191.2	3.6	19.6	42.2	91.1	121.4
EUROPE	**13 945.2**	**13 687.5**	**13 274.0**	**16 448.8**	**16 354.5**	**1 436.3**	**1 393.6**	**1 466.2**	**1 687.5**	**1 732.3**
Bulgaria	19.4	18.5	19.0	24.0	24.0	2.4	2.2	2.1	1.2	10.3
Croatia	-	-	-	-	-	4.9	-	-	-	-
Cyprus[2, 3]	1 194.7	1 368.5	1 346.1	1 448.8	1 237.7	93.5	154.6	111.7	69.6	63.0
Malta	355.7	334.2	398.4	542.1	511.8	3.6	7.6	4.2	1.2	83.6
Romania	-	1.1	-	-3.6	1.1	7.3	5.4	5.3	15.6	9.2
Russian Federation	1 274.8	1 276.0	1 391.4	1 803.8	1 913.2	104.4	115.5	129.7	119.9	115.6
Ukraine	144.5	148.1	149.7	158.3	154.6	48.6	44.6	19.0	20.4	53.8
AFRICA	**10.9**	**16.3**	**17.9**	**25.2**	**29.8**	**-**	**-**	**1.1**	**1.2**	**1.1**
Northern Africa	-	-	-	-	-	-	-	-	-	-
Algeria	-	-	-	-	-	-	-	-	-	-
Egypt	-	-	-	-	-	-	-	-	-	-
Libya	-	-	-	-	-	-	-	-	-	-
Morocco	-	-	-	-	-	-	-	-	-	-
Tunisia	-	-	-	-	-	-	-	-	-	-
Other African countries	10.9	16.3	17.9	25.2	28.6	-	-	1.1	-	1.1
Nigeria	-	-	-	-	-	-	-	-	-	-
South Africa	-	4.4	1.1	-	8.0	-	-	-	-	-
AMERICA	**358.2**	**345.1**	**345.7**	**308.2**	**375.5**	**29.1**	**42.5**	**72.7**	**130.7**	**148.8**
Northern America	207.6	182.9	218.2	188.3	204.9	4.9	20.7	42.2	91.1	122.5
Central America and Caribbean countries	150.5	162.2	127.5	119.9	168.3	23.1	21.8	30.6	38.4	26.3
Bahamas	-	-	-	-	-	-	1.1	-	-	-
Bermuda	-	-	17.9	10.8	10.3	-	-	-	-	-
Cayman Islands	13.4	4.4	6.3	10.8	18.3	-	-	-	-	-
Costa Rica	-	-	-	-	-	-	-	-	-	-
El Salvador	-	-	-	-	-	-	-	-	-	-
Guatemala	-	-	-	-	-	-	-	-	-	-
Honduras	-	-	-	-	-	-	-	-	-	-
Nicaragua	-	-	-	-	-	-	-	-	-	-
Panama	14.6	12.0	9.5	4.8	3.4	-	-	-	-	-
Virgin Islands, U.S.	-	-	-	-	-	-	-	-	-	-
South America	-	-	-	-	1.1	-	-	1.1	1.2	1.1
Argentina	-	-	-	-	-	-	-	-	-	-
Bolivia	-	-	-	-	-	-	-	-	-	-
Brazil	-	-	-	-	-	-	-	1.1	1.2	-
Colombia	-	-	-	-	-	-	-	-	-	-
Ecuador	-	-	-	-	-	-	-	-	-	-
Paraguay	-	-	-	-	-	-	-	-	-	-
Peru	-	-	-	-	1.1	-	-	-	-	-
Uruguay	-	-	-	-	-	-	-	-	-	-
Venezuela	-	-	-	-	-	-	-	-	-	-

Table 2. Foreign direct investment positions by country *(cont.)*

At year end

Million US dollars

	Inward					Outward				
	2014	2015	2016	2017	2018	2014	2015	2016	2017	2018
ASIA	**392.2**	**418.1**	**416.4**	**446.2**	**452.3**	**36.4**	**92.5**	**86.4**	**76.8**	**63.0**
Near and Middle East	145.7	148.1	121.2	131.9	166.0	18.2	67.5	62.2	55.2	38.9
Gulf Arabian countries	27.9	15.2	2.1	-	12.6	-	39.2	29.5	12.0	21.8
Kuwait	-	-	-	-	-	-	-	-	-	-
Qatar	-	-	-	-	-	-	-	-	-	-
Saudi Arabia	20.6	14.2	-	-2.4	-	-	-	-	-	-
United Arab Emirates	8.5	-	3.2	2.4	12.6	-	39.2	29.5	12.0	21.8
Other Near and Middle East	116.6	133.9	119.1	131.9	153.4	18.2	28.3	31.6	42.0	17.2
Jordan	-	-	-	-	-	-	-	-	-	-
Other Asian countries	246.5	270.0	294.1	313.0	286.2	18.2	25.0	24.2	21.6	24.0
China	72.8	76.2	81.2	93.5	67.6	-	-	1.1	1.2	-
Hong Kong, China	2.4	3.3	1.1	2.4	4.6	-	-	-	-	-
India	-	1.1	1.1	3.6	2.3	-	-	-	-	-
Indonesia	-	-	-	-	-	-	-	-	-	-
Iran, Islamic Republic of	-	-	-	-	-	-	-	-	-	-
Malaysia	-	-	-	-	-	-	-	1.1	1.2	1.1
Philippines	-	-	-	-	-	-	-	-	-	-
Singapore	48.6	64.2	65.4	79.2	74.4	-	-	-	-	-1.1
Chinese Taipei	-	-	-	-	-	-	-	-	-	-
Thailand	-	-	-	-	-	-	-	-	6.0	10.3
Viet Nam	-	-	11.6	20.4	25.2	-	-	-	-	-
AUSTRALIA, OCEANIA AND POLAR REGIONS	**52.2**	**42.5**	**29.5**	**31.2**	**27.5**	-	-	-	-	-
WORLD unallocated and confidential	**359.4**	**219.9**	**233.0**	**283.0**	**166.0**	**-8.5**	**25.0**	**7.4**	**33.6**	**61.8**
European Union (EU28)	**11 181.9**	**11 078.9**	**10 472.2**	**13 595.6**	**13 251.7**	**978.6**	**1 027.8**	**1 095.2**	**1 336.1**	**1 368.2**
G20 countries excl. European Union	**3 167.6**	**3 084.4**	**3 047.3**	**3 644.8**	**3 683.3**	**167.5**	**201.4**	**246.7**	**317.8**	**320.6**
G20 OECD countries	**1 799.3**	**1 711.5**	**1 572.7**	**1 745.0**	**1 691.1**	**63.1**	**84.9**	**115.9**	**195.5**	**204.9**
G20 Non-OECD countries	**1 368.3**	**1 372.9**	**1 473.6**	**1 899.7**	**1 992.2**	**104.4**	**116.5**	**130.7**	**122.3**	**115.6**
MENA countries	**29.1**	**15.2**	**2.1**	-	**13.7**	-	**39.2**	**30.6**	**13.2**	**21.8**
ASEAN countries	**49.8**	**65.3**	**78.0**	**99.5**	**99.6**	-	-	**1.1**	**7.2**	**11.5**

- Nil

Note: Detailed metadata at: *http://stats.oecd.org/OECDStat_Metadata/ShowMetadata.ashx?Dataset=FDI_CTRY_IND_SUMM.*

1. Information on data for Israel: *http://oe.cd/israel-disclaimer.*
2. Note by Turkey: The information in this document with reference to "Cyprus" relates to the southern part of the Island. There is no single authority representing both Turkish and Greek Cypriot people on the Island. Turkey recognises the Turkish Republic of Northern Cyprus (TRNC). Until a lasting and equitable solution is found within the context of the United Nations, Turkey shall preserve its position concerning the "Cyprus issue".
3. Note by all the European Union Member States of the OECD and the European Union: The Republic of Cyprus is recognised by all members of the United Nations with the exception of Turkey. The information in this document relates to the area under the effective control of the Government of the Republic of Cyprus.

Source: OECD International Direct Investment Statistics (database): https://doi.org/10.1787/idi-data-en

Table 3. Foreign direct investment income by country

Million US dollars

	Inward					Outward				
	2014	2015	2016	2017	2018	2014	2015	2016	2017	2018
WORLD	**1 040.2**	**1 154.7**	**1 186.6**	**1 398.9**	**1 871.8**	**54.4**	**154.2**	**117.2**	**216.4**	**158.1**
OECD COUNTRIES	**761.6**	**711.0**	**809.5**	**878.1**	**1 122.4**	**5.3**	**54.4**	**61.9**	**101.5**	**126.3**
Australia	-	-	-	-	-	-	-	-	-	-
Austria	38.5	28.8	18.8	24.8	29.5	-	-	.. c	-	-
Belgium	2.7	-	3.3	.. c	3.5	-	-	-	-	-
Canada	-2.7	-1.1	-	1.1	1.2	.. c	-	-	-	-
Chile	-	-	-	-	-	-	-	-	-	-
Czech Republic	.. c	4.4	6.6	-	9.4	.. c	-	.. c	.. c	-
Denmark	43.8	33.3	54.2	60.9	56.7	.. c	.. c	.. c	.. c	.. c
Estonia	42.5	74.3	89.6	112.7	146.3	4.0	-1.1	-1.1	11.3	10.6
Finland	21.2	21.1	23.2	33.8	46.0	5.3	5.5	6.6	-	1.2
France	10.6	5.5	5.5	7.9	8.3	-	-	.. c	.. c	-
Germany	67.7	58.8	47.6	57.5	46.0	-	-	-	-1.1	-
Greece	-	-	-	-	-	-	-	-	-	-
Hungary	8.0	.. c	-	-	-	-	-	-	-	-
Iceland	9.3	-	10.0	7.9	-1.2	-	-	-	-	-
Ireland	-	-	-	5.6	1.2	-	-	-	-	-
Israel[1]	-1.3	-1.1	-1.1	-	-1.2	-	-	-	-	-
Italy	.. c	3.3	6.6	10.1	7.1	-	-	-	-	-
Japan	-	-	-	-	-	-	-	-	-	-
Korea	9.3	7.8	6.6	.. c	-	-	-	-	-	-
Latvia	-	-	-	-	-	-	-	-	-	-
Lithuania	35.8	21.1	25.4	59.7	56.7	29.2	39.9	18.8	32.7	30.7
Luxembourg	21.2	41.0	45.3	120.6	81.4	5.3	-6.7	.. c	.. c	-4.7
Mexico	-	-	-	-	-	-	-	-	-	-
Netherlands	92.9	68.8	54.2	83.4	103.9	-	-	-	-	.. c
New Zealand	-	.. c	-	-	-	-	-	-	-	-
Norway	78.3	62.1	91.8	81.2	62.6	-	-	-	-	-
Poland	-2.7	2.2	6.6	9.0	15.3	-2.7	12.2	26.5	27.1	35.4
Portugal	-	-	-	-	-	-	.. c	-	-	-
Slovak Republic	-	-	-	-	-	.. c	.. c	.. c	.. c	.. c
Slovenia	-	-	-	-	-	-	-	-	-	-
Spain	.. c	.. c	2.2	1.1	11.8	.. c	.. c	5.5	.. c	-
Sweden	290.6	277.3	291.9	239.0	385.9	8.0	8.9	11.1	11.3	3.5
Switzerland	13.3	12.2	14.4	7.9	17.7	-4.0	23.3	8.8	9.0	.. c
Turkey	-1.3	-	-	3.4	4.7	-	-	-	-	-
United Kingdom	4.0	2.2	21.0	4.5	20.1	-8.0	-6.7	-3.3	1.1	.. c
United States	6.6	2.2	12.2	4.5	9.4	-	-	.. c	.. c	-
EUROPE	**932.7**	**925.1**	**1 043.9**	**1 197.2**	**1 491.8**	**54.4**	**109.8**	**89.6**	**140.9**	**132.2**
Bulgaria	-	-	.. c	2.3	-	-	.. c	-	-	-
Croatia	-	-	-	-	-	-	-	-	-	-
Cyprus[2, 3]	90.2	76.5	95.1	161.2	194.7	-	15.5	16.6	5.6	-1.2
Malta	45.1	65.4	33.2	34.9	34.2	-	.. c	.. c	-	-
Romania	-	-	-	-	-	-	-	-	-	-
Russian Federation	9.3	48.8	87.4	59.7	136.9	14.6	5.5	-6.6	5.6	3.5
Ukraine	5.3	12.2	12.2	1.1	8.3	-	-5.5	-5.5	-5.6	-
AFRICA	**-**	**-**	**-**	**-**	**-**	**-**	**-**	**-**	**-**	**-**
Northern Africa	-	-	-	-	-	-	-	-	-	-
Algeria	-	-	-	-	-	-	-	-	-	-
Egypt	-	-	-	-	-	-	-	-	-	-
Libya	-	-	-	-	-	-	-	-	-	-
Morocco	-	-	-	-	-	-	-	-	-	-
Tunisia	-	-	-	-	-	-	-	-	-	-
Other African countries	-	-	-	-	-	-	-	-	-	-
Nigeria	-	-	-	-	-	-	-	-	-	-
South Africa	-	-	-	-	-	-	-	-	-	-
AMERICA	**9.3**	**3.3**	**14.4**	**-11.3**	**-29.5**	**-4.0**	**-**	**1.1**	**2.3**	**-**
Northern America	4.0	1.1	12.2	5.6	10.6	.. c	-	.. c	.. c	-
Central America and Caribbean countries	5.3	2.2	2.2	-15.8	-40.1	-	-	-	-	-
Bahamas	-	-	-	-	-	-	-	-	-	-
Bermuda	-	-	-	-	-	-	-	-	-	-
Cayman Islands	.. c	.. c	-	-	.. c	-	-	-	-	-
Costa Rica	-	-	-	-	-	-	-	-	-	-
El Salvador	-	-	-	-	-	-	-	-	-	-
Guatemala	-	-	-	-	-	-	-	-	-	-
Honduras	-	-	-	-	-	-	-	-	-	-
Nicaragua	-	-	-	-	-	-	-	-	-	-
Panama	-	-	-	-	-	-	-	-	-	-
Virgin Islands, U.S.	-	-	-	-	-	-	-	-	-	-
South America	-	-	-	-	-	-	-	-	-	-
Argentina	-	-	-	-	-	-	-	-	-	-
Bolivia	-	-	-	-	-	-	-	-	-	-
Brazil	-	-	-	-	-	-	-	-	-	-
Colombia	-	-	-	-	-	-	-	-	-	-
Ecuador	-	-	-	-	-	-	-	-	-	-
Paraguay	-	-	-	-	-	-	-	-	-	-
Peru	-	-	-	-	-	-	-	-	-	-
Uruguay	-	-	-	-	-	-	-	-	-	-
Venezuela	-	-	-	-	-	-	-	-	-	-

Table 3. Foreign direct investment income by country *(cont.)*

Million US dollars

	Inward					Outward				
	2014	2015	2016	2017	2018	2014	2015	2016	2017	2018
ASIA	**5.3**	**10.0**	**4.4**	**-**	**2.4**	**-**	**25.5**	**11.1**	**21.4**	**1.2**
Near and Middle East	-2.7	-2.2	-3.3	-3.4	-3.5	-	15.5	13.3	22.5	-
Gulf Arabian countries	-	-	-	1.1	3.5	-	-	.. c	.. c	.. c
Kuwait	-	-	-	-	-	-	-	-	-	-
Qatar	-	-	-	-	-	-	-	-	-	-
Saudi Arabia	-	-	-	-	-	-	-	-	-	-
United Arab Emirates	-	-	-	1.1	3.5	-	-	.. c	.. c	.. c
Other Near and Middle East	-2.7	-2.2	-3.3	-4.5	-7.1	-	14.4	11.1	21.4	-
Jordan	-	-	-	-	-	-	-	-	-	-
Other Asian countries	8.0	12.2	7.7	3.4	7.1	-	11.1	-2.2	-	1.2
China	-	-	-1.1	-	-	-	-	.. c	-	-
Hong Kong, China	-	1.1	-	-	-	-	-	-	-	-
India	-	-	-	-	-	-	-	-	-	-
Indonesia	-	-	-	-	-	-	-	-	-	-
Iran, Islamic Republic of	-	-	-	-	-	-	-	-	-	-
Malaysia	-	-	-	-	-	-	-	-	-	-
Philippines	-	-	-	-	-	-	-	-	-	-
Singapore	1.3	3.3	3.3	2.3	5.9	-	-	-	-	-
Chinese Taipei	-	-	-	-	-	-	-	-	-	-
Thailand	-	-	-	-	-	-	-	-	-	-
Viet Nam	-	-	-	-	-	-	-	-	-	-
AUSTRALIA, OCEANIA AND POLAR REGIONS	**-**	**.. c**	**-**	**-**	**-**	**-**	**-**	**-**	**-**	**-**
WORLD unallocated and confidential	**92.9**	**.. d**	**123.9**	**213.1**	**407.2**	**4.0**	**18.9**	**15.5**	**51.9**	**24.8**
European Union (EU28)	**822.6**	**788.7**	**829.4**	**1 033.7**	**1 253.4**	**41.1**	**84.3**	**88.5**	**128.5**	**120.4**
G20 countries excl. European Union	**106.1**	**126.5**	**184.7**	**149.9**	**234.9**	**2.7**	**-2.2**	**-16.6**	**9.0**	**4.7**
G20 OECD countries	**96.9**	**77.6**	**99.5**	**90.2**	**96.8**	**-11.9**	**-6.7**	**-7.7**	**3.4**	**1.2**
G20 Non-OECD countries	**9.3**	**48.8**	**86.3**	**59.7**	**136.9**	**14.6**	**5.5**	**-7.7**	**5.6**	**3.5**
MENA countries	**-**	**-**	**-**	**1.1**	**3.5**	**-**	**-**	**.. c**	**.. c**	**.. c**
ASEAN countries	**1.3**	**3.3**	**3.3**	**2.3**	**5.9**	**-**	**-**	**-**	**-**	**-**

- Nil; .. Not available; c Confidential data; d Secondary Confidentiality

Note: Detailed metadata at: *http://stats.oecd.org/OECDStat_Metadata/ShowMetadata.ashx?Dataset=FDI_CTRY_IND_SUMM.*

1. Information on data for Israel: *http://oe.cd/israel-disclaimer.*
2. Note by Turkey: The information in this document with reference to "Cyprus" relates to the southern part of the Island. There is no single authority representing both Turkish and Greek Cypriot people on the Island. Turkey recognises the Turkish Republic of Northern Cyprus (TRNC). Until a lasting and equitable solution is found within the context of the United Nations, Turkey shall preserve its position concerning the "Cyprus issue".
3. Note by all the European Union Member States of the OECD and the European Union: The Republic of Cyprus is recognised by all members of the United Nations with the exception of Turkey. The information in this document relates to the area under the effective control of the Government of the Republic of Cyprus.

Source: OECD International Direct Investment Statistics (database): https://doi.org/10.1787/idi-data-en

Table 4. Foreign direct investment flows by industrial sector

Million US dollars

	Inward					Outward				
	2014	2015	2016	2017	2018	2014	2015	2016	2017	2018
All FDI activities	**894.3**	**734.3**	**257.7**	**666.2**	**993.7**	**517.4**	**67.7**	**147.1**	**130.8**	**190.0**
Agriculture, forestry and fishing	**49.1**	**13.3**	**14.4**	**33.8**	**16.5**	-	-	.. c	-	-
Mining and quarrying	**17.2**	**7.8**	**1.1**	**12.4**	-	-	-	-	-	-
Extraction activities	17.2	7.8	1.1	12.4	-	-	-	-	-	-
Manufacturing	**34.5**	**-53.2**	**22.1**	**32.7**	**173.5**	**49.1**	**23.3**	**73.0**	**25.9**	**10.6**
of which:										
Food products, beverages and tobacco	-47.8	-28.8	-16.6	-37.2	126.3	-	-	-	-	-
Textiles, wood and paper products; printing	50.4	-69.9	22.1	59.7	2.4	11.9	6.7	56.4	9.0	16.5
Chemical, rubber, plastic, non-metallic mineral products	8.0	-2.2	5.5	-20.3	48.4	.. c	.. c	.. c	-18.0	9.4
Metal and machinery products, except electrical equipment	37.2	25.5	4.4	14.7	13.0	-	-1.1	-	-	.. c
Motor vehicles, trailers, semi-trailers, other transport equipment	5.3	10.0	5.5	22.5	22.4	-	-	-	-	-
Other manufacturing	-18.6	12.2	1.1	-6.8	-38.9	1.3	-8.9	.. c	.. c	-16.5
Electricity, gas, steam and air conditioning supply	**-33.2**	**-24.4**	**24.3**	**-73.3**	**-24.8**	**.. c**	**.. c**	**-1.1**	**.. c**	-
Water supply; sewerage, waste management and remediation activities	**-9.3**	**1.1**	-	**-1.1**	**-1.2**	**.. c**	-	-	-	-
Construction	**39.8**	**24.4**	**18.8**	**91.3**	**67.3**	**-2.7**	**2.2**	**29.9**	**.. c**	**3.5**
Services	**463.0**	**484.7**	**81.8**	**427.2**	**555.9**	**475.0**	**17.7**	**39.8**	**83.4**	**126.3**
Wholesale and retail trade; repair of motor vehicles and motorcycles	-345.0	61.0	265.4	58.6	329.3	17.2	8.9	33.2	9.0	90.9
Transportation and storage	-83.6	57.7	64.1	50.7	30.7	4.0	-21.1	-	1.1	1.2
Accommodation and food service activities	31.8	-13.3	4.4	24.8	-22.4	.. c	.. c	-	-	-
Information and communication	-8.0	5.5	33.2	-42.8	-2.4	-	-	4.4	-	8.3
Financial and insurance activities	696.6	352.7	-206.8	314.5	187.7	359.6	26.6	-15.5	67.6	36.6
Activities of holding companies	252.1	84.3	-5.5	29.3	44.8	151.3	-41.0	-17.7	2.3	11.8
Real estate activities	-23.9	-77.6	-73.0	109.3	178.2	-	.. c	8.8	.. c	9.4
Professional, scientific and technical activities	189.7	91.0	-21.0	-111.6	-178.2	90.2	7.8	15.5	5.6	-17.7
Administrative and support service activities	-5.3	-2.2	3.3	14.7	-1.2	-	-	-	-1.1	3.5
Public administration; activities of households and of extraterritorial organisations	-	-	-	-	-	-	-	-	-	-
Education	.. c	-	-	-	3.5	-	-	.. c	-	-
Human health and social work activities	.. c	-	4.4	-	1.2	-	-	-	-	-
Arts, entertainment and recreation	8.0	10.0	5.5	9.0	29.5	-	1.1	.. c	-	.. c
Other services	.. c	-	-	-	-	-	-	-	-	-
Not allocated and confidential	**.. c**	**.. c**	**.. c**	**.. c**	**.. c**	**.. c**	**.. c**	**.. c**	**.. c**	**44.8**
Private real estate activities	**.. c**	**.. c**	**.. c**	**.. c**	**.. c**	**9.3**	**25.5**	**2.2**	**6.8**	**4.7**

- Nil; c Confidential data

Note: Detailed metadata at: *http://stats.oecd.org/OECDStat_Metadata/ShowMetadata.ashx?Dataset=FDI_CTRY_IND_SUMM.*

Source: *OECD International Direct Investment Statistics (database): https://doi.org/10.1787/idi-data-en*

Table 5. Foreign direct investment positions by industrial sector

At year end

Million US dollars

	Inward					Outward				
	2014	2015	2016	2017	2018	2014	2015	2016	2017	2018
All FDI activities	**15 118.0**	**14 729.5**	**14 316.4**	**17 542.6**	**17 405.5**	**1 493.3**	**1 553.6**	**1 633.8**	**1 929.7**	**2 007.1**
Agriculture, forestry and fishing	**639.8**	**673.9**	**606.1**	**735.2**	**668.7**	-	**-3.3**	**3.2**	**3.6**	-
Mining and quarrying	**115.3**	**124.1**	**121.2**	**148.7**	**167.2**	-	-	-	-	-
Extraction activities	115.3	124.1	121.2	148.7	167.2	-	-	-	-	-
Manufacturing	**1 836.9**	**1 669.0**	**1 689.7**	**1 970.5**	**2 041.4**	**105.6**	**121.9**	**205.5**	**248.3**	**241.6**
of which:										
Food products, beverages and tobacco	239.2	231.9	267.7	261.5	312.6	-13.4	.. c	1.1	.. c	1.1
Textiles, wood and paper products; printing	545.1	512.8	529.1	629.6	706.4	59.5	58.8	113.8	133.1	140.8
Chemical, rubber, plastic, non-metallic mineral products	150.5	101.3	80.1	88.8	156.9	32.8	27.2	50.6	27.6	40.1
Metal and machinery products, except electrical equipment	180.9	187.3	172.9	236.3	196.9	7.3	1.1	4.2	3.6	5.7
Motor vehicles, trailers, semi-trailers, other transport equipment	85.0	62.1	98.0	124.7	140.8	-	-	-	-	-
Other manufacturing	636.2	573.8	541.8	629.6	527.8	19.4	38.1	35.8	82.8	55.0
Electricity, gas, steam and air conditioning supply	**632.5**	**548.7**	**521.8**	**686.0**	**636.6**	-	-	-	-	-
Water supply; sewerage, waste management and remediation activities	**21.9**	**15.2**	**11.6**	**4.8**	**6.9**	-	-	-	-	-
Construction	**540.3**	**635.8**	**680.9**	**710.0**	**815.2**	**6.1**	**13.1**	**40.1**	**48.0**	**53.8**
Services	**10 197.2**	**10 068.6**	**9 749.1**	**12 120.4**	**11 992.2**	**1 380.4**	**1 374.0**	**1 364.0**	**1 565.1**	**1 612.1**
Wholesale and retail trade; repair of motor vehicles and motorcycles	1 919.5	1 879.2	2 112.4	2 475.4	2 782.2	364.2	360.4	335.2	365.8	447.7
Transportation and storage	587.6	541.1	587.1	1 039.8	901.1	49.8	4.4	7.4	8.4	6.9
Accommodation and food service activities	216.1	147.0	137.0	217.1	164.9	17.0	-	-	-	-
Information and communication	440.7	435.5	457.5	596.1	559.9	2.4	7.6	7.4	9.6	8.0
Financial and insurance activities	4 244.5	4 218.8	3 736.7	4 233.6	4 179.1	768.5	832.9	835.9	951.1	877.0
Activities of holding companies	723.6	757.8	769.5	550.5	641.2	178.5	188.4	201.3	201.5	313.7
Real estate activities	2 079.8	1 911.8	1 869.9	2 533.0	2 657.4	19.4	32.7	41.1	48.0	41.2
Professional, scientific and technical activities	372.7	568.3	529.1	687.2	298.8	131.1	120.8	124.4	159.5	180.9
Administrative and support service activities	194.3	229.7	185.5	172.7	208.4	20.6	8.7	7.4	16.8	50.4
Public administration; activities of households and of extraterritorial organisations	-	-	-	-	-	-	-	-	-	-
Education	4.9	3.3	10.5	7.2	28.6	2.4	-	2.1	1.2	1.1
Human health and social work activities	12.1	6.5	10.5	7.2	10.3	-	-	-	-	-
Arts, entertainment and recreation	116.6	107.8	108.6	147.5	199.2	4.9	5.4	4.2	4.8	1.1
Other services	8.5	19.6	2.1	3.6	1.1	-	-	-	-	-
Not allocated and confidential	**367.9**	**229.7**	**194.0**	**261.5**	**183.2**	**-9.7**	**6.5**	**-7.4**	**25.2**	**58.4**
Private real estate activities	**766.1**	**764.3**	**742.1**	**905.5**	**894.2**	**10.9**	**41.4**	**28.5**	**39.6**	**41.2**

- Nil; c Confidential data

Note: Detailed metadata at: *http://stats.oecd.org/OECDStat_Metadata/ShowMetadata.ashx?Dataset=FDI_CTRY_IND_SUMM.*

Source: OECD International Direct Investment Statistics (database): https://doi.org/10.1787/idi-data-en

Table 6. Foreign direct investment income by industrial sector

Million US dollars

	Inward					Outward				
	2014	2015	2016	2017	2018	2014	2015	2016	2017	2018
All FDI activities	**1 040.2**	**1 154.7**	**1 186.6**	**1 398.9**	**1 871.8**	**54.4**	**154.2**	**117.2**	**216.4**	**158.1**
Agriculture, forestry and fishing	**2.7**	**7.8**	**-**	**12.4**	**8.3**	**-**	**-**	**-**	**-**	**-**
Mining and quarrying	**10.6**	**11.1**	**12.2**	**16.9**	**14.2**	**-**	**-**	**-**	**-**	**-**
Extraction activities	10.6	11.1	12.2	16.9	14.2	-	-	-	-	-
Manufacturing	**161.9**	**99.8**	**139.3**	**228.8**	**254.9**	**2.7**	**2.2**	**1.1**	**6.8**	**2.4**
of which:										
Food products, beverages and tobacco	25.2	-1.1	8.8	30.4	33.0	-	-	-	-	-
Textiles, wood and paper products; printing	91.5	65.4	97.3	143.2	151.1	-	-	1.1	1.1	.. c
Chemical, rubber, plastic, non-metallic mineral products	-2.7	1.1	1.1	1.1	8.3	.. c	.. c	-	.. c	-
Metal and machinery products, except electrical equipment	4.0	-	5.5	7.9	11.8	-	-	-	-	-
Motor vehicles, trailers, semi-trailers, other transport equipment	9.3	7.8	13.3	13.5	10.6	-	-	-	-	-
Other manufacturing	33.2	26.6	13.3	32.7	40.1	-	-	-	-	-
Electricity, gas, steam and air conditioning supply	**35.8**	**38.8**	**54.2**	**39.5**	**31.9**	**.. c**	**.. c**	**.. c**	**.. c**	**-**
Water supply; sewerage, waste management and remediation activities	**-**	**-**	**-**	**-**	**-**	**.. c**	**-**	**-**	**-**	**-**
Construction	**2.7**	**4.4**	**-3.3**	**1.1**	**-4.7**	**-**	**-**	**-1.1**	**-**	**-**
Services	**735.0**	**784.2**	**881.3**	**901.8**	**1 174.3**	**47.8**	**137.5**	**106.2**	**163.5**	**144.0**
Wholesale and retail trade; repair of motor vehicles and motorcycles	199.0	187.5	217.8	250.3	397.7	-1.3	45.5	26.5	28.2	18.9
Transportation and storage	42.5	34.4	28.8	55.2	30.7	6.6	1.1	-	1.1	1.2
Accommodation and food service activities	1.3	1.1	1.1	10.1	-2.4	.. c	.. c	-	-	-
Information and communication	54.4	35.5	44.2	83.4	108.6	-	.. c	-	-	8.3
Financial and insurance activities	360.9	439.3	503.2	400.2	521.7	37.2	82.1	79.6	129.6	116.8
Activities of holding companies	45.1	71.0	37.6	39.5	66.1	8.0	18.9	2.2	19.2	8.3
Real estate activities	23.9	38.8	28.8	42.8	83.8	-	-	-3.3	-	-1.2
Professional, scientific and technical activities	8.0	12.2	15.5	7.9	-24.8	4.0	5.5	5.5	4.5	4.7
Administrative and support service activities	6.6	1.1	2.2	15.8	10.6	-	-	-	-	-
Public administration; activities of households and of extraterritorial organisations	-	-	-	-	-	-	-	-	-	-
Education	.. c	-	-	-	-	-	-	-	-	-
Human health and social work activities	-	-	-	-	-	-	-	-	-	-
Arts, entertainment and recreation	37.2	33.3	39.8	34.9	48.4	.. c	-	.. c	-	.. c
Other services	.. c	-	-	-	-	-	-	-	-	-
Not allocated and confidential	**91.5**	**208.5**	**102.8**	**198.4**	**393.0**	**.. c**	**.. c**	**.. c**	**.. c**	**11.8**
Private real estate activities	**-**	**-**	**-**	**-**	**-**	**-**	**-**	**-**	**-**	**-**

- Nil; c Confidential data

Note: Detailed metadata at: *http://stats.oecd.org/OECDStat_Metadata/ShowMetadata.ashx?Dataset=FDI_CTRY_IND_SUMM.*

Source: *OECD International Direct Investment Statistics (database): https://doi.org/10.1787/idi-data-en*

LITHUANIA

Table 1. Foreign direct investment flows by country

Million US dollars

	Inward					Outward				
	2014	2015	2016	2017	2018	2014	2015	2016	2017	2018
WORLD	**-183.0**	**1 053.7**	**436.0**	**1 027.4**	**1 092.9**	**9.0**	**369.0**	**51.3**	**68.4**	**671.5**
OECD COUNTRIES	**-750.7**	**1 176.7**	**-54.6**	**1 104.7**	**683.7**	**63.5**	**201.2**	**-90.5**	**-174.9**	**574.8**
Australia	-3.3	1.6	-3.3	0.1	7.8	-	-	-	-	.. c
Austria	7.8	8.9	31.4	-39.6	3.5	0.0	0.0	.. c	0.3	0.2
Belgium	-7.1	6.3	-47.9	9.3	9.9	.. d	.. d	.. d	.. d	.. d
Canada	-30.1	1.2	-0.3	19.1	-55.9	-	0.8	.. c	.. d	0.1
Chile	-	.. c	.. d	.. d	- d	-	-	-	-	-
Czech Republic	0.4	3.0	-2.3	0.9	-7.1	0.1	1.2	0.6	4.9	0.6
Denmark	-167.2	-36.2	46.1	51.9	59.3	.. d	.. d	-2.1	-1.1	-0.1
Estonia	-28.6	93.5	167.0	203.1	242.9	13.6	97.7	-30.8	187.9	122.8
Finland	12.0	17.0	67.0	-38.3	-56.7	-15.6	0.6	0.4	0.5	-0.5
France	6.9	32.6	21.0	162.0	-76.6	3.3	-6.1	3.5	6.6	-0.5
Germany	-180.8	111.0	-146.2	13.9	241.4	-3.3	-10.5	5.2	3.0	-1.1
Greece	.. d	.. d	1.3	.. d	.. d	0.9	1.4	1.1	1.0	0.5
Hungary	-0.2	0.4	3.0	-4.3	5.0	0.3	16.6	-1.0	-2.6	-0.2
Iceland	-5.7	-7.0	2.0	1.5	-0.8	-	-	.. d	.. c	-
Ireland	0.9	20.7	5.0	4.6	18.7	.. c	.. c	.. d	143.5	-94.3
Israel[1]	-6.0	9.9	15.3	13.7	17.9	-	-	.. c	-	.. c
Italy	1.0	-3.7	18.7	4.6	10.9	-0.9	.. d	1.6	1.3	1.4
Japan	.. d	.. d	-0.6	0.3	-0.8	-	.. c	-	-	-
Korea	.. c	.. d	-0.2	-0.1	.. d	-	-	-	-	.. c
Latvia	234.1	17.6	6.4	20.5	7.4	99.5	190.4	53.4	28.8	123.6
Lithuania	-	-	-	-	-	-	-	-	-	-
Luxembourg	-15.3	-38.4	-69.0	-25.3	130.9	.. c	.. d	.. c	.. c	.. d
Mexico	.. d	.. d	-0.2	.. d	.. d	-	-	-	-	-
Netherlands	439.7	242.6	530.7	170.7	131.9	-3.7	46.7	-81.7	-10.5	-31.0
New Zealand	.. c	.. c	.. c	.. d	.. d	-	-	-	-	.. c
Norway	50.7	90.1	108.2	-627.1	53.1	2.3	0.3	-0.1	1.3	-0.7
Poland	-770.9	-85.4	287.0	-66.1	101.2	-7.9	4.9	4.1	16.8	191.6
Portugal	-0.1	.. d	0.8	0.3	0.7	-	0.2	-	.. c	.. d
Slovak Republic	.. d	.. d	.. d	2.2	0.3	0.7	-0.8	1.3	0.1	-0.5
Slovenia	.. d	.. d	-1.4	3.9	0.4	0.2	0.1	0.3	-0.1	0.2
Spain	-41.3	30.3	7.7	7.8	20.3	7.5	.. d	4.1	2.2	1.6
Sweden	-293.0	290.1	-609.0	1 097.0	157.5	1.4	33.6	-1.4	-11.4	246.8
Switzerland	67.2	245.9	-276.8	40.9	72.8	-0.1	.. c	.. d	.. c	-0.4
Turkey	.. d	.. d	-0.1	-0.2	0.4	.. c	.. c	0.6	.. c	.. d
United Kingdom	180.5	124.6	-258.7	6.4	-338.0	2.7	2.6	1.3	-5.3	-4.3
United States	31.0	3.8	41.4	71.7	-74.5	.. d	.. d	2.7	0.1	8.2
EUROPE	**-171.8**	**1 027.3**	**117.5**	**757.9**	**1 277.4**	**15.8**	**371.9**	**29.7**	**36.8**	**658.0**
Bulgaria	7.1	-2.4	4.2	-0.9	2.5	3.4	20.0	1.9	-22.4	-4.1
Croatia	.. d	.. d	.. d	.. d	.. d	1.1	0.9	0.6	0.4	0.5
Cyprus[2, 3]	343.7	-225.0	228.8	171.0	79.6	-90.8	-61.1	93.3	165.7	99.4
Malta	365.7	4.3	-28.7	-432.7	340.8	.. c	-	0.1	.. c	.. d
Romania	-4.6	8.0	1.0	1.2	.. d	0.1	6.7	4.7	7.7	-2.7
Russian Federation	-362.3	41.1	44.1	-15.2	-7.2	-51.6	3.9	26.0	-4.4	18.4
Ukraine	3.0	6.5	-7.3	13.8	25.1	-26.2	2.1	-19.6	26.9	24.0
AFRICA	**-2.7**	**-0.9**	**-0.5**	**-4.8**	**2.0**	**0.1**	**.. c**	**.. c**	**.. d**	**.. d**
Northern Africa	.. d	0.7	-2.0	-2.7	.. d	-	-	-	-	-
Algeria	0.0	0.0	-	-	-	-	-	-	-	-
Egypt	.. d	0.7	-2.0	-2.8	-0.1	-	-	-	-	-
Libya	-	-	-	0.0	0.1	-	-	-	-	-
Morocco	-	-	-	-	-	-	-	-	-	-
Tunisia	-	-	-	-	.. d	-	-	-	-	-
Other African countries	.. d	-1.6	1.5	-2.0	.. d	0.1	.. c	.. c	.. d	.. d
Nigeria	-	-	.. c	.. c	.. d	-	-	-	.. c	.. c
South Africa	.. d	.. d	.. d	.. d	.. d	-	-	-	-	-
AMERICA	**4.3**	**-11.8**	**44.1**	**89.6**	**-420.2**	**.. d**	**.. d**	**2.8**	**-1.0**	**8.6**
Northern America	0.9	5.0	41.1	90.8	-130.4	.. d	.. d	2.7	0.2	8.3
Central America and Caribbean countries	.. d	.. d	2.9	-1.6	-289.9	.. c	-	.. d	.. c	.. d
Bahamas	.. c	.. c	.. c	-	-	-	-	-	-	-
Bermuda	.. c	.. c	.. d	.. d	.. c	-	-	-	-	-
Cayman Islands	.. d	.. d	.. d	.. d	-0.7	-	-	-	-	-
Costa Rica	-	.. c	.. c	.. c	-	-	-	-	-	-
El Salvador	-	0.1	-	-	-	-	-	-	-	-
Guatemala	-	-	-	-	-	-	-	-	-	-
Honduras	0.0	-	-	-	-	-	-	-	-	-
Nicaragua	-	-	-	-	-	-	-	-	-	-
Panama	9.6	-1.1	.. d	-5.4	-1.3	-	-	-	-	.. c
Virgin Islands, U.S.	.. c	-	.. c	-	-	-	-	-	-	-
South America	.. d	.. d	0.1	0.3	0.1	-	-	- d	.. c	.. c
Argentina	.. c	.. c	-	-	-	-	-	-	-	-
Bolivia	-	-	-	-	-	-	-	-	-	-
Brazil	.. d	0.6	.. d	.. d	0.1	-	-	-	-	-
Colombia	.. c	.. c	.. c	.. c	.. c	-	-	- d	-	- d
Ecuador	-	-	-	-	0.0	-	-	-	-	-
Paraguay	-	-	-	-	-	-	-	-	-	-
Peru	-	.. c	.. c	.. d	-	-	-	-	-	-
Uruguay	-	-	-	-	-	-	-	-	.. c	.. c
Venezuela	-	0.0	0.0	-	-	-	-	-	-	-

Table 1. Foreign direct investment flows by country *(cont.)*

Million US dollars

	Inward					Outward				
	2014	2015	2016	2017	2018	2014	2015	2016	2017	2018
ASIA	**.. d**	**.. d**	**.. d**	**171.3**	**175.2**	**9.1**	**-4.3**	**18.7**	**32.4**	**4.2**
Near and Middle East	-3.1	9.9	17.3	16.3	20.2	5.4	-6.7	2.7	4.7	1.7
Gulf Arabian countries	0.7	0.6	-0.1	1.1	1.7	.. d	.. d	.. d	.. d	.. d
Kuwait	-	-	-	-	-	-	-	-	-	-
Qatar	.. c	.. c	-	-	-	-	-	-	-	-
Saudi Arabia	.. c	.. c	-	-	- d	-	-	-	-	-
United Arab Emirates	.. d	0.2	0.3	0.9	1.6	.. c	.. d	.. d	.. c	-0.4
Other Near and Middle East	-3.8	9.3	17.5	15.2	18.5	.. d	.. d	.. d	.. d	.. d
Jordan	-	0.1	-	-	-	-	-	-	-	-
Other Asian countries	.. d	.. d	.. d	155.0	155.0	3.7	2.4	16.1	27.7	2.5
China	-1.7	0.5	2.3	2.9	-2.1	.. d	.. d	.. d	20.8	.. d
Hong Kong, China	0.3	13.3	311.1	144.5	195.3	-	-	-	-	0.0
India	0.6	-0.3	0.0	-0.2	-0.5	-	-	-	-	-
Indonesia	-	-	-	-	0.0	-	.. c	.. c	.. c	.. c
Iran, Islamic Republic of	.. d	.. d	-0.1	0.1	0.0	-	-	-	-	-
Malaysia	-	.. d	.. d	.. c	-0.4	-	-	-	-	-
Philippines	-	.. c	.. c	-0.1	0.1	-	-	-	-	-
Singapore	.. d	22.0	-2.1	0.6	-28.6	-	-	-	0.7	0.1
Chinese Taipei	.. c	.. d	0.0	0.1	-0.2	-	-	-	-	-
Thailand	-11.5	-12.9	-61.1	4.8	-7.9	-	.. c	.. c	-	.. c
Viet Nam	-	-	0.1	-	-	-	-	-	-	-
AUSTRALIA, OCEANIA AND POLAR REGIONS	**.. d**	**.. d**	**.. d**	**0.0**	**7.7**	**- d**	**-**	**- d**	**- d**	**.. c**
WORLD unallocated and confidential	**.. d**	**.. d**	**.. d**	**13.4**	**50.9**	**.. d**	**.. d**	**- d**	**- d**	**- d**
European Union (EU28)	**93.9**	**631.7**	**265.4**	**1 324.8**	**1 115.9**	**73.0**	**356.5**	**6.7**	**-25.4**	**616.6**
G20 countries excl. European Union	**-361.8**	**315.4**	**-282.2**	**264.8**	**-296.4**	**-45.7**	**-5.7**	**57.1**	**25.9**	**22.8**
G20 OECD countries	**2.3**	**273.6**	**-328.6**	**277.5**	**-286.1**	**2.5**	**-10.5**	**14.9**	**6.0**	**2.5**
G20 Non-OECD countries	**-364.1**	**41.8**	**46.4**	**-12.7**	**-10.3**	**-48.2**	**4.8**	**42.2**	**19.8**	**20.3**
MENA countries	**1.6**	**.. d**	**-2.4**	**-1.9**	**1.5**	**.. d**	**.. d**	**.. d**	**.. d**	**.. d**
ASEAN countries	**-11.9**	**9.1**	**-63.1**	**5.2**	**-36.8**	**-**	**.. c**	**.. c**	**3.9**	**0.5**

- Nil; .. Not available; c Confidential data; d Secondary Confidentiality

Note: Detailed metadata at: *http://stats.oecd.org/OECDStat_Metadata/ShowMetadata.ashx?Dataset=FDI_CTRY_IND_SUMM.*

1. Information on data for Israel: *http://oe.cd/israel-disclaimer.*
2. Note by Turkey: The information in this document with reference to "Cyprus" relates to the southern part of the Island. There is no single authority representing both Turkish and Greek Cypriot people on the Island. Turkey recognises the Turkish Republic of Northern Cyprus (TRNC). Until a lasting and equitable solution is found within the context of the United Nations, Turkey shall preserve its position concerning the "Cyprus issue".
3. Note by all the European Union Member States of the OECD and the European Union: The Republic of Cyprus is recognised by all members of the United Nations with the exception of Turkey. The information in this document relates to the area under the effective control of the Government of the Republic of Cyprus.

Source: OECD International Direct Investment Statistics (database): https://doi.org/10.1787/idi-data-en

Table 2. Foreign direct investment positions by country
At year end

Million US dollars

	Inward					Outward				
	2014	2015	2016	2017	2018	2014	2015	2016	2017	2018
WORLD	**16 700.4**	**15 846.1**	**16 047.7**	**19 555.1**	**19 500.5**	**3 516.1**	**3 532.5**	**3 542.6**	**4 137.5**	**4 642.8**
OECD COUNTRIES	..	**12 075.7**	**13 790.7**	**15 739.5**	**16 343.0**	**2 275.0**	**2 218.4**	**2 737.8**	**2 973.3**	**3 407.5**
Australia	..	.. d	.. d	.. d	6.9	-	-	-	-	.. c
Austria	..	155.9	160.7	170.0	152.7	0.1	0.1	0.1	0.4	0.6
Belgium	..	181.3	230.6	311.0	226.3	2.6	1.7	-0.8	4.5	5.9
Canada	..	361.2	356.8	463.3	365.7	-	0.8	0.6	0.8	0.8
Chile	..	0.0	0.0	0.1	0.1	-	-	-	-	-
Czech Republic	..	12.4	13.0	15.1	5.2	1.6	1.9	2.5	7.1	6.1
Denmark	..	766.7	808.3	911.8	913.7	8.9	2.1	0.3	0.8	-1.6
Estonia	..	819.1	1 081.1	1 396.7	1 513.8	277.7	346.0	369.7	627.6	729.1
Finland	..	562.0	580.6	703.5	646.4	2.6	2.9	3.2	4.7	1.8
France	..	393.3	414.3	467.4	460.7	1.8	-4.3	-1.3	5.9	5.6
Germany	..	1 034.8	1 081.4	1 309.6	1 286.7	20.9	10.6	12.0	20.4	19.4
Greece	..	0.6	0.7	1.1	1.4	4.3	5.4	6.2	8.2	8.3
Hungary	..	5.2	6.0	5.6	6.3	7.5	20.7	20.0	20.1	21.2
Iceland	..	39.8	36.9	42.0	30.9	-	-	0.2	0.3	0.3
Ireland	..	42.3	42.8	52.0	59.4	0.5	0.7	-49.4	96.5	0.3
Israel[1]	..	.. d	.. d	163.1	-178.0	-	-	.. c	.. c	-1.5
Italy	..	39.2	43.4	61.2	65.9	27.6	26.9	9.1	11.4	12.2
Japan	..	94.3	23.2	19.9	20.4	-	.. c	.. c	.. c	.. c
Korea	..	0.2	0.1	0.1	-	-	-	-	-	.. c
Latvia	..	185.9	270.5	388.8	368.8	459.1	601.6	674.4	836.7	931.0
Lithuania	..	1 481.5	315.6	434.4	790.1	-	-	-	-	-
Luxembourg	..	160.0	135.5	166.8	171.5	.. c	528.3	511.5	-1.2	10.4
Mexico	..	.. d	.. d	.. d	.. d	-	-	-	-	-
Netherlands	..	582.7	934.9	1 280.7	1 467.7	946.7	867.6	765.9	852.7	808.0
New Zealand	..	.. d	.. d	.. d	.. d	-	-	-	-	.. c
Norway	..	1 118.4	1 064.4	486.3	462.0	3.1	6.5	4.3	6.9	5.9
Poland	..	470.4	679.8	849.9	935.8	353.8	313.3	307.0	365.1	522.2
Portugal	..	0.8	1.3	2.4	9.1	-	0.2	0.2	0.3	0.4
Slovak Republic	..	7.4	8.2	11.8	10.4	7.6	7.4	9.4	9.5	8.8
Slovenia	..	0.4	0.8	.. d	18.2	0.6	0.6	0.9	0.9	1.1
Spain	..	60.3	69.0	82.0	74.7	8.4	4.5	8.2	11.8	13.4
Sweden	..	3 671.2	3 138.9	3 369.0	3 366.7	3.4	34.9	38.5	35.7	250.6
Switzerland	..	291.9	406.3	422.4	432.8	.. d	.. d	0.0	0.0	-0.4
Turkey	..	.. d	-0.7	-0.6	1.5	1.1	0.3	2.2	.. c	0.9
United Kingdom	..	252.4	1 488.9	1 638.7	1 959.3	18.6	34.7	34.4	31.7	26.4
United States	..	968.3	655.2	922.6	663.4	5.2	4.9	8.4	12.3	20.2
EUROPE	..	**13 743.3**	**14 350.1**	**17 185.4**	**17 718.8**	**3 515.2**	**3 533.9**	**3 526.0**	**4 078.0**	**4 572.7**
Bulgaria	..	4.1	4.0	0.8	1.7	80.7	90.2	89.6	77.8	73.7
Croatia	..	0.0	0.1	0.2	0.3	3.6	4.4	4.8	5.9	6.0
Cyprus[2, 3]	..	395.8	500.9	449.5	241.2	440.8	338.4	423.5	651.2	754.6
Malta	..	15.1	25.9	25.1	31.8	0.0	0.0	0.1	-0.2	-45.3
Romania	..	0.6	0.8	2.9	2.9	5.2	14.8	18.3	28.9	17.6
Russian Federation	..	526.3	345.3	468.2	389.8	85.9	94.0	112.4	107.4	137.2
Ukraine	..	247.6	232.1	288.8	272.8	49.5	69.4	27.1	75.8	75.1
AFRICA	..	**16.2**	**15.9**	**14.4**	**.. d**	**0.1**	**0.2**	**0.3**	**0.4**	**1.0**
Northern Africa	..	3.0	1.0	0.7	0.5	-	-	-	-	-
Algeria	..	-	-	-	-	-	-	-	-	-
Egypt	..	2.9	1.0	0.7	0.4	-	-	-	-	-
Libya	..	-	-	0.0	0.1	-	-	-	-	-
Morocco	..	-	-	-	-	-	-	-	-	-
Tunisia	..	0.0	0.0	0.0	-	-	-	-	-	-
Other African countries	..	13.3	14.9	13.7	.. d	0.1	0.2	0.3	0.4	1.0
Nigeria	..	0.0	-	0.0	0.2	-	-	-	.. c	.. c
South Africa	..	.. d	.. d	5.5	7.1	-	-	-	-	-
AMERICA	..	**1 757.8**	**1 423.3**	**1 888.1**	**1 521.3**	**6.1**	**6.5**	**9.9**	**15.2**	**23.2**
Northern America	..	1 329.5	1 012.1	1 385.9	1 029.1	5.2	5.7	9.0	13.0	21.0
Central America and Caribbean countries	..	427.7	410.6	501.5	491.6	0.9	0.8	0.9	.. d	2.2
Bahamas	..	.. c	.. c	-	.. c	-	-	-	-	-
Bermuda	..	.. c	.. c	.. c	.. c	- d	- d	-	-	-
Cayman Islands	..	322.0	332.6	.. c	.. c	-	-	-	-	-
Costa Rica	..	-	-	-	-	-	-	-	-	-
El Salvador	..	0.1	0.1	0.1	0.1	-	-	-	-	-
Guatemala	..	-	-	-	-	-	-	-	-	-
Honduras	..	0.0	0.0	0.0	0.0	-	-	-	-	-
Nicaragua	..	-	-	-	-	-	-	-	-	-
Panama	..	34.3	.. d	.. d	.. d	.. c	.. c	.. c	.. c	.. c
Virgin Islands, U.S.	..	-	-	-	-	-	-	-	-	-
South America	..	0.5	0.6	0.7	0.6	-	-	-	.. c	-
Argentina	..	0.2	0.2	0.2	.. d	-	-	-	-	-
Bolivia	..	-	-	-	-	-	-	-	-	-
Brazil	..	0.1	0.2	0.2	.. d	-	-	-	-	-
Colombia	..	0.1	0.1	0.1	0.1	-	-	-	-	-
Ecuador	..	-	-	-	-	-	-	-	-	-
Paraguay	..	-	-	-	-	-	-	-	-	-
Peru	..	0.1	0.1	0.1	0.1	-	-	-	-	-
Uruguay	..	-	-	-	-	-	-	-	.. c	-
Venezuela	..	0.0	-	-	-	-	-	-	-	-

Table 2. Foreign direct investment positions by country *(cont.)*

At year end

Million US dollars

	Inward					Outward				
	2014	2015	2016	2017	2018	2014	2015	2016	2017	2018
ASIA	..	**.. d**	**199.2**	**379.4**	**162.4**	**-5.3**	**-8.1**	**6.5**	**43.9**	**.. d**
Near and Middle East	..	.. d	57.0	182.0	-158.2	11.1	4.8	5.7	13.8	14.9
Gulf Arabian countries	..	.. d	.. d	.. d	.. d	6.8	3.0	7.0	11.0	11.6
Kuwait	..	-	-	-	-	-	-	-	-	-
Qatar	..	-	-	-	-	-	-	-	-	-
Saudi Arabia	..	.. d	.. d	.. d	.. d	- d	- d	- d	- d	- d
United Arab Emirates	..	.. d	5.5	6.0	6.5	3.0	5.4	8.5	12.0	11.2
Other Near and Middle East	..	-35.2	.. d	.. d	.. d	4.2	1.9	-1.3	2.8	3.3
Jordan	..	-1.7	0.0	0.0	.. d	-	-	-	-	-
Other Asian countries	..	270.5	142.2	197.4	320.5	-16.4	-13.0	0.8	30.0	.. d
China	..	17.4	21.1	42.7	49.7	9.6	12.2	25.9	52.1	50.6
Hong Kong, China	..	-4.9	5.5	15.3	131.9	.. c	.. c	.. c	.. c	0.0
India	..	.. d	.. d	3.6	5.8	-	-	-	-	-
Indonesia	..	-	-	.. c	.. c	-	.. c	.. c	.. c	.. c
Iran, Islamic Republic of	..	.. d	.. d	0.4	0.3	-	-	-	-	-
Malaysia	..	.. d	.. d	0.1	0.1	-	-	-	-	-
Philippines	..	-	-	-	0.0	-	-	-	-	-
Singapore	..	12.1	2.3	5.2	12.9	.. c	.. c	.. c	-0.1	-0.1
Chinese Taipei	..	0.1	0.1	0.1	.. d	-	-	-	-	-
Thailand	..	139.7	77.1	.. d	.. d	.. c	.. c	.. c	-28.4	-27.7
Viet Nam	..	0.1	0.1	0.2	0.2	-	-	-	-	-
AUSTRALIA, OCEANIA AND POLAR REGIONS	..	**.. d**	**5.4**	**4.3**	**.. d**	**-**	**-**	**-**	**-**	**.. c**
WORLD unallocated and confidential	..	**.. d**	**53.8**	**83.5**	**.. d**	**0.0**	**-**	**-**	**0.0**	**.. d**
European Union (EU28)	..	**11 301.5**	**12 037.9**	**14 114.9**	**14 788.6**	**3 255.0**	**3 255.4**	**3 259.6**	**3 716.1**	**4 189.8**
G20 countries excl. European Union	..	**3 718.4**	**4 453.9**	**5 424.5**	**5 316.2**	**170.6**	**180.4**	**204.2**	**248.6**	**278.4**
G20 OECD countries	..	**3 165.1**	**4 079.3**	**4 900.9**	**4 857.4**	**75.1**	**73.9**	**65.5**	**85.1**	**85.7**
G20 Non-OECD countries	..	**553.3**	**374.6**	**523.7**	**458.8**	**95.5**	**106.4**	**138.7**	**163.5**	**192.6**
MENA countries	..	**.. d**	**10.1**	**11.2**	**.. d**	**6.8**	**3.0**	**7.0**	**11.0**	**11.6**
ASEAN countries	..	**.. d**	**79.6**	**103.2**	**101.4**	**.. c**	**-27.3**	**-26.1**	**-25.0**	**-23.4**

\- Nil; .. Not available; c Confidential data; d Secondary Confidentiality

Note: Inward FDI positions are allocated according to the ultimate investing country. Detailed metadata at: *http://stats.oecd.org/OECDStat_Metadata/ShowMetadata.ashx?Dataset=FDI_CTRY_IND_SUMM*.

1. Information on data for Israel: *http://oe.cd/israel-disclaimer*.
2. Note by Turkey: The information in this document with reference to "Cyprus" relates to the southern part of the Island. There is no single authority representing both Turkish and Greek Cypriot people on the Island. Turkey recognises the Turkish Republic of Northern Cyprus (TRNC). Until a lasting and equitable solution is found within the context of the United Nations, Turkey shall preserve its position concerning the "Cyprus issue".
3. Note by all the European Union Member States of the OECD and the European Union: The Republic of Cyprus is recognised by all members of the United Nations with the exception of Turkey. The information in this document relates to the area under the effective control of the Government of the Republic of Cyprus.

Source: OECD International Direct Investment Statistics (database): https://doi.org/10.1787/idi-data-en

Table 3. Foreign direct investment income by country

Million US dollars

	Inward					Outward				
	2014	2015	2016	2017	2018	2014	2015	2016	2017	2018
WORLD	**684.3**	**1 642.2**	**1 721.9**	**1 980.4**	**2 241.6**	**119.8**	**134.9**	**145.1**	**149.8**	**300.1**
OECD COUNTRIES	**470.2**	**1 490.9**	**1 497.4**	**1 716.0**	**..**	**45.6**	**92.4**	**116.9**	**153.3**	**..**
Australia	-	-	-	0.1	..	-	-	-	-	..
Austria	9.0	6.6	7.4	4.2	..	-	-	-	-	..
Belgium	9.5	8.2	6.8	20.1	..	0.5	0.6	-1.2	3.9	..
Canada	-9.4	6.5	4.8	-4.8	..	-	-	0.0	0.0	..
Chile	-	-	-	-	..	-	-	-	-	..
Czech Republic	-0.1	0.7	0.5	2.7	..	-0.2	.. d	.. d	4.6	..
Denmark	127.8	57.4	16.9	62.3	..	0.0	0.3	0.3	1.8	..
Estonia	260.5	110.1	133.6	149.7	..	37.0	62.3	70.0	97.4	..
Finland	51.2	64.0	59.2	38.1	..	0.0	-	0.2	0.1	..
France	16.8	20.6	20.0	57.9	..	.. d	1.9	2.1	1.2	..
Germany	129.0	67.7	82.5	113.0	..	-1.0	2.6	1.2	1.1	..
Greece	.. c	.. c	-	.. c	..	0.1	0.3	0.3	0.1	..
Hungary	0.2	1.0	0.9	1.2	..	0.1	3.8	-0.4	-2.5	..
Iceland	2.2	2.6	0.8	2.2	..	-	-	-	0.0	..
Ireland	4.8	7.7	4.1	3.8	..	-	.. c	.. d	.. d	..
Israel[1]	0.3	0.5	2.7	1.8	..	-	-	-	-	..
Italy	2.9	2.7	3.7	4.6	..	-0.4	-0.1	0.0	-0.3	..
Japan	-	-	-	-	..	-	-	-	-	..
Korea	.. c	.. c	-	-	..	-	-	-	-	..
Latvia	57.0	45.0	51.2	53.0	..	41.3	33.0	19.9	12.3	..
Lithuania	-	-	-	-	..	-	-	-	-	..
Luxembourg	18.7	55.5	12.4	48.9	..	.. c	.. c	.. c	.. d	..
Mexico	-	-	-	.. c	..	-	-	-	-	..
Netherlands	141.6	168.2	213.5	248.2	..	2.3	8.6	19.1	28.5	..
New Zealand	-	-	-	-	..	-	-	-	-	..
Norway	71.3	83.6	61.3	93.3	..	0.2	0.7	0.4	0.3	..
Poland	-906.9	236.7	305.4	288.3	..	-5.8	-0.5	-6.1	4.6	..
Portugal	-	.. c	0.5	0.1	..	-	-	0.0	0.1	..
Slovak Republic	.. c	.. c	.. c	1.3	..	.. c	0.1	1.3	1.1	..
Slovenia	.. c	.. c	1.9	1.8	..	-	0.1	0.1	0.0	..
Spain	-11.3	-3.4	1.9	0.9	..	0.2	.. d	0.2	-0.3	..
Sweden	406.8	391.3	402.5	397.2	..	0.2	0.4	0.8	-0.9	..
Switzerland	78.9	107.1	40.2	61.4	..	-	-	-	-	..
Turkey	-1.0	-0.3	-0.4	-0.3	..	.. c	.. c	0.6	.. c	..
United Kingdom	35.9	56.9	19.3	26.2	..	0.9	3.1	5.3	0.6	..
United States	30.8	38.7	42.1	38.7	..	.. d	.. d	-1.2	-0.5	..
EUROPE	**671.6**	**1 583.5**	**1 604.1**	**1 822.6**	**..**	**117.9**	**138.0**	**146.4**	**149.7**	**..**
Bulgaria	-	0.6	-0.3	0.3	..	-1.2	0.3	6.2	0.1	..
Croatia	.. c	.. c	.. c	.. c	..	-	-0.1	0.1	-	..
Cyprus[2, 3]	120.0	48.0	85.7	70.8	..	42.6	-1.2	-2.9	3.2	..
Malta	11.8	17.0	17.7	11.0	..	-	-	-	.. c	..
Romania	-0.1	.. c	-	.. c	..	.. d	0.8	1.4	-0.4	..
Russian Federation	11.3	6.7	16.4	6.5	..	-6.9	-6.1	14.4	-12.2	..
Ukraine	1.8	1.4	3.1	14.5	..	-20.1	2.8	1.8	-2.7	..
AFRICA	**1.6**	**0.2**	**.. d**	**-1.4**	**..**	**.. d**	**.. d**	**0.1**	**0.1**	**..**
Northern Africa	.. c	0.3	0.0	0.0	..	-	-	-	-	..
Algeria	-	-	-	-	..	-	-	-	-	..
Egypt	.. c	0.3	0.0	0.0	..	-	-	-	-	..
Libya	-	-	-	-	..	-	-	-	-	..
Morocco	-	-	-	-	..	-	-	-	-	..
Tunisia	-	-	-	-	..	-	-	-	-	..
Other African countries	.. d	0.0	.. d	-1.4	..	.. d	.. d	0.1	0.1	..
Nigeria	-	-	-	-	..	-	-	-	-	..
South Africa	.. c	.. c	.. c	-	..	-	-	-	-	..
AMERICA	**16.2**	**47.1**	**45.5**	**33.4**	**..**	**.. d**	**.. d**	**-1.2**	**-1.6**	**..**
Northern America	21.5	45.2	46.9	33.9	..	.. d	.. d	-1.2	-0.5	..
Central America and Caribbean countries	.. d	.. d	-1.5	-0.4	..	0.9	.. c	0.0	.. d	..
Bahamas	-0.5	.. d	.. d	-	..	-	-	-	-	..
Bermuda	.. c	.. c	.. c	.. c	..	-	-	-	- d	..
Cayman Islands	-	.. c	.. c	.. c	..	-	-	-	-	..
Costa Rica	-	-	-	-	..	-	-	-	-	..
El Salvador	-	-	-	-	..	-	-	-	-	..
Guatemala	-	-	-	-	..	-	-	-	-	..
Honduras	-	-	-	-	..	-	-	-	-	..
Nicaragua	-	-	-	-	..	-	-	-	-	..
Panama	1.9	2.2	0.0	-1.1	..	.. c	.. c	.. c	.. c	..
Virgin Islands, U.S.	-	-	-	-	..	-	-	-	-	..
South America	.. c	.. c	-	-	..	-	- d	-	.. c	..
Argentina	.. c	.. c	-	-	..	-	-	-	-	..
Bolivia	-	-	-	-	..	-	-	-	-	..
Brazil	-	-	-	-	..	-	-	-	-	..
Colombia	-	-	-	-	..	-	-	-	-	..
Ecuador	-	-	-	-	..	-	-	-	-	..
Paraguay	-	-	-	-	..	-	-	-	-	..
Peru	-	-	-	-	..	-	-	-	-	..
Uruguay	-	-	-	-	..	-	-	-	.. c	..
Venezuela	-	-	-	-	..	-	-	-	-	..

Table 3. Foreign direct investment income by country *(cont.)*

Million US dollars

	Inward					Outward				
	2014	2015	2016	2017	2018	2014	2015	2016	2017	2018
ASIA	**.. d**	**.. d**	**.. d**	**119.2**	**..**	**0.8**	**-3.4**	**-0.1**	**1.6**	**..**
Near and Middle East	.. d	.. d	2.8	2.5	..	-0.7	-4.3	0.1	1.1	..
Gulf Arabian countries	.. d	.. d	0.3	0.1	..	.. d	-1.9	0.6	1.1	..
Kuwait	-	-	-	-	..	-	-	-	-	..
Qatar	-	-	-	-	..	-	-	-	-	..
Saudi Arabia	.. c	.. c	- d	-	..	- d	- d	- d	- d	..
United Arab Emirates	.. c	0.0	0.3	0.1	..	0.2	0.2	0.3	.. d	..
Other Near and Middle East	0.2	0.3	2.5	2.4	..	.. d	-2.4	-0.4	0.0	..
Jordan	-	-	-	-	..	-	-	-	-	..
Other Asian countries	-10.7	4.0	61.6	116.6	..	1.4	0.9	-0.2	0.5	..
China	-0.1	0.2	0.4	0.5	..	.. c	0.8	0.1	-0.5	..
Hong Kong, China	0.0	0.2	45.1	102.8	..	-	-	-	-	..
India	0.0	0.0	-0.6	0.0	..	-	-	-	-	..
Indonesia	-	-	-	-	..	-	-	-	.. c	..
Iran, Islamic Republic of	.. c	0.0	0.0	0.0	..	-	-	-	-	..
Malaysia	-	-	-	-	..	-	-	-	-	..
Philippines	-	-	-	-	..	-	-	-	-	..
Singapore	.. d	0.2	-3.8	4.4	..	.. c	.. c	.. c	.. d	..
Chinese Taipei	-	-	-	-	..	-	-	-	-	..
Thailand	.. d	4.2	.. d	9.8	..	.. c	.. c	.. c	.. d	..
Viet Nam	-	-	-	-	..	-	-	-	-	..
AUSTRALIA, OCEANIA AND POLAR REGIONS	**.. d**	**.. d**	**0.0**	**0.0**	**..**	**-**	**-**	**-**	**-**	**..**
WORLD unallocated and confidential	**.. d**	**.. d**	**.. d**	**6.6**	**..**	**.. d**	**- d**	**0.0**	**-**	**..**
European Union (EU28)	**485.5**	**1 363.1**	**1 449.1**	**1 605.9**	**..**	**127.9**	**124.1**	**121.9**	**155.6**	**..**
G20 countries excl. European Union	**217.2**	**200.1**	**188.4**	**242.4**	**..**	**-2.7**	**2.8**	**22.6**	**-10.2**	**..**
G20 OECD countries	**205.1**	**192.5**	**172.1**	**235.4**	**..**	**1.6**	**8.1**	**8.0**	**2.5**	**..**
G20 Non-OECD countries	**12.1**	**7.6**	**16.3**	**7.0**	**..**	**-4.3**	**-5.3**	**14.6**	**-12.7**	**..**
MENA countries	**0.7**	**0.7**	**0.1**	**-0.2**	**..**	**-0.4**	**-1.9**	**0.6**	**1.1**	**..**
ASEAN countries	**-10.9**	**4.4**	**14.2**	**14.3**	**..**	**.. c**	**-1.2**	**-1.1**	**-0.5**	**..**

- Nil; .. Not available; c Confidential data; d Secondary Confidentiality

Note: Detailed metadata at: *http://stats.oecd.org/OECDStat_Metadata/ShowMetadata.ashx?Dataset=FDI_CTRY_IND_SUMM.*

1. Information on data for Israel: *http://oe.cd/israel-disclaimer.*
2. Note by Turkey: The information in this document with reference to "Cyprus" relates to the southern part of the Island. There is no single authority representing both Turkish and Greek Cypriot people on the Island. Turkey recognises the Turkish Republic of Northern Cyprus (TRNC). Until a lasting and equitable solution is found within the context of the United Nations, Turkey shall preserve its position concerning the "Cyprus issue".
3. Note by all the European Union Member States of the OECD and the European Union: The Republic of Cyprus is recognised by all members of the United Nations with the exception of Turkey. The information in this document relates to the area under the effective control of the Government of the Republic of Cyprus.

Source: OECD International Direct Investment Statistics (database): https://doi.org/10.1787/idi-data-en

Table 4. Foreign direct investment flows by industrial sector

Million US dollars

	Inward					Outward				
	2014	2015	2016	2017	2018	2014	2015	2016	2017	2018
All FDI activities	**-183.0**	**1 053.7**	**436.0**	**1 027.4**	**1 092.9**	**9.0**	**369.0**	**51.3**	**68.4**	**671.5**
Agriculture, forestry and fishing	**10.2**	**-3.4**	**57.4**	**57.9**	**-24.5**	**-1.9**	**.. d**	**.. d**	**.. d**	**2.7**
Mining and quarrying	**-26.4**	**-6.3**	**-8.4**	**-13.0**	**1.4**	**-2.1**	**.. d**	**.. d**	**.. d**	**0.8**
Extraction activities	.. c	.. c	.. c	.. c	.. c	-	-	-	-	-
Manufacturing	**-690.3**	**453.4**	**-487.4**	**525.8**	**35.7**	**-0.5**	**-0.2**	**-36.7**	**0.4**	**22.0**
of which:										
Food products, beverages and tobacco	39.1	258.4	-109.1	69.0	34.2	.. d	1.0	4.2	5.9	4.3
Textiles, wood and paper products; printing	59.1	18.0	-51.4	82.9	58.2	-8.5	-1.9	0.3	-5.1	-1.7
Chemical, rubber, plastic, non-metallic mineral products	-903.2	92.1	-357.4	250.2	-213.0	5.8	5.2	-51.9	-0.9	16.1
Metal and machinery products, except electrical equipment	68.8	14.6	47.1	64.8	22.1	5.4	-0.6	5.6	6.9	0.2
Motor vehicles, trailers, semi-trailers, other transport equipment	53.4	72.7	-94.3	2.6	103.5	.. c	.. c	.. d	.. c	0.0
Other manufacturing	-7.5	-2.4	77.6	56.4	30.6	-0.3	.. d	.. d	.. d	3.0
Electricity, gas, steam and air conditioning supply	**.. d**	**-7.2**	**0.4**	**4.2**	**.. d**	**-14.9**	**.. d**	**.. d**	**.. d**	**.. d**
Water supply; sewerage, waste management and remediation activities	**.. d**	**-6.5**	**-0.7**	**7.2**	**.. d**	**0.0**	**.. d**	**.. d**	**.. d**	**.. d**
Construction	**49.5**	**34.9**	**82.7**	**37.2**	**-96.5**	**-46.7**	**14.4**	**33.0**	**7.3**	**5.7**
Services	**823.5**	**558.0**	**765.0**	**383.0**	**1 096.4**	**68.5**	**344.9**	**58.9**	**64.3**	**625.7**
Wholesale and retail trade; repair of motor vehicles and motorcycles	103.2	67.0	229.5	149.4	193.7	68.6	115.5	70.7	78.1	305.0
Transportation and storage	82.5	18.0	21.2	14.2	49.7	-93.6	-54.0	7.1	32.3	54.2
Accommodation and food service activities	0.7	1.0	-12.0	18.7	-10.8	0.9	.. d	1.2	-2.5	1.9
Information and communication	-548.2	426.0	50.6	7.7	23.5	-7.3	31.2	8.9	-3.7	24.0
Financial and insurance activities	980.7	-8.3	325.1	-94.0	184.8	-12.7	50.7	32.8	69.2	-233.0
Activities of holding companies	660.1	-181.0	.. d	-327.8	-50.5	34.4	9.4	43.6	1.7	53.5
Real estate activities	50.6	91.5	27.1	51.5	89.4	69.0	23.3	-60.0	47.9	16.8
Professional, scientific and technical activities	184.1	-50.3	115.2	196.3	511.6	39.5	160.4	-54.7	-188.9	473.8
Administrative and support service activities	-30.5	6.0	6.0	31.0	55.6	2.5	20.4	37.8	29.4	-13.5
Public administration; activities of households and of extraterritorial organisations	- d	- d	-	-	-	-	- d	- d	- d	-
Education	.. d	.. d	-0.1	-0.2	0.1	.. c	-	.. d	1.6	-3.5
Human health and social work activities	-1.2	1.2	-0.5	5.6	3.2	.. c	-0.2	.. d	0.2	0.1
Arts, entertainment and recreation	2.1	4.5	2.9	2.9	-5.3	.. c	.. c	.. d	0.7	.. d
Other services	-0.3	1.0	0.1	-0.1	0.7	.. d	0.2	.. d	.. d	-0.5
Not allocated and confidential	**.. d**	**0.0**	**-**	**0.0**	**- d**	**0.0**	**.. d**	**.. d**	**.. d**	**- d**
Private real estate activities	**43.3**	**30.9**	**27.0**	**25.1**	**62.2**	**6.7**	**6.4**	**2.4**	**3.7**	**-0.1**

- Nil; .. Not available; c Confidential data; d Secondary Confidentiality

Note: Detailed metadata at: *http://stats.oecd.org/OECDStat_Metadata/ShowMetadata.ashx?Dataset=FDI_CTRY_IND_SUMM.*

Source: OECD International Direct Investment Statistics (database): https://doi.org/10.1787/idi-data-en

Table 5. Foreign direct investment positions by industrial sector
At year end

Million US dollars

	Inward					Outward				
	2014	2015	2016	2017	2018	2014	2015	2016	2017	2018
All FDI activities	**16 700.4**	**15 846.1**	**16 047.7**	**19 555.1**	**19 500.5**	**3 516.1**	**3 532.5**	**3 542.6**	**4 137.5**	**4 642.8**
Agriculture, forestry and fishing	**191.6**	**173.8**	**238.1**	**359.1**	**332.5**	**-1.9**	**-4.2**	**28.8**	**32.6**	**33.8**
Mining and quarrying	**99.6**	**79.0**	**66.4**	**65.1**	**61.7**	**0.0**	**6.2**	**-0.5**	**-1.1**	**-0.3**
Extraction activities	.. c	.. c	.. c	.. c	.. c	-	-	-	-	-
Manufacturing	**3 006.4**	**3 076.7**	**2 579.6**	**3 500.7**	**3 353.5**	**508.2**	**488.0**	**397.6**	**422.6**	**443.4**
of which:										
Food products, beverages and tobacco	365.8	586.8	511.9	653.7	638.5	3.0	13.0	27.6	23.3	35.9
Textiles, wood and paper products; printing	488.2	439.7	386.7	535.5	577.0	16.0	1[illegible].0	5.5	1.7	3.1
Chemical, rubber, plastic, non-metallic mineral products	1 441.2	1 321.5	977.8	1 367.6	1 077.8	448.4	429.7	328.3	356.6	339.7
Metal and machinery products, except electrical equipment	172.1	169.1	198.7	304.2	345.6	20.0	14.7	21.0	29.3	29.9
Motor vehicles, trailers, semi-trailers, other transport equipment	162.1	213.4	107.2	125.2	203.2	-	12.6	.. c	9.3	9.0
Other manufacturing	377.1	346.3	397.3	514.4	511.4	20.8	7.0	.. d	2.3	25.8
Electricity, gas, steam and air conditioning supply	**326.3**	**294.2**	**297.5**	**337.1**	**304.3**	**-0.1**	**-0.9**	**2.1**	**0.9**	**23.2**
Water supply; sewerage, waste management and remediation activities	**19.8**	**1.9**	**3.6**	**13.9**	**11.8**	**2.7**	**-0.7**	**0.2**	**-2.2**	**-2.5**
Construction	**415.5**	**393.2**	**467.1**	**603.9**	**469.6**	**13.6**	**32.7**	**63.6**	**75.8**	**75.6**
Services	**12 275.9**	**11 471.9**	**12 007.5**	**14 190.6**	**14 431.3**	**2 896.0**	**2 916.8**	**2 956.2**	**3 497.5**	**3 963.5**
Wholesale and retail trade; repair of motor vehicles and motorcycles	1 728.4	1 653.7	1 854.2	2 277.1	2 284.9	354.0	560.8	603.6	809.9	1 063.1
Transportation and storage	378.5	359.2	391.5	452.6	455.4	96.0	24.0	28.5	70.1	119.3
Accommodation and food service activities	73.8	71.9	44.2	72.5	129.4	6.8	2.3	1.9	0.0	2.9
Information and communication	928.0	1 229.7	1 134.2	1 287.8	1 309.8	57.9	8[illegible].8	101.1	95.0	117.0
Financial and insurance activities	5 447.0	4 628.8	5 037.3	5 729.0	5 508.2	439.5	373.4	939.2	1 200.4	926.1
Activities of holding companies	1 317.9	925.5	1 520.2	1 410.9	1 332.7	317.9	243.0	294.2	386.1	411.0
Real estate activities	2 199.1	2 211.3	2 126.3	2 544.8	2 464.2	175.1	263.8	213.5	256.2	257.5
Professional, scientific and technical activities	1 186.9	1 019.4	1 093.7	1 424.5	1 863.1	1 747.0	1 544.5	938.8	896.1	1 337.7
Administrative and support service activities	289.2	248.2	276.3	332.6	358.0	21.3	67.4	112.8	147.8	126.3
Public administration; activities of households and of extraterritorial organisations	-	-	-	-	-	-	-	-	-	-
Education	1.5	1.6	0.8	0.9	1.0	0.5	0.1	14.4	17.8	12.0
Human health and social work activities	24.8	26.1	23.4	41.3	37.4	1.0	0.7	0.5	0.9	0.8
Arts, entertainment and recreation	17.1	19.5	22.1	24.3	16.8	-3.5	-2.8	1.8	3.3	1.5
Other services	1.7	2.4	3.2	3.3	3.3	0.5	0.6	0.1	0.1	-0.7
Not allocated and confidential	**0.0**	-	-	-	-	-	-	-	**0.0**	-
Private real estate activities	**365.3**	**355.3**	**387.9**	**484.8**	**535.8**	**97.6**	**94.5**	**94.6**	**111.4**	**106.2**

- Nil; .. Not available; c Confidential data; d Secondary Confidentiality

Note: Detailed metadata at: *http://stats.oecd.org/OECDStat_Metadata/ShowMetadata.ashx?Dataset=FDI_CTRY_IND_SUMM.*

Source: *OECD International Direct Investment Statistics (database): https://doi.org/10.1787/idi-data-en*

Table 6. Foreign direct investment income by industrial sector

Million US dollars

	Inward					Outward				
	2014	2015	2016	2017	2018	2014	2015	2016	2017	2018
All FDI activities	**684.3**	**1 642.2**	**1 721.9**	**1 980.4**	**2 241.6**	**119.8**	**134.9**	**145.1**	**149.8**	**300.1**
Agriculture, forestry and fishing	**-3.9**	**-7.3**	**-2.8**	**16.7**	**-5.0**	**0.0**	**-0.1**	**-0.2**	**0.0**	**2.5**
Mining and quarrying	**-26.5**	**-19.3**	**1.2**	**-6.1**	**8.6**	**-**	**-0.1**	**-0.4**	**-0.5**	**0.8**
Extraction activities	.. c	.. c	.. c	.. c	.. c	-	-	-	-	-
Manufacturing	**-555.4**	**617.3**	**688.1**	**669.4**	**680.1**	**-0.5**	**4.0**	**4.3**	**-7.2**	**16.5**
of which:										
Food products, beverages and tobacco	68.0	50.1	45.8	50.4	34.8	1.5	-1.2	1.4	3.7	-1.6
Textiles, wood and paper products; printing	60.8	35.2	35.3	50.4	50.7	-10.0	-2.5	1.0	-1.9	-0.6
Chemical, rubber, plastic, non-metallic mineral products	-782.9	441.1	495.0	454.2	456.7	3.7	4.0	0.7	.. d	19.2
Metal and machinery products, except electrical equipment	32.5	44.3	43.9	49.7	90.3	2.3	2.1	2.4	5.1	1.3
Motor vehicles, trailers, semi-trailers, other transport equipment	19.7	12.5	12.4	15.6	22.6	-	.. c	0.0	.. c	-0.1
Other manufacturing	46.5	34.1	55.7	49.2	25.0	2.0	.. d	-1.3	.. d	-1.6
Electricity, gas, steam and air conditioning supply	**36.8**	**10.6**	**28.0**	**27.8**	**30.0**	**.. d**	**.. d**	**.. d**	**-0.3**	**-4.9**
Water supply; sewerage, waste management and remediation activities	**14.3**	**2.5**	**0.9**	**2.8**	**1.1**	**.. c**	**.. c**	**.. d**	**1.1**	**0.9**
Construction	**35.5**	**15.5**	**48.5**	**57.7**	**32.6**	**-3.8**	**-0.2**	**7.3**	**1.5**	**6.9**
Services	**1 183.6**	**1 022.8**	**958.0**	**1 211.9**	**1 494.2**	**125.1**	**127.8**	**131.2**	**154.2**	**276.3**
Wholesale and retail trade; repair of motor vehicles and motorcycles	196.3	132.0	211.5	249.4	300.5	33.4	44.0	57.3	31.7	84.2
Transportation and storage	102.5	45.9	23.7	70.2	99.0	11.2	-2.8	12.9	18.8	10.8
Accommodation and food service activities	0.5	5.3	5.6	13.9	9.6	-0.5	-0.3	-1.1	-2.0	.. d
Information and communication	147.5	167.2	171.7	198.0	204.1	7.5	8.3	21.4	11.6	25.7
Financial and insurance activities	389.7	322.9	283.2	300.4	437.9	9.5	5.0	-5.7	1.8	7.2
Activities of holding companies	34.2	17.1	3.3	0.4	25.3	12.0	7.1	3.3	3.6	16.5
Real estate activities	115.0	173.2	129.2	158.1	165.4	7.7	4.8	0.2	21.9	35.9
Professional, scientific and technical activities	170.7	130.1	84.1	175.7	188.8	41.8	70.0	32.8	52.2	104.8
Administrative and support service activities	55.4	39.6	41.2	36.1	74.5	14.8	-0.3	13.6	16.6	8.8
Public administration; activities of households and of extraterritorial organisations	-	-	-	-	-	-	-	- d	-	- d
Education	0.4	0.3	0.2	0.0	0.1	-	-	.. c	1.6	0.2
Human health and social work activities	1.2	2.7	6.6	7.9	10.7	.. c	-	0.1	0.1	-
Arts, entertainment and recreation	4.8	3.6	0.9	2.2	2.0	.. c	-1.1	-1.1	-0.1	.. d
Other services	-0.4	-0.1	0.0	0.1	1.6	.. c	0.2	-0.2	-0.1	-0.6
Not allocated and confidential	**-**	**-**	**0.0**	**0.0**	**-**	**.. c**	**.. c**	**.. d**	**-**	**-**
Private real estate activities	**-**	**-**	**-**	**-**	**-**	**0.7**	**0.8**	**1.0**	**1.2**	**1.1**

- Nil; .. Not available; c Confidential data; d Secondary Confidentiality

Note: Detailed metadata at: *http://stats.oecd.org/OECDStat_Metadata/ShowMetadata.ashx?Dataset=FDI_CTRY_IND_SUMM.*

Source: OECD International Direct Investment Statistics (database): https://doi.org/10.1787/idi-data-en

LUXEMBOURG

Table 1. Foreign direct investment flows by country

Million US dollars

	Inward					Outward				
	2014	2015	2016	2017	2018	2014	2015	2016	2017	2018
WORLD	**204 201.9**	**606 571.3**	**210 228.9**	**89 655.1**	**-386 474.7**	**241 829.6**	**713 728.2**	**170 862.5**	**250 751.9**	**-365 790.2**
OECD COUNTRIES	**156 258.5**	**582 746.5**	**142 000.4**	**-328 496.2**	**-264 916.8**	**196 162.9**	**710 400.4**	**101 990.5**	**239 864.7**	**-336 020.3**
Australia	3 010.5	8 012.2	207.9	540.0	1 077.5	624.9	5 399.9	1 346.9	-1 510.5	-1 163.7
Austria	2 207.8	1 084.9	194.6	1 010.0	44.8	2 880.5	1 271.3	1 102.5	489.2	2 194.0
Belgium	6 308.9	-4 607.9	-4 462.0	36 783.9	-12 072.5	29 806.3	-27 860.2	-11 571.4	11 041.6	-4 919.2
Canada	19 310.1	19 727.1	26 750.0	13 386.3	6 554.9	5 557.9	-4 548.0	10 619.3	384.4	12 348.6
Chile	-14.6	-389.4	82.9	-147.7	20.1	510.8	-1 130.3	1 234.1	-1 170.1	643.2
Czech Republic	2 551.4	-87.6	-185.8	-219.8	-2 006.4	8 104.0	1 456.5	1 848.9	5 100.9	-1 940.3
Denmark	84.9	569.1	331.7	90.2	4 297.2	1 539.1	986.1	1 819.1	-543.3	2 014.6
Estonia	10.6	-256.2	26.5	10.1	-4.7	29.2	-7.8	14.4	-10.1	420.2
Finland	318.4	1 157.0	130.5	-1 606.4	-429.6	67.7	-195.2	9 544.4	1 994.1	1 530.7
France	10 301.2	9 516.4	-18 427.5	1 003.3	803.7	38 442.4	8 761.0	8 332.4	2 212.8	20 478.0
Germany	14 557.5	4 713.3	3 671.3	18 023.9	-5 214.2	8 602.9	5 026.1	11 283.9	2 154.2	456.7
Greece	78.3	24.4	48.7	-12.4	64.9	-463.0	274.0	-337.3	-119.5	489.8
Hungary	3 143.2	11 074.9	-13 275.5	-24 134.8	93.2	-717.8	-1 253.5	21 430.9	-2 973.7	-28 429.1
Iceland	-743.0	-3 372.2	3 081.9	-845.5	745.9	211.0	-1 318.9	-3 072.0	275.1	1 095.2
Ireland	50 127.4	218 776.5	90 021.0	-41 249.0	-60 762.4	-15 794.1	133 454.2	16 661.5	369 546.8	-5 696.9
Israel[1]	155.2	216.3	123.9	316.8	-881.6	1 194.1	-250.7	-179.1	126.3	1 172.0
Italy	2 831.4	71.0	27 740.8	9 585.2	-1 321.8	6 090.0	1 868.0	-564.0	2 446.2	-8 536.5
Japan	3 049.0	555.7	368.2	-790.2	839.1	2 284.7	51.0	-3.3	57.5	1 500.1
Korea	1 021.6	-32.2	68.6	94.7	-211.3	814.6	379.4	92.9	332.5	50.7
Latvia	-11.9	255.1	22.1	-63.1	-11.8	25.2	17.7	2.2	-34.9	-4.7
Lithuania	-11.9	13.3	-230.0	-3.4	-4.7	-4.0	43.3	10.0	-116.1	140.4
Luxembourg	-	-	-	-	-	-	-	-	-	-
Mexico	2 581.9	-1 921.2	-1 019.6	-1 306.5	61.4	5 086.9	2 022.2	-677.9	-1.1	-872.2
Netherlands	55 948.0	-15 783.7	27 296.3	-49 797.1	-128 018.4	34 446.1	45 895.7	55 690.6	63 971.4	-78 058.5
New Zealand	309.1	898.5	-293.0	-2 059.5	-828.5	240.1	799.8	-600.5	-242.4	-38.9
Norway	1 762.0	2 177.5	1 788.1	339.3	-997.3	-39.8	1 417.6	-559.5	166.8	-786.0
Poland	1 403.7	-1 419.9	-224.5	900.7	-1 222.7	3 127.2	-3 245.7	1 797.0	6 017.4	817.9
Portugal	1 338.7	-848.6	74.1	38.3	702.2	14 887.9	6 672.2	-346.1	-399.1	1 418.6
Slovak Republic	437.8	-7.8	-529.7	-151.1	-542.9	2 405.5	147.5	-644.7	299.9	-33.0
Slovenia	-14.6	32.2	31.0	68.8	-9.4	88.9	198.6	158.1	89.1	528.7
Spain	2 685.4	1 559.6	9 394.0	-1 210.7	-2 509.1	14 941.0	-575.7	13 300.9	10 268.3	10 609.0
Sweden	3 960.5	-3 662.8	-1 908.7	-1 899.4	2 705.1	3 395.3	5 080.4	4 845.7	-2 218.5	-4 876.7
Switzerland	25 807.4	3 142.5	10 995.2	-13 163.1	-16 059.2	3 799.9	56 767.6	13 964.4	34 755.9	-22 740.5
Turkey	143.3	-261.8	179.1	-489.2	118.0	1 157.0	2 086.5	-739.8	-1 166.7	-323.4
United Kingdom	-67 114.2	135 211.3	-26 024.5	-27 654.2	5 477.4	-28 622.8	274 278.5	-20 537.4	45 856.2	-90 308.0
United States	8 703.7	196 877.4	5 721.6	-243 887.9	-55 413.7	51 466.1	196 672.3	-33 263.3	-307 328.4	-145 201.2
EUROPE	**140 164.5**	**381 520.8**	**99 697.0**	**-109 883.9**	**-238 252.1**	**159 816.9**	**508 505.8**	**134 731.8**	**518 018.3**	**-202 223.5**
Bulgaria	-21.2	-2.2	44.2	-3.4	9.4	-91.5	175.3	56.4	25.9	642.0
Croatia	-1.3	7.8	-76.3	-1.1	1.2	88.9	341.7	-10.0	408.1	153.4
Cyprus[2, 3]	282.6	-3 690.5	-890.2	-487.0	1 061.0	2 929.5	-2 756.5	-4 280.7	-21 696.5	-8 213.1
Malta	1 943.7	-3 053.8	3 080.8	986.4	-2 513.9	6 539.7	-681.1	-105.1	3 173.3	221.9
Romania	378.1	8.9	142.7	31.6	-3.5	356.9	307.3	345.0	281.8	-74.4
Russian Federation	-1 410.4	18 485.9	-277.6	-3 753.8	7 794.2	812.0	308.4	-65.2	-8 096.0	-2 441.9
Ukraine	..	..	..	..	..	..	..	..	..	..
AFRICA	**1 130.4**	**-1 789.2**	**-915.6**	**1 081.1**	**164.1**	**2 390.9**	**-22.2**	**-17 328.3**	**-3 080.8**	**-915.9**
Northern Africa	79.6	590.1	-24.3	-7.9	146.3	26.5	145.3	246.6	-2 447.3	53.1
Algeria	..	..	..	..	..	..	..	..	..	..
Egypt	61.0	535.8	-1.1	-11.3	-10.6	17.2	62.1	192.4	1 077.7	30.7
Libya	..	..	..	..	..	..	..	..	..	..
Morocco	8.0	51.0	23.2	-4.5	99.1	180.4	69.9	67.5	-3 520.5	14.2
Tunisia	..	..	..	..	..	..	..	..	..	..
Other African countries	1 052.1	-2 378.3	-892.4	1 088.9	16.5	2 364.3	-166.4	-17 574.9	-633.5	-969.0
Nigeria	-	2.2	-3.3	-2.3	-18.9	-112.8	1.1	8.8	28.2	3.5
South Africa	10.6	-468.1	-31.0	41.7	-1 921.4	1 922.5	-379.5	-15 902.9	-844.3	-256.1
AMERICA	**60 191.1**	**212 503.6**	**40 339.5**	**189 918.8**	**-137 618.3**	**61 992.8**	**205 714.9**	**-8 946.1**	**-333 699.7**	**-98 458.6**
Northern America	28 013.8	216 604.5	32 471.5	-230 500.5	-48 858.7	57 024.0	192 065.4	-22 645.1	-306 944.0	-132 852.6
Central America and Caribbean countries	32 251.6	-11 772.6	10 003.3	424 235.1	-94 067.0	5 292.6	12 087.6	3 278.8	-28 145.6	30 725.8
Bahamas	..	..	..	..	..	..	..	..	..	..
Bermuda	..	..	..	..	..	..	..	..	..	..
Cayman Islands	..	..	..	..	..	..	..	..	..	..
Costa Rica	..	..	..	..	..	..	..	..	..	..
El Salvador	..	..	..	..	..	..	..	..	..	..
Guatemala	..	..	..	..	..	..	..	..	..	..
Honduras	..	..	..	..	..	..	..	..	..	..
Nicaragua	..	..	..	..	..	..	..	..	..	..
Panama	..	..	..	..	..	..	..	..	..	..
Virgin Islands, U.S.	..	..	..	..	..	..	..	..	..	..
South America	-73.0	7 670.5	-2 134.2	-3 815.8	5 306.3	-323.7	1 561.8	10 420.2	1 391.0	3 668.1
Argentina	-19.9	-38.8	39.8	-28.2	-31.9	1.3	290.6	-305.2	375.4	-203.0
Bolivia	..	..	..	..	..	..	..	..	..	..
Brazil	256.1	8 196.3	-2 248.1	-2 670.5	1 791.6	-1 801.8	-326.1	8 030.5	3 346.9	2 293.2
Colombia	..	..	..	..	..	..	..	..	..	..
Ecuador	..	..	..	..	..	..	..	..	..	..
Paraguay	..	..	..	..	..	..	..	..	..	..
Peru	..	..	..	..	..	..	..	..	..	..
Uruguay	-1.3	-322.8	-267.6	-1 641.3	3 788.5	648.8	1 218.0	-69.7	-288.6	403.6
Venezuela	-43.8	10.0	3.3	11.3	-	-350.3	38.8	10.0	20.3	-21.2

Table 1. Foreign direct investment flows by country *(cont.)*

Million US dollars

	Inward					Outward				
	2014	2015	2016	2017	2018	2014	2015	2016	2017	2018
ASIA	**-745.7**	**5 642.8**	**71 597.9**	**9 776.8**	**-10 981.9**	**16 397.8**	**-6 675.5**	**61 707.4**	**71 241.1**	**-62 851.4**
Near and Middle East	-1 946.4	10 690.0	-2 177.4	5 608.2	330.5	1 505.9	48.8	6 746.7	1 147.6	-3 528.9
Gulf Arabian countries	-2 004.8	10 247.4	-2 265.8	5 139.2	1 175.5	-124.7	174.2	6 409.4	583.9	-4 853.1
Kuwait	..	..	..	..	..	..	..	..	..	..
Qatar	..	..	..	..	..	..	..	..	..	..
Saudi Arabia	..	..	..	..	..	..	..	..	..	..
United Arab Emirates	..	..	..	..	..	..	..	..	..	..
Other Near and Middle East	58.4	442.6	88.5	468.9	-845.0	1 630.6	-124.2	337.3	564.8	1 325.4
Jordan	..	..	..	..	..	..	..	..	..	..
Other Asian countries	1 200.7	-5 047.1	73 775.3	4 168.6	-11 312.4	14 890.5	-6 725.5	54 960.7	70 092.4	-59 322.6
China	241.5	3 224.6	1 714.0	-4 019.8	2 355.7	-1 752.7	-84.3	1 239.6	-296.5	984.3
Hong Kong, China	-168.5	-11 713.8	3 968.8	49 342.8	1 310.0	7 691.4	-6 026.6	13 272.1	17 158.2	-710.5
India	175.1	-1 592.9	1 285.0	-111.6	-7.1	21.2	450.4	-801.7	976.2	-5.9
Indonesia	-18.6	-178.6	3 266.6	-53.0	94.4	452.4	91.0	280.9	125.1	70.8
Iran, Islamic Republic of	..	..	..	..	..	..	..	..	..	..
Malaysia	108.8	3 015.0	-157.0	39.5	316.3	127.4	-379.4	-1 583.5	96.9	101.5
Philippines	-29.2	-17.7	44.2	-6.8	-	-17.2	-25.5	-32.1	-22.5	-9.4
Singapore	-2 976.0	1 900.2	62 401.9	-39 960.5	-15 987.3	4 561.5	-1 466.4	41 560.3	50 418.2	-61 288.8
Chinese Taipei	17.2	-28.8	-32.1	13.5	-49.6	366.2	7.8	13.3	58.6	46.0
Thailand	-79.6	58.8	1 037.3	-263.8	40.1	360.9	64.3	82.9	308.9	13.0
Viet Nam	..	..	..	..	..	..	..	..	..	..
AUSTRALIA, OCEANIA AND POLAR REGIONS	**3 461.6**	**8 692.2**	**-491.0**	**-1 237.7**	**214.8**	**1 231.3**	**6 205.2**	**697.8**	**-1 727.0**	**-1 340.7**
WORLD unallocated and confidential	**-**	**1.1**	**1.1**	**-**	**-1.2**	**-**	**-**	**-**	**-**	**-**
European Union (EU28)	**93 720.3**	**350 654.5**	**96 017.9**	**-79 959.4**	**-201 386.8**	**133 100.7**	**449 558.5**	**109 844.1**	**497 263.0**	**-188 974.4**
G20 countries excl. European Union	**..**	**..**	**..**	**..**	**..**	**..**	**..**	**..**	**..**	**..**
G20 OECD countries	**-1 604.1**	**372 469.2**	**19 235.9**	**-231 494.8**	**-47 228.8**	**91 504.6**	**491 876.9**	**-24 110.4**	**-256 563.0**	**-211 570.9**
G20 Non-OECD countries	**..**	**..**	**..**	**..**	**..**	**..**	**..**	**..**	**..**	**..**
MENA countries	**..**	**..**	**..**	**..**	**..**	**..**	**..**	**..**	**..**	**..**
ASEAN countries	**-3 062.2**	**4 777.6**	**66 591.8**	**-40 330.3**	**-15 550.6**	**5 303.2**	**-1 723.8**	**41 298.2**	**51 882.5**	**-61 182.6**

- Nil; .. Not available

Note: Detailed metadata at: *http://stats.oecd.org/OECDStat_Metadata/ShowMetadata.ashx?Dataset=FDI_CTRY_IND_SUMM.*

1. Information on data for Israel: *http://oe.cd/israel-disclaimer.*
2. Note by Turkey: The information in this document with reference to "Cyprus" relates to the southern part of the Island. There is no single authority representing both Turkish and Greek Cypriot people on the Island. Turkey recognises the Turkish Republic of Northern Cyprus (TRNC). Until a lasting and equitable solution is found within the context of the United Nations, Turkey shall preserve its position concerning the "Cyprus issue".
3. Note by all the European Union Member States of the OECD and the European Union: The Republic of Cyprus is recognised by all members of the United Nations with the exception of Turkey. The information in this document relates to the area under the effective control of the Government of the Republic of Cyprus.

Source: OECD International Direct Investment Statistics (database): https://doi.org/10.1787/idi-data-en

Table 2. Foreign direct investment positions by country

At year end

Million US dollars

	Inward					Outward				
	2014	2015	2016	2017	2018	2014	2015	2016	2017	2018
WORLD	**3 258 954.0**	**3 705 702.8**	**3 812 960.9**	**4 289 898.1**	**3 758 983.3**	**3 975 378.6**	**4 516 753.4**	**4 603 600.7**	**5 140 522.9**	**4 602 940.2**
OECD COUNTRIES	**2 397 774.7**	**2 872 659.8**	**2 940 050.6**	**2 842 351.9**	**2 529 452.7**	**3 460 972.9**	**4 027 277.1**	**4 083 565.9**	**4 528 400.1**	**4 094 139.0**
Australia	-1 138.8	6 773.0	7 031.7	8 064.3	8 579.1	10 010.3	14 957.0	15 499.1	17 489.8	17 388.4
Austria	6 588.9	8 668.5	8 696.1	11 373.2	9 958.8	14 478.1	14 314.6	14 535.7	16 966.9	17 609.3
Belgium	97 306.5	93 423.0	84 242.6	132 145.6	119 768.7	177 366.7	130 850.3	121 490.5	143 456.5	123 047.9
Canada	186 919.2	195 659.2	205 626.6	219 531.1	223 256.2	113 637.3	94 957.0	94 844.5	102 013.7	105 807.2
Chile	520.8	124.1	208.7	61.2	80.1	2 580.0	1 388.1	2 371.7	659.6	679.0
Czech Republic	995.6	813.3	608.2	472.5	-1 275.5	10 846.8	10 419.2	11 122.6	19 185.7	17 000.2
Denmark	3 183.4	1 576.5	1 329.2	1 193.3	4 574.1	12 365.6	11 636.4	13 318.2	13 714.3	13 960.4
Estonia	282.9	24.0	49.5	64.8	37.8	170.0	148.1	132.8	136.7	532.4
Finland	343.6	1 470.9	1 559.0	100.7	-162.6	10 888.0	2 527.5	11 487.3	14 239.6	15 811.8
France	11 526.7	18 952.6	-75.9	2 699.7	-2 202.9	109 310.3	107 695.2	110 270.9	129 072.9	138 110.8
Germany	73 988.5	74 818.7	77 649.4	108 521.2	102 180.0	123 415.7	116 448.6	126 991.7	145 809.5	142 760.5
Greece	122.6	86.0	143.4	170.3	202.7	5 020.3	4 252.6	3 824.2	4 161.7	4 439.0
Hungary	29 792.8	38 949.4	25 331.5	479.7	380.1	19 851.7	16 308.1	37 760.1	36 382.8	8 918.0
Iceland	339.9	-3 075.7	-41.1	-929.5	-174.0	8 615.3	6 497.6	2 909.2	3 499.6	4 460.7
Ireland	215 675.2	428 173.1	515 381.0	520 647.6	455 170.6	211 936.9	348 204.7	358 916.4	734 654.6	731 323.6
Israel[1]	-559.7	-72.9	125.4	427.0	-429.4	4 165.6	2 366.9	2 331.6	2 164.8	3 531.0
Italy	-6 330.3	-5 630.9	20 633.5	31 939.3	29 949.6	77 360.0	76 620.6	75 576.1	87 044.9	76 710.6
Japan	3 990.7	3 279.3	3 789.4	3 972.2	4 402.3	6 269.6	5 626.6	5 147.0	5 316.6	6 581.2
Korea	-1 518.8	-1 854.1	-1 992.2	-1 982.5	-2 200.6	604.6	878.6	940.2	1 384.0	1 406.0
Latvia	-257.4	-5.4	14.8	-49.2	-58.4	103.2	112.1	126.5	103.1	100.8
Lithuania	530.6	487.8	-4.2	-7.2	-12.6	142.1	156.8	162.3	66.0	206.1
Luxembourg	-	-	-	-	-	-	-	-	-	-
Mexico	-4 027.2	-5 456.7	-5 941.8	-7 010.1	-6 941.8	13 894.2	14 838.3	15 755.2	15 616.5	14 764.1
Netherlands	520 318.3	493 296.7	500 100.1	481 716.2	352 722.7	681 876.2	676 733.8	728 111.1	840 130.7	712 597.9
New Zealand	2 362.6	6 236.3	5 479.1	4 892.1	4 349.7	451.6	1 217.8	627.2	379.0	290.8
Norway	2 822.8	4 385.4	5 720.5	6 851.8	5 549.6	12 295.2	12 623.8	11 853.1	12 913.2	12 259.0
Poland	4 101.2	4 186.2	2 191.4	3 889.4	1 931.5	20 177.1	16 972.1	16 684.9	23 876.2	23 597.4
Portugal	3 048.6	2 347.3	2 173.5	2 126.4	2 966.6	15 188.4	20 634.7	19 774.4	22 664.9	24 016.5
Slovak Republic	-339.9	-313.6	-807.4	-1 080.6	-1 558.3	4 883.1	4 535.7	3 586.0	4 352.4	4 071.4
Slovenia	-83.8	-42.5	-11.6	60.0	28.6	275.6	417.5	523.9	664.4	1 124.3
Spain	-12 332.8	-10 545.5	-3 170.7	-5 140.3	-5 367.5	58 444.3	53 882.4	60 198.2	73 761.1	83 558.5
Sweden	25 390.5	20 843.8	15 429.5	15 202.7	15 306.8	45 850.5	48 414.8	50 808.5	46 409.2	40 302.3
Switzerland	108 823.4	107 589.5	123 804.2	120 605.7	95 764.8	310 442.9	372 522.6	386 257.0	429 583.8	392 137.6
Turkey	229.5	-116.5	3.2	-399.4	-262.2	9 276.9	9 947.7	10 836.9	10 127.1	5 283.9
United Kingdom	429 623.9	538 447.5	490 215.0	512 064.0	495 502.6	495 405.0	772 187.3	728 330.3	855 159.5	732 942.5
United States	695 806.8	849 644.0	854 554.7	669 667.8	617 435.3	873 620.2	1 056 277.1	1 040 621.9	715 303.4	616 807.9
EUROPE	**1 849 320.8**	**2 155 923.8**	**2 178 883.7**	**2 268 923.0**	**1 972 110.1**	**2 704 486.7**	**3 080 775.2**	**3 157 912.9**	**3 888 943.4**	**3 541 797.6**
Bulgaria	-58.3	-55.5	-10.5	-15.6	-5.7	513.6	627.1	754.7	865.9	1 946.4
Croatia	-51.0	-38.1	-110.7	-128.3	-121.4	1 816.3	2 096.9	2 035.4	2 717.7	2 702.1
Cyprus[2, 3]	18 380.3	13 478.5	12 652.1	13 130.2	11 730.0	112 062.6	110 145.9	108 172.2	85 556.5	76 943.0
Malta	13 875.9	10 361.5	12 114.5	14 007.0	11 463.2	18 908.4	13 832.3	13 913.8	17 107.2	15 439.7
Romania	-38.9	-159.0	-11.6	20.4	-18.3	1 056.3	1 350.0	1 584.3	1 954.9	1 757.5
Russian Federation	-59 098.7	-39 469.8	-41 404.0	-39 601.8	-32 259.0	23 728.4	21 405.6	20 643.0	15 133.1	12 268.1
Ukraine	-91.1	-44.6	-40.1	-16.8	-16.0	432.2	487.2	561.8	710.0	559.9
AFRICA	**2 584.8**	**868.8**	**-1 516.8**	**-428.2**	**-695.0**	**27 357.3**	**27 155.1**	**10 512.3**	**11 516.0**	**10 658.3**
Northern Africa	-223.4	331.0	307.8	315.4	435.1	1 052.6	1 218.3	939.2	1 770.2	2 031.1
Algeria	64.3	56.6	62.2	78.0	79.0	23.1	16.3	11.6	10.8	8.0
Egypt	-424.9	103.4	113.8	103.1	91.6	775.8	878.6	578.7	1 527.9	1 450.7
Libya	-	-	-48.5	-55.2	-	-	-	-	-	-
Morocco	138.4	172.0	180.2	190.7	264.5	236.7	296.1	325.7	215.9	554.2
Tunisia	-	-1.1	-1.1	-	-	15.8	27.2	23.2	15.6	19.5
Other African countries	2 808.2	537.8	-1 824.6	-743.6	-1 130.1	26 304.7	25 936.9	9 573.1	9 745.7	8 627.2
Nigeria	-9.7	-6.5	-9.5	-13.2	-33.2	68.0	38.1	40.1	64.8	63.0
South Africa	1 361.0	1 018.0	539.7	368.2	-2 001.4	21 489.6	21 051.7	6 240.1	5 823.9	4 984.0
AMERICA	**1 294 522.0**	**1 432 650.0**	**1 452 071.3**	**1 814 172.5**	**1 596 997.9**	**1 152 185.8**	**1 318 975.5**	**1 308 018.3**	**1 023 541.6**	**903 820.7**
Northern America	882 726.0	1 045 303.2	1 060 181.3	889 200.0	840 691.6	987 257.6	1 151 228.1	1 135 465.4	817 315.9	722 616.2
Central America and Caribbean countries	410 159.4	379 516.6	385 655.1	921 855.4	751 543.4	102 952.0	109 065.9	105 306.2	126 739.0	113 323.8
Bahamas	56 925.5	39 407.7	42 337.9	52 796.8	50 043.5	-976.1	-1 223.7	-983.5	612.9	562.2
Bermuda	195 589.1	185 045.2	188 839.5	557 113.2	510 406.5	53 362.1	73 261.8	66 579.5	81 220.9	57 271.6
Cayman Islands	110 365.3	103 854.1	93 280.3	236 533.9	126 014.4	31 739.0	18 886.2	16 833.6	17 592.9	16 662.5
Costa Rica	-4.9	-3.3	-2.1	-3.6	-3.4	187.0	368.0	360.5	361.0	1 327.0
El Salvador	-2.4	3.3	79.1	90.0	139.7	24.3	156.8	152.8	18.0	18.3
Guatemala	-	-4.4	13.7	19.2	18.3	46.1	450.7	404.8	28.8	53.8
Honduras	103.2	-3.3	-	-	-	31.6	24.0	25.3	32.4	33.2
Nicaragua	-46.1	-2.2	-3.2	-2.4	-	7.3	7.6	-	73.2	73.3
Panama	1 021.1	1 922.7	5 080.6	4 718.2	3 722.2	1 538.3	1 706.0	2 214.6	984.6	934.3
Virgin Islands, U.S.	25.5	-	-	-2.4	-17.2	4.9	-	218.2	492.9	9 448.1
South America	1 636.6	7 830.2	6 234.8	3 117.1	4 763.0	61 976.2	58 680.5	67 246.8	79 485.5	67 880.7
Argentina	-69.2	-101.3	-44.3	-82.8	-117.9	6 586.5	4 075.1	5 092.2	4 859.7	4 781.3
Bolivia	-3.6	-3.3	6.3	10.8	12.6	103.2	103.9	112.8	110.3	69.8
Brazil	2 628.5	9 347.9	7 648.4	5 711.2	4 068.0	47 246.7	46 385.5	52 078.6	67 281.1	54 974.8
Colombia	-259.8	-46.8	22.1	624.9	121.4	860.8	937.4	834.8	916.3	1 107.2
Ecuador	-1.2	-	-	-6.0	-6.9	26.7	32.7	36.9	39.6	421.3
Paraguay	1.2	-4.4	-13.7	-14.4	-14.9	163.9	164.4	161.3	218.3	218.7
Peru	-78.9	-78.4	108.6	206.3	442.0	1 500.6	1 910.7	3 336.1	2 798.0	2 839.5
Uruguay	-1 069.6	-1 386.0	-1 683.4	-3 392.9	177.5	2 859.2	3 650.5	3 192.8	2 140.8	2 325.4
Venezuela	-32.8	-21.8	-17.9	-1.2	-1.1	49.8	25.0	28.5	50.4	48.1

Table 2. Foreign direct investment positions by country *(cont.)*
At year end

Million US dollars

	Inward					Outward				
	2014	2015	2016	2017	2018	2014	2015	2016	2017	2018
ASIA	**109 964.7**	**102 251.5**	**170 413.2**	**193 300.6**	**177 155.9**	**80 247.2**	**73 053.9**	**110 518.6**	**197 997.1**	**128 453.2**
Near and Middle East	30 659.7	38 255.9	36 630.1	44 291.2	42 391.8	5 442.8	3 860.6	10 741.0	11 439.2	8 754.3
Gulf Arabian countries	30 651.2	37 613.5	35 879.6	43 059.5	42 040.3	-25.5	140.4	6 563.7	6 965.7	3 192.1
Kuwait	-	-	-	-	-	-	2.2	-	3.6	3.4
Qatar	13 823.7	21 511.2	15 709.9	18 480.5	16 324.7	3.6	3.3	2.1	4.8	4.6
Saudi Arabia	1 742.2	1 550.4	2 633.1	4 258.8	4 224.9	88.6	99.1	127.5	133.1	123.7
United Arab Emirates	14 340.9	13 627.7	16 474.1	17 777.6	17 793.7	-162.7	37.0	6 411.9	6 800.2	3 029.5
Other Near and Middle East	9.7	641.3	750.5	1 231.7	351.5	5 467.1	3 720.2	4 177.3	4 473.5	5 562.2
Jordan	-	-	-	-1.2	-1.1	64.3	3.3	142.3	491.7	421.3
Other Asian countries	79 305.0	63 995.6	133 782.0	149 008.2	134 764.1	74 804.3	69 193.3	99 777.6	186 557.9	119 698.9
China	2 310.4	4 829.6	6 291.8	4 878.9	7 107.9	9 671.5	9 304.3	10 090.7	10 030.0	11 219.4
Hong Kong, China	52 313.1	36 174.2	35 913.4	89 821.3	87 453.6	9 314.6	4 420.3	10 354.2	30 358.6	24 495.1
India	-8.5	-1 577.6	-301.5	-430.6	-403.0	2 366.3	2 911.3	2 871.3	4 170.1	3 581.4
Indonesia	-3 183.4	-3 362.0	-182.4	-241.1	-142.0	591.3	651.1	886.5	977.5	972.1
Iran, Islamic Republic of	-	-	-	-	-	26.7	14.2	-	-	-
Malaysia	74.1	1 340.2	1 187.9	1 225.7	1 420.9	1 912.2	2 455.1	985.6	1 354.0	1 229.7
Philippines	-6.1	-22.9	20.0	13.2	12.6	163.9	170.9	153.9	141.5	114.5
Singapore	24 499.3	25 081.1	88 175.4	50 718.4	35 933.1	42 738.7	41 288.0	66 203.2	129 236.0	66 518.2
Chinese Taipei	29.1	-1.1	-34.8	-21.6	-68.7	316.9	327.7	328.9	373.0	348.1
Thailand	-75.3	-7.6	989.8	831.1	846.1	698.1	699.0	722.0	1 057.8	1 101.4
Viet Nam	-4.9	-4.4	-5.3	-8.4	-26.3	381.2	393.0	1 176.3	2 377.1	2 513.2
AUSTRALIA, OCEANIA AND POLAR REGIONS	**2 560.5**	**14 008.7**	**13 110.6**	**13 931.4**	**13 414.2**	**11 101.7**	**16 793.7**	**16 639.6**	**18 524.8**	**18 209.3**
WORLD unallocated and confidential	**1.2**	**-**	**-1.1**	**-1.2**	**-**	**-**	**-**	**-1.1**	**-**	**1.1**
European Union (EU28)	**1 435 583.4**	**1 733 611.3**	**1 766 311.8**	**1 845 603.3**	**1 603 094.8**	**2 229 711.6**	**2 561 511.2**	**2 620 192.9**	**3 320 218.3**	**3 011 528.5**
G20 countries excl. European Union	**1 334 752.4**	**1 646 751.2**	**1 626 674.4**	**1 521 928.5**	**1 450 175.2**	**1 944 573.0**	**2 376 312.5**	**2 322 843.9**	**2 192 746.5**	**1 951 467.8**
G20 OECD countries	**1 389 070.0**	**1 674 516.1**	**1 651 493.6**	**1 547 067.6**	**1 469 697.7**	**1 832 804.1**	**2 270 427.9**	**2 224 814.0**	**2 084 338.0**	**1 858 563.1**
G20 Non-OECD countries	**-54 317.6**	**-27 764.8**	**-24 819.2**	**-25 139.1**	**-19 522.6**	**111 768.8**	**105 884.6**	**98 029.9**	**108 408.5**	**92 904.7**
MENA countries	**31 000.8**	**38 664.1**	**36 909.5**	**44 179.7**	**43 220.7**	**1 998.4**	**2 258.0**	**9 034.5**	**10 688.4**	**7 023.1**
ASEAN countries	**21 975.2**	**23 023.4**	**90 184.5**	**52 867.6**	**38 568.8**	**46 531.6**	**45 707.1**	**70 178.1**	**135 207.5**	**72 506.3**

- Nil

Note: Detailed metadata at: *http://stats.oecd.org/OECDStat_Metadata/ShowMetadata.ashx?Dataset=FDI_CTRY_IND_SUMM.*

1. Information on data for Israel: *http://oe.cd/israel-disclaimer.*
2. Note by Turkey: The information in this document with reference to "Cyprus" relates to the southern part of the Island. There is no single authority representing both Turkish and Greek Cypriot people on the Island. Turkey recognises the Turkish Republic of Northern Cyprus (TRNC). Until a lasting and equitable solution is found within the context of the United Nations, Turkey shall preserve its position concerning the "Cyprus issue".
3. Note by all the European Union Member States of the OECD and the European Union: The Republic of Cyprus is recognised by all members of the United Nations with the exception of Turkey. The information in this document relates to the area under the effective control of the Government of the Republic of Cyprus.

Source: OECD International Direct Investment Statistics (database): https://doi.org/10.1787/idi-data-en

Table 3. Foreign direct investment income by country

Million US dollars

	Inward					Outward				
	2014	2015	2016	2017	2018	2014	2015	2016	2017	2018
WORLD	**72 524.9**	**49 914.6**	**55 099.0**	**54 408.7**	**48 114.0**	**80 830.6**	**75 208.0**	**77 250.9**	**80 172.5**	**71 511.9**
OECD COUNTRIES	**55 800.7**	**34 792.0**	**44 117.0**	**35 150.5**	**32 569.3**	**68 888.2**	**66 825.3**	**65 835.5**	**65 471.8**	**58 227.3**
Australia	..	..	..	..	..	..	..	..	..	..
Austria	..	..	..	..	..	..	..	..	..	..
Belgium	..	..	..	..	..	..	..	..	..	..
Canada	..	..	..	..	..	..	..	..	..	..
Chile	..	..	..	..	..	..	..	..	..	..
Czech Republic	..	..	..	..	..	..	..	..	..	..
Denmark	..	..	..	..	..	..	..	..	..	..
Estonia	..	..	..	..	..	..	..	..	..	..
Finland	..	..	..	..	..	..	..	..	..	..
France	..	..	..	..	..	..	..	..	..	..
Germany	..	..	..	..	..	..	..	..	..	..
Greece	..	..	..	..	..	..	..	..	..	..
Hungary	..	..	..	..	..	..	..	..	..	..
Iceland	..	..	..	..	..	..	..	..	..	..
Ireland	..	..	..	..	..	..	..	..	..	..
Israel[1]	..	..	..	..	..	..	..	..	..	..
Italy	..	..	..	..	..	..	..	..	..	..
Japan	..	..	..	..	..	..	..	..	..	..
Korea	..	..	..	..	..	..	..	..	..	..
Latvia	..	..	..	..	..	..	..	..	..	..
Lithuania	..	..	..	..	..	..	..	..	..	..
Luxembourg	..	..	..	..	..	..	..	..	..	..
Mexico	..	..	..	..	..	..	..	..	..	..
Netherlands	..	..	..	..	..	..	..	..	..	..
New Zealand	..	..	..	..	..	..	..	..	..	..
Norway	..	..	..	..	..	..	..	..	..	..
Poland	..	..	..	..	..	..	..	..	..	..
Portugal	..	..	..	..	..	..	..	..	..	..
Slovak Republic	..	..	..	..	..	..	..	..	..	..
Slovenia	..	..	..	..	..	..	..	..	..	..
Spain	..	..	..	..	..	..	..	..	..	..
Sweden	..	..	..	..	..	..	..	..	..	..
Switzerland	..	..	..	..	..	..	..	..	..	..
Turkey	..	..	..	..	..	..	..	..	..	..
United Kingdom	..	..	..	..	..	..	..	..	..	..
United States	..	..	..	..	..	..	..	..	..	..
EUROPE	**41 501.9**	**28 642.3**	**35 963.7**	**33 395.3**	**27 114.4**	**57 696.7**	**55 421.0**	**62 307.9**	**62 930.9**	**55 195.3**
Bulgaria	..	..	..	..	..	..	..	..	..	..
Croatia	..	..	..	..	..	..	..	..	..	..
Cyprus[2, 3]	..	..	..	..	..	..	..	..	..	..
Malta	..	..	..	..	..	..	..	..	..	..
Romania	..	..	..	..	..	..	..	..	..	..
Russian Federation	..	..	..	..	..	..	..	..	..	..
Ukraine	..	..	..	..	..	..	..	..	..	..
AFRICA	**-66.3**	**-54.4**	**-18.8**	**-9.0**	**-2.4**	**1 878.7**	**-647.8**	**691.1**	**164.6**	**217.2**
Northern Africa	25.2	18.9	21.0	28.2	38.9	203.0	-242.9	227.8	126.3	132.2
Algeria	..	..	..	..	..	..	..	..	..	..
Egypt	..	..	..	..	..	..	..	..	..	..
Libya	..	..	..	..	..	..	..	..	..	..
Morocco	..	..	..	..	..	..	..	..	..	..
Tunisia	..	..	..	..	..	..	..	..	..	..
Other African countries	-91.5	-73.2	-39.8	-37.2	-41.3	1 675.7	-404.9	464.4	38.3	85.0
Nigeria	..	..	..	..	..	..	..	..	..	..
South Africa	..	..	..	..	..	..	..	..	..	..
AMERICA	**28 406.5**	**18 969.5**	**17 569.4**	**17 819.9**	**18 088.0**	**17 549.4**	**17 794.8**	**8 843.3**	**11 603.0**	**10 675.1**
Northern America	14 881.3	8 932.9	9 908.2	6 690.3	9 867.8	14 017.5	15 115.9	6 821.9	7 780.4	5 923.5
Central America and Caribbean countries	13 305.0	9 889.1	7 960.9	10 914.2	8 160.0	2 908.3	2 804.2	1 592.4	2 514.9	3 419.1
Bahamas	..	..	..	..	..	..	..	..	..	..
Bermuda	..	..	..	..	..	..	..	..	..	..
Cayman Islands	..	..	..	..	..	..	..	..	..	..
Costa Rica	..	..	..	..	..	..	..	..	..	..
El Salvador	..	..	..	..	..	..	..	..	..	..
Guatemala	..	..	..	..	..	..	..	..	..	..
Honduras	..	..	..	..	..	..	..	..	..	..
Nicaragua	..	..	..	..	..	..	..	..	..	..
Panama	..	..	..	..	..	..	..	..	..	..
Virgin Islands, U.S.	..	..	..	..	..	..	..	..	..	..
South America	220.2	146.4	-299.7	215.3	60.2	623.6	-124.2	429.1	1 306.5	1 332.5
Argentina	..	..	..	..	..	..	..	..	..	..
Bolivia	..	..	..	..	..	..	..	..	..	..
Brazil	..	..	..	..	..	..	..	..	..	..
Colombia	..	..	..	..	..	..	..	..	..	..
Ecuador	..	..	..	..	..	..	..	..	..	..
Paraguay	..	..	..	..	..	..	..	..	..	..
Peru	..	..	..	..	..	..	..	..	..	..
Uruguay	..	..	..	..	..	..	..	..	..	..
Venezuela	..	..	..	..	..	..	..	..	..	..

Table 3. Foreign direct investment income by country *(cont.)*

Million US dollars

	Inward					Outward				
	2014	2015	2016	2017	2018	2014	2015	2016	2017	2018
ASIA	**2 656.2**	**1 564.1**	**1 579.1**	**2 954.6**	**2 832.5**	**3 508.0**	**2 104.3**	**5 116.7**	**5 191.1**	**5 218.9**
Near and Middle East	831.9	691.1	868.1	1 111.5	1 111.8	222.9	138.7	29.9	196.1	136.9
Gulf Arabian countries	790.8	619.0	817.2	1 067.5	1 053.9	57.1	48.8	60.8	6.8	10.6
Kuwait	..	..	..	..	..	..	..	..	..	..
Qatar	..	..	..	..	..	..	..	..	..	..
Saudi Arabia	..	..	..	..	..	..	..	..	..	..
United Arab Emirates	..	..	..	..	..	..	..	..	..	..
Other Near and Middle East	42.5	72.1	50.9	44.0	59.0	165.8	89.9	-31.0	189.4	127.5
Jordan	..	..	..	..	..	..	..	..	..	..
Other Asian countries	1 824.3	873.0	711.0	1 843.1	1 720.8	3 285.1	1 965.6	5 086.8	4 994.9	5 082.0
China	..	..	..	..	..	..	..	..	..	..
Hong Kong, China	..	..	..	..	..	..	..	..	..	..
India	..	..	..	..	..	..	..	..	..	..
Indonesia	..	..	..	..	..	..	..	..	..	..
Iran, Islamic Republic of	..	..	..	..	..	..	..	..	..	..
Malaysia	..	..	..	..	..	..	..	..	..	..
Philippines	..	..	..	..	..	..	..	..	..	..
Singapore	..	..	..	..	..	..	..	..	..	..
Chinese Taipei	..	..	..	..	..	..	..	..	..	..
Thailand	..	..	..	..	..	..	..	..	..	..
Viet Nam	..	..	..	..	..	..	..	..	..	..
AUSTRALIA, OCEANIA AND POLAR REGIONS	**26.5**	**794.2**	**6.6**	**246.9**	**80.3**	**197.7**	**535.8**	**291.9**	**282.9**	**204.2**
WORLD unallocated and confidential	**-**	**-1.1**	**-1.1**	**1.1**	**1.2**	**-**	**-**	**-**	**-**	**1.2**
European Union (EU28)	**33 618.2**	**20 536.9**	**31 769.3**	**25 108.8**	**19 733.3**	**48 584.3**	**47 401.0**	**55 002.8**	**48 878.4**	**43 330.6**
G20 countries excl. European Union	..	..	..	..	..	..	..	..	..	..
G20 OECD countries	..	..	..	..	..	..	..	..	..	..
G20 Non-OECD countries	..	..	..	..	..	..	..	..	..	..
MENA countries	..	..	..	..	..	..	..	..	..	..
ASEAN countries	**794.7**	**445.9**	**327.3**	**664.0**	**414.3**	**1 276.4**	**870.8**	**576.1**	**2 285.0**	**1 900.2**

- Nil; .. Not available

Note: Detailed metadata at: *http://stats.oecd.org/OECDStat_Metadata/ShowMetadata.ashx?Dataset=FDI_CTRY_IND_SUMM.*

1. Information on data for Israel: *http://oe.cd/israel-disclaimer.*
2. Note by Turkey: The information in this document with reference to "Cyprus" relates to the southern part of the Island. There is no single authority representing both Turkish and Greek Cypriot people on the Island. Turkey recognises the Turkish Republic of Northern Cyprus (TRNC). Until a lasting and equitable solution is found within the context of the United Nations, Turkey shall preserve its position concerning the "Cyprus issue".
3. Note by all the European Union Member States of the OECD and the European Union: The Republic of Cyprus is recognised by all members of the United Nations with the exception of Turkey. The information in this document relates to the area under the effective control of the Government of the Republic of Cyprus.

Source: OECD International Direct Investment Statistics (database): https://doi.org/10.1787/idi-data-en

Table 4. Foreign direct investment flows by industrial sector

Million US dollars

	Inward					Outward				
	2014	2015	2016	2017	2018	2014	2015	2016	2017	2018
All FDI activities	**204 201.9**	**606 571.3**	**210 228.9**	**89 655.1**	**-386 474.7**	**241 829.6**	**713 728.2**	**170 862.5**	**250 751.9**	**-365 790.2**
Agriculture, forestry and fishing	**-**	**-**	**-**	**-**	**-**	**29.2**	**106.5**	**-60.8**	**-224.3**	**-89.7**
Mining and quarrying	**1.3**	**1.1**	**2.2**	**2.3**	**2.4**	**4 720.7**	**-3 970.1**	**-7 304.0**	**-7 682.3**	**812.0**
Extraction activities	-	-	-	-	-	1 504.6	-3 485.3	-5 963.7	-5 208.0	224.2
Manufacturing	**4 662.3**	**-766.5**	**3 504.4**	**1 108.1**	**585.4**	**53 811.9**	**8 672.2**	**7 321.7**	**-8 691.2**	**3 835.7**
of which:										
Food products, beverages and tobacco	-15.9	-6.7	-	1.1	-1.2	9 426.8	2 057.0	790.7	-7 414.0	635.0
Textiles, wood and paper products; printing	-630.2	-1 466.4	639.2	781.2	-512.2	993.8	2 256.2	-1 037.3	36.1	435.5
Chemical, rubber, plastic, non-metallic mineral products	43.8	-278.4	1 238.5	-290.8	-195.9	6 931.1	2 880.8	3 351.8	-92.4	1 713.7
Metal and machinery products, except electrical equipment	5 108.1	886.3	1 544.8	573.8	1 267.6	24 999.3	-126.5	4 569.3	3 783.1	3 060.3
Motor vehicles, trailers, semi-trailers, other transport equipment	-5.3	11.1	6.6	33.8	18.9	10 017.2	494.7	-530.8	-3 990.5	-2 266.0
Other manufacturing	161.9	86.5	74.1	9.0	8.3	1 443.5	1 115.9	176.9	-1 013.4	257.3
Electricity, gas, steam and air conditioning supply	**-66.3**	**-32.2**	**-88.5**	**56.4**	**-**	**-199.0**	**1 393.2**	**-504.3**	**-11.3**	**87.3**
Water supply; sewerage, waste management and remediation activities	**9.3**	**10.0**	**3.3**	**10.1**	**9.4**	**35.8**	**116.5**	**49.8**	**22.5**	**27.1**
Construction	**19.9**	**-39.9**	**-3.3**	**23.7**	**28.3**	**1 505.9**	**1 558.5**	**-947.7**	**-412.6**	**-29.5**
Services	**199 519.7**	**607 422.1**	**206 689.2**	**88 454.5**	**-387 100.2**	**181 287.0**	**705 179.1**	**171 403.3**	**266 710.6**	**-371 187.3**
Wholesale and retail trade; repair of motor vehicles and motorcycles	4 862.7	25 386.6	-5 288.1	-5 236.2	-42 443.1	16 461.5	5 259.0	-10 656.9	-3 696.3	1 923.8
Transportation and storage	-55.7	-451.5	55.3	-192.8	86.2	2 571.3	144.2	-865.9	-844.3	426.1
Accommodation and food service activities	541.3	-183.0	142.7	6 774.9	-2 289.6	53.1	295.1	-434.6	-587.3	-118.0
Information and communication	2 542.1	-62.1	3 201.4	-5 642.0	19 432.3	15 487.6	5 587.4	3 002.3	-2 039.2	8 871.7
Financial and insurance activities	184 738.0	582 305.0	215 550.1	111 904.0	-369 627.1	50 494.9	682 990.6	154 887.8	411 346.0	-325 678.0
Activities of holding companies	175 798.1	536 296.2	199 542.2	108 339.5	-379 335.5	45 027.2	680 962.8	161 029.5	410 392.3	-321 118.8
Real estate activities	363.5	786.5	261.0	-2 657.0	16.5	2 096.3	3 576.3	1 994.9	-3 548.6	620.8
Professional, scientific and technical activities	808.0	677.8	-2 848.6	-12 272.6	2 269.6	96 652.5	65 878.0	20 013.3	-133 010.9	-56 675.3
Administrative and support service activities	5 650.8	-1 010.5	-4 381.3	-4 234.0	5 449.1	-2 589.9	-58 625.6	3 346.2	-689.9	-590.1
Public administration; activities of households and of extraterritorial organisations	-	-21.1	-	-	-	-	-	-	-	-
Education	-	-	-	-	-	50.4	124.2	-42.0	-22.5	-11.8
Human health and social work activities	70.3	-1.1	-2.2	12.4	5.9	-142.0	-28.8	39.8	-13.5	10.6
Arts, entertainment and recreation	-2.7	-	-	-	-	-70.3	24.4	118.3	48.5	43.7
Other services	-	-4.4	-1.1	-	-	224.2	-45.5	1.1	-231.1	-9.4
Not allocated and confidential	..	..	..	..	..	..	..	..	..	..
Private real estate activities	..	..	..	..	..	..	..	..	..	..

- Nil; .. Not available

Note: Detailed metadata at: *http://stats.oecd.org/OECDStat_Metadata/ShowMetadata.ashx?Dataset=FDI_CTRY_IND_SUMM.*

Source: *OECD International Direct Investment Statistics (database): https://doi.org/10.1787/idi-data-en*

Table 5. Foreign direct investment positions by industrial sector
At year end

Million US dollars

	Inward					Outward				
	2014	2015	2016	2017	2018	2014	2015	2016	2017	2018
All FDI activities	**3 258 954.0**	**3 705 702.8**	**3 812 960.9**	**4 289 898.1**	**3 758 983.3**	**3 975 378.6**	**4 516 753.4**	**4 603 600.7**	**5 140 522.9**	**4 602 940.2**
Agriculture, forestry and fishing	**-**	**-**	**-**	**-**	**-**	**1 630.5**	**1 625.5**	**1 624.3**	**1 572.3**	**1 455.2**
Mining and quarrying	**4.9**	**5.4**	**5.3**	**7.2**	**8.0**	**27 914.6**	**22 509.5**	**18 079.5**	**11 283.3**	**11 145.0**
Extraction activities	-	-	-	-	-	19 840.8	15 762.7	12 314.7	7 934.8	7 807.4
Manufacturing	**4 172.9**	**1 817.1**	**3 270.8**	**4 977.2**	**3 697.0**	**137 878.1**	**124 250.4**	**130 612.4**	**128 933.8**	**122 332.3**
of which:										
Food products, beverages and tobacco	-47.4	-41.4	-44.3	-51.6	-52.7	16 306.6	15 715.8	16 964.3	10 287.8	9 679.4
Textiles, wood and paper products; printing	1 811.4	273.3	664.1	1 091.4	482.0	5 618.9	7 242.2	5 968.2	6 357.6	6 104.9
Chemical, rubber, plastic, non-metallic mineral products	2 150.2	1 377.2	2 362.2	3 709.5	2 915.0	40 577.7	38 165.5	39 163.1	42 871.2	41 031.6
Metal and machinery products, except electrical equipment	132.3	86.0	162.3	66.0	198.1	53 220.1	42 201.4	47 510.3	48 683.1	47 082.7
Motor vehicles, trailers, semi-trailers, other transport equipment	3.6	9.8	15.8	36.0	34.3	13 521.4	12 406.1	12 717.4	12 649.3	10 992.7
Other manufacturing	121.4	112.1	110.7	127.1	120.2	8 634.7	8 518.2	8 288.2	8 084.7	7 442.2
Electricity, gas, steam and air conditioning supply	**4.9**	**-30.5**	**-113.8**	**-73.2**	**-74.4**	**4 618.4**	**5 701.7**	**5 077.5**	**5 474.9**	**4 823.7**
Water supply; sewerage, waste management and remediation activities	**-**	**12.0**	**13.7**	**15.6**	**14.9**	**154.2**	**246.1**	**290.9**	**316.6**	**287.4**
Construction	**216.1**	**153.5**	**125.4**	**133.1**	**123.7**	**5 198.8**	**6 128.5**	**4 917.3**	**4 967.6**	**4 656.5**
Services	**3 254 554.1**	**3 703 744.1**	**3 809 659.5**	**4 284 839.3**	**3 755 213.0**	**3 784 117.8**	**4 343 245.5**	**4 429 505.6**	**4 971 516.0**	**4 441 795.3**
Wholesale and retail trade; repair of motor vehicles and motorcycles	46 361.6	65 107.2	60 562.9	57 977.9	14 790.5	87 483.2	85 338.1	79 454.0	77 349.5	73 667.3
Transportation and storage	1 222.6	822.0	834.8	768.8	881.6	15 411.8	13 753.9	12 476.0	12 251.1	11 837.6
Accommodation and food service activities	468.6	212.3	305.7	7 584.6	4 890.1	2 087.0	2 104.5	1 663.3	1 884.1	1 749.5
Information and communication	1 891.6	2 049.0	5 299.9	3 153.0	25 787.7	27 880.6	31 540.6	31 997.5	30 467.7	39 564.9
Financial and insurance activities	3 143 201.7	3 577 710.4	3 691 717.1	4 183 956.6	3 678 967.3	3 088 935.1	3 678 577.0	3 757 454.4	4 390 758.0	3 931 506.8
Activities of holding companies	3 149 557.5	3 542 377.8	3 649 827.1	4 132 485.0	3 619 559.2	3 012 565.8	3 609 409.9	3 692 714.2	4 323 466.1	3 869 362.3
Real estate activities	1 626.9	2 226.5	2 893.4	135.5	64.1	10 542.0	12 732.7	13 500.6	11 054.2	10 646.9
Professional, scientific and technical activities	35 028.0	33 544.9	31 845.7	21 541.1	22 127.3	467 406.6	494 951.6	504 615.8	420 439.0	348 169.2
Administrative and support service activities	24 652.3	21 981.5	16 110.5	9 613.8	7 599.0	82 872.0	22 872.1	26 903.1	25 925.9	23 310.1
Public administration; activities of households and of extraterritorial organisations	-	-	-	-	-	-	-	-	-	-
Education	-	-	-	-	-	85.0	190.5	147.6	154.7	147.7
Human health and social work activities	66.8	63.1	64.3	79.2	80.1	919.1	764.3	776.9	861.1	820.9
Arts, entertainment and recreation	27.9	25.0	24.2	27.6	26.3	189.4	189.4	286.7	345.4	348.1
Other services	4.9	1.1	-	-	-	307.2	229.7	231.9	26.4	26.3
Not allocated and confidential	**1.2**	**1.1**	**-**	**-1.2**	**1.1**	**1.2**	**-1.1**	**-1.1**	**-1.2**	**-**
Private real estate activities	**-**	**-**	**-**	**-**	**-**	**13 865.0**	**13 047.4**	**13 494.3**	**16 459.6**	**16 444.9**

- Nil

Note: Detailed metadata at: *http://stats.oecd.org/OECDStat_Metadata/ShowMetadata.ashx?Dataset=FDI_CTRY_IND_SUMM.*

Source: *OECD International Direct Investment Statistics (database): https://doi.org/10.1787/idi-data-en*

Table 6. Foreign direct investment income by industrial sector

Million US dollars

	Inward					Outward				
	2014	2015	2016	2017	2018	2014	2015	2016	2017	2018
All FDI activities	**72 524.9**	**49 914.6**	**55 099.0**	**54 408.7**	**48 114.0**	**80 830.6**	**75 208.0**	**77 250.9**	**80 172.5**	**71 511.9**
Agriculture, forestry and fishing	-	-	-	-	-	**-31.8**	**25.5**	**5.5**	**10.1**	**-22.4**
Mining and quarrying	-	**1.1**	**1.1**	**1.1**	**1.2**	**-372.8**	**-2 460.3**	**-1 403.3**	**-394.5**	**-263.2**
Extraction activities	-	-	-	-	-	-403.3	-2 448.1	-1 123.5	-527.6	-364.7
Manufacturing	**-142.0**	**992.8**	**2 054.6**	**577.2**	**1 121.2**	**6 787.8**	**5 241.3**	**5 977.0**	**6 584.4**	**7 578.2**
of which:										
Food products, beverages and tobacco	2.7	-6.7	5.5	3.4	2.4	530.7	409.3	603.8	588.4	603.1
Textiles, wood and paper products; printing	-574.5	-46.6	279.8	9.0	98.0	80.9	129.8	457.8	468.9	363.5
Chemical, rubber, plastic, non-metallic mineral products	124.7	317.2	165.9	-163.5	-201.8	3 326.3	1 641.7	2 038.0	1 465.4	1 477.6
Metal and machinery products, except electrical equipment	120.7	630.1	1 509.5	689.9	1 138.9	1 719.5	2 092.1	1 572.5	2 892.6	3 692.9
Motor vehicles, trailers, semi-trailers, other transport equipment	13.3	14.4	17.7	20.3	64.9	362.2	412.6	609.3	537.7	745.9
Other manufacturing	169.8	84.3	76.3	18.0	18.9	768.2	555.7	695.6	632.4	695.1
Electricity, gas, steam and air conditioning supply	**5.3**	**4.4**	-	**4.5**	**4.7**	**-167.2**	**-102.1**	**2.2**	**116.1**	**90.9**
Water supply; sewerage, waste management and remediation activities	**6.6**	**-2.2**	**4.4**	**12.4**	**13.0**	**19.9**	**128.7**	**45.3**	**94.7**	**46.0**
Construction	**11.9**	**21.1**	**31.0**	**59.7**	**60.2**	**217.6**	**104.3**	**143.8**	**95.8**	**98.0**
Services	**72 641.6**	**48 871.9**	**53 004.5**	**53 749.3**	**46 909.0**	**74 229.8**	**72 145.3**	**72 346.6**	**73 521.6**	**63 823.9**
Wholesale and retail trade; repair of motor vehicles and motorcycles	2 122.9	1 731.6	937.7	2 210.6	1 699.5	5 163.9	5 117.0	6 138.5	7 412.9	6 500.6
Transportation and storage	-5.3	-137.5	102.8	34.9	66.1	810.7	230.7	648.0	1 309.9	954.8
Accommodation and food service activities	-5.3	37.7	46.4	30.4	31.9	-25.2	7.8	13.3	-27.1	-29.5
Information and communication	-29.2	-410.4	1 016.3	47.3	611.4	485.6	563.5	456.7	290.8	330.5
Financial and insurance activities	67 561.4	44 748.8	48 164.3	49 189.5	43 035.5	60 414.0	61 034.9	54 347.0	54 619.5	52 091.3
Activities of holding companies	65 800.7	42 135.3	43 660.3	45 169.7	40 015.3	56 071.4	58 230.7	51 862.2	51 464.3	50 033.0
Real estate activities	185.8	22.2	359.4	651.6	9.4	794.7	505.8	713.3	412.6	424.9
Professional, scientific and technical activities	1 869.4	1 824.7	1 603.5	1 098.0	1 233.3	5 940.0	4 177.5	10 105.1	8 717.2	3 050.9
Administrative and support service activities	927.4	1 047.1	764.1	473.5	205.4	655.4	434.8	-81.8	776.7	491.0
Public administration; activities of households and of extraterritorial organisations	-	-	-	-	-	-	-	-	-	-
Education	-	-	-	-	-	-2.7	5.5	-2.2	-7.9	-8.3
Human health and social work activities	13.3	5.5	6.6	9.0	10.6	30.5	54.4	-1.1	-3.4	-1.2
Arts, entertainment and recreation	4.0	4.4	3.3	4.5	4.7	37.2	12.2	17.7	28.2	28.3
Other services	-1.3	-1.1	-1.1	-	-	-73.0	1.1	-7.7	-10.1	-10.6
Not allocated and confidential	..	..	..	..	..	..	..	..	..	..
Private real estate activities	..	..	..	..	..	..	..	..	..	..

- Nil; .. Not available

Note: Detailed metadata at: *http://stats.oecd.org/OECDStat_Metadata/ShowMetadata.ashx?Dataset=FDI_CTRY_IND_SUMM.*

Source: *OECD International Direct Investment Statistics (database): https://doi.org/10.1787/idi-data-en*

MEXICO

Table 1. Foreign direct investment flows by country

Million US dollars

	Inward					Outward				
	2014	2015	2016	2017	2018	2014	2015	2016	2017	2018
WORLD	**30 261.5**	**35 647.9**	**30 644.0**	**33 596.5**	**33 615.3**	**6 331.6**	**10 663.0**	**627.6**	**3 833.0**	**7 831.0**
OECD COUNTRIES	..	..	..	..	..	..	..	..	..	..
Australia	20.8	685.6	97.1	1 374.8	598.9	..	..	..	..	..
Austria	2.2	69.5	50.1	83.3	109.6	..	..	..	..	..
Belgium	1 269.6	826.9	1 111.8	1 029.4	11.6	..	..	..	..	..
Canada	2 965.2	1 093.5	2 294.9	2 822.5	4 147.9	..	..	..	..	..
Chile	72.2	125.6	13.5	34.6	90.4	..	..	..	..	..
Czech Republic	0.2	0.0	0.3	0.1	1.9	..	..	..	..	..
Denmark	32.4	33.1	56.5	58.5	26.8	..	..	..	..	..
Estonia	0.0	-	-	0.0	0.1	..	..	..	..	..
Finland	108.6	203.5	-98.0	11.8	107.9	..	..	..	..	..
France	1 158.9	960.5	446.1	516.5	510.9	..	..	..	..	..
Germany	2 136.9	1 220.1	2 752.4	2 619.2	2 818.8	..	..	..	..	..
Greece	0.0	-	0.2	-	1.8	..	..	..	..	..
Hungary	0.1	0.1	0.1	0.2	0.6	..	..	..	..	..
Iceland	0.0	-	-	0.0	0.0	..	..	..	..	..
Ireland	35.3	-10.9	41.2	8.5	33.5	..	..	..	..	..
Israel[1]	8.8	-1.6	2 015.2	2.4	1.8	..	..	..	..	..
Italy	282.8	606.9	805.1	1 862.9	1 527.0	..	..	..	..	..
Japan	2 433.0	2 206.0	1 945.4	2 433.2	2 221.9	..	..	..	..	..
Korea	611.2	1 009.7	1 027.4	252.5	708.1	..	..	..	..	..
Latvia	-	-	0.0	-	0.1	..	..	..	..	..
Lithuania	0.2	0.0	-	0.0	0.0	..	..	..	..	..
Luxembourg	-19.9	4.7	9.6	3.4	52.6	..	..	..	..	..
Mexico	-	-	-	-	-	..	..	..	..	..
Netherlands	745.9	349.9	226.6	-123.6	505.9	..	..	..	..	..
New Zealand	75.6	1.8	1.1	-7.0	0.3	..	..	..	..	..
Norway	-23.4	66.7	11.2	45.7	67.4	..	..	..	..	..
Poland	0.1	0.1	0.4	0.6	-0.5	..	..	..	..	..
Portugal	1.2	0.3	7.3	11.5	26.9	..	..	..	..	..
Slovak Republic	0.0	0.1	0.0	0.9	0.2	..	..	..	..	..
Slovenia	-	-	-	0.2	0.1	..	..	..	..	..
Spain	4 451.1	3 897.7	3 552.2	3 385.3	4 146.0	..	..	..	..	..
Sweden	115.0	-37.9	84.8	-42.9	158.9	..	..	..	..	..
Switzerland	296.8	405.6	582.3	300.4	607.2	..	..	..	..	..
Turkey	0.4	0.0	0.0	1.9	0.2	..	..	..	..	..
United Kingdom	230.5	467.8	452.0	443.4	766.6	..	..	..	..	..
United States	10 347.2	19 466.1	10 820.3	15 187.8	12 398.4	..	..	..	..	..
EUROPE	**10 825.9**	**9 066.3**	**10 111.2**	**10 246.3**	**11 524.7**	..	..	..	..	..
Bulgaria	0.0	-	0.0	0.1	1.4	..	..	..	..	..
Croatia	-	-	-	0.1	0.1	..	..	..	..	..
Cyprus[2, 3]	-	-	0.0	12.8	9.0	..	..	..	..	..
Malta	0.0	0.1	16.6	0.0	0.1	..	..	..	..	..
Romania	0.0	0.1	0.0	0.4	0.1	..	..	..	..	..
Russian Federation	0.7	0.8	1.9	14.9	31.8	..	..	..	..	..
Ukraine	0.0	0.6	0.3	0.7	0.2	..	..	..	..	..
AFRICA	**5.1**	**3.1**	**6.3**	**2.4**	**16.7**	..	..	..	..	..
Northern Africa	0.3	0.0	0.0	0.1	0.0	..	..	..	..	..
Algeria	0.3	-	-	0.1	-	..	..	..	..	..
Egypt	-	0.0	0.0	-	0.0	..	..	..	..	..
Libya	-	-	-	-	-	..	..	..	..	..
Morocco	-	0.0	0.0	-	-	..	..	..	..	..
Tunisia	-	0.0	-	-	-	..	..	..	..	..
Other African countries	4.8	3.1	6.3	2.3	16.7	..	..	..	..	..
Nigeria	-	0.0	-	-	0.0	..	..	..	..	..
South Africa	4.8	3.0	3.4	2.0	16.3	..	..	..	..	..
AMERICA	**14 573.8**	**22 627.5**	**14 628.3**	**18 404.5**	**17 917.1**	..	..	..	..	..
Northern America	13 312.5	20 559.6	13 115.2	18 010.4	16 546.3	..	..	..	..	..
Central America and Caribbean countries	60.2	86.2	40.1	54.8	101.2	..	..	..	..	..
Bahamas	-	-	-	-	-	..	..	..	..	..
Bermuda	-	-0.5	-	-	-	..	..	..	..	..
Cayman Islands	-	-	-	-	0.0	..	..	..	..	..
Costa Rica	-0.4	0.1	1.5	2.0	-1.4	..	..	..	..	..
El Salvador	44.1	10.6	35.0	26.6	0.1	..	..	..	..	..
Guatemala	5.5	6.4	0.6	1.5	0.7	..	..	..	..	..
Honduras	0.1	0.7	0.3	0.8	0.5	..	..	..	..	..
Nicaragua	3.6	4.8	-	3.5	0.1	..	..	..	..	..
Panama	4.8	62.9	-1.3	16.6	49.8	..	..	..	..	..
Virgin Islands, U.S.	-	-	-	-	-	..	..	..	..	..
South America	1 211.9	1 997.8	1 473.0	339.4	1 269.6	..	..	..	..	..
Argentina	354.3	517.9	287.2	349.7	1 045.0	..	..	..	..	..
Bolivia	0.1	0.5	0.1	0.0	0.2	..	..	..	..	..
Brazil	629.0	1 145.3	912.6	-131.0	96.6	..	..	..	..	..
Colombia	100.2	113.9	213.1	71.5	-2.9	..	..	..	..	..
Ecuador	-7.8	43.9	2.8	0.1	0.0	..	..	..	..	..
Paraguay	-	0.0	0.0	0.3	-	..	..	..	..	..
Peru	15.2	2.9	6.9	8.3	30.4	..	..	..	..	..
Uruguay	28.1	37.3	23.5	-1.2	28.2	..	..	..	..	..
Venezuela	20.8	10.6	13.3	7.1	-18.2	..	..	..	..	..

Table 1. Foreign direct investment flows by country *(cont.)*

Million US dollars

	Inward					Outward				
	2014	2015	2016	2017	2018	2014	2015	2016	2017	2018
ASIA	**3 276.2**	**3 452.5**	**5 276.0**	**3 110.4**	**3 397.1**	..	..	..	..	..
Near and Middle East	23.3	0.8	2 017.7	2.5	9.9	..	..	..	..	..
Gulf Arabian countries	14.3	2.4	2.5	0.1	8.2	..	..	..	..	..
Kuwait	-	-	-	-	-	..	..	..	..	..
Qatar	-	-	-	0.0	0.0	..	..	..	..	..
Saudi Arabia	4.4	-	-	0.1	-6.4	..	..	..	..	..
United Arab Emirates	9.9	2.4	2.5	-	14.5	..	..	..	..	..
Other Near and Middle East	9.0	-1.6	2 015.2	2.4	1.8	..	..	..	..	..
Jordan	-	-	-	-	-	..	..	..	..	..
Other Asian countries	3 253.0	3 451.8	3 258.2	3 107.9	3 387.2	..	..	..	..	..
China	100.7	52.9	68.6	203.5	247.8	..	..	..	..	..
Hong Kong, China	34.7	29.7	84.1	73.5	153.0	..	..	..	..	..
India	14.9	23.5	27.2	47.6	23.3	..	..	..	..	..
Indonesia	12.8	10.1	18.0	33.0	37.0	..	..	..	..	..
Iran, Islamic Republic of	0.0	-	-	-	-0.1	..	..	..	..	..
Malaysia	0.0	-13.0	86.8	81.0	4.0	..	..	..	..	..
Philippines	-	0.0	-131.9	1.8	0.8	..	..	..	..	..
Singapore	-5.9	97.9	93.8	13.4	33.0	..	..	..	..	..
Chinese Taipei	50.1	34.5	36.3	-33.0	-42.7	..	..	..	..	..
Thailand	1.0	0.2	-	0.1	0.1	..	..	..	..	..
Viet Nam	-	-	2.6	1.2	0.8	..	..	..	..	..
AUSTRALIA, OCEANIA AND POLAR REGIONS	**96.3**	**687.4**	**98.3**	**1 367.8**	**599.2**	..	..	..	..	..
WORLD unallocated and confidential	**1 484.1**	**-188.9**	**524.0**	**465.0**	**160.5**	..	..	..	..	..
European Union (EU28)	**10 551.2**	**8 592.6**	**9 515.4**	**9 882.6**	**10 817.8**	..	..	..	..	..
G20 countries excl. European Union	**21 308.5**	**29 469.6**	**21 959.6**	**28 034.5**	**27 190.1**	..	..	..	..	..
G20 OECD countries	**20 187.0**	**27 716.2**	**20 640.7**	**27 514.7**	**25 698.6**	..	..	..	..	..
G20 Non-OECD countries	**1 121.5**	**1 753.5**	**1 318.9**	**519.8**	**1 491.5**	..	..	..	..	..
MENA countries	**14.7**	**2.4**	**2.5**	**0.2**	**8.2**	..	..	..	..	..
ASEAN countries	**7.9**	**95.3**	**69.3**	**130.5**	**75.6**	..	..	..	..	..

- Nil; .. Not available

Note: Data excludes resident Special Purpose Entities (SPEs). Detailed metadata at: *http://stats.oecd.org/OECDStat_Metadata/ShowMetadata.ashx?Dataset=FDI_CTRY_IND_SUMM.*

1. Information on data for Israel: *http://oe.cd/israel-disclaimer.*
2. Note by Turkey: The information in this document with reference to "Cyprus" relates to the southern part of the Island. There is no single authority representing both Turkish and Greek Cypriot people on the Island. Turkey recognises the Turkish Republic of Northern Cyprus (TRNC). Until a lasting and equitable solution is found within the context of the United Nations, Turkey shall preserve its position concerning the "Cyprus issue".
3. Note by all the European Union Member States of the OECD and the European Union: The Republic of Cyprus is recognised by all members of the United Nations with the exception of Turkey. The information in this document relates to the area under the effective control of the Government of the Republic of Cyprus.

Source: OECD International Direct Investment Statistics (database): https://doi.org/10.1787/idi-data-en

Table 2. Foreign direct investment positions by country

At year end

Million US dollars

	Inward					Outward				
	2014	2015	2016	2017	2018	2014	2015	2016	2017	2018
WORLD	**491 707.3**	**501 999.4**	**473 423.6**	**490 574.0**	**511 275.4**	**150 084.8**	**144 619.2**	**146 169.0**	**175 036.4**	**153 575.7**
OECD COUNTRIES	..	..	..	..	..	..	..	..	..	..
Australia	416.3	849.8	869.3	948.8	588.3	-	-	-	-	-
Austria	607.6	535.2	471.7	629.6	703.6	2 800.0	.. c	1 763.1	2 949.7	2 441.9
Belgium	2 712.5	1 419.6	2 204.6	1 515.2	985.3	.. c	.. c	.. c	.. c	.. c
Canada	20 164.4	20 819.1	17 749.2	18 033.7	18 390.0	1 187.6	1 014.6	500.0	1 190.7	1 183.6
Chile	1 790.4	2 027.5	1 824.1	1 870.4	2 146.2	3 565.6	2 798.5	2 052.3	2 675.6	2 816.2
Czech Republic	12.4	13.8	23.2	22.4	21.0	.. c	.. c	.. c	.. c	.. c
Denmark	914.1	907.5	883.1	880.9	1 213.9	.. c	.. c	.. c	.. c	.. c
Estonia	.. c	.. c	.. c	.. c	.. c	-	-	-	-	-
Finland	61.7	41.9	39.7	35.6	82.1	-	-	-	-	-
France	5 795.7	6 167.4	5 822.0	5 870.0	6 946.6	.. c	.. c	.. c	.. c	-
Germany	12 942.7	12 322.1	12 177.9	15 488.4	17 299.6	180.5	-25.0	-51.6	62.4	112.0
Greece	1.4	1.4	1.4	1.4	1.3	-	-	-	-	-
Hungary	6.6	6.8	6.6	25.6	4.4	2 026.5	2 048.3	2 121.1	2 015.5	2 086.2
Iceland	9.0	9.2	8.7	8.7	8.7	-	-	-	-	-
Ireland	359.6	430.2	346.5	416.0	589.8	.. c	.. c	.. c	-14.3	.. c
Israel[1]	256.1	262.9	251.4	259.0	277.5	-	-	-	-	-
Italy	1 995.6	2 029.4	1 812.8	2 377.4	3 698.1	-	-	-	-	-
Japan	12 601.0	13 313.0	13 672.1	12 634.3	13 994.1	-	-	-	-	-
Korea	3 892.1	4 939.9	4 909.4	4 497.2	4 259.7	-	-	-	-	-
Latvia	.. c	.. c	.. c	.. c	.. c	.. c	.. c	.. c	.. c	-
Lithuania	0.3	0.3	0.3	0.3	0.3	-	-	-	-	-
Luxembourg	12 885.9	14 771.6	13 894.1	14 922.4	14 911.2	-	-	-	.. c	.. c
Mexico	-	-	-	-	-	-	-	-	-	-
Netherlands	84 808.0	92 830.0	88 032.1	83 213.7	70 376.3	37 072.3	38 232.9	35 648.9	36 631.8	30 274.0
New Zealand	161.5	227.6	244.1	244.0	259.4	-	-	-	-	-
Norway	282.3	284.3	283.0	314.7	305.4	-	-	-	-	-
Poland	9.9	10.1	8.4	28.0	39.2	.. c	.. c	.. c	.. c	.. c
Portugal	223.0	232.5	245.7	327.3	291.1	-	-	-	-	-
Slovak Republic	28.4	25.2	27.5	37.4	42.5	.. c	.. c	.. c	.. c	.. c
Slovenia	17.1	21.4	17.7	29.2	23.3	-	-	-	-	-
Spain	60 310.1	56 794.9	56 611.1	53 482.9	63 162.5	6 083.0	7 603.6	7 405.4	8 541.3	9 646.6
Sweden	2 927.4	3 186.0	2 809.7	2 792.5	3 052.1	-	-	-	-	-
Switzerland	11 425.1	9 173.5	8 927.1	9 617.1	11 153.5	1 417.7	308.3	828.1	327.0	233.2
Turkey	15.8	16.6	16.6	5.5	20.0	.. c	.. c	.. c	.. c	.. c
United Kingdom	23 057.5	22 167.0	21 575.5	23 845.2	30 800.6	6 842.7	5 602.6	8 138.4	10 392.0	5 678.5
United States	211 770.6	215 897.5	198 867.4	215 899.0	226 333.1	52 057.1	48 575.3	56 190.2	75 404.4	63 769.2
EUROPE	**221 696.6**	**223 675.1**	**216 573.3**	**216 258.1**	**226 167.4**	**59 192.6**	**58 733.1**	**58 510.1**	**63 650.9**	**52 144.2**
Bulgaria	2.3	2.3	2.8	2.8	11.5	-	-	-	-	-
Croatia	-	-	-	-	-	.. c	.. c	-	.. c	.. c
Cyprus[2, 3]	37.7	37.7	38.5	37.6	38.0	-	-	-	-	-
Malta	33.9	31.4	82.9	104.3	138.3	-	-	-	-	-
Romania	4.2	4.1	4.8	8.0	3.2	-	-	-	-	-
Russian Federation	21.4	22.2	22.2	24.2	25.4	-	-	-	.. c	.. c
Ukraine	0.4	0.3	0.3	0.3	0.3	-	-	-	-	-
AFRICA	**451.5**	**407.2**	**397.7**	**390.2**	**368.5**	**-**	**-**	**-**	**-**	**-**
Northern Africa	7.3	7.5	7.5	8.0	8.3	-	-	-	-	-
Algeria	6.4	6.7	6.7	7.2	7.5	-	-	-	-	-
Egypt	0.9	0.9	0.8	0.8	0.8	-	-	-	-	-
Libya	.. c	.. c	.. c	.. c	.. c	-	-	-	-	-
Morocco	0.0	0.0	0.0	0.0	0.0	-	-	-	-	-
Tunisia	.. c	.. c	.. c	.. c	.. c	-	-	-	-	-
Other African countries	431.9	390.7	381.7	375.8	351.5	-	-	-	-	-
Nigeria	0.3	0.3	0.3	0.3	0.3	-	-	-	-	-
South Africa	30.0	24.3	27.0	11.5	9.8	-	-	-	-	-
AMERICA	**247 193.3**	**252 755.0**	**231 074.0**	**249 459.7**	**259 608.9**	**90 338.7**	**84 410.0**	**86 357.2**	**110 720.1**	**100 977.4**
Northern America	231 935.0	236 716.6	216 616.6	233 932.7	244 723.1	53 244.7	49 589.9	56 690.2	76 595.1	64 952.8
Central America and Caribbean countries	6 103.3	7 212.2	6 840.0	8 168.6	7 992.5	10 904.2	13 354.7	11 034.6	3 180.4	4 268.7
Bahamas	360.2	456.2	490.7	563.6	556.6	-	.. c	.. c	.. c	.. c
Bermuda	664.1	424.0	362.6	323.8	302.7	.. c	.. c	.. c	.. c	.. c
Cayman Islands	1 496.3	1 161.3	1 126.7	1 341.7	1 399.5	-	-	-	-	.. c
Costa Rica	85.8	68.0	54.1	61.5	52.7	1 688.5	1 918.6	1 750.2	874.9	864.1
El Salvador	13.8	13.7	14.8	14.4	14.1	1 078.7	1 067.9	1 124.3	625.8	823.2
Guatemala	117.7	128.6	130.2	901.7	606.3	1 102.7	1 619.8	1 411.9	577.0	586.7
Honduras	12.7	13.0	11.8	7.3	3.9	1 053.2	1 009.0	962.1	362.3	358.8
Nicaragua	38.5	40.3	39.0	47.1	60.6	616.9	696.7	695.4	-325.9	693.3
Panama	2 177.1	2 398.1	2 164.0	1 995.4	1 859.1	359.9	708.6	668.6	490.7	434.2
Virgin Islands, U.S.	511.1	507.7	492.9	517.9	383.2	-	-	-	-	-
South America	9 135.3	8 805.6	7 596.7	7 330.0	6 863.5	26 059.0	21 078.4	18 284.9	22 950.9	23 365.4
Argentina	3 140.3	3 078.4	2 877.0	2 497.8	1 402.5	-776.5	-412.2	-982.9	609.9	1 425.7
Bolivia	4.1	4.4	4.4	4.6	5.3	.. c	.. c	.. c	.. c	.. c
Brazil	2 167.1	1 455.1	780.1	906.3	1 220.3	19 291.6	14 434.1	12 018.0	9 525.2	9 104.0
Colombia	839.7	1 087.3	906.2	990.2	1 025.8	705.3	987.2	1 353.3	4 907.9	4 517.9
Ecuador	57.1	36.4	34.6	34.8	34.9	2 024.9	2 379.1	2 469.9	2 046.7	1 544.3
Paraguay	1.5	1.3	1.2	1.1	1.1	.. c	.. c	.. c	.. c	.. c
Peru	286.3	304.9	311.4	323.8	331.4	1 065.3	778.7	1 153.3	3 182.6	3 942.3
Uruguay	587.5	571.3	633.5	477.8	475.6	.. c	.. c	.. c	.. c	6.1
Venezuela	248.1	214.5	206.3	211.8	202.8	182.7	113.1	221.0	2.9	8.9

Table 2. Foreign direct investment positions by country *(cont.)*

At year end

Million US dollars

	Inward					Outward				
	2014	2015	2016	2017	2018	2014	2015	2016	2017	2018
ASIA	**21 416.6**	**23 796.9**	**24 096.3**	**23 121.1**	**24 124.6**	**720.8**	**-**	**796.7**	**747.0**	**216.7**
Near and Middle East	351.8	384.8	397.7	431.7	617.6	-	-	-	-	-
Gulf Arabian countries	92.9	119.0	143.6	169.8	328.4	-	-	-	-	-
Kuwait	.. c	.. c	.. c	.. c	.. c	-	-	-	-	-
Qatar	1.7	1.9	1.9	2.3	141.3	-	-	-	-	-
Saudi Arabia	0.3	0.3	0.3	0.3	0.3	-	-	-	-	-
United Arab Emirates	90.9	116.9	141.4	167.2	186.8	-	-	-	-	-
Other Near and Middle East	258.9	265.8	254.1	261.9	289.2	-	-	-	-	-
Jordan	0.0	0.0	0.0	0.0	0.0	-	-	-	-	-
Other Asian countries	21 061.2	23 408.3	23 696.7	22 687.5	23 502.8	672.5	-	183.3	166.3	168.5
China	537.1	634.0	636.4	730.5	1 324.7	-	-	-	-	-
Hong Kong, China	1 274.1	1 868.2	2 051.4	2 118.1	1 769.7	-	-	-	-	-
India	189.7	203.3	211.9	258.4	305.9	.. c	-	183.3	166.3	168.5
Indonesia	1.5	0.4	0.4	0.4	0.4	-	-	-	-	-
Iran, Islamic Republic of	0.9	0.8	0.7	0.8	0.9	-	-	-	-	-
Malaysia	9.5	8.5	8.9	5.3	15.1	.. c	-	-	-	-
Philippines	65.4	46.6	45.9	46.5	22.4	672.5	-	.. c	.. c	.. c
Singapore	1 416.3	1 368.8	1 178.8	1 333.4	936.7	.. c	-	.. c	.. c	.. c
Chinese Taipei	1 038.5	983.2	938.8	1 013.6	823.9	-	-	-	-	-
Thailand	27.2	33.5	34.1	40.4	39.9	-	-	-	-	-
Viet Nam	0.8	0.8	0.8	0.8	0.9	-	-	-	-	-
AUSTRALIA, OCEANIA AND POLAR REGIONS	**773.0**	**1 221.1**	**1 250.0**	**1 367.7**	**1 000.4**	**-**	**-**	**-**	**-**	**-**
WORLD unallocated and confidential	**176.3**	**144.2**	**32.3**	**-22.8**	**5.6**	**-167.4**	**1 476.1**	**505.0**	**-81.6**	**237.4**
European Union (EU28)	**209 755.7**	**213 989.9**	**207 140.7**	**206 094.2**	**214 435.6**	**55 005.0**	**53 462.4**	**55 025.2**	**60 578.3**	**50 239.2**
G20 countries excl. European Union	**298 739.0**	**303 939.7**	**282 027.5**	**304 028.9**	**326 619.2**	**78 783.0**	**69 189.4**	**75 995.3**	**97 351.0**	**81 441.6**
G20 OECD countries	**292 651.7**	**298 521.7**	**277 472.2**	**299 599.5**	**322 330.0**	**60 267.9**	**55 167.5**	**64 776.9**	**87 049.5**	**70 743.3**
G20 Non-OECD countries	**6 087.3**	**5 418.0**	**4 555.3**	**4 429.4**	**4 289.2**	**18 515.1**	**14 021.9**	**11 218.4**	**10 301.5**	**10 698.3**
MENA countries	**102.5**	**129.0**	**153.4**	**180.3**	**348.1**	**-**	**-**	**-**	**-**	**-**
ASEAN countries	**1 521.1**	**1 459.0**	**1 269.1**	**1 427.1**	**1 015.8**	**672.5**	**-**	**-**	**-**	**-**

- Nil; .. Not available; c Confidential data

Note: Data excludes resident Special Purpose Entities (SPEs). Detailed metadata at: *http://stats.oecd.org/OECDStat_Metadata/ShowMetadata.ashx?Dataset=FDI_CTRY_IND_SUMM.*

1. Information on data for Israel: *http://oe.cd/israel-disclaimer.*
2. Note by Turkey: The information in this document with reference to "Cyprus" relates to the southern part of the Island. There is no single authority representing both Turkish and Greek Cypriot people on the Island. Turkey recognises the Turkish Republic of Northern Cyprus (TRNC). Until a lasting and equitable solution is found within the context of the United Nations, Turkey shall preserve its position concerning the "Cyprus issue".
3. Note by all the European Union Member States of the OECD and the European Union: The Republic of Cyprus is recognised by all members of the United Nations with the exception of Turkey. The information in this document relates to the area under the effective control of the Government of the Republic of Cyprus.

Source: OECD International Direct Investment Statistics (database): https://doi.org/10.1787/idi-data-en

Table 4. Foreign direct investment flows by industrial sector

Million US dollars

	Inward					Outward				
	2014	2015	2016	2017	2018	2014	2015	2016	2017	2018
All FDI activities	**30 261.5**	**35 647.9**	**30 644.0**	**33 596.5**	**33 615.3**	**6 331.6**	**10 663.0**	**627.6**	**3 833.0**	**7 831.0**
Agriculture, forestry and fishing	**177.8**	**168.9**	**89.1**	**137.8**	**49.9**	..	..	..	..	..
Mining and quarrying	**2 679.3**	**1 581.7**	**918.8**	**1 363.7**	**1 505.8**	..	..	..	..	..
Extraction activities	374.3	1 489.5	231.7	659.0	931.9	..	..	..	..	..
Manufacturing	**18 757.6**	**17 704.1**	**17 862.4**	**15 352.9**	**16 317.6**	..	..	..	..	..
of which:										
Food products, beverages and tobacco	3 450.1	2 780.3	2 652.4	2 005.8	1 075.9	..	..	..	..	..
Textiles, wood and paper products; printing	937.9	341.9	827.8	447.0	430.8	..	..	..	..	..
Chemical, rubber, plastic, non-metallic mineral products	4 527.0	2 021.0	5 240.6	1 555.2	1 704.5	..	..	..	..	..
Metal and machinery products, except electrical equipment	2 637.9	2 507.7	2 562.5	2 450.2	4 067.4	..	..	..	..	..
Motor vehicles, trailers, semi-trailers, other transport equipment	5 917.9	7 052.5	5 566.2	7 786.1	7 858.4	..	..	..	..	..
Other manufacturing	1 286.9	3 000.6	1 012.9	1 108.6	1 180.6	..	..	..	..	..
Electricity, gas, steam and air conditioning supply	**695.1**	**1 081.3**	**1 293.8**	**2 153.1**	**4 957.2**	..	..	..	..	..
Water supply; sewerage, waste management and remediation activities	**6.0**	**-10.8**	**7.7**	**10.4**	**-6.9**	..	..	..	..	..
Construction	**886.0**	**2 027.9**	**1 012.8**	**3 020.1**	**1 530.7**	..	..	..	..	..
Services	**7 059.7**	**13 095.0**	**9 459.5**	**11 558.5**	**9 261.0**	..	..	..	..	..
Wholesale and retail trade; repair of motor vehicles and motorcycles	1 951.9	2 653.8	1 797.9	2 951.5	2 770.2	..	..	..	..	..
Transportation and storage	2 021.7	2 904.6	1 852.3	3 345.9	1 309.7	..	..	..	..	..
Accommodation and food service activities	953.5	534.1	601.5	873.6	1 104.9	..	..	..	..	..
Information and communication	-3 875.1	2 531.2	981.5	669.1	1 121.0	..	..	..	..	..
Financial and insurance activities	4 823.3	3 465.7	3 498.7	2 412.2	2 122.2	..	..	..	..	..
Activities of holding companies	-	-	-	-	-	..	..	..	..	..
Real estate activities	541.5	109.5	320.2	464.3	220.3	..	..	..	..	..
Professional, scientific and technical activities	253.9	568.0	206.8	294.5	334.0	..	..	..	..	..
Administrative and support service activities	292.0	173.8	141.2	332.8	187.5	..	..	..	..	..
Public administration; activities of households and of extraterritorial organisations	-	-	-	-	-	..	..	..	..	..
Education	4.1	21.2	0.0	30.2	55.9	..	..	..	..	..
Human health and social work activities	-1.2	16.4	11.9	10.4	3.4	..	..	..	..	..
Arts, entertainment and recreation	111.9	114.9	37.8	155.8	13.5	..	..	..	..	..
Other services	-17.8	1.6	9.5	18.2	18.3	..	..	..	..	..
Not allocated and confidential	-	**0.0**	**0.0**	**0.0**	-	**6 331.6**	**10 663.0**	**627.6**	**3 833.0**	**7 831.0**
Private real estate activities	-	-	-	-	-	..	..	..	..	..

- Nil; .. Not available

Note: Data excludes resident Special Purpose Entities (SPEs). Detailed metadata at: *http://stats.oecd.org/OECDStat_Metadata/ShowMetadata.ashx?Dataset=FDI_CTRY_IND_SUMM.*

Source: *OECD International Direct Investment Statistics (database): https://doi.org/10.1787/idi-data-en*

Table 5. Foreign direct investment positions by industrial sector

At year end

Million US dollars

	Inward					Outward				
	2014	2015	2016	2017	2018	2014	2015	2016	2017	2018
All FDI activities	**491 707.3**	**501 999.4**	**473 423.6**	**490 574.0**	**511 275.4**	**150 084.8**	**144 619.2**	**146 169.0**	**175 036.4**	**153 575.7**
Agriculture, forestry and fishing	..	..	..	..	..	..	..	..	..	..
Mining and quarrying	..	..	..	..	..	..	..	..	..	..
Extraction activities	..	..	..	..	..	..	..	..	..	..
Manufacturing	..	..	..	..	..	..	..	..	..	..
of which:										
Food products, beverages and tobacco	..	..	..	..	..	..	..	..	..	..
Textiles, wood and paper products; printing	..	..	..	..	..	..	..	..	..	..
Chemical, rubber, plastic, non-metallic mineral products	..	..	..	..	..	..	..	..	..	..
Metal and machinery products, except electrical equipment	..	..	..	..	..	..	..	..	..	..
Motor vehicles, trailers, semi-trailers, other transport equipment	..	..	..	..	..	..	..	..	..	..
Other manufacturing	..	..	..	..	..	..	..	..	..	..
Electricity, gas, steam and air conditioning supply	..	..	..	..	..	..	..	..	..	..
Water supply; sewerage, waste management and remediation activities	..	..	..	..	..	..	..	..	..	..
Construction	..	..	..	..	..	..	..	..	..	..
Services	..	..	..	..	..	..	..	..	..	..
Wholesale and retail trade; repair of motor vehicles and motorcycles	..	..	..	..	..	..	..	..	..	..
Transportation and storage	..	..	..	..	..	..	..	..	..	..
Accommodation and food service activities	..	..	..	..	..	..	..	..	..	..
Information and communication	..	..	..	..	..	..	..	..	..	..
Financial and insurance activities	..	..	..	..	..	..	..	..	..	..
Activities of holding companies	..	..	..	..	..	..	..	..	..	..
Real estate activities	..	..	..	..	..	..	..	..	..	..
Professional, scientific and technical activities	..	..	..	..	..	..	..	..	..	..
Administrative and support service activities	..	..	..	..	..	..	..	..	..	..
Public administration; activities of households and of extraterritorial organisations	..	..	..	..	..	..	..	..	..	..
Education	..	..	..	..	..	..	..	..	..	..
Human health and social work activities	..	..	..	..	..	..	..	..	..	..
Arts, entertainment and recreation	..	..	..	..	..	..	..	..	..	..
Other services	..	..	..	..	..	..	..	..	..	..
Not allocated and confidential	491 707.3	501 999.4	473 423.6	490 574.0	511 275.4	150 084.8	144 619.2	146 169.0	175 036.4	153 575.7
Private real estate activities	..	..	..	..	..	..	..	..	..	..

.. Not available

Note: Data excludes resident Special Purpose Entities (SPEs). Detailed metadata at: *http://stats.oecd.org/OECDStat_Metadata/ShowMetadata.ashx?Dataset=FDI_CTRY_IND_SUMM.*

Source: OECD International Direct Investment Statistics (database): https://doi.org/10.1787/idi-data-en

Table 1. Foreign direct investment flows by country

Million US dollars

	Inward					Outward				
	2014	2015	2016	2017	2018	2014	2015	2016	2017	2018
WORLD	**44 975.5**	**178 949.5**	**30 667.9**	**60 349.5**	**114 234.6**	**59 357.8**	**247 681.6**	**156 468.0**	**46 801.9**	**-18 831.6**
OECD COUNTRIES	**32 596.5**	**144 417.1**	**.. d**	**.. d**	**.. d**	**41 917.2**	**198 736.5**	**.. d**	**.. d**	**.. d**
Australia	423.2	-311.7	.. d	-18.0	656.2	8 602.9	6 298.4	3 495.5	598.6	11 935.6
Austria	-522.8	632.3	5 198.5	2 215.1	1 443.4	975.2	.. d	.. d	1 101.3	280.9
Belgium	1 584.2	24 487.0	3 798.5	2 065.2	-698.7	-1 720.8	1 364.4	-12 878.5	-7 180.7	-2 091.3
Canada	-597.1	321.7	.. d	.. d	.. d	1 658.5	-2 699.9	8 811.2	2 352.6	2 449.0
Chile	4.0	12.2	2.2	177.0	38.9	26.5	-275.1	24.3	1 008.9	541.7
Czech Republic	-39.8	-154.2	196.8	84.5	-1.2	179.1	78.8	-252.1	-2 877.9	357.6
Denmark	-319.8	269.6	953.2	666.2	1 140.1	337.0	2 427.1	2 219.4	880.4	636.1
Estonia	5.3	.. d	7.7	.. d	2.4	8.0	-1.1	-48.7	.. d	.. d
Finland	-90.2	-256.2	118.3	134.1	.. d	-1 573.6	640.0	.. d	311.1	.. d
France	7 851.9	5 818.1	2 812.1	9 558.1	19 401.6	5 575.2	3 292.3	-2 139.8	10 054.1	1 061.0
Germany	2 588.6	931.8	-23 753.2	-9 864.7	-10 558.2	1 848.2	9 468.7	-320.7	10 887.2	2 295.5
Greece	139.3	-229.6	.. d	-3.4	-13.0	207.0	266.2	220.1	96.9	151.1
Hungary	-87.6	31.1	80.7	-6.8	164.1	-652.8	726.6	-1 711.8	-5 713.0	-442.6
Iceland	30.5	.. d	.. d	.. d	.. d	-5.3	.. d	.. d	.. d	.. d
Ireland	-62.4	8 181.9	-9 937.0	7 052.2	7 043.6	2 469.2	2 433.7	9 342.0	42 026.8	5 372.4
Israel[1]	-107.5	194.1	.. d	.. d	-2 878.6	62.4	-92.1	-172.5	722.6	257.3
Italy	2 428.0	3 202.4	-2 142.0	-178.1	5 650.9	2 256.9	12 528.0	9 249.1	-7 045.4	2 461.9
Japan	1 072.0	49.9	2 794.4	897.3	-3 810.9	518.8	-345.0	-352.8	1 596.2	1 530.7
Korea	416.6	92.1	-352.8	55.2	504.0	-211.0	1 401.0	-17.7	468.9	-899.3
Latvia	2.7	.. d	3.3	- d	.. d	-1.3	93.2	-108.4	91.3	239.6
Lithuania	9.3	8.9	32.1	5.6	-34.2	-6.6	3.3	27.6	58.6	2.4
Luxembourg	6 022.3	54 648.9	37 168.0	-4 492.2	14 193.3	11 350.7	37 411.0	-24 029.6	-13 233.0	-34 098.9
Mexico	1 443.5	6 982.8	8 625.5	3 898.1	2 613.0	3 372.7	9 401.0	1 045.0	536.6	5 371.2
Netherlands	-	-	-	-	-	-	-	-	-	-
New Zealand	22.6	.. d	-15.5	-4.5	116.8	204.3	718.8	-33.2	315.6	1 084.6
Norway	-	472.5	2 002.7	556.9	1 439.9	1 045.5	752.1	1 361.3	-525.3	-227.8
Poland	43.8	4.4	-63.0	312.3	160.5	-820.0	642.3	-347.2	1 342.6	1 888.4
Portugal	-205.7	.. d	5.5	-3 810.2	-96.8	-408.7	.. d	816.1	37.2	258.5
Slovak Republic	-	3.3	67.5	5.6	-4.7	199.0	225.2	-91.8	76.7	38.9
Slovenia	-1.3	-	3.3	6.8	.. d	-2.7	.. d	117.2	.. d	.. d
Spain	494.9	553.5	6 030.1	-343.8	-1 943.8	1 536.4	1 961.2	3 195.8	-2 225.2	2 656.7
Sweden	-851.8	15.5	214.5	2 388.7	3 534.8	391.4	1 263.5	6 330.9	4 856.3	6 308.3
Switzerland	4 381.1	29 121.5	2 728.1	9 296.6	27 509.7	1 988.9	5 832.5	50 120.5	-38 188.5	53 252.7
Turkey	325.1	502.5	152.6	111.6	-354.1	879.7	885.2	786.2	223.2	861.6
United Kingdom	10 656.8	-16 751.0	-18 554.7	50 178.1	79 026.3	8 053.6	59 021.6	40 241.1	18 986.6	-95 421.9
United States	-4 467.3	26 127.6	-52 723.7	-38 080.3	-21 176.7	-6 452.2	40 418.2	-15 097.9	22 325.6	8 655.7
EUROPE	**36 671.1**	**115 736.0**	**1 311.5**	**65 504.5**	**147 292.6**	**39 925.7**	**146 049.9**	**109 442.7**	**-225.5**	**-52 711.0**
Bulgaria	2.7	-1.1	5.5	.. d	.. d	-61.0	24.4	151.5	146.5	37.8
Croatia	-15.9	-53.2	58.6	.. d	-1.2	122.1	-83.2	393.7	113.9	20.1
Cyprus[2, 3]	1 085.3	4 353.9	-346.1	-781.2	-1 739.6	485.6	823.1	4 721.9	-1 544.4	.. d
Malta	5.3	.. d	.. d	4.5	.. d	-1.3	.. d	3 055.4	.. d	.. d
Romania	-4.0	-22.2	334.0	-36.1	40.1	193.7	266.2	130.5	286.3	712.9
Russian Federation	1 095.9	-2 806.4	-4 626.8	-64.3	845.0	-631.6	1 333.3	2 184.0	-4 334.3	1 510.7
Ukraine	82.3	..	..	..	..	-348.9	..	..	..	..
AFRICA	**1 037.5**	**904.0**	**32 885.1**	**-2 163.2**	**1 922.6**	**2 822.1**	**22 071.0**	**-3 546.4**	**231.1**	**-2 772.3**
Northern Africa	15.9	17.7	29 634.0	-57.5	378.9	197.7	-2 800.9	5 816.7	1 378.7	-575.9
Algeria	-	..	..	..	..	18.6	..	..	..	..
Egypt	4.0	.. d	.. d	75.5	269.1	209.6	-4 764.3	1 643.3	1 228.7	-267.9
Libya	-	..	..	..	..	-1.3	..	..	..	..
Morocco	8.0	8.9	2.2	-	1.2	-29.2	17.7	6.6	18.0	30.7
Tunisia	-	..	..	..	..	-2.7	..	..	..	..
Other African countries	1 021.6	886.3	3 250.0	-2 105.7	1 544.9	2 624.4	24 871.9	-9 363.0	-1 148.7	-2 197.6
Nigeria	948.7	.. d	.. d	13.5	.. d	1 868.1	1 066.0	466.7	1 667.2	620.8
South Africa	-8.0	.. d	.. d	.. d	-142.8	122.1	21 531.9	-13 716.7	1 236.6	-1 544.9
AMERICA	**5 028.5**	**59 315.6**	**-21 712.9**	**-8 961.8**	**-39 500.8**	**1 322.8**	**56 687.7**	**58 314.7**	**26 021.9**	**18 723.0**
Northern America	-5 064.3	26 449.3	-52 139.8	-37 739.8	-20 466.2	-4 791.0	37 722.7	-6 682.5	24 689.4	11 104.7
Central America and Caribbean countries	9 688.2	32 094.3	32 467.1	21 684.1	-12 307.3	5 753.0	12 671.1	41 123.5	-1 321.2	12 675.6
Bahamas	22.6	..	..	..	..	801.4	..	..	..	..
Bermuda	6 972.3	..	..	..	..	3 068.9	..	..	..	..
Cayman Islands	1 982.2	..	..	..	..	-1 910.6	..	..	..	..
Costa Rica	11.9	..	..	..	..	-50.4	..	..	..	..
El Salvador	-1.3	..	..	..	..	13.3	..	..	..	..
Guatemala	5.3	..	..	..	..	-	..	..	..	..
Honduras	-	..	..	..	..	-4.0	..	..	..	..
Nicaragua	-	..	..	..	..	-4.0	..	..	..	..
Panama	10.6	..	..	..	..	17.2	..	..	..	..
Virgin Islands, U.S.	-	..	..	..	..	1.3	..	..	..	..
South America	404.7	772.0	-2 040.3	7 095.0	-6 727.3	359.6	6 294.0	23 873.7	2 654.7	-5 058.4
Argentina	6.6	-378.3	211.2	-24.8	-70.8	134.0	1 105.9	1 134.6	289.7	1 212.1
Bolivia	-1.3	..	..	..	..	6.6	..	..	..	..
Brazil	236.2	-412.6	-2 682.7	5 945.2	-8 271.0	-41.1	3 571.8	22 704.9	-701.2	-7 247.7
Colombia	1.3	..	..	..	..	-46.4	..	..	..	..
Ecuador	-	..	..	..	..	-4.0	..	..	..	..
Paraguay	5.3	..	..	..	..	-17.2	..	..	..	..
Peru	1.3	..	..	..	..	-38.5	..	..	..	..
Uruguay	19.9	.. d	52.0	709.1	-88.5	2.7	.. d	-267.6	71.0	403.6
Venezuela	118.1	.. d	.. d	27.1	69.6	333.0	-42.2	232.2	-64.3	254.9

Table 1. Foreign direct investment flows by country *(cont.)*

Million US dollars

	Inward					Outward				
	2014	2015	2016	2017	2018	2014	2015	2016	2017	2018
ASIA	**1 800.5**	**3 302.3**	**17 862.4**	**5 980.2**	**3 749.6**	**6 194.8**	**15 537.4**	**-11 196.5**	**19 834.3**	**4 994.7**
Near and Middle East	660.7	-166.4	14 800.4	1 626.6	1 299.4	4 619.9	4 300.6	4 479.7	2 599.5	731.7
Gulf Arabian countries	793.4	-364.9	452.3	1 512.8	4 182.7	4 485.9	4 468.1	4 205.5	1 486.9	385.9
Kuwait	5.3	..	..	..	..	-5.3	..	..	..	..
Qatar	498.9	..	..	..	..	2 166.6	..	..	..	..
Saudi Arabia	118.1	..	..	..	..	-147.3	..	..	..	..
United Arab Emirates	-21.2	..	..	..	..	881.0	..	..	..	..
Other Near and Middle East	-134.0	198.6	14 348.1	115.0	-2 882.1	132.7	-165.2	273.1	1 113.7	344.6
Jordan	-23.9	..	..	..	..	57.1	..	..	..	..
Other Asian countries	1 138.4	3 469.8	3 062.0	4 351.3	2 450.1	1 574.9	11 234.6	-15 675.1	17 234.8	4 261.8
China	459.1	942.9	108.4	236.7	110.9	1 166.2	3 175.8	1 801.4	512.9	1 824.6
Hong Kong, China	-1 959.7	1 752.6	304.1	4 626.3	2 106.7	-693.9	-613.4	96.2	1 701.0	1 418.6
India	169.8	.. d	.. d	.. d	.. d	546.6	1 237.9	274.2	1 070.9	1 862.4
Indonesia	63.7	.. d	.. d	-81.2	139.3	234.8	844.1	3 533.1	1 936.6	-256.1
Iran, Islamic Republic of	4.0	..	..	..	..	10.6	..	..	..	..
Malaysia	-509.5	-487.0	65.2	-1 233.2	-1 278.2	-57.1	343.9	-19 817.5	-1 745.0	234.9
Philippines	-26.5	-57.7	65.2	-78.9	23.6	-102.2	792.0	-479.9	-414.8	265.5
Singapore	1 241.9	1 129.2	-168.1	.. d	4 938.0	-341.0	2 198.6	-4 370.2	13 190.2	-2 288.4
Chinese Taipei	13.3	46.6	-19.9	.. d	.. d	33.2	-24.4	226.7	62.0	356.4
Thailand	14.6	.. d	-3.3	-36.1	68.5	-193.7	150.9	-3.3	22.5	310.4
Viet Nam	1.3	..	..	..	..	208.3	..	..	..	..
AUSTRALIA, OCEANIA AND POLAR REGIONS	**448.5**	**-306.2**	**322.9**	**-9.0**	**769.5**	**8 809.9**	**7 066.0**	**3 457.9**	**933.4**	**12 941.1**
WORLD unallocated and confidential	**-10.6**	**-2.2**	**-1.1**	**-1.1**	**1.2**	**282.6**	**269.6**	**-4.4**	**6.8**	**-7.1**
European Union (EU28)	**30 736.4**	**85 394.3**	**2 324.5**	**55 168.5**	**117 294.9**	**30 954.0**	**137 559.6**	**49 818.6**	**51 477.8**	**-108 282.8**
G20 countries excl. European Union	..	.. d	.. d	.. d	.. d	..	..	..	..	..
G20 OECD countries	**22 146.7**	**26 966.2**	.. d	.. d	.. d	**26 108.5**	**139 669.4**	**45 699.4**	**60 984.1**	**-59 699.0**
G20 Non-OECD countries	..	.. d	.. d	.. d	.. d	..	..	..	..	..
MENA countries	..	.. d	.. d	..	..	..	..	..	..	..
ASEAN countries	**789.4**	**698.8**	**153.7**	**-1 997.5**	**3 952.6**	**-249.4**	**4 585.7**	**-20 570.6**	**13 220.6**	**-1 340.7**

\- Nil; .. Not available; d Secondary Confidentiality

Note: Data excludes resident Special Purpose Entities (SPEs). Detailed metadata at: *http://stats.oecd.org/OECDStat_Metadata/ShowMetadata.ashx?Dataset=FDI_CTRY_IND_SUMM.*

1. Information on data for Israel: *http://oe.cd/israel-disclaimer.*
2. Note by Turkey: The information in this document with reference to "Cyprus" relates to the southern part of the Island. There is no single authority representing both Turkish and Greek Cypriot people on the Island. Turkey recognises the Turkish Republic of Northern Cyprus (TRNC). Until a lasting and equitable solution is found within the context of the United Nations, Turkey shall preserve its position concerning the "Cyprus issue".
3. Note by all the European Union Member States of the OECD and the European Union: The Republic of Cyprus is recognised by all members of the United Nations with the exception of Turkey. The information in this document relates to the area under the effective control of the Government of the Republic of Cyprus.

Source: OECD International Direct Investment Statistics (database): https://doi.org/10.1787/idi-data-en

NETHERLANDS

Table 2. Foreign direct investment positions by country

At year end

Million US dollars

	Inward					Outward				
	2014	2015	2016	2017	2018	2014	2015	2016	2017	2018
WORLD	**1 082 570.5**	**1 398 628.2**	**1 411 220.6**	**1 692 687.7**	**1 685 057.2**	**1 612 101.4**	**2 031 456.7**	**2 205 837.5**	**2 531 181.3**	**2 380 453.4**
OECD COUNTRIES	**933 153.6**	**1 198 410.5**	**.. d**	**.. d**	**.. d**	**1 330 478.8**	**1 541 775.7**	**.. d**	**.. d**	**.. d**
Australia	.. d	.. d	1 555.8	2 048.5	2 544.1	28 545.9	28 387.6	43 996.0	45 971.5	53 708.5
Austria	2 883.5	2 516.1	7 245.7	11 128.6	12 695.2	8 552.1	12 135.0	31 185.8	40 119.9	33 053.6
Belgium	67 251.4	83 909.6	71 095.2	85 869.5	94 237.5	104 693.1	99 675.6	91 123.6	95 225.5	97 249.8
Canada	1 466.6	3 048.4	3 416.3	.. d	.. d	38 540.4	33 325.0	37 483.9	49 606.6	55 902.2
Chile	.. d	39.2	42.2	211.1	.. d	2 100.4	1 350.0	1 226.9	2 443.0	2 020.8
Czech Republic	.. d	148.1	133.9	231.5	207.2	5 085.9	5 777.9	7 327.9	7 329.1	7 367.8
Denmark	15 926.6	9 328.3	7 749.6	10 704.0	11 324.7	7 239.7	8 013.1	9 159.9	12 381.9	12 279.6
Estonia	.. d	.. d	.. d	.. d	.. d	269.5	196.0	95.9	34.8	.. d
Finland	6 847.5	3 685.4	2 762.7	2 913.2	3 129.2	4 931.7	5 874.8	5 005.8	6 936.9	5 558.7
France	64 425.0	98 143.7	50 452.2	86 649.1	102 530.3	137 704.4	91 136.6	80 302.5	115 585.3	108 871.1
Germany	97 895.3	154 713.1	110 959.2	130 352.6	132 959.7	192 839.1	128 557.4	107 389.1	160 946.3	129 010.8
Greece	344.8	.. d	202.4	.. d	180.9	2 110.1	1 461.1	2 191.4	2 804.0	2 818.9
Hungary	.. d	260.2	335.2	387.4	527.8	4 430.3	6 859.0	8 111.1	7 622.9	5 788.9
Iceland	.. d	.. d	.. d	.. d	.. d	.. d	.. d	.. d	.. d	.. d
Ireland	22 673.3	36 161.1	26 201.1	37 367.5	62 097.6	16 201.0	16 597.7	28 811.0	68 467.3	72 672.3
Israel[1]	.. d	.. d	.. d	.. d	.. d	1 828.4	1 794.2	10 429.0	11 358.8	10 834.7
Italy	9 758.9	59 138.8	51 527.4	58 030.7	63 454.3	44 606.0	89 242.2	92 188.3	108 823.5	97 463.9
Japan	18 969.1	18 138.3	15 786.9	18 924.2	22 457.1	10 418.2	12 052.3	14 306.9	16 976.5	18 880.2
Korea	2 689.2	.. d	.. d	.. d	.. d	5 978.2	12 769.7	10 761.0	13 556.0	13 052.4
Latvia	.. d	.. d	.. d	.. d	.. d	.. d	.. d	6.3	141.5	453.4
Lithuania	.. d	.. d	.. d	.. d	.. d	52.2	138.3	162.3	176.3	182.0
Luxembourg	140 986.1	228 251.5	250 156.0	255 175.1	239 521.4	97 973.0	155 419.7	151 210.1	127 125.2	116 237.7
Mexico	7 905.0	13 393.6	21 133.1	40 009.6	25 199.2	22 853.0	49 578.7	39 748.1	44 376.3	49 705.7
Netherlands	-	-	-	-	-	-	-	-	-	-
New Zealand	.. d	.. d	.. d	.. d	.. d	1 069.6	3 382.7	3 610.2	4 709.8	5 448.8
Norway	440.7	11 237.9	10 935.0	.. d	.. d	5 247.3	6 064.2	7 779.1	7 868.8	7 563.5
Poland	567.0	1 147.5	986.6	1 565.1	1 699.1	8 485.3	8 248.2	9 423.4	12 728.5	14 546.6
Portugal	474.7	443.1	2 301.0	.. d	.. d	2 175.7	3 711.5	4 927.8	5 846.7	6 394.6
Slovak Republic	.. d	35.9	40.1	42.0	32.1	892.4	1 081.1	1 608.5	2 011.3	2 105.6
Slovenia	.. d	.. d	.. d	.. d	.. d	55.8	338.6	563.9	723.2	719.0
Spain	10 003.0	8 006.5	20 399.5	27 547.4	24 606.1	27 919.4	32 516.1	33 712.4	40 868.3	41 741.5
Sweden	13 233.7	11 164.9	8 481.1	12 525.8	16 739.2	6 743.1	8 507.3	13 205.4	27 794.4	28 852.8
Switzerland	56 646.3	97 062.6	97 585.1	131 342.0	139 761.9	196 883.3	193 982.6	242 478.1	240 470.1	264 982.8
Turkey	1 575.9	.. d	.. d	.. d	.. d	4 645.1	9 315.2	10 041.1	10 135.5	10 942.3
United Kingdom	253 370.5	139 073.5	126 866.2	203 810.3	243 570.0	186 247.8	221 479.6	308 583.3	337 166.0	248 733.7
United States	126 111.0	182 235.2	258 446.3	249 033.3	206 315.5	152 976.6	292 867.7	376 177.9	409 136.5	356 843.4
EUROPE	**810 453.0**	**989 061.5**	**887 338.5**	**1 102 294.3**	**1 191 305.2**	**1 087 463.3**	**1 136 504.1**	**1 286 362.4**	**1 478 606.4**	**1 355 688.1**
Bulgaria	.. d	.. d	.. d	.. d	.. d	236.7	377.8	514.4	669.2	699.6
Croatia	.. d	.. d	.. d	.. d	.. d	202.8	1 740.9	1 771.9	1 887.7	1 975.0
Cyprus[2, 3]	16 720.6	13 829.1	9 571.0	6 716.2	4 678.3	9 903.4	10 898.2	9 753.3	11 559.1	9 451.6
Malta	.. d	.. d	.. d	.. d	.. d	.. d	.. d	.. d	.. d	2 656.3
Romania	.. d	101.3	229.8	202.7	206.1	1 917.1	2 946.1	4 072.9	5 125.9	5 981.2
Russian Federation	2 384.5	3 998.9	-884.4	.. d	.. d	5 544.8	12 424.6	14 496.7	11 524.3	13 102.8
Ukraine	.. d	.. d	.. d	.. d	.. d	758.8	1 264.0	.. d	.. d	.. d
AFRICA	**1 911.0**	**4 282.0**	**6 331.8**	**5 233.9**	**5 532.4**	**31 814.3**	**84 774.1**	**54 397.6**	**60 393.4**	**78 553.9**
Northern Africa	106.8	646.7	647.2	740.0	1 202.2	10 130.5	16 855.7	15 038.5	18 295.8	42 641.4
Algeria	.. d	.. d	.. d	.. d	.. d	227.0	1 160.6	-414.3	.. d	.. d
Egypt	.. d	.. d	.. d	.. d	.. d	9 427.5	13 049.5	12 365.3	15 762.8	24 361.1
Libya	.. d	.. d	.. d	.. d	.. d	8.5	.. d	.. d	.. d	.. d
Morocco	.. d	.. d	26.4	.. d	.. d	207.6	177.5	166.5	217.1	243.9
Tunisia	.. d	.. d	.. d	.. d	.. d	.. d	.. d	640.9	.. d	713.3
Other African countries	1 804.2	3 635.3	5 684.6	4 492.7	4 330.2	21 682.6	67 919.4	39 359.1	42 098.8	35 911.4
Nigeria	.. d	.. d	.. d	.. d	.. d	11 691.8	13 748.5	11 704.4	11 705.4	11 717.4
South Africa	.. d	.. d	.. d	.. d	.. d	2 036.0	44 911.3	19 033.4	24 311.6	18 631.8
AMERICA	**220 368.9**	**326 748.0**	**426 499.4**	**475 897.1**	**347 356.3**	**305 692.2**	**586 562.9**	**646 745.0**	**736 278.5**	**689 145.9**
Northern America	127 578.8	185 283.6	261 861.5	252 706.9	210 375.5	191 526.7	326 509.5	413 659.7	458 747.9	412 749.0
Central America and Caribbean countries	91 407.2	150 807.8	179 638.5	226 189.7	169 789.3	81 407.8	140 218.8	135 836.4	154 104.1	173 873.4
Bahamas	.. d	.. d	.. d	.. d	.. d	.. d	.. d	.. d	.. d	.. d
Bermuda	54 737.7	.. d	.. d	.. d	.. d	44 011.1	.. d	37 572.5	31 373.2	31 165.6
Cayman Islands	10 656.2	.. d	.. d	.. d	.. d	4 248.1	15 846.5	.. d	.. d	.. d
Costa Rica	.. d	.. d	.. d	.. d	.. d	154.2	291.8	268.8	287.8	267.9
El Salvador	.. d	.. d	.. d	.. d	.. d	51.0	59.9	.. d	.. d	.. d
Guatemala	.. d	.. d	.. d	.. d	.. d	19.4	139.4	.. d	.. d	.. d
Honduras	.. d	.. d	.. d	.. d	.. d	.. d	176.4	143.4	.. d	.. d
Nicaragua	.. d	.. d	.. d	.. d	- d	.. d	.. d	9.5	.. d	.. d
Panama	80.1	.. d	.. d	.. d	.. d	200.3	22 280.9	.. d	.. d	.. d
Virgin Islands, U.S.	-	.. d	- d	.. d	.. d	.. d	.. d	.. d	.. d	- d
South America	1 381.6	-9 343.5	-15 001.6	-2 998.3	-32 808.6	32 756.4	119 835.6	97 248.9	123 427.7	102 523.5
Argentina	.. d	.. d	351.0	335.8	223.3	3 399.5	35 593.9	3 447.9	4 152.1	4 244.3
Bolivia	.. d	.. d	.. d	.. d	.. d	.. d	.. d	.. d	48.0	60.7
Brazil	558.5	-12 909.1	-18 457.9	-8 948.2	-39 560.3	22 766.8	74 165.5	85 475.9	108 382.1	89 102.4
Colombia	.. d	.. d	.. d	.. d	.. d	644.7	834.0	.. d	.. d	.. d
Ecuador	.. d	.. d	.. d	.. d	.. d	136.0	1 061.5	1 096.2	.. d	.. d
Paraguay	.. d	.. d	.. d	.. d	.. d	43.7	.. d	46.4	218.3	124.8
Peru	.. d	.. d	.. d	.. d	.. d	269.5	1 084.4	.. d	.. d	.. d
Uruguay	85.0	80.6	93.8	.. d	.. d	143.3	1 635.3	1 450.4	1 187.3	1 566.3
Venezuela	.. d	265.7	.. d	.. d	.. d	3 132.4	3 945.6	2 974.6	2 433.4	1 241.1

Table 2. Foreign direct investment positions by country *(cont.)*

At year end

Million US dollars

	Inward					Outward				
	2014	2015	2016	2017	2018	2014	2015	2016	2017	2018
ASIA	**48 227.7**	**76 994.0**	**89 411.8**	**106 813.4**	**137 862.4**	**156 679.6**	**191 223.7**	**169 962.1**	**204 412.3**	**197 275.0**
Near and Middle East	16 761.9	36 610.8	47 149.8	60 630.8	86 846.8	13 872.3	19 086.6	25 953.4	30 195.5	29 767.6
Gulf Arabian countries	10 108.6	8 376.7	8 813.1	12 243.9	18 639.8	11 345.8	16 594.4	14 885.6	18 354.5	18 375.3
Kuwait	.. d	.. d	.. d	.. d	.. d	.. d	.. d	.. d	.. d	.. d
Qatar	.. d	.. d	.. d	.. d	.. d	2 807.0	2 024.0	.. d	.. d	.. d
Saudi Arabia	.. d	.. d	.. d	.. d	.. d	2 465.8	5 086.6	6 261.2	8 161.4	8 352.4
United Arab Emirates	.. d	.. d	.. d	.. d	.. d	2 987.9	.. d	.. d	.. d	.. d
Other Near and Middle East	6 650.8	28 234.1	38 336.7	48 386.9	68 207.0	2 525.3	2 492.1	11 068.8	11 841.0	11 391.1
Jordan	.. d	.. d	.. d	.. d	.. d	296.2	.. d	.. d	.. d	.. d
Other Asian countries	31 465.8	40 383.2	42 262.0	46 182.5	51 015.6	142 806.1	172 137.2	144 008.6	174 216.8	167 507.4
China	1 647.5	2 859.0	2 161.9	1 884.1	1 649.9	16 099.0	17 563.4	13 651.3	14 641.4	14 567.2
Hong Kong, China	.. d	6 468.2	6 297.0	11 402.0	10 848.4	11 102.9	14 950.5	13 727.2	16 412.8	16 756.4
India	.. d	.. d	.. d	.. d	.. d	4 232.4	5 479.6	9 206.3	11 178.9	13 279.1
Indonesia	298.7	.. d	.. d	.. d	.. d	3 326.6	4 825.3	4 691.7	5 834.7	4 832.8
Iran, Islamic Republic of	.. d	.. d	.. d	.. d	.. d	.. d	.. d	.. d	.. d	.. d
Malaysia	2 485.3	3 531.8	6 481.5	997.8	399.6	1 658.5	2 893.8	2 616.2	3 142.2	3 362.7
Philippines	.. d	.. d	.. d	.. d	.. d	2 199.9	1 937.4	2 050.2	1 581.9	1 631.6
Singapore	2 618.8	3 927.1	3 849.5	3 479.3	6 319.0	64 781.9	67 917.8	33 773.6	49 851.3	38 161.2
Chinese Taipei	.. d	.. d	.. d	.. d	.. d	2 314.1	2 207.4	5 004.7	6 127.4	10 866.7
Thailand	.. d	.. d	.. d	.. d	.. d	1 620.8	2 033.8	4 186.8	4 332.0	1 785.0
Viet Nam	.. d	.. d	.. d	.. d	.. d	1 523.7	2 458.4	2 204.1	2 477.8	2 557.8
AUSTRALIA, OCEANIA AND POLAR REGIONS	**1 812.7**	**1 539.5**	**1 639.1**	**2 445.4**	**2 997.5**	**29 716.3**	**31 875.9**	**47 859.2**	**50 889.9**	**59 274.1**
WORLD unallocated and confidential	**-202.8**	**3.3**	**-**	**3.6**	**3.4**	**735.7**	**516.1**	**511.2**	**600.9**	**516.4**
European Union (EU28)	**724 519.0**	**850 549.8**	**747 996.2**	**934 695.4**	**1 017 271.6**	**871 630.3**	**914 229.7**	**1 005 014.2**	**1 202 970.7**	**1 052 941.4**
G20 countries excl. European Union	**.. d**	**.. d**	**.. d**	**.. d**	**.. d**	**..**	**1 168 762.1**	**1 277 242.5**	**1 500 466.5**	**1 309 227.2**
G20 OECD countries	**.. d**	**.. d**	**.. d**	**.. d**	**.. d**	**476 530.6**	**968 712.0**	**1 120 978.2**	**1 312 279.9**	**1 143 114.3**
G20 Non-OECD countries	**.. d**	**.. d**	**.. d**	**.. d**	**.. d**	**..**	**200 050.1**	**156 264.4**	**188 186.6**	**166 112.9**
MENA countries	**.. d**	**.. d**	**.. d**	**.. d**	**.. d**	**.. d**	**.. d**	**.. d**	**.. d**	**.. d**
ASEAN countries	**6 026.8**	**8 444.2**	**11 551.6**	**5 907.9**	**8 457.8**	**77 423.2**	**83 725.6**	**51 153.2**	**68 956.6**	**54 093.2**

- Nil; .. Not available; d Secondary Confidentiality

Note: Data excludes resident Special Purpose Entities (SPEs). Detailed metadata at: *http://stats.oecd.org/OECDStat_Metadata/ShowMetadata.ashx?Dataset=FDI_CTRY_IND_SUMM.*

1. Information on data for Israel: *http://oe.cd/israel-disclaimer*.
2. Note by Turkey: The information in this document with reference to "Cyprus" relates to the southern part of the Island. There is no single authority representing both Turkish and Greek Cypriot people on the Island. Turkey recognises the Turkish Republic of Northern Cyprus (TRNC). Until a lasting and equitable solution is found within the context of the United Nations, Turkey shall preserve its position concerning the "Cyprus issue".
3. Note by all the European Union Member States of the OECD and the European Union: The Republic of Cyprus is recognised by all members of the United Nations with the exception of Turkey. The information in this document relates to the area under the effective control of the Government of the Republic of Cyprus.

Source: OECD International Direct Investment Statistics (database): https://doi.org/10.1787/idi-data-en

NETHERLANDS

Table 3. Foreign direct investment income by country

Million US dollars

	Inward					Outward				
	2014	2015	2016	2017	2018	2014	2015	2016	2017	2018
WORLD	**43 655.3**	**72 777.6**	**69 363.0**	**64 354.6**	**69 427.6**	**59 978.8**	**102 728.8**	**87 990.7**	**104 394.1**	**116 101.7**
OECD COUNTRIES	**39 661.7**	**66 648.9**	**.. d**	**.. d**	**.. d**	**43 427.1**	**67 636.2**	**.. d**	**.. d**	**.. d**
Australia	4.0	8.9	.. d	7.9	5.9	1 344.0	1 060.5	1 471.9	1 765.3	1 493.0
Austria	67.7	165.3	38.7	348.3	338.7	127.4	.. d	.. d	1 524.1	1 438.7
Belgium	6 101.9	3 458.7	2 451.6	1 374.1	3 190.1	5 445.1	4 650.0	3 733.3	8 123.1	3 682.3
Canada	73.0	36.6	.. d	.. d	.. d	1 219.3	-2 782.0	212.3	2 543.1	6 972.7
Chile	-1.3	-	1.1	-1.1	2.4	123.4	-56.6	98.4	157.8	2 009.9
Czech Republic	1.3	2.2	2.2	2.3	2.4	281.3	300.6	541.9	385.5	559.4
Denmark	34.5	129.8	212.3	102.6	50.7	261.4	1 183.6	194.6	145.4	409.5
Estonia	-1.3	-	-	- d	-	9.3	5.5	-37.6	.. d	.. d
Finland	225.6	15.5	516.4	644.8	.. d	163.2	1 332.2	.. d	83.4	.. d
France	4 795.0	2 841.9	2 065.7	1 326.8	3 034.3	1 730.1	6 559.1	3 933.4	3 839.5	3 259.8
Germany	4 801.6	10 827.5	3 704.5	6 994.7	11 170.8	3 396.6	3 364.4	3 584.0	3 981.5	5 535.2
Greece	-	3.3	.. d	4.5	7.1	51.7	1.1	43.1	122.9	96.8
Hungary	1.3	2.2	2.2	1.1	-	107.5	135.3	158.1	175.9	203.0
Iceland	62.4	46.6	.. d	.. d	.. d	5.3	.. d	.. d	.. d	- d
Ireland	388.7	495.8	669.0	1 167.9	1 019.7	603.7	1 185.8	1 442.0	2 263.6	2 584.7
Israel[1]	19.9	1.1	-121.6	.. d	21.2	13.3	45.5	33.2	90.2	67.3
Italy	209.6	-2 699.9	628.1	3 038.0	5 312.2	723.1	2 036.6	729.8	839.8	1 442.2
Japan	869.0	1 746.0	1 580.2	2 269.2	3 341.2	595.7	251.8	766.3	479.1	1 552.0
Korea	74.3	61.0	56.4	16.9	18.9	107.5	213.0	228.9	180.4	681.0
Latvia	-1.3	-	-	- d	- d	-1.3	95.4	-63.0	90.2	98.0
Lithuania	-1.3	-	1.1	4.5	2.4	1.3	3.3	4.4	1.1	2.4
Luxembourg	3 049.0	13 805.9	36 715.7	9 632.5	6 715.4	1 625.3	1 453.1	2 265.8	7 956.3	-234.9
Mexico	-448.5	1 368.8	-165.9	792.5	951.3	561.2	2 099.8	1 195.4	1 904.0	3 381.3
Netherlands	-	-	-	-	-	-	-	-	-	-
New Zealand	-1.3	- d	1.1	-	-1.2	179.1	-68.8	52.0	404.7	657.4
Norway	1.3	112.0	320.7	-	86.2	107.5	74.3	175.8	156.7	131.0
Poland	13.3	11.1	8.8	11.3	11.8	874.4	397.1	575.0	1 241.1	1 188.5
Portugal	-272.0	.. d	2.2	14.7	-3.5	80.9	.. d	305.2	320.1	341.1
Slovak Republic	-	1.1	1.1	1.1	1.2	55.7	67.7	82.9	96.9	160.5
Slovenia	-1.3	1.1	-	-	-	-	.. d	24.3	.. d	29.5
Spain	598.4	1 148.1	1 286.1	2 132.8	3 145.3	1 004.4	1 434.3	1 144.5	1 532.0	1 705.4
Sweden	549.3	531.3	316.3	1 012.3	1 527.2	431.2	1 264.6	913.4	874.8	1 219.2
Switzerland	4 359.8	4 297.3	3 942.3	8 293.3	5 515.2	7 637.0	20 341.7	11 930.8	11 331.3	14 491.9
Turkey	159.2	39.9	133.8	94.7	-7.1	100.8	270.7	334.0	279.6	362.3
United Kingdom	9 113.7	12 038.8	7 847.0	15 127.9	18 053.8	12 140.1	9 511.9	7 806.0	10 397.9	7 778.8
United States	4 791.0	16 148.6	4 998.3	6 965.4	2 320.3	2 299.3	10 419.3	7 977.4	4 976.9	23 993.9
EUROPE	**36 358.0**	**48 797.6**	**62 055.7**	**52 926.4**	**61 045.7**	**38 066.9**	**58 612.3**	**43 607.2**	**57 609.1**	**48 779.7**
Bulgaria	-	1.1	1.1	- d	.. d	17.2	16.6	67.5	64.3	30.7
Croatia	-	-	-	-	-	1.3	4.4	19.9	18.0	26.0
Cyprus[2, 3]	1 119.8	1 141.4	508.7	179.2	-37.8	869.0	632.3	471.1	287.5	.. d
Malta	5.3	.. d	- d	1.1	.. d	-	.. d	3.3	.. d	.. d
Romania	-	-	4.4	10.1	4.7	152.6	303.9	257.7	266.0	291.5
Russian Federation	-27.9	-333.9	-69.7	174.7	-24.8	180.4	837.5	922.3	703.4	663.3
Ukraine	-	..	..	..	..	-222.9	..	..	..	..
AFRICA	**11.9**	**125.3**	**-203.5**	**-1 402.3**	**40.1**	**3 550.5**	**1 340.0**	**3 240.1**	**6 501.0**	**4 841.3**
Northern Africa	-1.3	112.0	130.5	4.5	93.2	249.4	591.2	890.2	3 183.4	2 845.5
Algeria	-1.3	..	..	..	..	51.7	..	..	..	..
Egypt	-	- d	- d	-	-	228.2	461.5	227.8	2 381.9	1 657.0
Libya	-	..	..	..	..	-2.7	..	..	..	..
Morocco	-	-	-	-	1.2	-14.6	18.9	7.7	5.6	5.9
Tunisia	-	..	..	..	..	-17.2	..	..	..	..
Other African countries	11.9	13.3	-334.0	-1 408.0	-53.1	3 301.0	748.8	2 351.0	3 317.6	1 995.8
Nigeria	2.7	.. d	.. d	3.4	.. d	2 873.8	851.9	1 269.5	2 831.7	1 494.2
South Africa	1.3	.. d	.. d	-1 433.9	-105.0	49.1	64.3	98.4	119.5	139.3
AMERICA	**5 442.5**	**21 294.5**	**5 346.7**	**10 053.0**	**4 512.0**	**10 041.1**	**25 308.9**	**23 961.1**	**21 175.7**	**44 580.4**
Northern America	4 864.0	16 185.2	5 154.3	7 051.1	2 368.7	3 509.4	7 625.1	8 184.2	7 517.8	30 964.2
Central America and Caribbean countries	573.2	3 988.9	2 041.4	4 075.1	3 796.8	4 999.3	11 447.6	7 273.0	8 014.9	6 599.8
Bahamas	34.5	..	..	..	..	43.8	..	..	..	..
Bermuda	582.5	..	..	..	..	4 212.6	..	..	..	..
Cayman Islands	524.1	..	..	..	..	-329.0	..	..	..	..
Costa Rica	-1.3	..	..	..	..	-14.6	..	..	..	..
El Salvador	-1.3	..	..	..	..	19.9	..	..	..	..
Guatemala	-	..	..	..	..	-4.0	..	..	..	..
Honduras	-1.3	..	..	..	..	-9.3	..	..	..	..
Nicaragua	-	..	..	..	..	-1.3	..	..	..	..
Panama	-	..	..	..	..	-1.3	..	..	..	..
Virgin Islands, U.S.	-	..	..	..	..	-	..	..	..	..
South America	4.0	1 120.4	-1 850.1	-1 073.2	-1 654.7	1 532.4	6 237.4	8 502.7	5 643.1	7 015.2
Argentina	-1.3	-	1.1	1.1	-	126.0	242.9	45.3	358.5	705.8
Bolivia	-	..	..	..	..	18.6	..	..	..	..
Brazil	-	867.4	-1 853.4	-1 149.8	-1 784.5	943.3	6 170.8	8 196.4	4 571.1	3 604.4
Colombia	-1.3	..	..	..	..	-54.4	..	..	..	..
Ecuador	-	..	..	..	..	29.2	..	..	..	..
Paraguay	-	..	..	..	..	13.3	..	..	..	..
Peru	-	..	..	..	..	-11.9	..	..	..	..
Uruguay	-	- d	-	23.7	27.1	35.8	.. d	60.8	53.0	188.8
Venezuela	-1.3	- d	- d	1.1	1.2	294.5	-215.2	39.8	155.6	-22.4

Table 3. Foreign direct investment income by country *(cont.)*

Million US dollars

	Inward					Outward				
	2014	2015	2016	2017	2018	2014	2015	2016	2017	2018
ASIA	**1 836.3**	**2 550.2**	**2 155.3**	**2 772.0**	**3 823.9**	**7 216.4**	**16 162.0**	**15 596.6**	**16 877.5**	**15 683.9**
Near and Middle East	441.8	359.4	173.6	454.3	564.1	2 684.1	2 751.0	1 454.2	2 282.7	1 081.1
Gulf Arabian countries	420.6	357.2	293.0	458.8	542.9	2 704.0	3 005.0	928.9	1 799.1	935.9
Kuwait	-	..	..	..	..	96.9	..	..	..	..
Qatar	1.3	..	..	..	..	1 375.9	..	..	..	..
Saudi Arabia	411.3	..	..	..	..	200.3	..	..	..	..
United Arab Emirates	4.0	..	..	..	..	262.7	..	..	..	..
Other Near and Middle East	21.2	2.2	-119.4	-4.5	22.4	-19.9	-254.0	525.3	484.7	146.3
Jordan	-	..	..	..	..	-47.8	..	..	..	..
Other Asian countries	1 393.1	2 190.8	1 981.6	2 316.5	3 258.6	4 532.3	13 409.9	14 142.4	14 594.7	14 602.9
China	38.5	52.1	54.2	62.0	72.0	1 095.9	2 038.8	2 052.4	1 943.4	2 679.1
Hong Kong, China	106.1	231.8	211.2	-122.9	-312.8	773.5	1 584.0	1 341.4	1 462.1	2 266.0
India	-	- d	.. d	- d	- d	107.5	198.6	233.3	350.6	299.8
Indonesia	4.0	.. d	.. d	3.4	3.5	489.6	320.6	1 055.0	1 681.9	1 066.9
Iran, Islamic Republic of	1.3	..	..	..	..	10.6	..	..	..	..
Malaysia	262.7	55.5	31.0	31.6	48.4	224.2	464.8	591.6	122.9	285.6
Philippines	-1.3	-	-	-	2.4	496.2	284.0	613.7	379.9	607.8
Singapore	21.2	25.5	31.0	.. d	59.0	595.7	6 785.4	5 824.4	6 222.5	2 578.8
Chinese Taipei	5.3	7.8	8.8	.. d	.. d	226.9	265.1	249.9	384.4	443.8
Thailand	-	- d	-	-	1.2	73.0	246.3	400.3	354.0	391.8
Viet Nam	-	..	..	..	..	41.1	..	..	..	..
AUSTRALIA, OCEANIA AND POLAR REGIONS	**6.6**	**11.1**	**8.8**	**6.8**	**5.9**	**1 527.1**	**1 005.0**	**1 541.5**	**2 176.8**	**2 159.8**
WORLD unallocated and confidential	**-**	**-1.1**	**-**	**-1.1**	**-**	**-423.2**	**300.6**	**44.2**	**54.1**	**56.7**
European Union (EU28)	**30 817.3**	**43 927.9**	**56 985.5**	**43 134.9**	**54 366.8**	**30 165.8**	**36 803.1**	**29 576.5**	**44 594.7**	**32 577.6**
G20 countries excl. European Union	**..**	**.. d**	**.. d**	**.. d**	**.. d**	**..**	**..**	**..**	**..**	**..**
G20 OECD countries	**24 450.0**	**42 418.2**	**.. d**	**.. d**	**.. d**	**24 224.5**	**33 005.0**	**28 239.5**	**31 187.0**	**56 452.3**
G20 Non-OECD countries	**..**	**.. d**	**.. d**	**.. d**	**.. d**	**..**	**..**	**..**	**..**	**..**
MENA countries	**..**	**.. d**	**.. d**	**..**	**..**	**..**	**..**	**..**	**..**	**..**
ASEAN countries	**293.2**	**88.7**	**67.5**	**69.9**	**118.0**	**1 917.2**	**8 384.9**	**8 908.5**	**9 310.1**	**5 753.6**

- Nil; .. Not available; d Secondary Confidentiality

Note: Data excludes resident Special Purpose Entities (SPEs). Detailed metadata at: *http://stats.oecd.org/OECDStat_Metadata/ShowMetadata.ashx?Dataset=FDI_CTRY_IND_SUMM.*

1. Information on data for Israel: *http://oe.cd/israel-disclaimer*.
2. Note by Turkey: The information in this document with reference to "Cyprus" relates to the southern part of the Island. There is no single authority representing both Turkish and Greek Cypriot people on the Island. Turkey recognises the Turkish Republic of Northern Cyprus (TRNC). Until a lasting and equitable solution is found within the context of the United Nations, Turkey shall preserve its position concerning the "Cyprus issue".
3. Note by all the European Union Member States of the OECD and the European Union: The Republic of Cyprus is recognised by all members of the United Nations with the exception of Turkey. The information in this document relates to the area under the effective control of the Government of the Republic of Cyprus.

Source: OECD International Direct Investment Statistics (database): https://doi.org/10.1787/idi-data-en

NETHERLANDS

Table 4. Foreign direct investment flows by industrial sector

Million US dollars

	Inward					Outward				
	2014	2015	2016	2017	2018	2014	2015	2016	2017	2018
All FDI activities	**44 975.5**	**178 949.5**	**30 667.9**	**60 349.5**	**114 234.6**	**59 357.8**	**247 681.6**	**156 468.0**	**46 801.9**	**-18 831.6**
Agriculture, forestry and fishing	**-**	**-**	**-**	**-**	**-**	**-**	**-**	**-**	**-**	**397.7**
Mining and quarrying	**272.0**	**704.4**	**7 675.6**	**-1 802.5**	**-1 405.6**	**-640.8**	**8 859.7**	**43 852.7**	**1 214.1**	**-11 244.0**
Extraction activities	266.7	717.7	-892.4	-189.4	482.7	-652.8	..	..	..	..
Manufacturing	**36 891.3**	**80 125.3**	**-63 707.8**	**26 708.4**	**42 931.7**	**47 138.1**	**124 883.0**	**23 716.7**	**20 804.9**	**-22 386.4**
of which:										
Food products, beverages and tobacco	7 278.8	14 658.9	-6 261.2	28 888.5	23 166.5	3 425.8	..	..	..	..
Textiles, wood and paper products; printing	110.1	110.9	-29.9	-413.7	93.2	264.0	..	..	..	..
Chemical, rubber, plastic, non-metallic mineral products	25 778.2	46 602.3	-75 256.0	-16 378.1	10 953.6	38 021.8	76 424.8	-19 147.4	-32 891.4	14 161.5
Metal and machinery products, except electrical equipment	1 520.5	9 021.6	26 067.7	14 415.5	7 122.6	5 235.5	..	..	..	..
Motor vehicles, trailers, semi-trailers, other transport equipment	744.3	9 479.8	-7 786.1	588.4	182.9	293.2	3 413.2	4 951.9	1 138.5	1 246.3
Other manufacturing	1 460.8	251.8	-442.3	-391.2	1 412.7	-106.1	..	..	..	..
Electricity, gas, steam and air conditioning supply	**1 342.7**	**1 131.4**	**-15 501.5**	**-2 095.6**	**1 687.7**	**2 503.6**	**-245.1**	**1 386.7**	**-3 040.2**	**2 811.3**
Water supply; sewerage, waste management and remediation activities	**-9.3**	**763.2**	**-63.0**	**-474.6**	**-38.9**	**-106.1**	**-26.6**	**2.2**	**-1.1**	**-80.3**
Construction	**938.0**	**761.0**	**369.3**	**-359.6**	**-43.7**	**1 030.9**	**2 442.6**	**4 105.9**	**-178.1**	**585.4**
Services	**5 539.3**	**95 466.4**	**101 966.2**	**38 372.2**	**71 103.5**	**9 345.9**	**111 556.3**	**83 638.2**	**28 145.6**	**11 039.8**
Wholesale and retail trade; repair of motor vehicles and motorcycles	-1 321.5	2 198.6	-771.9	19 341.7	14 326.7	2 140.1	33 044.9	13 996.5	9 362.0	6 733.2
Transportation and storage	-309.1	1 572.9	6 827.4	-843.2	3 196.0	386.1	2 508.0	4 117.0	6 537.0	5 622.6
Accommodation and food service activities	-108.8	59.9	50.9	37.2	-56.7	-1.3	1 118.1	1 973.9	44.0	100.3
Information and communication	12 763.7	-13 966.7	-14 428.8	1 116.0	-1 013.8	348.9	28 848.6	30 069.7	1 220.8	-1 085.8
Financial and insurance activities	-9 468.0	97 482.0	112 291.3	12 197.0	34 954.6	-2 430.7	41 570.7	24 748.4	5 560.8	11 989.9
Activities of holding companies	-	..	..	..	..	-1.3	..	..	..	..
Real estate activities	5 130.7	3 034.9	-1 539.3	6 077.1	16 192.6	1 532.4	..	..	..	..
Professional, scientific and technical activities	-520.1	1 606.2	1 917.5	-149.9	80.3	516.1	-521.4	2 534.6	-335.9	-20 299.8
Administrative and support service activities	-627.6	3 477.5	-2 380.8	596.3	3 423.8	6 858.2	..	..	..	..
Public administration; activities of households and of extraterritorial organisations	..	..	..	..	..	..	..	..	..	..
Education	-	-	-	-	-	-	..	..	..	..
Human health and social work activities	-	-	-	-	-	-	..	..	..	..
Arts, entertainment and recreation	-	-	-	-	-	-1.3	-	-2.2	-	-
Other services	-	-	-	-	-	-9.3	..	..	..	..
Not allocated and confidential	**..**	**-2.2**	**-70.8**	**1.1**	**-**	**..**	**211.9**	**-234.4**	**-143.2**	**44.8**
Private real estate activities	**-**	**-**	**-**	**-**	**..**	**82.3**	**..**	**..**	**..**	**..**

- Nil; .. Not available

Note: Data excludes resident Special Purpose Entities (SPEs). Detailed metadata at: *http://stats.oecd.org/OECDStat_Metadata/ShowMetadata.ashx?Dataset=FDI_CTRY_IND_SUMM.*

Source: *OECD International Direct Investment Statistics (database): https://doi.org/10.1787/idi-data-en*

Table 5. Foreign direct investment positions by industrial sector

At year end

Million US dollars

	Inward					Outward				
	2014	2015	2016	2017	2018	2014	2015	2016	2017	2018
All FDI activities	**1 082 570.5**	**1 398 628.2**	**1 411 220.6**	**1 692 687.7**	**1 685 057.2**	**1 612 101.4**	**2 031 456.7**	**2 205 837.5**	**2 531 181.3**	**2 380 453.4**
Agriculture, forestry and fishing	-	-	-	-	-	-	-	-	-	**802.6**
Mining and quarrying	**5 943.0**	**3 724.6**	**11 600.1**	**12 781.2**	**10 930.8**	**1 766.5**	**130 572.7**	**142 915.6**	**145 694.4**	**149 396.6**
Extraction activities	5 818.0	3 663.6	4 374.4	6 102.2	5 946.9	1 738.6	..	..	..	..
Manufacturing	**563 581.6**	**427 442.6**	**378 008.9**	**557 193.6**	**620 344.6**	**892 423.0**	**1 001 727.8**	**1 100 549.2**	**1 256 331.3**	**1 156 244.6**
of which:										
Food products, beverages and tobacco	212 252.6	118 596.6	101 236.4	142 581.0	176 896.0	148 080.1	..	..	..	..
Textiles, wood and paper products; printing	1 295.4	869.9	727.3	299.8	373.3	5 320.2	..	..	..	..
Chemical, rubber, plastic, non-metallic mineral products	253 912.0	228 710.9	196 414.0	299 781.7	337 000.2	603 547.3	581 739.8	580 851.7	608 671.1	658 441.7
Metal and machinery products, except electrical equipment	84 837.7	59 426.2	74 124.6	106 171.7	97 228.1	127 612.8	..	..	..	..
Motor vehicles, trailers, semi-trailers, other transport equipment	9 465.1	17 212.8	3 007.3	4 045.3	3 915.7	5 672.3	33 290.1	37 460.7	46 724.6	51 684.2
Other manufacturing	1 819.9	2 626.0	2 498.2	4 315.2	4 931.3	2 189.0	..	..	..	..
Electricity, gas, steam and air conditioning supply	**25 068.7**	**39 527.5**	**18 429.4**	**17 374.7**	**19 350.8**	**26 479.5**	**15 984.8**	**22 709.0**	**26 083.0**	**27 082.7**
Water supply; sewerage, waste management and remediation activities	**2 576.3**	**964.6**	**327.8**	**515.7**	**487.7**	**155.4**	**141.5**	**123.3**	**135.5**	**58.4**
Construction	**7 857.7**	**5 834.5**	**4 900.4**	**5 788.0**	**4 052.0**	**92 582.4**	**33 820.4**	**5 371.6**	**7 693.7**	**7 457.1**
Services	**477 544.4**	**921 134.5**	**997 954.0**	**1 099 033.3**	**1 029 891.2**	**581 806.4**	**832 290.7**	**917 529.3**	**1 072 968.3**	**1 013 047.9**
Wholesale and retail trade; repair of motor vehicles and motorcycles	226 928.6	128 964.6	113 356.2	112 052.1	129 125.3	204 498.1	231 707.1	276 894.7	261 246.1	247 122.7
Transportation and storage	54 261.8	35 653.8	34 776.0	48 785.1	44 040.5	51 809.3	34 339.7	30 248.8	43 610.0	53 487.5
Accommodation and food service activities	1 948.6	1 127.9	800.0	1 074.6	1 013.3	633.8	2 553.1	4 334.4	301.0	403.0
Information and communication	73 689.8	36 712.0	28 222.8	30 267.5	26 906.3	63 061.6	146 251.5	158 586.5	141 584.3	125 744.2
Financial and insurance activities	55 251.3	656 847.0	751 340.8	810 255.5	712 256.7	208 711.1	348 504.1	361 550.5	509 559.8	464 297.0
Activities of holding companies	-	..	..	..	..	-	..	..	..	..
Real estate activities	42 895.4	43 460.0	44 820.3	64 874.1	82 246.4	2 593.3	..	..	..	..
Professional, scientific and technical activities	6 724.9	2 845.9	10 717.8	13 108.7	14 384.0	27 227.4	26 454.0	40 154.9	46 572.3	41 822.8
Administrative and support service activities	15 845.2	15 523.1	13 919.0	18 616.0	19 919.9	22 789.9	..	..	..	..
Public administration; activities of households and of extraterritorial organisations	..	..	..	..	..	..	..	..	..	..
Education	-	-	-	-	-	-	..	..	..	..
Human health and social work activities	-	-	-	-	-	-1.2	..	..	..	..
Arts, entertainment and recreation	-	-	-	-	-	-1.2	3.3	1.1	2.4	3.4
Other services	-	-	-	-	-	477.1	..	..	..	..
Not allocated and confidential	..	-	-	**1.2**	-	..	**16 918.9**	**16 639.6**	**22 275.1**	**26 363.6**
Private real estate activities	-	-	-	-	..	**16 885.7**	..	..	..	..

- Nil; .. Not available

Note: Data excludes resident Special Purpose Entities (SPEs). Detailed metadata at: *http://stats.oecd.org/OECDStat_Metadata/ShowMetadata.ashx?Dataset=FDI_CTRY_IND_SUMM.*

1. National Bank of Netherlands note on the existence of a breaks in series between 2014 and 2015: *http://stats.oecd.org/OECDStat_Metadata/ShowMetadata.ashx?Dataset=FDI_CTRY_IND_SUMM&Lang=en&Coords=[MEASURE].[USD],[ECO_ACT].[FDI_T],[COU].[NLD],[FDI_TYPE].[LE_FA_F],[TIME].[2015],[MEASURE_PRINCIPLE].[DO]*

   Detailed metadata at: *http://stats.oecd.org/OECDStat_Metadata/ShowMetadata.ashx?Dataset=FDI_CTRY_IND_SUMM.*

Source: OECD International Direct Investment Statistics (database): https://doi.org/10.1787/idi-data-en

NETHERLANDS

Table 6. Foreign direct investment income by industrial sector

Million US dollars

	Inward					Outward				
	2014	2015	2016	2017	2018	2014	2015	2016	2017	2018
All FDI activities	**43 655.3**	**72 777.6**	**69 363.0**	**64 354.6**	**69 427.6**	**59 978.8**	**102 728.8**	**87 990.7**	**104 394.1**	**116 101.7**
Agriculture, forestry and fishing	-	-	-	-	-	-	-	-	-	**135.7**
Mining and quarrying	**1 023.0**	**56.6**	**125.0**	**320.1**	**92.1**	**10.6**	**4 448.1**	**9 031.3**	**5 952.0**	**5 687.5**
Extraction activities	992.4	42.2	90.7	377.6	92.1	-1.3	..	..	..	..
Manufacturing	**18 721.0**	**22 092.1**	**10 031.0**	**22 769.7**	**23 396.7**	**35 381.5**	**51 387.7**	**41 031.7**	**60 523.1**	**67 870.9**
of which:										
Food products, beverages and tobacco	5 981.2	7 464.2	1 978.3	7 397.1	7 532.2	5 271.3	..	..	..	..
Textiles, wood and paper products; printing	42.5	116.5	18.8	55.2	-2.4	106.1	..	..	..	..
Chemical, rubber, plastic, non-metallic mineral products	10 740.3	11 789.2	5 666.3	11 055.1	9 723.8	27 196.5	32 194.1	21 101.4	38 173.8	36 760.3
Metal and machinery products, except electrical equipment	1 247.2	1 794.8	1 415.5	1 861.1	3 239.7	2 649.6	..	..	..	..
Motor vehicles, trailers, semi-trailers, other transport equipment	589.1	875.2	520.8	780.1	943.0	123.4	103.2	1 573.6	209.7	282.1
Other manufacturing	122.1	52.1	432.4	1 621.0	1 960.3	29.2	..	..	..	..
Electricity, gas, steam and air conditioning supply	**2 134.8**	**2 109.8**	**2 064.6**	**836.4**	**838.0**	**1 077.4**	**506.9**	**761.9**	**988.6**	**1 251.0**
Water supply; sewerage, waste management and remediation activities	**37.2**	**762.1**	**-91.8**	**-64.3**	**-3.5**	**-86.2**	**-6.7**	**2.2**	**-1.1**	**2.4**
Construction	**793.4**	**726.6**	**332.9**	**189.4**	**-37.8**	**1 332.1**	**3 391.0**	**849.3**	**692.1**	**580.7**
Services	**20 946.0**	**47 030.5**	**56 901.5**	**40 304.4**	**45 141.0**	**22 262.2**	**41 344.4**	**34 788.2**	**34 230.6**	**38 440.9**
Wholesale and retail trade; repair of motor vehicles and motorcycles	6 729.5	10 558.0	5 316.8	7 859.3	6 579.7	3 351.5	11 670.5	8 761.5	5 177.5	5 846.8
Transportation and storage	2 780.9	2 545.8	2 984.6	2 534.1	1 012.6	1 549.7	2 320.6	2 773.4	3 026.7	2 777.1
Accommodation and food service activities	43.8	59.9	107.3	154.4	155.8	9.3	49.9	87.4	20.3	40.1
Information and communication	1 911.9	2 409.3	1 241.8	2 809.2	2 269.6	1 495.3	3 691.6	6 484.6	3 893.6	3 510.0
Financial and insurance activities	2 762.4	24 515.8	43 052.1	17 487.3	22 000.5	12 698.7	20 105.4	13 346.2	18 657.4	22 962.4
Activities of holding companies	-	..	..	..	..	-1.3	..	..	..	..
Real estate activities	3 033.0	2 403.8	1 912.0	2 781.0	4 436.4	1 142.4	..	..	..	..
Professional, scientific and technical activities	214.9	7.8	54.2	113.9	119.2	919.5	956.2	1 641.0	1 314.4	1 218.0
Administrative and support service activities	3 470.9	4 530.2	2 232.7	6 565.2	8 566.0	1 114.5	..	..	..	..
Public administration; activities of households and of extraterritorial organisations	..	..	..	..	..	..	..	..	..	..
Education	-	-	-	-	-	-	..	..	..	..
Human health and social work activities	-	-	-	-	-	-	..	..	..	..
Arts, entertainment and recreation	-	-	-	-	-	-	-	-	-	-
Other services	-	-	-	-	-	-23.9	..	..	..	..
Not allocated and confidential	..	-	-	**-1.1**	**1.2**	..	**1 657.2**	**1 526.0**	**2 008.8**	**2 132.7**
Private real estate activities	-	-	-	-	..	-	..	..	..	..

- Nil; .. Not available

Note: Data excludes resident Special Purpose Entities (SPEs). Detailed metadata at: *http://stats.oecd.org/OECDStat_Metadata/ShowMetadata.ashx?Dataset=FDI_CTRY_IND_SUMM.*

Source: OECD International Direct Investment Statistics (database): https://doi.org/10.1787/idi-data-en

NEW ZEALAND

Table 1. Foreign direct investment flows by country

Million US dollars

	Inward					Outward				
	2014	2015	2016	2017	2018	2014	2015	2016	2017	2018
WORLD	**2 493.8**	**-373.7**	**2 910.8**	**2 538.0**	**1 945.2**	**72.7**	**99.7**	**62.2**	**-222.5**	**424.9**
OECD COUNTRIES	**2 077.9**	**-1 022.4**	**.. c**	**2 320.2**	**811.0**	**-158.1**	**-756.4**	**.. c**	**-102.4**	**424.7**
Australia	359.3	35.7	2 709.7	1 869.2	-460.0	-476.0	-1 111.7	7.9	205.2	456.2
Austria	.. c	.. c	.. c	.. c	.. c	.. c	..	..	..	.. c
Belgium	-59.4	.. c	.. c	-13.8	.. c	.. c	.. c	.. c	.. c	.. c
Canada	1 782.3	456.4	-1 033.0	223.2	-3.7	11.7	-2.9	-33.5	-40.5	43.7
Chile	.. c	.. c	.. c	0.0	..	.. c	.. c	.. c	.. c	.. c
Czech Republic	.. c	.. c	.. c	.. c	.. c	..	..	..	..	..
Denmark	-0.6	.. c	.. c	1.2	.. c	0.1	0.0	..	..	..
Estonia	..	..	..	-	-	..	..	..	..	..
Finland	.. c	-0.1	.. c	1.0	.. c	11.8	-3.8	0.2	-0.1	-7.1
France	-38.2	14.1	35.1	-28.9	31.5	2.7	.. c	8.8	17.8	-34.1
Germany	-31.9	-24.2	-49.0	779.8	-53.2	0.5	.. c	20.8	-6.3	.. c
Greece	..	..	..	..	..	..	..	..	..	..
Hungary	.. c	.. c	.. c	.. c	..	0.6	..	..	..	..
Iceland	..	..	..	..	..	..	..	..	..	..
Ireland	-130.4	.. c	-41.1	-30.8	62.0	-26.0	.. c	.. c	1.0	-57.8
Israel[1]	..	..	.. c	.. c	.. c	..	..	..	..	..
Italy	-2.2	0.0	8.0	-0.2	.. c	.. c	.. c	.. c	.. c	.. c
Japan	1 012.7	-5.0	280.9	194.9	265.7	-16.2	-12.2	6.1	8.3	0.0
Korea	15.3	16.0	-13.8	5.7	5.3	-1.2	5.8	0.2	-27.9	.. c
Latvia	..	..	..	..	..	..	..	..	..	..
Lithuania	..	..	..	..	.. c	..	..	..	..	..
Luxembourg	-9.5	34.7	-13.6	-8.0	177.8	.. c	.. c	.. c	.. c	..
Mexico	.. c	.. d	-0.1	.. c	.. c	.. c	-1.1	14.4	.. c	.. c
Netherlands	-99.9	526.9	28.8	-75.9	156.2	159.5	41.0	-40.6	-107.0	.. c
New Zealand	-	-	-	0.0	-	-	-	-	0.0	-
Norway	.. c	12.5	.. c	.. c	.. c	..	..	..	..	..
Poland	.. c	.. c	0.0	0.0	.. c	..	..	..	..	..
Portugal	..	..	..	..	..	..	..	..	..	..
Slovak Republic	..	.. c	.. c	.. c	.. c	..	..	..	..	..
Slovenia	..	..	..	..	-	..	..	..	..	..
Spain	0.1	.. c	.. c	.. c	.. c	.. c	.. c	.. c	.. c	.. c
Sweden	.. c	11.1	-15.8	.. c	.. c	.. c	.. c	.. c	.. c	.. c
Switzerland	31.4	-67.2	69.2	29.4	16.5	0.0	0.0	0.0	0.1	..
Turkey	.. c	.. c	.. c	.. d	.. c	.. c	.. c	.. c	.. c	.. c
United Kingdom	64.9	-596.7	112.0	-485.7	342.0	11.0	56.9	48.4	9.8	-42.4
United States	-870.7	-22.9	353.3	-106.4	-227.9	268.1	367.0	-95.8	-282.6	-331.2
EUROPE	**-253.1**	**-1 466.5**	**454.6**	**144.6**	**1 245.6**	**119.5**	**10.9**	**106.8**	**29.1**	**-156.0**
Bulgaria	..	..	..	..	..	..	..	..	..	..
Croatia	..	-	..	-	0.0	..	..	..	..	..
Cyprus[2, 3]	..	..	..	..	..	.. c	.. c	..	..	..
Malta	.. c	.. c	.. c	.. c	..	..	..	..	..	..
Romania	..	..	.. c	.. c	.. c	..	..	..	..	..
Russian Federation	.. c	.. c	..	..	..	.. c	.. c	.. c	.. c	.. c
Ukraine	..	..	..	..	..	..	..	..	..	..
AFRICA	**-0.1**	**-17.5**	**.. c**	**.. c**	**.. c**	**-5.0**	**.. c**	**.. c**	**0.6**	**-10.9**
Northern Africa	-0.1	..	.. c	..	..	..	.. c	..	..	..
Algeria	..	..	..	..	..	..	..	..	..	..
Egypt	.. c	0.1	.. c	.. c	.. c	..	.. c	..	..	..
Libya	..	..	..	..	..	..	..	..	..	..
Morocco	..	..	..	..	..	..	..	..	..	..
Tunisia	..	..	..	..	..	..	..	..	..	..
Other African countries	0.0	.. c	.. c	..	..	-5.0	.. c	.. c	..	..
Nigeria	.. c	..	..	..	..	..	..	..	..	..
South Africa	.. c	.. c	0.1	.. c	.. c	.. c	..	..	.. c	.. c
AMERICA	**1 081.3**	**133.8**	**.. c**	**.. d**	**.. d**	**186.6**	**375.4**	**.. c**	**-288.2**	**170.0**
Northern America	911.5	..	..	..	..	279.8	..	..	..	..
Central America and Caribbean countries	146.0	.. c	.. c	..	..	-82.3	..	..	..	..
Bahamas	.. c	.. c	.. c	.. c	.. c	..	..	..	..	..
Bermuda	-85.5	-57.5	24.0	52.3	.. c	.. c	4.7	0.5	27.2	13.8
Cayman Islands	-60.2	-176.0	25.2	-248.7	-215.8	..	..	..	..	.. c
Costa Rica	..	..	..	..	..	..	..	..	..	..
El Salvador	..	..	..	..	..	..	..	..	..	..
Guatemala	..	..	..	..	..	..	..	..	..	..
Honduras	..	..	..	..	..	..	..	..	..	..
Nicaragua	..	..	..	..	..	..	..	..	..	..
Panama	.. c	.. c	..	..	..	-0.2	-0.3	0.2	1.1	..
Virgin Islands, U.S.	.. c	..	..	..	..	..	..	..	..	..
South America	23.7	.. c	.. c	..	..	-11.0	.. c	.. c	..	..
Argentina	.. c	.. c	.. c	-0.1	.. c	-0.7	0.6	.. c	.. c	.. c
Bolivia	..	..	..	..	..	..	..	..	.. c	.. c
Brazil	.. c	0.1	.. c	0.0	.. c	0.1	.. c	.. c	.. c	3.1
Colombia	.. c	.. c	.. c	.. c	.. c	..	..	..	.. c	.. c
Ecuador	..	-	..	..	..	..	..	..	..	..
Paraguay	..	..	..	..	..	..	..	..	..	..
Peru	..	..	..	..	..	.. c	0.9	2.0	.. c	.. c
Uruguay	..	..	..	..	..	.. c	.. c	.. c	.. c	.. c
Venezuela	.. c	.. c	.. c	.. c	..	.. c	1.7	-1.1	0.1	-0.2

Table 1. Foreign direct investment flows by country *(cont.)*

Million US dollars

	Inward					Outward				
	2014	2015	2016	2017	2018	2014	2015	2016	2017	2018
ASIA	**1 310.4**	**962.0**	**402.4**	**607.4**	**1 056.7**	**252.5**	**.. d**	**-23.3**	**-117.3**	**-111.4**
Near and Middle East	-2.8	.. c	.. c	..	..	..	.. c	..	..	..
Gulf Arabian countries	-2.8	.. c	.. c	..	..	28.6	.. c	..	..	..
Kuwait	..	..	..	..	..	..	..	..	..	..
Qatar	..	..	..	..	..	..	..	..	..	..
Saudi Arabia	..	..	..	..	-	.. c	2.1	-2.9	6.2	-12.8
United Arab Emirates	..	.. c	.. c	.. c	.. c	.. c	.. c	-9.4	.. c	-24.4
Other Near and Middle East	-	..	.. c	..	..	..	..	..	..	..
Jordan	..	..	-	..	..	..	..	..	..	..
Other Asian countries	1 313.1	.. c	.. c	..	..	223.9	.. c	.. c	..	..
China	.. c	0.5	33.7	128.9	4.9	10.0	13.0	-68.5	26.7	-21.1
Hong Kong, China	901.7	-14.7	549.4	685.4	1 103.8	86.3	913.8	-22.7	131.6	144.9
India	1.1	-0.4	0.9	.. d	0.3	.. c	.. c	.. c	.. c	.. c
Indonesia	-0.1	0.5	.. c	0.2	0.4	.. c	.. c	.. c	-21.9	-14.1
Iran, Islamic Republic of	..	..	..	..	..	..	..	..	..	..
Malaysia	-52.1	-86.3	.. c	-53.3	-24.9	160.3	.. c	0.3	-0.5	.. c
Philippines	.. c	1.4	2.2	6.7	.. c	0.1	.. c	.. c	.. c	.. c
Singapore	-587.4	1 053.4	-498.5	-338.6	-643.3	-29.1	-162.7	59.5	-164.7	-13.4
Chinese Taipei	.. c	0.2	-0.6	0.4	.. c	2.3	-7.1	-4.5	2.5	-0.8
Thailand	.. c	.. c	.. c	3.9	.. c	.. c	.. c	16.6	.. c	6.8
Viet Nam	.. c	.. c	.. c	2.1	.. c	.. c	.. c	-0.2	..	-6.9
AUSTRALIA, OCEANIA AND POLAR REGIONS	**363.2**	**36.6**	**2 708.3**	**1 864.0**	**-467.2**	**-480.9**	**-1 117.5**	**8.3**	**201.0**	**440.8**
WORLD unallocated and confidential	**-7.8**	**-22.1**	**-28.3**	**-29.5**	**686.2**	**0.1**	**78.1**	**77.9**	**-47.8**	**92.5**
European Union (EU28)	**-280.2**	**-1 449.8**	**400.8**	**88.2**	**1 201.7**	**94.9**	**-26.2**	**164.9**	**21.8**	**-153.5**
G20 countries excl. European Union	**2 311.2**	**-126.6**	**2 437.0**	**2 582.3**	**-91.5**	**-181.2**	**-634.8**	**-134.2**	**-83.1**	**38.7**
G20 OECD countries	**2 291.2**	**-126.6**	**2 403.0**	**2 451.6**	**-100.5**	**-215.1**	**-689.4**	**-24.2**	**-102.5**	**77.5**
G20 Non-OECD countries	**.. c**	**0.1**	**34.0**	**130.7**	**9.0**	**34.0**	**54.6**	**-110.0**	**19.4**	**-38.8**
MENA countries	**.. c**	**.. c**	**-0.3**	**.. c**	**.. d**	**.. c**	**.. c**	**-12.2**	**.. c**	**-37.2**
ASEAN countries	**-637.0**	**968.8**	**-448.5**	**-380.6**	**-324.6**	**142.0**	**-86.9**	**76.5**	**-212.5**	**-204.7**

- Nil; .. Not available; c Confidential data; d Secondary Confidentiality

Note: Detailed metadata at: *http://stats.oecd.org/OECDStat_Metadata/ShowMetadata.ashx?Dataset=FDI_CTRY_IND_SUMM.*

1. Information on data for Israel: *http://oe.cd/israel-disclaimer.*
2. Note by Turkey: The information in this document with reference to "Cyprus" relates to the southern part of the Island. There is no single authority representing both Turkish and Greek Cypriot people on the Island. Turkey recognises the Turkish Republic of Northern Cyprus (TRNC). Until a lasting and equitable solution is found within the context of the United Nations, Turkey shall preserve its position concerning the "Cyprus issue".
3. Note by all the European Union Member States of the OECD and the European Union: The Republic of Cyprus is recognised by all members of the United Nations with the exception of Turkey. The information in this document relates to the area under the effective control of the Government of the Republic of Cyprus.

Source: OECD International Direct Investment Statistics (database): https://doi.org/10.1787/idi-data-en

Table 2. Foreign direct investment positions by country

At year end

Million US dollars

	Inward					Outward				
	2014	2015	2016	2017	2018	2014	2015	2016	2017	2018
WORLD	**76 669.8**	**66 837.9**	**70 403.0**	**76 027.5**	**75 158.1**	**19 002.5**	**18 034.8**	**16 740.0**	**17 158.8**	**17 277.6**
OECD COUNTRIES	**62 219.1**	**53 071.1**	**.. c**	**60 092.1**	**58 702.8**	**15 755.7**	**14 012.7**	**.. c**	**13 252.2**	**13 655.4**
Australia	40 598.8	34 507.5	37 060.6	40 037.9	37 562.6	10 240.6	8 225.5	8 186.6	8 573.6	8 637.4
Austria	.. c	.. c	.. c	.. c	.. c	.. c	..	..	..	.. c
Belgium	.. c	.. c	.. c	427.8	72.8	.. c	.. c	-6.2	.. c	.. c
Canada	3 064.6	3 184.1	1 877.4	2 563.8	2 952.4	.. c	126.7	112.0	57.2	103.7
Chile	..	.. c	.. c	..	..	.. c	.. c	.. c	.. c	435.5
Czech Republic	.. c	..	.. c	..	.. c	..	..	..	..	..
Denmark	.. c	.. c	.. c	1.1	0.7	-	..	..	..	..
Estonia	..	..	..	..	..	..	..	..	..	..
Finland	.. c	.. c	.. c	.. c	.. c	11.4	7.2	7.5	7.6	..
France	105.1	72.5	75.5	75.0	93.3	.. c	.. c	43.6	70.5	.. c
Germany	-228.7	-183.9	-184.2	539.4	451.9	.. c	.. c	46.8	44.0	.. c
Greece	..	..	..	..	..	..	..	..	..	..
Hungary	.. c	.. c	.. c	.. c	.. c	..	..	..	..	..
Iceland	..	..	..	..	..	..	..	..	..	..
Ireland	-31.1	24.5	-56.0	-81.6	-2.0	.. c	.. c	.. c	58.8	.. c
Israel[1]	..	..	.. c	.. c	.. c	..	..	..	..	..
Italy	.. c	.. c	.. c	.. c	0.4	.. c	.. c	.. c	.. c	.. c
Japan	3 796.8	3 319.1	3 639.5	3 937.7	3 781.1	-9.3	-15.2	-10.1	-1.0	73.8
Korea	.. c	.. c	.. c	.. c	.. c	.. c	.. c	.. c	.. c	.. c
Latvia	..	..	..	..	..	..	..	..	..	..
Lithuania	..	..	..	..	..	..	..	..	..	..
Luxembourg	-22.4	224.8	226.4	335.8	483.9	.. c	.. c	.. c	.. c	.. c
Mexico	.. c	.. c	..	.. c	.. c	.. c	-0.9	.. c	18.7	39.5
Netherlands	2 671.7	2 906.5	2 821.4	2 748.3	2 908.2	.. c	333.6	289.1	.. c	.. c
New Zealand	-	-	-	0.0	-	-	-	-	0.0	-
Norway	143.3	.. c	.. c	.. c	.. c	..	..	..	..	..
Poland	.. c	0.0	0.0	0.0	.. c	..	..	..	..	..
Portugal	..	..	..	..	..	..	..	..	..	..
Slovak Republic	.. c	..	.. c	..	.. c	..	..	..	..	..
Slovenia	..	..	..	..	..	..	..	..	..	..
Spain	.. c	.. c	.. c	.. c	.. c	.. c	.. c	.. c	.. c	.. c
Sweden	.. c	36.3	.. c	.. c	.. c	.. c	.. c	.. c	.. c	.. c
Switzerland	414.7	297.2	362.4	443.2	438.0	-	-0.1	-0.1	..	..
Turkey	.. c	.. c	.. c	.. c	.. c	.. c	.. c	.. c	.. c	.. c
United Kingdom	5 652.5	2 881.6	3 735.6	3 334.0	4 311.2	1 061.7	1 038.4	850.3	951.2	885.0
United States	6 091.0	5 481.1	5 628.2	5 584.6	4 930.5	.. c	3 000.4	2 527.5	2 434.8	2 356.6
EUROPE	**9 237.8**	**7 230.1**	**8 147.4**	**8 624.7**	**10 096.2**	**2 203.4**	**2 697.9**	**1 967.3**	**2 161.9**	**2 005.2**
Bulgaria	..	..	..	..	..	..	..	..	..	..
Croatia	..	..	..	..	0.0	..	..	..	..	..
Cyprus[2, 3]	..	..	..	..	..	.. c	..	..	..	..
Malta	.. c	.. c	.. c	..	..	..	..	..	..	..
Romania	..	..	.. c	.. c	.. c	..	..	..	..	..
Russian Federation	.. c	..	..	..	..	.. c	.. c	.. c	.. c	.. c
Ukraine	..	..	..	..	..	..	..	..	..	..
AFRICA	**-0.2**	**.. c**	**.. c**	**.. c**	**.. c**	**-20.1**	**.. c**	**.. c**	**.. c**	**.. c**
Northern Africa	-0.1	..	.. c	..	..	..	..	..	..	..
Algeria	.. c	..	..	..	..	..	..	..	..	..
Egypt	.. c	..	.. c	.. c	.. c	..	..	..	..	..
Libya	..	..	..	..	..	..	..	..	..	..
Morocco	..	..	..	..	..	..	..	..	..	..
Tunisia	..	..	..	..	..	..	..	..	..	..
Other African countries	-0.1	.. c	.. c	..	..	-20.1	.. c	.. c	..	..
Nigeria	..	..	..	..	..	..	..	..	..	..
South Africa	.. c	.. c	-0.7	.. c	.. c	..	..	..	.. c	.. c
AMERICA	**11 358.6**	**.. d**	**.. c**	**10 511.5**	**.. d**	**3 548.2**	**.. d**	**.. c**	**.. d**	**.. d**
Northern America	9 155.6	..	..	..	..	3 338.8	..	..	..	..
Central America and Caribbean countries	2 203.3	.. c	.. c	..	..	42.1	..	.. c	..	..
Bahamas	.. c	.. c	.. c	.. c	.. c	..	..	..	..	..
Bermuda	.. c	.. c	.. c	.. c	.. c	223.6	199.0	203.2	207.7	210.0
Cayman Islands	981.4	723.8	715.5	829.3	897.1	..	..	..	..	.. c
Costa Rica	..	..	..	..	..	..	..	..	..	..
El Salvador	..	..	..	..	..	..	..	..	..	..
Guatemala	..	..	..	..	..	..	..	..	..	..
Honduras	..	..	..	..	..	..	..	..	..	..
Nicaragua	..	..	..	..	..	..	..	..	..	..
Panama	.. c	..	..	..	..	.. c	-1.0	-1.0	..	..
Virgin Islands, U.S.	..	..	..	..	..	..	..	..	..	..
South America	-0.2	.. c	.. c	..	..	167.3	.. c	.. c	..	..
Argentina	.. c	.. c	.. c	.. c	.. c	2.3	.. c	.. c	.. c	.. c
Bolivia	..	..	..	..	..	..	..	..	.. c	.. c
Brazil	.. c	.. c	.. c	.. c	.. c	.. c	.. c	.. c	.. c	16.2
Colombia	.. c	.. c	..	..	.. c	..	..	..	.. c	.. c
Ecuador	..	..	..	..	..	..	..	..	..	..
Paraguay	..	..	..	..	..	..	..	..	..	..
Peru	..	..	..	..	..	.. c	5.2	6.1	.. c	.. c
Uruguay	..	..	..	..	..	.. c	.. c	.. c	.. c	.. c
Venezuela	.. c	.. c	.. c	..	..	.. c	0.5	-0.8	-0.7	-0.8

Table 2. Foreign direct investment positions by country *(cont.)*
At year end

Million US dollars

	Inward					Outward				
	2014	2015	2016	2017	2018	2014	2015	2016	2017	2018
ASIA	**12 269.7**	**11 606.7**	**12 296.1**	**13 481.6**	**14 947.4**	**2 724.5**	**3 359.2**	**3 256.0**	**3 259.7**	**3 006.3**
Near and Middle East	..	.. c	.. c	..	..	..	.. c	.. c	..	..
Gulf Arabian countries	35.7	.. c	.. c	..	..	44.4	.. c	.. c	..	..
Kuwait	..	..	..	..	..	..	..	..	..	..
Qatar	..	..	..	..	..	..	..	..	..	..
Saudi Arabia	..	..	..	..	..	-5.1	-1.7	.. c	-0.1	27.3
United Arab Emirates	.. c	.. c	.. c	.. c	.. c	.. c	.. c	.. c	.. d	34.4
Other Near and Middle East	..	..	.. c	..	..	..	..	..	..	..
Jordan	..	..	..	..	..	..	..	..	..	..
Other Asian countries	12 234.0	.. c	.. c	..	..	2 680.1	.. c	.. c	..	..
China	509.8	.. d	.. c	898.8	945.3	64.7	68.4	4.8	32.7	44.7
Hong Kong, China	4 215.7	3 506.4	3 983.2	5 095.3	7 433.1	507.3	1 358.5	1 425.8	1 559.6	1 608.5
India	.. c	.. c	.. c	.. c	.. c	.. c	.. c	.. c	.. c	.. c
Indonesia	.. c	.. c	.. c	.. c	.. c	.. c	.. c	.. c	.. c	.. c
Iran, Islamic Republic of	..	..	..	..	..	..	..	..	..	..
Malaysia	.. c	173.9	.. c	.. c	.. c	707.7	.. c	.. c	.. c	.. c
Philippines	.. c	.. c	.. c	.. c	.. c	.. c	.. c	.. c	0.3	.. c
Singapore	3 312.2	3 971.2	3 556.9	3 126.4	2 044.4	1 339.8	1 131.9	1 036.8	966.5	556.4
Chinese Taipei	.. c	.. c	-0.4	.. c	.. c	10.8	2.8	-1.3	1.6	10.7
Thailand	.. c	2.9	-0.3	3.6	.. c	-9.9	0.5	.. c	-10.1	-0.8
Viet Nam	.. c	.. c	.. c	.. c	.. c	.. c	.. c	..	..	..
AUSTRALIA, OCEANIA AND POLAR REGIONS	**40 642.3**	**34 501.9**	**37 053.1**	**40 025.1**	**37 543.4**	**10 304.4**	**8 274.2**	**8 233.6**	**8 614.2**	**8 662.0**
WORLD unallocated and confidential	**3 161.5**	**2 064.9**	**2 531.7**	**3 384.7**	**2 614.4**	**242.0**	**372.6**	**431.4**	**399.9**	**219.3**
European Union (EU28)	**8 089.8**	**6 105.7**	**7 117.8**	**7 485.3**	**8 978.3**	**2 178.9**	**2 637.1**	**1 969.1**	**2 156.8**	**2 000.2**
G20 countries excl. European Union	**59 690.0**	**49 858.3**	**52 668.0**	**57 071.0**	**55 136.9**	**14 859.2**	**12 631.3**	**11 835.7**	**12 220.7**	**12 298.5**
G20 OECD countries	**59 105.6**	**49 295.1**	**51 858.3**	**56 100.3**	**54 118.5**	**14 736.7**	**12 478.0**	**11 805.6**	**12 170.6**	**12 177.1**
G20 Non-OECD countries	**584.4**	**563.2**	**809.6**	**970.7**	**1 018.4**	**122.5**	**153.2**	**30.0**	**50.2**	**121.4**
MENA countries	**.. c**	**.. c**	**.. c**	**.. c**	**.. d**	**.. c**	**.. c**	**16.7**	**.. d**	**61.7**
ASEAN countries	**3 603.2**	**4 149.4**	**3 809.6**	**3 404.1**	**2 637.9**	**2 077.5**	**1 872.7**	**1 784.6**	**1 681.9**	**1 137.8**

- Nil; .. Not available; c Confidential data; d Secondary Confidentiality

Note: Detailed metadata at: *http://stats.oecd.org/OECDStat_Metadata/ShowMetadata.ashx?Dataset=FDI_CTRY_IND_SUMM.*

1. Information on data for Israel: *http://oe.cd/israel-disclaimer.*
2. Note by Turkey: The information in this document with reference to "Cyprus" relates to the southern part of the Island. There is no single authority representing both Turkish and Greek Cypriot people on the Island. Turkey recognises the Turkish Republic of Northern Cyprus (TRNC). Until a lasting and equitable solution is found within the context of the United Nations, Turkey shall preserve its position concerning the "Cyprus issue".
3. Note by all the European Union Member States of the OECD and the European Union: The Republic of Cyprus is recognised by all members of the United Nations with the exception of Turkey. The information in this document relates to the area under the effective control of the Government of the Republic of Cyprus.

Source: OECD International Direct Investment Statistics (database): https://doi.org/10.1787/idi-data-en

NEW ZEALAND

Table 3. Foreign direct investment income by country

Million US dollars

	Inward					Outward				
	2014	2015	2016	2017	2018	2014	2015	2016	2017	2018
WORLD	**7 411.2**	**5 867.8**	**5 437.8**	**7 091.6**	**6 951.9**	**707.1**	**491.6**	**741.9**	**522.7**	**372.1**
OECD COUNTRIES	**6 984.0**	**5 428.0**	**.. c**	**6 571.4**	**6 263.5**	**682.3**	**34[illegible].1**	**.. c**	**478.3**	**308.4**
Australia	5 568.2	4 469.2	4 201.4	5 062.1	4 918.2	522.2	221.5	387.8	265.9	244.3
Austria	.. c	.. c	.. c	.. c	.. c	.. c	..	..	-	..
Belgium	.. c	..	.. c	0.8	.. c	.. c	.. c	0.4	.. c	.. c
Canada	156.3	104.3	136.5	158.6	201.6	17.8	-2.0	-25.8	-19.1	0.7
Chile	..	..	..	-	..	.. c	.. c	.. c	.. c	.. c
Czech Republic	..	..	..	..	..	..	..	..	..	..
Denmark	..	..	..	..	..	..	..	..	..	..
Estonia	..	..	..	..	..	..	..	..	..	..
Finland	.. c	.. c	.. c	.. c	.. c	0.2	0.1	0.0	0.0	0.0
France	30.2	28.7	22.5	30.5	12.2	.. c	.. c	-7.7	-0.7	-7.0
Germany	-18.2	.. d	20.4	68.5	9.8	.. c	.. c	-0.8	0.5	.. c
Greece	..	..	..	..	..	..	..	..	..	..
Hungary	..	..	..	..	..	0.0	..	..	..	..
Iceland	..	..	..	..	..	..	..	..	..	..
Ireland	8.0	.. c	.. c	2.3	3.3	-1.2	.. c	.. c	1.0	-0.1
Israel[1]	..	..	..	..	..	..	..	..	..	..
Italy	..	..	..	-	..	.. c	.. c	.. c	.. c	.. c
Japan	132.3	.. d	125.8	174.4	167.1	0.4	.. d	.. c	.. c	.. c
Korea	.. c	.. c	.. c	17.6	17.7	.. c	0.7	4.0	2.5	.. c
Latvia	..	..	..	..	..	..	..	..	..	..
Lithuania	..	..	..	..	..	..	..	..	..	..
Luxembourg	0.9	.. d	-0.8	.. c	21.3	.. c	.. c	.. c	.. c	..
Mexico	..	..	..	-	..	.. c	.. c	2.8	.. c	.. c
Netherlands	185.9	115.4	167.6	241.6	224.5	.. c	4.0	0.2	.. c	.. c
New Zealand	-	-	-	-	-	-	-	-	-	-
Norway	.. c	.. c	.. c	.. c	.. c	..	..	..	-	..
Poland	..	..	..	..	..	..	..	..	..	..
Portugal	..	..	..	..	..	..	..	..	..	..
Slovak Republic	..	..	..	..	..	..	..	..	..	..
Slovenia	..	..	..	..	..	..	..	..	..	..
Spain	..	..	.. c	.. c	.. c	.. c	.. c	.. c	.. c	.. c
Sweden	.. c	.. c	.. c	.. c	.. c	.. c	.. c	.. c	.. c	.. c
Switzerland	.. c	.. c	52.7	.. c	41.7	..	..	..	0.0	..
Turkey	..	..	..	-	..	.. c	.. c	.. c	.. c	.. c
United Kingdom	500.3	189.0	158.8	351.5	363.2	67.9	-13.8	32.7	-18.0	17.1
United States	316.8	341.6	232.9	362.6	238.2	60.9	186.4	51.6	132.0	59.8
EUROPE	**768.6**	**509.1**	**539.5**	**828.8**	**750.0**	**74.2**	**-85.7**	**150.5**	**96.1**	**16.3**
Bulgaria	..	..	..	..	..	..	..	..	..	..
Croatia	..	..	..	..	..	..	..	..	..	..
Cyprus[2, 3]	..	..	..	..	..	..	..	..	..	..
Malta	..	..	..	..	..	..	..	..	..	..
Romania	..	..	..	..	..	..	..	..	..	..
Russian Federation	..	..	..	..	..	.. c	.. c	.. c	.. c	.. c
Ukraine	..	..	..	..	..	..	..	..	..	..
AFRICA	**-**	**.. c**	**.. c**	**.. c**	**.. c**	**1.0**	**.. c**	**.. c**	**0.8**	**.. c**
Northern Africa	..	..	..	..	..	..	..	..	..	..
Algeria	..	..	..	..	..	..	..	..	..	..
Egypt	..	..	..	..	..	..	..	..	..	..
Libya	..	..	..	..	..	..	..	..	..	..
Morocco	..	..	..	..	..	..	..	..	..	..
Tunisia	..	..	..	..	..	..	..	..	..	..
Other African countries	..	.. c	.. c	..	..	..	.. c	.. c	..	..
Nigeria	..	..	..	..	..	..	..	..	..	..
South Africa	..	..	..	-	..	..	..	..	.. c	.. c
AMERICA	**610.7**	**.. d**	**.. c**	**.. d**	**.. d**	**54.1**	**.. d**	**.. c**	**151.6**	**.. d**
Northern America	..	..	..	..	..	..	..	..	..	..
Central America and Caribbean countries	137.7	.. c	.. c	..	..	-27.0	.. c	..	..	..
Bahamas	.. c	.. c	.. c	.. c	.. c	..	..	..	-	..
Bermuda	38.0	28.9	18.9	65.0	88.1	36.9	31.5	46.9	40.6	14.1
Cayman Islands	46.0	35.5	23.5	.. c	.. c	..	..	..	-	.. c
Costa Rica	..	..	..	..	..	..	..	..	..	..
El Salvador	..	..	..	..	..	..	..	..	..	..
Guatemala	..	..	..	..	..	..	..	..	..	..
Honduras	..	..	..	..	..	..	..	..	..	..
Nicaragua	..	..	..	..	..	..	..	..	..	..
Panama	.. c	.. c	..	-	..	0.0	0.0	0.0	0.0	..
Virgin Islands, U.S.	..	..	..	..	..	..	..	..	..	..
South America	-	..	..	..	..	2.4	.. c	.. c	..	..
Argentina	..	..	..	-	..	..	.. c	.. c	.. c	.. c
Bolivia	..	..	..	-	..	..	..	..	.. c	.. c
Brazil	..	..	..	-	..	0.2	.. c	.. c	.. c	.. c
Colombia	..	..	..	-	..	..	..	..	.. c	.. c
Ecuador	..	..	..	..	..	..	..	..	..	..
Paraguay	..	..	..	..	..	..	..	..	..	..
Peru	..	..	..	-	..	.. c	..	-0.4	.. c	.. c
Uruguay	..	..	..	-	..	.. c	.. c	.. c	.. c	.. c
Venezuela	..	..	..	-	..	..	0.0	0.0	0.0	0.0

NEW ZEALAND

Table 3. Foreign direct investment income by country *(cont.)*

Million US dollars

	Inward					Outward				
	2014	2015	2016	2017	2018	2014	2015	2016	2017	2018
ASIA	**456.9**	**360.5**	**269.7**	**555.9**	**690.7**	**55.7**	**125.9**	**121.0**	**5.7**	**30.7**
Near and Middle East	..	.. c	.. c	..	..	..	.. c	.. c	..	..
Gulf Arabian countries	1.1	.. c	.. c	..	..	2.5	.. c	.. c	..	..
Kuwait	..	..	..	..	..	..	..	..	..	..
Qatar	..	..	..	..	..	..	..	..	..	..
Saudi Arabia	..	..	..	-	..	0.0	.. d	0.0	-0.1	0.0
United Arab Emirates	.. c	.. c	.. c	.. c	.. c	.. c	.. c	.. c	17.1	.. c
Other Near and Middle East	..	..	..	..	..	..	..	..	..	..
Jordan	..	..	..	..	..	..	..	..	..	..
Other Asian countries	455.7	.. c	.. c	..	..	53.3	.. c	.. c	..	..
China	.. c	.. c	.. c	.. d	29.6	9.7	4.7	3.9	4.7	2.9
Hong Kong, China	191.9	158.6	153.3	269.7	288.4	.. c	-8.9	-2.0	15.8	-5.3
India	.. c	.. c	.. c	.. c	.. c	.. c	.. c	.. c	.. c	.. c
Indonesia	..	..	.. c	..	..	..	..	..	..	..
Iran, Islamic Republic of	..	..	..	..	..	..	..	..	..	..
Malaysia	.. c	.. c	.. c	.. c	.. c	.. c	.. c	.. c	0.4	-1.5
Philippines	.. c	.. c	.. c	.. c	.. c	.. c	.. c	.. c	.. c	.. c
Singapore	88.4	37.1	-41.3	76.9	189.6	36.1	100.1	85.4	.. c	.. c
Chinese Taipei	..	..	..	-	.. c	0.2	.. d	0.4	0.5	.. c
Thailand	..	..	..	-	..	.. c	.. c	.. c	0.3	.. c
Viet Nam	..	..	..	..	..	..	..	..	..	..
AUSTRALIA, OCEANIA AND POLAR REGIONS	**5 575.0**	**4 469.2**	**4 201.4**	**5 062.1**	**4 918.2**	**522.1**	**231.4**	**391.2**	**268.6**	**248.1**
WORLD unallocated and confidential	**-**	**18.7**	**-11.0**	**21.0**	**..**	**-**	**4.1**	**4.3**	**-**	**..**
European Union (EU28)	**700.4**	**428.3**	**458.8**	**748.8**	**671.8**	**73.2**	**-86.8**	**151.5**	**95.5**	**18.3**
G20 countries excl. European Union	**6 732.0**	**5 283.4**	**4 915.1**	**6 236.6**	**5 958.1**	**694.8**	**400.6**	**454.4**	**371.0**	**303.4**
G20 OECD countries	**6 728.9**	**5 284.6**	**4 913.8**	**6 225.9**	**5 928.0**	**684.3**	**395.6**	**447.3**	**365.7**	**299.9**
G20 Non-OECD countries	**3.1**	**-1.2**	**1.3**	**10.7**	**.. d**	**10.5**	**5.0**	**7.1**	**5.3**	**3.5**
MENA countries	**.. c**	**.. c**	**.. c**	**.. c**	**.. c**	**.. c**	**27.7**	**.. c**	**17.0**	**.. c**
ASEAN countries	**85.3**	**45.8**	**-26.9**	**82.9**	**185.5**	**39.8**	**100.8**	**86.6**	**-35.9**	**35.7**

- Nil; .. Not available; c Confidential data; d Secondary Confidentiality

Note: Detailed metadata at: *http://stats.oecd.org/OECDStat_Metadata/ShowMetadata.ashx?Dataset=FDI_CTRY_IND_SUMM.*

1. Information on data for Israel: *http://oe.cd/israel-disclaimer.*
2. Note by Turkey: The information in this document with reference to "Cyprus" relates to the southern part of the Island. There is no single authority representing both Turkish and Greek Cypriot people on the Island. Turkey recognises the Turkish Republic of Northern Cyprus (TRNC). Until a lasting and equitable solution is found within the context of the United Nations, Turkey shall preserve its position concerning the "Cyprus issue".
3. Note by all the European Union Member States of the OECD and the European Union: The Republic of Cyprus is recognised by all members of the United Nations with the exception of Turkey. The information in this document relates to the area under the effective control of the Government of the Republic of Cyprus.

Source: OECD International Direct Investment Statistics (database): https://doi.org/10.1787/idi-data-en

NEW ZEALAND

Table 4. Foreign direct investment flows by industrial sector

Million US dollars

	Inward					Outward				
	2014	2015	2016	2017	2018	2014	2015	2016	2017	2018
All FDI activities	**2 493.8**	**-373.7**	**2 910.8**	**2 538.0**	**1 945.2**	**72.7**	**99.7**	**62.2**	**-222.5**	**424.9**
Agriculture, forestry and fishing	..	..	..	..	..	..	..	..	..	..
Mining and quarrying	..	..	..	..	..	..	..	..	..	..
Extraction activities	..	..	..	..	..	..	..	..	..	..
Manufacturing	..	..	..	..	..	..	..	..	..	..
of which:										
Food products, beverages and tobacco	..	..	..	..	..	..	..	..	..	..
Textiles, wood and paper products; printing	..	..	..	..	..	..	..	..	..	..
Chemical, rubber, plastic, non-metallic mineral products	..	..	..	..	..	..	..	..	..	..
Metal and machinery products, except electrical equipment	..	..	..	..	..	..	..	..	..	..
Motor vehicles, trailers, semi-trailers, other transport equipment	..	..	..	..	..	..	..	..	..	..
Other manufacturing	..	..	..	..	..	..	..	..	..	..
Electricity, gas, steam and air conditioning supply	..	..	..	..	..	..	..	..	..	..
Water supply; sewerage, waste management and remediation activities	..	..	..	..	..	..	..	..	..	..
Construction	..	..	..	..	..	..	..	..	..	..
Services	..	..	..	..	..	..	..	..	..	..
Wholesale and retail trade; repair of motor vehicles and motorcycles	..	..	..	..	..	..	..	..	..	..
Transportation and storage	..	..	..	..	..	..	..	..	..	..
Accommodation and food service activities	..	..	..	..	..	..	..	..	..	..
Information and communication	..	..	..	..	..	..	..	..	..	..
Financial and insurance activities	..	..	..	..	..	..	..	..	..	..
Activities of holding companies	..	..	..	..	..	..	..	..	..	..
Real estate activities	..	..	..	..	..	..	..	..	..	..
Professional, scientific and technical activities	..	..	..	..	..	..	..	..	..	..
Administrative and support service activities	..	..	..	..	..	..	..	..	..	..
Public administration; activities of households and of extraterritorial organisations	..	..	..	..	..	..	..	..	..	..
Education	..	..	..	..	..	..	..	..	..	..
Human health and social work activities	..	..	..	..	..	..	..	..	..	..
Arts, entertainment and recreation	..	..	..	..	..	..	..	..	..	..
Other services	..	..	..	..	..	..	..	..	..	..
Not allocated and confidential	**2 493.8**	..	..	**2 538.0**	**1 945.2**	**72.7**	..	..	**-222.5**	**424.9**
Private real estate activities	..	..	..	..	..	..	..	..	..	..

.. Not available

Note: Detailed metadata at: *http://stats.oecd.org/OECDStat_Metadata/ShowMetadata.ashx?Dataset=FDI_CTRY_IND_SUMM.*

Source: *OECD International Direct Investment Statistics (database): https://doi.org/10.1787/idi-data-en*

Table 5. Foreign direct investment positions by industrial sector
At year end

Million US dollars

	Inward					Outward				
	2014	2015	2016	2017	2018	2014	2015	2016	2017	2018
All FDI activities	**76 669.8**	**66 837.9**	**70 403.0**	**76 027.5**	**75 158.1**	**19 002.5**	**18 034.8**	**16 740.0**	**17 158.8**	**17 277.6**
Agriculture, forestry and fishing	**4 572.1**	**4 240.5**	**5 004.1**	**5 802.1**	**6 222.6**	**.. c**	**.. c**	**.. c**	**.. c**	**.. c**
Mining and quarrying	**1 685.4**	**1 039.8**	**504.2**	**380.8**	**1 507.1**	**.. c**	**.. c**	**.. c**	**.. c**	**.. c**
Extraction activities	..	..	..	..	..	..	..	..	..	..
Manufacturing	**11 420.7**	**9 564.9**	**10 848.0**	**10 995.0**	**10 988.6**	**7 877.9**	**7 927.7**	**6 260.4**	**6 543.6**	**6 772.8**
of which:										
Food products, beverages and tobacco	..	..	..	..	..	..	..	..	..	..
Textiles, wood and paper products; printing	..	..	..	..	..	..	..	..	..	..
Chemical, rubber, plastic, non-metallic mineral products	..	..	..	..	..	..	..	..	..	..
Metal and machinery products, except electrical equipment	..	..	..	..	..	..	..	..	..	..
Motor vehicles, trailers, semi-trailers, other transport equipment	..	..	..	..	..	..	..	..	..	..
Other manufacturing	..	..	..	..	..	..	..	..	..	..
Electricity, gas, steam and air conditioning supply	**3 711.6**	**1 773.5**	**1 804.7**	**1 880.9**	**1 793.6**	**407.1**	**474.1**	**.. c**	**.. c**	**.. c**
Water supply; sewerage, waste management and remediation activities	**..**	**..**	**..**	**..**	**..**	**..**	**..**	**..**	**..**	**..**
Construction	**381.2**	**351.4**	**374.9**	**432.8**	**428.0**	**.. c**	**.. c**	**.. c**	**.. c**	**.. c**
Services	**54 898.8**	**38 721.2**	**40 524.9**	**44 983.5**	**42 788.8**	**9 369.2**	**7 535.2**	**7 807.8**	**7 643.6**	**6 580.8**
Wholesale and retail trade; repair of motor vehicles and motorcycles	8 186.6	7 331.3	7 773.9	7 871.9	8 415.1	3 258.3	3 860.3	4 058.2	4 266.8	4 314.9
Transportation and storage	215.3	166.1	541.7	466.9	502.1	860.0	854.6	.. c	.. c	.. c
Accommodation and food service activities	617.3	470.9	566.4	801.5	846.6	.. c	.. c	.. c	.. c	.. c
Information and communication	1 828.0	1 840.5	1 657.9	1 605.4	1 462.2	.. c	.. c	.. c	.. c	.. c
Financial and insurance activities	24 218.8	22 899.5	24 833.9	27 777.9	25 933.6	838.1	1 503.7	1 743.2	1 269.1	.. c
Activities of holding companies	..	..	..	..	..	..	..	..	..	..
Real estate activities	3 172.6	2 918.0	2 307.9	2 447.5	2 555.9	.. c	.. c	.. c	.. c	.. c
Professional, scientific and technical activities	2 079.1	1 511.5	1 102.8	2 024.5	2 033.4	.. c	76.0	51.8	106.9	87.0
Administrative and support service activities	208.9	518.2	702.3	693.1	227.6	.. c	.. c	.. c	.. c	.. c
Public administration; activities of households and of extraterritorial organisations	.. c	101.4	.. c	.. c	.. c	..	..	..	-	..
Education	..	..	..	..	..	..	..	..	..	..
Human health and social work activities	1 409.4	782.6	842.6	1 061.4	1 094.9	.. c	.. c	.. c	.. c	.. c
Arts, entertainment and recreation	..	..	..	-	..	.. c	350.4	380.4	223.7	380.1
Other services	.. c	91.0	.. c	.. c	.. c	..	..	..	-	..
Not allocated and confidential	**0.0**	**11 146.5**	**11 537.8**	**11 552.4**	**11 429.3**	**1 348.3**	**2 097.8**	**10 479.6**	**2 971.6**	**.. c**
Private real estate activities	**..**	**..**	**..**	**..**	**..**	**..**	**..**	**..**	**..**	**..**

- Nil; .. Not available; c Confidential data

Note: Detailed metadata at: *http://stats.oecd.org/OECDStat_Metadata/ShowMetadata.ashx?Dataset=FDI_CTRY_IND_SUMM.*

Source: *OECD International Direct Investment Statistics (database): https://doi.org/10.1787/idi-data-en*

Table 6. Foreign direct investment income by industrial sector

Million US dollars

	Inward					Outward				
	2014	2015	2016	2017	2018	2014	2015	2016	2017	2018
All FDI activities	**7 411.2**	**5 867.8**	**5 437.8**	**7 091.6**	**6 951.9**	**707.1**	**491.6**	**741.9**	**522.7**	**372.1**
Agriculture, forestry and fishing	..	..	..	..	..	..	..	..	..	..
Mining and quarrying	..	..	..	..	..	..	..	..	..	..
Extraction activities	..	..	..	..	..	..	..	..	..	..
Manufacturing	..	..	..	..	..	..	..	..	..	..
of which:										
Food products, beverages and tobacco	..	..	..	..	..	..	..	..	..	..
Textiles, wood and paper products; printing	..	..	..	..	..	..	..	..	..	..
Chemical, rubber, plastic, non-metallic mineral products	..	..	..	..	..	..	..	..	..	..
Metal and machinery products, except electrical equipment	..	..	..	..	..	..	..	..	..	..
Motor vehicles, trailers, semi-trailers, other transport equipment	..	..	..	..	..	..	..	..	..	..
Other manufacturing	..	..	..	..	..	..	..	..	..	..
Electricity, gas, steam and air conditioning supply	..	..	..	..	..	..	..	..	..	..
Water supply; sewerage, waste management and remediation activities	..	..	..	..	..	..	..	..	..	..
Construction	..	..	..	..	..	..	..	..	..	..
Services	..	..	..	..	..	..	..	..	..	..
Wholesale and retail trade; repair of motor vehicles and motorcycles	..	..	..	..	..	..	..	..	..	..
Transportation and storage	..	..	..	..	..	..	..	..	..	..
Accommodation and food service activities	..	..	..	..	..	..	..	..	..	..
Information and communication	..	..	..	..	..	..	..	..	..	..
Financial and insurance activities	..	..	..	..	..	..	..	..	..	..
Activities of holding companies	..	..	..	..	..	..	..	..	..	..
Real estate activities	..	..	..	..	..	..	..	..	..	..
Professional, scientific and technical activities	..	..	..	..	..	..	..	..	..	..
Administrative and support service activities	..	..	..	..	..	..	..	..	..	..
Public administration; activities of households and of extraterritorial organisations	..	..	..	..	..	..	..	..	..	..
Education	..	..	..	..	..	..	..	..	..	..
Human health and social work activities	..	..	..	..	..	..	..	..	..	..
Arts, entertainment and recreation	..	..	..	..	..	..	..	..	..	..
Other services	..	..	..	..	..	..	..	..	..	..
Not allocated and confidential	**7 411.2**	..	..	**7 091.6**	**6 951.9**	**707.1**	..	..	**522.7**	**372.1**
Private real estate activities	..	..	..	..	..	..	..	..	..	..

.. Not available

Note: Detailed metadata at: *http://stats.oecd.org/OECDStat_Metadata/ShowMetadata.ashx?Dataset=FDI_CTRY_IND_SUMM.*

Source: OECD International Direct Investment Statistics (database): https://doi.org/10.1787/idi-data-en

NORWAY

Table 1. Foreign direct investment flows by country

Million US dollars

	Inward					Outward				
	2014	2015	2016	2017	2018	2014	2015	2016	2017	2018
WORLD	**20 184.4**	**-3 070.8**	**-3 979.3**	**-5 758.3**	**-2 141.7**	**32 025.1**	**31 782.4**	**2 329.3**	**-6 865.8**	**9 084.1**
OECD COUNTRIES	..	..	.. d	..	.. d	..	..	.. d	..	.. d
Australia	..	..	..	..	.. d	..	..	..	.. d	..
Austria	..	..	..	.. d	..	..	..	..	..	..
Belgium	..	..	..	..	..	..	..	..	..	..
Canada	..	..	..	..	..	..	..	..	..	..
Chile	.. d	..	.. d	..	.. d	..	..	..	..	.. d
Czech Republic	.. d	..	.. d	..	..	..	.. d	..	..	..
Denmark	..	..	..	..	..	..	..	..	..	..
Estonia	.. d	..	..	.. d	..	..	..	..	..	.. d
Finland	..	..	..	..	..	..	..	..	..	..
France	..	..	..	..	..	..	..	..	..	..
Germany	..	..	..	..	..	..	..	..	..	..
Greece	..	.. d	.. d	.. d	.. d	..	..	..	..	..
Hungary	.. d	.. d	..	..	..	..	.. d	.. d	..	.. d
Iceland	..	..	..	..	..	..	..	..	..	..
Ireland	..	..	..	..	..	..	..	..	..	..
Israel[1]	.. d	.. d	.. d	.. d	.. d	.. d	.. d	..	..	.. d
Italy	..	..	..	..	..	..	.. d	.. d	.. d	..
Japan	..	..	..	..	.. d	..	..	..	..	..
Korea	.. d	.. d	..	..	..	..	..	..	..	..
Latvia	..	..	..	..	..	..	..	..	..	.. d
Lithuania	..	..	..	.. d	..	..	..	..	..	..
Luxembourg	..	..	..	..	..	..	..	..	..	..
Mexico	..	.. d	..	..	..	..	..	..	..	..
Netherlands	..	..	..	..	..	..	..	..	..	..
New Zealand	.. d	.. d	..	..	.. d	.. d	.. d	..	..	..
Norway	..	..	..	..	..	..	..	..	..	..
Poland	..	..	..	..	..	..	..	..	..	..
Portugal	..	.. d	..	..	..	.. d	..	..	..	..
Slovak Republic	..	.. d	.. d	.. d	..	..	..	..	..	..
Slovenia	..	.. d	.. d	.. d	- d	..	.. d	.. d	.. d	.. d
Spain	..	..	..	..	..	..	..	..	..	..
Sweden	..	..	..	..	..	..	..	..	..	..
Switzerland	..	..	..	..	..	..	..	..	..	..
Turkey	..	.. d	..	..	..	.. d	..	..	..	..
United Kingdom	..	..	..	..	..	..	..	..	..	..
United States	..	..	..	..	..	..	..	..	..	..
EUROPE	..	..	..	..	..	..	..	..	..	..
Bulgaria	.. d	.. d	..	..	- d	.. d	.. d	..	.. d	.. d
Croatia	.. d	.. d	..	.. d	.. d	.. d	..	..	.. d	.. d
Cyprus[2, 3]	..	..	..	..	..	..	..	..	..	..
Malta	.. d	..	.. d	.. d	.. d	..	..	.. d	.. d	..
Romania	.. d	.. d	.. d	.. d	.. d	.. d	..	.. d	.. d	..
Russian Federation	..	..	..	..	..	..	..	..	..	..
Ukraine	.. d	.. d	.. d	..	..	..	..	..	.. d	..
AFRICA	..	..	..	..	..	..	..	.. d	..	..
Northern Africa	.. d	..	..	..	..	..	..	..	..	..
Algeria	- d	.. d	- d	.. d	.. d	..	.. d	.. d	.. d	.. d
Egypt	.. d	..	..	..	..	..	..	..	..	..
Libya	.. d	- d	.. d	..	- d	..	.. d	.. d	..	.. d
Morocco	.. d	.. d	.. d	.. d	.. d	..	..	.. d	..	..
Tunisia	..	- d	- d	- d	- d	.. d	.. d	.. d	.. d	.. d
Other African countries	..	..	..	..	..	..	..	.. d	..	..
Nigeria	..	.. d	.. d	..	..	..	..	.. d	.. d	.. d
South Africa	.. d	..	..	..	..	..	.. d	.. d	.. d	.. d
AMERICA	..	..	..	..	..	..	..	..	..	..
Northern America	..	..	..	..	..	..	..	..	..	..
Central America and Caribbean countries	..	..	..	..	..	..	..	..	..	..
Bahamas	.. d	.. d	.. d	.. d	..	.. d	.. d	..	.. d	.. d
Bermuda	..	..	..	..	..	..	..	.. d	.. d	.. d
Cayman Islands	..	.. d	..	..	..	.. d	.. d	.. d	.. d	..
Costa Rica	..	..	..	.. d	.. d	..	.. d	.. d	.. d	.. d
El Salvador	- d	..	..	..	..	..	..	..	..	- d
Guatemala	..	..	..	..	..	.. d	.. d	.. d	.. d	.. d
Honduras	..	..	..	.. d	.. d	..	.. d	.. d	.. d	.. d
Nicaragua	..	..	..	..	..	..	..	.. d	.. d	.. d
Panama	.. d	.. d	.. d	.. d	.. d	.. d	.. d	.. d	.. d	..
Virgin Islands, U.S.	..	..	- d	- d	..	..	..	..	..	..
South America	..	..	..	..	..	..	..	..	..	..
Argentina	- d	- d	.. d	..	.. d	..	..	..	.. d	.. d
Bolivia	.. d	- d	- d	- d	- d	..	.. d	.. d	.. d	.. d
Brazil	..	..	..	..	..	..	..	..	..	..
Colombia	.. d	.. d	.. d	.. d	..	.. d	.. d	.. d	.. d	.. d
Ecuador	..	.. d	..	.. d	.. d	- d	..	.. d	..	.. d
Paraguay	- d	.. d	.. d	- d	.. d	..	..	..	..	..
Peru	.. d	.. d	.. d	.. d	.. d	.. d	.. d	.. d	.. d	.. d
Uruguay	.. d	.. d	.. d	.. d	.. d	.. d	.. d	.. d	.. d	.. d
Venezuela	- d	..	.. d	- d	.. d	..	.. d	.. d	.. d	.. d

Table 1. Foreign direct investment flows by country *(cont.)*

Million US dollars

	Inward					Outward				
	2014	2015	2016	2017	2018	2014	2015	2016	2017	2018
ASIA	..	..	..	..	..	..	..	..	..	..
Near and Middle East	..	..	..	..	..	..	.. d	..	..	.. d
Gulf Arabian countries	..	..	..	..	..	..	..	..	..	..
Kuwait	.. d	- d	.. d	.. d	.. d	..	..	.. d	.. d	..
Qatar	.. d	.. d	.. d	.. d	..	..	- d	.. d	..	.. d
Saudi Arabia	.. d	.. d	..	..	..	..	..	.. d	.. d	..
United Arab Emirates	..	..	..	..	..	..	..	..	..	..
Other Near and Middle East	.. d	.. d	.. d	..	..	..	.. d	..	.. d	.. d
Jordan	- d	- d	..	- d	- d	.. d	.. d	.. d	.. d	.. d
Other Asian countries	.. d	..	..	..	..	.. d	..	..	..	..
China	..	..	..	..	..	..	..	..	..	..
Hong Kong, China	..	..	..	..	..	.. d	..	..	..	..
India	..	.. d	.. d	..	..	..	..	..	..	..
Indonesia	..	..	.. d	..	..	..	..	..	.. d	..
Iran, Islamic Republic of	..	..	..	.. d	- d	.. d	.. d	.. d	..	..
Malaysia	.. d	..	..	.. d	.. d	..	..	.. d	..	..
Philippines	..	..	..	..	..	..	..	..	.. d	..
Singapore	..	..	..	..	..	..	..	..	..	..
Chinese Taipei	.. d	- d	.. d	.. d	.. d	.. d	..	..	.. d	.. d
Thailand	.. d	.. d	.. d	.. d	..	.. d	.. d	..	..	.. d
Viet Nam	..	.. d	..	..	..	.. d	..	.. d	.. d	.. d
AUSTRALIA, OCEANIA AND POLAR REGIONS	..	..	..	..	..	..	..	..	.. d	..
WORLD unallocated and confidential	..	..	..	..	..	..	..	.. d	.. d	..
European Union (EU28)	..	..	..	..	..	..	..	..	..	..
G20 countries excl. European Union	..	..	..	..	..	..	..	..	..	..
G20 OECD countries	..	..	..	..	..	..	..	..	..	..
G20 Non-OECD countries	..	..	..	..	..	..	..	..	..	..
MENA countries	..	..	..	..	..	..	..	..	..	..
ASEAN countries	..	..	..	..	..	..	..	..	..	..

- Nil; .. Not available; d Secondary Confidentiality

Note: Data excludes resident Special Purpose Entities (SPEs). Detailed metadata at: *http://stats.oecd.org/OECDStat_Metadata/ShowMetadata.ashx?Dataset=FDI_CTRY_IND_SUMM.*

1. Information on data for Israel: *http://oe.cd/israel-disclaimer.*
2. Note by Turkey: The information in this document with reference to "Cyprus" relates to the southern part of the Island. There is no single authority representing both Turkish and Greek Cypriot people on the Island. Turkey recognises the Turkish Republic of Northern Cyprus (TRNC). Until a lasting and equitable solution is found within the context of the United Nations, Turkey shall preserve its position concerning the "Cyprus issue".
3. Note by all the European Union Member States of the OECD and the European Union: The Republic of Cyprus is recognised by all members of the United Nations with the exception of Turkey. The information in this document relates to the area under the effective control of the Government of the Republic of Cyprus.

Source: OECD International Direct Investment Statistics (database): https://doi.org/10.1787/idi-data-en

Table 2. Foreign direct investment positions by country

At year end

Million US dollars

	Inward					Outward				
	2014	2015	2016	2017	2018	2014	2015	2016	2017	2018
WORLD	**173 127.2**	**147 486.5**	**147 524.4**	**145 487.8**	**134 927.8**	**162 027.9**	**172 431.7**	**192 013.0**	**200 887.5**	**196 080.1**
OECD COUNTRIES	**138 910.4**	**123 286.9**	**121 549.8**	**118 490.0**	**.. d**	**120 221.8**	**132 086.0**	**155 164.8**	**162 795.7**	**156 210.2**
Australia	183.6	220.0	113.9	-78.6	49.1	167.8	1 318.7	942.6	753.0	821.2
Austria	3 082.6	2 694.1	3 144.9	2 405.2	1 643.4	165.5	152.2	222.7	211.9	243.7
Belgium	10 340.0	9 358.9	7 263.2	7 344.3	3 892.4	17 066.4	8 045.2	5 357.7	-535.9	-281.8
Canada	1 882.1	750.9	1 191.4	4 717.7	428.8	1 117.1	1 224.2	1 172.7	2 013.8	1 903.6
Chile	.. c	2.4	-5.7	4.1	-13.0	823.8	1 211.5	1 294.0	1 217.1	1 090.0
Czech Republic	163.4	149.0	190.4	269.4	85.0	107.0	89.4	228.4	218.9	240.5
Denmark	8 056.8	5 511.0	5 906.3	8 161.4	6 122.6	11 291.0	12 156.6	11 599.2	13 278.0	12 805.6
Estonia	78.1	-72.1	.. c	5.0	121.2	772.9	675.9	658.9	486.4	212.4
Finland	2 212.2	3 332.5	3 279.1	2 451.3	6 398.0	1 416.4	521.1	1 435.4	1 783.9	1 597.7
France	10 633.4	7 326.1	7 331.1	6 638.4	5 428.9	4 092.1	3 406.7	2 750.2	4 606.3	4 926.9
Germany	8 166.9	6 982.2	8 057.8	6 461.5	5 892.4	1 859.0	1 663.2	2 111.8	2 533.3	3 082.6
Greece	-	.. c	.. c	0.2	.. c	41.3	45.1	10.7	28.7	35.0
Hungary	1.8	-3.4	2.3	1.9	-0.5	780.4	255.8	416.6	1 461.6	174.3
Iceland	317.8	84.3	50.1	214.4	179.3	179.1	157.7	367.5	412.1	311.3
Ireland	-419.9	1.6	-309.5	-59.4	532.8	1 908.2	1 318.5	2 180.9	2 201.9	2 044.4
Israel[1]	.. c	.. c	.. c	.. c	.. c	.. c	-0.5	2.1	-0.6	5.2
Italy	757.1	872.5	740.4	387.3	721.9	208.5	-9.6	228.2	229.1	180.0
Japan	1 423.0	955.4	1 028.1	1 388.7	1 119.0	91.4	118.2	112.6	572.8	538.7
Korea	206.5	-119.8	-259.7	-252.1	-241.7	284.5	559.6	1 055.8	886.7	807.8
Latvia	0.9	-8.6	-6.4	0.5	0.6	679.9	722.1	651.2	588.9	375.6
Lithuania	-1.3	-19.8	-20.3	76.6	-2.3	868.1	859.9	871.0	465.2	454.2
Luxembourg	15 118.7	12 193.6	13 070.7	12 330.2	11 252.7	430.1	508.5	.. c	.. c	7 412.5
Mexico	.. c	.. c	-19.5	-1.6	4.8	42.9	94.2	65.1	112.5	93.7
Netherlands	14 107.3	26 861.1	20 664.7	15 704.3	14 201.4	25 179.5	33 311.5	34 458.7	34 517.8	27 468.6
New Zealand	.. c	.. c	-22.9	-4.0	3.9	28.1	45.4	6.5	23.6	43.2
Norway	-	-	-	-	-	-	-	-	-	-
Poland	1 030.7	738.9	488.2	652.4	599.7	1 433.0	1 178.5	948.1	1 567.4	1 610.4
Portugal	9.4	113.2	.. c	.. c	2.5	18.4	18.6	21.3	31.9	73.4
Slovak Republic	.. c	8.3	-1.6	11.2	.. c	112.8	197.7	170.5	184.5	209.4
Slovenia	.. c	.. c	.. c	.. c	-	4.8	4.5	-6.1	1.8	-9.7
Spain	278.3	363.7	456.0	306.5	706.7	6 017.5	5 954.7	7 912.1	7 241.8	7 493.7
Sweden	27 145.8	27 732.1	31 404.2	32 143.6	29 901.2	20 671.3	25 913.3	25 640.0	27 733.7	25 165.1
Switzerland	3 898.5	3 095.8	2 932.1	2 713.8	3 626.5	774.8	-214.2	456.5	393.9	-72.8
Turkey	13.6	1.5	17.5	6.2	3.0	1 283.6	1 193.1	1 811.9	1 168.3	1 070.2
United Kingdom	16 834.1	7 554.8	7 269.5	7 360.4	9 091.7	6 227.6	9 742.5	12 983.9	18 532.3	14 621.7
United States	13 278.9	6 623.8	7 603.2	7 060.5	8 985.0	15 622.3	21 227.9	31 156.4	30 254.9	39 461.9
EUROPE	**128 377.0**	**120 245.4**	**116 565.9**	**110 452.4**	**105 260.6**	**107 194.9**	**112 592.7**	**123 598.1**	**131 532.9**	**116 409.6**
Bulgaria	.. c	.. c	-2.2	-2.6	-0.1	123.0	.. c	.. c	.. c	9.0
Croatia	.. c	.. c	-	.. c	-2.2	151.0	114.8	116.5	124.0	90.2
Cyprus[2, 3]	1 884.0	1 411.9	1 012.9	979.2	804.7	810.0	1 354.9	729.8	1 095.4	1 180.1
Malta	221.9	206.4	353.4	242.3	533.3	1 511.7	2 133.8	1 408.9	1 513.3	1 892.3
Romania	.. c	-61.1	-216.8	48.2	.. c	-73.2	96.1	110.6	116.8	121.1
Russian Federation	133.9	189.9	177.5	105.1	101.7	515.5	402.6	348.1	404.5	388.7
Ukraine	.. c	-	.. c	4.0	.. c	11.8	13.6	36.7	47.0	34.5
AFRICA	**75.5**	**113.4**	**-230.7**	**-125.1**	**-47.5**	**8 146.8**	**7 242.0**	**5 167.5**	**4 448.0**	**3 637.7**
Northern Africa	-4.6	-11.8	-17.1	-13.2	-6.8	1 266.2	1 335.5	1 303.9	1 212.7	969.7
Algeria	.. c	.. c	.. c	-	.. c	876.2	1 165.3	1 118.0	1 014.9	806.3
Egypt	-0.8	-8.2	-16.6	-12.8	-6.6	154.4	50.5	55.9	64.6	62.1
Libya	.. c	.. c	-	-	.. c	227.5	.. c	.. c	.. c	.. c
Morocco	.. c	.. c	.. c	-0.2	-0.1	5.1	6.9	11.4	14.0	.. c
Tunisia	-	.. c	-0.1	.. c	.. c	.. c	.. c	.. c	.. c	.. c
Other African countries	80.1	125.2	-213.7	-111.9	-40.9	6 880.6	5 906.4	3 863.7	3 235.2	2 667.8
Nigeria	-1.5	.. c	.. c	.. c	.. c	-150.6	-89.0	-1 063.3	.. c	-685.7
South Africa	-1.6	5.4	4.3	-3.5	-4.7	19.7	52.0	83.6	85.1	133.4
AMERICA	**26 999.3**	**16 708.2**	**17 355.1**	**19 010.7**	**15 445.9**	**25 550.6**	**31 305.0**	**40 921.3**	**41 439.2**	**53 390.1**
Northern America	15 161.0	7 374.7	8 794.7	11 778.1	9 413.7	16 767.0	22 481.6	32 344.1	32 270.5	41 375.9
Central America and Caribbean countries	11 792.1	9 358.6	8 660.1	6 919.4	5 820.0	3 808.1	4 132.9	2 502.7	1 782.5	2 165.2
Bahamas	.. c	39.3	20.5	177.8	95.9	27.6	27.1	.. c	.. c	34.1
Bermuda	5 611.2	4 885.4	4 241.5	3 308.9	3 074.0	3 211.3	3 455.5	2 153.2	1 418.3	1 758.8
Cayman Islands	4 737.6	3 701.1	3 514.6	2 541.5	1 623.5	350.5	258.6	222.2	154.8	178.8
Costa Rica	-	-	-	.. c	.. c	.. c	.. c	.. c	16.2	13.9
El Salvador	-	-	-	-	-	-	-	-	-	.. c
Guatemala	-	-	-	-	-	.. c	.. c	.. c	.. c	.. c
Honduras	-	-	.. c	.. c	.. c	-	.. c	.. c	.. c	.. c
Nicaragua	-	-	-	-	-	-	-	.. c	.. c	19.9
Panama	-3.9	.. c	-0.9	-0.7	-3.6	314.1	336.2	76.5	59.1	56.6
Virgin Islands, U.S.	-	-	.. c	-	-	-	-	-	-	-
South America	46.3	-25.1	-99.5	313.4	212.2	4 975.5	4 690.5	6 074.6	7 386.2	9 848.9
Argentina	-	-	-0.1	-0.7	.. c	76.6	72.5	149.2	140.4	115.2
Bolivia	.. c	.. c	.. c	.. c	-0.1	-	.. c	.. c	.. c	.. c
Brazil	-56.0	-101.0	-118.1	-94.5	-97.7	3 713.1	2 936.3	4 176.5	5 660.5	8 247.2
Colombia	.. c	-0.3	-0.3	.. c	-0.9	11.4	.. c	227.5	153.1	190.8
Ecuador	.. c	.. c	-0.2	-2.7	-0.5	.. c	-	.. c	.. c	.. c
Paraguay	.. c	.. c	.. c	.. c	.. c	-	-	-	-	-
Peru	.. c	.. c	.. c	.. c	.. c	354.5	393.3	216.1	190.1	201.7
Uruguay	.. c	.. c	12.5	8.3	.. c	.. c	.. c	.. c	8.9	-8.3
Venezuela	.. c	0.1	-	-	.. c	-4.0	-5.0	4.5	11.1	.. c

Table 2. Foreign direct investment positions by country *(cont.)*

At year end

Million US dollars

	Inward					Outward				
	2014	2015	2016	2017	2018	2014	2015	2016	2017	2018
ASIA	**8 673.6**	**3 018.3**	**5 349.9**	**6 911.3**	**5 031.3**	**17 463.5**	**15 866.6**	**17 510.2**	**18 018.0**	**17 003.3**
Near and Middle East	149.5	51.4	-33.9	402.6	367.1	2 125.2	793.1	1 065.4	1 591.2	1 851.6
Gulf Arabian countries	26.4	50.9	-28.3	338.5	320.0	353.6	278.3	727.1	1 049.3	1 010.0
Kuwait	.. c	.. c	0.7	.. c	.. c	1.9	0.9	0.7	-0.1	2.2
Qatar	.. c	0.1	-0.2	.. c	13.9	1.5	1.0	5.3	2.2	2.3
Saudi Arabia	-2.2	0.7	-1.7	-0.4	-0.9	49.1	48.2	57.4	56.8	61.1
United Arab Emirates	30.6	51.8	-15.5	20.6	16.9	245.0	137.2	207.9	169.8	161.8
Other Near and Middle East	.. c	0.6	-5.6	64.2	47.0	1 771.7	514.8	338.3	541.9	841.5
Jordan	.. c	-	-	.. c	-	.. c	.. c	.. c	.. c	.. c
Other Asian countries	.. c	2 966.9	5 383.8	6 508.8	4 664.2	.. c	15 073.6	16 444.8	16 426.8	15 151.8
China	4 656.4	813.5	2 630.6	1 392.6	770.9	921.9	-1 327.5	535.6	162.7	971.6
Hong Kong, China	171.5	3.3	-12.9	.. c	.. c	100.4	77.4	144.0	152.7	94.2
India	8.1	1.8	-13.7	31.9	24.6	453.4	275.5	189.2	213.6	349.3
Indonesia	11.8	-1.1	0.3	-1.1	-2.0	84.3	77.4	120.8	158.5	136.5
Iran, Islamic Republic of	-	-	-	.. c	.. c	-24.0	-30.3	.. c	.. c	.. c
Malaysia	688.4	210.0	702.8	619.6	46.0	306.9	304.1	223.1	275.8	246.6
Philippines	0.3	0.1	0.6	-1.3	-0.6	87.2	27.7	26.1	33.1	36.4
Singapore	889.5	1 053.8	267.7	124.7	-74.3	11 906.5	13 398.6	12 848.0	12 496.0	10 495.6
Chinese Taipei	.. c	-	0.3	0.1	-	4.3	5.8	10.4	16.0	7.9
Thailand	450.1	59.8	.. c	2 824.2	2 698.4	851.3	836.2	826.2	987.6	990.6
Viet Nam	-1.9	0.6	.. c	36.7	7.9	119.0	80.4	97.9	118.8	85.7
AUSTRALIA, OCEANIA AND POLAR REGIONS	**797.3**	**589.0**	**471.9**	**492.9**	**192.9**	**134.1**	**1 554.4**	**1 124.5**	**794.2**	**1 018.1**
WORLD unallocated and confidential	**8 204.4**	**6 812.3**	**8 012.3**	**8 745.6**	**9 044.6**	**3 538.0**	**3 870.9**	**3 691.3**	**4 655.2**	**4 621.3**
European Union (EU28)	**119 511.3**	**113 247.4**	**110 041.0**	**103 995.3**	**97 818.6**	**103 874.3**	**110 625.1**	**120 184.5**	**128 586.6**	**113 429.2**
G20 countries excl. European Union	**58 069.2**	**32 046.0**	**35 752.8**	**35 117.5**	**32 220.6**	**36 830.3**	**43 075.8**	**60 051.7**	**68 545.3**	**77 911.2**
G20 OECD countries	**53 318.7**	**31 136.9**	**33 073.7**	**33 688.2**	**31 482.9**	**30 996.9**	**40 538.8**	**54 391.3**	**61 663.1**	**67 508.4**
G20 Non-OECD countries	**4 750.5**	**909.1**	**2 679.2**	**1 429.4**	**737.7**	**5 833.5**	**2 537.0**	**5 660.6**	**6 882.2**	**10 402.9**
MENA countries	**24.1**	**39.7**	**-45.1**	**325.2**	**313.3**	**1 626.0**	**1 622.6**	**2 063.5**	**2 293.3**	**2 013.0**
ASEAN countries	**2 038.2**	**1 320.5**	**2 012.2**	**3 602.7**	**2 675.6**	**13 368.4**	**14 727.0**	**14 170.1**	**14 098.7**	**12 022.6**

- Nil; .. Not available; c Confidential data; d Secondary Confidentiality

Note: Data excludes resident Special Purpose Entities (SPEs). Detailed metadata at: *http://stats.oecd.org/OECDStat_Metadata/ShowMetadata.ashx?Dataset=FDI_CTRY_IND_SUMM.*

1. Information on data for Israel: *http://oe.cd/israel-disclaimer.*
2. Note by Turkey: The information in this document with reference to "Cyprus" relates to the southern part of the Island. There is no single authority representing both Turkish and Greek Cypriot people on the Island. Turkey recognises the Turkish Republic of Northern Cyprus (TRNC). Until a lasting and equitable solution is found within the context of the United Nations, Turkey shall preserve its position concerning the "Cyprus issue".
3. Note by all the European Union Member States of the OECD and the European Union: The Republic of Cyprus is recognised by all members of the United Nations with the exception of Turkey. The information in this document relates to the area under the effective control of the Government of the Republic of Cyprus.

Source: OECD International Direct Investment Statistics (database): https://doi.org/10.1787/idi-data-en

NORWAY

Table 3. Foreign direct investment income by country

Million US dollars

	Inward					Outward				
	2014	2015	2016	2017	2018	2014	2015	2016	2017	2018
WORLD	**7 795.1**	**6 207.2**	**6 312.1**	**11 105.4**	**12 865.1**	**13 637.3**	**9 061.4**	**6 709.1**	**8 328.7**	**12 001.4**
OECD COUNTRIES	**7 743.9**	**6 111.0**	**6 268.1**	**11 101.1**	**.. d**	**7 890.3**	**8 174.4**	**5 698.7**	**6 079.8**	**.. d**
Australia	-242.5	1.0	-34.4	-10.4	-2.7	19.4	69.7	-34.8	-24.4	-17.0
Austria	93.1	-207.7	33.9	148.1	260.6	207.1	-17.5	-30.5	-28.8	-15.9
Belgium	309.7	286.1	188.6	165.9	91.2	849.9	258.3	261.1	-200.3	22.3
Canada	584.9	448.3	-139.6	-102.6	39.5	57.6	318.8	153.6	306.4	106.0
Chile	0.6	1.1	.. c	.. c	.. c	54.7	68.8	-81.5	96.2	181.0
Czech Republic	29.0	16.4	14.2	35.2	.. c	8.9	7.7	45.8	21.9	17.9
Denmark	2 071.9	1 098.0	1 218.4	1 531.4	1 745.6	548.2	893.7	236.3	772.8	1 226.0
Estonia	-18.1	.. c	-9.0	13.9	-	121.7	39.8	35.4	88.4	33.7
Finland	177.9	-29.6	150.1	-27.0	1 062.5	385.3	91.4	77.7	60.9	-105.7
France	1 400.2	723.3	531.3	922.3	1 034.6	108.9	165.7	114.4	175.2	406.4
Germany	209.9	-346.7	584.7	494.3	319.0	820.5	197.4	952.0	101.1	208.7
Greece	-	-	-	-	-	8.3	20.2	-0.1	0.6	0.1
Hungary	-	.. c	-	.. c	.. c	133.3	101.3	107.3	12.3	64.8
Iceland	17.9	13.8	4.5	.. c	1.8	24.3	23.8	-2.0	5.9	12.3
Ireland	12.5	17.5	23.8	76.9	52.7	-57.9	-247.1	-15.6	29.5	323.3
Israel[1]	25.4	-	-	.. c	.. c	1.4	.. c	-1.8	.. c	.. c
Italy	91.6	107.9	-4.4	-108.2	3.7	-43.3	29.1	1.2	-12.8	5.0
Japan	89.7	.. c	-4.2	34.0	67.1	-3.7	29.6	0.4	3.5	2.8
Korea	-262.1	-188.6	.. c	48.1	.. c	73.8	185.9	86.3	32.4	132.9
Latvia	-5.6	-0.6	-0.2	.. c	.. c	63.9	89.8	78.3	132.0	125.0
Lithuania	0.5	.. c	-0.4	-0.2	.. c	33.2	37.2	50.0	53.7	84.9
Luxembourg	239.3	1 035.8	-52.0	534.5	315.2	10.2	-16.7	-11.2	49.2	87.2
Mexico	-1.6	.. c	.. c	.. c	.. c	-1.6	38.2	6.1	-7.6	-2.6
Netherlands	-335.9	798.5	452.8	1 519.6	1 323.1	535.4	2 040.0	1 813.1	2 081.0	824.6
New Zealand	-1.1	.. c	-2.5	.. c	.. c	7.5	6.6	7.4	9.7	16.4
Norway	-	-	-	-	-	-	-	-	-	-
Poland	-115.2	-44.3	-27.4	53.4	51.5	141.2	142.2	62.0	13.3	118.9
Portugal	-0.2	.. c	.. c	.. c	-0.2	-0.6	3.1	0.8	1.1	1.6
Slovak Republic	3.3	.. c	.. c	.. c	.. c	43.0	18.0	-3.3	13.1	22.1
Slovenia	-	-	-	-	-	0.5	1.4	.. c	.. c	-1.7
Spain	-5.7	18.7	18.2	78.5	161.3	-131.4	51.3	-1.2	7.5	-226.9
Sweden	2 459.6	2 999.4	2 951.7	4 732.6	3 822.0	2 728.1	2 404.2	1 779.7	1 437.2	993.8
Switzerland	282.8	-384.4	62.0	376.5	224.2	-301.8	51.1	0.2	-18.0	-0.9
Turkey	-	-	.. c	.. c	.. c	9.4	30.9	28.8	-159.1	30.0
United Kingdom	-78.1	-290.0	26.9	-122.7	1 007.3	587.6	818.5	-54.3	512.0	2 587.9
United States	704.9	110.4	396.4	651.2	753.1	944.5	348.6	88.3	566.3	579.9
EUROPE	**7 425.7**	**6 136.2**	**6 088.8**	**10 489.5**	**12 227.1**	**6 999.3**	**6 954.6**	**5 734.3**	**5 357.9**	**6 776.1**
Bulgaria	-	-	.. c	-	-	89.2	.. c	.. c	.. c	.. c
Croatia	-	-	-	.. c	-	-2.9	-0.5	3.5	3.6	1.6
Cyprus[2, 3]	84.1	147.4	-13.7	-57.8	66.1	-175.8	-522.3	-58.7	-74.4	-383.3
Malta	21.6	-18.8	24.0	-4.4	.. c	223.7	71.9	160.2	25.0	160.4
Romania	-0.5	0.1	1.7	.. c	.. c	-3.2	22.4	-0.5	11.6	8.0
Russian Federation	-5.1	.. c	2.1	.. c	.. c	36.7	42.7	56.1	50.9	30.1
Ukraine	-	-	-	-	-	-0.5	2.6	3.8	0.7	2.0
AFRICA	**4.8**	**2.1**	**5.7**	**-0.5**	**16.0**	**1 978.0**	**-612.8**	**272.6**	**2 142.8**	**3 417.3**
Northern Africa	-	-	-	.. c	-	541.9	39.4	26.9	235.2	723.9
Algeria	-	-	-	-	-	438.6	42.2	45.8	203.2	618.2
Egypt	-	-	-	.. c	-	10.6	9.7	-11.3	9.6	6.9
Libya	-	-	-	-	-	92.7	-12.3	-5.7	.. c	.. c
Morocco	-	-	-	-	-	0.8	0.4	-1.5	.. c	.. c
Tunisia	-	-	-	-	-	-1.0	.. c	.. c	.. c	.. c
Other African countries	4.8	2.1	5.7	-0.5	16.0	1 436.1	-652.3	245.7	1 907.6	2 693.5
Nigeria	-	-	.. c	.. c	.. c	265.6	.. c	.. c	.. c	.. c
South Africa	-	.. c	-	-	-	11.7	39.3	16.2	-8.3	24.0
AMERICA	**1 268.3**	**552.8**	**594.2**	**46.1**	**777.2**	**1 113.0**	**-69.9**	**-80.1**	**900.3**	**1 206.1**
Northern America	1 289.8	558.6	256.8	548.4	792.5	1 003.8	669.4	240.0	873.1	686.6
Central America and Caribbean countries	-22.1	-7.1	344.6	-507.4	-11.4	191.5	79.4	28.2	-7.9	48.9
Bahamas	3.8	8.6	.. c	-1.9	.. c	-0.2	.. c	.. c	.. c	2.3
Bermuda	-49.5	58.4	101.9	84.8	-49.7	136.6	10.8	46.3	-11.0	51.5
Cayman Islands	-25.9	-111.5	209.8	-613.7	-15.4	27.9	14.4	-36.8	-0.4	-21.4
Costa Rica	-	-	-	-	-	1.7	.. c	.. c	.. c	1.0
El Salvador	-	-	-	-	-	-	-	-	-	.. c
Guatemala	-	-	-	-	-	1.0	.. c	.. c	.. c	.. c
Honduras	-	-	-	-	-	-	.. c	.. c	.. c	.. c
Nicaragua	-	-	-	-	-	-	-	.. c	.. c	.. c
Panama	-	.. c	-	-	-	26.2	19.3	3.8	6.9	7.9
Virgin Islands, U.S.	-	-	-	-	-	-	-	-	-	-
South America	0.6	1.1	-7.3	5.1	-3.9	-82.2	-818.7	-348.4	35.1	470.6
Argentina	-	.. c	.. c	.. c	.. c	18.7	13.0	21.1	23.9	13.9
Bolivia	-	-	-	.. c	-	-	.. c	.. c	.. c	.. c
Brazil	2.9	-8.3	-13.5	-0.4	1.0	-166.3	-913.5	-280.8	-49.9	285.3
Colombia	-	-	-	.. c	-	-0.5	.. c	-16.2	-40.7	-25.4
Ecuador	-	.. c	-	-	-	-	.. c	.. c	-	.. c
Paraguay	0.2	-	-	-	-	-	-	-	-	-
Peru	-	.. c	-	.. c	.. c	15.9	3.8	1.2	-2.9	19.8
Uruguay	-2.9	.. c	.. c	.. c	.. c	-	.. c	.. c	0.1	-11.8
Venezuela	-	-	-	-	-	-4.9	.. c	8.2	.. c	.. c

Table 3. Foreign direct investment income by country *(cont.)*

Million US dollars

	Inward					Outward				
	2014	2015	2016	2017	2018	2014	2015	2016	2017	2018
ASIA	**-443.2**	**-441.8**	**-396.4**	**503.4**	**-166.2**	**3 477.5**	**2 608.9**	**860.6**	**-85.6**	**600.0**
Near and Middle East	15.1	-0.7	-0.7	.. c	50.3	2 167.6	1 290.9	168.8	214.8	484.5
Gulf Arabian countries	-10.2	-0.7	-0.7	.. c	45.7	60.3	57.5	87.9	86.0	117.2
Kuwait	-	.. c	-	.. c	.. c	1.0	.. c	-	-	0.5
Qatar	-	-	-	.. c	-	-0.3	1.2	-1.1	0.4	0.4
Saudi Arabia	-	-	-	-	.. c	16.2	21.2	.. c	.. c	18.9
United Arab Emirates	-10.2	-0.7	-0.7	-3.5	-4.7	38.9	-10.2	49.0	45.5	90.6
Other Near and Middle East	25.2	-	-	.. c	.. c	2 107.3	.. c	81.0	128.9	367.3
Jordan	-	-	-	-	-	-	.. c	.. c	.. c	.. c
Other Asian countries	-458.3	-441.1	-395.7	442.5	-216.5	1 309.8	1 318.0	691.8	-300.4	115.6
China	-259.3	17.6	46.3	47.9	26.7	22.2	208.9	23.6	79.6	261.3
Hong Kong, China	-57.6	-30.9	.. c	.. c	.. c	38.4	20.0	73.3	13.9	21.1
India	-	-	-	.. c	.. c	24.9	24.4	19.6	5.9	6.1
Indonesia	-	-	.. c	.. c	.. c	-1.3	-76.0	10.2	21.6	13.0
Iran, Islamic Republic of	-	-	-	-	-	-2.1	.. c	-4.6	-0.6	1.0
Malaysia	66.3	78.2	4.3	.. c	-2.7	64.7	74.0	41.0	-10.5	32.0
Philippines	-	-	.. c	.. c	.. c	2.5	5.3	2.4	0.7	1.1
Singapore	-40.5	-286.7	-375.7	305.3	-407.3	707.2	396.1	87.5	-823.1	-957.2
Chinese Taipei	-	.. c	.. c	.. c	-	-	6.0	.. c	1.6	2.2
Thailand	5.4	.. c	45.6	42.6	40.6	15.2	13.0	15.8	9.4	62.7
Viet Nam	-	.. c	.. c	.. c	.. c	6.7	25.0	18.8	24.8	.. c
AUSTRALIA, OCEANIA AND POLAR REGIONS	**-460.7**	**-42.0**	**12.1**	**31.9**	**-36.8**	**22.2**	**72.4**	**-86.9**	**-14.3**	**-0.7**
WORLD unallocated and confidential	**0.2**	**-**	**7.7**	**34.9**	**47.8**	**47.3**	**108.3**	**8.7**	**27.7**	**2.7**
European Union (EU28)	**6 645.3**	**6 280.6**	**6 104.6**	**9 995.2**	**11 410.6**	**7 233.2**	**6 790.9**	**5 701.8**	**5 384.5**	**6 551.1**
G20 countries excl. European Union	**2 235.4**	**535.1**	**1 284.7**	**1 885.3**	**3 332.5**	**2 535.9**	**1 592.3**	**1 233.7**	**1 640.2**	**4 692.9**
G20 OECD countries	**2 497.0**	**522.9**	**1 249.6**	**1 806.1**	**3 269.8**	**2 573.0**	**2 232.3**	**1 341.8**	**1 492.8**	**4 040.2**
G20 Non-OECD countries	**-261.7**	**12.2**	**35.0**	**79.2**	**62.7**	**-37.1**	**-640.0**	**-108.1**	**147.4**	**652.8**
MENA countries	**-10.2**	**-0.7**	**-0.7**	**.. c**	**45.7**	**603.2**	**97.0**	**116.0**	**323.2**	**843.4**
ASEAN countries	**31.4**	**-193.6**	**-326.2**	**302.3**	**-369.6**	**798.6**	**444.7**	**182.3**	**-774.5**	**-783.4**

- Nil; .. Not available; c Confidential data; d Secondary Confidentiality

Note: Data excludes resident Special Purpose Entities (SPEs). Detailed metadata at: *http://stats.oecd.org/OECDStat_Metadata/ShowMetadata.ashx?Dataset=FDI_CTRY_IND_SUMM.*

1. Information on data for Israel: *http://oe.cd/israel-disclaimer.*
2. Note by Turkey: The information in this document with reference to "Cyprus" relates to the southern part of the Island. There is no single authority representing both Turkish and Greek Cypriot people on the Island. Turkey recognises the Turkish Republic of Northern Cyprus (TRNC). Until a lasting and equitable solution is found within the context of the United Nations, Turkey shall preserve its position concerning the "Cyprus issue".
3. Note by all the European Union Member States of the OECD and the European Union: The Republic of Cyprus is recognised by all members of the United Nations with the exception of Turkey. The information in this document relates to the area under the effective control of the Government of the Republic of Cyprus.

Source: OECD International Direct Investment Statistics (database): https://doi.org/10.1787/idi-data-en

Table 4. Foreign direct investment flows by industrial sector

Million US dollars

	Inward					Outward				
	2014	2015	2016	2017	2018	2014	2015	2016	2017	2018
All FDI activities	**20 184.4**	**-3 070.8**	**-3 979.3**	**-5 758.3**	**-2 141.7**	**32 025.1**	**31 782.4**	**2 329.3**	**-6 865.8**	**9 084.1**
Agriculture, forestry and fishing	**.. d**	**.. d**	**.. d**	**..**	**..**	**.. d**	**.. d**	**.. d**	**..**	**.. d**
Mining and quarrying	**..**	**..**	**..**	**..**	**..**	**..**	**..**	**..**	**..**	**..**
Extraction activities	..	..	..	..	..	..	..	..	..	..
Manufacturing	**..**	**..**	**..**	**..**	**..**	**..**	**..**	**..**	**..**	**..**
of which:										
Food products, beverages and tobacco	..	..	..	..	..	..	..	..	..	..
Textiles, wood and paper products; printing	..	..	..	..	.. d	..	..	..	..	..
Chemical, rubber, plastic, non-metallic mineral products	..	..	..	..	..	..	..	..	.. d	.. d
Metal and machinery products, except electrical equipment	..	..	..	..	..	..	..	..	..	..
Motor vehicles, trailers, semi-trailers, other transport equipment	.. d	..	..	..	..	..	..	..	..	..
Other manufacturing	..	..	..	..	..	..	..	..	..	..
Electricity, gas, steam and air conditioning supply	**..**	**..**	**..**	**..**	**..**	**..**	**..**	**..**	**..**	**..**
Water supply; sewerage, waste management and remediation activities	**..**	**.. d**	**..**	**..**	**.. d**	**..**	**.. d**	**..**	**..**	**.. d**
Construction	**..**	**..**	**..**	**..**	**..**	**..**	**..**	**..**	**..**	**..**
Services	**..**	**..**	**..**	**..**	**..**	**..**	**..**	**..**	**..**	**..**
Wholesale and retail trade; repair of motor vehicles and motorcycles	..	..	..	..	..	..	..	..	..	..
Transportation and storage	..	..	..	..	..	..	..	..	..	..
Accommodation and food service activities	.. d	.. d	.. d	..	.. d	.. d	..	..	.. d	.. d
Information and communication	..	..	..	..	..	..	..	..	..	..
Financial and insurance activities	..	..	..	..	..	..	..	..	..	..
Activities of holding companies	.. d	.. d	.. d	.. d	.. d	..	..	..	..	.. d
Real estate activities	..	..	..	..	..	..	..	..	..	..
Professional, scientific and technical activities	..	..	..	..	..	..	..	..	..	..
Administrative and support service activities	..	..	..	..	..	..	..	..	..	..
Public administration; activities of households and of extraterritorial organisations	..	..	.. d	..	..	.. d	.. d	.. d	.. d	..
Education	..	.. d	..	..	.. d	.. d	.. d	.. d	.. d	.. d
Human health and social work activities	..	..	..	..	..	..	..	.. d	..	..
Arts, entertainment and recreation	..	.. d	..	.. d	.. d	.. d	.. d	.. d	.. d	.. d
Other services	..	..	..	.. d	.. d	.. d	.. d	.. d	.. d	.. d
Not allocated and confidential	**.. d**	**.. d**	**.. d**	**.. d**	**.. d**	**.. d**	**.. d**	**.. d**	**..**	**.. d**
Private real estate activities	**.. d**	**.. d**	**.. d**	**.. d**	**.. d**	**..**	**..**	**..**	**..**	**..**

.. Not available; d Secondary Confidentiality

Note: Data excludes resident Special Purpose Entities (SPEs). Detailed metadata at: *http://stats.oecd.org/OECDStat_Metadata/ShowMetadata.ashx?Dataset=FDI_CTRY_IND_SUMM.*

Source: OECD International Direct Investment Statistics (database): https://doi.org/10.1787/idi-data-en

Table 5. Foreign direct investment positions by industrial sector

At year end

Million US dollars

	Inward					Outward				
	2014	2015	2016	2017	2018	2014	2015	2016	2017	2018
All FDI activities	**173 127.2**	**147 486.5**	**147 524.4**	**145 487.8**	**134 927.8**	**162 027.9**	**172 431.7**	**192 013.0**	**200 887.5**	**196 080.1**
Agriculture, forestry and fishing	**.. c**	**651.2**	**155.2**	**256.6**	**258.2**	**1 447.2**	**1 999.4**	**2 147.1**	**2 157.7**	**2 267.7**
Mining and quarrying	**62 281.8**	**43 882.2**	**42 126.1**	**40 306.0**	**30 993.6**	**42 659.0**	**44 231.4**	**48 846.6**	**41 749.5**	**48 761.5**
Extraction activities	62 281.8	43 882.2	42 126.1	40 306.0	30 993.6	42 659.0	44 231.4	48 846.6	41 749.5	48 761.5
Manufacturing	**27 620.5**	**21 115.3**	**20 981.3**	**21 158.6**	**21 391.4**	**29 370.3**	**26 799.4**	**27 429.9**	**30 918.6**	**30 426.7**
of which:										
Food products, beverages and tobacco	1 689.9	1 293.9	2 892.5	2 879.8	2 402.5	2 475.2	2 432.7	2 625.1	3 050.9	2 916.3
Textiles, wood and paper products; printing	256.3	183.7	96.3	193.8	496.3	1 498.7	1 334.5	1 301.9	1 402.7	1 290.0
Chemical, rubber, plastic, non-metallic mineral products	13 219.1	9 713.8	9 560.1	10 370.8	11 899.0	9 570.8	8 144.0	9 490.4	10 545.2	11 813.1
Metal and machinery products, except electrical equipment	5 484.1	4 481.4	3 848.7	3 903.8	3 421.1	11 932.4	11 188.5	11 372.0	13 317.7	12 672.8
Motor vehicles, trailers, semi-trailers, other transport equipment	3 338.6	3 066.1	2 576.5	1 520.6	1 276.8	2 656.4	2 483.9	1 476.5	1 449.9	751.9
Other manufacturing	3 632.6	2 376.6	2 007.3	2 289.8	1 895.9	1 236.7	1 2[illegible]5.8	1 164.2	1 152.4	982.5
Electricity, gas, steam and air conditioning supply	**761.0**	**794.6**	**1 052.3**	**1 426.7**	**1 923.2**	**6 841.2**	**5 521.1**	**6 061.1**	**4 304.3**	**4 760.8**
Water supply; sewerage, waste management and remediation activities	**590.3**	**145.6**	**138.6**	**164.4**	**90.6**	**6.2**	**3.7**	**0.5**	**.. c**	**7.6**
Construction	**1 978.2**	**1 597.0**	**1 797.2**	**2 149.2**	**2 157.4**	**898.1**	**920.0**	**1 121.3**	**1 231.4**	**1 025.8**
Services	**67 856.7**	**62 762.3**	**69 383.9**	**67 789.4**	**67 490.1**	**59 072.4**	**71 457.1**	**81 890.7**	**93 976.6**	**85 567.0**
Wholesale and retail trade; repair of motor vehicles and motorcycles	14 771.1	11 421.9	12 247.8	12 957.1	12 374.3	4 413.6	4 237.5	4 496.2	4 714.4	4 875.5
Transportation and storage	11 375.8	8 775.5	8 922.4	10 352.0	10 645.9	9 684.4	9 776.7	10 227.4	11 244.5	8 331.3
Accommodation and food service activities	217.5	511.1	617.1	484.0	451.8	197.2	252.9	311.0	359.2	321.6
Information and communication	7 640.5	8 350.5	8 848.0	8 946.9	7 577.1	11 016.4	13 941.5	14 052.4	17 793.8	15 306.8
Financial and insurance activities	14 675.2	15 219.0	17 826.5	12 194.2	14 266.5	10 925.2	17 443.4	16 624.6	17 016.4	16 048.4
Activities of holding companies	-	.. c	.. c	.. c	.. c	871.7	1 045.6	481.7	.. c	-
Real estate activities	6 720.7	8 016.3	9 141.6	11 731.1	11 043.2	8 205.7	8 104.5	7 521.6	8 218.1	7 986.5
Professional, scientific and technical activities	6 951.3	4 500.0	5 653.8	3 889.5	3 862.5	7 573.1	3 467.2	5 620.8	5 838.6	5 753.5
Administrative and support service activities	4 558.5	4 782.2	4 960.9	5 939.8	6 135.3	1 888.2	4 139.2	4 141.5	3 241.0	4 635.2
Public administration; activities of households and of extraterritorial organisations	-	.. c	-	-	-	.. c	.. c	.. c	.. c	.. c
Education	.. c	.. c	29.4	.. c	.. c	19.7	38.8	15.1	24.5	33.9
Human health and social work activities	575.8	656.9	666.1	810.4	704.9	143.9	92.4	116.1	170.3	132.0
Arts, entertainment and recreation	138.6	401.7	326.2	385.4	372.6	36.1	[illegible]9.5	12.4	.. c	21.5
Other services	210.5	.. c	144.0	72.1	36.9	.. c	.. c	139.2	159.8	149.7
Not allocated and confidential	**.. c**	**9 335.2**	**3 984.9**	**3 654.0**	**1 589.0**	**1 731.5**	**1 995.2**	**3 320.0**	**.. c**	**287.3**
Private real estate activities	**8 189.4**	**7 203.1**	**7 904.8**	**8 582.9**	**9 034.4**	**20 002.0**	**19 504.2**	**21 195.7**	**23 200.7**	**22 975.8**

- Nil; c Confidential data

Note: Data excludes resident Special Purpose Entities (SPEs). Detailed metadata at: *http://stats.oecd.org/OECDStat_Metadata/ShowMetadata.ashx?Dataset=FDI_CTRY_IND_SUMM.*

Source: *OECD International Direct Investment Statistics (database): https://doi.org/10.1787/idi-data-en*

Table 6. Foreign direct investment income by industrial sector

Million US dollars

	Inward					Outward				
	2014	2015	2016	2017	2018	2014	2015	2016	2017	2018
All FDI activities	**7 795.1**	**6 207.2**	**6 312.1**	**11 105.4**	**12 865.1**	**13 637.3**	**9 061.4**	**6 709.1**	**8 328.7**	**12 001.4**
Agriculture, forestry and fishing	**145.8**	**47.5**	**9.5**	**32.5**	**25.8**	**194.4**	**111.4**	**127.0**	**56.8**	**141.5**
Mining and quarrying	**3 131.1**	**-293.0**	**945.5**	**4 062.5**	**5 190.8**	**1 966.4**	**-1 407.3**	**143.7**	**2 190.1**	**4 692.7**
Extraction activities	3 131.1	2 374.7	945.5	4 062.5	5 190.8	1 966.4	-1 594.6	143.7	2 190.1	4 692.7
Manufacturing	**978.0**	**2 108.9**	**1 110.8**	**683.6**	**2 156.4**	**3 998.5**	**2 595.9**	**2 588.3**	**2 957.7**	**2 167.1**
of which:										
Food products, beverages and tobacco	90.4	29.6	262.7	223.7	187.1	406.7	457.8	296.1	204.9	96.6
Textiles, wood and paper products; printing	-2.7	-84.6	-10.1	11.5	-8.2	74.6	-4.2	123.1	36.5	106.9
Chemical, rubber, plastic, non-metallic mineral products	205.2	260.5	1 255.1	1 404.5	1 799.9	2 259.8	1 840.3	977.5	1 822.5	1 424.7
Metal and machinery products, except electrical equipment	637.1	466.1	-372.7	-159.0	24.2	875.0	299.8	1 122.1	578.5	528.6
Motor vehicles, trailers, semi-trailers, other transport equipment	5.2	116.6	-365.0	-1 099.7	-68.3	233.3	-36.8	-10.7	171.4	-158.1
Other manufacturing	42.8	376.0	340.9	302.6	221.8	149.0	62.4	80.4	143.8	168.3
Electricity, gas, steam and air conditioning supply	**-38.9**	**36.5**	**-98.5**	**30.7**	**287.8**	**944.2**	**191.2**	**217.7**	**-383.6**	**1 828.6**
Water supply; sewerage, waste management and remediation activities	**158.4**	**.. c**	**9.5**	**14.0**	**8.1**	**0.2**	**.. c**	**0.8**	**.. c**	**.. c**
Construction	**119.5**	**181.4**	**127.3**	**127.6**	**-20.5**	**134.2**	**55.1**	**108.6**	**104.7**	**-64.4**
Services	**3 315.3**	**4 184.0**	**4 144.8**	**6 129.2**	**5 199.6**	**6 381.3**	**7 592.7**	**3 354.9**	**3 416.2**	**3 254.4**
Wholesale and retail trade; repair of motor vehicles and motorcycles	749.3	960.4	1 441.5	1 679.2	1 092.5	842.6	903.4	326.4	494.4	305.6
Transportation and storage	-563.5	-577.6	-377.0	82.2	107.4	553.0	107.8	104.6	142.3	510.6
Accommodation and food service activities	13.5	14.8	19.4	30.2	37.1	-43.3	-21.6	14.5	64.4	22.4
Information and communication	65.2	741.8	437.6	1 279.0	831.9	2 463.4	2 533.5	1 673.9	1 378.2	1 156.8
Financial and insurance activities	3 126.2	2 390.8	2 305.7	1 929.2	2 092.5	45.9	114.8	479.8	346.5	587.5
Activities of holding companies	-	0.2	3.6	7.3	3.9	-1.9	138.6	26.9	0.5	-
Real estate activities	511.8	154.6	448.4	1 231.5	550.8	847.2	1 498.2	613.2	668.0	145.5
Professional, scientific and technical activities	-311.5	61.8	-266.9	17.9	245.7	1 981.3	2 208.9	-31.2	161.5	482.0
Administrative and support service activities	-290.2	-9.2	94.9	-179.5	183.9	-318.6	151.3	155.7	123.2	-14.5
Public administration; activities of households and of extraterritorial organisations	-	-	-	-	-	5.2	2.1	10.5	21.6	47.2
Education	-0.6	-	2.6	1.8	2.3	1.6	3.1	3.0	0.7	7.7
Human health and social work activities	16.8	14.5	13.8	8.5	28.2	-0.5	4.5	5.4	15.0	8.1
Arts, entertainment and recreation	15.2	29.4	16.9	26.0	30.5	1.7	-1.6	-0.7	.. c	.. c
Other services	-16.8	12.0	8.0	23.3	-3.1	1.9	0.5	-	-1.7	-1.4
Not allocated and confidential	**-14.1**	**1.9**	**63.2**	**25.3**	**17.1**	**18.2**	**-9.1**	**168.1**	**.. c**	**.. c**
Private real estate activities	-	-	-	-	-	-	-	-	-	-

- Nil; c Confidential data

Note: Data excludes resident Special Purpose Entities (SPEs). Detailed metadata at: *http://stats.oecd.org/OECDStat_Metadata/ShowMetadata.ashx?Dataset=FDI_CTRY_IND_SUMM.*

Source: OECD International Direct Investment Statistics (database): https://doi.org/10.1787/idi-data-en

POLAND

Table 1. Foreign direct investment flows by country

Million US dollars

	Inward					Outward				
	2014	2015	2016	2017	2018	2014	2015	2016	2017	2018
WORLD	**14 269.8**	**15 268.0**	**15 706.8**	**9 172.4**	**13 948.2**	**2 898.3**	**4 994.6**	**11 598.3**	**2 169.5**	**-405.9**
OECD COUNTRIES	**12 432.2**	**14 175.7**	**15 111.8**	**7 065.9**	**10 639.4**	**-1 409.7**	**1 909.5**	**12 059.8**	**3 491.4**	**-1 217.3**
Australia	-25.8	11.4	-1.7	-4.7	4.6	-7.3	-10.0	4.0	1.3	-6.9
Austria	-1 196.7	808.3	1 115.1	1 311.2	-447.8	86.2	-68.2	7.0	67.7	5.7
Belgium	1 608.9	596.0	753.0	-99.6	206.6	6.7	6.2	16.7	31.8	59.7
Canada	78.8	33.8	-29.8	17.2	24.6	147.3	611.2	3 150.6	457.9	-1 557.9
Chile	-2.6	-0.6	0.9	-0.7	-8.5	0.2	145.7	229.2	159.9	43.1
Czech Republic	-67.4	403.3	104.6	754.2	559.7	40.7	98.5	113.8	-172.5	1 201.7
Denmark	-11.0	167.1	-99.0	-34.0	123.7	15.4	-68.6	283.1	50.7	-399.3
Estonia	-91.9	6.5	3.5	-5.0	-5.7	6.4	-1.5	16.0	-23.3	64.5
Finland	-42.5	-38.8	-40.0	50.4	37.9	4.9	28.0	37.9	-1.3	7.2
France	1 601.8	-83.1	1 652.8	-913.9	-155.3	602.7	30.8	-28.4	-490.8	-357.7
Germany	1 305.8	2 789.0	3 624.3	3 763.9	1 865.8	377.4	145.0	295.7	226.8	105.0
Greece	-12.3	2.7	8.8	-10.2	9.2	0.1	0.3	6.3	6.4	1.3
Hungary	-85.1	132.2	-89.3	1 000.7	-324.0	5.9	162.0	927.9	173.2	328.4
Iceland	-0.7	0.4	7.1	6.0	-0.3	0.4	0.0	-0.4	-0.3	0.0
Ireland	516.2	70.4	-577.5	225.5	-391.5	-3.2	46.5	-208.7	55.1	-2.4
Israel[1]	48.9	114.2	77.2	-134.1	39.2	-7.1	10.7	8.2	-101.7	2.2
Italy	431.6	121.0	-468.6	-2 184.3	225.3	5.2	35.9	6.1	-67.9	29.0
Japan	-95.5	-109.6	97.5	183.1	132.3	-18.1	-7.6	0.5	-4.4	5.3
Korea	19.5	86.1	4.0	184.3	101.5	2.9	-1.7	-8.3	-15.3	3.2
Latvia	38.6	13.1	12.3	27.0	16.9	70.8	9.6	24.1	24.5	3.1
Lithuania	55.1	15.6	14.9	27.0	125.4	179.0	59.1	239.8	1.1	57.8
Luxembourg	6 257.3	2 031.2	2 140.1	2 159.1	2 060.8	-282.9	-112.1	5 724.4	627.9	1 827.7
Mexico	12.6	2.3	-41.1	-12.7	11.2	-1.1	11.9	5.5	-27.2	14.6
Netherlands	4 685.1	3 498.4	4 819.8	-1 739.1	8 754.3	-74.2	236.9	296.4	39.0	-105.2
New Zealand	0.2	-0.2	-0.1	0.5	0.1	0.3	-0.1	0.0	-0.1	-0.3
Norway	92.4	-7.7	201.2	170.0	181.0	185.0	-297.0	-116.2	258.7	206.1
Poland	-	-	-	-	-	-	-	-	-	-
Portugal	9.1	-215.5	79.4	-6.5	216.9	11.3	14.8	1.3	-3.1	40.3
Slovak Republic	-69.9	-246.9	-35.1	102.3	164.3	36.7	11.6	83.3	68.3	134.1
Slovenia	8.2	-6.8	-6.6	3.5	-10.0	-1.8	6.8	5.9	1.8	6.0
Spain	131.7	996.7	-203.6	498.1	-1 994.6	111.5	65.3	80.8	130.3	182.5
Sweden	-1 399.0	769.1	13.2	622.8	-691.8	-2 831.3	-448.9	984.8	1 927.6	-1 393.7
Switzerland	-618.8	427.6	909.6	448.1	492.1	10.7	1 133.8	314.6	-55.9	-1 685.4
Turkey	26.7	-9.7	33.0	14.8	-6.8	17.8	24.5	31.9	8.5	-1.5
United Kingdom	202.7	2 636.1	916.4	-63.2	-388.5	122.2	150.4	-218.7	42.4	40.8
United States	-886.3	-809.4	130.3	731.5	-288.9	19.5	-51.6	-15.5	95.5	-76.1
EUROPE	**14 960.8**	**15 790.9**	**15 537.7**	**8 046.7**	**13 690.6**	**2 667.6**	**4 354.2**	**8 091.2**	**1 403.2**	**1 306.6**
Bulgaria	-8.6	-7.3	62.3	-31.3	-9.2	2.7	11.8	139.3	-18.4	70.8
Croatia	-1.7	12.0	18.6	-3.0	7.6	11.5	32.8	114.0	54.0	5.9
Cyprus[2, 3]	1 419.0	1 168.9	437.2	1 601.0	1 382.6	3 805.5	2 997.5	-1 616.2	-1 835.5	365.9
Malta	227.0	-230.1	46.1	290.2	1 666.3	256.6	101.6	182.2	-68.1	64.6
Romania	1.1	6.0	12.7	0.8	-34.5	-9.4	-75.4	132.0	102.6	232.6
Russian Federation	95.0	10.2	11.7	75.1	45.3	-103.2	53.2	17.0	74.5	-3.0
Ukraine	-32.0	-54.6	-27.0	-7.6	-14.8	-45.0	-24.0	57.3	122.3	143.2
AFRICA	**-14.7**	**-5.1**	**39.2**	**34.2**	**-7.6**	**-50.7**	**9.9**	**67.2**	**52.5**	**-138.9**
Northern Africa	1.8	-14.1	20.5	14.9	-5.0	7.2	7.9	4.2	10.9	1.8
Algeria	3.5	0.0	2.6	0.1	-0.5	0.2	-	0.1	0.0	-0.1
Egypt	-4.7	-5.2	19.2	9.2	5.1	3.8	0.3	2.3	0.7	0.1
Libya	-	0.0	-	-	-	-10.3	0.0	-	0.2	1.2
Morocco	0.2	-6.7	0.8	2.6	-6.4	13.2	0.8	2.7	11.7	1.3
Tunisia	2.8	-2.1	-2.1	3.0	-3.2	0.4	6.8	-0.9	-1.7	-0.7
Other African countries	-16.4	9.0	18.8	19.3	-2.8	-58.0	2.0	63.0	41.7	-139.5
Nigeria	-0.2	0.5	-0.4	-0.1	-0.1	-0.1	0.3	0.8	1.1	0.4
South Africa	15.4	0.8	-2.4	-1.6	-3.0	-2.7	0.5	65.4	37.4	-105.1
AMERICA	**-780.2**	**-758.1**	**14.5**	**785.6**	**-311.9**	**172.4**	**733.3**	**3 449.7**	**743.1**	**-1 535.0**
Northern America	-807.4	-775.5	100.5	748.7	-264.3	166.8	559.6	3 135.1	553.4	-1 634.1
Central America and Caribbean countries	29.4	10.2	-90.9	35.9	-37.7	-4.7	20.7	93.4	8.8	10.7
Bahamas	0.7	-	-	-0.1	-0.7	-3.1	42.2	86.1	47.8	0.5
Bermuda	-5.8	-36.2	-2.0	41.4	17.4	-	-	0.0	-	-
Cayman Islands	8.8	-1.8	25.5	6.7	-48.2	-	-	0.1	-1.0	-
Costa Rica	0.2	0.5	-0.4	-	-0.4	-0.4	-	-	-	-
El Salvador	0.1	-0.1	0.0	0.0	-	-	-	-	-	-
Guatemala	-	-	-0.3	-	0.2	-	-	-	-	-
Honduras	-	-	-	-	-	-	-	0.1	-	-
Nicaragua	0.2	0.1	0.3	0.2	0.2	-	-	-	-	-
Panama	2.6	2.3	-0.5	0.3	0.7	1.4	0.3	-0.4	-9.3	-3.9
Virgin Islands, U.S.	-	-	-	-	-	-	-	-	-	-
South America	-2.2	7.3	4.9	1.1	-9.9	10.3	153.0	221.2	179.3	88.2
Argentina	0.1	-1.2	3.0	-2.6	7.3	-0.9	-0.5	0.3	2.5	0.2
Bolivia	-	-	-	0.1	-0.2	-	-0.1	-	-	-
Brazil	-3.4	7.6	3.5	0.6	-3.2	9.5	3.5	-8.0	17.9	-2.0
Colombia	0.4	-0.3	-1.4	2.1	-2.7	-0.3	-0.3	-0.5	-0.4	47.4
Ecuador	0.7	0.1	-	-	-0.1	-	-	-	-	-
Paraguay	-	-	-	-	-	-	-	-	-	-
Peru	1.1	1.2	-1.2	0.2	-0.2	1.9	-0.2	0.1	-0.4	-0.4
Uruguay	1.1	0.6	0.1	1.8	-2.6	-	0.0	0.1	-0.3	-
Venezuela	-0.1	-0.2	0.1	-0.3	0.3	-0.2	-	-	-	-

Table 1. Foreign direct investment flows by country *(cont.)*

Million US dollars

	Inward					Outward				
	2014	2015	2016	2017	2018	2014	2015	2016	2017	2018
ASIA	**107.5**	**254.0**	**116.8**	**316.2**	**570.6**	**121.0**	**-92.6**	**-13.8**	**-30.5**	**-31.3**
Near and Middle East	110.0	123.0	59.0	-108.9	81.8	60.6	5.1	34.5	-77.9	60.1
Gulf Arabian countries	63.8	12.1	-15.2	25.6	41.9	69.4	-5.3	24.9	25.3	54.5
Kuwait	49.0	-0.3	1.2	-0.1	-0.8	-	-	-	-	-
Qatar	-1.1	0.7	0.2	-0.2	0.4	-	0.0	0.0	-	-
Saudi Arabia	0.1	2.2	-1.8	-1.4	24.1	-1.0	0.1	0.1	-0.4	-1.2
United Arab Emirates	13.9	9.4	4.7	27.2	18.6	60.8	3.8	23.6	25.1	55.7
Other Near and Middle East	46.2	110.9	74.2	-134.5	39.9	-8.7	10.3	9.6	-103.2	5.6
Jordan	-	0.0	-2.8	2.8	-0.5	0.0	-	-0.1	-	0.1
Other Asian countries	-1.1	131.1	57.8	425.1	488.9	60.4	-97.7	-48.4	47.4	-91.4
China	83.9	-2.2	13.8	56.9	87.8	0.7	-15.7	9.8	-7.2	4.3
Hong Kong, China	17.7	159.1	-79.6	-25.7	28.6	1.5	-3.3	0.5	7.2	15.9
India	15.3	6.4	18.9	20.1	-13.1	31.5	-9.4	4.9	22.4	22.1
Indonesia	1.8	0.4	-2.1	-0.2	0.7	-0.8	6.4	-0.6	-0.4	4.1
Iran, Islamic Republic of	-	0.0	0.4	-0.2	-0.2	-	-	-	4.2	-0.5
Malaysia	-1.6	-14.3	-1.1	0.2	0.4	5.5	-56.9	-0.3	-4.4	2.0
Philippines	0.7	0.6	1.0	-82.3	-29.9	1.3	-1.0	-0.4	0.0	0.4
Singapore	-54.4	-11.0	-12.0	54.1	110.7	-5.4	1.2	-1.3	14.3	-137.6
Chinese Taipei	-1.7	13.7	-0.9	-1.4	20.9	0.2	0.0	-0.2	0.2	0.0
Thailand	-1.5	0.1	-3.0	46.3	57.9	1.4	0.3	6.2	-0.1	4.3
Viet Nam	0.5	2.7	12.4	-11.2	-2.4	0.1	6.0	-6.5	36.2	-0.8
AUSTRALIA, OCEANIA AND POLAR REGIONS	**-0.9**	**10.3**	**-1.5**	**-8.5**	**-1.1**	**-12.0**	**-10.1**	**4.1**	**1.3**	**-7.2**
WORLD unallocated and confidential	**-2.7**	**-24.1**	**-**	**-1.7**	**7.5**	**0.1**	**0.0**	**0.0**	**-0.1**	**0.0**
European Union (EU28)	**15 513.2**	**15 415.3**	**14 315.4**	**7 347.4**	**12 970.1**	**2 556.4**	**3 476.6**	**7 646.8**	**950.3**	**2 576.2**
G20 countries excl. European Union	**2 880.4**	**4 692.0**	**5 961.9**	**1 862.7**	**1 671.5**	**1 201.7**	**981.9**	**3 312.2**	**373.4**	**-1 882.9**
G20 OECD countries	**2 672.0**	**4 667.9**	**5 917.2**	**1 715.8**	**1 525.7**	**1 268.5**	**938.9**	**3 223.4**	**226.7**	**-1 802.2**
G20 Non-OECD countries	**208.4**	**24.1**	**44.7**	**146.8**	**145.8**	**-66.8**	**42.9**	**88.8**	**146.7**	**-80.7**
MENA countries	**62.8**	**-5.1**	**2.6**	**40.4**	**36.9**	**76.5**	**2.7**	**29.0**	**36.1**	**56.3**
ASEAN countries	**-54.4**	**-22.7**	**-2.7**	**6.7**	**135.9**	**2.1**	**-43.3**	**-3.8**	**42.3**	**-127.4**

- Nil

Note: Detailed metadata at: *http://stats.oecd.org/OECDStat_Metadata/ShowMetadata.ashx?Dataset=FDI_CTRY_IND_SUMM.*

1. Information on data for Israel: *http://oe.cd/israel-disclaimer.*
2. Note by Turkey: The information in this document with reference to "Cyprus" relates to the southern part of the Island. There is no single authority representing both Turkish and Greek Cypriot people on the Island. Turkey recognises the Turkish Republic of Northern Cyprus (TRNC). Until a lasting and equitable solution is found within the context of the United Nations, Turkey shall preserve its position concerning the "Cyprus issue".
3. Note by all the European Union Member States of the OECD and the European Union: The Republic of Cyprus is recognised by all members of the United Nations with the exception of Turkey. The information in this document relates to the area under the effective control of the Government of the Republic of Cyprus.

Source: OECD International Direct Investment Statistics (database): https://doi.org/10.1787/idi-data-en

Table 2. Foreign direct investment positions by country

At year end

Million US dollars

	Inward					Outward				
	2014	2015	2016	2017	2018	2014	2015	2016	2017	2018
WORLD	**211 496.0**	**185 986.4**	**188 760.6**	**240 382.2**	**228 501.2**	**29 966.0**	**27 935.3**	**28 307.2**	**29 615.0**	**24 594.4**
OECD COUNTRIES	**181 660.9**	**181 896.6**	**166 906.9**	**210 833.9**	**200 170.8**	**15 847.9**	**14 439.6**	**19 546.2**	**21 753.3**	**18 131.2**
Australia	180.7	227.5	341.8	424.4	699.3	3.1	-4.8	7.6	5.4	0.2
Austria	6 460.1	6 044.5	5 591.3	7 722.7	7 530.2	390.1	234.5	237.3	338.5	336.6
Belgium	3 472.1	1 869.7	1 810.1	2 961.0	2 812.2	614.6	694.1	-45.9	-150.7	-72.9
Canada	2 715.7	2 466.5	1 627.5	2 078.3	2 003.9	152.4	753.0	1 960.6	1 862.3	-218.6
Chile	0.9	0.7	1.5	0.9	0.8	5.4	147.7	482.3	522.3	566.2
Czech Republic	777.0	1 012.5	917.0	1 279.1	1 557.2	1 757.8	1 823.4	2 038.3	3 495.6	2 767.4
Denmark	3 180.8	3 426.7	2 994.7	3 564.4	3 488.8	42.6	-5.2	299.0	414.1	40.2
Estonia	11.2	15.2	11.2	18.4	14.6	12.8	9.4	9.8	-12.2	49.7
Finland	2 165.1	2 036.8	1 924.5	2 208.7	2 029.3	7.6	39.7	97.6	111.9	113.5
France	23 160.0	24 032.8	19 054.9	23 780.8	23 779.3	-173.7	-21.2	707.6	307.9	-86.4
Germany	39 031.6	34 696.4	37 405.8	47 930.0	45 938.2	1 392.3	1 2[illegible]7.0	1 305.8	1 639.5	1 611.3
Greece	23.9	605.5	213.9	236.9	226.5	0.1	0.3	7.6	14.3	15.8
Hungary	188.0	188.5	149.9	269.6	212.9	404.9	522.8	1 366.7	1 659.4	1 820.7
Iceland	36.1	68.7	22.7	39.2	45.4	-0.1	-0.1	-0.4	-0.7	0.1
Ireland	1 885.1	607.6	642.2	757.3	871.6	-10.5	28.0	-178.9	80.7	52.3
Israel[1]	799.8	841.9	792.8	943.2	984.3	145.7	178.3	269.8	152.8	138.3
Italy	12 965.9	10 635.5	7 641.2	4 916.3	4 934.5	63.2	1[illegible]2.4	107.1	138.8	136.8
Japan	3 883.0	3 759.9	4 118.6	6 167.7	5 312.9	-6.6	-[illegible]2.1	-3.0	-6.5	-1.0
Korea	1 349.8	1 949.1	1 208.6	1 747.0	1 900.5	7.7	3.9	-7.7	-15.7	-17.7
Latvia	53.7	78.3	60.1	85.9	103.1	97.7	93.7	109.8	144.5	133.5
Lithuania	156.2	133.2	249.8	292.9	500.2	961.0	869.4	1 057.2	1 074.2	1 107.4
Luxembourg	2 279.7	2 651.8	1 824.6	2 338.2	2 350.7	7 438.3	6 820.8	7 656.0	6 259.6	7 490.2
Mexico	2.1	0.4	-5.1	-8.3	14.7	0.9	[illegible]1.8	16.1	-6.2	6.5
Netherlands	7 030.6	18 276.2	16 044.0	23 052.9	20 945.7	2 763.9	2 368.8	2 204.6	2 394.2	2 519.0
New Zealand	5.6	4.9	3.0	4.1	3.9	0.6	0.4	0.4	0.4	-
Norway	1 307.9	852.1	832.4	1 669.3	1 718.2	1 079.0	5[illegible]3.9	409.8	553.3	593.7
Poland	8 813.2	7 269.2	9 691.0	10 769.0	9 164.2	-	-	-	-	-
Portugal	3 659.3	2 361.3	2 236.6	2 949.5	2 904.1	39.5	[illegible]5.6	47.5	60.7	73.5
Slovak Republic	301.0	3.1	264.5	658.9	677.0	355.7	335.3	419.5	562.3	651.3
Slovenia	123.9	78.4	66.9	71.4	70.7	6.3	[illegible]0.7	15.9	18.6	21.0
Spain	11 113.4	8 556.2	8 476.1	11 721.2	10 647.3	-241.9	-63.8	70.8	-37.9	128.0
Sweden	3 755.0	4 938.4	3 647.5	4 625.5	4 926.3	-5 759.4	-5 803.1	-4 684.3	-3 312.8	-4 542.4
Switzerland	4 837.1	6 384.0	5 045.7	6 308.3	6 143.4	3 343.3	2 279.1	2 558.7	2 376.4	591.5
Turkey	65.2	74.7	85.0	111.7	105.7	258.1	271.6	273.3	271.4	258.0
United Kingdom	12 172.0	12 323.9	11 723.0	13 863.9	11 991.5	1 001.8	1 096.0	892.6	1 101.9	1 100.3
United States	23 907.8	23 636.0	20 441.6	25 566.4	23 561.6	752.4	831.5	894.3	809.1	747.2
EUROPE	**150 669.9**	**150 591.4**	**139 486.0**	**176 173.8**	**166 285.9**	**27 752.3**	**24 935.3**	**23 425.6**	**24 822.6**	**22 111.5**
Bulgaria	4.4	6.5	8.1	21.4	24.4	48.2	57.4	92.4	83.6	145.7
Croatia	23.2	30.4	44.8	59.8	61.7	75.9	105.0	148.4	223.0	218.6
Cyprus[2, 3]	-	-	-	-	-	9 546.2	9 221.5	3 643.9	1 854.0	1 608.5
Malta	-	336.7	-	-	-	437.7	593.3	815.8	822.6	791.2
Romania	-1.6	1.7	-3.0	-8.4	-13.0	594.4	5[illegible]0.1	599.6	803.0	965.8
Russian Federation	1 416.8	1 048.0	841.4	991.1	791.8	793.2	681.3	720.7	913.1	708.7
Ukraine	112.3	-91.2	-49.4	-230.3	-305.8	83.0	[illegible]8.4	15.1	122.5	222.9
AFRICA	**1 621.8**	**211.8**	**1 173.4**	**544.7**	**617.2**	**199.2**	**226.0**	**280.9**	**311.6**	**213.3**
Northern Africa	8.3	6.7	5.9	10.7	8.4	24.8	30.5	57.2	73.5	73.4
Algeria	-	-	-	-	-	0.1	0.1	0.2	0.2	0.1
Egypt	-	-	-	-	-	-26.0	-23.3	2.8	1.6	0.9
Libya	-	-	-	-	-	-1.5	-0.7	-0.7	-0.6	0.5
Morocco	8.3	6.7	5.9	10.7	8.4	51.7	47.8	49.6	66.7	65.7
Tunisia	-	-	-	-	-	0.4	6.6	5.4	5.6	6.2
Other African countries	1 613.5	205.1	1 167.5	534.0	608.8	174.5	195.5	223.7	238.1	140.0
Nigeria	-	-	-	-	-	0.6	3.5	4.5	4.9	5.3
South Africa	1 530.8	133.3	1 167.5	534.0	608.8	2.3	1.5	64.1	117.5	8.3
AMERICA	**26 640.3**	**26 197.5**	**22 069.1**	**27 639.1**	**25 585.3**	**1 005.5**	**1 847.9**	**3 537.5**	**3 438.3**	**1 389.3**
Northern America	26 623.6	26 102.5	22 069.1	27 644.7	25 565.4	904.7	1 584.5	2 854.9	2 671.4	528.6
Central America and Caribbean countries	12.7	91.9	-3.7	-6.7	16.3	65.4	80.8	174.6	198.2	207.6
Bahamas	-	-	-	-	-	34.9	73.6	161.3	214.5	212.1
Bermuda	8.8	56.7	-	-	-	-	-	-	-	-
Cayman Islands	-	-	-	-	-	-	-	0.0	-	-
Costa Rica	-	-	-	-	-	-	-	-	-	-
El Salvador	-	-	-	-	-	-	-	-	-	-
Guatemala	-	-	-	-	-	-	-	-	-	-
Honduras	-	-	-	-	-	-	-	-	-	-
Nicaragua	-	-	-	-	-	-	-	-	-	-
Panama	-	8.5	-	-	-	10.6	10.7	10.5	4.2	3.7
Virgin Islands, U.S.	-	-	-	-	-	-	-	-	-	-
South America	4.1	3.1	3.7	1.0	3.6	35.3	132.6	508.0	569.3	653.7
Argentina	-	-	-	-	-	1.2	1.1	0.9	0.7	1.1
Bolivia	-	-	-	-	-	-	-0.1	-	-	-
Brazil	-	-	0.0	0.1	-0.7	26.5	32.3	23.8	45.5	41.7
Colombia	-	-	-	-	-	-0.4	-0.7	-1.1	-1.4	44.0
Ecuador	-	-	-	-	-	-	-	-	-	-
Paraguay	-	-	-	-	-	-	-	-	-	-
Peru	-	-	-	-	-	2.6	2.3	1.8	2.2	0.7
Uruguay	3.2	2.4	2.3	-	3.4	0.1	0.1	0.3	-	0.0
Venezuela	-	-	-	-	-	-	-	-	-	-

Table 2. Foreign direct investment positions by country *(cont.)*

At year end

Million US dollars

	Inward					Outward				
	2014	2015	2016	2017	2018	2014	2015	2016	2017	2018
ASIA	**7 907.5**	**9 112.8**	**8 323.8**	**11 571.6**	**11 521.9**	**1 004.8**	**930.4**	**1 055.1**	**1 036.7**	**880.2**
Near and Middle East	1 129.7	1 125.0	1 027.8	1 198.2	1 232.1	283.2	320.7	441.7	356.0	354.7
Gulf Arabian countries	306.1	259.2	213.3	230.7	223.0	137.0	141.0	169.2	201.6	210.8
Kuwait	74.0	49.6	46.5	49.9	42.9	0.0	0.0	0.0	0.0	0.0
Qatar	190.7	167.8	137.5	169.1	158.6	-	-	-	-	-
Saudi Arabia	12.9	40.6	25.1	1.0	17.7	0.8	0.8	0.9	0.5	0.1
United Arab Emirates	28.5	1.2	4.3	10.7	3.9	127.3	141.5	168.6	200.9	210.6
Other Near and Middle East	823.6	865.8	814.5	967.5	1 009.1	146.2	179.7	272.5	154.4	143.8
Jordan	-	-	-	-	-	-	-	-0.1	-0.1	-
Other Asian countries	6 777.8	7 987.8	7 296.0	10 373.4	10 289.8	721.6	609.6	613.4	680.7	525.4
China	501.9	927.5	707.2	847.8	941.8	86.8	80.1	87.5	83.9	82.4
Hong Kong, China	295.9	517.8	412.2	454.1	275.9	6.4	5.4	8.7	1.3	15.2
India	184.0	206.6	251.5	271.8	276.9	256.9	235.1	236.1	250.6	247.1
Indonesia	-	-	-	-	-	19.1	26.3	26.2	22.9	27.1
Iran, Islamic Republic of	-	-	5.9	12.6	6.2	-	-	-	6.0	5.2
Malaysia	17.5	10.7	259.2	246.3	639.1	82.9	27.5	28.2	26.3	26.6
Philippines	23.0	52.8	44.6	51.3	46.4	8.6	7.3	8.2	8.1	8.2
Singapore	171.2	234.8	24.4	235.1	511.0	96.0	97.0	122.7	126.3	-10.6
Chinese Taipei	287.6	295.8	234.4	268.1	281.4	-1.8	0.1	-0.1	0.4	-1.5
Thailand	63.9	32.9	26.8	63.8	98.8	11.9	10.6	15.8	17.8	21.9
Viet Nam	-	-	2.5	2.2	-1.2	12.4	16.4	0.1	44.8	18.9
AUSTRALIA, OCEANIA AND POLAR REGIONS	**187.4**	**232.4**	**344.8**	**428.5**	**702.9**	**3.7**	**-4.3**	**8.1**	**5.9**	**0.2**
WORLD unallocated and confidential	**26 443.8**	**593.8**	**18 353.6**	**25 134.1**	**23 788.0**	**0.5**	**0.0**	**-**	**-**	**-**
European Union (EU28)	**142 804.9**	**142 217.0**	**132 690.3**	**166 147.5**	**157 749.4**	**21 867.2**	**20 916.0**	**19 041.6**	**20 089.2**	**19 196.4**
G20 countries excl. European Union	**123 080.4**	**116 158.7**	**106 635.5**	**129 224.2**	**122 878.3**	**4 638.3**	**5 317.7**	**7 314.5**	**7 542.9**	**4 653.0**
G20 OECD countries	**119 433.9**	**113 802.8**	**103 643.0**	**126 578.4**	**120 242.0**	**3 451.6**	**4 259.1**	**6 154.3**	**6 108.1**	**3 536.6**
G20 Non-OECD countries	**3 646.5**	**2 355.9**	**2 992.6**	**2 645.8**	**2 636.3**	**1 186.7**	**1 058.5**	**1 160.2**	**1 434.8**	**1 116.4**
MENA countries	**338.1**	**289.8**	**235.1**	**257.0**	**246.5**	**161.3**	**171.6**	**226.5**	**275.0**	**284.3**
ASEAN countries	**275.6**	**331.1**	**357.6**	**598.7**	**1 294.1**	**231.0**	**185.8**	**201.2**	**242.6**	**92.2**

- Nil

Note: Inward FDI positions are allocated according to the ultimate investing country. Detailed metadata at: *http://stats.oecd.org/OECDStat_Metadata/ShowMetadata.ashx?Dataset=FDI_CTRY_IND_SUMM.*

1. Information on data for Israel: *http://oe.cd/israel-disclaimer.*
2. Note by Turkey: The information in this document with reference to "Cyprus" relates to the southern part of the Island. There is no single authority representing both Turkish and Greek Cypriot people on the Island. Turkey recognises the Turkish Republic of Northern Cyprus (TRNC). Until a lasting and equitable solution is found within the context of the United Nations, Turkey shall preserve its position concerning the "Cyprus issue".
3. Note by all the European Union Member States of the OECD and the European Union: The Republic of Cyprus is recognised by all members of the United Nations with the exception of Turkey. The information in this document relates to the area under the effective control of the Government of the Republic of Cyprus.

Source: OECD International Direct Investment Statistics (database): https://doi.org/10.1787/idi-data-en

Table 3. Foreign direct investment income by country

Million US dollars

	Inward					Outward				
	2014	2015	2016	2017	2018	2014	2015	2016	2017	2018
WORLD	**20 330.2**	**17 905.4**	**20 777.9**	**21 490.7**	**23 952.6**	**1 596.7**	**814.8**	**1 004.5**	**2 286.9**	**2 265.6**
OECD COUNTRIES	**19 673.1**	**17 773.7**	**20 062.0**	**20 394.5**	**22 817.6**	**862.6**	**106.6**	**421.2**	**1 495.3**	**1 579.4**
Australia	2.4	1.9	2.0	1.9	-2.1	-1.4	-5.7	-2.0	-1.3	0.0
Austria	686.7	707.0	503.1	795.3	662.5	20.8	19.5	6.5	-1.7	-1.8
Belgium	488.5	442.9	399.8	371.6	312.7	12.8	12.8	7.3	-2.4	-6.9
Canada	29.6	32.1	29.2	25.3	23.4	1.6	12.0	-1 722.5	552.5	28.7
Chile	0.0	0.0	0.0	-	-	-1.5	-1.5	31.5	39.3	47.5
Czech Republic	-16.6	100.8	116.8	94.8	129.5	84.2	110.3	170.1	234.7	221.2
Denmark	198.9	350.9	271.9	307.1	317.7	1.0	18.5	2.7	-1.1	-6.6
Estonia	3.9	2.4	2.2	-8.3	-10.9	0.9	0.8	1.4	0.0	-0.6
Finland	184.3	185.6	168.4	221.4	284.6	-2.3	-0.1	11.1	8.8	4.3
France	2 114.2	1 730.5	1 672.3	1 991.5	1 896.9	-8.5	-14.1	6.7	2.9	-25.9
Germany	4 192.7	3 635.0	4 030.0	4 479.1	4 651.3	109.8	76.0	230.2	156.2	300.0
Greece	-16.0	5.5	5.8	2.3	2.2	0.1	-0.1	0.0	-0.5	0.3
Hungary	42.3	28.1	28.1	79.0	44.0	-26.3	41.4	58.5	93.7	249.7
Iceland	1.4	1.8	-0.4	1.3	0.6	-	-	-	-	-
Ireland	205.4	60.5	134.9	129.9	147.2	-2.9	-0.8	-0.2	0.3	3.1
Israel[1]	4.8	0.8	4.0	13.9	9.9	8.4	9.3	9.0	1.1	0.4
Italy	1 069.7	882.7	897.5	731.6	687.2	7.8	-2.8	0.1	-85.5	-21.8
Japan	80.9	30.2	37.3	193.6	63.4	-0.4	-	-	-	-
Korea	139.8	73.9	59.3	89.4	80.5	0.7	0.7	-0.1	-0.2	-1.3
Latvia	33.7	16.2	27.3	50.3	59.0	-0.1	11.0	9.6	13.0	17.1
Lithuania	15.8	11.5	6.8	17.8	-16.2	-90.5	332.3	286.8	323.1	104.4
Luxembourg	1 742.3	1 958.3	2 812.0	2 351.8	3 355.0	381.8	-61.7	1 727.8	128.7	321.6
Mexico	0.2	0.2	0.1	0.4	0.8	-	-0.6	-2.8	-0.4	3.3
Netherlands	4 467.9	4 027.0	4 807.1	4 606.6	6 109.3	-162.7	-6.7	30.3	84.4	60.7
New Zealand	0.2	-0.1	0.0	-0.1	-0.2	-	-	-	-	-
Norway	89.4	102.0	14.2	135.2	158.4	26.4	71.1	-10.8	213.9	208.6
Poland	-	-	-	-	-	-	-	-	-	-
Portugal	148.1	138.8	116.0	117.6	139.3	6.6	7.8	6.9	1.1	1.6
Slovak Republic	-33.8	24.9	17.2	13.2	27.3	463.8	47.2	58.5	69.0	104.4
Slovenia	10.8	7.8	7.2	7.6	7.1	0.9	2.5	3.0	1.9	1.4
Spain	778.1	710.9	736.7	821.4	802.2	-36.6	-18.3	19.0	10.8	16.6
Sweden	831.9	863.5	661.7	360.1	436.9	-99.6	-116.4	-111.4	-82.8	-140.8
Switzerland	546.0	505.5	676.0	704.0	702.7	76.3	42.9	31.5	78.0	35.7
Turkey	6.4	0.5	0.6	-3.4	-2.6	-16.7	2.0	28.4	4.2	1.9
United Kingdom	1 061.1	972.4	902.6	1 197.5	1 282.9	-5.5	4.8	-190.5	-4.3	52.7
United States	611.5	189.4	920.8	511.8	455.0	23.0	-143.9	11.4	-18.8	-0.1
EUROPE	**19 187.7**	**17 546.8**	**19 706.8**	**20 591.3**	**23 212.1**	**1 560.2**	**924.6**	**2 661.2**	**1 656.8**	**2 101.4**
Bulgaria	-4.3	-0.1	-4.8	-5.4	2.5	1.6	6.2	3.1	15.7	19.9
Croatia	3.5	4.2	3.2	6.5	7.7	1.3	-0.6	3.0	8.6	14.6
Cyprus[2, 3]	117.1	95.1	588.0	915.2	971.6	867.4	286.3	133.4	57.7	30.4
Malta	246.9	-15.7	58.6	95.7	42.3	-13.8	44.3	22.4	82.4	224.9
Romania	-2.6	-2.1	0.2	1.6	2.2	9.8	-53.2	-30.7	51.6	79.4
Russian Federation	12.6	4.0	24.9	19.4	13.6	21.1	41.0	33.5	57.9	37.0
Ukraine	-26.6	-15.9	-14.1	-13.7	-14.7	-89.3	5.3	80.9	93.0	129.0
AFRICA	**210.5**	**-12.7**	**1.2**	**2.2**	**3.5**	**-50.3**	**3.3**	**-5.1**	**8.0**	**6.2**
Northern Africa	1.2	-0.3	0.2	0.8	0.7	3.8	3.8	4.6	4.5	2.8
Algeria	-	-0.1	-0.1	-	-	-	-	-	-	-
Egypt	-	-	-	-	-	3.6	0.2	2.3	0.7	0.0
Libya	-	-	-	-	-	-1.8	0.1	-0.1	0.1	0.4
Morocco	1.2	-0.3	0.2	0.8	0.7	1.6	3.6	3.2	5.4	3.1
Tunisia	-	-	-	-	-	0.4	-0.1	-0.8	-1.7	-0.7
Other African countries	209.3	-12.4	1.0	1.4	2.7	-54.1	-0.5	-9.7	3.5	3.5
Nigeria	-	-	-	-	-	0.1	0.1	0.0	0.1	0.2
South Africa	209.6	-	-	-	0.3	-2.2	-0.2	-2.6	1.8	0.2
AMERICA	**657.8**	**220.8**	**912.8**	**544.3**	**500.8**	**26.9**	**-128.9**	**-1 681.2**	**570.2**	**85.8**
Northern America	641.1	221.6	950.1	537.1	478.4	24.7	-131.9	-1 711.1	533.7	28.5
Central America and Caribbean countries	15.6	-0.3	-37.1	7.3	22.6	3.7	3.8	-2.8	-3.0	10.5
Bahamas	-	-	-	1.6	-	2.4	4.4	0.9	7.4	10.6
Bermuda	-1.7	-3.1	-6.5	0.1	17.4	-	-	-	-	-
Cayman Islands	8.8	3.1	-33.5	-3.9	1.2	-	-	-	-0.9	-
Costa Rica	-	-	-	-	-	-	-	-	-	-
El Salvador	-	-	-	-	-	-	-	-	-	-
Guatemala	-	-	-	-	-	-	-	-	-	-
Honduras	-	-	-	-	-	-	-	-	-	-
Nicaragua	0.2	0.1	0.1	0.2	0.2	-	-	-	-	-
Panama	0.4	0.1	0.3	-0.1	-0.1	1.6	0.2	-0.5	-9.7	-3.5
Virgin Islands, U.S.	-	-	-	-	-	-	-	-	-	-
South America	1.1	-0.4	-0.2	-	-0.2	-1.5	-0.9	32.7	39.5	46.7
Argentina	-	-	-	-	-	0.3	-0.4	0.0	0.2	0.1
Bolivia	-	-	-	-	-	-	-	-	-	-
Brazil	0.5	-	-	-	0.0	-0.3	1.2	1.3	0.2	-
Colombia	-	-	-	-	-	0.0	-0.1	-0.2	-0.1	-0.8
Ecuador	0.8	-	-	-	-	-	-	-	-	-
Paraguay	-	-	-	-	-	-	-	-	-	-
Peru	-	-	-	-	-	-	-0.1	-0.1	-0.1	-0.1
Uruguay	-0.2	-0.5	-0.2	-	-0.2	-	0.0	0.1	-0.1	-
Venezuela	-	-	-	-	-	-	-	-	-	-

Table 3. Foreign direct investment income by country *(cont.)*

Million US dollars

	Inward					Outward				
	2014	2015	2016	2017	2018	2014	2015	2016	2017	2018
ASIA	**271.3**	**148.7**	**155.0**	**352.9**	**238.7**	**66.4**	**21.4**	**31.6**	**53.4**	**72.5**
Near and Middle East	19.1	23.3	16.9	27.9	26.5	32.7	29.7	41.9	25.2	49.0
Gulf Arabian countries	15.7	25.2	12.7	17.0	17.4	25.3	20.5	33.1	24.1	48.5
Kuwait	0.3	1.2	1.0	1.9	0.9	-	-	-	-	-
Qatar	-	-	-	-	-	-	-	-	-	-
Saudi Arabia	-	-	-0.2	-0.3	-0.1	0.1	-	-	-0.1	-0.4
United Arab Emirates	13.3	20.1	11.9	15.4	16.6	22.4	23.4	33.6	24.2	48.9
Other Near and Middle East	3.4	-1.9	4.2	10.9	9.1	7.4	9.2	8.8	1.1	0.4
Jordan	-	-	-	-	-	-	-	-	-	-
Other Asian countries	252.2	125.4	138.1	325.0	212.2	33.7	-8.3	-10.4	28.2	23.5
China	6.9	-2.3	5.2	8.2	14.8	-0.4	-4.2	-4.4	-4.4	-5.8
Hong Kong, China	8.4	9.8	0.6	17.9	18.7	-1.0	-2.0	-0.6	-5.8	2.9
India	13.9	10.2	17.3	17.5	13.0	16.9	14.9	14.1	12.8	25.8
Indonesia	-	-	-	-	-	-0.7	0.6	-2.0	-1.0	0.6
Iran, Islamic Republic of	-	-	0.3	-	-	-	-	-	0.0	0.1
Malaysia	1.0	1.0	0.9	-0.1	-0.4	-0.1	-1.2	-1.0	0.2	-0.7
Philippines	-	-	-0.1	-	0.1	-	-	0.6	0.1	0.0
Singapore	0.6	0.1	5.8	-3.0	19.8	-0.1	8.6	10.5	29.1	9.1
Chinese Taipei	-2.2	0.8	2.2	2.3	-1.6	-	-	0.0	0.0	0.0
Thailand	1.7	1.1	-	0.4	3.8	0.5	1.9	2.0	-1.3	0.9
Viet Nam	1.0	0.6	9.5	-1.1	0.2	0.0	-	-	0.2	3.2
AUSTRALIA, OCEANIA AND POLAR REGIONS	**2.9**	**1.8**	**2.1**	**-0.5**	**-3.1**	**-6.5**	**-5.7**	**-2.0**	**-1.3**	**0.0**
WORLD unallocated and confidential	**0.1**	**0.0**	**-**	**0.5**	**0.6**	**0.0**	**0.0**	**0.0**	**-0.2**	**-0.3**
European Union (EU28)	**18 570.7**	**16 944.4**	**18 970.6**	**19 752.6**	**22 354.0**	**1 521.8**	**746.7**	**2 465.7**	**1 166.2**	**1 624.0**
G20 countries excl. European Union	**9 551.9**	**7 560.7**	**8 599.2**	**9 263.2**	**9 178.2**	**145.3**	**-18.7**	**-1 601.1**	**672.7**	**395.0**
G20 OECD countries	**9 308.6**	**7 548.8**	**8 551.9**	**9 218.6**	**9 136.6**	**110.6**	**-71.7**	**-1 641.1**	**605.3**	**337.5**
G20 Non-OECD countries	**243.4**	**11.9**	**47.3**	**44.6**	**41.5**	**34.7**	**52.9**	**40.0**	**67.4**	**57.5**
MENA countries	**15.6**	**22.1**	**13.1**	**14.9**	**17.6**	**29.1**	**24.3**	**37.7**	**28.6**	**51.3**
ASEAN countries	**4.3**	**2.8**	**15.9**	**-3.8**	**23.5**	**-0.3**	**9.9**	**10.1**	**24.1**	**13.5**

- Nil

Note: Detailed metadata at: *http://stats.oecd.org/OECDStat_Metadata/ShowMetadata.ashx?Dataset=FDI_CTRY_IND_SUMM.*

1. Information on data for Israel: *http://oe.cd/israel-disclaimer.*
2. Note by Turkey: The information in this document with reference to "Cyprus" relates to the southern part of the Island. There is no single authority representing both Turkish and Greek Cypriot people on the Island. Turkey recognises the Turkish Republic of Northern Cyprus (TRNC). Until a lasting and equitable solution is found within the context of the United Nations, Turkey shall preserve its position concerning the "Cyprus issue".
3. Note by all the European Union Member States of the OECD and the European Union: The Republic of Cyprus is recognised by all members of the United Nations with the exception of Turkey. The information in this document relates to the area under the effective control of the Government of the Republic of Cyprus.

Source: OECD International Direct Investment Statistics (database): https://doi.org/10.1787/idi-data-en

POLAND

Table 4. Foreign direct investment flows by industrial sector

Million US dollars

	Inward					Outward				
	2014	2015	2016	2017	2018	2014	2015	2016	2017	2018
All FDI activities	**14 269.8**	**15 268.0**	**15 706.8**	**9 172.4**	**13 948.2**	**2 898.3**	**4 954.6**	**11 598.3**	**2 169.5**	**-405.9**
Agriculture, forestry and fishing	**95.0**	**31.4**	**67.6**	**142.5**	**-22.5**	**-3.1**	**-0.6**	**-13.1**	**-8.4**	**5.9**
Mining and quarrying	**-563.2**	**-82.2**	**43.1**	**86.8**	**168.3**	**433.1**	**1 245.1**	**3 287.1**	**918.4**	**488.6**
Extraction activities	-215.2	-89.8	-3.4	12.6	112.4	-148.0	89.1	466.0	323.7	207.1
Manufacturing	**3 675.1**	**3 155.4**	**3 829.9**	**4 679.8**	**5 956.4**	**-926.6**	**-280.4**	**52.1**	**96.1**	**2 349.5**
of which:										
Food products, beverages and tobacco	32.5	465.0	1 102.8	606.4	591.7	11.6	-97.0	-33.5	54.6	236.5
Textiles, wood and paper products; printing	1 131.4	586.3	-221.4	640.1	466.2	69.1	54.5	241.6	-44.5	20.5
Chemical, rubber, plastic, non-metallic mineral products	611.1	-257.5	-255.6	802.0	1 025.0	-1 295.2	-235.7	-238.2	-262.3	1 659.6
Metal and machinery products, except electrical equipment	847.7	528.9	1 222.8	947.6	1 408.3	93.2	-6.1	283.7	244.7	505.9
Motor vehicles, trailers, semi-trailers, other transport equipment	1 332.6	1 231.4	1 258.7	1 052.2	989.9	143.3	66.2	-274.2	110.9	-131.7
Other manufacturing	-280.2	601.3	722.7	631.5	1 475.2	51.4	-84.4	72.8	-7.2	58.8
Electricity, gas, steam and air conditioning supply	**575.0**	**-71.5**	**-478.1**	**-1 382.1**	**260.3**	**-1 007.0**	**-401.9**	**1.9**	**524.5**	**-202.1**
Water supply; sewerage, waste management and remediation activities	**5.2**	**14.8**	**5.3**	**26.8**	**14.6**	**5.2**	**1.0**	**4.8**	**11.5**	**17.9**
Construction	**1 239.7**	**338.4**	**889.2**	**953.6**	**992.9**	**-6.5**	**133.3**	**446.5**	**-12.8**	**49.6**
Services	**9 174.4**	**11 629.4**	**12 067.6**	**5 310.5**	**7 262.1**	**2 923.3**	**3 714.8**	**7 691.5**	**836.9**	**-2 657.7**
Wholesale and retail trade; repair of motor vehicles and motorcycles	755.0	2 883.7	2 369.8	-1 434.0	3 870.0	43.0	226.3	1 153.5	515.4	105.6
Transportation and storage	69.2	294.1	-11.1	583.4	716.7	-19.1	197.6	114.3	65.5	29.4
Accommodation and food service activities	28.4	39.7	2.1	89.1	195.2	5.3	198.2	154.1	103.6	40.6
Information and communication	3 852.6	1 737.8	3 330.6	1 875.1	-1 491.2	30.2	-396.4	1 750.0	1 010.2	73.8
Financial and insurance activities	-38.0	1 675.4	1 377.2	2 960.4	858.1	2 207.2	4 784.5	-1 055.5	-455.6	-2 379.8
Activities of holding companies	-41.0	1 034.6	854.9	4 159.7	276.4	2 346.4	4 165.7	-225.6	-298.8	-2 170.6
Real estate activities	1 756.7	1 862.6	1 670.1	1 640.5	754.3	-146.9	445.3	840.2	-150.5	-181.5
Professional, scientific and technical activities	2 134.2	2 874.2	3 118.0	-822.2	1 794.4	1 121.2	-1 635.2	2 816.1	-371.9	-5.1
Administrative and support service activities	487.7	171.2	106.8	302.8	337.2	-429.9	-70.9	2 049.8	124.8	-342.9
Public administration; activities of households and of extraterritorial organisations	-8.8	-1.8	-	-	-	-	-	-	-4.2	-
Education	1.6	-5.0	8.4	2.0	-4.5	7.7	4.9	-17.1	-3.4	0.2
Human health and social work activities	62.4	77.0	51.9	46.9	83.6	-1.2	1.3	-0.4	2.4	17.2
Arts, entertainment and recreation	86.1	5.9	36.6	40.7	144.4	5.8	1.4	2.9	2.7	-2.9
Other services	-12.7	14.6	7.0	25.8	4.0	100.0	-42.1	-116.5	-2.1	-12.4
Not allocated and confidential	**68.6**	**252.3**	**-717.7**	**-645.5**	**-684.0**	**1 479.9**	**583.5**	**127.6**	**-196.7**	**-457.7**
Private real estate activities	-	-	-	-	-	-	-	-	-	-

- Nil

Note: Detailed metadata at: *http://stats.oecd.org/OECDStat_Metadata/ShowMetadata.ashx?Dataset=FDI_CTRY_IND_SUMM.*

Source: *OECD International Direct Investment Statistics (database): https://doi.org/10.1787/idi-data-en*

Table 5. Foreign direct investment positions by industrial sector

At year end

Million US dollars

	Inward					Outward				
	2014	2015	2016	2017	2018	2014	2015	2016	2017	2018
All FDI activities	**211 496.0**	**185 986.4**	**188 760.6**	**240 382.2**	**228 501.2**	**29 966.0**	**27 935.3**	**28 307.2**	**29 615.0**	**24 594.4**
Agriculture, forestry and fishing	**1 018.3**	**992.3**	**979.8**	**1 220.4**	**1 100.9**	**18.3**	**11.8**	**4.2**	**4.2**	**21.0**
Mining and quarrying	**757.9**	**569.3**	**512.5**	**592.1**	**748.5**	**1 467.4**	**2 516.1**	**2 903.6**	**2 937.0**	**1 187.9**
Extraction activities	355.8	224.1	70.4	95.9	224.8	724.8	624.5	1 012.3	1 306.7	1 243.5
Manufacturing	**61 908.5**	**60 201.9**	**59 236.6**	**77 743.9**	**71 669.4**	**3 724.4**	**3 876.0**	**4 213.9**	**5 382.8**	**5 425.6**
of which:										
Food products, beverages and tobacco	11 435.2	11 079.0	11 805.9	15 861.6	13 422.7	269.3	734.9	689.8	705.9	946.8
Textiles, wood and paper products; printing	6 447.0	6 623.1	5 937.7	7 479.9	7 004.0	190.8	247.2	366.3	308.8	267.4
Chemical, rubber, plastic, non-metallic mineral products	11 760.7	10 946.1	9 490.6	12 591.5	11 099.2	1 377.2	1 346.0	1 312.6	2 089.6	1 748.1
Metal and machinery products, except electrical equipment	11 757.5	10 651.0	10 902.1	14 251.4	13 913.2	842.1	836.0	1 063.9	1 387.2	1 739.0
Motor vehicles, trailers, semi-trailers, other transport equipment	11 035.7	11 253.6	11 594.5	14 940.1	14 443.9	750.0	556.2	497.0	589.3	480.1
Other manufacturing	9 472.3	9 649.2	9 505.8	12 619.3	11 786.2	294.9	155.6	284.4	302.1	244.1
Electricity, gas, steam and air conditioning supply	**6 799.3**	**6 631.3**	**5 438.8**	**5 206.9**	**4 878.0**	**-1 454.3**	**-1 496.8**	**-1 329.4**	**-926.1**	**-1 054.2**
Water supply; sewerage, waste management and remediation activities	**477.2**	**414.0**	**418.0**	**528.9**	**482.6**	**0.3**	**2.6**	**20.2**	**36.2**	**39.8**
Construction	**9 431.2**	**9 218.0**	**9 028.9**	**12 178.6**	**11 996.2**	**-83.5**	**-20.3**	**443.8**	**601.3**	**495.7**
Services	**124 196.7**	**107 959.6**	**114 115.0**	**145 042.2**	**134 630.0**	**24 009.0**	**22 809.3**	**21 557.4**	**21 164.4**	**18 120.2**
Wholesale and retail trade; repair of motor vehicles and motorcycles	29 697.0	28 551.3	28 387.8	33 784.8	33 352.9	2 158.0	1 597.9	2 786.1	3 513.9	2 941.8
Transportation and storage	3 225.3	2 619.9	2 184.1	3 097.5	3 404.2	335.8	542.5	620.0	724.0	515.6
Accommodation and food service activities	719.0	974.7	968.2	1 438.9	1 671.7	-90.1	99.2	197.7	346.6	499.5
Information and communication	12 383.0	10 302.0	12 560.0	15 416.5	12 206.7	-1 698.4	-1 933.8	-25.1	640.5	704.4
Financial and insurance activities	47 729.3	33 638.0	34 432.9	49 361.0	42 343.5	13 165.8	14 161.9	9 756.5	9 075.4	7 807.2
Activities of holding companies	2 073.3	2 759.2	3 631.0	8 155.9	7 340.1	9 720.5	10 488.8	6 729.7	5 511.8	5 047.9
Real estate activities	14 301.0	15 376.2	16 680.8	21 103.9	21 919.6	552.4	551.5	787.2	466.7	381.9
Professional, scientific and technical activities	12 306.8	12 711.7	15 524.7	16 479.5	15 332.3	5 086.6	3 480.0	5 856.4	4 755.8	4 369.6
Administrative and support service activities	2 658.1	2 558.7	2 347.9	3 004.6	2 935.2	3 890.7	3 802.5	1 221.1	1 260.7	566.2
Public administration; activities of households and of extraterritorial organisations	28.2	23.2	-	-	-	0.7	0.6	0.6	0.7	0.7
Education	17.4	15.7	13.5	12.2	19.9	32.2	30.0	8.0	-3.7	-4.3
Human health and social work activities	781.4	804.5	764.6	970.4	968.8	3.9	4.2	4.7	-8.3	10.6
Arts, entertainment and recreation	260.6	265.2	137.9	202.3	325.6	42.0	50.4	37.0	45.2	39.0
Other services	89.6	118.5	112.6	170.7	149.7	529.4	422.4	307.2	346.7	288.1
Not allocated and confidential	**6 906.9**	**0.0**	**-968.9**	**-2 130.8**	**2 995.4**	**2 284.3**	**236.5**	**493.5**	**415.3**	**358.5**
Private real estate activities	-	-	-	-	-	-	-	-	-	-

- Nil

Note: Detailed metadata at: *http://stats.oecd.org/OECDStat_Metadata/ShowMetadata.ashx?Dataset=FDI_CTRY_IND_SUMM.*

Source: OECD International Direct Investment Statistics (database): https://doi.org/10.1787/idi-data-en

Table 6. Foreign direct investment income by industrial sector

Million US dollars

	Inward					Outward				
	2014	2015	2016	2017	2018	2014	2015	2016	2017	2018
All FDI activities	**20 330.2**	**17 905.4**	**20 777.9**	**21 490.7**	**23 952.6**	**1 596.7**	**814.8**	**1 004.5**	**2 286.9**	**2 265.6**
Agriculture, forestry and fishing	**74.8**	**82.1**	**85.7**	**35.4**	**49.0**	**-0.7**	**0.0**	**0.7**	**0.4**	**1.6**
Mining and quarrying	**-273.9**	**-130.2**	**-69.1**	**-41.4**	**33.8**	**-138.3**	**68.4**	**-1 659.0**	**784.4**	**284.0**
Extraction activities	-266.1	-134.1	-41.2	-41.3	4.2	-136.2	46.5	-20.7	193.0	198.5
Manufacturing	**8 313.1**	**7 474.9**	**7 876.9**	**8 380.4**	**9 251.7**	**25.4**	**246.3**	**638.2**	**595.3**	**439.1**
of which:										
Food products, beverages and tobacco	1 376.8	1 140.6	1 303.0	1 392.7	1 461.0	9.4	8.4	49.1	42.6	31.0
Textiles, wood and paper products; printing	904.9	895.5	792.1	873.0	1 054.2	-21.0	6.0	103.4	31.3	88.2
Chemical, rubber, plastic, non-metallic mineral products	1 506.2	1 100.1	1 300.9	1 432.7	1 777.5	-77.2	167.8	325.8	392.6	117.8
Metal and machinery products, except electrical equipment	1 688.0	1 558.0	1 733.4	1 640.2	1 842.5	62.6	56.9	105.8	76.3	156.0
Motor vehicles, trailers, semi-trailers, other transport equipment	1 505.6	1 346.2	1 509.4	1 880.7	1 760.8	37.0	7.9	46.9	44.8	37.2
Other manufacturing	1 331.6	1 434.5	1 238.0	1 161.0	1 355.7	14.7	-0.7	7.0	7.7	8.8
Electricity, gas, steam and air conditioning supply	**534.1**	**256.2**	**-59.4**	**376.2**	**466.8**	**-46.7**	**-45.4**	**-46.3**	**-20.5**	**-25.7**
Water supply; sewerage, waste management and remediation activities	**28.0**	**31.4**	**45.6**	**52.5**	**40.8**	**2.5**	**0.0**	**0.9**	**0.4**	**0.4**
Construction	**249.3**	**384.2**	**742.6**	**481.1**	**745.1**	**27.2**	**30.2**	**3.5**	**-38.3**	**16.1**
Services	**11 404.5**	**9 808.9**	**12 152.5**	**12 205.9**	**13 364.5**	**1 700.9**	**508.9**	**2 059.4**	**960.4**	**1 492.6**
Wholesale and retail trade; repair of motor vehicles and motorcycles	3 490.6	2 841.1	3 418.7	4 169.8	4 703.3	126.4	206.6	167.6	386.7	486.7
Transportation and storage	602.9	510.9	547.7	652.0	809.7	-50.0	5.9	8.5	0.9	51.2
Accommodation and food service activities	27.7	46.8	87.2	96.8	90.4	-20.3	18.2	31.7	38.0	63.4
Information and communication	1 501.5	1 740.3	1 482.2	2 096.5	1 054.2	36.0	48.5	37.4	43.0	99.0
Financial and insurance activities	3 524.2	2 591.6	2 514.3	2 435.6	3 118.2	745.2	188.5	-93.2	55.6	458.9
Activities of holding companies	-118.2	101.0	94.4	283.1	272.8	714.2	84.8	-40.4	-48.6	295.3
Real estate activities	865.6	852.6	1 718.0	962.9	1 683.2	-74.3	-14.0	82.5	52.9	89.7
Professional, scientific and technical activities	1 071.0	1 137.7	1 553.4	1 285.1	1 425.5	843.7	23.9	2.7	147.4	27.7
Administrative and support service activities	259.3	40.7	778.0	441.6	383.6	43.4	41.8	1 814.2	191.1	162.2
Public administration; activities of households and of extraterritorial organisations	3.8	2.4	-	-	-	-	-	-	-	-
Education	6.4	-1.3	5.6	-3.0	-2.3	1.8	2.5	2.4	-0.1	-0.3
Human health and social work activities	21.7	29.6	35.6	52.8	58.6	-1.0	-1.0	-1.1	0.6	1.7
Arts, entertainment and recreation	9.7	-6.9	-11.7	-4.7	15.4	-3.9	-4.7	2.7	1.5	0.0
Other services	20.1	23.3	23.6	20.7	24.8	53.9	-7.4	3.9	42.9	52.3
Not allocated and confidential	**0.4**	**-2.1**	**3.1**	**0.6**	**0.8**	**26.6**	**6.3**	**7.1**	**4.9**	**57.4**
Private real estate activities	-	-	-	-	-	-	-	-	-	-

- Nil

Note: Detailed metadata at: *http://stats.oecd.org/OECDStat_Metadata/ShowMetadata.ashx?Dataset=FDI_CTRY_IND_SUMM.*

Source: OECD International Direct Investment Statistics (database): https://doi.org/10.1787/idi-data-en

PORTUGAL

Table 1. Foreign direct investment flows by country

Million US dollars

	Inward					Outward				
	2014	2015	2016	2017	2018	2014	2015	2016	2017	2018
WORLD	**4 890.5**	**7 628.4**	**5 127.7**	**6 830.1**	**5 977.8**	**-3 721.6**	**5 224.6**	**1 008.5**	**-923.2**	**-66.1**
OECD COUNTRIES	..	..	..	..	..	..	..	..	..	..
Australia	4.0	4.4	-6.6	4.5	-3.5	39.8	136.4	102.8	-27.1	7.1
Austria	62.4	65.4	-35.4	801.5	114.5	-19.9	-5.5	1.1	-19.2	-1.2
Belgium	-891.6	-36.6	33.2	396.8	240.8	10.6	-42.2	44.2	-13.5	-409.5
Canada	14.6	-24.4	10.0	-9.0	-11.8	5.3	3.3	76.3	-5.6	-15.3
Chile	6.6	7.8	-	10.1	2.4	1.3	5.5	-	192.8	1.2
Czech Republic	8.0	1.1	3.3	-	-9.4	4.0	-2.2	-16.6	-21.4	18.9
Denmark	39.8	-8.9	29.9	111.6	250.2	1.3	-5.5	-8.8	6.8	4.7
Estonia	-	-	..	-	-	..	..	..	..	-
Finland	-2.7	2.2	12.2	-44.0	29.5	-1.3	-35.5	21.0	37.2	-64.9
France	963.2	853.0	107.3	852.2	332.8	-29.2	-238.5	-97.3	109.3	-93.2
Germany	205.7	-282.9	526.4	-160.1	51.9	766.9	-139.8	-197.9	-109.3	38.9
Greece	..	-	..	..	..	..	..	-	..	..
Hungary	-1.3	-1.1	-1.1	-1.1	-2.4	-359.6	-62.1	-12.2	-22.5	-41.3
Iceland	-	-	-	-	..	-	-	-	-	-
Ireland	-394.1	240.7	-279.8	11.3	-220.7	-27.9	2.2	-234.4	-103.7	-171.1
Israel[1]	..	..	..	..	-	..	..	..	..	-
Italy	-1 216.7	244.0	-55.3	197.3	381.2	14.6	321.7	-10.0	37.2	-75.5
Japan	22.6	1.1	-4.4	103.7	16.5	63.7	16.6	-92.9	-192.8	-5.9
Korea	2.7	-2.2	15.5	55.2	2.4	-	-	-	-	-1.2
Latvia	-	-	2.2	-	-	-	-	-	-	-
Lithuania	-	-	..	..	..	-	-	-	-	-
Luxembourg	2 389.5	7 205.8	2 171.8	2 357.1	139.3	934.1	-64.3	110.6	-676.4	151.1
Mexico	-10.6	-11.1	16.6	7.9	-11.8	-25.2	189.7	-12.2	7.9	23.6
Netherlands	-2 920.3	-1 077.1	673.4	-131.9	799.0	-4 273.6	4 033.3	-143.8	-3 447.2	1 213.3
New Zealand	1.3	3.3	1.1	-	-	-	-	-	-	-
Norway	42.5	-17.7	-14.4	4.5	7.1	-6.6	-	-	3.4	2.4
Poland	14.6	6.7	14.4	-54.1	28.3	-9.3	-342.8	-19.9	-91.3	53.1
Portugal	-	-	-	-	-	-	-	-	-	-
Slovak Republic	..	-	-	..	-	..	..	..	..	..
Slovenia	..	-	-	-	-	-	-	-	-	-
Spain	-500.2	-950.6	676.8	122.9	1 362.0	-325.1	705.5	535.2	1 455.3	56.7
Sweden	116.8	42.2	362.7	550.1	-27.1	6.6	7.8	11.1	36.1	24.8
Switzerland	195.0	104.3	269.8	156.7	20.1	42.5	79.9	7.7	33.8	-54.3
Turkey	1.3	16.6	4.4	81.2	-14.2	-1.3	-2.2	3.3	11.3	-2.4
United Kingdom	662.1	1 145.9	-73.0	-28.2	199.5	-83.6	402.7	268.7	170.2	103.9
United States	-122.1	326.1	69.7	62.0	175.9	-17.2	-159.7	1.1	-483.6	-94.4
EUROPE	**-1 066.7**	**7 840.3**	**4 612.4**	**4 927.3**	**3 832.2**	**-3 464.2**	**4 664.4**	**243.3**	**-2 619.8**	**618.4**
Bulgaria	1.3	-	-	-7.9	9.4	1.3	-	1.1	5.6	-3.5
Croatia	..	..	-	-	-	..	-	-	-	-
Cyprus[2, 3]	8.0	-22.2	55.3	-25.9	40.1	-	-	-17.7	4.5	-
Malta	71.6	280.6	-17.7	-250.3	74.4	26.5	61.0	7.7	20.3	-114.5
Romania	4.0	-5.5	7.7	-15.8	-4.7	-34.5	1.1	-10.0	-7.9	-
Russian Federation	54.4	1.1	10.0	11.3	23.6	-1.3	-	-	-45.1	-4.7
Ukraine	4.0	5.5	3.3	-1.1	18.9	-4.0	-2.2	-7.7	-1.1	-
AFRICA	**999.1**	**391.6**	**-465.6**	**-**	**470.9**	**-265.4**	**439.3**	**-113.9**	**1 263.7**	**-210.1**
Northern Africa	74.3	-15.5	16.6	30.4	-7.1	51.7	28.8	89.6	307.7	-2.4
Algeria	17.2	12.2	8.8	2.3	-	-95.5	-13.3	-56.4	-25.9	-16.5
Egypt	..	..	..	..	..	..	..	..	..	..
Libya	..	-	..	..	..	-	..	-	-	-
Morocco	38.5	-35.5	8.8	1.1	9.4	10.6	-18.9	-7.7	-7.9	1.2
Tunisia	-2.7	21.1	16.6	19.2	-4.7	14.6	4.4	-8.8	7.9	-9.4
Other African countries	..	..	..	..	..	..	..	..	..	..
Nigeria	-39.8	247.4	-215.6	1.1	1.2	47.8	57.7	-57.5	67.6	-
South Africa	8.0	-1.1	11.1	-18.0	34.2	2.7	-44.4	24.3	16.9	-
AMERICA	**1 724.8**	**-510.3**	**637.0**	**279.6**	**511.0**	**163.2**	**-535.8**	**761.9**	**543.3**	**13.0**
Northern America	-107.5	301.7	80.7	53.0	164.1	-11.9	-156.4	77.4	-489.2	-109.8
Central America and Caribbean countries	-1 265.8	279.5	325.1	130.8	-5.9	-2 320.6	28.8	232.2	720.3	-245.5
Bahamas	..	..	..	..	..	-	..	..	..	-
Bermuda	-	..	..	..	..	-	-	-	..	..
Cayman Islands	..	..	..	..	..	..	..	..	..	..
Costa Rica	-	-	1.1	-	1.2	-	-1.1	-	-3.4	-
El Salvador	-	-	-	-	-	-	-	-	-	-
Guatemala	-	-	-	-	-	-	..	-	-	-
Honduras	-	-	-	..	-	-	-	-	-	-
Nicaragua	-	-	-	-	-	-	-	-	-	-
Panama	..	..	..	..	..	..	..	..	..	..
Virgin Islands, U.S.	..	..	-	-	-	-	-	-	-	-
South America	3 098.1	-1 092.6	231.1	95.8	352.9	2 497.0	-407.1	451.2	312.3	368.2
Argentina	2.7	-	-1.1	-	1.2	-	-5.5	-1.1	6.8	-2.4
Bolivia	-	-	..	-	-	..	..	..	-	..
Brazil	3 054.3	-890.7	158.1	86.8	335.2	2 527.5	-412.6	274.2	138.7	259.6
Colombia	-	-1.1	14.4	-2.3	-2.4	1.3	4.4	1.1	10.1	1.2
Ecuador	-	..	..	-	..	-	-	-	-	-
Paraguay	-	-	-	..	..	-	-	..	..	-
Peru	-	-	-	-	..	..	..	..	..	..
Uruguay	-1.3	1.1	-	2.3	3.5	8.0	-1.1	6.6	1.1	-14.2
Venezuela	35.8	-208.5	56.4	-	14.2	-66.3	11.1	165.9	-40.6	-29.5

Table 1. Foreign direct investment flows by country *(cont.)*

Million US dollars

	Inward					Outward				
	2014	2015	2016	2017	2018	2014	2015	2016	2017	2018
ASIA	**2 859.2**	**1 449.8**	**958.8**	**1 155.5**	**1 105.9**	**272.0**	**105.4**	**-13.3**	**-301.0**	**-26.0**
Near and Middle East	..	..	..	..	..	..	..	..	..	..
Gulf Arabian countries	..	..	..	..	..	..	..	-	..	..
Kuwait	5.3	22.2	-1.1	7.9	3.5	-	-	-	-	22.4
Qatar	..	..	..	..	..	..	..	..	..	..
Saudi Arabia	..	..	..	..	..	..	-	..	..	..
United Arab Emirates	9.3	51.0	77.4	94.7	66.1	-1.3	-2.2	-4.4	-9.0	-3.5
Other Near and Middle East	..	..	..	..	..	..	..	..	..	..
Jordan	..	..	..	..	..	-	-	..	..	..
Other Asian countries	..	..	..	..	..	..	..	..	..	..
China	948.7	529.1	562.9	432.9	421.3	-35.8	5.5	10.0	-6.8	-47.2
Hong Kong, China	1 902.6	736.6	-47.6	210.8	249.0	..	..	-	..	..
India	5.3	-26.6	1.1	39.5	23.6	1.3	-1.1	-11.1	12.4	8.3
Indonesia	..	..	..	..	..	..	..	..	..	..
Iran, Islamic Republic of	-	..	..	..	..	-	-	-	-	-
Malaysia	..	..	..	..	..	-	..	-	..	..
Philippines	-	..	-	..	..	-	-	-	-	-
Singapore	..	..	..	..	..	-	-	-	-	-
Chinese Taipei	-	-	..	-	..	-	-	..	..	-
Thailand	..	..	..	..	..	-	-	..	..	..
Viet Nam	..	..	..	..	..	-	-	-	..	..
AUSTRALIA, OCEANIA AND POLAR REGIONS	**5.3**	**7.8**	**-7.7**	**5.6**	**-2.4**	**39.8**	**136.4**	**102.8**	**-27.1**	**7.1**
WORLD unallocated and confidential	..	..	..	..	..	..	..	..	..	..
European Union (EU28)	..	..	..	..	..	..	..	..	..	..
G20 countries excl. European Union	..	..	..	..	..	..	..	..	..	..
G20 OECD countries	..	..	..	..	..	..	..	..	..	..
G20 Non-OECD countries	..	..	..	..	..	..	..	..	..	..
MENA countries	..	..	..	..	..	..	..	..	..	..
ASEAN countries	..	..	..	..	..	..	..	..	..	..

- Nil; .. Not available

Note: Data excludes resident Special Purpose Entities (SPEs). Detailed metadata at: *http://stats.oecd.org/OECDStat_Metadata/ShowMetadata.ashx?Dataset=FDI_CTRY_IND_SUMM.*

1. Information on data for Israel: *http://oe.cd/israel-disclaimer.*
2. Note by Turkey: The information in this document with reference to "Cyprus" relates to the southern part of the Island. There is no single authority representing both Turkish and Greek Cypriot people on the Island. Turkey recognises the Turkish Republic of Northern Cyprus (TRNC). Until a lasting and equitable solution is found within the context of the United Nations, Turkey shall preserve its position concerning the "Cyprus issue".
3. Note by all the European Union Member States of the OECD and the European Union: The Republic of Cyprus is recognised by all members of the United Nations with the exception of Turkey. The information in this document relates to the area under the effective control of the Government of the Republic of Cyprus.

Source: OECD International Direct Investment Statistics (database): https://doi.org/10.1787/idi-data-en

Table 2. Foreign direct investment positions by country

At year end

Million US dollars

	Inward					Outward				
	2014	2015	2016	2017	2018	2014	2015	2016	2017	2018
WORLD	**140 065.9**	**136 652.2**	**135 156.5**	**164 862.1**	**155 906.8**	**64 754.0**	**65 306.5**	**64 076.1**	**69 935.2**	**62 012.8**
OECD COUNTRIES	..	..	..	..	..	..	..	..	..	..
Australia	14.6	17.4	7.4	16.8	13.7	117.8	210.1	285.7	266.3	257.6
Austria	1 153.4	638.0	542.8	2 486.2	2 460.5	178.5	149.2	154.9	152.3	145.4
Belgium	3 491.8	3 089.8	3 175.9	4 092.1	4 185.9	279.2	240.6	569.2	400.6	9.2
Canada	809.8	693.5	682.0	759.2	712.2	82.6	79.5	151.8	40.8	24.0
Chile	-2.4	5.4	6.3	22.8	24.0	35.2	29.4	30.6	220.7	207.2
Czech Republic	9.7	9.8	11.6	12.0	3.4	49.8	28.3	27.4	57.6	72.1
Denmark	590.1	526.9	538.6	726.8	935.4	217.3	170.9	153.9	188.3	186.6
Estonia	..	..	..	..	..	..	..	..	..	..
Finland	86.2	80.6	89.6	52.8	77.9	20.6	-17.4	-4.2	36.0	-21.8
France	6 817.2	6 540.0	6 856.8	8 933.8	8 594.0	993.1	971.1	1 267.0	1 498.0	1 267.5
Germany	5 900.5	4 872.1	4 943.6	5 664.4	5 522.1	977.4	754.5	1 232.2	1 326.5	1 360.2
Greece	..	..	..	..	..	..	..	..	..	..
Hungary	34.0	29.4	27.4	30.0	26.3	281.7	170.9	140.2	136.7	89.3
Iceland	..	..	..	..	..	-	-	-	-	-
Ireland	2 183.0	2 263.5	1 924.7	2 166.0	1 853.7	1 516.4	1 430.6	1 186.9	1 260.5	1 039.6
Israel[1]	..	..	..	..	..	..	..	..	..	..
Italy	911.8	1 037.6	849.6	1 163.3	1 482.7	344.8	627.1	575.5	692.0	574.8
Japan	389.7	345.1	326.8	486.9	480.9	145.7	150.2	170.8	130.7	128.2
Korea	128.7	114.3	122.3	188.3	182.0	-	-	-1.1	-	-1.1
Latvia	7.3	6.5	6.3	7.2	6.9	1.2	1.1	1.1	-	-
Lithuania	..	..	..	..	-	-	-	-	-	-
Luxembourg	15 822.2	21 026.7	21 182.7	27 124.0	25 738.5	1 561.3	2 452.9	3 230.7	3 129.0	2 899.0
Mexico	-	-12.0	-2.1	7.2	-4.6	46.1	76.2	37.9	60.0	83.6
Netherlands	32 738.2	31 325.0	31 755.0	36 945.3	32 714.7	13 318.7	17 856.3	17 631.5	15 868.3	13 707.4
New Zealand	3.6	6.5	7.4	15.6	13.7	-	-	-	-	-
Norway	193.0	159.0	136.0	190.7	188.9	7.3	10.9	11.6	16.8	17.2
Poland	43.7	40.3	52.7	-7.2	21.8	2 565.4	1 465.4	1 263.8	2 000.5	1 907.5
Portugal	-	-	-	-	-	-	-	-	-	-
Slovak Republic	..	..	..	..	..	..	..	..	..	..
Slovenia	..	..	..	..	..	-	-	-	-	-
Spain	23 988.2	20 985.3	22 209.3	26 151.4	27 806.3	10 559.0	11 449.1	10 625.1	13 681.9	13 079.9
Sweden	669.0	651.1	964.5	1 773.8	1 668.2	231.9	224.3	205.5	231.5	235.9
Switzerland	2 352.9	2 211.2	2 409.6	2 910.8	2 774.2	162.7	194.9	138.1	112.7	59.5
Turkey	27.9	42.5	46.4	137.9	119.1	68.0	62.1	63.2	63.6	53.8
United Kingdom	9 402.0	10 467.1	9 986.3	11 208.9	10 730.5	2 445.2	2 742.5	2 645.7	2 925.2	2 911.6
United States	1 478.8	1 715.8	1 695.0	1 799.0	1 885.7	1 501.8	1 511.2	1 573.7	1 053.0	1 425.5
EUROPE	**109 215.6**	**108 867.7**	**110 706.2**	**135 050.4**	**130 140.8**	**36 682.8**	**41 800.8**	**41 879.4**	**44 649.8**	**40 382.4**
Bulgaria	4.9	4.4	5.3	-2.4	6.9	30.4	27.2	26.4	36.0	30.9
Croatia	..	..	..	..	..	..	-	-	-	..
Cyprus[2, 3]	653.2	569.4	605.0	675.2	669.8	23.1	20.7	5.3	8.4	9.2
Malta	956.7	1 231.4	1 265.9	1 304.9	1 291.5	418.9	369.1	350.0	407.8	368.7
Romania	-	-6.5	1.1	-14.4	-18.3	240.4	215.6	194.0	208.7	201.5
Russian Federation	176.0	159.0	163.4	196.7	211.8	29.1	26.1	31.6	37.2	24.0
Ukraine	12.1	16.3	19.0	20.4	36.6	4.9	8.7	3.2	3.6	3.4
AFRICA	**3 059.5**	**3 063.7**	**1 964.8**	**2 957.5**	**3 122.3**	**10 391.5**	**8 974.4**	**7 459.7**	**9 829.7**	**7 944.8**
Northern Africa	127.5	95.8	109.6	157.1	144.3	1 112.1	1 174.7	1 223.8	1 644.3	1 573.2
Algeria	9.7	19.6	27.4	34.8	33.2	286.5	278.7	249.8	261.5	241.6
Egypt	..	..	..	..	..	..	..	..	..	..
Libya	..	..	..	..	..	..	..	..	..	..
Morocco	32.8	-7.6	3.2	1.2	9.2	166.3	194.9	186.6	200.3	193.5
Tunisia	83.8	95.8	108.6	146.3	135.1	36.4	86.0	69.6	82.8	66.4
Other African countries	..	..	..	..	..	..	..	..	..	..
Nigeria	-32.8	221.0	5.3	7.2	6.9	-43.7	3.3	-32.7	21.6	20.6
South Africa	150.5	135.0	141.2	146.3	172.9	234.3	197.1	249.8	284.2	251.9
AMERICA	**7 253.0**	**6 294.0**	**5 088.0**	**5 947.5**	**6 158.7**	**8 000.9**	**6 173.1**	**6 660.7**	**6 652.7**	**6 407.1**
Northern America	2 288.6	2 410.5	2 376.9	2 558.2	2 597.9	1 583.2	1 590.6	1 724.5	1 093.8	1 449.5
Central America and Caribbean countries	675.0	897.1	-109.6	75.6	61.8	1 050.2	975.5	1 007.7	1 207.7	916.0
Bahamas	..	..	..	..	..	..	..	..	..	..
Bermuda	..	..	..	..	..	..	..	..	..	..
Cayman Islands	..	..	..	..	..	..	..	..	..	..
Costa Rica	3.6	3.3	2.1	2.4	3.4	8.5	6.5	6.3	6.0	5.7
El Salvador	-	-	-	-	-	-	-	-	-	-
Guatemala	-	-	-	-	-	..	..	..	..	..
Honduras	-	-	-	..	..	..	..	..	-	..
Nicaragua	-	-	-	-	-	..	-	-	-	-
Panama	..	..	..	..	..	..	..	..	..	..
Virgin Islands, U.S.	..	..	..	..	..	-	-	-	-	-
South America	4 289.4	2 986.4	2 819.6	3 313.7	3 499.0	5 367.5	3 607.0	3 928.5	4 351.2	4 042.8
Argentina	-	-	-1.1	-1.2	-1.1	23.1	18.5	20.0	31.2	25.2
Bolivia	-	-	..	..	..	..	..	..	..	..
Brazil	4 045.4	2 945.0	2 761.7	3 229.8	3 398.2	4 932.9	3 328.3	3 475.3	3 672.3	3 533.3
Colombia	-1.2	-2.2	11.6	9.6	6.9	13.4	9.8	13.7	24.0	24.0
Ecuador	-	..	-	-	..	..	..	..	-	-
Paraguay	-	-	..	-	..	..	..	..	..	..
Peru	-	-	..	..	..	..	..	..	..	..
Uruguay	2.4	3.3	3.2	6.0	9.2	18.2	18.5	25.3	28.8	14.9
Venezuela	244.0	34.8	33.7	37.2	51.5	269.5	137.2	294.1	280.6	1.1

Table 2. Foreign direct investment positions by country *(cont.)*

At year end

Million US dollars

	Inward					Outward				
	2014	2015	2016	2017	2018	2014	2015	2016	2017	2018
ASIA	**4 138.9**	**5 218.3**	**5 831.1**	**7 921.6**	**8 457.8**	**1 708.2**	**1 716.9**	**1 835.1**	**1 874.6**	**1 831.9**
Near and Middle East	..	..	..	..	..	..	..	..	..	..
Gulf Arabian countries	..	..	..	..	..	..	..	..	..	..
Kuwait	48.6	69.7	64.3	66.0	66.4	-	-	-	-	22.9
Qatar	..	..	..	..	..	..	..	..	..	..
Saudi Arabia	..	..	..	..	..	..	..	..	..	..
United Arab Emirates	65.6	303.8	367.9	527.7	567.9	26.7	20.7	15.8	9.6	6.9
Other Near and Middle East	..	..	..	..	..	..	..	..	..	..
Jordan	..	..	..	..	..	-	-	..	..	..
Other Asian countries	..	..	..	..	..	..	..	..	..	..
China	1 057.5	1 356.6	1 849.9	2 570.2	2 861.2	55.8	53.3	55.9	58.8	17.2
Hong Kong, China	1 981.4	2 496.5	2 225.2	2 763.3	2 707.8	..	..	..	..	..
India	3.6	-21.8	-20.0	22.8	44.7	91.1	87.1	68.5	69.6	74.4
Indonesia	..	..	..	..	..	..	..	..	..	..
Iran, Islamic Republic of	-	..	..	..	..	..	..	..	..	..
Malaysia	..	..	..	..	..	..	..	..	..	..
Philippines	-	..	..	..	..	-	-	-	-	-
Singapore	..	..	..	..	..	..	..	..	..	..
Chinese Taipei	-	-	..	-	..	..	..	..	..	..
Thailand	..	..	..	..	..	..	..	..	..	..
Viet Nam	..	..	..	..	..	-	-	-	..	..
AUSTRALIA, OCEANIA AND POLAR REGIONS	**41.3**	**43.5**	**32.7**	**51.6**	**46.9**	**117.8**	**210.1**	**285.7**	**267.5**	**259.9**
WORLD unallocated and confidential	..	..	..	..	..	..	..	..	..	..
European Union (EU28)	..	..	..	..	..	..	..	..	..	..
G20 countries excl. European Union	..	..	..	..	..	..	..	..	..	..
G20 OECD countries	..	..	..	..	..	..	..	..	..	..
G20 Non-OECD countries	..	..	..	..	..	..	..	..	..	..
MENA countries	..	..	..	..	..	..	..	..	..	..
ASEAN countries	..	..	..	..	..	..	..	..	..	..

- Nil; .. Not available

Note: Data excludes resident Special Purpose Entities (SPEs). Detailed metadata at: *http://stats.oecd.org/OECDStat_Metadata/ShowMetadata.ashx?Dataset=FDI_CTRY_IND_SUMM.*

1. Information on data for Israel: *http://oe.cd/israel-disclaimer.*
2. Note by Turkey: The information in this document with reference to "Cyprus" relates to the southern part of the Island. There is no single authority representing both Turkish and Greek Cypriot people on the Island. Turkey recognises the Turkish Republic of Northern Cyprus (TRNC). Until a lasting and equitable solution is found within the context of the United Nations, Turkey shall preserve its position concerning the "Cyprus issue".
3. Note by all the European Union Member States of the OECD and the European Union: The Republic of Cyprus is recognised by all members of the United Nations with the exception of Turkey. The information in this document relates to the area under the effective control of the Government of the Republic of Cyprus.

Source: OECD International Direct Investment Statistics (database): https://doi.org/10.1787/idi-data-en

Table 3. Foreign direct investment income by country

Million US dollars

	Inward					Outward				
	2014	2015	2016	2017	2018	2014	2015	2016	2017	2018
WORLD	**4 622.5**	**5 343.3**	**5 732.6**	**6 342.0**	**6 791.0**	**2 085.7**	**2 118.7**	**2 715.9**	**3 883.4**	**3 030.8**
OECD COUNTRIES	..	..	..	..	..	..	..	..	..	..
Australia	-	-	-	..	-	..	..	..	..	..
Austria	..	..	..	..	..	..	..	..	..	..
Belgium	..	..	..	..	..	..	..	..	..	..
Canada	-	..	..	..	..	..	..	..	..	-
Chile	-	-	-	..	-	-	..	..	..	..
Czech Republic	-	-	-	-	-	-	-	..	..	..
Denmark	..	..	..	..	..	..	..	..	..	-
Estonia	-	..	-	..	-	-	..	..	-	-
Finland	..	-	..	..	..	-	-	-	-	-
France	..	..	..	..	..	..	..	..	..	..
Germany	..	..	..	..	..	..	..	..	..	..
Greece	-	-	-	-	-	-	-	-	-	-
Hungary	-	-	..	..	-	..	..	..	..	..
Iceland	-	-	-	-	-	-	-	-	-	-
Ireland	..	..	..	..	..	..	..	..	..	..
Israel[1]	-	-	-	..	-	-	-	-	-	-
Italy	..	..	..	..	..	..	..	..	..	..
Japan	..	..	..	..	..	-	..	..	..	..
Korea	-	..	..	..	-	-	-	-	-	-
Latvia	-	-	-	-	-	-	-	-	-	-
Lithuania	-	-	-	-	-	-	-	-	-	-
Luxembourg	..	..	..	..	..	..	..	..	..	..
Mexico	-	-	-	-	-	..	..	..	..	..
Netherlands	..	..	..	..	..	..	..	..	..	..
New Zealand	-	-	-	-	-	-	-	-	-	-
Norway	-	..	..	..	..	-	..	-	..	..
Poland	-	..	..	..	..	..	..	..	..	..
Portugal	-	-	-	-	-	-	-	-	-	-
Slovak Republic	-	-	-	-	..	-	-	-	-	-
Slovenia	-	-	-	-	-	-	-	-	-	-
Spain	..	..	..	..	..	..	..	..	..	..
Sweden	..	..	..	..	..	..	..	..	..	..
Switzerland	..	..	..	..	..	..	..	..	..	..
Turkey	-	..	..	..	-	..	..	..	..	..
United Kingdom	..	..	..	..	..	..	..	..	..	..
United States	..	..	..	..	..	..	..	..	..	..
EUROPE	..	..	..	..	..	..	..	..	..	..
Bulgaria	-	..	..	-	..	-	-	-	..	-
Croatia	-	-	-	-	-	-	-	-	-	-
Cyprus[2, 3]	..	..	..	..	..	..	..	..	..	-
Malta	..	..	..	..	..	..	..	..	..	..
Romania	-	-	-	-	-	-	..	..	..	..
Russian Federation	-	-	-	-	-	-	-	-	..	..
Ukraine	-	-	-	-	-	-	..	-	-	-
AFRICA	..	..	..	..	..	..	..	..	..	..
Northern Africa	-	..	..	..	-	..	..	..	..	..
Algeria	-	-	-	..	-	..	..	..	..	-
Egypt	-	-	-	-	-	..	..	..	..	..
Libya	-	-	-	-	-	-	-	-	-	-
Morocco	-	..	-	..	-	..	..	..	..	..
Tunisia	-	..	..	..	-	..	..	..	..	..
Other African countries	..	..	..	..	..	..	..	..	..	..
Nigeria	-	..	-	-	-	-	-	..	..	-
South Africa	-	..	..	..	-	-	-	-	..	..
AMERICA	..	..	..	..	..	..	..	..	..	..
Northern America	..	..	..	..	..	..	..	..	..	..
Central America and Caribbean countries	..	..	..	..	..	..	..	..	..	..
Bahamas	..	..	..	..	..	-	..	-	..	-
Bermuda	-	-	-	-	-	-	-	-	-	-
Cayman Islands	-	..	..	-	-	..	..	..	..	..
Costa Rica	-	..	-	-	-	-	..	-	..	-
El Salvador	-	-	-	-	-	-	-	-	-	-
Guatemala	-	-	-	-	-	-	..	-	-	-
Honduras	-	-	-	-	-	-	-	-	-	-
Nicaragua	-	-	-	-	-	-	-	-	-	-
Panama	-	..	..	..	-	-	..	..	..	..
Virgin Islands, U.S.	-	-	-	-	-	-	-	-	-	-
South America	..	..	..	..	..	..	..	..	..	..
Argentina	-	-	-	-	-	-	..	..	..	-
Bolivia	-	-	-	-	-	-	-	-	..	-
Brazil	..	..	..	..	..	..	..	..	..	..
Colombia	-	-	-	-	-	-	-	..	..	-
Ecuador	-	-	-	-	-	-	-	-	-	-
Paraguay	-	-	-	-	-	-	-	-	-	-
Peru	-	-	-	-	-	-	-	..	..	..
Uruguay	-	-	..	-	-	..	..	..	..	-
Venezuela	-	-	-	-	-	..	..	..	..	-

Table 3. Foreign direct investment income by country *(cont.)*

Million US dollars

	Inward					Outward				
	2014	2015	2016	2017	2018	2014	2015	2016	2017	2018
ASIA	..	..	..	..	..	..	..	..	..	..
Near and Middle East	-	..	..	..	..	..	..	..	..	..
Gulf Arabian countries	-	..	..	..	..	-	..	..	..	..
Kuwait	-	..	..	..	-	-	-	-	-	-
Qatar	-	-	-	..	-	-	..	..	..	..
Saudi Arabia	-	..	..	-	-	-	..	..	..	-
United Arab Emirates	-	-	..	..	..	-	..	..	-	-
Other Near and Middle East	-	-	..	..	-	..	..	..	..	..
Jordan	-	-	-	-	-	-	-	-	-	-
Other Asian countries	..	..	..	..	..	..	..	..	..	..
China	-	..	..	..	..	..	..	..	..	..
Hong Kong, China	-	..	..	..	..	-	..	..	..	..
India	-	..	-	-	-	-	..	..	..	..
Indonesia	-	-	-	-	-	..	..	..	-	..
Iran, Islamic Republic of	-	-	-	-	-	-	-	-	-	-
Malaysia	-	-	-	-	-	-	..	-	-	-
Philippines	-	-	-	-	-	-	-	-	-	-
Singapore	-	..	..	..	..	-	..	-	-	-
Chinese Taipei	-	-	-	-	-	-	-	-	-	-
Thailand	-	-	-	-	-	-	-	..	-	-
Viet Nam	-	-	-	-	-	-	-	-	-	-
AUSTRALIA, OCEANIA AND POLAR REGIONS	-	-	..	..	-	..	..	..	..	..
WORLD unallocated and confidential	..	..	..	..	..	..	..	..	..	..
European Union (EU28)	..	..	..	..	..	..	..	..	..	..
G20 countries excl. European Union	..	..	..	..	..	..	..	..	..	..
G20 OECD countries	..	..	..	..	..	..	..	..	..	..
G20 Non-OECD countries	..	..	..	..	..	..	..	..	..	..
MENA countries	-	..	..	..	..	..	..	..	..	..
ASEAN countries	-	..	..	..	..	..	..	..	-	..

- Nil; .. Not available

Note: Data excludes resident Special Purpose Entities (SPEs). Detailed metadata at: *http://stats.oecd.org/OECDStat_Metadata/ShowMetadata.ashx?Dataset=FDI_CTRY_IND_SUMM.*

1. Information on data for Israel: *http://oe.cd/israel-disclaimer.*
2. Note by Turkey: The information in this document with reference to "Cyprus" relates to the southern part of the Island. There is no single authority representing both Turkish and Greek Cypriot people on the Island. Turkey recognises the Turkish Republic of Northern Cyprus (TRNC). Until a lasting and equitable solution is found within the context of the United Nations, Turkey shall preserve its position concerning the "Cyprus issue".
3. Note by all the European Union Member States of the OECD and the European Union: The Republic of Cyprus is recognised by all members of the United Nations with the exception of Turkey. The information in this document relates to the area under the effective control of the Government of the Republic of Cyprus.

Source: OECD International Direct Investment Statistics (database): https://doi.org/10.1787/idi-data-en

PORTUGAL

Table 4. Foreign direct investment flows by industrial sector

Million US dollars

	Inward					Outward				
	2014	2015	2016	2017	2018	2014	2015	2016	2017	2018
All FDI activities	**4 890.5**	**7 628.4**	**5 127.7**	**6 830.1**	**5 977.8**	**-3 721.6**	**5 224.6**	**1 008.5**	**-923.2**	**-66.1**
Agriculture, forestry and fishing	..	..	..	..	..	..	..	..	..	..
Mining and quarrying	..	..	..	..	..	..	..	..	..	..
Extraction activities	-	-	-	-	-	-	-	-	-	-
Manufacturing	**-240.1**	**327.2**	**251.0**	**-28.2**	**231.3**	**-1 149.0**	**-890.7**	**-140.4**	**227.7**	**-393.0**
of which:										
Food products, beverages and tobacco	..	..	..	..	..	..	..	..	..	..
Textiles, wood and paper products; printing	..	..	..	..	..	..	..	..	..	..
Chemical, rubber, plastic, non-metallic mineral products	..	..	..	..	..	..	..	..	..	..
Metal and machinery products, except electrical equipment	..	..	..	..	..	..	..	..	..	..
Motor vehicles, trailers, semi-trailers, other transport equipment	..	..	..	..	..	..	..	..	..	..
Other manufacturing	..	..	..	..	..	..	..	..	..	..
Electricity, gas, steam and air conditioning supply	..	..	..	..	..	..	..	..	..	..
Water supply; sewerage, waste management and remediation activities	..	..	..	..	..	..	..	..	..	..
Construction	**-212.3**	**-291.7**	**-389.3**	**251.4**	**480.3**	**-536.0**	**236.3**	**-575.0**	**162.3**	**-341.1**
Services	**3 161.7**	**5 773.7**	**2 722.5**	**4 975.8**	**2 793.6**	**-1 756.7**	**6 237.4**	**416.9**	**766.5**	**-370.6**
Wholesale and retail trade; repair of motor vehicles and motorcycles	582.5	-1 287.9	190.2	1 043.9	126.3	183.1	484.7	533.0	-171.3	-335.2
Transportation and storage	..	..	..	..	..	..	..	..	..	..
Accommodation and food service activities	..	..	..	..	..	..	..	..	..	..
Information and communication	-2 924.2	5 693.8	10.0	-69.9	-335.2	286.6	28.8	8.8	-42.8	110.9
Financial and insurance activities	6 124.5	652.2	1 528.3	1 497.0	1 038.6	-11 389.1	3 777.0	-112.8	-542.2	-623.2
Activities of holding companies	..	..	..	..	..	..	..	..	..	..
Real estate activities	628.9	934.0	675.7	925.5	487.4	132.7	1 124.8	809.5	108.2	31.9
Professional, scientific and technical activities	-1 594.8	-583.5	94.0	680.9	1 253.4	9 153.5	840.8	-1 032.8	1 180.3	935.9
Administrative and support service activities	..	..	..	..	..	..	..	..	..	..
Public administration; activities of households and of extraterritorial organisations	-	-	-	-	-	..	-	-	-	-
Education	-	-	-	..	..	-	..	..	..	-
Human health and social work activities	-	..	..	..	..	..	..	..	..	..
Arts, entertainment and recreation	-	..	..	..	..	-	..	-	..	..
Other services	-	..	..	..	..	..	..	..	..	..
Not allocated and confidential	..	..	..	..	..	..	..	..	..	..
Private real estate activities	-	-	-	-	-	-	-	-	-	-

- Nil; .. Not available

Note: Data excludes resident Special Purpose Entities (SPEs). Detailed metadata at: *http://stats.oecd.org/OECDStat_Metadata/ShowMetadata.ashx?Dataset=FDI_CTRY_IND_SUMM.*

Source: OECD International Direct Investment Statistics (database): https://doi.org/10.1787/idi-data-en

Table 5. Foreign direct investment positions by industrial sector

At year end

Million US dollars

	Inward					Outward				
	2014	2015	2016	2017	2018	2014	2015	2016	2017	2018
All FDI activities	**140 065.9**	**136 652.2**	**135 156.5**	**164 862.1**	**155 906.8**	**64 754.0**	**65 306.5**	**64 076.1**	**69 935.2**	**62 012.8**
Agriculture, forestry and fishing	..	..	..	..	..	..	..	..	..	..
Mining and quarrying	..	..	..	..	..	..	..	..	..	..
Extraction activities	-	-	-	-	-	-	-	-	-	-
Manufacturing	**9 473.6**	**8 875.3**	**9 178.9**	**9 177.3**	**8 971.8**	**3 941.0**	**3 022.3**	**3 320.3**	**3 391.7**	**3 069.6**
of which:										
Food products, beverages and tobacco	..	..	..	..	..	..	..	..	..	..
Textiles, wood and paper products; printing	..	..	..	..	..	..	..	..	..	..
Chemical, rubber, plastic, non-metallic mineral products	..	..	..	..	..	..	..	..	..	..
Metal and machinery products, except electrical equipment	..	..	..	..	..	..	..	..	..	..
Motor vehicles, trailers, semi-trailers, other transport equipment	..	..	..	..	..	..	..	..	..	..
Other manufacturing	..	..	..	..	..	..	..	..	..	..
Electricity, gas, steam and air conditioning supply	..	..	..	..	..	..	..	..	..	..
Water supply; sewerage, waste management and remediation activities	..	..	..	..	..	..	..	..	..	..
Construction	**4 308.8**	**3 757.2**	**3 164.3**	**3 612.4**	**3 626.1**	**4 472.7**	**4 473.6**	**3 471.1**	**4 395.5**	**3 354.7**
Services	**104 331.3**	**102 303.8**	**99 785.0**	**123 298.2**	**113 338.7**	**57 673.4**	**57 735.4**	**55 955.5**	**62 750.1**	**55 161.4**
Wholesale and retail trade; repair of motor vehicles and motorcycles	15 081.6	12 331.0	11 623.3	15 801.2	14 326.8	4 317.3	4 443.1	4 123.5	4 407.5	3 583.7
Transportation and storage	..	..	..	..	..	..	..	..	..	..
Accommodation and food service activities	..	..	..	..	..	..	..	..	..	..
Information and communication	2 284.9	7 598.3	7 219.4	8 268.2	1 498.7	-165.1	-92.5	-42.2	-137.9	-134.0
Financial and insurance activities	39 149.9	33 572.1	32 243.1	38 660.4	51 047.6	31 894.4	25 713.7	22 617.3	23 857.0	24 184.8
Activities of holding companies	..	..	..	..	..	..	..	..	..	..
Real estate activities	6 945.9	7 988.0	8 275.5	10 201.5	10 146.6	2 118.6	2 966.8	3 530.1	4 309.2	4 220.3
Professional, scientific and technical activities	28 949.0	29 451.3	29 792.3	37 529.4	25 752.2	15 800.3	21 437.1	22 263.1	26 847.0	21 720.9
Administrative and support service activities	..	..	..	..	..	..	..	..	..	..
Public administration; activities of households and of extraterritorial organisations	-	-	-	-	-	..	..	..	..	..
Education	..	..	..	..	..	..	..	..	..	..
Human health and social work activities	..	..	..	..	..	..	..	..	..	..
Arts, entertainment and recreation	..	..	..	..	..	..	..	..	..	..
Other services	..	..	..	..	..	..	..	..	..	..
Not allocated and confidential	..	..	..	..	..	..	..	..	..	..
Private real estate activities	-	-	-	-	-	-	-	-	-	-

- Nil; .. Not available

Note: Data excludes resident Special Purpose Entities (SPEs). Detailed metadata at: *http://stats.oecd.org/OECDStat_Metadata/ShowMetadata.ashx?Dataset=FDI_CTRY_IND_SUMM.*

Source: OECD International Direct Investment Statistics (database): https://doi.org/10.1787/idi-data-en

PORTUGAL

Table 6. Foreign direct investment income by industrial sector

Million US dollars

	Inward					Outward				
	2014	2015	2016	2017	2018	2014	2015	2016	2017	2018
All FDI activities	**4 622.5**	**5 343.3**	**5 732.6**	**6 342.0**	**6 791.0**	**2 085.7**	**2 118.7**	**2 715.9**	**3 883.4**	**3 030.8**
Agriculture, forestry and fishing	..	..	..	..	..	..	..	..	..	..
Mining and quarrying	..	..	..	..	..	-	..	..	..	..
Extraction activities	-	-	-	-	-	-	-	-	-	-
Manufacturing	..	..	..	..	..	..	..	..	..	..
of which:										
Food products, beverages and tobacco	..	..	..	..	..	..	..	..	..	..
Textiles, wood and paper products; printing	..	..	..	..	..	..	..	..	..	..
Chemical, rubber, plastic, non-metallic mineral products	..	..	..	..	..	..	..	..	..	..
Metal and machinery products, except electrical equipment	..	..	..	..	..	..	..	..	..	..
Motor vehicles, trailers, semi-trailers, other transport equipment	..	..	..	..	..	-	..	..	-	..
Other manufacturing	..	..	..	..	..	..	..	..	..	..
Electricity, gas, steam and air conditioning supply	..	..	..	..	..	..	..	..	..	..
Water supply; sewerage, waste management and remediation activities	..	..	..	..	..	-	..	..	..	-
Construction	..	..	..	..	..	..	..	..	..	..
Services	..	..	..	..	..	..	..	..	..	..
Wholesale and retail trade; repair of motor vehicles and motorcycles	..	..	..	..	..	..	..	..	..	..
Transportation and storage	..	..	..	..	..	..	..	..	..	..
Accommodation and food service activities	..	..	..	..	..	..	..	..	..	..
Information and communication	..	..	..	..	..	..	..	..	-	..
Financial and insurance activities	..	..	..	..	..	..	..	..	..	..
Activities of holding companies	..	..	..	..	..	..	..	..	..	..
Real estate activities	..	..	..	..	..	..	..	..	..	..
Professional, scientific and technical activities	..	..	..	..	..	..	..	..	..	..
Administrative and support service activities	..	..	..	..	..	..	..	..	..	..
Public administration; activities of households and of extraterritorial organisations	-	-	-	-	-	..	-	-	-	-
Education	-	..	-	..	-	-	-	-	-	-
Human health and social work activities	..	..	..	..	..	-	..	..	..	-
Arts, entertainment and recreation	-	..	..	..	..	-	..	..	..	..
Other services	..	..	..	..	..	..	..	..	..	..
Not allocated and confidential	..	..	..	..	..	..	..	..	..	..
Private real estate activities	-	-	-	-	-	-	-	-	-	-

- Nil; .. Not available

Note: Data excludes resident Special Purpose Entities (SPEs). Detailed metadata at: *http://stats.oecd.org/OECDStat_Metadata/ShowMetadata.ashx?Dataset=FDI_CTRY_IND_SUMM.*

Source: OECD International Direct Investment Statistics (database): https://doi.org/10.1787/idi-data-en

SLOVAK REPUBLIC

Table 1. Foreign direct investment flows by country

Million US dollars

	Inward					Outward				
	2014	2015	2016	2017	2018	2014	2015	2016	2017	2018
WORLD	**-331.5**	**..**	**805.1**	**4 008.2**	**1 183.2**	**-123.4**	**..**	**95.5**	**1 322.6**	**234.1**
OECD COUNTRIES	**180.9**	**..**	**1 407.7**	**4 534.0**	**1 440.1**	**-139.6**	**..**	**121.3**	**1 252.5**	**194.6**
Australia	3.6	..	.. c	1.2	-3.3	-	..	.. c	.. c	4.2
Austria	-156.9	..	163.0	-152.3	279.5	4.2	..	82.9	1.0	52.6
Belgium	53.7	..	38.4	342.5	292.6	44.5	..	-	-	-
Canada	1.2	..	.. c	2.3	0.4	0.0	..	.. c	.. c	.. c
Chile	0.0	..	.. c	-1.7	0.6	0.8	..	.. c	.. c	.. c
Czech Republic	855.6	..	667.5	1 172.7	509.2	-136.2	..	-23.6	1 148.8	-94.4
Denmark	5.1	..	-82.4	76.7	-10.7	0.1	..	.. c	.. c	.. c
Estonia	0.4	..	.. c	2.8	-0.4	-	..	-	-	-
Finland	-2.6	..	.. c	38.3	34.2	0.4	..	.. c	.. c	0.7
France	-77.6	..	-76.1	193.4	493.5	0.0	..	.. c	6.8	8.3
Germany	-258.6	..	446.9	901.5	-558.8	17.0	..	.. c	-1.5	6.9
Greece	-4.3	..	.. c	4.1	-4.2	-	..	-	-	-
Hungary	197.9	..	159.0	-13.4	65.3	-9.1	..	47.1	0.2	-2.4
Iceland	-2.4	..	.. c	-0.2	-0.2	-	..	.. c	.. c	.. c
Ireland	-134.2	..	.. c	65.8	-121.1	-	..	.. c	-	.. c
Israel[1]	-1.1	..	.. c	22.1	0.3	-	..	-	-	-
Italy	62.0	..	-864.4	179.7	134.4	3.9	..	.. c	2.0	0.9
Japan	-24.4	..	.. c	36.6	25.9	-	..	-	-	-0.3
Korea	263.8	..	-14.1	48.7	150.7	-	..	.. c	-	0.6
Latvia	0.2	..	.. c	0.6	18.2	-	..	.. c	.. c	.. c
Lithuania	0.2	..	.. c	0.8	.. c	0.7	..	.. c	.. c	.. c
Luxembourg	-304.8	..	-408.2	322.9	-190.2	-71.4	..	.. c	-31.8	-33.3
Mexico	0.3	..	.. c	-2.1	-46.1	-	..	-	-	-
Netherlands	-419.6	..	1 796.9	-798.9	-248.5	-5.9	..	.. c	-98.9	58.9
New Zealand	-1.8	..	-11.4	-12.4	0.1	-	..	-	-	-
Norway	77.9	..	.. c	-20.9	-5.6	-	..	.. c	.. c	.. c
Poland	-47.8	..	21.4	158.1	98.0	6.2	..	-51.8	109.0	89.7
Portugal	-8.7	..	.. c	0.8	-0.7	-	..	.. c	.. c	.. c
Slovak Republic	-	..	..	-	-	-	..	-	-	-
Slovenia	1.6	..	.. c	3.2	-4.7	0.5	..	.. c	-0.6	0.6
Spain	2.7	..	52.4	145.4	-20.9	0.0	..	.. c	.. c	-0.4
Sweden	-29.8	..	119.0	689.6	58.9	-	..	-	-	-
Switzerland	-75.7	..	-75.5	178.5	122.9	-0.2	..	.. c	-0.3	1.4
Turkey	6.6	..	.. c	20.1	-10.4	0.0	..	.. c	.. c	.. c
United Kingdom	8.0	..	2.3	705.7	501.2	1.1	..	.. c	70.6	91.3
United States	190.7	..	-413.9	222.4	-119.9	4.5	..	.. c	.. c	6.2
EUROPE	**-664.9**	**..**	**1 086.8**	**3 789.3**	**1 226.2**	**-121.4**	**..**	**88.6**	**1 275.5**	**206.7**
Bulgaria	-2.6	..	.. c	-2.7	9.6	0.0	..	.. c	-0.4	0.8
Croatia	-5.3	..	.. c	1.3	4.8	-0.3	..	.. c	2.2	1.7
Cyprus[2, 3]	-255.9	..	-182.2	-148.2	-198.4	26.0	..	-39.1	4.6	13.1
Malta	0.6	..	.. c	31.4	129.3	-	..	.. c	.. c	2.9
Romania	-0.5	..	.. c	7.2	-45.3	-0.2	..	-9.2	2.3	-1.1
Russian Federation	-87.5	..	.. c	10.8	55.6	0.1	..	.. c	5.6	4.3
Ukraine	-0.8	..	.. c	-1.0	-2.6	6.0	..	-3.1	-6.9	5.1
AFRICA	**-2.8**	**..**	**.. c**	**-0.2**	**10.4**	**-0.6**	**..**	**.. c**	**.. c**	**-0.7**
Northern Africa	-21.6	..	.. c	2.4	5.7	-0.6	..	.. c	.. c	.. c
Algeria	0.5	..	-	-	-	-	..	-	-	-
Egypt	-20.5	..	.. c	4.4	1.6	-	..	-	-	-
Libya	-	..	-	-	-	-	..	-	-	-
Morocco	-1.0	..	.. c	-3.4	1.7	-0.6	..	.. c	.. c	.. c
Tunisia	-0.5	..	.. c	1.5	2.3	-	..	.. c	-	-
Other African countries	18.8	..	.. c	-2.6	4.7	-	..	.. c	.. c	.. c
Nigeria	-0.5	..	.. c	-0.1	-0.1	-	..	.. c	.. c	.. c
South Africa	0.9	..	.. c	-3.7	2.6	-	..	-	-	-
AMERICA	**165.3**	**..**	**-332.1**	**242.5**	**-147.4**	**5.2**	**..**	**3.9**	**9.1**	**7.9**
Northern America	192.0	..	-405.6	224.7	-119.5	4.4	..	-2.1	0.4	7.0
Central America and Caribbean countries	-25.2	..	81.4	16.4	-30.5	-	..	-	-	-
Bahamas	-	..	.. c	.. c	.. c	-	..	-	-	-
Bermuda	-	..	-	.. c	.. c	-	..	-	-	-
Cayman Islands	-0.5	..	.. c	24.4	10.7	-	..	-	-	-
Costa Rica	-0.7	..	.. c	.. c	.. c	-	..	-	-	-
El Salvador	-	..	.. c	.. c	-	-	..	-	-	-
Guatemala	-	..	-	.. c	-	-	..	-	-	-
Honduras	-	..	-	-	-	-	..	-	-	-
Nicaragua	-	..	-	-	-	-	..	-	-	-
Panama	-15.0	..	.. c	-0.2	1.9	-	..	-	-	-
Virgin Islands, U.S.	-	..	-	-	-	-	..	-	-	-
South America	-1.5	..	-8.0	1.3	2.6	0.8	..	.. c	8.7	0.9
Argentina	0.1	..	0.7	-0.1	0.4	-	..	.. c	.. c	.. c
Bolivia	-	..	-	-	-	-	..	-	-	-
Brazil	-0.9	..	.. c	3.0	1.5	-	..	.. c	.. c	.. c
Colombia	0.2	..	.. c	0.0	0.1	-	..	-	-	-
Ecuador	0.1	..	.. c	0.0	0.0	-	..	-	-	-
Paraguay	-	..	-	-	-	-	..	-	-	-
Peru	-0.8	..	.. c	0.1	0.0	-	..	-	-	-
Uruguay	0.0	..	.. c	-	-	-	..	-	-	-
Venezuela	0.0	..	-	.. c	-	-	..	-	-	-

SLOVAK REPUBLIC

Table 1. Foreign direct investment flows by country *(cont.)*

Million US dollars

	Inward					Outward				
	2014	2015	2016	2017	2018	2014	2015	2016	2017	2018
ASIA	**169.1**	..	**80.4**	**-12.0**	**97.3**	**-6.7**	..	**.. c**	**37.5**	**16.0**
Near and Middle East	2.4	..	.. c	21.9	6.7	0.0	..	.. c	.. c	.. c
Gulf Arabian countries	3.4	..	.. c	0.1	6.4	-	..	-	-	-
Kuwait	-	..	.. c	.. c	.. c	-	..	-	-	-
Qatar	0.0	..	.. c	-0.9	1.0	-	..	-	-	-
Saudi Arabia	0.7	..	.. c	-0.4	-0.7	-	..	-	-	-
United Arab Emirates	2.7	..	.. c	1.4	6.1	-	..	-	-	-
Other Near and Middle East	-1.0	..	.. c	21.9	0.3	0.0	..	.. c	.. c	.. c
Jordan	0.0	..	.. c	-0.1	0.0	-	..	-	-	-
Other Asian countries	166.7	..	78.6	-34.0	90.6	-6.7	..	.. c	37.3	15.8
China	-2.7	..	.. c	6.4	0.9	0.0	..	.. c	31.4	13.5
Hong Kong, China	-2.8	..	.. c	2.6	-14.6	-	..	.. c	.. c	0.0
India	-1.4	..	.. c	1.3	-5.1	0.0	..	.. c	.. c	.. c
Indonesia	-0.9	..	.. c	-4.7	4.8	-	..	-	-	-
Iran, Islamic Republic of	-	..	.. c	.. c	-	-	..	-	-	-
Malaysia	-10.8	..	.. c	-8.3	-7.4	-6.7	..	-	-	-
Philippines	0.0	..	.. c	-	-0.2	-	..	-	-	-
Singapore	-9.2	..	.. c	-65.2	-30.9	-	..	.. c	.. c	2.0
Chinese Taipei	-41.6	..	.. c	-67.7	-24.2	-	..	-	-	-
Thailand	-13.3	..	.. c	1.9	-3.6	-	..	-	-	-
Viet Nam	9.8	..	.. c	14.5	-5.6	0.2	..	.. c	.. c	-0.1
AUSTRALIA, OCEANIA AND POLAR REGIONS	**1.8**	..	**-24.6**	**-11.3**	**-3.4**	**-**	..	**.. c**	**.. c**	**4.2**
WORLD unallocated and confidential	**-**	..	**.. d**	**0.0**	**0.0**	**0.0**	..	**- d**	**.. d**	**0.0**
European Union (EU28)	**-521.3**	..	**1 727.9**	**3 929.2**	**1 224.5**	**-118.6**	..	**72.0**	**1 275.4**	**195.2**
G20 countries excl. European Union	**83.7**	..	**-892.6**	**2 322.2**	**627.8**	**26.6**	..	**-8.7**	**128.1**	**139.7**
G20 OECD countries	**175.6**	..	**-858.0**	**2 309.6**	**567.6**	**26.4**	..	**-28.2**	**80.1**	**121.6**
G20 Non-OECD countries	**-91.9**	..	**-34.7**	**12.6**	**60.1**	**0.2**	..	**19.5**	**48.0**	**18.0**
MENA countries	**-18.2**	..	**2.6**	**2.4**	**12.0**	**-0.6**	..	**.. c**	**.. c**	**-0.6**
ASEAN countries	**-24.4**	..	**31.2**	**-61.8**	**-43.0**	**-6.5**	..	**.. c**	**.. c**	**1.8**

- Nil; .. Not available; c Confidential data; d Secondary Confidentiality

Note: Detailed metadata at: *http://stats.oecd.org/OECDStat_Metadata/ShowMetadata.ashx?Dataset=FDI_CTRY_IND_SUMM.*

1. Information on data for Israel: *http://oe.cd/israel-disclaimer.*
2. Note by Turkey: The information in this document with reference to "Cyprus" relates to the southern part of the Island. There is no single authority representing both Turkish and Greek Cypriot people on the Island. Turkey recognises the Turkish Republic of Northern Cyprus (TRNC). Until a lasting and equitable solution is found within the context of the United Nations, Turkey shall preserve its position concerning the "Cyprus issue".
3. Note by all the European Union Member States of the OECD and the European Union: The Republic of Cyprus is recognised by all members of the United Nations with the exception of Turkey. The information in this document relates to the area under the effective control of the Government of the Republic of Cyprus.

Source: OECD International Direct Investment Statistics (database): https://doi.org/10.1787/idi-data-en

SLOVAK REPUBLIC

Table 2. Foreign direct investment positions by country
At year end

Million US dollars

	Inward					Outward				
	2014	2015	2016	2017	2018	2014	2015	2016	2017	2018
WORLD	**49 740.8**	**46 015.8**	**47 591.7**	**59 510.3**	**58 441.2**	**2 820.2**	**2 462.3**	**2 631.0**	**4 589.9**	**4 585.5**
OECD COUNTRIES	**48 018.1**	**44 605.1**	**46 192.4**	**58 505.6**	**57 390.7**	**2 161.9**	**1 948.1**	**2 199.9**	**4 045.3**	**4 009.2**
Australia	-17.6	12.5	-3.4	-2.6	-6.8	.. c	.. c	1.3	.. c	.. c
Austria	7 795.7	7 714.3	6 860.6	7 651.6	6 756.4	69.1	50.3	124.1	168.9	186.6
Belgium	2 489.4	2 165.4	2 340.4	2 995.0	3 081.5	-	-	-	-	-
Canada	28.0	20.0	25.0	33.0	25.5	.. c	.. c	.. c	.. c	.. c
Chile	-0.1	-0.8	.. c	-1.6	-0.9	.. c	.. c	.. c	.. c	.. c
Czech Republic	5 117.2	4 537.1	5 423.3	7 731.1	7 512.7	988.9	948.7	900.1	2 388.7	2 191.3
Denmark	492.2	430.8	407.5	521.6	469.6	.. c	.. c	.. c	49.9	48.7
Estonia	17.0	15.6	15.6	16.7	16.5	-	-	-	-	-
Finland	100.8	116.9	107.7	155.7	182.6	.. c	.. c	.. c	.. c	.. c
France	1 165.0	917.1	881.9	817.5	1 336.7	.. c	66.7	64.7	73.4	69.6
Germany	4 255.7	3 076.0	2 666.1	4 558.9	4 189.0	37.4	27.5	40.5	41.4	36.9
Greece	1.7	5.8	-1.1	2.7	10.1	.. c	.. c	-	-	-
Hungary	2 681.7	2 613.3	2 597.3	2 999.6	3 059.4	74.0	83.1	135.1	162.3	151.4
Iceland	9.4	.. c	.. c	0.3	0.2	.. c	.. c	.. c	.. c	.. c
Ireland	610.8	519.7	421.4	547.5	438.5	.. c	.. c	-	-	-1.7
Israel[1]	5.9	-1.9	-1.0	5.3	4.9	-	-	-	-	-
Italy	3 191.1	3 399.9	2 311.4	2 791.2	2 845.4	34.0	26.1	26.4	31.9	31.3
Japan	43.8	44.2	72.1	127.9	144.1	-	-	-	-	-0.2
Korea	3 184.2	3 230.4	3 060.2	3 446.1	3 384.4	.. c	.. c	-	-	0.6
Latvia	4.4	5.6	-0.1	-0.7	27.7	.. c	.. c	11.4	14.8	13.0
Lithuania	-0.8	-1.0	-2.2	-1.7	-0.8	.. c	.. c	.. c	.. c	.. c
Luxembourg	4 152.7	3 872.2	3 303.8	4 018.9	3 954.3	.. c	73.3	80.3	77.2	40.3
Mexico	0.4	-62.4	-1.7	-4.8	-49.1	.. c	.. c	.. c	.. c	.. c
Netherlands	9 818.0	9 077.4	13 231.4	15 300.2	14 966.9	78.5	190.2	253.1	193.5	255.0
New Zealand	27.0	24.1	5.7	-0.1	0.0	-	-	-	-	-
Norway	150.6	150.1	147.6	138.6	127.1	.. c	-	.. c	.. c	.. c
Poland	71.2	316.8	196.3	471.5	455.9	265.2	229.7	156.1	299.5	368.6
Portugal	4.6	4.0	-1.3	-0.8	-1.8	.. c	.. c	.. c	.. c	.. c
Slovak Republic	-	-	..	-	-	-	-	..	-	-
Slovenia	16.7	15.0	8.8	11.9	7.0	.. c	17.3	17.1	18.9	16.9
Spain	613.5	587.4	650.9	837.8	795.0	.. c	.. c	.. c	.. c	.. c
Sweden	294.5	257.7	351.2	823.1	840.4	-	-	-	.. c	.. c
Switzerland	845.5	718.2	593.7	842.4	874.4	.. c	6.1	11.2	12.9	12.1
Turkey	6.0	-3.3	-13.2	5.6	-4.2	.. c	149.3	146.1	164.5	154.4
United Kingdom	540.6	492.0	545.6	1 441.6	1 793.3	.. c	7.9	138.3	232.8	310.5
United States	305.1	331.5	-11.4	222.6	155.1	.. c	14.9	11.9	10.8	16.5
EUROPE	**45 519.0**	**41 801.5**	**43 701.0**	**54 881.7**	**53 964.5**	**2 705.3**	**2 388.2**	**2 517.4**	**4 423.3**	**4 396.3**
Bulgaria	5.1	12.2	22.7	22.9	32.1	4.4	4.4	4.4	4.9	5.5
Croatia	3.4	4.5	-1.5	-4.2	2.8	13.4	9.9	12.2	16.0	13.7
Cyprus[2, 3]	1 367.1	1 383.2	1 809.1	1 795.1	1 728.6	158.5	147.4	87.8	95.7	143.0
Malta	117.2	106.2	77.9	150.0	268.6	.. c	.. c	.. c	.. c	.. c
Romania	5.4	6.6	25.4	36.5	-8.1	21.4	18.8	7.5	11.4	10.3
Russian Federation	-375.5	-182.8	-225.4	-243.6	-181.8	21.0	28.9	35.3	45.9	46.5
Ukraine	-3.2	-0.4	-2.6	-3.4	-6.0	137.8	122.5	113.7	121.6	111.0
AFRICA	**44.7**	**45.9**	**31.8**	**48.7**	**56.3**	**6.2**	**5.6**	**.. c**	**.. c**	**.. c**
Northern Africa	-11.1	-1.9	-1.2	-0.5	5.2	6.2	5.6	.. c	.. c	.. c
Algeria	.. c	-	-	-	-	-	-	-	-	-
Egypt	-12.1	-2.0	-4.2	-0.3	-0.4	-	-	-	-	-
Libya	-	-	-	-	-	-	-	-	-	-
Morocco	0.6	-0.5	-0.7	-6.0	-2.1	.. c	.. c	.. c	.. c	.. c
Tunisia	0.4	0.8	3.7	5.8	7.8	.. c	.. c	-	-	-
Other African countries	55.8	47.8	33.0	49.2	51.1	-	-	.. c	.. c	.. c
Nigeria	.. c	.. c	0.0	-0.2	-0.2	-	-	.. c	.. c	.. c
South Africa	-2.6	-1.7	-9.8	-15.3	-11.9	-	-	-	-	-
AMERICA	**588.7**	**546.7**	**322.4**	**671.8**	**655.3**	**53.6**	**28.9**	**52.2**	**66.2**	**71.0**
Northern America	333.1	351.6	13.6	255.6	180.6	16.3	15.0	12.2	11.9	18.3
Central America and Caribbean countries	115.1	68.5	123.0	209.7	206.3	12.9	10.9	.. c	.. c	.. c
Bahamas	0.4	27.2	.. c	.. c	.. c	-	-	-	-	-
Bermuda	-	-	-	.. c	.. c	-	-	-	-	-
Cayman Islands	.. c	.. c	.. c	82.5	104.1	-	-	-	-	-
Costa Rica	1.0	0.4	.. c	.. c	.. c	-	-	-	-	-
El Salvador	-	-	.. c	-	-	-	-	-	-	-
Guatemala	-	-	-	.. c	-	-	-	-	-	-
Honduras	-	-	-	-	-	-	-	-	-	-
Nicaragua	-	-	-	-	-	-	-	-	-	-
Panama	2.8	2.5	1.8	73.1	90.1	-	-	-	-	-
Virgin Islands, U.S.	-	-	-	-	-	-	-	-	-	-
South America	140.5	126.6	185.8	206.4	268.4	24.4	2.9	26.2	38.6	37.7
Argentina	130.6	118.9	182.0	208.0	269.6	.. c	.. c	.. c	.. c	.. c
Bolivia	-	-	-	-	-	-	-	-	-	-
Brazil	10.1	8.6	4.9	1.0	0.5	.. c	2.9	8.6	18.1	17.7
Colombia	.. c	-	-0.8	-0.9	-0.8	-	-	-	-	-
Ecuador	-	-0.1	0.0	.. c	.. c	-	-	-	-	-
Paraguay	-	-	-	-	-	-	-	-	-	-
Peru	.. c	-	.. c	0.0	0.0	-	-	-	-	-
Uruguay	.. c	.. c	.. c	.. c	.. c	-	-	-	-	-
Venezuela	.. c	.. c	.. c	.. c	.. c	-	-	-	-	-

Table 2. Foreign direct investment positions by country *(cont.)*
At year end

Million US dollars

	Inward					Outward				
	2014	2015	2016	2017	2018	2014	2015	2016	2017	2018
ASIA	**3 579.0**	**3 585.1**	**3 534.1**	**3 910.9**	**3 772.2**	**54.5**	**39.6**	**54.7**	**93.1**	**110.7**
Near and Middle East	17.1	2.1	4.0	8.6	15.1	8.2	.. c	.. c	.. c	.. c
Gulf Arabian countries	7.7	1.3	2.4	0.5	7.6	-	-	-	-	-
Kuwait	-	-	.. c	.. c	-	-	-	-	-	-
Qatar	-	-	0.0	-1.0	-	-	-	-	-	-
Saudi Arabia	.. c	12.1	.. c	10.8	10.1	-	-	-	-	-
United Arab Emirates	-5.6	-10.9	-9.1	-9.2	-2.5	-	-	-	-	-
Other Near and Middle East	9.4	0.9	1.6	8.0	7.5	8.2	.. c	.. c	.. c	.. c
Jordan	.. c	-0.1	.. c	-0.2	-0.2	-	-	-	-	-
Other Asian countries	3 561.9	3 583.0	3 530.1	3 902.3	3 757.2	46.3	39.3	54.2	92.3	109.7
China	38.0	15.0	26.7	36.1	35.3	.. c	24.1	23.9	52.6	63.5
Hong Kong, China	6.2	5.8	24.7	30.2	14.7	.. c	.. c	.. c	.. c	.. c
India	-2.1	-4.6	-3.4	-2.7	-6.8	.. c	6.2	9.2	13.7	12.8
Indonesia	-0.3	1.0	4.5	0.0	4.7	-	-	-	-	-
Iran, Islamic Republic of	-	-	-	-	-	-	-	-	-	-
Malaysia	98.9	83.1	76.1	77.0	65.0	.. c	.. c	.. c	.. c	.. c
Philippines	0.0	-	0.3	0.2	0.0	-	-	-	-	-
Singapore	107.4	73.8	103.1	51.2	19.9	.. c	.. c	.. c	.. c	.. c
Chinese Taipei	58.9	74.3	79.6	18.1	-6.3	-	-	-	-	-
Thailand	6.5	2.2	3.0	6.8	0.8	-	-	-	-	-
Viet Nam	20.5	57.9	81.0	112.0	101.5	.. c	.. c	.. c	.. c	.. c
AUSTRALIA, OCEANIA AND POLAR REGIONS	**9.4**	**36.6**	**2.3**	**-2.8**	**-7.1**	**0.7**	**.. c**	**1.3**	**.. c**	**.. c**
WORLD unallocated and confidential	**-**	**0.0**	**0.0**	**0.0**	**0.0**	**-**	**- d**	**- d**	**.. d**	**.. d**
European Union (EU28)	**44 931.8**	**41 651.8**	**44 250.0**	**55 691.5**	**54 760.1**	**2 162.7**	**1 982.1**	**2 123.2**	**3 975.3**	**3 977.6**
G20 countries excl. European Union	**12 513.6**	**11 424.5**	**9 523.7**	**13 431.5**	**13 933.1**	**387.3**	**365.5**	**520.4**	**703.6**	**782.3**
G20 OECD countries	**12 702.1**	**11 458.0**	**9 532.6**	**13 437.2**	**13 813.4**	**343.2**	**303.5**	**443.3**	**573.2**	**641.7**
G20 Non-OECD countries	**-188.6**	**-33.5**	**-8.9**	**-5.7**	**119.7**	**44.0**	**61.9**	**77.0**	**130.4**	**140.6**
MENA countries	**0.1**	**.. c**	**.. c**	**3.0**	**15.6**	**6.2**	**.. c**	**.. c**	**.. c**	**.. c**
ASEAN countries	**232.9**	**.. c**	**267.9**	**247.2**	**191.9**	**20.5**	**.. c**	**17.9**	**23.2**	**.. c**

- Nil; .. Not available; c Confidential data; d Secondary Confidentiality

Note: Detailed metadata at: *http://stats.oecd.org/OECDStat_Metadata/ShowMetadata.ashx?Dataset=FDI_CTRY_IND_SUMM.*

1. Information on data for Israel: *http://oe.cd/israel-disclaimer.*
2. Note by Turkey: The information in this document with reference to "Cyprus" relates to the southern part of the Island. There is no single authority representing both Turkish and Greek Cypriot people on the Island. Turkey recognises the Turkish Republic of Northern Cyprus (TRNC). Until a lasting and equitable solution is found within the context of the United Nations, Turkey shall preserve its position concerning the "Cyprus issue".
3. Note by all the European Union Member States of the OECD and the European Union: The Republic of Cyprus is recognised by all members of the United Nations with the exception of Turkey. The information in this document relates to the area under the effective control of the Government of the Republic of Cyprus.

Source: OECD International Direct Investment Statistics (database): https://doi.org/10.1787/idi-data-en

Table 3. Foreign direct investment income by country

Million US dollars

	Inward					Outward				
	2014	2015	2016	2017	2018	2014	2015	2016	2017	2018
WORLD	**4 375.2**	**..**	**4 411.3**	**4 330.4**	**4 773.8**	**201.7**	**..**	**205.8**	**391.1**	**371.1**
OECD COUNTRIES	**4 464.5**	**..**	**4 485.3**	**4 421.3**	**4 764.4**	**124.8**	**..**	**167.3**	**354.9**	**307.8**
Australia	-	..	-	-	-	-	..	-	-	0.0
Austria	823.5	..	744.7	698.1	593.2	1.0	..	19.4	11.9	11.0
Belgium	217.2	..	223.8	211.8	265.8	0.0	..	-	-	-
Canada	-2.7	..	2.8	.. c	.. c	-	..	0.1	0.2	.. c
Chile	-	..	-	-	-	0.8	..	0.4	.. c	0.4
Czech Republic	643.3	..	195.5	314.7	320.0	36.6	..	47.6	229.7	215.3
Denmark	5.3	..	46.0	61.6	.. c	-	..	3.0	.. c	.. c
Estonia	0.7	..	0.0	.. c	2.4	-	..	-	-	-
Finland	2.3	..	3.2	6.4	-9.7	0.0	..	-	-	-
France	115.7	..	128.3	151.8	134.7	0.0	..	6.9	.. c	8.4
Germany	476.4	..	576.9	524.3	512.3	0.1	..	3.1	14.0	5.1
Greece	-0.1	..	-	.. c	.. c	-	..	-	-	-
Hungary	124.9	..	247.1	182.9	484.6	3.1	..	20.7	-1.2	-1.0
Iceland	0.3	..	0.1	-	-	-	..	-	-	-
Ireland	4.2	..	25.6	22.1	6.6	-	..	-	-	-
Israel[1]	0.0	..	0.2	1.7	0.7	-	..	-	-	-
Italy	184.4	..	349.2	260.3	193.7	0.4	..	0.1	.. c	.. c
Japan	0.1	..	2.7	-19.5	0.7	-	..	-	-	-
Korea	732.6	..	398.1	401.4	519.1	-	..	-0.8	-	-
Latvia	-	..	-	.. c	.. c	-	..	-	-	-
Lithuania	-	..	0.0	.. c	.. c	-	..	-	-	-
Luxembourg	84.5	..	283.3	257.2	441.7	60.9	..	-1.2	.. c	-4.7
Mexico	-	..	-	-	-	-	..	-	-	-
Netherlands	744.7	..	946.3	1 056.1	1 170.7	12.5	..	17.4	24.4	13.2
New Zealand	-	..	0.6	-	-	-	..	-	-	-
Norway	80.8	..	-1.5	15.3	7.0	-	..	-	-	-
Poland	101.1	..	29.6	21.5	2.0	0.6	..	4.0	34.8	43.7
Portugal	0.1	..	-	-	0.0	-	..	-	-	2.1
Slovak Republic	-	..	..	-	-	-	..	..	-	-
Slovenia	0.5	..	-0.4	-0.6	-0.9	1.1	..	-	-	-
Spain	23.2	..	77.1	50.8	80.9	-	..	-	.. c	-
Sweden	0.0	..	24.4	33.0	17.1	-	..	-	-	-
Switzerland	-2.2	..	43.6	104.6	9.2	0.4	..	-	-1.3	-1.1
Turkey	0.0	..	0.8	.. c	.. c	6.1	..	37.3	.. c	-0.4
United Kingdom	98.7	..	139.6	80.5	42.9	1.2	..	9.2	.. c	11.6
United States	5.0	..	-2.6	-21.3	-35.7	-	..	-	1.6	1.5
EUROPE	**3 247.7**	**..**	**4 006.6**	**4 027.0**	**4 301.2**	**197.4**	**..**	**200.6**	**380.7**	**361.6**
Bulgaria	0.0	..	0.4	0.5	.. c	-	..	0.1	.. c	-
Croatia	-	..	.. c	0.3	.. c	0.0	..	6.3	.. c	.. c
Cyprus[2, 3]	-95.6	..	-27.2	29.4	46.8	36.6	..	19.1	19.1	19.9
Malta	3.3	..	4.3	25.4	30.2	-	..	1.5	1.9	.. c
Romania	0.0	..	-	.. c	.. c	-	..	0.0	.. c	.. c
Russian Federation	0.4	..	-2.6	-2.8	3.3	0.8	..	4.1	5.5	9.6
Ukraine	-0.2	..	-0.4	-0.4	-0.6	45.8	..	0.7	0.4	23.0
AFRICA	**3.9**	**..**	**-0.8**	**6.9**	**2.9**	**-**	**..**	**-**	**.. c**	**-**
Northern Africa	-	..	-	-	-	-	..	-	.. c	-
Algeria	-	..	-	-	-	-	..	-	-	-
Egypt	-	..	-	-	-	-	..	-	-	-
Libya	-	..	-	-	-	-	..	-	-	-
Morocco	-	..	-	-	-	-	..	-	.. c	-
Tunisia	-	..	-	-	-	-	..	-	-	-
Other African countries	3.9	..	-0.8	6.9	2.9	-	..	-	-	-
Nigeria	-	..	-	-	-	-	..	-	-	-
South Africa	-	..	-	.. c	.. c	-	..	-	-	-
AMERICA	**0.1**	**..**	**-0.6**	**-21.1**	**-28.5**	**-**	**..**	**0.6**	**.. c**	**2.5**
Northern America	0.1	..	0.2	-21.6	-36.1	-	..	0.1	1.8	1.7
Central America and Caribbean countries	-	..	-0.1	0.0	9.6	-	..	-	-	-
Bahamas	-	..	-	-	-	-	..	-	-	-
Bermuda	-	..	-	.. c	.. c	-	..	-	-	-
Cayman Islands	0.0	..	-0.1	-0.1	.. c	-	..	-	-	-
Costa Rica	-	..	-	-	-	-	..	-	-	-
El Salvador	-	..	-	-	-	-	..	-	-	-
Guatemala	-	..	-	-	-	-	..	-	-	-
Honduras	-	..	-	-	-	-	..	-	-	-
Nicaragua	-	..	-	-	-	-	..	-	-	-
Panama	-	..	-0.1	-0.1	.. c	-	..	-	-	-
Virgin Islands, U.S.	-	..	-	-	-	-	..	-	-	-
South America	-	..	-0.7	0.6	-1.9	-	..	0.5	.. c	0.8
Argentina	0.2	..	0.5	0.5	-1.8	-	..	-	-	-
Bolivia	-	..	-	-	-	-	..	-	-	-
Brazil	-	..	-1.2	0.1	-0.1	-	..	0.1	0.4	.. c
Colombia	-	..	-	-	-	-	..	-	-	-
Ecuador	-	..	-	-	-	-	..	-	-	-
Paraguay	-	..	-	-	-	-	..	-	-	-
Peru	-	..	-	-	-	-	..	-	-	-
Uruguay	-	..	-	-	-	-	..	-	-	-
Venezuela	-	..	-	-	-	-	..	-	-	-

Table 3. Foreign direct investment income by country *(cont.)*

Million US dollars

	Inward					Outward				
	2014	2015	2016	2017	2018	2014	2015	2016	2017	2018
ASIA	**728.7**	**..**	**405.6**	**317.6**	**498.1**	**-6.7**	**..**	**4.5**	**7.7**	**7.0**
Near and Middle East	-	..	-0.3	1.3	-0.2	-	..	-	-	-
Gulf Arabian countries	-	..	-0.2	.. c	.. c	-	..	-	-	-
Kuwait	-	..	-	-	-	-	..	-	-	-
Qatar	-	..	-	-	-	-	..	-	-	-
Saudi Arabia	-	..	-0.2	.. c	.. c	-	..	-	-	-
United Arab Emirates	-	..	-	-	-	-	..	-	-	-
Other Near and Middle East	-	..	-0.1	1.5	0.4	-	..	-	-	-
Jordan	-	..	-	-	-	-	..	-	-	-
Other Asian countries	728.7	..	405.9	316.3	498.2	-6.7	..	4.5	7.7	7.0
China	0.4	..	-0.8	-1.2	2.7	-	..	5.0	8.0	7.3
Hong Kong, China	0.2	..	0.4	.. c	.. c	-	..	0.4	.. c	-
India	0.0	..	-	-	0.0	-	..	-	-0.3	-0.2
Indonesia	-	..	-	-	-	-	..	-	-	-
Iran, Islamic Republic of	-	..	-	-	-	-	..	-	-	-
Malaysia	0.1	..	0.2	.. c	.. c	-6.7	..	-	-	-
Philippines	-	..	-	-	-	-	..	-	-	-
Singapore	-3.9	..	4.7	-66.2	-17.8	-	..	-	-	-
Chinese Taipei	-	..	0.0	.. c	.. c	-	..	-	-	-
Thailand	0.3	..	0.1	.. c	.. c	-	..	-	-	-
Viet Nam	-	..	0.6	.. c	.. c	0.0	..	0.0	.. c	.. c
AUSTRALIA, OCEANIA AND POLAR REGIONS	**-**	**..**	**0.6**	**-**	**.. c**	**-**	**..**	**-**	**-**	**0.0**
WORLD unallocated and confidential	**394.9**	**..**	**-**	**0.0**	**.. d**	**11.0**	**..**	**-**	**.. d**	**0.0**
European Union (EU28)	**3 558.1**	**..**	**4 018.1**	**3 994.8**	**4 350.7**	**200.1**	**..**	**157.5**	**362.0**	**330.0**
G20 countries excl. European Union	**1 611.4**	**..**	**1 591.4**	**1 373.8**	**1 360.7**	**8.6**	**..**	**65.1**	**65.4**	**43.6**
G20 OECD countries	**1 610.4**	**..**	**1 595.8**	**1 377.4**	**1 357.2**	**7.8**	**..**	**56.0**	**51.8**	**26.6**
G20 Non-OECD countries	**1.1**	**..**	**-4.4**	**-3.6**	**3.5**	**0.8**	**..**	**9.1**	**13.6**	**17.1**
MENA countries	**-**	**..**	**-0.5**	**.. c**	**-0.8**	**-**	**..**	**-**	**.. c**	**-**
ASEAN countries	**-3.9**	**..**	**.. c**	**-64.9**	**-23.5**	**-6.7**	**..**	**0.0**	**.. c**	**-0.1**

- Nil; .. Not available; c Confidential data; d Secondary Confidentiality

Note: Detailed metadata at: *http://stats.oecd.org/OECDStat_Metadata/ShowMetadata.ashx?Dataset=FDI_CTRY_IND_SUMM.*

1. Information on data for Israel: *http://oe.cd/israel-disclaimer.*
2. Note by Turkey: The information in this document with reference to "Cyprus" relates to the southern part of the Island. There is no single authority representing both Turkish and Greek Cypriot people on the Island. Turkey recognises the Turkish Republic of Northern Cyprus (TRNC). Until a lasting and equitable solution is found within the context of the United Nations, Turkey shall preserve its position concerning the "Cyprus issue".
3. Note by all the European Union Member States of the OECD and the European Union: The Republic of Cyprus is recognised by all members of the United Nations with the exception of Turkey. The information in this document relates to the area under the effective control of the Government of the Republic of Cyprus.

Source: OECD International Direct Investment Statistics (database): https://doi.org/10.1787/idi-data-en

SLOVAK REPUBLIC

Table 4. Foreign direct investment flows by industrial sector

Million US dollars

	Inward					Outward				
	2014	2015	2016	2017	2018	2014	2015	2016	2017	2018
All FDI activities	**-331.5**	..	**805.1**	**4 008.2**	**1 183.2**	**-123.4**	..	**95.5**	**1 322.6**	**234.1**
Agriculture, forestry and fishing	..	..	**-40.1**	**14.3**	..	..	..	.. c	.. c	..
Mining and quarrying	..	..	**-41.0**	**21.9**	..	..	..	**0.3**	**243.5**	..
Extraction activities	..	..	49.5	12.2	..	..	..	.. c	.. c	..
Manufacturing	..	..	**845.9**	**1 883.0**	..	..	..	**78.9**	**74.6**	..
of which:										
Food products, beverages and tobacco	..	..	-10.7	-13.0	..	..	..	7.8	5.9	..
Textiles, wood and paper products; printing	..	..	93.9	62.7	..	..	..	62.7	8.7	..
Chemical, rubber, plastic, non-metallic mineral products	..	..	257.3	132.1	..	..	..	-0.4	8.4	..
Metal and machinery products, except electrical equipment	..	..	-124.8	511.4	..	..	..	-23.8	6.0	..
Motor vehicles, trailers, semi-trailers, other transport equipment	..	..	355.5	788.3	..	..	..	8.3	-2.2	..
Other manufacturing	..	..	274.7	401.5	..	..	..	24.4	47.8	..
Electricity, gas, steam and air conditioning supply	..	..	**12.7**	**-106.1**	..	..	..	**4.7**	**0.2**	..
Water supply; sewerage, waste management and remediation activities	..	..	**-2.5**	**17.5**	..	..	..	.. c	**2.0**	..
Construction	..	..	**12.5**	**46.8**	..	..	..	**-103.7**	**23.8**	..
Services	..	..	**17.6**	**2 130.8**	..	..	..	**106.4**	**980.1**	..
Wholesale and retail trade; repair of motor vehicles and motorcycles	..	..	292.9	141.5	..	..	..	47.4	44.6	..
Transportation and storage	..	..	54.7	83.4	..	..	..	54.8	-4.3	..
Accommodation and food service activities	..	..	-38.3	-0.6	..	..	..	.. c	.. c	..
Information and communication	..	..	-202.1	189.3	..	..	..	33.0	127.1	..
Financial and insurance activities	..	..	701.8	229.4	..	..	..	1.2	-98.3	..
Activities of holding companies	..	..	3.4	-96.0	..	..	..	3.7	-53.3	..
Real estate activities	..	..	-109.3	507.6	..	..	..	1.8	303.8	..
Professional, scientific and technical activities	..	..	-132.5	1 173.0	..	..	..	-114.4	137.0	..
Administrative and support service activities	..	..	-586.2	-339.8	..	..	..	.. c	6.7	..
Public administration; activities of households and of extraterritorial organisations	..	..	-	-	..	..	..	-	.. c	..
Education	..	..	.. c	.. c	..	..	..	-	-	..
Human health and social work activities	..	..	-8.5	199.8	..	..	..	.. c	.. c	..
Arts, entertainment and recreation	..	..	81.3	-50.1	..	..	..	27.7	.. c	..
Other services	..	..	-36.3	-2.7	..	..	..	54.6	.. c	..
Not allocated and confidential	**-331.5**	..	-	**0.0**	**1 183.2**	**-123.4**	..	.. c	.. c	**234.1**
Private real estate activities	..	..	-	-	..	..	..	-	-	..

- Nil; .. Not available; c Confidential data

Note: Detailed metadata at: *http://stats.oecd.org/OECDStat_Metadata/ShowMetadata.ashx?Dataset=FDI_CTRY_IND_SUMM.*

Source: OECD International Direct Investment Statistics (database): https://doi.org/10.1787/idi-data-en

SLOVAK REPUBLIC

Table 5. Foreign direct investment positions by industrial sector

At year end

Million US dollars

	Inward					Outward				
	2014	2015	2016	2017	2018	2014	2015	2016	2017	2018
All FDI activities	**49 740.8**	**46 015.8**	**47 591.7**	**59 510.3**	**58 441.2**	**2 820.2**	**2 462.3**	**2 631.0**	**4 589.9**	**4 585.5**
Agriculture, forestry and fishing	**190.6**	**164.2**	**150.4**	**181.2**	..	.. c	**1.7**	**13.2**	**6.2**	..
Mining and quarrying	**254.9**	**111.5**	**94.5**	**76.1**	..	.. c	.. c	**70.6**	**413.0**	..
Extraction activities	.. c	9.6	.. d	-18.8	..	.. c	.. c	.. c	.. c	..
Manufacturing	**16 620.9**	**15 301.7**	**15 358.3**	**19 091.0**	..	**540.0**	**515.8**	**471.8**	**600.4**	..
of which:										
Food products, beverages and tobacco	837.0	884.7	637.7	670.5	..	35.8	20.4	35.9	48.0	..
Textiles, wood and paper products; printing	716.8	628.1	676.7	809.4	..	43.8	76.2	118.3	146.2	..
Chemical, rubber, plastic, non-metallic mineral products	.. c	3 528.0	3 587.1	4 115.7	..	.. c	-	61.5	76.6	..
Metal and machinery products, except electrical equipment	5 326.0	4 845.5	4 830.7	5 673.6	..	180.0	80.7	89.3	107.2	..
Motor vehicles, trailers, semi-trailers, other transport equipment	3 514.2	3 275.4	3 383.9	5 411.5	..	.. c	66.6	68.4	70.6	..
Other manufacturing	2 510.9	2 139.9	2 242.2	2 410.4	..	81.5	87.9	98.4	151.8	..
Electricity, gas, steam and air conditioning supply	**1 846.2**	**1 948.8**	**3 484.1**	**3 919.6**	..	**43.9**	**5.7**	**19.2**	**24.5**	..
Water supply; sewerage, waste management and remediation activities	**120.4**	**126.5**	**121.3**	**154.4**	..	.. c	**2.2**	**0.8**	**3.2**	..
Construction	**526.5**	**477.1**	**608.9**	**765.1**	..	**132.1**	**87.8**	**54.0**	**86.9**	..
Services	**30 181.2**	**27 885.9**	**27 774.2**	**35 322.9**	..	**2 099.0**	**1 778.9**	**2 001.4**	**3 455.8**	..
Wholesale and retail trade; repair of motor vehicles and motorcycles	4 512.0	4 137.5	4 344.0	5 091.3	..	588.9	469.1	485.8	603.8	..
Transportation and storage	1 414.6	1 856.1	1 833.5	2 149.4	..	24.1	65.7	133.1	153.7	..
Accommodation and food service activities	302.7	69.1	124.9	158.6	..	.. c	.. c	.. c	3.9	..
Information and communication	1 933.4	2 369.6	2 142.0	2 632.1	..	126.2	106.5	133.9	290.7	..
Financial and insurance activities	12 197.6	11 235.6	11 048.2	12 869.9	..	280.9	361.1	261.3	214.5	..
Activities of holding companies	.. c	124.0	-120.5	-541.8	..	150.8	81.5	.. d	80.7	..
Real estate activities	3 871.4	3 289.5	3 004.2	4 369.4	..	82.1	410.3	386.3	754.7	..
Professional, scientific and technical activities	1 973.8	1 598.9	1 636.3	3 315.4	..	344.7	146.8	381.6	598.1	..
Administrative and support service activities	3 747.8	2 882.5	3 158.4	4 019.4	..	481.1	17.9	.. d	23.3	..
Public administration; activities of households and of extraterritorial organisations	-	-	-	-	..	-	-	-	.. c	..
Education	1.6	1.5	.. c	.. c	..	-	-	-	-	..
Human health and social work activities	137.2	134.3	126.4	421.8	..	.. c	.. c	.. c	.. c	..
Arts, entertainment and recreation	71.5	166.1	252.0	181.2	..	.. c	39.5	49.8	57.7	..
Other services	13.6	145.0	103.3	113.2	..	-	14.9	.. c	.. c	..
Not allocated and confidential	-	**0.1**	**0.0**	**0.0**	**58 441.2**	.. c	.. c	-	**0.0**	**4 585.5**
Private real estate activities	-	-	-	-	..	-	-	-	-	..

- Nil; .. Not available; c Confidential data; d Secondary Confidentiality

Note: Detailed metadata at: *http://stats.oecd.org/OECDStat_Metadata/ShowMetadata.ashx?Dataset=FDI_CTRY_IND_SUMM.*

Source: OECD International Direct Investment Statistics (database): https://doi.org/10.1787/idi-data-en

Table 6. Foreign direct investment income by industrial sector

Million US dollars

	Inward					Outward				
	2014	2015	2016	2017	2018	2014	2015	2016	2017	2018
All FDI activities	**4 375.2**	..	**4 411.3**	**4 330.4**	**4 773.8**	**201.7**	..	**205.8**	**391.1**	**371.1**
Agriculture, forestry and fishing	..	..	**6.6**	**21.1**	..	..	..	**.. c**	**-3.5**	..
Mining and quarrying	..	..	**40.7**	**40.2**	..	..	..	**.. c**	**-44.2**	..
Extraction activities	..	..	36.7	.. c	..	..	..	.. c	.. c	..
Manufacturing	..	..	**2 233.4**	**2 049.3**	..	..	..	**29.9**	**28.2**	..
of which:										
Food products, beverages and tobacco	..	..	89.0	49.1	..	..	..	.. c	0.2	..
Textiles, wood and paper products; printing	..	..	101.5	85.2	..	..	..	16.6	.. c	..
Chemical, rubber, plastic, non-metallic mineral products	..	..	616.1	530.5	..	..	..	1.0	.. c	..
Metal and machinery products, except electrical equipment	..	..	601.1	505.7	..	..	..	0.3	5.1	..
Motor vehicles, trailers, semi-trailers, other transport equipment	..	..	664.1	688.0	..	..	..	3.3	.. c	..
Other manufacturing	..	..	161.5	190.7	..	..	..	8.2	11.7	..
Electricity, gas, steam and air conditioning supply	..	..	**81.0**	**30.1**	..	..	..	**0.9**	**2.6**	..
Water supply; sewerage, waste management and remediation activities	..	..	**5.0**	**15.0**	..	..	..	**0.1**	**0.3**	..
Construction	..	..	**21.0**	**63.6**	..	..	..	**3.7**	**25.2**	..
Services	..	..	**2 023.7**	**2 111.0**	..	..	..	**170.4**	**382.5**	..
Wholesale and retail trade; repair of motor vehicles and motorcycles	..	..	495.7	627.7	..	..	..	53.4	156.8	..
Transportation and storage	..	..	116.3	100.1	..	..	..	11.1	-5.6	..
Accommodation and food service activities	..	..	-16.7	9.6	..	..	..	.. c	.. c	..
Information and communication	..	..	286.3	335.9	..	..	..	10.8	32.1	..
Financial and insurance activities	..	..	1 003.3	864.7	..	..	..	28.9	34.5	..
Activities of holding companies	..	..	-19.9	-30.8	..	..	..	8.6	10.7	..
Real estate activities	..	..	105.6	86.1	..	..	..	21.6	69.4	..
Professional, scientific and technical activities	..	..	74.9	-7.0	..	..	..	33.0	34.0	..
Administrative and support service activities	..	..	-8.2	37.4	..	..	..	.. c	.. c	..
Public administration; activities of households and of extraterritorial organisations	..	..	-	-	..	..	..	-	.. c	..
Education	..	..	.. c	0.0	..	..	..	-	-	..
Human health and social work activities	..	..	0.9	-1.5	..	..	..	.. c	.. c	..
Arts, entertainment and recreation	..	..	17.4	77.0	..	..	..	2.8	.. c	..
Other services	..	..	-51.9	.. c	..	..	..	.. c	.. c	..
Not allocated and confidential	**4 375.2**	..	**0.0**	**0.0**	**4 773.8**	**201.7**	..	**.. c**	**0.0**	**371.1**
Private real estate activities	..	..	-	-	..	..	..	-	-	..

- Nil; .. Not available; c Confidential data

Note: Detailed metadata at: *http://stats.oecd.org/OECDStat_Metadata/ShowMetadata.ashx?Dataset=FDI_CTRY_IND_SUMM.*

Source: *OECD International Direct Investment Statistics (database): https://doi.org/10.1787/idi-data-en*

SLOVENIA

Table 1. Foreign direct investment flows by country

Million US dollars

	Inward					Outward				
	2014	2015	2016	2017	2018	2014	2015	2016	2017	2018
WORLD	**1 049.9**	**1 674.7**	**1 244.7**	**895.8**	**1 368.3**	**275.2**	**267.3**	**289.6**	**337.7**	**267.4**
OECD COUNTRIES	**799.6**	**1 491.9**	**1 149.2**	**624.1**	**1 204.1**	**240.2**	**119.7**	**-11.7**	**195.9**	**50.5**
Australia	-0.6	-0.7	0.8	1.3	-15.3	6.3	7.6	2.7	3.1	-4.1
Austria	-200.1	295.9	148.6	435.0	262.8	93.9	3.4	-45.5	-4.6	10.6
Belgium	0.9	12.7	18.1	18.3	-18.2	-0.7	0.1	-0.3	-0.3	0.4
Canada	-0.1	-0.6	-2.0	-1.1	-0.5	2.7	-0.6	2.4	-0.6	9.3
Chile	0.0	0.0	0.0	0.0	0.0	-	-	1.0	2.3	2.2
Czech Republic	39.2	92.7	47.3	31.2	4.2	31.4	-3.3	19.7	-7.9	3.6
Denmark	-5.0	0.1	-3.5	1.7	0.0	-8.6	3.1	-4.9	1.1	3.3
Estonia	1.3	0.5	-0.2	-0.1	-1.3	-	-	-	-	-
Finland	0.8	1.0	-10.9	3.9	-6.2	-0.3	0.2	-3.5	1.7	4.9
France	-44.9	1.4	-22.6	63.1	-28.8	-0.4	-7.3	0.3	-7.4	1.6
Germany	502.6	151.7	35.4	54.4	189.4	51.2	-42.7	-21.2	129.2	22.0
Greece	-0.7	-1.6	0.4	2.3	1.6	3.5	0.7	2.7	8.8	6.4
Hungary	8.0	3.7	6.4	9.7	30.7	-6.5	-0.8	1.0	2.8	-2.0
Iceland	0.0	0.0	-	0.0	0.0	-	-	-	0.0	-
Ireland	-16.2	15.3	31.6	-5.8	-0.7	0.6	0.2	4.2	0.6	0.1
Israel[1]	-0.9	0.3	1.3	2.5	1.6	0.1	-	-	-	-
Italy	36.6	62.3	91.2	-128.2	45.2	9.4	-2.3	13.6	39.0	-3.1
Japan	-1.6	25.7	-0.9	-27.4	-28.2	-0.4	0.0	-0.9	-0.4	0.1
Korea	0.4	-1.7	1.0	1.3	-0.5	0.5	0.1	0.1	-0.3	-0.7
Latvia	0.8	1.0	0.5	0.3	0.3	-0.1	0.0	0.0	0.0	-0.1
Lithuania	0.3	0.2	0.1	0.1	0.0	-0.3	-0.2	0.0	0.2	-0.2
Luxembourg	169.4	222.7	469.8	-11.2	463.5	1.3	-3.2	3.7	-3.4	0.0
Mexico	-0.2	0.2	-0.2	0.0	-0.7	5.7	1.4	-3.7	1.7	-1.1
Netherlands	240.7	325.1	135.8	54.4	98.2	32.2	15.1	17.1	-8.2	27.4
New Zealand	0.5	0.1	0.0	0.0	-0.1	-	-	0.0	0.1	-0.1
Norway	5.5	-0.2	-0.6	1.0	-0.1	-	-	-	0.0	-
Poland	2.8	7.9	8.5	-5.6	9.6	7.4	-1.6	2.3	0.5	-3.0
Portugal	-0.3	-0.1	0.1	0.6	0.4	1.0	0.9	-0.5	2.6	-1.7
Slovak Republic	12.3	-3.2	3.3	6.3	-1.3	4.6	-2.7	-5.5	-0.1	-3.7
Slovenia	-	-	-	-	-	-	-	-	-	-
Spain	1.0	0.1	1.9	2.3	-3.9	3.1	2.6	16.9	9.3	1.2
Sweden	8.9	33.6	81.8	7.8	-17.0	-6.4	10.9	-1.5	7.9	1.1
Switzerland	80.8	182.5	68.5	97.0	119.8	-14.1	152.3	-5.6	0.1	-1.3
Turkey	0.5	-3.5	-7.1	14.4	16.2	2.9	-2.5	0.1	15.7	-3.6
United Kingdom	-55.2	72.3	43.3	-0.1	16.9	5.5	0.3	-11.5	-15.3	-0.5
United States	13.5	-4.1	1.8	-5.2	66.6	14.4	-12.3	5.1	17.9	-18.4
EUROPE	**1 064.1**	**1 655.4**	**1 235.5**	**913.3**	**1 359.8**	**234.4**	**252.5**	**261.5**	**301.2**	**250.4**
Bulgaria	0.4	4.6	1.6	1.9	2.9	-7.7	5.4	-0.2	-0.1	-1.3
Croatia	328.1	132.0	-27.2	62.3	35.3	64.8	-15.6	105.6	176.5	134.4
Cyprus[2, 3]	-28.0	37.6	15.0	-12.3	62.0	-8.2	2.7	10.1	-9.6	1.5
Malta	-3.8	1.7	51.6	11.3	6.7	0.0	0.0	0.0	-0.5	0.4
Romania	0.3	0.5	-1.4	3.3	-4.4	-0.6	-6.0	2.2	3.5	-10.8
Russian Federation	-25.7	-6.5	6.8	116.8	16.2	114.6	48.7	17.3	28.5	20.0
Ukraine	-0.3	5.8	-1.8	-2.2	1.1	-20.0	9.7	4.5	7.9	3.4
AFRICA	**3.3**	**1.6**	**-2.4**	**-0.4**	**1.6**	**-7.7**	**-13.6**	**-11.1**	**-1.2**	**-2.7**
Northern Africa	3.2	1.2	0.9	-0.6	2.3	3.2	1.3	0.7	2.9	0.6
Algeria	0.2	-0.4	0.6	0.0	0.0	0.1	-	-	0.0	0.0
Egypt	2.9	1.0	0.0	-0.7	0.9	0.0	0.0	-	-	-
Libya	-	0.0	0.0	-	-	3.2	1.4	0.7	2.3	0.5
Morocco	0.5	0.3	0.3	0.0	1.6	0.0	0.0	0.0	0.6	0.0
Tunisia	-0.5	0.2	0.1	0.1	-0.3	-	-	-	-	-
Other African countries	0.1	0.3	-3.3	0.3	-0.7	-10.9	-14.9	-11.8	-4.1	-3.3
Nigeria	-0.1	0.1	-	-	-	-	-	-	-	-
South Africa	0.1	0.0	-0.2	0.2	-0.6	2.6	3.3	1.0	-0.7	2.0
AMERICA	**16.5**	**-4.9**	**3.5**	**-1.1**	**71.0**	**20.2**	**-11.6**	**5.3**	**23.2**	**-5.4**
Northern America	13.3	-4.8	-0.2	-6.3	66.1	17.1	-12.9	7.5	17.3	-9.1
Central America and Caribbean countries	3.7	-0.1	4.8	5.7	4.2	5.7	1.4	-3.6	1.7	-1.1
Bahamas	-0.3	0.0	0.0	-	-	-	-	-	-	-
Bermuda	0.0	0.0	-	0.0	0.0	-	-	-	-	-
Cayman Islands	28.6	0.0	0.0	-	-	-	-	-	-	-
Costa Rica	-	-	-	-0.1	-	-	0.0	-	-	-
El Salvador	-	-	-	-	-	-	-	-	-	-
Guatemala	0.0	0.0	0.0	0.0	-	-	-	-	-	-
Honduras	-	-	-	-	-	-	-	-	-	-
Nicaragua	-	-	-	-	-	-	-	-	-	-
Panama	-0.2	-0.6	0.1	-2.2	-0.2	-	0.0	0.0	0.0	0.0
Virgin Islands, U.S.	-	-	-	-	-	-	-	-	-	-
South America	-0.5	0.0	-1.1	-0.5	0.7	-2.6	-0.1	1.5	4.1	4.8
Argentina	-0.5	-0.3	-0.6	-0.4	-0.1	-	-	-	1.4	2.3
Bolivia	-	-	-	0.0	-	-	-	-	-	-
Brazil	0.1	0.2	-0.5	0.1	0.8	-0.7	0.0	0.9	-1.9	0.3
Colombia	-	0.0	0.0	0.0	0.0	-0.5	-	0.4	0.1	-0.2
Ecuador	-	-	-	-	0.0	-1.4	-0.1	-1.1	0.0	0.0
Paraguay	-	-	0.0	-	-	-	-	-	-	-
Peru	0.0	0.0	-	0.0	0.0	-	-	0.3	2.3	0.3
Uruguay	-	-	0.0	0.0	-	-	-	-	-	-
Venezuela	-	0.0	0.0	-0.1	-	-	-	-	-	-

Table 1. Foreign direct investment flows by country *(cont.)*

Million US dollars

	Inward					Outward				
	2014	2015	2016	2017	2018	2014	2015	2016	2017	2018
ASIA	**9.8**	**31.1**	**6.4**	**-13.3**	**-8.0**	**12.1**	**14.8**	**14.5**	**-1.9**	**15.0**
Near and Middle East	1.7	4.2	13.0	21.0	14.9	1.3	1.4	-0.8	-1.6	1.8
Gulf Arabian countries	2.7	3.0	11.7	18.7	13.9	1.2	1.3	-0.8	-1.6	1.8
Kuwait	-0.2	0.0	0.0	-0.1	-0.5	-	-	-	-	-
Qatar	-0.2	0.0	-0.1	0.1	0.0	-	-	-	-	-
Saudi Arabia	1.1	1.3	0.4	0.5	0.4	0.0	-0.2	0.2	-0.1	0.0
United Arab Emirates	1.9	1.7	11.5	18.2	14.1	1.2	1.6	-1.0	-1.5	1.7
Other Near and Middle East	-1.0	1.2	1.3	2.3	1.0	0.1	0.1	-	0.0	0.0
Jordan	-0.2	0.9	0.0	-0.1	-0.5	0.0	0.0	-	-	-
Other Asian countries	8.2	26.9	-6.7	-34.3	-22.9	10.8	13.4	15.3	-0.3	13.3
China	1.5	4.8	6.2	2.2	0.5	6.0	9.4	11.8	1.0	13.4
Hong Kong, China	3.2	-3.3	-7.1	-4.4	4.9	2.2	2.1	0.4	1.8	-2.9
India	2.1	-2.1	2.3	-1.2	-3.3	0.3	-0.5	-0.4	0.2	0.2
Indonesia	-	-	-	-	0.0	-	-	0.1	-0.1	0.0
Iran, Islamic Republic of	-	-	0.0	0.0	0.0	-	0.0	-0.1	-0.2	0.1
Malaysia	0.5	0.0	-0.7	-1.0	2.1	-0.5	0.1	0.1	0.1	0.1
Philippines	0.1	-0.1	0.0	0.0	0.0	-	-	-	-	-
Singapore	0.9	4.9	-5.2	-1.6	0.5	0.0	0.1	0.1	-0.6	0.9
Chinese Taipei	0.0	-0.1	0.0	0.0	0.0	-	-	-	0.0	-
Thailand	0.0	0.0	0.0	0.0	-0.5	0.5	0.0	-	-0.1	-0.3
Viet Nam	0.0	0.0	0.0	-	0.0	-	-	-	-	-
AUSTRALIA, OCEANIA AND POLAR REGIONS	**-0.2**	**-0.6**	**0.8**	**1.3**	**-15.4**	**6.3**	**7.6**	**2.7**	**3.1**	**-4.2**
WORLD unallocated and confidential	**-43.7**	**-7.9**	**0.9**	**-4.0**	**-40.7**	**9.9**	**17.6**	**16.7**	**13.2**	**14.3**
European Union (EU28)	**999.9**	**1 471.5**	**1 126.3**	**606.9**	**1 147.7**	**270.0**	**-40.0**	**105.0**	**326.2**	**192.3**
G20 countries excl. European Union	**429.6**	**300.3**	**155.1**	**90.7**	**274.2**	**220.4**	**2.2**	**17.7**	**211.1**	**39.7**
G20 OECD countries	**450.9**	**302.9**	**140.8**	**-27.5**	**260.3**	**97.7**	**-58.3**	**-13.1**	**182.7**	**1.5**
G20 Non-OECD countries	**-21.3**	**-2.6**	**14.4**	**118.1**	**13.8**	**122.7**	**60.6**	**30.8**	**28.4**	**38.2**
MENA countries	**5.6**	**5.2**	**12.7**	**17.9**	**15.6**	**4.4**	**2.7**	**-0.1**	**1.3**	**2.3**
ASEAN countries	**1.6**	**4.7**	**-6.0**	**-2.6**	**2.1**	**0.0**	**0.2**	**0.2**	**-0.7**	**0.7**

- Nil

Note: Detailed metadata at: *http://stats.oecd.org/OECDStat_Metadata/ShowMetadata.ashx?Dataset=FDI_CTRY_IND_SUMM.*

1. Information on data for Israel: *http://oe.cd/israel-disclaimer*.
2. Note by Turkey: The information in this document with reference to "Cyprus" relates to the southern part of the Island. There is no single authority representing both Turkish and Greek Cypriot people on the Island. Turkey recognises the Turkish Republic of Northern Cyprus (TRNC). Until a lasting and equitable solution is found within the context of the United Nations, Turkey shall preserve its position concerning the "Cyprus issue".
3. Note by all the European Union Member States of the OECD and the European Union: The Republic of Cyprus is recognised by all members of the United Nations with the exception of Turkey. The information in this document relates to the area under the effective control of the Government of the Republic of Cyprus.

Source: OECD International Direct Investment Statistics (database): https://doi.org/10.1787/idi-data-en

SLOVENIA

Table 2. Foreign direct investment positions by country
At year end

Million US dollars

	Inward					Outward				
	2014	2015	2016	2017	2018	2014	2015	2016	2017	2018
WORLD	**12 385.8**	**12 642.4**	**13 671.8**	**16 738.8**	**17 348.3**	**6 477.2**	**5 997.2**	**6 051.6**	**7 159.3**	**6 940.9**
OECD COUNTRIES	..	..	..	**14 011.5**	**13 594.8**	**961.6**	**969.9**	**924.9**	**1 245.2**	**1 205.3**
Australia	..	..	..	-	-	11.4	17.7	20.5	26.3	20.2
Austria	..	..	..	2 539.1	2 337.0	193.4	179.6	120.9	129.2	133.2
Belgium	..	..	..	142.1	115.2	3.0	2.9	2.7	2.8	3.0
Canada	..	..	..	-	-	7.9	6.1	8.6	8.6	17.0
Chile	..	..	..	-	-	-	-	1.0	3.4	5.4
Czech Republic	..	..	..	258.0	230.7	81.4	66.9	75.6	82.7	85.0
Denmark	..	..	..	-	-	14.1	15.6	10.5	13.1	15.6
Estonia	..	..	..	-	-	-	-	-	-	-
Finland	..	..	..	-	-	0.7	0.8	1.3	3.3	7.9
France	..	..	..	815.5	793.2	21.2	15.3	14.3	9.2	9.5
Germany	..	..	..	2 526.3	2 607.7	144.4	84.0	61.7	209.0	174.4
Greece	..	..	..	-	-	6.3	6.5	9.1	19.4	25.2
Hungary	..	..	..	-	-	21.6	20.5	24.4	25.8	32.1
Iceland	..	..	..	-	-	-	-	-	-	-
Ireland	..	..	..	-	-	1.2	1.2	5.2	6.2	6.0
Israel[1]	..	..	..	-	-	-	-	-	-	-
Italy	..	..	..	1 568.4	1 500.7	74.7	62.0	79.3	127.4	120.3
Japan	..	..	..	409.0	388.7	2.5	2.5	1.6	1.3	1.4
Korea	..	..	..	-	-	5.5	4.8	4.8	5.1	4.7
Latvia	..	..	..	-	-	0.6	0.5	0.4	0.4	0.3
Lithuania	..	..	..	-	-	0.3	0.1	0.2	0.4	0.2
Luxembourg	..	..	..	313.9	274.2	3.3	2.1	5.6	3.8	3.6
Mexico	..	..	..	259.5	237.6	7.6	8.3	5.0	12.3	10.5
Netherlands	..	..	..	701.3	595.4	246.2	234.1	243.0	269.0	287.0
New Zealand	..	..	..	-	-	-	-	0.0	0.1	0.0
Norway	..	..	..	-	-	-	-	-	0.0	0.0
Poland	..	..	..	81.4	33.7	78.3	69.0	70.0	89.7	82.8
Portugal	..	..	..	-	-	4.1	4.6	3.9	7.2	5.2
Slovak Republic	..	..	..	-	-	20.6	16.5	13.9	15.3	11.1
Slovenia	..	..	..	314.0	363.2	-	-	-	-	-
Spain	..	..	..	-	-	27.7	29.0	43.0	58.3	56.0
Sweden	..	..	..	165.7	181.0	2.3	11.9	9.9	12.9	13.3
Switzerland	..	..	..	1 335.1	1 400.6	-117.7	25.2	20.3	15.7	13.4
Turkey	..	..	..	-	-	15.7	10.3	8.4	24.1	16.2
United Kingdom	..	..	..	438.0	838.1	26.6	24.7	14.6	-4.8	-5.6
United States	..	..	..	2 144.2	1 697.7	57.8	47.8	45.6	68.7	50.3
EUROPE	..	..	..	**12 841.8**	**13 088.9**	**5 852.1**	**5 388.9**	**5 524.1**	**6 533.9**	**6 409.5**
Bulgaria	..	..	..	-	-	6.4	12.1	12.5	13.0	10.7
Croatia	..	..	..	744.2	873.4	1 818.9	1 619.1	1 714.3	2 181.0	2 234.0
Cyprus[2, 3]	..	..	..	163.8	242.0	33.1	32.5	40.3	37.3	30.0
Malta	..	..	..	-	-	-	0.0	0.0	-0.5	-0.1
Romania	..	..	..	-	-	34.2	24.7	27.2	33.2	21.6
Russian Federation	..	..	..	599.7	539.6	373.8	332.4	413.2	465.6	408.5
Ukraine	..	..	..	-	-	22.5	30.8	32.4	46.5	49.4
AFRICA	..	..	..	**-**	**-**	**264.5**	**244.3**	**131.3**	**135.2**	**24.9**
Northern Africa	..	..	..	-	-	4.6	5.5	5.9	9.5	9.6
Algeria	..	..	..	-	-	0.1	0.1	0.0	0.0	0.0
Egypt	..	..	..	-	-	0.0	-	-	-	-
Libya	..	..	..	-	-	4.5	5.4	5.9	8.9	9.0
Morocco	..	..	..	-	-	0.1	0.0	0.0	0.6	0.6
Tunisia	..	..	..	-	-	-	-	-	-	-
Other African countries	..	..	..	-	-	259.9	238.9	125.4	125.7	15.3
Nigeria	..	..	..	-	-	-	-	-	-	-
South Africa	..	..	..	-	-	26.0	22.1	25.9	28.0	29.4
AMERICA	..	..	..	**2 403.7**	**1 935.3**	**79.1**	**67.5**	**65.2**	**100.3**	**93.1**
Northern America	..	..	..	2 144.2	1 697.7	65.7	53.9	54.3	77.3	67.4
Central America and Caribbean countries	..	..	..	259.5	237.6	10.5	11.0	7.6	15.3	13.5
Bahamas	..	..	..	-	-	-	-	-	-	-
Bermuda	..	..	..	-	-	-	-	-	-	-
Cayman Islands	..	..	..	-	-	-	-	-	-	-
Costa Rica	..	..	..	-	-	-	-	-	-	-
El Salvador	..	..	..	-	-	-	-	-	-	-
Guatemala	..	..	..	-	-	-	-	-	-	-
Honduras	..	..	..	-	-	-	-	-	-	-
Nicaragua	..	..	..	-	-	-	-	-	-	-
Panama	..	..	..	-	-	3.0	2.7	2.6	0.8	0.8
Virgin Islands, U.S.	..	..	..	-	-	-	-	-	-	-
South America	..	..	..	-	-	2.9	2.6	3.3	7.7	12.3
Argentina	..	..	..	-	-	-	-	-	1.5	3.7
Bolivia	..	..	..	-	-	-	-	-	-	-
Brazil	..	..	..	-	-	2.7	2.4	2.5	0.5	0.7
Colombia	..	..	..	-	-	0.0	-	0.4	0.5	0.3
Ecuador	..	..	..	-	-	0.2	0.2	-0.9	-0.9	-0.9
Paraguay	..	..	..	-	-	-	-	-	-	-
Peru	..	..	..	-	-	-	-	0.3	2.7	3.0
Uruguay	..	..	..	-	-	-	-	-	-	-
Venezuela	..	..	..	-	-	-	-	-	-	-

Table 2. Foreign direct investment positions by country *(cont.)*

At year end

Million US dollars

	Inward					Outward				
	2014	2015	2016	2017	2018	2014	2015	2016	2017	2018
ASIA	..	..	..	**411.2**	**797.3**	**51.3**	**63.4**	**75.5**	**82.1**	**94.4**
Near and Middle East	..	..	..	-	-	2.5	3.3	3.6	2.3	2.5
Gulf Arabian countries	..	..	..	-	-	2.5	3.3	3.5	2.2	2.5
Kuwait	..	..	..	-	-	-	-	-	-	-
Qatar	..	..	..	-	-	-	-	-	-	-
Saudi Arabia	..	..	..	-	-	0.3	0.0	0.2	0.1	0.1
United Arab Emirates	..	..	..	-	-	2.3	3.2	3.3	2.1	2.3
Other Near and Middle East	..	..	..	-	-	0.0	0.1	0.1	0.1	0.0
Jordan	..	..	..	-	-	0.0	-	-	-	-
Other Asian countries	..	..	..	411.2	797.3	48.8	60.1	72.0	79.8	91.9
China	..	..	..	2.2	408.7	29.7	38.3	46.1	53.9	66.0
Hong Kong, China	..	..	..	-	-	2.5	4.5	4.6	6.5	4.0
India	..	..	..	-	-	0.4	-0.1	-0.4	0.5	0.7
Indonesia	..	..	..	-	-	-	-	0.1	0.0	0.0
Iran, Islamic Republic of	..	..	..	-	-	0.0	0.0	-0.1	-0.3	-0.2
Malaysia	..	..	..	-	-	0.6	0.5	0.6	1.2	1.2
Philippines	..	..	..	-	-	-	-	-	-	-
Singapore	..	..	..	-	-	0.1	0.0	1.7	1.3	2.2
Chinese Taipei	..	..	..	-	-	-	-	-	-	-
Thailand	..	..	..	-	-	1.5	1.3	1.3	0.2	-0.1
Viet Nam	..	..	..	-	-	-	-	-	-	-
AUSTRALIA, OCEANIA AND POLAR REGIONS	..	..	..	-	-	**11.4**	**17.7**	**20.5**	**26.4**	**20.2**
WORLD unallocated and confidential	..	..	..	**1 082.1**	**1 526.8**	**218.7**	**215.4**	**234.9**	**281.4**	**298.8**
European Union (EU28)	..	..	..	**10 771.6**	**10 985.6**	**2 864.6**	**2 536.2**	**2 603.7**	**3 344.1**	**3 362.2**
G20 countries excl. European Union	..	..	..	**8 762.8**	**9 011.9**	**807.9**	**678.7**	**751.9**	**1 037.4**	**928.4**
G20 OECD countries	..	..	..	**8 160.9**	**8 063.7**	**375.1**	**283.5**	**264.3**	**487.2**	**419.1**
G20 Non-OECD countries	..	..	..	**601.9**	**948.3**	**432.8**	**395.2**	**487.5**	**550.2**	**509.3**
MENA countries	..	..	..	-	-	**7.1**	**8.7**	**9.5**	**11.7**	**12.0**
ASEAN countries	..	..	..	-	-	**2.2**	**1.9**	**3.7**	**2.7**	**3.3**

- Nil; .. Not available

Note: Inward FDI positions are allocated according to the ultimate investing country. Inward FDI positions by immediate counterpart country are available for more years in the *OECD FDI database according to BMD4*. Detailed metadata at: *http://stats.oecd.org/OECDStat_Metadata/ShowMetadata.ashx?Dataset=FDI_CTRY_IND_SUMM*.

1. Information on data for Israel: *http://oe.cd/israel-disclaimer*.
2. Note by Turkey: The information in this document with reference to “Cyprus” relates to the southern part of the Island. There is no single authority representing both Turkish and Greek Cypriot people on the Island. Turkey recognises the Turkish Republic of Northern Cyprus (TRNC). Until a lasting and equitable solution is found within the context of the United Nations, Turkey shall preserve its position concerning the “Cyprus issue”.
3. Note by all the European Union Member States of the OECD and the European Union: The Republic of Cyprus is recognised by all members of the United Nations with the exception of Turkey. The information in this document relates to the area under the effective control of the Government of the Republic of Cyprus.

Source: OECD International Direct Investment Statistics (database): https://doi.org/10.1787/idi-data-en

SLOVENIA

Table 3. Foreign direct investment income by country

Million US dollars

	Inward					Outward				
	2014	2015	2016	2017	2018	2014	2015	2016	2017	2018
WORLD	**-48.9**	**1 078.2**	**1 252.3**	**1 254.8**	**1 567.5**	**-87.2**	**55.2**	**176.5**	**219.7**	**346.4**
OECD COUNTRIES	**-6.2**	**1 027.2**	**1 240.3**	**1 310.9**	**1 436.8**	**61.1**	**15.3**	**27.0**	**52.6**	**61.0**
Australia	-1.1	-0.5	0.1	1.2	-0.6	0.1	-1.7	-4.7	-2.4	-1.8
Austria	-582.4	367.6	426.5	458.2	489.0	45.3	2.9	4.7	3.4	2.6
Belgium	19.9	18.7	21.5	18.6	19.7	-0.5	-0.6	0.0	0.3	0.3
Canada	0.0	-0.1	-0.1	-	-	-0.1	-0.1	0.0	0.5	-2.5
Chile	-	-	-	-	-	-	-	-	0.0	0.0
Czech Republic	-7.8	10.6	16.0	20.6	15.5	8.3	5.1	9.8	7.6	12.4
Denmark	23.4	19.8	20.6	15.4	18.8	0.5	0.5	0.7	0.7	1.3
Estonia	0.1	0.1	0.1	0.0	-	-	-	-	-	-
Finland	6.4	5.0	4.1	2.4	4.9	-0.7	-1.3	0.1	-0.4	0.1
France	76.0	48.3	103.5	105.7	135.4	-0.8	-1.3	0.2	-1.5	1.0
Germany	137.6	172.6	172.6	180.0	170.4	9.8	-1.2	7.3	13.3	3.0
Greece	0.2	0.0	0.9	2.7	3.1	0.6	0.2	0.0	0.3	0.0
Hungary	20.9	13.2	6.7	11.9	12.3	-1.6	0.1	3.7	5.0	4.9
Iceland	-	-	-	-	-	-	-	-	-	-
Ireland	0.4	0.7	-6.9	-0.1	0.6	-0.1	0.8	0.7	0.3	0.5
Israel[1]	0.0	0.5	-0.1	0.0	0.2	-	-	-	-	-
Italy	38.8	57.2	96.1	60.9	103.9	-6.7	-1.7	0.4	11.6	3.3
Japan	1.7	2.6	4.0	0.2	3.0	0.0	-0.1	-0.5	-0.1	0.0
Korea	0.6	0.4	0.0	-0.3	-0.2	0.9	0.8	0.8	0.8	-0.3
Latvia	0.1	0.1	0.1	0.2	0.1	0.1	0.1	0.1	0.1	0.1
Lithuania	0.1	0.1	0.2	-	-	0.2	0.1	0.2	0.2	0.2
Luxembourg	34.6	45.5	102.9	62.0	18.2	0.0	-0.4	-	0.5	-
Mexico	-	-	-	-	-	-0.3	-2.1	-3.0	-1.3	-0.9
Netherlands	-11.6	41.1	56.6	127.2	145.9	0.9	3.5	3.5	3.8	26.2
New Zealand	0.0	0.0	0.0	-	-	-	-	-	-	-
Norway	0.7	0.5	0.2	1.2	1.0	-	-	-	-	0.0
Poland	0.1	1.3	4.9	3.7	3.3	7.6	7.4	7.0	9.5	10.2
Portugal	-	-	-	-	-	0.1	0.3	0.3	0.3	0.3
Slovak Republic	2.1	2.5	6.2	7.4	-0.6	-1.2	0.4	-0.4	-0.7	0.0
Slovenia	-	-	-	-	-	-	-	-	-	-
Spain	0.2	-0.4	0.0	1.7	1.1	3.2	0.9	2.0	1.3	-0.4
Sweden	10.2	8.0	11.5	33.2	34.1	1.2	2.3	0.6	0.9	0.4
Switzerland	149.5	162.9	124.6	137.4	196.6	-12.1	-1.7	-3.3	0.0	0.6
Turkey	-3.4	-0.7	-0.3	0.5	-2.1	1.7	-0.2	0.3	1.5	2.1
United Kingdom	65.2	37.4	50.3	48.2	39.6	1.7	2.2	-0.1	-0.3	2.8
United States	11.4	12.2	17.8	10.7	23.3	3.0	0.4	-3.2	-2.1	-5.4
EUROPE	**-78.4**	**1 064.1**	**1 236.4**	**1 246.7**	**1 524.1**	**-93.5**	**66.1**	**184.1**	**223.0**	**362.4**
Bulgaria	0.4	1.4	1.0	0.1	0.6	-0.6	0.5	1.0	-2.1	-0.4
Croatia	-32.3	29.7	-29.7	-103.6	59.7	-93.7	-21.2	-13.7	35.1	86.7
Cyprus[2, 3]	-29.2	20.1	14.7	5.9	9.0	-1.0	0.5	9.1	-8.8	0.8
Malta	1.1	3.9	11.7	11.9	9.2	-	0.0	0.0	-0.5	0.4
Romania	-0.3	-0.5	0.1	-	0.2	1.6	1.5	1.4	1.0	1.3
Russian Federation	-1.0	-12.7	-3.5	-3.4	-2.4	12.3	5.0	23.7	23.3	31.2
Ukraine	-0.3	-0.3	-0.9	0.2	-0.1	-2.7	10.3	12.1	4.5	7.9
AFRICA	**0.1**	**1.5**	**-2.9**	**0.0**	**-0.1**	**-3.8**	**-13.2**	**-11.2**	**-0.3**	**-2.5**
Northern Africa	0.0	1.2	0.1	0.0	-0.1	3.7	1.3	0.7	2.2	0.5
Algeria	0.0	0.0	0.0	-	-	-	-	-	0.0	0.0
Egypt	0.2	1.2	0.0	0.0	-0.1	-	-	-	-	-
Libya	-	0.0	0.0	-	-	3.7	1.4	0.7	2.3	0.5
Morocco	0.3	0.3	0.3	-	-	0.0	0.0	0.0	-0.1	0.0
Tunisia	-0.5	-0.3	-0.1	-	-	-	-	-	-	-
Other African countries	0.1	0.2	-3.0	-	-	-7.5	-14.6	-11.9	-2.5	-3.0
Nigeria	-	-	-	-	-	-	-	-	-	-
South Africa	-	-	0.0	-	-	3.2	3.2	0.8	-0.5	2.0
AMERICA	**22.3**	**11.4**	**17.9**	**7.4**	**27.0**	**1.7**	**-2.8**	**-7.4**	**-3.0**	**-8.8**
Northern America	11.4	12.1	17.7	10.7	23.3	2.9	0.2	-3.3	-1.6	-7.9
Central America and Caribbean countries	10.9	-0.7	0.2	-3.3	3.7	-0.3	-2.1	-3.0	-1.3	-0.9
Bahamas	0.0	0.0	0.0	-	-	-	-	-	-	-
Bermuda	-	-	-	-	-	-	-	-	-	-
Cayman Islands	4.1	0.0	0.0	-	-	-	-	-	-	-
Costa Rica	-	-	-	-	-	-	-	-	-	-
El Salvador	-	-	-	-	-	-	-	-	-	-
Guatemala	-	-	-	-	-	-	-	-	-	-
Honduras	-	-	-	-	-	-	-	-	-	-
Nicaragua	-	-	-	-	-	-	-	-	-	-
Panama	0.5	0.2	0.1	-2.2	-0.2	-	-	-	-	-
Virgin Islands, U.S.	-	-	-	-	-	-	-	-	-	-
South America	0.0	0.0	0.0	-	-	-0.9	-0.9	-1.2	-0.1	0.0
Argentina	0.0	0.0	0.0	-	-	-	-	-	0.0	0.0
Bolivia	-	-	-	-	-	-	-	-	-	-
Brazil	-	-	-	-	-	-0.1	-0.8	-0.1	-0.1	0.0
Colombia	-	-	-	-	-	-0.4	-	-	-	-
Ecuador	-	-	-	-	-	-0.4	-0.2	-1.0	0.0	-
Paraguay	-	-	-	-	-	-	-	-	-	-
Peru	-	-	-	-	-	-	-	-	0.0	0.0
Uruguay	-	-	-	-	-	-	-	-	-	-
Venezuela	-	-	-	-	-	-	-	-	-	-

Table 3. Foreign direct investment income by country *(cont.)*

Million US dollars

	Inward					Outward				
	2014	2015	2016	2017	2018	2014	2015	2016	2017	2018
ASIA	**4.5**	**1.3**	**0.0**	**-0.5**	**17.0**	**8.3**	**6.9**	**15.8**	**2.5**	**-2.9**
Near and Middle East	1.3	1.6	2.8	0.8	14.5	-0.6	-0.7	1.3	-1.6	1.0
Gulf Arabian countries	1.3	1.2	3.0	0.8	14.3	-0.6	-0.7	1.3	-1.6	1.0
Kuwait	0.0	0.0	-0.1	0.0	0.0	-	-	-	-	-
Qatar	-	-	-	-	-	-	-	-	-	-
Saudi Arabia	0.2	0.4	0.4	0.9	0.4	0.0	0.0	-0.1	0.0	-
United Arab Emirates	1.2	0.8	2.7	-0.1	13.9	-0.6	-0.7	1.4	-1.6	1.0
Other Near and Middle East	0.0	0.5	-0.2	0.0	0.2	-	-	-	0.0	0.0
Jordan	0.0	0.0	0.0	-	-	-	-	-	-	-
Other Asian countries	3.2	-0.3	-2.8	-1.3	2.5	8.8	7.5	14.4	4.1	-3.9
China	0.0	0.1	0.2	-0.1	-0.3	5.6	6.5	9.1	1.8	-4.6
Hong Kong, China	0.3	-3.6	-6.9	-1.0	0.1	2.1	2.1	4.3	1.3	1.3
India	0.0	0.0	0.0	0.0	0.0	-0.1	-0.2	-0.2	0.1	0.3
Indonesia	-	-	-	-	-	-	-	-	-	-
Iran, Islamic Republic of	-	-	-	-	-	-	0.0	-0.1	-0.1	-
Malaysia	-	-	-	-	0.0	-	-	-	0.0	-
Philippines	0.1	0.0	0.0	-	-	-	-	-	-	-
Singapore	0.5	0.3	0.0	0.0	0.1	0.0	0.1	0.0	0.0	0.0
Chinese Taipei	-0.1	-0.1	0.0	-	-	-	-	-	-	-
Thailand	-	-	0.0	-	-	0.0	-	-	-	-0.9
Viet Nam	-	-	-	-	-	-	-	-	-	-
AUSTRALIA, OCEANIA AND POLAR REGIONS	**-1.1**	**-0.4**	**0.1**	**1.2**	**-0.6**	**0.1**	**-1.7**	**-4.7**	**-2.4**	**-1.8**
WORLD unallocated and confidential	**3.8**	**0.2**	**0.8**	**0.1**	**0.0**	**0.0**	**-**	**0.0**	**0.0**	**0.0**
European Union (EU28)	**-225.6**	**903.8**	**1 091.9**	**1 074.2**	**1 294.1**	**-25.7**	**1.6**	**38.6**	**80.7**	**157.9**
G20 countries excl. European Union	**326.0**	**317.3**	**441.1**	**404.4**	**470.5**	**30.3**	**8.7**	**30.9**	**44.4**	**30.2**
G20 OECD countries	**326.8**	**329.5**	**444.0**	**407.1**	**472.9**	**9.4**	**-5.1**	**-2.5**	**19.9**	**1.4**
G20 Non-OECD countries	**-0.8**	**-12.2**	**-3.0**	**-2.7**	**-2.3**	**20.9**	**13.8**	**33.3**	**24.5**	**28.8**
MENA countries	**1.3**	**2.4**	**3.1**	**0.8**	**14.2**	**3.1**	**0.7**	**2.0**	**0.5**	**1.5**
ASEAN countries	**0.6**	**0.3**	**0.0**	**0.0**	**0.1**	**0.0**	**0.1**	**0.0**	**0.0**	**-0.9**

- Nil

Note: Detailed metadata at: *http://stats.oecd.org/OECDStat_Metadata/ShowMetadata.ashx?Dataset=FDI_CTRY_IND_SUMM.*

1. Information on data for Israel: *http://oe.cd/israel-disclaimer*.
2. Note by Turkey: The information in this document with reference to "Cyprus" relates to the southern part of the Island. There is no single authority representing both Turkish and Greek Cypriot people on the Island. Turkey recognises the Turkish Republic of Northern Cyprus (TRNC). Until a lasting and equitable solution is found within the context of the United Nations, Turkey shall preserve its position concerning the "Cyprus issue".
3. Note by all the European Union Member States of the OECD and the European Union: The Republic of Cyprus is recognised by all members of the United Nations with the exception of Turkey. The information in this document relates to the area under the effective control of the Government of the Republic of Cyprus.

Source: OECD International Direct Investment Statistics (database): https://doi.org/10.1787/idi-data-en

SLOVENIA

Table 4. Foreign direct investment flows by industrial sector

Million US dollars

	Inward					Outward				
	2014	2015	2016	2017	2018	2014	2015	2016	2017	2018
All FDI activities	**1 049.9**	**1 674.7**	**1 244.7**	**895.8**	**1 368.3**	**275.2**	**267.3**	**289.6**	**337.7**	**267.4**
Agriculture, forestry and fishing	**-0.9**	**-0.2**	**3.5**	**0.3**	**0.4**	**-1.4**	**10.0**	**3.7**	**2.4**	**4.1**
Mining and quarrying	**-3.0**	**-0.4**	**0.1**	**5.8**	**9.9**	**0.7**	**-0.7**	**5.1**	**16.5**	**3.4**
Extraction activities	-1.3	0.1	0.6	6.0	-1.6	-	-	-	-	-
Manufacturing	**374.9**	**809.1**	**508.3**	**254.7**	**819.4**	**151.1**	**108.2**	**120.3**	**244.9**	**36.0**
of which:										
Food products, beverages and tobacco	11.9	405.5	207.7	129.8	-1.3	-51.7	3.4	6.1	16.5	-9.2
Textiles, wood and paper products; printing	-28.5	12.7	33.0	59.6	37.4	-4.3	-2.2	1.3	0.6	-1.4
Chemical, rubber, plastic, non-metallic mineral products	107.6	159.2	140.6	11.4	125.0	151.8	18.0	41.4	124.7	55.1
Metal and machinery products, except electrical equipment	70.9	106.0	80.4	17.5	94.9	2.7	3.6	55.9	62.6	10.5
Motor vehicles, trailers, semi-trailers, other transport equipment	134.1	20.6	-20.0	-3.9	175.7	-31.7	52.5	4.6	-14.6	0.5
Other manufacturing	78.9	105.2	66.6	40.2	387.6	84.4	33.0	11.0	55.1	-19.5
Electricity, gas, steam and air conditioning supply	**9.6**	**14.0**	**-20.7**	**29.8**	**42.0**	**0.6**	**25.4**	**14.0**	**40.3**	**24.1**
Water supply; sewerage, waste management and remediation activities	**2.3**	**0.0**	**-0.8**	**1.0**	**3.4**	**0.7**	**-0.1**	**0.0**	**1.1**	**-0.4**
Construction	**-67.4**	**-11.6**	**28.7**	**45.4**	**-16.2**	**-2.7**	**-10.7**	**6.5**	**6.1**	**-9.6**
Services	**723.2**	**844.1**	**715.0**	**557.1**	**485.2**	**77.6**	**95.3**	**81.0**	**-47.5**	**131.1**
Wholesale and retail trade; repair of motor vehicles and motorcycles	716.3	67.9	31.6	85.8	220.9	116.4	4.3	68.8	23.1	32.0
Transportation and storage	327.0	40.6	19.9	-6.8	1.7	-17.5	-22.1	-12.8	2.0	8.9
Accommodation and food service activities	1.3	45.5	1.1	-11.5	-10.8	-8.1	-7.2	-3.5	6.7	0.0
Information and communication	238.5	211.9	38.2	27.4	59.3	-10.7	11.6	13.4	-108.6	-2.8
Financial and insurance activities	-168.1	512.7	445.9	255.2	114.3	-22.6	147.6	21.2	25.3	73.3
Activities of holding companies	-28.8	105.0	22.8	190.0	-7.1	-68.4	0.8	4.6	-20.8	12.2
Real estate activities	-509.2	-57.3	101.0	110.9	51.8	-0.2	4.6	4.9	5.6	4.5
Professional, scientific and technical activities	109.6	3.2	47.1	74.4	31.1	34.9	4.5	-2.9	0.1	8.7
Administrative and support service activities	7.3	3.4	-15.6	17.8	14.5	-16.9	-26.5	-10.0	-6.8	4.6
Public administration; activities of households and of extraterritorial organisations	0.0	0.0	0.0	-	-	-	-	-	-	-
Education	-0.3	-0.3	-0.4	0.2	-	-0.1	-0.1	0.0	0.0	0.0
Human health and social work activities	-0.8	6.2	-0.2	1.1	1.6	2.4	-	-	-	-
Arts, entertainment and recreation	0.1	8.9	45.6	2.9	1.4	-0.8	-21.7	0.5	1.1	-0.9
Other services	1.4	1.4	0.9	0.0	-0.7	0.8	0.2	1.4	4.1	2.9
Not allocated and confidential	**11.3**	**19.6**	**10.7**	**1.7**	**24.2**	**48.5**	**40.0**	**59.0**	**73.9**	**78.8**
Private real estate activities	-	-	-	-	-	-	-	-	-	-

- Nil

Note: Detailed metadata at: *http://stats.oecd.org/OECDStat_Metadata/ShowMetadata.ashx?Dataset=FDI_CTRY_IND_SUMM.*

Source: OECD International Direct Investment Statistics (database): https://doi.org/10.1787/idi-data-en

SLOVENIA

Table 5. Foreign direct investment positions by industrial sector

At year end

Million US dollars

	Inward					Outward				
	2014	2015	2016	2017	2018	2014	2015	2016	2017	2018
All FDI activities	**12 385.8**	**12 642.4**	**13 671.8**	**16 738.8**	**17 348.3**	**6 477.2**	**5 997.2**	**6 051.6**	**7 159.3**	**6 940.9**
Agriculture, forestry and fishing	**19.2**	**17.4**	**19.8**	**26.4**	**25.6**	**22.0**	**29.3**	**40.3**	**49.3**	**51.0**
Mining and quarrying	**50.6**	**46.9**	**46.0**	**61.9**	**68.5**	**21.0**	**18.4**	**26.0**	**42.5**	**43.8**
Extraction activities	33.4	32.3	33.7	44.8	41.1	-	-	-	-	-
Manufacturing	**4 012.6**	**4 323.9**	**4 446.8**	**5 567.8**	**6 221.2**	**1 585.0**	**1 533.9**	**1 509.5**	**1 903.6**	**1 782.3**
of which:										
Food products, beverages and tobacco	205.2	577.3	522.0	733.6	704.0	287.5	260.7	216.1	266.9	243.7
Textiles, wood and paper products; printing	469.7	425.1	446.3	552.9	535.0	13.7	8.7	6.5	11.6	10.8
Chemical, rubber, plastic, non-metallic mineral products	1 477.4	1 508.9	1 602.9	1 904.6	1 943.2	493.1	415.2	562.3	754.4	683.8
Metal and machinery products, except electrical equipment	577.5	591.7	639.3	852.3	927.9	177.1	151.6	183.3	324.2	298.7
Motor vehicles, trailers, semi-trailers, other transport equipment	601.5	512.7	393.5	451.6	576.3	94.0	206.6	161.6	81.9	115.1
Other manufacturing	681.2	708.1	842.9	1 073.0	1 534.8	519.7	491.1	379.8	464.6	430.2
Electricity, gas, steam and air conditioning supply	**405.7**	**379.1**	**350.6**	**439.5**	**448.4**	**143.8**	**151.5**	**143.4**	**198.6**	**248.3**
Water supply; sewerage, waste management and remediation activities	**69.5**	**63.5**	**61.3**	**69.9**	**92.5**	**15.1**	**9.9**	**12.4**	**16.2**	**15.0**
Construction	**103.9**	**96.4**	**162.3**	**262.3**	**225.6**	**27.7**	**14.9**	**62.0**	**109.6**	**35.6**
Services	**7 457.1**	**7 456.3**	**8 307.0**	**9 960.9**	**9 846.6**	**3 503.8**	**3 159.5**	**3 089.2**	**3 385.4**	**3 271.9**
Wholesale and retail trade; repair of motor vehicles and motorcycles	2 828.7	2 681.1	2 629.6	2 968.1	3 094.5	1 409.2	1 306.6	1 303.2	1 451.4	1 376.3
Transportation and storage	456.9	305.4	307.3	328.3	294.5	349.1	314.6	192.6	192.2	89.2
Accommodation and food service activities	34.3	94.2	102.9	122.7	134.7	62.9	38.9	41.0	53.3	50.7
Information and communication	674.4	774.1	790.1	945.4	929.2	296.2	282.2	171.9	213.0	195.0
Financial and insurance activities	1 927.3	2 241.3	3 080.7	3 682.9	3 368.2	910.1	909.7	1 016.0	1 050.8	1 110.5
Activities of holding companies	144.4	261.4	264.4	440.9	374.1	302.9	250.1	398.0	308.0	306.4
Real estate activities	910.0	760.1	834.8	1 089.7	1 161.0	154.5	140.1	311.8	328.9	330.3
Professional, scientific and technical activities	464.4	430.9	429.5	664.6	665.2	200.1	175.1	52.6	83.8	89.8
Administrative and support service activities	133.7	128.6	77.6	98.7	142.5	59.7	-49.4	-41.2	-17.4	-9.6
Public administration; activities of households and of extraterritorial organisations	0.0	0.0	0.0	-	-	-	-	-	-	-
Education	-0.1	-0.3	-0.9	-	-	-0.2	-0.2	-0.2	-0.1	-0.1
Human health and social work activities	2.1	8.0	7.4	10.2	10.5	2.2	2.0	1.9	2.2	2.1
Arts, entertainment and recreation	4.4	13.1	27.7	27.7	25.5	27.4	11.1	10.4	-3.4	5.2
Other services	21.0	19.9	20.2	22.5	20.8	32.4	28.9	29.2	30.6	32.4
Not allocated and confidential	**267.2**	**258.9**	**278.0**	**350.0**	**420.0**	**1 158.8**	**1 080.0**	**1 168.8**	**1 454.0**	**1 493.0**
Private real estate activities	-	-	-	-	-	-	-	-	-	-

- Nil

Note: Detailed metadata at: *http://stats.oecd.org/OECDStat_Metadata/ShowMetadata.ashx?Dataset=FDI_CTRY_IND_SUMM.*

Source: OECD *International Direct Investment Statistics (database): https://doi.org/10.1787/idi-data-en*

Table 6. Foreign direct investment income by industrial sector

Million US dollars

	Inward					Outward				
	2014	2015	2016	2017	2018	2014	2015	2016	2017	2018
All FDI activities	**-48.9**	**1 078.2**	**1 252.3**	**1 254.8**	**1 567.5**	**-87.2**	**55.2**	**176.5**	**219.7**	**346.4**
Agriculture, forestry and fishing	**1.0**	**2.6**	**1.1**	**0.7**	**1.1**	**-1.4**	**1.9**	**1.4**	**2.9**	**4.6**
Mining and quarrying	**-1.1**	**-1.0**	**0.0**	**-0.9**	**1.4**	**-0.6**	**-0.2**	**0.2**	**1.9**	**4.0**
Extraction activities	-2.3	-1.6	-1.1	-1.4	-1.9	-	-	-	-	-
Manufacturing	**489.5**	**518.4**	**565.5**	**566.8**	**527.5**	**6.8**	**55.8**	**87.2**	**94.9**	**99.6**
of which:										
Food products, beverages and tobacco	20.8	29.3	46.7	59.7	74.8	17.8	16.4	21.6	25.1	15.7
Textiles, wood and paper products; printing	27.9	41.9	45.1	29.2	27.7	-1.1	-0.2	-0.4	0.8	0.5
Chemical, rubber, plastic, non-metallic mineral products	236.7	232.3	183.4	194.4	236.3	22.9	21.8	30.6	38.2	47.6
Metal and machinery products, except electrical equipment	63.5	67.8	92.4	42.3	95.6	-10.0	5.2	20.9	38.1	32.2
Motor vehicles, trailers, semi-trailers, other transport equipment	43.4	74.1	62.6	90.9	76.4	-50.7	-1.8	-1.1	-30.5	-9.5
Other manufacturing	97.0	73.0	135.3	150.3	16.7	28.0	14.4	15.6	23.2	13.2
Electricity, gas, steam and air conditioning supply	**-0.9**	**7.2**	**-5.7**	**6.7**	**-1.4**	**6.4**	**7.2**	**4.4**	**2.3**	**8.4**
Water supply; sewerage, waste management and remediation activities	**8.9**	**6.4**	**7.2**	**8.1**	**9.7**	**-0.8**	**-0.1**	**0.3**	**1.1**	**0.2**
Construction	**-70.7**	**-7.2**	**0.7**	**3.4**	**27.4**	**-9.3**	**-3.9**	**1.7**	**0.3**	**-3.3**
Services	**-475.7**	**551.8**	**683.4**	**670.0**	**1 001.9**	**-88.4**	**-5.5**	**80.9**	**116.1**	**231.2**
Wholesale and retail trade; repair of motor vehicles and motorcycles	184.0	267.4	207.6	127.9	362.4	-21.2	45.3	55.0	19.3	70.2
Transportation and storage	22.7	32.5	35.7	27.2	-4.8	-10.9	-18.3	-11.5	-2.2	-2.9
Accommodation and food service activities	0.4	-7.6	3.3	4.4	9.0	-8.7	-1.2	-0.1	-0.2	1.7
Information and communication	81.2	96.6	64.7	69.2	87.5	9.5	11.7	9.1	10.2	10.9
Financial and insurance activities	-340.8	26.1	273.5	276.1	362.8	-11.6	-12.2	59.2	97.5	131.3
Activities of holding companies	-6.2	4.7	21.4	-2.8	12.0	6.2	-1.8	12.1	-6.7	24.6
Real estate activities	-466.4	94.4	65.6	89.5	91.7	-34.2	-10.5	-37.1	-12.6	5.2
Professional, scientific and technical activities	37.8	31.5	40.4	60.7	79.2	3.5	4.2	6.4	5.2	8.5
Administrative and support service activities	2.9	6.8	-18.1	12.5	10.2	-15.9	-25.2	-2.6	-5.7	3.1
Public administration; activities of households and of extraterritorial organisations	0.0	-	0.0	-	-	-	-	-	-	-
Education	-0.2	-0.2	-0.4	-	-	-0.1	-0.1	0.0	0.0	0.0
Human health and social work activities	0.1	1.4	0.7	1.1	1.6	-	-	-	-	-
Arts, entertainment and recreation	0.0	0.2	8.6	-0.7	0.7	0.4	0.6	1.2	1.3	0.8
Other services	2.6	2.9	1.7	2.2	1.6	0.6	0.2	1.3	3.2	2.4
Not allocated and confidential	**0.0**	**0.0**	**0.0**	**0.0**	**0.0**	**0.0**	**0.1**	**0.5**	**0.2**	**1.7**
Private real estate activities	-	-	-	-	-	-	-	-	-	-

- Nil

Note: Detailed metadata at: *http://stats.oecd.org/OECDStat_Metadata/ShowMetadata.ashx?Dataset=FDI_CTRY_IND_SUMM.*

Source: *OECD International Direct Investment Statistics (database): https://doi.org/10.1787/idi-data-en*

SPAIN

Table 1. Foreign direct investment flows by country

Million US dollars

	Inward					Outward				
	2014	2015	2016	2017	2018	2014	2015	2016	2017	2018
WORLD	**22 571.3**	**8 556.9**	**31 538.2**	**38 723.9**	**44 981.7**	**36 742.7**	**41 916.8**	**43 902.5**	**52 237.6**	**27 057.7**
OECD COUNTRIES	**18 905.4**	**3 863.6**	**29 570.9**	**37 079.2**	**41 693.6**	**19 793.0**	**29 547.4**	**31 354.6**	**41 750.6**	**18 446.8**
Australia	.. c	.. c	.. c	-69.9	-105.0	.. d	86.5	.. d	.. d	.. d
Austria	.. d	.. c	.. c	.. c	.. d	.. c	.. d	.. d	366.4	.. d
Belgium	.. c	1 104.8	-613.7	-860.1	766.0	825.3	472.5	496.5	.. c	.. c
Canada	.. d	.. d	.. d	.. d	-226.6	.. d	.. c	.. d	.. d	.. d
Chile	.. d	.. c	.. c	.. c	.. c	9 246.4	2 327.2	2 945.9	-9 885.0	.. c
Czech Republic	.. d	.. c	.. c	86.8	.. c	.. c	.. d	.. d	.. d	140.4
Denmark	.. d	407.1	.. d	.. d	.. d	.. d	.. d	.. d	-845.5	.. d
Estonia	.. c	.. c	.. c	.. c	.. c	.. c	.. c	.. c	.. c	.. c
Finland	.. c	.. c	.. d	.. d	.. c	.. c	.. c	.. c	.. c	509.9
France	5 794.1	5 733.8	3 236.8	2 097.8	2 002.8	-6 383.2	2 692.2	1 638.8	4 001.8	1 533.1
Germany	225.6	455.9	4 997.2	4 927.3	7 649.0	-222.9	1 487.5	1 946.3	838.7	-2 207.0
Greece	.. c	.. c	.. c	.. c	.. c	.. d	.. c	.. d	.. d	.. d
Hungary	.. d	-59.9	-327.3	.. c	.. d	.. d	.. c	.. c	.. d	250.2
Iceland	.. c	.. c	.. c	.. c	.. c	.. c	.. c	.. c	.. c	.. c
Ireland	-776.2	-487.0	125.0	5 828.0	-266.7	8 097.4	905.2	-2 992.4	3 220.6	652.7
Israel[1]	.. c	.. c	.. c	.. c	.. c	.. c	.. c	.. c	.. c	.. c
Italy	2 386.9	.. c	273.1	-7 800.7	7 739.9	398.0	-607.9	1 299.3	1 107.0	-729.4
Japan	.. d	.. d	.. d	.. d	.. c	.. c	.. c	.. c	.. c	.. d
Korea	.. d	.. d	56.4	.. d	.. d	.. c	.. d	.. d	.. c	.. c
Latvia	.. c	.. c	.. c	.. c	.. c	.. c	.. c	.. c	.. c	.. c
Lithuania	.. c	.. c	.. c	.. c	.. c	.. c	.. c	.. c	.. c	.. c
Luxembourg	14 861.4	-1 273.4	3 083.0	5 442.5	12 230.6	-1 653.2	-555.7	4 707.5	-1 810.4	4 127.2
Mexico	.. d	.. d	.. d	.. d	.. d	2 568.7	3 667.2	4 497.4	2 633.3	2 981.2
Netherlands	-11 406.4	-2 909.6	6 856.1	14 784.1	.. d	-2 182.6	.. d	-11 090.3	200.7	1 043.3
New Zealand	.. d	.. c	.. c	.. c	.. c	.. c	.. c	.. c	.. c	.. c
Norway	.. d	.. d	.. d	.. d	.. d	.. d	146.4	.. d	258.1	.. d
Poland	.. c	.. d	.. d	.. c	.. d	805.4	621.2	339.5	715.8	.. d
Portugal	894.3	.. d	498.7	.. d	155.8	841.2	-1 520.8	.. c	735.0	1 446.9
Slovak Republic	.. c	.. c	.. c	.. c	.. c	91.5	.. c	267.6	.. c	.. d
Slovenia	.. c	.. c	.. c	.. c	.. c	.. c	.. c	.. c	.. c	.. c
Spain	-	-	-	-	-	-	-	-	-	-
Sweden	1 909.2	1 008.3	531.9	358.5	.. d	.. d	.. d	.. d	.. c	.. d
Switzerland	1 000.4	1 223.5	517.5	760.9	-1 390.3	1 093.3	.. d	.. c	.. d	.. d
Turkey	.. c	.. c	.. c	.. c	.. c	.. d	.. d	.. d	.. d	.. d
United Kingdom	1 038.9	-2 814.2	6 699.1	3 206.0	.. d	2 860.6	7 553.0	.. d	18 778.0	2 635.4
United States	-261.4	-2 931.8	.. d	7 098.4	2 584.7	6 407.1	4 604.5	14 355.9	14 962.2	3 820.4
EUROPE	**18 275.2**	**5 021.6**	**26 952.3**	**28 554.8**	**35 353.5**	**2 548.8**	**9 505.3**	**9 039.0**	**32 055.0**	**12 445.4**
Bulgaria	.. c	.. c	.. c	.. c	.. c	.. c	.. c	.. c	.. c	.. c
Croatia	.. c	.. c	.. c	.. c	.. c	.. c	.. c	.. c	.. c	.. c
Cyprus[2, 3]	.. c	.. c	.. c	.. d	.. c	.. c	.. c	.. c	.. c	.. d
Malta	.. d	.. d	288.6	.. d	.. c	.. c	.. c	.. c	.. c	.. c
Romania	.. c	.. d	.. d	-272.8	.. c	.. d	.. d	.. c	.. c	.. c
Russian Federation	.. d	.. d	.. d	.. d	.. d	.. c	.. d	.. d	.. d	.. d
Ukraine	.. c	.. c	.. c	.. c	.. c	.. c	.. c	.. c	.. c	.. c
AFRICA	**.. c**	**.. c**	**.. d**	**-100.3**	**-231.3**	**370.2**	**.. d**	**426.8**	**.. d**	**.. d**
Northern Africa	.. c	.. c	.. c	-67.6	.. c	.. d	.. d	212.3	.. d	.. d
Algeria	.. c	.. c	.. c	.. c	.. c	.. d	.. d	.. d	.. d	.. d
Egypt	.. c	.. c	.. c	.. c	.. c	.. d	.. d	.. c	.. c	.. d
Libya	.. c	.. c	.. c	.. c	.. c	.. c	.. c	.. c	.. c	.. c
Morocco	.. c	.. c	.. c	.. c	.. c	.. d	.. d	.. d	.. d	.. d
Tunisia	.. c	.. c	.. c	.. c	.. c	.. c	.. c	.. c	.. c	.. c
Other African countries	.. c	.. c	.. d	.. c	-177.0	.. d	.. d	.. d	.. d	.. d
Nigeria	.. c	.. c	.. c	.. c	.. c	.. c	.. c	.. c	.. c	.. c
South Africa	.. c	.. c	.. c	.. c	.. c	.. d	.. c	.. c	.. d	.. d
AMERICA	**.. d**	**1 269.0**	**2 522.4**	**9 599.8**	**-2 727.5**	**32 213.1**	**33 926.8**	**.. d**	**17 214.5**	**11 557.9**
Northern America	94.2	-2 604.5	308.5	7 157.0	.. d	6 663.1	15 013.9	14 870.1	17 123.2	.. d
Central America and Caribbean countries	2 933.5	.. d	2 995.7	-924.4	-2 443.1	7 079.7	4 289.5	5 592.2	2 749.4	3 078.0
Bahamas	.. c	.. c	.. c	.. c	.. c	.. c	.. c	.. c	.. c	.. c
Bermuda	.. c	.. c	.. c	.. c	.. c	.. c	.. d	.. d	.. c	106.2
Cayman Islands	.. c	.. d	.. d	.. d	.. d	.. c	74.3	.. d	.. d	.. d
Costa Rica	.. c	.. c	.. c	.. c	.. c	.. d	.. d	74.1	.. d	.. d
El Salvador	.. c	.. c	.. c	.. c	.. c	.. d	.. c	-60.8	.. c	.. c
Guatemala	.. c	.. c	.. c	.. c	.. c	.. d	.. d	.. d	.. d	.. d
Honduras	.. c	.. c	.. c	.. c	.. c	.. c	.. c	.. c	.. c	.. c
Nicaragua	.. c	.. c	.. c	.. c	.. c	107.5	.. c	.. c	.. c	.. c
Panama	.. c	.. d	.. d	.. c	.. d	.. d	.. c	.. d	.. d	.. d
Virgin Islands, U.S.	.. c	.. c	.. c	.. c	.. c	.. c	.. c	.. c	.. c	.. c
South America	116.8	2 094.3	.. d	3 367.2	-2 643.7	18 471.5	14 623.4	12 134.2	-2 657.0	7 126.2
Argentina	.. d	.. d	801.7	.. c	.. d	335.7	.. d	.. d	1 551.1	.. d
Bolivia	.. c	.. c	.. c	.. c	.. c	.. d	.. d	141.5	.. d	.. d
Brazil	-703.2	330.6	-1 172.2	307.7	-2 554.0	6 251.8	8 139.8	3 517.6	.. d	.. d
Colombia	.. d	.. d	.. d	162.3	.. d	.. c	356.1	1 375.7	527.6	-468.5
Ecuador	.. c	.. c	.. c	.. c	.. c	.. d	.. d	.. c	.. d	.. d
Paraguay	.. c	.. c	.. c	.. c	.. c	.. d	.. c	.. c	.. c	.. d
Peru	-534.7	.. d	.. c	.. c	.. c	.. d	.. c	899.0	.. c	.. d
Uruguay	1 601.4	-675.5	.. d	2 785.5	-85.0	.. d	.. d	.. d	.. d	.. d
Venezuela	.. d	.. d	-219.0	.. d	.. d	4 008.2	-232.9	.. d	.. d	.. d

Table 1. Foreign direct investment flows by country *(cont.)*

Million US dollars

	Inward					Outward				
	2014	2015	2016	2017	2018	2014	2015	2016	2017	2018
ASIA	**816.0**	**2 095.4**	**.. d**	**.. d**	**12 362.8**	**.. d**	**.. d**	**2 088.9**	**.. d**	**3 570.2**
Near and Middle East	.. d	564.6	.. d	.. d	3 436.8	.. d	.. d	90.7	.. d	.. d
Gulf Arabian countries	.. d	531.3	.. d	.. d	.. d	.. d	.. c	98.4	.. d	.. d
Kuwait	.. c	.. c	.. c	.. c	.. c	.. c	.. c	.. c	.. c	60.2
Qatar	.. d	.. c	.. c	.. c	.. c	.. c	.. c	.. d	.. c	.. c
Saudi Arabia	.. c	.. c	.. c	.. c	.. c	.. d	.. c	80.7	288.6	.. d
United Arab Emirates	.. d	.. d	.. d	.. d	.. d	.. c	.. c	.. c	.. c	.. c
Other Near and Middle East	.. c	.. c	.. c	.. c	.. c	.. c	.. c	.. c	58.6	.. d
Jordan	.. c	.. c	.. c	.. c	.. c	.. c	.. c	.. c	.. c	.. c
Other Asian countries	.. d	1 530.8	.. d	.. d	.. d	.. d	.. d	.. d	.. d	1 539.0
China	634.2	.. c	.. d	.. d	.. c	.. d	.. d	.. d	.. d	.. d
Hong Kong, China	.. d	.. d	.. c	.. c	396.6	.. d	.. d	.. d	.. d	.. d
India	.. c	100.9	.. d	.. c	.. c	.. d	.. d	.. d	.. d	.. d
Indonesia	.. c	.. c	.. c	.. c	.. c	.. c	.. c	.. c	.. c	.. c
Iran, Islamic Republic of	.. c	.. c	.. c	.. c	.. c	.. c	.. c	.. c	.. c	.. c
Malaysia	.. c	.. c	.. c	.. d	.. c	.. d	.. d	.. d	.. d	.. c
Philippines	.. c	.. c	.. c	.. c	.. c	.. c	.. c	.. c	.. c	.. c
Singapore	.. d	.. d	.. d	.. c	.. d	.. d	.. c	.. d	.. d	.. c
Chinese Taipei	.. c	.. c	.. c	.. c	.. c	.. c	.. c	.. c	.. c	.. c
Thailand	.. c	.. c	.. c	.. c	.. c	.. c	.. c	.. c	.. c	.. c
Viet Nam	.. c	.. c	.. c	.. c	.. c	.. c	.. c	.. c	.. c	.. c
AUSTRALIA, OCEANIA AND POLAR REGIONS	**.. d**	**.. c**	**.. d**	**.. c**	**-85.0**	**.. d**	**87.6**	**.. d**	**.. d**	**.. d**
WORLD unallocated and confidential	**.. d**	**.. d**	**.. d**	**.. d**	**309.2**	**.. d**	**.. d**	**.. d**	**.. d**	**.. d**
European Union (EU28)	**15 917.5**	**3 517.5**	**26 679.2**	**27 674.4**	**36 656.4**	**.. c**	**5 427.6**	**7 327.2**	**27 664.3**	**10 666.8**
G20 countries excl. European Union	**.. d**	**.. d**	**.. d**	**.. d**	**.. d**	**.. d**	**.. d**	**.. d**	**.. d**	**.. d**
G20 OECD countries	**.. d**	**.. d**	**.. d**	**.. d**	**.. d**	**.. d**	**.. d**	**.. d**	**.. d**	**.. d**
G20 Non-OECD countries	**.. d**	**.. d**	**.. d**	**.. d**	**.. d**	**.. d**	**.. d**	**.. d**	**.. d**	**.. d**
MENA countries	**.. d**	**.. d**	**.. d**	**.. d**	**.. d**	**.. d**	**.. d**	**.. d**	**.. d**	**.. d**
ASEAN countries	**.. d**	**768.7**	**-214.5**	**.. d**	**.. d**	**.. d**	**.. d**	**.. d**	**.. d**	**.. d**

- Nil; .. Not available; c Confidential data; d Secondary Confidentiality

Note: Detailed metadata at: *http://stats.oecd.org/OECDStat_Metadata/ShowMetadata.ashx?Dataset=FDI_CTRY_IND_SUMM.*

1. Information on data for Israel: *http://oe.cd/israel-disclaimer*.
2. Note by Turkey: The information in this document with reference to "Cyprus" relates to the southern part of the Island. There is no single authority representing both Turkish and Greek Cypriot people on the Island. Turkey recognises the Turkish Republic of Northern Cyprus (TRNC). Until a lasting and equitable solution is found within the context of the United Nations, Turkey shall preserve its position concerning the "Cyprus issue".
3. Note by all the European Union Member States of the OECD and the European Union: The Republic of Cyprus is recognised by all members of the United Nations with the exception of Turkey. The information in this document relates to the area under the effective control of the Government of the Republic of Cyprus.

Source: OECD International Direct Investment Statistics (database): https://doi.org/10.1787/idi-data-en

SPAIN

Table 2. Foreign direct investment positions by country
At year end

Million US dollars

	Inward					Outward				
	2014	2015	2016	2017	2018	2014	2015	2016	2017	2018
WORLD	**596 701.0**	**561 589.5**	**591 484.1**	**702 018.5**	**721 877.7**	**523 853.8**	**512 970.1**	**536 713.4**	**604 725.4**	**578 268.8**
OECD COUNTRIES	**546 451.8**	**486 835.1**	**500 669.3**	**630 915.1**	**651 254.9**	**383 525.7**	**391 384.9**	**397 723.2**	**454 105.3**	**433 716.5**
Australia	.. c	528.0	541.8	.. c	.. c	794.0	795.9	749.4	1 422.4	1 620.1
Austria	2 116.2	2 462.7	2 773.3	2 757.3	2 681.5	217.3	1 561.2	741.0	1 513.6	1 657.9
Belgium	15 926.6	12 694.6	10 892.8	14 574.2	14 961.1	5 580.0	5 065.9	5 179.7	4 809.3	4 485.9
Canada	.. d	.. d	.. d	.. d	.. d	.. d	.. d	.. d	.. d	.. d
Chile	.. c	.. c	363.7	164.3	.. c	24 340.3	24 655.4	29 014.4	21 084.2	19 791.6
Czech Republic	.. c	234.1	267.7	182.3	226.7	1 337.9	878.7	862.2	1 092.6	1 142.7
Denmark	3 429.8	2 880.8	3 714.6	5 087.6	5 237.0	1 605.0	1 693.0	1 919.5	600.9	670.9
Estonia	.. c	131.7	127.5	.. c	.. c	.. c	.. c	.. c	.. c	.. c
Finland	373.9	688.1	668.3	467.7	423.6	299.9	142.6	138.1	.. c	545.0
France	62 744.7	49 139.9	49 944.1	75 380.2	73 945.5	11 457.5	13 467.6	14 496.7	20 436.6	21 090.0
Germany	45 310.2	39 033.2	42 411.7	62 896.4	67 621.9	13 168.1	19 597.2	22 436.0	26 458.4	23 725.7
Greece	199.1	217.7	235.1	123.5	164.9	1 063.6	869.9	809.5	777.2	803.8
Hungary	821.9	766.5	290.9	199.1	.. c	.. c	.. c	.. c	1 140.6	1 316.7
Iceland	.. c	139.4	107.5	.. c	.. c	.. c	.. c	.. c	.. c	.. c
Ireland	7 600.3	5 358.7	4 721.2	13 281.4	13 780.6	15 050.0	13 765.9	10 065.4	13 971.0	11 309.8
Israel[1]	.. c	240.6	237.2	.. c	.. c	.. c	.. c	.. c	.. c	430.5
Italy	42 713.3	36 819.8	32 802.8	34 941.2	40 132.8	10 614.9	9 176.9	9 398.1	12 070.0	11 365.9
Japan	1 719.2	1 934.7	2 525.6	2 710.5	6 881.2	348.4	389.8	366.8	394.6	156.9
Korea	730.9	706.6	741.0	862.3	936.6	546.3	347.3	476.4	518.1	1 876.6
Latvia	.. c	238.4	250.9	.. c	.. c	.. c	.. c	.. c	.. c	.. c
Lithuania	.. c	133.9	134.9	.. c	.. c	.. c	.. c	.. c	.. c	.. c
Luxembourg	81 542.6	74 101.3	75 552.9	94 206.0	101 804.4	6 155.5	6 378.9	7 147.7	7 188.8	9 946.2
Mexico	6 086.3	7 552.5	8 237.6	9 137.7	9 214.6	38 168.9	36 186.2	35 245.1	41 691.1	40 135.1
Netherlands	143 472.6	117 213.9	125 141.8	138 404.9	136 923.5	10 016.3	3 727.8	-5 369.5	-7 511.4	-4 236.3
New Zealand	514.8	480.1	529.1	782.0	766.0	.. c	.. c	.. c	.. c	.. c
Norway	4 471.5	4 641.3	4 875.1	5 729.2	5 838.1	1 431.4	2 275.6	2 430.7	3 145.8	3 336.4
Poland	-2 820.4	-2 467.1	-2 449.7	-3 800.7	-602.2	10 804.3	8 338.6	7 588.3	11 122.6	11 072.8
Portugal	13 279.8	11 309.7	11 488.4	17 977.9	17 492.6	27 879.4	24 051.2	24 401.8	26 321.7	21 755.2
Slovak Republic	.. c	.. c	.. c	.. c	.. c	333.9	288.5	554.4	736.4	957.2
Slovenia	.. c	.. c	.. c	.. c	.. c	.. c	.. c	.. c	.. c	.. c
Spain	-	-	-	-	-	-	-	-	-	-
Sweden	9 935.0	7 139.9	7 136.1	12 799.2	12 942.5	2 566.6	1 683.2	1 189.0	1 312.1	1 145.0
Switzerland	20 021.7	19 392.5	18 878.5	20 821.5	18 700.5	16 150.0	14 706.6	14 572.6	15 147.5	14 455.0
Turkey	.. c	117.6	157.1	.. c	.. c	7 884.4	7 573.3	6 945.3	9 534.7	6 282.3
United Kingdom	60 163.5	68 239.5	72 232.5	86 613.1	86 063.7	86 912.6	96 595.5	90 076.9	120 250.7	116 458.7
United States	23 708.9	22 885.1	23 206.5	32 341.1	33 137.2	67 057.2	65 670.1	77 630.4	100 135.5	94 377.1
EUROPE	**522 631.2**	**463 316.3**	**475 622.4**	**596 749.8**	**612 390.7**	**250 932.6**	**253 675.6**	**244 902.5**	**277 332.7**	**265 862.1**
Bulgaria	.. c	.. c	.. c	.. c	.. c	373.9	333.2	425.8	707.6	681.2
Croatia	.. c	.. c	.. c	.. c	.. c	.. c	.. c	.. c	146.3	135.1
Cyprus[2, 3]	.. c	305.9	372.1	832.3	445.4	610.7	862.3	577.6	663.2	529.0
Malta	743.0	1 455.6	1 671.8	1 027.8	981.2	774.6	827.4	492.3	478.5	538.1
Romania	.. c	-189.4	-355.2	.. c	.. c	1 307.6	1 156.2	1 119.4	1 176.5	1 080.8
Russian Federation	2 463.4	6 848.1	7 344.8	3 331.7	3 473.8	881.4	687.0	952.9	1 414.0	802.6
Ukraine	-157.8	.. c	.. c	-321.4	-360.7	.. c	.. c	.. c	.. c	.. c
AFRICA	**914.2**	**1 759.4**	**2 172.4**	**1 113.0**	**724.8**	**6 571.9**	**6 124.1**	**5 432.7**	**6 487.2**	**6 083.1**
Northern Africa	870.5	1 333.7	1 347.1	807.1	649.2	4 618.4	4 377.8	3 537.5	4 254.0	3 954.7
Algeria	.. c	555.3	528.1	.. c	.. c	715.1	374.5	247.7	380.2	535.8
Egypt	.. c	.. c	.. c	.. c	.. c	1 118.2	1 679.9	855.9	892.3	950.3
Libya	.. c	.. c	.. c	.. c	.. c	.. c	.. c	.. c	.. c	.. c
Morocco	.. c	236.3	253.0	.. c	.. c	2 376.0	2 182.9	2 284.2	2 621.7	2 425.0
Tunisia	.. c	.. c	.. c	.. c	.. c	.. d	.. d	.. d	.. d	.. d
Other African countries	.. c	425.7	825.3	305.8	.. c	1 953.5	1 746.3	1 894.2	2 233.1	.. d
Nigeria	.. c	.. c	.. c	.. c	.. c	.. c	.. c	.. c	.. c	.. c
South Africa	.. c	.. c	.. c	.. c	.. c	1 204.4	892.8	1 041.4	1 217.3	1 147.2
AMERICA	**56 748.2**	**58 386.5**	**59 992.6**	**82 108.4**	**76 535.4**	**254 653.8**	**240 939.6**	**273 982.3**	**306 248.5**	**288 702.8**
Northern America	25 715.9	25 010.3	25 235.6	34 474.7	34 989.7	73 994.5	80 902.6	92 409.6	118 421.7	110 077.9
Central America and Caribbean countries	11 123.6	13 585.2	15 693.1	17 432.2	.. d	50 726.3	47 525.3	47 441.8	54 293.6	.. d
Bahamas	.. c	.. c	397.4	361.0	340.1	.. c	.. c	.. c	.. c	225.6
Bermuda	.. c	.. c	.. c	.. c	.. c	.. c	.. c	.. c	.. c	.. c
Cayman Islands	.. c	254.8	202.4	171.5	265.6	3 176.1	1 686.4	1 640.1	2 601.3	258.8
Costa Rica	365.4	319.0	235.1	231.5	225.6	1 193.5	1 279.4	1 708.7	1 920.1	2 057.5
El Salvador	.. c	.. c	.. c	.. c	.. c	860.8	766.5	734.7	704.0	689.3
Guatemala	.. c	.. c	.. c	.. c	.. c	636.2	575.9	788.4	887.5	904.5
Honduras	.. c	.. c	.. c	.. c	.. c	156.6	142.6	145.5	.. c	.. c
Nicaragua	.. c	.. c	.. c	.. c	.. c	240.4	360.4	227.7	214.7	186.6
Panama	1 004.1	1 172.6	1 845.7	2 175.6	2 244.1	2 043.3	2 335.3	2 640.5	2 222.4	2 744.4
Virgin Islands, U.S.	.. c	.. c	.. c	.. c	.. c	.. c	.. c	.. c	.. c	.. c
South America	19 908.8	19 791.0	19 064.0	30 201.5	26 220.5	129 933.0	112 511.7	134 130.9	133 533.2	126 582.3
Argentina	390.9	521.5	531.3	490.5	332.0	18 092.5	18 258.0	17 689.5	21 599.9	18 392.5
Bolivia	.. c	.. c	.. c	.. c	.. c	1 217.7	1 993.5	2 052.3	2 176.8	2 076.9
Brazil	6 796.5	6 607.5	5 098.6	8 656.8	5 885.0	54 191.4	43 924.9	59 134.6	61 021.8	59 441.3
Colombia	4 157.1	3 571.0	3 576.5	4 248.0	4 387.5	7 881.9	6 402.8	7 202.5	8 234.6	7 106.7
Ecuador	.. c	.. c	.. c	124.7	117.9	3 679.9	3 810.6	3 900.1	4 042.9	4 197.4
Paraguay	.. c	.. c	.. c	.. c	.. c	511.1	434.5	638.8	616.5	531.3
Peru	490.5	512.8	608.2	654.8	589.7	6 076.6	4 739.2	4 715.9	5 187.1	3 907.7
Uruguay	7 203.3	6 783.9	6 980.1	11 601.1	10 873.6	5 124.7	4 943.9	5 172.3	5 882.7	7 174.3
Venezuela	733.3	1 659.2	1 910.0	.. c	.. c	8 770.7	3 224.8	4 546.2	3 601.6	3 855.0

Table 2. Foreign direct investment positions by country *(cont.)*

At year end

Million US dollars

	Inward					Outward				
	2014	2015	2016	2017	2018	2014	2015	2016	2017	2018
ASIA	**9 335.2**	**12 938.5**	**14 606.3**	**13 198.6**	**23 707.4**	**11 100.5**	**11 409.9**	**11 614.8**	**13 175.8**	**15 948.0**
Near and Middle East	6 111.8	7 053.9	6 956.9	5 737.6	.. d	1 412.0	1 555.8	1 436.7	1 934.5	.. d
Gulf Arabian countries	6 043.8	6 545.5	6 427.7	5 647.6	.. d	1 351.3	1 487.2	1 391.4	1 761.8	3 200.1
Kuwait	.. c	766.5	807.4	.. c	.. c	.. c	133.9	.. c	134.3	122.5
Qatar	.. c	509.5	239.3	.. c	.. c	244.0	237.3	140.2	.. c	143.1
Saudi Arabia	.. c	301.6	347.8	.. c	.. c	745.5	810.0	793.7	1 007.4	1 027.0
United Arab Emirates	.. c	4 596.6	4 476.7	4 853.7	4 364.6	230.7	292.9	250.9	309.4	1 793.0
Other Near and Middle East	.. c	508.4	528.1	.. c	.. c	.. c	.. c	.. c	172.7	503.8
Jordan	.. c	.. c	.. c	.. c	.. c	.. c	.. c	.. c	.. c	.. c
Other Asian countries	3 223.4	5 884.6	7 649.4	7 461.0	15 051.5	9 688.5	9 854.1	10 177.1	11 241.3	12 244.1
China	.. c	430.0	1 272.3	1 363.6	2 500.6	3 059.5	2 942.8	3 073.7	3 402.5	3 455.5
Hong Kong, China	535.4	804.6	1 067.8	910.3	1 249.1	2 930.8	2 112.1	2 307.4	2 618.1	2 225.8
India	-225.8	.. c	.. c	.. c	.. c	746.7	2 212.3	1 810.9	1 703.0	2 363.2
Indonesia	.. c	.. c	.. c	.. c	.. c	.. c	.. c	.. c	.. c	151.1
Iran, Islamic Republic of	.. c	.. c	.. c	.. c	.. c	.. c	.. c	.. c	.. c	.. c
Malaysia	.. c	.. c	.. c	289.0	267.9	1 107.3	975.5	1 037.2	1 156.2	1 114.0
Philippines	.. c	.. c	.. c	.. c	.. c	.. c	.. c	.. c	470.1	.. c
Singapore	290.2	1 834.5	1 782.4	1 381.6	3 164.6	264.7	186.2	412.1	585.3	521.0
Chinese Taipei	.. c	.. c	.. c	.. c	.. c	.. c	.. c	.. c	.. c	.. c
Thailand	.. c	.. c	.. c	.. c	.. c	.. c	.. c	.. c	.. c	120.2
Viet Nam	.. c	.. c	.. c	.. c	.. c	.. c	.. c	.. c	.. c	.. c
AUSTRALIA, OCEANIA AND POLAR REGIONS	**919.1**	**1 130.1**	**1 086.8**	**835.9**	**717.9**	**801.3**	**803.5**	**779.0**	**1 450.0**	**1 643.0**
WORLD unallocated and confidential	**6 153.1**	**298.3**	**276.2**	**8 012.7**	**7 801.7**	**-206.4**	**17.4**	**2.1**	**31.2**	**29.8**
European Union (EU28)	**493 623.9**	**428 099.1**	**440 206.6**	**565 328.6**	**583 020.4**	**222 719.4**	**226 789.3**	**218 177.5**	**245 827.5**	**238 479.5**
G20 countries excl. European Union	**.. d**	**.. d**	**.. d**	**.. d**	**.. d**	**.. d**	**.. d**	**.. d**	**.. d**	**.. d**
G20 OECD countries	**.. d**	**.. d**	**.. d**	**.. d**	**.. d**	**.. d**	**.. d**	**.. d**	**.. d**	**.. d**
G20 Non-OECD countries	**.. d**	**.. d**	**.. d**	**.. d**	**.. d**	**.. d**	**.. d**	**.. d**	**.. d**	**86 780.4**
MENA countries	**.. d**	**.. d**	**.. d**	**.. d**	**.. d**	**.. d**	**.. d**	**.. d**	**.. d**	**.. d**
ASEAN countries	**291.4**	**1 787.7**	**1 685.5**	**1 565.1**	**3 386.8**	**1 958.3**	**1 762.7**	**2 034.4**	**2 437.0**	**2 008.2**

- Nil; .. Not available; c Confidential data; d Secondary Confidentiality

Note: Detailed metadata at: *http://stats.oecd.org/OECDStat_Metadata/ShowMetadata.ashx?Dataset=FDI_CTRY_IND_SUMM.*

1. Information on data for Israel: *http://oe.cd/israel-disclaimer.*
2. Note by Turkey: The information in this document with reference to "Cyprus" relates to the southern part of the Island. There is no single authority representing both Turkish and Greek Cypriot people on the Island. Turkey recognises the Turkish Republic of Northern Cyprus (TRNC). Until a lasting and equitable solution is found within the context of the United Nations, Turkey shall preserve its position concerning the "Cyprus issue".
3. Note by all the European Union Member States of the OECD and the European Union: The Republic of Cyprus is recognised by all members of the United Nations with the exception of Turkey. The information in this document relates to the area under the effective control of the Government of the Republic of Cyprus.

Source: OECD International Direct Investment Statistics (database): https://doi.org/10.1787/idi-data-en

Table 3. Foreign direct investment income by country

Million US dollars

	Inward					Outward				
	2014	2015	2016	2017	2018	2014	2015	2016	2017	2018
WORLD	**24 009.6**	**22 030.0**	**23 652.5**	**27 419.7**	**25 196.5**	**35 392.1**	**31 693.8**	**33 708.9**	**34 204.7**	**36 001.4**
OECD COUNTRIES	**22 936.2**	**20 645.6**	**22 342.1**	**25 629.6**	**23 726.0**	**23 346.2**	**22 210.8**	**22 331.1**	**24 096.5**	**27 290.2**
Australia	.. c	.. c	.. c	.. c	.. c	.. c	.. c	.. d	.. d	.. d
Austria	.. d	.. d	.. d	.. d	.. d	.. d	.. d	.. d	.. d	.. d
Belgium	.. d	.. d	.. d	.. d	.. d	.. d	155.1	.. d	.. d	.. d
Canada	.. d	.. d	.. c	.. c	.. c	.. d	.. d	.. d	.. d	.. c
Chile	.. c	.. c	.. c	.. c	.. c	.. d	.. d	.. d	.. d	.. d
Czech Republic	.. c	.. c	.. c	.. c	.. c	.. d	.. d	.. d	.. d	.. d
Denmark	.. d	.. d	.. d	.. d	.. d	.. d	.. d	.. d	.. c	.. d
Estonia	.. c	.. c	.. c	.. c	.. c	.. c	.. c	.. c	.. c	.. c
Finland	.. c	.. c	.. d	.. c	.. c	.. c	.. c	.. c	.. c	.. c
France	.. d	.. d	.. d	.. d	.. d	.. d	609.0	.. d	1 232.1	.. d
Germany	.. d	2 318.4	.. d	2 466.5	2 581.1	.. d	.. d	.. d	.. d	.. d
Greece	.. c	.. c	.. c	.. c	.. c	.. d	.. c	.. d	.. d	.. d
Hungary	.. c	.. d	.. c	.. c	.. c	-1 160.9	.. d	.. c	.. d	.. d
Iceland	.. c	.. c	.. c	.. c	.. c	.. c	.. c	.. c	.. c	.. c
Ireland	.. d	.. d	.. d	.. d	.. d	326.4	597.9	549.6	428.4	529.9
Israel[1]	.. c	.. c	.. c	.. c	.. c	.. c	.. c	.. c	.. c	.. c
Italy	.. d	.. d	.. d	.. d	.. d	-92.9	.. d	.. d	.. d	.. d
Japan	.. d	.. d	.. d	.. d	.. d	.. c	.. c	.. c	.. c	.. c
Korea	.. c	.. c	.. c	.. c	.. c	.. c	.. c	.. c	.. c	.. c
Latvia	.. c	.. c	.. c	.. c	.. c	.. c	.. c	.. c	.. c	.. c
Lithuania	.. c	.. c	.. c	.. c	.. c	.. c	.. c	.. c	.. c	.. c
Luxembourg	2 883.1	1 843.6	723.2	.. d	2 097.3	671.4	-118.7	.. c	443.0	256.1
Mexico	-67.7	.. c	.. d	.. d	.. d	.. d	.. d	.. d	.. d	.. d
Netherlands	5 354.9	.. d	.. d	5 620.6	4 753.9	1 809.7	1 913.5	990.8	326.9	2 496.2
New Zealand	.. d	.. c	.. c	.. c	.. c	.. c	.. c	.. c	.. c	.. c
Norway	.. c	.. d	.. d	.. d	.. d	.. c	.. d	.. d	.. d	.. c
Poland	.. d	.. d	.. d	.. d	.. d	.. d	.. d	.. d	.. d	.. d
Portugal	.. c	.. c	.. d	.. d	.. d	.. d	.. d	.. d	.. d	.. d
Slovak Republic	.. c	.. c	.. c	.. c	.. c	.. c	.. c	56.4	.. d	.. c
Slovenia	.. c	.. c	.. c	.. c	.. c	.. c	.. c	.. c	.. c	.. c
Spain	-	-	-	-	-	-	-	-	-	-
Sweden	.. d	.. d	.. d	.. d	.. d	.. d	.. d	.. d	.. d	.. d
Switzerland	.. d	.. d	.. d	.. d	.. d	.. d	.. d	.. d	.. d	.. d
Turkey	.. c	.. c	.. c	.. c	.. c	.. d	.. d	.. d	.. d	.. d
United Kingdom	2 382.9	2 948.4	.. d	2 930.9	2 960.0	.. d	.. d	4 732.9	.. d	.. d
United States	.. d	.. d	.. d	.. d	.. d	2 051.2	1 403.2	.. d	.. d	.. d
EUROPE	**21 813.7**	**19 446.5**	**20 403.6**	**23 854.1**	**21 987.5**	**15 344.3**	**15 306.7**	**14 131.4**	**15 534.9**	**18 071.5**
Bulgaria	.. c	.. c	.. c	.. c	.. c	.. c	.. c	.. c	.. c	.. c
Croatia	.. c	.. c	.. c	.. c	.. c	.. c	.. c	.. c	.. c	.. c
Cyprus[2, 3]	.. c	.. c	.. c	.. c	.. c	.. c	.. c	.. c	.. d	.. c
Malta	.. d	.. c	.. c	.. c	.. c	.. c	.. c	.. c	.. c	.. c
Romania	.. c	.. c	.. c	.. c	.. c	.. c	.. c	.. d	.. c	.. c
Russian Federation	.. c	.. c	.. c	.. c	.. c	.. d	.. c	.. d	.. d	.. d
Ukraine	.. c	.. c	.. c	.. c	.. c	.. c	.. c	.. c	.. c	.. c
AFRICA	**.. d**	**.. d**	**.. d**	**.. d**	**.. d**	**.. d**	**.. d**	**.. d**	**.. d**	**.. d**
Northern Africa	.. d	.. d	.. d	.. d	.. d	.. d	.. d	.. d	.. d	.. d
Algeria	.. c	.. d	.. c	64.3	.. c	.. c	.. c	.. c	.. c	.. c
Egypt	.. c	.. c	.. c	.. c	.. c	.. d	.. c	.. c	.. c	.. c
Libya	.. c	.. c	.. c	.. c	.. c	.. c	.. c	.. c	.. c	.. c
Morocco	.. c	.. c	.. c	.. c	.. c	.. d	.. d	.. d	.. d	.. d
Tunisia	.. c	.. c	.. c	.. c	.. c	.. c	.. c	.. c	.. c	.. c
Other African countries	.. c	.. c	.. c	.. c	.. c	.. c	.. c	.. d	.. d	.. d
Nigeria	.. c	.. c	.. c	.. c	.. c	.. c	.. c	.. c	.. c	.. c
South Africa	.. c	.. c	.. c	.. c	.. c	.. d	.. c	.. d	.. d	.. d
AMERICA	**2 319.2**	**1 884.6**	**2 119.9**	**2 581.4**	**2 316.8**	**18 370.7**	**15 937.9**	**17 964.2**	**16 809.8**	**.. d**
Northern America	.. d	.. d	.. d	.. d	.. d	2 532.8	2 589.0	.. d	.. d	.. d
Central America and Caribbean countries	-79.6	-84.3	.. d	.. d	.. d	.. d	.. d	.. d	.. d	.. d
Bahamas	.. c	.. c	.. c	.. c	.. c	.. c	.. c	.. c	.. c	.. c
Bermuda	.. c	.. c	.. c	.. c	.. c	.. c	.. c	.. c	.. c	.. c
Cayman Islands	.. c	.. c	.. c	.. c	.. c	.. c	.. c	.. d	.. d	.. c
Costa Rica	.. c	.. c	.. c	.. c	.. c	.. c	.. d	.. d	.. d	.. d
El Salvador	.. c	.. c	.. c	.. c	.. c	.. c	.. d	.. d	.. d	.. d
Guatemala	.. c	.. c	.. c	.. c	.. c	.. d	.. d	.. c	.. d	.. d
Honduras	.. c	.. c	.. c	.. c	.. c	.. c	.. c	.. c	.. c	.. c
Nicaragua	.. c	.. c	.. c	.. c	.. c	.. c	.. c	.. c	.. c	.. c
Panama	.. c	.. d	.. d	.. c	.. c	.. d	.. d	.. d	.. d	.. d
Virgin Islands, U.S.	.. c	.. c	.. c	.. c	.. c	.. c	.. c	.. c	.. c	.. c
South America	1 291.0	748.8	188.0	1 010.0	736.5	.. d	.. d	.. d	.. d	.. d
Argentina	.. c	.. c	.. c	.. d	.. d	.. d	.. d	.. d	.. d	.. d
Bolivia	.. c	.. c	.. c	.. c	.. c	.. d	.. d	.. c	.. c	.. c
Brazil	546.6	.. c	.. c	73.3	110.9	.. d	.. d	.. d	.. d	.. d
Colombia	.. c	-56.6	-108.4	.. c	.. c	.. c	.. d	.. d	.. c	.. c
Ecuador	.. c	.. c	.. c	.. c	.. c	.. d	.. d	.. d	.. d	.. d
Paraguay	.. c	.. c	.. c	.. c	.. c	.. d	.. d	.. d	.. d	.. d
Peru	.. c	.. c	.. c	.. c	.. c	.. d	.. d	.. d	.. d	.. d
Uruguay	.. d	.. d	.. d	.. d	.. d	.. d	.. d	.. c	.. d	.. d
Venezuela	.. c	.. c	.. c	.. c	.. c	.. d	.. c	.. d	.. d	.. d

Table 3. Foreign direct investment income by country *(cont.)*

Million US dollars

	Inward					Outward				
	2014	2015	2016	2017	2018	2014	2015	2016	2017	2018
ASIA	**.. d**	**.. d**	**.. d**	**.. d**	**.. d**	**.. d**	**.. d**	**.. d**	**.. d**	**.. d**
Near and Middle East	.. c	.. d	.. d	.. d	.. d	.. c	.. c	.. c	.. d	.. d
Gulf Arabian countries	.. c	.. d	.. d	.. d	.. d	.. c	.. c	.. c	.. d	.. d
Kuwait	.. c	.. c	.. c	.. c	.. c	.. c	.. c	.. c	.. c	.. c
Qatar	.. c	.. c	.. c	.. c	.. d	.. c	.. c	.. c	.. c	.. c
Saudi Arabia	.. c	.. c	.. c	.. c	.. c	.. c	.. c	.. d	.. c	.. d
United Arab Emirates	.. c	.. c	.. c	.. c	.. c	.. c	.. c	.. c	.. c	.. c
Other Near and Middle East	.. c	.. c	.. c	.. c	.. c	.. c	.. c	.. c	.. c	.. c
Jordan	.. c	.. c	.. c	.. c	.. c	.. c	.. c	.. c	.. c	.. c
Other Asian countries	.. d	.. d	.. d	.. d	.. d	.. d	.. d	.. d	.. d	.. d
China	.. c	.. c	.. c	.. c	.. c	.. d	.. c	.. d	.. d	.. d
Hong Kong, China	.. c	.. c	.. c	.. c	.. c	.. d	.. d	.. d	.. c	.. d
India	.. c	.. c	.. c	.. c	.. c	.. d	.. d	.. c	.. c	.. d
Indonesia	.. c	.. c	.. c	.. c	.. c	.. c	.. c	.. c	.. c	.. c
Iran, Islamic Republic of	.. c	.. c	.. c	.. c	.. c	.. c	.. c	.. c	.. c	.. c
Malaysia	.. c	.. c	.. c	.. c	.. c	.. c	.. d	.. c	.. c	.. c
Philippines	.. c	.. c	.. c	.. c	.. c	.. c	.. c	.. c	.. c	.. c
Singapore	.. c	.. c	.. c	.. c	.. c	.. c	.. c	.. c	.. d	.. c
Chinese Taipei	.. c	.. c	.. c	.. c	.. c	.. c	.. c	.. c	.. c	.. c
Thailand	.. c	.. c	.. c	.. c	.. c	.. c	.. c	.. c	.. c	.. c
Viet Nam	.. c	.. c	.. c	.. c	.. c	.. c	.. c	.. c	.. c	.. c
AUSTRALIA, OCEANIA AND POLAR REGIONS	**.. d**	**.. c**	**.. c**	**.. c**	**.. c**	**.. c**	**.. c**	**.. d**	**.. d**	**.. d**
WORLD unallocated and confidential	**- d**	**.. d**	**.. d**	**.. d**	**.. d**	**.. d**	**- d**	**.. d**	**.. d**	**.. d**
European Union (EU28)	**20 298.5**	**17 997.8**	**19 122.0**	**22 234.2**	**20 506.3**	**13 780.0**	**13 038.3**	**11 260.6**	**12 726.9**	**15 655.6**
G20 countries excl. European Union	**.. d**	**.. d**	**.. d**	**.. d**	**.. d**	**.. d**	**.. d**	**.. d**	**.. d**	**.. d**
G20 OECD countries	**.. d**	**.. d**	**.. d**	**.. d**	**.. d**	**.. d**	**.. d**	**.. d**	**.. d**	**.. d**
G20 Non-OECD countries	**.. d**	**.. d**	**.. d**	**.. d**	**.. d**	**.. d**	**.. d**	**.. d**	**.. d**	**.. d**
MENA countries	**.. d**	**.. d**	**.. d**	**.. d**	**.. d**	**.. d**	**.. d**	**.. d**	**.. d**	**.. d**
ASEAN countries	**.. c**	**.. c**	**.. c**	**.. c**	**.. c**	**.. c**	**.. d**	**.. c**	**.. c**	**.. c**

- Nil; .. Not available; c Confidential data; d Secondary Confidentiality

Note: Detailed metadata at: *http://stats.oecd.org/OECDStat_Metadata/ShowMetadata.ashx?Dataset=FDI_CTRY_IND_SUMM.*

1. Information on data for Israel: *http://oe.cd/israel-disclaimer.*
2. Note by Turkey: The information in this document with reference to "Cyprus" relates to the southern part of the Island. There is no single authority representing both Turkish and Greek Cypriot people on the Island. Turkey recognises the Turkish Republic of Northern Cyprus (TRNC). Until a lasting and equitable solution is found within the context of the United Nations, Turkey shall preserve its position concerning the "Cyprus issue".
3. Note by all the European Union Member States of the OECD and the European Union: The Republic of Cyprus is recognised by all members of the United Nations with the exception of Turkey. The information in this document relates to the area under the effective control of the Government of the Republic of Cyprus.

Source: OECD International Direct Investment Statistics (database): https://doi.org/10.1787/idi-data-en

Table 4. Foreign direct investment flows by industrial sector

Million US dollars

	Inward					Outward				
	2014	2015	2016	2017	2018	2014	2015	2016	2017	2018
All FDI activities	**22 571.3**	**8 556.9**	**31 538.2**	**38 723.9**	**44 981.7**	**36 742.7**	**41 9[illegible]6.8**	**43 902.5**	**52 237.6**	**27 057.7**
Agriculture, forestry and fishing	**428.6**	**68.8**	**.. c**	**59.7**	..	**.. c**	**.. c**	**.. c**	**.. c**	..
Mining and quarrying	**-2 680.1**	**206.3**	**-358.3**	**-1 306.5**	..	**-1 939.8**	**10 266.2**	**266.5**	**1 923.1**	..
Extraction activities	-2 600.5	69.9	.. c	-164.6	..	-1 955.7	10 163.1	726.5	2 011.0	..
Manufacturing	**-2 035.3**	**746.5**	**-2 464.9**	**9 391.3**	..	**1 095.9**	**3 988.9**	**-748.6**	**-733.9**	..
of which:										
Food products, beverages and tobacco	871.7	807.5	-1 177.7	-782.3	..	496.2	1 2[illegible]9.1	633.6	-383.3	..
Textiles, wood and paper products; printing	-678.0	-424.8	295.3	.. c	..	-976.5	-1[illegible]4.3	231.1	-67.6	..
Chemical, rubber, plastic, non-metallic mineral products	1 915.9	731.0	1 594.6	-411.5	..	1 529.8	8[illegible]4.2	1 200.9	-1 573.7	..
Metal and machinery products, except electrical equipment	.. d	-619.0	-3 493.3	.. d	..	346.3	4[illegible]4.9	-705.5	-1 707.8	..
Motor vehicles, trailers, semi-trailers, other transport equipment	.. c	-970.6	-92.9	1 668.4	..	-509.5	1 251.2	-2 930.4	942.4	..
Other manufacturing	3 133.9	1 223.5	409.2	10 005.6	..	209.6	402.7	821.6	2 057.3	..
Electricity, gas, steam and air conditioning supply	**-1 325.5**	**-4 239.6**	**832.7**	**-11 759.7**	..	**5 230.2**	**303.9**	**368.2**	**-8 098.3**	..
Water supply; sewerage, waste management and remediation activities	**471.0**	**519.1**	**.. c**	**.. c**	..	**-99.5**	**.. c**	**.. c**	**289.7**	..
Construction	**1 212.7**	**2 132.0**	**295.3**	**-311.1**	..	**1 034.9**	**2 128.7**	**1 733.9**	**2 522.8**	..
Services	**23 245.3**	**6 988.4**	**29 775.5**	**38 074.6**	..	**31 052.1**	**26 1[illegible]7.6**	**42 472.6**	**56 548.3**	..
Wholesale and retail trade; repair of motor vehicles and motorcycles	769.5	2 686.6	13 212.4	-8 010.4	..	.. c	2 208.5	10 753.1	6 342.0	..
Transportation and storage	104.8	2 553.5	2 358.7	521.9	..	1 373.2	5 690.5	4 328.2	5 007.3	..
Accommodation and food service activities	590.4	640.0	-1 012.9	.. c	..	-128.7	157.5	564.0	612.1	..
Information and communication	11 192.8	747.6	1 185.4	1 603.0	..	147.3	6 185.2	240.0	1 238.9	..
Financial and insurance activities	5 206.3	-5 765.9	9 786.6	37 921.3	..	17 627.7	9 843.6	21 005.2	39 290.9	..
Activities of holding companies	735.0	-5 101.5	10 160.3	39 513.0	..	3 748.2	-6 806.4	12 830.9	29 247.0	..
Real estate activities	2 853.9	3 737.1	2 976.9	.. c	..	350.3	1 152.5	2 537.9	-744.0	..
Professional, scientific and technical activities	-143.3	1 315.6	429.1	2 929.8	..	8 646.7	2 208.5	3 624.9	4 533.9	..
Administrative and support service activities	1 769.9	1 282.3	230.0	2 088.8	..	2 206.4	-1 289.0	-776.3	144.3	..
Public administration; activities of households and of extraterritorial organisations	.. c	.. c	.. c	.. c	..	.. c	.. c	.. c	.. c	..
Education	.. c	.. c	.. c	-224.3	..	.. c	.. c	.. c	.. c	..
Human health and social work activities	-597.1	74.3	.. c	140.9	..	.. c	96.5	.. c	.. c	..
Arts, entertainment and recreation	234.8	164.2	433.5	968.3	..	-172.5	.. c	-183.6	.. c	..
Other services	1 222.0	109.8	.. c	126.3	..	1 283.0	-1[illegible]8.7	164.8	66.5	..
Not allocated and confidential	..	..	..	..	**44 981.7**	..	..	..	..	**27 057.7**
Private real estate activities	..	..	..	..	..	..	..	..	..	..

.. Not available; c Confidential data; d Secondary Confidentiality

Note: Detailed metadata at: *http://stats.oecd.org/OECDStat_Metadata/ShowMetadata.ashx?Dataset=FDI_CTRY_IND_SUMM.*

Source: *OECD International Direct Investment Statistics (database): https://doi.org/10.1787/idi-data-en*

Table 5. Foreign direct investment positions by industrial sector
At year end

Million US dollars

	Inward					Outward				
	2014	2015	2016	2017	2018	2014	2015	2016	2017	2018
All FDI activities	**596 701.0**	**561 589.5**	**591 484.1**	**702 018.5**	**721 877.7**	**523 853.8**	**512 970.1**	**536 713.4**	**604 725.4**	**578 268.8**
Agriculture, forestry and fishing	**842.6**	**1 027.8**	**1 230.1**	**1 507.6**	..	**367.9**	**396.3**	**419.5**	**471.3**	..
Mining and quarrying	**6 183.4**	**6 542.2**	**5 794.2**	**5 046.8**	..	**9 949.5**	**15 517.7**	**10 424.8**	**13 569.2**	..
Extraction activities	490.5	557.4	639.8	582.9	..	8 932.1	12 853.6	8 508.5	11 688.7	..
Manufacturing	**139 052.1**	**122 152.4**	**94 135.1**	**113 578.8**	..	**92 569.1**	**94 196.0**	**68 722.5**	**77 676.9**	..
of which:										
Food products, beverages and tobacco	22 720.7	21 696.2	18 415.7	17 240.3	..	10 035.8	11 018.0	8 972.3	10 079.2	..
Textiles, wood and paper products; printing	4 365.9	3 391.4	3 730.4	3 770.7	..	2 685.6	2 620.6	2 963.0	3 246.6	..
Chemical, rubber, plastic, non-metallic mineral products	36 639.1	29 817.1	30 986.6	34 678.6	..	17 931.0	24 003.3	25 403.2	24 959.2	..
Metal and machinery products, except electrical equipment	26 432.2	23 859.6	19 487.7	22 188.8	..	20 861.9	17 482.9	16 233.8	15 573.3	..
Motor vehicles, trailers, semi-trailers, other transport equipment	8 232.8	11 835.6	8 158.5	12 453.8	..	2 580.0	4 212.3	5 934.4	8 872.6	..
Other manufacturing	40 661.4	31 553.6	13 357.2	23 246.6	..	38 476.0	34 857.9	9 215.8	14 946.0	..
Electricity, gas, steam and air conditioning supply	**66 937.0**	**58 351.7**	**58 542.2**	**55 206.3**	..	**39 315.0**	**34 352.7**	**30 709.4**	**25 602.1**	..
Water supply; sewerage, waste management and remediation activities	**1 682.7**	**1 473.1**	**2 374.8**	**2 712.9**	..	**1 731.3**	**1 845.4**	**1 686.5**	**1 959.7**	..
Construction	**8 618.9**	**10 317.9**	**9 787.1**	**11 422.4**	..	**16 324.8**	**21 097.4**	**27 245.7**	**30 798.8**	..
Services	**236 101.2**	**225 635.3**	**280 366.8**	**338 571.6**	..	**331 252.6**	**316 141.5**	**371 641.2**	**424 798.5**	..
Wholesale and retail trade; repair of motor vehicles and motorcycles	38 008.6	37 812.7	50 711.5	47 930.0	..	34 074.9	30 121.9	35 279.9	39 435.1	..
Transportation and storage	9 880.3	10 135.0	13 258.1	18 893.0	..	5 680.8	9 750.7	10 227.7	14 130.5	..
Accommodation and food service activities	3 956.8	3 985.8	4 384.9	5 550.5	..	4 845.5	5 788.8	5 221.9	6 584.3	..
Information and communication	31 465.8	29 326.1	29 932.5	32 843.6	..	58 145.7	49 477.4	51 140.5	57 261.9	..
Financial and insurance activities	91 971.7	80 270.0	114 767.6	150 653.6	..	201 906.0	194 900.4	232 360.1	266 589.1	..
Activities of holding companies	31 928.4	31 645.1	68 059.5	101 166.9	..	24 847.8	29 771.4	67 731.6	73 263.4	..
Real estate activities	17 621.4	21 436.0	25 382.1	28 491.2	..	8 174.5	9 325.0	12 273.6	14 374.0	..
Professional, scientific and technical activities	18 561.2	17 907.5	16 563.7	21 939.3	..	8 714.8	7 587.4	17 833.9	18 865.4	..
Administrative and support service activities	20 361.7	20 765.4	19 543.6	24 931.6	..	7 455.8	7 200.9	5 960.8	5 322.6	..
Public administration; activities of households and of extraterritorial organisations	.. c	.. c	.. c	.. c	..	.. c	.. c	.. c	.. c	..
Education	.. c	.. c	.. c	.. c	..	.. c	.. c	.. c	.. c	..
Human health and social work activities	571.8	636.9	644.0	987.0	..	154.2	153.5	.. c	.. c	..
Arts, entertainment and recreation	2 068.8	1 935.8	2 761.7	3 677.1	..	-139.6	-145.9	-906.5	-783.2	..
Other services	534.2	387.6	632.4	738.8	..	1 274.8	1 083.3	1 243.8	1 921.3	..
Not allocated and confidential	..	..	..	..	**721 877.7**	..	..	..	..	**578 268.8**
Private real estate activities	..	..	..	..	..	..	..	..	..	..

.. Not available; c Confidential data

Note: Detailed metadata at: *http://stats.oecd.org/OECDStat_Metadata/ShowMetadata.ashx?Dataset=FDI_CTRY_IND_SUMM.*

Source: OECD International Direct Investment Statistics (database): https://doi.org/10.1787/idi-data-en

SPAIN

Table 6. Foreign direct investment income by industrial sector

Million US dollars

	Inward					Outward				
	2014	2015	2016	2017	2018	2014	2015	2016	2017	2018
All FDI activities	**24 009.6**	**22 030.0**	**23 652.5**	**27 419.7**	**25 196.5**	**35 392.1**	**31 693.8**	**33 708.9**	**34 204.7**	**36 001.4**
Agriculture, forestry and fishing	.. c	.. c	.. c	.. c	..	.. c	.. c	.. c	.. c	..
Mining and quarrying	**111.5**	**246.3**	.. c	**544.5**	..	**306.5**	**881.9**	**204.6**	**363.0**	..
Extraction activities	.. c	73.2	65.2	.. c	..	196.4	732.1	.. c	86.8	..
Manufacturing	**6 680.4**	**6 403.8**	**7 193.4**	**7 279.9**	..	**2 820.8**	**2 636.7**	**3 889.2**	**2 747.2**	..
of which:										
Food products, beverages and tobacco	1 011.0	938.4	1 038.4	716.9	..	727.1	828.6	498.7	534.3	..
Textiles, wood and paper products; printing	171.2	.. c	338.4	262.7	..	.. c	56.6	200.2	.. d	..
Chemical, rubber, plastic, non-metallic mineral products	2 140.1	2 896.3	3 777.5	2 583.7	..	802.7	982.8	1 353.5	740.6	..
Metal and machinery products, except electrical equipment	1 487.3	.. d	-299.7	918.7	..	1 897.3	881.9	731.0	634.7	..
Motor vehicles, trailers, semi-trailers, other transport equipment	1 125.1	1 610.6	1 639.9	1 823.9	..	-98.2	-280.6	434.6	.. c	..
Other manufacturing	745.7	471.4	697.8	974.0	..	.. d	166.4	671.2	603.1	..
Electricity, gas, steam and air conditioning supply	**3 297.1**	**1 105.9**	**1 967.3**	**2 505.9**	..	**3 169.7**	**1 426.5**	**1 954.0**	**1 765.3**	..
Water supply; sewerage, waste management and remediation activities	.. c	.. c	.. c	**232.2**	..	**84.9**	**267.3**	**257.7**	**310.0**	..
Construction	**249.4**	**97.6**	.. c	**115.0**	..	**313.1**	**259.6**	**-65.2**	**933.4**	..
Services	**10 948.7**	**11 828.1**	**12 222.7**	**14 387.3**	..	**28 227.4**	**25 449.8**	**27 612.5**	**27 706.0**	..
Wholesale and retail trade; repair of motor vehicles and motorcycles	2 028.7	2 728.8	3 728.9	2 599.5	..	2 471.8	2 538.0	3 333.0	4 054.8	..
Transportation and storage	317.1	406.0	442.3	784.6	..	817.3	2 002.2	1 433.2	1 661.6	..
Accommodation and food service activities	177.8	343.9	179.1	541.1	..	351.6	429.3	399.2	462.2	..
Information and communication	594.4	816.4	1 112.5	1 268.2	..	4 294.8	2 086.5	3 974.3	1 781.1	..
Financial and insurance activities	5 012.6	5 646.1	4 803.7	6 455.9	..	18 053.6	18 234.1	16 065.5	18 018.3	..
Activities of holding companies	1 005.7	2 021.1	2 276.9	3 626.4	..	1 617.4	2 995.0	3 442.4	2 918.5	..
Real estate activities	548.0	438.2	679.0	1 042.7	..	.. c	196.3	289.7	263.8	..
Professional, scientific and technical activities	1 158.3	342.8	253.2	634.7	..	1 829.6	-605.7	1 683.1	1 209.6	..
Administrative and support service activities	904.9	1 074.9	948.8	780.1	..	483.0	582.4	384.8	311.1	..
Public administration; activities of households and of extraterritorial organisations	.. c	.. c	.. c	.. c	..	.. c	.. c	.. c	.. c	..
Education	.. c	.. c	.. c	.. c	..	.. c	.. c	.. c	.. c	..
Human health and social work activities	90.2	.. c	.. c	.. c	..	.. c	.. c	.. c	.. c	..
Arts, entertainment and recreation	74.3	.. c	.. c	.. c	..	-111.5	-63.2	-73.0	-62.0	..
Other services	.. c	.. c	.. c	186.0	..	.. c	.. c	.. c	72.1	..
Not allocated and confidential	..	..	..	..	**25 196.5**	..	..	..	..	**36 001.4**
Private real estate activities	..	..	..	..	..	..	..	..	..	..

.. Not available; c Confidential data; d Secondary Confidentiality

Note: Detailed metadata at: *http://stats.oecd.org/OECDStat_Metadata/ShowMetadata.ashx?Dataset=FDI_CTRY_IND_SUMM.*

Source: *OECD International Direct Investment Statistics (database): https://doi.org/10.1787/idi-data-en*

SWEDEN

Table 1. Foreign direct investment flows by country

Million US dollars

	Inward					Outward				
	2014	2015	2016	2017	2018	2014	2015	2016	2017	2018
WORLD	**4 018.7**	**8 382.1**	**19 149.8**	**14 262.3**	**3 356.3**	**9 179.4**	**12 760.1**	**4 726.5**	**25 537.5**	**16 774.3**
OECD COUNTRIES	**3 827.8**	**17 392.7**	**17 325.5**	**12 573.2**	**3 418.8**	**7 597.6**	**8 682.2**	**4 995.4**	**20 787.1**	**13 000.4**
Australia	-1 519.6	.. c	.. c	-29.8	-177.3	582.2	44.1	112.0	-	242.5
Austria	400.4	117.6	20.7	758.2	145.1	262.7	48.5	76.2	183.5	72.0
Belgium	-4 426.2	-627.0	401.3	-394.8	-17.4	-721.9	-3 365.3	4 275.2	-13 935.9	-6 872.9
Canada	-121.6	4 214.7	104.7	-72.1	-11.3	124.5	376.8	1 241.7	966.8	-44.0
Chile	.. c	.. c	.. c	-	.. c	74.1	-203.9	-24.3	145.1	-3.7
Czech Republic	141.3	23.7	1.4	2.8	-18.2	-15.9	13.6	1 781.1	-111.3	32.3
Denmark	1 029.3	-31.1	809.2	1 585.4	1 938.2	1 026.7	1 608.1	-191.2	1 118.9	3 332.9
Estonia	30.5	2.3	13.2	19.3	7.2	597.1	-219.0	265.5	709.3	239.1
Finland	1 295.2	-4 317.6	1 149.9	301.9	348.4	2 520.4	1 993.9	2 433.2	-900.0	877.1
France	436.5	87.8	112.3	2 543.6	368.9	-338.9	311.9	1 202.7	384.5	954.4
Germany	11 175.2	5 579.1	-424.1	-266.1	752.1	1 148.4	1 547.3	249.6	9 190.6	-6 495.2
Greece	-	-	.. c	-	-	11.1	3.3	-13.8	6.2	4.9
Hungary	.. c	.. c	.. c	1.2	-4.7	102.8	87.4	113.2	-10.1	-70.3
Iceland	-23.0	-18.5	-55.5	-3.0	-7.6	-15.0	0.1	-0.6	-5.7	15.1
Ireland	-1 579.5	704.1	-3 636.1	2 461.0	1 986.1	-327.4	359.1	670.6	3 269.0	11 409.7
Israel[1]	26.5	.. c	6.4	4.8	-	-311.7	18.7	40.1	17.4	74.1
Italy	116.8	97.3	62.1	94.1	794.1	2 115.6	140.0	-2 255.5	651.5	1 838.4
Japan	1 136.3	2 661.1	352.4	920.2	1 077.9	-437.0	342.9	231.6	214.7	379.5
Korea	.. c	.. c	.. c	42.7	32.1	-41.8	-27.4	158.6	-258.6	-235.9
Latvia	5.7	-1.2	-7.9	.. c	-5.3	189.7	23.1	-424.1	841.6	142.3
Lithuania	8.9	-18.9	3.3	.. c	.. c	-250.7	-308.9	-371.1	1 159.8	392.3
Luxembourg	-8 121.4	7 585.2	164.0	-1 961.7	-3 690.7	449.0	837.9	-6 890.9	-3 792.7	1 106.0
Mexico	.. c	.. c	.. c	-7.5	26.1	205.8	97.8	1 681.1	-1 419.1	-345.6
Netherlands	4 936.5	-6 221.5	9 550.5	-1 426.3	-4 133.2	5 167.7	-1 665.7	-5 138.8	15 380.3	-6 005.9
New Zealand	.. c	.. c	.. c	-	0.2	-42.7	24.0	3.6	28.0	17.7
Norway	1 211.8	1 143.4	-1 095.0	1 773.6	-197.3	1 344.9	2 405.9	1 644.1	4 665.1	3 700.3
Poland	.. c	.. c	.. c	760.7	476.8	-714.6	-657.9	1 196.4	440.3	-316.3
Portugal	1.7	-0.7	-2.8	.. c	.. c	237.6	132.9	119.3	119.2	94.9
Slovak Republic	7.3	-1.7	3.9	13.9	-15.3	-29.4	-21.5	324.8	205.1	-59.4
Slovenia	.. c	.. c	.. c	.. c	.. c	-6.0	31.4	49.7	41.3	41.2
Spain	451.2	-16.6	37.2	-99.8	16.7	381.8	-92.3	814.9	1 406.9	127.2
Sweden	-	-	-	-	-	-	-	-	-	-
Switzerland	-401.9	549.6	364.9	3 199.6	-252.3	2 138.1	1 246.7	1 465.1	611.2	178.7
Turkey	15.7	3.3	1.9	1.6	-4.1	-38.9	67.6	59.5	137.4	56.7
United Kingdom	-947.0	3 589.1	3 813.2	6 012.6	1 310.2	-3 599.9	-1 632.0	-514.0	-2 234.2	2 341.3
United States	-5 642.4	2 109.3	6 011.7	-3 668.3	2 538.7	-4 251.8	4 827.3	238.5	2 721.0	5 779.0
EUROPE	**7 360.7**	**8 173.0**	**11 682.8**	**14 989.7**	**-1 101.0**	**10 513.4**	**3 119.2**	**1 289.0**	**21 727.6**	**8 150.0**
Bulgaria	.. c	-	.. c	.. c	.. c	69.7	84.8	106.0	47.9	96.0
Croatia	.. c	.. c	.. c	.. c	.. c	12.2	21.8	-58.9	50.8	31.1
Cyprus[2, 3]	-1 271.7	-366.5	425.8	-480.8	-1 248.4	.. c	-148.5	.. c	-19.9	204.2
Malta	187.6	35.7	-98.4	.. c	109.4	219.7	20.6	-313.4	960.2	487.2
Romania	.. c	-	.. c	-	.. c	124.3	29.4	145.4	34.5	38.7
Russian Federation	69.2	1.3	11.0	3.4	-19.2	286.7	-11.9	115.6	834.6	696.1
Ukraine	.. c	.. c	0.5	.. c	.. c	-34.5	24.2	101.4	31.2	104.5
AFRICA	**.. c**	**.. c**	**.. c**	**5.9**	**2.6**	**-336.0**	**1 849.4**	**-445.9**	**28.5**	**413.8**
Northern Africa	0.6	.. c	.. c	1.4	-2.5	-240.5	-180.2	-53.6	-20.5	26.5
Algeria	-	.. c	.. c	-	-	15.0	7.5	-14.5	-2.5	12.8
Egypt	0.6	0.2	-1.3	1.4	-0.1	-62.4	-30.4	-49.7	.. c	23.7
Libya	-	-	-	-	-2.5	-	-	-	-	4.6
Morocco	-	-	-	0.1	-	-202.0	-164.1	7.6	-0.9	-17.5
Tunisia	-	-	-	-	-	8.7	6.8	.. c	0.1	2.9
Other African countries	.. c	.. c	.. c	4.4	5.2	-95.5	2 029.5	-392.2	49.0	387.2
Nigeria	14.6	0.7	1.5	0.5	-2.8	-24.8	3.0	.. c	-7.6	24.4
South Africa	.. c	.. c	.. c	-0.8	7.9	82.5	130.5	94.7	400.4	184.5
AMERICA	**-3 104.9**	**-3 922.3**	**6 334.5**	**-7 382.9**	**2 250.5**	**-2 641.3**	**5 506.0**	**3 530.6**	**2 614.7**	**6 738.1**
Northern America	-5 763.9	6 324.0	6 116.4	-3 740.4	2 527.5	-4 125.9	5 205.2	1 478.1	3 687.5	5 738.6
Central America and Caribbean countries	2 211.0	-9 528.1	421.1	.. c	-233.6	444.6	26.5	1 682.8	-1 424.4	-170.1
Bahamas	-	-	-0.5	-1.6	-	7.1	1.7	-	-0.8	0.8
Bermuda	.. c	.. c	.. c	59.7	9.0	.. c	-22.5	-3.6	26.0	.. c
Cayman Islands	234.8	.. c	10.8	.. c	.. c	35.7	-18.9	2.5	-31.6	27.8
Costa Rica	-	-	-	-	-	.. c	.. c	2.7	-15.2	.. c
El Salvador	-	-	-	-	-	.. c	.. c	.. c	.. c	.. c
Guatemala	-	-	-	-	-	.. c	.. c	4.6	-2.8	.. c
Honduras	-	-	-	-	-	.. c	.. c	.. c	.. c	.. c
Nicaragua	-	-	-	-	-	.. c	.. c	-	-	-
Panama	-	-	-	-	-	5.4	9.4	8.4	4.6	.. c
Virgin Islands, U.S.	-	-	-	-	-	-	-	-	.. c	-
South America	.. c	.. c	.. c	2.7	-43.4	1 040.0	274.4	369.8	351.7	1 169.5
Argentina	.. c	.. c	.. c	-	-	164.1	126.8	136.3	180.4	245.4
Bolivia	-	-	-	-	-	123.2	19.5	-111.6	-172.1	253.0
Brazil	5.2	.. c	.. c	2.7	11.2	548.0	171.0	222.3	94.4	591.2
Colombia	.. c	.. c	.. c	-	-	40.7	36.7	38.8	53.8	-8.9
Ecuador	.. c	.. c	.. c	-	-	1.2	7.9	-	4.4	0.1
Paraguay	-	-	-	-	-	0.3	-1.5	-0.1	-1.1	.. c
Peru	.. c	.. c	.. c	-	-	26.2	80.1	105.7	42.2	60.2
Uruguay	.. c	.. c	.. c	-	.. c	19.5	2.6	13.8	-0.9	14.8
Venezuela	.. c	.. c	.. c	-	-	42.6	35.4	-14.5	5.4	17.4

Table 1. Foreign direct investment flows by country (cont.)

Million US dollars

	Inward					Outward				
	2014	2015	2016	2017	2018	2014	2015	2016	2017	2018
ASIA	**1 171.3**	**3 921.7**	**1 765.9**	**6 680.7**	**2 381.6**	**1 104.4**	**2 220.1**	**243.7**	**1 145.1**	**1 212.3**
Near and Middle East	-121.0	-48.3	.. c	.. c	.. c	-353.4	79.2	112.8	16.5	118.5
Gulf Arabian countries	.. c	-47.5	.. c	.. c	.. c	-50.0	3.6	75.0	4.4	42.1
Kuwait	-	-	-	-	-	2.5	2.0	0.7	0.5	1.4
Qatar	-	-	-	-	-	-	-	-0.2	-0.2	-1.2
Saudi Arabia	.. c	-52.0	.. c	.. c	.. c	-11.7	-36.4	19.4	8.2	-23.9
United Arab Emirates	2.3	3.7	-1.2	0.1	-0.3	-47.4	47.2	56.2	-6.2	52.8
Other Near and Middle East	.. c	.. c	.. c	4.8	-	-303.4	75.6	37.6	12.1	76.4
Jordan	-	-	-	-	-	0.4	6.3	0.2	0.4	0.1
Other Asian countries	1 292.3	3 970.0	1 930.0	6 780.3	2 474.3	1 457.7	2 140.9	131.0	1 128.6	1 093.7
China	309.9	865.7	1 473.1	5 375.9	1 667.4	962.8	1 934.4	711.2	671.7	28.8
Hong Kong, China	.. c	.. c	.. c	26.3	-291.4	493.6	-122.4	-864.0	343.4	209.8
India	-5.2	2.6	-0.1	16.8	0.2	138.3	-501.8	350.5	568.0	390.2
Indonesia	.. c	.. c	.. c	-	-	-78.3	-53.1	33.7	7.6	36.5
Iran, Islamic Republic of	-	-0.6	-	-	1.8	-34.3	.. c	.. c	.. c	-86.6
Malaysia	.. c	.. c	6.1	31.2	-	78.4	77.1	96.8	34.4	24.7
Philippines	-	.. c	.. c	-	-	53.2	60.6	77.7	-44.1	-67.3
Singapore	-28.4	-65.5	.. c	.. c	-11.9	411.2	76.8	-113.7	-583.8	126.1
Chinese Taipei	.. c	1.1	-1.9	0.2	0.7	-269.1	88.7	-0.6	-19.2	-11.7
Thailand	.. c	.. c	.. c	0.5	-	109.0	79.1	52.4	55.8	132.0
Viet Nam	7.0	-1.5	3.6	1.1	-1.2	-1.5	74.0	5.0	9.5	18.6
AUSTRALIA, OCEANIA AND POLAR REGIONS	**-1 479.6**	**.. c**	**.. c**	**-29.8**	**-177.1**	**538.9**	**65.5**	**115.6**	**28.0**	**260.2**
WORLD unallocated and confidential	**.. d**	**.. d**	**.. d**	**-1.2**	**-0.3**	**-**	**-0.1**	**-6.5**	**-6.4**	**-0.1**
European Union (EU28)	**6 733.6**	**7 357.7**	**12 611.7**	**10 073.7**	**-690.8**	**8 354.3**	**-790.3**	**-2 430.2**	**15 194.9**	**4 051.6**
G20 countries excl. European Union	**6 437.4**	**17 776.3**	**11 198.5**	**10 864.9**	**8 282.2**	**-2 439.2**	**7 855.8**	**4 089.5**	**13 119.7**	**6 619.9**
G20 OECD countries	**5 869.9**	**17 558.6**	**9 472.4**	**5 571.1**	**6 707.3**	**-4 532.0**	**6 096.1**	**2 405.9**	**10 354.4**	**4 471.1**
G20 Non-OECD countries	**567.5**	**217.7**	**1 725.9**	**5 293.8**	**1 575.0**	**2 092.7**	**1 759.7**	**1 683.6**	**2 765.3**	**2 148.8**
MENA countries	**.. c**	**-46.7**	**.. c**	**.. c**	**.. c**	**-283.1**	**-178.8**	**17.2**	**-23.4**	**66.2**
ASEAN countries	**.. c**	**102.4**	**.. c**	**.. c**	**-13.0**	**569.1**	**265.1**	**167.5**	**-525.2**	**298.8**

- Nil; .. Not available; c Confidential data; d Secondary Confidentiality

Note: Detailed metadata at: *http://stats.oecd.org/OECDStat_Metadata/ShowMetadata.ashx?Dataset=FDI_CTRY_IND_SUMM.*

1. Information on data for Israel: *http://oe.cd/israel-disclaimer.*
2. Note by Turkey: The information in this document with reference to "Cyprus" relates to the southern part of the Island. There is no single authority representing both Turkish and Greek Cypriot people on the Island. Turkey recognises the Turkish Republic of Northern Cyprus (TRNC). Until a lasting and equitable solution is found within the context of the United Nations, Turkey shall preserve its position concerning the "Cyprus issue".
3. Note by all the European Union Member States of the OECD and the European Union: The Republic of Cyprus is recognised by all members of the United Nations with the exception of Turkey. The information in this document relates to the area under the effective control of the Government of the Republic of Cyprus.

Source: OECD International Direct Investment Statistics (database): https://doi.org/10.1787/idi-data-en

Table 2. Foreign direct investment positions by country
At year end

Million US dollars

	Inward					Outward				
	2014	2015	2016	2017	2018	2014	2015	2016	2017	2018
WORLD	**320 593.8**	**317 407.1**	**315 873.3**	**367 705.7**	**342 276.0**	**402 098.5**	**355 227.1**	**348 463.4**	**384 598.9**	**374 513.3**
OECD COUNTRIES	**300 713.8**	**297 404.6**	**298 763.8**	**344 042.0**	**321 378.2**	**343 451.9**	**303 418.3**	**304 518.3**	**323 276.2**	**331 122.4**
Australia	662.4	967.0	334.6	225.1	202.4	2 564.0	2 350.8	2 190.7	2 864.8	2 641.6
Austria	2 369.8	2 256.5	2 668.0	2 866.8	2 573.1	4 142.9	3 191.9	1 329.1	1 891.1	1 053.9
Belgium	2 825.1	1 213.9	1 976.7	4 714.5	1 031.9	16 933.8	12 966.2	18 130.1	-707.6	806.5
Canada	2 798.0	3 566.6	2 403.1	1 786.9	2 287.7	2 993.3	3 053.9	3 702.9	4 883.4	5 070.9
Chile	.. c	.. c	.. c	.. c	.. c	1 910.2	1 442.9	1 320.0	1 547.1	1 546.8
Czech Republic	47.4	183.3	61.5	48.0	68.7	1 400.8	1 047.3	2 206.2	3 373.3	2 952.9
Denmark	26 702.9	25 593.8	23 463.7	24 358.1	25 332.4	25 066.8	19 869.6	21 135.7	21 306.4	24 017.2
Estonia	259.0	393.2	101.9	29.5	156.2	5 316.1	4 403.6	4 280.4	5 538.5	5 588.5
Finland	31 826.8	28 602.7	28 031.2	32 591.1	28 941.5	38 234.1	34 445.7	38 931.8	27 011.7	24 881.8
France	3 939.9	5 490.4	4 734.2	6 956.5	7 230.5	7 868.7	7 160.8	7 608.5	9 168.1	8 853.9
Germany	24 019.9	30 921.2	30 561.2	35 412.3	31 604.4	23 016.9	17 635.9	10 989.6	21 151.1	20 083.4
Greece	-	-5.3	.. c	.. c	-2.6	163.4	131.9	175.7	182.5	133.7
Hungary	-88.0	-60.8	41.3	30.5	217.4	922.5	616.9	595.2	687.0	371.5
Iceland	.. c	121.1	.. c	.. c	.. c	42.8	32.5	37.3	88.8	259.9
Ireland	993.5	3 554.4	-1 888.2	1 212.5	4 771.6	2 344.8	1 882.6	2 211.1	11 977.6	12 163.9
Israel[1]	.. c	.. c	.. c	.. c	.. c	466.1	1 015.4	654.8	523.1	434.1
Italy	927.8	842.0	966.4	1 130.0	1 496.3	6 861.4	6 843.8	5 694.5	7 472.1	7 903.9
Japan	2 637.6	3 040.8	2 991.3	4 590.9	5 142.5	2 656.6	3 054.8	3 414.1	3 671.1	3 910.0
Korea	.. c	113.7	187.7	280.9	285.5	2 261.3	2 503.8	2 566.0	2 525.0	2 690.0
Latvia	8.3	.. c	89.6	11.8	32.2	3 023.7	2 792.3	2 221.0	3 358.9	3 167.4
Lithuania	46.5	45.0	19.0	10.7	168.2	3 377.0	3 163.0	2 484.3	4 324.6	4 447.8
Luxembourg	46 174.2	49 006.1	46 425.5	52 702.0	46 477.4	27 782.6	24 887.7	18 691.7	15 251.5	12 783.5
Mexico	.. c	.. c	.. c	143.8	.. c	1 293.5	1 771.0	3 467.6	1 624.0	1 281.6
Netherlands	64 319.2	51 513.0	56 945.3	59 077.7	56 963.4	33 700.8	22 604.1	21 408.5	34 453.1	34 863.2
New Zealand	.. c	.. c	.. c	.. c	.. c	75.2	136.1	130.9	189.6	184.8
Norway	20 658.9	22 318.5	25 059.4	28 045.9	27 810.8	27 163.0	27 778.4	31 239.8	28 314.6	27 886.5
Poland	-4 620.7	-6 061.2	-3 138.9	-2 827.9	-3 447.9	6 370.9	5 759.1	6 247.4	8 396.7	6 899.4
Portugal	.. c	.. c	.. c	.. c	-24.3	4 742.1	1 307.7	1 325.2	1 608.2	1 522.6
Slovak Republic	45.9	48.6	47.2	29.5	36.0	167.9	113.6	280.0	953.9	821.3
Slovenia	.. c	-	.. c	.. c	.. c	46.5	58.8	189.9	226.0	256.1
Spain	2 370.8	1 301.7	1 681.5	1 784.0	1 571.6	10 860.5	9 660.6	10 563.8	13 932.1	14 959.9
Sweden	-	-	-	-	-	-	-	-	-	-
Switzerland	8 363.1	9 962.0	8 140.0	8 797.4	7 511.1	8 112.7	9 610.9	10 130.4	11 839.4	10 928.2
Turkey	-25.2	-20.4	-7.6	-6.5	2.8	1 308.0	1 225.5	1 131.2	1 630.1	1 338.6
United Kingdom	39 557.2	40 672.7	37 130.2	50 735.7	47 985.1	27 110.8	22 791.3	20 680.1	22 338.6	22 328.2
United States	22 361.9	20 357.0	29 357.0	29 039.8	24 797.9	49 550.9	52 063.3	49 637.2	54 004.4	62 088.7
EUROPE	**281 287.1**	**277 701.0**	**271 255.5**	**319 233.9**	**297 572.7**	**307 097.3**	**259 335.3**	**251 207.8**	**278 149.7**	**261 990.9**
Bulgaria	.. c	-	.. c	.. c	.. c	269.0	269.1	369.0	373.7	519.9
Croatia	-	-	-	.. c	.. c	286.0	369.5	336.9	392.9	628.4
Cyprus[2, 3]	6 444.2	6 609.2	6 509.0	8 470.4	7 128.5	1 562.1	1 127.0	1 543.0	1 505.4	1 501.0
Malta	577.7	656.8	285.5	514.1	607.7	1 495.3	619.8	762.4	1 573.5	370.4
Romania	.. c	.. c	.. c	.. c	.. c	615.7	560.1	662.6	756.9	619.9
Russian Federation	205.0	115.9	188.8	70.4	62.1	7 436.1	5 663.6	6 596.7	7 401.4	6 145.8
Ukraine	.. c	-	-	-	.. c	408.9	123.7	137.3	216.5	352.2
AFRICA	**72.3**	**166.2**	**97.8**	**32.7**	**159.9**	**3 867.8**	**4 195.1**	**4 336.9**	**4 536.7**	**4 537.1**
Northern Africa	52.1	16.5	-24.9	.. c	35.1	1 312.9	989.1	697.2	546.8	470.3
Algeria	-	-26.2	-	-	-	.. c	125.3	.. c	.. c	.. c
Egypt	-30.2	-32.7	-24.8	.. c	-	442.4	387.8	246.9	96.9	93.0
Libya	-	-	-	-	35.1	-	-	-	-	-49.1
Morocco	.. c	.. c	.. c	.. c	-	.. c	417.5	383.5	389.9	359.1
Tunisia	-	-	-	-	-	.. c	.. c	.. c	.. c	.. c
Other African countries	20.3	149.7	122.8	33.3	124.9	2 554.9	3 206.0	3 639.7	3 989.9	4 066.8
Nigeria	65.5	40.3	87.0	-	92.7	102.0	94.7	34.8	.. c	-5.4
South Africa	-137.1	.. c	.. c	-18.6	-19.3	818.9	747.7	1 122.1	1 696.4	1 612.8
AMERICA	**31 672.6**	**28 803.2**	**34 778.9**	**32 794.0**	**28 883.2**	**64 929.0**	**66 073.0**	**65 408.5**	**69 980.8**	**77 679.3**
Northern America	25 159.8	23 923.6	31 760.1	30 826.8	27 085.6	52 564.0	55 137.0	53 357.0	58 964.3	67 236.3
Central America and Caribbean countries	5 602.4	4 384.5	2 821.7	1 679.0	1 688.7	1 852.8	2 377.5	4 115.8	2 253.4	1 509.8
Bahamas	-	.. c	.. c	.. c	-	.. c	.. c	.. c	.. c	.. c
Bermuda	1 363.1	.. c	461.8	502.2	580.9	288.5	309.1	223.6	233.4	-87.0
Cayman Islands	.. c	2 116.7	2 094.7	946.8	353.9	49.5	34.4	143.3	95.8	86.5
Costa Rica	-	-	-	-	-	.. c	4.0	11.0	-4.1	-5.0
El Salvador	-	-	-	.. c	-	.. c	.. c	.. c	.. c	.. c
Guatemala	-	-	-	-	-	.. c	.. c	.. c	.. c	.. c
Honduras	-	-	-	-	-	.. c	.. c	.. c	.. c	.. c
Nicaragua	-	-	-	-	-	-	-	-	-	-
Panama	-	-	-	-	-	39.2	53.8	75.4	81.8	7.9
Virgin Islands, U.S.	-	-	-	-	-	-	-	.. c	.. c	.. c
South America	910.4	495.1	197.2	288.3	109.0	10 512.2	8 558.5	7 935.7	8 762.9	8 933.3
Argentina	.. c	.. c	.. c	.. c	.. c	657.4	461.0	451.1	577.9	570.1
Bolivia	.. c	-	-	-	-	1 502.3	1 700.0	.. c	1 077.2	.. c
Brazil	-77.0	-100.3	130.9	165.8	.. c	5 281.0	3 977.2	4 280.6	4 608.8	4 546.3
Colombia	.. c	.. c	-	-	-	384.6	298.1	229.2	288.7	240.1
Ecuador	.. c	.. c	-	-	-	.. c	115.2	62.1	84.2	68.1
Paraguay	-	-	-	-	-	.. c	24.9	.. c	.. c	.. c
Peru	.. c	.. c	-	-	-	331.0	372.0	377.6	440.8	447.0
Uruguay	.. c	.. c	-	-	-	118.4	77.5	91.0	77.4	77.5
Venezuela	.. c	.. c	-	.. c	.. c	156.7	89.8	116.4	50.2	27.4

Table 2. Foreign direct investment positions by country *(cont.)*

At year end

Million US dollars

	Inward					Outward				
	2014	2015	2016	2017	2018	2014	2015	2016	2017	2018
ASIA	**6 715.1**	**9 540.7**	**9 267.7**	**15 246.5**	**15 294.5**	**23 562.9**	**23 134.4**	**25 188.6**	**28 877.3**	**27 479.7**
Near and Middle East	615.9	920.8	336.1	425.4	.. c	1 006.9	1 675.4	1 190.7	1 002.8	1 021.2
Gulf Arabian countries	.. c	769.4	254.8	.. c	.. c	487.5	576.1	512.3	465.3	575.5
Kuwait	-	-	-	-	-	.. c	.. c	.. c	.. c	.. c
Qatar	-	-	-	-	-	.. c	.. c	.. c	.. c	1.2
Saudi Arabia	.. c	.. c	.. c	.. c	.. c	191.5	16[illegible].8	145.7	170.7	157.2
United Arab Emirates	-15.3	-41.1	-24.3	-2.6	.. c	222.2	308.1	284.3	228.7	346.7
Other Near and Middle East	.. c	.. c	.. c	.. c	.. c	519.3	1 099.3	678.3	537.5	445.7
Jordan	-	-	-	-	-	.. c	.. c	.. c	.. c	.. c
Other Asian countries	6 099.3	8 619.9	8 931.6	14 821.0	15 131.6	22 555.9	21 459.0	23 997.9	27 874.5	26 458.5
China	.. c	4 535.4	5 198.3	9 156.1	8 424.2	9 411.0	8 170.3	10 669.4	13 182.6	11 205.8
Hong Kong, China	35.9	29.7	54.7	564.0	635.0	1 090.5	1 414.2	508.8	511.3	1 110.7
India	68.9	147.6	102.3	104.7	-7.6	2 165.8	1 739.2	2 261.8	2 909.6	2 620.8
Indonesia	.. c	.. c	-	.. c	.. c	191.9	119.8	267.4	305.3	265.8
Iran, Islamic Republic of	11.0	.. c	-	-	.. c	.. c	.. c	.. c	.. c	.. c
Malaysia	.. c	-	.. c	.. c	-5.8	979.4	898.0	715.7	858.1	750.2
Philippines	.. c	-9.2	.. c	.. c	.. c	240.1	370.7	359.8	296.3	151.1
Singapore	535.2	725.3	267.8	18.8	606.3	898.2	1 336.5	1 082.1	725.6	744.6
Chinese Taipei	20.8	31.9	29.1	24.6	.. c	240.8	370.9	204.8	239.9	335.9
Thailand	-109.0	.. c	.. c	-21.8	-	1 448.9	1 370.0	1 414.7	1 888.4	1 820.5
Viet Nam	32.4	34.6	42.3	38.0	49.8	-20.6	2.6	-5.2	0.9	7.1
AUSTRALIA, OCEANIA AND POLAR REGIONS	**701.2**	**1 048.1**	**334.5**	**222.7**	**202.3**	**2 641.6**	**2 489.3**	**2 321.5**	**3 054.3**	**2 826.3**
WORLD unallocated and confidential	**145.5**	**147.9**	**138.9**	**175.9**	**163.2**	**-0.1**	**-**	**0.1**	**0.1**	**-**
European Union (EU28)	**250 038.8**	**244 085.4**	**236 821.3**	**281 411.4**	**260 861.9**	**261 000.1**	**213 776.7**	**201 053.5**	**227 551.5**	**214 499.9**
G20 countries excl. European Union	**102 323.5**	**112 774.5**	**114 665.0**	**140 032.0**	**129 881.0**	**153 639.4**	**141 495.6**	**136 877.1**	**162 185.3**	**165 315.5**
G20 OECD countries	**98 249.6**	**107 339.7**	**108 767.6**	**130 295.7**	**121 191.0**	**127 485.6**	**120 455.1**	**111 082.3**	**131 332.7**	**138 190.9**
G20 Non-OECD countries	**4 073.9**	**5 434.8**	**5 897.4**	**9 736.4**	**8 690.0**	**26 153.7**	**21 040.5**	**25 794.8**	**30 852.6**	**27 124.7**
MENA countries	**609.0**	**905.8**	**229.7**	**.. c**	**188.8**	**1 849.7**	**1 640.5**	**1 224.1**	**1 003.0**	**1 028.6**
ASEAN countries	**347.8**	**700.3**	**356.2**	**96.1**	**653.4**	**3 825.6**	**4 146.1**	**3 894.9**	**4 125.4**	**3 880.1**

\- Nil; c Confidential data

Note: Detailed metadata at: *http://stats.oecd.org/OECDStat_Metadata/ShowMetadata.ashx?Dataset=FDI_CTRY_IND_SUMM.*

1. Information on data for Israel: *http://oe.cd/israel-disclaimer.*
2. Note by Turkey: The information in this document with reference to "Cyprus" relates to the southern part of the Island. There is no single authority representing both Turkish and Greek Cypriot people on the Island. Turkey recognises the Turkish Republic of Northern Cyprus (TRNC). Until a lasting and equitable solution is found within the context of the United Nations, Turkey shall preserve its position concerning the "Cyprus issue".
3. Note by all the European Union Member States of the OECD and the European Union: The Republic of Cyprus is recognised by all members of the United Nations with the exception of Turkey. The information in this document relates to the area under the effective control of the Government of the Republic of Cyprus.

Source: OECD International Direct Investment Statistics (database): https://doi.org/10.1787/idi-data-en

Table 3. Foreign direct investment income by country

Million US dollars

	Inward					Outward				
	2014	2015	2016	2017	2018	2014	2015	2016	2017	2018
WORLD	**23 598.2**	**22 048.3**	**21 831.1**	**22 161.0**	**24 099.7**	**36 103.3**	**26 788.9**	**25 589.9**	**30 696.6**	**32 906.9**
OECD COUNTRIES	**24 127.0**	**20 688.0**	**20 089.5**	**20 065.8**	**22 016.7**	**29 403.8**	**22 429.7**	**21 645.9**	**25 321.0**	**26 536.3**
Australia	91.1	-0.8	-0.9	-5.4	-7.5	332.1	194.4	207.7	248.9	132.3
Austria	475.2	244.0	236.4	250.3	326.7	385.9	323.9	155.6	217.7	202.5
Belgium	105.0	75.6	309.1	246.3	-7.4	1 369.0	500.0	933.8	1 091.5	1 347.3
Canada	488.8	250.0	200.5	549.6	152.2	315.7	444.4	367.6	276.8	208.7
Chile	14.4	8.3	.. c	.. c	4.3	127.0	-112.0	149.4	150.7	80.0
Czech Republic	138.9	22.9	0.5	-	0.2	208.5	196.2	242.5	302.9	217.5
Denmark	1 504.2	875.5	1 582.7	1 378.6	1 286.6	2 702.8	1 689.5	1 690.3	1 680.1	1 695.3
Estonia	9.3	1.1	7.7	17.4	10.9	941.3	342.5	462.9	486.6	540.3
Finland	2 952.4	2 125.6	2 020.3	1 916.9	2 357.2	3 025.4	1 886.3	2 512.1	4 206.3	3 723.3
France	491.3	179.6	526.0	624.9	454.6	314.3	430.0	526.7	1 077.7	889.1
Germany	2 325.4	2 270.7	1 546.1	1 930.7	1 975.1	2 428.3	2 695.2	220.0	1 231.9	1 560.9
Greece	-	-	-	-	-	17.6	10.8	14.0	12.8	17.5
Hungary	-8.6	.. c	.. c	.. c	-1.4	129.3	50.3	41.6	93.5	77.7
Iceland	-22.3	-17.8	-55.5	-3.0	-7.6	4.4	0.8	0.6	-7.6	15.5
Ireland	278.1	226.4	-3.7	184.9	112.9	161.1	141.6	199.4	296.4	478.2
Israel[1]	26.5	-0.8	6.4	4.8	-	-222.0	12.2	27.3	38.5	119.0
Italy	118.8	101.6	109.3	115.4	-52.7	209.8	417.7	327.4	435.4	310.6
Japan	210.1	521.3	511.7	456.9	540.9	211.7	92.5	425.4	277.5	208.9
Korea	23.0	19.1	14.0	41.3	35.4	148.0	133.9	124.4	408.9	305.7
Latvia	5.8	-	-9.5	.. c	-	449.3	289.5	308.4	463.7	428.3
Lithuania	-	-20.0	-	.. c	-1.3	502.6	225.3	332.6	470.6	542.2
Luxembourg	1 204.5	907.1	959.3	1 317.3	2 216.9	1 697.0	408.6	1 145.9	636.8	433.8
Mexico	.. c	.. c	.. c	-5.9	21.4	139.1	194.9	158.6	213.1	228.9
Netherlands	3 803.3	3 593.8	3 539.6	4 450.9	3 522.3	5 149.5	2 381.7	2 361.8	2 512.0	3 467.4
New Zealand	.. c	.. c	.. c	.. c	0.2	-0.9	17.7	18.2	16.3	13.0
Norway	2 857.0	1 824.2	1 623.4	1 465.7	1 556.2	2 878.5	2 178.6	3 297.4	3 207.4	2 800.0
Poland	-7.3	18.9	-65.2	-25.2	-51.4	607.3	430.9	462.3	267.8	333.0
Portugal	-	-	.. c	-	-	130.9	134.4	86.5	101.8	163.9
Slovak Republic	-	-	-	-	-	28.6	32.0	27.2	35.8	29.2
Slovenia	-	-	-	-	-	10.2	13.8	3.5	9.4	23.1
Spain	253.4	234.7	249.3	86.2	320.8	331.1	608.1	558.9	522.6	754.4
Sweden	-	-	-	-	-	-	-	-	-	-
Switzerland	1 188.2	1 169.7	811.5	802.4	1 004.4	1 286.2	1 240.2	1 701.0	1 137.7	1 159.1
Turkey	-	-	-	-	-	63.3	54.6	55.7	91.4	75.4
United Kingdom	4 405.6	4 957.0	3 934.0	2 963.6	3 994.1	1 023.8	1 391.9	259.7	296.4	1 035.5
United States	1 199.0	1 081.8	2 033.1	1 300.6	2 252.4	3 249.8	3 891.9	2 572.1	3 282.6	2 919.2
EUROPE	**21 555.4**	**19 121.0**	**17 590.0**	**18 073.6**	**19 459.1**	**27 743.8**	**18 991.6**	**18 982.9**	**22 162.5**	**23 849.9**
Bulgaria	-	-	-	-	-	51.6	31.1	51.7	48.0	41.3
Croatia	-	-	.. c	-	-	35.1	17.7	18.9	9.6	46.6
Cyprus[2, 3]	-825.1	52.6	78.4	205.1	202.6	16.5	3.7	78.4	89.6	117.9
Malta	363.1	235.3	103.0	80.6	219.1	273.3	123.5	156.4	181.0	196.7
Romania	.. c	-	.. c	.. c	.. c	64.3	53.1	34.7	32.9	71.8
Russian Federation	-	-	-1.2	-	-	836.2	367.2	511.3	763.5	887.8
Ukraine	-	-	-	-	-	18.2	33.8	85.2	32.8	91.4
AFRICA	**.. c**	**.. c**	**-3.3**	**4.8**	**.. c**	**123.5**	**-61.9**	**242.5**	**231.3**	**345.7**
Northern Africa	-	-	-	-	-	-220.7	-141.1	49.9	14.7	19.1
Algeria	-	-	-	-	-	15.0	20.2	4.2	-2.5	12.8
Egypt	-	-	-	-	-	-55.0	-12.0	28.2	3.0	11.9
Libya	-	-	-	-	-	-	-	-	-	-
Morocco	-	-	-	-	-	-189.5	-155.8	14.7	14.0	-8.5
Tunisia	-	-	-	-	-	8.7	6.5	2.8	0.1	2.9
Other African countries	.. c	.. c	-3.3	4.8	.. c	344.3	79.0	192.6	216.5	326.6
Nigeria	-	-	-	-	-	8.6	4.2	-0.5	-7.0	19.3
South Africa	.. c	.. c	.. c	-	-	170.6	66.9	91.9	99.7	160.5
AMERICA	**1 555.6**	**1 574.4**	**2 579.9**	**1 860.5**	**2 416.5**	**5 180.5**	**5 087.5**	**3 791.2**	**4 671.5**	**4 690.3**
Northern America	1 687.8	1 331.8	2 233.6	1 850.0	2 404.6	3 567.0	4 338.0	2 941.5	3 559.1	3 131.5
Central America and Caribbean countries	-150.6	274.5	371.2	5.3	-4.5	282.9	218.9	209.3	288.1	324.7
Bahamas	-	-	-0.5	-1.6	-	7.1	1.7	-	0.5	0.8
Bermuda	32.5	19.7	29.7	54.4	67.7	53.2	-21.2	14.5	21.9	10.8
Cayman Islands	-63.8	238.3	288.7	24.5	3.3	47.4	32.7	32.1	18.7	74.1
Costa Rica	-	-	-	-	-	1.3	1.9	-14.6	4.4	-3.7
El Salvador	-	-	-	-	-	0.4	1.4	1.1	0.8	1.5
Guatemala	-	-	-	-	-	2.3	0.8	-7.9	14.3	-7.0
Honduras	-	-	-	-	-	-	0.2	0.9	0.2	0.7
Nicaragua	-	-	-	-	-	.. c	-	-	-	-
Panama	-	-	-	-	-	8.6	14.5	7.1	4.8	-
Virgin Islands, U.S.	-	-	-	-	-	-	-	-	-	-
South America	18.4	.. c	-24.9	5.1	16.5	1 330.6	530.8	640.3	824.3	1 234.1
Argentina	.. c	.. c	.. c	-	-	183.5	154.6	180.0	184.0	170.8
Bolivia	-	-	-	-	-	324.8	270.5	204.2	218.1	452.8
Brazil	3.4	-37.8	-20.9	4.7	12.1	423.5	57.2	7.6	200.0	462.5
Colombia	.. c	.. c	.. c	-	-	35.0	27.9	11.7	-0.4	9.2
Ecuador	.. c	.. c	.. c	-	-	5.1	5.2	-0.6	4.1	3.3
Paraguay	-	-	-	-	-	-0.3	-0.1	-1.2	-1.4	-1.2
Peru	.. c	.. c	.. c	.. c	.. c	58.9	79.8	79.1	40.7	40.3
Uruguay	-	.. c	.. c	-	-	31.1	11.6	25.8	22.5	-0.7
Venezuela	.. c	0.9	.. c	-	-	142.0	36.1	-15.8	6.0	17.4

Table 3. Foreign direct investment income by country *(cont.)*

Million US dollars

	Inward					Outward				
	2014	2015	2016	2017	2018	2014	2015	2016	2017	2018
ASIA	**401.5**	**1 359.9**	**1 664.1**	**2 226.9**	**2 230.7**	**2 724.7**	**2 560.9**	**2 347.5**	**3 366.1**	**3 875.8**
Near and Middle East	26.8	61.0	.. c	.. c	.. c	-147.8	113.9	107.9	76.8	195.0
Gulf Arabian countries	-	61.8	.. c	.. c	.. c	59.3	80.3	66.4	37.8	68.9
Kuwait	-	-	-	-	-	3.5	2.0	2.0	1.2	1.4
Qatar	-	-	-	-	-	-	-	-0.2	-0.2	-1.2
Saudi Arabia	-	61.8	.. c	.. c	.. c	0.4	15.9	17.3	11.2	14.6
United Arab Emirates	-	.. c	-	-	.. c	27.3	35.6	33.5	15.2	41.7
Other Near and Middle East	26.8	-0.8	6.7	4.8	-	-207.1	33.5	41.5	38.8	126.1
Jordan	-	-	-	-	-	0.4	6.3	0.2	0.4	0.1
Other Asian countries	374.8	1 298.9	1 639.8	2 207.9	2 220.3	2 872.5	2 447.1	2 239.6	3 289.5	3 680.7
China	157.7	860.9	1 081.6	1 629.8	1 613.5	757.6	1 029.5	821.9	1 585.0	1 480.5
Hong Kong, China	3.1	-5.9	-8.8	26.6	7.2	940.5	388.1	229.9	182.9	667.2
India	-15.0	-1.3	1.1	14.6	1.6	323.3	163.1	247.5	474.1	401.7
Indonesia	.. c	.. c	.. c	.. c	.. c	10.5	-2.4	24.9	16.7	34.1
Iran, Islamic Republic of	-	-	-	-	-	-27.0	18.0	15.3	-16.7	-69.5
Malaysia	.. c	.. c	7.0	35.2	.. c	134.0	115.2	65.1	75.6	80.5
Philippines	-	.. c	.. c	.. c	.. c	35.7	20.4	36.6	22.2	21.4
Singapore	9.5	-87.9	26.1	4.1	21.5	117.2	132.2	3.4	-86.8	91.6
Chinese Taipei	.. c	.. c	.. c	-	.. c	78.6	39.6	32.7	62.0	89.8
Thailand	.. c	.. c	.. c	.. c	.. c	70.8	98.0	99.5	154.3	164.1
Viet Nam	-	-	-	-	-	10.2	17.0	18.8	13.8	21.2
AUSTRALIA, OCEANIA AND POLAR REGIONS	**91.7**	**1.1**	**-0.2**	**-5.4**	**-7.2**	**330.6**	**210.8**	**225.9**	**265.1**	**145.3**
WORLD unallocated and confidential	**.. d**	**.. d**	**0.6**	**0.6**	**.. d**	**0.1**	**-**	**-**	**0.1**	**-0.1**
European Union (EU28)	**17 593.8**	**16 099.7**	**15 123.2**	**15 744.8**	**16 886.7**	**22 268.1**	**14 852.9**	**13 217.1**	**16 814.9**	**18 749.8**
G20 countries excl. European Union	**9 483.2**	**10 252.2**	**9 943.6**	**9 635.1**	**11 003.6**	**11 141.4**	**11 793.6**	**7 147.3**	**11 174.7**	**11 487.4**
G20 OECD countries	**9 353.9**	**9 380.9**	**8 875.1**	**7 971.7**	**9 366.0**	**8 435.8**	**9 941.8**	**5 245.0**	**7 840.4**	**7 875.1**
G20 Non-OECD countries	**129.3**	**871.2**	**1 068.3**	**1 663.4**	**1 637.8**	**2 705.6**	**1 851.9**	**1 902.3**	**3 334.3**	**3 612.3**
MENA countries	**-**	**61.8**	**.. c**	**.. c**	**.. c**	**-148.3**	**-51.1**	**116.1**	**48.0**	**84.6**
ASEAN countries	**-3.8**	**-95.0**	**29.5**	**39.4**	**21.6**	**377.7**	**391.5**	**261.4**	**198.0**	**458.2**

- Nil; .. Not available; c Confidential data; d Secondary Confidentiality

Note: Detailed metadata at: *http://stats.oecd.org/OECDStat_Metadata/ShowMetadata.ashx?Dataset=FDI_CTRY_IND_SUMM.*

1. Information on data for Israel: *http://oe.cd/israel-disclaimer.*
2. Note by Turkey: The information in this document with reference to "Cyprus" relates to the southern part of the Island. There is no single authority representing both Turkish and Greek Cypriot people on the Island. Turkey recognises the Turkish Republic of Northern Cyprus (TRNC). Until a lasting and equitable solution is found within the context of the United Nations, Turkey shall preserve its position concerning the "Cyprus issue".
3. Note by all the European Union Member States of the OECD and the European Union: The Republic of Cyprus is recognised by all members of the United Nations with the exception of Turkey. The information in this document relates to the area under the effective control of the Government of the Republic of Cyprus.

Source: OECD International Direct Investment Statistics (database): https://doi.org/10.1787/idi-data-en

Table 4. Foreign direct investment flows by industrial sector

Million US dollars

	Inward					Outward				
	2014	2015	2016	2017	2018	2014	2015	2016	2017	2018
All FDI activities	**4 018.7**	**8 382.1**	**19 149.8**	**14 262.3**	**3 356.3**	**9 179.4**	**12 760.1**	**4 726.5**	**25 537.5**	**16 774.3**
Agriculture, forestry and fishing	**-20.8**	**29.3**	**30.3**	**3.7**	**2.8**	**.. c**	**3.8**	**-0.5**	**5.4**	**8.4**
Mining and quarrying	**275.5**	**25.2**	**1 394.1**	**412.2**	**684.1**	**-393.3**	**-434.0**	**1 562.7**	**544.3**	**177.0**
Extraction activities	282.9	21.1	1 372.6	398.4	687.9	-231.5	-458.3	779.8	311.0	-18.0
Manufacturing	**6 004.0**	**6 731.6**	**818.0**	**5 787.8**	**5 590.8**	**4 430.5**	**6 724.0**	**4 417.3**	**11 346.8**	**13 688.3**
of which:										
Food products, beverages and tobacco	-3 015.9	-709.5	-128.8	441.6	292.6	-2 530.6	-168.7	-964.3	679.7	476.5
Textiles, wood and paper products; printing	53.5	-498.3	-68.5	-504.6	-160.5	486.6	-451.8	321.4	.. c	.. c
Chemical, rubber, plastic, non-metallic mineral products	-29.0	2 659.8	511.9	1 995.3	-373.5	-3 677.9	-597.4	-338.5	285.0	-1 568.6
Metal and machinery products, except electrical equipment	-1 420.4	-217.1	422.7	1 575.3	3 707.7	8 219.7	-122.3	323.6	5 261.6	11 541.4
Motor vehicles, trailers, semi-trailers, other transport equipment	10 260.2	4 325.9	.. c	-115.1	2 333.3	1 483.4	4 661.4	4 414.5	1 084.1	2 906.7
Other manufacturing	155.8	1 170.8	-316.3	2 395.3	-208.9	449.4	3 402.9	660.3	-912.5	-205.2
Electricity, gas, steam and air conditioning supply	**-2 618.7**	**-3 793.2**	**105.4**	**-2 095.1**	**-1 296.4**	**.. c**	**.. c**	**.. c**	**.. c**	**.. c**
Water supply; sewerage, waste management and remediation activities	**-31.9**	**65.0**	**-23.3**	**15.2**	**33.6**	**-4.1**	**-31.0**	**-134.6**	**76.4**	**46.7**
Construction	**-226.5**	**-531.0**	**370.6**	**134.0**	**-309.3**	**.. c**	**.. c**	**.. c**	**.. c**	**.. c**
Services	**-1 506.6**	**3 739.6**	**16 489.8**	**8 369.4**	**3 039.6**	**8 547.4**	**6 727.8**	**-2 342.7**	**12 259.5**	**3 136.3**
Wholesale and retail trade; repair of motor vehicles and motorcycles	2 986.2	2 102.1	15 379.3	4 397.4	-3 688.8	8 428.5	-877.2	-2 116.4	2 146.3	-587.9
Transportation and storage	-277.7	539.1	285.2	38.8	472.1	248.7	865.3	.. c	-1 200.9	777.4
Accommodation and food service activities	146.8	-30.8	-254.5	105.5	10.5	50.0	178.4	476.8	74.4	14.5
Information and communication	3 618.1	-109.3	-1 050.5	-2 263.8	-806.3	1 752.8	309.3	-1 722.4	-412.0	853.8
Financial and insurance activities	-5 323.8	-1 262.1	3 348.7	2 399.3	52.5	-3 549.3	2 556.0	-656.6	721.2	-2 458.2
Activities of holding companies	.. c	-123.0	3 648.7	-94.3	-1 446.3	-1 435.6	.. c	.. c	-31.2	-2 968.3
Real estate activities	-487.6	-409.2	-1 200.0	-956.6	1 838.2	982.5	.. c	288.0	2 243.6	1 763.1
Professional, scientific and technical activities	-832.2	3 052.6	-498.7	1 992.3	2 354.6	-614.3	2 087.6	59.0	2 795.1	763.4
Administrative and support service activities	-1 230.0	-91.8	573.7	2 748.2	1 794.2	636.6	455.2	1 345.6	5 377.8	1 776.2
Public administration; activities of households and of extraterritorial organisations	-	-	-	-	-	28.7	-	78.2	527.7	98.2
Education	11.2	-2.0	0.2	8.4	8.5	.. c	-	0.6	5.3	18.9
Human health and social work activities	-356.9	.. c	-119.2	-107.9	.. c	.. c	.. c	80.6	156.9	131.8
Arts, entertainment and recreation	.. c	-8.7	-9.4	-7.4	24.2	626.1	80.0	-50.6	22.1	25.7
Other services	97.4	-28.5	35.3	15.1	2.0	0.1	-0.1	43.0	-198.0	-40.4
Not allocated and confidential	**1 992.3**	**1 987.5**	**-149.4**	**1 531.4**	**-4 705.4**	**.. c**	**.. c**	**.. c**	**.. c**	**.. c**
Private real estate activities	**151.5**	**128.1**	**114.2**	**103.8**	**316.7**	**-11.7**	**323.0**	**-28.5**	**589.4**	**127.7**

- Nil; c Confidential data

Note: Detailed metadata at: *http://stats.oecd.org/OECDStat_Metadata/ShowMetadata.ashx?Dataset=FDI_CTRY_IND_SUMM.*

Source: *OECD International Direct Investment Statistics (database): https://doi.org/10.1787/idi-data-en*

Table 5. Foreign direct investment positions by industrial sector

At year end

Million US dollars

	Inward					Outward				
	2014	2015	2016	2017	2018	2014	2015	2016	2017	2018
All FDI activities	**320 593.8**	**317 407.1**	**315 873.3**	**367 705.7**	**342 276.0**	**402 098.5**	**355 227.1**	**348 463.4**	**384 598.9**	**374 513.3**
Agriculture, forestry and fishing	**.. c**	**401.5**	**87.0**	**27.2**	**.. c**	**.. c**	**-232.9**	**315.9**	**267.3**	**476.5**
Mining and quarrying	**1 551.4**	**1 677.2**	**1 400.2**	**1 696.9**	**1 577.9**	**2 949.5**	**2 369.4**	**3 560.5**	**3 596.7**	**3 953.5**
Extraction activities	.. c	.. c	959.3	1 298.9	1 236.0	2 458.4	.. c	.. c	.. c	.. c
Manufacturing	**139 418.8**	**137 035.4**	**126 855.4**	**143 295.8**	**132 695.6**	**165 442.3**	**152 650.5**	**143 849.8**	**157 396.9**	**158 828.1**
of which:										
Food products, beverages and tobacco	27 818.8	23 432.1	22 480.4	23 642.7	21 676.2	8 307.4	6 604.6	4 965.9	4 359.0	4 827.4
Textiles, wood and paper products; printing	17 345.6	15 360.4	14 300.8	15 442.4	14 309.8	10 343.5	11 848.0	.. c	.. c	.. c
Chemical, rubber, plastic, non-metallic mineral products	52 757.1	51 258.6	46 418.3	53 826.8	51 458.8	38 661.5	37 211.8	35 800.1	41 282.7	38 390.8
Metal and machinery products, except electrical equipment	14 480.5	13 066.9	13 125.1	16 100.0	16 189.5	57 396.1	55 824.9	46 384.3	47 357.7	48 345.3
Motor vehicles, trailers, semi-trailers, other transport equipment	17 735.3	21 588.5	20 459.8	21 700.8	19 201.3	33 334.6	.. c	.. c	.. c	40 956.3
Other manufacturing	9 281.4	12 328.9	10 071.0	12 583.1	9 860.0	17 399.4	8 176.2	8 946.2	10 120.2	11 633.8
Electricity, gas, steam and air conditioning supply	**26 054.9**	**24 155.9**	**22 630.4**	**24 152.0**	**20 912.9**	**.. c**	**.. c**	**.. c**	**.. c**	**.. c**
Water supply; sewerage, waste management and remediation activities	**672.0**	**601.8**	**768.6**	**875.2**	**855.9**	**745.0**	**550.4**	**.. c**	**.. c**	**.. c**
Construction	**2 926.2**	**1 947.3**	**1 823.4**	**2 306.9**	**1 367.2**	**4 010.6**	**4 508.9**	**3 772.2**	**4 089.2**	**4 658.0**
Services	**133 558.4**	**134 601.5**	**145 536.8**	**171 678.9**	**160 773.5**	**176 356.7**	**158 311.9**	**168 696.7**	**176 821.9**	**170 264.7**
Wholesale and retail trade; repair of motor vehicles and motorcycles	25 896.5	30 055.8	34 316.8	45 380.8	40 702.0	33 026.5	36 019.7	36 711.7	42 604.2	37 443.3
Transportation and storage	5 449.7	4 972.4	3 500.7	4 980.3	6 348.0	6 634.0	6 226.7	6 627.9	6 245.4	6 792.5
Accommodation and food service activities	1 694.2	1 114.6	897.5	1 697.2	529.7	.. c	578.4	.. c	585.2	.. c
Information and communication	13 567.3	14 436.0	13 554.8	15 140.6	11 852.7	25 880.1	14 139.7	17 386.6	23 408.4	26 720.3
Financial and insurance activities	49 340.1	46 374.2	59 826.0	63 977.0	64 381.3	76 464.8	72 985.7	74 760.7	57 176.2	45 079.1
Activities of holding companies	6 976.5	16 455.1	24 801.6	23 556.7	28 397.2	4 012.3	7 050.0	7 495.9	9 367.6	11 651.7
Real estate activities	15 664.2	18 024.1	17 034.6	19 253.7	17 076.2	12 770.3	8 482.5	11 045.6	16 808.1	18 357.3
Professional, scientific and technical activities	15 164.7	14 675.1	10 890.4	12 126.3	13 654.1	10 590.2	10 991.4	8 528.9	13 016.7	16 348.9
Administrative and support service activities	5 316.7	4 296.7	4 791.9	8 348.4	4 598.3	8 456.8	7 981.5	8 803.3	12 815.8	13 905.7
Public administration; activities of households and of extraterritorial organisations	-	-	-	-	-	.. c	-	.. c	.. c	.. c
Education	29.5	.. c	.. c	.. c	139.3	.. c	-	.. c	.. c	.. c
Human health and social work activities	1 065.7	318.3	282.4	.. c	1 095.3	-91.1	.. c	1 162.3	2 479.9	2 760.4
Arts, entertainment and recreation	.. c	.. c	.. c	.. c	371.6	523.3	.. c	.. c	588.5	.. c
Other services	202.3	.. c	233.7	214.5	25.0	.. c	.. c	.. c	.. c	.. c
Not allocated and confidential	**.. c**	**3 961.8**	**4 151.2**	**8 549.5**	**.. c**	**.. c**	**.. c**	**.. c**	**.. c**	**.. c**
Private real estate activities	**10 161.9**	**13 024.7**	**12 620.3**	**15 123.3**	**14 196.1**	**20 318.7**	**20 437.3**	**20 236.9**	**25 655.1**	**24 175.2**

- Nil; c Confidential data

Note: Detailed metadata at: *http://stats.oecd.org/OECDStat_Metadata/ShowMetadata.ashx?Dataset=FDI_CTRY_IND_SUMM.*

Source: OECD International Direct Investment Statistics (database): https://doi.org/10.1787/idi-data-en

Table 6. Foreign direct investment income by industrial sector

Million US dollars

	Inward					Outward				
	2014	2015	2016	2017	2018	2014	2015	2016	2017	2018
All FDI activities	**23 598.2**	**22 048.3**	**21 831.1**	**22 161.0**	**24 099.7**	**36 103.3**	**26 788.9**	**25 589.9**	**30 696.6**	**32 906.9**
Agriculture, forestry and fishing	**-20.8**	**35.8**	**30.3**	**3.7**	**2.8**	**24.1**	**5.2**	**-0.5**	**5.4**	**8.9**
Mining and quarrying	**-288.8**	**64.7**	**363.0**	**463.6**	**329.6**	**-132.2**	**-28.6**	**554.5**	**659.9**	**476.0**
Extraction activities	-300.2	21.1	310.1	436.1	333.4	-176.4	-262.9	297.0	304.9	140.6
Manufacturing	**10 431.6**	**10 519.3**	**11 210.4**	**11 192.6**	**12 926.8**	**14 399.0**	**13 087.1**	**11 593.5**	**14 395.6**	**15 628.4**
of which:										
Food products, beverages and tobacco	843.9	304.4	962.3	661.9	665.6	1 041.0	495.3	1 325.8	832.9	814.2
Textiles, wood and paper products; printing	585.9	350.8	149.1	498.1	618.7	-12.5	1 221.3	663.6	1 388.8	985.7
Chemical, rubber, plastic, non-metallic mineral products	5 734.9	5 040.4	5 323.7	4 225.3	5 870.0	290.4	1 124.2	159.3	1 425.8	370.4
Metal and machinery products, except electrical equipment	1 201.3	1 468.6	1 113.4	1 714.1	1 311.4	7 372.7	6 847.2	5 249.6	6 131.4	7 506.7
Motor vehicles, trailers, semi-trailers, other transport equipment	1 184.0	2 286.8	2 822.4	3 255.9	3 320.9	3 093.2	1 715.0	2 516.2	3 852.8	4 576.8
Other manufacturing	881.6	1 068.4	839.5	837.4	1 140.0	2 614.2	1 684.2	1 679.2	763.9	1 374.6
Electricity, gas, steam and air conditioning supply	**1 450.0**	**870.9**	**186.9**	**204.4**	**153.4**	**812.5**	**734.3**	**108.5**	**596.2**	**361.4**
Water supply; sewerage, waste management and remediation activities	**44.8**	**65.0**	**3.0**	**15.2**	**34.2**	**0.4**	**-21.6**	**-32.8**	**77.8**	**60.6**
Construction	**314.3**	**-58.0**	**162.6**	**458.5**	**109.5**	**312.4**	**404.8**	**198.8**	**-59.9**	**115.3**
Services	**10 747.1**	**10 079.8**	**9 764.4**	**9 519.5**	**9 907.9**	**20 193.2**	**11 961.5**	**12 640.6**	**14 402.8**	**15 642.8**
Wholesale and retail trade; repair of motor vehicles and motorcycles	2 510.1	2 564.7	3 090.3	3 042.5	2 853.8	4 895.4	2 908.9	3 394.6	4 078.3	3 980.1
Transportation and storage	78.4	559.8	339.0	207.3	-130.1	971.0	278.3	-20.9	57.4	-5.5
Accommodation and food service activities	93.6	131.7	37.7	132.1	60.3	65.0	191.1	126.3	99.9	18.1
Information and communication	2 081.2	1 183.8	1 209.5	703.1	1 635.5	3 432.4	1 535.8	1 874.8	2 300.7	3 108.8
Financial and insurance activities	4 007.9	3 680.7	3 218.3	3 142.4	3 443.2	8 403.3	4 438.6	4 242.3	5 120.0	4 560.9
Activities of holding companies	69.5	1 192.6	642.4	264.0	390.2	51.3	172.6	314.1	197.8	295.3
Real estate activities	887.0	568.1	310.5	537.1	189.3	583.5	653.6	245.1	167.1	366.2
Professional, scientific and technical activities	890.5	1 018.1	1 119.1	1 219.8	1 331.0	887.9	980.6	1 283.8	941.5	1 603.1
Administrative and support service activities	406.3	421.6	484.0	541.5	448.9	668.5	828.4	1 114.2	1 201.0	1 683.2
Public administration; activities of households and of extraterritorial organisations	-	-	-	-	-	28.7	-	78.2	170.7	144.5
Education	11.5	-2.0	0.2	8.4	8.5	3.5	-	0.6	5.3	18.9
Human health and social work activities	-269.1	-9.6	-77.0	-27.3	41.4	13.0	17.2	89.3	79.8	-18.8
Arts, entertainment and recreation	-11.1	-8.7	-9.4	-7.4	24.2	240.7	129.0	138.3	119.8	147.5
Other services	60.8	-28.5	42.0	19.8	2.0	0.1	-0.1	74.2	61.7	35.8
Not allocated and confidential	**879.8**	**440.4**	**-3.0**	**105.4**	**424.0**	**438.2**	**536.6**	**383.1**	**381.7**	**423.6**
Private real estate activities	**40.2**	**30.5**	**113.6**	**198.1**	**211.5**	**55.7**	**109.6**	**144.2**	**237.2**	**189.9**

- Nil

Note: Detailed metadata at: *http://stats.oecd.org/OECDStat_Metadata/ShowMetadata.ashx?Dataset=FDI_CTRY_IND_SUMM.*

Source: OECD International Direct Investment Statistics (database): https://doi.org/10.1787/idi-data-en

SWITZERLAND

Table 1. Foreign direct investment flows by country

Million US dollars

	Inward					Outward				
	2014	2015	2016	2017	2018	2014	2015	2016	2017	2018
WORLD	**9 351.8**	**75 289.0**	**88 618.5**	**107 321.0**	**-53 150.2**	**-46.6**	**88 758.7**	**122 101.3**	**30 144.2**	**60 780.8**
OECD COUNTRIES	**25 688.5**	**65 220.3**	**81 521.3**	**65 134.8**	**-29 280.3**	**1 204.5**	**91 331.5**	**140 593.9**	**-31 673.3**	**43 933.4**
Australia	.. c	.. c	.. c	.. c	.. c	-2 777.6	7 562.9	-71.2	-1 583.5	-8 511.9
Austria	-788.1	-78.7	10 231.0	-1 124.1	11 252.1	770.8	79.7	249.4	-276.7	-465.0
Belgium	-1 724.8	1 662.6	-1 125.3	-1 112.3	-1 102.7	297.6	3 203.3	-1 645.8	-4 318.2	-3 167.0
Canada	-157.4	259.3	-137.6	2 989.7	51.0	2 866.3	-1 782.0	-2 965.1	950.4	-5 989.4
Chile	.. c	.. c	.. c	.. c	.. c	47.0	-3 418.5	-466.8	-47.0	3 679.4
Czech Republic	.. c	.. c	.. c	.. c	.. c	220.5	-527.9	-753.9	543.3	176.0
Denmark	-169.8	-2 869.0	-373.1	1 515.9	245.4	492.5	-287.4	-413.4	135.8	144.2
Estonia	.. c	.. c	.. c	.. c	.. c	.. c	-99.8	354.9	-327.6	20.3
Finland	-38.2	.. c	.. c	.. c	.. c	157.7	-39.3	173.5	-430.2	163.9
France	-1 604.7	120.5	-2 933.5	528.9	10 279.2	-1 301.7	23 296.8	2 938.0	-908.0	9 228.9
Germany	-1 527.6	885.8	2 355.3	1 364.9	-7 473.6	2 200.5	1 994.8	7 347.9	5 976.9	11 069.0
Greece	.. c	.. c	.. c	.. c	.. c	100.1	1.9	-357.9	437.1	-35.5
Hungary	.. c	1 980.5	4 529.9	2 557.8	-3 103.3	-73.8	335.6	4 023.8	394.8	388.4
Iceland	.. c	.. c	.. c	.. c	.. c	.. c	.. c	.. c	.. c	.. c
Ireland	.. c	13 893.8	-7 503.5	11 032.5	23 007.5	-2 019.4	39 418.8	36 492.0	-42 926.0	18 632.7
Israel[1]	-148.3	51.3	-200.0	-177.3	-26.1	153.1	160.9	919.7	-147.7	53.4
Italy	-285.0	425.1	535.4	25.7	-1 405.1	1 815.8	-513.0	819.8	591.5	1 200.2
Japan	-45.3	543.1	-441.9	-1 935.9	797.4	-378.8	262.6	2 284.5	4 507.7	2 412.6
Korea	.. c	.. c	.. c	.. c	.. c	369.7	255.5	-835.2	304.3	-2.6
Latvia	.. c	.. c	.. c	.. c	.. c	.. c	0.2	3.5	96.2	37.7
Lithuania	.. c	.. c	.. c	.. c	.. c	.. c	-5.9	-0.4	-19.2	76.0
Luxembourg	6 866.3	7 346.5	7 699.8	44 047.1	-21 054.7	2 950.5	9 652.8	8 639.8	-6 200.7	15 133.4
Mexico	.. c	.. c	.. c	.. c	.. c	-3 345.4	388.0	864.0	714.1	1 071.0
Netherlands	5 897.3	28 229.1	50 032.0	47 931.0	-41 870.4	11 650.2	14 872.9	27 253.9	8 645.9	-3 473.1
New Zealand	.. c	.. c	.. c	.. c	.. c	30.4	30.4	39.7	-18.5	41.2
Norway	.. c	.. c	.. c	.. c	.. c	351.2	-213.0	2 386.5	-332.9	-258.5
Poland	.. c	.. c	.. c	.. c	.. c	149.4	-252.8	533.9	811.1	785.9
Portugal	.. c	.. c	.. c	.. c	.. c	238.3	465.8	231.3	359.8	252.0
Slovak Republic	.. c	.. c	.. c	.. c	.. c	58.1	109.3	71.3	268.9	209.3
Slovenia	.. c	.. c	.. c	.. c	.. c	.. c	.. c	.. c	.. c	.. c
Spain	-1 010.4	134.5	-563.5	-53.1	-1 572.2	99.0	-309.7	-225.4	330.1	1 023.7
Sweden	-1 161.3	2 087.1	-103.7	800.5	595.5	61.8	-478.2	-1 008.7	1 078.2	151.0
Switzerland	..	..	..	..	..	..	..	..	..	..
Turkey	.. c	.. c	.. c	.. c	.. c	585.8	631.9	694.2	415.6	303.1
United Kingdom	21 634.3	14 326.0	6 064.1	-26 374.0	39 763.9	-9 535.5	-13 426.6	13 511.9	-15 367.7	11 886.7
United States	2 351.8	-2 713.8	13 510.2	-17 478.2	-38 009.8	-5 238.2	9 805.7	39 403.9	14 738.1	-12 367.7
EUROPE	**4 402.6**	**61 166.0**	**74 206.8**	**89 331.9**	**33 702.9**	**-1 489.9**	**73 445.0**	**106 340.7**	**10 270.5**	**65 761.4**
Bulgaria	.. c	.. c	.. c	.. c	.. c	91.7	22.5	-15.2	38.4	-25.0
Croatia	.. c	.. c	.. c	.. c	.. c	42.7	-4.5	18.7	58.8	0.1
Cyprus[2, 3]	.. c	-1 920.1	-487.9	1 298.6	-625.7	.. c	-777.4	-1 387.2	49 541.0	-501.0
Malta	.. c	.. c	.. c	.. c	.. c	.. c	.. c	.. c	.. c	.. c
Romania	.. c	.. c	.. c	.. c	.. c	49.0	-116.9	-24.3	439.3	271.6
Russian Federation	.. c	.. c	.. c	.. c	.. c	844.1	785.0	1 619.3	4 851.3	2 937.0
Ukraine	.. c	.. c	.. c	.. c	.. c	228.5	-148.4	-81.9	774.5	602.8
AFRICA	**.. c**	**.. c**	**.. c**	**.. c**	**.. c**	**320.5**	**3 132.6**	**283.0**	**-1 408.2**	**-396.9**
Northern Africa	.. c	.. c	.. c	.. c	.. c	.. c	526.7	-600.6	-105.2	-43.6
Algeria	.. c	.. c	.. c	.. c	.. c	.. c	.. c	.. c	.. c	.. c
Egypt	.. c	.. c	.. c	.. c	.. c	57.8	522.0	-415.4	-113.3	-72.4
Libya	.. c	.. c	.. c	.. c	.. c	.. c	.. c	.. c	.. c	.. c
Morocco	.. c	.. c	.. c	.. c	.. c	-17.6	-3.5	-228.6	-21.0	15.3
Tunisia	.. c	.. c	.. c	.. c	.. c	3.4	-15.2	2.4	12.7	13.8
Other African countries	.. c	.. c	.. c	.. c	.. c	.. c	2 605.9	883.6	-1 303.0	-353.3
Nigeria	.. c	.. c	.. c	.. c	.. c	-29.4	244.6	162.8	35.0	-2.7
South Africa	.. c	.. c	.. c	.. c	.. c	224.0	-199.1	683.7	-67.1	-368.9
AMERICA	**4 606.4**	**18 223.3**	**13 294.5**	**17 885.7**	**-89 030.8**	**-7 749.5**	**-2 997.9**	**15 557.0**	**12 011.6**	**150.9**
Northern America	2 194.4	-2 454.5	13 372.5	-14 488.5	-37 958.6	-2 371.9	8 023.7	36 438.7	15 688.5	-18 357.1
Central America and Caribbean countries	.. c	.. c	.. c	.. c	.. c	-7 378.3	-6 682.2	-20 977.3	-4 355.1	9 795.9
Bahamas	.. c	.. c	.. c	.. c	.. c	.. c	.. c	.. c	.. c	.. c
Bermuda	.. c	.. c	.. c	.. c	.. c	.. c	-27 216.8	-253.8	-6 333.5	14 118.5
Cayman Islands	.. c	.. c	.. c	.. c	.. c	.. c	.. c	.. c	.. c	.. c
Costa Rica	.. c	.. c	.. c	.. c	.. c	52.1	93.2	79.5	153.6	259.3
El Salvador	.. c	.. c	.. c	.. c	.. c	.. c	.. c	.. c	.. c	.. c
Guatemala	.. c	.. c	.. c	.. c	.. c	38.8	26.7	19.8	-57.2	2.2
Honduras	.. c	.. c	.. c	.. c	.. c	.. c	.. c	.. c	.. c	.. c
Nicaragua	.. c	.. c	.. c	.. c	.. c	.. c	.. c	.. c	.. c	.. c
Panama	.. c	.. c	.. c	.. c	.. c	.. c	-2 159.0	-3 793.5	4 032.2	-224.7
Virgin Islands, U.S.	.. c	.. c	.. c	.. c	.. c	.. c	.. c	.. c	.. c	.. c
South America	.. c	.. c	.. c	.. c	.. c	2 000.7	-4 339.4	95.6	678.2	8 712.0
Argentina	.. c	.. c	.. c	.. c	.. c	333.2	228.3	-424.6	108.9	313.0
Bolivia	.. c	.. c	.. c	.. c	.. c	0.0	2.6	-15.6	11.5	8.0
Brazil	.. c	.. c	.. c	.. c	.. c	1 410.0	-1 136.0	43.3	-262.1	1 243.3
Colombia	.. c	.. c	.. c	.. c	.. c	145.1	21.7	6.6	299.9	3 543.6
Ecuador	.. c	.. c	.. c	.. c	.. c	59.6	35.5	-12.7	37.2	90.1
Paraguay	.. c	.. c	.. c	.. c	.. c	.. c	.. c	.. c	.. c	.. c
Peru	.. c	.. c	.. c	.. c	.. c	21.7	109.1	-1.2	315.4	-216.0
Uruguay	.. c	.. c	.. c	.. c	.. c	346.3	46.1	664.1	60.3	101.4
Venezuela	.. c	.. c	.. c	.. c	.. c	-360.3	-224.7	304.5	137.7	-45.1

Table 1. Foreign direct investment flows by country *(cont.)*

Million US dollars

	Inward					Outward				
	2014	2015	2016	2017	2018	2014	2015	2016	2017	2018
ASIA	**-518.9**	**.. c**	**.. c**	**.. c**	**.. c**	**11 358.3**	**7 201.1**	**-847.5**	**11 193.6**	**4 975.4**
Near and Middle East	.. c	.. c	.. c	.. c	.. c	.. c	76.4	-3 250.8	-592.8	-2 808.7
Gulf Arabian countries	.. c	.. c	.. c	.. c	.. c	2 212.5	.. c	.. c	.. c	.. c
Kuwait	.. c	.. c	.. c	.. c	.. c	.. c	.. c	.. c	.. c	.. c
Qatar	.. c	.. c	.. c	.. c	.. c	.. c	5.7	-3.1	4.7	0.2
Saudi Arabia	.. c	.. c	.. c	.. c	.. c	111.7	-1.9	93.9	90.7	192.2
United Arab Emirates	.. c	.. c	.. c	.. c	.. c	1 993.2	44.8	-3 869.3	-530.7	-3 402.4
Other Near and Middle East	.. c	.. c	.. c	.. c	.. c	172.8	.. c	.. c	.. c	.. c
Jordan	.. c	.. c	.. c	.. c	.. c	.. c	-29.1	45.0	47.9	-5.1
Other Asian countries	.. c	.. c	.. c	.. c	.. c	.. c	7 124.6	2 403.3	11 786.4	7 784.1
China	.. c	.. c	.. c	.. c	.. c	3 675.8	1 542.3	1 505.6	3 217.4	3 012.9
Hong Kong, China	.. c	.. c	.. c	.. c	.. c	761.8	1 017.5	-306.7	709.9	-125.8
India	.. c	.. c	.. c	.. c	.. c	524.9	798.9	160.6	1 056.4	831.4
Indonesia	.. c	.. c	.. c	.. c	.. c	2 087.0	1 878.2	2 063.0	1 977.9	1 891.6
Iran, Islamic Republic of	.. c	.. c	.. c	.. c	.. c	.. c	.. c	.. c	.. c	.. c
Malaysia	.. c	.. c	.. c	.. c	.. c	568.8	45.3	164.0	621.2	-2 811.2
Philippines	.. c	.. c	.. c	.. c	.. c	74.5	467.7	-18.1	770.3	-186.8
Singapore	.. c	.. c	.. c	.. c	.. c	415.3	448.2	-2 512.0	-1 398.5	2 519.5
Chinese Taipei	.. c	.. c	.. c	.. c	.. c	188.3	243.7	124.2	206.7	113.7
Thailand	.. c	.. c	.. c	.. c	.. c	131.4	141.9	-38.1	143.3	205.1
Viet Nam	.. c	.. c	.. c	.. c	.. c	70.3	78.5	89.1	72.7	-8.5
AUSTRALIA, OCEANIA AND POLAR REGIONS	**.. c**	**.. c**	**.. c**	**.. c**	**.. c**	**-2 722.1**	**7 686.8**	**-9.9**	**-1 504.6**	**-8 552.1**
WORLD unallocated and confidential	**.. d**	**-4 694.8**	**1 759.1**	**2 216.5**	**1 406.5**	**236.0**	**291.1**	**778.0**	**-418.7**	**-1 157.8**
European Union (EU28)	**23 276.5**	**65 440.5**	**71 371.2**	**80 296.7**	**6 301.5**	**8 305.9**	**76 608.6**	**97 057.4**	**-702.4**	**63 308.3**
G20 countries excl. European Union	**19 259.3**	**12 161.4**	**18 849.4**	**-35 286.2**	**195.1**	**-5 528.3**	**32 372.2**	**69 737.4**	**21 312.8**	**20 352.3**
G20 OECD countries	**20 327.9**	**.. c**	**.. c**	**.. c**	**.. c**	**-14 739.1**	**28 476.6**	**63 992.6**	**10 339.5**	**10 299.9**
G20 Non-OECD countries	**-1 068.7**	**.. c**	**.. c**	**.. c**	**.. c**	**9 210.7**	**3 895.7**	**5 744.8**	**10 973.3**	**10 052.4**
MENA countries	**147.1**	**.. c**	**.. c**	**.. c**	**.. c**	**2 256.0**	**513.2**	**-4 782.8**	**-549.2**	**-2 900.5**
ASEAN countries	**76.1**	**.. c**	**.. c**	**.. c**	**.. c**	**3 353.4**	**3 050.0**	**-261.7**	**2 187.6**	**1 679.1**

.. Not available; c Confidential data; d Secondary Confidentiality

Note: Detailed metadata at: *http://stats.oecd.org/OECDStat_Metadata/ShowMetadata.ashx?Dataset=FDI_CTRY_IND_SUMM.*

1. Information on data for Israel: *http://oe.cd/israel-disclaimer.*
2. Note by Turkey: The information in this document with reference to "Cyprus" relates to the southern part of the Island. There is no single authority representing both Turkish and Greek Cypriot people on the Island. Turkey recognises the Turkish Republic of Northern Cyprus (TRNC). Until a lasting and equitable solution is found within the context of the United Nations, Turkey shall preserve its position concerning the "Cyprus issue".
3. Note by all the European Union Member States of the OECD and the European Union: The Republic of Cyprus is recognised by all members of the United Nations with the exception of Turkey. The information in this document relates to the area under the effective control of the Government of the Republic of Cyprus.

Source: OECD International Direct Investment Statistics (database): https://doi.org/10.1787/idi-data-en

SWITZERLAND

Table 2. Foreign direct investment positions by country

At year end

Million US dollars

	Inward					Outward				
	2014	2015	2016	2017	2018	2014	2015	2016	2017	2018
WORLD	**812 908.1**	**890 483.5**	**1 119 934.6**	**1 352 536.5**	**1 354 535.3**	**1 077 238.6**	**1 131 401.8**	**1 307 515.6**	**1 438 450.5**	**1 494 721.1**
OECD COUNTRIES	**702 621.6**	**781 032.0**	**970 270.2**	**1 172 834.0**	**1 144 052.6**	**745 954.5**	**838 339.4**	**1 016 897.7**	**1 077 991.4**	**1 126 184.4**
Australia	.. c	3 502.7	1 940.5	2 079.6	2 512.1	16 421.0	17 596.4	16 878.5	15 748.8	6 657.5
Austria	5 256.5	7 755.5	7 194.8	8 849.3	10 402.8	8 566.0	7 847.3	8 585.9	10 083.2	9 419.6
Belgium	6 726.4	7 053.7	5 524.9	4 912.9	3 504.9	12 830.2	14 937.6	15 460.1	13 433.0	9 795.1
Canada	32 808.3	38 515.4	34 915.7	37 968.4	30 541.9	41 696.1	46 319.5	45 514.4	40 064.7	31 707.5
Chile	.. c	.. c	.. c	.. c	.. c	2 101.8	-1 521.6	-2 047.4	-2 007.9	1 768.7
Czech Republic	.. c	.. c	.. c	.. c	.. c	5 598.2	4 423.6	3 430.7	4 268.3	4 404.2
Denmark	5 630.4	3 202.6	2 447.4	4 075.3	4 341.5	2 270.5	1 712.9	1 547.5	1 670.3	1 605.9
Estonia	.. c	.. c	.. c	.. c	.. c	.. c	57.0	422.1	114.7	159.1
Finland	415.0	.. c	.. c	.. c	.. c	783.2	587.7	787.0	554.7	950.0
France	44 948.7	43 161.5	38 499.6	44 185.0	49 454.0	34 060.4	56 069.5	57 878.9	59 973.3	64 794.4
Germany	32 897.4	32 442.7	30 031.2	44 849.7	40 692.4	36 002.7	37 620.6	40 499.1	48 507.0	59 063.6
Greece	.. c	.. c	.. c	.. c	.. c	2 163.0	2 006.0	1 630.7	2 307.0	2 167.6
Hungary	.. c	677.5	1 029.8	2 158.6	1 221.9	2 017.9	2 008.4	5 851.4	5 944.5	5 769.7
Iceland	.. c	.. c	.. c	.. c	.. c	.. c	.. c	.. c	.. c	.. c
Ireland	.. c	108 101.8	116 412.3	118 166.4	163 579.5	29 052.8	69 389.6	132 031.7	98 663.4	119 519.3
Israel[1]	1 548.7	1 560.9	1 911.8	1 628.2	1 721.2	1 113.3	1 174.2	1 509.3	1 572.0	1 552.0
Italy	5 417.7	6 013.1	6 456.2	6 565.9	3 962.8	16 796.1	15 748.7	15 681.2	18 173.7	18 091.6
Japan	9 664.2	11 113.6	24 229.3	26 129.7	28 035.4	8 002.3	9 276.9	11 537.6	14 526.4	16 868.7
Korea	.. c	.. c	.. c	.. c	.. c	4 393.9	4 358.0	3 308.1	3 951.0	3 896.0
Latvia	.. c	.. c	.. c	.. c	.. c	.. c	37.0	40.3	142.1	172.6
Lithuania	.. c	.. c	.. c	.. c	.. c	.. c	305.2	392.6	397.6	479.7
Luxembourg	43 215.5	25 940.6	25 780.5	28 116.8	19 968.6	138 974.8	155 062.0	176 411.5	195 540.5	194 161.4
Mexico	.. c	12 916.4	12 901.1	12 632.0	11 291.2	7 731.2	7 477.5	5 455.3	5 844.3	6 617.4
Netherlands	51 559.6	72 628.9	75 748.2	70 600.8	56 252.4	98 835.3	108 127.0	129 189.4	159 429.8	159 419.9
New Zealand	.. c	.. c	.. c	.. c	.. c	438.5	425.3	605.9	393.1	374.8
Norway	.. c	.. c	.. c	.. c	.. c	3 204.9	1 963.0	5 000.0	4 631.5	4 743.7
Poland	.. c	.. c	.. c	.. c	.. c	6 025.1	5 252.4	5 377.9	6 805.2	6 990.2
Portugal	.. c	.. c	.. c	.. c	.. c	1 300.6	1 491.1	1 227.6	1 495.1	1 386.0
Slovak Republic	.. c	.. c	.. c	.. c	.. c	458.1	528.5	507.8	804.9	943.2
Slovenia	.. c	.. c	.. c	.. c	.. c	.. c	.. c	.. c	.. c	.. c
Spain	5 320.9	6 446.0	5 999.5	6 713.0	6 770.7	8 856.6	8 865.0	9 044.9	9 892.3	10 669.1
Sweden	5 125.4	10 303.6	10 116.7	12 231.3	12 762.1	7 975.8	7 385.9	6 073.3	7 619.1	8 312.0
Switzerland	..	..	..	..	..	..	..	..	..	..
Turkey	.. c	.. c	.. c	.. c	.. c	2 866.6	2 604.6	2 634.4	2 603.4	2 368.1
United Kingdom	24 906.3	34 199.7	49 449.3	67 484.0	66 954.3	59 220.7	49 593.4	57 795.0	56 489.9	79 525.7
United States	307 592.9	320 103.1	475 221.2	625 315.0	571 242.9	184 329.8	198 165.8	255 192.6	286 906.6	289 971.3
EUROPE	**353 052.5**	**408 473.5**	**467 168.6**	**517 180.8**	**578 378.4**	**517 998.7**	**590 995.9**	**734 926.1**	**828 712.4**	**883 774.7**
Bulgaria	.. c	.. c	.. c	.. c	.. c	366.5	312.9	281.1	340.4	244.7
Croatia	.. c	.. c	.. c	.. c	.. c	383.3	342.5	365.7	446.8	437.3
Cyprus[2, 3]	.. c	.. c	.. c	.. c	.. c	.. c	2 706.9	8 522.8	58 934.2	59 069.3
Malta	.. c	.. c	.. c	.. c	.. c	.. c	.. c	.. c	.. c	.. c
Romania	.. c	.. c	.. c	.. c	.. c	2 564.1	2 217.2	2 142.0	2 730.6	2 621.2
Russian Federation	.. c	5 486.0	21 016.8	28 394.1	29 004.2	9 529.9	8 654.6	19 932.0	22 401.0	23 916.5
Ukraine	.. c	.. c	.. c	.. c	.. c	1 161.2	457.5	603.9	1 522.0	2 132.9
AFRICA	**.. c**	**.. c**	**.. c**	**.. c**	**.. c**	**10 963.3**	**13 362.4**	**13 128.9**	**11 842.7**	**11 503.6**
Northern Africa	.. c	.. c	.. c	.. c	.. c	.. c	2 519.3	1 379.2	1 278.5	1 200.0
Algeria	.. c	.. c	.. c	.. c	.. c	.. c	.. c	.. c	.. c	.. c
Egypt	.. c	.. c	.. c	.. c	.. c	1 413.6	1 864.1	779.7	638.7	621.0
Libya	.. c	.. c	.. c	.. c	.. c	.. c	.. c	.. c	.. c	.. c
Morocco	.. c	.. c	.. c	.. c	.. c	603.8	558.3	334.8	342.2	380.0
Tunisia	.. c	.. c	.. c	.. c	.. c	57.2	44.8	35.0	41.3	46.4
Other African countries	.. c	.. c	.. c	.. c	.. c	.. c	10 843.1	11 749.7	10 564.2	10 303.6
Nigeria	.. c	.. c	.. c	.. c	.. c	397.2	599.0	468.1	440.7	422.9
South Africa	.. c	.. c	.. c	.. c	.. c	2 850.4	2 170.0	2 660.1	2 597.2	2 637.6
AMERICA	**400 880.5**	**422 245.5**	**577 694.2**	**743 747.1**	**681 112.2**	**422 168.7**	**397 993.7**	**428 914.5**	**456 889.8**	**463 680.0**
Northern America	340 401.2	358 618.5	510 136.9	663 283.2	601 784.9	226 025.9	244 485.3	300 707.0	326 971.3	321 678.8
Central America and Caribbean countries	.. c	.. c	.. c	.. c	.. c	170 827.3	135 650.8	110 271.5	110 552.7	116 558.1
Bahamas	.. c	.. c	.. c	.. c	.. c	.. c	.. c	.. c	.. c	.. c
Bermuda	.. c	.. c	.. c	.. c	.. c	.. c	42 253.8	39 716.6	48 475.8	62 690.5
Cayman Islands	.. c	.. c	.. c	.. c	.. c	.. c	.. c	.. c	.. c	.. c
Costa Rica	.. c	.. c	.. c	.. c	.. c	618.7	652.4	784.2	940.0	1 095.2
El Salvador	.. c	.. c	.. c	.. c	.. c	.. c	.. c	.. c	.. c	.. c
Guatemala	.. c	.. c	.. c	.. c	.. c	218.7	215.5	204.6	193.6	193.5
Honduras	.. c	.. c	.. c	.. c	.. c	.. c	.. c	.. c	.. c	.. c
Nicaragua	.. c	.. c	.. c	.. c	.. c	.. c	.. c	.. c	.. c	.. c
Panama	.. c	.. c	.. c	.. c	.. c	.. c	3 037.1	262.3	4 020.5	3 131.7
Virgin Islands, U.S.	.. c	.. c	.. c	.. c	.. c	.. c	.. c	.. c	.. c	.. c
South America	.. c	.. c	.. c	.. c	.. c	25 315.5	17 857.6	17 936.0	19 365.9	25 443.0
Argentina	.. c	.. c	.. c	.. c	.. c	4 370.0	4 974.5	4 070.7	4 024.2	3 091.9
Bolivia	.. c	.. c	.. c	.. c	.. c	66.7	72.9	58.1	69.2	75.1
Brazil	.. c	.. c	.. c	.. c	.. c	13 098.4	9 346.7	10 761.5	11 068.1	10 649.5
Colombia	.. c	.. c	.. c	.. c	.. c	1 022.2	842.7	898.2	1 252.1	4 749.3
Ecuador	.. c	.. c	.. c	.. c	.. c	338.6	352.4	303.4	325.2	417.3
Paraguay	.. c	.. c	.. c	.. c	.. c	.. c	.. c	.. c	.. c	.. c
Peru	.. c	.. c	.. c	.. c	.. c	596.8	660.9	656.4	331.2	27.3
Uruguay	.. c	.. c	.. c	.. c	.. c	1 771.9	1 819.7	2 259.7	2 324.0	2 428.6
Venezuela	.. c	.. c	.. c	.. c	.. c	1 760.9	1 210.9	877.5	1 793.9	2 057.5

Table 2. Foreign direct investment positions by country *(cont.)*

At year end

Million US dollars

	Inward					Outward				
	2014	2015	2016	2017	2018	2014	2015	2016	2017	2018
ASIA	**.. c**	**.. c**	**.. c**	**.. c**	**.. c**	**106 350.1**	**108 073.4**	**109 652.4**	**120 244.3**	**123 233.6**
Near and Middle East	.. c	.. c	.. c	.. c	.. c	.. c	25 275.5	23 581.1	23 602.1	20 840.9
Gulf Arabian countries	.. c	.. c	.. c	.. c	.. c	23 592.1	.. c	.. c	.. c	.. c
Kuwait	.. c	.. c	.. c	.. c	.. c	.. c	.. c	.. c	.. c	.. c
Qatar	.. c	.. c	.. c	.. c	.. c	.. c	46.4	58.6	60.3	162.4
Saudi Arabia	.. c	.. c	.. c	.. c	.. c	939.4	943.2	900.0	983.0	1 133.0
United Arab Emirates	.. c	1 768.0	837.9	793.8	738.9	20 796.1	20 908.9	18 484.5	18 255.6	14 898.6
Other Near and Middle East	.. c	.. c	.. c	.. c	.. c	1 583.0	.. c	.. c	.. c	.. c
Jordan	.. c	.. c	.. c	.. c	.. c	.. c	246.2	278.8	337.3	315.3
Other Asian countries	.. c	.. c	.. c	.. c	.. c	.. c	82 797.8	86 071.3	96 642.1	102 392.6
China	.. c	.. c	7 228.0	17 357.5	18 084.2	20 247.8	19 874.7	19 654.7	22 700.2	23 287.2
Hong Kong, China	.. c	.. c	.. c	.. c	.. c	6 074.9	6 273.9	5 990.4	7 720.7	7 350.4
India	.. c	1 597.2	1 881.8	1 856.2	2 337.7	4 569.7	4 870.1	4 718.4	6 209.9	6 343.6
Indonesia	.. c	.. c	.. c	.. c	.. c	5 549.9	6 453.1	6 828.0	7 087.7	6 625.8
Iran, Islamic Republic of	.. c	.. c	.. c	.. c	.. c	.. c	.. c	.. c	.. c	.. c
Malaysia	.. c	.. c	.. c	.. c	.. c	4 472.2	4 057.9	5 979.9	6 278.6	3 043.1
Philippines	.. c	.. c	.. c	.. c	.. c	1 107.3	1 414.4	1 427.3	2 201.0	1 894.7
Singapore	.. c	.. c	.. c	.. c	.. c	17 584.1	17 783.2	18 343.3	17 667.7	25 177.7
Chinese Taipei	.. c	.. c	.. c	.. c	.. c	1 749.2	1 775.0	1 826.3	1 944.6	1 832.8
Thailand	.. c	.. c	.. c	.. c	.. c	2 664.5	2 503.2	2 465.7	2 710.5	2 854.0
Viet Nam	.. c	.. c	.. c	.. c	.. c	537.5	605.6	629.8	707.0	692.7
AUSTRALIA, OCEANIA AND POLAR REGIONS	**.. c**	**.. c**	**.. c**	**.. c**	**.. c**	**16 915.3**	**18 145.0**	**17 592.0**	**16 336.4**	**7 142.4**
WORLD unallocated and confidential	**.. d**	**40 222.1**	**37 042.6**	**41 763.6**	**41 615.2**	**2 842.5**	**2 831.5**	**3 301.8**	**4 424.9**	**5 386.7**
European Union (EU28)	**307 666.0**	**357 873.6**	**376 580.5**	**423 622.6**	**445 233.5**	**481 186.1**	**556 226.4**	**682 898.0**	**767 033.7**	**822 570.8**
G20 countries excl. European Union	**520 810.3**	**545 502.7**	**734 578.5**	**938 569.7**	**879 605.4**	**472 676.2**	**502 117.9**	**581 900.3**	**629 860.6**	**657 246.7**
G20 OECD countries	**474 321.6**	**.. c**	**.. c**	**.. c**	**.. c**	**411 520.9**	**444 831.0**	**512 375.0**	**552 789.2**	**579 561.7**
G20 Non-OECD countries	**46 488.7**	**.. c**	**.. c**	**.. c**	**.. c**	**61 155.3**	**57 286.9**	**69 525.4**	**77 071.4**	**77 685.0**
MENA countries	**4 628.6**	**.. c**	**.. c**	**.. c**	**.. c**	**26 088.8**	**26 611.5**	**23 433.0**	**23 291.9**	**20 478.1**
ASEAN countries	**-982.5**	**.. c**	**.. c**	**.. c**	**.. c**	**31 999.0**	**32 888.5**	**35 701.5**	**36 732.9**	**40 432.5**

.. Not available; c Confidential data; d Secondary Confidentiality

Note: Inward FDI positions are allocated according to the ultimate investing country. Detailed metadata at: *http://stats.oecd.org/OECDStat_Metadata/ShowMetadata.ashx?Dataset=FDI_CTRY_IND_SUMM.*

1. Information on data for Israel: *http://oe.cd/israel-disclaimer.*
2. Note by Turkey: The information in this document with reference to "Cyprus" relates to the southern part of the Island. There is no single authority representing both Turkish and Greek Cypriot people on the Island. Turkey recognises the Turkish Republic of Northern Cyprus (TRNC). Until a lasting and equitable solution is found within the context of the United Nations, Turkey shall preserve its position concerning the "Cyprus issue".
3. Note by all the European Union Member States of the OECD and the European Union: The Republic of Cyprus is recognised by all members of the United Nations with the exception of Turkey. The information in this document relates to the area under the effective control of the Government of the Republic of Cyprus.

Source: OECD International Direct Investment Statistics (database): https://doi.org/10.1787/idi-data-en

SWITZERLAND

Table 3. Foreign direct investment income by country

Million US dollars

	Inward					Outward				
	2014	2015	2016	2017	2018	2014	2015	2016	2017	2018
WORLD	**73 369.0**	**59 799.7**	**70 912.0**	**98 750.6**	**105 009.9**	**90 613.8**	**91 017.9**	**90 756.2**	**99 840.3**	**106 142.4**
OECD COUNTRIES	**..**	**..c**	**..c**	**..c**	**..c**	**..**	**..c**	**..c**	**..c**	**..c**
Australia	..c	..c	..c	..c	..c	..c	..c	..c	..c	..c
Austria	..c	..c	..c	..c	..c	..c	..c	..c	..c	..c
Belgium	..c	..c	..c	..c	..c	..c	..c	..c	..c	..c
Canada	..c	..c	..c	..c	..c	..c	..c	..c	..c	..c
Chile	..c	..c	..c	..c	..c	..c	..c	..c	..c	..c
Czech Republic	..c	..c	..c	..c	..c	..c	..c	..c	..c	..c
Denmark	..c	..c	..c	..c	..c	..c	..c	..c	..c	..c
Estonia	..c	..c	..c	..c	..c	..c	..c	..c	..c	..c
Finland	..c	..c	..c	..c	..c	..c	..c	..c	..c	..c
France	..c	..c	..c	..c	..c	..c	..c	..c	..c	..c
Germany	..c	..c	..c	..c	..c	..c	..c	..c	..c	..c
Greece	..c	..c	..c	..c	..c	..c	..c	..c	..c	..c
Hungary	..c	..c	..c	..c	..c	..c	..c	..c	..c	..c
Iceland	..c	..c	..c	..c	..c	..c	..c	..c	..c	..c
Ireland	..c	..c	..c	..c	..c	..c	..c	..c	..c	..c
Israel[1]	..c	..c	..c	..c	..c	..c	..c	..c	..c	..c
Italy	..c	..c	..c	..c	..c	..c	..c	..c	..c	..c
Japan	..c	..c	..c	..c	..c	..c	..c	..c	..c	..c
Korea	..c	..c	..c	..c	..c	..c	..c	..c	..c	..c
Latvia	..c	..c	..c	..c	..c	..c	..c	..c	..c	..c
Lithuania	..c	..c	..c	..c	..c	..c	..c	..c	..c	..c
Luxembourg	..c	..c	..c	..c	..c	..c	..c	..c	..c	..c
Mexico	..c	..c	..c	..c	..c	..c	..c	..c	..c	..c
Netherlands	..c	..c	..c	..c	..c	..c	..c	..c	..c	..c
New Zealand	..c	..c	..c	..c	..c	..c	..c	..c	..c	..c
Norway	..c	..c	..c	..c	..c	..c	..c	..c	..c	..c
Poland	..c	..c	..c	..c	..c	..c	..c	..c	..c	..c
Portugal	..c	..c	..c	..c	..c	..c	..c	..c	..c	..c
Slovak Republic	..c	..c	..c	..c	..c	..c	..c	..c	..c	..c
Slovenia	..c	..c	..c	..c	..c	..c	..c	..c	..c	..c
Spain	..c	..c	..c	..c	..c	..c	..c	..c	..c	..c
Sweden	..c	..c	..c	..c	..c	..c	..c	..c	..c	..c
Switzerland	..	..	..	..	..	..	..	..	..	..
Turkey	..c	..c	..c	..c	..c	..c	..c	..c	..c	..c
United Kingdom	..c	..c	..c	..c	..c	..c	..c	..c	..c	..c
United States	..c	..c	..c	..c	..c	..c	..c	..c	..c	..c
EUROPE	**..c**	**..c**	**..c**	**..c**	**..c**	**..c**	**..c**	**..c**	**..c**	**..c**
Bulgaria	..c	..c	..c	..c	..c	..c	..c	..c	..c	..c
Croatia	..c	..c	..c	..c	..c	..c	..c	..c	..c	..c
Cyprus[2, 3]	..c	..c	..c	..c	..c	..c	..c	..c	..c	..c
Malta	..c	..c	..c	..c	..c	..c	..c	..c	..c	..c
Romania	..c	..c	..c	..c	..c	..c	..c	..c	..c	..c
Russian Federation	..c	..c	..c	..c	..c	..c	..c	..c	..c	..c
Ukraine	..c	..c	..c	..c	..c	..c	..c	..c	..c	..c
AFRICA	**..c**	**..c**	**..c**	**..c**	**..c**	**..c**	**..c**	**..c**	**..c**	**..c**
Northern Africa	..c	..c	..c	..c	..c	..c	..c	..c	..c	..c
Algeria	..c	..c	..c	..c	..c	..c	..c	..c	..c	..c
Egypt	..c	..c	..c	..c	..c	..c	..c	..c	..c	..c
Libya	..c	..	..	..	..	..c	..c	..c	..c	..c
Morocco	..c	..c	..c	..c	..c	..c	..c	..c	..c	..c
Tunisia	..c	..c	..c	..c	..c	..c	..c	..c	..c	..c
Other African countries	..c	..c	..c	..c	..c	..c	..c	..c	..c	..c
Nigeria	..c	..c	..c	..c	..c	..c	..c	..c	..c	..c
South Africa	..c	..c	..c	..c	..c	..c	..c	..c	..c	..c
AMERICA	**..c**	**..c**	**..c**	**..c**	**..c**	**..c**	**..c**	**..c**	**..c**	**..c**
Northern America	..c	..c	..c	..c	..c	..c	..c	..c	..c	..c
Central America and Caribbean countries	..c	..c	..c	..c	..c	..c	..c	..c	..c	..c
Bahamas	..c	..c	..c	..c	..c	..c	..c	..c	..c	..c
Bermuda	..c	..c	..c	..c	..c	..c	..c	..c	..c	..c
Cayman Islands	..c	..c	..c	..c	..c	..c	..c	..c	..c	..c
Costa Rica	..c	..c	..c	..c	..c	..c	..c	..c	..c	..c
El Salvador	..c	..c	..c	..c	..c	..c	..c	..c	..c	..c
Guatemala	..c	..c	..c	..c	..c	..c	..c	..c	..c	..c
Honduras	..c	..c	..c	..c	..c	..c	..c	..c	..c	..c
Nicaragua	..c	..c	..c	..c	..c	..c	..c	..c	..c	..c
Panama	..c	..c	..c	..c	..c	..c	..c	..c	..c	..c
Virgin Islands, U.S.	..c	..c	..c	..c	..c	..c	..c	..c	..c	..c
South America	..c	..c	..c	..c	..c	..c	..c	..c	..c	..c
Argentina	..c	..c	..c	..c	..c	..c	..c	..c	..c	..c
Bolivia	..c	..c	..c	..c	..c	..c	..c	..c	..c	..c
Brazil	..c	..c	..c	..c	..c	..c	..c	..c	..c	..c
Colombia	..c	..c	..c	..c	..c	..c	..c	..c	..c	..c
Ecuador	..c	..c	..c	..c	..c	..c	..c	..c	..c	..c
Paraguay	..c	..c	..c	..c	..c	..c	..c	..c	..c	..c
Peru	..c	..c	..c	..c	..c	..c	..c	..c	..c	..c
Uruguay	..c	..c	..c	..c	..c	..c	..c	..c	..c	..c
Venezuela	..c	..c	..c	..c	..c	..c	..c	..c	..c	..c

Table 3. Foreign direct investment income by country *(cont.)*

Million US dollars

	Inward					Outward				
	2014	2015	2016	2017	2018	2014	2015	2016	2017	2018
ASIA	.. c	.. c	.. c	.. c	.. c	.. c	.. c	.. c	.. c	.. c
Near and Middle East	.. c	.. c	.. c	.. c	.. c	.. c	.. c	.. c	.. c	.. c
Gulf Arabian countries	.. c	.. c	.. c	.. c	.. c	.. c	.. c	.. c	.. c	.. c
Kuwait	.. c	.. c	.. c	.. c	.. c	.. c	.. c	.. c	.. c	.. c
Qatar	.. c	.. c	.. c	.. c	.. c	.. c	.. c	.. c	.. c	.. c
Saudi Arabia	.. c	.. c	.. c	.. c	.. c	.. c	.. c	.. c	.. c	.. c
United Arab Emirates	.. c	.. c	.. c	.. c	.. c	.. c	.. c	.. c	.. c	.. c
Other Near and Middle East	.. c	.. c	.. c	.. c	.. c	.. c	.. c	.. c	.. c	.. c
Jordan	.. c	.. c	.. c	.. c	.. c	.. c	.. c	.. c	.. c	.. c
Other Asian countries	.. c	.. c	.. c	.. c	.. c	.. c	.. c	.. c	.. c	.. c
China	.. c	.. c	.. c	.. c	.. c	.. c	.. c	.. c	.. c	.. c
Hong Kong, China	.. c	.. c	.. c	.. c	.. c	.. c	.. c	.. c	.. c	.. c
India	.. c	.. c	.. c	.. c	.. c	.. c	.. c	.. c	.. c	.. c
Indonesia	.. c	.. c	.. c	.. c	.. c	.. c	.. c	.. c	.. c	.. c
Iran, Islamic Republic of	.. c	..	..	..	..	.. c	.. c	.. c	.. c	.. c
Malaysia	.. c	.. c	.. c	.. c	.. c	.. c	.. c	.. c	.. c	.. c
Philippines	.. c	.. c	.. c	.. c	.. c	.. c	.. c	.. c	.. c	.. c
Singapore	.. c	.. c	.. c	.. c	.. c	.. c	.. c	.. c	.. c	.. c
Chinese Taipei	.. c	.. c	.. c	.. c	.. c	.. c	.. c	.. c	.. c	.. c
Thailand	.. c	.. c	.. c	.. c	.. c	.. c	.. c	.. c	.. c	.. c
Viet Nam	.. c	.. c	.. c	.. c	.. c	.. c	.. c	.. c	.. c	.. c
AUSTRALIA, OCEANIA AND POLAR REGIONS	.. c	.. c	.. c	.. c	.. c	.. c	.. c	.. c	.. c	.. c
WORLD unallocated and confidential	.. d	59 799.7	70 912.0	98 750.6	105 009.9	.. d	91 017.9	90 756.2	99 840.3	106 142.4
European Union (EU28)	.. c	.. c	.. c	.. c	.. c	.. c	.. c	.. c	.. c	.. c
G20 countries excl. European Union	.. c	.. c	.. c	.. c	.. c	.. c	.. c	.. c	.. c	.. c
G20 OECD countries	.. c	.. c	.. c	.. c	.. c	.. c	.. c	.. c	.. c	.. c
G20 Non-OECD countries	.. c	.. c	.. c	.. c	.. c	.. c	.. c	.. c	.. c	.. c
MENA countries	.. c	.. c	.. c	.. c	.. c	.. c	.. c	.. c	.. c	.. c
ASEAN countries	.. c	.. c	.. c	.. c	.. c	.. c	.. c	.. c	.. c	.. c

.. Not available; c Confidential data; d Secondary Confidentiality

Note: Detailed metadata at: *http://stats.oecd.org/OECDStat_Metadata/ShowMetadata.ashx?Dataset=FDI_CTRY_IND_SUMM.*

1. Information on data for Israel: *http://oe.cd/israel-disclaimer.*
2. Note by Turkey: The information in this document with reference to "Cyprus" relates to the southern part of the Island. There is no single authority representing both Turkish and Greek Cypriot people on the Island. Turkey recognises the Turkish Republic of Northern Cyprus (TRNC). Until a lasting and equitable solution is found within the context of the United Nations, Turkey shall preserve its position concerning the "Cyprus issue".
3. Note by all the European Union Member States of the OECD and the European Union: The Republic of Cyprus is recognised by all members of the United Nations with the exception of Turkey. The information in this document relates to the area under the effective control of the Government of the Republic of Cyprus.

Source: OECD International Direct Investment Statistics (database): https://doi.org/10.1787/idi-data-en

SWITZERLAND

Table 4. Foreign direct investment flows by industrial sector

Million US dollars

	Inward					Outward				
	2014	2015	2016	2017	2018	2014	2015	2016	2017	2018
All FDI activities	**9 351.8**	**75 289.0**	**88 618.5**	**107 321.0**	**-53 150.2**	**-46.6**	**88 758.7**	**122 101.3**	**30 144.2**	**60 780.8**
Agriculture, forestry and fishing	..	..	..	..	..	..	.. c	.. c	.. c	.. c
Mining and quarrying	..	.. c	.. c	.. c	.. c	..	.. c	.. c	.. c	.. c
Extraction activities	..	.. c	.. c	.. c	.. c	..	.. c	.. c	.. c	.. c
Manufacturing	..	**13 326.5**	**5 158.7**	**58 765.6**	**-23 731.2**	..	**8 520.6**	**30 641.8**	**-8 413.6**	**12 745.5**
of which:										
Food products, beverages and tobacco	..	.. c	.. c	.. c	.. c	..	.. c	.. c	.. c	.. c
Textiles, wood and paper products; printing	..	.. c	.. c	.. c	.. c	..	.. c	.. c	.. c	.. c
Chemical, rubber, plastic, non-metallic mineral products	..	.. c	.. c	.. c	.. c	..	.. c	.. c	.. c	.. c
Metal and machinery products, except electrical equipment	..	.. c	.. c	.. c	.. c	..	.. c	.. c	.. c	.. c
Motor vehicles, trailers, semi-trailers, other transport equipment	..	.. c	.. c	.. c	.. c	..	.. c	.. c	.. c	.. c
Other manufacturing	..	.. c	.. c	.. c	.. c	..	.. c	.. c	.. c	.. c
Electricity, gas, steam and air conditioning supply	..	.. c	.. c	.. c	.. c	..	.. c	.. c	.. c	.. c
Water supply; sewerage, waste management and remediation activities	..	.. c	.. c	.. c	.. c	..	..	..	..	..
Construction	..	.. c	.. c	.. c	.. c	..	.. c	.. c	.. c	.. c
Services	..	**61 494.9**	**82 451.3**	**47 147.6**	**-28 407.3**	..	**75 273.3**	**91 968.0**	**38 628.5**	**48 443.9**
Wholesale and retail trade; repair of motor vehicles and motorcycles	..	4 015.9	11 478.5	11 863.0	15 302.3	..	23 498.8	14 484.4	-7 472.3	32 501.8
Transportation and storage	..	140.6	771.7	1 500.9	1 671.2	..	872.6	1 248.7	3 850.0	3 869.8
Accommodation and food service activities	..	-184.8	34.2	-273.9	-33.9	..	205.2	-134.6	85.9	-48.6
Information and communication	..	792.3	245.7	-741.7	-806.2	..	2 837.9	-218.5	-836.3	-73.9
Financial and insurance activities	..	18 121.8	48 505.3	52 018.4	-35 279.2	..	24 219.4	57 308.0	50 185.6	17 167.2
Activities of holding companies	..	312.8	33 247.5	48 490.4	18 787.2	..	3 914.2	27 085.6	51 517.0	15 433.1
Real estate activities	..	.. c	.. c	.. c	.. c	..	.. c	.. c	.. c	.. c
Professional, scientific and technical activities	..	21 957.3	19 743.8	-20 018.5	-2 168.9	..	24 123.7	13 950.6	-6 542.0	-2 556.1
Administrative and support service activities	..	.. c	.. c	.. c	.. c	..	.. c	.. c	.. c	.. c
Public administration; activities of households and of extraterritorial organisations	..	..	..	..	..	..	..	..	..	..
Education	..	.. c	.. c	.. c	.. c	..	..	..	..	..
Human health and social work activities	..	.. c	.. c	.. c	.. c	..	.. c	.. c	.. c	.. c
Arts, entertainment and recreation	..	.. c	.. c	.. c	.. c	..	.. c	.. c	.. c	.. c
Other services	..	.. c	.. c	.. c	.. c	..	.. c	.. c	.. c	.. c
Not allocated and confidential	**9 351.8**	.. c	.. c	.. c	.. c	**-46.6**	.. c	.. c	.. c	.. c
Private real estate activities	..	**455.8**	**271.6**	**51.7**	**53.7**	..	**291.1**	**778.2**	**-419.3**	**-1 157.8**

.. Not available; c Confidential data

Note: Detailed metadata at: *http://stats.oecd.org/OECDStat_Metadata/ShowMetadata.ashx?Dataset=FDI_CTRY_IND_SUMM.*

Source: OECD International Direct Investment Statistics (database): https://doi.org/10.1787/idi-data-en

Table 5. Foreign direct investment positions by industrial sector
At year end

Million US dollars

	Inward					Outward				
	2014	2015	2016	2017	2018	2014	2015	2016	2017	2018
All FDI activities	**812 908.1**	**890 483.5**	**1 119 934.6**	**1 352 536.5**	**1 354 535.3**	**1 077 238.6**	**1 131 401.8**	**1 307 515.6**	**1 438 450.5**	**1 494 721.1**
Agriculture, forestry and fishing	..	..	..	..	..	..	.. c	.. c	.. c	.. c
Mining and quarrying	.. c	.. c	.. c	.. c	.. c	.. c	.. c	.. c	.. c	.. c
Extraction activities	..	.. c	.. c	.. c	.. c	.. c	.. c	.. c	.. c	.. c
Manufacturing	**101 766.9**	**122 792.3**	**132 027.7**	**171 545.7**	**180 660.9**	**381 116.3**	**388 136.2**	**397 880.6**	**416 086.7**	**433 268.0**
of which:										
Food products, beverages and tobacco	.. c	.. c	.. c	.. c	.. c	.. c	.. c	.. c	.. c	.. c
Textiles, wood and paper products; printing	.. c	.. c	.. c	.. c	.. c	.. c	.. c	.. c	.. c	.. c
Chemical, rubber, plastic, non-metallic mineral products	.. c	.. c	.. c	.. c	.. c	.. c	.. c	.. c	.. c	.. c
Metal and machinery products, except electrical equipment	.. c	.. c	.. c	.. c	.. c	.. c	.. c	.. c	.. c	.. c
Motor vehicles, trailers, semi-trailers, other transport equipment	.. c	.. c	.. c	.. c	.. c	.. c	.. c	.. c	.. c	.. c
Other manufacturing	.. c	.. c	.. c	.. c	.. c	.. c	.. c	.. c	.. c	.. c
Electricity, gas, steam and air conditioning supply	.. c	.. c	.. c	.. c	.. c	..	.. c	.. c	.. c	.. c
Water supply; sewerage, waste management and remediation activities	.. c	.. c	.. c	.. c	.. c	.. c	.. c	.. c	.. c	.. c
Construction	.. c	.. c	.. c	.. c	.. c	.. c	.. c	.. c	.. c	.. c
Services	**669 648.4**	**725 685.8**	**945 988.4**	**1 135 632.0**	**1 130 665.6**	**681 980.3**	**725 079.3**	**891 740.2**	**1 001 150.7**	**1 039 785.8**
Wholesale and retail trade; repair of motor vehicles and motorcycles	152 448.3	158 848.0	174 365.0	194 221.9	211 275.1	111 983.3	128 014.8	145 482.5	137 390.5	158 281.2
Transportation and storage	7 378.2	7 525.0	8 466.5	10 437.7	11 732.0	19 692.0	19 986.6	20 104.8	24 219.4	28 692.6
Accommodation and food service activities	2 874.3	2 803.9	2 859.0	2 943.4	2 877.1	1 275.4	1 240.6	996.8	1 195.0	1 222.6
Information and communication	17 886.6	18 639.2	18 012.4	16 964.1	16 607.6	8 535.5	10 396.5	9 368.5	10 535.0	10 403.0
Financial and insurance activities	333 263.6	362 818.0	494 827.6	659 863.9	645 635.8	388 399.4	383 697.0	497 395.3	590 938.9	616 496.2
Activities of holding companies	174 569.8	185 639.3	284 941.7	385 029.9	420 421.3	214 632.1	198 039.4	278 631.0	364 500.8	397 433.0
Real estate activities	.. c	.. c	.. c	.. c	.. c	.. c	.. c	.. c	.. c	.. c
Professional, scientific and technical activities	150 690.0	151 634.8	216 036.8	215 938.2	216 213.0	142 232.3	171 560.2	201 733.8	221 368.8	210 128.0
Administrative and support service activities	.. c	.. c	.. c	.. c	.. c	.. c	.. c	.. c	.. c	.. c
Public administration; activities of households and of extraterritorial organisations	..	.. c	.. c	.. c	.. c	.. c	.. c	.. c	.. c	.. c
Education	..	.. c	.. c	.. c	.. c	.. c	.. c	.. c	.. c	.. c
Human health and social work activities	.. c	.. c	.. c	.. c	.. c	.. c	.. c	.. c	.. c	.. c
Arts, entertainment and recreation	.. c	.. c	.. c	.. c	.. c	.. c	.. c	.. c	.. c	.. c
Other services	..	.. c	.. c	.. c	.. c	.. c	.. c	.. c	.. c	.. c
Not allocated and confidential	.. c	.. c	.. c	.. c	.. c	.. c	.. c	.. c	.. c	.. c
Private real estate activities	**36.6**	**37 822.5**	**37 130.3**	**38 800.6**	**38 485.3**	..	**2 831.5**	**3 302.1**	**4 424.9**	**5 386.7**

.. Not available; c Confidential data

Note: Detailed metadata at: *http://stats.oecd.org/OECDStat_Metadata/ShowMetadata.ashx?Dataset=FDI_CTRY_IND_SUMM.*

Source: OECD International Direct Investment Statistics (database): https://doi.org/10.1787/idi-data-en

Table 6. Foreign direct investment income by industrial sector

Million US dollars

	Inward					Outward				
	2014	2015	2016	2017	2018	2014	2015	2016	2017	2018
All FDI activities	**73 369.0**	**59 799.7**	**70 912.0**	**98 750.6**	**105 009.9**	**90 613.8**	**91 017.9**	**90 756.2**	**99 840.3**	**106 142.4**
Agriculture, forestry and fishing	..	..	..	..	..	..	.. c	.. c	.. c	.. c
Mining and quarrying	..	.. c	.. c	.. c	.. c	..	.. c	.. c	.. c	.. c
Extraction activities	..	.. c	.. c	.. c	.. c	..	.. c	.. c	.. c	.. c
Manufacturing	..	**15 250.9**	**14 936.6**	**16 355.8**	**14 886.6**	..	**45 452.7**	**37 187.2**	**37 262.8**	**45 770.8**
of which:										
Food products, beverages and tobacco	..	.. c	.. c	.. c	.. c	..	.. c	.. c	.. c	.. c
Textiles, wood and paper products; printing	..	.. c	.. c	.. c	.. c	..	.. c	.. c	.. c	.. c
Chemical, rubber, plastic, non-metallic mineral products	..	.. c	.. c	.. c	.. c	..	.. c	.. c	.. c	.. c
Metal and machinery products, except electrical equipment	..	.. c	.. c	.. c	.. c	..	.. c	.. c	.. c	.. c
Motor vehicles, trailers, semi-trailers, other transport equipment	..	.. c	.. c	.. c	.. c	..	.. c	.. c	.. c	.. c
Other manufacturing	..	.. c	.. c	.. c	.. c	..	.. c	.. c	.. c	.. c
Electricity, gas, steam and air conditioning supply	..	.. c	.. c	.. c	.. c	..	.. c	.. c	.. c	.. c
Water supply; sewerage, waste management and remediation activities	..	.. c	.. c	.. c	.. c	..	..	..	..	..
Construction	..	.. c	.. c	.. c	.. c	..	.. c	.. c	.. c	.. c
Services	..	**44 583.4**	**55 721.5**	**82 191.1**	**89 990.1**	..	**45 517.0**	**53 714.9**	**61 986.2**	**59 341.3**
Wholesale and retail trade; repair of motor vehicles and motorcycles	..	13 440.7	15 466.8	28 346.3	24 855.6	..	4 387.4	9 711.5	7 494.9	6 463.7
Transportation and storage	..	628.6	1 042.2	1 217.1	1 391.0	..	1 450.7	1 483.9	2 114.1	1 650.7
Accommodation and food service activities	..	-47.7	165.1	72.5	46.5	..	130.8	-146.7	80.5	69.6
Information and communication	..	3 149.1	3 339.2	3 503.9	1 959.1	..	213.2	179.4	851.1	151.0
Financial and insurance activities	..	18 216.0	20 956.7	38 887.8	36 035.0	..	22 948.1	20 979.0	26 656.5	28 957.9
Activities of holding companies	..	5 617.3	1 581.5	17 962.5	22 218.2	..	11 457.5	7 020.4	16 461.2	15 319.1
Real estate activities	..	.. c	.. c	.. c	.. c	..	.. c	.. c	.. c	.. c
Professional, scientific and technical activities	..	8 982.2	14 319.6	10 822.0	27 312.7	..	15 979.6	20 011.6	23 274.0	21 333.4
Administrative and support service activities	..	.. c	.. c	.. c	.. c	..	.. c	.. c	.. c	.. c
Public administration; activities of households and of extraterritorial organisations	..	..	..	..	..	..	..	..	..	..
Education	..	.. c	.. c	.. c	.. c	..	..	..	..	..
Human health and social work activities	..	.. c	.. c	.. c	.. c	..	.. c	.. c	.. c	.. c
Arts, entertainment and recreation	..	.. c	.. c	.. c	.. c	..	.. c	.. c	.. c	.. c
Other services	..	.. c	.. c	.. c	.. c	..	.. c	.. c	.. c	.. c
Not allocated and confidential	**73 369.0**	.. c	.. c	.. c	.. c	**90 613.8**	.. c	.. c	.. c	.. c
Private real estate activities	..	..	..	..	..	..	..	..	..	..

.. Not available; c Confidential data

Note: Detailed metadata at: *http://stats.oecd.org/OECDStat_Metadata/ShowMetadata.ashx?Dataset=FDI_CTRY_IND_SUMM.*

Source: OECD International Direct Investment Statistics (database): https://doi.org/10.1787/idi-data-en

Table 1. Foreign direct investment flows by country

Million US dollars

	Inward					Outward				
	2014	2015	2016	2017	2018	2014	2015	2016	2017	2018
WORLD	**12 447.9**	**18 916.2**	**13 719.1**	**11 184.5**	**12 966.3**	**6 663.8**	**4 900.6**	**2 891.6**	**2 634.7**	**3 606.4**
OECD COUNTRIES	**6 831.7**	**11 504.5**	**6 939.7**	**4 217.9**	**5 724.3**	..	**3 965.4**	**2 180.2**	**1 920.0**	**3 205.2**
Australia	3.3	4.0	28.1	462.7	48.0	..	0.1	1.2	1.6	0.9
Austria	88.4	84.0	364.4	-1 152.9	455.0	..	44.0	3.0	10.4	38.6
Belgium	184.7	856.2	406.7	199.6	127.9	..	-102.4	2.8	11.2	19.8
Canada	14.6	33.1	117.9	41.7	33.6	..	15.6	12.9	12.8	10.4
Chile	0.0	-	5.6	1.9	-	..	-	0.1	0.1	-
Czech Republic	5.0	2.4	1.9	65.7	13.7	..	0.9	0.4	5.3	0.3
Denmark	66.4	43.6	63.6	31.0	221.7	..	0.9	1.8	0.7	0.4
Estonia	-	1.0	3.0	-	1.0	..	0.2	0.0	0.7	1.0
Finland	27.3	7.2	8.9	12.9	11.6	..	0.1	0.4	3.6	4.3
France	245.3	172.8	-123.9	396.7	451.5	..	17.4	28.8	28.9	26.3
Germany	1 058.4	654.5	644.7	362.9	267.4	..	220.5	13.3	189.9	52.3
Greece	65.5	51.1	7.0	1.3	20.1	..	0.8	2.4	19.0	21.5
Hungary	-	-0.1	3.9	1.1	1.2	..	3.5	5.9	15.2	-14.6
Iceland	0.2	-	-	-	-	..	-	-	-	-
Ireland	59.0	144.5	300.1	44.4	-168.3	..	0.1	-0.4	-0.9	0.9
Israel[1]	17.8	13.7	5.2	3.2	36.7	..	2.6	1.0	1.2	6.6
Italy	521.5	242.8	209.0	43.6	389.4	..	21.9	30.7	31.5	46.1
Japan	253.5	315.3	460.9	184.3	147.5	..	0.0	3.6	0.8	0.1
Korea	59.5	59.1	132.5	35.3	198.3	..	32.5	15.7	0.3	-7.5
Latvia	-11.2	1.0	3.2	0.0	1.2	..	2.6	1.2	8.6	0.9
Lithuania	-	1.0	1.0	1.0	1.0	..	0.4	-	0.1	1.1
Luxembourg	244.5	2 376.7	506.5	-265.9	443.3	..	136.9	57.8	-389.4	42.7
Mexico	-	-	-	-	-	..	0.0	1.1	4.1	3.9
Netherlands	1 985.3	1 625.8	1 634.9	1 674.9	1 149.5	..	1 507.0	716.2	697.8	1 664.7
New Zealand	-	-	-	4.8	2.0	..	-	0.1	-	0.2
Norway	285.9	49.8	10.9	61.8	224.7	..	89.0	-4.0	0.9	0.4
Poland	18.9	-3.0	1.5	8.0	7.9	..	1.6	1.5	3.0	6.8
Portugal	3.5	4.0	-0.5	1.1	1.3	..	0.2	2.3	49.5	13.8
Slovak Republic	3.4	6.4	1.6	2.0	1.0	..	0.0	0.2	-1.2	1.0
Slovenia	1.4	1.3	0.0	6.6	-	..	0.0	1.0	11.8	2.3
Spain	81.7	2 338.4	293.8	1 403.2	219.4	..	3.8	6.6	9.6	21.1
Sweden	64.4	50.9	44.7	42.7	87.6	..	0.4	49.0	38.9	16.4
Switzerland	188.1	192.7	343.9	13.0	146.1	..	11.5	54.7	23.2	106.5
Turkey	-	-	-	-	-	..	-	-	-	-
United Kingdom	904.4	598.0	952.5	296.7	680.6	..	621.7	337.8	334.9	340.6
United States	380.0	1 578.2	507.6	233.7	502.7	..	1 334.5	831.0	796.2	775.4
EUROPE	**9 127.0**	**12 054.5**	**8 535.1**	**6 377.5**	**7 166.3**	**..**	**3 009.4**	**1 473.8**	**1 187.7**	**2 616.1**
Bulgaria	8.4	16.4	13.2	4.8	21.5	..	31.8	4.1	43.7	8.9
Croatia	-	0.4	0.2	0.9	-	..	36.8	14.3	2.7	0.7
Cyprus[2, 3]	0.0	13.5	5.3	-	-	..	-	-	-	-0.8
Malta	-0.2	3.7	-39.7	0.9	21.1	..	80.4	19.8	15.6	30.9
Romania	2.1	3.3	4.0	1.0	7.1	..	27.6	53.1	12.3	21.8
Russian Federation	1 062.2	902.3	788.1	44.9	113.7	..	65.5	-59.2	30.9	20.1
Ukraine	23.0	49.0	35.1	18.0	53.5	..	13.0	12.2	-55.0	23.7
AFRICA	**93.8**	**144.5**	**86.2**	**124.2**	**239.2**	**..**	**34.5**	**91.1**	**105.2**	**64.6**
Northern Africa	49.4	128.0	72.4	59.4	188.8	..	14.2	60.6	78.3	44.6
Algeria	3.4	7.0	10.0	6.0	37.0	..	3.5	26.0	39.2	11.1
Egypt	17.0	35.0	36.0	32.2	71.8	..	7.4	24.9	30.8	3.8
Libya	26.0	82.0	22.6	20.0	66.0	..	0.1	-	-	0.4
Morocco	3.0	1.0	1.0	1.4	7.0	..	1.0	9.4	7.4	28.9
Tunisia	-	3.0	2.8	-0.2	7.0	..	2.2	0.4	1.0	0.5
Other African countries	44.5	16.5	13.8	64.9	50.5	..	20.4	30.4	26.9	20.0
Nigeria	-	-	-2.0	-	1.0	..	0.2	11.0	1.8	-
South Africa	42.5	-1.5	0.0	1.0	3.8	..	8.8	0.0	0.1	7.0
AMERICA	**391.1**	**1 626.3**	**644.2**	**340.7**	**622.7**	**..**	**1 338.7**	**870.8**	**821.7**	**806.7**
Northern America	394.6	1 611.3	625.6	275.4	536.3	..	1 350.0	843.9	809.0	785.8
Central America and Caribbean countries	-3.8	9.0	13.3	62.3	79.5	..	-12.8	8.8	7.6	7.3
Bahamas	-6.6	1.0	-	-	-	..	-	-	-	-
Bermuda	-	-	-	-	-	..	-8.8	7.0	-	-
Cayman Islands	0.4	3.7	0.2	1.3	-	..	-	-	2.7	-
Costa Rica	-	-	-	-	-	..	-	-	-	-
El Salvador	-	0.1	-		-	..	-	-	-	-
Guatemala	-	-	-	-	-	..	-	-	-	1.2
Honduras	-	-	-	-	-	..	-	-	-	-
Nicaragua	-	-	-	-	-	..	-	-	-	-
Panama	-	0.2	0.1	1.3	2.1	..	-	-	-	0.2
Virgin Islands, U.S.	-	-	-	7.0	0.3	..	-	0.3	-	-
South America	0.4	6.1	5.3	2.9	7.0	..	1.5	18.0	5.1	13.5
Argentina	-	-	-	1.0	-	..	-	-	-	-
Bolivia	-	-	-	-	-	..	-	-	-	-
Brazil	0.3	6.1	-0.3	-	1.0	..	1.2	0.1	0.8	1.1
Colombia	-	-	-	-	-	..	0.2	17.9	2.2	9.9
Ecuador	-	-	-	-	-	..	-	-	2.0	2.5
Paraguay	-	-	-	-	-	..	-	-	-	-
Peru	-	-	-	-	-	..	-	-	0.0	0.1
Uruguay	-	-	-	-	-	..	-	-	-	-
Venezuela	-	-	-	-	6.0	..	-	-	-	-

Table 1. Foreign direct investment flows by country *(cont.)*

Million US dollars

	Inward					Outward				
	2014	2015	2016	2017	2018	2014	2015	2016	2017	2018
ASIA	**3 163.6**	**5 086.8**	**4 425.7**	**3 874.7**	**4 888.0**	..	**518.0**	**454.6**	**518.5**	**117.9**
Near and Middle East	2 377.6	3 582.2	3 257.0	3 212.7	3 160.0	..	414.2	313.6	402.8	27.6
Gulf Arabian countries	1 123.8	2 059.7	1 499.3	1 369.2	1 872.6	..	115.2	72.0	125.4	-14.2
Kuwait	326.1	246.2	258.2	197.7	343.0	..	43.5	-1.6	-0.1	-0.2
Qatar	26.3	427.2	462.9	164.3	513.1	..	14.7	-4.7	-0.3	-3.0
Saudi Arabia	323.3	554.3	372.3	525.2	432.4	..	2.8	0.3	5.3	-4.0
United Arab Emirates	294.1	362.6	291.3	260.2	134.3	..	23.6	38.8	52.6	-15.2
Other Near and Middle East	1 253.8	1 522.5	1 757.7	1 843.5	1 287.5	..	299.0	241.6	277.5	41.8
Jordan	44.6	28.4	39.3	37.1	138.9	..	2.3	-0.1	1.2	-0.3
Other Asian countries	786.0	1 504.6	1 168.7	662.1	1 728.0	..	103.7	141.0	115.7	90.3
China	52.7	521.4	346.1	146.9	81.2	..	21.3	33.0	10.3	26.9
Hong Kong, China	60.7	29.8	-53.0	17.2	178.5	..	20.6	0.3	0.1	0.8
India	-4.7	2.4	-1.4	9.2	30.4	..	18.2	1.0	5.9	6.7
Indonesia	-	1.0	-5.4	1.0	1.0	..	0.5	5.1	0.0	9.2
Iran, Islamic Republic of	105.1	95.4	95.2	55.0	425.4	..	0.1	0.1	-4.0	2.2
Malaysia	24.9	317.5	13.1	34.9	2.4	..	0.2	0.1	6.9	5.7
Philippines	-	-	-	-	0.0	..	0.0	-	-	0.1
Singapore	135.2	12.1	32.5	21.8	10.8	..	0.1	0.3	1.6	2.3
Chinese Taipei	0.4	0.6	0.9	6.2	247.5	..	0.4	0.4	0.1	0.3
Thailand	-0.1	0.1	-6.4	54.1	68.5	..	4.4	0.5	0.4	0.9
Viet Nam	-	-	0.4	-	-	..	0.1	20.4	1.3	2.9
AUSTRALIA, OCEANIA AND POLAR REGIONS	**3.4**	**4.0**	**28.1**	**467.4**	**50.0**	..	**0.1**	**1.4**	**1.6**	**1.2**
WORLD unallocated and confidential	**-331.1**	**0.0**	**0.0**	**0.0**	-	..	**0.0**	**0.0**	-	-
European Union (EU28)	**5 627.9**	**9 297.8**	**5 311.2**	**3 184.1**	**4 434.4**	..	**2 659.1**	**1 354.0**	**1 153.1**	**2 369.8**
G20 countries excl. European Union	**4 916.7**	**5 643.8**	**4 428.6**	**2 786.7**	**3 382.4**	..	**2 382.5**	**1 256.5**	**1 454.3**	**1 315.3**
G20 OECD countries	**3 440.4**	**3 657.9**	**2 929.2**	**2 057.6**	**2 718.8**	..	**2 264.2**	**1 276.2**	**1 401.0**	**1 248.5**
G20 Non-OECD countries	**1 476.3**	**1 985.9**	**1 499.5**	**729.1**	**663.6**	..	**118.3**	**-19.8**	**53.3**	**66.8**
MENA countries	**1 269.8**	**2 257.5**	**1 761.0**	**1 504.5**	**2 311.4**	..	**131.6**	**132.8**	**205.6**	**31.3**
ASEAN countries	**160.0**	**330.7**	**34.2**	**111.8**	**82.7**	..	**5.3**	**26.4**	**10.1**	**21.1**

- Nil; .. Not available

Note: Detailed metadata at: *http://stats.oecd.org/OECDStat_Metadata/ShowMetadata.ashx?Dataset=FDI_CTRY_IND_SUMM.*

1. Information on data for Israel: *http://oe.cd/israel-disclaimer*.
2. Note by Turkey: The information in this document with reference to "Cyprus" relates to the southern part of the Island. There is no single authority representing both Turkish and Greek Cypriot people on the Island. Turkey recognises the Turkish Republic of Northern Cyprus (TRNC). Until a lasting and equitable solution is found within the context of the United Nations, Turkey shall preserve its position concerning the "Cyprus issue".
3. Note by all the European Union Member States of the OECD and the European Union: The Republic of Cyprus is recognised by all members of the United Nations with the exception of Turkey. The information in this document relates to the area under the effective control of the Government of the Republic of Cyprus.

Source: OECD International Direct Investment Statistics (database): https://doi.org/10.1787/idi-data-en

Table 2. Foreign direct investment positions by country
At year end

Million US dollars

	Inward					Outward				
	2014	2015	2016	2017	2018	2014	2015	2016	2017	2018
WORLD	**182 064.6**	**158 077.6**	**148 428.2**	**197 374.5**	**147 107.1**	**39 513.3**	**35 615.0**	**38 368.6**	**45 534.1**	**44 449.2**
OECD COUNTRIES	..	..	**113 130.5**	**150 106.9**	**104 597.2**	**22 480.6**	**19 879.9**	**22 665.3**	**26 945.2**	**29 517.0**
Australia	..	..	69.3	27.4	21.9	24.0	2.7	-2.8	-7.5	-12.1
Austria	..	..	9 231.8	4 197.7	2 204.7	956.2	1 206.5	1 251.5	1 831.6	1 916.5
Belgium	..	..	3 191.7	3 423.7	2 502.1	195.7	130.3	213.7	205.9	353.5
Canada	..	..	879.7	1 687.2	1 372.5	34.4	18.0	18.5	20.6	15.5
Chile	..	..	11.8	13.7	6.2	7.1	6.8	7.1	8.1	-
Czech Republic	..	..	151.0	626.2	210.7	-	-	-0.2	-0.1	-0.8
Denmark	..	..	541.8	896.2	829.7	1.0	0.0	0.0	-0.2	0.1
Estonia	..	..	0.2	0.3	0.1	1.1	0.4	-	-	-
Finland	..	..	2 440.4	2 375.3	1 345.2	1.1	0.3	0.4	1.8	2.7
France	..	..	6 174.8	8 572.4	5 483.6	167.1	60.7	106.6	137.4	98.4
Germany	..	..	15 383.4	20 402.4	13 387.7	1 526.6	1 216.7	1 356.5	1 729.5	1 683.5
Greece	..	..	152.9	180.7	101.9	54.0	24.3	26.3	42.0	41.3
Hungary	..	..	29.6	11.2	7.6	15.9	19.1	26.9	25.5	-0.2
Iceland	..	..	..	1.0	1.0	-	-	-	-	-
Ireland	..	..	728.4	788.3	398.9	607.5	598.5	647.7	659.0	584.7
Israel[1]	..	..	944.0	1 262.3	903.2	184.2	203.9	114.1	124.5	143.4
Italy	..	..	4 207.3	5 117.3	3 151.8	86.9	117.8	144.4	155.3	140.1
Japan	..	..	3 041.5	5 252.1	2 996.2	-	0.1	0.2	0.6	2.3
Korea	..	..	1 796.3	2 366.7	2 099.7	5.8	4.0	6.7	0.6	2.2
Latvia	..	..	..	1.0	1.0	3.4	23.0	4.8	-12.9	-15.1
Lithuania	..	..	0.6	-	0.0	0.1	-	-	-	-
Luxembourg	..	..	9 110.5	13 159.1	7 563.4	1 056.1	988.9	1 846.6	511.2	534.7
Mexico	..	..	..	0.1	1.5	0.5	-0.7	-8.0	7.9	-8.5
Netherlands	..	..	22 320.4	35 323.6	31 769.3	12 171.1	11 726.5	13 020.1	15 036.7	17 574.8
New Zealand	..	..	1.9	4.5	8.5	0.4	2.5	1.5	1.9	2.1
Norway	..	..	788.9	845.7	399.9	90.3	-0.3	-	-	-
Poland	..	..	29.7	47.7	47.1	17.6	8.1	37.3	74.9	52.6
Portugal	..	..	39.4	45.5	24.4	1.1	4.8	5.3	6.3	13.7
Slovak Republic	..	..	..	27.3	21.0	21.6	-0.2	-0.2	-2.2	-2.7
Slovenia	..	..	0.7	0.1	0.1	-0.7	0.5	-0.1	1.6	12.4
Spain	..	..	7 448.1	10 618.3	6 091.7	189.7	175.1	273.4	250.7	205.9
Sweden	..	..	460.6	472.7	418.3	0.1	8.0	4.1	52.2	42.3
Switzerland	..	..	5 046.1	7 065.9	5 279.3	417.8	161.9	165.6	184.8	205.4
Turkey	..	..	91.1	160.8	76.7	-	-	-	-	-
United Kingdom	..	..	12 756.6	16 288.2	10 089.1	2 637.4	1 626.9	1 570.9	3 890.6	4 113.0
United States	..	..	6 058.8	8 844.4	5 781.2	2 009.2	1 567.9	1 826.6	2 007.0	1 815.1
EUROPE	..	..	**111 203.1**	**143 842.3**	**107 699.4**	**24 346.7**	**25 793.9**	**29 278.9**	**35 693.6**	**36 638.9**
Bulgaria	..	..	5.0	2.0	3.9	116.4	141.7	267.5	291.9	291.6
Croatia	..	..	0.0	0.0	0.0	174.1	153.6	157.2	139.8	157.3
Cyprus[2, 3]	..	..	..	-	-	-	-	-	-	-
Malta	..	..	132.8	107.2	54.1	1 656.9	1 646.5	1 754.4	2 050.6	1 760.4
Romania	..	..	1.0	6.6	3.2	281.3	107.5	219.3	255.4	330.8
Russian Federation	..	..	10 415.2	12 732.4	16 055.1	564.4	594.1	467.5	428.7	694.5
Ukraine	..	..	7.5	0.1	0.2	128.2	59.1	124.7	115.3	176.7
AFRICA	..	..	**122.8**	**147.2**	**114.5**	**1 126.0**	**966.6**	**1 258.8**	**1 568.7**	**1 265.8**
Northern Africa	..	..	102.9	134.1	105.1	986.6	633.7	1 141.9	1 371.0	1 110.0
Algeria	..	..	..	-	-	234.4	181.1	632.3	1 174.1	908.2
Egypt	..	..	2.4	10.2	12.5	296.0	245.0	195.0	204.5	245.4
Libya	..	..	98.9	123.0	92.2	147.8	123.2	16.7	-119.4	-160.9
Morocco	..	..	1.6	0.7	0.2	146.3	33.5	247.9	72.3	88.5
Tunisia	..	..	0.0	0.2	0.2	162.2	50.9	50.1	39.4	28.8
Other African countries	..	..	19.9	13.1	9.4	139.5	332.9	116.9	197.7	155.8
Nigeria	..	..	..	-	-	21.2	70.9	64.9	80.3	23.2
South Africa	..	..	2.2	5.1	2.1	6.5	3.0	7.8	14.8	8.3
AMERICA	..	..	**8 356.1**	**12 739.5**	**8 510.1**	**3 236.1**	**3 052.4**	**2 868.3**	**3 322.3**	**2 240.2**
Northern America	..	..	6 938.5	10 531.6	7 153.7	2 043.6	1 585.9	1 845.1	2 027.5	1 830.6
Central America and Caribbean countries	..	..	1 188.5	1 931.7	1 231.8	1 076.5	1 415.6	966.4	1 237.4	370.0
Bahamas	..	..	4.6	138.7	114.5	2.6	2.6	2.6	2.6	2.6
Bermuda	..	..	50.5	181.7	91.5	12.8	1.9	3.7	7.8	7.4
Cayman Islands	..	..	255.5	421.3	283.1	0.0	706.2	831.7	1 055.8	540.8
Costa Rica	..	..	..	-	-	-	-	-	-	-
El Salvador	..	..	..	-	-	-	-	-	-	-
Guatemala	..	..	..	-	-	-	-	-	-	-
Honduras	..	..	..	-	-	-	-	-	-	-
Nicaragua	..	..	..	-	-	-	-	-	-	-
Panama	..	..	740.2	847.9	543.9	445.8	394.7	34.9	41.2	-261.5
Virgin Islands, U.S.	..	..	-	7.0	7.3	-	-	-	-	-
South America	..	..	229.1	276.2	124.5	115.9	51.0	56.8	57.4	39.6
Argentina	..	..	..	-	-	-	-	-	-	-
Bolivia	..	..	..	-	-	-	-	-	-	-
Brazil	..	..	217.3	262.5	118.3	78.9	16.6	-0.1	-0.6	-0.5
Colombia	..	..	..	-	-	30.0	27.6	47.4	49.9	40.0
Ecuador	..	..	..	-	-	-	-	2.3	-	-
Paraguay	..	..	..	-	-	-	-	-	-	-
Peru	..	..	..	-	-	-	-	-	-	0.1
Uruguay	..	..	..	-	-	-	-	-	-	-
Venezuela	..	..	..	-	-	-	-	-	-	-

Table 2. Foreign direct investment positions by country *(cont.)*
At year end

Million US dollars

	Inward					Outward				
	2014	2015	2016	2017	2018	2014	2015	2016	2017	2018
ASIA	..	..	**28 675.2**	**40 613.6**	**30 752.8**	**10 482.9**	**5 530.4**	**4 767.0**	**4 818.3**	**4 366.3**
Near and Middle East	..	..	21 226.3	28 190.3	22 365.2	8 599.4	3 359.5	2 526.8	2 466.3	2 621.6
Gulf Arabian countries	..	..	12 485.6	14 745.2	12 783.9	538.2	1 284.6	1 048.4	1 399.0	1 501.7
Kuwait	..	..	1 056.4	1 273.8	1 085.1	0.9	0.9	7.2	8.5	-83.0
Qatar	..	..	4 940.6	5 965.9	6 432.9	86.6	43.5	110.0	-252.9	101.2
Saudi Arabia	..	..	3 888.3	4 187.9	3 224.1	42.4	95.2	-0.8	-49.7	-47.4
United Arab Emirates	..	..	1 493.2	1 993.0	1 465.6	235.7	267.4	552.6	907.6	935.4
Other Near and Middle East	..	..	8 740.7	13 445.1	9 581.3	8 061.2	2 074.9	1 478.3	1 067.3	1 119.9
Jordan	..	..	70.4	83.5	44.2	14.7	15.2	22.6	13.7	13.2
Other Asian countries	..	..	7 448.9	12 423.4	8 387.6	1 883.5	2 170.9	2 240.3	2 352.0	1 744.7
China	..	..	492.4	1 561.8	1 136.5	119.5	143.6	181.1	260.9	190.8
Hong Kong, China	..	..	57.0	69.4	81.1	-2.5	0.6	0.1	10.5	21.5
India	..	..	65.6	143.2	144.5	148.9	130.4	111.9	124.0	200.9
Indonesia	..	..	0.6	0.3	0.2	91.4	111.2	-48.2	-54.2	-49.0
Iran, Islamic Republic of	..	..	176.0	89.1	103.9	437.2	503.0	408.2	394.2	387.3
Malaysia	..	..	951.2	1 463.6	644.5	201.2	145.8	142.6	193.6	186.9
Philippines	..	..	..	-	-	0.8	0.4	-0.7	-0.6	-1.0
Singapore	..	..	193.5	274.2	220.6	4.2	18.8	17.5	24.4	32.5
Chinese Taipei	..	..	14.5	52.4	49.2	-	0.1	0.2	0.3	0.1
Thailand	..	..	493.7	949.1	768.0	17.0	128.6	104.0	91.6	128.9
Viet Nam	..	..	..	-	-	-	-	-	0.2	-
AUSTRALIA, OCEANIA AND POLAR REGIONS	..	..	**71.1**	**31.9**	**30.3**	**321.6**	**271.6**	**195.5**	**131.3**	**-61.9**
WORLD unallocated and confidential	..	..	**0.0**	**0.0**	**0.0**	**0.0**	**-**	**-**	**0.0**	**-**
European Union (EU28)	..	..	**94 540.5**	**122 691.1**	**85 710.5**	**21 939.2**	**19 985.4**	**22 934.2**	**27 334.3**	**29 891.6**
G20 countries excl. European Union	..	..	**65 540.5**	**87 612.1**	**65 142.6**	**7 543.8**	**5 708.2**	**5 738.9**	**8 665.7**	**8 847.0**
G20 OECD countries	..	..	**50 458.9**	**68 719.0**	**44 461.8**	**6 491.9**	**4 614.2**	**5 019.7**	**7 941.9**	**7 849.4**
G20 Non-OECD countries	..	..	**15 081.6**	**18 893.1**	**20 680.8**	**1 051.9**	**1 094.0**	**719.2**	**723.8**	**997.6**
MENA countries	..	..	**13 467.0**	**15 854.1**	**13 535.3**	**1 582.7**	**1 941.7**	**2 213.4**	**2 788.0**	**2 625.0**
ASEAN countries	..	..	**1 639.0**	**2 687.1**	**1 633.3**	**314.5**	**404.8**	**215.2**	**255.0**	**298.2**

- Nil; .. Not available

Note: Inward FDI positions are allocated according to the ultimate investing country. Inward FDI positions by immediate counterpart country are available for more years in the *OECD FDI database according to BMD4*. Detailed metadata at: *http://stats.oecd.org/OECDStat_Metadata/ShowMetadata.ashx?Dataset=FDI_CTRY_IND_SUMM*.

1. Information on data for Israel: *http://oe.cd/israel-disclaimer*.
2. Note by Turkey: The information in this document with reference to "Cyprus" relates to the southern part of the Island. There is no single authority representing both Turkish and Greek Cypriot people on the Island. Turkey recognises the Turkish Republic of Northern Cyprus (TRNC). Until a lasting and equitable solution is found within the context of the United Nations, Turkey shall preserve its position concerning the "Cyprus issue".
3. Note by all the European Union Member States of the OECD and the European Union: The Republic of Cyprus is recognised by all members of the United Nations with the exception of Turkey. The information in this document relates to the area under the effective control of the Government of the Republic of Cyprus.

Source: OECD International Direct Investment Statistics (database): https://doi.org/10.1787/idi-data-en

Table 3. Foreign direct investment income by country

Million US dollars

	Inward					Outward				
	2014	2015	2016	2017	2018	2014	2015	2016	2017	2018
WORLD	**2 349.7**	**3 554.0**	**3 137.5**	**3 276.9**	**3 198.2**	**313.5**	**219.3**	**201.5**	**296.8**	**955.9**
OECD COUNTRIES	..	**3 290.7**	**2 887.2**	**3 146.9**	..	..	**109.8**	**86.7**	**124.6**	..
Australia	..	0.1	0.4	0.5	..	..	-	-	0.1	..
Austria	..	61.8	88.1	15.7	..	..	4.4	-	-	..
Belgium	..	121.7	82.8	56.4	..	..	-	-	0.1	..
Canada	..	0.5	4.9	3.8	..	..	-	0.2	-	..
Chile	..	-	5.6	4.9	..	..	-	-	-	..
Czech Republic	..	14.4	16.5	0.0	..	..	-	-	-	..
Denmark	..	2.6	5.4	3.9	..	..	-	-	-	..
Estonia	..	-	-	-	..	..	-	-	-	..
Finland	..	461.3	12.3	1.0	..	..	-	-	-	..
France	..	154.1	178.1	208.8	..	..	-	2.0	0.2	..
Germany	..	515.8	413.0	497.9	..	..	2.9	-2.4	-4.1	..
Greece	..	61.5	0.8	9.1	..	..	-	-	-	..
Hungary	..	-	6.0	12.5	..	..	-0.1	-0.1	-	..
Iceland	..	-	-	-	..	..	-	-	-	..
Ireland	..	2.8	11.5	0.6	..	..	-	0.0	-	..
Israel[1]	..	7.6	9.8	5.7	..	..	-	-	-	..
Italy	..	76.4	75.3	63.8	..	..	0.1	-	-	..
Japan	..	45.9	148.0	119.4	..	..	-	2.6	-	..
Korea	..	12.6	20.8	30.5	..	..	-	-	4.4	..
Latvia	..	-	-	-	..	..	-	2.6	3.3	..
Lithuania	..	-	-	-	..	..	-	-	-	..
Luxembourg	..	94.0	90.2	224.5	..	..	20.7	0.1	13.0	..
Mexico	..	-	-	-	..	..	-	-	-	..
Netherlands	..	419.5	486.1	463.8	..	..	57.0	46.2	92.4	..
New Zealand	..	-	-	-	..	..	-	-	-	..
Norway	..	7.3	18.1	20.3	..	..	-	0.0	-	..
Poland	..	-	0.0	0.6	..	..	-	0.4	0.7	..
Portugal	..	6.5	7.3	5.1	..	..	-	-	-	..
Slovak Republic	..	14.1	18.8	13.9	..	..	-	0.0	-	..
Slovenia	..	-	-	-	..	..	-	-	-	..
Spain	..	185.3	211.9	119.3	..	..	-	-	0.0	..
Sweden	..	6.0	5.8	195.8	..	..	-	0.0	-	..
Switzerland	..	154.6	251.6	331.9	..	..	0.0	0.5	4.6	..
Turkey	..	-	-	-	..	..	-	-	-	..
United Kingdom	..	481.1	618.3	643.8	..	..	9.8	24.1	-0.1	..
United States	..	383.4	100.3	93.6	..	..	15.0	10.6	10.0	..
EUROPE	..	**3 004.6**	**2 614.5**	**2 899.4**	..	..	**99.8**	**77.9**	**129.0**	..
Bulgaria	..	0.1	0.6	0.1	..	..	0.3	0.1	0.4	..
Croatia	..	1.1	-	-	..	..	-	-	-	..
Cyprus[2, 3]	..	-	-	-	..	..	-	-	-	..
Malta	..	1.3	11.1	7.3	..	..	-	0.7	9.7	..
Romania	..	0.1	0.0	0.0	..	..	0.1	-	-	..
Russian Federation	..	159.4	4.3	1.0	..	..	2.9	0.8	0.6	..
Ukraine	..	0.1	-	0.0	..	..	-	1.2	7.0	..
AFRICA	..	**1.6**	**5.5**	**0.5**	..	..	**5.1**	**3.2**	**5.5**	..
Northern Africa	..	1.6	5.5	0.5	..	..	5.0	3.1	5.5	..
Algeria	..	1.5	-	0.0	..	..	3.9	2.5	3.8	..
Egypt	..	0.1	0.1	0.1	..	..	0.5	0.6	1.7	..
Libya	..	-	5.3	0.4	..	..	-	-	-	..
Morocco	..	-	-	-	..	..	0.6	-	0.1	..
Tunisia	..	-	-	-	..	..	-	-	-	..
Other African countries	..	-	0.0	0.0	..	..	0.1	0.1	-	..
Nigeria	..	-	-	-	..	..	-	-	-	..
South Africa	..	-	-	-	..	..	-	-	-	..
AMERICA	..	**417.6**	**114.9**	**107.0**	..	..	**14.7**	**10.6**	**9.9**	..
Northern America	..	383.9	105.1	97.4	..	..	15.0	10.7	10.0	..
Central America and Caribbean countries	..	33.7	4.2	4.7	..	..	-0.3	-0.1	-0.1	..
Bahamas	..	-	-	-	..	..	-	-	-	..
Bermuda	..	-	-	4.3	..	..	-0.3	-	-	..
Cayman Islands	..	3.7	4.2	0.2	..	..	-	-	-	..
Costa Rica	..	-	-	-	..	..	-	-	-	..
El Salvador	..	-	-	-	..	..	-	-	-	..
Guatemala	..	-	-	-	..	..	-	-	-	..
Honduras	..	-	-	-	..	..	-	-	-	..
Nicaragua	..	-	-	-	..	..	-	-	-	..
Panama	..	-	-	-	..	..	-	-	-	..
Virgin Islands, U.S.	..	-	-	-	..	..	-	-	-	..
South America	..	0.0	5.6	4.9	..	..	-	0.0	-	..
Argentina	..	-	-	-	..	..	-	-	-	..
Bolivia	..	-	-	-	..	..	-	-	-	..
Brazil	..	-	-	-	..	..	-	-	-	..
Colombia	..	-	-	-	..	..	-	0.0	-	..
Ecuador	..	-	-	-	..	..	-	-	-	..
Paraguay	..	-	-	-	..	..	-	-	-	..
Peru	..	-	-	-	..	..	-	-	-	..
Uruguay	..	0.0	-	-	..	..	-	-	-	..
Venezuela	..	-	-	-	..	..	-	-	-	..

Table 3. Foreign direct investment income by country *(cont.)*

Million US dollars

	Inward					Outward				
	2014	2015	2016	2017	2018	2014	2015	2016	2017	2018
ASIA	..	**130.1**	**372.6**	**329.2**	..	..	**99.8**	**106.2**	**138.8**	..
Near and Middle East	..	28.2	153.5	133.7	..	..	95.1	83.3	95.1	..
Gulf Arabian countries	..	17.3	128.9	115.0	..	..	78.2	82.1	93.2	..
Kuwait	..	-	52.6	46.6	..	..	-	-	0.0	..
Qatar	..	0.8	43.3	37.6	..	..	-	-	-	..
Saudi Arabia	..	-	6.6	19.9	..	..	0.1	0.5	-	..
United Arab Emirates	..	16.6	26.4	10.8	..	..	13.1	0.3	0.1	..
Other Near and Middle East	..	10.9	24.6	18.7	..	..	16.9	1.2	1.9	..
Jordan	..	1.0	-	0.1	..	..	1.3	-	0.0	..
Other Asian countries	..	101.9	219.2	195.5	..	..	4.7	22.9	43.8	..
China	..	0.2	2.6	2.3	..	..	-	0.8	18.1	..
Hong Kong, China	..	20.1	5.4	0.3	..	..	0.3	-	0.0	..
India	..	0.3	1.0	0.4	..	..	-	-	0.2	..
Indonesia	..	-	1.0	0.4	..	..	-	-	-	..
Iran, Islamic Republic of	..	0.4	-	-	..	..	-	-	0.2	..
Malaysia	..	9.2	8.5	4.0	..	..	-	-	-	..
Philippines	..	-	-	-	..	..	-	-	-	..
Singapore	..	11.8	27.5	34.3	..	..	-	2.4	0.5	..
Chinese Taipei	..	1.3	2.5	3.2	..	..	-	-	-	..
Thailand	..	-	1.0	0.4	..	..	-	-	-	..
Viet Nam	..	-	-	-	..	..	-	-	-	..
AUSTRALIA, OCEANIA AND POLAR REGIONS	..	**0.1**	**0.4**	**0.5**	..	..	-	-	**0.1**	..
WORLD unallocated and confidential	..	-	**0.0**	**0.0**	..	..	**0.0**	-	**0.0**	..
European Union (EU28)	..	**2 681.3**	**2 339.6**	**2 543.7**	..	..	**95.2**	**73.6**	**115.7**	..
G20 countries excl. European Union	..	**1 829.5**	**1 574.4**	**1 686.0**	..	..	**30.7**	**39.1**	**29.4**	..
G20 OECD countries	..	**1 669.8**	**1 558.9**	**1 661.9**	..	..	**27.8**	**37.0**	**10.5**	..
G20 Non-OECD countries	..	**159.8**	**15.4**	**24.0**	..	..	**2.9**	**2.1**	**19.0**	..
MENA countries	..	**21.4**	**137.4**	**118.0**	..	..	**96.6**	**85.3**	**98.7**	..
ASEAN countries	..	**20.9**	**37.9**	**39.2**	..	..	-	**2.4**	**0.5**	..

- Nil; .. Not available

Note: Detailed metadata at: *http://stats.oecd.org/OECDStat_Metadata/ShowMetadata.ashx?Dataset=FDI_CTRY_IND_SUMM.*

1. Information on data for Israel: *http://oe.cd/israel-disclaimer.*
2. Note by Turkey: The information in this document with reference to “Cyprus” relates to the southern part of the Island. There is no single authority representing both Turkish and Greek Cypriot people on the Island. Turkey recognises the Turkish Republic of Northern Cyprus (TRNC). Until a lasting and equitable solution is found within the context of the United Nations, Turkey shall preserve its position concerning the “Cyprus issue”.
3. Note by all the European Union Member States of the OECD and the European Union: The Republic of Cyprus is recognised by all members of the United Nations with the exception of Turkey. The information in this document relates to the area under the effective control of the Government of the Republic of Cyprus.

Source: OECD International Direct Investment Statistics (database): https://doi.org/10.1787/idi-data-en

Table 4. Foreign direct investment flows by industrial sector

Million US dollars

	Inward					Outward				
	2014	2015	2016	2017	2018	2014	2015	2016	2017	2018
All FDI activities	**12 447.9**	**18 916.2**	**13 719.1**	**11 184.5**	**12 966.3**	**6 663.8**	**4 900.6**	**2 891.6**	**2 634.7**	**3 606.4**
Agriculture, forestry and fishing	**61.5**	**49.8**	**41.5**	**50.5**	**96.2**	..	**9.2**	**7.2**	**20.2**	**18.3**
Mining and quarrying	**309.1**	**221.3**	**161.7**	**453.9**	**67.0**	..	**1 800.2**	**1 068.3**	**1 036.1**	**835.1**
Extraction activities	286.5	159.5	125.7	443.1	24.0	..	1 760.5	1 074.2	994.5	819.8
Manufacturing	**2 613.0**	**4 463.6**	**2 410.2**	**1 190.8**	**2 076.8**	..	**819.9**	**397.7**	**373.6**	**476.9**
of which:										
Food products, beverages and tobacco	252.6	918.6	728.1	363.8	478.5	..	294.2	41.5	25.7	63.0
Textiles, wood and paper products; printing	193.9	470.9	168.0	137.3	175.0	..	93.1	71.6	143.6	190.1
Chemical, rubber, plastic, non-metallic mineral products	713.2	2 059.5	273.1	422.8	524.2	..	36.6	54.6	66.9	37.5
Metal and machinery products, except electrical equipment	228.0	410.3	721.7	118.7	99.5	..	109.1	60.7	22.5	47.3
Motor vehicles, trailers, semi-trailers, other transport equipment	105.4	152.0	168.6	30.7	352.8	..	6.7	13.0	18.9	1.3
Other manufacturing	1 119.9	452.3	350.8	117.6	446.8	..	280.3	156.3	95.9	137.8
Electricity, gas, steam and air conditioning supply	**1 199.7**	**1 576.2**	**629.5**	**-945.0**	**370.1**	..	**87.4**	**39.2**	**24.7**	**387.2**
Water supply; sewerage, waste management and remediation activities	**2.8**	**11.9**	**3.1**	**-5.3**	**4.0**	..	**0.2**	**0.6**	**0.7**	**0.3**
Construction	**296.2**	**39.1**	**270.7**	**568.9**	**187.3**	..	**305.0**	**39.6**	**144.5**	**67.3**
Services	**3 975.7**	**8 398.3**	**6 312.4**	**5 227.8**	**4 249.8**	..	**1 878.9**	**1 339.0**	**1 034.7**	**1 821.5**
Wholesale and retail trade; repair of motor vehicles and motorcycles	850.8	801.3	932.9	1 276.7	1 271.4	..	53.3	78.4	118.2	12.3
Transportation and storage	637.4	2 042.9	1 553.1	1 926.5	878.7	..	37.1	139.5	108.5	36.7
Accommodation and food service activities	9.3	9.5	258.2	91.2	422.0	..	44.1	47.9	123.7	-26.5
Information and communication	195.9	1 464.9	858.3	-171.6	203.4	..	647.3	84.7	38.8	16.1
Financial and insurance activities	1 625.4	3 522.2	1 856.8	1 252.2	1 138.7	..	647.0	481.8	-79.7	1 152.1
Activities of holding companies	160.6	205.9	126.5	-2.2	83.1	..	490.3	257.3	191.5	886.4
Real estate activities	259.3	190.7	367.8	303.6	93.4	..	378.1	367.7	567.3	430.4
Professional, scientific and technical activities	88.1	44.2	105.1	70.1	-35.3	..	13.5	13.9	19.0	112.3
Administrative and support service activities	50.4	218.9	149.0	323.5	54.5	..	20.5	2.5	19.1	8.9
Public administration; activities of households and of extraterritorial organisations	0.6	-	0.1	0.4	2.0	..	0.0	0.1	-0.8	-
Education	0.0	0.0	-74.1	-10.8	0.6	..	0.7	0.6	1.5	11.0
Human health and social work activities	168.8	81.6	315.0	126.2	95.5	..	19.5	85.3	4.3	4.1
Arts, entertainment and recreation	24.4	1.6	16.3	9.7	19.5	..	0.4	-0.6	2.6	1.2
Other services	65.3	20.7	-26.0	30.2	105.3	..	17.6	37.1	112.3	62.8
Not allocated and confidential	**-331.1**	**0.0**	**-**	**0.0**	**0.0**	**6 663.8**	**-0.3**	**0.0**	**0.3**	**0.0**
Private real estate activities	**4 321.0**	**4 156.0**	**3 890.0**	**4 643.0**	**5 915.0**	..	..	..	..	..

- Nil; .. Not available

Note: Detailed metadata at: *http://stats.oecd.org/OECDStat_Metadata/ShowMetadata.ashx?Dataset=FDI_CTRY_IND_SUMM.*

Source: OECD International Direct Investment Statistics (database): https://doi.org/10.1787/idi-data-en

Table 5. Foreign direct investment positions by industrial sector
At year end

Million US dollars

	Inward					Outward				
	2014	2015	2016	2017	2018	2014	2015	2016	2017	2018
All FDI activities	**182 064.6**	**158 077.6**	**148 428.2**	**197 374.5**	**147 107.1**	**39 513.3**	**35 615.0**	**38 368.6**	**45 534.1**	**44 449.2**
Agriculture, forestry and fishing	**1 071.9**	**806.3**	**748.0**	**1 399.7**	**724.1**	**14.4**	**3.3**	**8.8**	**29.6**	**32.2**
Mining and quarrying	**3 964.1**	**3 135.4**	**2 690.9**	**4 770.7**	**3 595.7**	**7 655.1**	**4 630.2**	**4 202.3**	**5 296.4**	**3 577.5**
Extraction activities	1 772.5	1 183.2	1 091.6	2 081.3	1 454.7	-	4 470.6	4 045.2	5 137.9	3 480.7
Manufacturing	**61 215.5**	**52 233.5**	**45 957.9**	**61 628.8**	**37 738.0**	**5 556.0**	**5 233.4**	**4 483.8**	**4 032.4**	**4 059.9**
of which:										
Food products, beverages and tobacco	12 746.2	11 320.5	9 858.9	12 306.0	6 945.4	3 036.4	1 771.7	2 051.6	709.2	787.9
Textiles, wood and paper products; printing	1 230.7	952.1	992.7	1 718.0	1 217.1	939.2	1 481.9	790.2	979.7	933.5
Chemical, rubber, plastic, non-metallic mineral products	14 231.3	16 424.6	13 787.1	19 186.3	13 544.8	597.5	962.5	641.6	813.5	643.5
Metal and machinery products, except electrical equipment	7 506.7	4 620.7	4 948.8	6 928.9	3 450.0	496.7	507.1	769.6	1 345.0	1 277.1
Motor vehicles, trailers, semi-trailers, other transport equipment	13 115.6	9 254.1	8 922.2	12 504.2	6 776.1	31.3	95.8	121.6	101.1	140.1
Other manufacturing	12 385.0	9 661.5	7 448.2	8 985.4	5 804.7	454.8	414.5	109.2	84.0	277.8
Electricity, gas, steam and air conditioning supply	**17 647.3**	**15 558.9**	**11 829.6**	**18 971.8**	**6 633.8**	**670.9**	**699.5**	**468.4**	**425.8**	**305.7**
Water supply; sewerage, waste management and remediation activities	**86.5**	**63.8**	**62.6**	**53.1**	**26.0**	**-**	**12.8**	**10.3**	**2.4**	**2.9**
Construction	**1 875.0**	**1 610.9**	**1 459.9**	**946.4**	**792.3**	**1 073.9**	**1 005.7**	**1 085.2**	**466.7**	**333.0**
Services	**96 204.5**	**84 668.9**	**85 679.5**	**109 604.1**	**97 597.3**	**24 543.0**	**24 030.2**	**28 109.9**	**35 280.8**	**36 138.0**
Wholesale and retail trade; repair of motor vehicles and motorcycles	22 986.4	26 398.6	32 069.7	40 520.1	38 722.1	1 983.3	934.6	1 574.7	2 057.0	2 709.1
Transportation and storage	3 583.2	2 918.6	3 359.9	7 086.5	4 752.1	779.9	1 169.8	1 433.2	2 826.7	1 399.5
Accommodation and food service activities	677.6	511.2	455.7	936.9	511.2	470.7	168.1	411.0	338.9	204.2
Information and communication	23 118.4	16 036.0	12 633.9	16 146.3	9 779.3	1 675.1	2 639.1	2 510.0	1 774.9	1 086.2
Financial and insurance activities	38 975.2	33 219.9	31 950.3	38 057.2	38 610.9	17 833.2	18 598.7	21 595.0	27 650.6	29 978.4
Activities of holding companies	3 677.2	4 750.9	3 999.7	5 187.8	3 353.4	10 616.7	11 891.5	13 266.3	18 980.4	21 067.0
Real estate activities	1 152.1	1 475.2	1 354.6	2 342.1	1 972.6	775.6	347.7	321.9	471.1	573.9
Professional, scientific and technical activities	377.6	305.9	315.8	692.6	498.9	2.6	46.1	45.4	52.6	5.4
Administrative and support service activities	2 435.2	1 859.6	1 569.8	2 104.2	1 574.4	404.4	13.3	60.4	12.2	27.9
Public administration; activities of households and of extraterritorial organisations	-	-	0.0	0.4	0.4	0.6	-	-	-0.8	-0.8
Education	125.1	60.9	11.6	13.6	10.0	18.8	6.0	5.6	4.8	2.5
Human health and social work activities	1 730.5	1 049.4	759.7	653.8	378.4	10.6	8.8	80.5	35.9	73.8
Arts, entertainment and recreation	154.7	112.3	572.4	129.1	96.1	259.6	2.4	24.6	26.2	59.8
Other services	888.5	721.4	626.2	921.2	690.9	328.7	75.7	47.6	30.6	18.1
Not allocated and confidential	**-0.1**	**-0.1**	**-0.1**	**-0.1**	**-0.1**	**0.0**	**-**	**-**	**0.0**	**-**
Private real estate activities	-	..	..	..	..	-	..	..	..	..

\- Nil; .. Not available

Note: Detailed metadata at: *http://stats.oecd.org/OECDStat_Metadata/ShowMetadata.ashx?Dataset=FDI_CTRY_IND_SUMM.*

Source: OECD International Direct Investment Statistics (database): https://doi.org/10.1787/idi-data-en

Table 6. Foreign direct investment income by industrial sector

Million US dollars

	Inward					Outward				
	2014	2015	2016	2017	2018	2014	2015	2016	2017	2018
All FDI activities	**2 349.7**	**3 554.0**	**3 137.5**	**3 276.9**	**3 198.2**	**313.5**	**219.3**	**201.5**	**296.8**	**955.9**
Agriculture, forestry and fishing	..	**0.3**	**22.9**	**12.7**	**13.3**	..	**0.2**	**0.2**	-	**0.1**
Mining and quarrying	..	**198.2**	**116.6**	**240.2**	**75.0**	..	**1.1**	**0.1**	**0.3**	**1.5**
Extraction activities	..	61.2	46.0	115.2	56.3	..	-	-	-	-
Manufacturing	..	**1 222.1**	**1 369.8**	**1 286.5**	**1 140.6**	..	**40.8**	**70.2**	**122.2**	**291.3**
of which:										
Food products, beverages and tobacco	..	391.3	496.8	483.4	337.9	..	-	13.3	23.6	24.4
Textiles, wood and paper products; printing	..	59.5	28.4	59.8	67.6	..	1.2	3.5	4.4	21.0
Chemical, rubber, plastic, non-metallic mineral products	..	147.6	350.2	196.2	168.4	..	21.9	29.3	34.4	30.5
Metal and machinery products, except electrical equipment	..	52.4	169.2	169.0	149.5	..	3.1	15.2	15.1	25.9
Motor vehicles, trailers, semi-trailers, other transport equipment	..	343.0	193.1	141.2	192.4	..	-	1.0	0.5	-
Other manufacturing	..	228.3	132.1	236.9	224.9	..	14.6	7.9	44.3	189.5
Electricity, gas, steam and air conditioning supply	..	**153.8**	**133.4**	**88.7**	**121.8**	..	**0.5**	**1.5**	**0.1**	**20.3**
Water supply; sewerage, waste management and remediation activities	..	-	**0.2**	**1.2**	**0.0**	..	-	-	-	-
Construction	..	**42.1**	**27.4**	**41.4**	**51.1**	..	**22.9**	**1.2**	**18.0**	**28.9**
Services	..	**1 937.6**	**1 467.1**	**1 606.4**	**1 796.4**	..	**153.8**	**128.3**	**157.2**	**613.8**
Wholesale and retail trade; repair of motor vehicles and motorcycles	..	410.1	517.0	453.1	366.6	..	3.6	4.5	5.2	14.9
Transportation and storage	..	193.0	313.2	193.5	358.0	..	4.8	0.1	4.9	11.2
Accommodation and food service activities	..	8.7	27.1	23.9	132.9	..	-	0.4	4.0	9.0
Information and communication	..	649.3	44.1	462.2	297.1	..	-0.3	-0.2	19.3	2.2
Financial and insurance activities	..	520.4	319.4	309.5	489.0	..	118.2	121.2	104.3	519.1
Activities of holding companies	..	14.5	18.1	9.7	56.3	..	26.9	3.4	2.1	261.1
Real estate activities	..	17.2	35.9	13.0	19.5	..	-	-0.1	3.4	1.2
Professional, scientific and technical activities	..	37.5	123.0	62.8	25.7	..	1.1	0.4	4.8	4.6
Administrative and support service activities	..	29.5	35.4	20.8	34.9	..	-	0.7	9.9	1.1
Public administration; activities of households and of extraterritorial organisations	..	-	-	-	0.0	..	-	-	-	-
Education	..	0.1	0.0	0.0	0.4	..	-	0.1	0.0	-
Human health and social work activities	..	34.5	28.1	7.1	4.9	..	23.7	-	0.4	45.1
Arts, entertainment and recreation	..	18.1	7.2	5.0	6.4	..	-	0.4	-	3.1
Other services	..	19.3	16.7	55.6	61.0	..	2.6	0.9	1.1	2.4
Not allocated and confidential	**2 349.7**	**0.0**	**0.0**	**0.0**	**0.0**	**313.5**	**0.0**	**0.0**	**-1.0**	**0.0**
Private real estate activities	..	..	..	..	..	..	..	..	..	..

- Nil; .. Not available

Note: Detailed metadata at: *http://stats.oecd.org/OECDStat_Metadata/ShowMetadata.ashx?Dataset=FDI_CTRY_IND_SUMM.*

Source: OECD International Direct Investment Statistics (database): https://doi.org/10.1787/idi-data-en

UNITED KINGDOM

Table 1. Foreign direct investment flows by country

Million US dollars

	Inward					Outward				
	2014	2015	2016	2017	2018	2014	2015	2016	2017	2018
WORLD	**45 831.4**	**38 669.2**	**196 503.4**	**78 511.5**	**83 854.9**	.. c	**-65 561.5**	**-22 310.4**	**106 692.0**	**84 616.5**
OECD COUNTRIES	**45 922.0**	**19 066.5**	**152 390.0**	**51 399.7**	**69 233.0**	.. c	**-65 795.3**	.. c	**111 666.2**	**55 126.1**
Australia	.. c	1 996.9	-2 159.2	3 026.0	935.0	.. c	186.4	1 215.9	-4 470.8	3 917.6
Austria	.. c	48.9	-101.2	-10.3	225.4	-209.1	.. c	114.7	385.0	146.7
Belgium	.. c	-825.1	.. c	-2 818.7	3 273.3	.. c	2 459.9	.. c	.. c	1 808.7
Canada	.. d	5 388.8	155.2	.. d	.. d	.. c	.. c	-1 391.4	137.8	.. c
Chile	.. c	-	-1.4	12.9	5.3	.. c	-812.8	274.0	-42.5	68.0
Czech Republic	.. c	32.1	-	-1.3	58.7	.. c	7.6	-66.1	218.9	-94.7
Denmark	.. c	689.1	36.4	534.4	621.6	.. c	-1 222.3	1 063.4	-464.8	.. c
Estonia	.. c	-	-	-	5.3	19.8	.. c	-112.0	43.8	-5.3
Finland	77.4	103.9	-55.3	34.8	277.4	-75.7	-65.7	62.1	82.4	-538.9
France	7 510.7	.. c	618.1	7 700.2	-21.3	.. c	1 657.8	697.7	-1 984.3	3 862.9
Germany	3 215.3	7 605.8	3 330.6	318.1	5 667.6	.. c	-2 397.3	-174.1	894.9	7 093.5
Greece	8.2	32.1	12.1	-55.4	5.3	.. c	244.5	.. c	148.1	73.4
Hungary	.. c	10.7	-13.5	43.8	14.7	.. c	-187.9	.. c	218.9	113.4
Iceland	.. c	35.1	56.7	-23.2	4.0	.. c	-	-1.4	2.6	84.0
Ireland	.. c	1 040.5	-948.7	673.4	-1 388.6	.. c	-123.8	-7 641.0	13 060.8	-5 646.3
Israel[1]	.. c	68.8	25.6	.. d	.. c	248.6	160.4	125.5	230.5	49.4
Italy	411.6	348.4	-755.7	1 862.0	420.2	.. c	.. c	430.5	-632.2	12.0
Japan	3 622.0	2 624.9	2 295.5	10 144.2	.. c	.. c	.. c	-27.0	.. c	-200.1
Korea	.. c	.. c	188.9	202.2	.. c	663.5	.. c	1 654.5	.. c	649.6
Latvia	.. c	-1.5	1.4	7.7	1.3	.. c	-13.8	-20.2	-	-13.3
Lithuania	.. c	-	1.4	.. c	2.7	.. c	4.6	-44.5	9.0	-9.3
Luxembourg	2 482.7	-1 298.7	29 121.5	5 499.6	-9 086.3	.. c	-12 168.1	2 112.0	7 078.3	164.1
Mexico	.. c	-18.3	6.7	7.7	.. c	956.5	1 066.5	569.5	1 129.3	956.4
Netherlands	.. c	-34 055.0	.. c	-2 319.1	-19 455.8	-12 935.5	-10 400.3	-17 797.6	.. c	6 434.6
New Zealand	42.8	29.0	55.3	-37.3	82.7	237.1	-195.6	14.8	155.8	288.1
Norway	1 918.0	.. c	.. c	461.0	.. c	.. c	1 563.0	1 376.5	.. c	-2 917.2
Poland	.. c	29.0	-1.4	67.0	52.0	.. c	1 715.8	-151.1	378.6	-1 001.7
Portugal	.. c	19.9	8.1	-27.0	-16.0	.. c	-516.4	-599.2	211.2	.. c
Slovak Republic	.. c	32.1	2.7	.. c	-20.0	-143.2	-18.3	-60.7	.. c	-66.7
Slovenia	.. c	-1.5	-	2.6	5.3	.. c	-9.2	13.5	-25.8	-8.0
Spain	.. c	3 495.8	2 531.7	-797.1	3 284.0	3 088.6	441.6	1 066.1	.. c	-3 174.6
Sweden	1 025.7	918.3	-13.5	1 070.0	1 024.4	.. c	728.8	3 170.0	866.6	731.0
Switzerland	2 914.1	670.7	1 144.4	5 114.6	.. c	3 571.0	2 021.4	-1 334.7	209.9	-2 036.8
Turkey	13.2	1.5	-10.8	39.9	.. c	.. c	-71.8	359.0	-316.8	440.2
United Kingdom	-	-	-	-	-	..	-	-	-	-
United States	25 044.5	32 258.2	25 049.9	20 392.7	73 990.9	4 695.4	-17 153.6	982.5	92 951.3	41 811.4
EUROPE	**6 628.3**	**-18 800.6**	**131 993.3**	**28 489.6**	**-15 226.1**	**-161 899.9**	**-18 453.8**	**-34 803.0**	**13 574.6**	**13 957.6**
Bulgaria	.. c	-3.1	-1.4	15.5	-2.7	34.6	39.7	-1.4	94.0	.. c
Croatia	.. c	.. d	-	.. c	4.0	.. c	38.2	-17.5	-32.2	.. c
Cyprus[2, 3]	324.3	592.8	103.9	.. c	650.9	.. c	38.2	.. c	-320.6	.. c
Malta	.. c	.. c	-44.5	-106.9	584.2	.. c	.. c	62.1	-1 344.3	-26.7
Romania	.. c	-	2.7	.. d	-2.7	.. c	125.3	.. c	166.1	.. c
Russian Federation	.. c	.. c	-64.8	-55.4	.. c	.. c	1 167.3	-583.0	-725.0	.. c
Ukraine	.. c	.. c	-2.7	11.6	5.3	.. c	.. c	-545.2	-83.7	.. c
AFRICA	**726.0**	**.. c**	**17.5**	**376.0**	**1 147.1**	**4 468.2**	**343.8**	**-8 461.5**	**.. c**	**15 459.5**
Northern Africa	.. c	22.9	5.4	2.6	6.7	423.1	-2 097.8	-1 596.5	.. c	.. c
Algeria	.. c	.. c	-	.. c	.. c	.. c	.. c	.. c	.. c	.. c
Egypt	.. c	-1.5	-	-1.3	-	941.7	-267.4	-399.5	.. c	.. c
Libya	.. c	.. c	5.4	.. c	-	.. c	.. c	.. c	.. c	.. c
Morocco	.. c	-	-	-1.3	2.7	.. c	.. c	-141.7	.. c	-8.0
Tunisia	.. c	-	-	.. c	.. c	.. c	149.7	-5.4	-	2.7
Other African countries	.. d	.. c	12.1	373.4	1 141.8	4 045.1	2 441.6	-6 865.0	-5 973.5	.. d
Nigeria	.. c	.. c	56.7	.. c	.. c	.. c	.. c	746.3	330.9	352.1
South Africa	691.5	539.3	-89.1	.. c	1 083.1	.. c	1 364.4	.. c	423.6	3 114.6
AMERICA	**27 634.2**	**42 771.6**	**28 348.2**	**28 581.0**	**78 571.4**	**14 488.0**	**-32 724.2**	**2 657.2**	**99 262.2**	**40 489.5**
Northern America	.. d	37 647.1	25 203.8	.. d	.. d	.. d	.. d	-406.2	93 089.1	.. d
Central America and Caribbean countries	.. c	5 129.1	3 129.6	6 847.8	1 959.5	5 737.6	2 308.6	2 086.4	5 270.4	.. c
Bahamas	316.1	7.6	-78.3	33.5	166.7	.. c	.. c	93.1	.. c	14.7
Bermuda	.. c	1 644.0	1 658.6	1 943.1	-799.0	.. c	-553.1	-547.9	-157.1	-1 164.5
Cayman Islands	-1 743.5	617.3	3 681.5	-16.7	-2 834.5	.. c	3 454.5	.. c	3 427.8	.. c
Costa Rica	-	-	-1.4	-	-	.. c	128.3	.. c	.. c	.. c
El Salvador	-	-	-	-	-	.. c	-7.5	.. c	.. c	1.3
Guatemala	525.2	111.5	44.5	158.4	-68.0	.. c	-7.5	-20.2	101.7	-20.0
Honduras	-	-	-	-	-	.. c	-7.6	-4.0	.. c	.. c
Nicaragua	-	-	-	-	-	.. c	.. c	-1.4	20.6	2.7
Panama	-31.3	-6.1	-2.7	6.4	-62.7	.. c	.. c	12.1	.. c	-2.7
Virgin Islands, U.S.	-	.. c	2.7	.. c	-6.7	-	-	1.4	-3.9	1.3
South America	.. c	-3.1	14.8	.. c	.. d	.. d	.. d	978.4	902.7	1 939.4
Argentina	.. c	1.5	-	-	-	.. c	693.7	.. c	.. c	292.1
Bolivia	-	-	-	-	-	.. c	-	-	1.3	-
Brazil	.. c	-3.1	16.2	.. c	4.0	2 838.3	1 451.5	466.9	261.4	.. c
Colombia	.. c	.. c	-	.. c	1.3	-13.2	-183.3	-167.3	.. c	237.4
Ecuador	.. c	.. c	-	.. c	-	.. c	6.1	.. c	18.0	-2.7
Paraguay	-	-	-	.. c	.. d	.. c	.. c	2.7	1.3	1.3
Peru	.. c	-	-	-	2.7	23.0	29.0	29.7	61.8	58.7
Uruguay	-	-	-	-	-	.. c	-153.9	.. c	1.3	.. c
Venezuela	.. c	-	-	-	-	212.4	-62.6	43.2	94.0	.. c

Table 1. Foreign direct investment flows by country *(cont.)*

Million US dollars

	Inward					Outward				
	2014	2015	2016	2017	2018	2014	2015	2016	2017	2018
ASIA	**10 339.2**	**12 022.9**	**37 720.6**	**19 660.1**	**18 311.3**	**16 371.4**	**-14 866.3**	**16 969.0**	**.. c**	**7 659.1**
Near and Middle East	544.9	.. c	.. c	891.1	.. c	2 840.0	.. c	.. c	.. d	-73.4
Gulf Arabian countries	.. d	.. c	.. c	844.7	-504.2	.. c	.. c	.. c	1 282.5	-8.0
Kuwait	.. c	-12.2	20.2	-9.0	-5.3	.. c	1.5	8.1	.. c	17.3
Qatar	.. c	6.1	4.0	16.7	-36.0	.. c	51.9	33.7	.. c	25.3
Saudi Arabia	.. c	-1.5	-74.2	3.9	-28.0	.. c	718.1	653.2	696.6	.. c
United Arab Emirates	.. c	.. c	.. c	645.1	-93.4	.. c	.. c	.. c	.. c	-1 240.5
Other Near and Middle East	.. c	76.4	27.0	47.6	.. c	.. c	.. c	655.9	.. d	-65.4
Jordan	.. c	.. c	-	.. d	2.7	.. c	33.6	.. c	.. c	.. c
Other Asian countries	9 794.2	.. d	.. d	18 769.0	.. c	13 531.4	.. d	.. d	5 329.6	7 732.4
China	961.5	702.8	552.0	1 357.2	-34.7	740.9	-1 233.0	1 526.3	-330.9	1 923.4
Hong Kong, China	.. c	1 416.3	.. c	2 724.7	.. c	.. c	5 112.3	3 859.6	2 978.4	3 764.2
India	.. c	.. c	-792.2	1 874.8	509.5	549.9	994.7	.. c	-441.7	-2 058.2
Indonesia	.. c	.. c	.. c	.. c	-	.. c	-250.6	1 081.0	-614.2	.. c
Iran, Islamic Republic of	.. c	-3.1	5.4	.. c	6.7	.. c	.. c	.. c	-1.3	-
Malaysia	207.4	38.2	-145.7	94.0	301.5	2 527.2	99.3	902.8	535.7	716.3
Philippines	.. c	.. c	2.7	23.2	-4.0	.. c	-58.1	43.2	65.7	.. c
Singapore	3 855.8	5 735.7	5 612.7	-664.4	-94.7	.. c	4 181.8	.. c	-387.6	-257.4
Chinese Taipei	13.2	3.1	-2.7	10.3	34.7	512.0	302.5	483.1	337.4	.. d
Thailand	57.6	.. c	-4.0	38.6	.. c	350.7	-48.9	790.8	-37.3	-197.4
Viet Nam	.. c	-	.. c	-	4.0	.. c	230.7	-54.0	.. c	735.0
AUSTRALIA, OCEANIA AND POLAR REGIONS	**.. c**	**2 016.8**	**-1 576.2**	**1 406.1**	**1 051.1**	**.. c**	**140.6**	**1 326.6**	**-4 567.3**	**7 052.2**
WORLD unallocated and confidential	**461.0**	**111.5**	**-**	**-1.3**	**-**	**.. c**	**-1.5**	**1.4**	**-2 468.5**	**..**
European Union (EU28)	**8 740.5**	**-21 095.5**	**124 186.2**	**10 816.4**	**-13 814.9**	**.. c**	**-20 478.2**	**-30 313.1**	**19 025.2**	**11 747.4**
G20 countries excl. European Union	**.. d**	**.. d**	**.. d**	**.. d**	**.. d**	**.. c**	**.. d**	**.. d**	**.. d**	**.. d**
G20 OECD countries	**.. d**	**.. d**	**28 719.3**	**.. d**	**.. d**	**.. c**	**.. d**	**4 317.1**	**.. d**	**.. d**
G20 Non-OECD countries	**.. c**	**.. d**	**.. d**	**.. d**	**.. d**	**.. c**	**4 906.0**	**.. d**	**.. d**	**.. d**
MENA countries	**.. c**	**.. d**	**.. d**	**.. d**	**.. d**	**.. c**	**.. d**	**.. d**	**.. d**	**.. d**
ASEAN countries	**4 326.6**	**5 890.0**	**5 261.8**	**23.2**	**-34.7**	**6 499.8**	**4 242.9**	**-1 083.7**	**-283.3**	**2 606.4**

- Nil; .. Not available; c Confidential data; d Secondary Confidentiality

Note: Detailed metadata at: *http://stats.oecd.org/OECDStat_Metadata/ShowMetadata.ashx?Dataset=FDI_CTRY_IND_SUMM.*

1. Information on data for Israel: *http://oe.cd/israel-disclaimer.*
2. Note by Turkey: The information in this document with reference to "Cyprus" relates to the southern part of the Island. There is no single authority representing both Turkish and Greek Cypriot people on the Island. Turkey recognises the Turkish Republic of Northern Cyprus (TRNC). Until a lasting and equitable solution is found within the context of the United Nations, Turkey shall preserve its position concerning the "Cyprus issue".
3. Note by all the European Union Member States of the OECD and the European Union: The Republic of Cyprus is recognised by all members of the United Nations with the exception of Turkey. The information in this document relates to the area under the effective control of the Government of the Republic of Cyprus.

Source: OECD International Direct Investment Statistics (database): https://doi.org/10.1787/idi-data-en

Table 2. Foreign direct investment positions by country
At year end

Million US dollars

	Inward					Outward				
	2014	2015	2016	2017	2018	2014	2015	2016	2017	2018
WORLD	**1 613 251.2**	**1 530 133.4**	**1 475 523.4**	**1 608 032.7**	**1 864 337.9**	**1 583 661.5**	**1 606 364.8**	**1 491 940.0**	**1 624 231.9**	**1 750 803.6**
OECD COUNTRIES	**1 350 049.9**	**1 174 173.1**	**1 199 040.5**	**1 302 699.6**	**1 502 476.8**	**1 133 338.5**	**1 132 488.1**	**1 082 914.3**	**1 228 098.9**	**1 319 841.3**
Australia	17 892.4	21 298.2	13 707.7	9 537.9	17 473.7	31 037.4	41 861.3	50 488.4	41 335.0	47 865.9
Austria	3 602.2	2 682.3	1 620.1	3 295.5	2 627.9	1 527.3	1 461.2	1 237.5	6 516.7	6 102.6
Belgium	39 931.4	31 358.9	32 478.8	21 928.1	142 987.2	17 046.8	23 441.0	18 363.9	16 087.0	17 326.4
Canada	.. d	25 080.0	.. d	25 777.6	17 383.5	44 953.2	25 497.9	25 920.8	30 636.4	.. d
Chile	.. c	.. c	64.0	177.0	113.0	2 076.4	1 886.5	1 504.5	1 364.7	1 451.1
Czech Republic	14.0	244.5	7.4	13.5	.. c	2 610.0	2 588.9	2 301.6	2 864.5	3 040.5
Denmark	10 517.9	9 629.5	8 335.6	9 085.3	10 730.0	10 939.2	8 965.6	8 488.1	6 949.1	8 413.1
Estonia	.. c	-	.. d	1.4	30.5	190.3	243.0	254.6	328.3	328.8
Finland	2 321.4	1 677.5	728.3	1 417.4	1 833.2	1 636.5	1 089.2	1 082.5	737.7	1 110.8
France	118 638.1	103 141.7	73 722.5	92 834.8	83 722.2	59 663.0	89 638.4	88 253.2	96 604.5	98 701.3
Germany	78 145.1	74 831.1	73 599.5	60 671.5	114 095.5	37 060.8	26 286.3	25 709.2	29 363.6	38 571.8
Greece	299.5	1 052.2	145.2	410.8	1 044.8	2 433.7	806.2	338.3	294.6	506.5
Hungary	.. c	213.4	-20.9	258.1	74.9	1 382.2	1 040.3	1 322.4	1 232.3	1 857.3
Iceland	477.4	297.9	.. d	320.2	.. d	35.9	4.4	.. c	9.5	.. d
Ireland	21 430.6	18 241.0	14 128.4	18 897.4	22 181.0	52 678.6	63 484.0	59 292.7	87 562.5	65 801.7
Israel[1]	901.7	.. d	585.6	702.6	.. c	883.0	869.9	.. d	1 299.8	.. d
Italy	6 925.1	11 338.2	6 223.4	11 594.4	7 500.3	15 494.5	16 227.0	15 318.0	13 023.9	20 227.2
Japan	59 644.3	61 144.0	57 189.1	66 968.0	117 392.4	6 382.2	6 664.2	5 411.5	7 213.9	8 933.6
Korea	3 539.8	2 720.8	2 278.3	3 025.3	2 554.3	7 450.9	5 112.6	7 549.5	8 779.9	7 153.7
Latvia	.. c	69.7	.. d	77.0	16.5	.. d	108.2	.. d	293.2	104.1
Lithuania	.. c	1.5	3.7	1.4	12.7	98.3	77.1	52.9	64.9	100.3
Luxembourg	122 987.5	103 286.9	141 221.6	157 273.3	146 397.1	168 620.9	139 059.0	138 730.5	138 135.4	149 007.2
Mexico	.. c	90.4	137.8	143.2	157.4	10 093.6	10 889.2	9 244.7	12 657.7	12 907.2
Netherlands	274 585.0	216 009.2	260 914.0	298 142.1	194 091.7	185 280.8	190 733.6	174 360.9	184 431.8	189 094.8
New Zealand	541.3	779.5	324.8	644.5	1 523.4	1 318.3	1 590.1	1 077.6	1 189.0	1 658.0
Norway	8 405.6	6 702.7	6 562.9	8 744.8	10 609.4	4 143.5	4 976.3	8 408.2	4 988.5	5 379.0
Poland	160.7	429.8	147.6	237.8	1 113.4	7 778.5	8 961.2	7 620.9	9 197.4	8 988.2
Portugal	730.1	806.2	513.0	936.4	1 439.6	3 943.8	4 503.6	4 139.5	4 961.5	5 943.9
Slovak Republic	6.2	237.1	13.5	-1.4	839.2	368.2	354.2	392.4	647.2	652.5
Slovenia	14.0	8.9	3.7	5.4	19.0	168.5	164.5	153.8	154.0	252.6
Spain	71 279.3	56 827.2	37 244.4	55 279.0	63 157.3	25 355.7	66 708.7	68 820.3	85 680.3	92 869.1
Sweden	14 984.4	14 073.8	9 070.0	13 673.8	11 221.3	28 121.7	24 265.0	22 833.1	26 604.5	25 384.0
Switzerland	62 160.7	57 891.2	55 736.3	61 018.8	86 045.4	22 945.4	26 704.2	27 217.4	38 721.8	54 607.1
Turkey	196.6	253.4	120.6	329.7	80.0	5 624.0	9 506.5	9 554.7	9 256.9	8 188.4
United Kingdom	-	-	-	-	-	-	-	-	-	-
United States	394 881.4	458 850.0	379 012.2	379 278.5	424 763.2	374 093.6	351 603.4	296 443.6	358 975.8	400 959.8
EUROPE	**949 558.5**	**806 748.7**	**831 161.3**	**948 009.7**	**1 041 642.8**	**740 121.7**	**791 412.3**	**761 980.6**	**838 956.9**	**884 034.5**
Bulgaria	9.4	7.4	48.0	129.7	34.3	215.3	131.9	66.4	198.6	297.1
Croatia	.. c	-	-	-	.. d	349.5	340.8	294.0	-40.5	25.4
Cyprus[2, 3]	5 784.7	6 157.4	5 212.2	5 080.4	6 802.1	814.4	770.6	3 973.4	3 026.6	4 110.7
Malta	979.7	938.1	830.4	968.8	1 273.3	.. c	3 236.5	.. c	1 871.4	2 357.5
Romania	.. d	13.3	7.4	8.1	14.0	1 313.6	1 310.0	1 216.6	824.2	727.4
Russian Federation	.. c	.. c	1 233.9	.. c	.. c	21 365.1	12 249.6	14 423.7	.. c	13 482.3
Ukraine	.. c	-	48.0	150.0	55.9	346.3	195.6	200.5	-448.6	-43.2
AFRICA	**4 666.1**	**3 608.5**	**2 405.0**	**4 437.2**	**3 258.9**	**66 249.6**	**57 590.4**	**55 471.8**	**44 658.8**	**44 029.5**
Northern Africa	.. c	.. c	253.4	.. c	.. c	16 326.1	.. c	.. c	.. c	10 135.8
Algeria	.. c	.. c	-	-	.. c	.. c	.. c	.. c	.. c	.. c
Egypt	.. c	25.2	22.1	35.1	12.7	9 794.1	.. c	.. c	.. c	.. c
Libya	.. c	.. c	228.8	.. c	.. c	.. c	.. c	-7.4	-8.1	.. c
Morocco	.. c	3.0	1.2	-	3.8	257.4	244.5	251.0	344.5	.. c
Tunisia	.. c	1.5	1.2	.. c	.. c	.. c	1 132.2	9.8	-	2.5
Other African countries	.. d	.. d	2 151.6	.. d	.. d	49 923.6	.. d	.. d	.. d	33 893.6
Nigeria	.. c	.. c	343.2	.. c	.. c	2 305.8	6 108.5	6 318.1	.. c	6 180.0
South Africa	3 455.5	2 279.2	1 283.1	2 995.5	1 930.9	19 755.1	17 138.4	16 511.3	12 221.3	13 250.0
AMERICA	**525 240.3**	**575 829.9**	**506 918.4**	**504 675.0**	**591 551.4**	**555 287.1**	**508 150.6**	**435 309.4**	**488 116.5**	**555 225.3**
Northern America	.. d	483 930.1	.. d	405 056.1	442 145.5	419 046.8	377 102.8	322 376.7	389 619.0	.. d
Central America and Caribbean countries	94 223.1	91 624.2	104 814.9	96 187.0	148 967.9	104 255.9	98 473.6	87 270.3	75 695.2	91 456.1
Bahamas	1 099.8	103.7	899.3	982.3	2 554.3	.. c	.. c	916.5	.. c	.. c
Bermuda	22 890.8	26 338.2	22 099.9	24 192.7	32 525.1	41 273.0	22 046.5	26 139.7	7 742.2	29 221.8
Cayman Islands	29 254.3	28 202.4	33 373.1	31 897.0	47 270.5	29 269.9	26 444.9	16 754.8	.. c	.. c
Costa Rica	-	-	-4.9	-	1.3	255.9	400.1	264.5	56.7	19.0
El Salvador	-	-	-	-	-	7.8	3.0	20.9	52.7	15.2
Guatemala	4 744.2	2 611.1	1 269.5	3 034.7	1 107.0	269.9	134.9	123.0	195.9	368.2
Honduras	-	-	-	-	-	.. c	.. d	.. c	.. c	.. c
Nicaragua	-	-	-	-	-	.. c	.. c	2.5	39.2	.. c
Panama	722.3	340.8	966.9	351.3	1 032.1	.. c	.. c	.. c	.. c	.. c
Virgin Islands, U.S.	-	.. c	11.1	.. c	8.9	-	-	1.2	-24.3	6.3
South America	.. d	277.1	.. d	3 432.0	438.0	31 984.4	32 574.1	25 663.7	22 802.3	.. d
Argentina	149.8	13.3	1.2	1.4	1.3	5 132.6	5 773.6	5 978.6	5 676.3	.. c
Bolivia	-	-	-	-	-	.. c	3.0	4.9	6.8	14.0
Brazil	.. c	211.9	.. c	.. c	312.3	22 937.6	23 184.6	16 604.7	14 784.5	13 333.8
Colombia	.. c	.. c	1.2	-	2.5	945.4	859.5	720.9	535.1	924.2
Ecuador	.. c	.. c	-	.. c	-	59.3	40.0	32.0	58.1	106.6
Paraguay	-	-	-	.. c	-	93.6	.. d	.. d	10.8	19.0
Peru	.. c	1.5	1.2	2.7	5.1	310.5	315.6	220.2	143.2	600.5
Uruguay	-	-	-	-	-	.. c	-81.5	40.6	63.5	90.1
Venezuela	.. c	-	-	-	-	404.1	503.9	479.8	156.7	120.6

Table 2. Foreign direct investment positions by country *(cont.)*

At year end

Million US dollars

	Inward					Outward				
	2014	2015	2016	2017	2018	2014	2015	2016	2017	2018
ASIA	**114 787.8**	**121 621.2**	**118 903.9**	**139 605.5**	**208 843.5**	**188 702.0**	**204 825.1**	**187 341.6**	**210 516.1**	**215 945.2**
Near and Middle East	9 884.6	9 328.7	8 028.0	9 832.5	27 544.8	21 386.9	24 358.3	29 862.2	48 280.0	39 551.9
Gulf Arabian countries	8 503.9	8 183.2	7 063.6	8 665.0	.. d	10 608.4	.. d	.. d	34 156.2	.. d
Kuwait	424.3	389.7	381.4	432.4	634.8	.. c	1.5	17.2	40.5	58.4
Qatar	.. c	143.7	62.7	145.9	.. c	143.5	168.9	200.5	.. c	209.5
Saudi Arabia	79.6	47.4	109.5	277.0	818.8	4 780.0	5 117.1	4 638.9	5 660.0	5 726.8
United Arab Emirates	6 318.3	.. c	5 274.9	6 481.6	6 262.5	2 879.9	2 347.4	6 256.6	8 308.3	13 220.8
Other Near and Middle East	1 380.7	1 147.0	963.2	1 167.4	.. c	10 778.5	.. c	.. c	14 123.8	.. c
Jordan	.. c	.. c	.. d	.. c	.. c	1 137.3	.. c	.. c	.. c	19.0
Other Asian countries	104 903.3	112 291.0	110 875.9	129 771.7	181 298.7	167 315.1	180 466.8	157 479.4	162 236.2	176 393.3
China	1 789.4	3 350.6	1 874.8	3 102.3	4 576.6	11 602.2	14 614.7	14 276.0	11 268.7	16 665.0
Hong Kong, China	19 887.7	16 135.2	.. c	27 569.2	27 753.0	81 641.2	81 575.3	75 429.9	.. c	90 990.2
India	3 316.7	3 916.7	1 830.5	10 772.9	3 022.7	4 893.9	17 956.4	16 223.4	17 726.0	18 456.3
Indonesia	.. c	.. c	.. c	-	-	7 060.8	6 779.8	7 229.7	6 170.8	6 781.8
Iran, Islamic Republic of	.. c	.. c	301.4	.. c	.. c	.. c	.. c	.. c	21.6	30.5
Malaysia	712.9	632.8	321.1	760.7	1 022.0	5 081.1	4 761.4	4 215.8	4 514.3	3 856.8
Philippines	.. c	.. c	98.4	.. d	69.8	252.7	265.3	.. d	370.2	889.9
Singapore	13 482.1	22 766.7	22 418.5	12 241.6	22 999.9	26 112.3	27 709.0	13 125.8	8 882.6	11 712.6
Chinese Taipei	207.5	143.7	76.3	197.3	137.1	3 631.8	3 586.2	3 667.1	5 042.6	4 353.2
Thailand	402.5	206.0	152.5	471.6	985.1	4 269.9	2 605.2	2 973.3	2 968.5	3 540.7
Viet Nam	.. c	1.5	.. c	-	5.1	.. c	90.4	238.7	206.7	.. c
AUSTRALIA, OCEANIA AND POLAR REGIONS	**18 998.4**	**22 323.7**	**16 136.1**	**11 305.2**	**19 041.5**	**33 301.1**	**44 385.0**	**51 836.6**	**41 982.2**	**51 569.1**
WORLD unallocated and confidential	-	**1.5**	**-1.2**	-	-	-	**1.5**	-	**1.4**	-
European Union (EU28)	**773 397.8**	**653 278.0**	**666 208.6**	**752 218.6**	**814 943.5**	**630 416.5**	**675 997.3**	**647 232.1**	**717 615.2**	**741 901.7**
G20 countries excl. European Union	.. d	.. d	.. d	.. d	.. d	**689 380.7**	**686 101.1**	**629 779.8**	.. d	.. d
G20 OECD countries	.. d	**758 747.8**	.. d	**650 160.8**	**785 122.5**	**591 853.4**	**583 286.9**	**533 893.5**	**607 847.6**	.. d
G20 Non-OECD countries	.. c	.. d	.. d	.. d	.. d	**97 527.3**	**102 814.2**	**95 886.3**	.. d	.. d
MENA countries	.. d	.. d	.. d	.. d	.. d	.. c	.. d	.. d	.. d	.. d
ASEAN countries	**15 296.4**	**24 398.3**	**24 397.8**	**14 764.2**	.. d	**44 482.1**	**43 375.8**	**29 233.6**	**25 014.2**	**29 560.7**

- Nil; .. Not available; c Confidential data; d Secondary Confidentiality

Note: Detailed metadata at: *http://stats.oecd.org/OECDStat_Metadata/ShowMetadata.ashx?Dataset=FDI_CTRY_IND_SUMM*.

1. Information on data for Israel: *http://oe.cd/israel-disclaimer*.
2. Note by Turkey: The information in this document with reference to "Cyprus" relates to the southern part of the Island. There is no single authority representing both Turkish and Greek Cypriot people on the Island. Turkey recognises the Turkish Republic of Northern Cyprus (TRNC). Until a lasting and equitable solution is found within the context of the United Nations, Turkey shall preserve its position concerning the "Cyprus issue".
3. Note by all the European Union Member States of the OECD and the European Union: The Republic of Cyprus is recognised by all members of the United Nations with the exception of Turkey. The information in this document relates to the area under the effective control of the Government of the Republic of Cyprus.

Source: OECD International Direct Investment Statistics (database): https://doi.org/10.1787/idi-data-en

UNITED KINGDOM

Table 3. Foreign direct investment income by country

Million US dollars

	Inward					Outward				
	2014	2015	2016	2017	2018	2014	2015	2016	2017	2018
WORLD	**86 183.7**	**73 579.8**	**70 274.0**	**67 481.3**	**92 655.7**	**108 019.4**	**87 384.3**	**68 005.4**	**95 923.3**	**119 289.0**
OECD COUNTRIES	**71 172.2**	**60 730.3**	**54 981.1**	**59 286.6**	**79 241.0**	**61 753.4**	**52 395.7**	**41 728.7**	**62 389.9**	**77 589.7**
Australia	624.0	-433.9	-835.4	-288.4	-540.2	4 306.9	3 436.2	2 580.3	5 269.1	4 906.0
Austria	278.2	48.9	108.0	96.6	104.0	.. c	18.3	226.7	283.3	213.4
Belgium	2 749.4	2 363.6	2 807.0	2 356.4	2 218.2	767.2	543.9	1 944.7	1 551.6	2 394.3
Canada	.. d	473.6	1 503.4	-324.5	.. d	.. c	.. d	2 603.2	.. d	3 183.9
Chile	.. c	3.1	6.7	5.2	1.3	153.1	136.0	183.5	445.5	262.8
Czech Republic	1.6	12.2	-	-1.3	.. c	293.1	203.2	117.4	39.9	206.7
Denmark	.. c	944.2	1 013.5	149.4	545.6	594.3	403.4	782.7	1 201.4	489.5
Estonia	.. c	-	-	-	-	24.7	16.8	1.4	3.9	1.3
Finland	230.5	116.1	-10.8	59.2	104.0	339.2	157.4	136.3	70.8	209.4
France	5 340.8	4 045.8	-156.5	1 604.4	4 236.4	.. c	3 916.0	3 175.4	3 847.5	3 193.3
Germany	9 328.3	6 540.9	7 066.1	3 416.2	10 262.8	.. c	3 703.6	2 916.3	4 402.5	3 161.3
Greece	112.0	81.0	64.8	28.3	64.0	116.9	3.1	32.4	70.8	88.0
Hungary	3.3	18.3	1.4	-18.0	-1.3	.. c	134.5	124.2	154.5	238.8
Iceland	37.9	.. d	.. d	.. d	12.0	3.3	-	1.4	-	-
Ireland	722.8	1 489.7	369.8	1 103.5	1 365.9	2 023.4	1 809.0	6 047.2	4 465.6	5 150.1
Israel[1]	87.3	.. d	.. d	29.6	.. c	344.1	.. d	.. d	.. d	218.8
Italy	910.4	417.1	390.0	600.1	428.2	1 109.6	1 113.8	628.9	920.7	417.5
Japan	3 368.5	2 450.7	4 247.0	8 593.9	7 249.6	648.7	470.6	1 346.8	819.0	496.2
Korea	.. c	45.8	133.6	212.5	.. c	931.8	351.4	620.8	892.4	943.0
Latvia	.. c	4.6	1.4	.. d	2.7	.. c	.. d	.. d	.. c	.. d
Lithuania	.. c	-	1.4	.. c	-	9.9	19.9	6.7	15.5	2.7
Luxembourg	2 528.8	1 798.3	1 638.3	2 259.9	1 163.1	3 585.8	1 680.7	.. c	3 274.5	3 266.6
Mexico	.. c	1.5	12.1	11.6	-	1 183.7	1 219.3	919.0	1 254.2	1 315.2
Netherlands	9 000.7	5 156.6	4 527.7	2 603.7	4 635.2	8 995.7	6 010.7	3 132.3	8 555.2	11 300.5
New Zealand	51.0	33.6	27.0	1.3	18.7	268.4	.. d	287.4	338.7	325.5
Norway	1 249.6	313.2	35.1	140.4	.. c	.. c	6.1	-242.9	631.0	956.4
Poland	13.2	15.3	5.4	11.6	16.0	1 024.0	547.0	642.4	920.7	720.3
Portugal	256.8	186.4	129.6	47.6	38.7	233.8	74.9	4.0	172.5	257.4
Slovak Republic	.. c	10.7	-	-	14.7	84.0	65.7	41.8	81.1	53.4
Slovenia	.. c	-	-	-	-	23.0	22.9	18.9	15.5	10.7
Spain	5 235.4	3 217.7	3 052.6	3 251.4	7 563.0	1 656.2	1 341.5	1 450.7	1 813.0	1 978.1
Sweden	1 468.6	999.2	743.6	1 220.7	621.6	2 920.6	3 107.7	3 263.2	1 746.1	.. c
Switzerland	1 236.4	2 158.9	2 731.4	5 923.3	5 204.7	1 906.5	3 749.4	3 824.6	2 472.3	2 862.5
Turkey	19.8	7.6	8.1	7.7	21.3	.. c	22.9	6.7	197.0	333.5
United Kingdom	-	-	-	-	-	-	-	-	-	-
United States	23 154.4	27 862.5	25 295.5	26 149.9	29 937.3	25 923.6	17 746.4	3 456.1	14 439.9	25 239.4
EUROPE	**44 879.8**	**33 566.1**	**29 561.4**	**28 839.8**	**45 442.2**	**33 847.5**	**33 760.1**	**33 303.6**	**41 867.1**	**48 578.1**
Bulgaria	.. c	-1.5	4.0	-1.3	1.3	34.6	22.9	9.4	14.2	2.7
Croatia	.. c	-	-	.. c	.. d	.. d	47.4	36.4	-5.2	.. d
Cyprus[2, 3]	503.8	433.9	465.6	479.0	1 025.7	.. c	10.7	-29.7	.. c	.. c
Malta	261.8	3.1	33.7	142.9	73.4	.. c	.. c	202.4	-33.5	20.0
Romania	-	1.5	-	.. d	-1.3	171.2	195.6	222.7	95.3	128.1
Russian Federation	.. c	.. c	-63.4	-18.0	.. c	2 132.0	1 816.7	1 047.2	1 035.3	.. c
Ukraine	.. c	-	5.4	5.2	1.3	.. c	-35.1	.. c	-12.9	74.7
AFRICA	**.. c**	**129.9**	**58.0**	**-240.8**	**105.4**	**6 172.2**	**1 969.4**	**3 757.1**	**4 222.3**	**6 378.6**
Northern Africa	.. c	.. c	6.7	5.2	-1.3	.. c	-554.6	.. d	.. d	.. d
Algeria	.. c	.. c	-	.. c	.. c	.. c	38.2	.. c	.. c	.. c
Egypt	1.6	1.5	2.7	1.3	-1.3	518.6	33.6	-36.4	-197.0	49.4
Libya	.. c	.. c	5.4	.. c	-	.. c	.. c	1.4	-	-1.3
Morocco	.. c	-	-	-	-	-123.5	-10.7	-67.5	1.3	-24.0
Tunisia	.. c	-	-	.. c	.. c	.. c	.. d	-1.4	-3.9	-
Other African countries	.. c	.. d	51.3	-245.9	105.4	.. d	2 525.6	.. d	.. d	.. d
Nigeria	.. c	.. c	48.6	.. c	.. c	1 121.2	.. c	237.5	339.9	490.9
South Africa	.. c	79.5	-39.1	-279.4	-8.0	2 558.4	2 635.6	2 261.8	2 868.9	2 118.2
AMERICA	**32 143.6**	**32 861.7**	**33 415.7**	**27 531.5**	**36 154.5**	**37 431.7**	**25 642.5**	**11 785.4**	**21 917.3**	**36 297.2**
Northern America	.. d	28 334.6	26 798.9	25 825.4	.. d	.. d	.. d	6 059.4	.. d	28 423.4
Central America and Caribbean countries	5 882.5	4 510.3	6 596.5	1 702.3	4 823.3	8 156.1	6 279.6	4 835.4	4 026.5	6 710.7
Bahamas	278.2	22.9	17.5	36.1	268.1	.. c	181.8	101.2	.. c	.. c
Bermuda	2 535.4	1 650.1	1 966.3	355.4	644.3	4 028.6	.. c	1 071.5	.. c	2 883.8
Cayman Islands	1 420.8	951.9	1 496.6	-21.9	2 048.8	1 969.0	2 562.3	1 504.7	1 568.4	.. c
Costa Rica	-	-	-1.4	-	-	51.0	.. c	13.5	.. c	-9.3
El Salvador	-	-	-	-	-	.. c	-	-	-1.3	1.3
Guatemala	324.3	162.0	95.8	81.1	58.7	14.8	16.8	-5.4	18.0	-5.3
Honduras	-	-	-	-	-	.. c	.. c	-2.7	2.6	.. c
Nicaragua	-	-	-	-	-	.. c	-6.1	-2.7	1.3	-
Panama	51.0	-12.2	33.7	-25.8	.. c	.. c	272.0	242.9	3.9	.. c
Virgin Islands, U.S.	.. c	.. c	-	.. c	-	-	-	1.4	-2.6	1.3
South America	.. d	15.3	18.9	5.2	.. d	.. d	.. d	889.3	.. d	1 163.1
Argentina	8.2	.. d	-	-	.. d	637.1	686.0	.. d	.. d	266.8
Bolivia	-	-	-	-	-	.. c	-	-	-	2.7
Brazil	6.6	10.7	12.1	-2.6	4.0	2 074.4	1 417.9	51.3	571.7	545.6
Colombia	.. c	-	-	.. c	-	.. c	-27.5	1.4	9.0	65.4
Ecuador	.. c	.. c	-	.. c	-	9.9	6.1	5.4	5.2	4.0
Paraguay	-	-	-	.. c	-	.. c	15.3	.. d	1.3	2.7
Peru	.. c	-	-	-	-	47.7	74.9	79.6	86.3	102.7
Uruguay	-	-	-	-	-	-95.5	-33.6	20.2	10.3	1.3
Venezuela	.. c	-	-	-	-	97.1	.. c	9.4	42.5	.. c

Table 3. Foreign direct investment income by country *(cont.)*

Million US dollars

	Inward					Outward				
	2014	2015	2016	2017	2018	2014	2015	2016	2017	2018
ASIA	**8 972.7**	**7 417.9**	**7 450.7**	**13 230.7**	**11 523.3**	**25 790.3**	**22 071.8**	**16 130.9**	**21 202.7**	**21 903.4**
Near and Middle East	870.9	1 318.6	187.6	206.0	.. c	4 084.6	2 495.0	1 673.4	3 423.9	3 434.7
Gulf Arabian countries	765.6	1 277.3	161.9	172.5	130.7	1 883.4	.. d	1 305.0	2 428.5	2 095.5
Kuwait	.. c	.. c	-5.4	1.3	4.0	.. c	.. c	.. c	.. c	.. c
Qatar	.. c	6.1	1.4	-2.6	146.7	19.8	33.6	33.7	.. c	22.7
Saudi Arabia	3.3	-	-2.7	-3.9	8.0	745.8	829.6	686.9	913.0	633.6
United Arab Emirates	727.7	1 252.9	148.4	161.0	33.3	770.5	490.5	377.9	.. c	765.6
Other Near and Middle East	105.4	42.8	25.6	33.5	.. c	2 201.2	.. c	368.4	995.4	1 339.2
Jordan	.. c	.. c	.. d	1.3	-	.. c	16.8	.. d	3.9	1.3
Other Asian countries	8 101.7	6 099.3	7 263.2	13 026.0	.. d	21 705.6	19 576.8	14 457.5	17 780.1	18 468.7
China	334.2	64.2	5.4	-56.7	-60.0	831.4	1 819.7	2 615.4	2 017.8	2 175.5
Hong Kong, China	1 569.0	2 429.3	2 129.6	.. c	.. c	7 823.5	7 793.7	4 365.7	8 338.9	7 084.2
India	289.8	226.1	558.7	2 146.5	422.8	2 240.7	2 395.7	1 523.6	1 276.1	1 756.7
Indonesia	.. c	.. c	.. c	.. c	-	1 297.3	635.6	885.3	256.2	1 004.4
Iran, Islamic Republic of	.. c	-	1.4	.. c	1.3	.. c	.. c	.. c	-	1.3
Malaysia	172.9	30.6	-141.7	20.6	1.3	1 595.3	1 544.7	697.7	1 198.8	992.4
Philippines	.. c	.. c	.. d	5.2	5.3	90.6	.. d	207.8	153.2	208.1
Singapore	.. c	741.0	542.5	391.5	124.1	2 751.1	1 954.2	310.4	834.4	1 684.7
Chinese Taipei	14.8	7.6	6.7	6.4	1.3	561.4	382.0	345.5	358.0	188.1
Thailand	39.5	.. c	8.1	6.4	28.0	498.8	310.2	276.7	381.1	270.8
Viet Nam	.. c	-	.. c	-	-	184.4	294.9	233.5	279.4	268.1
AUSTRALIA, OCEANIA AND POLAR REGIONS	**.. c**	**-395.7**	**-211.9**	**-1 880.0**	**-568.2**	**4 777.7**	**3 940.4**	**3 028.3**	**6 712.6**	**6 131.8**
WORLD unallocated and confidential	**-487.3**	**-**	**-**	**-**	**-1.3**	**-**	**-**	**-**	**1.3**	**-**
European Union (EU28)	**39 214.7**	**27 903.7**	**22 259.1**	**19 488.8**	**34 539.1**	**25 977.9**	**25 457.6**	**26 484.5**	**34 195.2**	**37 895.2**
G20 countries excl. European Union	**.. d**	**.. d**	**.. d**	**.. d**	**.. d**	**.. c**	**.. d**	**.. d**	**.. d**	**.. d**
G20 OECD countries	**.. d**	**41 411.8**	**37 664.0**	**39 983.3**	**.. d**	**.. c**	**.. d**	**18 253.7**	**.. d**	**43 189.3**
G20 Non-OECD countries	**.. c**	**.. d**	**.. d**	**.. d**	**.. d**	**12 517.3**	**12 236.8**	**.. d**	**.. d**	**.. d**
MENA countries	**.. d**	**.. d**	**.. d**	**.. d**	**.. d**	**.. c**	**.. d**	**.. d**	**.. d**	**.. d**
ASEAN countries	**.. c**	**864.8**	**201.1**	**445.5**	**.. d**	**6 898.3**	**4 968.7**	**2 637.0**	**3 145.8**	**4 717.9**

- Nil; .. Not available; c Confidential data; d Secondary Confidentiality

Note: Detailed metadata at: *http://stats.oecd.org/OECDStat_Metadata/ShowMetadata.ashx?Dataset=FDI_CTRY_IND_SUMM.*

1. Information on data for Israel: *http://oe.cd/israel-disclaimer*.
2. Note by Turkey: The information in this document with reference to “Cyprus” relates to the southern part of the Island. There is no single authority representing both Turkish and Greek Cypriot people on the Island. Turkey recognises the Turkish Republic of Northern Cyprus (TRNC). Until a lasting and equitable solution is found within the context of the United Nations, Turkey shall preserve its position concerning the “Cyprus issue”.
3. Note by all the European Union Member States of the OECD and the European Union: The Republic of Cyprus is recognised by all members of the United Nations with the exception of Turkey. The information in this document relates to the area under the effective control of the Government of the Republic of Cyprus.

Source: OECD International Direct Investment Statistics (database): https://doi.org/10.1787/idi-data-en

Table 4. Foreign direct investment flows by industrial sector

Million US dollars

	Inward					Outward				
	2014	2015	2016	2017	2018	2014	2015	2016	2017	2018
All FDI activities	**45 831.4**	**38 669.2**	**196 503.4**	**78 511.5**	**83 854.9**	**.. c**	**-65 561.5**	**-22 310.4**	**106 692.0**	**84 616.5**
Agriculture, forestry and fishing	**-107.0**	**.. d**	**.. d**	**..**	**..**	**24.7**	**155.8**	**.. d**	**..**	**..**
Mining and quarrying	**17 393.8**	**.. c**	**-5 006.7**	**..**	**..**	**.. c**	**-55 168.8**	**-10 352.2**	**..**	**..**
Extraction activities	17 497.5	.. c	-5 363.0	..	..	.. c	-31 489.7	-7 040.5	..	..
Manufacturing	**18 063.9**	**4 058.1**	**.. c**	**..**	**..**	**9 486.3**	**-2 756.3**	**-19 759.8**	**..**	**..**
of which:										
Food products, beverages and tobacco	10 131.7	913.7	.. c	..	..	.. c	-2 273.5	.. c	..	..
Textiles, wood and paper products; printing	490.6	631.0	-1 206.5	..	..	.. c	297.9	676.1	..	..
Chemical, rubber, plastic, non-metallic mineral products	.. c	-753.2	4 753.0	..	..	.. c	621.8	-20 716.6	..	..
Metal and machinery products, except electrical equipment	577.9	4 890.8	-3 666.7	..	..	-5 116.9	-293.4	-20.2	..	..
Motor vehicles, trailers, semi-trailers, other transport equipment	.. c	2 942.7	190.3	..	..	3 253.2	.. c	.. c	..	..
Other manufacturing	.. c	-4 568.4	.. c	..	..	6 867.0	.. d	-744.9	..	..
Electricity, gas, steam and air conditioning supply	**-4 993.4**	**2 145.1**	**948.7**	**..**	**..**	**.. c**	**-499.6**	**2 480.4**	**..**	**..**
Water supply; sewerage, waste management and remediation activities	**.. c**	**762.4**	**155.2**	**..**	**..**	**.. c**	**.. c**	**232.1**	**..**	**..**
Construction	**.. c**	**1 509.5**	**632.9**	**..**	**..**	**-2 133.7**	**-32.1**	**228.1**	**..**	**..**
Services	**.. c**	**59 229.9**	**90 098.5**	**..**	**..**	**.. c**	**.. c**	**4 178.1**	**..**	**..**
Wholesale and retail trade; repair of motor vehicles and motorcycles	-11 718.8	-5 778.5	-776.0	..	..	.. c	-5 064.9	2 920.4	..	..
Transportation and storage	.. c	5 110.8	4 045.9	..	..	875.9	1 951.1	2 446.7	..	..
Accommodation and food service activities	-382.0	2 187.9	556.0	..	..	.. c	4 288.8	3 863.7	..	..
Information and communication	-2 609.5	11 618.0	6 530.4	..	..	.. c	-2 939.6	-2 383.3	..	..
Financial and insurance activities	24 702.0	33 865.5	33 583.0	..	..	-34 257.5	-12 719.6	-2 970.3	..	..
Activities of holding companies	.. c	.. c	2 979.8	..	..	.. c	.. c	4 287.4	..	..
Real estate activities	.. c	.. c	691.0	..	..	568.0	2 019.9	.. c	..	..
Professional, scientific and technical activities	956.5	11 020.6	40 257.8	..	..	6 847.2	.. c	1 052.6	..	..
Administrative and support service activities	.. c	-1 709.7	5 153.8	..	..	3 003.0	935.1	414.3	..	..
Public administration; activities of households and of extraterritorial organisations	.. c	.. d	-5.4	..	..	.. c	.. c	.. c	..	..
Education	637.1	-162.0	16.2	..	..	.. c	.. c	577.6	..	..
Human health and social work activities	-56.0	759.4	36.4	..	..	.. c	59.6	.. c	..	..
Arts, entertainment and recreation	-847.9	22.9	484.5	..	..	.. c	90.1	-17.5	..	..
Other services	-112.0	13.8	-477.7	..	..	-3.3	29.0	-18.9	..	..
Not allocated and confidential	**.. d**	**.. c**	**.. c**	**78 511.5**	**..**	**.. d**	**.. c**	**.. d**	**106 692.0**	**..**
Private real estate activities	**.. c**	**-**	**975.7**	**..**	**..**	**.. c**	**.. c**	**354.9**	**..**	**..**

- Nil; .. Not available; c Confidential data; d Secondary Confidentiality

Note: Detailed metadata at: *http://stats.oecd.org/OECDStat_Metadata/ShowMetadata.ashx?Dataset=FDI_CTRY_IND_SUMM.*

Source: *OECD International Direct Investment Statistics (database): https://doi.org/10.1787/idi-data-en*

Table 5. Foreign direct investment positions by industrial sector

At year end

Million US dollars

	Inward					Outward				
	2014	2015	2016	2017	2018	2014	2015	2016	2017	2018
All FDI activities	**1 613 251.2**	**1 530 133.4**	**1 475 523.4**	**1 608 032.7**	**1 864 337.9**	**1 583 661.5**	**1 606 364.8**	**1 491 940.0**	**1 624 231.9**	**1 750 803.6**
Agriculture, forestry and fishing	**.. d**	**.. d**	**1 264.6**	..	..	**1 828.4**	**2 110.3**	**2 510.8**	..	..
Mining and quarrying	**153 784.7**	**119 963.0**	**132 329.9**	..	..	**297 151.3**	**253 109.1**	**202 806.0**	..	..
Extraction activities	151 895.5	118 995.3	130 880.8	..	..	263 034.3	249 428.0	212 398.8	..	..
Manufacturing	**325 931.4**	**276 431.5**	**334 730.0**	..	..	**276 259.0**	**278 878.2**	**258 536.1**	..	..
of which:										
Food products, beverages and tobacco	106 271.5	68 039.4	157 723.0	..	..	71 255.9	80 726.1	75 635.4	..	..
Textiles, wood and paper products; printing	13 528.9	11 218.1	6 014.3	..	..	2 042.1	1 132.2	3 001.6	..	..
Chemical, rubber, plastic, non-metallic mineral products	44 897.0	53 703.3	49 282.8	..	..	100 363.5	102 458.5	94 373.2	..	..
Metal and machinery products, except electrical equipment	76 341.7	68 149.1	54 824.7	..	..	30 190.3	26 689.4	22 262.3	..	..
Motor vehicles, trailers, semi-trailers, other transport equipment	26 953.2	22 302.9	18 538.6	..	..	20 464.9	21 032.9	18 020.7	..	..
Other manufacturing	57 939.2	53 020.2	48 346.7	..	..	51 942.3	46 840.5	45 243.0	..	..
Electricity, gas, steam and air conditioning supply	**73 655.2**	**66 665.7**	**54 853.0**	..	..	**12 890.8**	**.. c**	**.. c**	..	..
Water supply; sewerage, waste management and remediation activities	**4 535.1**	**4 198.3**	**3 333.7**	..	..	**1 447.7**	**.. c**	**1 987.9**	..	..
Construction	**21 212.2**	**11 510.1**	**11 789.9**	..	..	**2 363.5**	**2 036.2**	**1 732.1**	..	..
Services	**1 025 844.0**	**1 030 195.6**	**919 501.8**	..	..	**.. c**	**923 218.7**	**875 655.1**	..	..
Wholesale and retail trade; repair of motor vehicles and motorcycles	212 090.5	185 336.4	149 114.3	..	..	64 282.4	65 988.4	60 396.1	..	..
Transportation and storage	64 308.9	57 025.8	59 575.6	..	..	24 446.2	28 163.9	28 931.0	..	..
Accommodation and food service activities	11 589.7	28 366.9	26 292.3	..	..	43 429.0	39 589.5	34 191.2	..	..
Information and communication	134 363.5	127 621.5	98 525.0	..	..	154 358.8	163 784.8	151 643.5	..	..
Financial and insurance activities	436 567.9	477 211.0	443 907.0	..	..	576 968.8	526 796.1	518 002.2	..	..
Activities of holding companies	1 009.4	514.2	16.0	..	..	.. c	.. c	147 121.4	..	..
Real estate activities	7 096.7	8 867.8	7 582.7	..	..	11 475.8	9 930.4	12 874.9	..	..
Professional, scientific and technical activities	82 188.8	94 248.7	87 481.9	..	..	44 808.1	49 832.5	45 967.5	..	..
Administrative and support service activities	52 159.1	41 273.0	36 081.9	..	..	29 472.7	29 548.0	18 024.4	..	..
Public administration; activities of households and of extraterritorial organisations	1.6	3.0	1.2	..	..	386.9	.. d	.. c	..	..
Education	2 982.8	1 892.4	2 409.9	..	..	887.7	.. c	5 345.1	..	..
Human health and social work activities	4 803.4	2 249.6	1 675.5	..	..	160.7	280.1	654.4	..	..
Arts, entertainment and recreation	10 269.9	4 813.3	5 553.0	..	..	2 895.5	3 681.1	1 614.0	..	..
Other services	7 421.2	1 286.3	1 301.5	..	..	244.9	238.6	.. d	..	..
Not allocated and confidential	**8 288.6**	**.. c**	**-**	**1 608 032.7**	..	**.. d**	**.. c**	**.. c**	**1 624 231.9**	..
Private real estate activities	**.. c**	**.. c**	**17 720.5**	..	..	**.. c**	**.. c**	**130 103.3**	..	..

- Nil; .. Not available; c Confidential data; d Secondary Confidentiality

Note: Detailed metadata at: *http://stats.oecd.org/OECDStat_Metadata/ShowMetadata.ashx?Dataset=FDI_CTRY_IND_SUMM.*

Source: *OECD International Direct Investment Statistics (database): https://doi.org/10.1787/idi-data-en*

Table 6. Foreign direct investment income by industrial sector

Million US dollars

	Inward					Outward				
	2014	2015	2016	2017	2018	2014	2015	2016	2017	2018
All FDI activities	**86 183.7**	**73 579.8**	**70 274.0**	**67 481.3**	**92 655.7**	**108 019.4**	**87 384.3**	**68 005.4**	**95 923.3**	**119 289.0**
Agriculture, forestry and fishing	**.. d**	**.. d**	**44.5**	..	..	**130.1**	**162.0**	**.. d**	..	..
Mining and quarrying	**10 056.0**	**1 943.5**	**.. c**	..	..	**24 163.6**	**342.2**	**940.6**	..	..
Extraction activities	10 026.3	1 922.1	.. c	..	..	22 787.3	4 837.3	-2 183.5	..	..
Manufacturing	**15 095.5**	**12 991.6**	**13 948.7**	..	..	**24 807.4**	**29 524.8**	**21 915.0**	..	..
of which:										
Food products, beverages and tobacco	4 262.4	2 866.3	2 179.5	..	..	7 721.4	9 538.6	5 726.0	..	..
Textiles, wood and paper products; printing	727.7	485.9	539.8	..	..	.. c	470.6	847.5	..	..
Chemical, rubber, plastic, non-metallic mineral products	1 717.2	3 252.9	3 040.5	..	..	9 921.0	13 214.7	10 425.1	..	..
Metal and machinery products, except electrical equipment	2 607.8	1 949.6	1 851.6	..	..	2 362.5	2 129.9	1 893.4	..	..
Motor vehicles, trailers, semi-trailers, other transport equipment	4 874.9	3 223.8	2 913.6	..	..	2 100.8	2 328.5	2 164.6	..	..
Other manufacturing	905.5	1 213.1	3 422.4	..	..	.. d	1 841.1	857.0	..	..
Electricity, gas, steam and air conditioning supply	**4 730.0**	**4 909.1**	**4 485.8**	..	..	**.. c**	**.. c**	**1 290.1**	..	..
Water supply; sewerage, waste management and remediation activities	**214.0**	**357.5**	**.. c**	..	..	**.. c**	**137.5**	**230.8**	..	..
Construction	**1 094.8**	**628.0**	**-570.9**	..	..	**172.9**	**201.7**	**256.4**	..	..
Services	**.. c**	**52 531.7**	**50 503.4**	..	..	**.. c**	**53 902.2**	**41 396.8**	..	..
Wholesale and retail trade; repair of motor vehicles and motorcycles	10 271.7	9 196.3	9 179.5	..	..	824.8	1 861.0	3 870.4	..	..
Transportation and storage	5 293.1	5 778.5	5 427.8	..	..	1 101.4	965.6	1 021.6	..	..
Accommodation and food service activities	549.9	698.2	.. c	..	..	7 090.9	7 398.0	6 897.4	..	..
Information and communication	4 975.3	7 356.8	2 956.8	..	..	4 237.7	5 398.0	4 124.2	..	..
Financial and insurance activities	27 625.9	29 288.0	28 310.4	..	..	36 083.3	30 583.7	19 581.6	..	..
Activities of holding companies	.. c	.. c	2 558.7	..	..	.. c	.. c	5 160.6	..	..
Real estate activities	182.7	363.6	193.0	..	..	900.6	1 081.7	689.6	..	..
Professional, scientific and technical activities	3 427.7	-1 469.8	4 106.6	..	..	3 394.8	3 931.2	2 522.3	..	..
Administrative and support service activities	1 789.6	1 359.8	1 336.0	..	..	1 315.4	1 323.1	1 442.6	..	..
Public administration; activities of households and of extraterritorial organisations	.. c	-	.. d	..	..	.. c	.. c	.. c	..	..
Education	.. c	-59.6	-64.8	..	..	.. c	.. c	630.2	..	..
Human health and social work activities	357.3	58.1	8.1	..	..	.. c	-10.7	-1.4	..	..
Arts, entertainment and recreation	.. c	-77.9	20.2	..	..	322.7	302.5	161.9	..	..
Other services	181.1	39.7	78.3	..	..	19.8	27.5	.. d	..	..
Not allocated and confidential	**.. d**	**.. c**	**.. c**	**67 481.3**	..	**.. d**	**.. c**	**.. d**	**95 923.3**	..
Private real estate activities	**.. c**	**.. c**	**147.1**	..	..	**.. c**	**.. c**	**1 662.6**	..	..

- Nil; .. Not available; c Confidential data; d Secondary Confidentiality

Note: Detailed metadata at: *http://stats.oecd.org/OECDStat_Metadata/ShowMetadata.ashx?Dataset=FDI_CTRY_IND_SUMM.*

Source: OECD International Direct Investment Statistics (database): https://doi.org/10.1787/idi-data-en

UNITED STATES

Table 1. Foreign direct investment flows by country

Million US dollars

	Inward					Outward				
	2014	2015	2016	2017	2018	2014	2015	2016	2017	2018
WORLD	**201 733.0**	**467 625.0**	**471 792.0**	**277 258.0**	**253 561.0**	**333 014.0**	**264 359.0**	**289 261.0**	**300 378.0**	**-90 623.0**
OECD COUNTRIES	..	..	.. d	..	.. d	..	**181 055.0**	.. d	..	.. d
Australia	1 098.0	10 587.0	4 715.0	-905.0	3 204.0	17 489.0	271.0	6 739.0	-414.0	-2 992.0
Austria	983.0	198.0	3 482.0	1 788.0	-443.0	299.0	92.0	310.0	1 030.0	575.0
Belgium	11 410.0	-12 327.0	3 363.0	5 982.0	6 015.0	-663.0	3 014.0	2 522.0	1 318.0	9 937.0
Canada	23 479.0	58 887.0	67 053.0	71 904.0	47 469.0	30 691.0	10 114.0	13 822.0	18 624.0	19 695.0
Chile	67.0	158.0	92.0	123.0	445.0	617.0	1 450.0	346.0	-1 793.0	363.0
Czech Republic	-4.0	30.0	-4.0	11.0	-59.0	628.0	433.0	-497.0	246.0	1 394.0
Denmark	3 282.0	1 013.0	3 616.0	176.0	2 041.0	896.0	-122.0	1 758.0	-1 763.0	-1 114.0
Estonia	-	-	.. c	-	1.0	7.0	-2.0	-80.0	6.0	11.0
Finland	-1 455.0	655.0	-79.0	829.0	1 459.0	-111.0	-1 322.0	2 055.0	-444.0	-384.0
France	10 197.0	33 472.0	28 104.0	20 757.0	23 440.0	1 517.0	4 156.0	1 053.0	2 742.0	1 560.0
Germany	37 121.0	25 353.0	14 931.0	11 899.0	26 795.0	-115.0	1 691.0	4 424.0	2 148.0	2 632.0
Greece	-28.0	35.0	45.0	-24.0	.. c	42.0	1 054.0	45.0	62.0	100.0
Hungary	4 452.0	-5 312.0	-854.0	1 629.0	.. c	184.0	163.0	-476.0	510.0	1 212.0
Iceland	.. c	.. c	.. c	.. c	-40.0	25.0	131.0	.. c	68.0	.. c
Ireland	7 114.0	14 892.0	36 695.0	17 269.0	64 187.0	47 993.0	69 631.0	50 035.0	44 669.0	-10 522.0
Israel[1]	-1 198.0	952.0	116.0	-243.0	1 671.0	925.0	553.0	463.0	734.0	581.0
Italy	4 071.0	6 924.0	608.0	262.0	2 367.0	1 846.0	800.0	-74.0	705.0	7 551.0
Japan	44 891.0	32 997.0	31 610.0	43 868.0	22 200.0	-13 003.0	5 177.0	-1 398.0	9 653.0	3 289.0
Korea	9 024.0	1 302.0	3 392.0	10 392.0	5 218.0	4 795.0	2 225.0	1 902.0	1 693.0	-455.0
Latvia	.. c	.. c	.. c	.. c	.. c	24.0	8.0	11.0	10.0	8.0
Lithuania	.. c	.. c	.. c	.. c	.. c	27.0	-34.0	4.0	13.0	17.0
Luxembourg	27 943.0	172 740.0	57 398.0	2 477.0	-110 388.0	37 125.0	-365.0	30 833.0	33 444.0	37 632.0
Mexico	1 742.0	1 116.0	2 372.0	702.0	-260.0	8 218.0	7 255.0	5 212.0	6 334.0	7 180.0
Netherlands	29 685.0	33 318.0	47 186.0	17 770.0	83 614.0	24 320.0	41 337.0	44 203.0	34 542.0	-26 517.0
New Zealand	66.0	-317.0	-228.0	-39.0	615.0	-462.0	145.0	428.0	6.0	-336.0
Norway	3 549.0	8 130.0	-572.0	473.0	.. c	923.0	-235.0	285.0	-542.0	-1 960.0
Poland	-34.0	-6.0	175.0	449.0	-823.0	165.0	72.0	613.0	8.0	1 094.0
Portugal	50.0	6.0	-5.0	7.0	-74.0	528.0	15.0	75.0	-5.0	267.0
Slovak Republic	-11.0	.. c	-2.0	.. c	10.0	198.0	49.0	-286.0	247.0	51.0
Slovenia	.. c	-	.. c	.. c	9.0	67.0	18.0	17.0	14.0	1.0
Spain	4 671.0	4 956.0	3 294.0	4 078.0	3 843.0	3 160.0	1 387.0	1.0	388.0	4 124.0
Sweden	4 134.0	3 685.0	4 161.0	-265.0	550.0	-6 066.0	50.0	1 462.0	1 259.0	5 886.0
Switzerland	31 139.0	-5 732.0	56 155.0	21 082.0	25 576.0	19 291.0	17 059.0	20 732.0	30 026.0	2 994.0
Turkey	-26.0	46.0	271.0	203.0	294.0	181.0	333.0	312.0	481.0	778.0
United Kingdom	-94 851.0	50 294.0	57 267.0	43 694.0	1 326.0	29 112.0	14 426.0	33 469.0	23 093.0	8 618.0
United States	-	-	-	-	-	-	-	-	-	-
EUROPE	**.. c**	**338 653.0**	**.. c**	**.. c**	**.. c**	**157 721.0**	**.. c**	**.. c**	**.. c**	**.. c**
Bulgaria	.. c	.. c	.. c	.. c	.. c	74.0	49.0	33.0	47.0	43.0
Croatia	.. c	.. c	.. c	.. c	.. c	-21.0	-89.0	-1.0	26.0	-8.0
Cyprus[2, 3]	-71.0	151.0	-673.0	-1 290.0	-169.0	186.0	-69.0	-624.0	-537.0	-412.0
Malta	484.0	-257.0	600.0	.. c	-26.0	-49.0	61.0	-14.0	-6.0	-85.0
Romania	-7.0	25.0	10.0	-25.0	.. c	233.0	251.0	69.0	-327.0	217.0
Russian Federation	.. c	-376.0	132.0	-34.0	124.0	-1 661.0	539.0	1 175.0	-934.0	1 363.0
Ukraine	-	.. c	-1.0	-1.0	-	43.0	17.0	7.0	-56.0	87.0
AFRICA	**825.0**	**1 853.0**	**194.0**	**1 210.0**	**54.0**	**2 405.0**	**829.0**	**-2 109.0**	**332.0**	**353.0**
Northern Africa	.. c	.. c	.. c	.. c	.. c	2 515.0	176.0	-894.0	.. c	.. c
Algeria	.. c	.. c	-3.0	.. c	.. c	457.0	15.0	288.0	68.0	-135.0
Egypt	-	8.0	-36.0	106.0	-18.0	1 844.0	325.0	-801.0	-1 705.0	428.0
Libya	.. c	.. c	.. c	.. c	.. c	55.0	-112.0	-333.0	.. c	.. c
Morocco	-5.0	.. c	.. c	-4.0	-3.0	64.0	-10.0	-74.0	-14.0	-38.0
Tunisia	-4.0	1.0	-1.0	-2.0	15.0	95.0	-42.0	26.0	-36.0	-24.0
Other African countries	.. c	.. c	.. c	.. c	.. c	-110.0	653.0	-1 215.0	.. c	.. c
Nigeria	13.0	5.0	23.0	20.0	14.0	-1 232.0	1 094.0	-131.0	1 667.0	-92.0
South Africa	421.0	1 893.0	95.0	1 141.0	-116.0	191.0	-205.0	-318.0	596.0	847.0
AMERICA	**37 106.0**	**70 515.0**	**.. c**	**.. c**	**.. c**	**95 875.0**	**62 030.0**	**72 394.0**	**81 671.0**	**-108 797.0**
Northern America	23 479.0	58 887.0	.. c	.. c	.. c	30 743.0	10 113.0	13 821.0	18 623.0	19 694.0
Central America and Caribbean countries	.. c	.. c	.. c	.. c	.. c	53 610.0	50 016.0	55 841.0	65 193.0	-133 631.0
Bahamas	183.0	-128.0	-421.0	-534.0	588.0	1 742.0	-4 178.0	1 232.0	-510.0	-7 135.0
Bermuda	-1 962.0	-933.0	20 515.0	-3 750.0	12 109.0	15 429.0	25 106.0	31 015.0	30 031.0	-158 148.0
Cayman Islands	13 507.0	11 574.0	-1 213.0	2 065.0	3 234.0	25 821.0	20 608.0	11 148.0	25 731.0	21 923.0
Costa Rica	-32.0	20.0	82.0	-109.0	-88.0	509.0	70.0	66.0	194.0	42.0
El Salvador	-11.0	6.0	2.0	1.0	.. c	-50.0	-288.0	322.0	265.0	249.0
Guatemala	-11.0	6.0	17.0	-2.0	-	76.0	-49.0	-91.0	75.0	28.0
Honduras	2.0	3.0	24.0	-36.0	-28.0	20.0	425.0	9.0	98.0	-902.0
Nicaragua	.. c	.. c	.. c	.. c	.. c	39.0	8.0	-35.0	-23.0	-40.0
Panama	208.0	243.0	100.0	-280.0	335.0	59.0	-189.0	599.0	261.0	424.0
Virgin Islands, U.S.	..	..	..	..	..	..	..	..	..	..
South America	.. c	.. c	.. c	.. c	.. c	11 491.0	1 832.0	2 723.0	-2 139.0	5 144.0
Argentina	-35.0	-50.0	21.0	145.0	-146.0	1 743.0	813.0	223.0	1 414.0	2 396.0
Bolivia	29.0	.. c	.. c	.. c	.. c	-23.0	14.0	95.0	53.0	34.0
Brazil	-407.0	-750.0	-2 586.0	866.0	-361.0	6 773.0	448.0	3 796.0	2 576.0	2 410.0
Colombia	-239.0	169.0	77.0	-63.0	-71.0	600.0	770.0	-508.0	-66.0	768.0
Ecuador	-4.0	2.0	-3.0	18.0	7.0	250.0	-41.0	46.0	-203.0	160.0
Paraguay	.. c	.. c	-	1.0	-12.0	52.0	-9.0	.. c	.. c	.. c
Peru	-45.0	-3.0	19.0	19.0	20.0	1 009.0	-477.0	-154.0	551.0	-932.0
Uruguay	400.0	-299.0	58.0	-203.0	25.0	62.0	9.0	-55.0	.. c	-176.0
Venezuela	246.0	224.0	491.0	-154.0	911.0	161.0	-1 449.0	-1 154.0	-670.0	-292.0

Table 1. Foreign direct investment flows by country *(cont.)*

Million US dollars

	Inward					Outward				
	2014	2015	2016	2017	2018	2014	2015	2016	2017	2018
ASIA	**.. c**	**.. c**	**.. c**	**.. c**	**.. c**	**.. c**	**.. c**	**.. c**	**.. c**	**.. c**
Near and Middle East	-1 538.0	.. c	.. c	.. c	2 188.0	7 952.0	1 435.0	.. c	.. c	.. c
Gulf Arabian countries	-390.0	.. c	.. c	.. c	725.0	.. c	973.0	.. c	.. c	.. c
Kuwait	61.0	41.0	15.0	9.0	173.0	93.0	-56.0	-77.0	.. c	27.0
Qatar	.. c	.. c	.. c	204.0	-696.0	220.0	502.0	694.0	309.0	2 880.0
Saudi Arabia	-1 189.0	474.0	743.0	-161.0	943.0	375.0	1 322.0	729.0	482.0	335.0
United Arab Emirates	639.0	129.0	-32.0	1 630.0	327.0	6 145.0	-565.0	-2 437.0	3 117.0	627.0
Other Near and Middle East	-1 148.0	.. c	.. c	.. c	1 463.0	.. c	462.0	.. c	.. c	.. c
Jordan	28.0	.. c	.. c	.. c	-207.0	.. c	11.0	.. c	.. c	-18.0
Other Asian countries	.. c	.. c	.. c	.. c	.. c	.. c	.. c	26 633.0	.. c	.. c
China	2 201.0	5 127.0	25 445.0	-504.0	-754.0	11 033.0	6 029.0	8 561.0	9 850.0	7 592.0
Hong Kong, China	4 731.0	682.0	1 430.0	-568.0	3 493.0	6 171.0	4 988.0	466.0	5 374.0	1 242.0
India	1 287.0	298.0	-537.0	928.0	-223.0	4 092.0	3 820.0	3 786.0	4 238.0	2 080.0
Indonesia	339.0	173.0	-1 070.0	-244.0	29.0	3 443.0	176.0	-452.0	262.0	-3 051.0
Iran, Islamic Republic of	2.0	-3.0	-	-	-	-	-	-	-	-
Malaysia	235.0	118.0	-157.0	-30.0	182.0	2 940.0	2 054.0	-1 083.0	404.0	-88.0
Philippines	768.0	145.0	-432.0	3.0	-348.0	643.0	75.0	546.0	749.0	689.0
Singapore	3 911.0	2 660.0	2 013.0	-1 713.0	-477.0	25 117.0	21 390.0	10 945.0	17 219.0	-47 508.0
Chinese Taipei	1 387.0	760.0	665.0	432.0	2 480.0	774.0	751.0	543.0	471.0	529.0
Thailand	572.0	469.0	456.0	-4.0	-100.0	2 929.0	200.0	1 495.0	-3 357.0	44.0
Viet Nam	1 065.0	473.0	-1 412.0	-34.0	-61.0	240.0	88.0	157.0	61.0	344.0
AUSTRALIA, OCEANIA AND POLAR REGIONS	**.. c**	**.. c**	**.. c**	**.. c**	**.. c**	**.. c**	**620.0**	**7 284.0**	**.. c**	**.. c**
WORLD unallocated and confidential	**10 042.0**	**-1 035.0**	**2 893.0**	**1 116.0**	**22 639.0**	**64.0**	**-35.0**	**-8 275.0**	**3 027.0**	**-1 346.0**
European Union (EU28)	**49 204.0**	**329 844.0**	**259 250.0**	**127 893.0**	**121 685.0**	**141 607.0**	**136 756.0**	**170 941.0**	**143 443.0**	**43 887.0**
G20 countries excl. European Union	**.. d**	**227 767.0**	**232 566.0**	**204 913.0**	**131 549.0**	**106 720.0**	**59 390.0**	**82 961.0**	**83 543.0**	**61 828.0**
G20 OECD countries	**36 746.0**	**220 978.0**	**210 323.0**	**202 776.0**	**132 053.0**	**80 731.0**	**46 448.0**	**65 461.0**	**65 059.0**	**47 856.0**
G20 Non-OECD countries	**.. d**	**6 789.0**	**22 243.0**	**2 137.0**	**-504.0**	**25 989.0**	**12 942.0**	**17 500.0**	**18 484.0**	**13 972.0**
MENA countries	**.. d**	**.. d**	**..**	**.. d**	**.. d**	**.. d**	**.. d**	**.. d**	**.. d**	**.. d**
ASEAN countries	**.. d**	**.. d**	**..**	**.. d**	**.. d**	**35 295.0**	**23 996.0**	**.. d**	**15 352.0**	**.. d**

- Nil; .. Not available; c Confidential data; d Secondary Confidentiality

Note: Detailed metadata at: *http://stats.oecd.org/OECDStat_Metadata/ShowMetadata.ashx?Dataset=FDI_CTRY_IND_SUMM.*

1. Information on data for Israel: *http://oe.cd/israel-disclaimer.*
2. Note by Turkey: The information in this document with reference to “Cyprus” relates to the southern part of the Island. There is no single authority representing both Turkish and Greek Cypriot people on the Island. Turkey recognises the Turkish Republic of Northern Cyprus (TRNC). Until a lasting and equitable solution is found within the context of the United Nations, Turkey shall preserve its position concerning the “Cyprus issue”.
3. Note by all the European Union Member States of the OECD and the European Union: The Republic of Cyprus is recognised by all members of the United Nations with the exception of Turkey. The information in this document relates to the area under the effective control of the Government of the Republic of Cyprus.

Source: OECD International Direct Investment Statistics (database): https://doi.org/10.1787/idi-data-en

Table 2. Foreign direct investment positions by country

At year end

Million US dollars

	Inward					Outward				
	2014	2015	2016	2017	2018	2014	2015	2016	2017	2018
WORLD	**2 945 795.0**	**3 354 907.0**	**3 765 114.0**	**4 025 492.0**	**4 344 610.0**	**5 108 835.0**	**5 289 071.0**	**5 586 030.0**	**6 013 335.0**	**5 950 991.0**
OECD COUNTRIES	**.. d**	**.. d**	**.. d**	**.. d**	**.. d**	**.. d**	**.. d**	**.. d**	**..**	**4 483 364.0**
Australia	60 951.0	68 733.0	76 220.0	73 002.0	71 460.0	177 420.0	160 061.0	166 430.0	168 855.0	162 983.0
Austria	3 073.0	3 181.0	3 468.0	3 954.0	6 290.0	10 171.0	6 508.0	6 871.0	7 819.0	8 579.0
Belgium	44 257.0	47 192.0	71 223.0	80 352.0	84 661.0	48 242.0	48 096.0	51 589.0	54 954.0	64 051.0
Canada	328 089.0	394 814.0	457 557.0	523 761.0	588 399.0	370 220.0	361 954.0	365 375.0	391 208.0	401 874.0
Chile	1 287.0	2 394.0	2 531.0	2 674.0	3 483.0	28 843.0	28 134.0	28 959.0	25 884.0	26 146.0
Czech Republic	2.0	2.0	.. c	2.0	2.0	6 183.0	6 343.0	4 888.0	5 406.0	6 737.0
Denmark	13 188.0	14 534.0	17 588.0	17 541.0	19 572.0	16 497.0	15 794.0	17 018.0	13 873.0	13 205.0
Estonia	-5.0	-5.0	-5.0	-5.0	-5.0	173.0	160.0	71.0	72.0	76.0
Finland	7 678.0	8 750.0	8 197.0	8 741.0	9 978.0	2 765.0	1 258.0	3 200.0	3 318.0	2 482.0
France	218 339.0	255 524.0	272 149.0	301 540.0	326 437.0	77 738.0	81 274.0	80 739.0	85 572.0	86 863.0
Germany	327 995.0	356 982.0	371 148.0	405 552.0	474 472.0	114 421.0	120 519.0	133 696.0	136 128.0	140 331.0
Greece	978.0	978.0	1 057.0	1 028.0	889.0	-54.0	1 007.0	1 042.0	1 224.0	1 415.0
Hungary	109.0	108.0	108.0	108.0	123.0	5 582.0	7 625.0	7 223.0	7 131.0	7 811.0
Iceland	.. c	.. c	.. c	.. c	.. c	.. c	.. c	.. c	.. c	896.0
Ireland	136 291.0	260 047.0	320 089.0	328 671.0	385 322.0	273 247.0	337 831.0	391 264.0	446 383.0	442 167.0
Israel[1]	20 561.0	24 923.0	59 229.0	39 307.0	38 453.0	10 387.0	10 251.0	10 325.0	26 667.0	27 144.0
Italy	33 071.0	34 425.0	35 258.0	35 672.0	38 626.0	30 154.0	30 869.0	30 922.0	30 708.0	38 479.0
Japan	373 120.0	404 081.0	422 243.0	476 878.0	488 714.0	104 130.0	106 932.0	124 550.0	129 064.0	125 488.0
Korea	37 900.0	37 837.0	41 243.0	50 633.0	57 623.0	37 454.0	38 608.0	38 493.0	41 602.0	41 532.0
Latvia	-	-	-	-	.. c	40.0	39.0	69.0	71.0	70.0
Lithuania	-	-	.. c	-	-	145.0	109.0	120.0	154.0	171.0
Luxembourg	12 086.0	12 728.0	29 760.0	28 792.0	18 440.0	596 105.0	599 001.0	640 646.0	676 418.0	713 829.0
Mexico	33 302.0	34 390.0	34 783.0	35 408.0	37 234.0	94 482.0	101 326.0	100 734.0	109 671.0	114 877.0
Netherlands	131 678.0	165 597.0	189 873.0	169 155.0	228 144.0	753 546.0	829 693.0	898 495.0	936 728.0	883 188.0
New Zealand	1 210.0	509.0	529.0	1 039.0	1 310.0	9 011.0	11 427.0	11 948.0	11 938.0	11 289.0
Norway	33 408.0	29 477.0	26 950.0	27 661.0	28 413.0	34 808.0	31 697.0	29 230.0	29 187.0	27 913.0
Poland	.. c	.. c	.. c	.. c	.. c	13 122.0	11 872.0	11 863.0	12 604.0	12 977.0
Portugal	.. c	.. c	.. c	.. c	.. c	2 067.0	1 971.0	1 985.0	2 060.0	2 825.0
Slovak Republic	-1.0	-1.0	.. c	-1.0	-1.0	989.0	987.0	562.0	867.0	847.0
Slovenia	.. c	2.0	.. c	4.0	4.0	315.0	336.0	354.0	369.0	369.0
Spain	61 892.0	66 106.0	67 880.0	73 244.0	76 380.0	35 253.0	36 075.0	33 484.0	33 128.0	36 962.0
Sweden	43 566.0	48 137.0	54 418.0	54 150.0	55 424.0	33 516.0	32 593.0	31 723.0	34 622.0	39 307.0
Switzerland	154 550.0	143 403.0	180 893.0	201 867.0	222 491.0	142 886.0	171 342.0	187 048.0	249 968.0	278 044.0
Turkey	1 087.0	1 969.0	2 157.0	2 282.0	2 357.0	3 718.0	3 798.0	3 852.0	4 266.0	4 656.0
United Kingdom	520 463.0	558 931.0	572 206.0	614 865.0	597 219.0	631 666.0	632 327.0	686 048.0	747 571.0	757 781.0
United States	87 833.0	83 796.0	73 410.0	75 565.0	79 443.0	-	-	-	-	-
EUROPE	**1 760 609.0**	**2 023 546.0**	**2 239 293.0**	**2 369 767.0**	**2 594 926.0**	**.. c**	**.. c**	**.. c**	**.. c**	**.. c**
Bulgaria	-	.. c	5.0	.. c	.. c	740.0	684.0	711.0	848.0	928.0
Croatia	4.0	4.0	.. c	4.0	4.0	212.0	180.0	176.0	199.0	187.0
Cyprus[2, 3]	.. c	.. c	1 103.0	306.0	203.0	2 771.0	2 583.0	1 996.0	1 650.0	3 461.0
Malta	.. c	7.0	8.0	11.0	54.0	408.0	504.0	547.0	601.0	620.0
Romania	1.0	1.0	.. c	-	-	3 103.0	3 774.0	3 923.0	3 620.0	4 019.0
Russian Federation	6 015.0	4 111.0	4 289.0	4 157.0	3 876.0	9 764.0	10 259.0	14 520.0	13 881.0	14 795.0
Ukraine	1.0	3.0	3.0	4.0	6.0	620.0	498.0	476.0	398.0	402.0
AFRICA	**3 474.0**	**4 470.0**	**4 485.0**	**5 806.0**	**5 752.0**	**69 029.0**	**52 004.0**	**51 689.0**	**50 285.0**	**47 796.0**
Northern Africa	-39.0	-32.0	.. c	.. c	.. c	.. c	19 376.0	17 671.0	14 131.0	13 748.0
Algeria	-	-	-	-	-	3 014.0	2 698.0	2 986.0	3 030.0	3 571.0
Egypt	-19.0	-16.0	-3.0	35.0	28.0	.. c	14 068.0	12 561.0	9 352.0	8 384.0
Libya	2.0	5.0	.. c	.. c	.. c	2 599.0	1 820.0	1 373.0	1 058.0	1 134.0
Morocco	-22.0	-21.0	-21.0	-22.0	-22.0	529.0	493.0	434.0	412.0	408.0
Tunisia	-	-	-	-	-	447.0	297.0	317.0	279.0	251.0
Other African countries	3 513.0	4 502.0	.. c	.. c	.. c	.. c	32 628.0	34 018.0	36 154.0	34 048.0
Nigeria	.. c	.. c	.. c	.. c	.. c	4 884.0	5 872.0	4 349.0	5 774.0	5 630.0
South Africa	3 075.0	3 934.0	3 878.0	5 073.0	4 991.0	7 346.0	6 926.0	6 659.0	7 334.0	7 621.0
AMERICA	**544 799.0**	**638 071.0**	**694 668.0**	**771 976.0**	**874 700.0**	**1 268 684.0**	**1 264 600.0**	**1 294 838.0**	**1 399 292.0**	**1 334 198.0**
Northern America	415 929.0	478 615.0	530 969.0	599 326.0	667 838.0	370 224.0	361 958.0	365 379.0	391 212.0	401 878.0
Central America and Caribbean countries	.. c	.. c	107 605.0	112 795.0	147 445.0	747 890.0	770 364.0	791 098.0	871 182.0	790 843.0
Bahamas	355.0	123.0	168.0	179.0	378.0	27 301.0	22 737.0	23 647.0	23 387.0	18 518.0
Bermuda	32 139.0	30 555.0	33 237.0	35 920.0	60 750.0	283 019.0	303 244.0	314 853.0	346 804.0	249 386.0
Cayman Islands	.. c	11 559.0	12 295.0	13 398.0	20 895.0	304 005.0	303 438.0	306 512.0	331 391.0	334 477.0
Costa Rica	.. c	.. c	.. c	.. c	78.0	1 608.0	1 642.0	1 349.0	1 567.0	1 625.0
El Salvador	.. c	.. c	.. c	.. c	.. c	2 782.0	2 576.0	2 774.0	3 037.0	3 277.0
Guatemala	15.0	15.0	15.0	15.0	15.0	1 182.0	1 098.0	992.0	1 048.0	1 026.0
Honduras	2.0	2.0	2.0	2.0	2.0	848.0	1 274.0	1 283.0	1 405.0	504.0
Nicaragua	.. c	.. c	.. c	.. c	.. c	250.0	256.0	217.0	187.0	138.0
Panama	704.0	658.0	733.0	759.0	862.0	4 510.0	4 447.0	4 301.0	4 706.0	5 050.0
Virgin Islands, U.S.	..	..	..	..	..	..	..	..	..	..
South America	.. c	.. c	56 094.0	59 855.0	59 417.0	150 128.0	131 775.0	137 848.0	136 389.0	140 970.0
Argentina	5 090.0	5 134.0	4 937.0	4 608.0	4 896.0	14 727.0	14 624.0	14 057.0	14 907.0	15 196.0
Bolivia	9.0	9.0	9.0	9.0	9.0	492.0	481.0	552.0	598.0	618.0
Brazil	18 530.0	43 662.0	38 751.0	42 841.0	39 803.0	69 548.0	56 847.0	66 418.0	68 272.0	70 878.0
Colombia	2 126.0	2 443.0	2 679.0	2 591.0	3 242.0	8 280.0	7 750.0	7 467.0	7 222.0	7 737.0
Ecuador	-23.0	-23.0	-27.0	-27.0	3.0	971.0	913.0	1 036.0	779.0	898.0
Paraguay	-	-	-	-	-	209.0	.. c	207.0	179.0	148.0
Peru	244.0	240.0	247.0	260.0	280.0	8 097.0	7 573.0	5 742.0	6 370.0	6 403.0
Uruguay	264.0	326.0	353.0	367.0	381.0	2 232.0	2 239.0	2 178.0	1 556.0	1 314.0
Venezuela	4 326.0	4 558.0	4 742.0	4 801.0	5 728.0	10 803.0	9 825.0	7 364.0	6 632.0	6 478.0

Table 2. Foreign direct investment positions by country *(cont.)*
At year end

Million US dollars

	Inward					Outward				
	2014	2015	2016	2017	2018	2014	2015	2016	2017	2018
ASIA	.. c	.. c	.. c	.. c	.. c	.. c	.. c	.. c	.. c	.. c
Near and Middle East	62 256.0	65 601.0	100 744.0	84 331.0	.. c	.. c	.. c	.. c	.. c	.. c
Gulf Arabian countries	41 479.0	40 412.0	41 194.0	44 642.0	.. c	.. c	.. c	.. c	.. c	44 232.0
Kuwait	318.0	808.0	787.0	804.0	967.0	434.0	342.0	250.0	296.0	313.0
Qatar	2 440.0	2 784.0	2 809.0	3 494.0	2 447.0	9 898.0	7 252.0	7 938.0	8 183.0	10 636.0
Saudi Arabia	11 542.0	11 497.0	12 280.0	14 055.0	15 368.0	8 800.0	10 025.0	10 585.0	11 085.0	11 379.0
United Arab Emirates	26 208.0	24 978.0	24 990.0	26 011.0	26 738.0	17 466.0	16 205.0	13 568.0	16 785.0	17 303.0
Other Near and Middle East	20 777.0	25 189.0	59 550.0	39 689.0	.. c	.. c	.. c	.. c	.. c	.. c
Jordan	.. c	.. c	.. c	.. c	.. c	212.0	224.0	209.0	232.0	.. c
Other Asian countries	.. c	.. c	.. c	.. c	.. c	.. c	.. c	.. c	.. c	.. c
China	29 049.0	33 050.0	58 976.0	58 048.0	60 182.0	82 244.0	92 150.0	97 287.0	107 556.0	116 518.0
Hong Kong, China	13 012.0	14 567.0	15 009.0	14 996.0	16 888.0	64 741.0	69 367.0	68 944.0	81 234.0	82 546.0
India	11 514.0	11 647.0	12 155.0	13 123.0	13 734.0	33 241.0	35 361.0	38 634.0	44 458.0	45 984.0
Indonesia	438.0	504.0	527.0	585.0	689.0	15 674.0	15 717.0	14 944.0	15 171.0	11 140.0
Iran, Islamic Republic of	1.0	1.0	1.0	1.0	1.0	2.0	2.0	2.0	2.0	2.0
Malaysia	1 304.0	1 307.0	1 484.0	1 471.0	2 417.0	14 642.0	15 765.0	14 606.0	15 080.0	13 581.0
Philippines	.. c	856.0	892.0	975.0	377.0	4 073.0	5 992.0	6 325.0	7 116.0	7 645.0
Singapore	33 675.0	38 573.0	82 786.0	88 596.0	54 227.0	229 189.0	253 277.0	255 344.0	274 260.0	218 835.0
Chinese Taipei	9 439.0	10 249.0	10 924.0	11 306.0	14 093.0	15 942.0	15 295.0	15 935.0	17 031.0	17 530.0
Thailand	515.0	514.0	2 139.0	2 160.0	2 056.0	18 143.0	17 942.0	18 021.0	15 006.0	17 667.0
Viet Nam	11.0	11.0	11.0	12.0	10.0	1 746.0	1 816.0	1 956.0	2 010.0	2 358.0
AUSTRALIA, OCEANIA AND POLAR REGIONS	.. c	.. c	.. c	.. c	.. c	.. c	.. c	.. c	.. c	.. c
WORLD unallocated and confidential	2 430.0	689.0	694.0	27.0	51.0	23 127.0	20 854.0	21 694.0	28 228.0	23 529.0
European Union (EU28)	1 561 324.0	1 838 900.0	2 019 137.0	2 127 626.0	2 326 836.0	2 659 118.0	2 810 011.0	3 041 226.0	3 244 095.0	3 269 739.0
G20 countries excl. European Union	2 107 403.0	2 345 021.0	2 494 167.0	2 737 648.0	2 905 523.0	1 882 747.0	1 879 577.0	1 993 943.0	2 127 309.0	2 168 375.0
G20 OECD countries	2 022 150.0	2 231 482.0	2 358 374.0	2 595 158.0	2 761 984.0	1 641 403.0	1 637 668.0	1 730 839.0	1 844 645.0	1 874 864.0
G20 Non-OECD countries	85 253.0	113 539.0	135 793.0	142 490.0	143 539.0	241 344.0	241 909.0	263 104.0	282 664.0	293 511.0
MENA countries	.. d	.. d	.. d	.. d	.. d	.. d	.. d	.. d	.. d	.. d
ASEAN countries	.. d	.. d	.. d	.. d	.. d	283 583.0	310 640.0	311 348.0	328 809.0	.. d

- Nil; .. Not available; c Confidential data; d Secondary Confidentiality

Note: Inward FDI positions are allocated according to the ultimate investing country. Detailed metadata at: *http://stats.oecd.org/OECDStat_Metadata/ShowMetadata.ashx?Dataset=FDI_CTRY_IND_SUMM*.

1. Information on data for Israel: *http://oe.cd/israel-disclaimer*.
2. Note by Turkey: The information in this document with reference to "Cyprus" relates to the southern part of the Island. There is no single authority representing both Turkish and Greek Cypriot people on the Island. Turkey recognises the Turkish Republic of Northern Cyprus (TRNC). Until a lasting and equitable solution is found within the context of the United Nations, Turkey shall preserve its position concerning the "Cyprus issue".
3. Note by all the European Union Member States of the OECD and the European Union: The Republic of Cyprus is recognised by all members of the United Nations with the exception of Turkey. The information in this document relates to the area under the effective control of the Government of the Republic of Cyprus.

Source: OECD International Direct Investment Statistics (database): https://doi.org/10.1787/idi-data-en

UNITED STATES

Table 3. Foreign direct investment income by country

Million US dollars

	Inward					Outward				
	2014	2015	2016	2017	2018	2014	2015	2016	2017	2018
WORLD	**177 294.0**	**149 926.0**	**155 978.0**	**173 778.0**	**208 078.0**	**457 122.0**	**433 333.0**	**427 542.0**	**470 933.0**	**531 010.0**
OECD COUNTRIES	**..**	**..**	**..**	**..**	**.. d**	**299 164.0**	**300 546.0**	**297 512.0**	**..**	**348 717.0**
Australia	3 040.0	1 221.0	555.0	908.0	4 267.0	9 079.0	8 743.0	6 881.0	7 912.0	10 254.0
Austria	532.0	509.0	565.0	728.0	943.0	2 264.0	172.0	409.0	471.0	804.0
Belgium	4 748.0	2 616.0	3 289.0	8 339.0	6 262.0	3 483.0	3 244.0	4 343.0	6 166.0	5 713.0
Canada	15 032.0	14 732.0	14 485.0	22 273.0	27 330.0	31 718.0	21 096.0	19 077.0	27 354.0	30 619.0
Chile	69.0	69.0	84.0	-16.0	200.0	2 764.0	2 091.0	1 636.0	1 810.0	2 326.0
Czech Republic	-	-	-	1.0	6.0	767.0	596.0	481.0	473.0	560.0
Denmark	1 095.0	1 051.0	1 110.0	1 206.0	1 627.0	696.0	668.0	741.0	471.0	192.0
Estonia	.. c	-	-	-	-	6.0	2.0	2.0	7.0	12.0
Finland	612.0	398.0	466.0	320.0	846.0	65.0	109.0	126.0	285.0	115.0
France	10 774.0	15 808.0	12 017.0	10 999.0	11 277.0	4 084.0	1 445.0	2 820.0	3 010.0	1 587.0
Germany	17 595.0	12 872.0	14 683.0	13 043.0	23 422.0	2 850.0	6 322.0	4 851.0	6 156.0	6 810.0
Greece	.. c	.. c	.. c	.. c	.. c	130.0	19.0	127.0	130.0	200.0
Hungary	.. c	445.0	.. c	.. c	.. c	524.0	591.0	455.0	656.0	570.0
Iceland	.. c	.. c	268.0	292.0	.. c	51.0	43.0	47.0	74.0	83.0
Ireland	3 752.0	9 772.0	7 094.0	10 741.0	8 433.0	43 670.0	56 589.0	52 366.0	51 804.0	53 071.0
Israel[1]	302.0	-845.0	226.0	308.0	166.0	363.0	260.0	546.0	560.0	381.0
Italy	1 815.0	516.0	476.0	645.0	1 353.0	1 415.0	1 622.0	1 792.0	1 457.0	1 534.0
Japan	20 126.0	17 789.0	16 637.0	24 355.0	24 765.0	8 928.0	12 365.0	12 832.0	13 681.0	13 088.0
Korea	2 734.0	1 948.0	1 251.0	1 627.0	1 857.0	2 165.0	2 867.0	2 475.0	2 228.0	2 963.0
Latvia	-	-	-	-	1.0	7.0	8.0	11.0	10.0	8.0
Lithuania	-	-	-	-	-	4.0	-	-1.0	-	-1.0
Luxembourg	7 597.0	8 264.0	13 698.0	12 881.0	16 145.0	41 095.0	28 340.0	34 819.0	36 825.0	36 050.0
Mexico	1 858.0	1 352.0	1 208.0	1 269.0	1 417.0	7 057.0	7 351.0	6 514.0	8 962.0	8 562.0
Netherlands	20 740.0	16 069.0	18 645.0	15 546.0	19 187.0	70 382.0	70 573.0	72 130.0	76 083.0	86 618.0
New Zealand	21.0	-64.0	-124.0	-8.0	377.0	433.0	537.0	531.0	633.0	595.0
Norway	732.0	71.0	-638.0	442.0	2 121.0	4 062.0	1 750.0	854.0	1 630.0	1 505.0
Poland	.. c	22.0	.. c	.. c	.. c	748.0	601.0	1 060.0	666.0	1 096.0
Portugal	13.0	10.0	-2.0	23.0	-46.0	294.0	207.0	232.0	272.0	165.0
Slovak Republic	.. c	-	-	-	1.0	51.0	37.0	-27.0	20.0	-11.0
Slovenia	-2.0	-	-	-	-	15.0	22.0	20.0	17.0	12.0
Spain	1 079.0	2 105.0	1 518.0	1 571.0	3 111.0	2 595.0	3 088.0	1 958.0	3 229.0	3 257.0
Sweden	3 274.0	3 278.0	3 278.0	3 498.0	3 616.0	1 558.0	809.0	463.0	1 880.0	1 181.0
Switzerland	20 075.0	19 588.0	18 300.0	15 660.0	20 165.0	22 567.0	28 953.0	30 321.0	30 474.0	31 408.0
Turkey	.. c	.. c	115.0	71.0	.. c	312.0	412.0	320.0	577.0	639.0
United Kingdom	27 147.0	8 942.0	18 697.0	20 467.0	18 822.0	32 973.0	39 022.0	36 299.0	41 311.0	46 751.0
United States	-	-	-	-	-	-	-	-	-	-
EUROPE	**122 793.0**	**103 476.0**	**114 812.0**	**118 276.0**	**139 429.0**	**233 708.0**	**243 582.0**	**.. c**	**.. c**	**.. c**
Bulgaria	-	2.0	3.0	-1.0	7.0	73.0	71.0	58.0	63.0	64.0
Croatia	-	-	-	-	-	-6.0	-2.0	10.0	11.0	10.0
Cyprus[2, 3]	43.0	94.0	122.0	-10.0	-39.0	81.0	103.0	66.0	254.0	182.0
Malta	22.0	.. c	.. c	.. c	.. c	41.0	44.0	45.0	53.0	73.0
Romania	-	-	-	-	-	127.0	-60.0	-8.0	77.0	235.0
Russian Federation	-60.0	-286.0	-33.0	231.0	326.0	330.0	630.0	1 008.0	1 331.0	1 338.0
Ukraine	-	-	-	-	-	134.0	42.0	40.0	83.0	100.0
AFRICA	**488.0**	**189.0**	**-3.0**	**170.0**	**159.0**	**5 523.0**	**2 915.0**	**2 208.0**	**3 435.0**	**4 182.0**
Northern Africa	2.0	3.0	.. c	.. c	.. c	2 307.0	569.0	390.0	.. c	1 596.0
Algeria	-	-	-	-	-	1 125.0	477.0	460.0	564.0	467.0
Egypt	2.0	3.0	.. c	.. c	.. c	1 121.0	105.0	113.0	508.0	1 031.0
Libya	-	-	-	-	-	44.0	-27.0	-140.0	.. c	80.0
Morocco	-	-	-	-	-	-4.0	15.0	-43.0	1.0	-2.0
Tunisia	-	-	-	-	-	21.0	-1.0	-	3.0	20.0
Other African countries	486.0	186.0	.. c	.. c	.. c	3 216.0	2 346.0	1 818.0	.. c	2 586.0
Nigeria	.. c	.. c	.. c	8.0	.. c	1 101.0	1 120.0	696.0	821.0	452.0
South Africa	414.0	.. c	11.0	-21.0	-1.0	499.0	420.0	292.0	852.0	668.0
AMERICA	**23 867.0**	**23 292.0**	**21 319.0**	**26 663.0**	**33 721.0**	**117 230.0**	**103 307.0**	**102 961.0**	**113 471.0**	**131 947.0**
Northern America	15 032.0	14 732.0	14 485.0	22 273.0	27 330.0	31 717.0	21 095.0	19 076.0	27 353.0	30 618.0
Central America and Caribbean countries	7 778.0	7 648.0	6 609.0	4 033.0	5 488.0	73 721.0	75 015.0	77 781.0	77 210.0	90 884.0
Bahamas	86.0	66.0	-31.0	-23.0	8.0	4 145.0	2 818.0	717.0	592.0	223.0
Bermuda	1 965.0	2 718.0	1 358.0	104.0	989.0	34 806.0	38 357.0	41 554.0	32 341.0	35 178.0
Cayman Islands	3 939.0	3 143.0	3 896.0	2 234.0	2 389.0	24 338.0	23 664.0	26 279.0	33 235.0	41 804.0
Costa Rica	2.0	1.0	-1.0	1.0	-3.0	228.0	174.0	125.0	127.0	143.0
El Salvador	-	-	-	-	-	126.0	38.0	594.0	298.0	349.0
Guatemala	-	-	-	-	-	77.0	31.0	10.0	73.0	60.0
Honduras	-	-	-	-	-	16.0	61.0	111.0	68.0	-77.0
Nicaragua	-	-	-	-	-	1.0	-9.0	-24.0	-18.0	-24.0
Panama	148.0	301.0	116.0	13.0	132.0	107.0	308.0	474.0	603.0	618.0
Virgin Islands, U.S.	..	..	..	..	..	..	..	..	..	..
South America	1 057.0	912.0	225.0	357.0	903.0	11 776.0	7 189.0	6 095.0	8 912.0	10 450.0
Argentina	.. c	-88.0	-70.0	.. c	55.0	971.0	1 451.0	1 723.0	1 965.0	1 450.0
Bolivia	-	-	-	-	-	-	39.0	108.0	80.0	70.0
Brazil	175.0	12.0	-8.0	-55.0	-81.0	4 666.0	2 068.0	2 390.0	3 389.0	3 846.0
Colombia	74.0	19.0	21.0	23.0	25.0	811.0	286.0	343.0	731.0	1 139.0
Ecuador	1.0	1.0	.. c	3.0	7.0	183.0	99.0	147.0	125.0	60.0
Paraguay	-	-	-	-	-	22.0	9.0	21.0	.. c	22.0
Peru	.. c	.. c	.. c	.. c	.. c	1 183.0	151.0	321.0	484.0	741.0
Uruguay	46.0	67.0	27.0	9.0	15.0	50.0	8.0	-52.0	110.0	129.0
Venezuela	.. c	.. c	196.0	342.0	.. c	1 199.0	1 094.0	-475.0	51.0	261.0

Table 3. Foreign direct investment income by country *(cont.)*

Million US dollars

	Inward					Outward				
	2014	2015	2016	2017	2018	2014	2015	2016	2017	2018
ASIA	**.. c**	**.. c**	**19 367.0**	**.. c**	**.. c**	**.. c**	**73 941.0**	**.. c**	**.. c**	**.. c**
Near and Middle East	346.0	-244.0	1 053.0	877.0	.. c	.. c	9 343.0	.. c	.. c	.. c
Gulf Arabian countries	48.0	604.0	830.0	573.0	.. c	.. c	8 906.0	5 135.0	6 800.0	7 607.0
Kuwait	25.0	66.0	29.0	20.0	24.0	44.0	40.0	-28.0	32.0	9.0
Qatar	.. c	.. c	.. c	.. c	.. c	10 002.0	6 210.0	3 338.0	4 314.0	5 053.0
Saudi Arabia	.. c	.. c	.. c	.. c	.. c	1 893.0	1 355.0	1 105.0	1 147.0	1 020.0
United Arab Emirates	166.0	197.0	237.0	150.0	104.0	1 897.0	1 809.0	1 272.0	1 503.0	1 366.0
Other Near and Middle East	298.0	-848.0	223.0	304.0	.. c	.. c	437.0	.. c	.. c	.. c
Jordan	-4.0	-4.0	-4.0	-5.0	.. c	.. c	24.0	30.0	36.0	27.0
Other Asian countries	.. c	.. c	18 314.0	.. c	.. c	.. c	64 598.0	.. c	.. c	.. c
China	1 416.0	683.0	-248.0	454.0	811.0	13 593.0	10 674.0	12 106.0	13 417.0	13 073.0
Hong Kong, China	262.0	-284.0	-109.0	-748.0	564.0	5 237.0	5 663.0	4 407.0	6 056.0	7 867.0
India	657.0	477.0	120.0	353.0	174.0	3 239.0	3 110.0	4 112.0	4 983.0	4 482.0
Indonesia	25.0	20.0	28.0	.. c	27.0	2 231.0	989.0	1 161.0	1 472.0	3 483.0
Iran, Islamic Republic of	-	-	-	-	-	-	-	-	-	-
Malaysia	4.0	-	4.0	2.0	21.0	2 814.0	1 539.0	957.0	1 012.0	1 182.0
Philippines	.. c	.. c	1.0	2.0	3.0	703.0	435.0	814.0	1 096.0	837.0
Singapore	845.0	831.0	173.0	71.0	480.0	31 019.0	22 937.0	25 002.0	24 496.0	35 579.0
Chinese Taipei	618.0	554.0	382.0	622.0	738.0	1 332.0	1 177.0	1 334.0	1 407.0	1 493.0
Thailand	19.0	18.0	89.0	.. c	-54.0	1 645.0	1 315.0	1 675.0	2 298.0	2 575.0
Viet Nam	-	-	-	-	-2.0	52.0	79.0	111.0	58.0	248.0
AUSTRALIA, OCEANIA AND POLAR REGIONS	**.. c**	**.. c**	**483.0**	**.. c**	**.. c**	**.. c**	**9 587.0**	**.. c**	**.. c**	**10 939.0**
WORLD unallocated and confidential	**-128.0**	**2.0**	**-**	**170.0**	**471.0**	**3 856.0**	**1.0**	**-13 340.0**	**-6 725.0**	**1 884.0**
European Union (EU28)	**101 756.0**	**82 831.0**	**96 287.0**	**100 933.0**	**116 047.0**	**209 991.0**	**214 242.0**	**215 648.0**	**231 858.0**	**246 856.0**
G20 countries excl. European Union	**.. d**	**.. d**	**.. d**	**.. d**	**.. d**	**128 003.0**	**121 942.0**	**117 758.0**	**141 204.0**	**152 167.0**
G20 OECD countries	**.. d**	**.. d**	**80 124.0**	**95 657.0**	**.. d**	**100 581.0**	**101 245.0**	**93 861.0**	**112 648.0**	**122 807.0**
G20 Non-OECD countries	**.. d**	**.. d**	**.. d**	**.. d**	**.. d**	**27 422.0**	**20 697.0**	**23 897.0**	**28 556.0**	**29 360.0**
MENA countries	..	..	..	..	**.. d**	**.. d**	**.. d**	**.. d**	**.. d**	**.. d**
ASEAN countries	..	..	**295.0**	..	**.. d**	**38 476.0**	**27 306.0**	**29 732.0**	**30 441.0**	**.. d**

- Nil; .. Not available; c Confidential data; d Secondary Confidentiality

Note: Detailed metadata at: *http://stats.oecd.org/OECDStat_Metadata/ShowMetadata.ashx?Dataset=FDI_CTRY_IND_SUMM.*

1. Information on data for Israel: *http://oe.cd/israel-disclaimer.*
2. Note by Turkey: The information in this document with reference to "Cyprus" relates to the southern part of the Island. There is no single authority representing both Turkish and Greek Cypriot people on the Island. Turkey recognises the Turkish Republic of Northern Cyprus (TRNC). Until a lasting and equitable solution is found within the context of the United Nations, Turkey shall preserve its position concerning the "Cyprus issue".
3. Note by all the European Union Member States of the OECD and the European Union: The Republic of Cyprus is recognised by all members of the United Nations with the exception of Turkey. The information in this document relates to the area under the effective control of the Government of the Republic of Cyprus.

Source: OECD International Direct Investment Statistics (database): https://doi.org/10.1787/idi-data-en

Table 4. Foreign direct investment flows by industrial sector

Million US dollars

	Inward					Outward				
	2014	2015	2016	2017	2018	2014	2015	2016	2017	2018
All FDI activities	**201 733.0**	**467 625.0**	**471 792.0**	**277 258.0**	**253 561.0**	**333 014.0**	**264 359.0**	**289 261.0**	**300 378.0**	**-90 623.0**
Agriculture, forestry and fishing	**603.0**	**152.0**	**-194.0**	**379.0**	**804.0**	**931.0**	**172.0**	**183.0**	**233.0**	**105.0**
Mining and quarrying	**12 781.0**	**3 350.0**	**22 039.0**	**7 246.0**	**-1 666.0**	**15 213.0**	**416.0**	**-4 488.0**	**-16 672.0**	**-4 259.0**
Extraction activities	10 660.0	4 903.0	19 409.0	5 374.0	-861.0	11 711.0	-1 390.0	-3 376.0	-16 089.0	-5 006.0
Manufacturing	**162 123.0**	**230 981.0**	**204 441.0**	**95 575.0**	**166 889.0**	**55 037.0**	**43 502.0**	**52 609.0**	**77 073.0**	**50 911.0**
of which:										
Food products, beverages and tobacco	42 658.0	15 928.0	32 294.0	6 736.0	37 807.0	6 951.0	5 947.0	5 831.0	8 982.0	5 247.0
Textiles, wood and paper products; printing	987.0	666.0	.. c	.. c	3 938.0	2 478.0	470.0	818.0	2 868.0	807.0
Chemical, rubber, plastic, non-metallic mineral products	86 136.0	164 986.0	125 825.0	52 238.0	94 712.0	14 226.0	9 024.0	.. c	.. c	.. c
Metal and machinery products, except electrical equipment	24 875.0	22 071.0	32 242.0	19 059.0	21 329.0	23 894.0	14 926.0	18 561.0	34 497.0	22 230.0
Motor vehicles, trailers, semi-trailers, other transport equipment	8 014.0	21 511.0	7 505.0	11 668.0	9 415.0	4 591.0	11 282.0	7 446.0	9 160.0	3 375.0
Other manufacturing	-548.0	5 820.0	.. c	.. c	-311.0	2 897.0	1 853.0	.. c	.. c	.. c
Electricity, gas, steam and air conditioning supply	**.. c**	**.. c**	**.. c**	**.. c**	**.. c**	**4 648.0**	**1 140.0**	**1 377.0**	**1 376.0**	**-105.0**
Water supply; sewerage, waste management and remediation activities	**.. c**	**.. c**	**.. c**	**.. c**	**.. c**	**135.0**	**-29.0**	**-121.0**	**50.0**	**-48.0**
Construction	**4 735.0**	**2 563.0**	**670.0**	**636.0**	**-1 605.0**	**1 681.0**	**174.0**	**1 308.0**	**-450.0**	**-1 078.0**
Services	**12 309.0**	**231 243.0**	**.. c**	**167 233.0**	**81 036.0**	**255 368.0**	**218 985.0**	**238 391.0**	**238 768.0**	**-136 145.0**
Wholesale and retail trade; repair of motor vehicles and motorcycles	45 594.0	30 558.0	21 737.0	72 057.0	80 189.0	16 341.0	11 678.0	21 613.0	14 286.0	-14 102.0
Transportation and storage	19 227.0	7 609.0	21 746.0	4 251.0	4 996.0	2 630.0	3 021.0	3 947.0	10 232.0	-1 488.0
Accommodation and food service activities	174.0	2 174.0	1 881.0	11 415.0	1 010.0	3 306.0	774.0	1 781.0	-378.0	3 231.0
Information and communication	11 178.0	8 810.0	9 695.0	5 974.0	5 504.0	20 404.0	13 488.0	21 503.0	19 997.0	51 810.0
Financial and insurance activities	-99 305.0	152 978.0	.. c	54 425.0	40 523.0	178 231.0	168 550.0	163 795.0	169 729.0	-201 739.0
Activities of holding companies	-124 001.0	86 662.0	.. c	14 065.0	6 632.0	172 172.0	159 366.0	147 587.0	127 632.0	-318 145.0
Real estate activities	6 142.0	5 618.0	7 383.0	6 915.0	35 006.0	1 101.0	1 670.0	396.0	1 923.0	39.0
Professional, scientific and technical activities	18 802.0	22 593.0	.. c	6 522.0	-96 363.0	17 800.0	7 065.0	8 771.0	-1 853.0	9 597.0
Administrative and support service activities	9 629.0	-2 457.0	.. c	5 297.0	2 169.0	12 229.0	11 991.0	14 450.0	14 599.0	14 076.0
Public administration; activities of households and of extraterritorial organisations	..	..	..	..	..	..	..	..	..	..
Education	382.0	914.0	1 524.0	-883.0	-290.0	531.0	311.0	-283.0	641.0	337.0
Human health and social work activities	427.0	548.0	3 547.0	1 731.0	226.0	1 316.0	662.0	285.0	462.0	282.0
Arts, entertainment and recreation	101.0	893.0	434.0	441.0	7 463.0	309.0	-1 034.0	1 414.0	7 645.0	425.0
Other services	-42.0	1 005.0	1 791.0	-912.0	603.0	1 170.0	809.0	719.0	1 485.0	1 387.0
Not allocated and confidential	**9 254.0**	**-3 700.0**	**82 945.0**	..	**8 103.0**	-	**-1.0**	**-2.0**	..	**-4.0**
Private real estate activities	..	..	..	..	..	..	..	..	..	..

- Nil; .. Not available; c Confidential data

Note: Detailed metadata at: *http://stats.oecd.org/OECDStat_Metadata/ShowMetadata.ashx?Dataset=FDI_CTRY_IND_SUMM.*

Source: OECD International Direct Investment Statistics (database): https://doi.org/10.1787/idi-data-en

UNITED STATES

Table 5. Foreign direct investment positions by industrial sector
At year end

Million US dollars

	Inward					Outward				
	2014	2015	2016	2017	2018	2014	2015	2016	2017	2018
All FDI activities	**2 945 795.0**	**3 354 907.0**	**3 765 114.0**	**4 025 492.0**	**4 344 610.0**	**5 108 835.0**	**5 289 071 0**	**5 586 030.0**	**6 013 335.0**	**5 950 991.0**
Agriculture, forestry and fishing	**4 657.0**	**4 519.0**	**4 313.0**	**4 667.0**	**5 652.0**	**6 347.0**	**6 800 0**	**7 019.0**	**7 395.0**	**6 526.0**
Mining and quarrying	**126 961.0**	**117 142.0**	**127 161.0**	**132 270.0**	**132 061.0**	**214 287.0**	**180 418 0**	**169 643.0**	**159 493.0**	**156 795.0**
Extraction activities	91 775.0	83 594.0	91 209.0	94 988.0	91 773.0	159 792.0	133 823.0	127 422.0	117 920.0	114 814.0
Manufacturing	**1 114 540.0**	**1 359 812.0**	**1 541 897.0**	**1 607 209.0**	**1 771 552.0**	**654 335.0**	**693 847 0**	**735 648.0**	**870 099.0**	**902 555.0**
of which:										
Food products, beverages and tobacco	123 224.0	153 111.0	171 621.0	181 051.0	217 070.0	122 699.0	115 332.0	122 680.0	136 412.0	143 604.0
Textiles, wood and paper products; printing	14 586.0	18 105.0	.. c	22 179.0	26 145.0	19 852.0	20 834.0	20 272.0	23 262.0	24 049.0
Chemical, rubber, plastic, non-metallic mineral products	529 813.0	708 611.0	821 544.0	841 488.0	1 006 276.0	197 656.0	204 271.0	.. c	.. c	.. c
Metal and machinery products, except electrical equipment	267 770.0	277 034.0	315 552.0	332 494.0	357 080.0	232 451.0	260 665.0	269 274.0	321 162.0	351 402.0
Motor vehicles, trailers, semi-trailers, other transport equipment	116 026.0	131 842.0	137 475.0	149 571.0	151 914.0	54 198.0	62 087.0	73 112.0	84 912.0	86 189.0
Other manufacturing	63 122.0	71 109.0	.. c	80 427.0	13 069.0	27 480.0	30 659.0	.. c	.. c	.. c
Electricity, gas, steam and air conditioning supply	**.. c**	**.. c**	**.. c**	**.. c**	**.. c**	**15 795.0**	**16 274 0**	**14 108.0**	**16 287.0**	**15 303.0**
Water supply; sewerage, waste management and remediation activities	**.. c**	**.. c**	**.. c**	**.. c**	**.. c**	**1 683.0**	**1 251 0**	**1 228.0**	**1 224.0**	**1 305.0**
Construction	**20 970.0**	**23 178.0**	**24 299.0**	**23 290.0**	**22 440.0**	**4 255.0**	**4 075 0**	**5 616.0**	**5 215.0**	**4 506.0**
Services	**1 609 055.0**	**1 785 372.0**	**1 986 409.0**	**2 168 333.0**	**2 316 811.0**	**4 212 131.0**	**4 386 407 0**	**4 652 766.0**	**4 953 622.0**	**4 864 001.0**
Wholesale and retail trade; repair of motor vehicles and motorcycles	391 335.0	434 145.0	449 664.0	514 043.0	594 623.0	297 613.0	291 265.0	310 189.0	330 428.0	299 062.0
Transportation and storage	74 396.0	70 394.0	91 187.0	97 759.0	102 827.0	33 393.0	33 911.0	42 716.0	52 315.0	46 143.0
Accommodation and food service activities	15 059.0	17 766.0	19 774.0	31 389.0	43 630.0	18 918.0	18 671.0	26 968.0	27 267.0	29 678.0
Information and communication	147 618.0	168 281.0	172 933.0	184 168.0	180 441.0	179 689.0	198 689.0	207 182.0	226 576.0	286 330.0
Financial and insurance activities	728 412.0	806 094.0	.. c	.. c	970 639.0	3 378 448.0	3 516 420.0	3 715 424.0	3 935 016.0	3 801 657.0
Activities of holding companies	144 413.0	168 184.0	.. c	.. c	229 219.0	2 472 128.0	2 678 541.0	2 857 262.0	2 991 188.0	2 772 320.0
Real estate activities	45 842.0	52 755.0	58 866.0	67 197.0	105 620.0	38 420.0	39 505.0	39 806.0	42 497.0	43 536.0
Professional, scientific and technical activities	137 115.0	165 832.0	.. c	.. c	203 849.0	120 733.0	125 583.0	131 491.0	132 117.0	146 019.0
Administrative and support service activities	52 851.0	49 615.0	73 848.0	77 049.0	78 459.0	116 879.0	132 847.0	147 515.0	164 497.0	170 293.0
Public administration; activities of households and of extraterritorial organisations	..	..	..	..	..	..	..	..	..	..
Education	2 717.0	3 655.0	4 876.0	3 944.0	3 793.0	2 691.0	2 650.0	2 425.0	3 072.0	3 269.0
Human health and social work activities	9 284.0	9 697.0	13 195.0	15 005.0	16 043.0	7 315.0	7 841.0	8 158.0	8 675.0	6 564.0
Arts, entertainment and recreation	2 400.0	3 241.0	3 574.0	3 936.0	11 394.0	10 691.0	10 799.0	11 046.0	20 088.0	19 023.0
Other services	2 026.0	3 897.0	5 721.0	4 904.0	5 493.0	7 341.0	8 226.0	9 846.0	11 074.0	12 427.0
Not allocated and confidential	**67 067.0**	**66 389.0**	**621 938.0**	..	**96 094.0**	**12 534.0**	**12 838.0**	-	..	-
Private real estate activities	..	..	..	..	..	..	..	..	..	..

- Nil; .. Not available; c Confidential data

Note: Detailed metadata at: *http://stats.oecd.org/OECDStat_Metadata/ShowMetadata.ashx?Dataset=FDI_CTRY_IND_SUMM.*

Source: *OECD International Direct Investment Statistics (database): https://doi.org/10.1787/idi-data-en*

Table 6. Foreign direct investment income by industrial sector

Million US dollars

	Inward					Outward				
	2014	2015	2016	2017	2018	2014	2015	2016	2017	2018
All FDI activities	**177 294.0**	**149 926.0**	**155 978.0**	**173 778.0**	**208 078.0**	**457 122.0**	**433 333.0**	**427 542.0**	**470 933.0**	**531 010.0**
Agriculture, forestry and fishing	**186.0**	**65.0**	**192.0**	**142.0**	**166.0**	**452.0**	**290.0**	**516.0**	**274.0**	**206.0**
Mining and quarrying	**8 952.0**	**-518.0**	**-1 753.0**	**752.0**	**3 827.0**	**18 173.0**	**3 541.0**	**3 157.0**	**9 819.0**	**14 932.0**
Extraction activities	6 690.0	-1 130.0	-2 643.0	-1 045.0	2 401.0	13 671.0	1 143.0	-267.0	4 974.0	7 492.0
Manufacturing	**70 634.0**	**64 636.0**	**76 148.0**	**88 786.0**	**94 473.0**	**63 148.0**	**67 102.0**	**72 037.0**	**81 077.0**	**79 791.0**
of which:										
Food products, beverages and tobacco	8 679.0	5 461.0	9 532.0	13 704.0	11 703.0	10 358.0	7 840.0	7 703.0	10 173.0	10 049.0
Textiles, wood and paper products; printing	867.0	923.0	1 114.0	1 282.0	1 469.0	1 089.0	1 688.0	1 954.0	2 387.0	2 695.0
Chemical, rubber, plastic, non-metallic mineral products	34 569.0	35 449.0	37 376.0	45 161.0	48 980.0	19 787.0	22 245.0	25 974.0	27 160.0	24 927.0
Metal and machinery products, except electrical equipment	15 461.0	11 110.0	15 867.0	13 107.0	19 894.0	23 814.0	22 430.0	26 532.0	28 174.0	33 406.0
Motor vehicles, trailers, semi-trailers, other transport equipment	9 520.0	8 803.0	8 881.0	11 648.0	11 583.0	6 149.0	10 632.0	7 699.0	9 937.0	7 991.0
Other manufacturing	1 535.0	2 889.0	3 379.0	3 882.0	845.0	1 950.0	2 266.0	2 175.0	3 246.0	722.0
Electricity, gas, steam and air conditioning supply	**.. c**	**.. c**	**.. c**	**2 815.0**	**3 440.0**	**.. c**	**1 980.0**	**1 951.0**	**1 456.0**	**1 368.0**
Water supply; sewerage, waste management and remediation activities	**.. c**	**.. c**	**.. c**	**205.0**	**406.0**	**.. c**	**28.0**	**45.0**	**47.0**	**-8.0**
Construction	**1 593.0**	**1 458.0**	**951.0**	**-680.0**	**-803.0**	**1 136.0**	**823.0**	**275.0**	**-98.0**	**-343.0**
Services	**92 624.0**	**82 089.0**	**.. c**	**81 758.0**	**106 567.0**	**371 831.0**	**359 568.0**	**349 559.0**	**378 357.0**	**435 060.0**
Wholesale and retail trade; repair of motor vehicles and motorcycles	25 104.0	23 551.0	13 420.0	19 007.0	31 911.0	33 638.0	24 803.0	26 464.0	26 899.0	35 099.0
Transportation and storage	3 209.0	3 793.0	3 210.0	4 478.0	5 600.0	3 647.0	3 580.0	4 235.0	4 492.0	3 785.0
Accommodation and food service activities	876.0	987.0	1 526.0	1 238.0	1 314.0	2 036.0	2 627.0	2 778.0	3 019.0	2 762.0
Information and communication	3 608.0	2 611.0	1 836.0	3 037.0	6 233.0	16 333.0	14 756.0	17 485.0	17 566.0	16 781.0
Financial and insurance activities	50 252.0	38 939.0	45 997.0	40 635.0	47 240.0	286 326.0	280 867.0	262 109.0	283 832.0	342 692.0
Activities of holding companies	11 071.0	7 383.0	9 835.0	11 201.0	13 118.0	241 504.0	231 586.0	215 719.0	229 567.0	276 179.0
Real estate activities	1 228.0	1 546.0	1 957.0	1 958.0	2 346.0	-234.0	508.0	1 386.0	1 882.0	1 687.0
Professional, scientific and technical activities	3 775.0	5 602.0	4 779.0	4 707.0	4 146.0	11 818.0	12 830.0	14 173.0	14 997.0	11 630.0
Administrative and support service activities	3 942.0	4 427.0	.. c	5 833.0	6 370.0	15 870.0	17 861.0	18 849.0	22 347.0	17 166.0
Public administration; activities of households and of extraterritorial organisations	..	..	..	..	..	..	..	..	..	..
Education	-2.0	-141.0	-81.0	-275.0	-326.0	250.0	260.0	307.0	376.0	423.0
Human health and social work activities	636.0	754.0	863.0	910.0	910.0	180.0	215.0	151.0	374.0	221.0
Arts, entertainment and recreation	-99.0	-41.0	-24.0	172.0	585.0	872.0	375.0	730.0	980.0	1 335.0
Other services	95.0	61.0	-131.0	58.0	238.0	1 095.0	886.0	892.0	1 593.0	1 479.0
Not allocated and confidential	**3 229.0**	**2 261.0**	**4 587.0**	**..**	**2.0**	**-**	**1 417.0**	**1 737.0**	**..**	**4.0**
Private real estate activities	..	..	..	..	..	..	..	..	..	..

- Nil; .. Not available; c Confidential data

Note: Detailed metadata at: *http://stats.oecd.org/OECDStat_Metadata/ShowMetadata.ashx?Dataset=FDI_CTRY_IND_SUMM.*

Source: OECD International Direct Investment Statistics (database): https://doi.org/10.1787/idi-data-en

www.ingramcontent.com/pod-product-compliance
Lightning Source LLC
Chambersburg PA
CBHW061159240926
51846CB00006B/1060
9789264313248